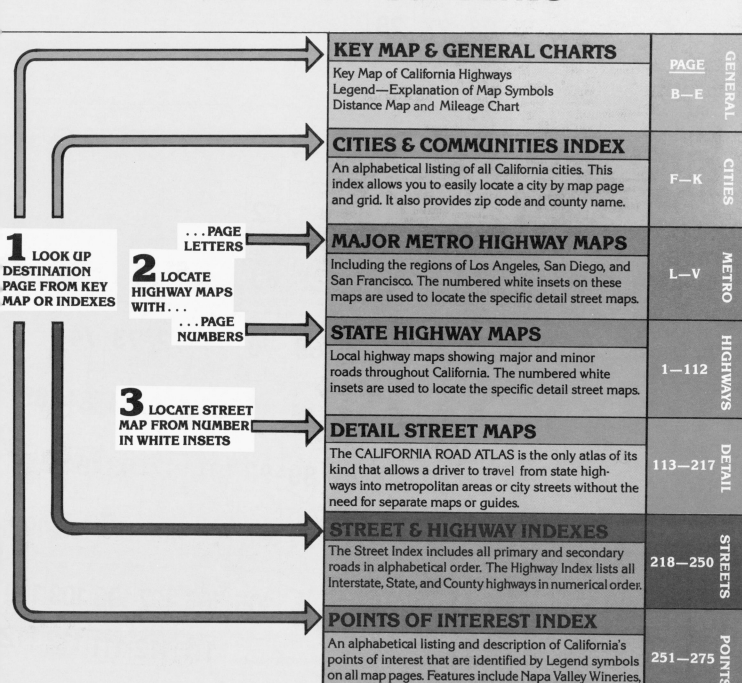

W9-CRO-427

*REVISED EDITION*

*Including Handy California State Foldout Map*

# CALIFORNIA
## R O A D   A T L A S
### THE COMPLETE DRIVER'S GUIDE FROM STATE ROADS TO CITY STREETS

# FOLLOW THE EASY-TO-USE
# 1-2-3 TABLE OF CONTENTS

**1 LOOK UP DESTINATION PAGE FROM KEY MAP OR INDEXES**

**2 LOCATE HIGHWAY MAPS WITH . . .**

. . . PAGE LETTERS

. . . PAGE NUMBERS

**3 LOCATE STREET MAP FROM NUMBER IN WHITE INSETS**

17731 Cowan, Irvine, CA 92714 (714) 863-1984
550 Jackson St., San Francisco, CA 94133 (415) 981-7520
603 West 7th St., Los Angeles, CA 90017 (213) 627-4018

**B**

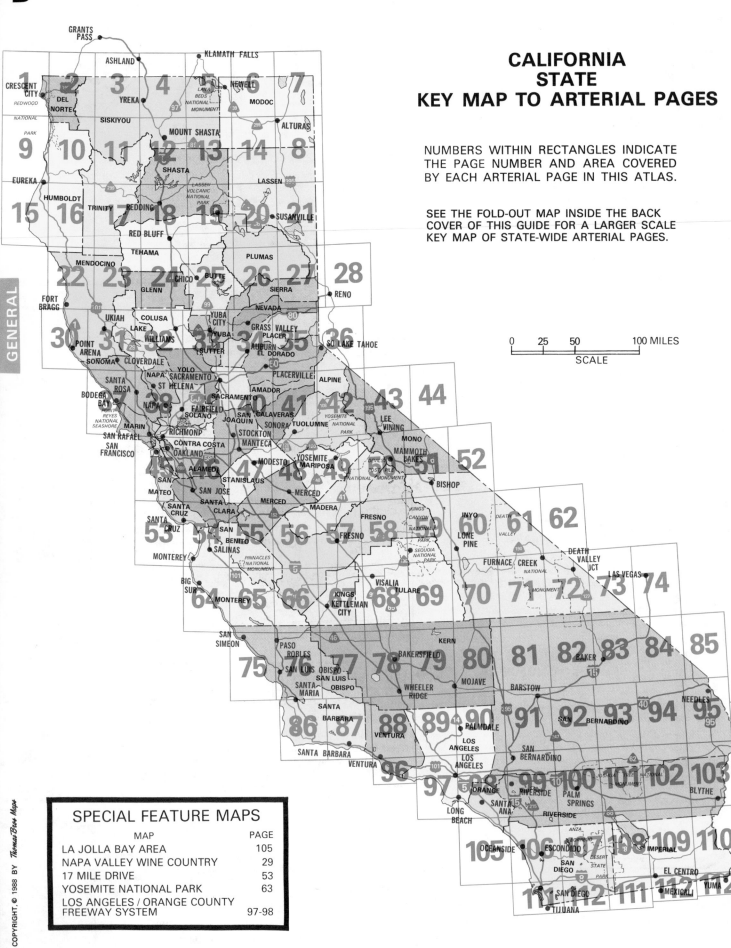

# CALIFORNIA STATE KEY MAP TO ARTERIAL PAGES

NUMBERS WITHIN RECTANGLES INDICATE THE PAGE NUMBER AND AREA COVERED BY EACH ARTERIAL PAGE IN THIS ATLAS.

SEE THE FOLD-OUT MAP INSIDE THE BACK COVER OF THIS GUIDE FOR A LARGER SCALE KEY MAP OF STATE-WIDE ARTERIAL PAGES.

| | | | |
|---|---|---|---|
| 0 | 25 | 50 | 100 MILES |

SCALE

GENERAL

## SPECIAL FEATURE MAPS

N

# LEGEND

## EXPLANATION OF MAP SYMBOLS

**DETAIL PAGES**

**ARTERIAL PAGES**

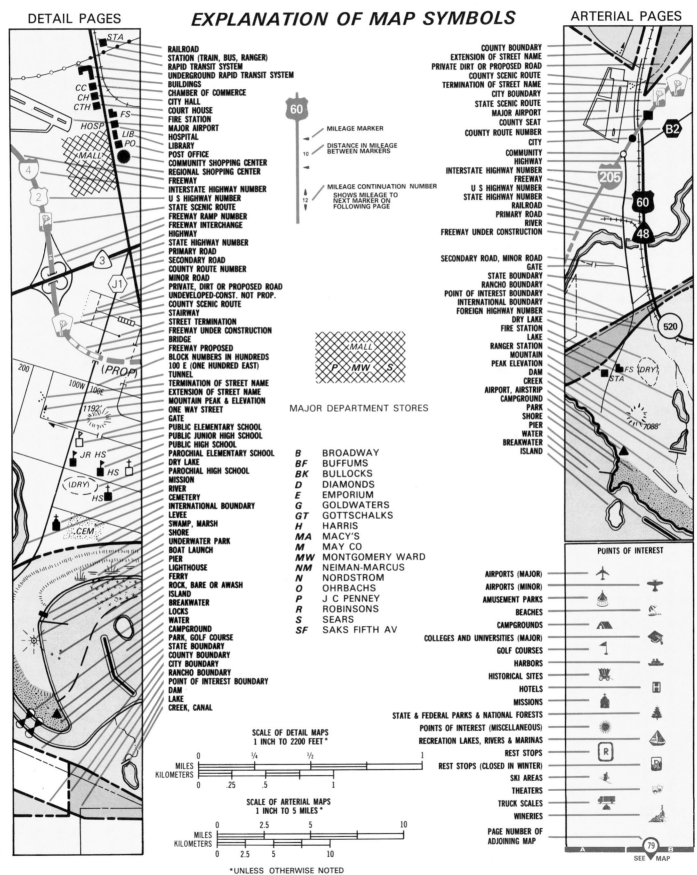

RAILROAD
STATION (TRAIN, BUS, RANGER)
RAPID TRANSIT SYSTEM
UNDERGROUND RAPID TRANSIT SYSTEM
BUILDINGS
CHAMBER OF COMMERCE
CITY HALL
COURT HOUSE
FIRE STATION
MAJOR AIRPORT
HOSPITAL
LIBRARY
POST OFFICE
COMMUNITY SHOPPING CENTER
REGIONAL SHOPPING CENTER
FREEWAY
INTERSTATE HIGHWAY NUMBER
U S HIGHWAY NUMBER
STATE SCENIC ROUTE
FREEWAY RAMP NUMBER
FREEWAY INTERCHANGE
HIGHWAY
STATE HIGHWAY NUMBER
PRIMARY ROAD
SECONDARY ROAD
COUNTY ROUTE NUMBER
MINOR ROAD
PRIVATE, DIRT OR PROPOSED ROAD
UNDEVELOPED-CONST. NOT PROP.
COUNTY SCENIC ROUTE
STAIRWAY
STREET TERMINATION
FREEWAY UNDER CONSTRUCTION
BRIDGE
FREEWAY PROPOSED
BLOCK NUMBERS IN HUNDREDS
100 E (ONE HUNDRED EAST)
TUNNEL
TERMINATION OF STREET NAME
EXTENSION OF STREET NAME
MOUNTAIN PEAK & ELEVATION
ONE WAY STREET
GATE
PUBLIC ELEMENTARY SCHOOL
PUBLIC JUNIOR HIGH SCHOOL
PUBLIC HIGH SCHOOL
PAROCHIAL ELEMENTARY SCHOOL
DRY LAKE
PAROCHIAL HIGH SCHOOL
MISSION
RIVER
CEMETERY
INTERNATIONAL BOUNDARY
LEVEE
SWAMP, MARSH
SHORE
UNDERWATER PARK
BOAT LAUNCH
PIER
LIGHTHOUSE
FERRY
ROCK, BARE OR AWASH
ISLAND
BREAKWATER
LOCKS
WATER
CAMPGROUND
PARK, GOLF COURSE
STATE BOUNDARY
COUNTY BOUNDARY
CITY BOUNDARY
RANCHO BOUNDARY
POINT OF INTEREST BOUNDARY
DAM
LAKE
CREEK, CANAL

MILEAGE MARKER

DISTANCE IN MILEAGE
BETWEEN MARKERS

MILEAGE CONTINUATION NUMBER
SHOWS MILEAGE TO
NEXT MARKER ON
FOLLOWING PAGE

MALL
P   MW   S

MAJOR DEPARTMENT STORES

| | |
|---|---|
| B | BROADWAY |
| BF | BUFFUMS |
| BK | BULLOCKS |
| D | DIAMONDS |
| E | EMPORIUM |
| G | GOLDWATERS |
| GT | GOTTSCHALKS |
| H | HARRIS |
| MA | MACY'S |
| M | MAY CO |
| MW | MONTGOMERY WARD |
| NM | NEIMAN-MARCUS |
| N | NORDSTROM |
| O | OHRBACHS |
| P | J C PENNEY |
| R | ROBINSONS |
| S | SEARS |
| SF | SAKS FIFTH AV |

COUNTY BOUNDARY
EXTENSION OF STREET NAME
PRIVATE DIRT OR PROPOSED ROAD
COUNTY SCENIC ROUTE
TERMINATION OF STREET NAME
CITY BOUNDARY
STATE SCENIC ROUTE
MAJOR AIRPORT
COUNTY SEAT
COUNTY ROUTE NUMBER
CITY
COMMUNITY
HIGHWAY
INTERSTATE HIGHWAY NUMBER
FREEWAY
U S HIGHWAY NUMBER
STATE HIGHWAY NUMBER
RAILROAD
PRIMARY ROAD
RIVER
FREEWAY UNDER CONSTRUCTION

SECONDARY ROAD, MINOR ROAD
GATE
STATE BOUNDARY
RANCHO BOUNDARY
POINT OF INTEREST BOUNDARY
INTERNATIONAL BOUNDARY
FOREIGN HIGHWAY NUMBER
DRY LAKE
FIRE STATION
LAKE
RANGER STATION
MOUNTAIN
PEAK ELEVATION
DAM
CREEK
AIRPORT, AIRSTRIP
CAMPGROUND
PARK
SHORE
PIER
WATER
BREAKWATER
ISLAND

GENERAL

### POINTS OF INTEREST

AIRPORTS (MAJOR)
AIRPORTS (MINOR)
AMUSEMENT PARKS
BEACHES
CAMPGROUNDS
COLLEGES AND UNIVERSITIES (MAJOR)
GOLF COURSES
HARBORS
HISTORICAL SITES
HOTELS
MISSIONS
STATE & FEDERAL PARKS & NATIONAL FORESTS
POINTS OF INTEREST (MISCELLANEOUS)
RECREATION LAKES, RIVERS & MARINAS
REST STOPS
REST STOPS (CLOSED IN WINTER)
SKI AREAS
THEATERS
TRUCK SCALES
WINERIES
PAGE NUMBER OF
ADJOINING MAP

SEE ▼ MAP

### SCALE OF DETAIL MAPS
1 INCH TO 2200 FEET *

MILES
0    ¼    ½    1
KILOMETERS
0    .25    .5    1

### SCALE OF ARTERIAL MAPS
1 INCH TO 5 MILES *

MILES
0    2.5    5    10
KILOMETERS
0    2.5    5    10

*UNLESS OTHERWISE NOTED

**D**

# DISTANCE MAP

DISTANCE BETWEEN POINTS GIVEN
IN MILES. MILEAGE DETERMINED
BY MOST DIRECT DRIVING ROUTE.

```
0    25    50          100 MILES
|────|────|────────────|
          SCALE
```

IN ADDITION TO THIS
DISTANCE MAP, MILEAGE
NUMBERS ARE INCLUDED
AS A SPECIAL FEATURE
ON INTERSTATE HIGHWAYS
THROUGHOUT THE BOOK.

GENERAL

# MILEAGE CHART

MILEAGE DETERMINED BY MOST DIRECT DRIVING ROUTE

| | BAKERSFIELD | CHICO | EUREKA | FRESNO | LAS VEGAS | LONG BEACH | LOS ANGELES | MERCED | MODESTO | OAKLAND | PALM SPRINGS | REDDING | RIVERSIDE | SACRAMENTO | SALINAS | SAN DIEGO | SAN FRANCISCO | SAN JOSE | SAN LUIS OBISPO | SANTA ANA | SANTA BARBARA | SANTA ROSA | SOUTH LAKE TAHOE | STOCKTON | VENTURA |
|---|---|---|---|---|---|---|---|---|---|---|---|---|---|---|---|---|---|---|---|---|---|---|---|---|---|
| ALTURAS | 577 | 207 | 292 | 470 | 624 | 705 | 650 | 415 | 374 | 379 | 720 | 142 | 645 | 297 | 471 | 741 | 360 | 392 | 577 | 683 | 737 | 367 | 241 | 342 | 692 |
| ANAHEIM | 138 | 505 | 718 | 245 | 274 | 24 | 30 | 302 | 341 | 443 | 100 | 577 | 42 | 415 | 346 | 86 | 449 | 403 | 235 | 4 | 128 | 485 | 490 | 370 | 102 |
| AUBURN | 306 | 90 | 321 | 199 | 601 | 441 | 420 | 143 | 106 | 115 | 518 | 175 | 473 | 34 | 207 | 539 | 121 | 151 | 339 | 452 | 444 | 131 | 86 | 70 | 421 |
| BAKERSFIELD | | 362 | 555 | 109 | 284 | 132 | 113 | 163 | 200 | 285 | 209 | 433 | 177 | 272 | 206 | 232 | 283 | 241 | 114 | 143 | 146 | 340 | 360 | 227 | 115 |
| BARSTOW | 129 | 491 | 684 | 236 | 155 | 123 | 131 | 292 | 330 | 414 | 123 | 559 | 78 | 401 | 335 | 180 | 412 | 385 | 264 | 116 | 205 | 469 | 395 | 356 | 174 |
| BENECIA | 292 | 144 | 287 | 177 | 578 | 429 | 396 | 123 | 84 | 37 | 510 | 187 | 466 | 58 | 106 | 513 | 43 | 49 | 236 | 456 | 341 | 61 | 164 | 74 | 374 |
| BISHOP | 222 | 360 | 553 | 235 | 284 | 308 | 277 | 223 | 252 | 314 | 308 | 396 | 242 | 265 | 347 | 360 | 335 | 321 | 357 | 301 | 327 | 382 | 176 | 240 | 296 |
| BLYTHE | 339 | 705 | 918 | 446 | 208 | 228 | 230 | 501 | 521 | 622 | 129 | 775 | 171 | 616 | 530 | 222 | 619 | 575 | 433 | 202 | 314 | 676 | 686 | 568 | 287 |
| BODEGA BAY | 404 | 189 | 266 | 249 | 632 | 491 | 451 | 194 | 156 | 74 | 568 | 246 | 527 | 141 | 165 | 594 | 64 | 109 | 294 | 516 | 400 | 23 | 256 | 152 | 431 |
| BURBANK | 104 | 465 | 659 | 210 | 294 | 31 | 9 | 266 | 304 | 383 | 111 | 536 | 67 | 376 | 304 | 127 | 377 | 334 | 200 | 45 | 93 | 421 | 446 | 330 | 64 |
| CHICO | 362 | | 218 | 254 | 620 | 498 | 475 | 198 | 160 | 172 | 575 | 73 | 543 | 89 | 264 | 638 | 180 | 212 | 389 | 509 | 490 | 166 | 170 | 134 | 477 |
| CLAREMONT | 135 | 497 | 691 | 308 | 246 | 47 | 26 | 298 | 336 | 415 | 79 | 568 | 23 | 408 | 336 | 107 | 409 | 366 | 226 | 23 | 118 | 453 | 469 | 360 | 88 |
| DAVIS | 287 | 83 | 282 | 180 | 582 | 422 | 399 | 134 | 87 | 66 | 499 | 155 | 454 | 15 | 158 | 520 | 74 | 102 | 320 | 433 | 425 | 83 | 127 | 60 | 402 |
| DEATH VALLEY | 238 | 530 | 703 | 395 | 213 | 229 | 206 | 393 | 422 | 484 | 306 | 566 | 262 | 435 | 475 | 407 | 505 | 491 | 352 | 324 | 366 | 552 | 346 | 410 | 336 |
| EL CENTRO | 322 | 706 | 872 | 427 | 303 | 219 | 213 | 482 | 520 | 615 | 110 | 775 | 154 | 618 | 536 | 110 | 601 | 561 | 413 | 201 | 308 | 660 | 596 | 554 | 279 |
| EUREKA | 555 | 218 | | 446 | 797 | 683 | 669 | 390 | 353 | 288 | 788 | 149 | 743 | 287 | 381 | 776 | 269 | 323 | 508 | 722 | 614 | 219 | 388 | 332 | 643 |
| FAIRFIELD | 278 | 132 | 276 | 171 | 561 | 412 | 391 | 118 | 79 | 45 | 489 | 173 | 457 | 43 | 132 | 554 | 55 | 78 | 260 | 423 | 362 | 57 | 150 | 51 | 389 |
| FORT BRAGG | 460 | 199 | 156 | 353 | 730 | 597 | 551 | 292 | 255 | 180 | 674 | 288 | 629 | 217 | 280 | 669 | 176 | 216 | 401 | 608 | 507 | 119 | 319 | 233 | 534 |
| FRESNO | 109 | 254 | 446 | | 284 | 239 | 220 | 56 | 93 | 178 | 316 | 325 | 272 | 165 | 134 | 339 | 185 | 151 | 140 | 250 | 245 | 233 | 251 | 120 | 222 |
| GRASS VALLEY | 329 | 78 | 320 | 222 | 624 | 464 | 443 | 166 | 129 | 138 | 541 | 163 | 496 | 57 | 230 | 562 | 144 | 174 | 362 | 475 | 467 | 154 | 115 | 93 | 444 |
| LAGUNA BEACH | 162 | 528 | 741 | 269 | 288 | 34 | 55 | 324 | 363 | 465 | 115 | 598 | 62 | 437 | 368 | 75 | 471 | 425 | 257 | 19 | 150 | 507 | 511 | 391 | 123 |
| LA JOLLA | 219 | 625 | 763 | 326 | 319 | 90 | 103 | 382 | 419 | 507 | 122 | 667 | 79 | 492 | 428 | 13 | 517 | 449 | 309 | 79 | 203 | 536 | 529 | 450 | 172 |
| LASSEN NATIONAL PARK | 437 | 102 | 202 | 329 | 695 | 573 | 550 | 273 | 235 | 247 | 650 | 45 | 618 | 164 | 339 | 713 | 255 | 287 | 459 | 584 | 562 | 241 | 199 | 209 | 552 |
| LAS VEGAS | 284 | 620 | 797 | 284 | | 276 | 286 | 446 | 484 | 567 | 276 | 640 | 231 | 567 | 488 | 332 | 568 | 524 | 414 | 269 | 354 | 610 | 466 | 510 | 323 |
| LONE PINE | 159 | 420 | 593 | 285 | 224 | 232 | 209 | 283 | 312 | 374 | 277 | 456 | 233 | 325 | 365 | 337 | 395 | 381 | 273 | 245 | 285 | 442 | 236 | 300 | 254 |
| LONG BEACH | 132 | 498 | 683 | 239 | 276 | | 24 | 294 | 333 | 417 | 118 | 568 | 60 | 407 | 338 | 103 | 427 | 383 | 218 | 25 | 120 | 477 | 479 | 361 | 93 |
| LOS ANGELES | 113 | 475 | 669 | 220 | 286 | 24 | | 276 | 314 | 393 | 103 | 546 | 56 | 386 | 314 | 119 | 387 | 344 | 204 | 35 | 96 | 431 | 456 | 340 | 66 |
| MAMMOTH LAKES | 262 | 320 | 513 | 195 | 324 | 348 | 317 | 283 | 212 | 274 | 348 | 356 | 217 | 225 | 307 | 400 | 295 | 281 | 397 | 341 | 367 | 342 | 130 | 200 | 336 |
| MANTECA | 215 | 147 | 345 | 108 | 499 | 348 | 329 | 54 | 15 | 63 | 425 | 219 | 380 | 44 | 99 | 447 | 73 | 65 | 248 | 382 | 354 | 123 | 144 | 13 | 330 |
| MARTINEZ | 288 | 146 | 290 | 172 | 571 | 424 | 391 | 118 | 79 | 28 | 507 | 191 | 460 | 61 | 101 | 509 | 38 | 47 | 233 | 453 | 338 | 64 | 168 | 70 | 369 |
| MERCED | 163 | 198 | 390 | 56 | 446 | 294 | 276 | | 37 | 123 | 368 | 269 | 326 | 109 | 105 | 395 | 130 | 115 | 195 | 305 | 300 | 172 | 194 | 64 | 278 |
| MODESTO | 200 | 160 | 353 | 93 | 484 | 333 | 314 | 37 | | 84 | 410 | 232 | 365 | 72 | 104 | 432 | 92 | 77 | 233 | 344 | 339 | 135 | 156 | 27 | 315 |
| MOJAVE | 62 | 424 | 617 | 169 | 229 | 117 | 94 | 225 | 262 | 347 | 162 | 495 | 118 | 334 | 268 | 213 | 345 | 303 | 190 | 130 | 116 | 402 | 351 | 289 | 87 |
| MONTEREY | 216 | 278 | 399 | 149 | 504 | 356 | 334 | 115 | 138 | 111 | 433 | 350 | 388 | 190 | 18 | 442 | 122 | 75 | 145 | 367 | 250 | 170 | 272 | 141 | 273 |
| NAPA | 331 | 150 | 255 | 224 | 613 | 463 | 439 | 169 | 130 | 46 | 540 | 191 | 495 | 61 | 145 | 566 | 56 | 88 | 270 | 492 | 363 | 36 | 168 | 69 | 390 |
| NEEDLES | 281 | 638 | 821 | 383 | 108 | 269 | 279 | 439 | 476 | 560 | 190 | 729 | 224 | 548 | 481 | 311 | 561 | 517 | 416 | 262 | 352 | 603 | 552 | 508 | 316 |
| NEVADA CITY | 334 | 83 | 325 | 227 | 629 | 469 | 448 | 171 | 134 | 143 | 546 | 168 | 501 | 62 | 235 | 567 | 149 | 179 | 367 | 480 | 472 | 159 | 110 | 98 | 449 |
| NEWPORT BEACH | 155 | 519 | 735 | 262 | 279 | 21 | 43 | 317 | 366 | 458 | 108 | 592 | 55 | 430 | 361 | 81 | 465 | 418 | 230 | 12 | 141 | 498 | 502 | 382 | 114 |
| OAKLAND | 285 | 172 | 288 | 178 | 567 | 417 | 393 | 123 | 84 | | 494 | 218 | 449 | 81 | 99 | 520 | 10 | 42 | 224 | 446 | 317 | 60 | 195 | 73 | 344 |
| ONTARIO | 141 | 493 | 696 | 247 | 222 | 44 | 37 | 303 | 341 | 420 | 77 | 573 | 21 | 413 | 341 | 125 | 414 | 371 | 232 | 33 | 123 | 458 | 483 | 367 | 103 |
| OXNARD | 122 | 485 | 650 | 229 | 316 | 85 | 59 | 271 | 322 | 351 | 165 | 555 | 117 | 395 | 252 | 178 | 379 | 329 | 142 | 97 | 38 | 421 | 478 | 349 | 7 |
| PALMDALE | 98 | 460 | 653 | 205 | 244 | 81 | 58 | 261 | 298 | 383 | 126 | 531 | 82 | 370 | 304 | 182 | 381 | 339 | 221 | 94 | 116 | 438 | 387 | 325 | 87 |
| PALM SPRINGS | 209 | 575 | 788 | 316 | 276 | 118 | 103 | 368 | 410 | 494 | | 658 | 56 | 484 | 415 | 135 | 504 | 460 | 306 | 96 | 199 | 554 | 435 | 438 | 172 |
| PALO ALTO | 261 | 213 | 302 | 171 | 544 | 403 | 364 | 135 | 97 | 43 | 480 | 251 | 433 | 120 | 74 | 482 | 33 | 20 | 205 | 426 | 311 | 89 | 223 | 92 | 342 |
| PASADENA | 109 | 475 | 688 | 216 | 259 | 31 | 7 | 271 | 310 | 394 | 104 | 554 | 52 | 384 | 315 | 134 | 404 | 360 | 210 | 42 | 95 | 454 | 463 | 338 | 68 |
| PLACERVILLE | 282 | 133 | 331 | 175 | 525 | 416 | 395 | 122 | 83 | 125 | 493 | 205 | 461 | 44 | 177 | 548 | 131 | 127 | 309 | 427 | 429 | 141 | 59 | 55 | 397 |
| REDDING | 433 | 73 | 149 | 325 | 640 | 568 | 546 | 269 | 232 | 218 | 658 | | 600 | 161 | 334 | 680 | 218 | 246 | 431 | 579 | 537 | 223 | 249 | 206 | 548 |
| RENO | 432 | 104 | 342 | 297 | 444 | 510 | 504 | 241 | 209 | 216 | 510 | 196 | 465 | 132 | 308 | 561 | 223 | 249 | 434 | 503 | 507 | 229 | 61 | 177 | 496 |
| RICHMOND | 299 | 163 | 276 | 192 | 581 | 431 | 407 | 137 | 98 | 14 | 508 | 204 | 462 | 74 | 113 | 534 | 24 | 56 | 238 | 460 | 331 | 50 | 181 | 82 | 358 |
| RIVERSIDE | 177 | 543 | 743 | 272 | 231 | 60 | 56 | 326 | 365 | 449 | 56 | 600 | | 439 | 367 | 92 | 463 | 413 | 259 | 43 | 147 | 509 | 379 | 406 | 125 |
| SACRAMENTO | 272 | 89 | 287 | 165 | 567 | 407 | 386 | 109 | 72 | 81 | 484 | 161 | 439 | | 173 | 505 | 87 | 117 | 305 | 418 | 410 | 97 | 107 | 45 | 387 |
| SALINAS | 206 | 264 | 381 | 134 | 488 | 338 | 314 | 105 | 104 | 99 | 415 | 334 | 367 | 173 | | 441 | 101 | 57 | 125 | 349 | 218 | 160 | 251 | 122 | 245 |
| SAN BERNARDINO | 167 | 534 | 714 | 269 | 228 | 63 | 59 | 325 | 362 | 439 | 57 | 595 | 13 | 436 | 360 | 104 | 444 | 401 | 260 | 48 | 154 | 486 | 436 | 389 | 123 |
| SAN DIEGO | 232 | 638 | 776 | 339 | 332 | 103 | 119 | 395 | 432 | 520 | 135 | 680 | 92 | 505 | 441 | | 530 | 462 | 322 | 84 | 216 | 549 | 542 | 493 | 185 |
| SAN FRANCISCO | 283 | 180 | 269 | 185 | 568 | 427 | 387 | 130 | 92 | 10 | 504 | 218 | 463 | 87 | 101 | 530 | | 45 | 230 | 452 | 336 | 56 | 192 | 88 | 367 |
| SAN JOSE | 241 | 212 | 323 | 151 | 524 | 383 | 344 | 115 | 77 | 42 | 460 | 246 | 413 | 117 | 57 | 462 | 45 | | 185 | 406 | 291 | 96 | 197 | 72 | 322 |
| SAN JUAN CAPISTRANO | 163 | 529 | 742 | 270 | 289 | 40 | 55 | 325 | 364 | 466 | 116 | 599 | 63 | 438 | 369 | 66 | 472 | 426 | 258 | 20 | 151 | 508 | 512 | 114 | 124 |
| SAN LUIS OBISPO | 114 | 384 | 508 | 140 | 414 | 218 | 204 | 195 | 233 | 224 | 306 | 431 | 259 | 305 | 125 | 322 | 230 | 185 | | 238 | 106 | 281 | 382 | 254 | 137 |
| SAN MATEO | 313 | 199 | 288 | 181 | 554 | 413 | 374 | 125 | 86 | 29 | 490 | 237 | 443 | 106 | 84 | 492 | 19 | 30 | 215 | 436 | 321 | 75 | 209 | 78 | 352 |
| SAN PEDRO | 134 | 496 | 690 | 242 | 285 | 9 | 22 | 298 | 336 | 415 | 126 | 568 | 68 | 408 | 336 | 118 | 409 | 366 | 213 | 37 | 108 | 454 | 478 | 362 | 75 |
| SAN RAFAEL | 306 | 167 | 260 | 199 | 588 | 438 | 414 | 144 | 105 | 21 | 515 | 243 | 470 | 83 | 121 | 559 | 18 | 64 | 246 | 470 | 339 | 39 | 181 | 94 | 366 |
| SANTA ANA | 143 | 509 | 722 | 250 | 269 | 25 | 35 | 305 | 344 | 446 | 96 | 579 | 43 | 418 | 349 | 84 | 452 | 406 | 238 | | 131 | 488 | 492 | 372 | 104 |
| SANTA BARBARA | 146 | 490 | 614 | 245 | 354 | 120 | 96 | 300 | 339 | 317 | 199 | 537 | 147 | 410 | 218 | 216 | 336 | 291 | 106 | 131 | | 387 | 490 | 374 | 31 |
| SANTA CRUZ | 239 | 230 | 354 | 150 | 524 | 379 | 344 | 116 | 109 | 75 | 456 | 275 | 411 | 146 | 33 | 462 | 74 | 29 | 162 | 390 | 268 | 129 | 229 | 101 | 300 |
| SANTA MARIA | 145 | 415 | 539 | 171 | 428 | 194 | 170 | 226 | 264 | 255 | 273 | 462 | 221 | 336 | 156 | 290 | 261 | 216 | 31 | 205 | 74 | 312 | 413 | 285 | 103 |
| SANTA ROSA | 340 | 166 | 219 | 233 | 610 | 477 | 431 | 172 | 135 | 60 | 554 | 223 | 509 | 97 | 160 | 549 | 56 | 96 | 281 | 488 | 387 | | 199 | 113 | 414 |
| SAUSALITO | 298 | 183 | 276 | 200 | 583 | 442 | 402 | 145 | 107 | 25 | 519 | 259 | 478 | 99 | 116 | 545 | 15 | 60 | 245 | 467 | 351 | 55 | 207 | 103 | 382 |
| SEQUOIA NATIONAL PK | 129 | 343 | 556 | 84 | 408 | 258 | 234 | 139 | 178 | 335 | 235 | 385 | 303 | 252 | 209 | 361 | 272 | 228 | 178 | 269 | 276 | 329 | 335 | 206 | 262 |
| SONOMA | 331 | 163 | 239 | 224 | 613 | 468 | 439 | 170 | 130 | 46 | 540 | 204 | 495 | 75 | 146 | 584 | 43 | 89 | 271 | 495 | 364 | 20 | 181 | 82 | 391 |
| SONORA | 215 | 189 | 387 | 108 | 498 | 380 | 366 | 52 | 42 | 105 | 420 | 261 | 391 | 86 | 157 | 447 | 115 | 107 | 247 | 357 | 352 | 165 | 139 | 55 | 330 |
| SOUTH LAKE TAHOE | 360 | 170 | 388 | 251 | 466 | 479 | 456 | 194 | 156 | 195 | 435 | 249 | 379 | 107 | 251 | 542 | 192 | 197 | 382 | 492 | 490 | 199 | | 131 | 471 |
| STOCKTON | 227 | 134 | 332 | 120 | 510 | 361 | 340 | 64 | 27 | 73 | 438 | 206 | 406 | 45 | 122 | 493 | 88 | 72 | 254 | 372 | 374 | 113 | 131 | | 342 |
| SUSANVILLE | 465 | 105 | 257 | 356 | 599 | 600 | 577 | 299 | 262 | 275 | 677 | 110 | 645 | 191 | 369 | 714 | 252 | 280 | 465 | 613 | 571 | 257 | 133 | 240 | 582 |
| UKIAH | 402 | 147 | 179 | 295 | 672 | 539 | 493 | 234 | 197 | 135 | 616 | 184 | 571 | 159 | 222 | 611 | 118 | 158 | 343 | 550 | 449 | 62 | 253 | 175 | 476 |
| VALLEJO | 310 | 147 | 265 | 203 | 592 | 442 | 418 | 131 | 92 | 25 | 519 | 186 | 474 | 57 | 124 | 545 | 35 | 67 | 249 | 471 | 342 | 46 | 266 | 65 | 370 |
| VENTURA | 115 | 477 | 643 | 222 | 323 | 93 | 66 | 278 | 315 | 344 | 172 | 548 | 125 | 387 | 245 | 185 | 367 | 322 | 137 | 104 | 31 | 414 | 471 | 342 | |
| YOSEMITE NATIONAL PK | 199 | 263 | 476 | 92 | 435 | 331 | 307 | 83 | 122 | 174 | 408 | 333 | 364 | 172 | 188 | 434 | 184 | 178 | 236 | 342 | 329 | 234 | 133 | 129 | 330 |
| YREKA | 531 | 171 | 205 | 427 | 698 | 657 | 638 | 372 | 335 | 307 | 747 | 98 | 689 | 263 | 423 | 756 | 317 | 346 | 534 | 668 | 630 | 325 | 315 | 297 | 645 |
| YUBA CITY | 313 | 48 | 290 | 206 | 608 | 448 | 427 | 150 | 113 | 122 | 525 | 133 | 480 | 41 | 214 | 546 | 128 | 158 | 346 | 459 | 451 | 201 | 145 | 86 | 428 |
| YUMA | 379 | 742 | 922 | 491 | 299 | 278 | 271 | 545 | 584 | 674 | 169 | 816 | 221 | 655 | 595 | 173 | 655 | 614 | 473 | 260 | 368 | 702 | 646 | 603 | 337 |

# CITIES AND COMMUNITIES INDEX

| COMMUNITY NAME | CO. | ZIP CODE | PAGE & GRID |
|---|---|---|---|
| **A** | | | |
| ACADEMY | FRCO | 93612 | 57 E2 |
| ACAMPO | SJCO | 95226 | 40 A4 |
| ACTIS | KER | 93501 | 80 A5 |
| ACTON | LACO | 93510 | 89 E4 |
| ADAMS | LAK | 95496 | 31 E4 |
| ADELAIDA | SLO | 93446 | 75 E1 |
| *ADELANTO | SBD | 92301 | 91 A3 |
| ADIN | MOD | 96006 | 14 D3 |
| AERIAL ACRES | KER | 93523 | 80 D5 |
| AETNA SPRINGS | NAPA | 94567 | 32 B5 |
| AFTON | GLE | 95920 | 25 A5 |
| AGATE BAY | PLA | 95711 | 35 E1 |
| AGOURA | LACO | 91301 | 97 A1 |
| *AGOURA HILLS | LACO | 91301 | 96 E1 |
| AGUA CALIENTE | SDCO | 92086 | 107 C2 |
| AGUA CALIENTE | SON | 95476 | 38 B3 |
| AGUA CALIENTE HOT SPGS | SDCO | 92036 | 107 E4 |
| AGUA DULCE | LACO | 91350 | 89 D4 |
| AGUANGA | RCO | 92302 | 107 A1 |
| AGUEREBERRY POINT | INY | 92328 | 71 D1 |
| AHWAHNEE | MAD | 93601 | 49 C4 |
| AINSWORTH CORNER | SIS | | 5 C2 |
| *ALAMEDA | ALA | 94501 | L D5 |
| ALAMO | CC | 94507 | M A4 |
| ALAMORIO | IMP | 92227 | 109 B4 |
| *ALBANY | ALA | 94706 | L D4 |
| ALBERHILL | RCO | 92303 | 99 A4 |
| ALBION | MEN | 95410 | 30 B1 |
| ALDERPOINT | HUM | 95411 | 16 D5 |
| ALDER SPRINGS | FRCO | 93602 | 58 A1 |
| ALDER SPRINGS | GLE | 95939 | 23 E3 |
| ALGODONES | BAJA | | 112 C5 |
| *ALHAMBRA | LACO | 91801 | R C3 |
| ALISO VIEJO | ORA | 92656 | 98 D5 |
| ALLEGHANY | SIE | 95910 | 26 D4 |
| ALLENSWORTH | TUL | 93219 | 68 A4 |
| ALMANOR | PLU | 95911 | 20 B4 |
| ALPAUGH | TUL | 93201 | 67 E4 |
| ALPINE | SDCO | 92001 | 107 B5 |
| ALPINE HEIGHTS | SDCO | 92001 | 107 B5 |
| ALPINE HIGHLANDS | SDCO | 92001 | 107 B5 |
| ALPINE HILLS | SDCO | 92001 | 107 B5 |
| ALPINE HILLS | SMCO | 94025 | N D3 |
| ALPINE MEADOWS | PLA | 95730 | 35 D2 |
| ALPINE PEAKS | PLA | 95730 | 35 D2 |
| ALTA | PLA | 95701 | 34 E1 |
| ALTADENA | LACO | 91001 | R C2 |
| ALTA LOMA | SBD | 91701 | U D2 |
| ALTAMONT | ALA | 94550 | M D5 |
| ALTAMONT | KLAM | | 5 C1 |
| ALTA SIERRA | KER | 93285 | 69 C5 |
| ALTAVILLE | CAL | 95221 | 41 B4 |
| ALTA VISTA | INY | 93514 | 51 C3 |
| ALTON | HUM | 95540 | 15 D2 |
| *ALTURAS | MOD | 96101 | 8 A1 |
| ALUM ROCK | SCL | 95127 | P C3 |
| ALVISO | SCL | 95002 | P B2 |
| *AMADOR CITY | AMA | 95601 | 40 D2 |
| AMARGOSA VALLEY | NYE | | 62 E4 |
| AMBLER | TUL | 93277 | 68 B1 |
| AMBOY | SBD | 92304 | 93 E3 |
| AMERICAN HOUSE | PLU | 95981 | 26 C3 |
| *ANAHEIM | ORA | 92801 | T D2 |
| ANAHEIM HILLS | ORA | 92807 | T E2 |
| *ANDERSON | SHA | 96007 | 18 C3 |
| ANDERSON SPRINGS | LAK | 95461 | 31 E4 |
| ANDRADE | IMP | 92283 | 112 C5 |
| *ANGELS CAMP | CAL | 95222 | 41 B4 |
| ANGELUS OAKS | SBD | 92305 | 99 E1 |
| ANGWIN | NAPA | 94508 | 38 C1 |
| ANNAPOLIS | SON | 95412 | 30 E5 |
| ANTELOPE | SAC | 95842 | 34 A5 |
| ANTELOPE ACRES | LACO | 93534 | 89 D2 |
| *ANTIOCH | CC | 94509 | M C3 |
| ANZA | RCO | 92306 | 100 C5 |
| APPLEGATE | PLA | 95703 | 34 D3 |
| APPLE VALLEY | SBD | 92307 | 91 C4 |
| APTOS | SCR | 95003 | 54 B2 |
| ARABIA | RCO | 92274 | 101 B5 |
| ARBUCKLE | COL | 95912 | 32 E3 |
| *ARCADIA | LACO | 91006 | R C3 |
| *ARCATA | HUM | 95521 | 9 E5 |
| ARDEN | CLK | | 74 D3 |
| ARDEN | SAC | 95864 | 40 A1 |
| ARGUS | SBD | 93562 | 71 B5 |
| ARLINGTON | RCO | 92503 | 99 A3 |
| ARMONA | KIN | 93202 | 67 D1 |
| ARNOLD | CAL | 95223 | 41 C3 |
| ARNOLD HEIGHTS | RCO | 92508 | 99 B3 |
| AROMAS | MON | 95004 | 54 C2 |
| ARROWBEAR LAKE | SBD | 92308 | 99 D1 |
| ARROWHEAD SPRINGS | SBD | 92404 | 99 C1 |
| *ARROYO GRANDE | SLO | 93420 | 76 B4 |
| *ARTESIA | LACO | 90701 | T A1 |
| ARTOIS | GLE | 95913 | 24 D4 |
| *ARVIN | KER | 93203 | 78 E4 |
| ASHFORD JUNCTION | INY | 92328 | 72 C4 |
| *ASHLAND | JKSN | | 3 E1 |
| ASPENDELL | INY | 93514 | 51 B5 |
| ASTI | SON | 95413 | 31 C5 |
| *ATASCADERO | SLO | 93422 | 76 A2 |
| *ATHERTON | SMCO | 94025 | N D2 |
| ATOLIA | SBD | 93558 | 80 E3 |
| *ATWATER | MCO | 95301 | 48 B4 |
| ATWOOD | ORA | 92670 | T E1 |
| *AUBURN | PLA | 95603 | 34 C3 |
| AUBURNDALE | RCO | 91760 | U E4 |
| *AVALON | LACO | 90704 | 97 E5 |
| AVENAL | KIN | 93204 | 66 E3 |
| AVERY | CAL | 95224 | 41 C3 |
| AVILA BEACH | SLO | 93424 | 76 A4 |
| AVON | CC | 94523 | 38 E4 |
| *AZUSA | LACO | 91702 | U A1 |
| **B** | | | |
| BABBITT | MIN | | 44 B1 |
| BADGER | TUL | 93603 | 58 D4 |
| BADWATER | INY | 92328 | 72 A2 |
| BAKER | SBD | 92309 | 83 B3 |
| *BAKERSFIELD | KER | 93301 | 78 D3 |
| BALBOA | ORA | 92661 | T C4 |
| BALBOA ISLAND | ORA | 92662 | T C4 |
| BALCH CAMP | FRCO | 93657 | 58 C2 |
| *BALDWIN PARK | LACO | 91706 | R D3 |
| BALLARAT | INY | 93562 | 71 C3 |
| BALLARD | SB | 93441 | 86 E3 |
| BALLENA | SDCO | 92065 | 107 B4 |
| BALLICO | MCO | 95303 | 48 A3 |
| BANGOR | BUT | 95914 | 25 E5 |
| BANKHEAD SPRINGS | SDCO | 92005 | 111 A4 |
| BANNER | SDCO | 92036 | 107 D4 |
| *BANNING | RCO | 92220 | 100 A3 |
| BARD | IMP | 92222 | 112 D5 |
| BARDSDALE | VEN | 93015 | 88 D4 |
| BARRETT JUNCTION | SDCO | 92017 | 112 B2 |
| BARSTOW | FRCO | 93702 | 57 B3 |
| *BARSTOW | SBD | 92311 | 91 E1 |
| BARTLETT | INY | 93545 | 60 B5 |
| BARTLETT SPRINGS | LAK | 95443 | 32 A2 |
| BARTON | AMA | 92309 | 41 B2 |
| BASSETT | LACO | 91746 | R D4 |
| BASSETTS | SIE | 96125 | 27 A4 |
| BASS LAKE | MAD | 93604 | 49 E4 |
| BAXTER | PLA | 95704 | 34 E1 |
| BAYSHORE | SMCO | 94005 | L C5 |
| BAYSIDE | HUM | 95524 | 9 E5 |
| BAYWOOD PARK | SLO | 93401 | 75 E3 |
| BEAR HARBOR | MEN | 95489 | 22 B2 |
| BEAR VALLEY | ALP | 95223 | 41 E2 |
| BEAR VALLEY | MPA | 95338 | 48 E3 |
| BEAR VALLEY | SDCO | 92027 | 106 E3 |
| BEAR VALLEY SPRINGS | KER | 93561 | 79 B4 |
| BEATTY | NYE | | 62 B2 |
| BEATTY JUNCTION | INYO | 92328 | 61 E4 |
| *BEAUMONT | RCO | 92223 | 99 E3 |
| BECKWOURTH | PLU | 96129 | 27 C2 |
| BEE ROCK | SLO | 93928 | 65 D5 |
| BEL AIRE | MAR | 94920 | L B4 |
| BEL AIR ESTATES | LACO | 90077 | Q B4 |
| BELDEN | PLU | 95915 | 26 A1 |
| *BELL | LACO | 90201 | R B5 |
| BELLA VISTA | KER | 93283 | 79 E1 |
| BELLA VISTA | SHA | 96008 | 18 D2 |
| *BELLFLOWER | LACO | 90706 | S E1 |
| *BELL GARDENS | LACO | 90201 | R B5 |
| BELLOTA | SJCO | 95236 | 40 C4 |
| BELL SPRINGS | MEN | 95440 | 22 D1 |
| BEL MARIN KEYS | MAR | 94947 | L B2 |
| *BELMONT | SMCO | 94002 | N C2 |
| *BELVEDERE | MAR | 94920 | L B4 |
| BELVEDERE GARDENS | MAR | 94920 | L B4 |
| BENBOW | HUM | 95440 | 22 C1 |
| BEND | TEH | 96008 | 18 D4 |
| *BENICIA | SOL | 94510 | L E2 |
| BEN LOMOND | SCR | 95005 | N E5 |
| BENTON | MNO | 93512 | 51 C1 |
| BERENDA | MAD | 93637 | 56 E1 |
| *BERKELEY | ALA | 94701 | L D4 |
| BERMUDA DUNES | RCO | 92201 | 101 A4 |
| BERRY CREEK | BUT | 95916 | 25 E3 |
| BERRYESSA HIGHLANDS | NAPA | 94558 | 38 D1 |
| BERRYESSA PINES | NAPA | 94567 | 38 C1 |
| BERTELEDA | DN | 95531 | 2 A4 |
| BERTSCH TERRACE | DN | 95531 | 1 E4 |
| BETHANY | SJCO | 95376 | M E5 |
| BETHEL ISLAND | CC | 94511 | M D3 |
| BETTERAVIA | SB | 93455 | 86 B1 |
| *BEVERLY HILLS | LACO | 90210 | Q C3 |
| BIEBER | LAS | 96009 | 14 B3 |
| BIG BAR | AMA | 95704 | 41 A2 |
| BIG BEAR CITY | SBD | 92314 | 92 A5 |
| *BIG BEAR LAKE | SBD | 92315 | 92 A5 |
| BIG BEND | SHA | 96011 | 13 A4 |
| BIG BEND | SON | 95476 | 38 B3 |
| BIG CREEK | FRCO | 93605 | 50 B5 |
| *BIGGS | BUT | 95917 | 25 B5 |
| BIG MEADOW | CAL | 95223 | 41 E2 |
| BIG OAK FLAT | TUO | 95305 | 48 D1 |
| BIG PINE | INY | 93513 | 51 E5 |
| BIG RIVER | SBD | 92242 | 104 A1 |
| BIG SPRINGS | SIS | | 4 C5 |
| BIG SUR | MON | 93920 | 64 B2 |
| BINGHAMTON | SOL | 95625 | 39 B2 |
| BIOLA | FRCO | 93606 | 57 B3 |
| BIRCH HILL | SDCO | 92060 | 107 A2 |
| BIRCHVILLE | NEV | | 34 C1 |
| BIRDS LANDING | SOL | 94512 | 39 B4 |
| *BISHOP | INY | 93514 | 51 D4 |
| BITTERWATER | SBT | 93930 | 65 C1 |
| BLACKHAWK | CC | 94526 | M B4 |
| BLACK POINT | MAR | 94947 | L B2 |
| BLACKWELLS CORNER | KER | 93249 | 77 C1 |
| BLAIRSDEN | PLU | 96103 | 27 A2 |
| BLOCKSBURG | HUM | 95414 | 16 D4 |
| BLOOMINGTON | SBD | 92316 | 99 A2 |
| BLOSSOM | TEH | 96080 | 18 B5 |
| BLOSSOM VALLEY | SDCO | 92021 | 107 A5 |
| BLUE DIAMOND | CLK | | 74 B3 |
| BLUE JAY | SBD | 92317 | 91 C5 |
| *BLUE LAKE | HUM | 95525 | 10 A5 |
| BLUE LAKES | LAK | 95493 | 31 C2 |
| *BLYTHE | RCO | 92225 | 103 D5 |
| BOCA | NEV | 95737 | 27 E5 |
| BODEGA | SON | 94922 | 37 C3 |
| BODEGA BAY | SON | 94923 | 37 C3 |
| BODFISH | KER | 93205 | 79 C1 |
| BODIE | MNO | 93517 | 43 D3 |
| BOLINAS | MAR | 94924 | 37 E5 |
| BOLSA KNOLLS | MON | 93906 | 54 C3 |
| BOMBAY BEACH | IMP | 92257 | 108 E2 |
| *BONANZA | KLAM | | 5 E1 |
| BONDS CORNER | IMP | 92250 | 112 C4 |
| BONITA | SDCO | 92002 | V D4 |
| BONNEFOY | AMA | 95642 | 41 A2 |
| BONSALL | SDCO | 92003 | 106 C2 |
| BOONVILLE | MEN | 95415 | 30 E3 |
| BOOTJACK | MPA | 95338 | 49 B3 |
| BORON | KER | 93516 | 80 E5 |
| BORREGO | SDCO | 92004 | 107 E3 |
| BORREGO SPRINGS | SDCO | 92004 | 107 E2 |
| BOSTONIA | SDCO | 92021 | V E2 |
| BOULDER CREEK | SCR | 95006 | N E5 |
| BOULDER OAKS | SDCO | 92062 | 112 D1 |
| BOULEVARD | SDCO | 92005 | 111 A4 |
| BOUSE | LPAZ | 92363 | 104 D3 |
| BOWLES | FRCO | 93725 | 57 C4 |
| BOWMAN | PLA | 95707 | 34 C3 |
| BOYES HOT SPRINGS | SON | 95476 | 38 B3 |
| BOYLE HEIGHTS | LACO | 90033 | R A4 |
| *BRADBURY | LACO | 91010 | R E3 |
| BRADLEY | MON | 93426 | 65 E4 |
| BRANSCOMB | MEN | 95417 | 22 D3 |
| *BRAWLEY | IMP | 92227 | 109 A4 |
| *BREA | ORA | 92621 | T D1 |
| BRENDA | LPAZ | | 104 D4 |
| *BRENTWOOD | CC | 94513 | M D3 |
| BRENTWOOD | LACO | 90049 | Q B4 |
| BRICEBURG | MPA | 95345 | 49 B2 |
| BRICELAND | HUM | 95440 | 16 B5 |
| BRIDGE HAVEN | SON | 95450 | 37 C2 |
| BRIDGE HOUSE | SAC | 95683 | 40 C2 |
| BRIDGEPORT | MPA | 95306 | 49 A4 |
| BRIDGEPORT | MNO | 93517 | 43 B3 |
| BRIDGEPORT | NEV | 95975 | 34 B1 |
| BRIDGEVIEW | JOS | | 2 D1 |
| BRIDGEVILLE | HUM | 95526 | 16 C3 |
| *BRISBANE | SMCO | 94005 | L C5 |
| BRITE VALLEY | KER | 93561 | 79 C4 |
| BRODERICK | YOL | 95605 | 39 D1 |
| BROOKDALE | SCR | 95007 | N E5 |
| BROOKINGS | CUR | | 1 D2 |
| BROOKS | YOL | 95606 | 32 D5 |
| BROWNS VALLEY | YUB | 95918 | 33 E1 |
| BROWNSVILLE | YUB | 95919 | 26 A4 |
| BRUCEVILLE | SAC | 95683 | 39 E3 |
| BRUSH CREEK | BUT | 95916 | 25 E3 |
| BRYN MAWR | SBD | 92318 | 99 C2 |
| BRYTE | YOL | 95605 | 39 D1 |
| BUCKEYE | ED | 95634 | 34 E3 |
| BUCKEYE | SHA | 96003 | 18 B2 |
| BUCKHORN | AMA | 95666 | 41 B2 |
| BUCKHORN SPRINGS | JKSN | | 4 B2 |
| BUCKMAN SPRINGS | SDCO | 92062 | 112 D1 |
| BUCK MEADOWS | MPA | 95321 | 49 A1 |
| BUCKS BAR | ED | 95684 | 35 A5 |
| BUCKS LAKE | PLU | 95971 | 26 B2 |
| BUELLTON | SB | 93427 | 86 D3 |
| BUENA | SDCO | 92083 | 106 C3 |
| *BUENA PARK | ORA | 90620 | T B1 |
| BUENA VISTA | AMA | 95640 | 40 D3 |
| BUHACH | MCO | 95340 | 48 B4 |
| BULLHEAD CITY | MOH | | 85 D4 |
| BUMMERVILLE | CAL | 95257 | 41 B2 |
| BUNTINGVILLE | LAS | 96114 | 21 B4 |
| *BURBANK | LACO | 91501 | Q E2 |
| BURDELL | MAR | 94947 | L A1 |
| *BURLINGAME | SMCO | 94010 | N C1 |
| BURNEY | SHA | 96013 | 13 C5 |
| BURNT RANCH | TRI | 95527 | 10 D5 |
| BURREL | FRCO | 93607 | 57 B5 |
| BURSON | CAL | 95225 | 40 D4 |
| BUTTE CITY | GLE | 95920 | 25 A5 |
| BUTTE MEADOWS | BUT | 95921 | 25 D1 |
| BUTTONWILLOW | KER | 93206 | 78 A3 |
| BYRON | CC | 94514 | M D4 |
| **C** | | | |
| CABAZON | RCO | 92230 | 100 B3 |
| CABBAGE PATCH | CAL | 95223 | 41 E2 |
| CADENASSO | YOL | 95607 | 32 E5 |
| CADIZ | SBD | 92319 | 94 B4 |
| CADWELL | SON | | 37 E2 |
| CAIRNS CORNER | TUL | 93247 | 68 C2 |
| CAJON JUNCTION | SBD | 92358 | 91 A5 |
| CAJON PASS | SBD | 92397 | 91 A5 |
| CALABASAS | LACO | 91302 | 97 B1 |
| CALAVERITAS | CAL | 95249 | 41 A3 |
| *CALEXICO | IMP | 92231 | 112 B4 |
| CALICO GHOST TOWN | SBD | 92398 | 82 A5 |
| CALIENTE | KER | 93518 | 79 B3 |
| *CALIFORNIA CITY | KER | 93505 | 80 B4 |
| CALIFORNIA HOT SPRINGS | TUL | 93207 | 69 B4 |
| CALIFORNIA VALLEY | SLO | 93453 | 77 B3 |
| CALIMESA | RCO | 92320 | 99 D2 |
| *CALIPATRIA | IMP | 92233 | 109 B3 |
| *CALISTOGA | NAPA | 94515 | 38 A1 |
| CALLAHAN | SIS | 96014 | 11 D2 |
| CALNEVA | LAS | 96113 | 21 E5 |
| CALPELLA | MEN | 95418 | 31 B1 |
| CALPINE | SIE | 96124 | 27 B3 |
| CALWA | FRCO | 93725 | 57 C3 |
| *CAMARILLO | VEN | 93010 | 96 C1 |
| CAMBRIA | SLO | 93428 | 75 C2 |
| CAMDEN | FRCO | 93656 | 57 C5 |
| CAMERON CORNERS | SDCO | 92006 | 112 D2 |
| CAMERON PARK | ED | 95682 | 34 C5 |
| CAMINO | ED | 95709 | 35 A4 |
| *CAMPBELL | SCL | 95008 | P B4 |
| CAMP CONIFER | TUL | 93271 | 59 A5 |
| CAMP CONNELL | CAL | 95223 | 41 D3 |
| CAMP KLAMATH | DN | 95548 | 2 A5 |
| CAMP MEEKER | SON | 95419 | 37 D2 |
| CAMPO | SDCO | 92006 | 112 D2 |
| CAMPO SECO | CAL | 95226 | 40 E3 |
| CAMP SIERRA | FRCO | 93634 | 50 B5 |
| CAMPTONVILLE | YUB | 95922 | 26 B5 |
| CANBY | MOD | 96015 | 14 D1 |
| CANE BRAKE | KER | 93255 | 70 B5 |
| CANOGA PARK | LACO | 91303 | Q A2 |
| CANTIL | KER | 93519 | 80 C3 |
| CANTUA CREEK | FRCO | 93608 | 56 D5 |
| CANYON CITY | SDCO | 92006 | 112 D2 |
| CANYON COUNTRY | LACO | 91351 | 89 C4 |
| CANYON CREST HEIGHTS | RCO | 92507 | 99 B2 |
| CANYON DAM | PLU | 95923 | 20 C5 |
| CANYON LAKE | RCO | 92380 | 99 C4 |
| CAPAY | YOL | 95607 | 32 E5 |
| CAPETOWN | HUM | 95536 | 15 C3 |
| CAPISTRANO BEACH | ORA | 92624 | 105 D1 |
| *CAPITOLA | SCR | 95010 | 54 A2 |
| CARBONDALE | AMA | 95640 | 40 C2 |
| CARDIFF-BY-THE-SEA | SDCO | 92007 | 106 B4 |
| CARL INN | TUO | 95321 | 49 C1 |
| CARLOTTA | HUM | 95528 | 16 A2 |
| *CARLSBAD | SDCO | 92008 | 106 B3 |
| *CARMEL | MON | 93921 | 54 A5 |
| CARMEL HIGHLANDS | MON | 93921 | 54 A5 |
| CARMEL VALLEY VILLAGE | MON | 93924 | 54 C5 |
| CARMET | SON | 94923 | 37 C2 |
| CARMICHAEL | SAC | 95608 | 34 A5 |
| CARNELIAN BAY | PLA | 95711 | 36 A1 |
| CARPENTERVILLE | CUR | | 1 C1 |
| *CARPINTERIA | SB | 93013 | 87 E4 |
| CARQUINEZ HEIGHTS | SOL | 94590 | 38 C4 |
| *CARSON | LACO | 90745 | S C2 |
| *CARSON CITY | CRSN | | 36 C2 |
| CARSON HILL | CAL | 95222 | 41 B4 |
| CARTAGO | INY | 93549 | 70 B1 |
| CARUTHERS | FRCO | 93609 | 57 C5 |
| CASA BLANCA | RCO | 92504 | 99 B3 |
| CASA DE ORO | SDCO | 92077 | V E3 |
| CASITAS SPRINGS | VEN | 93001 | 88 A4 |
| CASMALIA | SB | 93429 | 86 B1 |
| CASPER | MEN | 95420 | 22 B5 |
| CASSEL | SHA | 96016 | 13 D5 |
| CASTAIC | LACO | 91310 | 89 B4 |
| CASTELLA | SHA | 96017 | 12 C3 |
| CASTELLAMMARE | LACO | 90290 | Q A4 |
| CASTLE CRAG | SHA | 96013 | 12 C3 |
| CASTLE PARK | SDCO | 92011 | V D5 |
| CASTRO VALLEY | ALA | 94546 | L E5 |
| CASTROVILLE | MON | 95012 | 54 B3 |
| *CATHEDRAL CITY | RCO | 92234 | 100 D4 |
| CATHEYS VALLEY | MPA | 95306 | 49 A3 |
| CAVE JUNCTION | JOS | | 2 D1 |
| CAYTON | SHA | 96013 | 13 C4 |
| CAYUCOS | SLO | 93430 | 75 D2 |
| CAZADERO | SON | 95421 | 37 C1 |
| CECILVILLE | SIS | 96018 | 11 B3 |
| CEDAR BROOK | FRCO | 93641 | 58 D3 |
| CEDAR CREST | FRCO | 93605 | 50 C5 |
| CEDAR FLAT | PLA | 95711 | 35 E1 |
| CEDAR GLEN | SBD | 92321 | 91 D5 |
| CEDAR GROVE | ED | 95709 | 35 A4 |
| CEDAR GROVE | FRCO | 93641 | 59 B3 |
| CEDARPINES PARK | SBD | 92322 | 91 B5 |
| CEDAR RIDGE | TUO | 95370 | 41 D4 |
| CEDAR VALLEY | MAD | 93644 | 49 D4 |
| CEDARVILLE | MOD | 96104 | 7 D5 |
| CENTERVILLE | ALA | 94536 | P A2 |
| CENTERVILLE | DGL | | 36 C3 |
| CENTERVILLE | FRCO | 93654 | 57 E3 |
| CENTERVILLE | SHA | 96001 | 18 B2 |
| CENTRAL VALLEY | SHA | 96019 | 18 C1 |
| CENTURY CITY | LACO | 90067 | Q D4 |
| *CERES | STA | 95307 | 47 D3 |
| *CERRITOS | LACO | 90701 | T B1 |
| CHALFANT | MNO | 93514 | 51 D3 |
| CHALLENGE | YUB | 95925 | 26 B4 |
| CHAMBERS LODGE | PLA | 95718 | 35 E2 |
| CHARLESTON PARK | CLK | | 74 A2 |
| CHATSWORTH | LACO | 91311 | Q A1 |
| CHAWANAKEE | FRCO | 93602 | 50 A5 |
| CHEMEKETA PARK | SCL | 95030 | P A4 |
| CHEROKEE | BUT | 95965 | 25 D3 |
| CHEROKEE | NEV | 93602 | 26 C5 |
| CHERRY VALLEY | RCO | 92223 | 99 E2 |
| CHESTER | PLU | 96020 | 20 A4 |
| CHICAGO PARK | NEV | 95712 | 34 C2 |
| *CHICO | BUT | 95926 | 25 B3 |
| CHILCOOT | PLU | 96105 | 27 D2 |
| CHINATOWN | SFCO | 94108 | 142 D2 |
| CHINESE CAMP | TUO | 95309 | 41 B5 |
| *CHINO | SBD | 91710 | U D3 |
| CHINQUAPIN | MPA | 95389 | 49 D2 |
| CHIQUITA LAKE | ED | 95634 | 35 A3 |
| CHLORIDE CITY | INY | 92328 | 62 A4 |

*INDICATES INCORPORATED CITY

CITIES

# CITIES AND COMMUNITIES INDEX


| COMMUNITY NAME | CO. | ZIP CODE | PAGE & GRID |
|---|---|---|---|
| CHOCTAW VALLEY | KER | 93306 | 78 E2 |
| CHOLAME | SLO | 93431 | 66 D5 |
| *CHOWCHILLA | MAD | 93610 | 48 D5 |
| CHROME | GLE | 95963 | 24 A3 |
| CHUALAR | MON | 93925 | 54 D4 |
| *CHULA VISTA | SDCO | 92010 | V D4 |
| CIBOLA | LPAZ | | 110 D2 |
| CIENEGA SPRINGS | LPAZ | | 104 C1 |
| CIMA | SBD | 92323 | 84 B4 |
| CIRCLE OAKS | NAPA | 94599 | 38 D2 |
| CISCO | PLA | 95728 | 35 B1 |
| CITRUS HEIGHTS | SAC | 95610 | 34 A5 |
| CLAIREMONT | SDCO | 92117 | V B2 |
| CLARAVILLE | KER | 93283 | 79 D2 |
| *CLAREMONT | LACO | 91711 | U C2 |
| CLARK | STOR | | 28 E4 |
| CLARKSBURG | YOL | 95612 | 39 D2 |
| CLARKSVILLE | ED | 95682 | 34 C5 |
| CLAY | SAC | 95638 | 40 B3 |
| *CLAYTON | CC | 94517 | M B3 |
| CLEAR CREEK | SIS | 96039 | 2 E4 |
| *CLEARLAKE | LAK | 95422 | 32 A3 |
| CLEARLAKE KEYS | LAK | 95423 | 32 A3 |
| CLEARLAKE OAKS | LAK | 95423 | 32 A3 |
| CLEMENTS | SJCO | 95227 | 40 C3 |
| CLEONE | MEN | 95437 | 22 C4 |
| CLIFF HOUSE | TUO | 95321 | 49 B1 |
| CLINTON | AMA | 95232 | 41 A2 |
| CLIPPER GAP | PLA | 95703 | 34 C3 |
| CLIPPER MILLS | BUT | 95930 | 26 A4 |
| CLOVERDALE | SHA | 96007 | 18 B3 |
| *CLOVERDALE | SON | 95425 | 31 C4 |
| *CLOVIS | FRCO | 93612 | 57 D3 |
| CLYDE | CC | 94520 | M A3 |
| *COACHELLA | RCO | 92236 | 101 B4 |
| *COALINGA | FRCO | 93210 | 66 D3 |
| COALINGA MINERAL SPGS | FRCO | 93210 | 66 B2 |
| COARSEGOLD | MAD | 93614 | 49 C4 |
| COBB | LAK | 95426 | 31 E4 |
| COCKATOO GROVE | SDCO | 92010 | V E4 |
| CODORA | GLE | 95970 | 25 A5 |
| COFFEE CREEK | TRI | 96091 | 11 E3 |
| COHASSET | BUT | 95926 | 25 C1 |
| COLD SPRINGS | TUO | 95370 | 42 A3 |
| COLES STATION | ED | 95684 | 35 B5 |
| COLEVILLE | MNO | 96107 | 42 D1 |
| *COLFAX | PLA | 95713 | 34 D2 |
| COLLEGE CITY | COL | 95931 | 33 A3 |
| COLLEGEVILLE | SJCO | 95206 | 40 B5 |
| COLLIERVILLE | SJCO | 95220 | 40 B3 |
| COLLINSVILLE | SOL | 94585 | 39 B4 |
| *COLMA | SMCO | 94015 | L B5 |
| COLOMA | ED | 95613 | 34 D4 |
| *COLTON | SBD | 92324 | 99 B2 |
| COLUMBIA | TUO | 95310 | 41 C4 |
| *COLUSA | COL | 95932 | 32 E2 |
| *COMMERCE | LACO | 90040 | R B4 |
| COMPTCHE | MEN | 95427 | 30 C1 |
| *COMPTON | LACO | 90220 | S C1 |
| *CONCORD | CC | 94520 | M A3 |
| CONFIDENCE | TUO | 95370 | 41 D4 |
| CONSTANTIA | LAS | 96019 | 27 E1 |
| COOKS STATION | AMA | 95666 | 41 C1 |
| COOLIDGE SPRING | IMP | | 108 C1 |
| COPCO | SIS | 96044 | 4 C2 |
| COPPEROPOLIS | CAL | 95228 | 41 A5 |
| *CORCORAN | KIN | 93212 | 67 E3 |
| CORDELIA | SOL | 93063 | L E1 |
| *CORNING | TEH | 96021 | 24 D2 |
| *CORONA | RCO | 91720 | U E4 |
| CORONA DEL MAR | ORA | 92625 | T C5 |
| *CORONADO | SDCO | 92118 | V B4 |
| *CORTE MADERA | MAR | 94925 | L A3 |
| COSO JUNCTION | INY | 93542 | 70 C3 |
| *COSTA MESA | ORA | 92626 | T C4 |
| COSUMNES | SAC | 95683 | 40 B2 |
| *COTATI | SON | 94928 | 37 E3 |
| COTO DE CAZA | ORA | 92678 | 98 E4 |
| COTTAGE SPRINGS | CAL | 95223 | 41 D2 |
| COTTON CENTER | TUL | 93257 | 68 C3 |
| COTTONWOOD | SHA | 96022 | 18 C3 |
| COULTERVILLE | MPA | 95311 | 48 D2 |
| COURTLAND | SAC | 95615 | 39 D3 |
| COVELO | MEN | 95428 | 23 A3 |
| *COVINA | LACO | 91722 | U A2 |
| COVINGTON MILL | TRI | 96052 | 11 E5 |
| COWAN HEIGHTS | ORA | 92705 | 98 C4 |
| COW HOLLOW | SFCO | 94123 | 142 A2 |
| COYOTE | SCL | 95013 | P D4 |
| COYOTE WELLS | IMP | 92259 | 111 C3 |
| COZZENS CORNERS | SON | 95441 | 31 D5 |
| CRAFTON | SBD | 92373 | 99 D2 |
| CRANMORE | SUT | 95645 | 33 B3 |
| CRANNELL | HUM | 95530 | 9 E4 |
| *CRESCENT CITY | DN | 95531 | 1 D4 |
| CRESCENT MILLS | PLU | 95934 | 20 C5 |
| CRESSEY | MCO | 95312 | 48 A4 |
| CREST | SDCO | 92021 | 112 A1 |
| CRESTLINE | SBD | 92325 | 91 C5 |
| CRESTMORE | SBD | 92316 | 99 B2 |
| CRESTON | SLO | 93432 | 76 B2 |
| CRESTVIEW | MNO | 93514 | 50 D1 |
| CROCKETT | CC | 94525 | L D3 |
| CROMBERG | PLU | 96103 | 27 A2 |
| CROWN POINT | SDCO | 92109 | V A3 |
| CROWS LANDING | SIS | 95313 | 47 C4 |
| *CRYSTAL BAY | DGL | | 36 A1 |
| *CUDAHY | LACO | 90201 | R B5 |
| CUESTA BY THE SEA | SLO | 93402 | 75 D3 |
| *CULVER CITY | LACO | 90230 | Q D4 |
| CUMMINGS | MEN | 95477 | 22 D2 |
| CUMMINGS VALLEY | KER | 93561 | 79 B4 |
| CUNNINGHAM | SON | 95472 | 37 E2 |
| *CUPERTINO | SCL | 95014 | P A3 |
| CURRY VILLAGE | MPA | 95389 | 49 D2 |
| CUTLER | TUL | 93615 | 58 B5 |
| CUTTEN | HUM | 95534 | 15 E1 |
| CUYAMA | SB | 93214 | 87 D1 |
| CUYAMACA | SDCO | 92036 | 107 C4 |
| *CYPRESS | ORA | 90630 | T B2 |
| D | | | |
| DAGGETT | SBD | 92327 | 92 A1 |
| DAIRY | KLAM | | 5 D1 |
| DAIRYVILLE | TEH | 96080 | 18 D5 |
| DALES | TEH | 96080 | 18 E4 |
| *DALY CITY | SMCO | 94014 | L B5 |
| DANA | SHA | 96036 | 13 D3 |
| DANA POINT | ORA | 92629 | 105 D1 |
| *DANVILLE | CC | 94526 | M A4 |
| DARDANELLE | TUO | 95314 | 42 B2 |
| DARLINGTONIA | DN | 95543 | 2 A3 |
| DARRAH | MPA | 95338 | 49 C3 |
| DARWIN | INY | 93522 | 70 E2 |
| DATE CITY | IMP | 92250 | 112 C3 |
| DAULTON | MAD | 93653 | 57 B1 |
| DAVENPORT | SCR | | 53 D2 |
| *DAVIS | YOL | 95616 | 39 C1 |
| DAVIS CREEK | MOD | 96108 | 7 C4 |
| DAVIS DAM | MOH | | 85 D4 |
| DAY | MOD | 96056 | 13 E3 |
| DAYTON | BUT | 95926 | 25 B3 |
| DAYTON | LYON | | 36 D1 |
| DE BON | SIS | 96034 | 12 C1 |
| DEER PARK | NAPA | 94576 | 38 B1 |
| DEHESA | SDCO | 92021 | 112 A1 |
| *DELANO | KER | 93215 | 68 B5 |
| DEL CERRO | SDCO | 92120 | V D3 |
| DEL DIOS | SDCO | 92025 | 106 D3 |
| DELEVAN | COL | 95988 | 24 D5 |
| DELFT COLONY | TUL | 93619 | 58 A5 |
| DELHI | MCO | 95315 | 47 E4 |
| DEL LOMA | TRI | 96010 | 17 A1 |
| *DEL MAR | SDCO | 92014 | V A1 |
| DEL PASO HEIGHTS | SAC | 95838 | 33 E5 |
| DEL REY | FRCO | 93616 | 57 E4 |
| *DEL REY OAKS | MON | 93940 | 54 B4 |
| DEL RIO WOODS | SON | 95448 | 37 E1 |
| DEL ROSA | SBD | 92404 | 99 C1 |
| DELTA | SHA | 96051 | 12 B4 |
| DE LUZ | SDCO | 92055 | 106 B1 |
| DEMOCRAT HOT SPRINGS | KER | 93301 | 79 B2 |
| DENAIR | STA | 95316 | 47 E3 |
| DENNY | TRI | 95538 | 10 E5 |
| DENVERTON | SOL | 94585 | 39 A3 |
| DERBY ACRES | KER | 93268 | 77 E3 |
| DE SABLA | BUT | 95978 | 25 C2 |
| DESCANSO | SDCO | 92016 | 107 C5 |
| DESCANSO JUNCTION | SDCO | 92016 | 107 C5 |
| DESERT BEACH | RCO | 92254 | 101 D5 |
| DESERT HAVEN | RCO | 92240 | 100 D3 |
| *DESERT HOT SPRINGS | RCO | 92240 | 100 D2 |
| DESERT LAKE | KER | 93516 | 80 D5 |
| DESERT SHORES | IMP | 92274 | 108 C1 |
| DEVILS DEN | KER | 93204 | 67 B5 |
| DEVORE | SBD | 92405 | 99 B1 |
| DIABLO | CC | 94528 | M B4 |
| DIABLO CASA HOT SPGS | MNO | 93546 | 50 E2 |
| DIAMOND BAR | LACO | 91765 | U B3 |
| DIAMOND SPRINGS | ED | 95619 | 34 E5 |
| DI GIORGIO | KER | 93217 | 79 A3 |
| DILLON BEACH | MAR | 94929 | 37 D3 |
| DINKEY CREEK | FRCO | 93617 | 58 C1 |
| *DINUBA | TUL | 93618 | 58 A5 |
| DISCOVERY BAY | CC | 94514 | 39 D5 |
| DIXIELAND | IMP | 92251 | 108 D5 |
| *DIXON | SOL | 95620 | 39 B2 |
| DOBBINS | YUB | 95935 | 26 B5 |
| DOG TOWN | CAL | 95249 | 41 B4 |
| DOGTOWN | MPA | 95311 | 48 E2 |
| DOGTOWN | SJCO | 95220 | 40 C3 |
| DORRINGTON | CAL | 95223 | 41 D3 |
| *DORRIS | SIS | 96023 | 5 A2 |
| *DOS PALOS | MCO | 93620 | 56 B2 |
| DOS PALOS Y | MCO | 93620 | 56 A1 |
| DOS RIOS | MEN | 95429 | 23 A3 |
| DOUGLAS CITY | TRI | 96024 | 17 D2 |
| *DOWNEY | LACO | 90241 | R B5 |
| DOWNIEVILLE | SIE | 95936 | 26 D4 |
| DOYLE | LAS | 96019 | 27 E1 |
| DOYLES CORNER | SHA | 96040 | 13 D5 |
| DOZIER | SOL | 94535 | 39 B3 |
| DRYTOWN | AMA | 95699 | 40 E2 |
| *DUARTE | LACO | 91010 | R D3 |
| *DUBLIN | ALA | 94566 | M B5 |
| DUCOR | TUL | 93218 | 68 D4 |
| DULZURA | SDCO | 92017 | 112 B2 |
| DUNCANS MILLS | SON | 95430 | 37 C2 |
| DUNLAP | FRCO | 93621 | 58 C3 |
| DUNLAP | MEN | 95490 | 30 D1 |
| DUNMOVIN | INY | 93542 | 70 C3 |
| DUNNIGAN | YOL | 95937 | 33 A4 |
| *DUNSMUIR | SIS | 96025 | 12 D3 |
| DURHAM | BUT | 95938 | 25 B3 |
| DUSTIN ACRES | KER | 93268 | 78 A4 |
| DUTCH FLAT | PLA | 95714 | 34 D1 |
| DYER | ESM | | 52 B2 |
| E | | | |
| EAGLE LAKE RESORT | LAS | 96130 | 20 D2 |
| EAGLE MOUNTAIN | RCO | 92241 | 102 B3 |
| EAGLE ROCK | LACO | 90041 | R A3 |
| EAGLES NEST | SDCO | 92086 | 107 C2 |
| EAGLEVILLE | MOD | 96110 | 8 D2 |
| EARLIMART | TUL | 93219 | 68 B4 |
| EARP | SBD | 92242 | 104 B1 |
| EAST BAKERSFIELD | KER | 93307 | 78 D3 |
| EAST HIGHLANDS | SBD | 92346 | 99 C1 |
| EAST IRVINE | ORA | 92720 | T E4 |
| EAST LAKE | ORA | 92686 | T E1 |
| EAST NICOLAUS | SUT | 95622 | 33 D3 |
| EASTON | FRCO | 93706 | 57 C4 |
| EAST OROSI | TUL | 93647 | 58 B5 |
| *EAST PALO ALTO | SMCO | 94303 | N E2 |
| EAST QUINCY | PLU | 95971 | 26 D1 |
| EAST SAN DIEGO | SDCO | 92105 | V C3 |
| EASTSIDE ACRES | MAD | 93622 | 56 C3 |
| EASTSIDE RANCH | MAD | 93622 | 56 C3 |
| ECHO DELL | SDCO | 92016 | 107 C5 |
| ECHO LAKE | ED | 95721 | 35 B4 |
| EDEN GARDENS | SDCO | 92075 | 106 B4 |
| EDEN HOT SPRINGS | RCO | 92353 | 99 D3 |
| EDGEWOOD | SIS | 96094 | 12 C1 |
| EDISON | KER | 93220 | 78 E3 |
| EDNA | SLO | 93401 | 76 B4 |
| EDWARDS AIR FORCE BASE | KER | 93523 | 90 C1 |
| EEL ROCK | HUM | 95554 | 16 C4 |
| EHRENBERG | YUMA | | 103 E5 |
| EL BONITA | SON | 95446 | 37 C1 |
| *EL CAJON | SDCO | 92020 | V E3 |
| *EL CENTRO | IMP | 92243 | 109 A5 |
| *EL CERRITO | CC | 94530 | L C3 |
| ELDERS CORNERS | PLA | 95603 | 34 C3 |
| ELDERWOOD | TUL | 93286 | 58 C5 |
| EL DORADO | ED | 95623 | 34 D5 |
| EL DORADO HILLS | ED | 95630 | 34 C5 |
| ELDRIDGE | SON | 95431 | 38 B3 |
| ELECTRA | AMA | 95642 | 41 A2 |
| EL GRANADA | SMCO | 94018 | N B2 |
| ELIZABETH LAKE | LACO | 93550 | 89 D3 |
| ELK | MEN | 95432 | 30 C2 |
| ELK CREEK | GLE | 95939 | 24 A4 |
| ELK GROVE | SAC | 95624 | 39 E2 |
| ELK VALLEY | DN | 95543 | 2 C2 |
| ELLWOOD | SB | 93117 | 87 B4 |
| ELMIRA | SOL | 95625 | 39 B2 |
| EL MODENA | ORA | 92669 | T E2 |
| *EL MONTE | LACO | 91731 | R D3 |
| *ELMORE | IMP | 92227 | 108 D3 |
| ELM VIEW | FRCO | 93725 | 57 C4 |
| EL NIDO | MCO | 95317 | 56 C1 |
| *EL PASO DE ROBLES | SLO | 93446 | 76 A1 |
| EL PORTAL | MPA | 95318 | 49 C2 |
| EL PORVENIR | FRE | 93608 | 56 C5 |
| EL PRADO | SDCO | 92104 | V B3 |
| *EL SEGUNDO | LACO | 90245 | Q C5 |
| EL SERENO | LACO | 90031 | R A3 |
| EL SOBRANTE | CC | 94803 | L D3 |
| EL TORO | ORA | 92630 | 98 D4 |
| EL TORO MARINE BASE | ORA | 92709 | 98 D4 |
| EL VERANO | SON | 95433 | L B1 |
| ELVERTA | SAC | 95626 | 33 E5 |
| EMERALD BAY | ED | 95733 | 35 E3 |
| EMERALD BAY | ORA | 92651 | T D5 |
| *EMERYVILLE | ALA | 94608 | L C4 |
| EMIGRANT GAP | PLA | 95715 | 35 A1 |
| EMMATON | SAC | | M D2 |
| EMPIRE | STA | 95319 | 47 D2 |
| ENCANTO | SDCO | 92114 | V D4 |
| *ENCINITAS | SDCO | 92024 | 106 B4 |
| ENCINO | LACO | 91316 | Q B3 |
| ENGINEER SPRINGS | SDCO | 92017 | 112 B2 |
| ENTERPRISE | SHA | 96001 | 18 C2 |
| *ESCALON | SJCO | 95320 | 47 C1 |
| *ESCONDIDO | SDCO | 92025 | 106 D3 |
| ESPARTO | YOL | 95627 | 33 A5 |
| ESSEX | SBD | 92332 | 94 D2 |
| ESTRELLA | SLO | 93415 | 76 B1 |
| ETHEDA SPRINGS | FRCO | 93633 | 58 D4 |
| *ETNA | SIS | 96027 | 11 D1 |
| ETTERSBURG | HUM | 95440 | 16 A5 |
| EUCALYPTUS HILLS | SDCO | 92040 | V E2 |
| *EUREKA | HUM | 95501 | 15 E1 |
| EUREKA VALLEY | SFCO | 94114 | 45 B2 |
| EVELYN | INY | 92384 | 72 E2 |
| *EXETER | TUL | 93221 | 68 C1 |
| F | | | |
| *FAIRFAX | MAR | 94930 | L A3 |
| *FAIRFIELD | SOL | 94533 | M A1 |
| FAIRHAVEN | HUM | 95564 | 15 D1 |
| FAIRMEAD | MAD | 93610 | 56 D1 |
| FAIRMONT | LACO | 93534 | 89 C2 |
| FAIR OAKS | SAC | 95628 | 34 A5 |
| FAIR PLAY | ED | 95684 | 41 A1 |
| FAIRVIEW | TUL | 93238 | 69 C4 |
| FALES HOT SPRINGS | MNO | 93517 | 43 A2 |
| FALLBROOK | SDCO | 92028 | 106 C2 |
| FALLEN LEAF | ED | 95716 | 35 E4 |
| FALLON | MAR | 94932 | 37 D3 |
| FALL RIVER MILLS | SHA | 96028 | 13 E4 |
| FAMOSO | KER | 93250 | 78 C1 |
| *FARMERSVILLE | TUL | 93223 | 68 C1 |
| FAWNSKIN | SBD | 92333 | 91 E5 |
| FEATHER FALLS | BUT | 95940 | 26 A4 |
| FELLOWS | KER | 93224 | 77 E4 |
| FELIX | CAL | 95228 | 41 A4 |
| FELTON | SCR | 95018 | N E5 |
| FENNER | SBD | 92332 | 94 E2 |
| FERN | SHA | 96096 | 19 A1 |
| FERNBROOK | SDCO | 92065 | 107 A4 |
| *FERNDALE | HUM | 95536 | 15 D2 |
| FETTERS HOT SPRINGS | SON | 95476 | 38 B3 |
| FIDDLETOWN | AMA | 95629 | 40 E1 |
| FIELDBROOK | HUM | 95521 | 10 A4 |
| FIELDS LANDING | HUM | 95537 | 15 E1 |
| *FILLMORE | VEN | 93015 | 88 D4 |
| FINE GOLD | MAD | 93643 | 49 D5 |
| FINLEY | LAK | 95435 | 31 D3 |
| *FIREBAUGH | FRCO | 93622 | 56 C3 |
| FISH CAMP | MPA | 93623 | 49 D3 |
| FISH ROCK | MEN | 95445 | 30 D4 |
| FISH SPRINGS | INY | 93513 | 59 E1 |
| FIVE CORNERS | LAKE | | 7 B1 |
| FIVE CORNERS | SJCO | 95336 | 47 C1 |
| FIVE POINTS | FRCO | 93624 | 57 A5 |
| FIVE POINTS | LACO | 91732 | R D4 |
| FLEETRIDGE | SDCO | 92106 | V A3 |
| FLETCHER HILLS | SDCO | 92020 | V D2 |
| FLINN SPRINGS | SDCO | 92021 | 107 A5 |
| FLORIN | SAC | 95828 | 39 E2 |
| FLOURNOY | TEH | 96029 | 24 B2 |
| FLOWING WELLS | RCO | 92254 | 101 C5 |
| *FOLSOM | SAC | 95630 | 34 B5 |
| *FONTANA | SBD | 92335 | 99 B1 |
| FOOTHILL FARMS | SAC | 95841 | 34 A5 |
| FORBESTOWN | BUT | 95963 | 26 A4 |
| FORD CITY | KER | 93268 | 78 A4 |
| FOREST | SIE | 95910 | 26 D4 |
| FORESTA | MPA | 95389 | 49 C2 |
| FOREST FALLS | SBD | 92339 | 100 A2 |
| FOREST GLEN | TRI | 96030 | 17 A3 |
| FORESTHILL | PLA | 95631 | 34 D3 |
| FOREST HOME | AMA | 95640 | 40 C2 |
| FOREST KNOLLS | MAR | 94933 | 38 A5 |
| FOREST LAKE | LAK | 95461 | 32 A4 |
| FOREST RANCH | BUT | 95942 | 25 C2 |
| FOREST SPRINGS | NEV | 95945 | 34 C2 |
| FORESTVILLE | SON | 95436 | 37 D2 |
| FORKS OF SALMON | SIS | 96031 | 11 A2 |
| FORREST PARK | LACO | 91350 | 89 C4 |
| FORT BIDWELL | MOD | 96112 | 7 D3 |
| *FORT BRAGG | MEN | 95437 | 22 C5 |
| FORT DICK | DN | 95538 | 1 D3 |
| FORT IRWIN | SBD | 92311 | 82 B3 |
| *FORT JONES | SIS | 96032 | 3 D5 |
| FORT ORD VILLAGE | MON | 93941 | 54 B4 |
| FORT ROSS | SON | 95450 | 37 B1 |
| FORT SEWARD | HUM | 95438 | 16 D5 |
| *FORTUNA | HUM | 95540 | 15 E2 |
| FOSTER | SDCO | 92040 | V E1 |
| *FOSTER CITY | SMCO | 94404 | N D1 |
| FOSTER PARK | VEN | 93001 | 88 A5 |
| FOUNTAIN SPRINGS | TUL | 93257 | 68 E4 |
| *FOUNTAIN VALLEY | ORA | 92708 | T C3 |
| FOUR CORNERS | SHA | 96016 | 13 C4 |
| FOUTS SPRINGS | COL | 95979 | 24 A5 |
| *FOWLER | FRCO | 93625 | 57 D4 |
| FRANKLIN | SAC | 95639 | 39 E2 |
| FRAZIER PARK | KER | 93225 | 88 D1 |
| FREDALBA | SBD | 92382 | 99 D1 |
| FREDERICKSBURG | ALP | 96120 | 36 B4 |
| FREDS PLACE | ED | 95720 | 35 D4 |
| FREEDOM | SCR | 95019 | 54 B2 |
| FREEMAN | KER | 93527 | 80 C1 |
| FREEPORT | SAC | 95832 | 39 E2 |
| FREESTONE | SON | 95472 | 37 D2 |
| *FREMONT | ALA | 94536 | P A2 |
| FREMONT VALLEY | KER | 93519 | 80 B4 |
| FRENCH CAMP | SJCO | 95231 | 40 B5 |
| FRENCH CORRAL | NEV | 95975 | 34 B1 |
| FRENCH GULCH | SHA | 96033 | 18 A1 |
| FRESH POND | ED | 95725 | 35 B4 |
| FRESHWATER | HUM | 95504 | 16 A1 |
| *FRESNO | FRCO | 93706 | 57 C3 |
| FRIANT | FRCO | 93626 | 57 D2 |
| FROGTOWN | CAL | 95222 | 41 B4 |
| FRUITVALE | KER | 93308 | 78 C3 |
| FRUTO | GLE | 95988 | 24 B4 |
| FULLER ACRES | KER | 93307 | 78 E3 |
| *FULLERTON | ORA | 92631 | T C1 |
| FULTON | SON | 95439 | 37 E1 |
| FURNACE CREEK RANCH | INY | 92328 | 62 A5 |
| G | | | |
| GALLINAS | MAR | 94903 | L B3 |
| *GALT | SAC | 95632 | 40 A3 |
| GANNS | CAL | 95223 | 41 D2 |
| GARBERVILLE | HUM | 95440 | 16 C5 |
| *GARDENA | LACO | 90247 | S C1 |
| GARDEN FARMS | SLO | 93422 | 76 B2 |
| *GARDEN GROVE | ORA | 92640 | T C2 |
| GARDEN PARK | ED | 95633 | 34 D4 |
| GARDEN VALLEY | ED | 95633 | 34 D4 |
| GARDNERVILLE | DGL | | 36 C3 |
| GAREY | SB | 93454 | 86 C1 |
| GARFIELD | KER | 93240 | 79 C1 |
| GARLOCK | KER | 93519 | 80 D2 |
| GARNET | RCO | 92258 | 100 C3 |
| GASQUET | DN | 95543 | 2 A3 |
| GAVIOTA | SB | 93017 | 86 D4 |
| GAZELLE | SIS | 96034 | 4 B5 |
| GENESEE | PLU | 95983 | 26 E1 |
| GENOA | DGL | | 36 B3 |
| GEORGETOWN | ED | 95634 | 34 E3 |
| GERBER | TEH | 96035 | 24 E1 |
| GEYSERVILLE | SON | 95441 | 31 D5 |
| GIANT FOREST | TUL | 93271 | 59 A4 |
| GIBSONVILLE | SIE | 95981 | 26 D3 |
| GILMAN HOT SPRINGS | RCO | 92340 | 99 E3 |




*INDICATES INCORPORATED CITY

# CITIES AND COMMUNITIES INDEX

| COMMUNITY NAME | CO. | ZIP CODE | PAGE & GRID |
|---|---|---|---|
| *GILROY | SCL | 95020 | 54 D2 |
| GLAMIS | IMP | 92248 | 109 E4 |
| GLEN AVON | RCO | 92509 | 99 A2 |
| GLENBROOK | DGL | | 36 A2 |
| GLENBURN | SHA | 96036 | 13 D4 |
| GLENCOE | CAL | 95232 | 41 B2 |
| *GLENDALE | LACO | 91201 | Q E3 |
| *GLENDORA | LACO | 91740 | U A1 |
| GLEN ELLEN | SON | 95442 | 38 B2 |
| GLENHAVEN | LAK | 95443 | 31 E3 |
| GLENN | GLE | 95943 | 25 A4 |
| GLENNVILLE | KER | 93226 | 69 A5 |
| GLEN OAKS | SDCO | 92001 | 107 A5 |
| GLEN VALLEY | RCO | 92370 | 99 B3 |
| GLENVIEW | LAK | 95451 | 31 E4 |
| GLENVIEW | LACO | 90290 | Q A3 |
| GLENVIEW | SDCO | 92021 | 107 A5 |
| GOFFS | SBD | 92332 | 94 E1 |
| GOLDEN HILLS | KER | 93561 | 79 C4 |
| GOLDEN SHORES | MOH | 92363 | 95 E1 |
| GOLDEN VALLEY | WSH | | 28 B3 |
| GOLD HILL | ED | 95651 | 34 D4 |
| GOLD HILL | STOR | | 36 D1 |
| GOLD RUN | PLA | 95717 | 34 D2 |
| GOLD SPRINGS | TUO | 93570 | 41 C4 |
| GOLETA | SB | 93017 | 87 B4 |
| *GONZALES | MON | 93926 | 54 E5 |
| GONZALEZ ORTEGA | BAJA | | 112 C4 |
| GOOD HOPE | RCO | 92370 | 99 B4 |
| GOODSPRINGS | CLK | | 74 B4 |
| GOODYEARS BAR | SIE | 95944 | 26 D4 |
| GORDONS WELL | IMP | | 112 A5 |
| GORMAN | LACO | 93534 | 88 E2 |
| GOSHEN | TUL | 93227 | 68 A1 |
| GOTTVILLE | SIS | 96050 | 3 E3 |
| GOVERNMENT FLAT | TEH | 95939 | 23 D2 |
| GRAEAGLE | PLU | 96103 | 27 A3 |
| GRANADA HILLS | LACO | 91344 | Q A1 |
| *GRAND TERRACE | SBD | 92324 | 99 B2 |
| GRANGEVILLE | KIN | 93230 | 67 D1 |
| GRANITEVILLE | NEV | 95959 | 26 E5 |
| GRANTVILLE | SDCO | 92120 | V C3 |
| GRAPEVINE | KER | 93301 | 88 D1 |
| *GRASS VALLEY | NEV | 95945 | 34 C1 |
| GRATON | SON | 95444 | 37 D2 |
| GRAVESBORO | FRCO | 93657 | 58 A3 |
| GRAYSON | STA | 95363 | 47 B3 |
| GRAYS WELL | IMP | | 112 B5 |
| GREELEY HILL | MPA | 95311 | 48 E1 |
| GREENACRES | KER | 93308 | 78 C3 |
| GREEN ACRES | RCO | 92343 | 99 D4 |
| GREENBRAE | MAR | 94904 | L B3 |
| GREENFIELD | KER | 93309 | 78 D3 |
| *GREENFIELD | MON | 93927 | 65 B1 |
| GREEN POINT | MAR | 94947 | L B2 |
| GREEN VALLEY | LACO | 91350 | 89 C3 |
| GREEN VALLEY ESTATES | SOL | 94585 | 38 D3 |
| GREEN VALLEY FALLS | SDCO | 92016 | 107 C5 |
| GREEN VALLEY LAKE | SBD | 92341 | 91 D5 |
| GREENVIEW | SIS | 96037 | 3 D5 |
| GREENVILLE | PLU | 95947 | 20 C5 |
| GREENWOOD | ED | 95635 | 34 D3 |
| GRENADA | SIS | 96038 | 4 B4 |
| *GRIDLEY | BUT | 95948 | 25 C5 |
| GRIMES | COL | 95950 | 33 B2 |
| GRIZZLY FLAT | ED | 95636 | 35 B5 |
| GROSSMONT | SDCO | 92041 | V D3 |
| GROVELAND | TUO | 95321 | 48 E1 |
| *GROVER CITY | SLO | 93433 | 76 A4 |
| GROVERS HOT SPRINGS | ALP | 96120 | 36 B5 |
| *GUADALUPE | SB | 93434 | 76 B5 |
| GUALALA | MEN | 95445 | 30 D4 |
| GUASTI | SBD | 91743 | U E2 |
| GUATAY | SDCO | 92031 | 107 C5 |
| GUERNEVILLE | SON | 95446 | 37 C2 |
| GUERNEWOOD PARK | SON | 95446 | 37 C2 |
| GUINDA | YOL | 95637 | 32 D4 |
| *GUSTINE | MCO | 95322 | 47 C5 |
| H | | | |
| HACIENDA | SON | 95436 | 37 D1 |
| HACIENDA HEIGHTS | LACO | 91745 | R E5 |
| HAIGHT-ASHBURY | SFCO | 94117 | 142 A4 |
| *HALF MOON BAY | SMCO | 94019 | N C2 |
| HALLELUJAH JUNCTION | LAS | 96135 | 27 E2 |
| HALLWOOD | YUB | 95901 | 33 D2 |
| HAMBURG | SIS | 96045 | 3 C4 |
| HAMILTON BRANCH | PLU | 96137 | 20 C4 |
| HAMILTON CITY | GLE | 95951 | 24 E3 |
| HAMMOND | TUL | 93271 | 58 E5 |
| HAMMONTON | YUB | 95901 | 33 E2 |
| HAM'S STATION | AMA | 95666 | 41 C1 |
| *HANFORD | KIN | 93230 | 67 D1 |
| HAPPY CAMP | SIS | 96039 | 3 A4 |
| HARBIN SPRINGS | LAK | 95461 | 32 A4 |
| HARBISON CANYON | SDCO | 92021 | 107 A5 |
| HARBOR | CUR | | 1 D2 |
| HARBOR CITY | LACO | 90710 | S C2 |
| HARDWICK | KIN | 93230 | 67 D1 |
| HARMONY | SLO | 93435 | 75 C2 |
| HARMONY GROVE | SDCO | 92025 | 106 D3 |
| HARRIS | HUM | 95447 | 16 D5 |
| HARRISBURG | INY | 92328 | 71 C1 |
| HARRISON PARK | SDCO | 92036 | 107 C4 |
| HARTLEY | SOL | 95688 | 39 A2 |
| HART PARK | KER | 93306 | 78 E2 |
| HASKELL CREEK | SIE | 96124 | 27 B3 |
| HAT CREEK | SHA | 96040 | 13 D5 |
| HATFIELD | SIS | 96134 | 5 D2 |
| HAVILAH | KER | 93518 | 79 C2 |

| COMMUNITY NAME | CO. | ZIP CODE | PAGE & GRID |
|---|---|---|---|
| *HAWAIIAN GARDENS | LACO | 90716 | T A2 |
| HAWKINSVILLE | SIS | 96097 | 4 A4 |
| *HAWTHORNE | LACO | 90250 | Q D5 |
| HAWTHORNE | MIN | | 44 B1 |
| HAYFORK | TRI | 96041 | 17 B2 |
| *HAYWARD | ALA | 94544 | L E5 |
| HAZEL CREEK | SHA | 96017 | 12 C4 |
| *HEALDSBURG | SON | 95448 | 37 D1 |
| HEBER | IMP | 92249 | 112 A3 |
| HELENA | TRI | 96042 | 17 B1 |
| HELENDALE | SBD | 92342 | 91 B2 |
| HELLS GATE | INY | 92328 | 61 E3 |
| HELM | FRCO | 93627 | 57 A5 |
| HENDERSON | CLK | | 74 E3 |
| HENDERSON VILLAGE | SJCO | | 40 A4 |
| *HEMET | RCO | 92343 | 99 E4 |
| HENLEY | KLAM | | 5 C1 |
| HENLEY | SIS | 96044 | 4 A3 |
| HENLEYVILLE | TEH | 96021 | 24 C1 |
| HERALD | SAC | 95638 | 40 B3 |
| *HERCULES | CC | 94547 | L C3 |
| HERMIT VALLEY | ALP | 95314 | 42 B1 |
| *HERMOSA BEACH | LACO | 90254 | S A1 |
| HERNANDEZ | SBT | 95043 | 65 E1 |
| HERNDON | FRCO | 93711 | 57 B3 |
| HESPERIA | SBD | 92345 | 91 B4 |
| HESSEL | SON | 95472 | 37 E3 |
| HICKMAN | STA | 95323 | 47 E2 |
| HIDDEN GLEN | SDCO | 92001 | 112 B1 |
| *HIDDEN HILLS | LACO | 91302 | 97 A1 |
| HIDDEN MEADOWS | SDCO | 92026 | 106 D3 |
| HIDDEN VALLEY LAKE | LAK | 95461 | 32 B4 |
| HIDDEN VALLEY | PLA | 95650 | 34 B4 |
| HIGGINS CORNER | NEV | 95603 | 34 C3 |
| *HIGHLAND | SBD | 92346 | 99 C1 |
| HIGHLAND PARK | LACO | 90042 | R A3 |
| HIGHLANDS HARBOR | LAK | 95457 | 32 A3 |
| HIGHTS CORNER | KER | 93308 | 78 C2 |
| HIGHWAY CITY | FRCO | 93705 | 57 C3 |
| HIGHWAY HIGHLANDS | LACO | 91214 | Q E2 |
| HILLCREST | SHA | 96065 | 13 B5 |
| HILL HAVEN | MAR | 94920 | L B4 |
| *HILLSBOROUGH | SMCO | 94010 | N C1 |
| HILMAR | MCO | 95324 | 47 E4 |
| HILT | SIS | 96043 | 4 A2 |
| HINKLEY | SBD | 92347 | 91 C1 |
| HOAGLIN | TRI | 95495 | 16 E5 |
| HOBART MILLS | NEV | 95734 | 27 D5 |
| HOBERGS | LAK | 95496 | 31 E4 |
| HODSON | CAL | 95228 | 41 A5 |
| HOLLAND | JOS | | 2 D1 |
| *HOLLISTER | SBT | 95023 | 54 E3 |
| HOLLOW TREE | MEN | 95455 | 22 B2 |
| HOLLYWOOD | LACO | 90028 | Q D3 |
| HOLLYWOOD BEACH | VEN | 93043 | 96 A1 |
| HOLLYWOOD-BY-THE-SEA | VEN | 93043 | 96 A1 |
| HOLMES | HUM | 95569 | 16 B3 |
| HOLT | SJCO | 95234 | 39 E5 |
| *HOLTVILLE | IMP | 92250 | 109 B5 |
| HOLY CITY | SCL | 95026 | P B5 |
| HOME GARDENS | RCO | 91720 | 99 A3 |
| HOMELAND | RCO | 92348 | 99 D4 |
| HONCUT | BUT | 95965 | 33 D1 |
| HONEYDEW | HUM | 95545 | 15 E4 |
| HOOD | SAC | 95639 | 39 D2 |
| HOOPA | HUM | 95546 | 10 C4 |
| HOPE LANDING | SJCO | 95686 | 39 E3 |
| HOPETON | MCO | 95369 | 48 B3 |
| HOPE VLY FOREST CAMP | ALP | 96120 | 36 B5 |
| HOPLAND | MEN | 95449 | 31 B3 |
| HORNBROOK | SIS | 96044 | 4 B3 |
| HORNITOS | MPA | 95325 | 48 E3 |
| HORSE CREEK | SIS | 96045 | 3 C3 |
| HOT SPRINGS | KLAM | | 6 A1 |
| HOUGH SPRINGS | LAK | 95443 | 32 A2 |
| HOWLAND FLAT | SIE | 95981 | 26 D3 |
| HUASNA | SLO | 93420 | 76 D4 |
| *HUGHSON | STA | 95326 | 47 E2 |
| HULBURD GROVE | SDCO | 92016 | 107 C5 |
| HULLVILLE | LAK | 95469 | 23 C5 |
| HUME | FRCO | 93628 | 58 E3 |
| HUMPHREYS STATION | FRCO | 93612 | 58 A2 |
| *HUNTINGTON BEACH | ORA | 92646 | T B4 |
| HUNTINGTON LAKE | FRCO | 93634 | 50 B5 |
| *HUNTINGTON PARK | LACO | 90255 | R A5 |
| HURLETON | BUT | 95962 | 25 E4 |
| *HURON | FRCO | 93234 | 67 A2 |
| HYAMPOM | TRI | 96046 | 16 E2 |
| HYDESVILLE | HUM | 95547 | 15 E2 |
| I | | | |
| IDYLLWILD | RCO | 92349 | 100 B4 |
| IDYLWILD | SCL | 95030 | P B4 |
| IGNACIO | MAR | 94947 | L B2 |
| IGO | SHA | 96047 | 18 B3 |
| ILLINOIS VALLEY | JOS | | 2 C2 |
| *IMPERIAL | IMP | 92251 | 109 A5 |
| *IMPERIAL BEACH | SDCO | 92032 | V B5 |
| IMPERIAL GABLES | IMP | 92266 | 110 A3 |
| INCLINE | MPA | 95318 | 49 C2 |
| INCLINE VILLAGE | WSH | | 36 A1 |
| INDEPENDENCE | CAL | 95245 | 41 B2 |
| INDEPENDENCE | INY | 93526 | 60 A3 |
| INDIAN FALLS | PLU | 95952 | 26 C1 |
| INDIAN SPRINGS | SDCO | 92035 | 112 A1 |
| *INDIAN WELLS | RCO | 92260 | 100 E4 |
| *INDIO | RCO | 92201 | 101 A4 |
| *INDUSTRY | LACO | 91744 | R E4 |
| *INGLEWOOD | LACO | 90301 | Q D5 |
| INGOT | SHA | 96008 | 18 E1 |

| COMMUNITY NAME | CO. | ZIP CODE | PAGE & GRID |
|---|---|---|---|
| INSKIP | BUT | 95921 | 25 D1 |
| INVERNESS | MAR | 94937 | 37 D4 |
| INWOOD | SHA | 96088 | 19 A2 |
| INYOKERN | KER | 93527 | 80 D1 |
| *IONE | AMA | 95640 | 40 D2 |
| IOWA HILL | PLA | 95713 | 34 D2 |
| *IRVINE | ORA | 92715 | T E4 |
| IRVING'S CREST | SDCO | 92065 | 107 A4 |
| IRVINGTON | ALA | 94538 | P A2 |
| IRWIN | MCO | 95380 | 47 E4 |
| *IRWINDALE | LACO | 91706 | R E3 |
| ISLA VISTA | SB | 93017 | 87 B4 |
| *ISLETON | SAC | 95641 | M D2 |
| IVANHOE | TUL | 93235 | 68 B1 |
| IVANPAH | SBD | 92364 | 84 C3 |
| J | | | |
| *JACKSON | AMA | 95642 | 40 E2 |
| JACKSON GATE | AMA | 95642 | 40 E2 |
| JACUMBA | SDCO | 92034 | 111 B4 |
| JAMACHA | SDCO | 92035 | 106 E4 |
| JAMESBURG | MON | 93924 | 64 D1 |
| JAMESTOWN | TUO | 95327 | 41 C5 |
| JAMUL | SDCO | 92035 | 112 A1 |
| JANESVILLE | LAS | 96114 | 21 A4 |
| JARBO GAP | BUT | 95916 | 25 D3 |
| JENNER-BY-THE-SEA | SON | 95450 | 37 B2 |
| JENNY LIND | CAL | 95252 | 40 D4 |
| JESMOND DENE | SDCO | 92026 | 106 D3 |
| JIMGREY | SBD | 93516 | 81 A5 |
| JIMTOWN | SON | 95959 | 31 E5 |
| JOHANNESBURG | KER | 93528 | 80 D3 |
| JOHNSONDALE | TUL | 93236 | 69 C4 |
| JOHNSON PARK | SHA | 96013 | 13 C5 |
| JOHNSONS | HUM | 95546 | 10 B2 |
| JOHNSTONVILLE | LAS | 96130 | 21 A3 |
| JOHNSTOWN | SDCO | 92021 | 107 A5 |
| JOHNSVILLE | PLU | 95921 | 26 E3 |
| JOLON | MON | 93928 | 65 B4 |
| JONESVILLE | BUT | 95921 | 19 E5 |
| JOSHUA TREE | SBD | 92252 | 100 E1 |
| JULIAN | SDCO | 92036 | 107 C3 |
| JUNCTION CITY | TRI | 96048 | 17 C1 |
| JUNE LAKE | MNO | 93529 | 50 D1 |
| JUNE LAKE JUNCTION | MNO | 93529 | 50 D1 |
| JUNIPER FLATS | RCO | 92367 | 99 D3 |
| JUNIPER LAKE RESORT | LAS | 96020 | 20 A3 |
| K | | | |
| KAGEL CANYON | LACO | 91342 | Q D1 |
| KANE SPRING | IMP | 92227 | 108 D3 |
| KARNAK | SUT | 95676 | 33 C4 |
| KAWEAH | TUL | 93237 | 58 E5 |
| KEARNEY PARK | FRCO | 93706 | 57 B3 |
| KEARNY MESA | SDCO | | V B2 |
| KEARSARGE | INY | 93526 | 60 A3 |
| KEDDIE | PLU | 95952 | 26 C1 |
| KEELER | INY | 93530 | 60 C5 |
| KEENE | KER | 93531 | 79 B4 |
| KELLOGG | SON | 94515 | 31 E5 |
| KELSEY | ED | 95643 | 34 D4 |
| KELSEYVILLE | LAK | 95451 | 31 D3 |
| KELSO | SBD | 92351 | 83 E5 |
| KENO | KLAM | | 5 A1 |
| KENSINGTON | CC | 94708 | L D3 |
| KENSINGTON | SDCO | 92116 | V C3 |
| KENTFIELD | MAR | 94904 | L A3 |
| KENTWOOD IN THE PINES | SDCO | 92036 | 107 C4 |
| KENWOOD | SON | 95452 | 38 B2 |
| KEOUGH HOT SPRINGS | INY | 93514 | 51 D4 |
| KERBY | JOS | | 2 D1 |
| KERCKOFF POWERHOUSE | FRCO | 93602 | 57 E1 |
| *KERMAN | FRCO | 93630 | 57 A3 |
| KERN CITY | KER | 93309 | 78 C3 |
| KERNVALE | KER | 93240 | 79 C1 |
| KERNVILLE | KER | 93238 | 69 C5 |
| KESWICK | SHA | 96001 | 18 B2 |
| KETTLEMAN CITY | KIN | 93239 | 67 B3 |
| KEYES | STA | 95328 | 47 D3 |
| KILKARE | ALA | 94586 | P B1 |
| *KING CITY | MON | 93930 | 65 C2 |
| KING COLE | KLAM | | 4 D1 |
| KINGS BEACH | PLA | 95719 | 36 A1 |
| *KINGSBURG | FRCO | 93631 | 57 D5 |
| KINGSBURY | DGL | | 36 B3 |
| KINGS MOUNTAIN PARK | SMCO | 94062 | N C3 |
| KINGSVILLE | ED | 95623 | 34 D5 |
| KINGVALE | NEV | 95728 | 35 C1 |
| KINSLEY | MPA | 95311 | 49 B2 |
| KIRKVILLE | SUT | 95645 | 33 B3 |
| KIRKWOOD | ALP | 95646 | 36 A5 |
| KIRKWOOD | TEH | 96021 | 24 D2 |
| KIT CARSON | AMA | 95644 | 35 E5 |
| KLAMATH | DN | 95548 | 2 A5 |
| *KLAMATH FALLS | KLAM | | 5 B1 |
| KLAMATH GLEN | DN | 95548 | 2 A5 |
| KLAMATH RIVER | SIS | 96050 | 3 D3 |
| KLAU | SLO | 93465 | 75 D1 |
| KNEELAND | HUM | 95549 | 16 B1 |
| KNIGHTSEN | CC | 94548 | M D3 |
| KNIGHTS FERRY | STA | 95367 | 48 A1 |
| KNIGHTS LANDING | YOL | 95645 | 33 C4 |
| KNOB | SHA | 96076 | 17 C3 |
| KNOWLES | MAD | 93653 | 49 B5 |
| KNOWLES CORNER | SON | 95472 | 37 D2 |
| KNOXVILLE | NAPA | 95637 | 32 C4 |
| KONO TAYEE | LAK | 95458 | 31 E3 |
| KORBEL | HUM | 95550 | 10 B5 |
| KRAMER | SBD | 93516 | 80 E5 |
| KYBURZ | ED | 95720 | 35 D4 |

| COMMUNITY NAME | CO. | ZIP CODE | PAGE & GRID |
|---|---|---|---|
| L | | | |
| LA BARR MEADOWS | NEV | 95945 | 34 C2 |
| *LA CANADA FLINTRIDGE | LACO | 91011 | R B2 |
| LA CONCHITA | VEN | 93001 | 87 E5 |
| LA COSTA | SDCO | 92008 | 106 C3 |
| LA CRESCENTA | LACO | 91214 | R A2 |
| LADERA | SMCO | 94025 | N D3 |
| *LAFAYETTE | CC | 94549 | L E4 |
| LA GRANGE | STA | 95329 | 48 C2 |
| *LAGUNA BEACH | ORA | 92651 | T E5 |
| LAGUNA HILLS | ORA | 92653 | 98 D5 |
| LAGUNA NIGUEL | ORA | 92677 | 98 D5 |
| LAGUNITAS | MAR | 94938 | 38 A5 |
| *LA HABRA | ORA | 90631 | R E5 |
| *LA HABRA HEIGHTS | LACO | 90631 | R D5 |
| LA HONDA | SMCO | 94020 | 45 D4 |
| LA HONDA PARK | CAL | 94020 | 41 B4 |
| LAIRDS CORNER | TUL | 93257 | 68 B3 |
| LA JOLLA | SDCO | 92037 | 105 G3 |
| LA JOLLA AMAGO | SDCO | 92061 | 107 A2 |
| LAKE ALPINE | ALP | 95235 | 42 A1 |
| LAKE ARROWHEAD | SBD | 92352 | 91 C5 |
| LAKE BERRYESSA ESTATES | NAPA | 94567 | 32 C5 |
| LAKE CITY | MOD | 96115 | 7 D5 |
| LAKE CITY | NEV | 95959 | 26 D5 |
| *LAKE ELSINORE | RCO | 92330 | 99 B4 |
| LAKE FOREST | ORA | 92630 | 98 D4 |
| LAKE FOREST | PLA | 95730 | 35 E2 |
| LAKE HAVASU CITY | MOH | | 96 B4 |
| LAKEHEAD | SHA | 96051 | 12 C5 |
| LAKE HENSHAW | SDCO | 92070 | 107 B3 |
| LAKE HILLS EST | ED | 95630 | 34 C5 |
| LAKE HUGHES | LACO | 93532 | 89 C3 |
| LAKE ISABELLA | KER | 93240 | 79 C1 |
| LAKELAND VILLAGE | RCO | 92330 | 99 B5 |
| LAKE OF THE WOODS | KER | 93225 | 88 C2 |
| *LAKEPORT | LAK | 95453 | 31 D3 |
| LAKE RIVERSIDE | RCO | 92302 | 100 B5 |
| LAKESHORE | FRCO | 93634 | 50 C5 |
| LAKESHORE | SHA | 96051 | 12 B5 |
| LAKESIDE | SDCO | 92040 | V E2 |
| LAKESIDE PARK | LACO | 91304 | 97 B1 |
| LAKE TAMARISK | RCO | 92239 | 102 C4 |
| *LAKEVIEW | LAKE | | 7 C1 |
| LAKEVIEW | RCO | 92353 | 99 D3 |
| LAKEVIEW | SDCO | 92040 | 107 A5 |
| LAKEVIEW HOT SPRINGS | RCO | 92370 | 99 C3 |
| LAKEVIEW TERRACE | LACO | 91340 | Q D1 |
| LAKEVILLE | SON | 95452 | L B1 |
| *LAKEWOOD | LACO | 90712 | S E2 |
| LA LOMA | STA | 95354 | 47 D2 |
| *LA MESA | SDCO | 92041 | V D3 |
| *LA MIRADA | LACO | 90638 | T B1 |
| LA MOINE | SHA | 96017 | 12 C4 |
| LAMONT | KER | 93241 | 78 E3 |
| LANARE | FRCO | 93656 | 57 B5 |
| *LANCASTER | LACO | 93534 | 90 A3 |
| LANDERS | SBD | 92284 | 92 E5 |
| LANGELL VALLEY | KLAM | | 6 B2 |
| *LA PALMA | ORA | 90623 | T B2 |
| LA PLAYA | SDCO | 92106 | V A3 |
| LA PORTE | PLU | 95981 | 26 C3 |
| LA PRESA | SDCO | 92077 | V E4 |
| *LA PUENTE | LACO | 91744 | R E4 |
| *LA QUINTA | RCO | 92253 | 100 E4 |
| *LARKSPUR | MAR | 94939 | L A3 |
| LAS CRUCES | SB | 93017 | 86 D4 |
| LA SIERRA | RCO | 92505 | 99 A3 |
| LAS LOMAS | SON | 95728 | 31 B5 |
| LAS VEGAS | CLK | 89114 | 74 D2 |
| LATHROP | SJCO | 95330 | 47 B1 |
| LATON | FRCO | 93242 | 57 D5 |
| LATROBE | ED | 95682 | 40 C1 |
| LAUGHLIN | CLK | | 85 D4 |
| LAUREL HEIGHTS | SFCO | 94118 | 141 E3 |
| *LA VERNE | LACO | 91750 | U B2 |
| *LAWNDALE | LACO | 90260 | S B1 |
| LAYTONVILLE | MEN | 95454 | 22 D3 |
| LEBEC | KER | 93243 | 88 D1 |
| LEESVILLE | COL | 95987 | 32 B2 |
| LEE VINING | MNO | 93541 | 43 C5 |
| LEGGETT | MEN | 95455 | 22 C2 |
| LE GRAND | MCO | 95333 | 48 D5 |
| LELITER | KER | 93527 | 70 D5 |
| LEMONCOVE | TUL | 93244 | 68 D1 |
| *LEMON GROVE | SDCO | 92045 | V D3 |
| LEMON HEIGHTS | ORA | 92705 | T E3 |
| LEMON VALLEY | WSH | 96109 | 28 B3 |
| *LEMOORE | KIN | 93245 | 67 C1 |
| LENWOOD | SBD | 92311 | 91 D1 |
| LEUCADIA | SDCO | 92024 | 106 B3 |
| LEWISTON | TRI | 96052 | 17 D1 |
| LIBERTY FARMS | SOL | 95647 | 39 C3 |
| LIDO ISLE | ORA | 92663 | T C4 |
| LIKELY | MOD | 96116 | 8 B3 |
| LINCOLN | JKSN | | 4 C2 |
| *LINCOLN | PLA | 95648 | 34 A3 |
| LINCOLN ACRES | SDCO | 92050 | V D4 |
| LINCOLN VILLAGE | SJCO | 95207 | 40 A5 |
| LINDA | YUB | 95961 | 33 D2 |
| LINDA MAR | SMCO | 94044 | N B1 |
| LINDA VISTA | SDCO | 92111 | V B3 |
| LINDCOVE | TUL | 93221 | 68 C1 |
| LINDEN | SJCO | 95236 | 40 C5 |
| *LINDSAY | TUL | 93247 | 68 D2 |
| LINGARD | MCO | 95340 | 48 C5 |
| LITCHFIELD | LAS | 96117 | 21 C3 |
| LITTLE BORREGO | SDCO | 92004 | 108 A3 |
| LITTLE LAKE | INY | 93542 | 70 C4 |
| LITTLE RIVER | MEN | 95456 | 30 B1 |

*INDICATES INCORPORATED CITY

# CITIES AND COMMUNITIES INDEX


| COMMUNITY NAME | CO. | ZIP CODE | PAGE & GRID |
|---|---|---|---|
| LITTLEROCK | LACO | 93543 | 90 B3 |
| LITTLE SHASTA | SIS | 96064 | 4 C4 |
| LITTLE VALLEY | LAS | 96053 | 14 B5 |
| *LIVE OAK | SUT | 95953 | 33 C1 |
| LIVE OAK PARK | SDCO | 92028 | 106 C2 |
| LIVE OAK SPRINGS | SDCO | 92005 | 112 E1 |
| *LIVERMORE | ALA | 94550 | M C5 |
| *LIVINGSTON | MCO | 95334 | 48 A4 |
| LLANADA | SBT | 95043 | 55 D4 |
| LOCH LOMOND | LAK | 95426 | 31 E4 |
| LOCKE | SAC | 95649 | 39 D3 |
| LOCKEFORD | SJCO | 95237 | 40 B4 |
| LOCKWOOD | MON | 93932 | 65 C4 |
| LOCKWOOD VALLEY | VEN | 93225 | 88 C2 |
| LODGE POLE | TUL | 93271 | 59 B4 |
| *LODI | SJCO | 95240 | 40 A4 |
| LODOGA | COL | 95979 | 32 B1 |
| LOGAN HEIGHTS | SDCO | 92113 | V B4 |
| LOG CABIN | YUB | 95922 | 26 C5 |
| LOG SPRING | TEH | 96074 | 14 E4 |
| LOLETA | HUM | 95551 | 15 E2 |
| *LOMA LINDA | SBD | 92354 | 99 C2 |
| LOMA MAR | SMCO | 94021 | N C4 |
| LOMA PARK | KER | 93306 | 78 E3 |
| LOMA RICA | YUB | 95901 | 33 E1 |
| LOMA VERDE | MAR | 94947 | L A2 |
| *LOMITA | LACO | 90717 | S C2 |
| LOMO | BUT | 95942 | 25 C1 |
| *LOMPOC | SB | 93436 | 86 B3 |
| LONDON | TUL | 93631 | 58 A5 |
| LONE PINE | INY | 93545 | 60 B4 |
| LONG BARN | TUO | 95335 | 41 E4 |
| *LONG BEACH | LACO | 90801 | S D3 |
| LONGVALE | MEN | 95490 | 22 E4 |
| LONGVIEW | LACO | 93553 | 90 C4 |
| LOOKOUT | MOD | 96054 | 14 B3 |
| *LOOMIS | PLA | 95650 | 34 B4 |
| LOOMIS CORNERS | SHA | 96003 | 18 C2 |
| LORAINE | KER | 93518 | 79 D3 |
| LORELLA | KLAM | | 6 A1 |
| *LOS ALAMITOS | ORA | 90720 | T A2 |
| LOS ALAMOS | SB | 93440 | 86 C2 |
| *LOS ALTOS | SCL | 94022 | N E3 |
| *LOS ALTOS HILLS | SCL | 94022 | N E3 |
| *LOS ANGELES | LACO | 90001 | R A4 |
| *LOS BANOS | MCO | 93635 | 55 E1 |
| *LOS GATOS | SCL | 95030 | P A4 |
| LOS MOLINOS | TEH | 96055 | 24 E1 |
| LOS OLIVOS | SB | 93441 | 86 E3 |
| LOS OSOS | SLO | 93401 | 75 E3 |
| LOS RANCHITOS | MAR | 94903 | L A3 |
| LOS SERRANOS | SBD | 91710 | U C3 |
| LOST HILLS | KER | 93249 | 77 D1 |
| LOS TRANCOS WOODS | SMCO | 94025 | N D3 |
| LOTUS | ED | 95651 | 34 D4 |
| LOVELOCK | BUT | 95978 | 25 D2 |
| LOWER LAKE | LAK | 95457 | 32 A4 |
| *LOYALTON | SIE | 96118 | 27 C3 |
| LUCERNE | LAK | 95458 | 31 D2 |
| LUCERNE VALLEY | SBD | 92356 | 91 E4 |
| LUCIA | MON | 93920 | 64 D3 |
| LUDLOW | SBD | 92357 | 93 B2 |
| LUNDY | MNO | 93541 | 43 B4 |
| LUNING | MIN | | 44 E1 |
| *LYNWOOD | LACO | 90262 | S D1 |
| LYNWOOD HILLS | SDCO | 92010 | V D4 |
| LYONSVILLE | TEH | 96075 | 19 C4 |
| LYTLE CREEK | SBD | 92358 | 91 A5 |
| LYTTON | SON | 95448 | 31 D5 |
| M | | | |
| MACDOEL | SIS | 96058 | 4 E3 |
| MADELINE | LAS | 96119 | 8 B4 |
| *MADERA | MAD | 93637 | 57 A2 |
| MADISON | YOL | 95653 | 33 A5 |
| MAD RIVER | TRI | 95552 | 16 E3 |
| MADRONE | SCL | 95037 | P D5 |
| MAGALIA | BUT | 95954 | 25 C2 |
| MAGUNDEN | KER | 93306 | 78 E3 |
| MALAGA | FRCO | 93725 | 57 D4 |
| MALIBU BEACH | LACO | 90265 | 97 B2 |
| MALIN | KLAM | | 5 E2 |
| *MAMMOTH LAKES | MNO | 93546 | 50 D2 |
| MANCHESTER | MEN | 95459 | 30 C3 |
| *MANHATTAN BEACH | LACO | 90266 | S A1 |
| MANKAS CORNER | SOL | 94533 | L E1 |
| *MANTECA | SJCO | 95336 | 47 B1 |
| MANTON | TEH | 96059 | 19 A3 |
| MANZANITA | SDCO | 92005 | 111 A4 |
| MAPLE CREEK | HUM | 95550 | 16 B1 |
| MARCH FIELD | RCO | 92508 | 99 C3 |
| *MARICOPA | KER | 93252 | 78 A5 |
| *MARINA | MON | 93933 | 54 B4 |
| MARINA | SFCO | 94123 | 142 B1 |
| MARINA DEL REY | LACO | 90291 | Q B5 |
| MARIN CITY | MAR | 94965 | L B4 |
| MARINWOOD | MAR | 94903 | L A3 |
| MARIPOSA | MPA | 95338 | 49 B3 |
| MARIPOSA PINES | MPA | 95338 | 49 B2 |
| MARKLEEVILLE | ALP | 96120 | 36 C5 |
| MARK WEST SPRINGS | SON | 95492 | 37 E1 |
| MARSHALL STATION | FRCO | 93651 | 57 E2 |
| MARTELL | AMA | 95654 | 40 E2 |
| *MARTINEZ | CC | 94553 | L E3 |
| MARTINS FERRY | HUM | 95556 | 10 C3 |
| MAR VISTA | LACO | 90066 | Q C4 |
| *MARYSVILLE | YUB | 95901 | 33 D2 |
| MASONIC | MNO | 93517 | 43 C2 |
| MATHER | TUO | 95339 | 42 B5 |
| MAXWELL | COL | 95955 | 32 D1 |
| MAYFAIR | KER | 93307 | 78 E3 |
| *MAYWOOD | LACO | 90270 | R A4 |
| MCARTHUR | SHA | 96056 | 13 E4 |
| MCCANN | HUM | 95569 | 16 B4 |
| MCCAULEY | MPA | 93518 | 49 C2 |
| MCCLOUD | SIS | 96057 | 12 D2 |
| *MCFARLAND | KER | 93250 | 78 B1 |
| MCKAYS POINT | TUL | 93286 | 68 D1 |
| MCKEE BRIDGE | JKSN | | 3 C1 |
| MCKINLEYVILLE | HUM | 95521 | 9 E4 |
| MCKITTRICK | KER | 93251 | 77 D3 |
| MCMULLIN | FRCO | 93706 | 57 B4 |
| MEADOW LAKES | FRCO | 93602 | 58 A1 |
| MEADOW VALLEY | PLU | 95956 | 26 B2 |
| MEADOW VISTA | PLA | 95722 | 34 C3 |
| MECCA | RCO | 92254 | 101 C5 |
| MEEKS BAY | ED | 95723 | 35 E2 |
| MEINERS OAKS | VEN | 93023 | 88 A4 |
| MELOLAND | IMP | 92243 | 112 B3 |
| MENDOCINO | MEN | 95460 | 30 B1 |
| MENDOCINO COAST | MEN | 95459 | 30 C3 |
| *MENDOTA | FRCO | 93640 | 56 D3 |
| *MENLO PARK | SMCO | 94025 | N D2 |
| MENTONE | SBD | 92359 | 99 D2 |
| *MERCED | MCO | 95340 | 48 C4 |
| MERCED FALLS | MCO | 95369 | 48 D3 |
| MERCEY HOT SPRINGS | FRCO | 95043 | 55 E4 |
| MERIDIAN | SUT | 95957 | 33 B2 |
| *MERRILL | KLAM | | 5 D2 |
| MESA GRANDE | SDCO | 92070 | 107 B3 |
| MESQUITE SPRING | INY | 92328 | 61 B2 |
| METTLER | KER | 93301 | 78 E5 |
| MEXICALI | BAJA | | 112 B4 |
| MEYERS | ED | 95731 | 36 A4 |
| MICHIGAN BAR | SAC | 95683 | 40 C1 |
| MICHIGAN BLUFF | PLA | 95631 | 35 A2 |
| MIDDLE RIVER | SJCO | 95234 | 39 D5 |
| MIDDLETOWN | LAK | 95461 | 32 A5 |
| MIDLAND | KLAM | | 5 B1 |
| MIDLAND | RCO | 92255 | 103 B3 |
| MIDPINES | MPA | 95345 | 49 B3 |
| MIDWAY | ALA | 94550 | M E5 |
| MIDWAY | SHA | 96088 | 19 A2 |
| MIDWAY CITY | ORA | 92655 | T C3 |
| MIDWAY WELL | IMP | | 112 E3 |
| MILFORD | LAS | 96121 | 21 C5 |
| *MILLBRAE | SMCO | 94030 | N C1 |
| MILL CREEK | TEH | 96061 | 19 D4 |
| MILLERS CORNER | MAD | 93614 | 57 C1 |
| MILLS ORCHARDS | COL | 95955 | 32 C1 |
| *MILL VALLEY | MAR | 94942 | L A3 |
| MILLVILLE | SHA | 96062 | 18 D2 |
| MILO | TUL | 93265 | 68 E2 |
| *MILPITAS | SCL | 95035 | P B3 |
| MILTON | CAL | 95230 | 40 E4 |
| MINA | MIN | | 44 E2 |
| *MINDEN | DGL | | 36 C3 |
| MINERAL | TEH | 96063 | 19 C4 |
| MINERAL KING | TUL | 93271 | 59 B5 |
| MINKLER | FRCO | 93657 | 58 A3 |
| MINNESOTA | SHA | 96001 | 18 B2 |
| MINTER VILLAGE | KER | 93301 | 78 C2 |
| MIRACLE HOT SPRINGS | KER | 93288 | 79 C1 |
| MIRA LOMA | RCO | 91752 | 98 E2 |
| MIRAMAR | SDCO | 92145 | V B1 |
| MIRAMAR | SMCO | 94019 | N B2 |
| MIRA MESA | SDCO | 92126 | V B1 |
| MIRA MONTE | VEN | 93023 | 88 A4 |
| MIRAMONTE | FRCO | 93641 | 58 C3 |
| MIRANDA | HUM | 95553 | 16 C4 |
| MIRA VISTA | LAK | 95461 | 31 E4 |
| MISSION BEACH | SDCO | 92109 | V A3 |
| MISSION HIGHLANDS | SON | 95476 | 38 B3 |
| MISSION HILLS | SDCO | 92103 | V B3 |
| MISSION SAN JOSE | ALA | 94538 | P B2 |
| *MISSION VIEJO | ORA | 92675 | 98 D5 |
| MISSION VILLAGE | SDCO | 92123 | V C2 |
| MITCHELL MILL | CAL | 95255 | 41 B2 |
| MI-WUK VILLAGE | TUO | 95346 | 41 E4 |
| MOCCASIN | TUO | 95347 | 48 D1 |
| *MODESTO | STA | 95350 | 47 D2 |
| MODJESKA | ORA | 92705 | 98 E4 |
| MOJAVE | KER | 93501 | 80 A5 |
| MOKELUMNE HILL | CAL | 95245 | 41 A3 |
| MONMOUTH | FRCO | 93725 | 57 C4 |
| MONO CAMP | MPA | 95338 | 49 B3 |
| MONO CITY | MNO | 93541 | 43 C4 |
| MONO HOT SPRINGS | FRCO | 93642 | 50 D4 |
| MONO LAKE | MNO | 93541 | 43 C5 |
| MONOLITH | KER | 93548 | 79 D4 |
| MONO VISTA | TUO | 95370 | 41 D4 |
| *MONROVIA | LACO | 91016 | R D3 |
| MONSON | TUL | 93618 | 58 B5 |
| *MONTAGUE | SIS | 96064 | 4 B4 |
| MONTALVO | VEN | 93003 | 88 B5 |
| MONTARA | SMCO | 94037 | N B2 |
| *MONTCLAIR | SBD | 91763 | U C2 |
| *MONTEBELLO | LACO | 90640 | R C4 |
| MONTECITO | SB | 93108 | 87 D4 |
| MONTE MARIA | MAR | 94947 | L A2 |
| MONTE NIDO | LACO | 91302 | 97 B2 |
| *MONTEREY | MON | 93940 | 54 B4 |
| MONTEREY HILLS | LACO | 90032 | R B3 |
| *MONTEREY PARK | LACO | 91754 | R B4 |
| MONTE RIO | SON | 95462 | 37 C2 |
| *MONTE SERENO | SCL | 95030 | P A4 |
| MONTEZUMA | SOL | 94512 | 39 B4 |
| MONTGOMERY CREEK | SHA | 96065 | 13 A5 |
| MONTROSE | LACO | 91020 | Q E2 |
| MOONRIDGE | SBD | 92315 | 92 A5 |
| MOONSTONE | HUM | 95570 | 9 E4 |
| *MOORPARK | VEN | 93021 | 88 D5 |
| MOORPARK HOME ACRES | VEN | 93021 | 88 D5 |
| *MORAGA | CC | 94556 | L E4 |
| MORENA VILLAGE | SDCO | 92110 | 112 D1 |
| MORENO | SDCO | 92040 | 107 A5 |
| *MORENO VALLEY | RCO | 92360 | 99 D3 |
| MORETTIS | SDCO | 92070 | 107 B3 |
| *MORGAN HILL | SCL | 95037 | P D5 |
| MORMON BAR | MPA | 95338 | 49 B3 |
| MORONGO VALLEY | SBD | 92256 | 100 C2 |
| *MORRO BAY | SLO | 93442 | 75 E3 |
| MOSS BEACH | SMCO | 94038 | N B2 |
| MOSS LANDING | MON | 95036 | 54 B3 |
| MOUNTAIN CENTER | RCO | 92361 | 100 B4 |
| MOUNTAIN GATE | SHA | 96003 | 18 C1 |
| MOUNTAIN HOME VILLAGE | SBD | 92359 | 99 E1 |
| MOUNTAIN MESA | KER | 93240 | 79 D1 |
| MOUNTAIN RANCH | CAL | 95246 | 41 B3 |
| MOUNTAIN REST | FRCO | 93667 | 58 B1 |
| MOUNTAIN SPRINGS | CLK | | 74 A3 |
| MOUNTAIN VIEW | RCO | 92509 | 99 A2 |
| *MOUNTAIN VIEW | SCL | 94040 | N E3 |
| MOUNT AUKUM | ED | 95656 | 40 E1 |
| MOUNT BALDY VILLAGE | SBD | 91759 | 90 E5 |
| MOUNT BULLION | MPA | 95338 | 49 A3 |
| MOUNT HEBRON | SIS | 96066 | 5 A4 |
| MOUNT HELIX | SDCO | 92041 | V D3 |
| MOUNT HERMON | SCR | 95041 | P A5 |
| MOUNT LAGUNA | SDCO | 92048 | 107 E5 |
| *MOUNT SHASTA | SIS | 96067 | 12 C2 |
| MOUNT SIGNAL | IMP | 92231 | 112 A4 |
| MT VIEW | JKSN | | 4 C1 |
| MOUNT WILSON | LACO | 91023 | R C2 |
| MUGGINSVILLE | SIS | 96032 | 3 C5 |
| MUIR BEACH | MAR | 94965 | L A4 |
| MURPHYS | CAL | 95247 | 41 C4 |
| MURPHYS RANCH | CAL | 95247 | 41 C4 |
| MURRIETA | RCO | 92362 | 99 C5 |
| MURRIETA HOT SPRINGS | RCO | 92362 | 99 C5 |
| MUSCOY | SBD | 92405 | 99 B1 |
| MYERS FLAT | HUM | 95554 | 16 B4 |
| N | | | |
| NAIRN | MCO | 95340 | 48 B4 |
| NANCEVILLE | TUL | 93257 | 68 D3 |
| *NAPA | NAPA | 94558 | L D1 |
| NAPLES | LACO | 90803 | S E3 |
| NAPLES | SB | 93117 | 87 A4 |
| NASHVILLE | ED | 95675 | 40 E1 |
| *NATIONAL CITY | SDCO | 92050 | V C4 |
| NATOMA | SAC | 95630 | 34 B5 |
| NAVARRO | MEN | 95463 | 30 D2 |
| NAVELENCIA | FRCO | 93654 | 58 A4 |
| *NEEDLES | SBD | 92363 | 95 D2 |
| NEENACH | LACO | 93534 | 89 B2 |
| NELSON | BUT | 95958 | 25 B4 |
| NESTOR | SDCO | 92154 | V C5 |
| *NEVADA CITY | NEV | 95959 | 34 C1 |
| NEW ALMADEN | SCL | 95042 | P C4 |
| *NEWARK | ALA | 94560 | P A2 |
| NEW AUBERRY | FRCO | 93602 | 57 E1 |
| NEWBERRY SPRINGS | SBD | 92365 | 92 B2 |
| NEWBURY PARK | VEN | 91320 | 96 D1 |
| NEWCASTLE | PLA | 95658 | 34 C4 |
| NEW CUYAMA | SB | 93214 | 87 C1 |
| NEWELL | MOD | 96134 | 5 E3 |
| NEWHALL | LACO | 91321 | 89 C5 |
| NEWHALL RANCH | LACO | 91355 | 89 B4 |
| NEW IDAHO | LAKE | | 7 B1 |
| NEW IDRIA | SBT | 95027 | 66 A1 |
| *NEWMAN | STA | 95360 | 47 C4 |
| NEW PINE CREEK | MOD | 97635 | 7 C2 |
| *NEWPORT BEACH | ORA | 92660 | T C4 |
| NEWPORT CENTER | ORA | 92660 | T D4 |
| NEWTOWN | ED | 95709 | 35 A5 |
| NEWVILLE | GLE | 95963 | 24 B3 |
| NEW WASHOE CITY | WSH | 95611 | 36 C1 |
| NICASIO | MAR | 94946 | 37 E4 |
| NICE | LAK | 95464 | 31 C4 |
| NICHOLLS WARM SPRINGS | RCO | 92225 | 103 C5 |
| NICHOLS | CC | 94565 | 39 A4 |
| NICOLAUS | SUT | 95659 | 33 D3 |
| NILAND | IMP | 92257 | 109 B2 |
| NIPINNAWASSEE | MAD | 93601 | 49 C4 |
| NIPOMO | SLO | 93444 | 76 C5 |
| NIPTON | SBD | 92364 | 84 C2 |
| NIXON | WSH | 96109 | 28 E2 |
| NOB HILL | SFCO | 94108 | 142 D1 |
| NOE VALLEY | SFCO | 94114 | 142 A5 |
| *NORCO | RCO | 91760 | U E4 |
| NORD | BUT | 95926 | 25 A3 |
| NORDEN | NEV | 95724 | 35 C1 |
| NORMAN | GLE | 95988 | 24 D5 |
| NORTH BEACH | SFCO | 94133 | 142 D1 |
| NORTH BLOOMFIELD | NEV | 95959 | 26 D5 |
| NORTH COLUMBIA | NEV | 95959 | 26 C5 |
| NORTH EDWARDS | KER | 93523 | 80 D5 |
| NORTH FORK | MAD | 93643 | 49 E5 |
| NORTH HIGHLANDS | SAC | 95660 | 34 A5 |
| NORTH HOLLYWOOD | LACO | 91601 | Q C2 |
| NORTH JAMUL | SDCO | 92035 | 112 A1 |
| NORTH LAS VEGAS | CLK | | 74 D2 |
| NORTH LONG BEACH | LACO | 90805 | S D2 |
| NORTH RICHMOND | CC | 94807 | L C3 |
| NORTHRIDGE | LACO | 91324 | Q B2 |
| NORTH SAN JUAN | NEV | 95960 | 26 B5 |
| NORTH SHORE | RCO | 92254 | 101 D5 |
| NORTHSTAR | PLA | 95732 | 35 E1 |
| NORTHWOOD | ORA | 92720 | T E3 |
| NORTHWOOD | SON | 95462 | 37 C2 |
| NORTON AFB | SBD | 92409 | 99 C1 |
| *NORWALK | LACO | 90650 | T A1 |
| *NOVATO | MAR | 94947 | L A2 |
| NOYO | MEN | 95437 | 22 C5 |
| NUBIEBER | LAS | 96068 | 14 B3 |
| NUEVO | RCO | 92367 | 99 D3 |
| NYLAND | VEN | 93030 | 88 C5 |
| O | | | |
| *OAKDALE | STA | 95361 | 47 D1 |
| OAK GLEN | SBD | 92399 | 99 E2 |
| OAK GROVE VALLEY | SDCO | 92086 | 107 B1 |
| OAKGROVE | TUL | 93271 | 59 A5 |
| OAKHURST | MAD | 93644 | 49 D4 |
| *OAKLAND | ALA | 94601 | L D4 |
| OAKLEY | CC | 94561 | M D3 |
| OAK RUN | SHA | 96069 | 18 E1 |
| OAK VIEW | VEN | 93022 | 88 A4 |
| OAKVILLE | NAPA | 94562 | 38 B2 |
| OASIS | RCO | 92274 | 108 B1 |
| OATMAN | MOH | | 85 E5 |
| OBRIEN | JOS | | 2 C2 |
| O'BRIEN | SHA | 96070 | 12 C5 |
| OCCIDENTAL | SON | 95465 | 37 C2 |
| OCEAN BEACH | SDCO | 92107 | V A3 |
| OCEANO | SLO | 93445 | 76 B5 |
| *OCEANSIDE | SDCO | 92054 | 106 B3 |
| OCEAN VIEW | SON | 95450 | 37 C2 |
| OCOTILLO | IMP | 92259 | 111 C3 |
| OCOTILLO WELLS | SDCO | 92004 | 108 B3 |
| OGILBY | IMP | 92222 | 110 B5 |
| OILDALE | KER | 93308 | 78 D2 |
| *OJAI | VEN | 93023 | 88 B4 |
| OLANCHA | INY | 93549 | 70 B1 |
| OLD BOULEVARD | SDCO | 92005 | 111 A4 |
| OLD RIVER | KER | 93307 | 78 C3 |
| OLD STATION | SHA | 96071 | 19 D1 |
| OLD TOWN | LAS | 96137 | 20 C4 |
| OLEMA | MAR | 94950 | 37 E4 |
| OLENE | KLAM | | 5 C1 |
| OLINDA | ORA | 92621 | T D1 |
| OLINDA | SHA | 96007 | 18 C3 |
| OLINGHOUSE | WSH | | 28 E3 |
| OLIVE | ORA | 92665 | T D2 |
| OLIVEHURST | YUB | 95961 | 33 D2 |
| OLIVENHAIN | SDCO | 92067 | 106 C4 |
| OLIVE VIEW | LACO | 91342 | Q C1 |
| OLYMPIC VALLEY | PLA | 95730 | 35 D1 |
| OMO RANCH | ED | 95661 | 41 B1 |
| O'NEALS | MAD | 93645 | 57 D1 |
| ONO | SHA | 96072 | 18 A3 |
| *ONTARIO | SBD | 91761 | U D2 |
| ONYX | KER | 93255 | 69 E5 |
| OPHIR | PLA | 95603 | 34 C4 |
| *ORANGE | ORA | 92666 | T D2 |
| *ORANGE COVE | FRCO | 93646 | 58 B4 |
| ORANGE PARK ACRES | ORA | 92669 | T E2 |
| ORANGEVALE | SAC | 95662 | 34 B5 |
| ORCHARD SHORES | LAK | 95423 | 32 A3 |
| ORCUTT | SB | 93455 | 86 C1 |
| ORDBEND | GLE | 95943 | 25 A3 |
| OREGON HOUSE | YUB | 95962 | 26 A5 |
| ORICK | HUM | 95555 | 10 A2 |
| *ORINDA | CC | 94563 | L E4 |
| ORINDA VILLAGE | CC | 94563 | 45 D1 |
| *ORLAND | GLE | 95963 | 24 D3 |
| ORLEANS | HUM | 95556 | 10 D2 |
| ORO FINO | SIS | 96032 | 3 D5 |
| ORO GRANDE | SBD | 92368 | 91 B3 |
| ORO LOMA | FRCO | 93622 | 56 A2 |
| OROSI | TUL | 93647 | 58 B4 |
| *OROVILLE | BUT | 95965 | 25 C4 |
| ORR SPRINGS | MEN | 95482 | 31 A1 |
| OTAY | SDCO | 92011 | V C5 |
| OUTINGDALE | ED | 95684 | 34 E5 |
| *OXNARD | VEN | 93030 | 96 B1 |
| P | | | |
| PACHECO | CC | 94553 | L E3 |
| *PACIFICA | SMCO | 94044 | N B1 |
| PACIFIC BEACH | SDCO | 92109 | V A2 |
| *PACIFIC GROVE | MON | 93950 | 54 A4 |
| PACIFIC HEIGHTS | SFCO | 94115 | 142 B2 |
| PACIFIC HOUSE | ED | 95725 | 35 B4 |
| PACIFIC PALISADES | LACO | 90272 | Q B4 |
| PACOIMA | LACO | 91331 | Q C1 |
| PAHRUMP | NYE | | 73 C2 |
| PAICINES | SBT | 95043 | 55 B3 |
| PAINTED HILLS | RCO | 92282 | 100 C2 |
| PAINTERSVILLE | SAC | 95615 | 39 D3 |
| PAJARO | MON | 95076 | 54 C2 |
| PALA | SDCO | 92059 | 106 D2 |
| PALA MESA VILLAGE | SDCO | 92028 | 106 D2 |
| PALERMO | BUT | 95968 | 25 D5 |
| PALISADES HIGHLANDS | LACO | 90272 | Q B4 |
| PALM CITY | SDCO | 92154 | V C5 |
| *PALMDALE | LACO | 93550 | 90 A3 |
| PALMDALE EAST | LACO | 93550 | 90 A3 |
| *PALM DESERT | RCO | 92260 | 100 D4 |
| PALMS | LACO | 90034 | Q C4 |
| *PALM SPRINGS | RCO | 92262 | 100 D3 |
| *PALO ALTO | SCL | 94301 | N E2 |
| PALO CEDRO | SHA | 96073 | 18 D2 |
| PALOMA | CAL | 95252 | 40 E3 |
| PALOMAR MOUNTAIN | SDCO | 92060 | 107 A2 |
| *PALOS VERDES ESTATES | LACO | 90274 | S A2 |
| PALO VERDE | IMP | 92266 | 110 C1 |
| PALO VERDE | SDCO | 92001 | 107 B5 |
| PANAMA | KER | 93309 | 78 D3 |


***INDICATES INCORPORATED CITY**

# CITIES AND COMMUNITIES INDEX


| COMMUNITY NAME | CO. | ZIP CODE | PAGE & GRID |
|---|---|---|---|
| PANAMINT SPRINGS | INY | 93545 | 71 A1 |
| PANOCHE | SBT | 95043 | 55 D4 |
| PANORAMA CITY | LACO | 91402 | Q C2 |
| *PARADISE | BUT | 95969 | 25 C3 |
| PARADISE CAY | MAR | 94920 | 38 B5 |
| PARADISE VALLEY | SCL | 95037 | P D5 |
| PARAISO SPRINGS | MON | 93960 | 64 E1 |
| *PARAMOUNT | LACO | 90723 | S E1 |
| PARKFIELD | MON | 93451 | 66 C4 |
| PARKER | LPAZ | | 104 B1 |
| PARK VILLAGE | INY | 92328 | 62 A5 |
| *PARLIER | FRCO | 93648 | 57 E4 |
| *PASADENA | LACO | 91101 | R B3 |
| PASKENTA | TEH | 96074 | 24 B2 |
| PASO PICACHO | SDCO | 92036 | 107 C4 |
| *PASO ROBLES | SLO | 93446 | 76 A1 |
| PATRICK CREEK | DN | 95543 | 2 B3 |
| *PATTERSON | STA | 95363 | 47 B3 |
| PATTON VILLAGE | LAS | 96113 | 21 D5 |
| PAUMA VALLEY | SDCO | 92061 | 106 E2 |
| PAYNES CREEK | TEH | 96075 | 19 B4 |
| PAYNESVILLE | ALP | 96120 | 36 B4 |
| PEANUT | TRI | 96041 | 17 B3 |
| PEARBLOSSOM | LACO | 93553 | 90 C4 |
| PEARDALE | NEV | 95945 | 34 C1 |
| PEARLAND | LACO | 93550 | 90 B3 |
| PEARSONVILLE | INY | 93542 | 70 C5 |
| PEBBLE BEACH | MON | 93953 | 54 A4 |
| PECWAN | HUM | 95546 | 10 B2 |
| PEDLEY | RCO | 92509 | 99 A2 |
| PELICAN CITY | KLAM | | 5 B1 |
| PENNGROVE | SON | 94951 | 38 A3 |
| PENNINGTON | SUT | 95953 | 33 C1 |
| PENTZ | BUT | 95965 | 25 D3 |
| PEPPERWOOD | HUM | 95565 | 16 A3 |
| PERKINS | SAC | 95826 | 39 E1 |
| *PERRIS | RCO | 92370 | 99 C4 |
| PESCADERO | SMCO | 94060 | N C4 |
| *PETALUMA | SON | 94952 | L A1 |
| PETER PAM | TUO | 95335 | 41 E4 |
| PETERS | SJCO | 95236 | 40 C5 |
| PETROLIA | HUM | 95558 | 15 D4 |
| PHILLIPS | ED | 95735 | 35 E4 |
| PHILLIPSVILLE | HUM | 95558 | 16 B5 |
| PHILO | MEN | 95466 | 30 E3 |
| PICACHO | IMP | 92222 | 110 D4 |
| *PICO RIVERA | LACO | 90660 | R C4 |
| *PIEDMONT | ALA | 94611 | L D4 |
| PIERCY | MEN | 95467 | 22 C1 |
| PIKE | SIE | 95922 | 26 C5 |
| PILOT HILL | ED | 95664 | 34 C4 |
| PINE COVE | RCO | 92349 | 100 B4 |
| PINECREST | TUO | 95364 | 42 A3 |
| PINEDALE | FRCO | 93650 | 57 C3 |
| PINE FLAT | TUL | 93207 | 69 B4 |
| PINE GROVE | AMA | 95665 | 41 A2 |
| PINE GROVE | LAK | 95426 | 31 E4 |
| PINE GROVE | MEN | 95460 | 30 B1 |
| PINE GROVE | SHA | 96003 | 18 C2 |
| PINE HILLS | SDCO | 92036 | 107 C4 |
| PINEHURST | FRCO | 93641 | 58 D3 |
| PINEHURST | JKSN | | 4 C1 |
| PINELAND | PLA | 95718 | 35 E2 |
| PINE MEADOW | RCO | 92361 | 100 C5 |
| PINE MOUNTAIN CLUB | KER | 93225 | 88 B1 |
| PINE RIDGE | FRCO | 93602 | 58 B1 |
| PINE VALLEY | SDCO | 92062 | 107 D5 |
| PINO GRANDE | ED | 95634 | 35 A4 |
| *PINOLE | CC | 94564 | L C3 |
| PINOLE ESTATES | CC | 94564 | L D3 |
| PINON PINES | KER | 93225 | 88 C1 |
| PINYON PINES | RCO | 92361 | 100 D5 |
| PIONEER STATION | AMA | 95666 | 41 B2 |
| PIONEERTOWN | SBD | 92268 | 100 D1 |
| PIRU | VEN | 93040 | 88 E4 |
| *PISMO BEACH | SLO | 93449 | 76 B4 |
| *PITTSBURG | CC | 94565 | M B3 |
| PITTVILLE | SHA | 96056 | 13 E4 |
| PIXLEY | TUL | 93256 | 68 B4 |
| *PLACENTIA | ORA | 92670 | T D1 |
| *PLACERVILLE | ED | 95667 | 34 E5 |
| PLAINSBURG | MCO | 95333 | 48 D5 |
| PLAINVIEW | TUL | 93267 | 68 C2 |
| PLANADA | MCO | 95365 | 48 D4 |
| PLASSE | AMA | 95666 | 35 E5 |
| PLASTER CITY | IMP | 92269 | 108 D5 |
| PLATINA | SHA | 96076 | 17 D3 |
| PLAYA DEL REY | LACO | 90291 | 97 C2 |
| PLEASANT GROVE | SUT | 95668 | 33 D4 |
| *PLEASANT HILL | CC | 94523 | L E3 |
| *PLEASANTON | ALA | 94566 | M C5 |
| PLEASANT VALLEY | ED | 95709 | 35 A5 |
| *PLYMOUTH | AMA | 95669 | 40 D2 |
| *POINT ARENA | MEN | 95468 | 30 C4 |
| POINT LOMA | SDCO | 92106 | V A3 |
| POINT PLEASANT | SAC | 95624 | 39 D3 |
| POINT REYES STATION | MAR | 94956 | 37 D4 |
| POLLARD FLAT | SHA | 96017 | 12 C4 |
| POLLOCK PINES | ED | 95726 | 35 A4 |
| POMINS | ED | 95733 | 35 E2 |
| POMO | MEN | 95469 | 31 C1 |
| *POMONA | LACO | 91766 | U C2 |
| POND | KER | 93280 | 68 B5 |
| PONDEROSA | TUL | 93208 | 69 C3 |
| PONDEROSA BASIN | MPA | 95338 | 49 C3 |
| PONDEROSA SKY RANCH | TEH | | 19 B4 |
| PONDOSA | SIS | 96077 | 13 C3 |
| POPE VALLEY | NAPA | 94567 | 32 C5 |
| POPLAR | TUL | 93257 | 68 C3 |
| PORT COSTA | CC | 94569 | L D3 |
| PORTER RANCH | LACO | 91311 | Q A1 |
| *PORTERVILLE | TUL | 93257 | 68 D3 |
| *PORT HUENEME | VEN | 93041 | 96 B1 |
| *PORTOLA | PLU | 96122 | 27 B2 |
| *PORTOLA VALLEY | SMCO | 94025 | N D3 |
| POSEY | TUL | 93260 | 69 B5 |
| POSTON | LPAZ | | 104 A2 |
| POSTON 2 | LPAZ | | 104 A3 |
| POTRERO | SDCO | 92063 | 112 C2 |
| POTTER VALLEY | MEN | 95469 | 31 B1 |
| *POWAY | SDCO | 92064 | V D1 |
| POZO | SLO | 93453 | 76 D3 |
| PRATHER | FRCO | 93651 | 57 E1 |
| PRATTVILLE | PLU | 95923 | 20 B4 |
| PRESIDIO | SFCO | 94118 | 141 D2 |
| PRESIDIO OF SAN FRAN | SFCO | 94129 | 141 D2 |
| PRESTON | SON | 95425 | 31 C4 |
| PRIEST | TUO | 95305 | 48 D1 |
| PRINCETON | COL | 95970 | 25 A5 |
| PRINCETON BY THE SEA | SMCO | 94018 | N B2 |
| PROBERTA | TEH | 96078 | 24 D1 |
| PROGRESO | BAJA | | 112 A4 |
| PROJECT CITY | SHA | 96079 | 18 C1 |
| PRUNEDALE | MON | 93901 | 54 C3 |
| PUERTA LA CRUZ | SDCO | 92086 | 107 C2 |
| PULGA | BUT | 95965 | 25 D2 |
| PUMPKIN CENTER | KER | 93309 | 78 D3 |
| Q | | | |
| QUAIL VALLEY | RCO | 92380 | 99 C4 |
| QUAKING ASPEN | TUL | 93208 | 69 C3 |
| QUARTZ HILL | LACO | 93536 | 89 E3 |
| QUARTZSITE | LPAZ | | 104 B4 |
| QUINCY | PLU | 95971 | 26 C1 |
| QUINCY JUNCTION | PLU | 95971 | 26 D1 |
| R | | | |
| RACKERBY | YUB | 95972 | 25 E5 |
| RAFAEL VILLAGE | MAR | 94947 | L A2 |
| RAILROAD FLAT | CAL | 95248 | 41 B2 |
| RAINBOW | SDCO | 92028 | 106 D1 |
| RAISIN CITY | FRCO | 93652 | 57 B4 |
| RAMONA | SDCO | 92065 | 107 A4 |
| RAMSEY | LPAZ | | 104 D4 |
| RANCHITA | SDCO | 92066 | 107 D3 |
| RANCHO BERNARDO | SDCO | 92128 | 106 D4 |
| RANCHO CALIFORNIA | RCO | 92390 | 106 D1 |
| RANCHO CORDOVA | SAC | 95670 | 40 B1 |
| *RANCHO CUCAMONGA | SBD | 91730 | U D2 |
| *RANCHO MIRAGE | RCO | 92270 | 100 D4 |
| RANCHO MURIETA | SAC | 95683 | 40 C1 |
| *RANCHO PALOS VERDES | LACO | 90274 | S B3 |
| RANCHO PENASQUITOS | SDCO | 92129 | 106 D4 |
| RANCHO SAN DIEGO | SDCO | 92077 | V E3 |
| RANCHO SANTA FE | SDCO | 92067 | 106 C4 |
| RANCHO SANTA MARGARITA | ORA | 92688 | 98 E4 |
| RANCHO TEHAMA | TEH | 96021 | 24 C1 |
| RANDOLF | SIE | 96126 | 27 C4 |
| RANDSBURG | KER | 93554 | 80 D3 |
| RAVENDALE | LAS | 96123 | 8 C5 |
| RAYMOND | MAD | 93653 | 49 B5 |
| RED APPLE | CAL | 95224 | 41 C3 |
| REDBANK | TEH | 96080 | 18 B5 |
| *RED BLUFF | TEH | 96080 | 18 C5 |
| REDCREST | HUM | 95569 | 16 A3 |
| *REDDING | SHA | 96001 | 18 C2 |
| RED HILL | ORA | 92705 | T E3 |
| *REDLANDS | SBD | 92373 | 99 C2 |
| RED MOUNTAIN | SBD | 93558 | 80 E3 |
| *REDONDO BEACH | LACO | 90277 | S A2 |
| REDWAY | HUM | 95560 | 16 B5 |
| *REDWOOD CITY | SMCO | 94061 | N D2 |
| REDWOOD ESTATES | SCL | 95044 | P B4 |
| REDWOOD PARK | SMCO | 94062 | N C2 |
| REDWOOD SHORES | SMCO | 94065 | N D2 |
| REDWOOD VALLEY | MEN | 95470 | 31 B1 |
| *REEDLEY | FRCO | 93654 | 58 A4 |
| RENO | WSH | | 28 B4 |
| RENO-STEAD | WSH | | 28 B3 |
| REPRESA | SAC | 95671 | 34 B5 |
| REQUA | DN | 95561 | 1 E5 |
| RESCUE | ED | 95672 | 34 D5 |
| RESEDA | LACO | 91335 | Q B2 |
| REWARD | INY | 93526 | 60 B3 |
| RHEEM VALLEY | CC | 94570 | 45 E1 |
| *RIALTO | SBD | 92376 | 99 B1 |
| RICARDO | KER | 93519 | 80 B3 |
| RICE | SBD | 92280 | 103 B2 |
| RICHARDSON SPRINGS | BUT | 95978 | 25 B2 |
| RICH BAR | PLU | 95915 | 26 B1 |
| RICHFIELD | TEH | 96083 | 24 D1 |
| RICHGROVE | TUL | 93261 | 68 C5 |
| *RICHMOND | CC | 94801 | L C3 |
| RICHMOND | SFCO | 94121 | 141 B4 |
| RICHVALE | BUT | 95974 | 25 C4 |
| *RIDGECREST | KER | 93555 | 80 D1 |
| RIMFOREST | SBD | 92378 | 99 C1 |
| RIMROCK | SBD | 92268 | 100 D1 |
| RINCON | SDCO | 92082 | 106 E2 |
| RIO BRAVO | KER | 93306 | 78 E2 |
| *RIO DELL | HUM | 95562 | 15 E3 |
| RIO DELL | SON | 95486 | 37 D2 |
| RIO LINDA | SAC | 95673 | 33 E5 |
| RIO NIDO | SON | 95471 | 37 D1 |
| RIO OSO | SUT | 95674 | 33 D3 |
| *RIO VISTA | SOL | 94571 | M D2 |
| RIPLEY | RCO | 92272 | 103 D5 |
| *RIPON | SJCO | 95366 | 47 C2 |
| *RIVERBANK | STA | 95367 | 47 D2 |
| RIVERDALE | FRCO | 93656 | 57 B5 |
| RIVER KERN | KER | 93238 | 69 D5 |
| RIVER PINES | AMA | 95675 | 40 E1 |
| *RIVERSIDE | RCO | 92501 | 99 B2 |
| RIVERTON | ED | 95725 | 35 B4 |
| RIVIERA | MOH | | 85 D4 |
| RIVIERA HEIGHTS | LAK | 95443 | 31 D3 |
| RIVIERA WEST | LAK | 95422 | 31 E3 |
| ROADS END | TUL | 93236 | 69 C4 |
| ROBBINS | SUT | 95676 | 33 C4 |
| ROBINSONS CORNER | BUT | 95948 | 25 C5 |
| ROBLA | SAC | 95673 | 33 E5 |
| ROCKAWAY BEACH | SMCO | 94044 | N B1 |
| ROCK HAVEN | SDCO | 92065 | 106 E4 |
| *ROCKLIN | PLA | 95677 | 34 B4 |
| ROCKPORT | MEN | 95488 | 22 B3 |
| ROCKVILLE | SOL | 94585 | 38 E3 |
| RODEO | CC | 94572 | L D3 |
| ROGERS LANDING | MOH | | 85 D4 |
| *ROHNERT PARK | SON | 94928 | 38 A2 |
| ROHNERVILLE | HUM | 95540 | 15 E2 |
| ROLINDA | FRCO | 93705 | 57 B3 |
| *ROLLING HILLS | LACO | 90274 | S B3 |
| *ROLLING HILLS ESTATES | LACO | 90274 | S B2 |
| ROMOLAND | RCO | 92380 | 99 D4 |
| ROSAMOND | KER | 93560 | 90 A1 |
| ROSEDALE | KER | 93308 | 78 C3 |
| *ROSEMEAD | LACO | 91770 | R C3 |
| ROSEMONT | SDCO | 92065 | 106 E4 |
| *ROSEVILLE | PLA | 95678 | 34 A4 |
| ROSEVILLE | SDCO | 92106 | V A3 |
| ROSEWOOD | TEH | 96022 | 18 B4 |
| *ROSS | MAR | 94957 | L A3 |
| ROSSMOOR | ORA | 90720 | T A2 |
| ROUGH AND READY | NEV | 95975 | 34 B1 |
| ROUND MOUNTAIN | SHA | 96084 | 13 A5 |
| ROVANA | INY | 93514 | 51 B3 |
| ROWLAND HEIGHTS | LACO | 91745 | U A3 |
| RUBIDOUX | RCO | 92509 | 99 A2 |
| RUCH | JKSN | | 3 C1 |
| RUCKER | SCL | 95020 | P D5 |
| RUMSEY | YOL | 95679 | 32 D4 |
| RUNNING SPRINGS | SBD | 92382 | 99 D1 |
| RUSSIAN HILL | SFCO | 94133 | 142 C2 |
| RUTH | TRI | 95526 | 17 A4 |
| RUTHERFORD | NAPA | 94573 | 38 B2 |
| RYDE | SAC | 95680 | M E1 |
| S | | | |
| SABRE CITY | PLA | 95660 | 34 A5 |
| *SACRAMENTO | SAC | 95813 | 39 E1 |
| *SAINT HELENA | NAPA | 94574 | 38 B1 |
| SALIDA | STA | 95368 | 47 C2 |
| *SALINAS | MON | 93901 | 54 C4 |
| SALMON CREEK | SON | 94923 | 37 C2 |
| SALT CREEK LODGE | SHA | 96051 | 12 C5 |
| SALTDALE | KER | 93519 | 80 C3 |
| SALTON | RCO | 92257 | 108 D1 |
| SALTON CITY | IMP | 92274 | 108 C2 |
| SALTON SEA BEACH | IMP | 92274 | 108 C1 |
| SALVADOR | NAPA | 94558 | 38 C3 |
| SALYER | TRI | 95563 | 10 D5 |
| SAMOA | HUM | 95560 | 9 D5 |
| SAN ANDREAS | CAL | 95249 | 41 A3 |
| *SAN ANSELMO | MAR | 94960 | L A3 |
| SAN ANTONIO HEIGHTS | SBD | 91786 | U D1 |
| SAN ARDO | MON | 93450 | 65 D3 |
| SAN BENITO | SBT | 95023 | 55 C5 |
| *SAN BERNARDINO | SBD | 92402 | 99 C1 |
| SANBORN | KER | 93501 | 80 A5 |
| *SAN BRUNO | SMCO | 94066 | N C1 |
| SAN CARLOS | SDCO | 92119 | V D2 |
| *SAN CARLOS | SMCO | 94070 | N D2 |
| *SAN CLEMENTE | ORA | 92672 | 105 D1 |
| SANDBERG | LACO | 93532 | 89 A2 |
| *SAND CITY | MON | 93955 | 54 B4 |
| *SAN DIEGO | SDCO | 92101 | V B3 |
| SAN DIEGO COUNTRY EST | SDCO | 92065 | 107 B4 |
| *SAN DIMAS | LACO | 91773 | U B2 |
| SANDY | CLK | | 74 A5 |
| SAN FELIPE | SDCO | 92086 | 107 C3 |
| *SAN FERNANDO | LACO | 91341 | Q C1 |
| *SAN FRANCISCO | SFCO | 94101 | L B4 |
| *SAN GABRIEL | LACO | 91776 | R C3 |
| *SANGER | FRCO | 93657 | 57 E3 |
| SAN GERONIMO | MAR | 94963 | 38 A5 |
| SAN GORGONIO | RCO | 92282 | 100 B3 |
| SAN GREGORIO | SMCO | 94074 | N C3 |
| *SAN JACINTO | RCO | 92383 | 99 E3 |
| *SAN JOAQUIN | FRCO | 93660 | 56 E4 |
| *SAN JOSE | SCL | 95103 | P B3 |
| *SAN JUAN BAUTISTA | SBT | 95045 | 54 D3 |
| *SAN JUAN CAPISTRANO | ORA | 92675 | 98 D5 |
| SAN JUAN HOT SPRINGS | ORA | 92675 | 98 E5 |
| *SAN LEANDRO | ALA | 94577 | L E5 |
| SAN LORENZO | ALA | 94580 | L E5 |
| SAN LUCAS | MON | 93954 | 65 D3 |
| *SAN LUIS OBISPO | SLO | 93401 | 76 B3 |
| SAN LUIS REY | SDCO | 92068 | 106 B2 |
| SAN LUIS REY HEIGHTS | SDCO | 92028 | 106 C2 |
| *SAN MARCOS | SDCO | 92069 | 106 D3 |
| SAN MARIN | MAR | 94947 | L A2 |
| *SAN MARINO | LACO | 91108 | R C3 |
| SAN MARTIN | SCL | 95046 | P D5 |
| *SAN MATEO | SMCO | 94401 | N C1 |
| SAN MIGUEL | SLO | 93451 | 66 A5 |
| SAN ONOFRE | SDCO | 92672 | 105 E1 |
| *SAN PABLO | CC | 94806 | L C3 |
| SAN PASQUAL | SDCO | 92025 | 106 E3 |
| SAN PEDRO | LACO | 90731 | S C3 |
| SAN QUENTIN | MAR | 94964 | L B3 |
| *SAN RAFAEL | MAR | 94901 | L B3 |
| *SAN RAMON | CC | 94583 | M B4 |
| SAN SIMEON | SLO | 93452 | 75 B1 |
| *SANTA ANA | ORA | 92701 | T D3 |
| SANTA ANA GARDENS | ORA | 92704 | T D3 |
| *SANTA BARBARA | SB | 93101 | 87 C4 |
| *SANTA CLARA | SCL | 95050 | P B3 |
| *SANTA CRUZ | SCR | 95060 | 53 E2 |
| *SANTA FE SPRINGS | LACO | 90670 | R C5 |
| SANTA MARGARITA | SLO | 93453 | 76 B3 |
| *SANTA MARIA | SB | 93454 | 86 B1 |
| *SANTA MONICA | LACO | 90402 | Q B4 |
| *SANTA PAULA | VEN | 93060 | 88 C5 |
| SANTA RITA | ALA | 94566 | M C5 |
| SANTA RITA | MON | 93901 | 54 C3 |
| SANTA RITA PARK | MER | 93660 | 56 B1 |
| *SANTA ROSA | SON | 95401 | 37 E2 |
| SANTA SUSANA | VEN | 93065 | 89 A5 |
| SANTA SUSANA PARK | VEN | 93063 | 89 A5 |
| SANTA VENETIA | MAR | 94903 | L B3 |
| SANTA YNEZ | SB | 93460 | 86 E3 |
| SANTA YSABEL | SDCO | 92070 | 107 C3 |
| *SANTEE | SDCO | 92071 | V D2 |
| SAN YSIDRO | SDCO | 92073 | V D5 |
| *SARATOGA | SCL | 95070 | P A4 |
| SATICOY | VEN | 93003 | 88 C5 |
| SATTLEY | SIE | 96124 | 27 C3 |
| SAUGUS | LACO | 91350 | 89 B4 |
| *SAUSALITO | MAR | 94965 | L B4 |
| SAWYERS BAR | SIS | 96027 | 11 B2 |
| SCALES | SIE | 95981 | 26 C4 |
| SCHELLVILLE | SON | 95476 | L B1 |
| SCISSORS CROSSING | SDCO | 92036 | 107 D3 |
| SCOTIA | HUM | 95565 | 16 A3 |
| SCOTT BAR | SIS | 96085 | 3 C4 |
| SCOTT DAM | LAK | 95469 | 23 C5 |
| SCOTTS CORNER | ALA | 94586 | P B1 |
| *SCOTTS VALLEY | SCR | 95060 | P A5 |
| SCOTTYS CASTLE | INY | 92328 | 61 B1 |
| SCRIPPS MIRAMAR RANCH | SDCO | 92131 | V C1 |
| SEACLIFF | SFCO | 94121 | 141 C2 |
| SEA CLIFF | VEN | 93001 | 87 E5 |
| *SEAL BEACH | ORA | 90740 | T A3 |
| SEA RANCH | SON | 95412 | 30 E5 |
| SEARCHLIGHT | CLK | | 85 A2 |
| SEARCHLIGHT JUNCTION | SBD | 92332 | 95 B1 |
| SEARS POINT | SON | 94952 | L B2 |
| *SEASIDE | MON | 93955 | 54 B4 |
| *SEBASTOPOL | SON | 95472 | 37 E2 |
| SEDCO HILLS | RCO | 92330 | 99 C4 |
| SEELEY | IMP | 92273 | 108 E5 |
| SEIAD VALLEY | SIS | 96086 | 3 B3 |
| SEIGLER SPRINGS | LAK | 95426 | 31 E4 |
| *SELMA | FRCO | 93662 | 57 E4 |
| SENECA | PLU | 95923 | 20 C5 |
| SEPULVEDA | LACO | 91335 | Q B2 |
| SERENE LAKES | PLA | 95728 | 35 C1 |
| SERENO DEL MAR | SON | 94923 | 37 C2 |
| SERRA MESA | SDCO | 92123 | V C3 |
| SEVEN PINES | INY | 93526 | 59 E3 |
| SHADOW HILLS | LAK | 95461 | 32 A4 |
| SHADY DELL | SDCO | 92065 | V E1 |
| SHADY GLEN | PLA | 95713 | 34 D2 |
| *SHAFTER | KER | 93263 | 78 B2 |
| SHANDON | SLO | 93461 | 76 D1 |
| SHASTA | SHA | 96087 | 18 B2 |
| SHAVER LAKE HEIGHTS | FRCO | 93664 | 58 B1 |
| SHAVER LAKE POINT | FRCO | 93664 | 50 B5 |
| SHEEP RANCH | CAL | 95250 | 41 B3 |
| SHELL BEACH | SLO | 93449 | 76 B4 |
| SHELL TRACT | SON | | 39 A5 |
| SHELTER VALLEY RANCHOS | SDCO | 92036 | 107 D4 |
| SHERIDAN | SON | 95462 | 37 C2 |
| SHERMAN OAKS | LACO | 91403 | Q C3 |
| SHINGLE MILL | SON | 95480 | 31 A5 |
| SHINGLE SPRINGS | ED | 95682 | 34 D5 |
| SHINGLETOWN | SHA | 96088 | 19 A3 |
| SHIVELY | HUM | 95565 | 16 B3 |
| SHORE ACRES | CC | 94565 | 39 A4 |
| SHOSHONE | INY | 92384 | 73 A4 |
| SHUMWAY | LAS | | 21 B1 |
| SIERRA BROOKS | SIE | 96135 | 27 D3 |
| SIERRA CITY | SIE | 96125 | 27 A4 |
| *SIERRA MADRE | LACO | 91024 | R D2 |
| SIERRAVILLE | SIE | 96126 | 27 C4 |
| *SIGNAL HILL | LACO | 90806 | S D2 |
| SILVERADO CANYON | ORA | 92676 | 98 E4 |
| SILVER CITY | LYON | | 36 C1 |
| SILVER CITY | TUL | 93271 | 59 B5 |
| SILVER FORK | ED | 95728 | 35 C4 |
| SILVER LAKE | LACO | 90039 | Q E3 |
| SILVERPEAK | ESM | | 52 D1 |
| SILVER STRAND | VEN | 93030 | 96 B1 |
| *SIMI VALLEY | VEN | 93065 | 89 A5 |
| SIMMLER | SLO | 93453 | 77 B3 |
| SISQUOC | SB | 93454 | 86 C1 |
| SITES | COL | 95979 | 32 C1 |
| SKAGGS SPRINGS | SON | 95448 | 31 C5 |
| SKIDOO | INY | 92328 | 61 D5 |
| SKYFOREST | SBD | 92385 | 99 C1 |
| SKY LONDA | SMCO | 94062 | N D3 |
| SKY VALLEY | RCO | 92240 | 100 E3 |
| SLEEPY HOLLOW | MAR | 94960 | L A3 |
| SLEEPY VALLEY | LACO | 91350 | 89 D4 |
| SLIDE INN | TUO | 95335 | 41 E4 |
| SLOAN | CLK | | 74 D4 |
| SLOAT | PLU | 96127 | 26 E2 |
| SLOUGHHOUSE | SAC | 95683 | 40 B1 |
| SMARTVILLE | YUB | 95977 | 34 A2 |


*INDICATES INCORPORATED CITY

# CITIES AND COMMUNITIES INDEX


| COMMUNITY NAME | CO. | ZIP CODE | PAGE & GRID |
|---|---|---|---|
| SMITHFLAT | ED | 95727 | 34 E5 |
| SMITH RIVER | DN | 95567 | 1 E3 |
| SMITH STATION | TUO | 95321 | 49 A1 |
| SNELLING | MCO | 95369 | 48 C3 |
| SOBOBA HOT SPRINGS | RCO | 92383 | 99 E3 |
| SODA BAY | LAK | 95443 | 31 D3 |
| SODA SPRINGS | NEV | 95728 | 27 C5 |
| SODA SPRINGS | SON | 95728 | 31 A5 |
| *SOLANA BEACH | SDCO | 92075 | 106 B4 |
| *SOLEDAD | MON | 93960 | 55 A5 |
| *SOLVANG | SB | 93463 | 86 E3 |
| SOMERSET | ED | 95684 | 35 A5 |
| SOMES BAR | SIS | 95568 | 10 E2 |
| SOMIS | VEN | 93066 | 88 D5 |
| *SONOMA | SON | 95476 | L B1 |
| *SONORA | TUO | 95370 | 41 C5 |
| SONORA JUNCTION | MNO | 93517 | 42 E2 |
| SOQUEL | SCR | 95073 | 54 A2 |
| SORRENTO VALLEY | SDCO | 92121 | V B1 |
| SOULSBYVILLE | TUO | 95372 | 41 D5 |
| SOUTH BELRIDGE | KER | 93251 | 77 D2 |
| SOUTH DOS PALOS | MCO | 93665 | 56 A2 |
| *SOUTH EL MONTE | LACO | 91733 | R C4 |
| SOUTH FORK | MAD | | 49 E5 |
| SOUTH FORK | MPA | 95318 | 49 B2 |
| *SOUTH GATE | LACO | 90280 | R A5 |
| SOUTH LAGUNA | ORA | 92677 | T E5 |
| SOUTH LAKE | KER | 93283 | 79 D1 |
| *SOUTH LAKE TAHOE | ED | 95705 | 36 A3 |
| SOUTH OF MARKET | SFCO | 94103 | 143 C4 |
| SOUTH OROVILLE | BUT | 95965 | 25 D4 |
| SOUTH PARK | SON | 95404 | 38 A2 |
| *SOUTH PASADENA | LACO | 91030 | R B3 |
| SOUTHPORT | YOL | 95691 | 39 D1 |
| *SOUTH SAN FRANCISCO | SMCO | 94080 | N C1 |
| SOUTH SAN GABRIEL | LACO | 91770 | R B4 |
| SOUTH TAFT | KER | 93268 | 78 A4 |
| SPANISH CREEK | PLU | 95971 | 26 D1 |
| SPANISH FLAT WOODLANDS | NAPA | 94558 | 38 D1 |
| SPANISH RANCH | PLU | 95956 | 26 C1 |
| SPARKS | WSH | | 28 C4 |
| SPAULDING | LAS | 96130 | 20 D1 |
| SPENCEVILLE | NEV | 95945 | 34 B2 |
| SPRECKELS | MON | 93962 | 54 D4 |
| SPRING GARDEN | PLU | 95971 | 26 E2 |
| SPRING TOWN | ALA | 94550 | M C5 |
| SPRING VALLEY | SDCO | 92077 | V D3 |
| SPRINGVILLE | TUL | 93265 | 68 E2 |
| SPRINGVILLE | VEN | 93010 | 96 C1 |
| SQUAW VALLEY | FRCO | 93646 | 58 B3 |
| SQUIRREL MTN VALLEY | KER | 93240 | 79 D1 |
| STAFFORD | HUM | 95565 | 16 A3 |
| STAGECOACH | LYON | | 28 E5 |
| STANDARD | TUO | 95373 | 41 D5 |
| STANDISH | LAS | 96128 | 21 B3 |
| STANFIELD HILL | YUB | 95918 | 34 A1 |
| STANFORD | SCL | 94305 | N D2 |
| STANISLAUS | TUO | 95247 | 41 C4 |
| *STANTON | ORA | 90680 | T B2 |
| *STATELINE | WSH | | 36 B3 |
| STAUFFER | VEN | 93225 | 88 C2 |
| STENT | TUO | 95347 | 41 C5 |
| STEVINSON | MCO | 95374 | 47 E4 |
| STEWART | CRSN | | 36 C2 |
| STEWART-LENNOX | KLAM | | 5 B1 |
| STEWARTS POINT | SON | 95480 | 30 E5 |
| STINSON BEACH | MAR | 94970 | L A4 |
| STIRLING CITY | BUT | 95978 | 25 D2 |
| *STOCKTON | SJCO | 95201 | 40 B3 |
| STONYFORD | COL | 95979 | 24 B5 |
| STOVEPIPE WELLS | INY | 92328 | 61 D4 |
| STRATFORD | KIN | 93266 | 67 C2 |
| STRATHMORE | TUL | 93267 | 68 D2 |
| STRAWBERRY | ED | 95735 | 35 D4 |
| STRAWBERRY | TUO | 95375 | 42 A3 |
| STRAWBERRY VALLEY | YUB | 95981 | 26 A4 |
| STRONGHOLD | MOD | 96431 | 5 E3 |
| STUDIO CITY | LACO | 91604 | Q C3 |
| SUGAR LOAF | SBD | 92386 | 92 A5 |
| SUGARLOAF VILLAGE | TUL | 93260 | 69 B4 |
| SUGAR PINE | MAD | 95389 | 49 D3 |
| SUGARPINE | TUO | 95346 | 41 D4 |
| *SUISUN CITY | SOL | 94585 | M A1 |
| SULTANA | TUL | 93666 | 58 B5 |
| SUMMERHOME PARK | SON | 95436 | 37 D2 |
| SUMMERLAND | SB | 93067 | 87 D4 |
| SUMMIT | SBD | 92322 | 91 A5 |
| SUMMIT | VEN | 93023 | 88 C4 |
| SUMMIT CITY | SHA | 96089 | 18 B1 |
| SUN CITY | RCO | 92381 | 99 C4 |
| SUNLAND | LACO | 91040 | Q D1 |
| SUNNYBROOK | AMA | 95640 | 40 D2 |
| SUNNYSIDE | SDCO | 92002 | V D4 |
| SUNNYSLOPE | RCO | 93656 | 99 A2 |
| *SUNNYVALE | SCL | 94086 | P A3 |
| SUNNY VISTA | SDCO | 92010 | V D4 |
| SUNOL | ALA | 94586 | P B1 |
| SUNSET | SFCO | 94122 | 141 B5 |
| SUNSET BEACH | ORA | 90742 | T A3 |
| SUNSET ESTATES | PLA | 95678 | 33 E4 |
| SUN VALLEY | LACO | 91352 | Q D2 |
| SUN VALLEY | WSH | | 28 B4 |
| SURF | SB | 93436 | 86 A3 |
| SURFSIDE | ORA | 90743 | T A3 |

| COMMUNITY NAME | CO. | ZIP CODE | PAGE & GRID |
|---|---|---|---|
| *SUSANVILLE | LAS | 96130 | 20 E3 |
| SUTCLIFFE | WSH | | 28 C1 |
| SUTTER | SUT | 95982 | 33 C2 |
| *SUTTER CREEK | AMA | 95685 | 40 E2 |
| SWANSBORO COUNTRY | ED | 95727 | 35 A4 |
| SWANSEA | INY | 93545 | 60 C5 |
| SWEETBRIER | SHA | 96017 | 12 C3 |
| SWEETLAND | NEV | 95959 | 26 B5 |
| SWEETWATER | LYON | | 43 C1 |
| SYCAMORE | COL | 95957 | 33 A2 |
| SYLMAR | LACO | 91342 | Q B1 |
| SYLMAR SQUARE | LACO | 91342 | Q C1 |
| SYLVIA PARK | LACO | 90290 | Q A3 |
| T | | | |
| *TAFT | KER | 93268 | 78 A4 |
| TAFT HEIGHTS | KER | 93268 | 77 E4 |
| TAHOE CITY | PLA | 95730 | 35 E2 |
| TAHOE PINES | PLA | 95718 | 35 D2 |
| TAHOE VILLAGE | DGL | | 36 B3 |
| TAHOE VISTA | PLA | 95732 | 36 A1 |
| TAHOMA | PLA | 95733 | 35 E2 |
| TAKILMA | JOS | | 2 D2 |
| TALENT | JKSN | | 3 E1 |
| TALMAGE | MEN | 95481 | 31 B2 |
| TAMALPAIS VALLEY | MAR | 94941 | L A4 |
| TAMARACK | CAL | 95223 | 41 E2 |
| TANCRED | YOL | 95606 | 32 D5 |
| TARZANA | LACO | 91356 | Q A3 |
| TASSAJARA | CC | | 46 B1 |
| TASSAJARA HOT SPRGS | MON | 93924 | 64 D2 |
| TAYLORSVILLE | PLU | 95983 | 20 D5 |
| TECATE | BAJA | | 112 C2 |
| TECATE | SDCO | 92080 | 112 C2 |
| TECOPA | INY | 92389 | 73 A4 |
| TECOPA HOT SPRINGS | INY | 92389 | 73 A4 |
| *TEHACHAPI | KER | 93561 | 79 D4 |
| TEHACHAPI EAST | KER | 93561 | 79 D4 |
| *TEHAMA | TEH | 96090 | 24 D1 |
| TELEGRAPH CITY | CAL | 95228 | 40 E5 |
| TELEGRAPH HILL | SFCO | 94133 | 142 D1 |
| TEMECULA | RCO | 92390 | 106 C1 |
| *TEMPLE CITY | LACO | 91780 | R C3 |
| TEMPLETON | SLO | 93465 | 76 A2 |
| TENNANT | SIS | 96012 | 5 B5 |
| TERMINOUS | SJCO | 95240 | 39 E4 |
| TERMO | LAS | 96132 | 8 B5 |
| TERRA BELLA | TUL | 93270 | 68 D3 |
| TERRA LINDA | MAR | 94903 | L A3 |
| THE HIGHLANDS | SMCO | 94402 | N C2 |
| THE ISTHMUS | LACO | 90704 | 105 D5 |
| THE NARROWS | SDCO | 92004 | 108 A3 |
| THERMAL | RCO | 92274 | 101 B5 |
| THERMALANDS | PLA | 95648 | 34 B3 |
| THE WILLOWS | SDCO | 92001 | 107 B5 |
| THISBE | WSH | | 28 E4 |
| THORNE | MIN | | 44 B1 |
| THORNTON | SJCO | 95686 | 39 E3 |
| *THOUSAND OAKS | VEN | 91360 | 96 E1 |
| THOUSAND PALMS | RCO | 92276 | 100 E3 |
| THREE ARCH BAY | ORA | 92677 | 98 D5 |
| THREE RIVERS | TUL | 93271 | 58 D5 |
| *TIBURON | MAR | 94920 | L B4 |
| TIERRA BUENA | SUT | 95991 | 33 C2 |
| TIERRA DEL SOL | SDCO | 92005 | 112 E2 |
| TIERRASANTA | SDCO | 92124 | V C2 |
| TIJUANA | BAJA | | 111 D2 |
| TIMBER LODGE | MPA | 95345 | 49 B3 |
| TIPTON | TUL | 93272 | 68 B3 |
| TISDALE | SUT | 95957 | 33 B3 |
| TOBIN | PLU | 95965 | 26 A1 |
| TOLLHOUSE | FRCO | 93667 | 58 A2 |
| TOMALES | MAR | 94971 | 37 D3 |
| TOMS PLACE | MNO | 93546 | 50 B2 |
| TOPANGA | LACO | 90290 | Q A3 |
| TOPANGA PARK | LACO | 90290 | 97 B1 |
| TOPAZ | MNO | 96133 | 36 D5 |
| TOPOCK | MOH | | 95 E2 |
| *TORRANCE | LACO | 90505 | S B2 |
| TOWER HOUSE | SHA | 96095 | 18 A2 |
| TOYON | SHA | 96019 | 18 C1 |
| TRABUCO CANYON | ORA | 92678 | 98 E4 |
| *TRACY | SJCO | 95376 | 46 E2 |
| TRAIL PARK | ED | 95651 | 34 E4 |
| TRANQUILLITY | FRCO | 93668 | 56 D4 |
| TRAVER | TUL | 93673 | 57 E5 |
| TRAVIS AIR FORCE BASE | SOL | 94535 | 39 A3 |
| TRES PINOS | SBT | 95075 | 55 A3 |
| *TRINIDAD | HUM | 95570 | 9 E4 |
| TRINITY CENTER | TRI | 96091 | 11 E4 |
| TRIUNFO | VEN | 91362 | 96 E1 |
| TRONA | SBD | 93562 | 71 B5 |
| TROPICO | KER | 93560 | 89 E1 |
| TROWBRIDGE | SUT | 95659 | 33 D3 |
| TROY | PLA | 95728 | 35 B1 |
| TRUCKEE | NEV | 95734 | 27 D5 |
| TUDOR | SUT | 95991 | 33 C3 |
| TUJUNGA | LACO | 91042 | Q E1 |
| *TULARE | TUL | 93274 | 68 A2 |
| *TULELAKE | SIS | 96134 | 5 D2 |
| TUOLUMNE | TUO | 95379 | 41 D5 |
| TUOLUMNE MEADOWS | TUO | 95379 | 43 A5 |
| TUPMAN | KER | 93276 | 78 B3 |
| *TURLOCK | STA | 95380 | 47 E3 |
| TURTLE ROCK | ORA | 92715 | 98 C4 |

| COMMUNITY NAME | CO. | ZIP CODE | PAGE & GRID |
|---|---|---|---|
| *TUSTIN | ORA | 92680 | T E3 |
| TUTTLE | MCO | 95340 | 48 D4 |
| TWAIN | PLU | 95984 | 26 B1 |
| TWAIN HARTE | TUO | 95383 | 41 D4 |
| TWAIN HARTE VALLEY | TUO | 95383 | 41 D4 |
| TWENTYNINE PALMS | SBD | 92277 | 101 B1 |
| TWIN BRIDGES | ED | 95735 | 35 E4 |
| TWIN CITIES | SAC | 95632 | 40 A3 |
| TWIN OAKS | SDCO | 92083 | 106 C3 |
| TWIN PEAKS | SBD | 92391 | 91 C5 |
| TYNDALL LANDING | YOL | 95698 | 33 B4 |
| U | | | |
| *UKIAH | MEN | 95482 | 31 B2 |
| ULTRA | TUL | 93256 | 68 D3 |
| *UNION CITY | ALA | 94587 | P A1 |
| UNIVERSAL CITY | LACO | 91608 | Q D3 |
| UNIVERSITY CITY | SDCO | 92122 | V A2 |
| *UPLAND | SBD | 91786 | U D2 |
| UPPER LAKE | LAK | 95485 | 31 D2 |
| V | | | |
| VACATION BEACH | SON | 95446 | 37 C2 |
| *VACAVILLE | SOL | 95688 | 39 A2 |
| VALENCIA | LACO | 91355 | 89 B4 |
| VALERIE | RCO | 92274 | 101 A5 |
| VALINDA | LACO | 91744 | R E4 |
| VALLECITO | CAL | 95251 | 41 C4 |
| VALLECITO | SDCO | 92036 | 107 E4 |
| *VALLEJO | SOL | 94590 | L D2 |
| VALLEJO HEIGHTS | SOL | 94590 | 38 D4 |
| VALLE VISTA | RCO | 92343 | 99 E4 |
| VALLEY ACRES | KER | 93268 | 78 A4 |
| VALLEY CENTER | SDCO | 92082 | 106 E2 |
| VALLEY FORD | SON | 94972 | 37 D3 |
| VALLEY HOME | STA | 95384 | 47 D1 |
| VALLEY OF ENCHANTMENT | SBD | 92322 | 91 B5 |
| VALLEY SPRINGS | CAL | 95252 | 40 D3 |
| VALLEY WELLS | INY | 92366 | 71 C4 |
| VAL VERDE PARK | LACO | 91350 | 89 A4 |
| VAN NUYS | LACO | 91408 | Q C2 |
| VENICE | LACO | 90291 | Q B5 |
| VENTUCOPA | SB | 93252 | 87 E1 |
| VEN-TU PARK | VEN | 91320 | 96 D1 |
| *VENTURA | VEN | 93001 | 88 B5 |
| VERDEMONT | SBD | 92407 | 99 B1 |
| VERDI | WSH | | 28 A4 |
| VERDI SIERRA PINES | SIE | 95737 | 27 E4 |
| VERDUGO CITY | LACO | 91046 | Q E2 |
| *VERNON | LACO | 90058 | R A4 |
| VERONA | SUT | 95659 | 33 D4 |
| VICHY SPRINGS | MEN | 95482 | 31 B2 |
| VICTOR | SJCO | 95253 | 40 B4 |
| VICTORIA | SDCO | 92001 | 107 B5 |
| *VICTORVILLE | SBD | 92392 | 91 C3 |
| VIDAL | SBD | 92280 | 103 E1 |
| VIDAL JUNCTION | SBD | 92280 | 103 D1 |
| VILLA GRANDE | SON | 95486 | 37 C2 |
| *VILLA PARK | ORA | 92667 | T E2 |
| VINA | TEH | 96092 | 24 E2 |
| VINCENT | LACO | 93550 | 90 A4 |
| VINEBURG | SON | 95487 | L C1 |
| VINTON | PLU | 96135 | 27 D2 |
| VIOLA | SHA | 96088 | 19 C2 |
| VIRGILIA | PLU | 95984 | 26 B1 |
| *VIRGINIA CITY | STOR | | 36 D1 |
| VIRGINIA COLONY | VEN | 93021 | 88 E5 |
| *VISALIA | TUL | 93277 | 68 B1 |
| *VISTA | SDCO | 92083 | 106 C3 |
| VISTA VERDE | SMCO | 94025 | N D3 |
| VOLCANO | AMA | 95689 | 41 A2 |
| VOLCANOVILLE | ED | 95634 | 34 E3 |
| VOLLMERS | SHA | 96051 | 12 B4 |
| VOLTA | MER | 93635 | 55 D1 |
| VORDEN | SAC | 95690 | M E1 |
| W | | | |
| WAHTOKE PARK | FRCO | 93654 | 58 A4 |
| WALKER | MNO | 96107 | 42 E1 |
| WALLACE | ED | 95254 | 40 D3 |
| WALMORT | SAC | 95683 | 40 A2 |
| *WALNUT | LACO | 91789 | U A3 |
| *WALNUT CREEK | CC | 94595 | M A4 |
| WALNUT GROVE | SAC | 95690 | M E1 |
| WALSH LANDING | SON | 95450 | 37 A1 |
| WARM SPRING | LACO | 91310 | 89 B3 |
| WARM SPRINGS | ALA | 94538 | P B2 |
| WARNER SPRINGS | SDCO | 92086 | 107 C2 |
| *WASCO | KER | 93280 | 78 B1 |
| WASHINGTON | NEV | 95986 | 26 E5 |
| WASHOE | SON | 94952 | 37 E3 |
| WASHOE CITY | WSH | | 28 B5 |
| *WATERFORD | STA | 95386 | 48 A2 |
| WATERLOO | SJCO | 95201 | 40 B4 |
| *WATSONVILLE | SCR | 95076 | 54 C2 |
| WATTS | LACO | 90002 | Q E5 |
| WAWONA | MPA | 95389 | 49 D3 |
| WEAVERVILLE | TRI | 96093 | 17 D1 |
| *WEED | SIS | 96094 | 12 C1 |
| WEED PATCH | KER | 93307 | 78 E4 |
| WEIMAR | PLA | 95736 | 34 D3 |
| WEITCHPEC | HUM | 95546 | 10 C3 |
| WELDON | KER | 93283 | 79 D1 |
| WELLSONA | SLO | 93446 | 76 A1 |
| WENDEL | LAS | 96136 | 21 D3 |
| WENTWORTH SPRINGS | ED | 95725 | 35 C3 |
| WEOTT | HUM | 95571 | 16 B4 |

| COMMUNITY NAME | CO. | ZIP CODE | PAGE & GRID |
|---|---|---|---|
| WEST BRANCH | BUT | 95941 | 25 C1 |
| WEST BUTTE | SUT | 95953 | 33 B2 |
| *WEST COVINA | LACO | 91790 | U A2 |
| WESTERN ADDITION | SFCO | 94115 | 143 A4 |
| WEST HAVEN | FRCO | 93234 | 67 B2 |
| *WEST HOLLYWOOD | LACO | 90069 | Q D3 |
| *WESTLAKE VILLAGE | LACO | 91361 | 96 E1 |
| WESTLEY | STA | 95387 | 47 B3 |
| WEST LOS ANGELES | LACO | 90025 | Q C4 |
| *WESTMINSTER | ORA | 92683 | T B3 |
| *WESTMORELAND | IMP | 92281 | 109 A4 |
| WEST OF TWIN PEAKS | SFCO | 94122 | 141 D5 |
| WEST PITTSBURG | CC | 94565 | M B3 |
| WEST POINT | CAL | 95255 | 41 B2 |
| WESTPORT | MEN | 95488 | 22 C4 |
| *WEST SACRAMENTO | YOL | 95691 | 39 D1 |
| WEST SIDE | LAKE | | 7 B1 |
| WESTVILLE | PLA | 95631 | 35 A2 |
| WESTWOOD | LAS | 96137 | 20 C4 |
| WESTWOOD | LACO | 90024 | 97 C4 |
| *WHEATLAND | YUB | 95692 | 33 E3 |
| WHEATON SPRINGS | SBD | 92364 | 84 B2 |
| WHEATVILLE | FRCO | 93656 | 57 A5 |
| WHEELER RIDGE | KER | 93284 | 78 D5 |
| WHEELER SPRINGS | VEN | 93023 | 88 A4 |
| WHISKEYTOWN | SHA | 96095 | 18 A2 |
| WHISPERING PINES | LAK | 95461 | 32 A4 |
| WHITE HALL | ED | 95725 | 35 C4 |
| WHITE HORSE | MOD | 96054 | 13 E2 |
| WHITE PINES | CAL | 95223 | 41 C3 |
| WHITE RIVER | TUL | 93257 | 68 E4 |
| WHITETHORN | HUM | 95489 | 22 B1 |
| WHITEWATER | RCO | 92282 | 100 C3 |
| WHITE WOLF | TUO | 95389 | 42 D5 |
| WHITLEY GARDENS | SLO | 93436 | 76 C1 |
| WHITLOW | HUM | 95554 | 16 C4 |
| WHITMORE | SHA | 96096 | 19 A2 |
| *WHITTIER | LACO | 90605 | R D5 |
| WILBUR SPRINGS | COL | 95987 | 32 C3 |
| WILDOMAR | RCO | 92395 | 99 C5 |
| WILDROSE | INY | 93562 | 71 C2 |
| *WILLIAMS | COL | 95987 | 32 D2 |
| WILLIAMS | JOS | | 3 A1 |
| *WILLITS | MEN | 95490 | 23 A5 |
| WILLOW CREEK | HUM | 95573 | 10 D5 |
| WILLOW RANCH | MOD | 96138 | 7 C3 |
| *WILLOWS | GLE | 95988 | 24 D4 |
| WILLOW SPRINGS | KER | 93550 | 89 D1 |
| WILMINGTON | LACO | 90744 | S C2 |
| WILSEYVILLE | CAL | 95257 | 41 B2 |
| WILSONIA | TUL | 93633 | 58 E3 |
| WILTON | SAC | 95693 | 40 B2 |
| WINCHESTER | RCO | 92396 | 99 D4 |
| WINCHUCK | CUR | | 1 D2 |
| WINDSOR | SON | 95492 | 37 E1 |
| WINTER GARDENS | SDCO | 92040 | V E2 |
| WINTERHAVEN | IMP | 92283 | 112 C5 |
| *WINTERS | YOL | 95694 | 39 A1 |
| WINTERWARM | SDCO | 92028 | 106 C2 |
| WISHON | MAD | 93669 | 49 E4 |
| WITCH CREEK | SDCO | 92065 | 107 B3 |
| WITTER SPRINGS | LAK | 95493 | 31 D2 |
| WOFFORD HEIGHTS | KER | 93285 | 69 C5 |
| WOLF | NEV | 95945 | 34 B2 |
| WONDER VALLEY | FRCO | 93657 | 58 B3 |
| WOODACRE | MAR | 94973 | L A3 |
| WOODBRIDGE | ORA | 92714 | T E4 |
| WOODCREST | RCO | 92504 | 99 B3 |
| WOODFORD | KER | 96120 | 79 B4 |
| WOODFORDS | ALP | 96120 | 36 B4 |
| *WOODLAKE | TUL | 93286 | 58 D5 |
| *WOODLAND | YOL | 95695 | 33 B5 |
| WOODLAND HILLS | LACO | 91364 | Q A3 |
| *WOODSIDE | SMCO | 94062 | N D2 |
| WOODSIDE VILLAGE | LACO | 91792 | R E4 |
| WOODVILLE | TUL | 93257 | 68 C3 |
| WOODY | KER | 93287 | 69 A5 |
| WORDEN | KLAM | | 5 B2 |
| WRIGHTS LAKE | ED | 95720 | 35 D4 |
| WRIGHTWOOD | SBD | 92397 | 90 E5 |
| WYANDOTTE | BUT | 95965 | 25 D5 |
| WYNOLA | SDCO | 92036 | 107 C3 |
| Y | | | |
| YANKEE HILL | BUT | 95969 | 25 D3 |
| YANKEE JIMS | PLA | 95631 | 34 D3 |
| YERMO | SBD | 92398 | 92 A1 |
| YETTEM | TUL | 93670 | 58 B5 |
| YOLO | YOL | 95697 | 33 B5 |
| *YORBA LINDA | ORA | 92686 | T D1 |
| YORKVILLE | MEN | 95494 | 31 B4 |
| YOSEMITE FORKS | MAD | 93644 | 49 D4 |
| YOSEMITE VILLAGE | MPA | 95389 | 49 D1 |
| YOUNGSTOWN | SJCO | 95220 | 40 B4 |
| *YOUNTVILLE | NAPA | 94599 | 38 C2 |
| *YREKA | SIS | 96097 | 4 A4 |
| *YUBA CITY | SUT | 95991 | 33 C2 |
| YUCAIPA | SBD | 92399 | 99 D2 |
| YUCCA VALLEY | SBD | 92284 | 100 E1 |
| *YUMA | YUMA | | 112 D5 |
| Z | | | |
| ZAMORA | YOL | 95698 | 33 B4 |
| ZENIA | TRI | 95495 | 16 E4 |
| ZEPHYR COVE | DGL | | 36 A3 |








*INDICATES INCORPORATED CITY

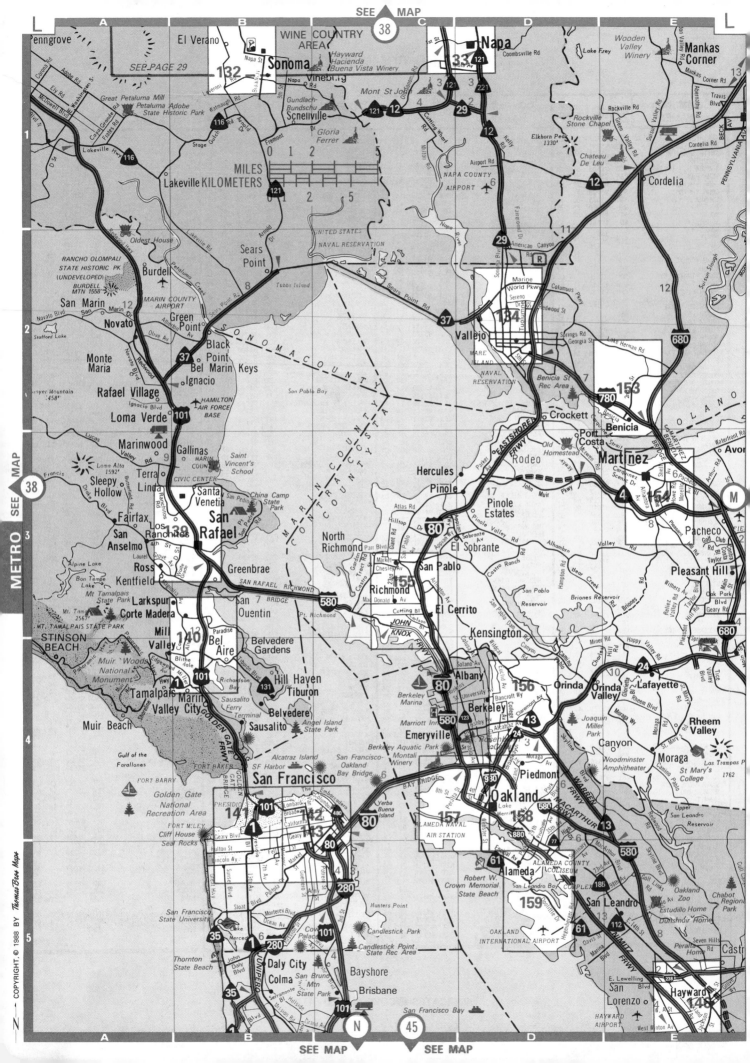

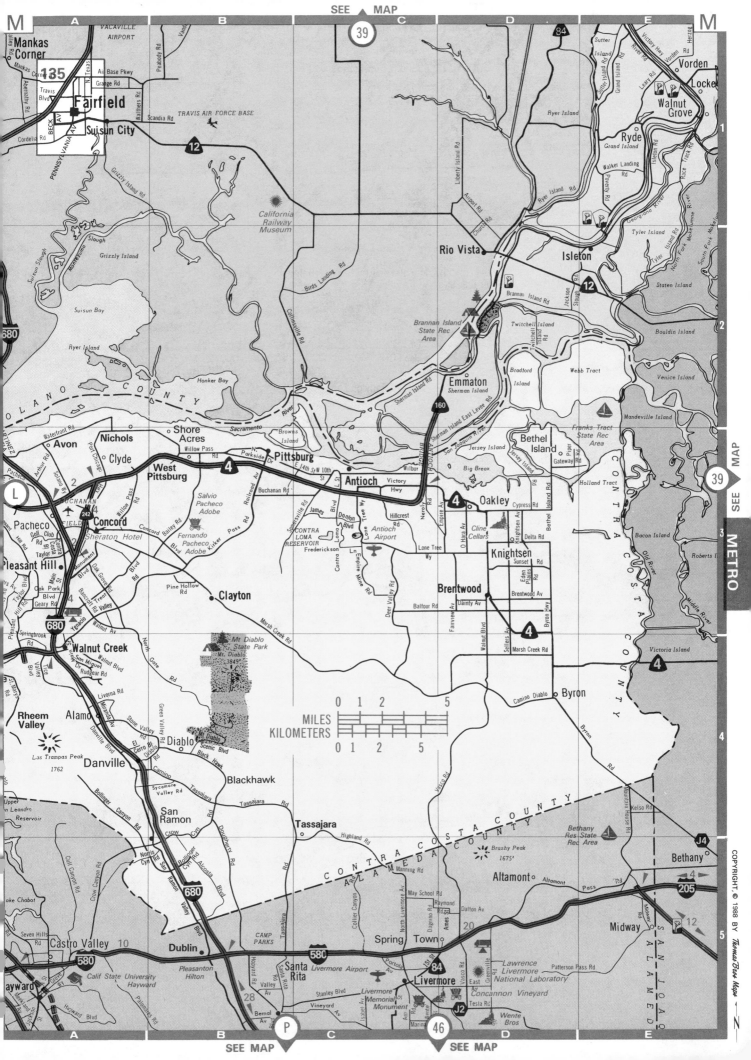

PACIFIC

Brisbane

35

101

SERRA FRWY

South San Francisco

82 380

San Bruno

35

144

Millbrae

Pacifica

SHARP PARK BEACH

Rockaway Beach

San Pedro Point

Linda Mar

DEVILS SLIDE

San Andreas Lake

San Francisco State Fish and Game Refuge

Hillsborough

Burlingame

San Mateo

SAN FRANCISCO INTERNATIONAL AIRPORT

San Francisco Airport Marriott

San Francisco Bay

SAN MATEO BRIDGE

YOUNGER FRWY

San Lorenzo

Hayward

HAYWARD AIRPORT

46

13

92

ALAMEDA COUNTY

Graywhale Cove State Beach

Montara State Beach

Montara Mountain

Montara

Moss Beach

Moss Beach

Pilarcitos Lake

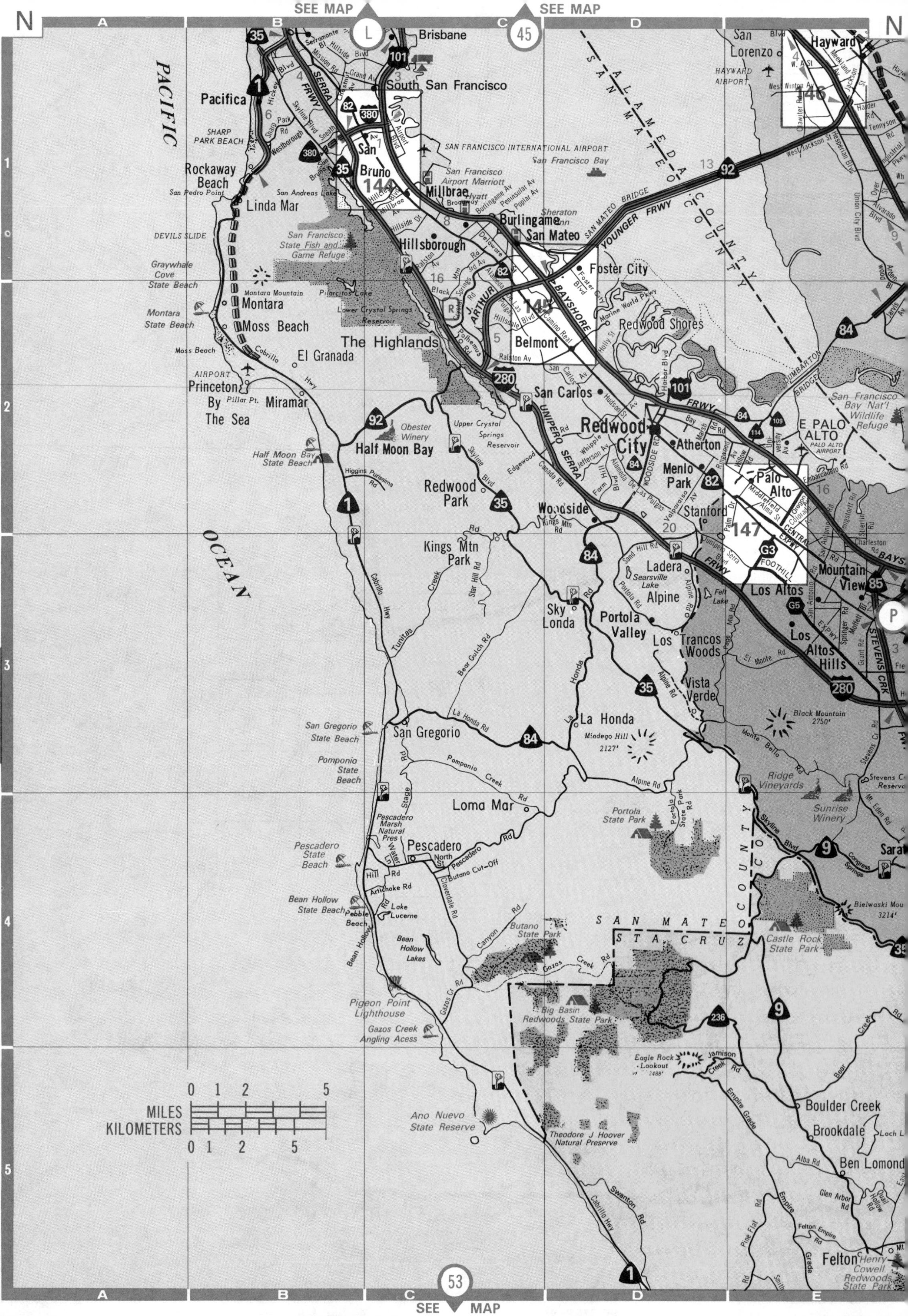

Lower Crystal Springs Reservoir

The Highlands

El Granada

J. ARTHUR

BAYSHORE

144

Foster City

Redwood Shores

Belmont

San Carlos

280

AIRPORT

Princeton By The Sea

Miramar

Pillar Pt.

92

Obester Winery

Upper Crystal Springs Reservoir

UNIPERO SERRA

101 FRWY

Redwood City

Atherton

Menlo Park

82

E PALO ALTO

Palo Alto

PALO ALTO AIRPORT

84

109

114

San Francisco Bay Nat'l Wildlife Refuge

DUMBARTON BRIDGE

Half Moon Bay

Half Moon Bay State Beach

Higgins Purissima Rd

1

Redwood Park

35

Woodside

84

Kings Mtn Park

Sky Londa

Ladera

Searsville Lake

Alpine

Stanford

147

G3 FOOTHILL

Mountain View

85

P

OCEAN

Portola Valley

Los Trancos Woods

Los Altos

G5

Los Altos Hills

280

STEVENS CRK

35

Vista Verde

Black Mountain 2750'

La Honda

Mindego Hill 2127'

San Gregorio State Beach

Pomponio State Beach

San Gregorio

84

La Honda Rd

Pomponio Creek

Alpine Rd

Ridge Vineyards

Sunrise Winery

Monte Bello

Stevens Cr Reservo

Loma Mar

Portola State Park

SAN MATEO COUNTY

Skyline Blvd

9

Sarato

Congress Springs

Pescadero Marsh Natural Pres

Pescadero State Beach

Pescadero

North St

Butano Cut-Off

Cloverdale Rd

Bean Hollow State Beach

Pebble Beach

Lake Lucerne

Bean Hollow Lakes

Butano State Park

Gazos Creek Rd

SAN MATEO
STA. CRUZ

Castle Rock State Park

Bielwaski Mou 3214'

9

Pigeon Point Lighthouse

Gazos Creek Angling Acess

Big Basin Redwoods State Park

236

Eagle Rock Lookout 2488'

Jamison Creek Rd

Boulder Creek

Brookdale

MILES

0 1 2 5

KILOMETERS

0 1 2 5

Ano Nuevo State Reserve

Theodore J Hoover Natural Preserve

Ben Lomond

Glen Arbor Rd

Felton

Henry Cowell Redwoods State Park

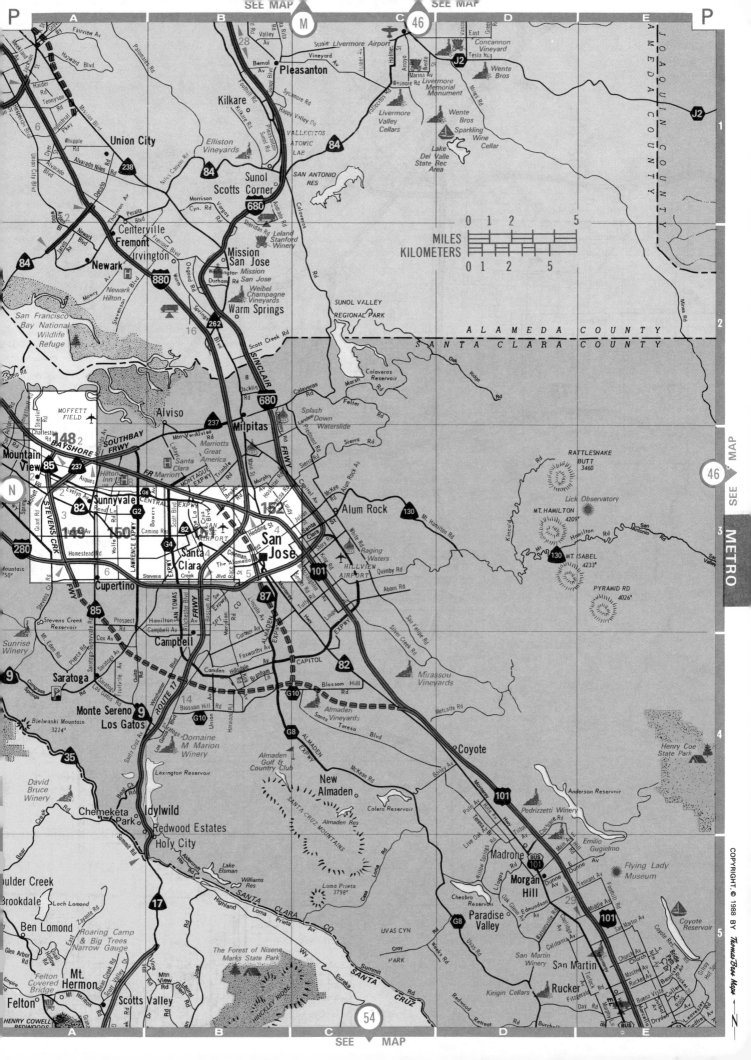

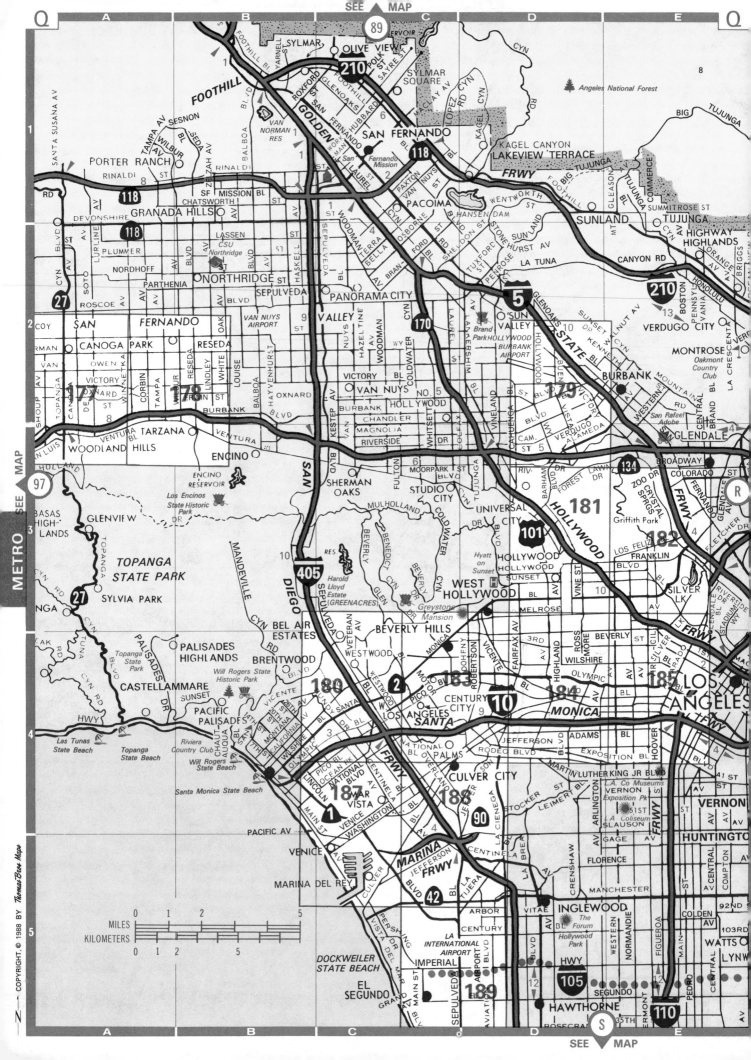

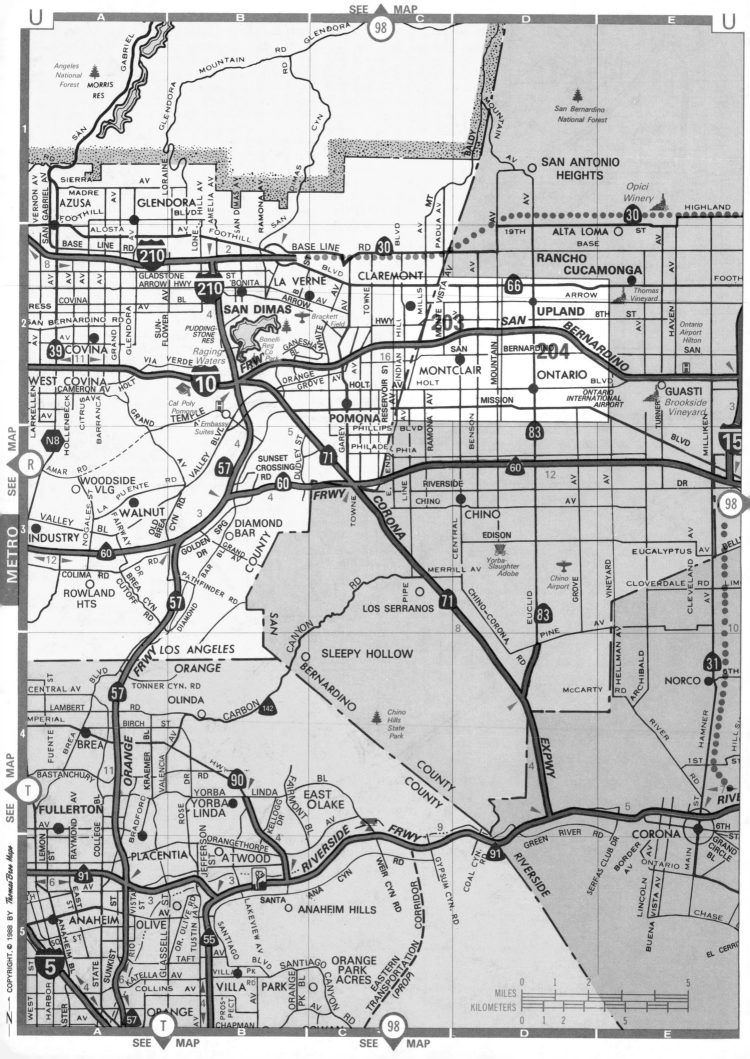

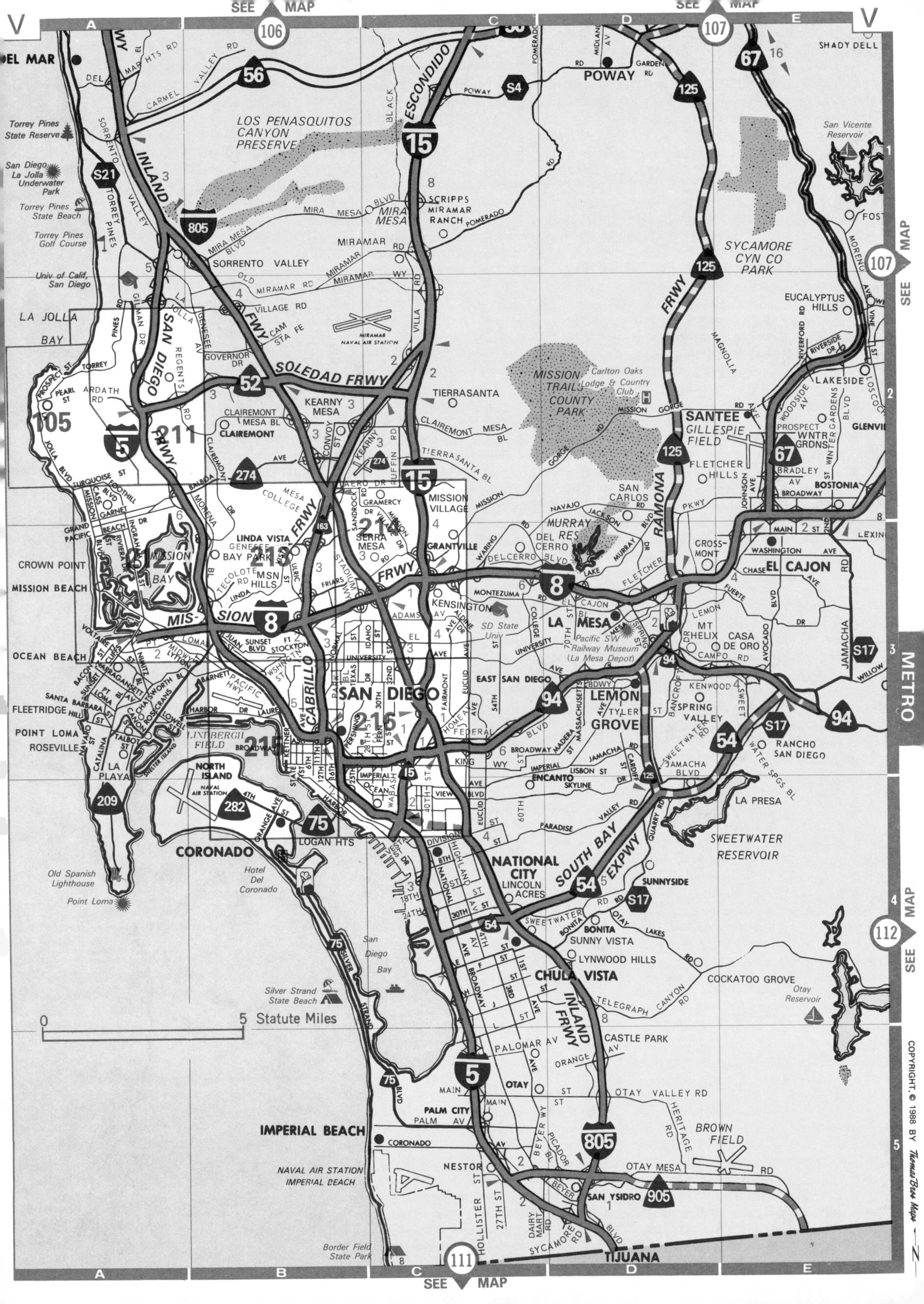

EL MAR

Torrey Pines State Reserve
San Diego La Jolla Underwater Park
Torrey Pines State Beach
Torrey Pines Golf Course
Univ of Calif, San Diego

LOS PENASQUITOS CANYON PRESERVE

56

POWAY

67 · 16 · SHADY DELL

125

San Vicente Reservoir

15

S4

POWAY

SYCAMORE CYN CO PARK

EUCALYPTUS HILLS

LAKESIDE

GLENVIEW

LA JOLLA BAY

INLAND FWY

SORRENTO VALLEY

MIRAMAR
MIRA MESA
SCRIPPS MIRAMAR RANCH
MIRAMAR NAVAL AIR STATION

805

SOLEDAD FRWY

52

SAN DIEGO FRWY

KEARNY MESA

TIERRASANTA

CLAIREMONT MESA

MISSION TRAILS COUNTY PARK
Carlton Oaks Lodge & Country Club

SANTEE
GILLESPIE FIELD
FLETCHER HILLS

BOSTONIA

67

125

RAMONA

105

211

274

CLAIREMONT

LINDA VISTA
BAY PARK
MSN HILLS
SERRA MESA
213

215

MISSION VILLAGE
GRANTVILLE

SAN CARLOS
DEL CERRO

GROSSMONT

EL CAJON

CASA DE ORO

MT HELIX

8

CROWN POINT
MISSION BEACH

212

OCEAN BEACH

MISSION BAY

KENSINGTON
SD State Univ
EAST SAN DIEGO
UNIVERSITY
Pacific SW Railway Museum (La Mesa Depot)

LA MESA

94

Santa Barbara
FLEETRIDGE
POINT LOMA
ROSEVILLE
LA PLAYA

CABRILLO FRWY

SAN DIEGO

215

LEMON GROVE
SPRING VALLEY

54

S17

94

RANCHO SAN DIEGO

209

LINDBERGH FIELD

282

NORTH ISLAND NAVAL AIR STATION

75

CORONADO

LOGAN HTS

ENCANTO
SKYLINE

SOUTH BAY
54 EXPWY

LA PRESA

SWEETWATER RESERVOIR

Hotel Del Coronado

NATIONAL CITY
LINCOLN ACRES

S17

SUNNYSIDE

Old Spanish Lighthouse
Point Loma

San Diego Bay

Silver Strand State Beach

75

SILVER STRAND

SWEETWATER

BONITA
SUNNY VISTA
LYNWOOD HILLS

CHULA VISTA

COCKATOO GROVE

Otay Reservoir

112

IMPERIAL BEACH

PALM CITY

INLAND FRWY

CASTLE PARK

5

OTAY

OTAY VALLEY RD

BROWN FIELD

805

NAVAL AIR STATION IMPERIAL BEACH

NESTOR

SAN YSIDRO

905

OTAY MESA

Border Field State Park

0 · 5 Statute Miles

METRO

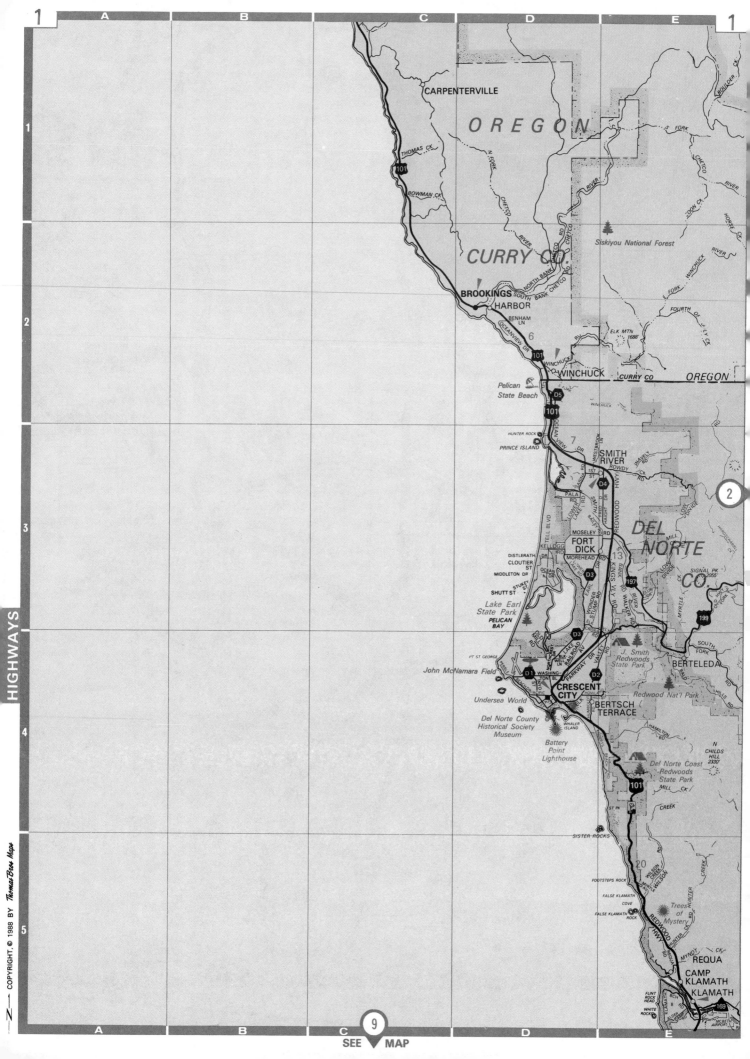

| | A | B | C | D | E | |

OREGON

CARPENTERVILLE

THOMAS CK.

BOWMAN CK.

CURRY CO.

Siskiyou National Forest

BROOKINGS
HARBOR

WINCHUCK

Pelican
State Beach

SMITH
RIVER

HUNTER ROCK
PRINCE ISLAND

DEL
NORTE
CO.

MOSELEY
FORT
DICK

DISTLERATH
CLOUTIER
ST
MIDDLETON DR

SHUTT ST

Lake Earl
State Park
PELICAN
BAY

PT ST GEORGE

John McNamara Field

J. Smith
Redwoods
State Park

BERTELEDA

Redwood Nat'l Park

Undersea World

CRESCENT
CITY
BERTSCH
TERRACE

Del Norte County
Historical Society
Museum

WHALER
ISLAND

Battery
Point
Lighthouse

Del Norte Coast
Redwoods
State Park

SISTER ROCKS

FOOTSTEPS ROCK

FALSE KLAMATH
COVE
FALSE KLAMATH
ROCK

Trees
of
Mystery

REQUA
CAMP
KLAMATH
KLAMATH

FLINT
ROCK
HEAD

WHITE
ROCK

HIGHWAYS

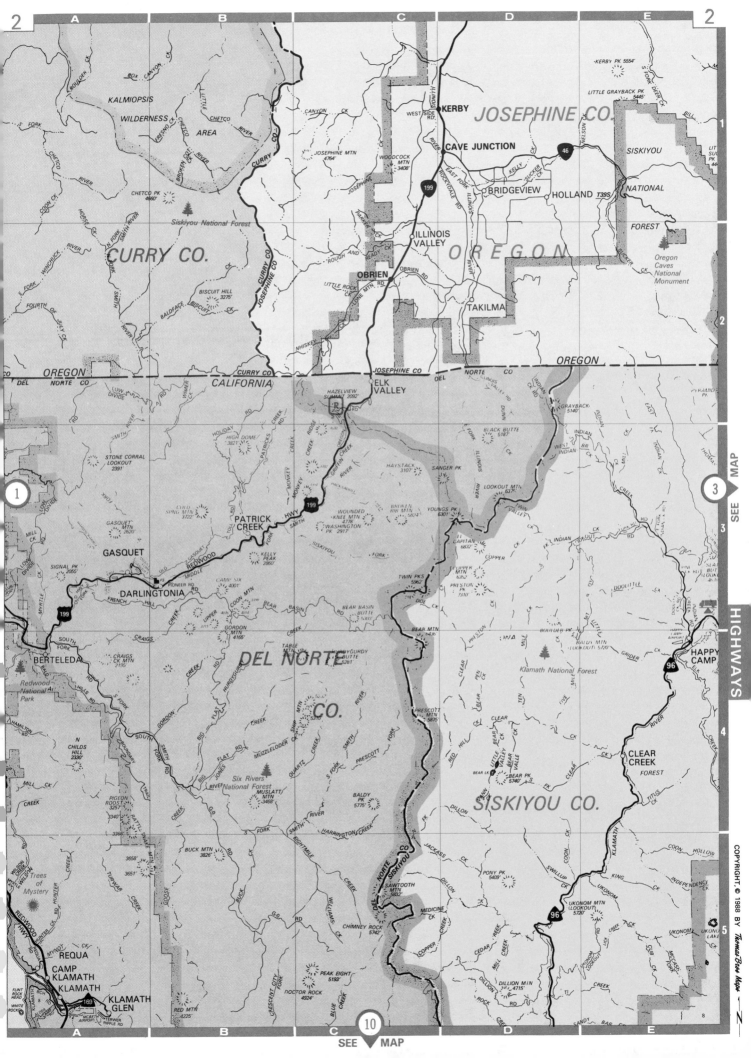

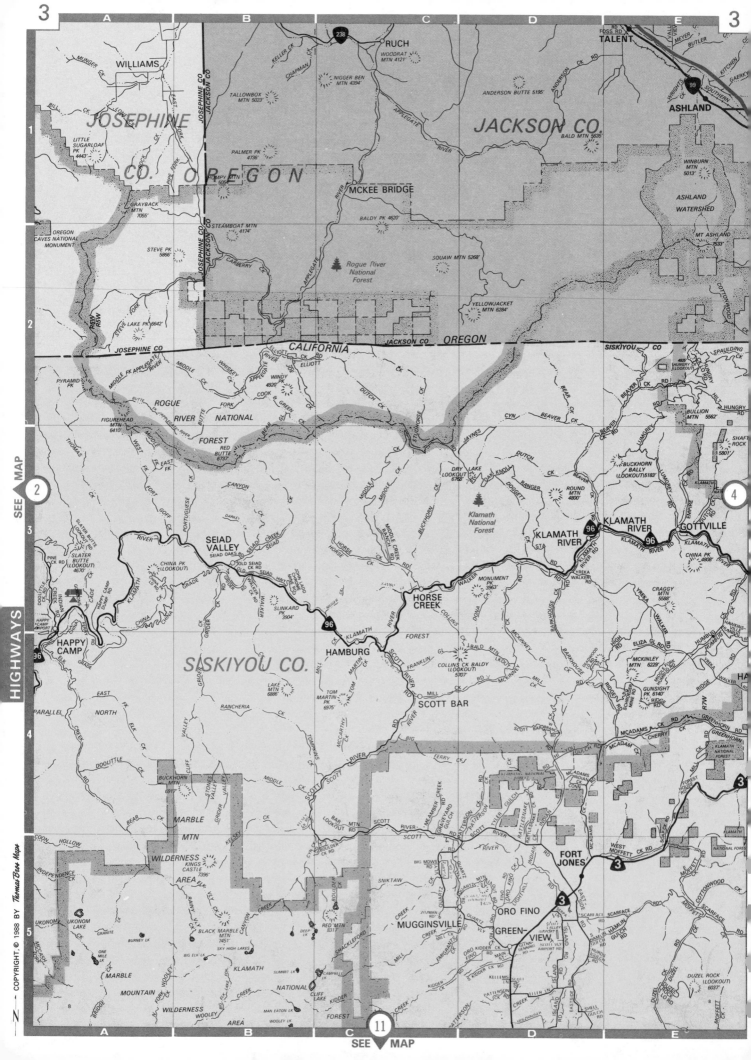

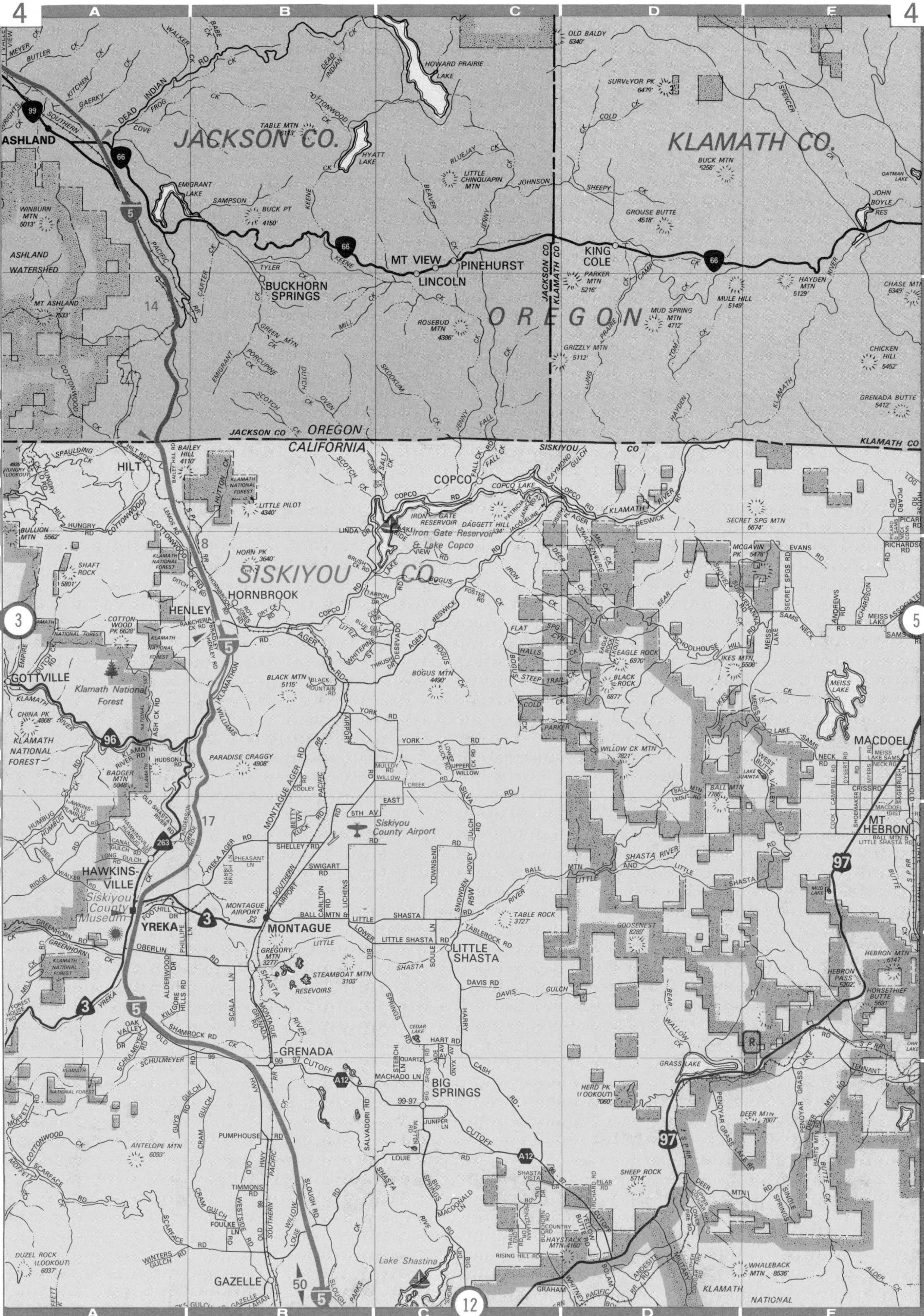

JACKSON CO.

KLAMATH CO.

OREGON

ASHLAND

SISKIYOU CO.

CALIFORNIA

KLAMATH NATIONAL FOREST

Klamath National Forest

YREKA

MONTAGUE

HAWKINS-VILLE

GOTTVILLE

HENLEY

HORNBROOK

HILT

COPCO

Iron Gate Reservoir & Lake Copco

KING COLE

MT VIEW

PINEHURST

LINCOLN

BUCKHORN SPRINGS

LITTLE SHASTA

GRENADA

BIG SPRINGS

GAZELLE

MACDOEL

MT HEBRON

Siskiyou County Airport

Siskiyou County Museum

Lake Shastina

SEE MAP

HIGHWAYS

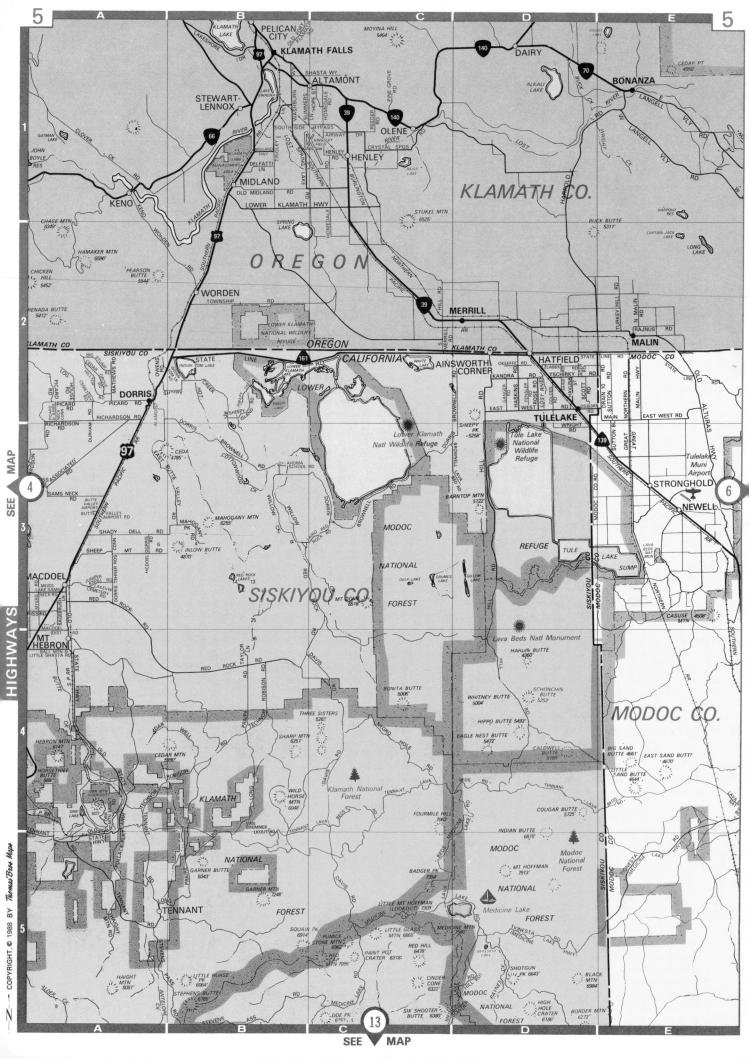

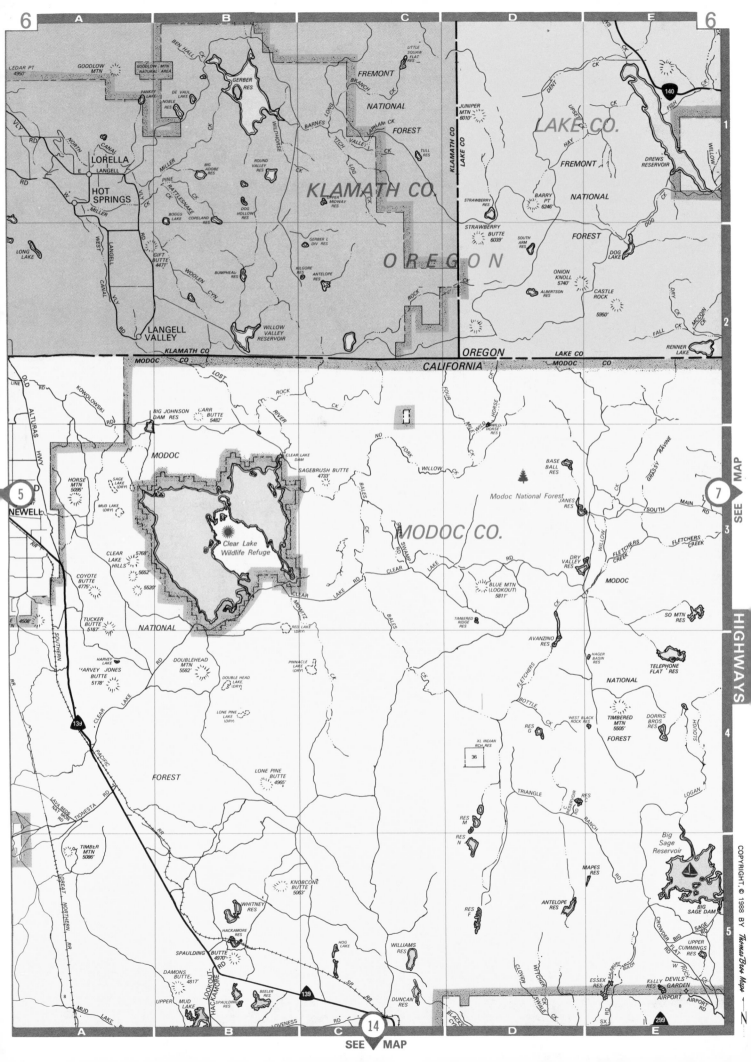

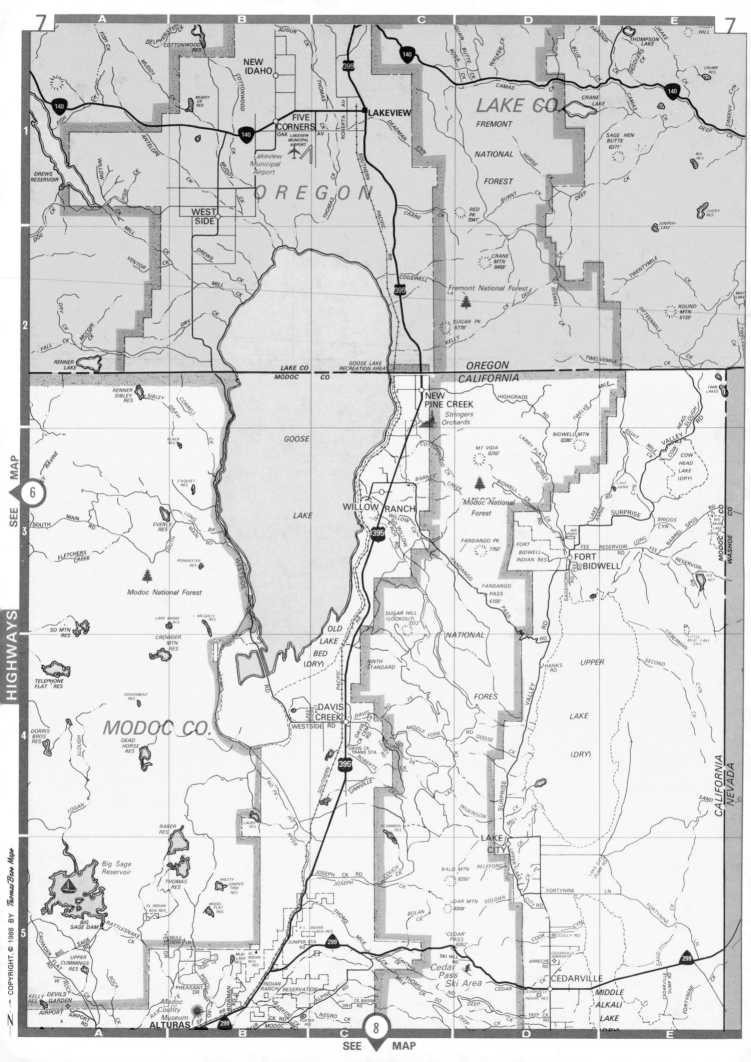

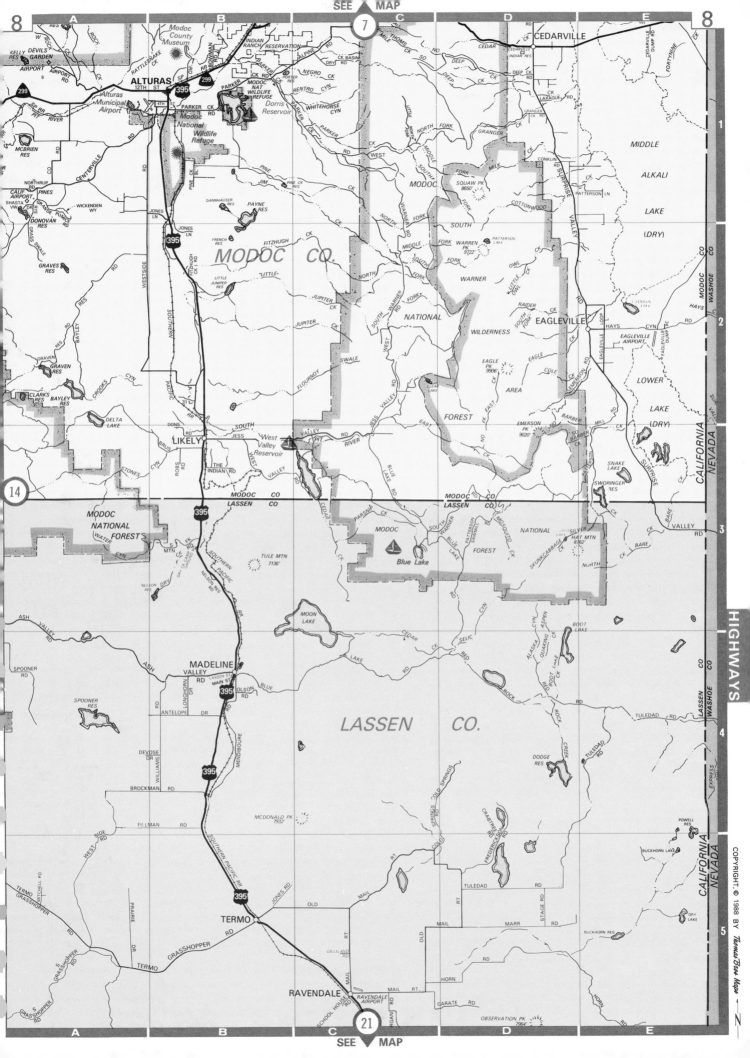

FLINT
ROCK
HEAD

WHITE
ROCK

101

RED
PARK
RD

PRAIRIE
CREEK
REDWOOD
STATE
PARK

DAVIDSON RD

101

ORICK

FRESHWATER
ROCKS

FRESHWATER
LAGOON

SHARP PT

Humboldt Lagoons
State Park

Harry A.
Merlo
State
St. Rec.
Area

10

DRY
LAGOON
BEACH
STATE
PARK

BIG
LAGOON

PITCHER    CK

101

HUM.
CO.

22

REDWOOD HWY

GRAY

Patricks
Point
State Park

WESTGATE AV

R

Trinidad
State
Beach

STUMPTOWN
RD

TRINIDAD

R

MOON-
STONE

TRINIDAD SCENIC DR

ADAM

CRANNELL

Little River
State Beach

CRANNELL
RD

LITTLE
RIVER

Arcata
Airport

12

MURRAY RD

MCKINLEY-
OVILLE

AIRPORT
RD

MCKINLEYVILLE
CENTRAL AV

Azalea
State
Reserve

Camp
Curtis

101   200

LANPHERE
RD

GUINTOLI
LN

FOSTER
AV

SPEAR AV

JACKSON
RD

BASE RD

ST LOUIS
RD

ARCATA

255

9
FRWY

SUNNY
BRAE
LN
GOLF
COURSE
RD

ARCATA
BAY

BAY-
SIDE

JACOBY CK RD

SAMOA

Humboldt
HUM County
CO   Airport

FAIR-
HAVEN

EUREKA
AIRPORT

5TH ST

PARKER
RD

QUAKER ST

REDMOND
RD

EUREKA

HARRIS   ST

MYRTLE

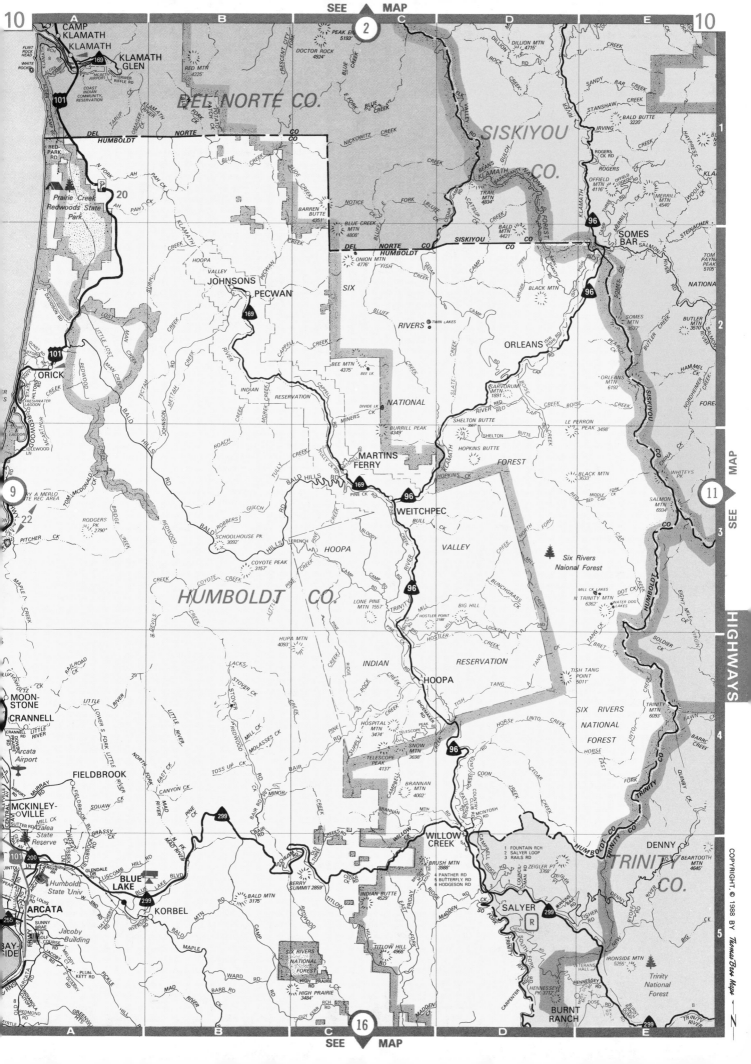

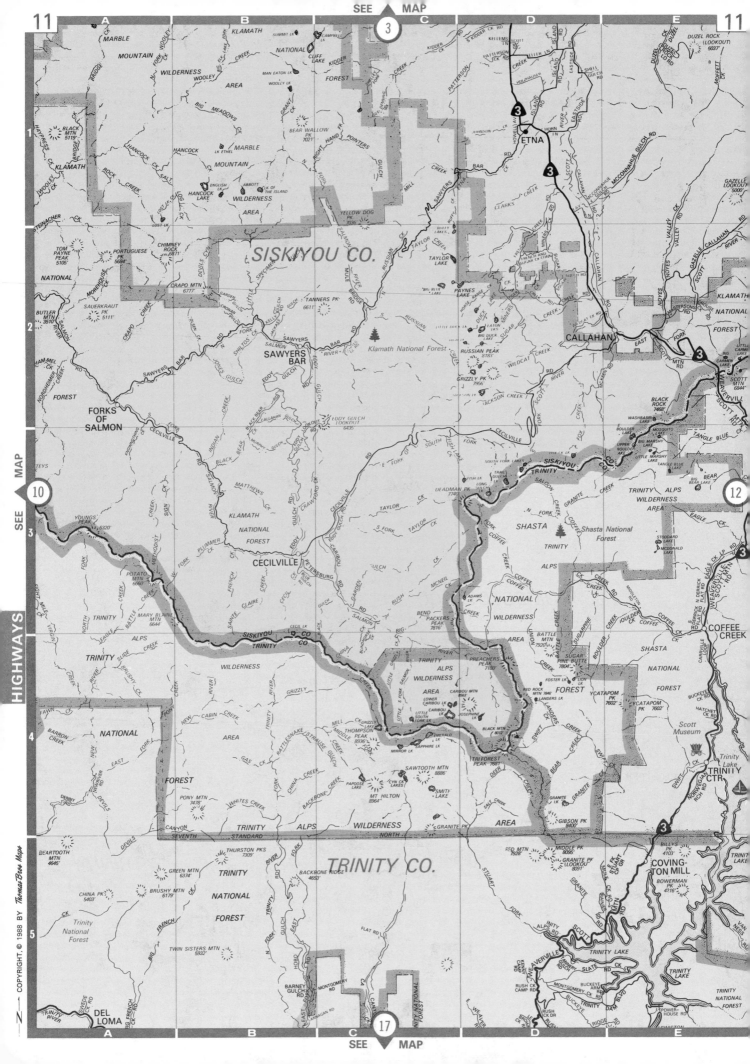

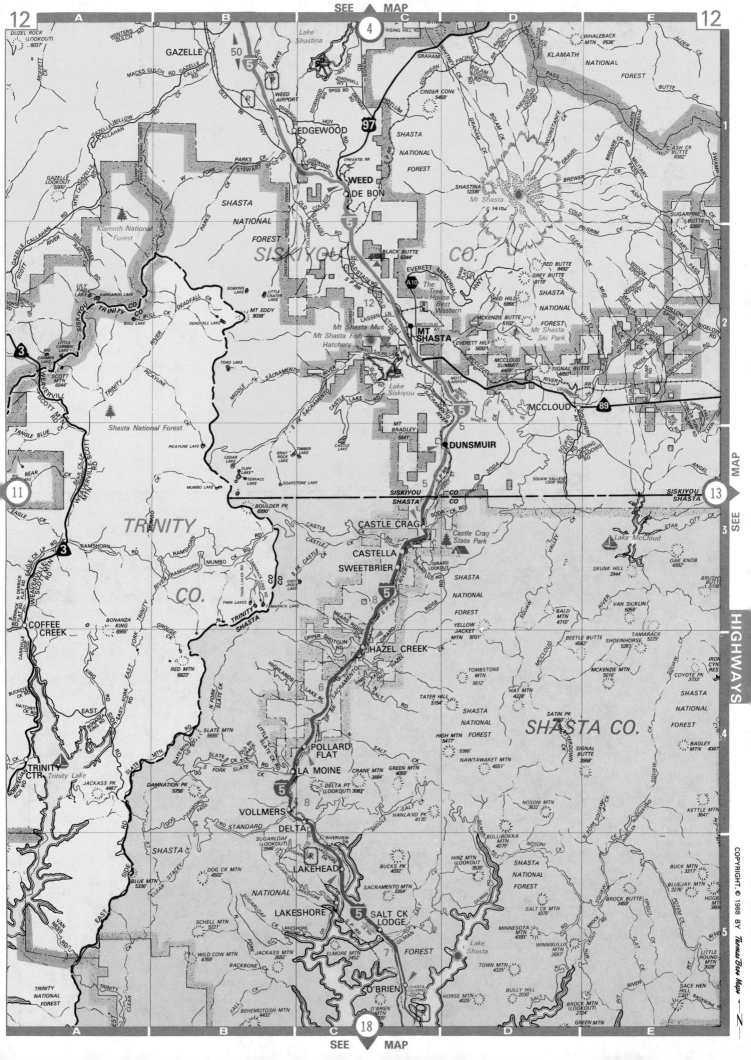

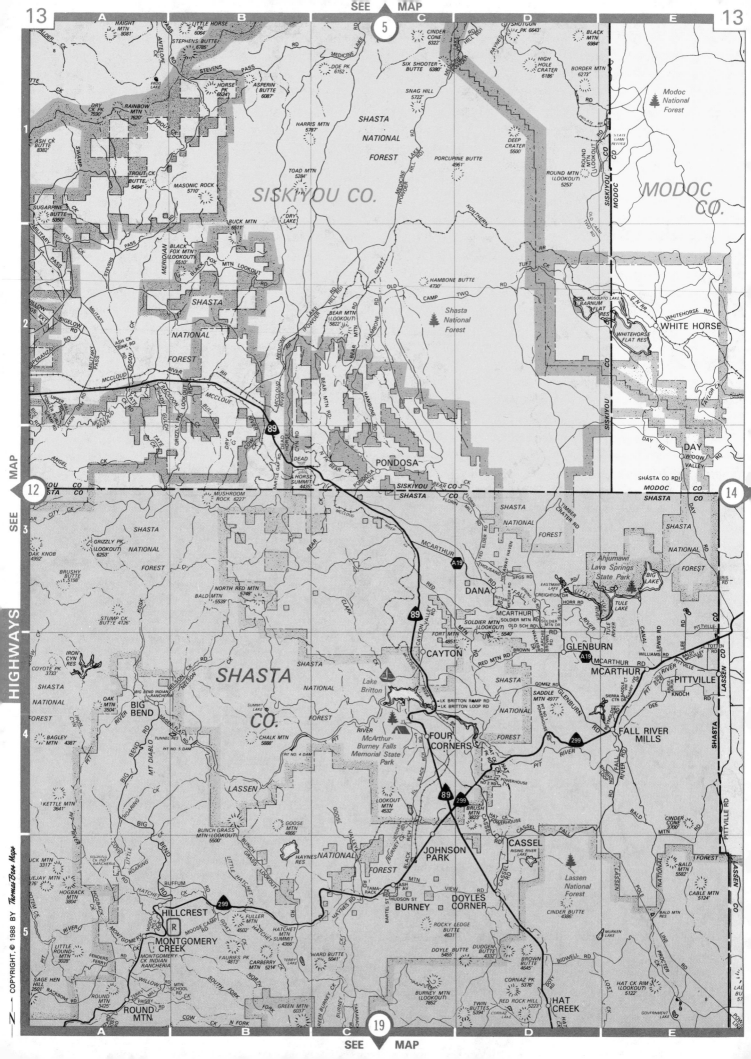

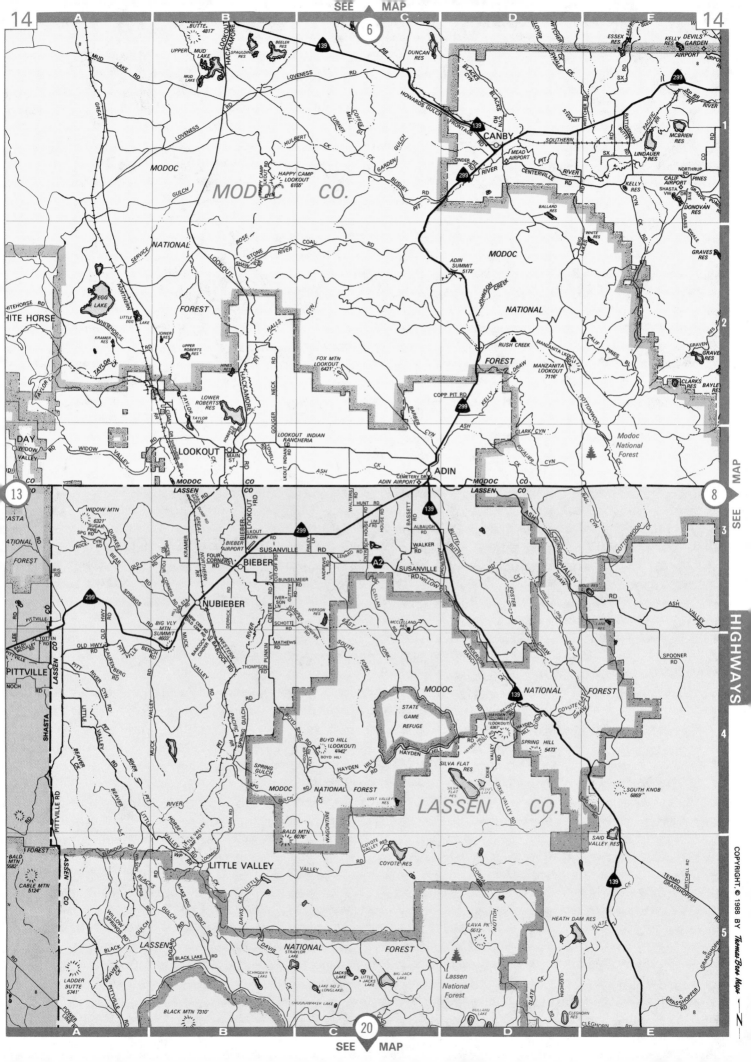

SEE MAP
9

SAMOA

FAIR-HAVEN
EUREKA AIRPORT

HUMBOLDT CO AIRPORT

EUREKA

CUT-TEN

7

HUMBOLDT BAY

S JETTY RD

FIELDS LANDING

6

WRIGLEY RD

N FORK ELK RIVER

ELK RIVER

PACIFIC

TABLE BLUFF

SALMON CK

CANNIBAL

LOLETA

101

OCEAN

3

CENTERVILLE RD

RUSS LN

FERNDALE

2

PALMER CK RD

FORTUNA

ROHNER-VILLE

4

211

PACIFIC

GRIZZLY BLUFF

WILLIAMS CK RD

WILLIAMS LN

ANDERSON LN

REGLI LN

HARBERS LN

LAWSON LN

PLEASANT
McCAHILL

CHURCH

DRAKE RD

36

HYDES-VILLE

ALTON

FALSE CAPE

MATTOLE

BEAR RIVER RIDGE

BEAR RIVER

5

RIO DELL

SCOT

16

211

CAPE MENDOCINO

SUGAR LOAF ISLAND

UPPER BEAR RIVER

CAPETOWN

HUMBOLDT CO

LOWER RD

3

CENTENNIAL RD

MONUMENT RD

MT PIERCE LOOKOUT

MT PIERCE 3188'

N FK MATTOLE RIVER

MATTOLE RIVER

TAYLOR PK 3390

BIG HILL 3040'

OLD MATTOLE RD

211

N FORK

CLARK FORK RD

PETROLIA

CHAMBERS RD

CONKLIN CK RD

MOORE HILL 1245'

MATTOLE

MATTOLE

LIGHTHOUSE RD

PRICHETT RD

ROSCOE RD

LINDLEY

MATTOLE RIVER

CATHEYS PK 3070'

4

LITTLE CHAPARRAL MTN 2650'

COOSKIE MTN 2951'

BURRELL RD

HONEYDEW

KING RANGE

NATIONAL

CONSERVATION AREA

SQUAW CK

211

EAST FK

WILDER RIDGE

OAT HILL 2350'

HONEYDEW CO

UPPER BEAR CK

211

KINGS PK 4087

NORTH SLIDE PK 3517

HADLEY PK 3020

King Range National Conservation Area

SHUBRICK PK 2797

5

SADDLE MTN 3290'

BEAR

HORSE MTN 1929'

KINGS PK RD

HIGHWAYS

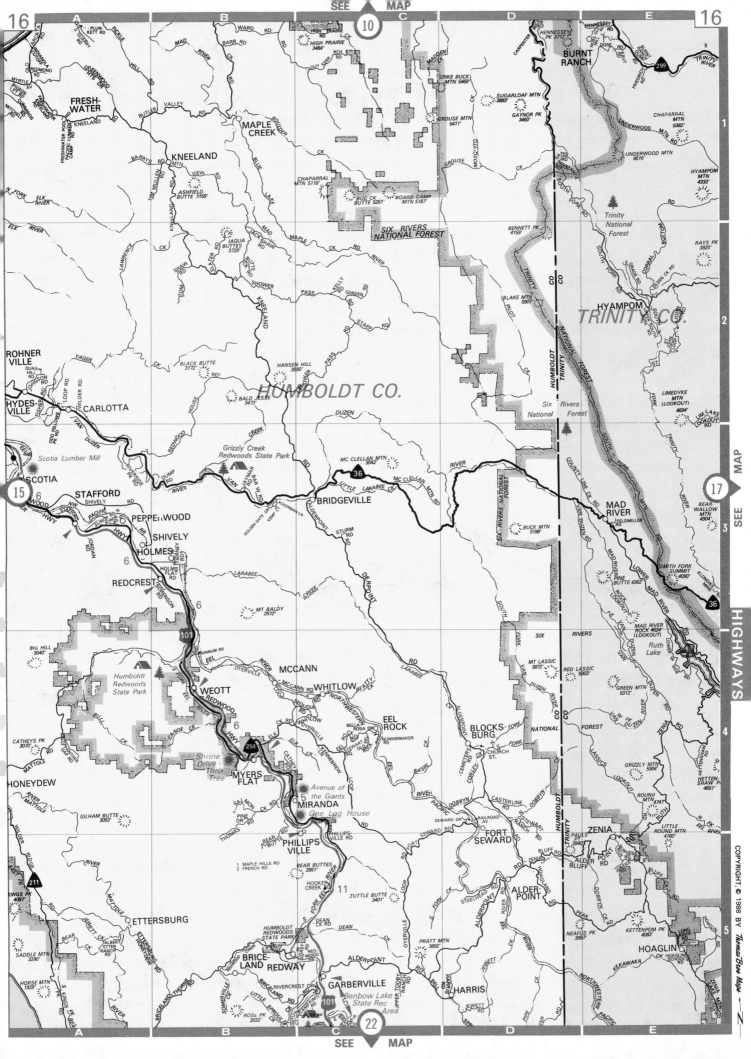

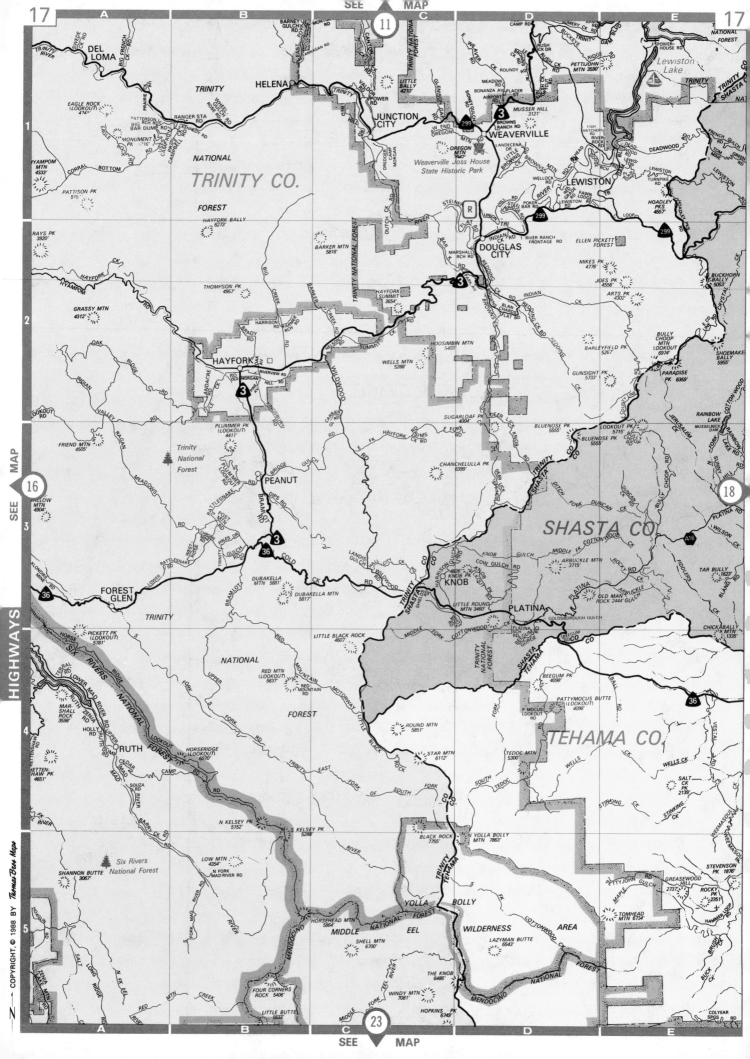

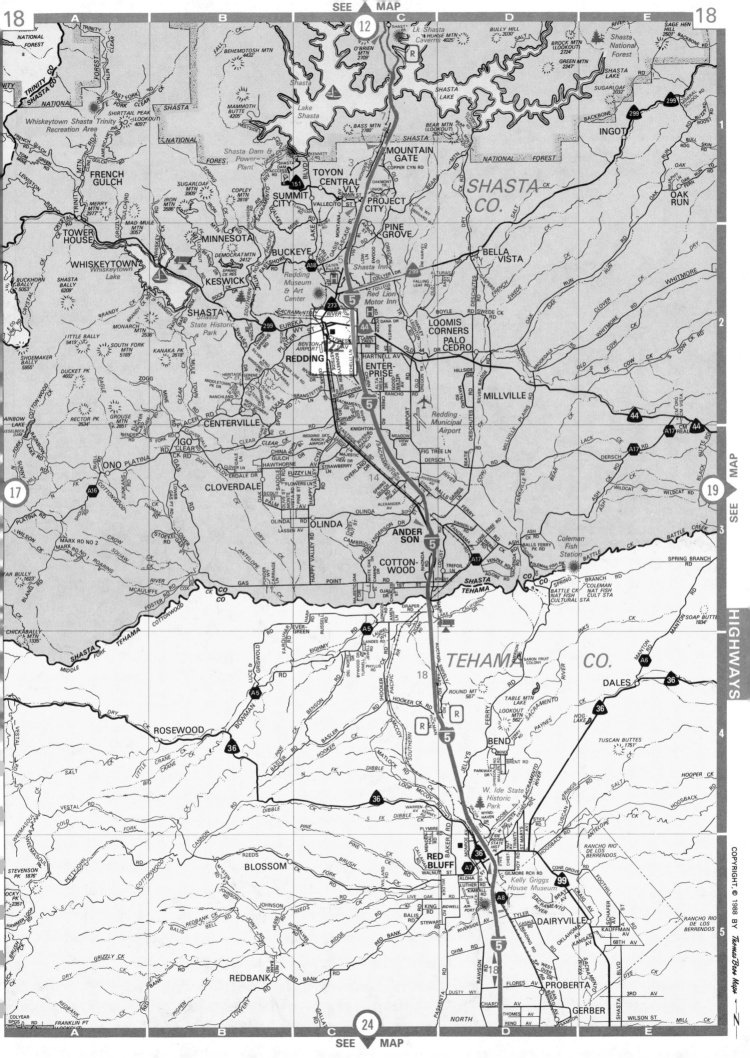

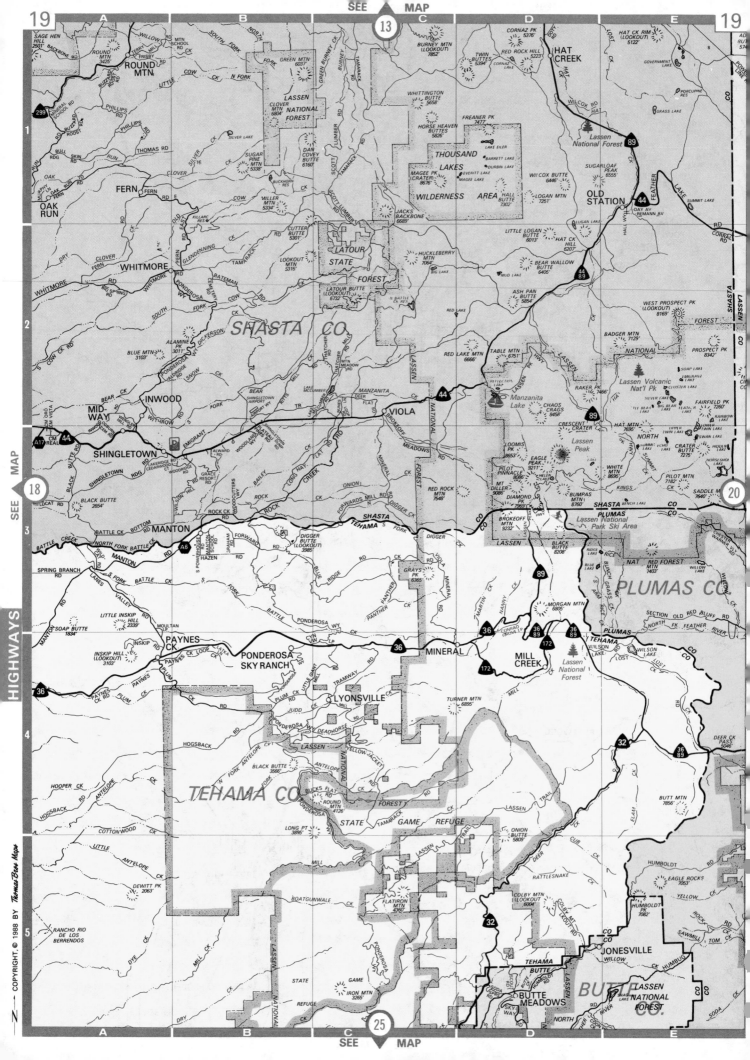

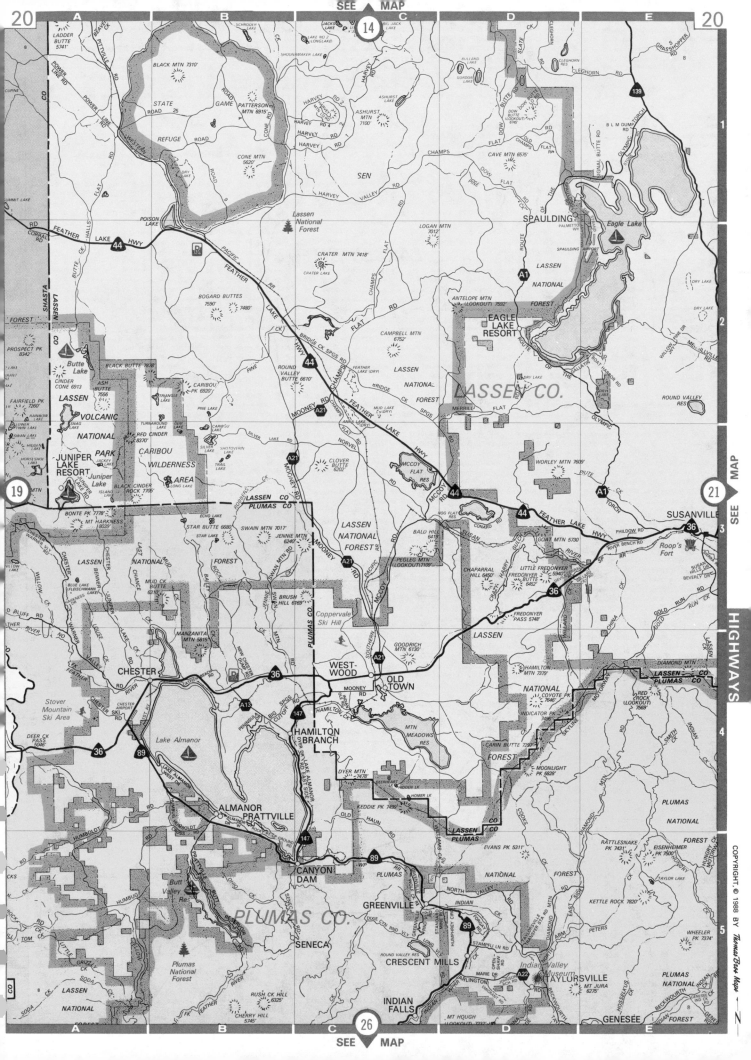

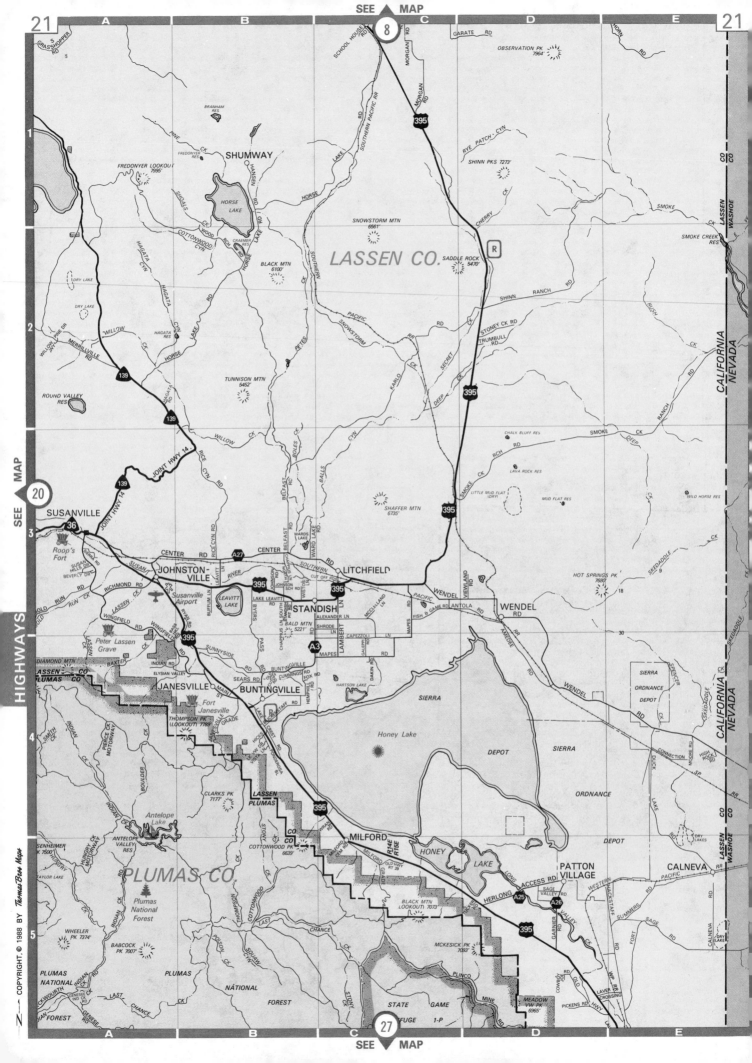

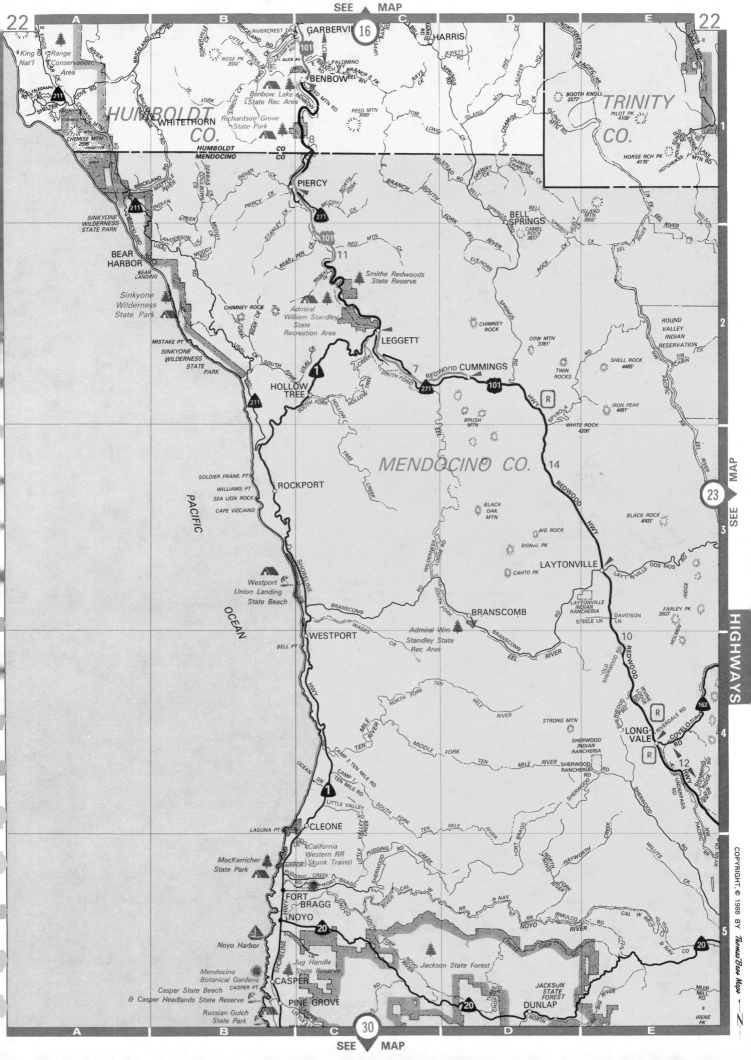

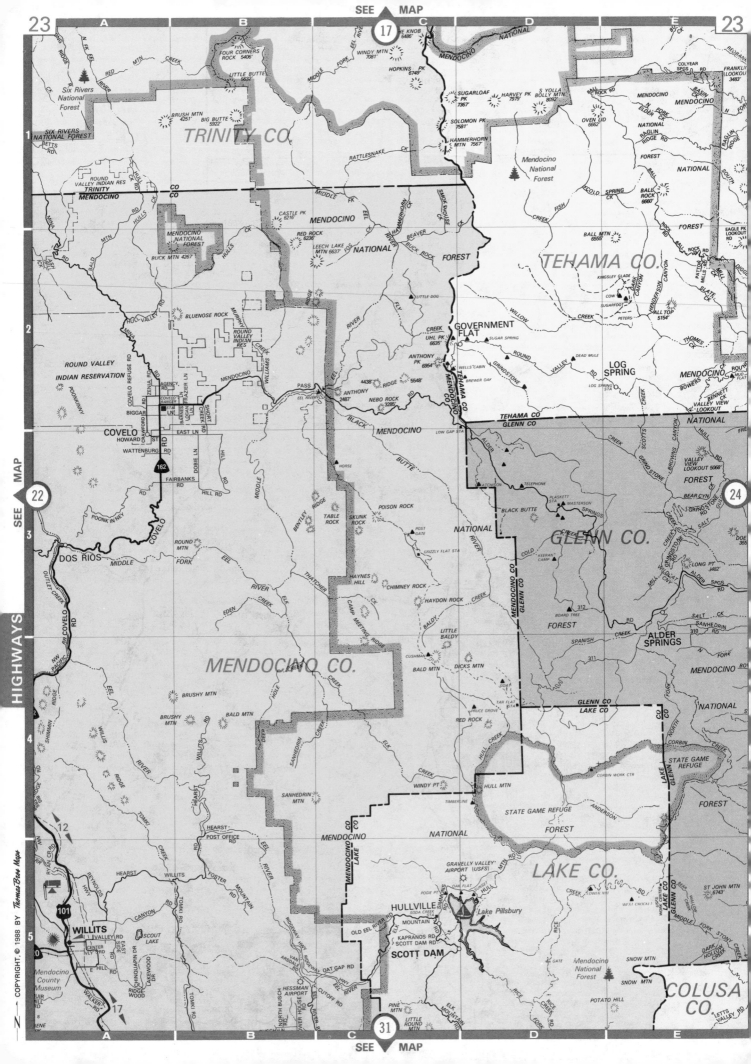

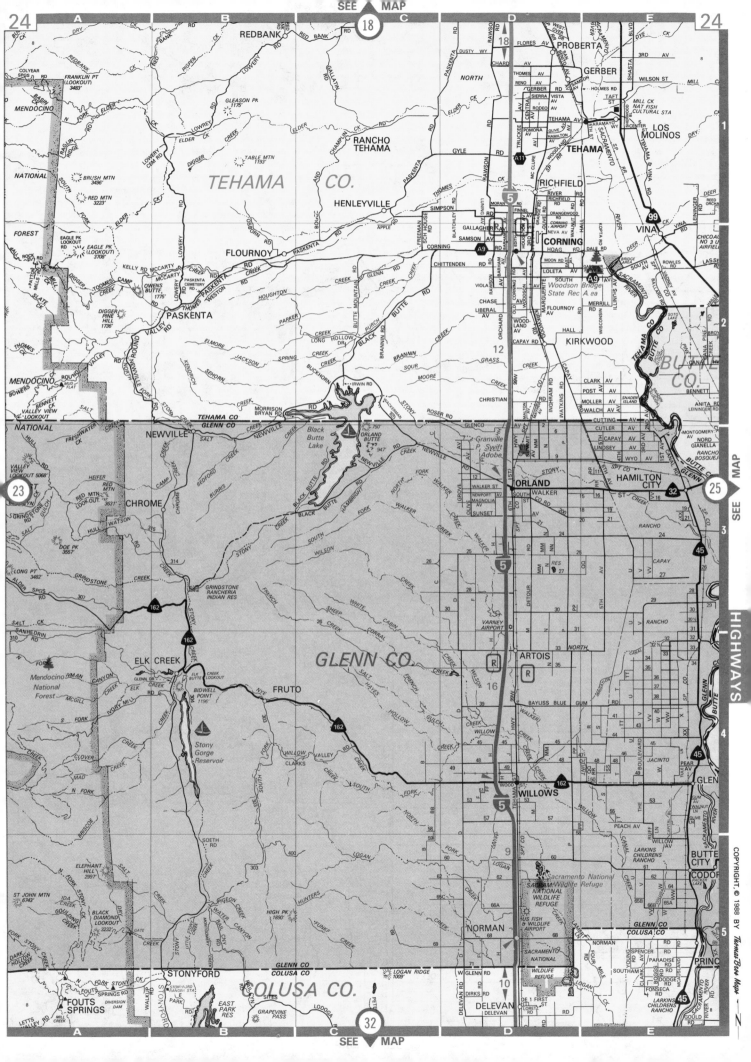

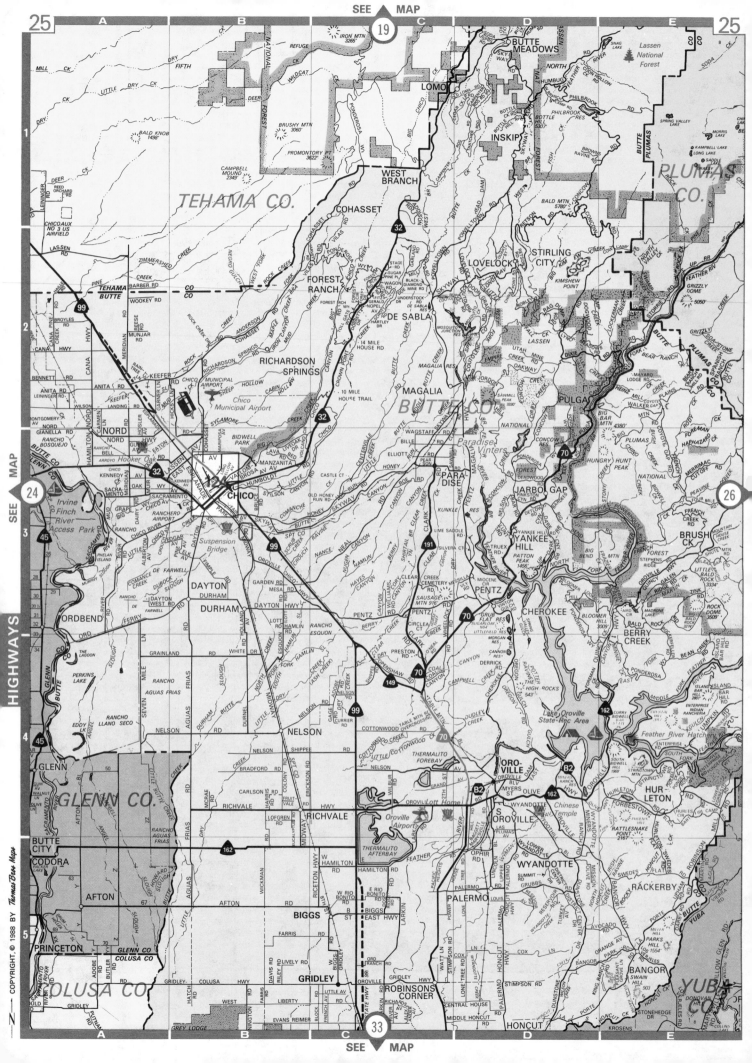

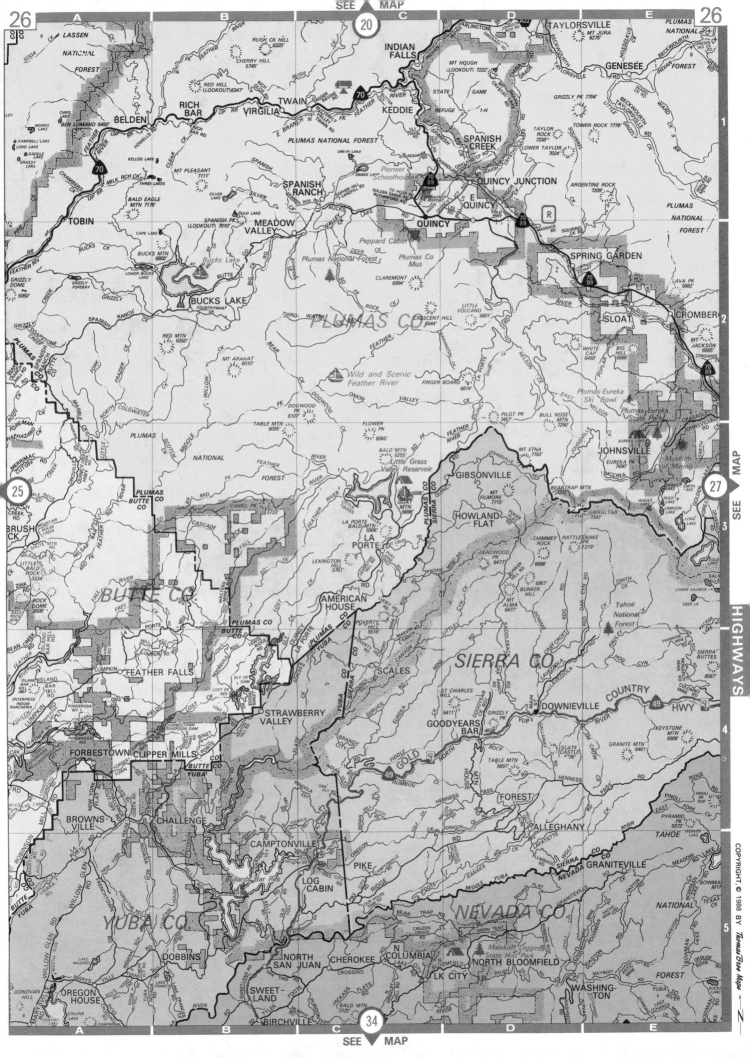

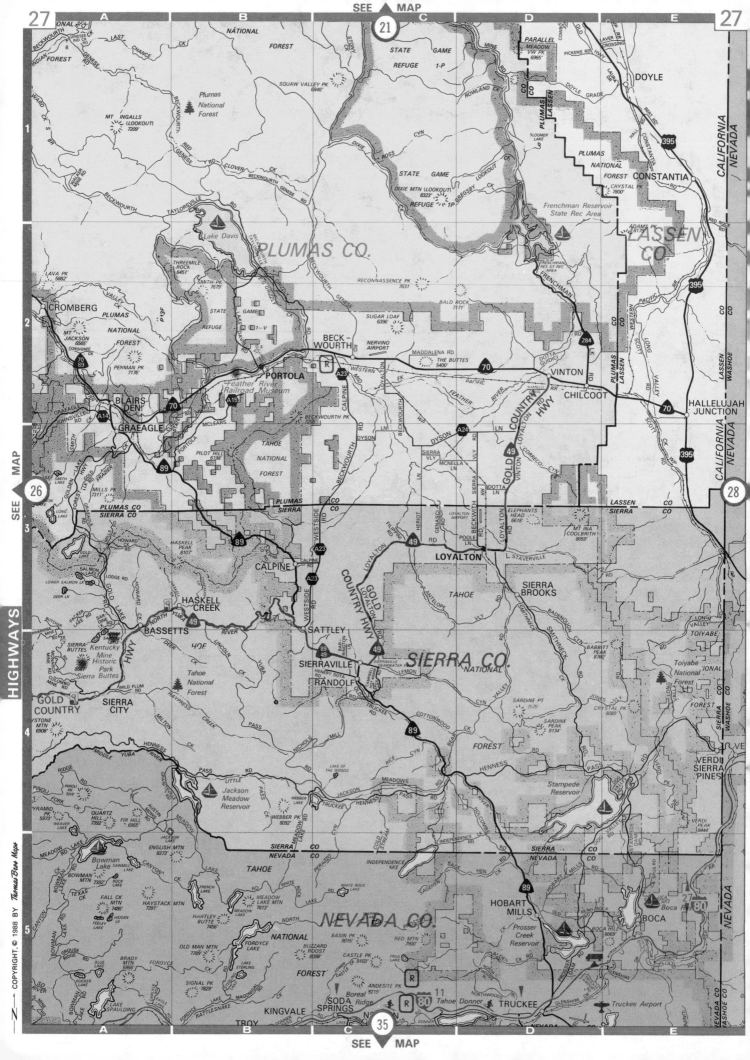

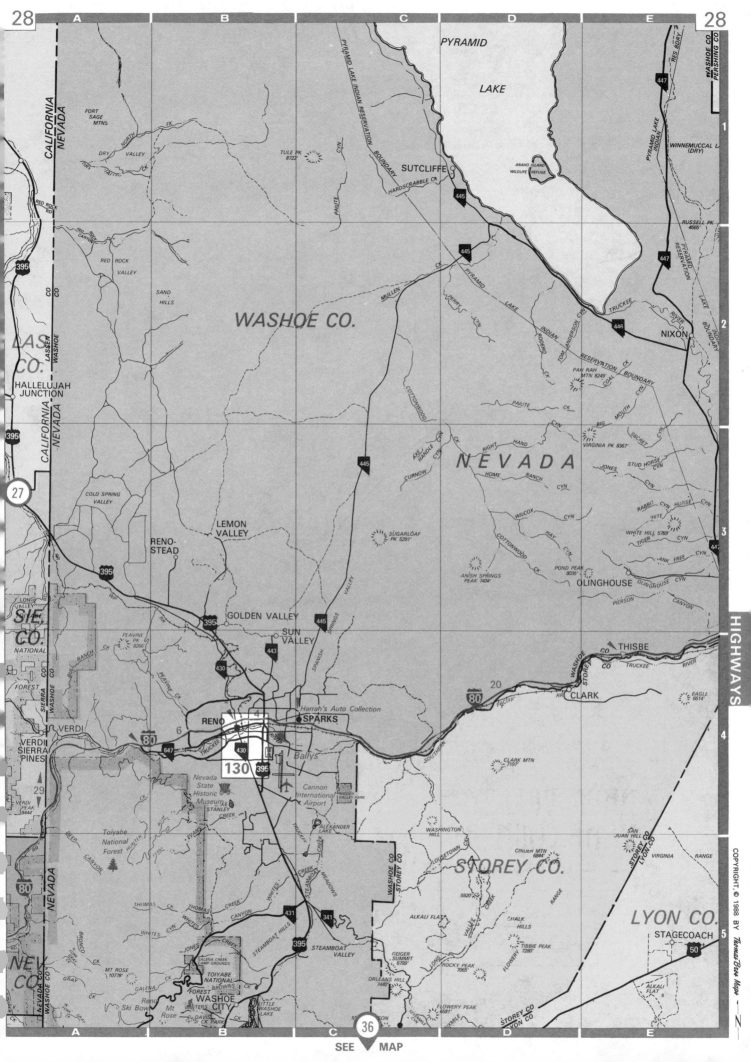

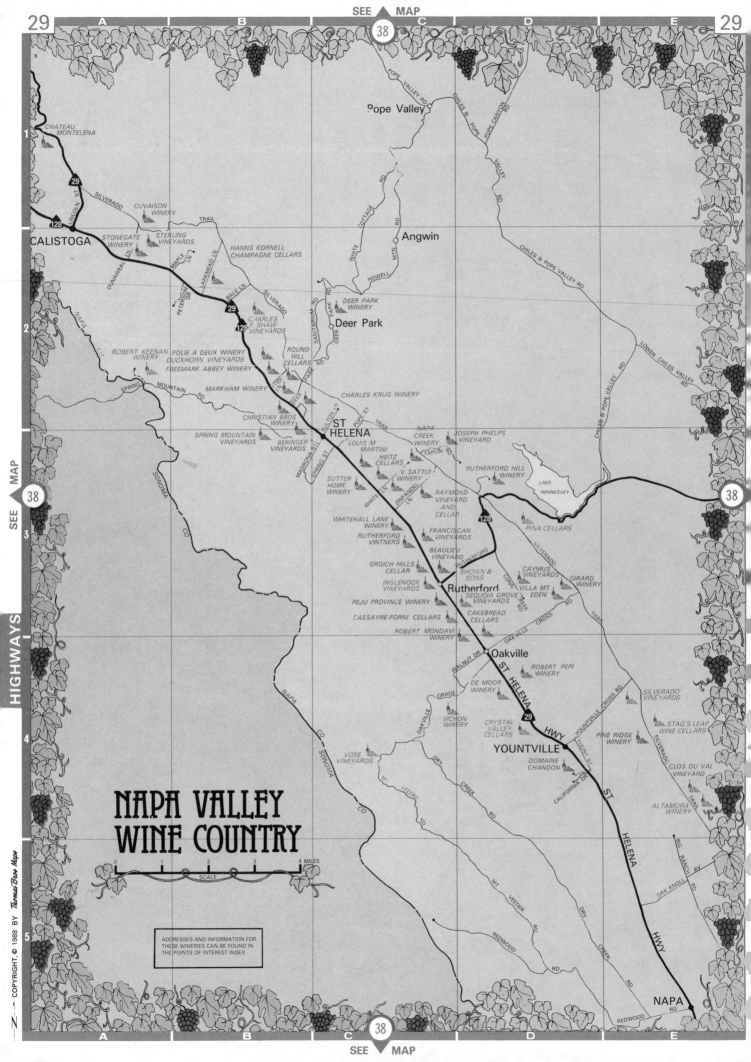

A   B   C   D   E

Pope Valley

POPE VALLEY RD
CHILES & POPE VALLEY RD
POPE CANYON RD
VALLEY RD
CHILES & POPE VALLEY RD
LOWER CHILES VALLEY RD
CHILES & POPE VALLEY RD

CHATEAU MONTELENA

29

SILVERADO
LINCOLN ST
CUVAISON WINERY
TRAIL

128
CALISTOGA
STONEGATE WINERY
STERLING VINEYARDS
DUNAWEAL LN
MAPLE LN
LARKMEAD LN
PETERSON DR
BALE LN
SILVERADO

HANNS KORNELL CHAMPAGNE CELLARS

Angwin

WHITE COTTAGE RD
WHITE MTN RD
HOWELL MTN RD

29
128
CHARLES F. SHAW VINEYARDS

DEER PARK WINERY

SANITARIUM RD
DEER PARK RD

Deer Park

ROBERT KEENAN WINERY
FOLIE A DEUX WINERY
DUCKHORN VINEYARDS
FREEMARK ABBEY WINERY

ROUND HILL CELLARS
DEER PARK RD

SPRING   MOUNTAIN RD
MARKHAM WINERY

CHARLES KRUG WINERY

SONOMA CO

CHRISTIAN BROS WINERY
SPRING MOUNTAIN VINEYARDS
BERINGER VINEYARDS
MADRONA ST
SPRING ST

ST HELENA
FULTON LN
POPE ST
TRAIL

NAPA CREEK WINERY

JOSEPH PHELPS VINEYARD

LOUIS M MARTINI
HEITZ CELLARS
V SATTUI WINERY
WHITE LN
ZINFANDEL LN
SUTTER HOME WINERY

TAPLIN RD

RUTHERFORD HILL WINERY

Lake Hennessey

WHITEHALL LANE WINERY
RUTHERFORD VINTNERS

RAYMOND VINEYARD AND CELLAR

128

FRANCISCAN VINEYARDS

PINA CELLARS

BEAULIEU VINEYARD
RUTHERFORD

GRGICH HILLS CELLAR

SHOWN & SONS

SILVERADO
CAYMUS VINEYARDS
VILLA MT EDEN
GIRARD WINERY

INGLENOOK VINEYARDS
Rutherford
SEQUOIA GROVE VINEYARDS

CONN CREEK RD

PEJU PROVINCE WINERY
CASSAYRE-FORNI CELLARS
CAKEBREAD CELLARS

CONN CREEK RD
TRAIL

ROBERT MONDAVI WINERY

OAKVILLE CROSS RD

Oakville
WALNUT DR
ST HELENA

ROBERT PEPI WINERY

SILVERADO VINEYARDS

DE MOOR WINERY

YOUNTVILLE CROSS RD

GRADE
VICHON WINERY
OAKVILLE

CRYSTAL VALLEY CELLARS

29
HWY

STAG'S LEAP WINE CELLARS

YOUNTVILLE

PINE RIDGE WINERY

SILVERADO TRAIL

VOSE VINEYARDS

DOMAINE CHANDON
CALIFORNIA DR
YOUNT ST

CLOS DU VAL VINEYARD

ST HELENA

ALTAMURA WINERY

NAPA CO SONOMA CO
MT VEEDER RD
DRY CREEK RD

# NAPA VALLEY WINE COUNTRY

0   1   2   3   4 MILES
SCALE

BIG RANCH RD
OAK KNOLL RD

ST HELENA HWY

MT VEEDER RD
DRY CREEK RD
REDWOOD RD

NAPA
REDWOOD RD

A   B   C   D   E

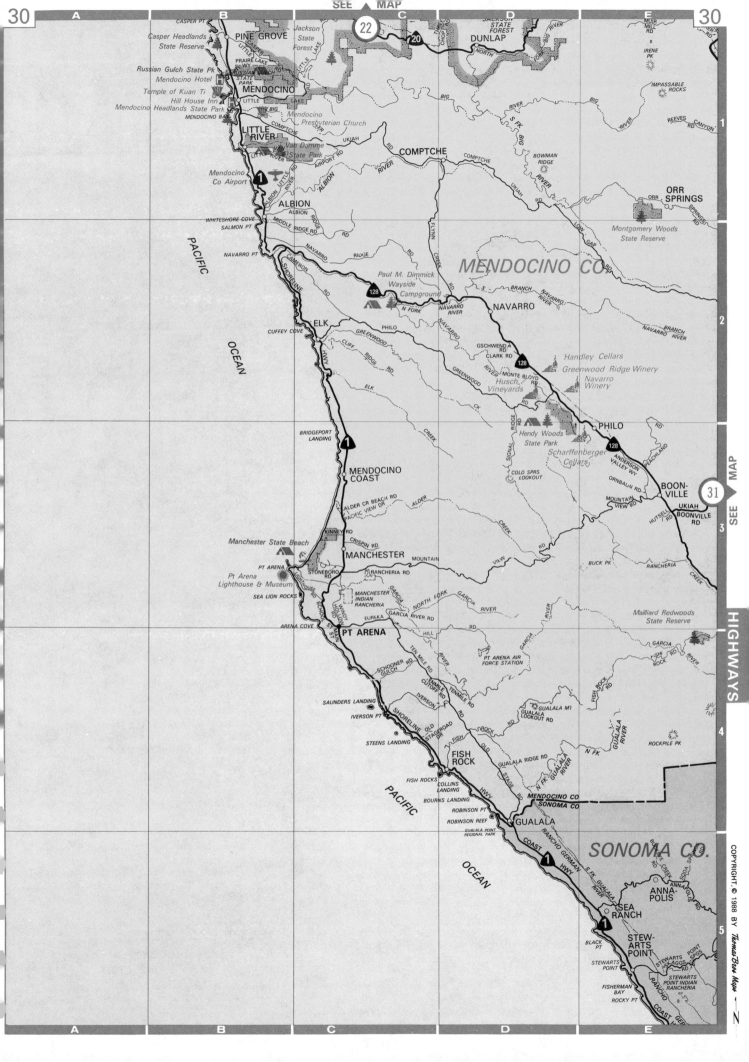

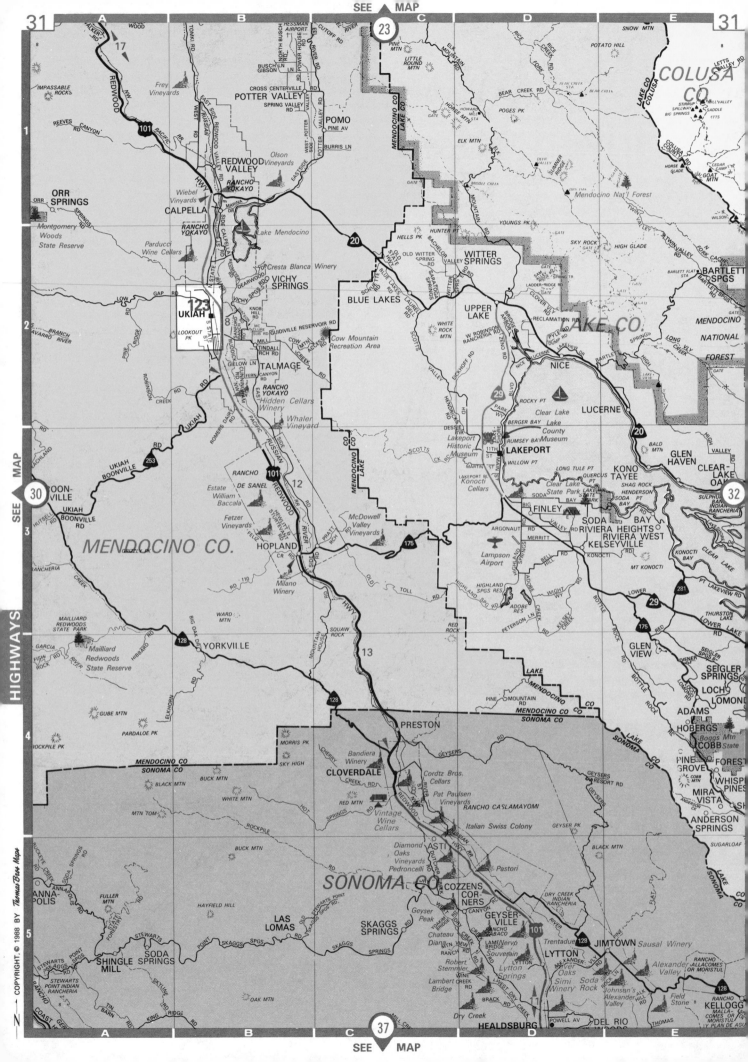

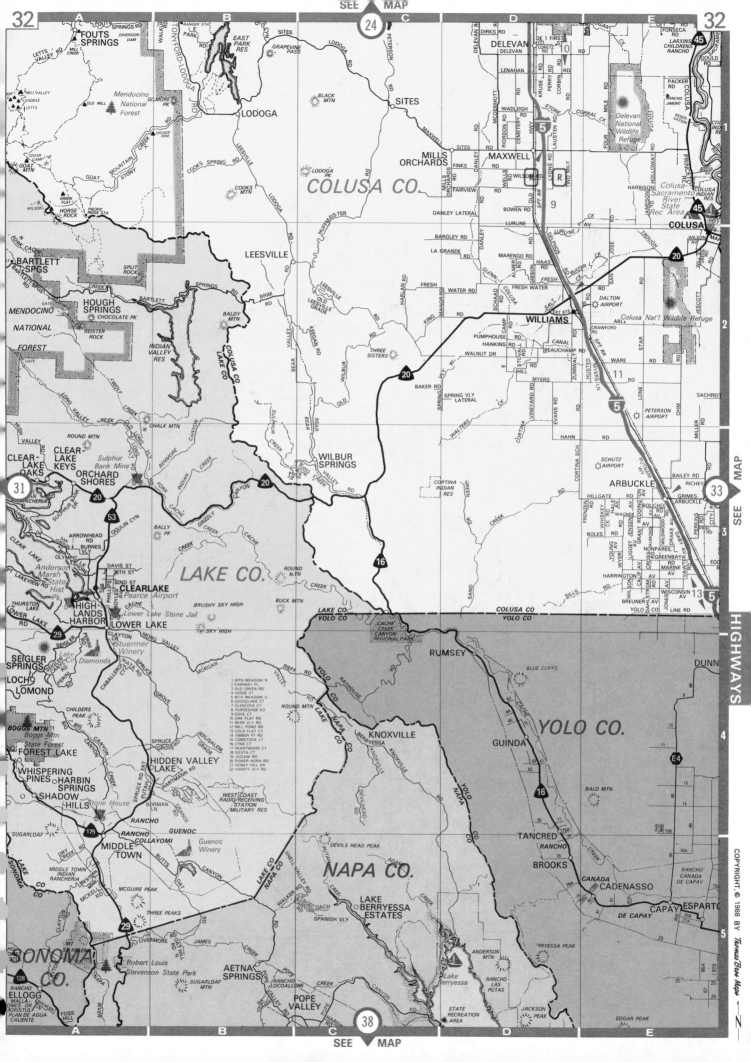

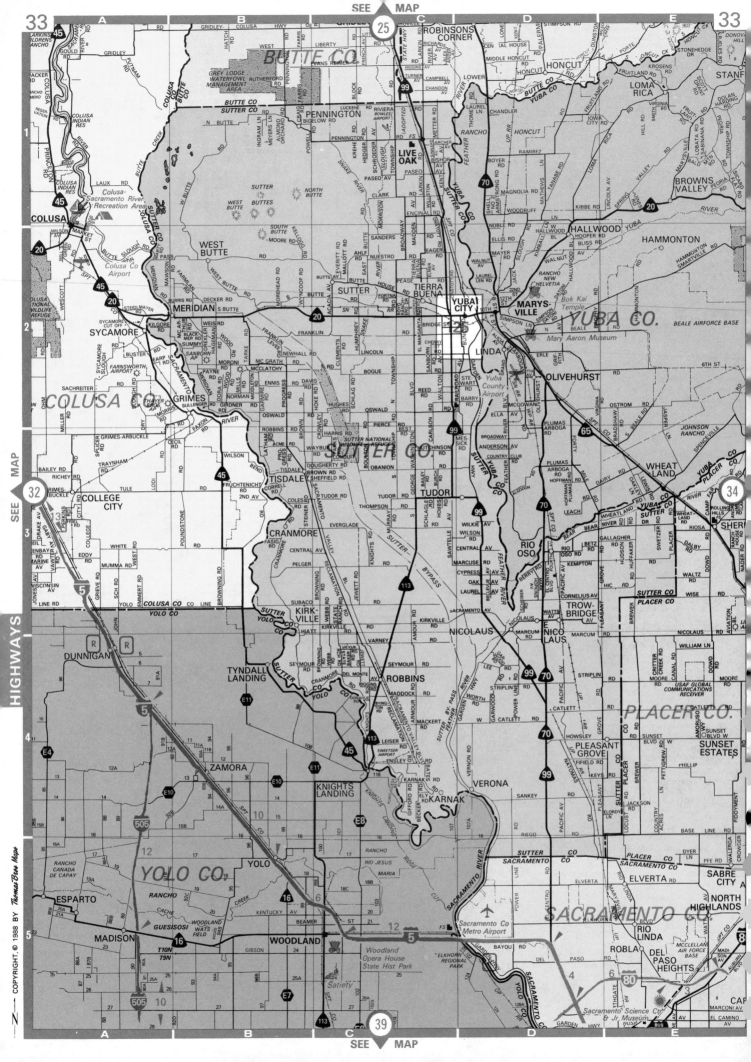

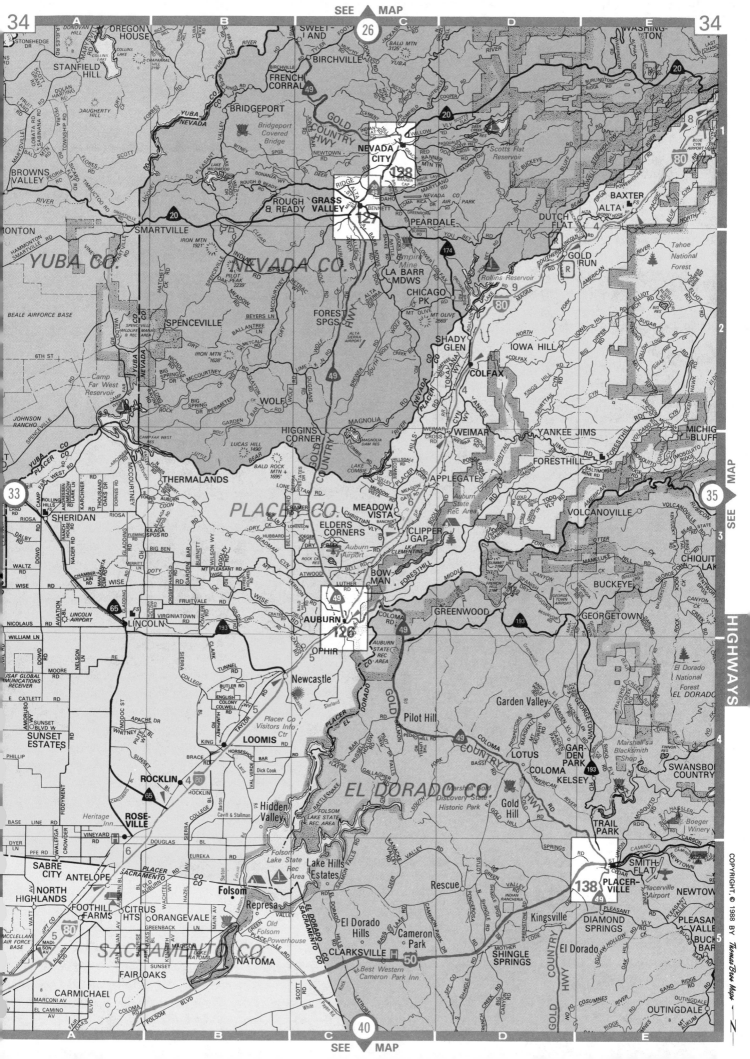

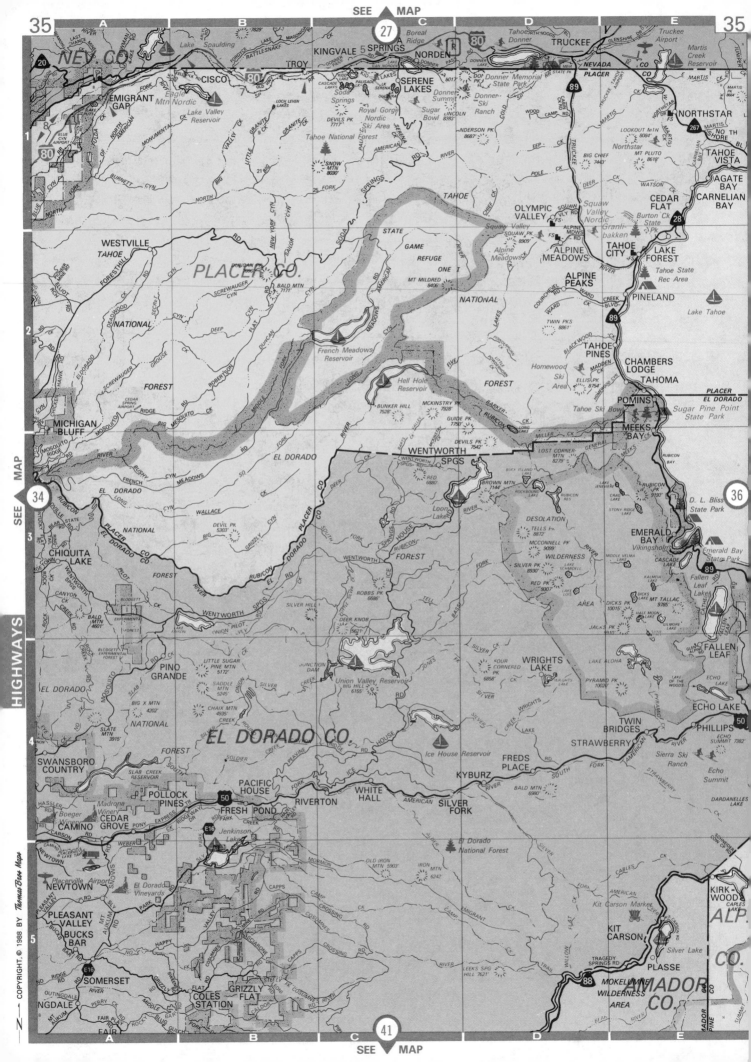

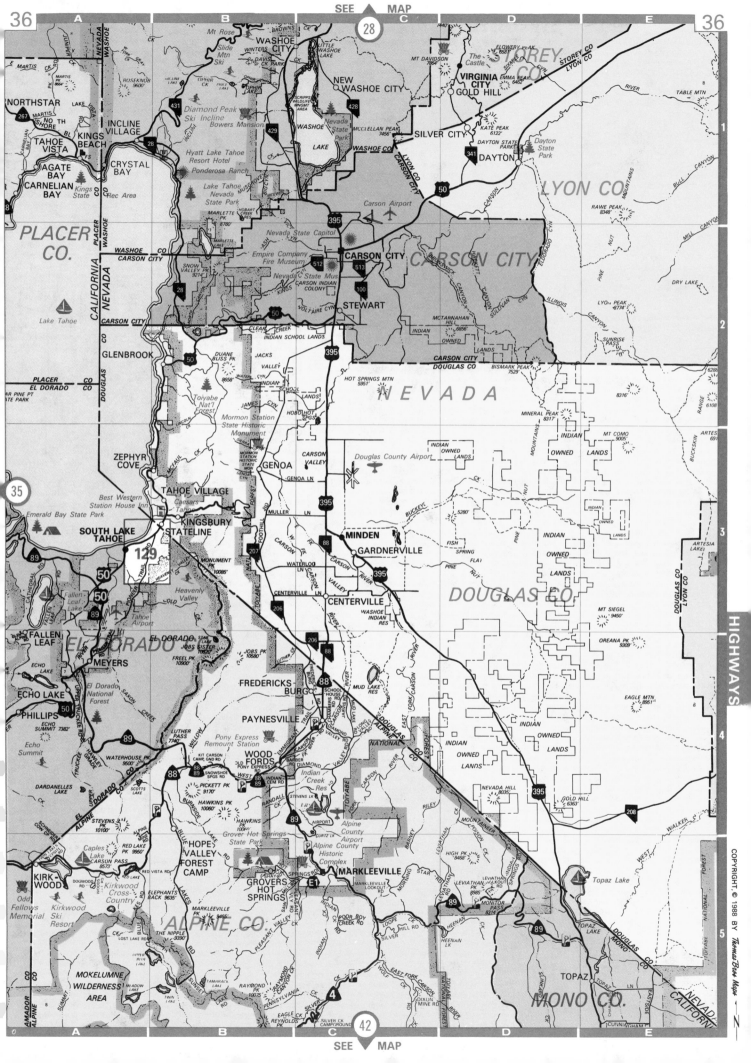

A   B   C   D   E

PACIFIC OCEAN

MARIN CO.

DRAKES BAY

**Labels (west/coast region):**

RCHO INDIAN RANCHERIA
COAST HWY
GERMAN
Kruse Rhododendron State Reserve
FISK MILL COVE
Salt Point State Park
TABLE MTN
OAK MTN
Austin Creek State Rec Area
SALT PT GERSTLE COVE
KRUSE RANCH RD
SEAVIEW
SALT POINT STATE PARK
WALSH LANDING
GUALALA RIVER
OCEAN COVE STILLWATER COVE
TIMBER COVE WINDERMERE PT
Ft Ross State Historic Park
FORT ROSS
FORT ROSS COVE
BIG OAT MTN
FOX MTN
Armstrong Redwoods State Reserve
ROCKY MT
MT JACKSON
Korbel Champagne Cellars
CAZADERO
EL BONITA
RIO NIDO
HACIENDA
MEYERS GRADE RD
RANCHO MUNIZ
BLACK MTN
POLE MTN
BOHAN DILLON
SEAVIEW QUARRY RD
NIESTRIATH
ROSS
KING
RIDGE
KING
RD
CAZADERO HWY
ARM WOODS RD
GUERNEWOOD PARK
VACATION BEACH
GUERNE
GUERNEVILLE
RIO DELL
SUMMER HOME PARK
VILLA GRANDE
NORTH WOOD
MONTE RIO
FORESTVILLE
JENNER-BY-THE-SEA
GOAT ROCK
116 HWY
DUNCANS MILLS
BRIDGE HAVEN
RED HILL
OCEAN VIEW
Rancho Bodega
CAMP MEEKER
GRATON
SERENO DEL MAR
DUNCAN POINT
CARMET
OCCIDENTAL
Graton Rancho Canada De Jonive
Sebastopol Indian Rancheria
IRISH HILL
Sonoma Coast State Beach
SALMON CREEK
Rancho Bodega
RANCHO ESTERO AMERICANO
FREESTONE
SEBASTOPOL
BODEGA BAY
MUSSEL PT
BODEGA
VALLEY FORD
Saint Teresa's Church
1 HWY
KNOWLES CORNER
CUNNINGHAM
CADWELL
HESSEL
Doran Regional Park
BODEGA HEAD
Bodega Harbor
WASHOE
FALLON
DILLON BEACH
TOMALES BLUFF
TOMALES
BIRD ROCK
DILLON BEACH RD
TWO ROCK
PETALUMA RD
RANCHO SAN ANTONIO
MCCLURES BEACH
PIERCE POINT
RANCHO NICASIO
TOMS PT
TOMALES BAY
SHORELINE HWY
POINT REYES BEACH
Tomales Bay State Park
INVERNESS
PT REYES STATION
DRAKES ESTERO
POINT REYES
OLEMA
NICASIO
S.P. TAYLOR STATE PARK
FOREST KNOLLS
LAGUNITAS
PT REYES
SEA LION COVE
CHIMNEY ROCK
Point Reyes
PT RESISTANCE
National Seashore
Golden Gate Nat'l Rec Area
KENT LAKE
RANCHO TOMALES
DOUBLE PT
ABALONE PT
MILLERS PT
MESA RD
BOLINAS
SHORELINE HWY

**Labels (east region):**

HEALDSBURG MUNICIPAL AIRPORT
WEST DRY CREEK RD
CREEK RD
BRACK
Simi Winery
RANCHO SOTOYOMY
DEL RIO WOODS
EXANGER VALLEY
CHALK HILL RD
Field Stone
KELLOGG
MALLA-COMES OR MORISTINI Y PLAN DE AGUA CALIENTE
128
HEALDSBURG
Mill Creek Vineyards
POWELL AV
William Wheeler Winery
Stephen Zellerbach
Mill Creek Vineyards
WALLACE
FOPPIANO
Clos Du Bois
White Oak Vineyards
J.W. Morris Winery
Cambiaso Vineyards
MARK WEST SPRINGS
Piper Sonoma Cellars
Belvedere Winery
WINDSOR
RIVER RD
Hop Kiln
Rodney Strong
Landmark Vineyards
SWEETWATER SPRINGS
Rochipli Vineyards
MARK W STATION
IMARK W STATION
AIRPORT
FULTON
PORTER CREEK RD
De Loach Vineyards
Topolos at Russian River
Dehlinger
PINER
RANCHO SAN MIGUEL
BADGER
SANTA ROSA
COLLEGE AV
12
13
SOUTH PARK
RANCHO LLANO DE SANTA ROSA
STONY PT
REDWOOD HWY
SANTA ROSA AV
8
RANCHO COTATE
116
ROHNERT PARK
38
COTATI
ROBLAR
RANCHO BLUCHER
RANCHO ROBLAR DE LA MISERIA
MIDDLE TWO ROCK RD
SPRING HILL RD
CHILENO VLY RD
RED HILL RD
RANCHO NICASIO
RANCHO ROBLAR DE LA MISERIA
101

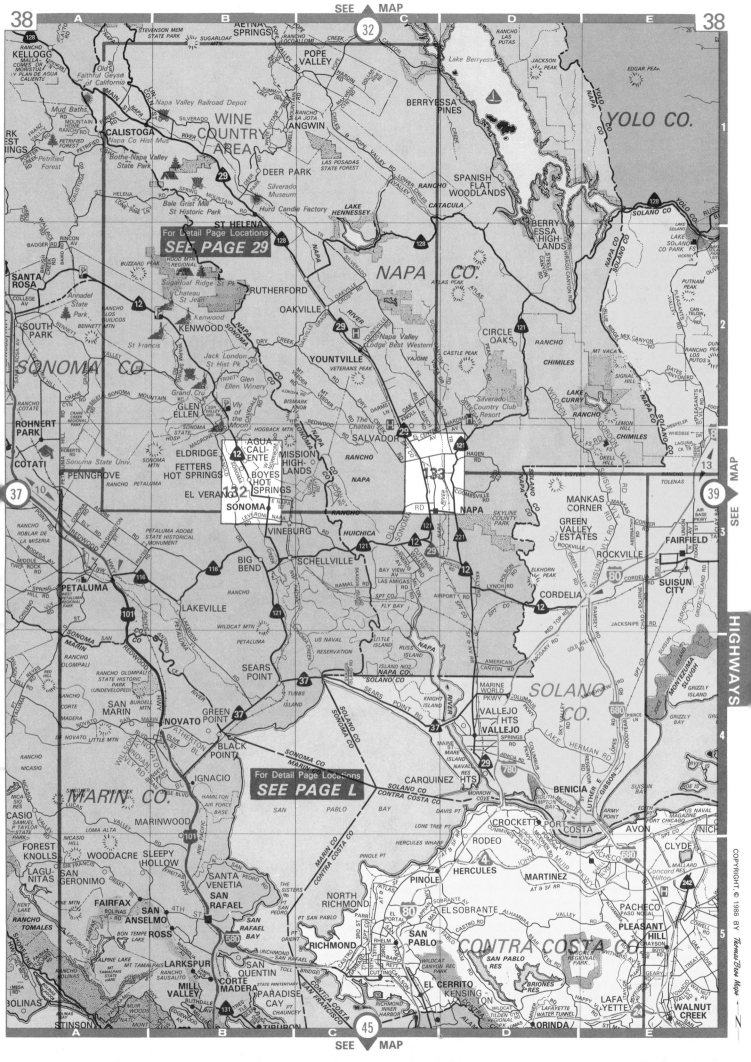

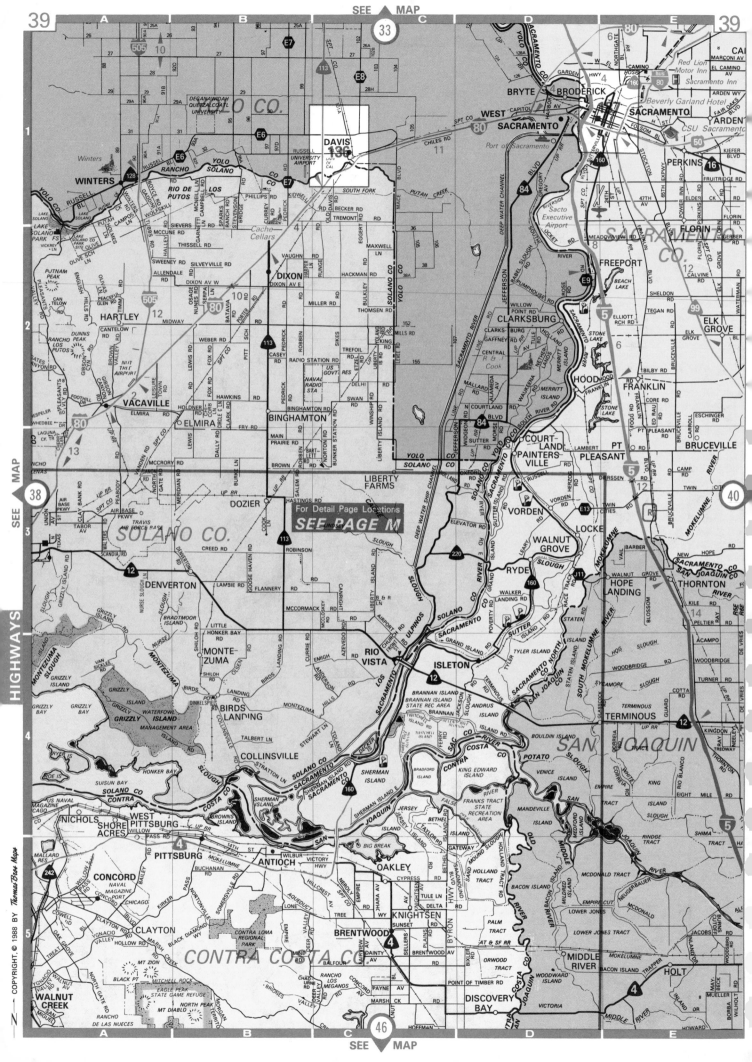

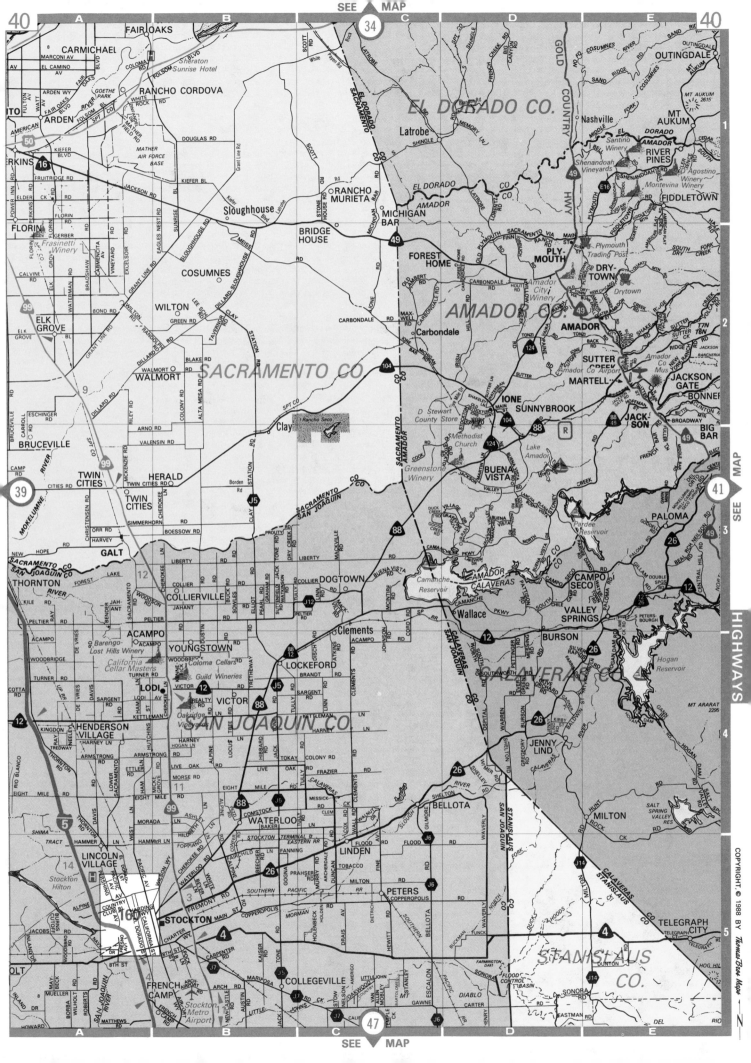

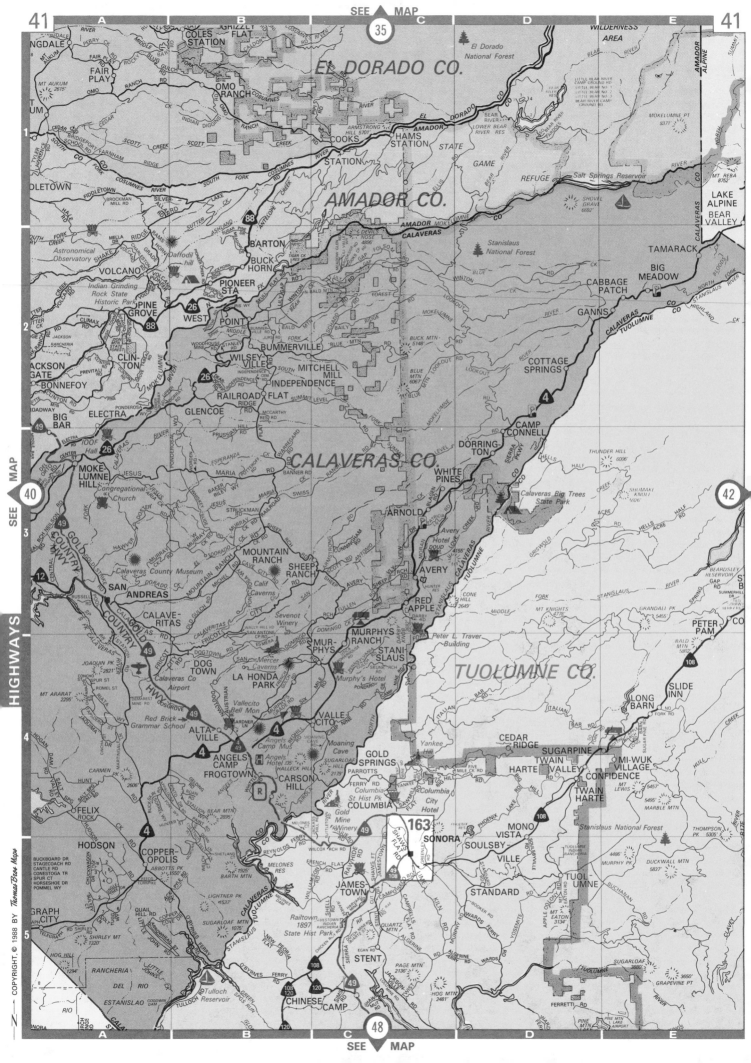

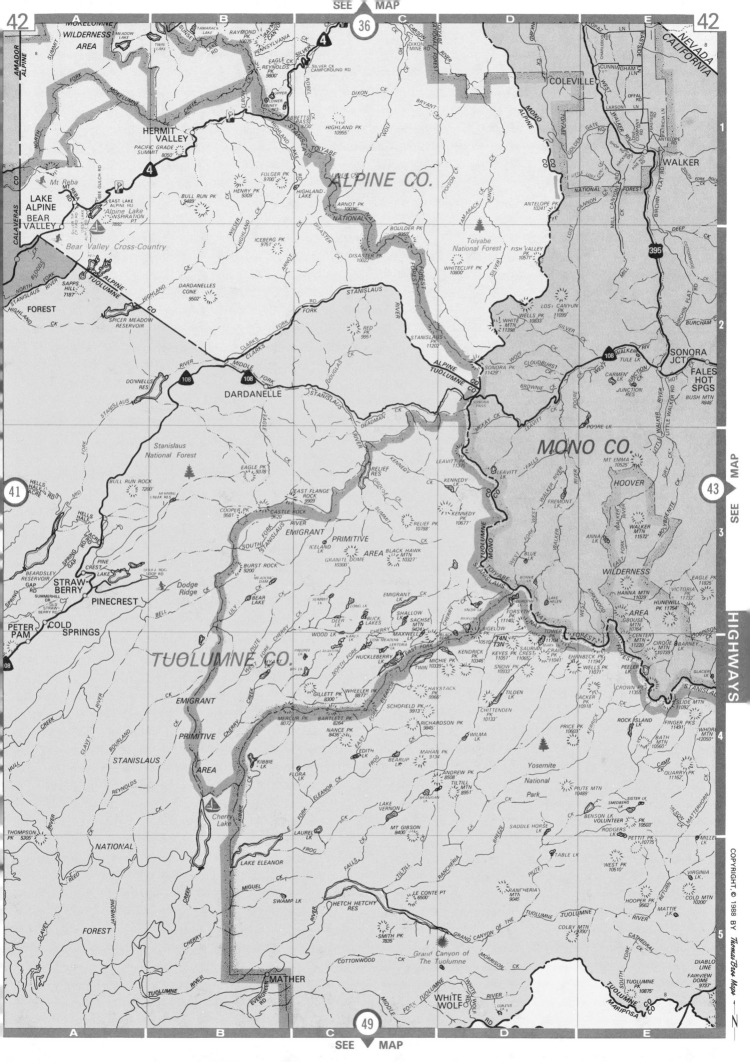

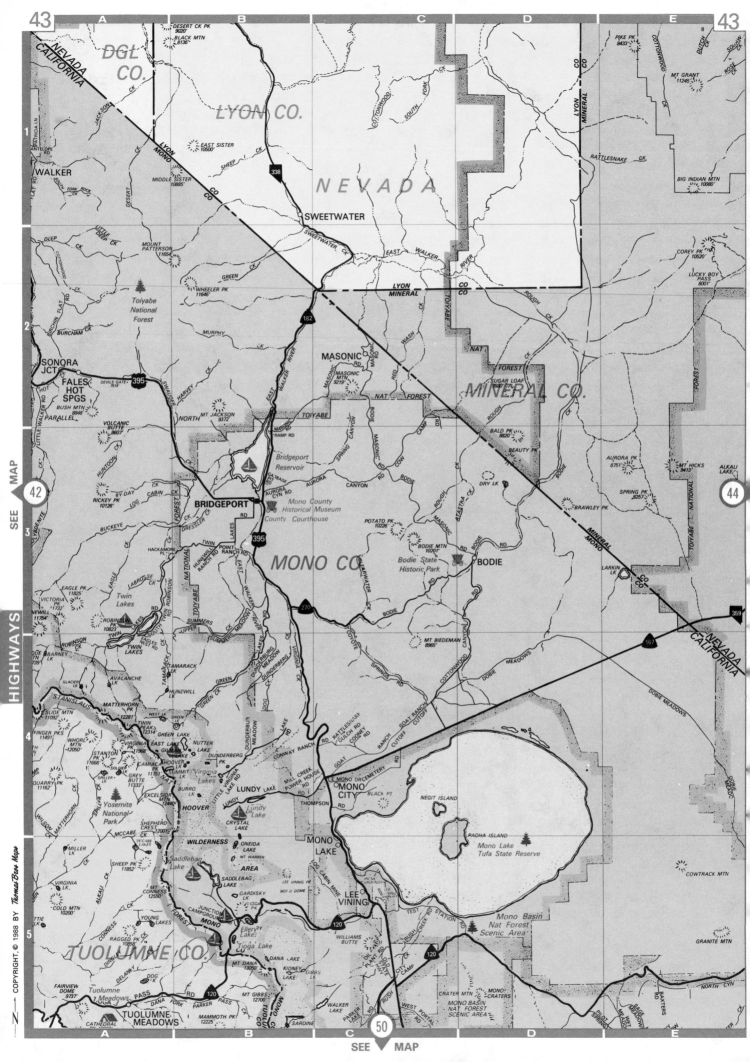

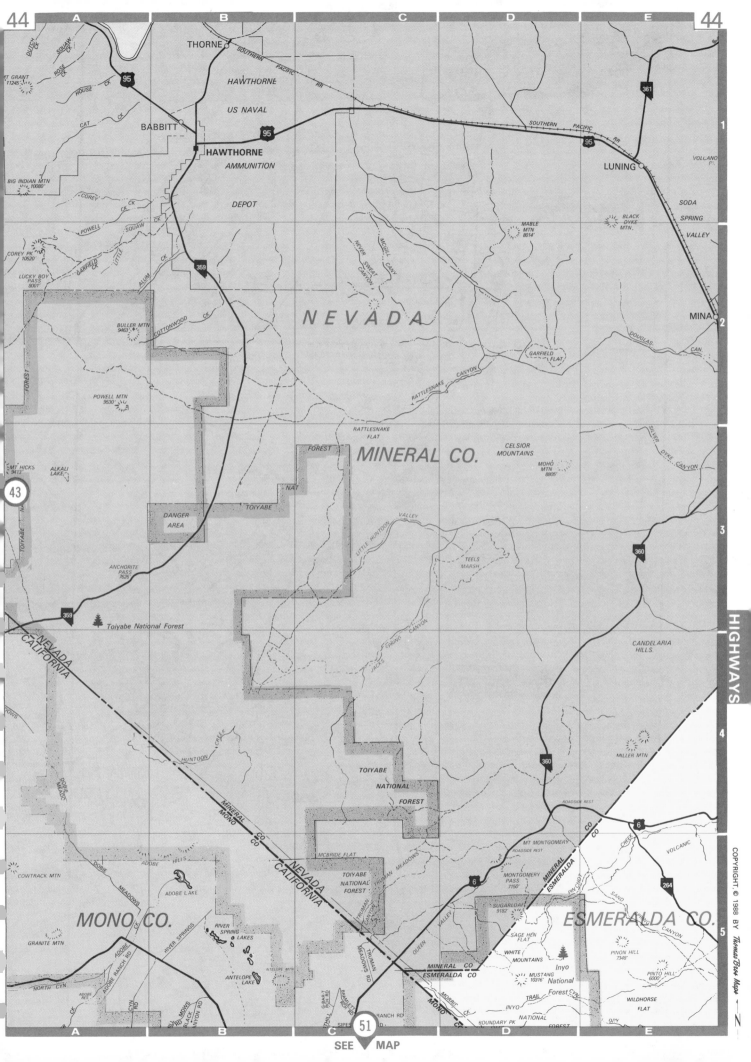

DUTCH CK
SQUAW CK
MT GRANT 11245'
ROSE CK
HOUSE CK
CAT CK

THORNE

SOUTHERN PACIFIC RR

HAWTHORNE

US NAVAL

**95**

BABBITT

HAWTHORNE

AMMUNITION

DEPOT

SOUTHERN PACIFIC RR

**95**

LUNING

VOLCANO PK.

SODA

SPRING

VALLEY

BIG INDIAN MTN 10080'

COREY CK

POWELL CK

SQUAW CK

COREY PK 10520'

GARFIELD CK

LITTLE

ALUM CK

LUCKY BOY PASS 8001'

**359**

BULLER MTN 9463'

COTTONWOOD CK

NEVADA

NEVER SWEAT CANYON

McGILL CANY

MABLE MTN 8014'

BLACK DYKE MTN.

MINA

DOUGLAS CAN.

POWELL MTN 9530'

GARFIELD FLAT

RATTLESNAKE CANYON

SILVER DYKE CANYON

RATTLESNAKE FLAT

FOREST

**MINERAL CO.**

CELSIOR MOUNTAINS

MT HICKS 9413'

ALKALI LAKE

NAT

MOHO MTN 8805'

**43**

DANGER AREA

TOIYABE

LITTLE HUNTOON VALLEY

TEELS MARSH

**360**

TOIYABE NAT

ANCHORITE PASS 7626'

**359**

Toiyabe National Forest

JACKS SPRING CANYON

CANDELARIA HILLS

NEVADA CALIFORNIA

MINERAL MONO CO CO

HUNTOON CREEK

MILLER MTN

**360**

DOBIE MEADOWS

TOIYABE

NATIONAL

FOREST

ROADSIDE REST

MINERAL CO ESMERALDA CO

**6**

COWTRACK MTN

ADOBE HILLS

ADOBE LAKE

McBRIDE FLAT

TOIYABE NATIONAL FOREST

TRUMAN MEADOWS

MT MONTGOMERY
ROADSIDE REST

**6**

MONTGOMERY PASS 7150'

MINERAL CO

ESMERALDA CO

PINCHOT

VOLCANIC

SAND SPRING CANYON

**264**

**MONO CO.**

GRANITE MTN

RIVER SPRINGS

RIVER SPRING LAKES

ADOBE CK

ANTELOPE LAKE

ANTELOPE MTN

TRUMAN CANYON

TRUMAN MEADOWS RD

QUEEN VALLEY

SUGARLOAF 9182'

**ESMERALDA CO.**

PINON HILL 7348'

PINTO HILL 6000'

SAGE HEN FLAT

WHITE

MOUNTAINS

Inyo

MUSTANG 10316'

National

WILDHORSE FLAT

NORTH CYN

ADOBE RANCH RD

HILL RD

BLACK CANYON RD

GIBART BCH RD

BRAMLETTE RICH RD

BRANCH RD

SIPES RD

MINERAL CO
ESMERALDA CO

MONO CO

MORRIS CK

INYO NATIONAL FOREST

BOUNDARY PK 7343'

DRY

HIGHWAYS

**HIGHWAYS**

STINSON BEACH

MUIR BEACH

MARIN CO.

MARIN CITY

SAUSALITO

VALLEY

TIBURON

BELVEDERE

PARADISE CAY

CONTRA COSTA CO.

SAN FRANCISCO CO.

San Francisco Bay

SAN FRANCISCO

GOLDEN GATE BRIDGE

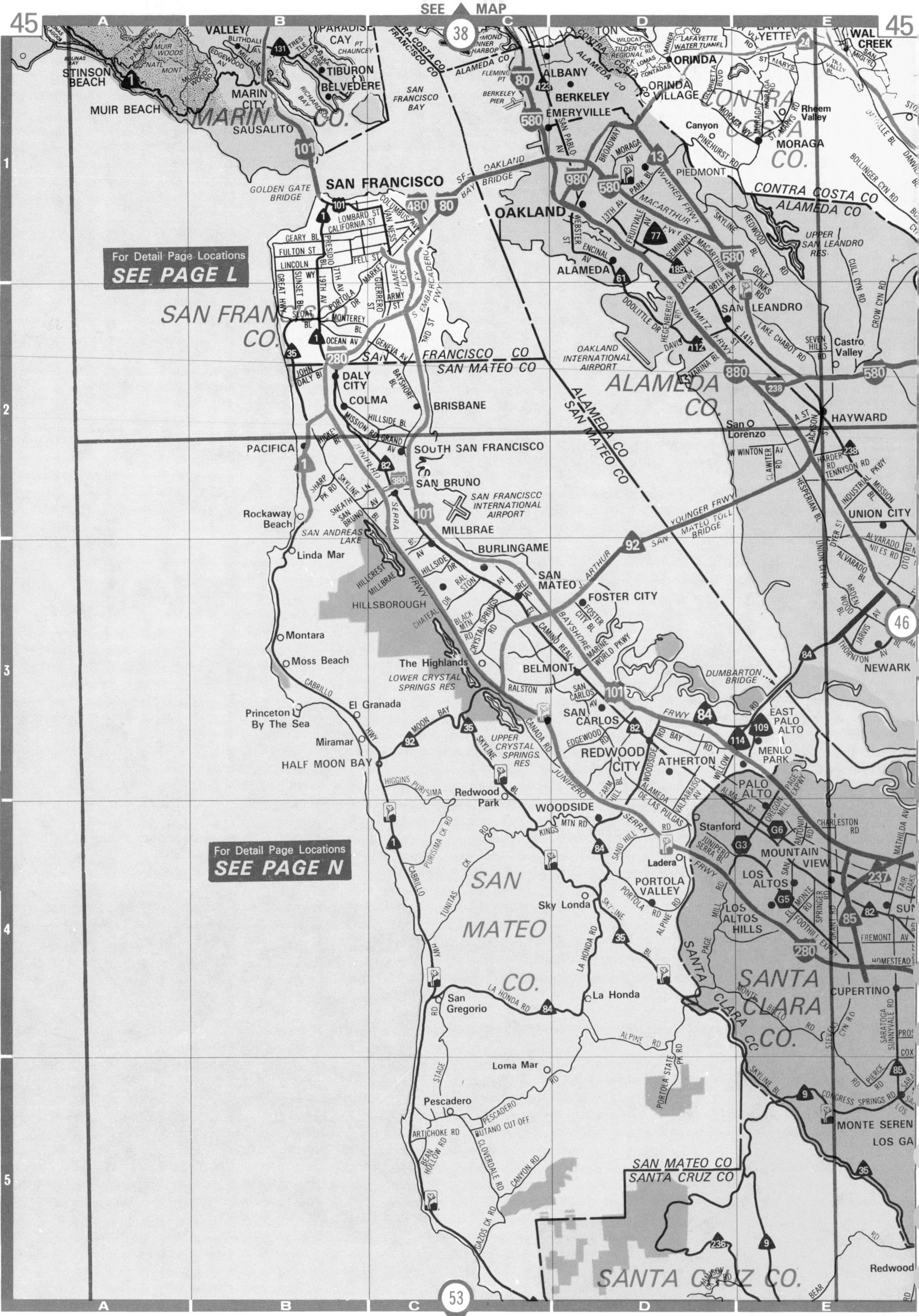

For Detail Page Locations **SEE PAGE L**

SAN FRANCISCO CO.

ORINDA

ORINDA VILLAGE

ALBANY

BERKELEY

EMERYVILLE

WALNUT CREEK

MORAGA

CONTRA COSTA CO.

ALAMEDA CO.

OAKLAND

PIEDMONT

ALAMEDA

Oakland International Airport

SAN LEANDRO

Castro Valley

ALAMEDA CO.

San Lorenzo

HAYWARD

DALY CITY

COLMA

BRISBANE

PACIFICA

SOUTH SAN FRANCISCO

SAN BRUNO

San Francisco International Airport

MILLBRAE

BURLINGAME

SAN MATEO CO.

SAN MATEO

FOSTER CITY

Rockaway Beach

San Andreas Lake

Linda Mar

HILLSBOROUGH

The Highlands

BELMONT

UNION CITY

NEWARK

Dumbarton Bridge

EAST PALO ALTO

MENLO PARK

SAN CARLOS

REDWOOD CITY

ATHERTON

PALO ALTO

Stanford

MOUNTAIN VIEW

LOS ALTOS

LOS ALTOS HILLS

CUPERTINO

Montara

Moss Beach

Princeton By The Sea

El Granada

Miramar

HALF MOON BAY

For Detail Page Locations **SEE PAGE N**

SAN MATEO CO.

Redwood Park

WOODSIDE

Sky Londa

PORTOLA VALLEY

Ladera

SANTA CLARA CO.

MONTE SERENO

San Gregorio

La Honda

Loma Mar

Pescadero

SAN MATEO CO.

SANTA CRUZ CO.

SANTA CRUZ CO.

Redwood

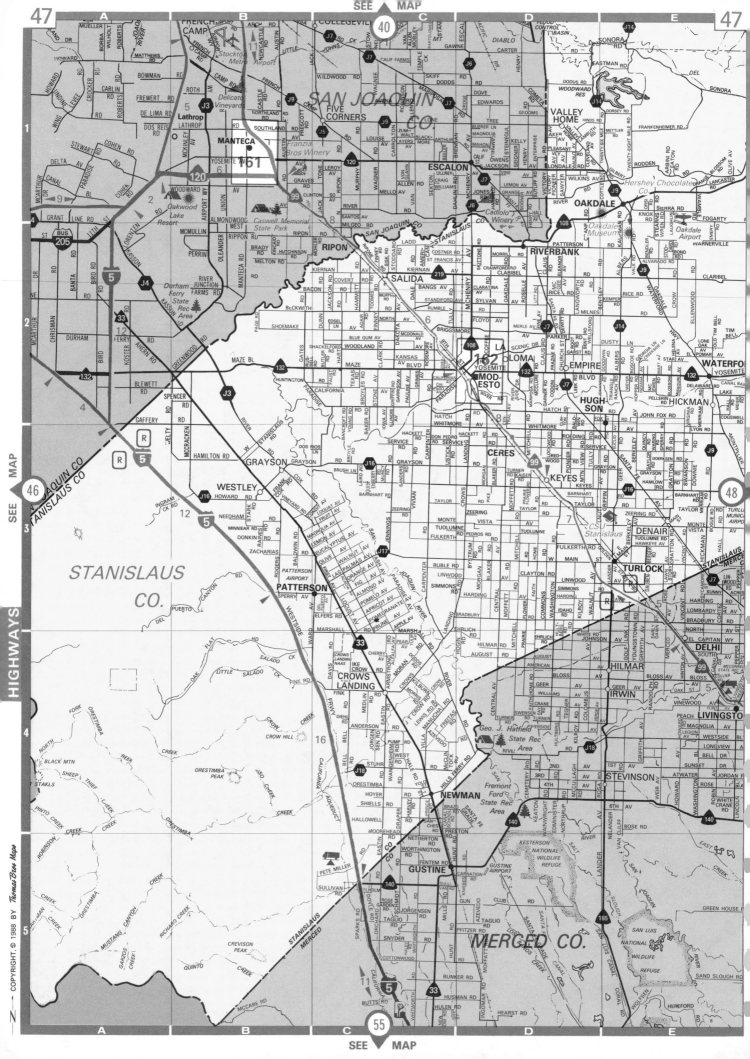

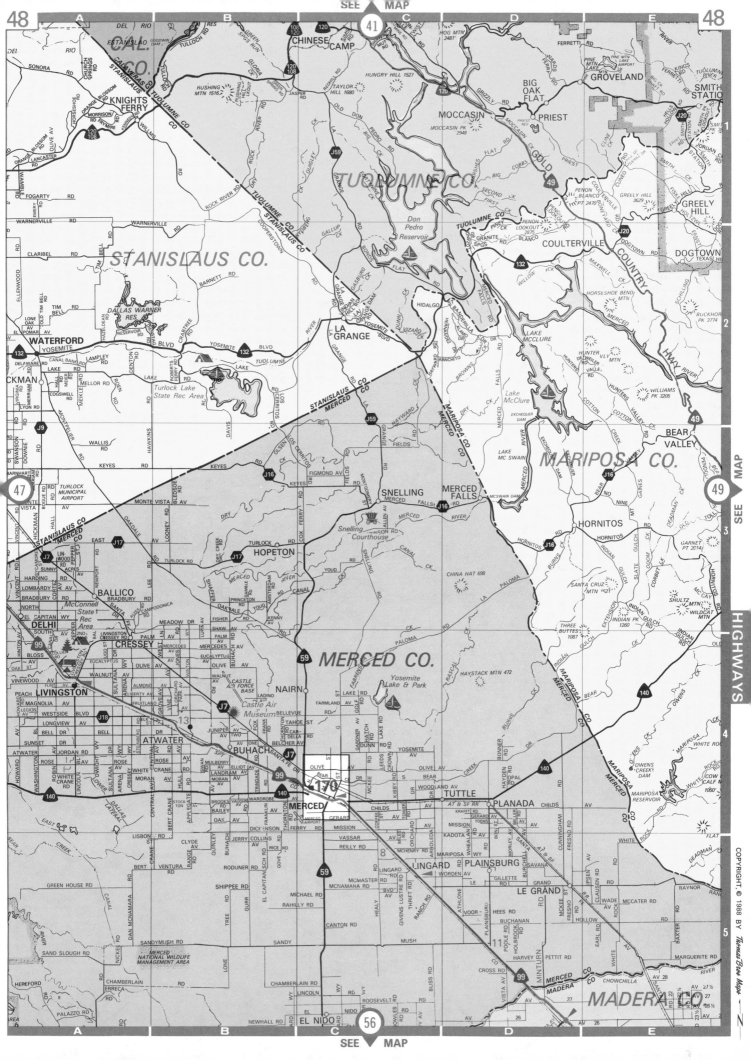

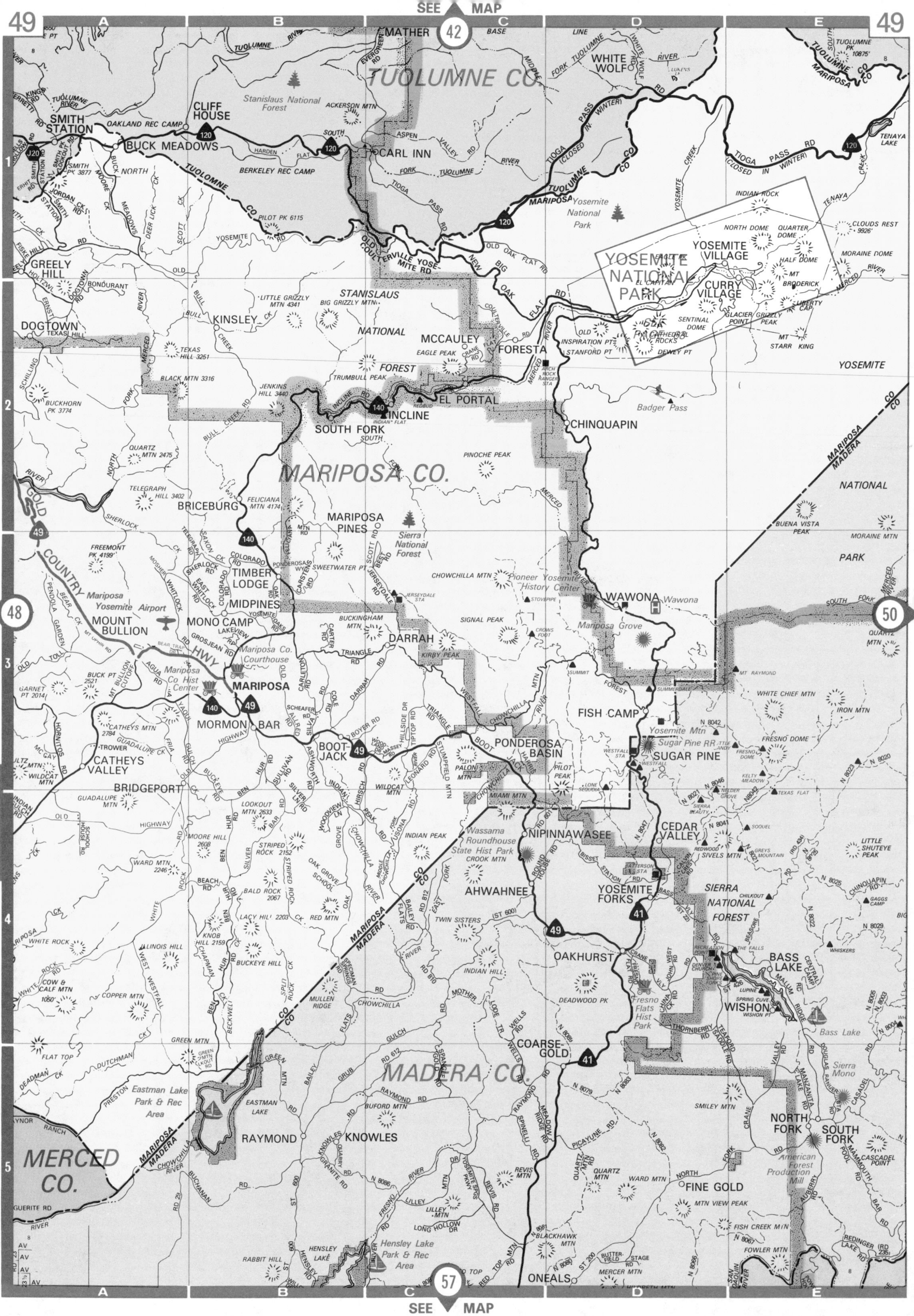

TUOLUMNE CO.

Stanislaus National Forest

MATHER
WHITE WOLF
CLIFF HOUSE
SMITH STATION
BUCK MEADOWS
CARL INN
OAKLAND REC CAMP
Berkeley Rec Camp
120

TUOLUMNE CO.
MARIPOSA CO.
TENAYA LAKE
TUOLUMNE PK 10875'

GREELY HILL
DOGTOWN
Texas Hill
KINSLEY

STANISLAUS
NATIONAL
FOREST

McCAULEY
FORESTA
Eagle Peak
Trumbull Peak

YOSEMITE NATIONAL PARK

INDIAN ROCK
NORTH DOME
QUARTER DOME
CLOUDS REST 9926'
YOSEMITE VILLAGE
HALF DOME
MORAINE DOME
MT BRODERICK
CURRY VILLAGE
LIBERTY CAP
GLACIER POINT
GRIZZLY PEAK
MT STARR KING

Yosemite National Park

EL PORTAL
INCLINE
140
SOUTH FORK

CHINQUAPIN
Badger Pass

MARIPOSA CO.

BRICEBURG
140
MARIPOSA PINES
Sierra National Forest

PINOCHE PEAK

YOSEMITE

NATIONAL
PARK

BUENA VISTA PEAK
MORAINE MTN

GOLD
COUNTRY
49

TIMBER LODGE
MIDPINES
MONO CAMP

Mariposa Yosemite Airport
MOUNT BULLION

Mariposa Co. Courthouse
MARIPOSA
140  49
MORMON BAR

CHOWCHILLA MTN
Pioneer Yosemite History Center
WAWONA
Wawona
Mariposa Grove

DARRAH
Triangle Rd

SIGNAL PEAK
CROWS FOOT
LONE SEQUOIA

FISH CAMP

MT RAYMOND
SUMMERDALE
WHITE CHIEF MTN
IRON MTN

BOOT JACK
49

PONDEROSA BASIN

Yosemite Mtn Sugar Pine RR
SUGAR PINE
WESTFALL
FRESNO DOME
KELTY MEADOW
TEXAS FLAT

CATHEYS VALLEY
BRIDGEPORT

LOOKOUT MTN 2633
Moore Hill 2608
WARD MTN 2246

MIAMI MTN

NIPINNAWASEE
CEDAR VALLEY
REDWOOD
SIVELS MTN
GREYS MOUNTAIN

LITTLE SHUTEYE PEAK

HIGHWAYS

AHWAHNEE
Wassama Roundhouse State Hist Park
CROOK MTN

YOSEMITE FORKS
41
SIERRA NATIONAL FOREST
CHILKOOT MTN
GAGGS CAMP
CHINQUAPIN MTN

OAKHURST
Fresno Flats Hist Park

BASS LAKE
Bass Lake

COARSE-GOLD
41

MADERA CO.

WISHON

Sierra Mono

MERCED CO.

Eastman Lake Park & Rec Area
EASTMAN LAKE

RAYMOND
KNOWLES

NORTH FORK
SOUTH FORK
American Forest Production Mill

FINE GOLD

Hensley Lake Park & Rec Area
Hensley Lake

CASCADEL POINT

ONEALS

COPYRIGHT © 1988 BY Thomas Bros. Maps

SEE MAP 43

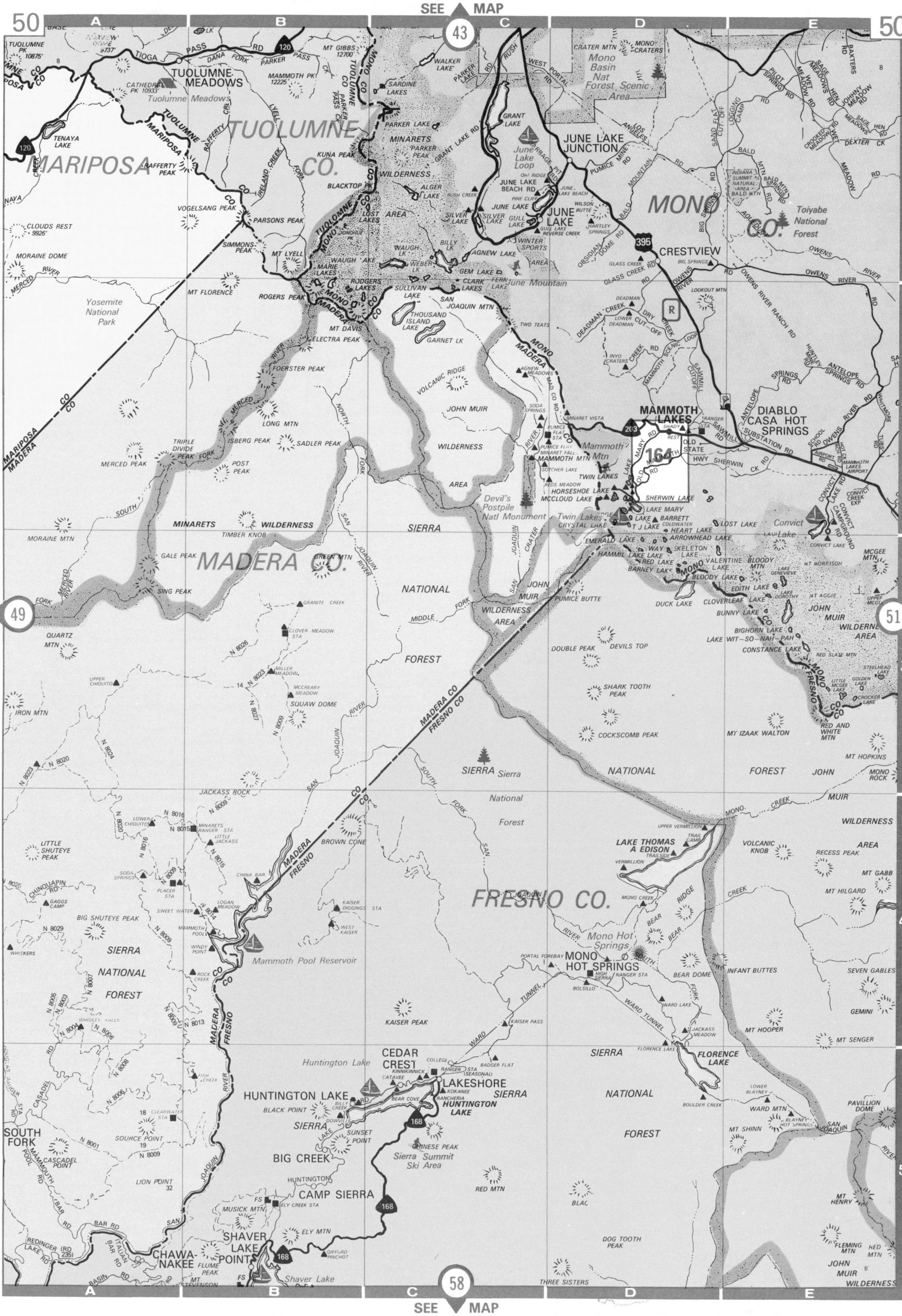

A B C D E
1 2 3 4 5
TUOLUMNE MEADOWS
Tuolumne Meadows
TIOGA PASS RD
TUOLUMNE CO.
MARIPOSA
MONO CO.
Mono Basin Natl Forest Scenic Area
JUNE LAKE JUNCTION
June Lake Loop
JUNE LAKE
CRESTVIEW
Toiyabe National Forest
June Mountain
Yosemite National Park
MINARETS WILDERNESS
JOHN MUIR WILDERNESS
MAMMOTH LAKES
DIABLO CASA HOT SPRINGS
Devil's Postpile Natl Monument
MADERA CO.
SIERRA NATIONAL FOREST
MADERA CO
FRESNO CO
FRESNO CO.
LAKE THOMAS A EDISON
MONO HOT SPRINGS
FLORENCE LAKE
Mammoth Pool Reservoir
CEDAR CREST
Huntington Lake
HUNTINGTON LAKE
LAKESHORE
BIG CREEK
Sierra Summit Ski Area
CAMP SIERRA
SHAVER LAKE POINT
Shaver Lake
CHAWANAKEE
SOUTH FORK
KAISER PEAK
RED MTN
DOG TOOTH PEAK
THREE SISTERS


SEE MAP 49

SEE MAP 51

HIGHWAYS



SEE MAP 58

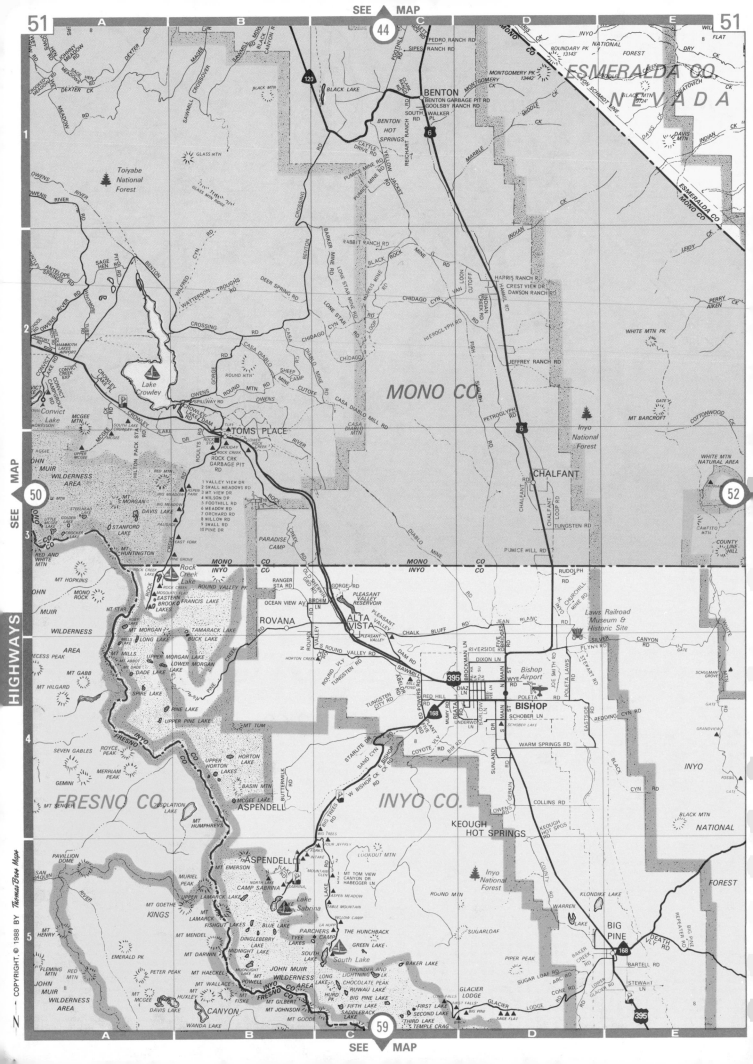

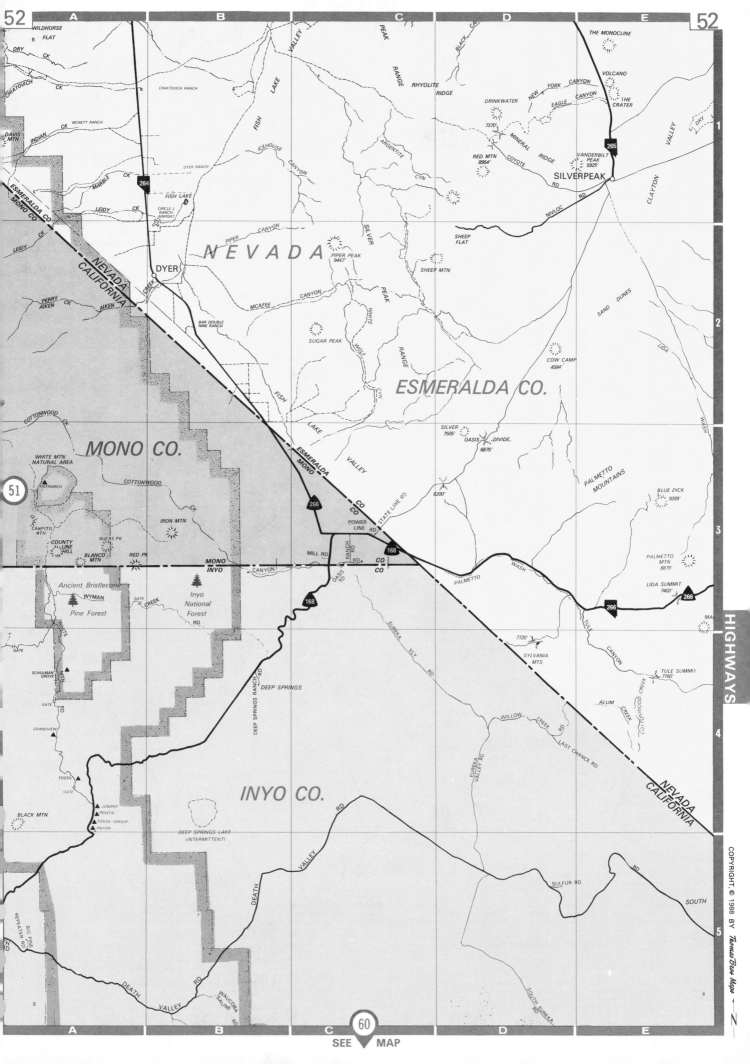

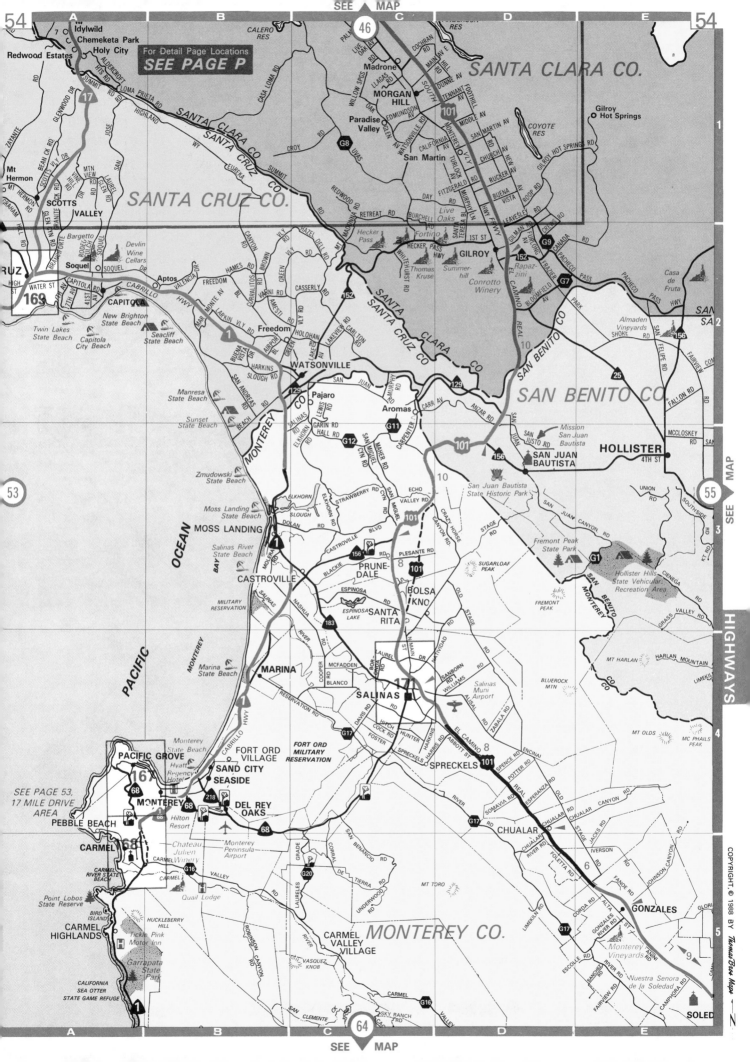

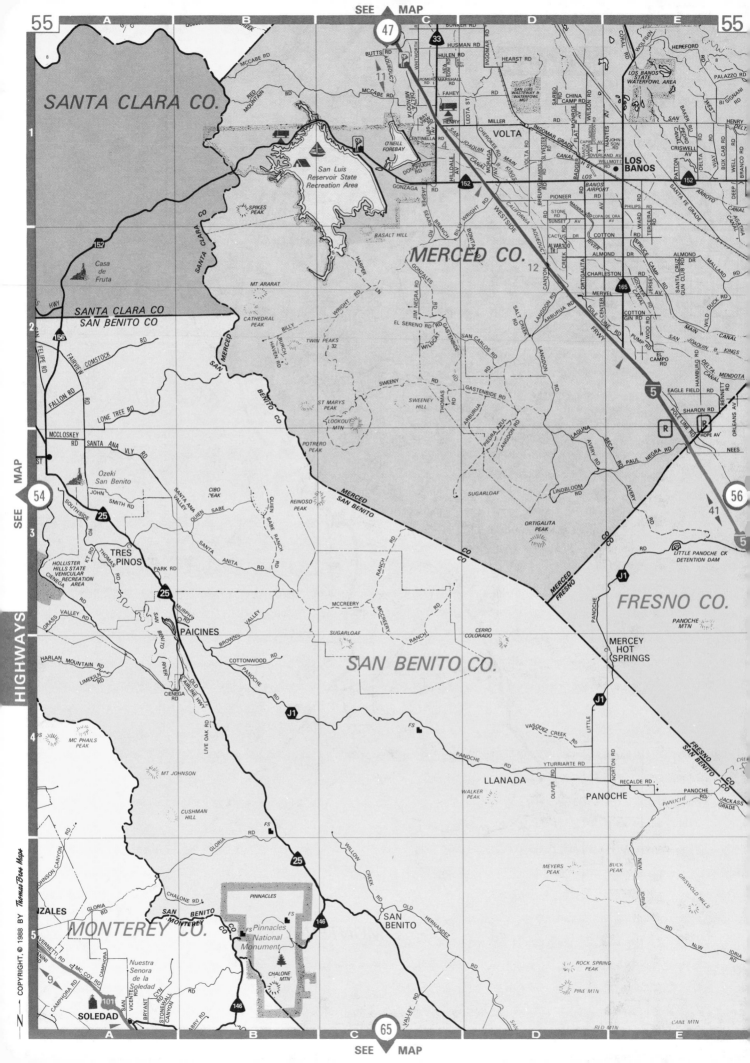

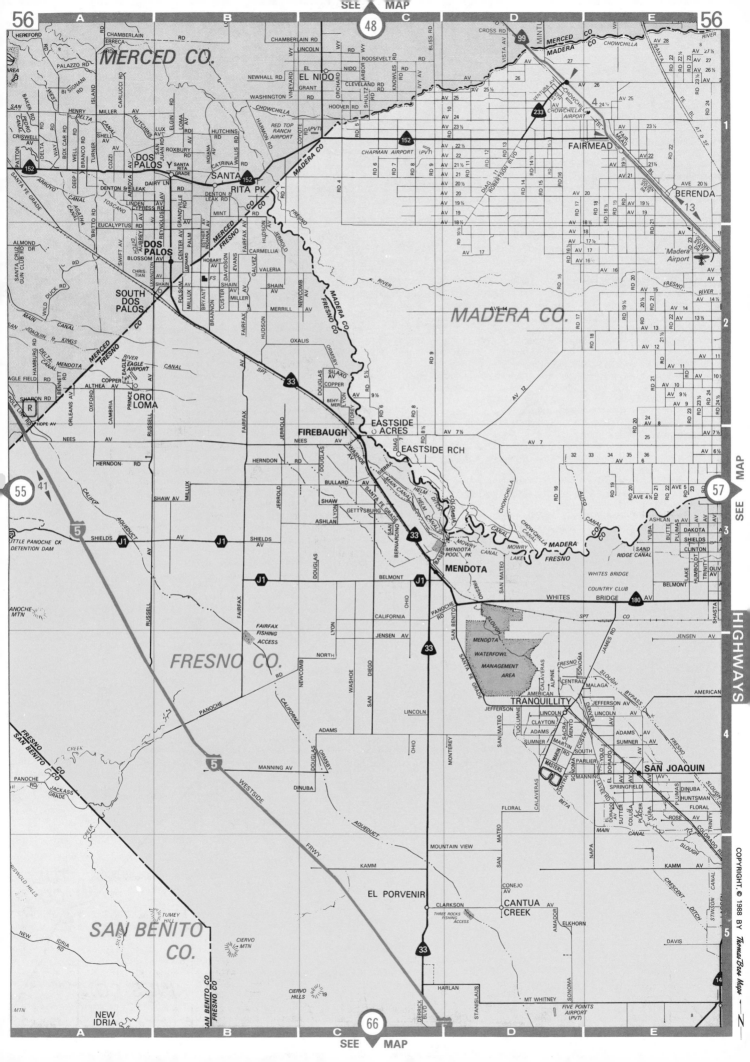

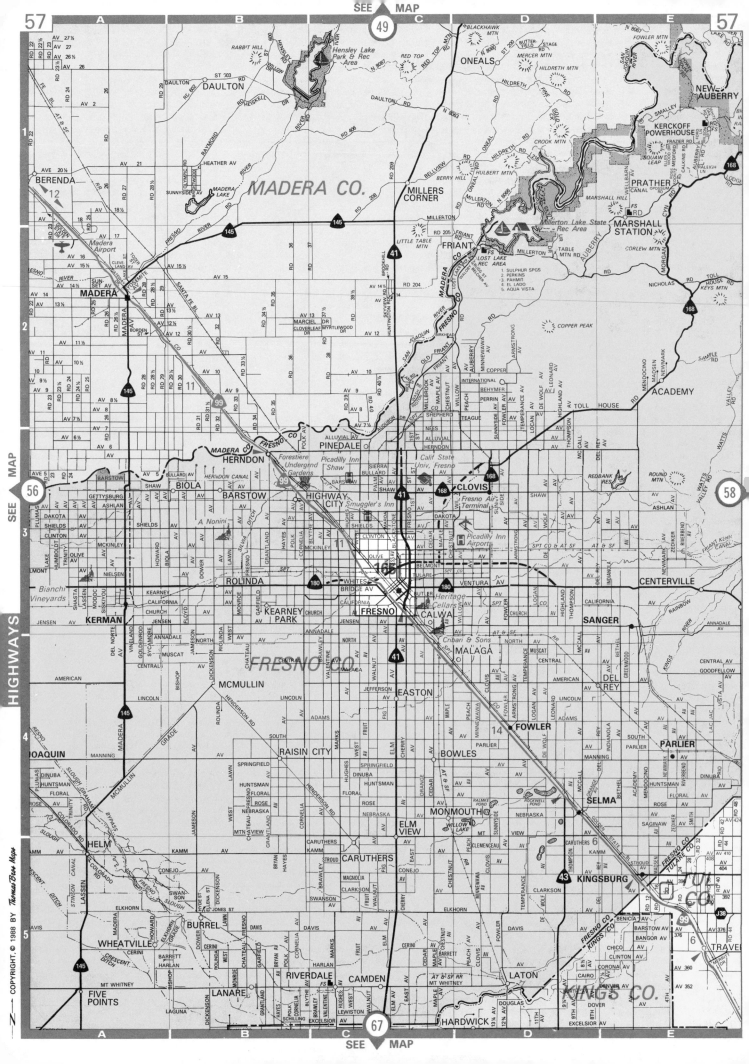

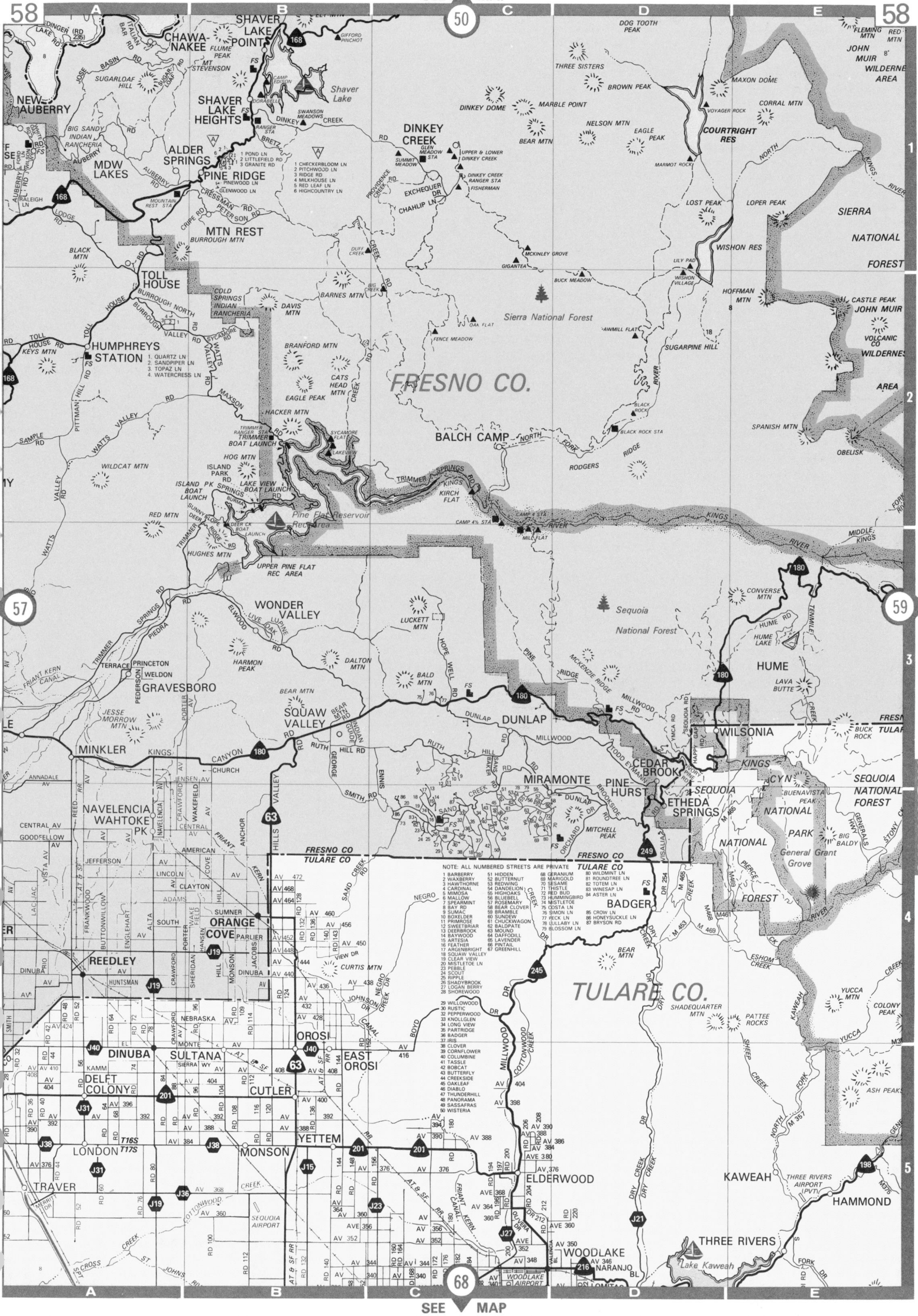

# Major Place Names

NEW AUBERRY · CHAWANAKEE · SHAVER LAKE POINTS · SHAVER LAKE HEIGHTS · ALDER SPRINGS · PINE RIDGE · MDW LAKES · MTN REST · TOLL HOUSE · HUMPHREYS STATION · DINKEY CREEK · BALCH CAMP · WONDER VALLEY · GRAVESBORO · SQUAW VALLEY · MINKLER · DUNLAP · MIRAMONTE · PINEHURST · CEDAR BROOK · BETHEDA SPRINGS · WILSONIA · HUME · BADGER · NAVELENCIA WAHTOKE PK · REEDLEY · ORANGE COVE · DINUBA · SULTANA · DELFT COLONY · CUTLER · OROSI · EAST OROSI · MONSON · YETTEM · LONDON · TRAVER · ELDERWOOD · WOODLAKE · NARANJO · KAWEAH · HAMMOND · THREE RIVERS

FRESNO CO. · TULARE CO. · SIERRA NATIONAL FOREST · SEQUOIA NATIONAL FOREST · SEQUOIA NATIONAL PARK · JOHN MUIR WILDERNESS AREA · JOHN MUIR VOLCANIC WILDERNESS AREA · General Grant Grove · Shaver Lake · Pine Flat Reservoir Rec Area · Lake Kaweah · Courtright Res · Wishon Res · Hume Lake

## NOTE: ALL NUMBERED STREETS ARE PRIVATE

| | | |
|---|---|---|
| 1 BARBERRY | 30 RUSTIC | 59 BRAMBLE |
| 2 WAXBERRY | 31 PEPPERWOOD | 60 SUNDEW |
| 3 HAWTHORNE | 32 KNOLLGLEN | 61 CHUCKWAGON |
| 4 CARDINAL | 33 LONG VIEW | 62 BALDPATE |
| 5 MIMOSA | 34 LONG VIEW | 63 MOUND |
| 6 MALLOW | 35 PARTRIDGE | 64 DAFFODIL |
| 7 SPEARMINT | 36 BADGER | 65 LAVENDER |
| 8 BAY RD | 37 IRIS | 66 PINTAIL |
| 9 SUMAC | 38 CLOVER | 67 GREENHILL |
| 10 BOXELDER | 39 CORNFLOWER | 68 GERANIUM |
| 11 PRIMROSE | 40 COLUMBINE | 69 MARIGOLD |
| 12 SWEETBRIAR | 41 TASSLE | 70 SESAME |
| 13 DEERBROOK | 42 BOBCAT | 71 THISTLE |
| 14 BAYWOOD | 43 BUTTERFLY | 72 RED BUD |
| 15 ARTESIA | 44 CREEKSIDE | 73 HUMMINGBIRD |
| 16 FEATHER | 45 OAKLEAF | 74 MISTLETOE |
| 17 ARGENBRIGHT | 46 DIABLO | 75 COSTA LN |
| 18 SQUAW VALLEY | 47 THUNDERHILL | 76 SIMON LN |
| 19 CLEAR VIEW | 48 PANORAMA | 77 PECK LN |
| 20 MISTLETOE LN | 49 SASSAFRAS | 78 LULLABY LN |
| 21 PEBBLE | 50 WISTERIA | 79 BLOSSOM LN |
| 22 SCOUT | 51 HIDDEN | 80 WILDMINT LN |
| 23 RIPPLE | 52 BUTTERNUT | 81 ROUNDTREE LN |
| 24 SHADYBROOK | 53 REDWING | 82 TOTEM LN |
| 25 LOGAN BERRY | 54 DANDELION | 83 WINESAP LN |
| 26 SHOREWOOD | 55 HIGHOAKS | 84 ASTER LN |
| 29 WILLOWOOD | 56 BLUEBELL | 85 CROW LN |
| | 57 ROSEMARY | 86 HONEYSUCKLE LN |
| | 58 BEAR CLOVER | 87 BRYSON RD |

PINE RIDGE
1 POND LN
2 LITTLEFIELD RD
3 GRANITE RD
4 MILKHOUSE LN
5 RED LEAF LN
6 HIGHCOUNTRY LN

CHECKERBLOOM LN
PITCHWOOD LN
RIDGE RD

HUMPHREYS STATION
1 QUARTZ LN
2 SANDPIPER LN
3 TOPAZ LN
4 WATERCRESS LN

HIGHWAYS

59 | A B C D E | 59

HIGHWAYS

© COPYRIGHT 1988 BY Thomas Bros. Maps

**Fresno Co.**

JOHN MUIR WILDERNESS AREA
PETER PEAK
MT HAECKEL
MT WALLACE
MT POWELL
MT FISKE
MT HUXLEY
DAVIS LAKE
MT MCGEE
RED MTN
WANDA LAKE
BLACK GIANT
MT GODDARD
LANGILLE PEAK
SOLOMONS MT
SCYLIA
MT REINSTEIN
BLACKCAP MTN
THE CITADEL
MT MCDUFFIE
WHEEL MTN
BLUE CANYON PEAK
FINGER PEAK
MT WOODWORTH
GREAT CLIFFS
OBSERVATION PEAK

CANYON
INYO FRESNO CO.
MT JOHNSON
MT GOODE
MT WINCHELL
NORTH PALISADE
COLUMBINE PEAK
MT SILL
RAUD PEAK
LONG LAKE
LIGHTNING
CHOCOLAT
RUWAU LAKE
BIG PINE LAKE
SADDLEBACK LAKE
HURD PK
FIFTH LAKE

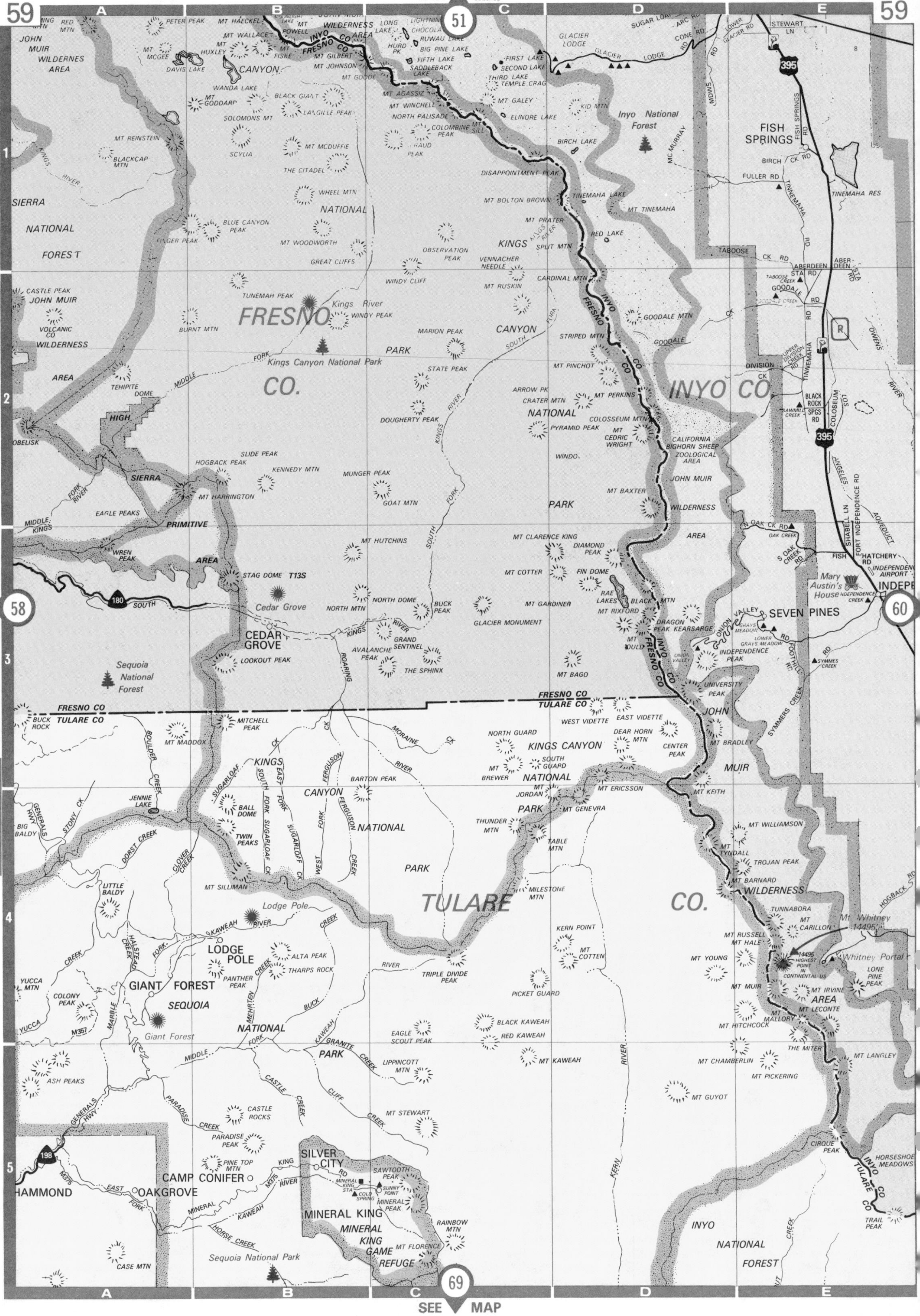

SUGAR LOAF
GLACIER LODGE
CONE RD
ARC RD
LOWER GLACIER RD
STEWART LN
395
FIRST LAKE
SECOND LAKE
THIRD LAKE
TEMPLE CRAG
MT GALEY
ELINORE LAKE
KID MTN
BIRCH LAKE
Inyo National Forest

FISH SPRINGS
BIRCH CK RD
FULLER RD
TINEMAHA RES

SIERRA NATIONAL FOREST

MT AGASSIZ
DISAPPOINTMENT PEAK
MT BOLTON BROWN
TINEMAHA LAKE
MT TINEMAHA
MT PRATER
MAGS RIVER
RED LAKE
SPLIT MTN
TABOOSE
ABERDEEN
TABOOSE CREEK RD
GOODALE
GOODALE MTN
GOODALE CK

NATIONAL FOREST

CASTLE PEAK
JOHN MUIR
VOLCANIC CO WILDERNESS AREA
TUNEMAH PEAK
Kings River
WINDY PEAK
BURNT MTN
MARION PEAK
STATE PEAK
WINDY CLIFF
MT RUSKIN
CARDINAL MTN
STRIPED MTN
MT PINCHOT
DIVISION
BLACK ROCK SPGS RD
AWMILL CREEK
UPPER DIPPER CREEK RD

**FRESNO**

**PARK**

**CO.**

**KINGS CANYON**

HIGH
OBELISK
TEHIPITE DOME
SIERRA PRIMITIVE AREA
HOGBACK PEAK
SLIDE PEAK
KENNEDY MTN
MUNGER PEAK
GOAT MTN
MT HARRINGTON
EAGLE PEAKS
MIDDLE KINGS FORK RIVER
WREN PEAK
STAG DOME T13S
180 SOUTH
CEDAR GROVE

DOUGHERTY PEAK
PYRAMID PEAK
ARROW PK
CRATER MTN
MT PERKINS
COLOSSEUM MTN
MT CEDRIC WRIGHT
WINDO
CALIFORNIA BIGHORN SHEEP ZOOLOGICAL AREA
MT BAXTER
JOHN MUIR WILDERNESS AREA

INYO CO
NATIONAL PARK

MT HUTCHINS
MT CLARENCE KING
DIAMOND PEAK
MT COTTER
FIN DOME
RAE LAKES
MT GARDINER
BLACK MTN
MT RIXFORD
DRAGON PEAK
GLACIER MONUMENT
KEARSARGE
GOULD
 GROUSE VALLEY
GRAYS MEADOW
LOWER GRAYS MEADOW
INDEPENDENCE PEAK
UNION VALLEY
SEVEN PINES
Mary Austin's House
INDEPENDENCE
INDEPENDENCE AIRPORT
SYMMES CREEK

CEDAR GROVE
LOOKOUT PEAK
NORTH DOME
NORTH MTN
BUCK PEAK
GRAND SENTINEL
AVALANCHE PEAK
THE SPHINX
MT BAGO
UNIVERSITY PEAK
FRESNO CO TULARE CO

Sequoia National Forest

FRESNO CO / TULARE CO
BUCK ROCK
MITCHELL PEAK
MT MADDOX
NORTH GUARD
SOUTH GUARD
MT BREWER
WEST VIDETTE
EAST VIDETTE
DEER HORN MTN
CENTER PEAK
MT BRADLEY
JOHN MUIR WILDERNESS
MT KEITH

**KINGS CANYON NATIONAL PARK**

BOULDER CREEK
SUGARLOAF
BALL DOME
TWIN PEAKS
JENNIE LAKE
BARTON PEAK
MORAINE
MT JORDAN
MT ERICSSON
MT GENEVRA
THUNDER MTN
TABLE MTN
MT WILLIAMSON
MT TYNDALL
TROJAN PEAK
MT BARNARD
WILDERNESS AREA
TUNNABORA

GENERALS HWY
BIG BALDY
STONY CK
LITTLE BALDY
MT SILLIMAN
Lodge Pole
LODGE POLE
DORST CREEK
CLOVER CREEK
KAWEAH RIVER
ALTA PEAK
THARPS ROCK
MILESTONE MTN
KERN POINT
MT COTTEN
TUNNABORA
MT CARILLON
Mt Whitney 14495
MT RUSSELL
MT HALE
14495 HIGHEST POINT IN CONTINENTAL US
Whitney Portal
LONE PINE PEAK

**TULARE**   **CO.**

YUCCA MTN
COLONY PEAK
YUCCA
M357
GIANT FOREST
SEQUOIA
Giant Forest
PANTHER PEAK
MEHRTEN CREEK
BUCK CREEK
TRIPLE DIVIDE PEAK
PICKET GUARD
MT YOUNG
MT MUIR
MT IRVINE
LE CONTE
MT MALLORY
MT HITCHCOCK
THE MITER
AREA

**NATIONAL**   **PARK**
EAGLE SCOUT PEAK
LIPPINCOTT MTN
BLACK KAWEAH
RED KAWEAH
MT KAWEAH
GRANITE CREEK
KAWEAH FORK
MIDDLE FORK
MT STEWART
CASTLE CREEK
CLIFF CREEK
MT CHAMBERLIN
MT PICKERING
MT LANGLEY

ASH PEAKS
CASTLE ROCKS
PARADISE CREEK
PARADISE PEAK
PINE TOP MTN
SILVER CITY
SAWTOOTH PEAK
MT GUYOT
CIRQUE PEAK
HORSESHOE MEADOWS
198
M375
HAMMOND
OAKGROVE
CAMP CONIFER
EAST FORK
MINERAL
KAWEAH
HORSE CREEK
MINERAL KING RD
COLD SPRING
SUNNY POINT
MINERAL PEAK
RAINBOW MTN
MINERAL KING GAME REFUGE
MT FLORENCE
Sequoia National Park

SEQUOIA NATIONAL FOREST

KERN RIVER
INYO NATIONAL FOREST
TRAIL PEAK
INYO TULARE CO

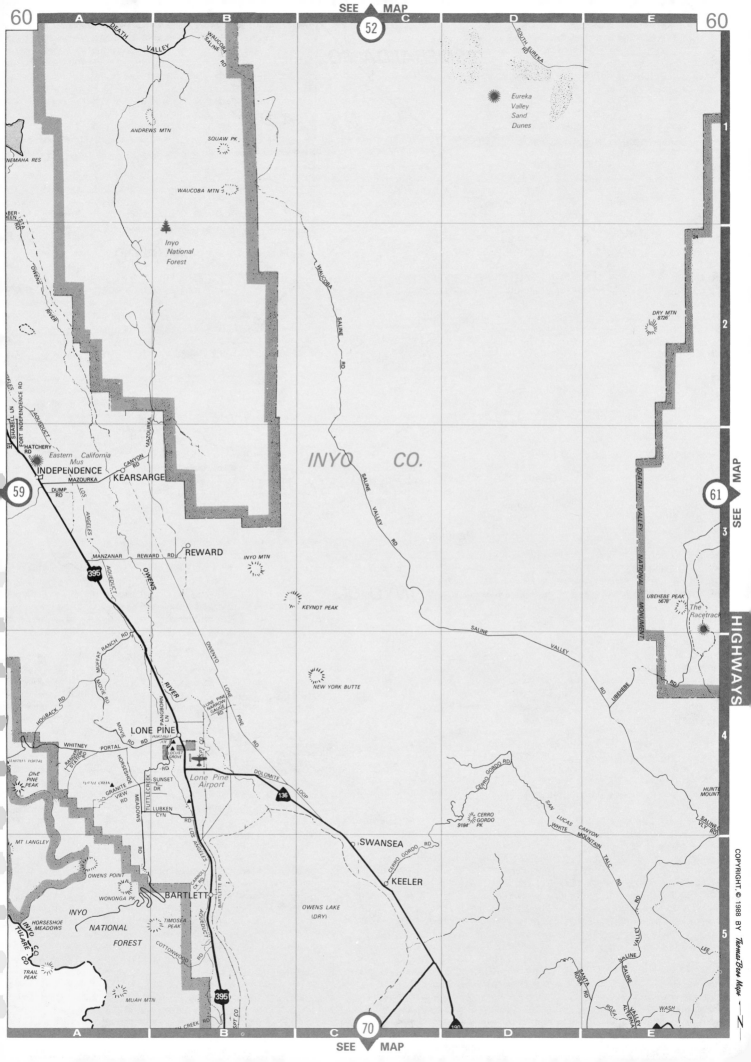

SEE MAP
52

SEE MAP
70

SEE MAP

59

61

HIGHWAYS

DEATH VALLEY

WAUCOBA SALINE RD

South Eureka RD

Eureka
Valley Sand
Dunes

ANDREWS MTN

SQUAW PK

WAUCOBA MTN

Inyo
National
Forest

DRY MTN
8726'

NEMAHA RES

OWENS RIVER

WAUCOBA SALINE RD

INYO CO.

DEATH VALLEY NATIONAL MONUMENT

FORT INDEPENDENCE RD

HATCHERY RD
Eastern California Mus
INDEPENDENCE

MAZOURKA CANYON RD

KEARSARGE

SALINE VALLEY RD

UBEHEBE PEAK
5678'

The Racetrack

DUMP RD

LOS ANGELES AQUEDUCT

395

MANZANAR

REWARD RD

REWARD

INYO MTN

SALINE VALLEY

UBEHEBE RD

OWENS

KEYNOT PEAK

OWENVO

LONE PINE RD

NEW YORK BUTTE

RIVER

HOGBACK RD

MOVIE RD

MUFFAT RANCH RD

LONE PINE NARROW GAUGE RD

PANGBORN LN

LONE PINE

PORTAGE

CERRO GORDO RD

WHITNEY PORTAL
RANGER STATION

MOVIE RD

LOCUST GROVE

DOLOMITE LOOP

CERRO GORDO PK
9184'

SAN LUCAS CANYON

HUNTER MOUNT

ONE PINE PEAK

HORSESHOE

TUTTLE CREEK

SUNSET DR

Lone Pine
Airport

136

SWANSEA

WHITE MOUNTAIN TALC RD

SALINE VLY RD

GRANITE VIEW RD

LUBKEN CYN RD

CERRO GORDO RD

KEELER

MT LANGLEY

TUTTLE CREEK MEADOWS

LOS ANGELES AQUEDUCT

CA RD HQ

OWENS LAKE
(DRY)

OWENS POINT

CARROLL

BARTLETTE RD

WONONGA PK

BARTLETT

SALINE VALLEY ALTERNA

INYO

TIMOSEA PEAK

SANTA ROSA RD

HORSESHOE MEADOWS

NATIONAL

COTTONWOOD RD

SALINE

ROSA RD

LEE

WASH

TRAIL PEAK

FOREST

INYO CO
TULARE CO

MUAH MTN

COTTONWOOD CREEK RD

395

SPT CO

100

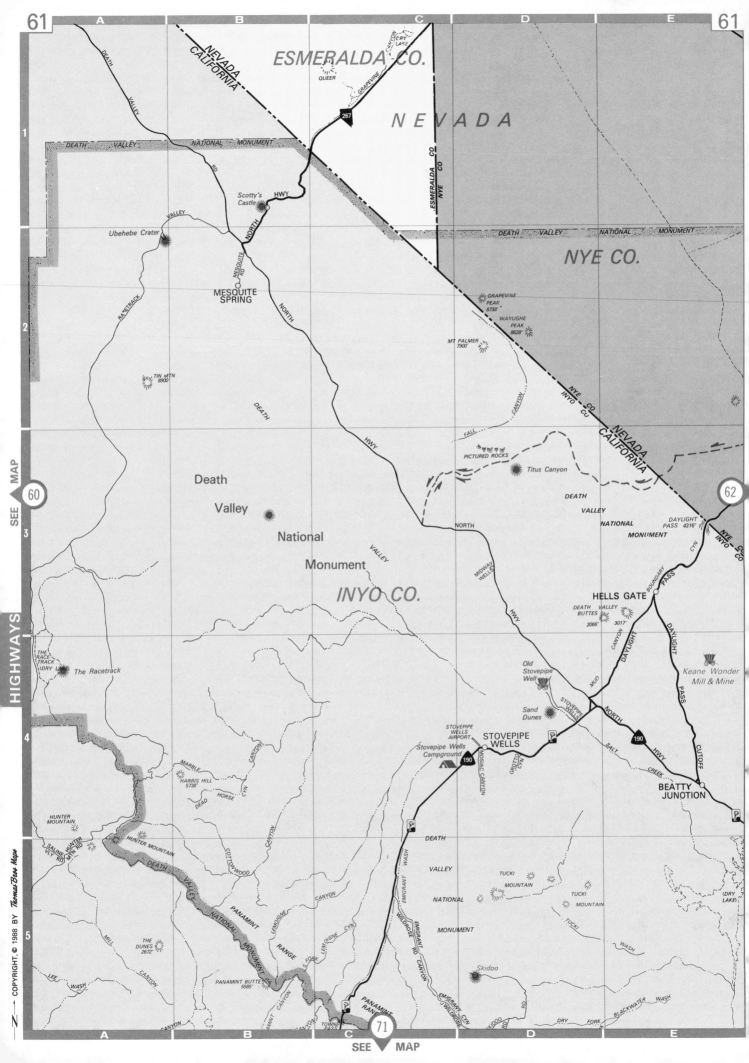

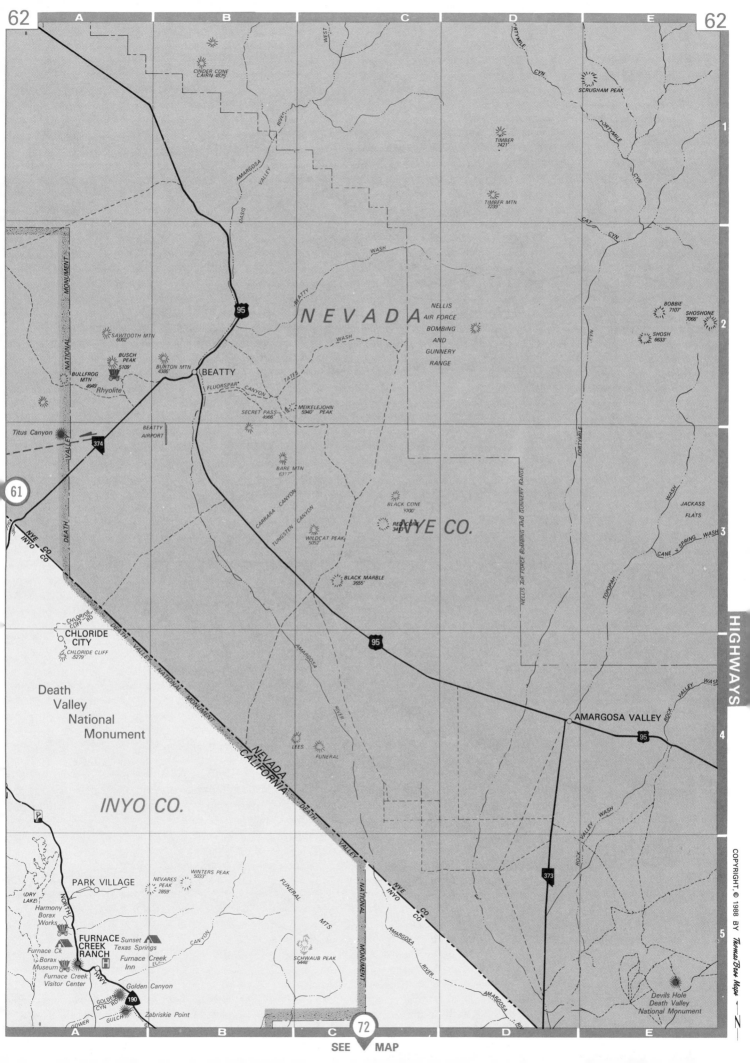

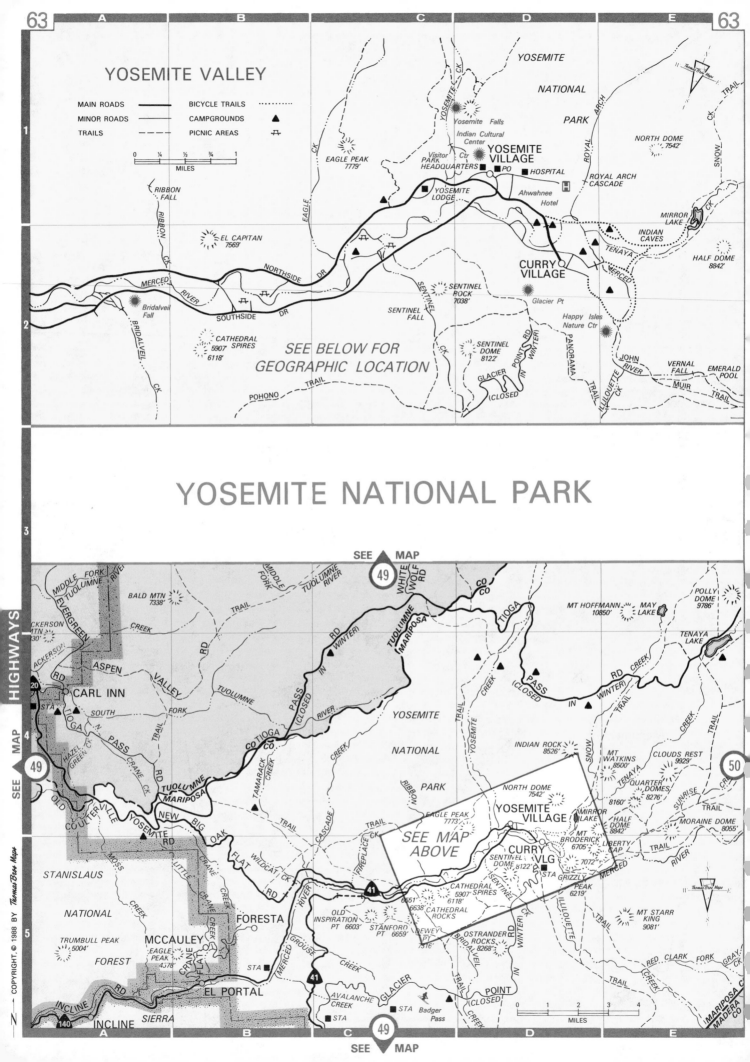

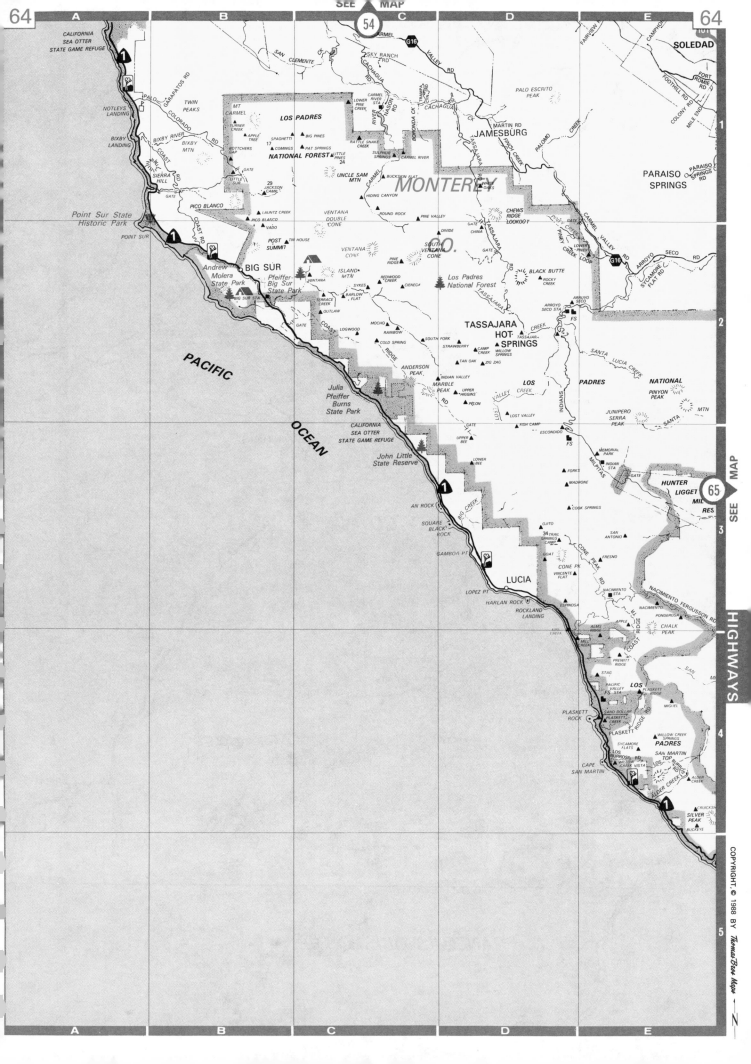

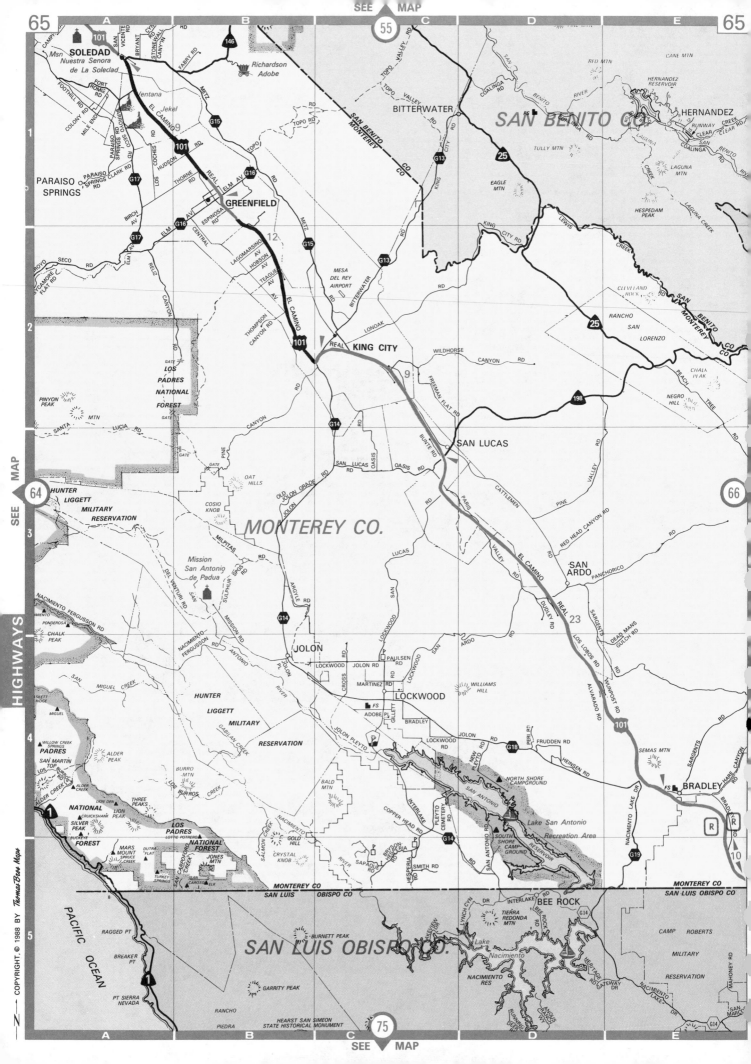

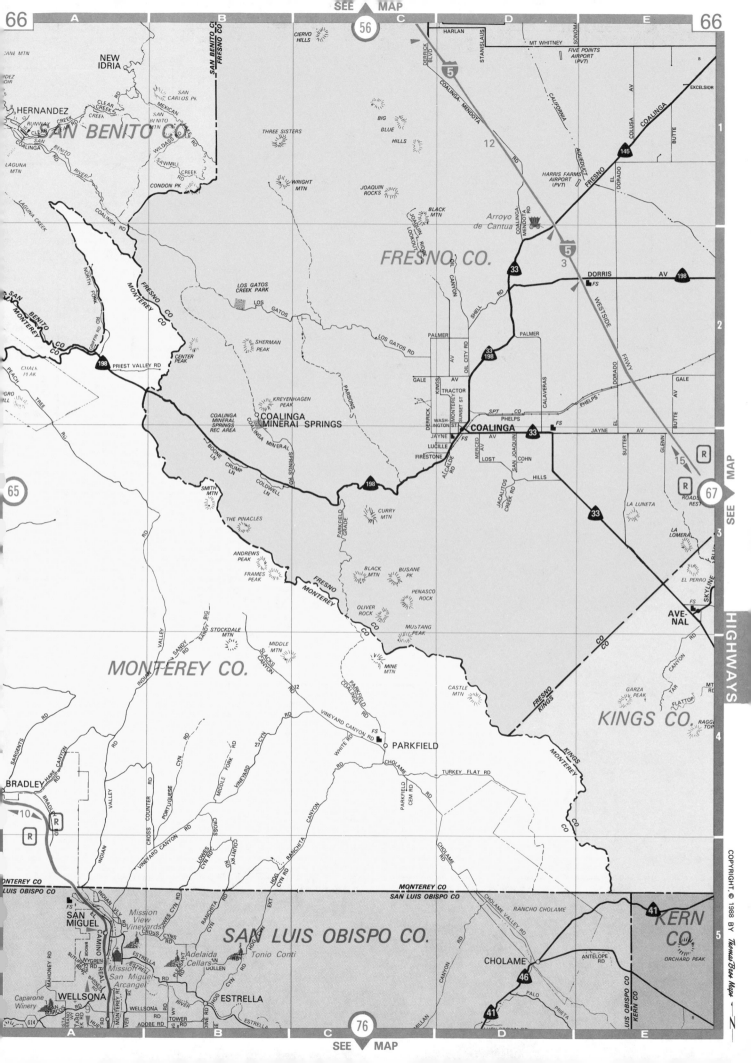

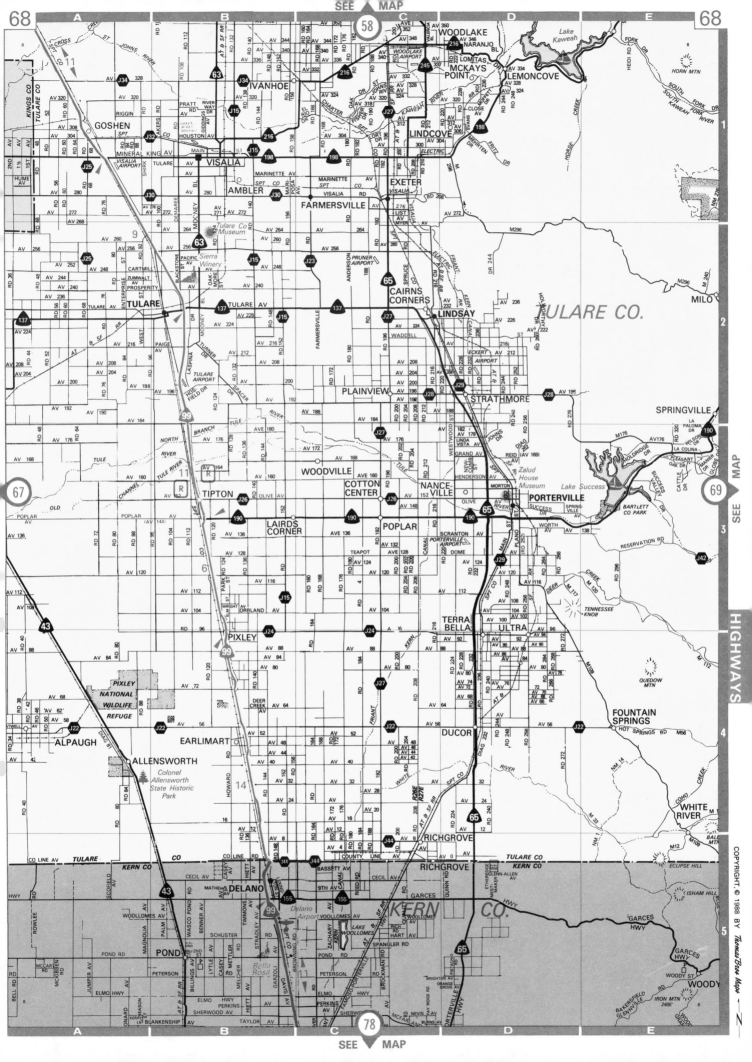

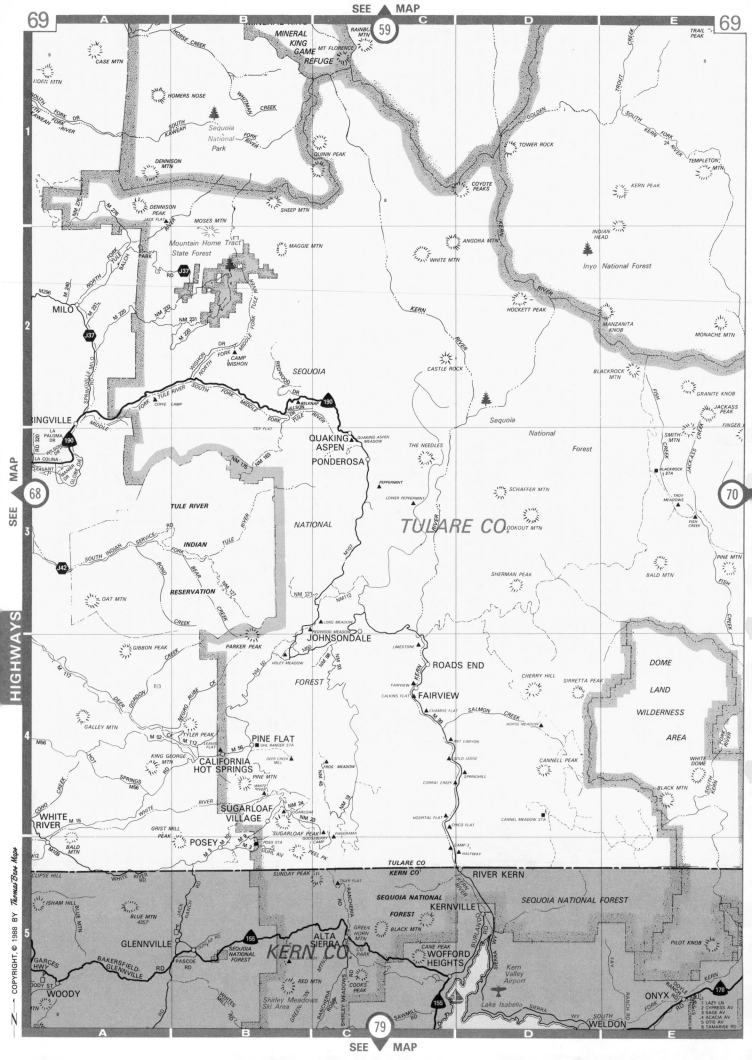

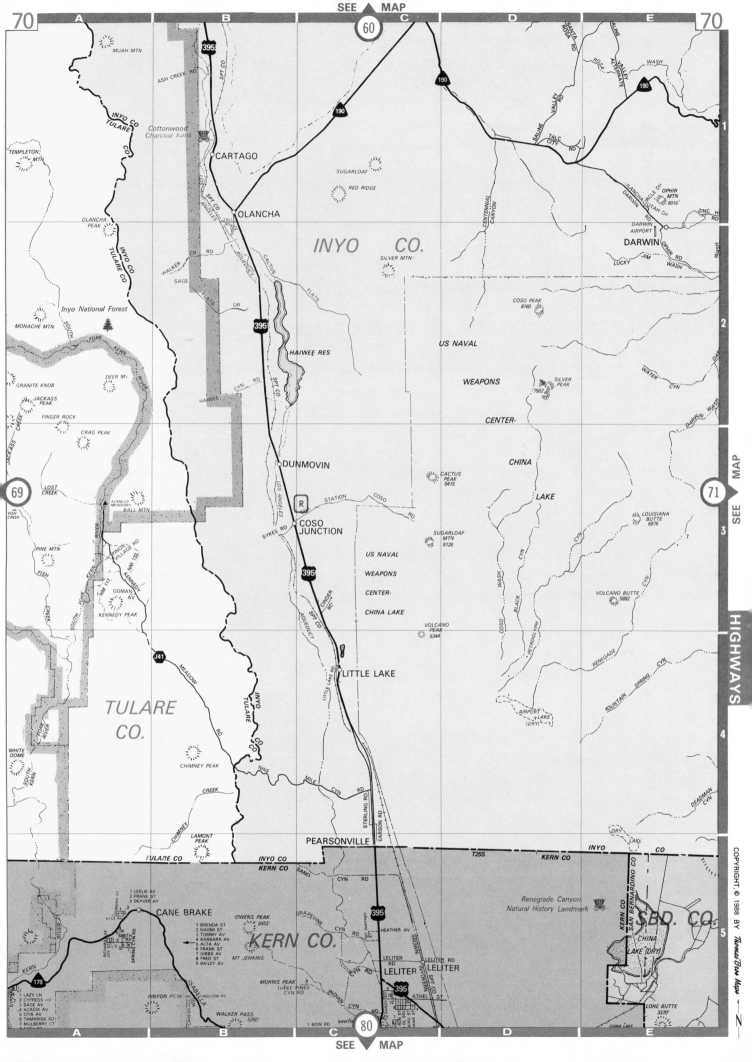

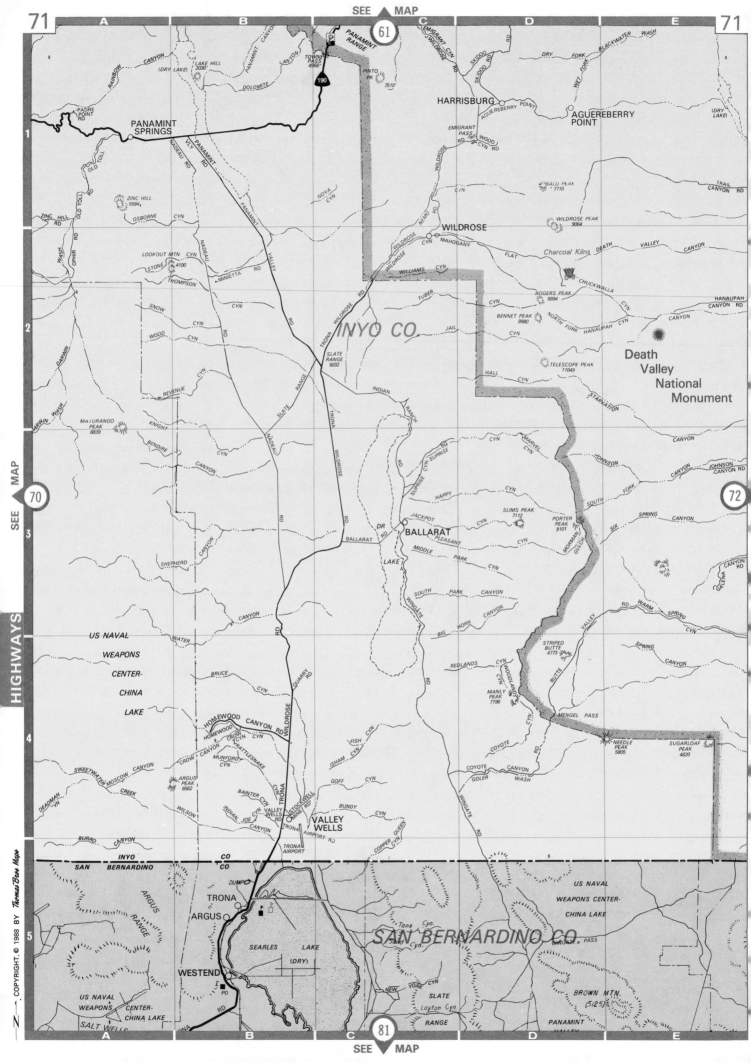

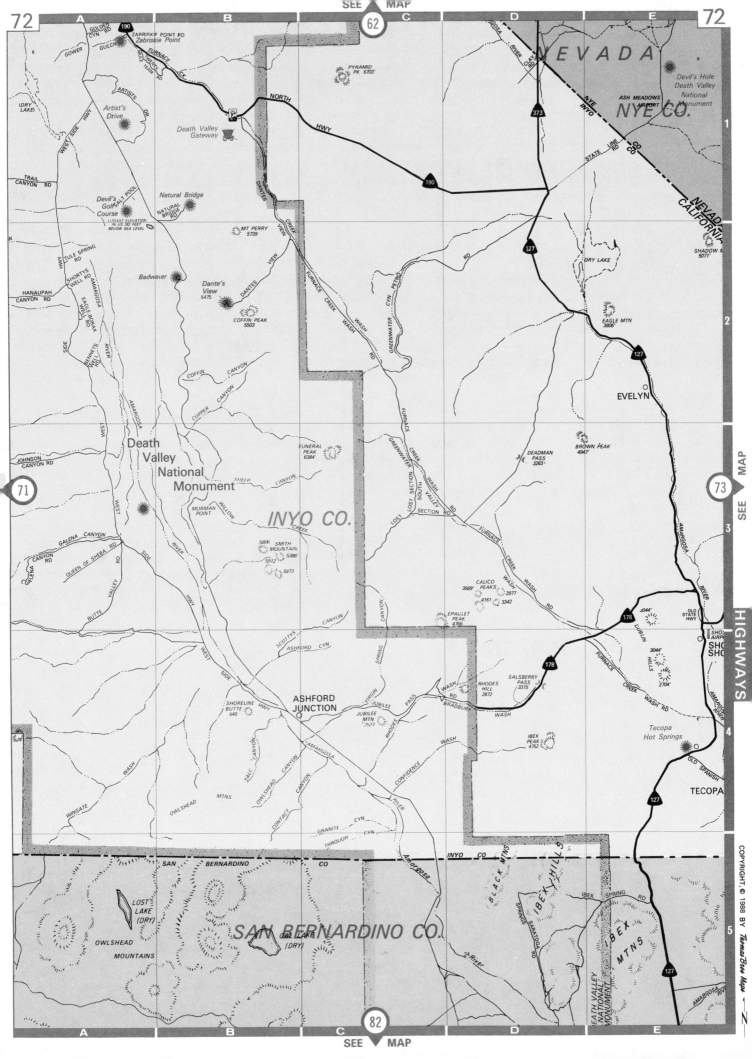

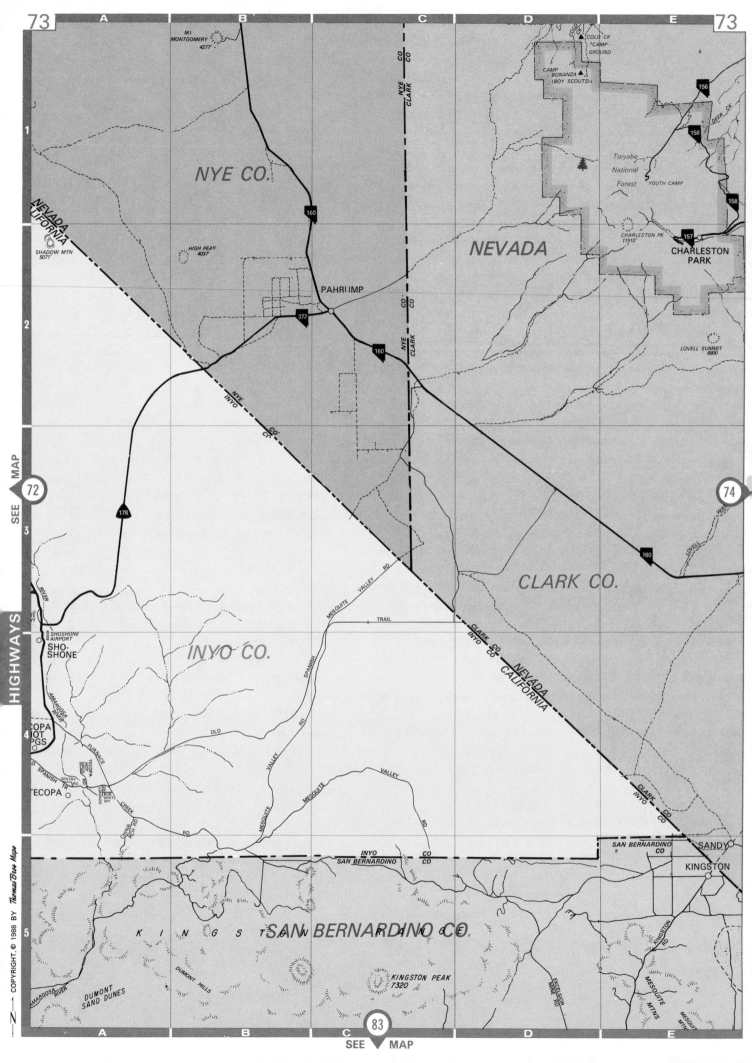

A   B   C   D   E

1

2

SEE MAP 72

3

HIGHWAYS

4

5

NYE CO.

NEVADA

NEVADA
CALIFORNIA

M†
MONTGOMERY
4277'

160

HIGH PEAK
4037'

SHADOW MTN
5071'

PAHRUMP

372

160

NYE
CLARK
CO.
CO.

NYE
INYO
CO
CO

CLARK CO.

178

SHOSHONE
AIRPORT
SHO-
SHONE

INYO CO.

MESQUITE    VALLEY    RD.

TRAIL

SPANISH

AMARGOSA   RIVER

COPA
HOT
PGS

FURNACE

TECOPA
HOT
SPGS

TECOPA

OLD  SPANISH

GENTRY
TR

OLD

VALLEY

OLD
808
WHITE
WY

CHINA
RCH RD

RD.

CREEK

RD.

MESQUITE

VALLEY

MESQUITE

VALLEY

RD.

MESQUITE

CLARK   CO
INYO   CO

NEVADA
CALIFORNIA

CLARK
INYO
CO

INYO      CO
SAN BERNARDINO   CO

SAN BERNARDINO
CO

SANDY

KINGSTON

160

Toiyabe

National

Forest   YOUTH CAMP

CHARLESTON PK
11910'

CHARLESTON
PARK

LOVELL SUMMIT
6800

COLD CK

COLD CK
CAMP-
GROUND

CAMP
BONANZA
(BOY SCOUTS)

156

158

158

157

LOVELL  WASH

EXCELSIOR
MINE RD

KINGSTON
RD

MESQUITE

MTNS

MESQUI

MTN

K   I   N   G   S   T   O   N      R   A   N   G   E

SAN BERNARDINO CO.

AMARGOSA   RIVER

DUMONT
SAND DUNES

DUMONT HILLS

KINGSTON PEAK
7320

SEE MAP 74

SEE MAP 83

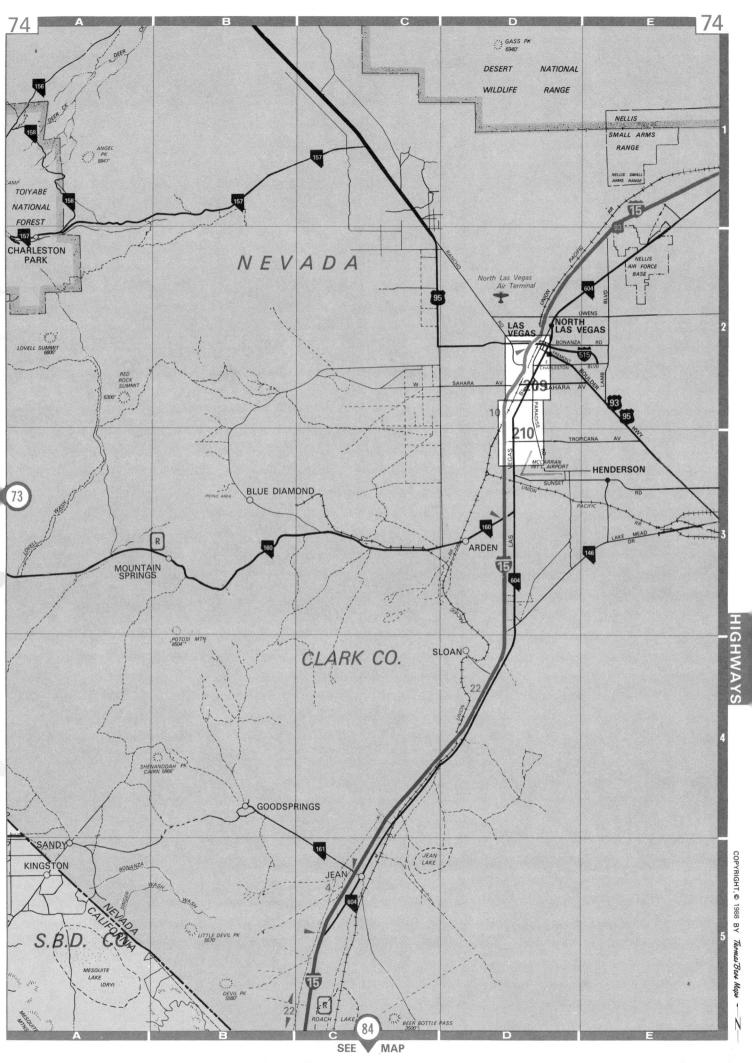

A     B     C     D     E

156

158

157

GASS PK
6940'

DESERT NATIONAL

WILDLIFE RANGE

NELLIS

SMALL ARMS

RANGE

1

NELLIS SMALL
ARMS RANGE

CAMP
TOIYABE

NATIONAL

FOREST

158

157

157

N E V A D A

RANCHO

North Las Vegas
Air Terminal

95

RR

15

93

PACIFIC

UNION

NELLIS
AIR FORCE
BASE

604

OWENS

BLVD

157

CHARLESTON
PARK

LAS
VEGAS

NORTH
LAS VEGAS

BONANZA   RD

515

2

LOVELL SUMMIT
6800'

95

E

FREMONT

CHARLESTON

BLVD

BOULDER

LAMB

RED
ROCK SUMMIT

6300'

W

SAHARA   AV

209

SAHARA   AV

93

95

HWY

10

BLVD

PARADISE

210

TROPICANA   AV

73

BLUE DIAMOND

PICNIC AREA

VEGAS

McCARRAN
INT'L AIRPORT

HENDERSON

SUNSET

UNION

RD

160

ARDEN

PACIFIC

LAKE   MEAD
DR

RR

3

R

MOUNTAIN
SPRINGS

160

160

146

WASH

LOVELL

15

604

POTOSI MTN
8504'

CLARK CO.

SLOAN

PACIFIC

HIGHWAYS

SHENANDOAH PK
CAIRN 5866'

22

UNION

4

SANDY

KINGSTON

GOODSPRINGS

BONANZA

SINGER

WASH

WASH

161

JEAN
4

JEAN
LAKE

604

N E V A D A
CALIFORNIA

LITTLE DEVIL PK
5570'

S.B.D. CO.

5

MESQUITE
LAKE
(DRY)

DEVIL PK
5580'

22

15

R

ROACH   LAKE

BEER BOTTLE PASS
3500'

MESQUITE
MTNS

84

A     B     C     D     E

SEE ▼ MAP

SEE MAP
65

PT SIERRA NEVADA

GARRITY PEAK

RANCHO PIEDRA BLANCA

Hearst San Simeon State Historic Monument

PINE MTN

NACIMIENTO RES

RD GATEWAY DR

NACIMIENTO LAKE

SAN MARCOS

W

CABRILLO

PT PIEDRAS BLANCAS

BLACK OAK MTN ROCKY BUTTE

RED MTN

SAN SIMEON CK RD

ANGELES HWY

LAKEVIEW DR

RUNNING DEER RD

614

SAN MARCOS

**1**

SAN SIMEON

SAN SIMEON PT

SAN SIMEON BAY

Best Western Cavalier Inn

HWY

VAN GORDON CK RD

RANCHO SAN SIMEON

CHIMNEY

LIME MTN

CYPRESS MTN DR

KLAU MINE RD

MTN DR

CHIMNEY

CYPRESS

ADELAIDA

CHIMNEY ROCK

ADELAIDA

PEACHY

CYN

KILER

Wm. Randolph Hearst State Beach

San Simeon State Beach

SIMEON

**SAN LUIS OBISPO CO.**

CYPRESS MTN

KLAU

VINEYARD DR

JENSEN RD

WILLOW

NIDEVER RD

LANDER

CAMBRIA

SCOTT ROCK

SANTA

NORTHERLY BRANCH GREEN VLY RD

ROSA

CREEK

BLACK MTN RD

York Mountain

DOVER CYN

PASO DE

**46**

PASO DE

JACK CREEK RD

Pesenti

Moonstone Inn Motel
Mariners Inn

MAIN ST

RANCHO

GREEN

SANTA ROSA

YORK MTN RD

DOVER CYN RD

SHADOW CYN RD

YORK MTN

OAKDALE RD

PACIFIC

OCEAN

CAMBRIA AIR FORCE STA

HARMONY VLY RD

RANCHO SAN

VILLA CREEK RD

PICACHO

THUNDER CYN RD

COTTONTAIL CK RD

SANTA

RITA

RANCHO

ASUNCION

SAN GREGORIO

HARMONY

GERONIMO

WHALE ROCK RES

CREEK

OLD

SANTA

TORO CREEK

PARK RANGE PEAK

**1** CAYUCOS

Cayucos State Beach

Morro Strand State Beach

MONTECITO RD

RANCHO MORO Y CAYUCOS

LOS

Breakers Motel

Atascadero State Beach

ESTERO

SAN BERNARDINO CK RD

**76**

Morro Rock

**MORRO BAY**

CABRILLO HWY

SAN CK RD

LU

Morro Bay Aquarium

MORRO BAY

HOLLISTER PEAK

**1**

CABRILLO HWY

Morro Bay Museum Of Natural History

BAY

9TH ST

SANTA YSABEL RD

SANTA YSABEL RD

**BAYWOOD PARK**

RANCHO CANADA DE LOS Y PECHO Y IS

Morro Bay State Park

LOS OSOS

**LOS OSOS**

**CUESTA BY-THE-SEA**

Los Osos Oaks State Reserve

LOS OSOS VALLEY RD

PREFUMO CYN RD

PECHO RD

PACIFIC

Montana De Oro State Park

CHURCH RD

SEE CYN RD

RANCHO

CANADA DE

SADDLE PEAK

LOS OSOS

GREEN PEAK

PG&E NUCLEAR POWER PLANT

Y PECHO

Y ISLAY

BALD RANCHO

SAN LUIS HILL

PT SAN LUIS

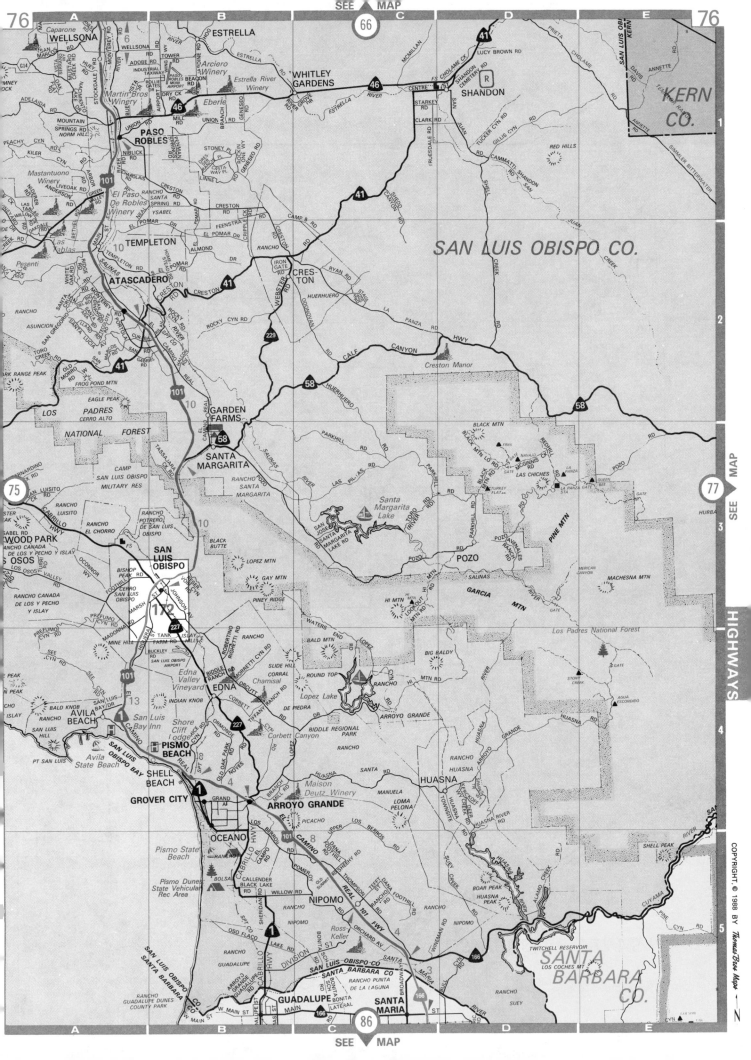

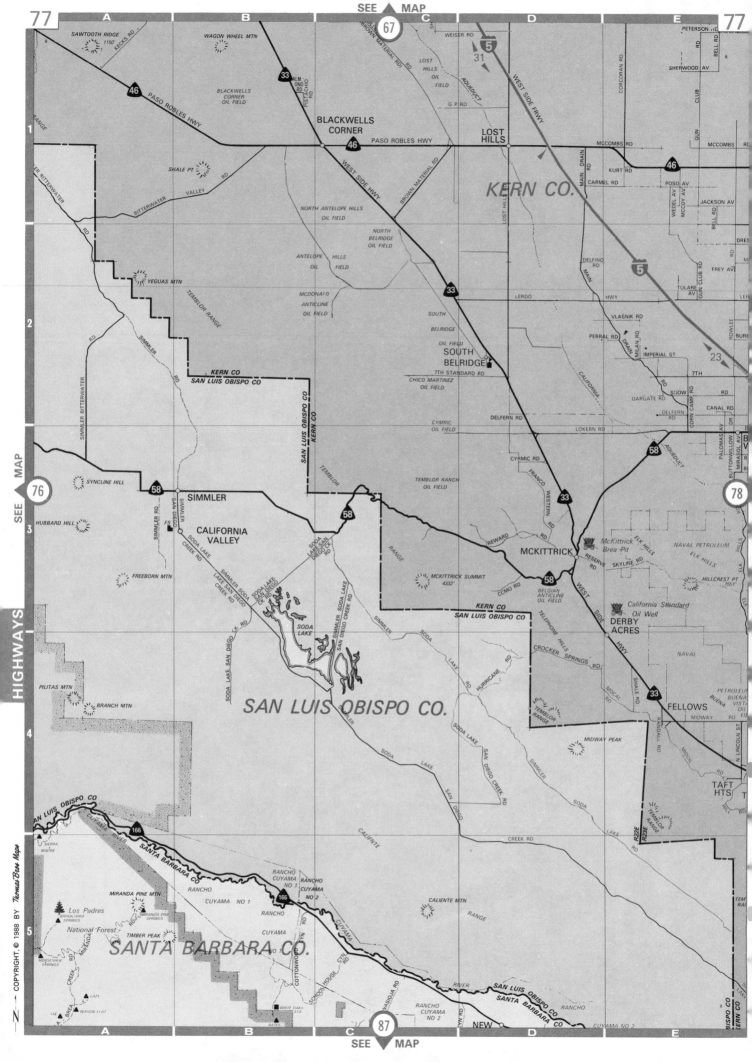

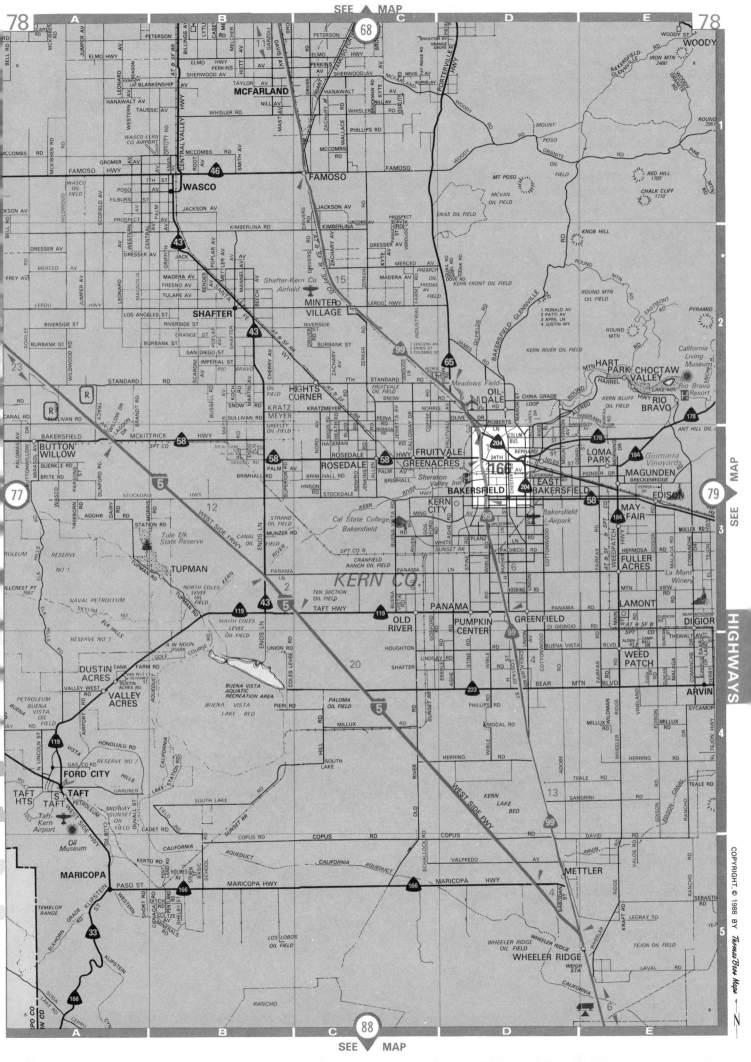

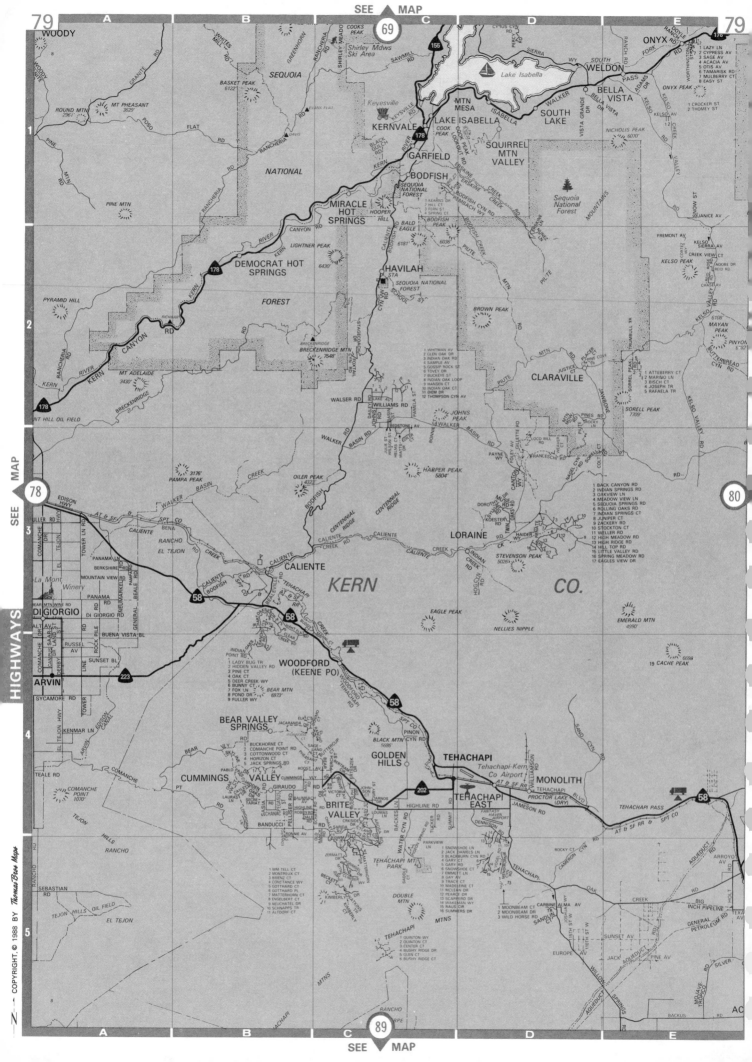

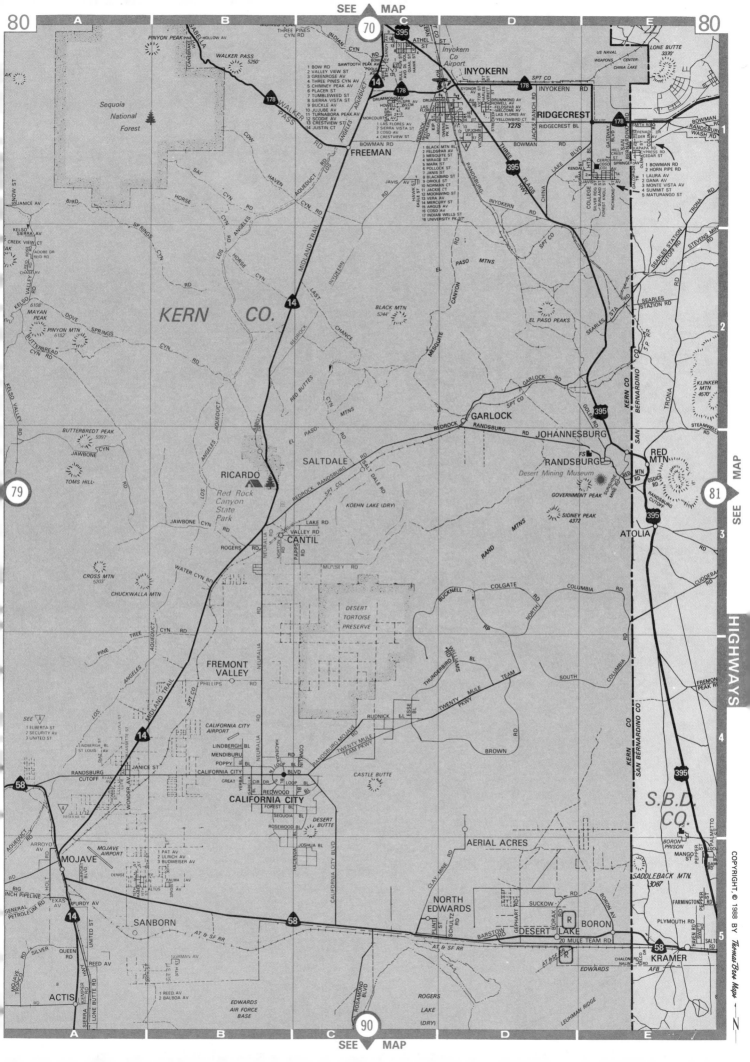

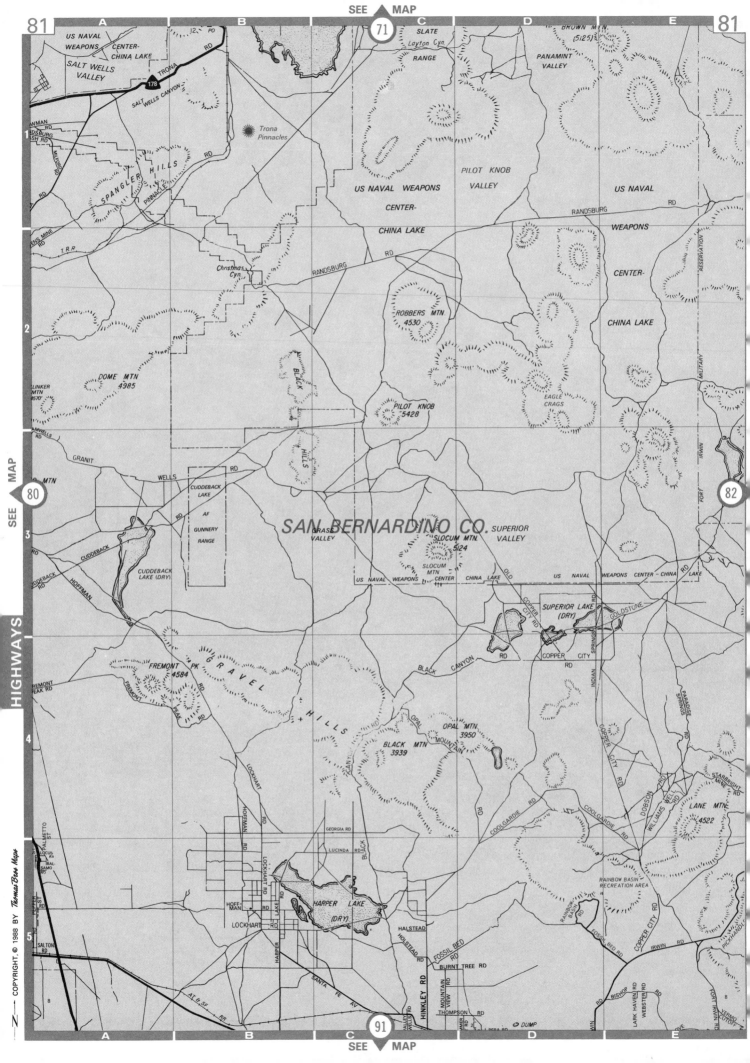

SEE MAP 71

SEE MAP 80

SEE MAP 82

91

SEE MAP

HIGHWAYS

US NAVAL
WEAPONS
CENTER-
CHINA LAKE

SALT WELLS
VALLEY

SALT WELLS CANYON

TRONA

178

Trona Pinnacles

SPANGLER HILLS

PINNACLE

BOWMAN RD

RDSBURG
WASH RD

MILFORD RD

RD

STEVENS MINE RD

T.R.R.

Christmas Cyn.

RANDSBURG

RD

SLATE
Layton Cyn.

RANGE

BROWN MTN.
(5125)

PANAMINT
VALLEY

PILOT KNOB
VALLEY

US NAVAL WEAPONS
CENTER-
CHINA LAKE

RANDSBURG RD

US NAVAL
WEAPONS
CENTER-
CHINA LAKE

RESERVATION

ROBBERS MTN.
4530

DOME MTN
4985

LINKER
MTN
4570'

BLACK

HILLS

PILOT KNOB
5428

EAGLE
CRAGS

MILITARY

AMWELLS RD

GRANIT

WELLS     RD

RD

MTN

CUDDEBACK
LAKE

AF
GUNNERY
RANGE

SAN BERNARDINO CO.

GRASS
VALLEY

SLOCUM MTN.
5124

SUPERIOR
VALLEY

SLOCUM
MTN

US NAVAL WEAPONS  CENTER  CHINA LAKE

OLD

US  NAVAL  WEAPONS CENTER - CHINA  LAKE

FORT  IRWIN

CUDDEBACK

CUDDEBACK RD

HOFMAN

CUDDEBACK
LAKE (DRY)

RD

COPPER
CITY RD

SUPERIOR LAKE
(DRY)

COPPER CITY RD

GOLDSTONE

COPPER CITY RD

INDIAN SPRINGS RD

FREMONT PK
4584

GRAVEL

HILLS

FREMONT

FREMONT PEAK RD

PEAK

RD

BLACK CANYON     RD

COPPER CITY RD

PARADISE SPRINGS RD

FREMONT
PEAK RD

OPAL
RD

OPAL MTN.
3950

BLACK MTN
3939

BLACK

MOUNTAIN

RD

COOLGARDIE     RD

COOLGARDIE  RD

DOBSON  RD

WILLIAMS WELL RD

STARBRIGHT
MINE RD

LANE MTN.
4522

LOCKHART

RD

HOFMAN RD

GEORGIA RD

LUCINDA  RD

BLACK

RAINBOW BASIN
RECREATION AREA

RAINBOW
BASIN

PALMETTO
ST

LOCUST AV

BAL
SAMO
RD

LOCKHART RD

HARPER

LAKE RD

HOFF-
MAN
RD

HARPER LAKE
(DRY)

HALSTEAD

FOSSIL BED

RAINBOW BASIN RD

FOSSIL BED RD

PEPPER
ST

LOCKHART

HOLSTEAD

RD

IRWIN     RD

COPPER CITY RD

PICKHANDLE

SALTON
RD

8

HARPER

SANTA FE AV

AT & SF    RR

HINKLEY  RD

MOUNTAIN
VIEW RD

THOMPSON   RD

FOSSIL BED

BURNT TREE RD

WIN

FORT IRWIN CUTOFF

VERMO

DUMP

LARK HAVEN RD

BISHOP RD

WEBSTER RD

WELLS RD

HAMER
RD 2

LBERA RD

8

N

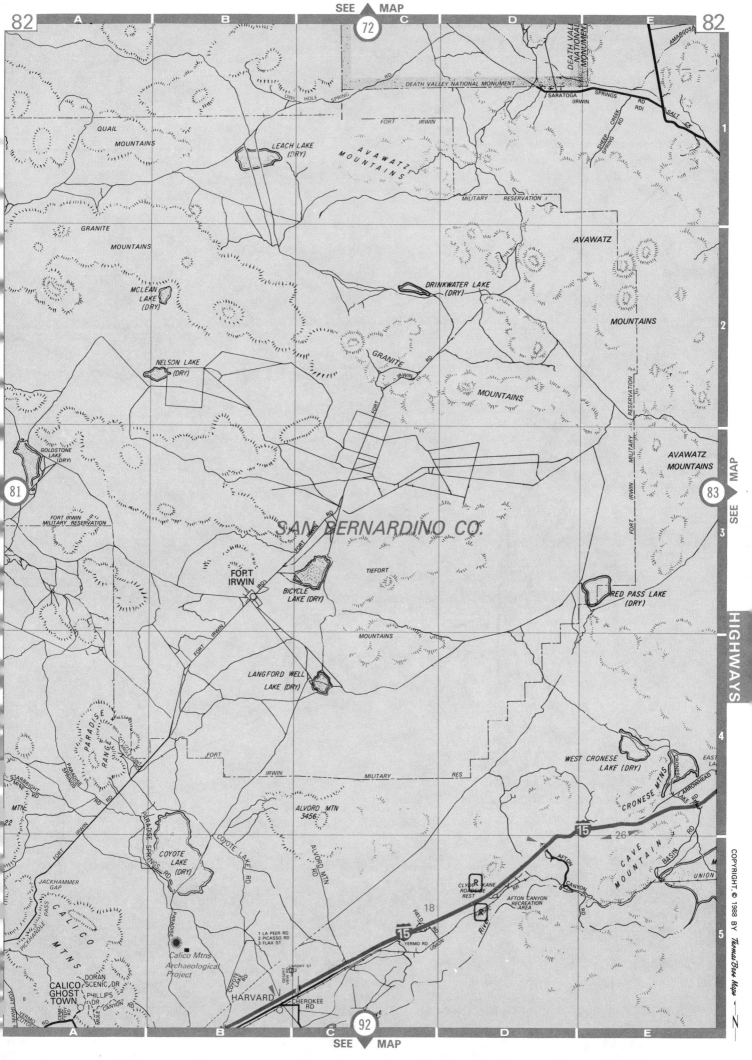

QUAIL
MOUNTAINS

LEACH LAKE
(DRY)

DEATH VALLEY NATIONAL MONUMENT

AVAWATZ
MOUNTAINS

FORT    IRWIN

SARATOGA
(IRWIN

SHEEP
SPRING
RD

SPRINGS    RD

SALT CK

CREEK RD (RD)

AMARGOSA

MILITARY    RESERVATION

AVAWATZ

1

GRANITE

MOUNTAINS

DRINKWATER LAKE
(DRY)

MOUNTAINS

MCLEAN
LAKE
(DRY)

NELSON LAKE
(DRY)

GRANITE

MOUNTAINS

FORT
IRWIN
RD

MILITARY    RESERVATION

AVAWATZ
MOUNTAINS

2

SEE MAP
81

GOLDSTONE
LAKE
(DRY)

FORT IRWIN
MILITARY RESERVATION

FORT IRWIN RD

SAN BERNARDINO CO.

FORT    IRWIN    MILITARY    RESERVATION

SEE MAP
83

3

FORT
IRWIN
RD

FORT IRWIN

BICYCLE
LAKE (DRY)

TIEFORT

MOUNTAINS

RED PASS LAKE
(DRY)

PARADISE    RANGE

PARADISE SPRINGS

PARADISE SPRINGS RD

ANGELO RD

FORT IRWIN RD

LANGFORD WELL
LAKE (DRY)

FORT

IRWIN    MILITARY    RES

WEST CRONESE
LAKE (DRY)

CRONESE MTNS

EAST
LA

ARROWHEAD

LAKE RD

4

STARBRIGHT
MINE
RD

MTN

22

PICKHANDLE PASS

PARADISE RD

PARADISE SPRINGS RD

COYOTE
LAKE
(DRY)

COYOTE LAKE RD

ALVORD MTN
3456

ALVORD MTN
RD

15

26

CAVE    MOUNTAIN

BASIN

UNION

COPYRIGHT © 1988 BY   Thomas Bros Maps

JACKHAMMER
GAP

CALICO
MTNS

DORAN
SCENIC DR

PHILLIPS
DR

CALICO CANYON RD

Calico Mtns
Archaeological
Project

PARADISE RD

COYOTE LAKE RD

1 LA PEER RD
2 PICASSO RD
3 FLAX ST

FIELD RD

UNION RD

18

CLYDE   KANE
ROADSIDE
REST

PACIFIC

AFTON CANYON
RECREATION
AREA

AFTON

CANYON

RR

R

River

15

HIGHWAYS

5

CALICO
GHOST
TOWN

VERMO RD

CEMETERY RD

COYOTE RD

CARDIFF ST

DESERT
VIEW RD

2

HARVARD

CHEROKEE
RD

YERMO RD

VERMO RD

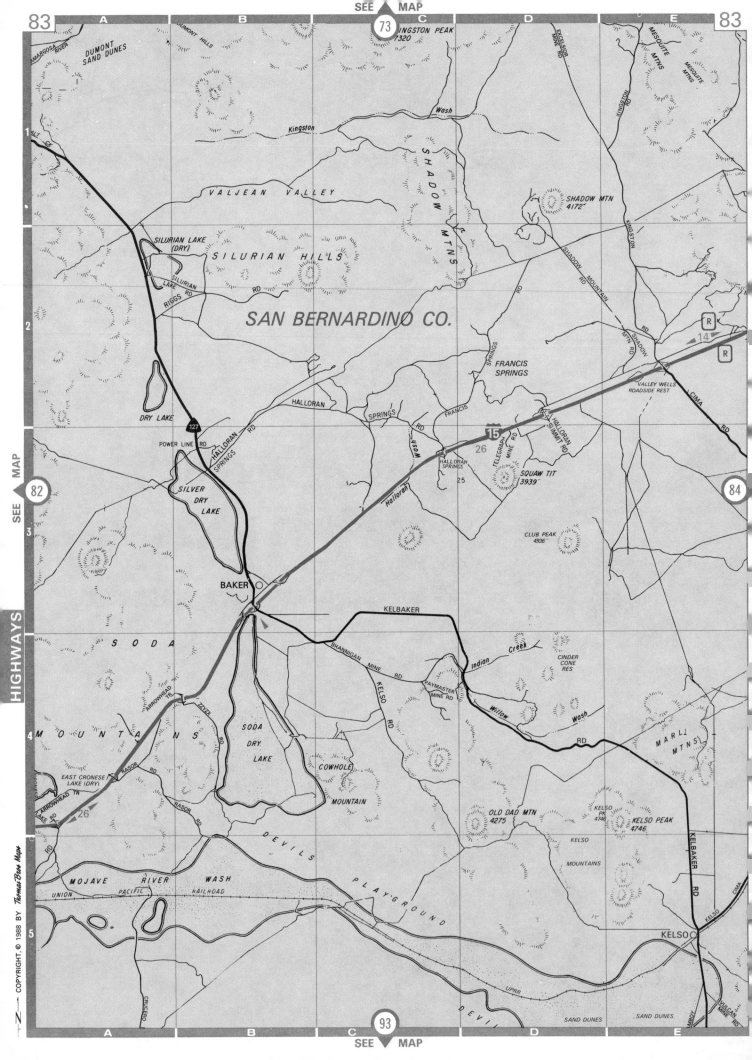

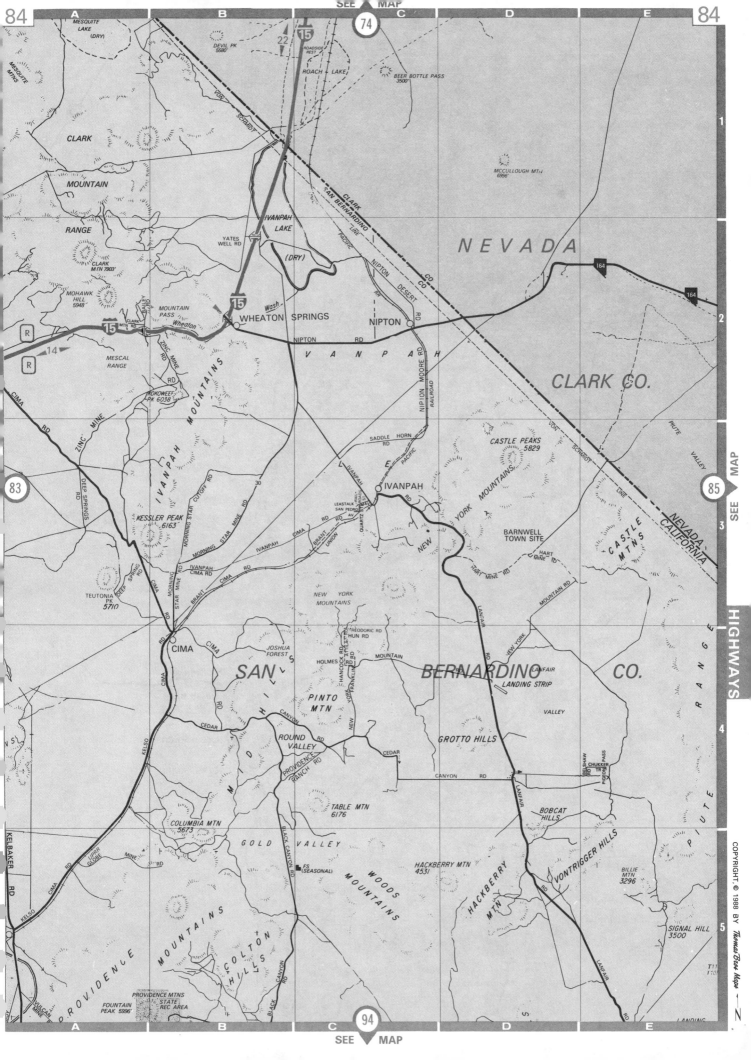

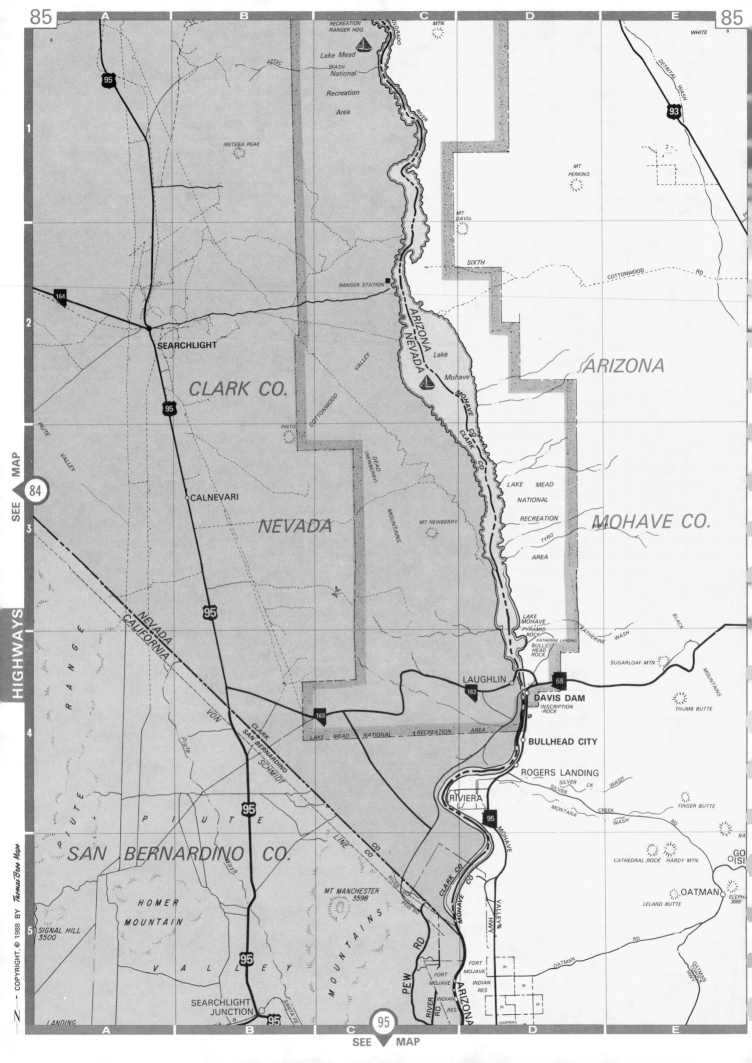

A B C D E

1

WHITE

95

RECREATION
RANGER HDQ

Lake Mead

WASH

National

Recreation

Area

MTN

DETRITAL WASH

93

MT
PERKINS

2

164

AZTEC

SEARCHLIGHT

RANGER STATION

ARIZONA
NEVADA

Lake

Mohave

ARIZONA

MT
DAVIS

SIXTH

COTTONWOOD          RD

CLARK CO.

IRETEBA PEAK

95

VALLEY

COTTONWOOD

MOHAVE CO.

SEE MAP

84

PIUTE

VALLEY

PINTO

DEAD
(NEWBERRY)

MT NEWBERRY

LAKE

MEAD

NATIONAL

RECREATION

TYRO

AREA

WASH

MOHAVE CO.

3

CALNEVARI

NEVADA

MOUNTAINS

HIGHWAYS

95

LAKE
MOHAVE
PYRAMID
ROCK
KATHERINE LANDING
BULLS
HEAD
ROCK

KATHERINE

WASH

BLACK

SUGARLOAF MTN

MOUNTAINS

RANGE

VON

NEVADA
CALIFORNIA

SCHMIDT

CLARK
SAN BERNARDINO

LINE    CO.

PIUTE

LAUGHLIN

163

68

DAVIS DAM

INSCRIPTION
ROCK

THUMB BUTTE

4

163

LAKE    MEAD    NATIONAL    RECREATION    AREA

BULLHEAD CITY

ROGERS LANDING

SILVER    CK    WASH

SILVER

95

RIVIERA

95

MONTANA    CREEK

WASH

FINGER BUTTE

SAN    BERNARDINO    CO.

PIUTE

WASH

RIVER    RD

PEW RD

MT MANCHESTER
3598

MOUNTAINS

CLARK    CO.

MOHAVE    CO.

MOHAVE
HWY

BA

CATHEDRAL ROCK    HARDY MTN

GO
O (SI

HOMER

MOUNTAIN

SIGNAL HILL
3500

95

VALLEY

SEARCHLIGHT
JUNCTION

95

SANTA FE

PEW RD

FORT
MOJAVE

FORT
MOJAVE
INDIAN
RES

IR

IR

FORT MOJAVE
INDIAN
RES

IR

IR

HARPERS

OATMAN

LELAND BUTTE

OATMAN

ELEPHA
3666

OATMAN
HWY

RD

ARIZONA

5

LANDING

A B C D E

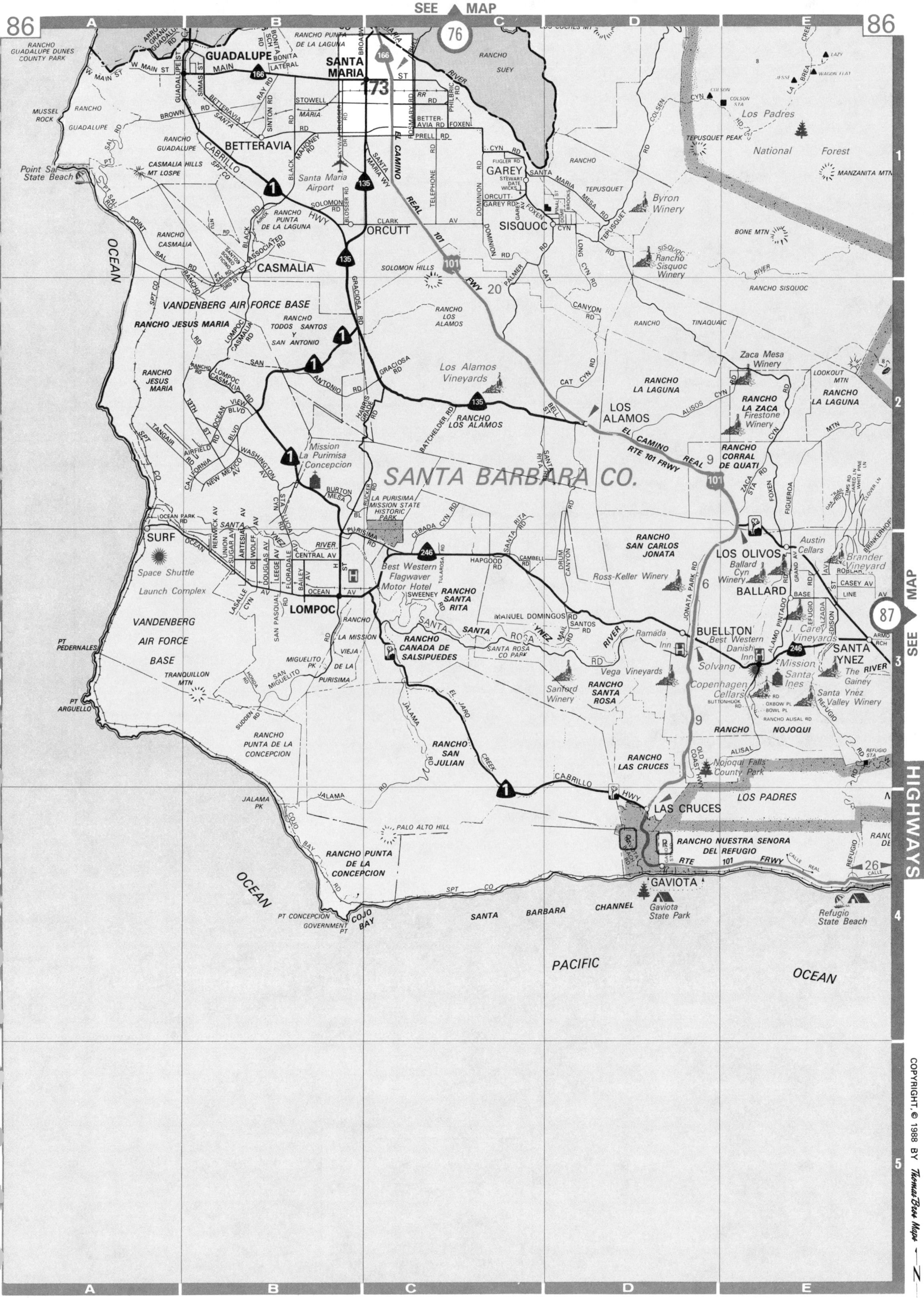

SANTA BARBARA CO.

GUADALUPE
SANTA MARIA
BETTERAVIA
ORCUTT
CASMALIA
SISQUOC
GAREY
LOS ALAMOS
LOMPOC
SURF
BUELLTON
LOS OLIVOS
BALLARD
SANTA YNEZ
LAS CRUCES
GAVIOTA

VANDENBERG AIR FORCE BASE

Los Padres National Forest

Point Sal State Beach
Rancho Guadalupe Dunes County Park
Mussel Rock

OCEAN

PACIFIC OCEAN

SANTA BARBARA CHANNEL

PT PEDERNALES
PT ARGUELLO
PT CONCEPCION

Space Shuttle Launch Complex
Mission La Purisima Concepcion
La Purisima Mission State Historic Park

Byron Winery
Zaca Mesa Winery
Firestone Winery
Sanford Winery
Vega Vineyards
Gainey Winery
Santa Ynez Valley Winery
Ross-Keller Winery

Best Western Flagwaver Motor Hotel
Best Western Danish Inn
Mission Santa Ines
Copenhagen Cellars
Solvang

Nojoqui Falls County Park
Gaviota State Park
Refugio State Beach

SEE MAP 76
SEE MAP 87
HIGHWAYS

SEE MAP

S.L.O. CO.

KERN CO.

SAN LUIS OBISPO CO
SANTA BARBARA CO

Rancho Cuyama No 2

NEW CUYAMA

CUYAMA

Cuyama No 2

SODA LAKE RD

166

CEHN CYN

STUBBLEFIELD RD

FOOTHILL

ALISO CYN RD

PERKINS RD

WASIOJA RD

WASHINGTON ST

JOHNSON ST
CUYAMA ST
WYLIE ST

SCHAEFFER RD

SANTA

KERN CO
BARBARA CO VENTURA CO

BALLINGER CYN

33

1

PEAK MTN

MC PHERSON PEAK

WHITE OAKS STA

BATES CANYON

BRANCH CANYON STA

FOOTHILL

BELL RD

KIRSCHENMANN RD

SANTA BARBARA CYN RD

CUYAMA

VENTUCOPA

LA PANZA AV
EL POBLAR AV

QUATAL CYN

RIVER

LOS PA

SAN RAFAEL WILDERNESS

WHEAT PEAK

SAN RAFAEL WILDERNESS

BALD MTN

ZACA LAKE

LOS PADRES NATIONAL FOREST

CATWAY RD

FIGUEROA MTN

DAVY BROWN

PINO ALTO

FIGUEROA STA

NIRA

LOST VALLEY

CACHUMA RD

CACHUMA MTN

Montgomery Potrero

FOX MTN

Los Padres National Forest

SISQUOC CONDOR SANCTUARY

SAMON PEAK

Upper Tinta

CUYAMA PEAK

MORRO HILL

CUYAMA

VEN CO.

RIVER

2

RANCHO LA LAGUNA (GUTIERREZ)

FIGUEROA MTN RD

SAGE HILL SADDLE STA

MCKINLEY MTN

SAN RAFAEL

SAN RAFAEL MTN

LOS PADRES

BIG PINE MTN

MADULCE PEAK

LIZARD HEAD

DEAL JUNCTION

BRINKERHOFF AV

CLOVER LN

WILDERNESS

SANTA BARBARA CO.

SEE MAP 86

RANCHO DE CANADA LOS PINOS

LINDA VISTA DR

AV
AV
AV

RANCHO SAN MARCOS

LITTLE PINE MTN

NATIONAL

LOMA PELONA

CREEK

HILDRETH PEAK

MINE CAMP

SEE MAP 88

3

ANCHO LOMAS LA PURIFICACION

ARMOUR RCH RD

ALISOS AV

HAPPY CYN RD

RANCHO TEQUEPIS

RANCHO TEQUEPIS

Lake Cachuma Recreation Area

CACHUMA CO PK

154

LOMA ALTA

NINETEEN OAKS

HIDDEN POTRERO

ARROYO BURRO

FOREST RANCHO LOS PRIETOS Y NAJALAYEGUA

CAMUESA PEAK

REDROCK

GIBRALTAR RD

BIG CALIENTE

LOWER CALIENTE

MONTE ARIDO

OLD MAN MTN

SANTA YNEZ

VENTURA

MATILIJA

MURIETTA

A RIVER

REFUGIO STA

CAMINO CIELO

SANTA YNEZ PEAK

SANTA YNEZ RIVER

SAN MARCOS PASS RD

SANTA STAGECOACH RD

PARADISE RD

SANTA YNEZ RIVER

GIBRALTAR

FALLS

SANTA LIVE YNEZ OAK

NORTH PORTAL

GIBRALTAR DAM

GIBRALTAR TUNNEL

GIBRALTAR RES

SANTA

P BAR FLATS

AGUA CALIENTE

GATE

PENDOLA STA

JAMESON LAKE

JUNCAL RD

UPPER SANTA YNEZ RIVER

WHITE LEDGE PE

MATILIJA

NATIONAL FOREST

BROADCAST PEAK

CONDOR PEAK

W CAMINO CIELO

WATER TUNNEL

KINEVAN RD

154

PAINTED CAVE RD

HIDDEN VLY RD

Chumash Painted Caves State Hist Park

CAMINO

CIELO

MATIAS POTRERO

FORBUSH FLAT

BLUE CANYON

UPPER BLUE CANYON RD

BARBARA

MONTECITO PEAK

DIVIDE PEAK

NOON PARK

CHISMAHOO MTN

RANCHO CANADA DEL CORRAL

26

CALLE QUEBRADA

AVD DEL CAPITAN

CALLE REAL

RANCHO LOS DOS PUEBLOS

CATHEDRAL PEAK

ROMERO CYN

DAULTON MILL RD

BARBARA WATER TUNNEL

CIELO

GATE

SNOWBALL MTN

LA GRANADA

4

El Capitan State

NAPLES

ELLWOOD

GOLETA

101

Univ of Calif Santa Barbara

HOLLISTER

Sta Barbara Airport

ISLA VISTA

Isla Vista Co Beach Park

GLEN ANNIE RD

FAIRVIEW AV

PATTERSON AV

SAN

217

Goleta Beach County Park

GOLETA PT

225

Arroyo Burro Beach County Park

Pepper Tree Inn

FOOTHILL RD

STATE ST

8

SANTA BARBARA

192

144

225

SYCAMORE

Clark Bird Refuge

174

Sheraton Santa Barbara Hotel

MONTECITO

Valley RD

Montecito Inn

12

SUMMER- LAND

Marriott's Santa Barbara Biltmore

Carpinteria State Beach

SNOWBALL MTN

192

101

CARPINTERIA

8

150

RANCHO EL RINCON

224

W CASITAS PASS RD

RINCON MTN

10

SANTA

BARBARA

PACIFIC

CHANNEL

RINCON PT

PUNTA GORDA

LA CONCHITA

SEA CLIFF

VENTURA

OCEAN

PITAS PT

Channel Islands National Park

SAN MIGUEL ISL

SANTA ROSA ISL

SANTA CRUZ ISL

SANTA BARBARA ISL

INSET NOT TO SCALE

HIGHWAYS

N

COPYRIGHT, © 1988 BY Thomas Bros Maps

5

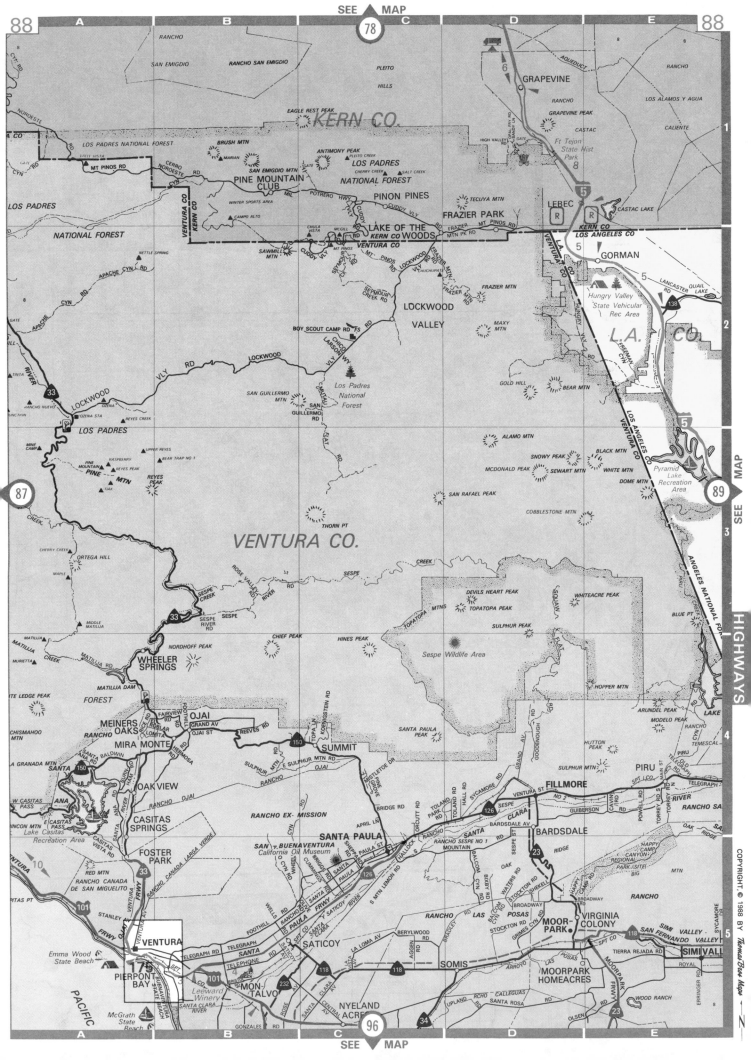

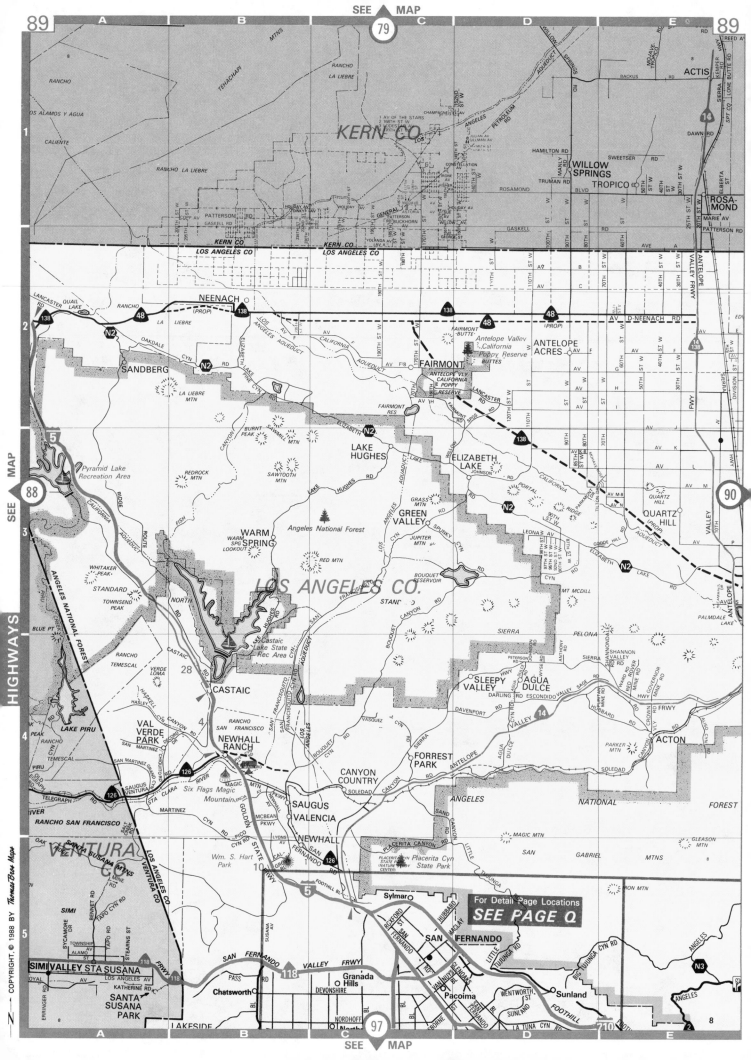

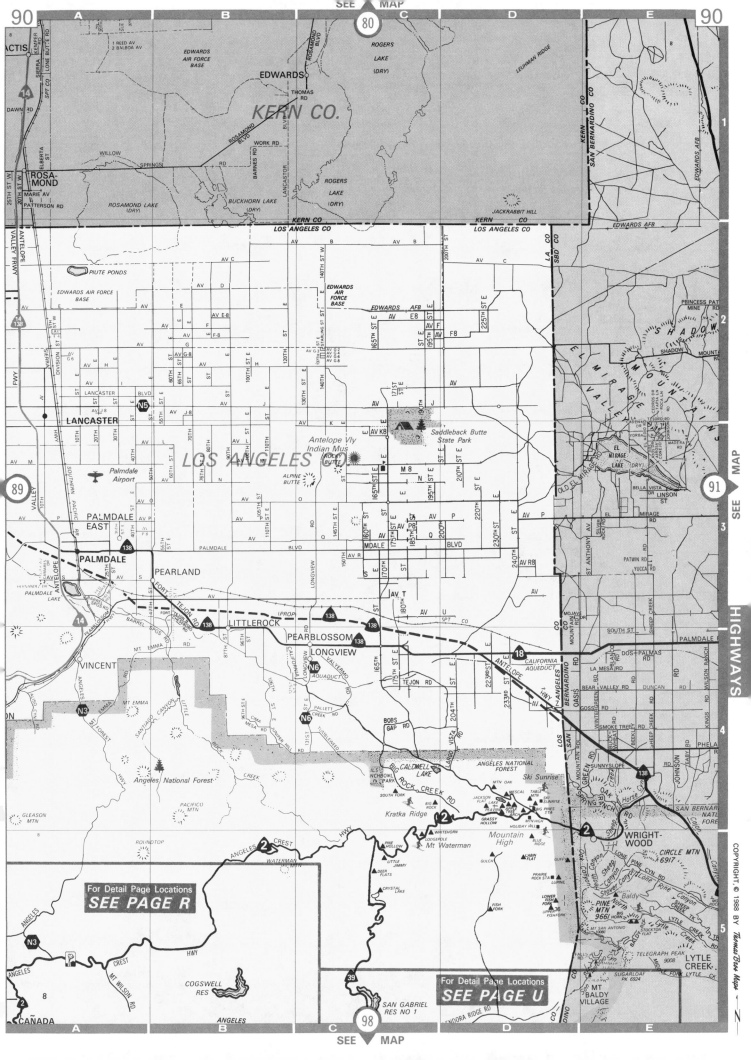

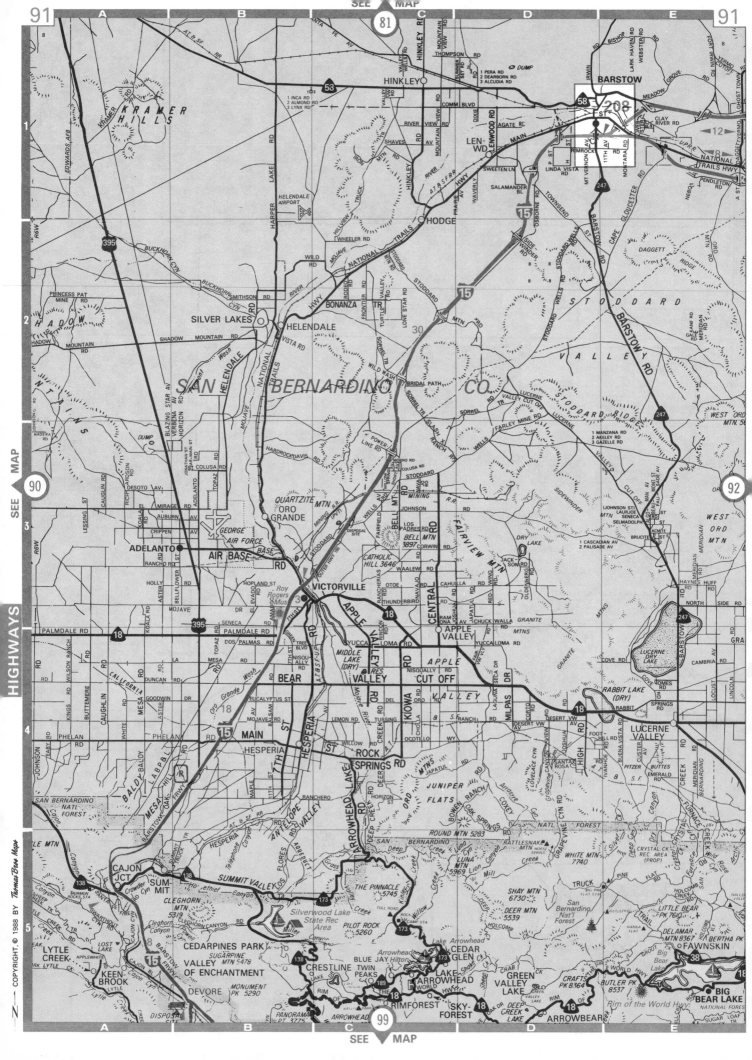

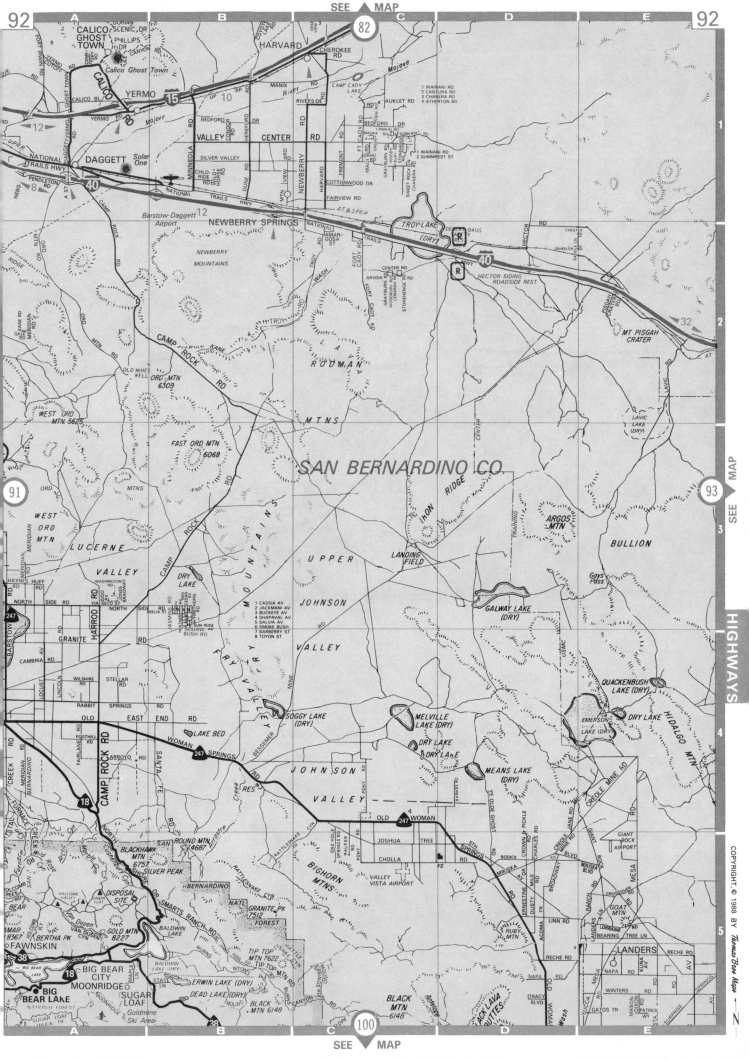

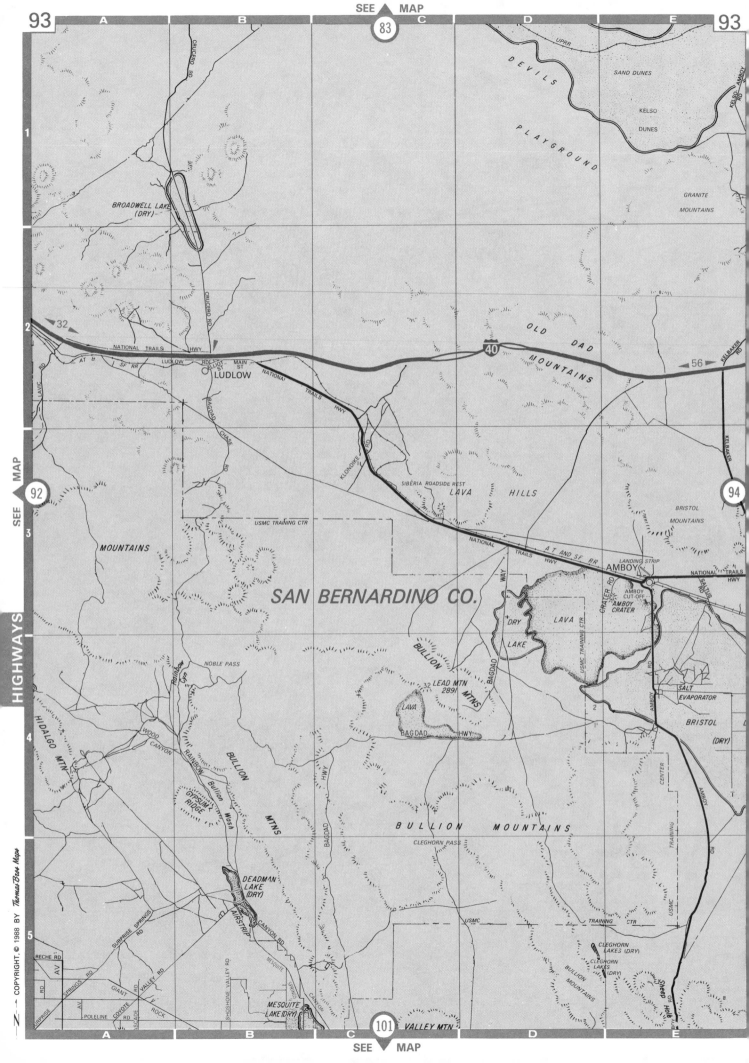

A    B    C    D    E

1

DEVILS

SAND DUNES

KELSO
DUNES

P L A Y G R O U N D

BROADWELL LAKE
(DRY)

GRANITE
MOUNTAINS

CRUCERO RD

2

32

OLD  DAD

40

MOUNTAINS

56

KELBAKER RD

NATIONAL TRAILS     HWY

LUDLOW  HD
AT &  SF RR  ELLIOT  MAIN
ST     ST
LUDLOW

NATIONAL

TRAILS

HWY

KELBAKER RD

LAVIC RD

3

BAGDAD CHASE RD

KLONDIKE RD

SIBERIA ROADSIDE REST

LAVA    HILLS

BRISTOL
MOUNTAINS

MOUNTAINS

USMC TRAINING CTR

NATIONAL     TRAILS     AT AND SF  RR

LANDING STRIP

AMBOY

SAN BERNARDINO CO.

WAY

DRY

LAVA

CRATER RD

AMBOY
CUT-OFF

AMBOY
CRATER

NATIONAL   TRAILS
HWY

SALTUS RD

LAKE

USMC TRAINING CTR

AMBOY RD

SALT
EVAPORATOR

NOBLE PASS

BULLION

MTNS

LEAD MTN
2891
32

LAVA

BAGDAD

BRISTOL

(DRY)

RAINBOW CYN

2

4

HIDALGO MTN.

WOOD
CANYON

RAINBOW

BULLION
Bullion Wash

GYPSUM
RIDGE

BULLION

MTNS

BAGDAD        HWY

BAGDAD   HWY

B U L L I O N     M O U N T A I N S

CENTER

CLEGHORN PASS

AMBOY RD

DEADMAN
LAKE
(DRY)

AIRSTRIP
CANYON RD

USMC

TRAINING

TRAINING     CTR

USMC

Sheep Hole

5

SURPRISE SPRINGS
RD

MESQUITE
SPRING CANYON

CLEGHORN
LAKES (DRY)

CLEGHORN
LAKES
(DRY)

BULLION
MOUNTAINS

8

RECHE RD

SURPRISE    AV
RD

SPRINGS RD

GIANT
ROCK

VALLEY RD

SHOSHONE VALLEY RD

COYOTE

CASCADE

POLELINE

AV

MESQUITE
LAKE (DRY)

VALLEY MTN.

A    B    C    D    E

SEE ► MAP

84

FENNER

FOUNTAIN
PEAK 5996'

MITCHELL CAVERNS
NATURAL PRESERVE

Providence
Mtn's State
Rec Area

PROVIDENCE

HILLS

BLACK CANYON

VALLEY

GOFFS

FENNER HILLS

MOUNTAIN SPRINGS RD

LANFAIR RD

1

CLIPPER

HALFWAY HILL
2996

BLIND
HILLS

ESSEX RD

HIDDEN HILLS RD

HIDDEN          HILLS        RD

HORSE
HILLS

HIDDEN HILL RD

HIDDEN HILLS

VALLEY

◄ 25 ►

◄ 56

KELBAKER RD

KELBAKER RD

CLIPPER

MOUNTAINS

CASTLE DOME
3299

85

40

ROADSIDE
REST

R

R

GOFFS RD

LANDING STRIP

OLD       NATIONAL       TRAILS       HWY

ESSEX RD HWY

ESSEX

SUNFLOWER

NATIONAL        TRAILS         HWY

PIUTE

MOUNTAINS

2

93

VAN
WINKLE
MTN

KELBAKER RD

MARBLE

MOUNTAINS

FENNER

VALLEY

DANBY RD

MERCURY
MTN

SPRINGS

OLD
WOMAN
MTNS

SUNFLOWER

LITTLE
PIUTE
MTNS

95

SEE ► MAP

**SAN BERNARDINO CO.**

CADIZ
SUMMIT
ROADSIDE REST

NATIONAL TRAILS HWY

RR

COLTON

SPRINGS RD

WASH

PILOT PK
3727

SUNFLOWER

SUNFLOWER SPRINGS SPUR

WASH

3

NATIONAL TRAILS
HWY

SALTUS

BOLO RD

CHAMBLESS ROADSIDE REST

CADIZ RD

TRILOBITES

AT & SF

AT & SF

CADIZ

SHIP

MOUNTAINS

O L D

W O M A N

M O U N T A I N S

HIGHWAYS

4

PORATOR

RISTOL

LAKE

(DRY)

CALUMET

MOUNTAINS

CADIZ

VALLEY

SAND

DUNES

CADIZ RD

CADIZ RD

KILBECK

HILLS

OLD

WOMAN

MTNS

WARD

VALLEY

COPYRIGHT, © 1988 BY  Thomas Bros Maps

AMBOY

RD

SAND
DUNES

CADIZ
LAKE
(DRY)

SAND
DUNES

SAND

DUNES

SAND
DUNES

CADIZ RD

DANBY LAKE

5

A · B · C · D · E

SEE ▼ MAP

102

N

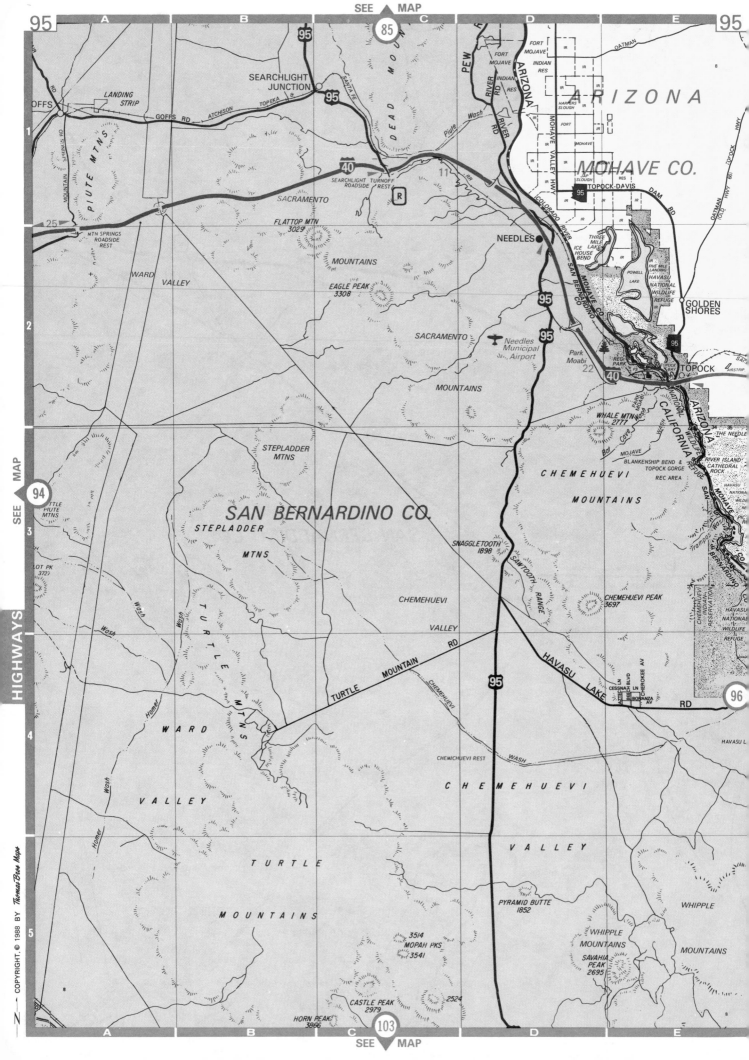

A | B | C | D | E

OFFS

LANDING STRIP

SHINNS RD

PIUTE MTNS

GOFFS RD        ATCHISON    TOPEKA  &

SANTA FE

SEARCHLIGHT JUNCTION

**95**

DEAD MOUNTAINS

PEW R?

FORT MOJAVE RIVER RD

FORT MOJAVE INDIAN RES

MOJAVE INDIAN RES

FORT MOJAVE

ARIZONA

A R I Z O N A

OATMAN

IR

IR

IR

MOHAVE VALLEY HWY

HARPERS SLOUGH

MOHAVE CO.

TOPOCK-DAVIS DAM RD

OATMAN (OLD HWY 66) HWY

TOPOCK HWY

25

MTN SPRINGS ROADSIDE REST

**40**

SEARCHLIGHT TURNOFF ROADSIDE REST

R

SACRAMENTO

FLATTOP MTN 3029

11

PIUTE WASH

COLORADO RIVER

RR

IR

95 TOPOCK-DAVIS

IR

IR

IR

NEEDLES

SAN BERNARDINO CO

MOHAVE CO

THREE MILE LAKE

ICE HOUSE BEND

FIVE MILE LANDING

POWELL LAKE

HAVASU NATIONAL WILDLIFE REFUGE

GOLDEN SHORES

WARD VALLEY

MOUNTAINS

EAGLE PEAK 3308

SACRAMENTO

MOUNTAINS

Needles Municipal Airport

**95**

**95**

Park Moabi

PARK MOABI RD

REG PARK FS

22

TOPOCK

95

**40**

AIRSTRIP

SEE MAP 94

TTLE PIUTE MTNS

STEPLADDER MTNS

STEPLADDER MTNS

**SAN BERNARDINO CO.**

WHALE MTN 2777

Bat Cove Wash

MOJAVE PARK MOABI

CHEMEHUEVI MOUNTAINS

CALIFORNIA

ARIZONA

THE NEEDLE

BLANKENSHIP BEND & TOPOCK GORGE REC AREA

RIVER ISLAND CATHEDRAL ROCK

NATIONAL WILDLIFE REFUGE

HAVASU NATIONAL WILDLIFE

SAN BERNARDINO CO

PIC

LOT PK 3727

Wash

Wash

Wash

Homer

TURTLE MTNS

CHEMEHUEVI

VALLEY

SNAGGLETOOTH 1898

SAWTOOTH RANGE

CHEMEHUEVI PEAK 3697

CHEMEHUEVI INDIAN RESERVATION

HAVASU NATIONAL WILDLIFE REFUGE

TURTLE MOUNTAIN RD

CHEMEHUEVI

**95**

HAVASU LAKE

CESSNAT BLVD

ASTER LN

DATE LN

CHEROKEE AV

TO BONANZA

BONANZA AV

RD

**96**

Homer

Wash

WARD

VALLEY

CHEMICHUEVI REST

WASH

C H E M E H U E V I

HAVASU L

Homer

TURTLE

MOUNTAINS

V A L L E Y

PYRAMID BUTTE 1852

WHIPPLE

MOUNTAINS

WHIPPLE MOUNTAINS

MOUNTAINS

3514 MOPAH PKS 3541

SAVAHIA PEAK 2695

CASTLE PEAK 2979

2524

HORN PEAK 3866

A | B | C | D | E

HIGHWAYS

N

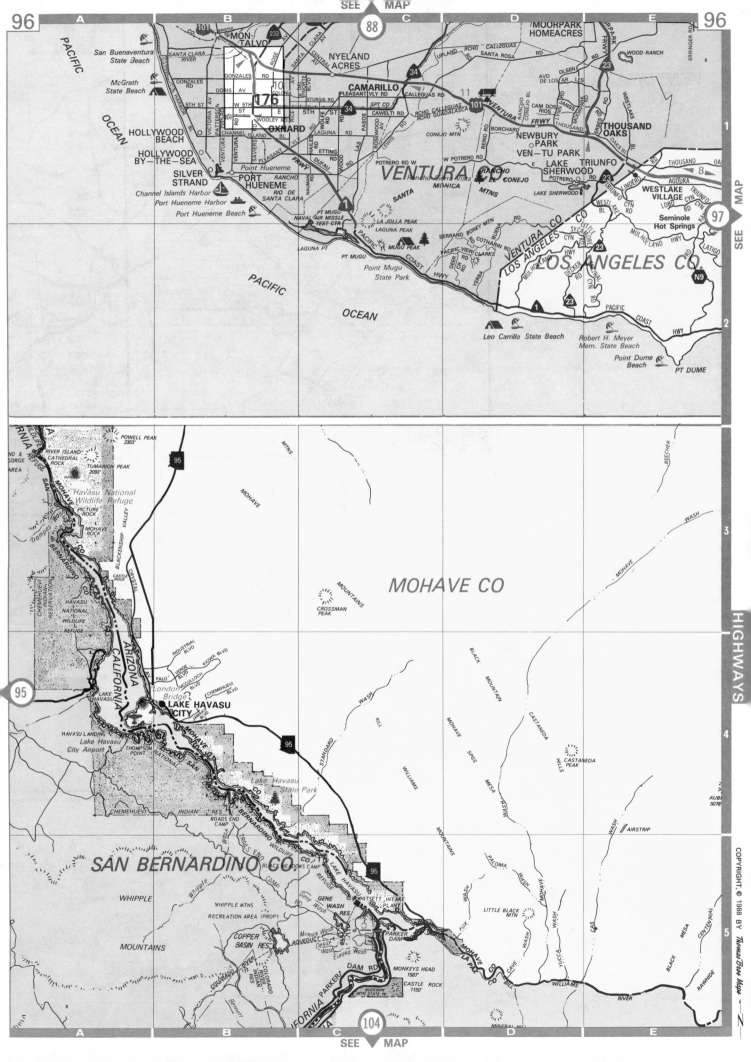

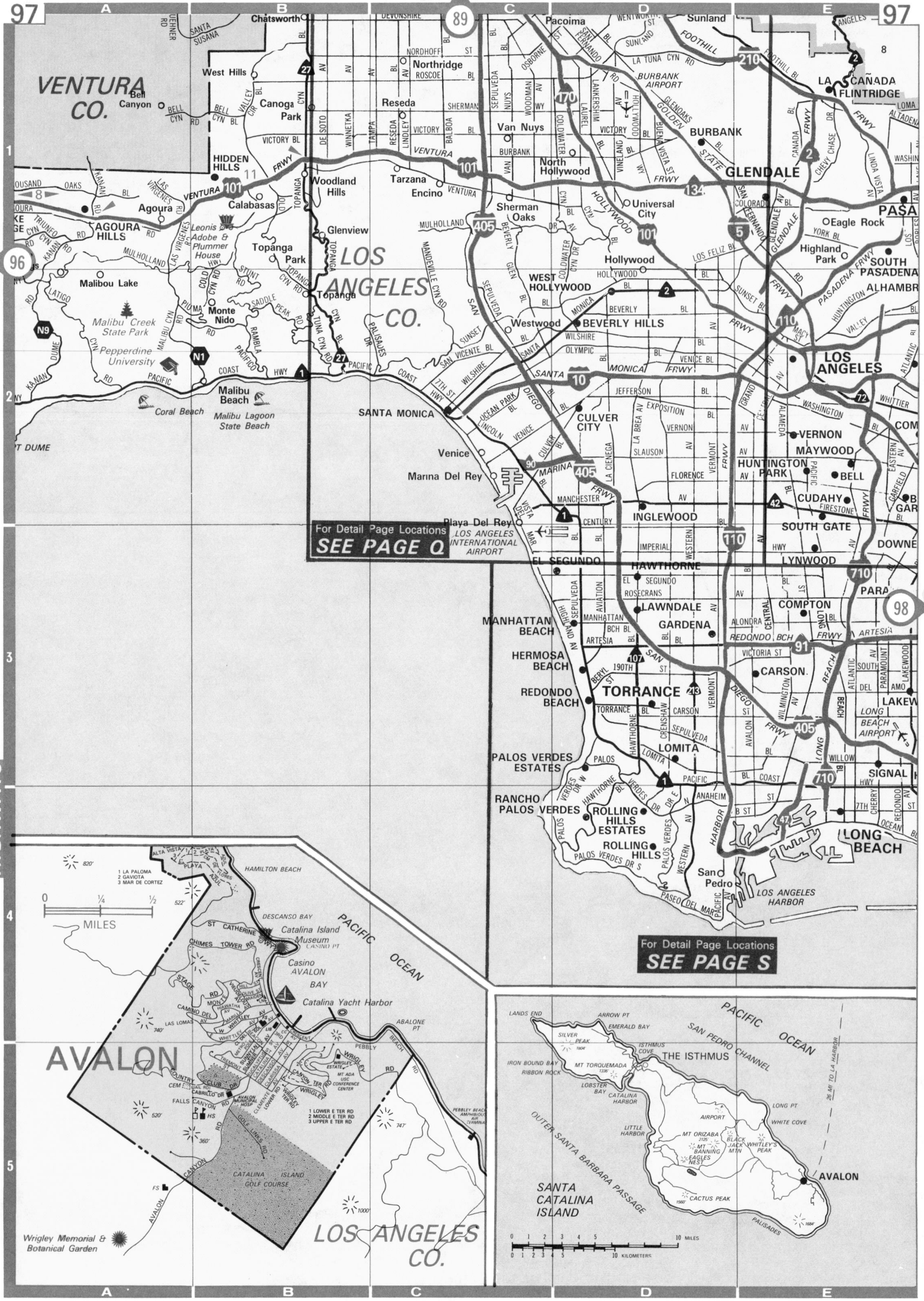

**97** ... **97**

SEE MAP

HIGHWAYS

VENTURA CO.

LOS ANGELES CO.

Chatsworth · West Hills · Canoga Park · Northridge · Reseda · Van Nuys · North Hollywood · Burbank · GLENDALE · LA CAÑADA FLINTRIDGE · PASA(DENA)

Bell Canyon · Hidden Hills · Woodland Hills · Tarzana · Encino · Sherman Oaks · Universal City · Eagle Rock · Highland Park · SOUTH PASADENA · ALHAMBR(A)

AGOURA HILLS · Agoura · Calabasas · Glenview · Topanga Park · Hollywood · WEST HOLLYWOOD · Westwood · BEVERLY HILLS · LOS ANGELES

Malibou Lake · Malibu Creek State Park · Pepperdine University · Monte Nido · Topanga · Culver City · Santa Monica · Venice · Marina Del Rey · Playa Del Rey · Inglewood · Vernon · Maywood · HUNTINGTON PARK · BELL · CUDAHY · SOUTH GATE · DOWNE(Y)

Coral Beach · Malibu Beach · Malibu Lagoon State Beach · PT DUME

For Detail Page Locations SEE PAGE Q

LOS ANGELES INTERNATIONAL AIRPORT · EL SEGUNDO · HAWTHORNE · LAWNDALE · GARDENA · COMPTON · LYNWOOD · PARA(MOUNT)

MANHATTAN BEACH · HERMOSA BEACH · REDONDO BEACH · TORRANCE · CARSON · LAKEW(OOD) · Long Beach Airport · SIGNAL

PALOS VERDES ESTATES · RANCHO PALOS VERDES · ROLLING HILLS ESTATES · ROLLING HILLS · LOMITA · San Pedro · LONG BEACH

For Detail Page Locations SEE PAGE S

LOS ANGELES HARBOR

AVALON

1 LA PALOMA 2 GAVIOTA 3 MAR DE CORTEZ

Descanso Bay · Catalina Island Museum · Casino · AVALON BAY · Catalina Yacht Harbor · Hamilton Beach · PACIFIC OCEAN · Abalone Pt · Pebbly Beach

MILES 0 ¼ ½

Catalina Island Golf Course · Wrigley Memorial & Botanical Garden

LOS ANGELES CO.

SANTA CATALINA ISLAND · PACIFIC OCEAN · Lands End · Arrow Pt · Emerald Bay · Silver Peak · Isthmus Cove · THE ISTHMUS · San Pedro Channel · Iron Bound Bay · Ribbon Rock · MT Torquemada · Lobster Bay · Catalina Harbor · Little Harbor · Airport · White Cove · MT Orizaba · MT Banning · Eagles Nest · Black Jack Mtn · Whitley's Peak · Long Pt · AVALON · Cactus Peak · Outer Santa Barbara Passage

0 1 2 3 4 5 10 MILES

COPYRIGHT © 1988 BY Thomas Bros Maps

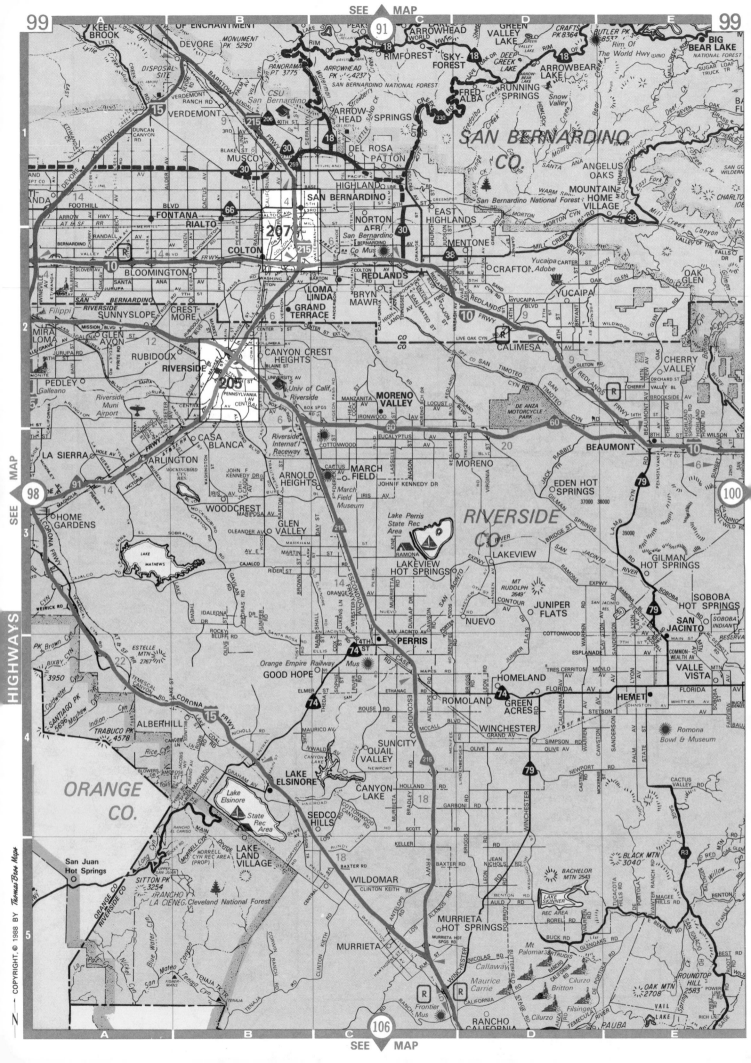

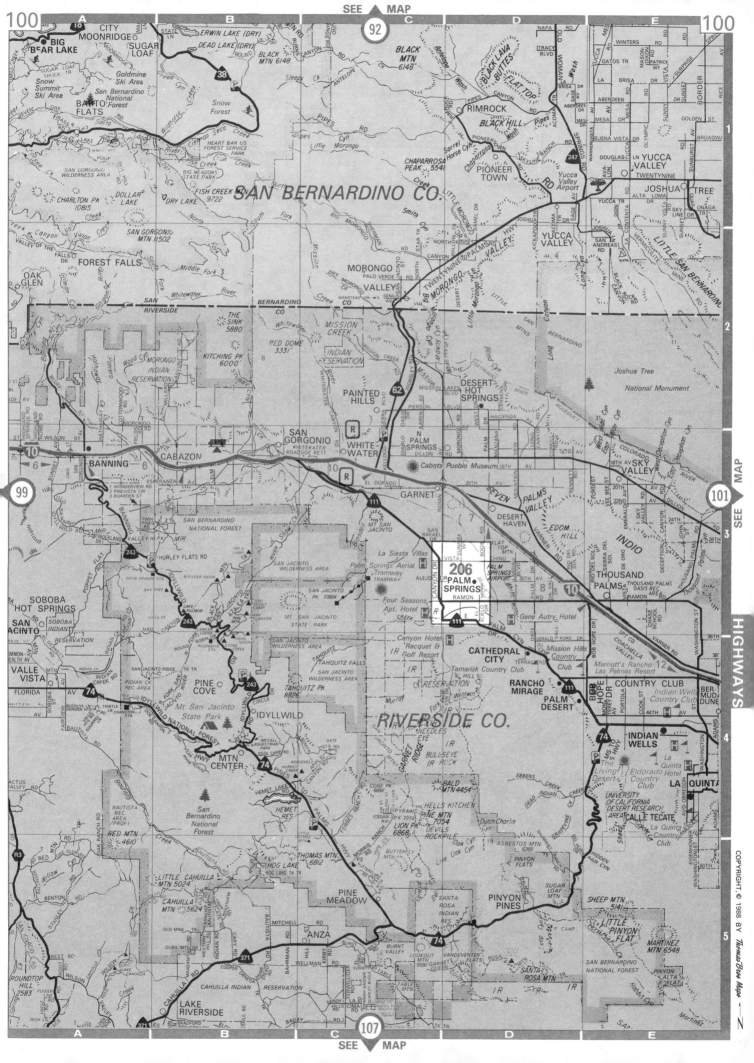

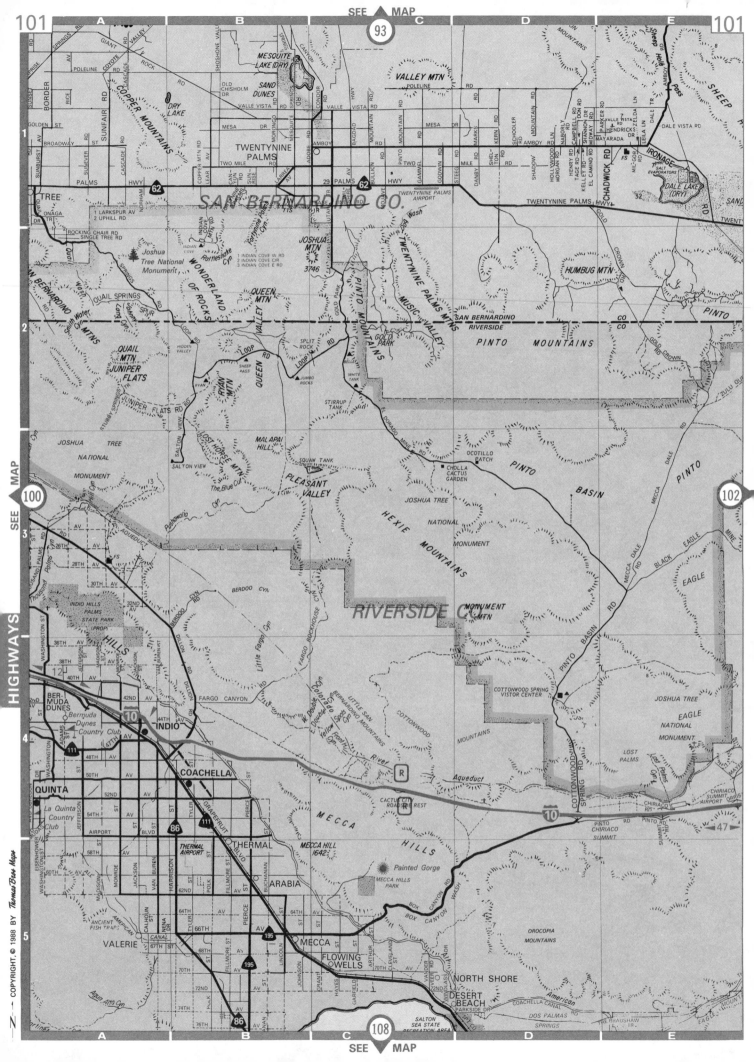

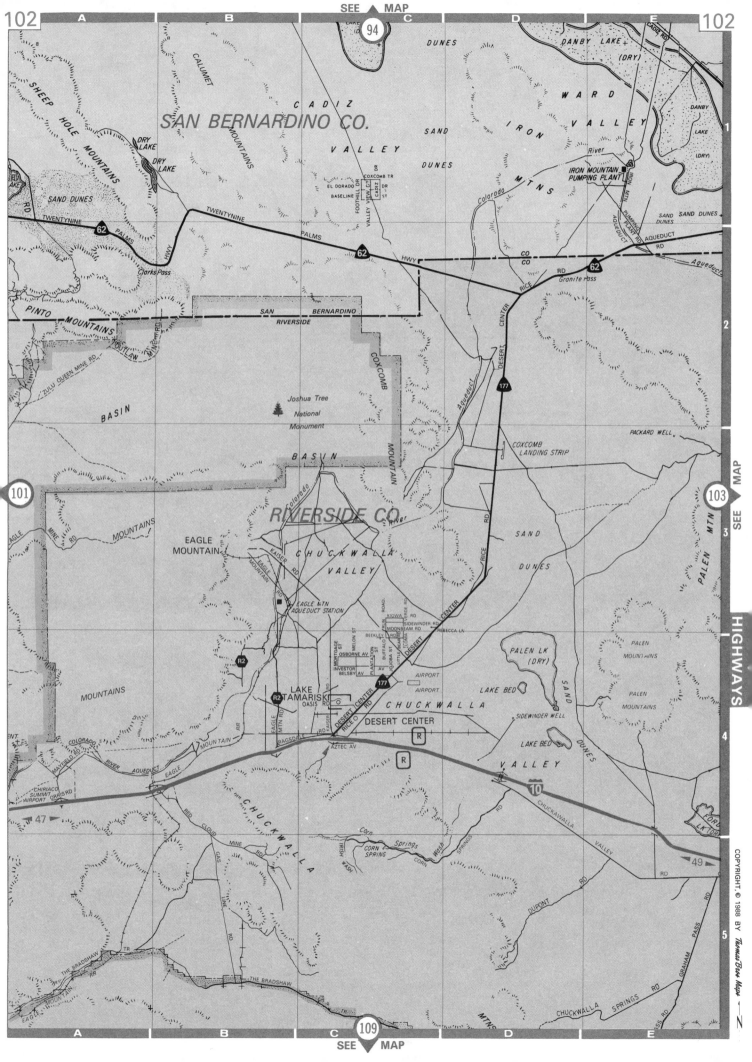

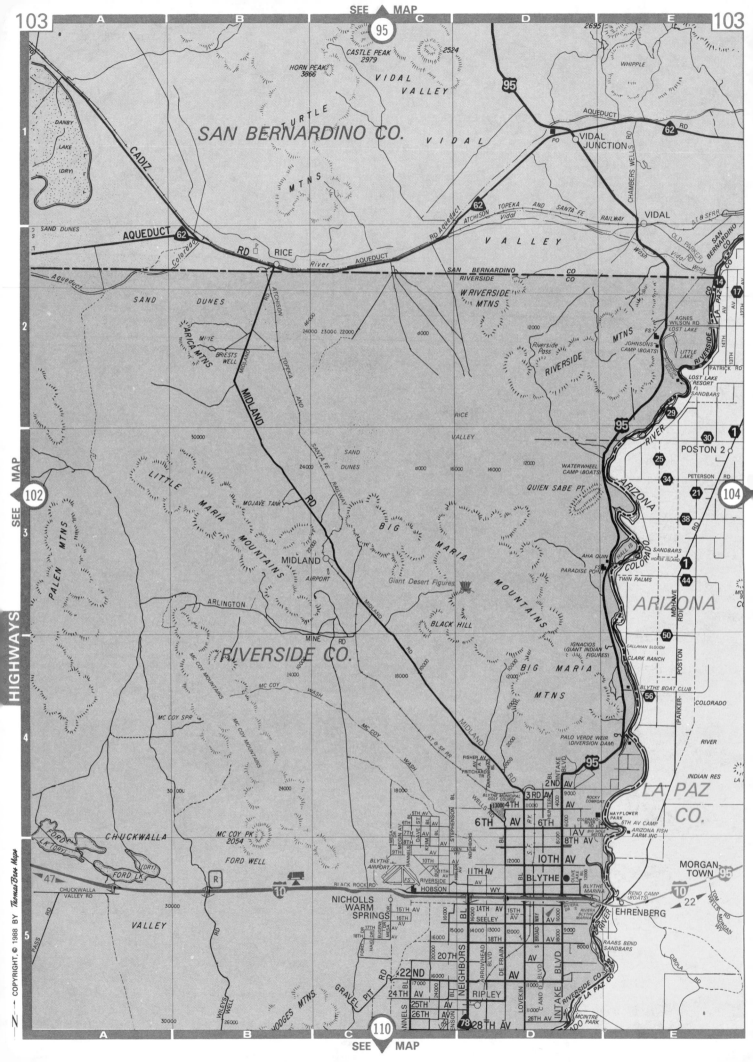

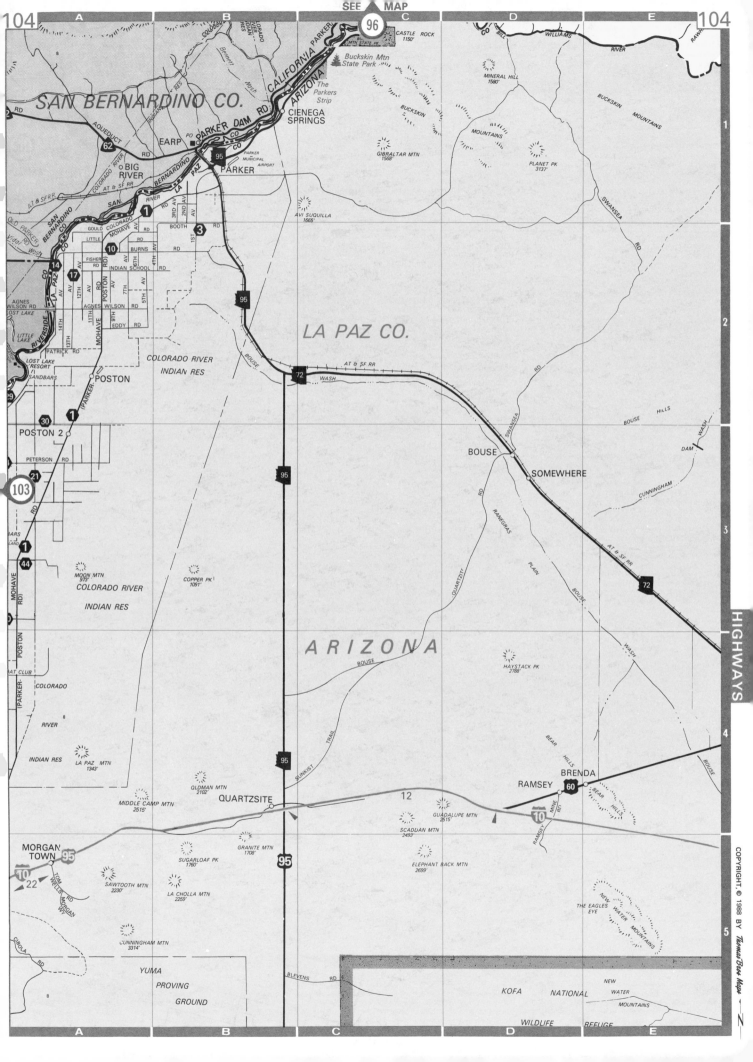

SEE MAP

98

SEE MAP

V

SAN JUAN CAPISTRANO

202

ORANGE CO.

South Laguna

Three Arch Bay

Ritz Carlton Hotel

Dana Point

Capistrano Beach

San Clemente

San Clemente State Beach

San Onofre Visitor's Ctr

San Onofre State Park

SAN DIEGO CO.

106

SAN ONOFRE

San Onofre State Beach

LA JOLLA SHORES

ECOLOGICAL STUDY AREA

LA JOLLA AREA

LA JOLLA BAY

San Diego - La Jolla Underwater Park

PT LA JOLLA

ELLEN SCRIPPS PARK

Boomer Beach

SHELL BEACH

1 UNION PL

Colonial Inn

Wipeout Beach

Hotel La Jolla

COAST BLVD PK

Casa Beach

WHISPERING SANDS

NICHOLSON PT PARK

Marine Street Beach

VISTA DE LA PLAYA

Windansea Beach

PLAYA

PLAYA DEL SUR

KOLMAR ST

ROSEMONT

LA JOLLA STRAND PARK

WINAMAR

HERMOSA TERRACE

BIG ROCK REEF

La Jolla Caves

Spindrift Golf Course

PROSPECT RD

La Jolla Country Club

SR H.S. LA JOLLA

MUIRLANDS DR

NAUTILUS ST

LA JOLLA SCENIC DR

SOLEDAD MTN RD

SAN DIEGO

PACIFIC OCEAN

SR H.S. LA JOLLA

NEWKIRK DR

Bird Rock

La Jolla Hermosa Park

Cortez Pl

KATE O SESSIONS MEMORIAL PARK

TURQUOISE

TOURMALINE

OPAL

LORING

BERYL

HIGHWAYS

211

SEE MAP

212

SEE MAP

N

COPYRIGHT © 1988 BY Thomas Bros Maps

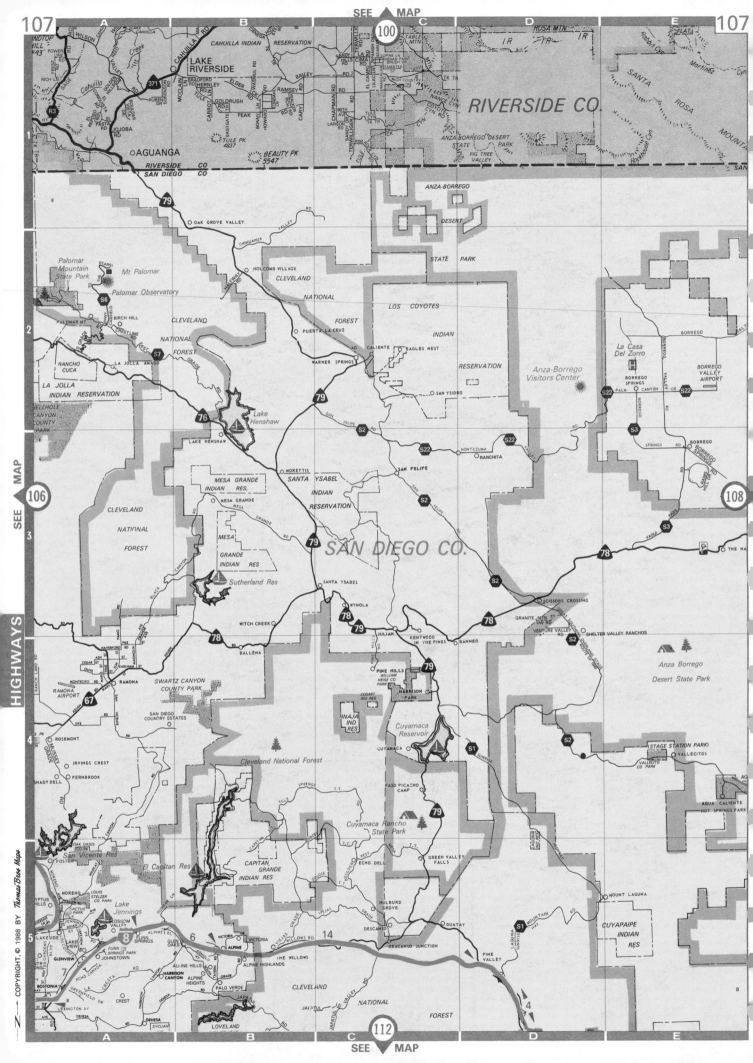

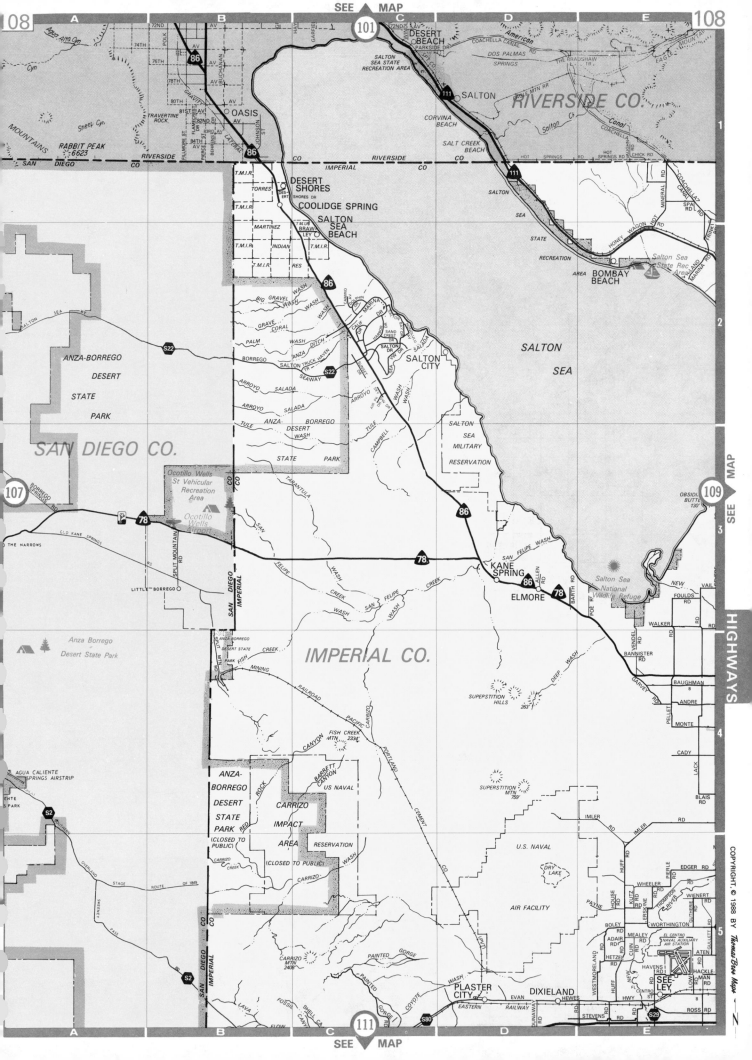

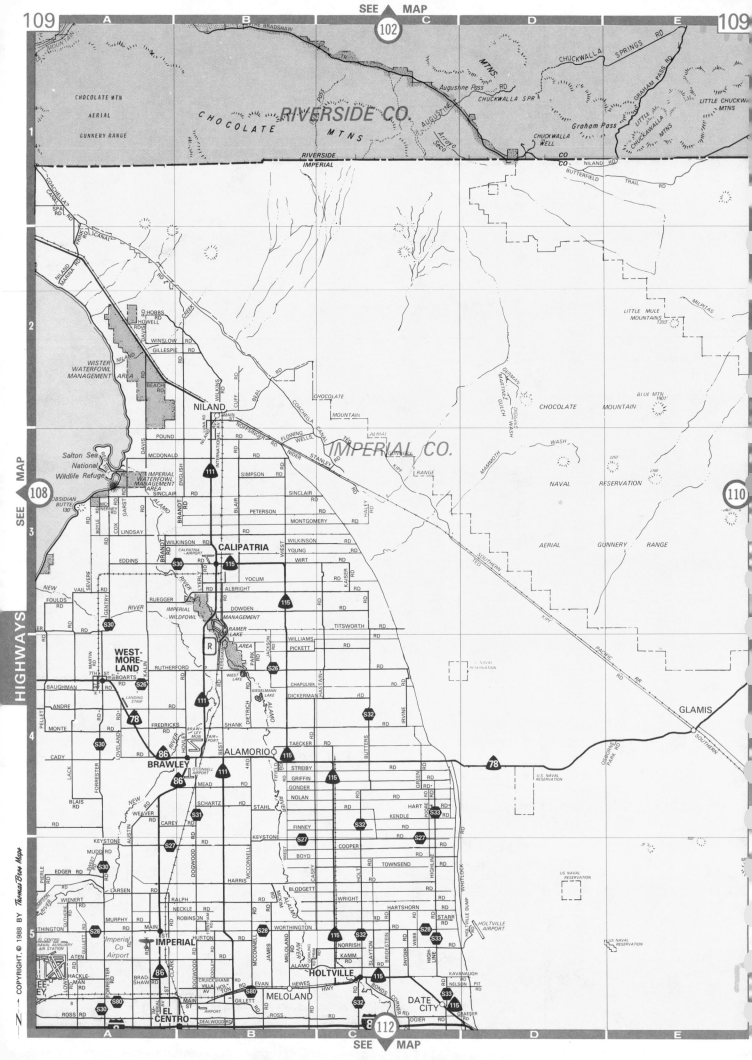

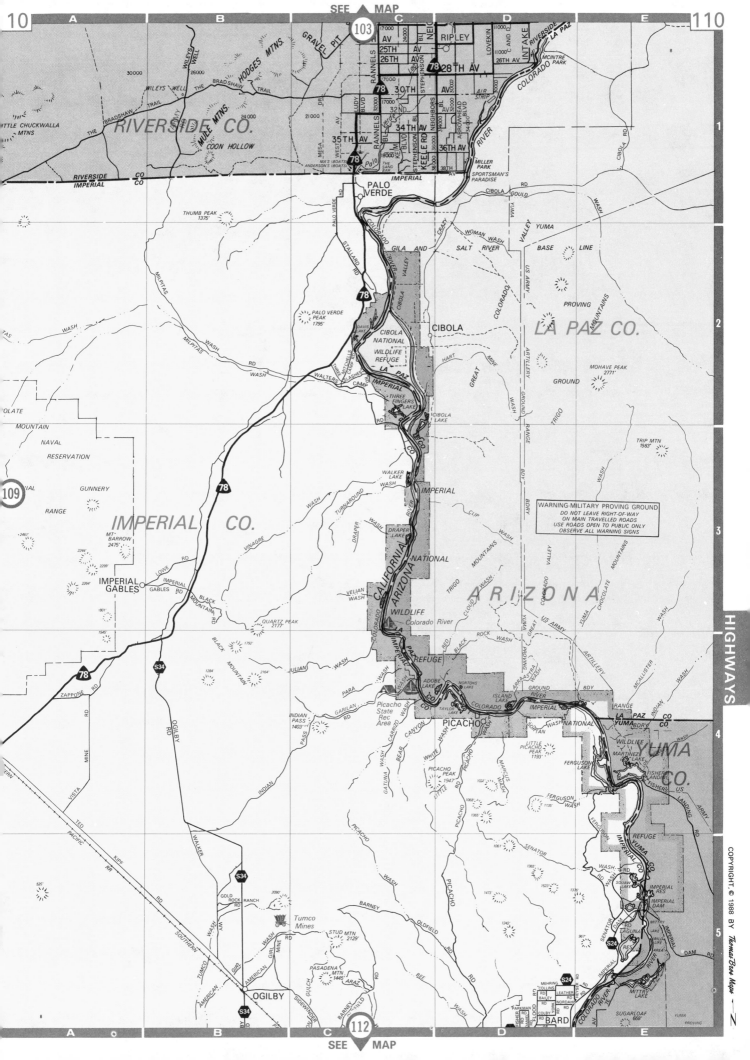

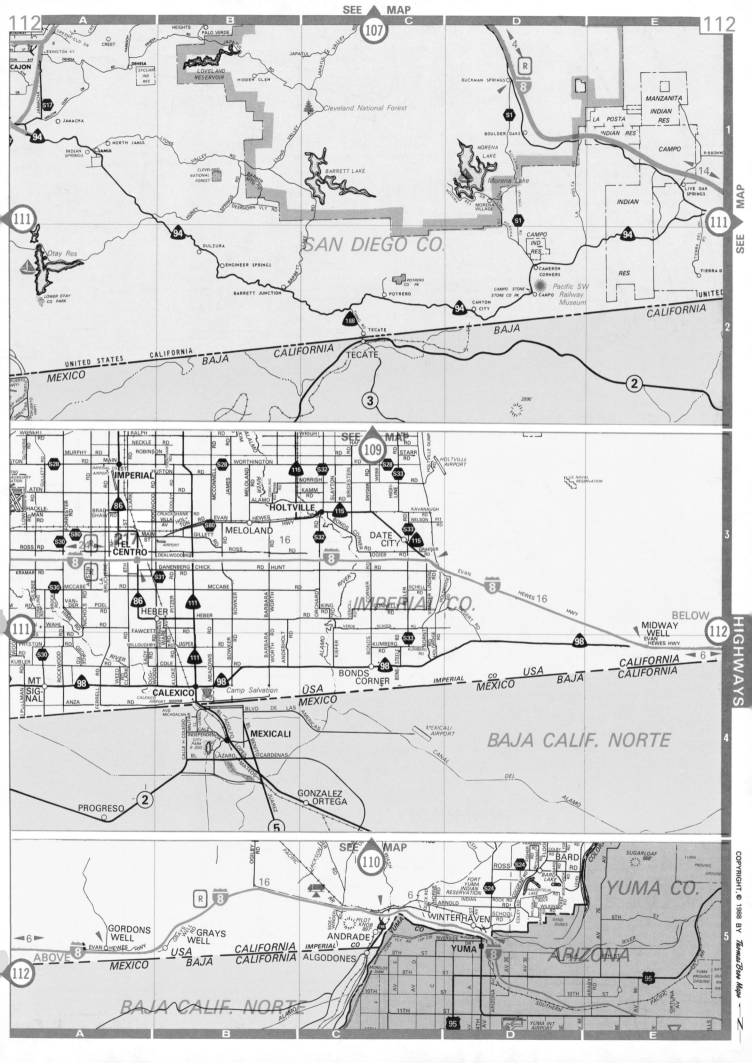

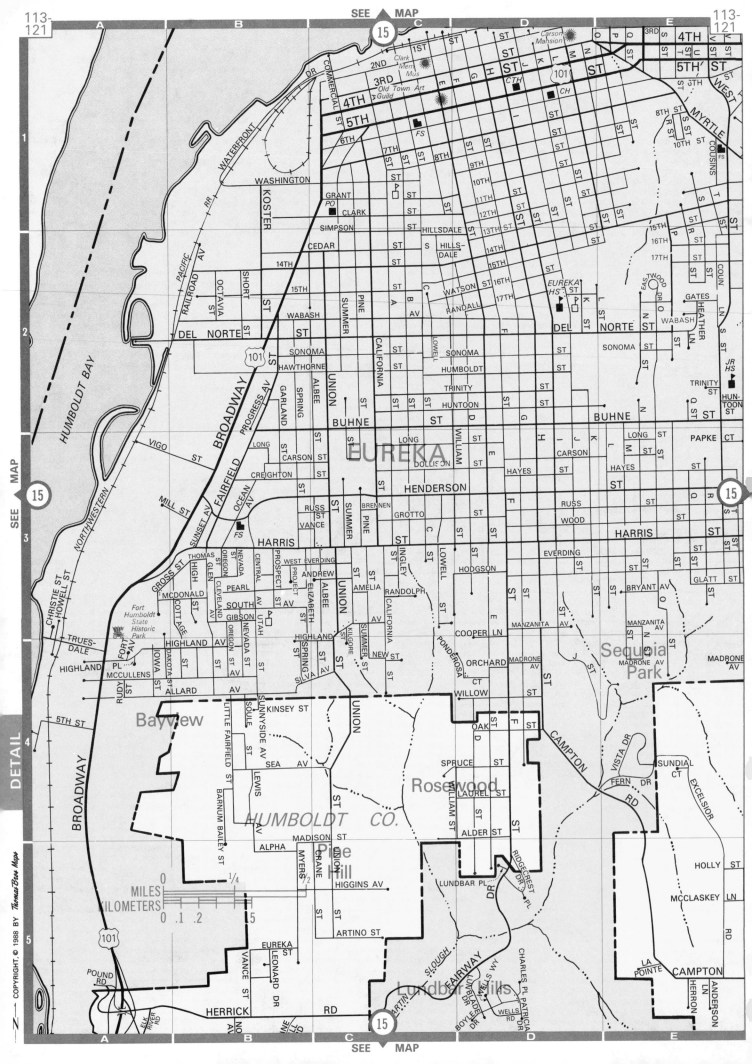

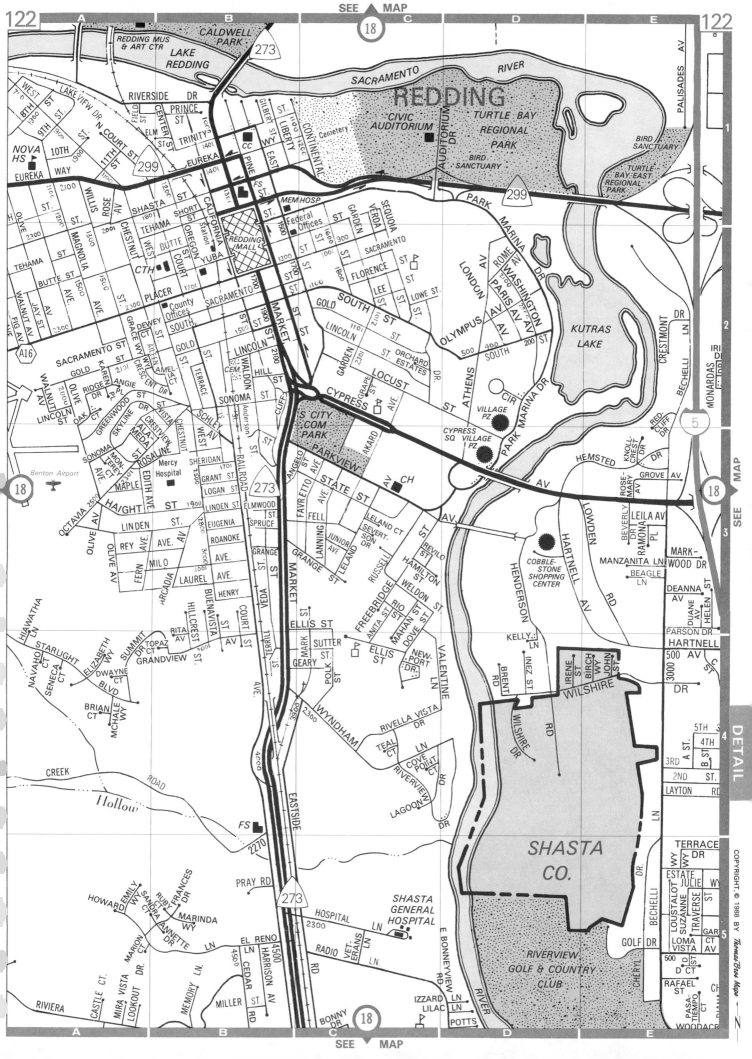

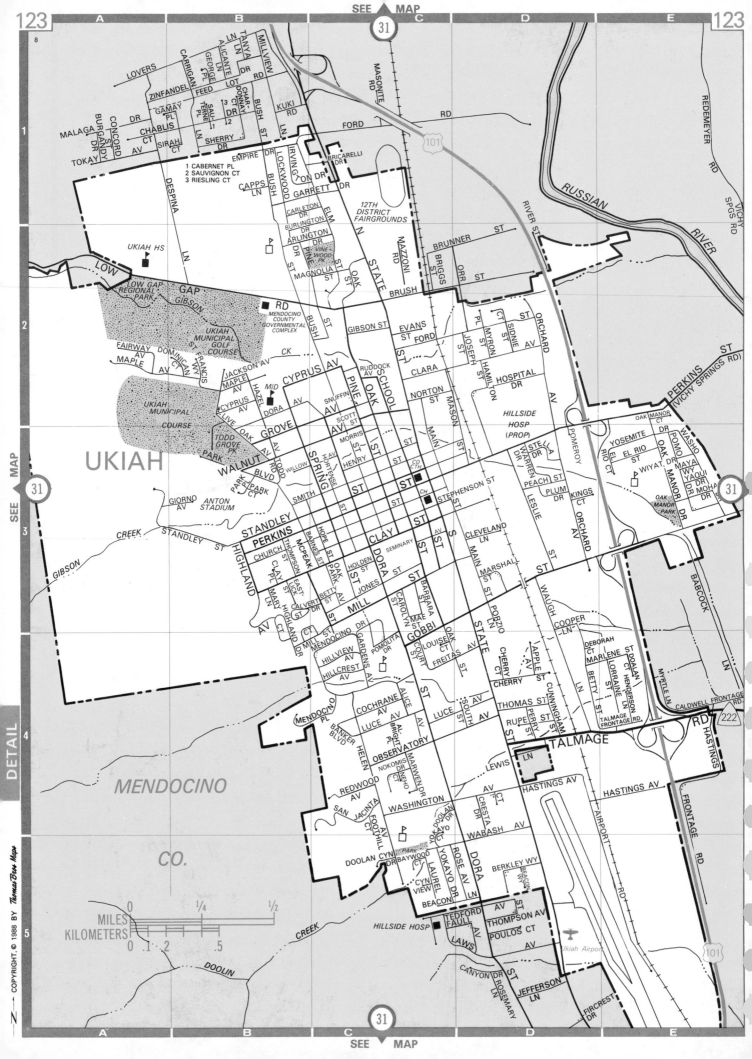

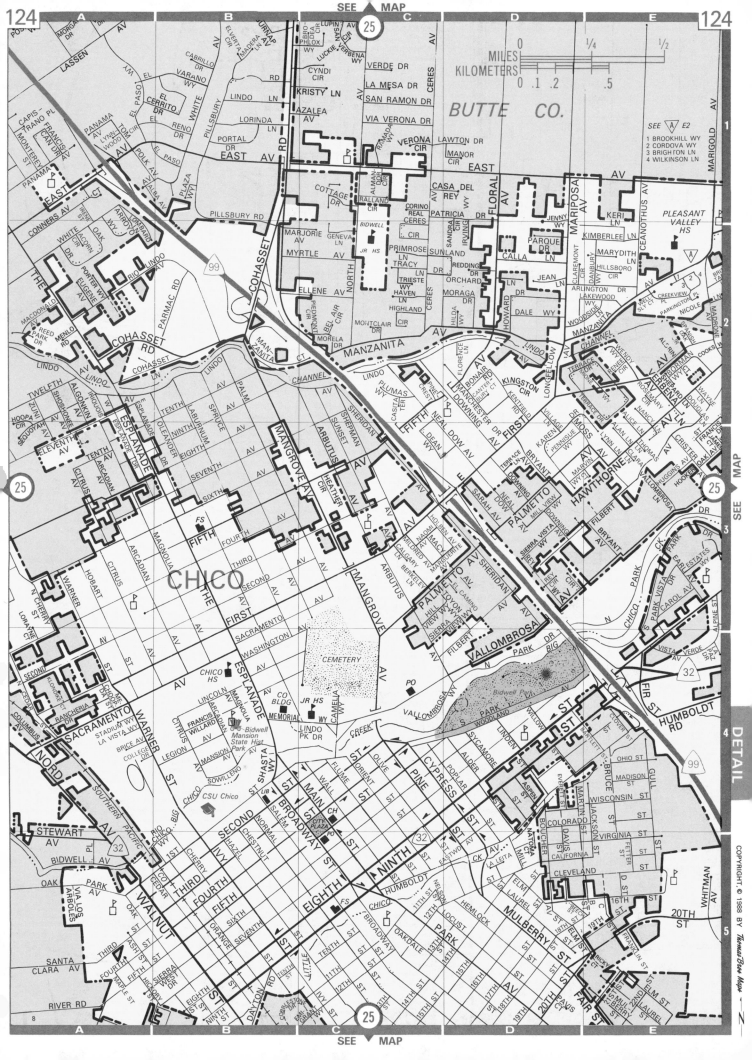

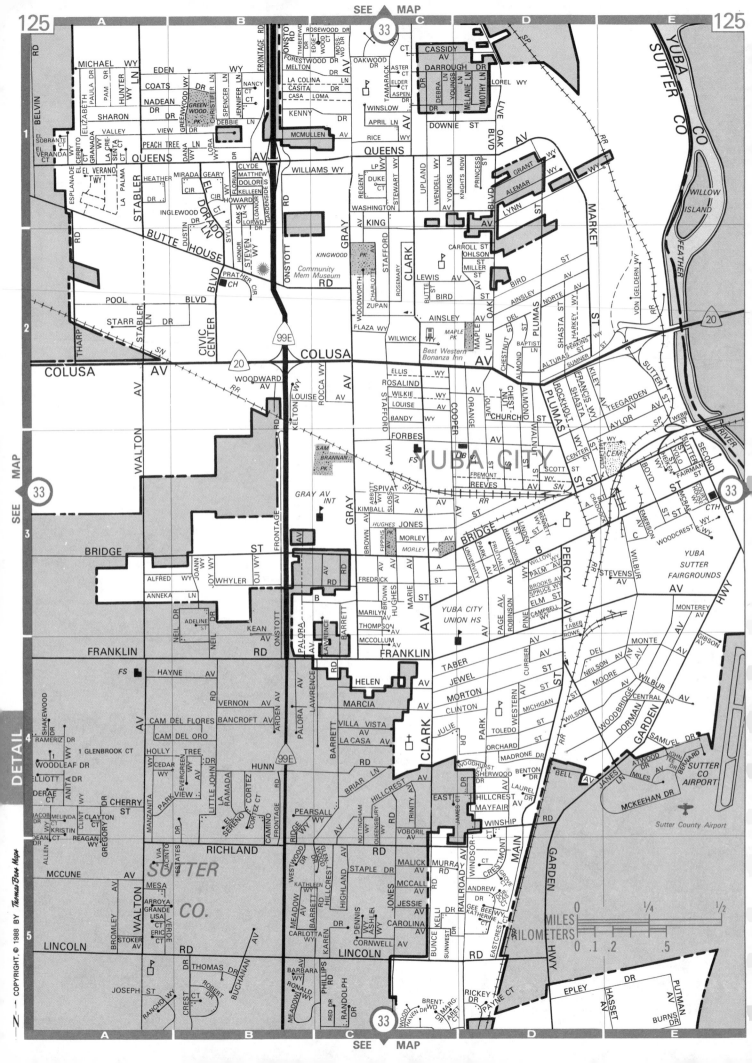

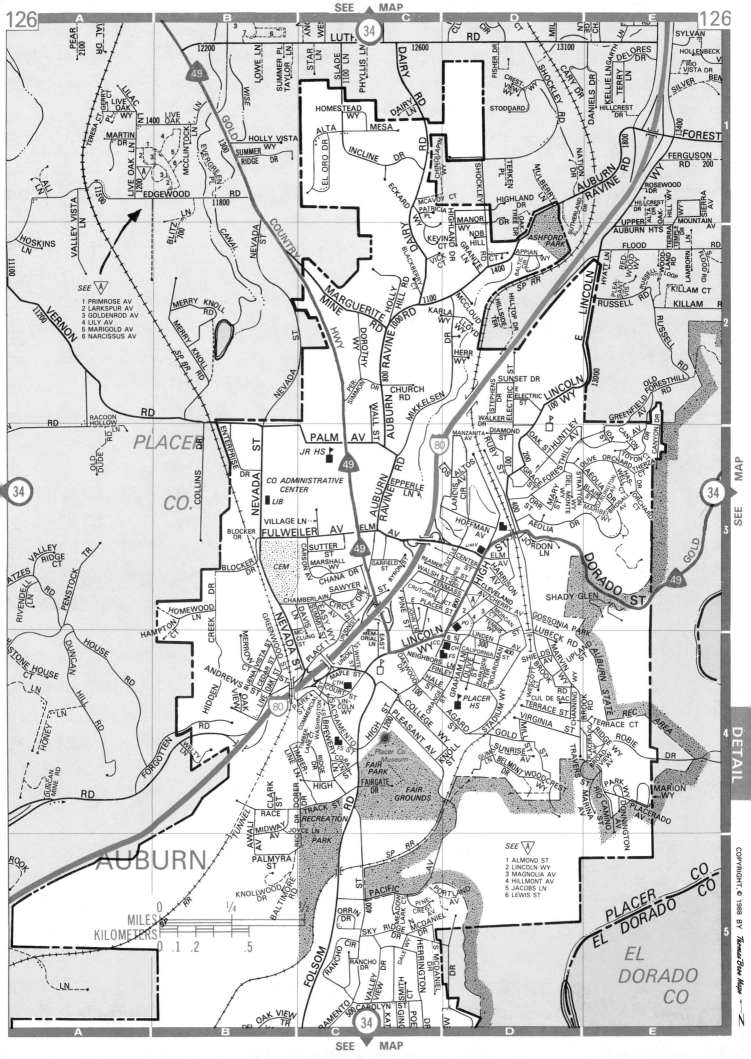

34

SEE A
1 PRIMROSE AV
2 LARKSPUR AV
3 GOLDENROD AV
4 LILY AV
5 MARIGOLD AV
6 NARCISSUS AV

PLACER CO.

PLACER
CO.

AUBURN

SEE A
1 ALMOND ST
2 LINCOLN WY
3 MAGNOLIA AV
4 HILLMONT AV
5 JACOBS LN
6 LEWIS ST

EL DORADO CO

MILES
KILOMETERS
0    .1  .2      .5

DETAIL

34

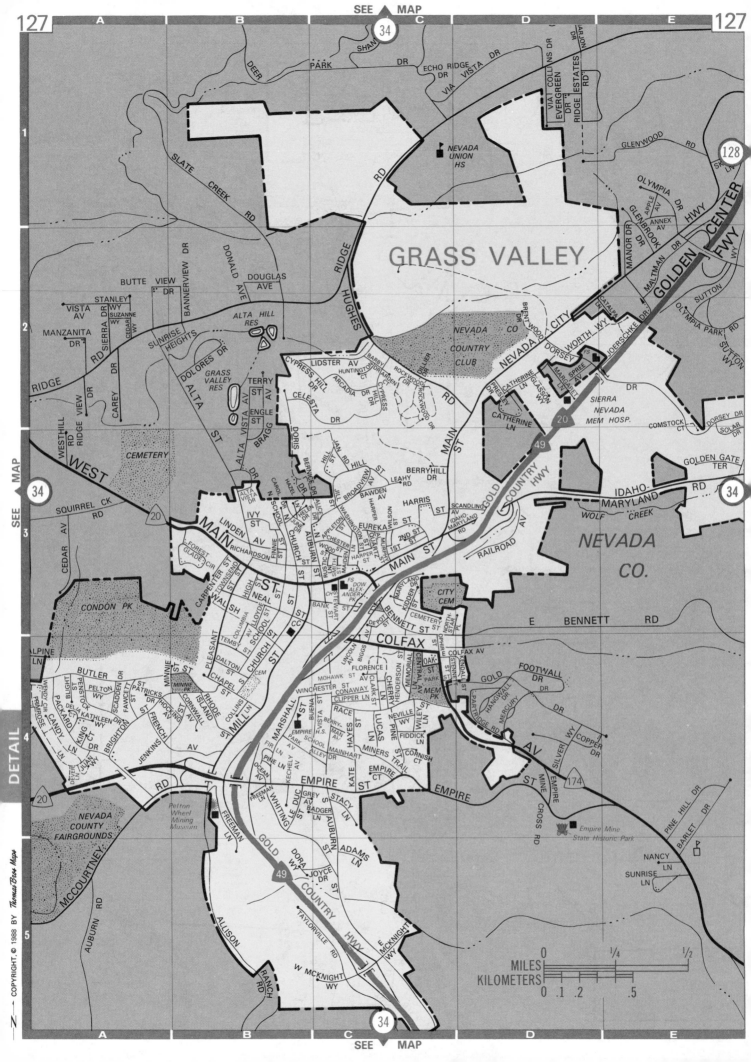

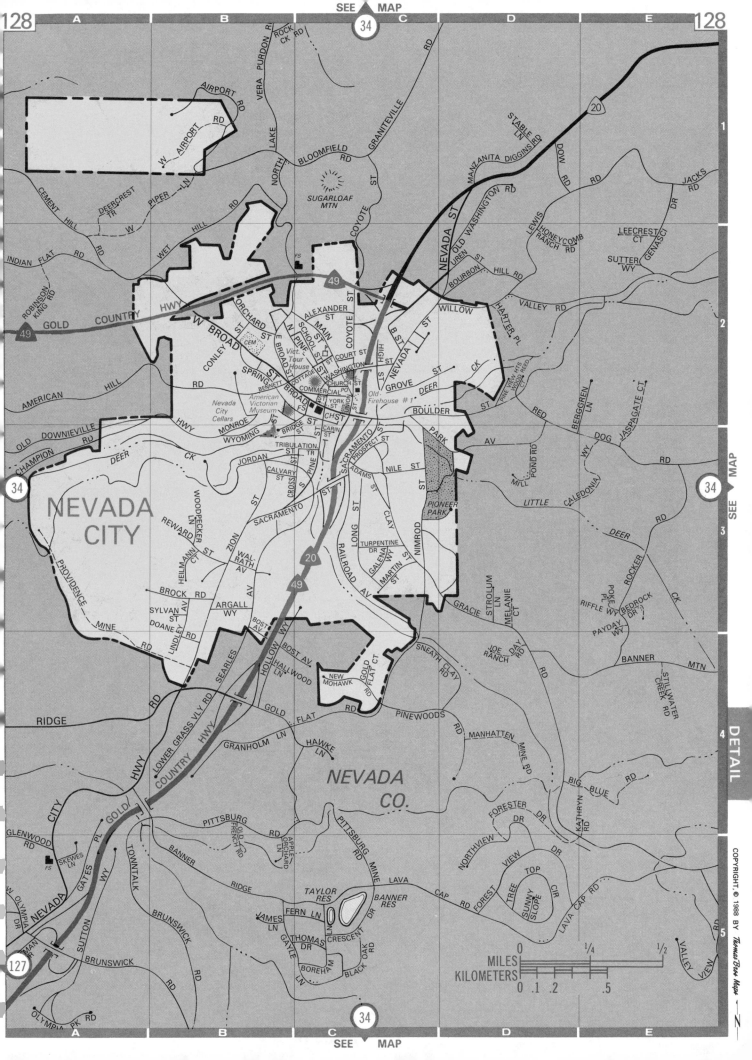

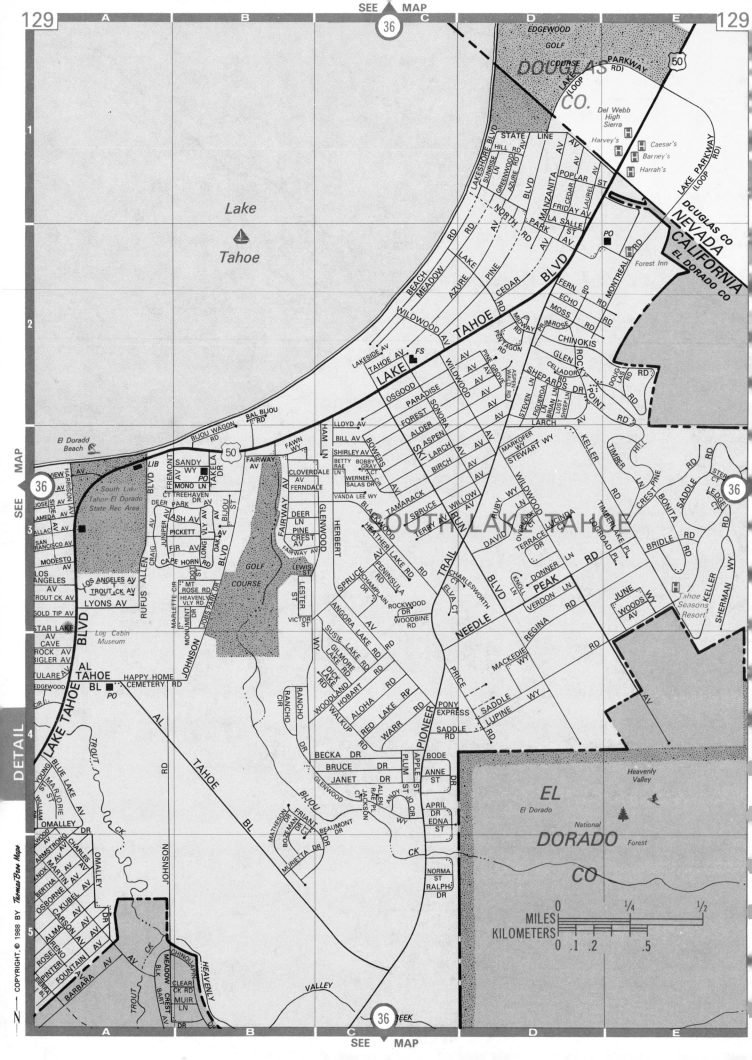

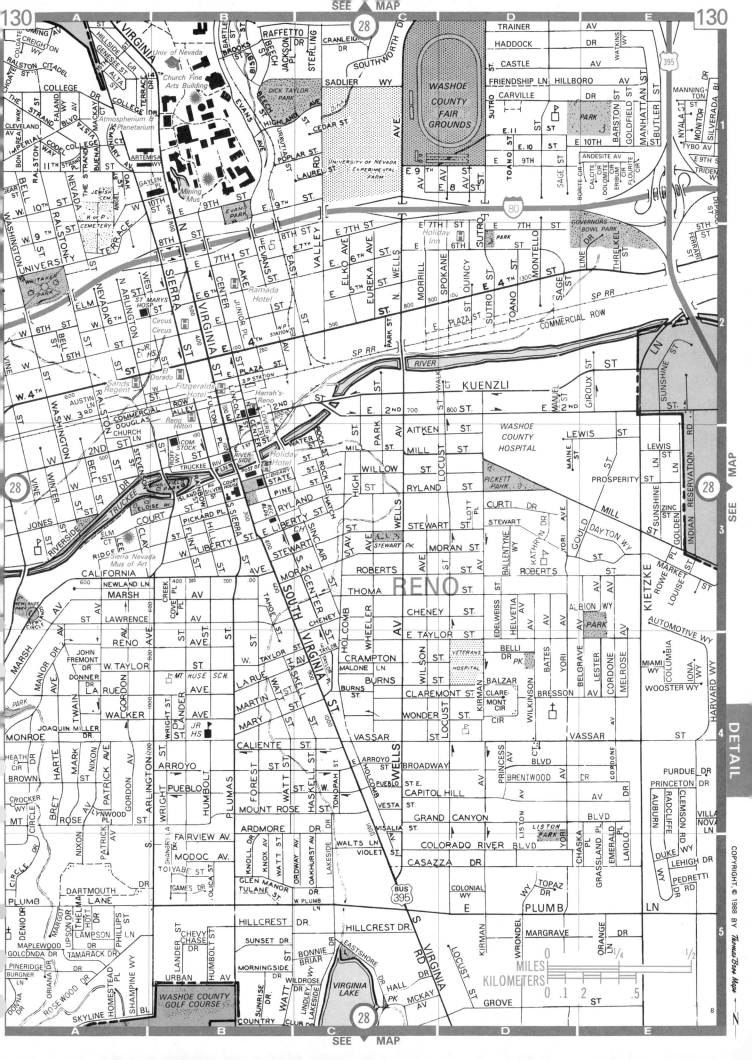

SEE MAP

37

SEE MAP

37

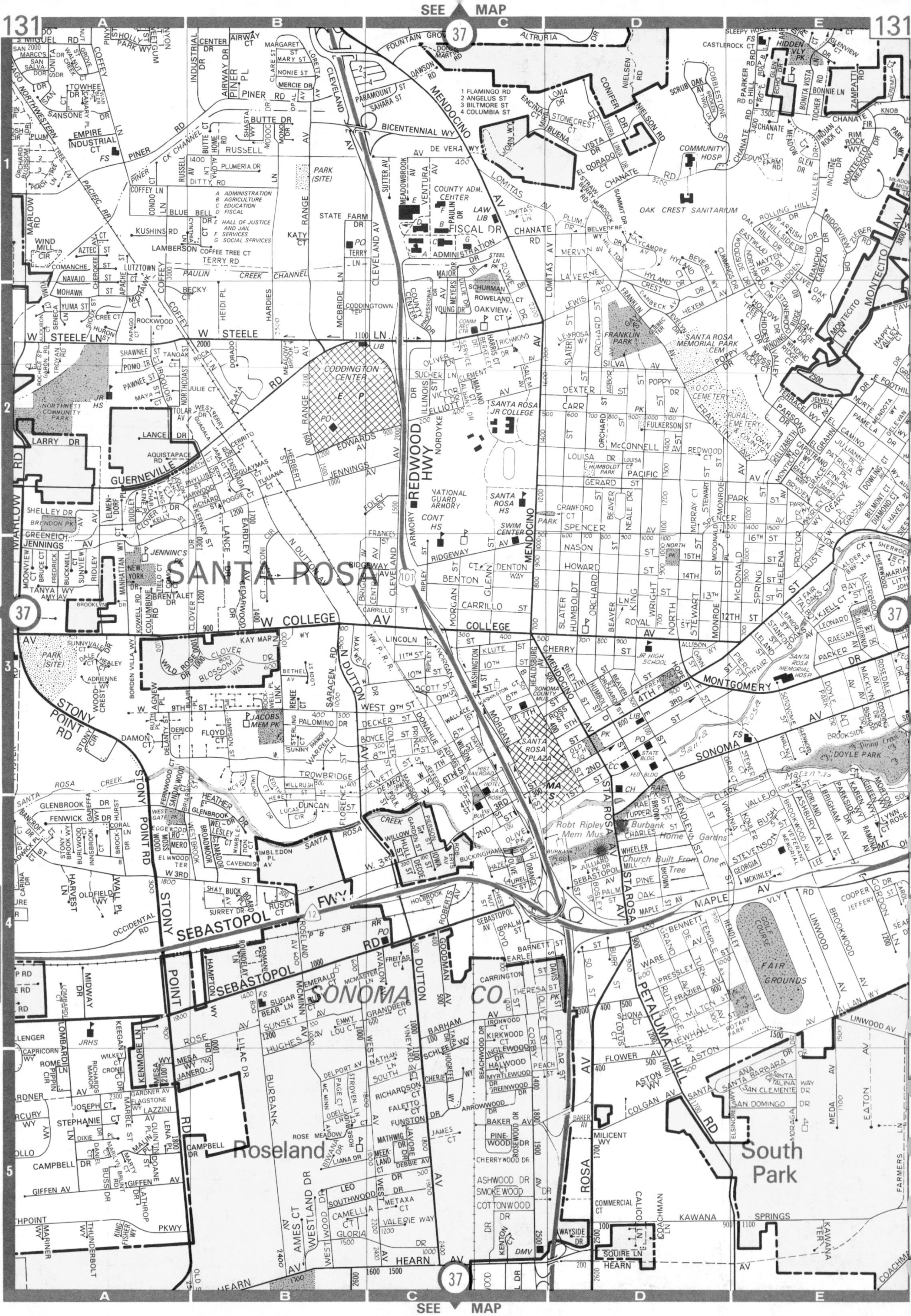

**SANTA ROSA**

SONOMA CO.

Roseland

South Park

DETAIL

1 FLAMINGO RD
2 ANGELUS ST
3 BILTMORE ST
4 COLUMBIA ST

A ADMINISTRATION
B AGRICULTURE
C EDUCATION
D FISCAL
E HALL OF JUSTICE AND JAIL
F SERVICES
G SOCIAL SERVICES

COUNTY ADM. CENTER

CODDINGTON CENTER

SANTA ROSA JR COLLEGE

SANTA ROSA HS

NATIONAL GUARD ARMORY

SANTA ROSA PLAZA

FAIR GROUNDS

DOYLE PARK

COMMUNITY HOSP

OAK CREST SANITARIUM

SANTA ROSA MEMORIAL PARK CEM

SANTA ROSA MEMORIAL HOSP

BURBANK

Robt Ripley Mem Mus

Charles Burbank Home & Gardens

Church Built From One Tree

REDWOOD HWY

SEBASTOPOL FWY

STONY POINT RD

SEE MAP

37

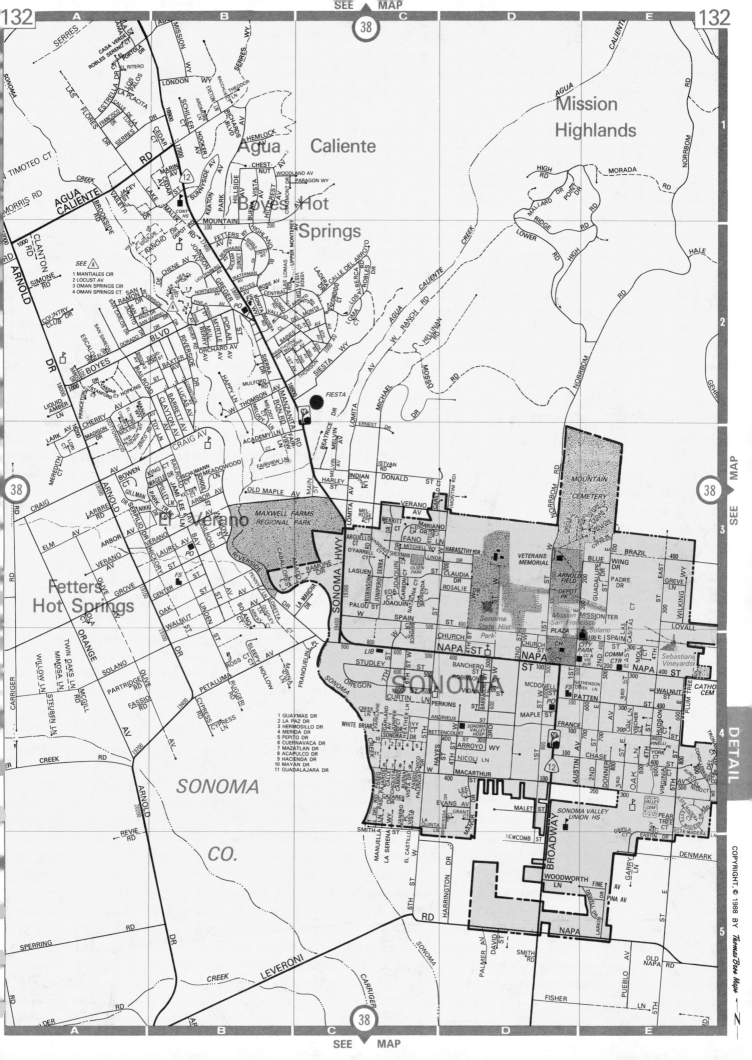

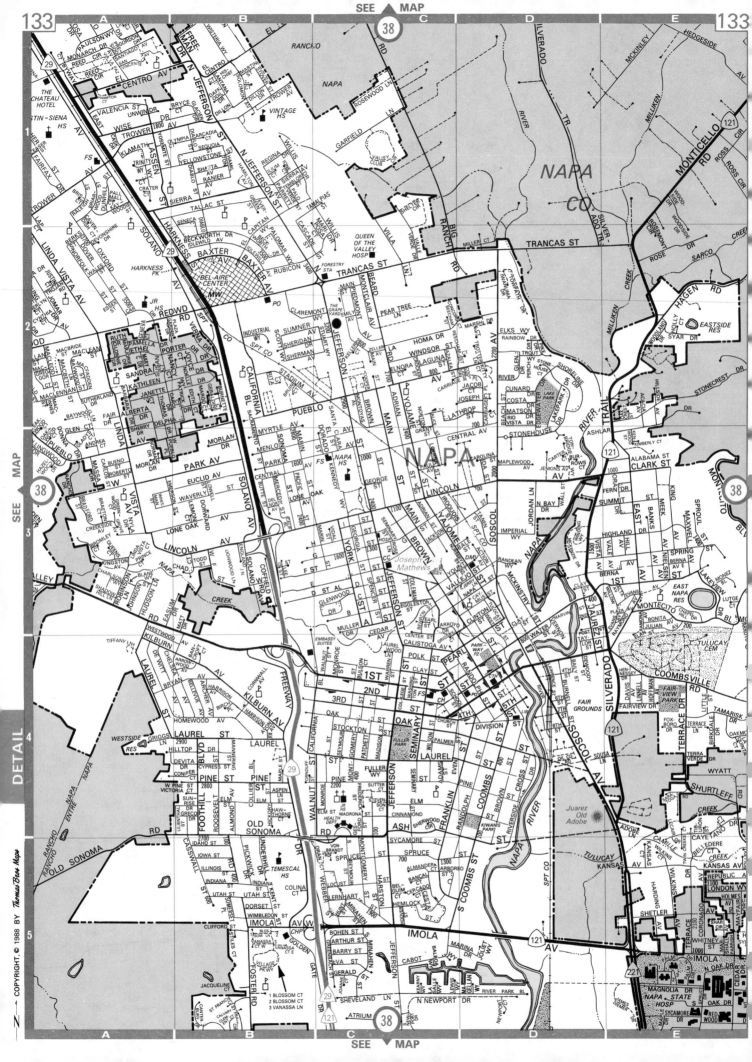

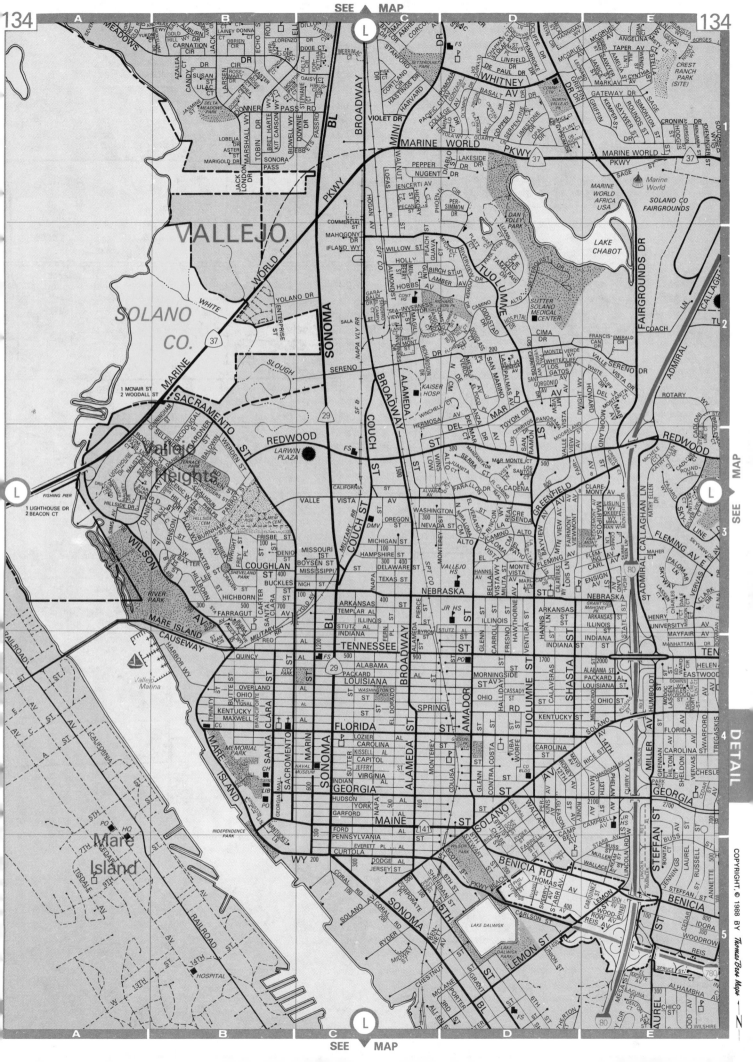

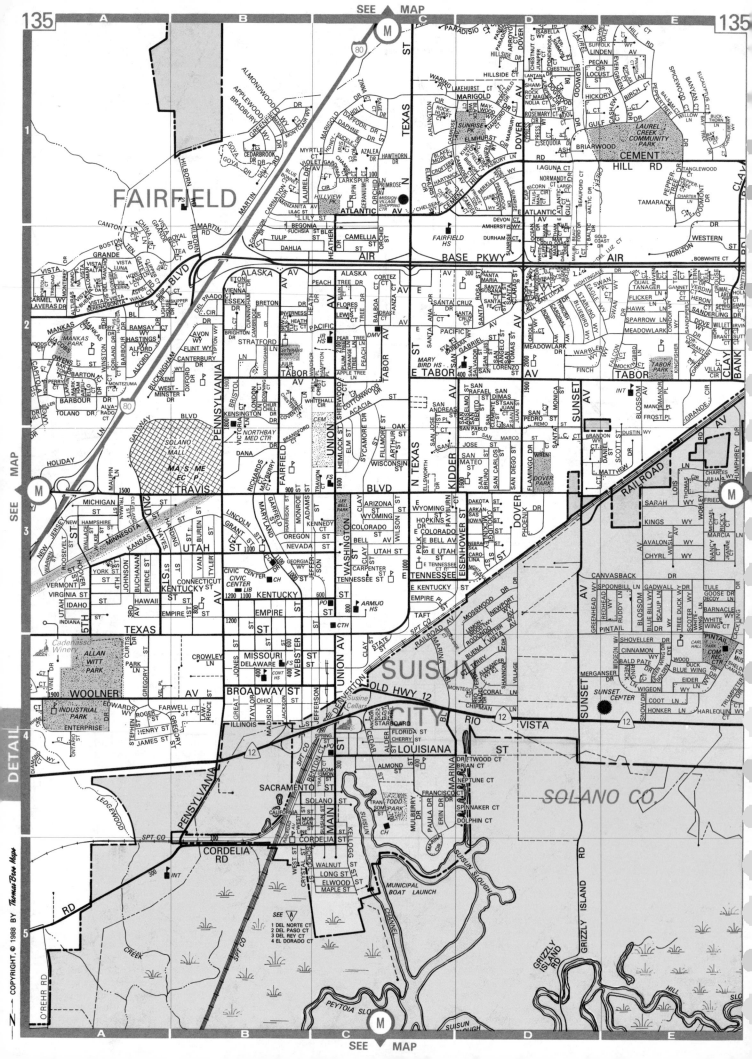

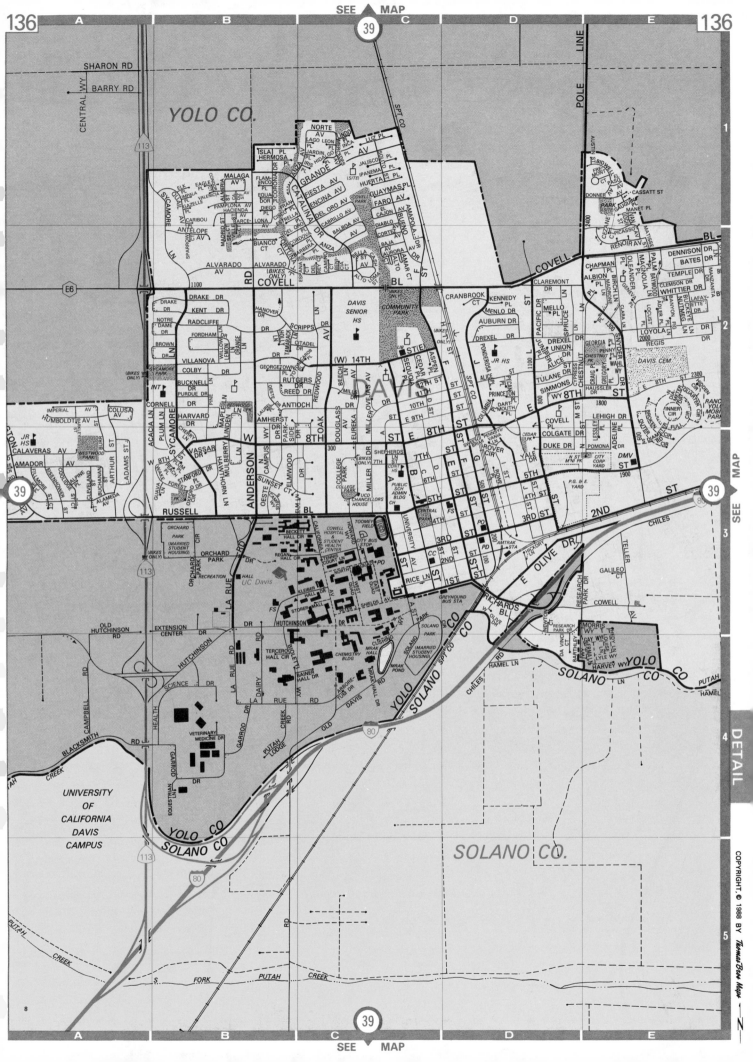

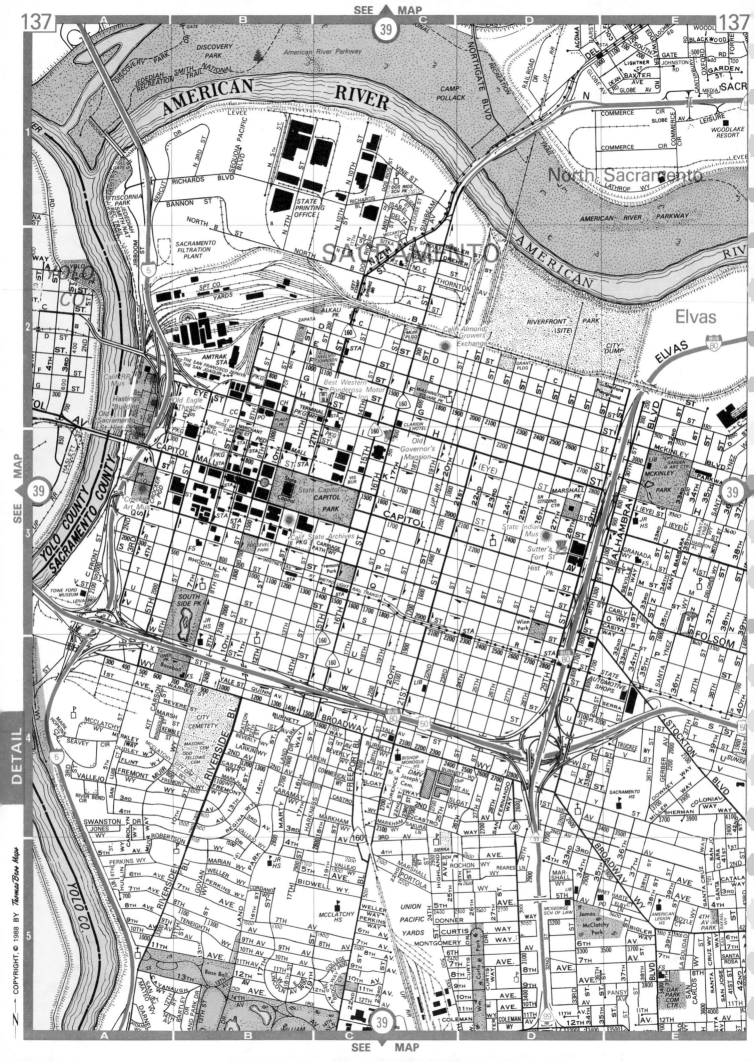

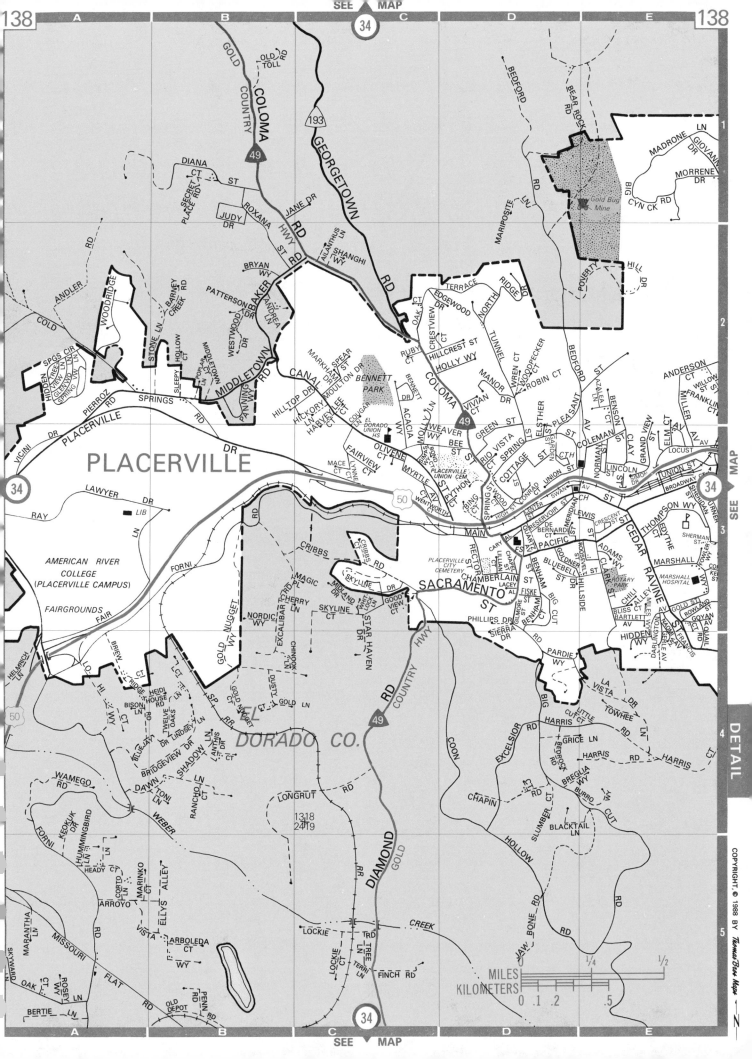

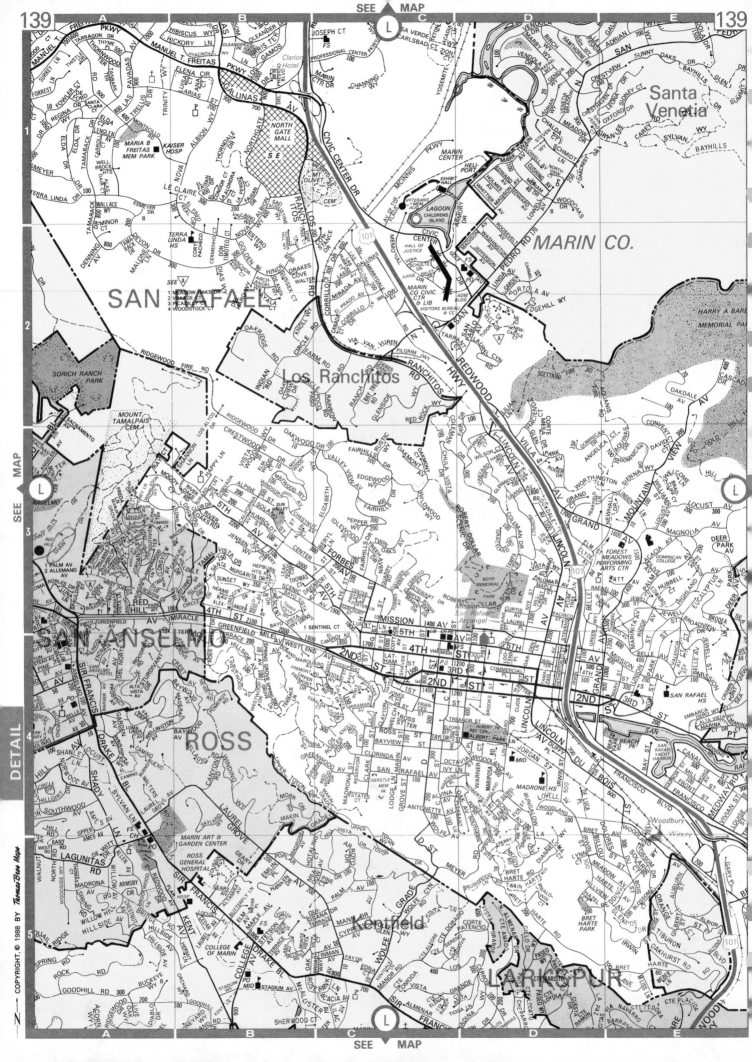

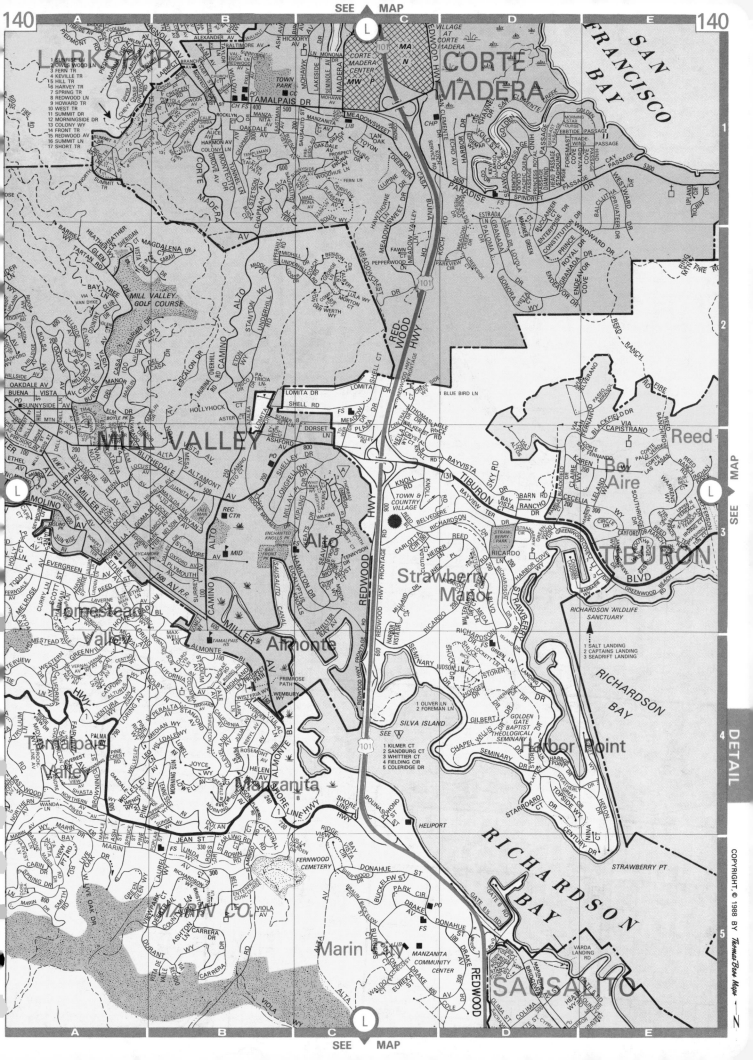

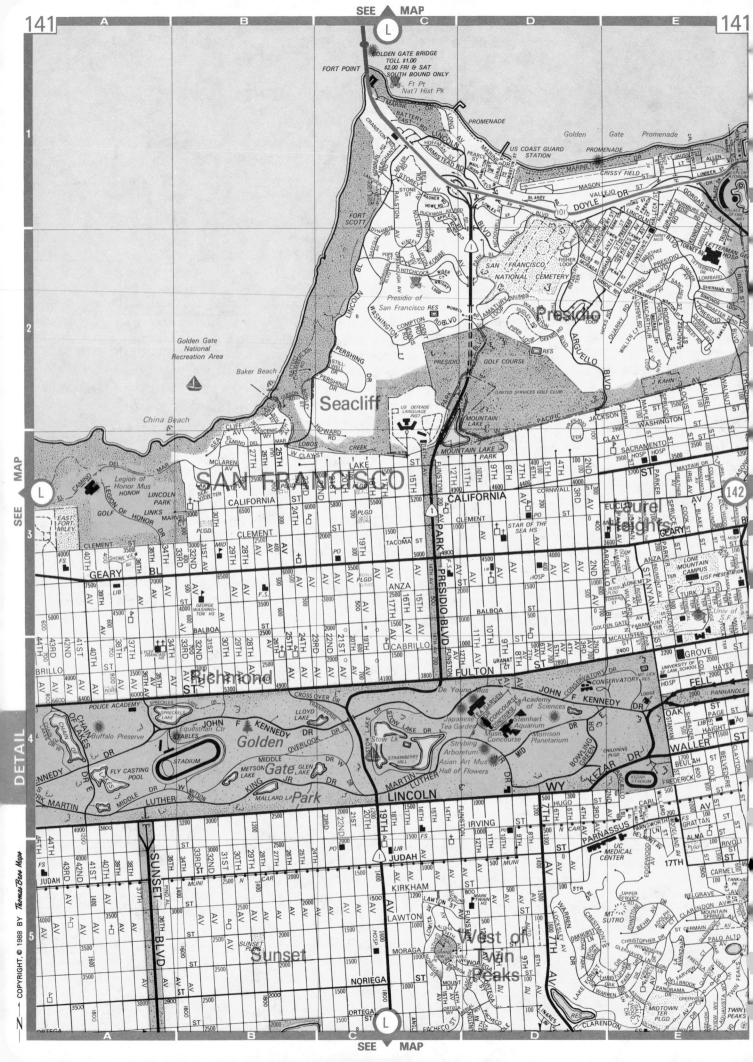

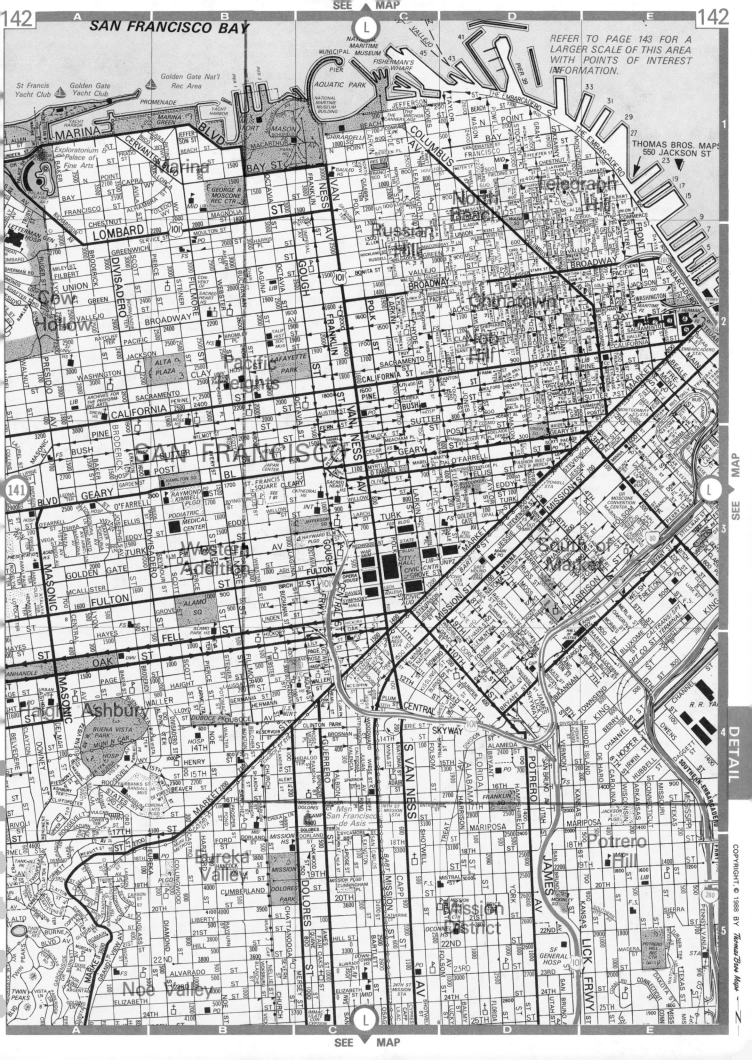

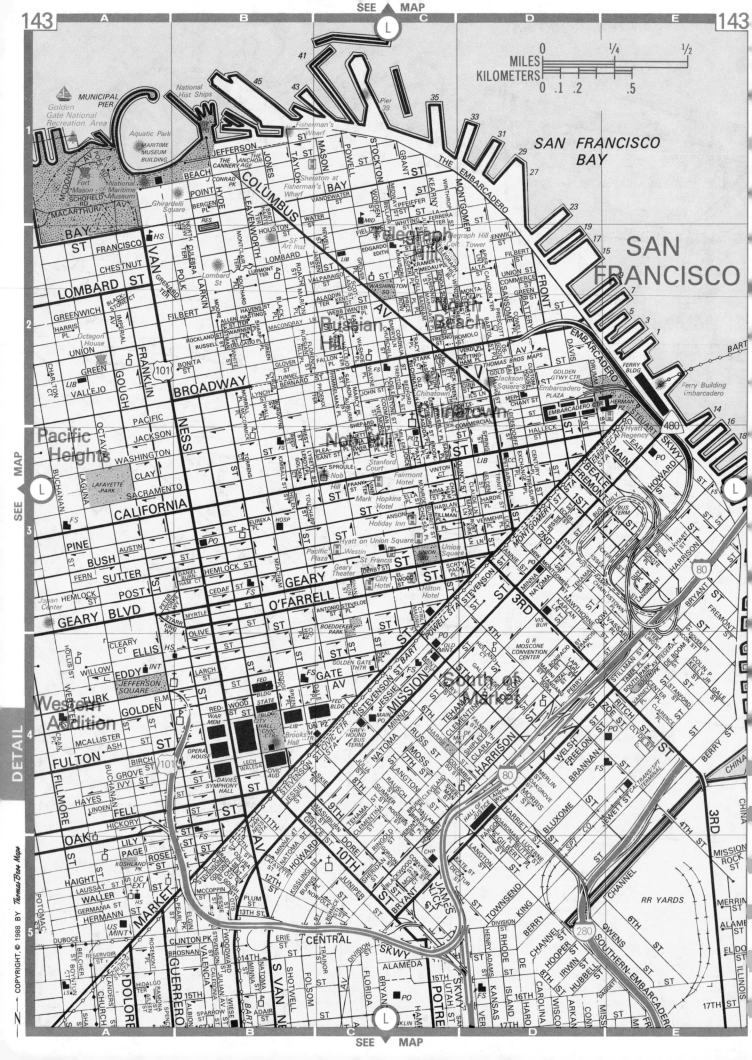

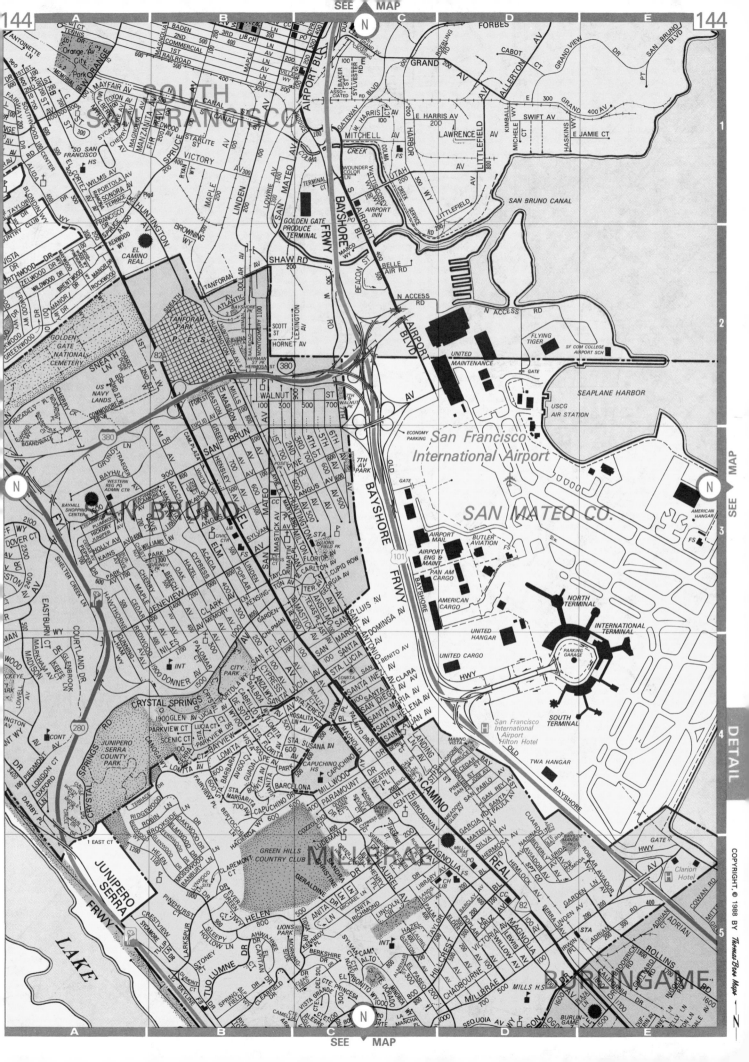

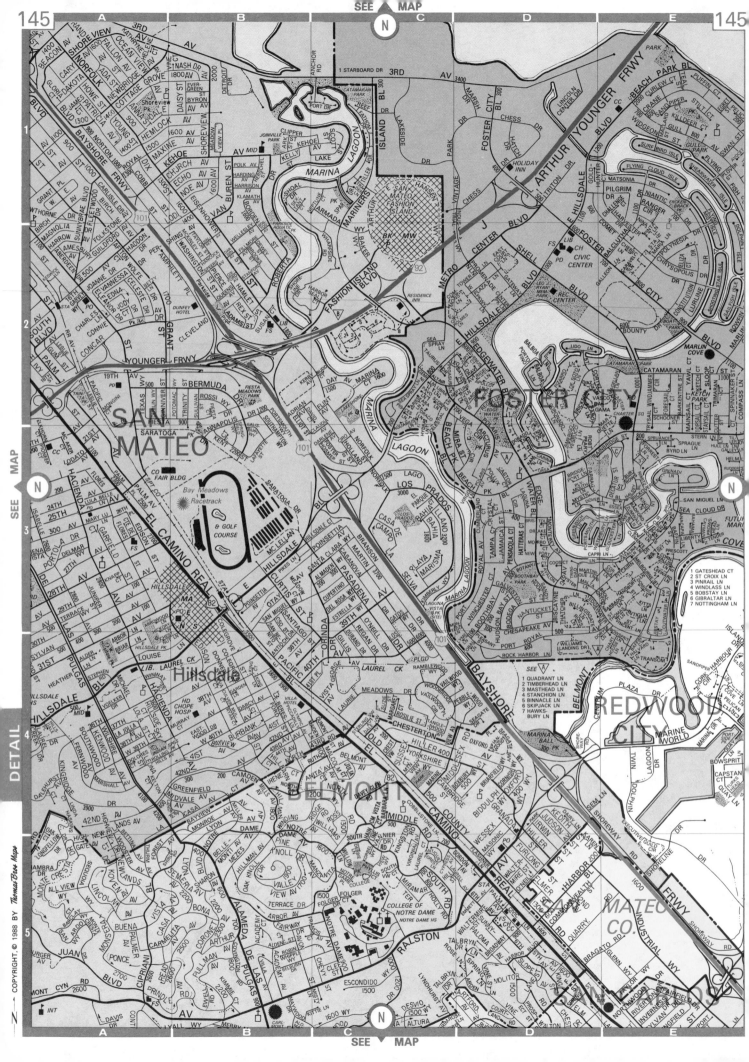

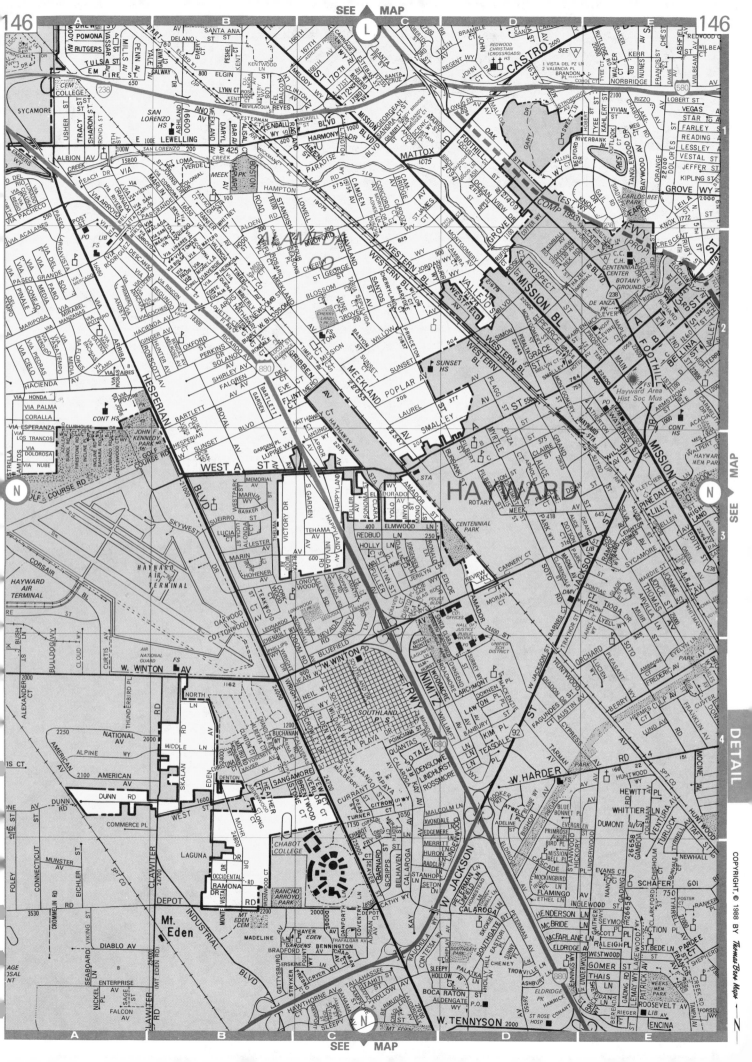

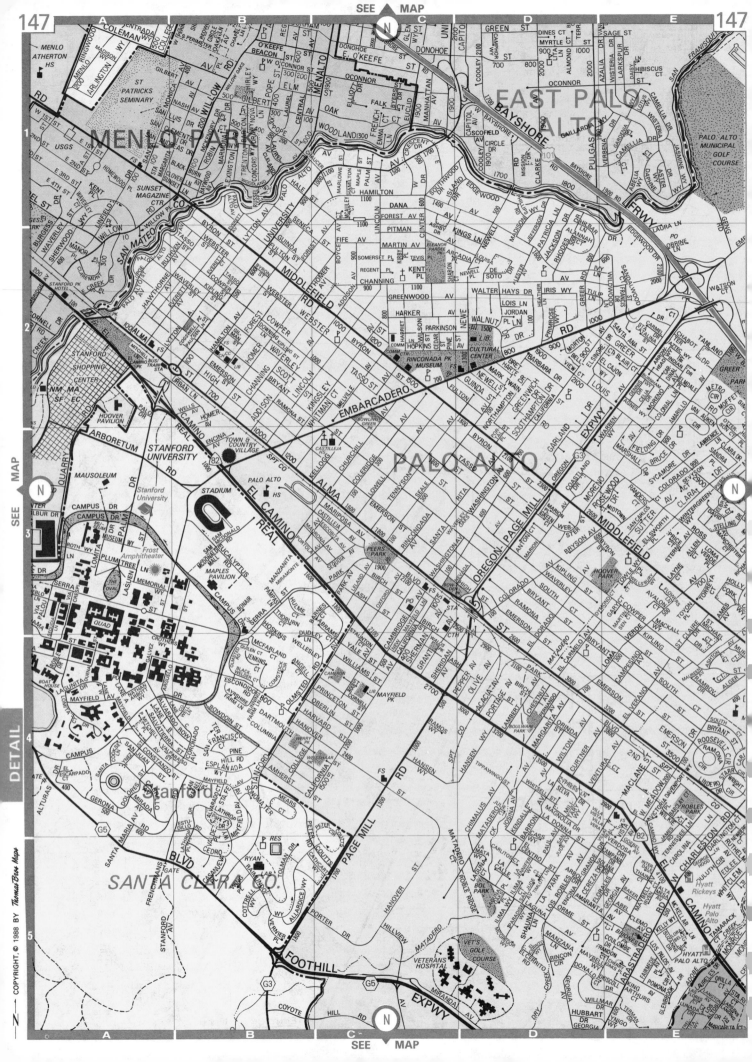

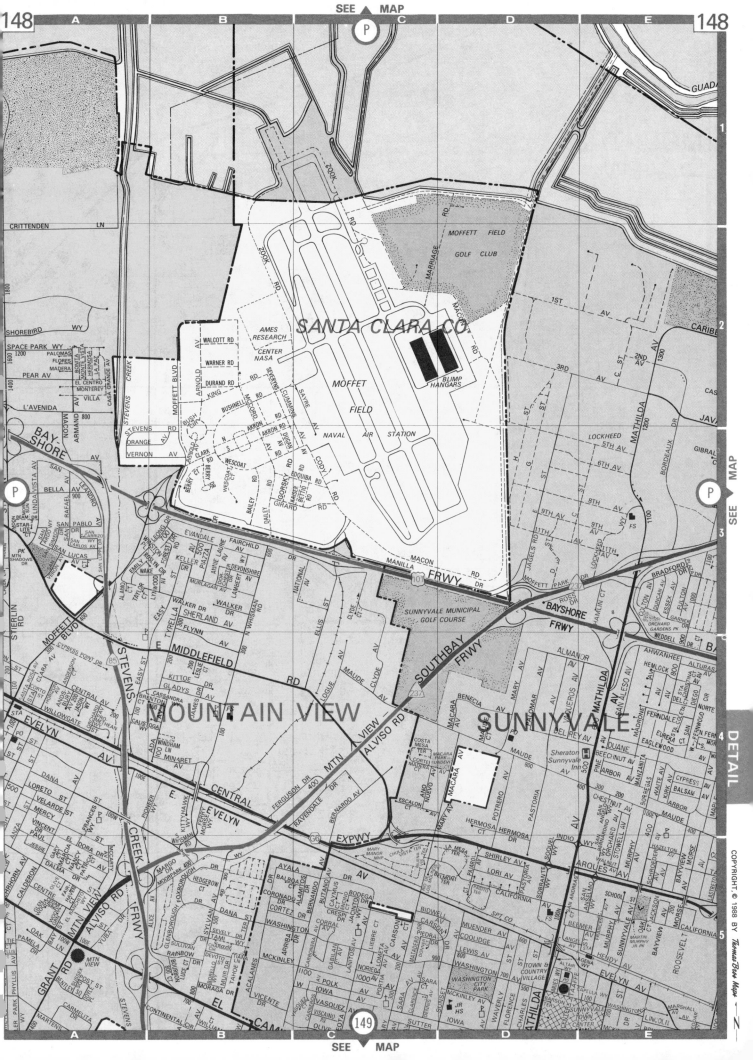

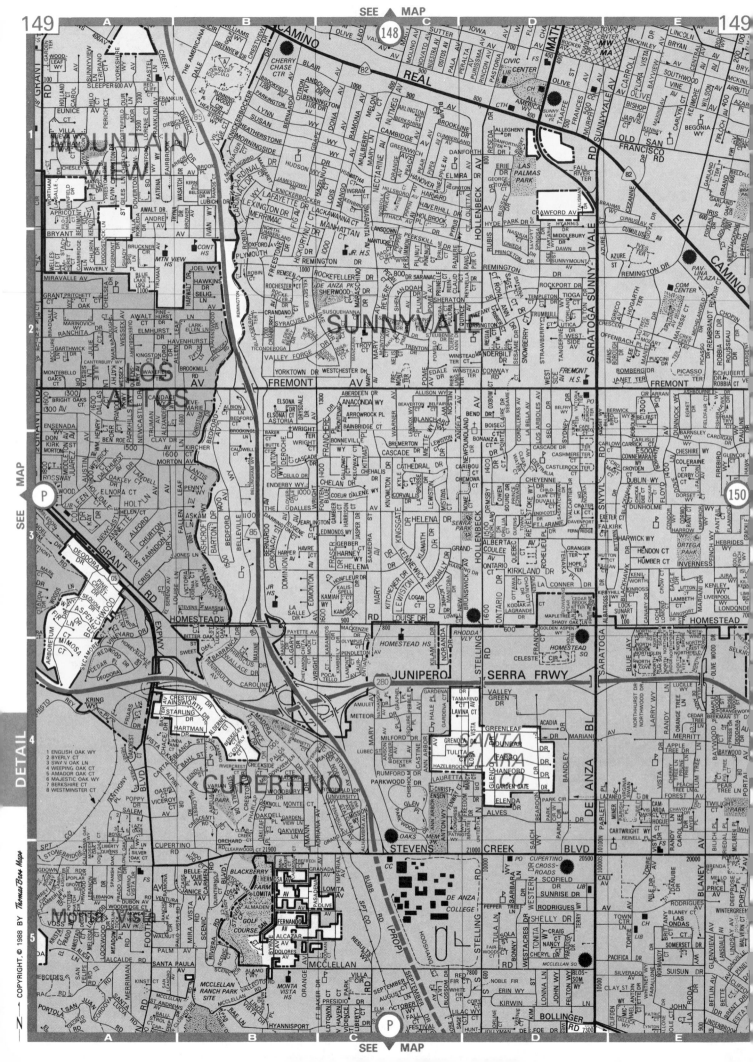

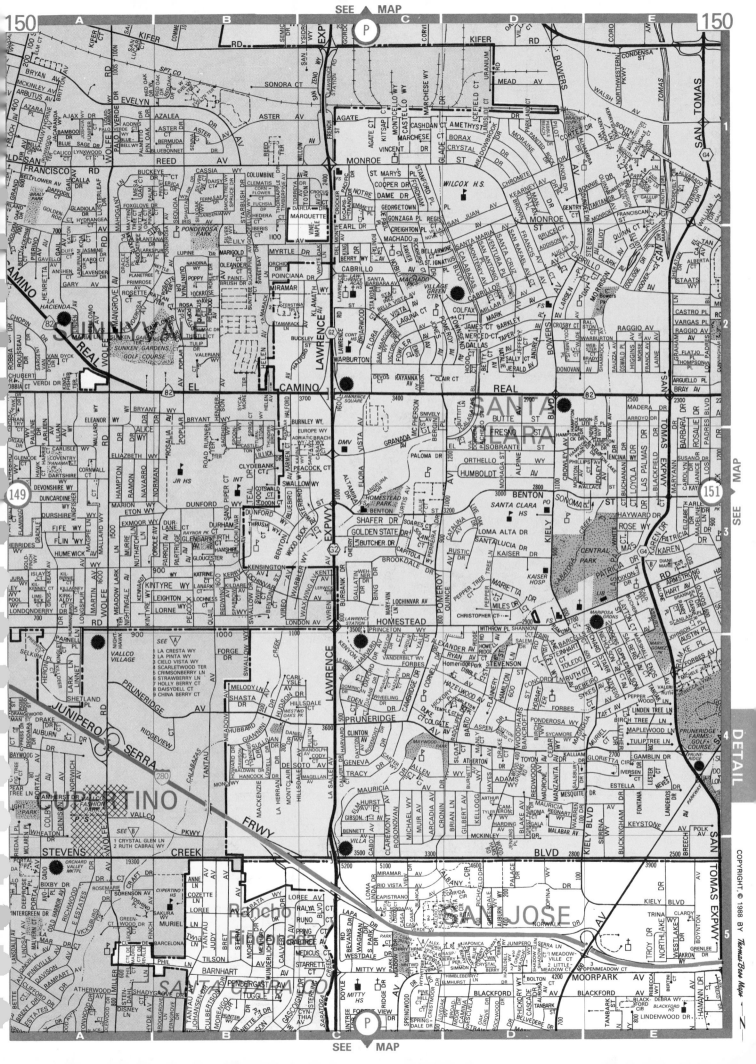

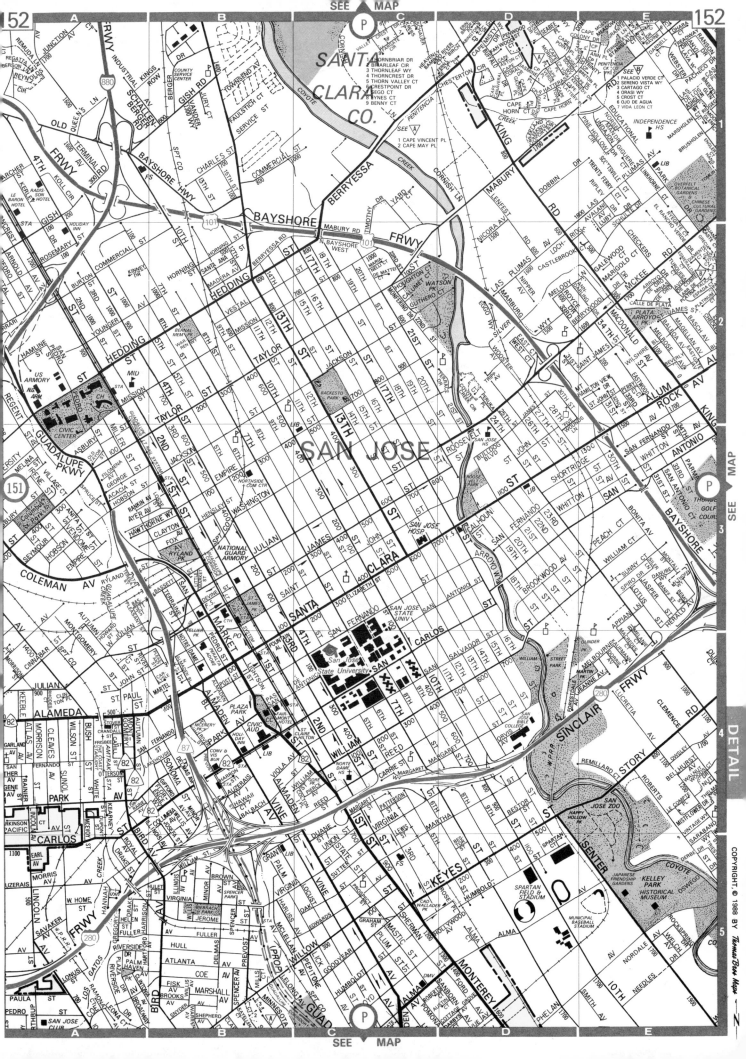

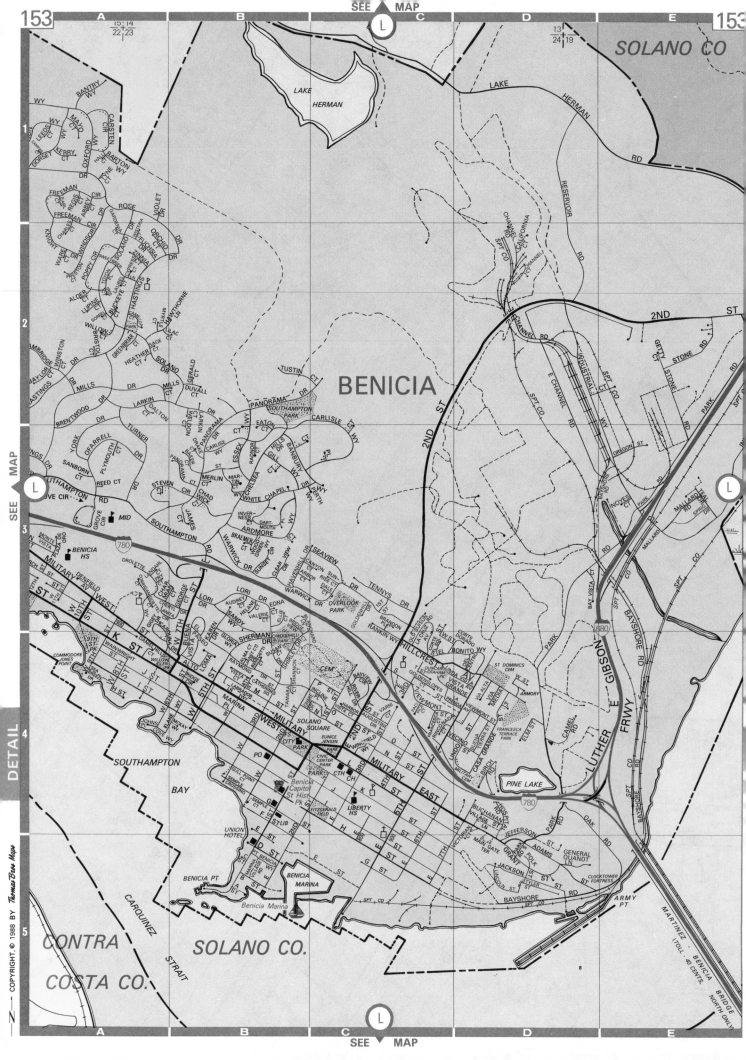

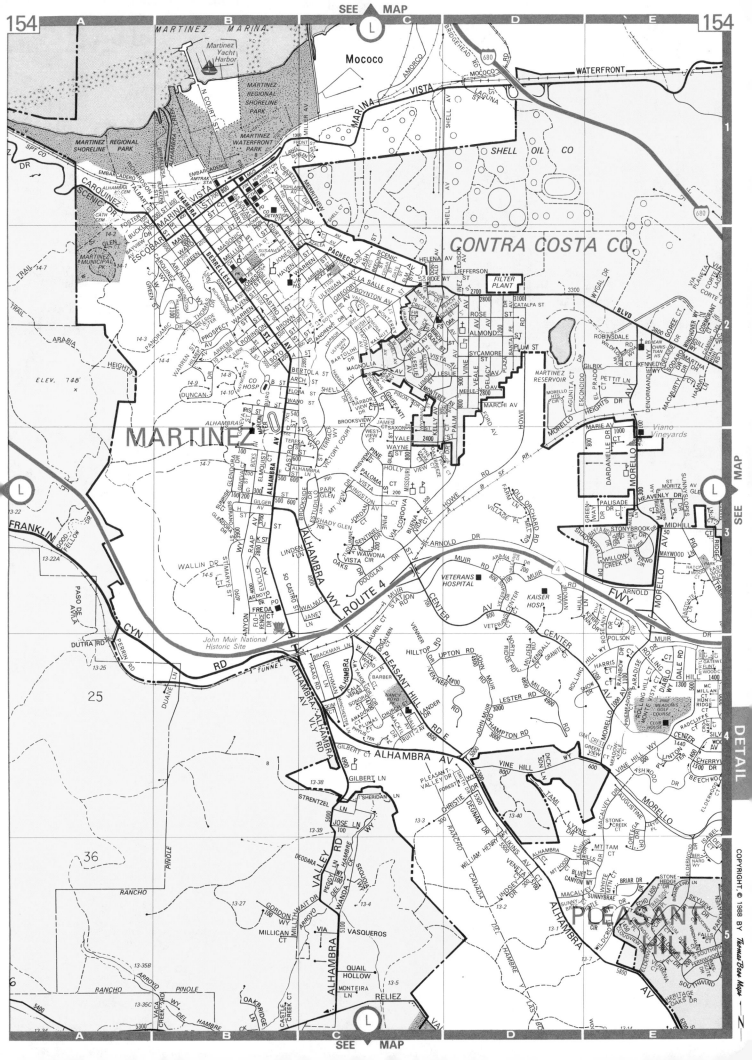

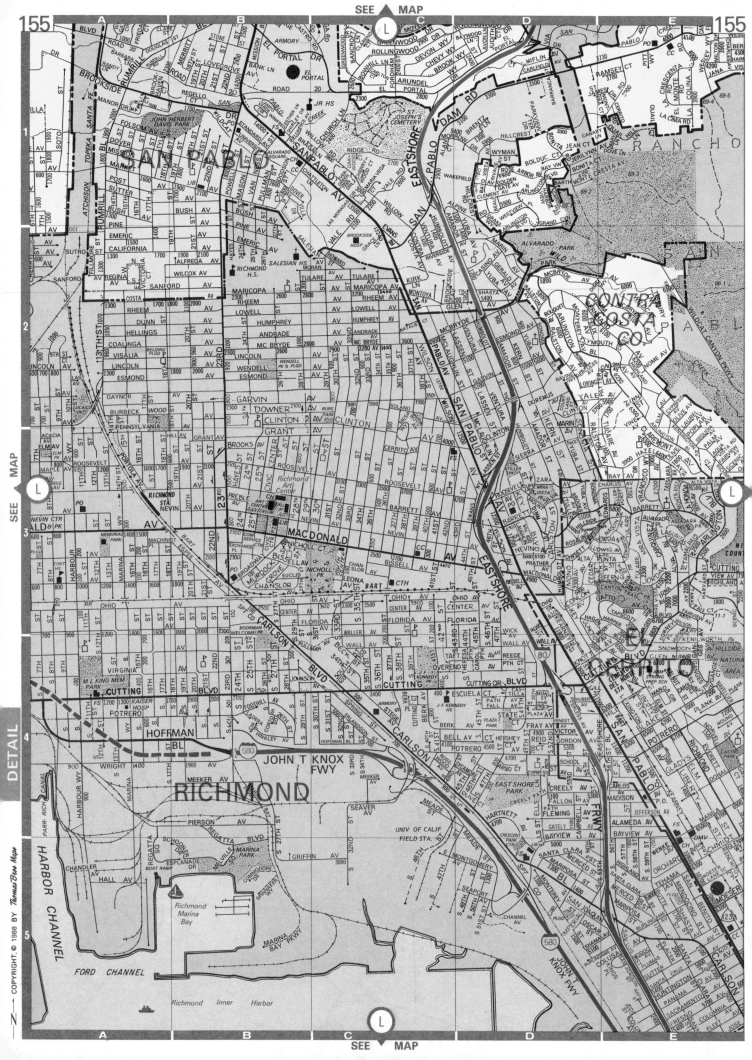

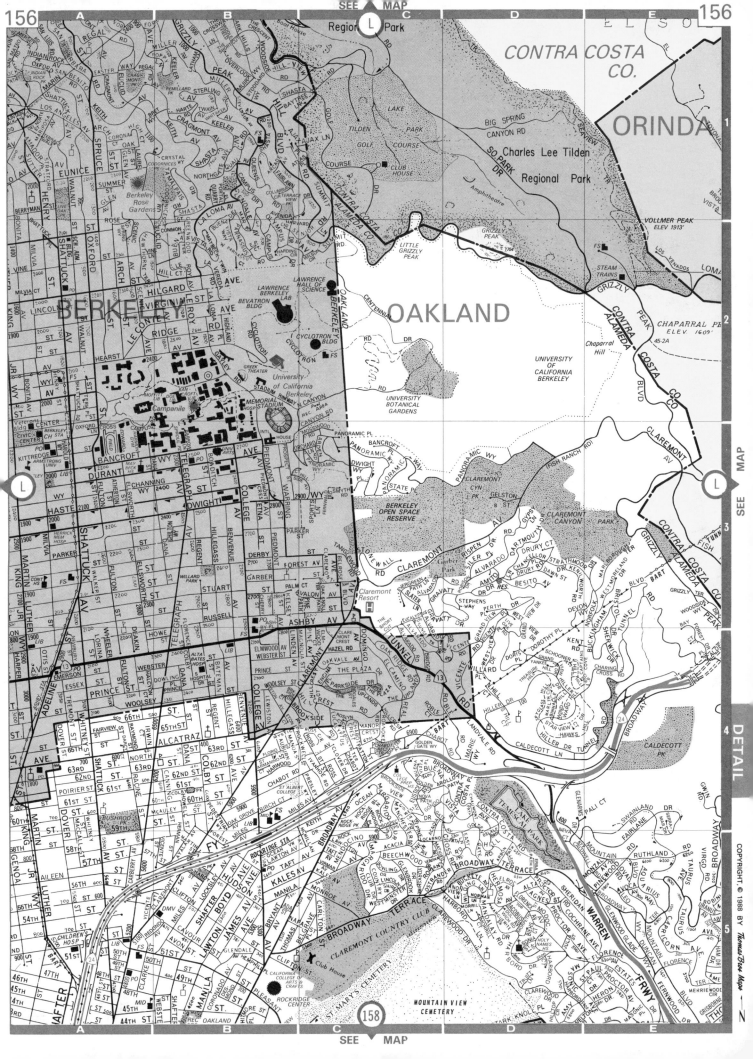

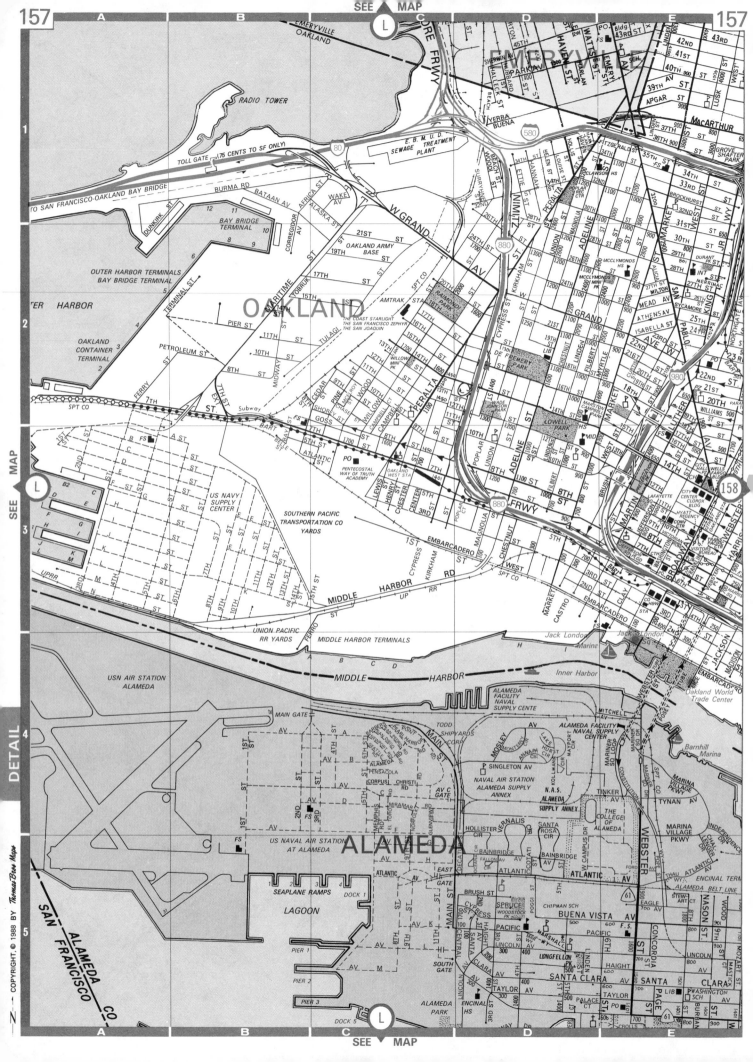

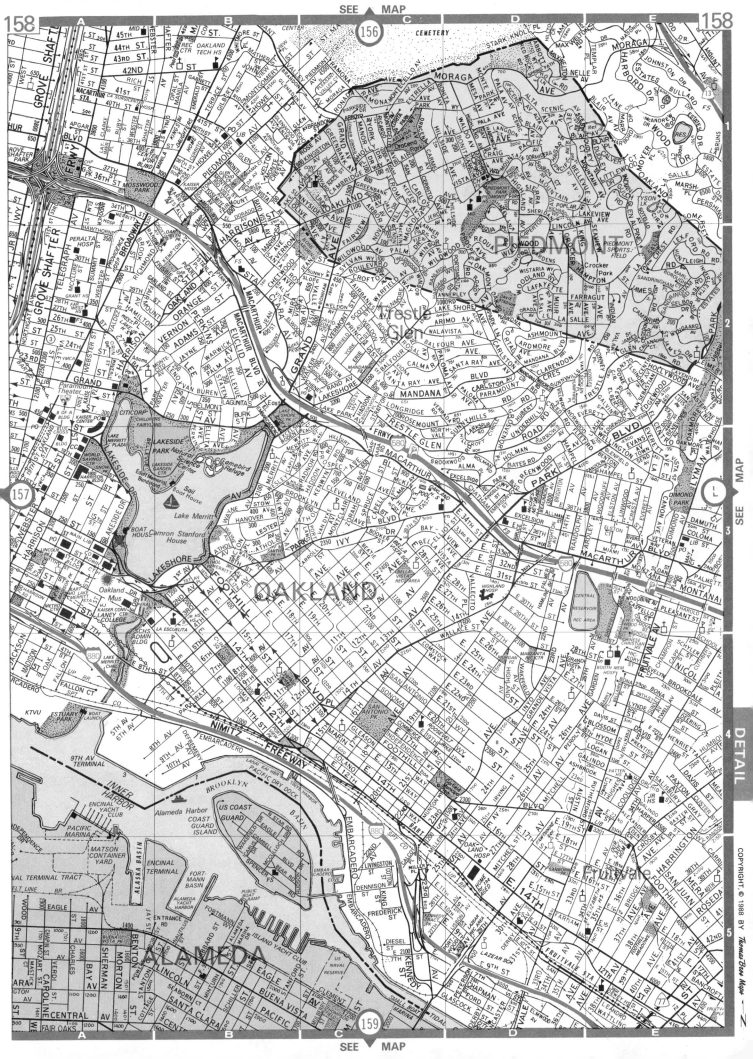

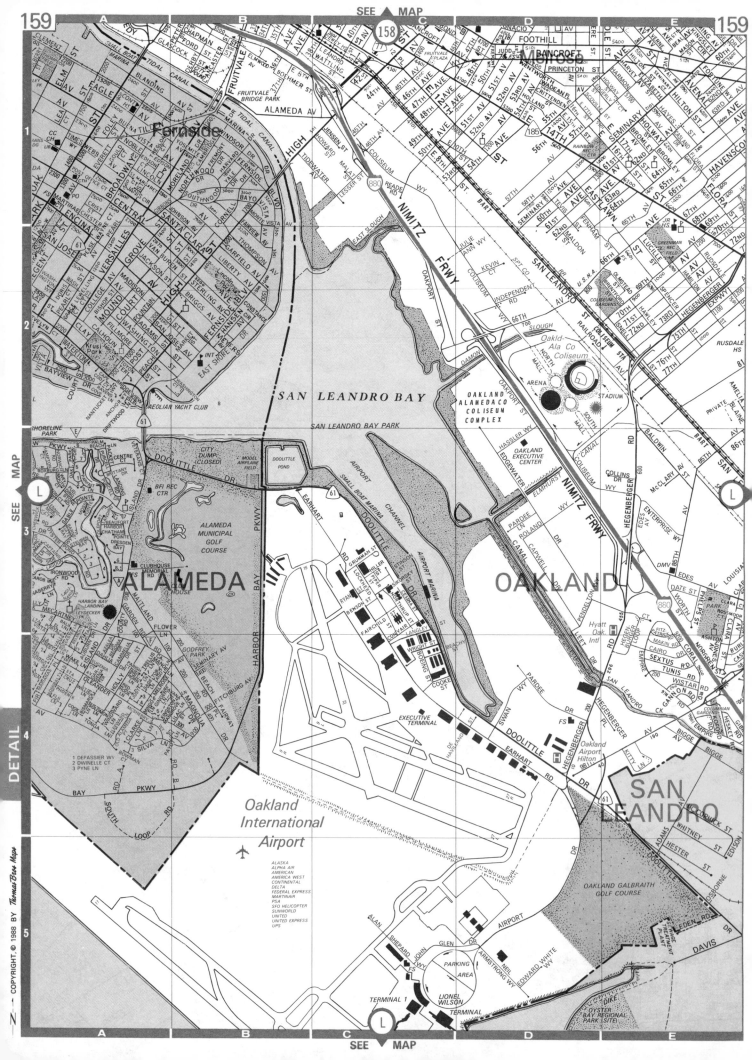

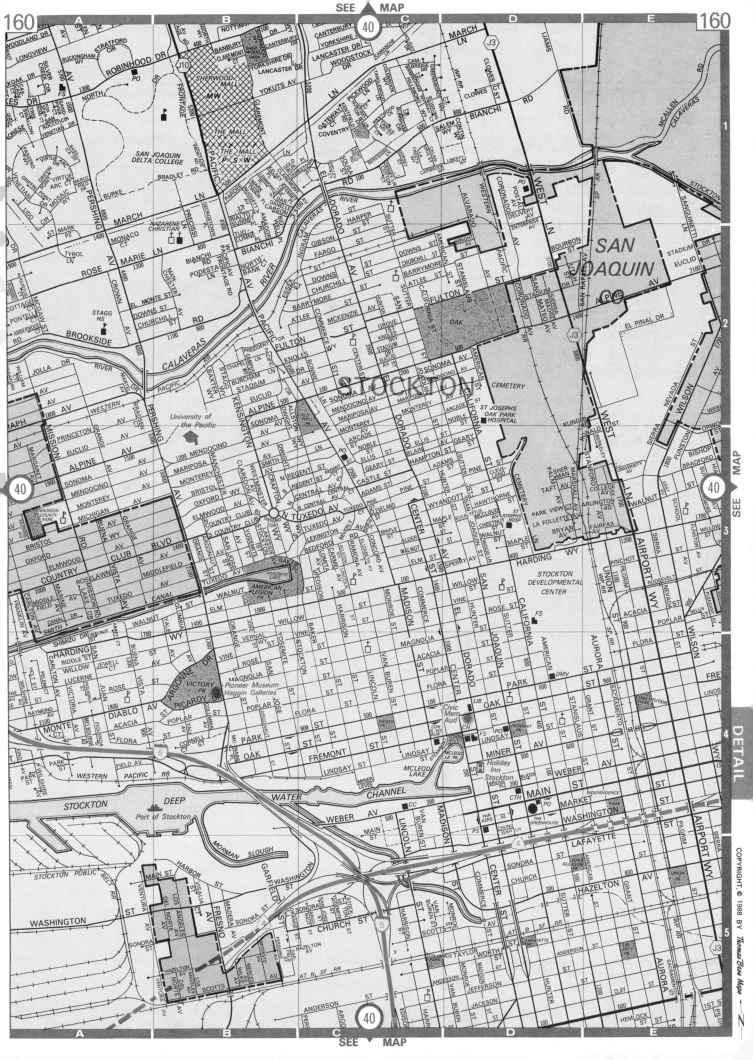

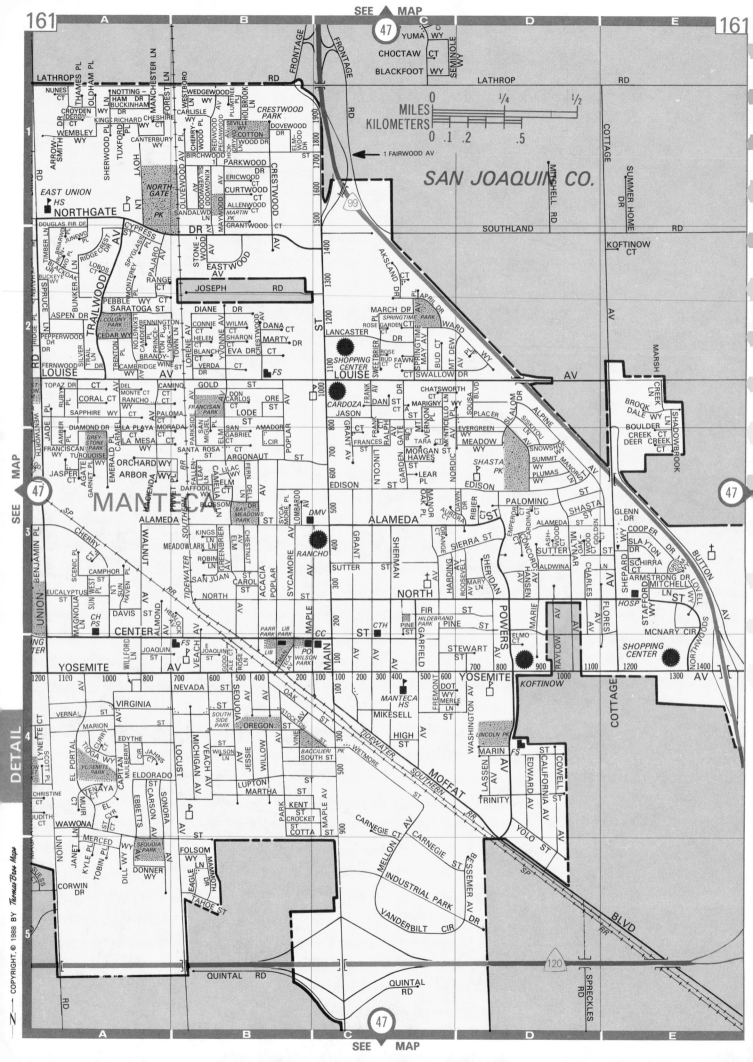

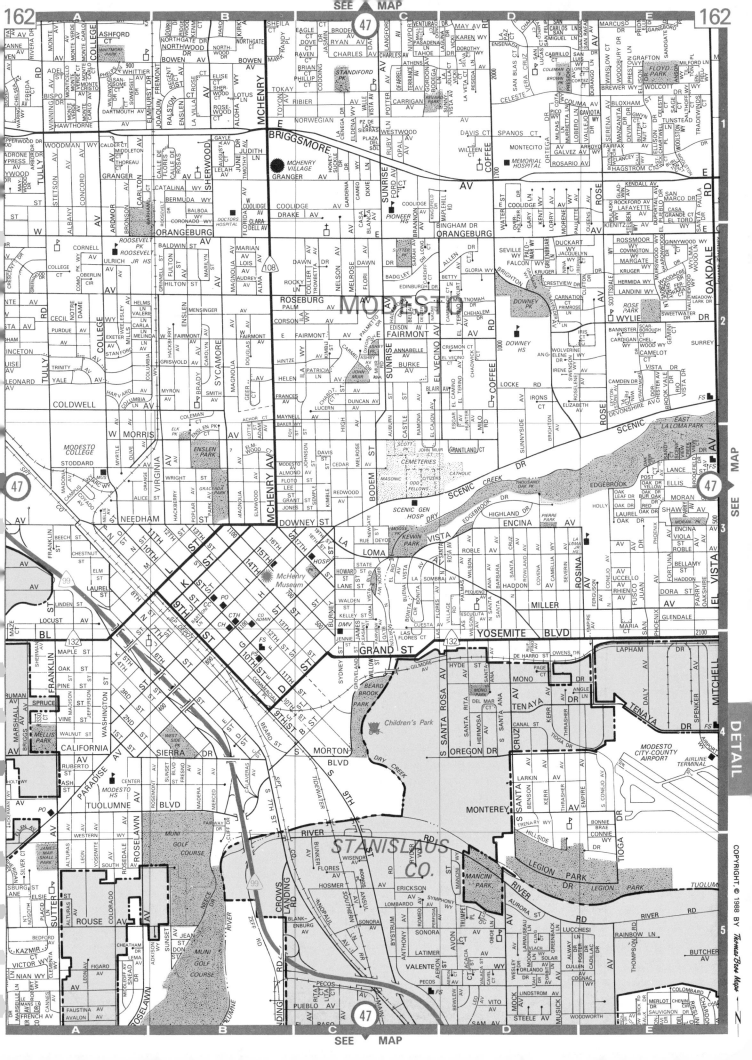

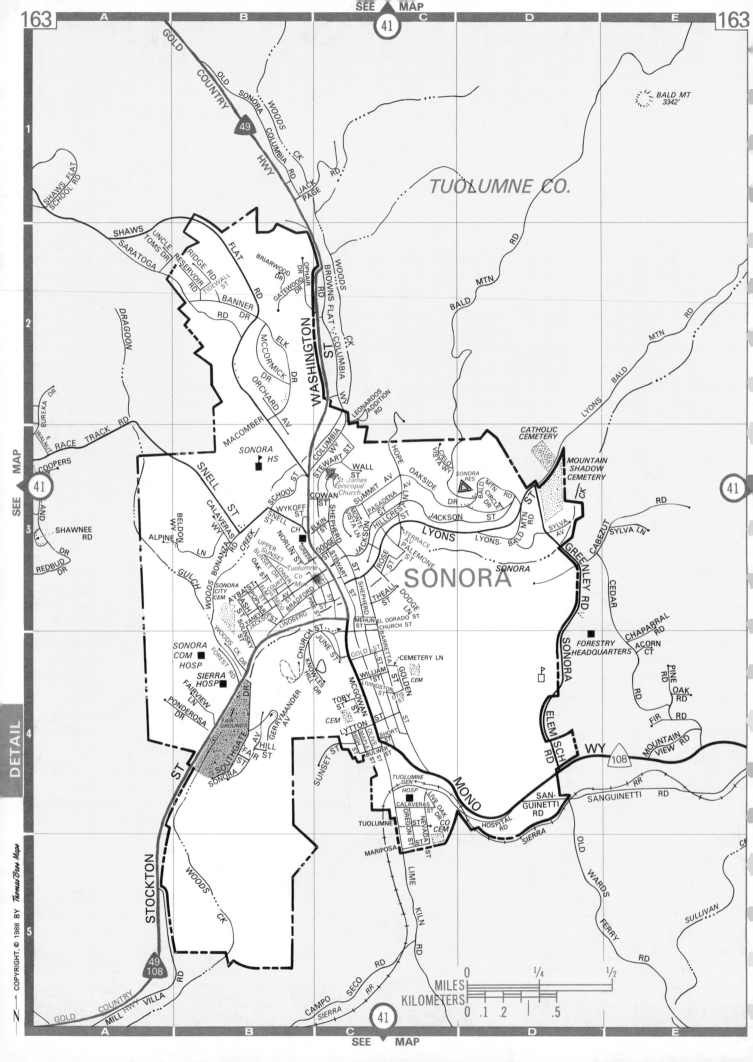

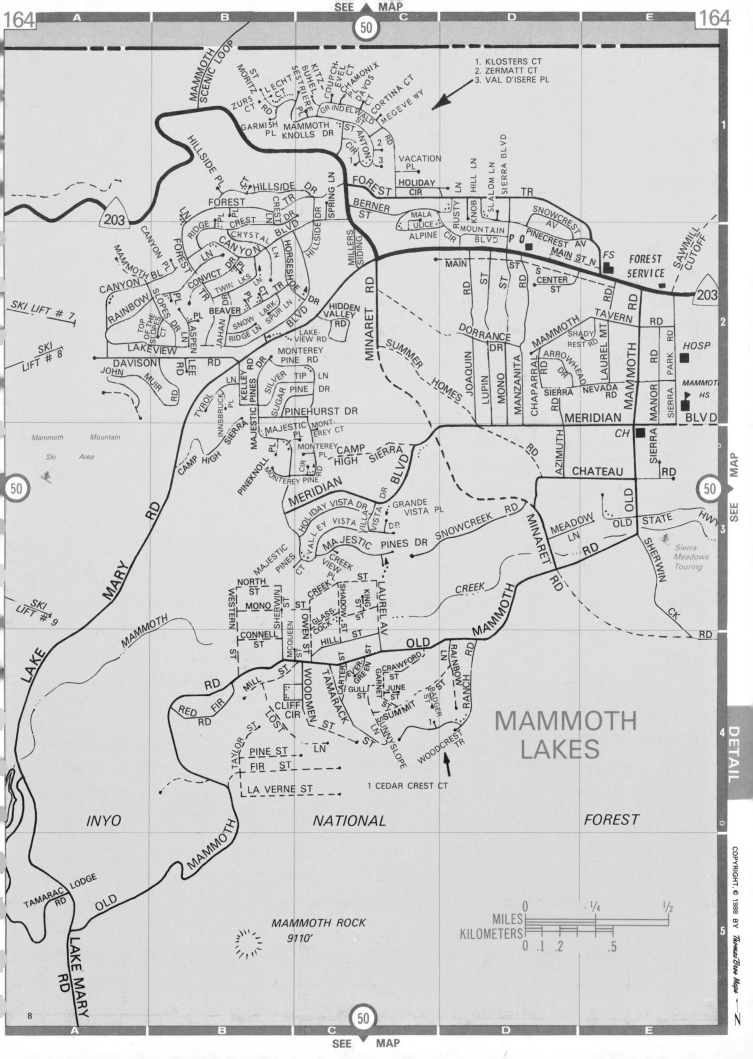

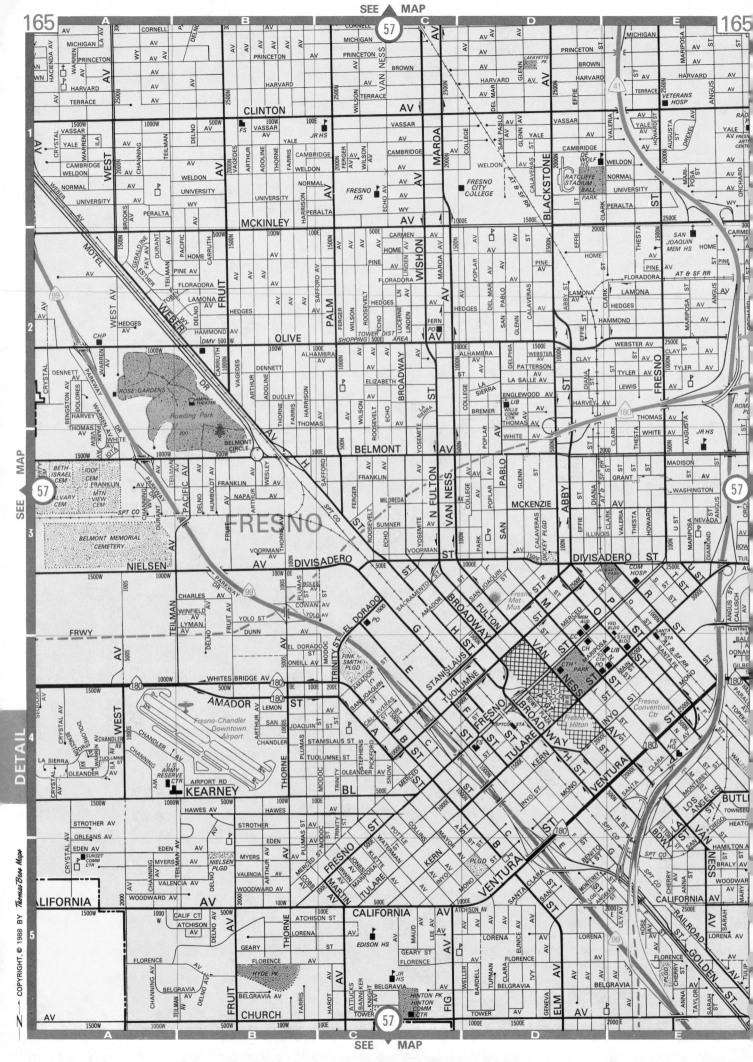

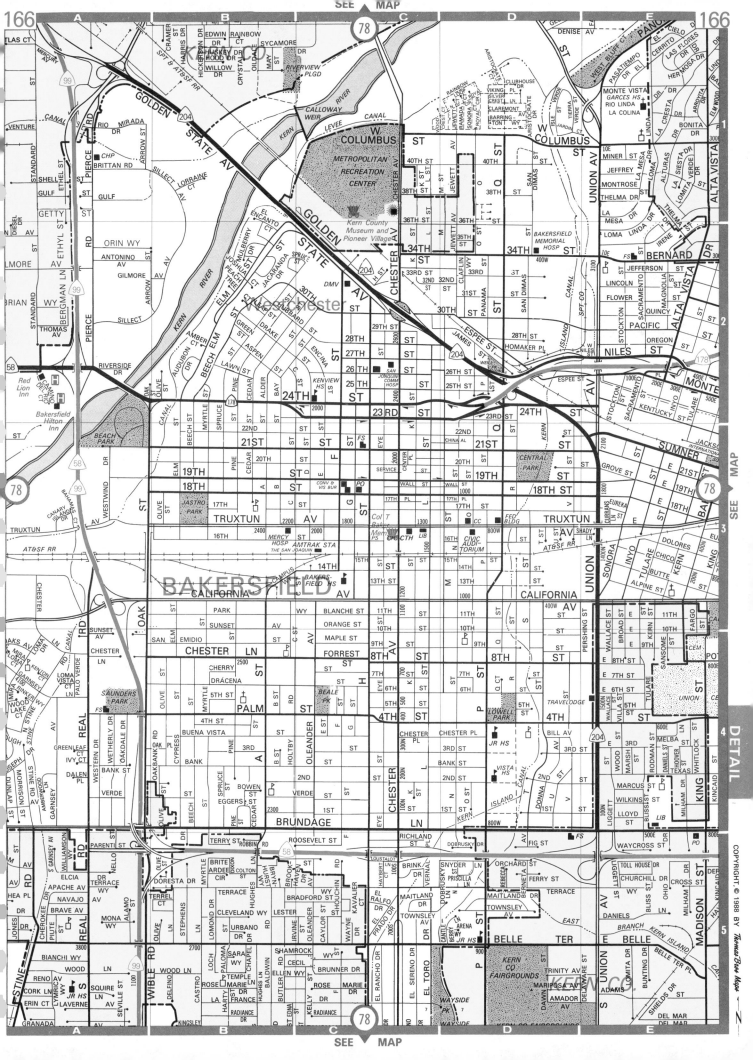

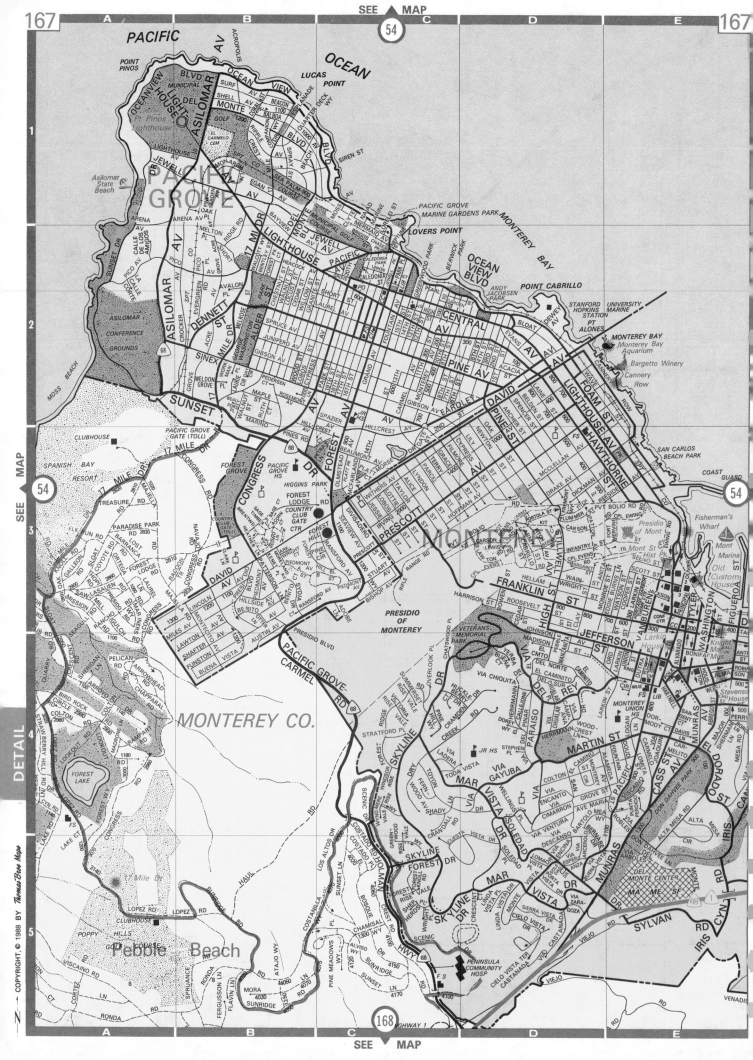

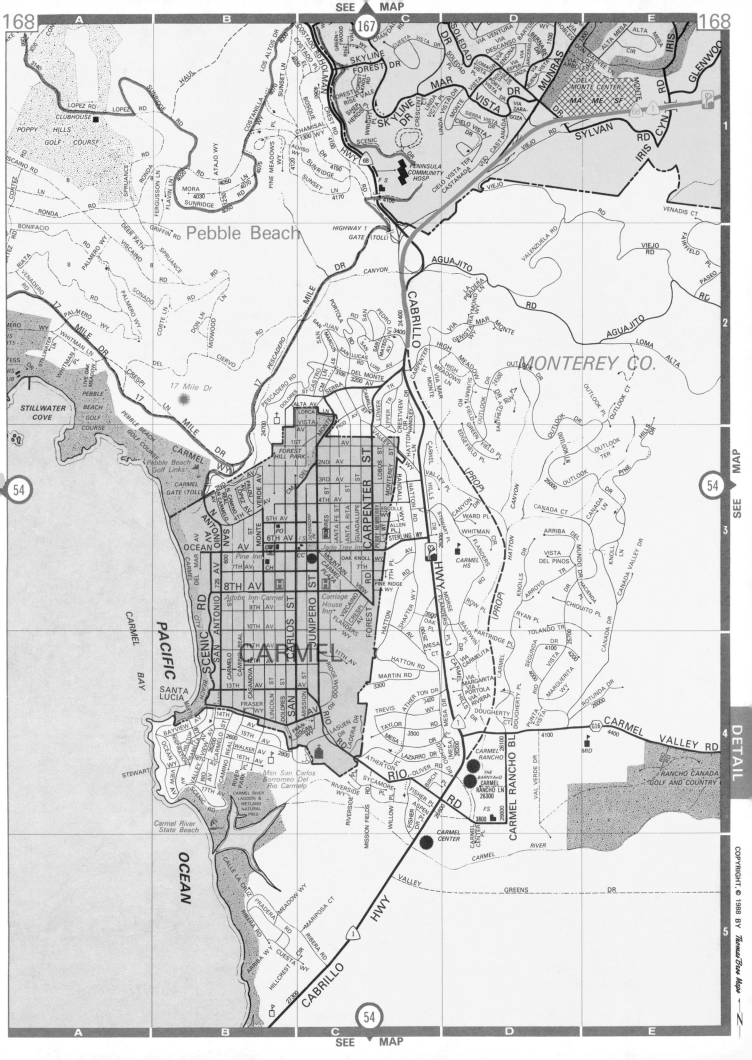

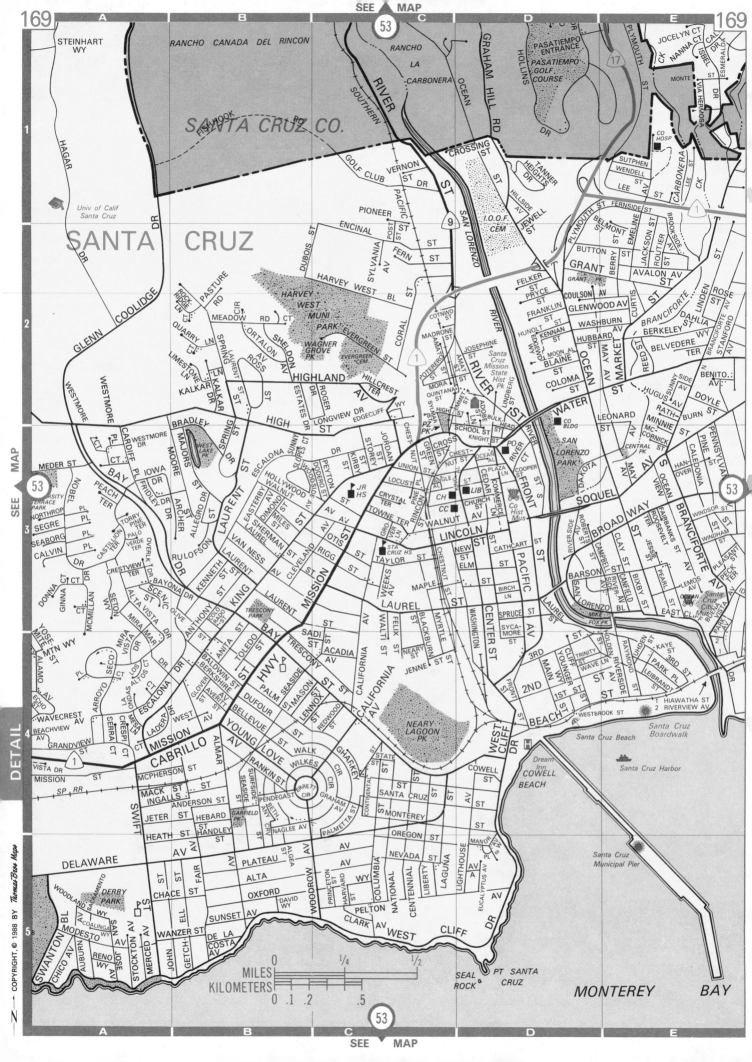

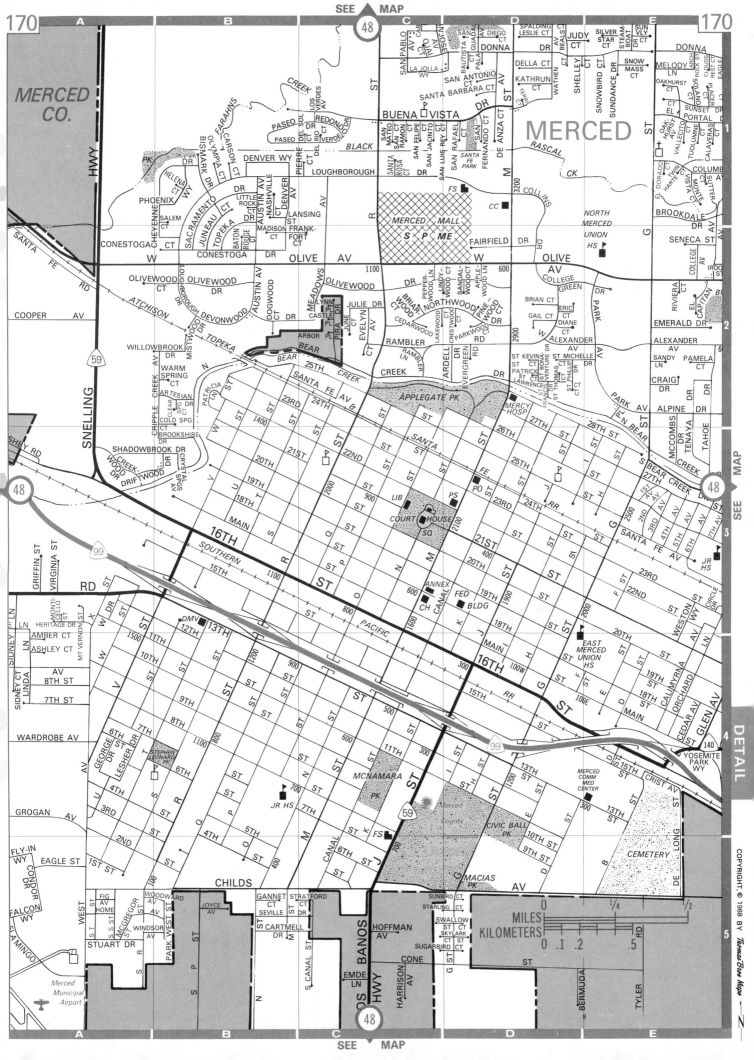

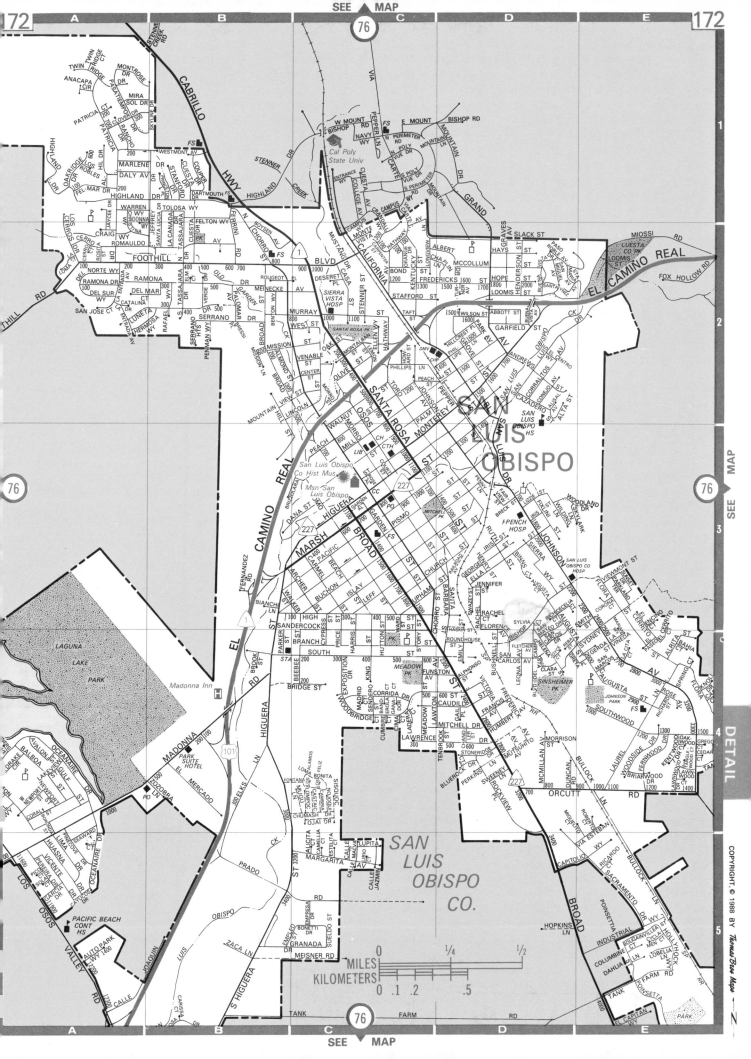

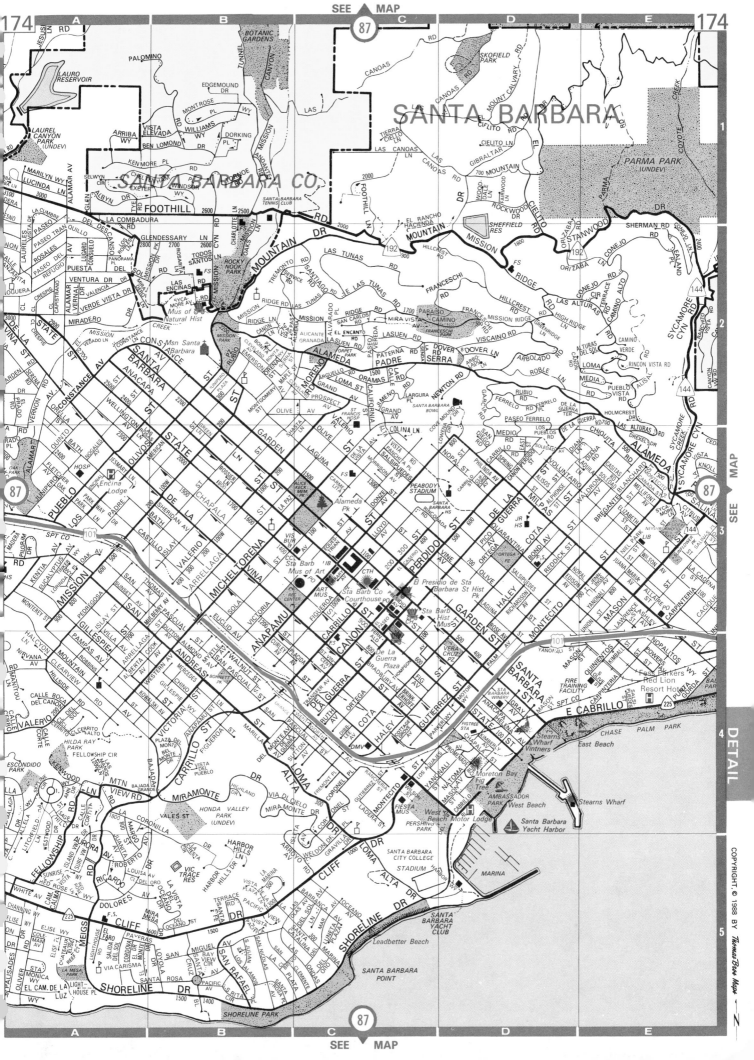

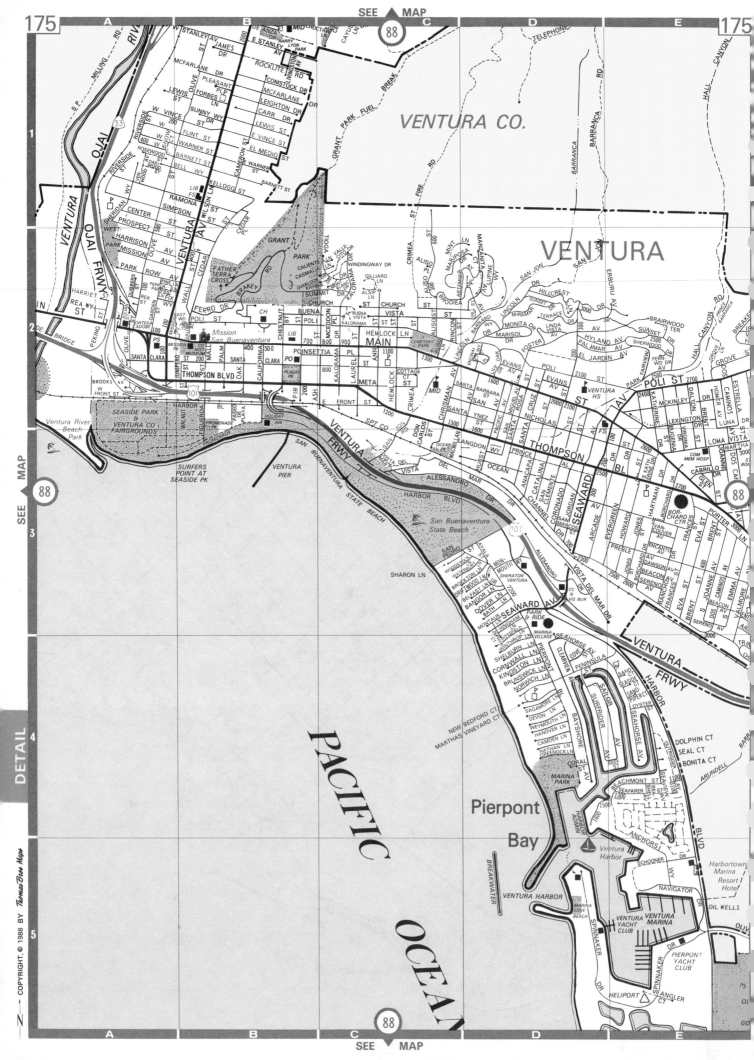

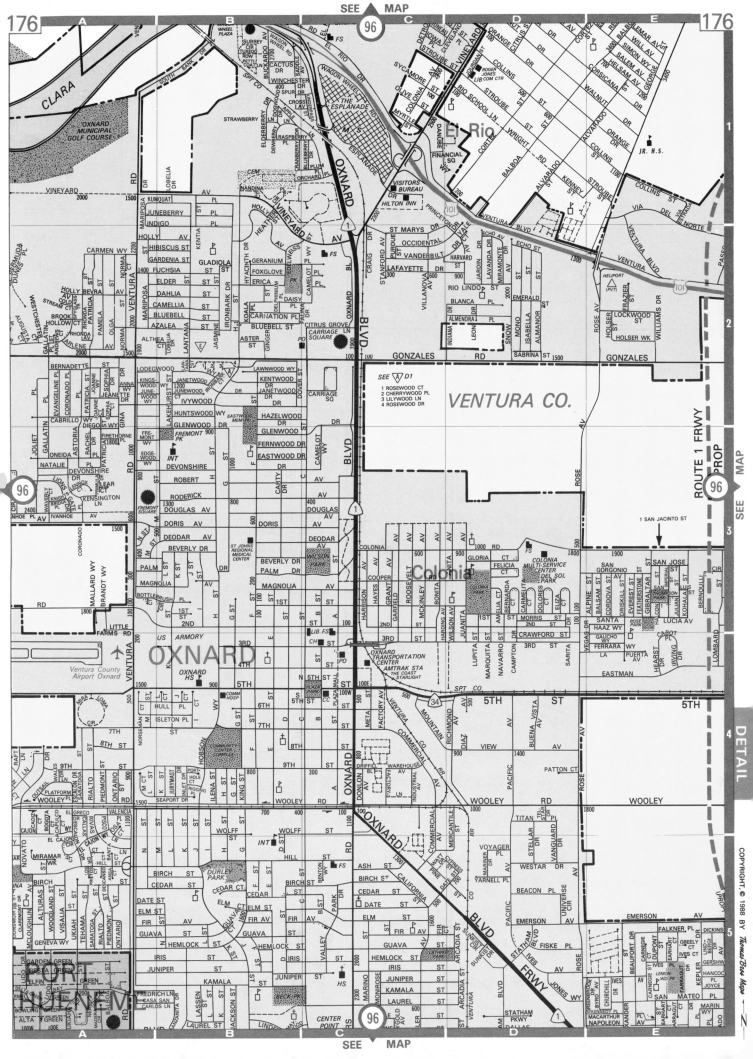

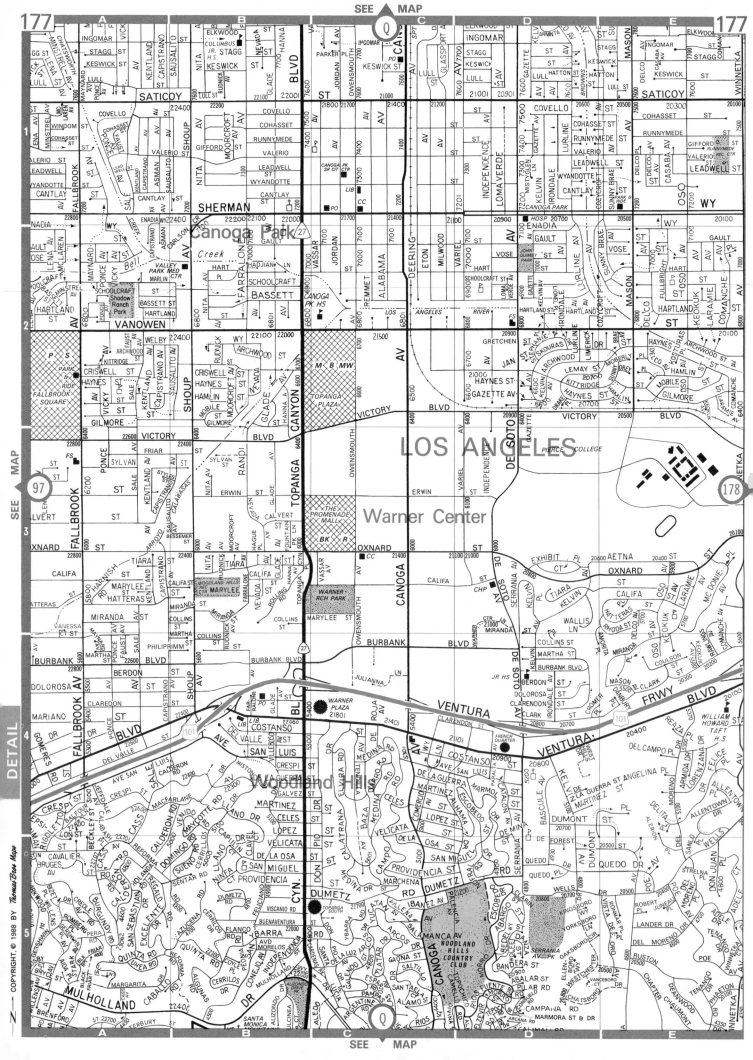

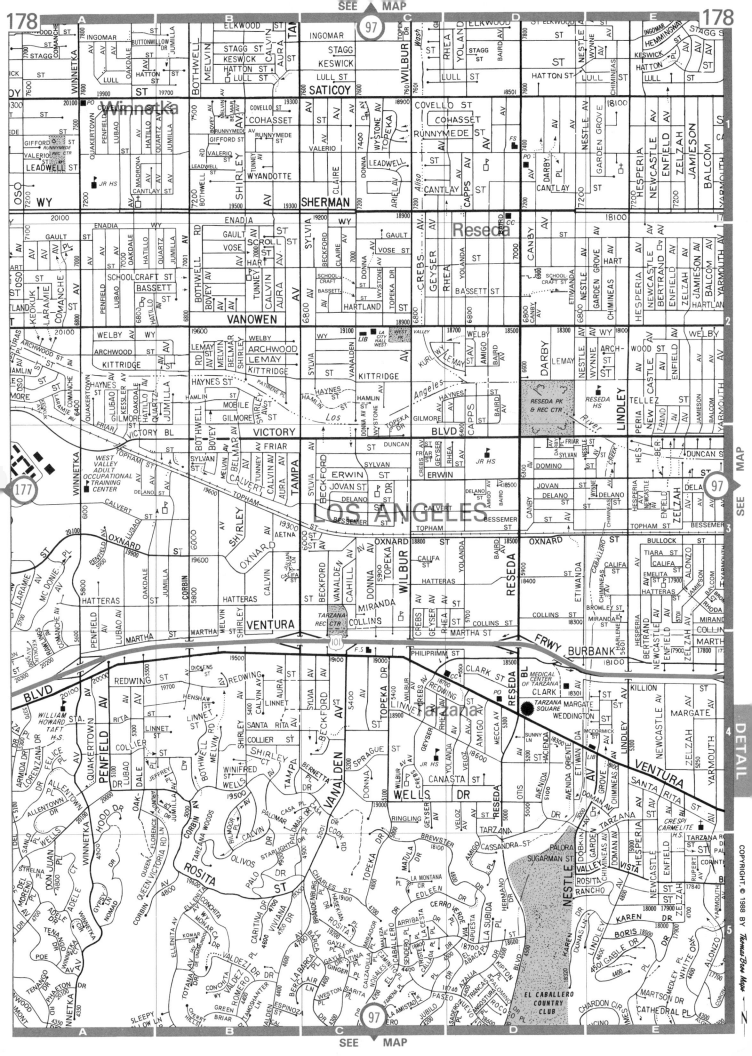

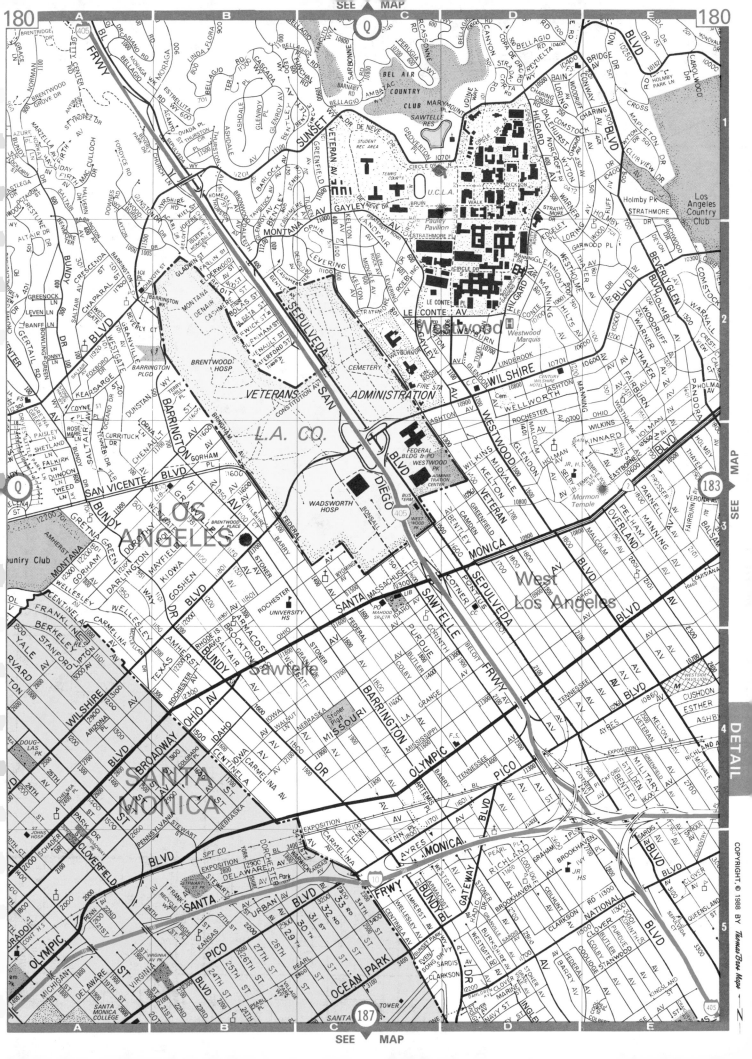

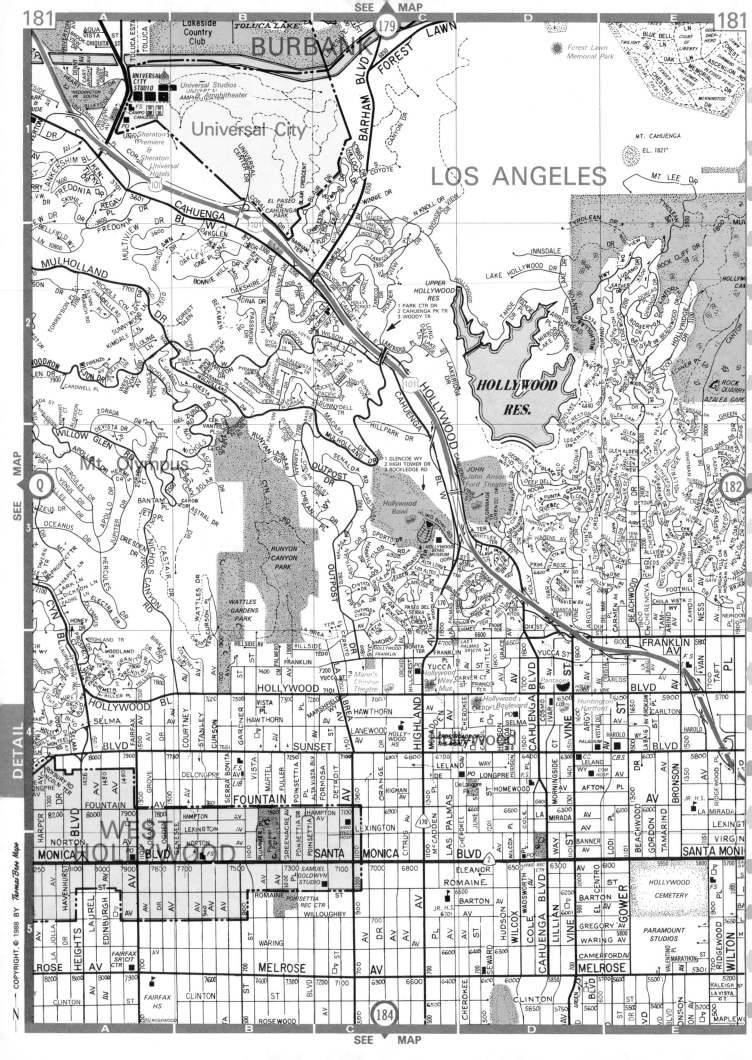

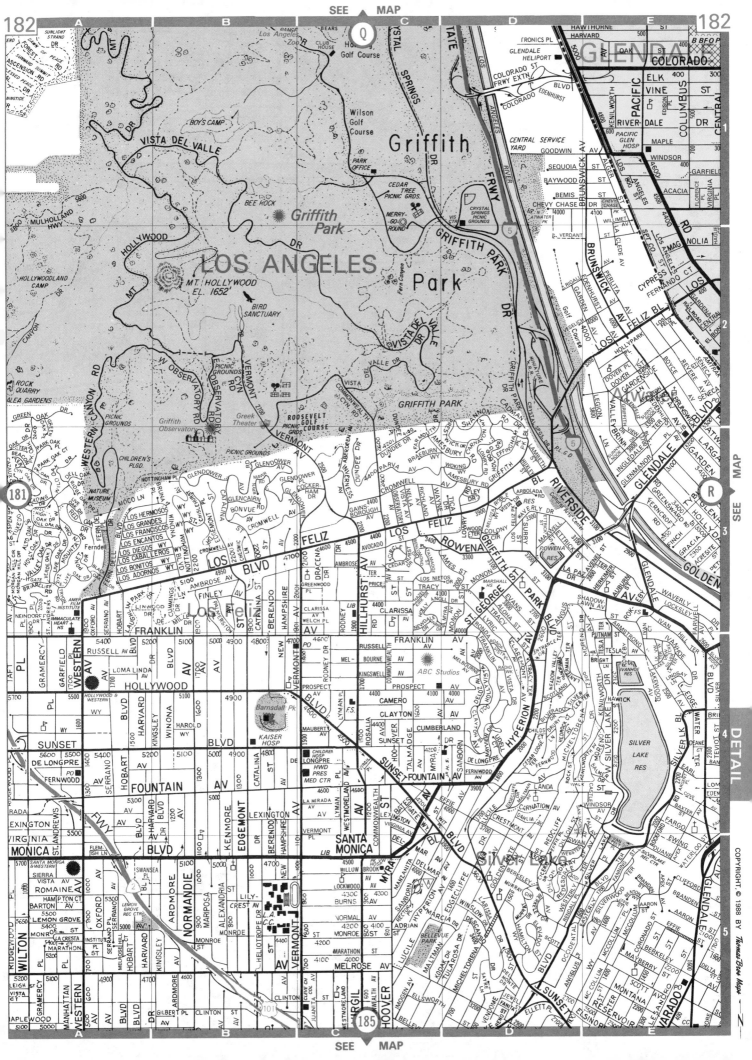

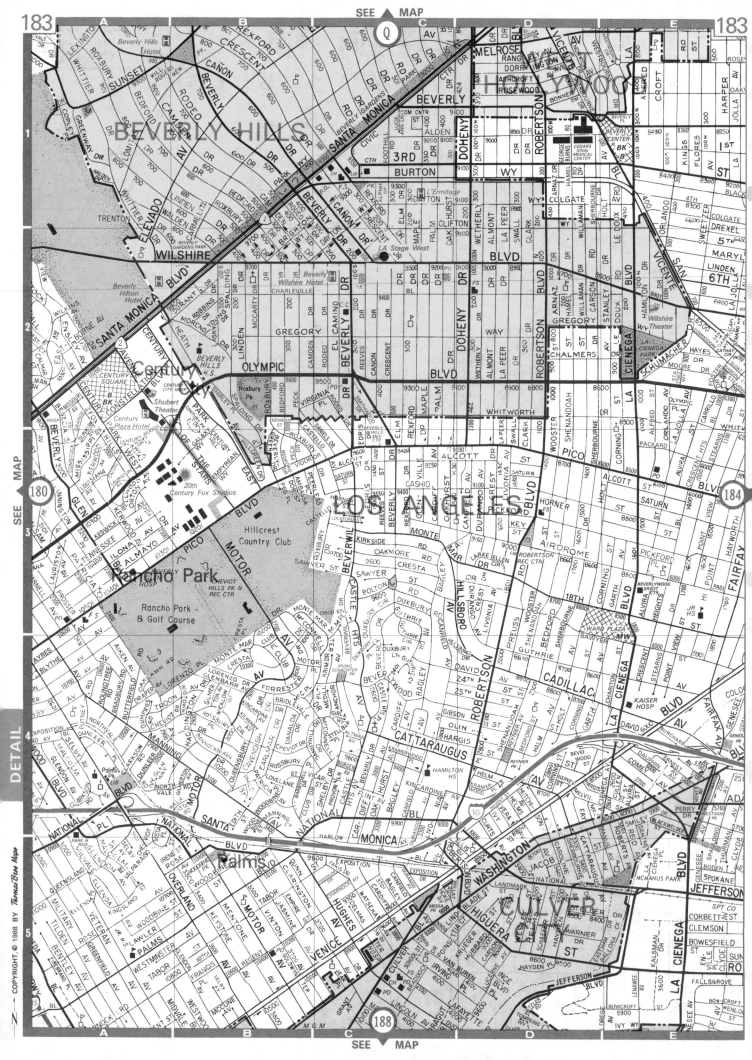

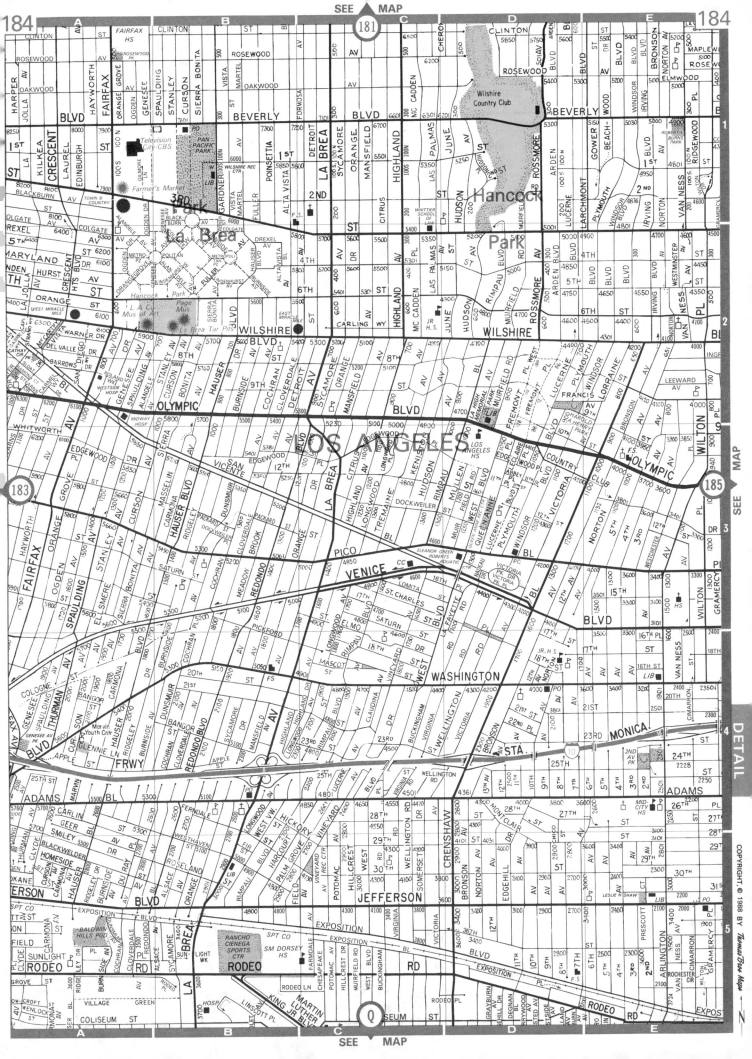

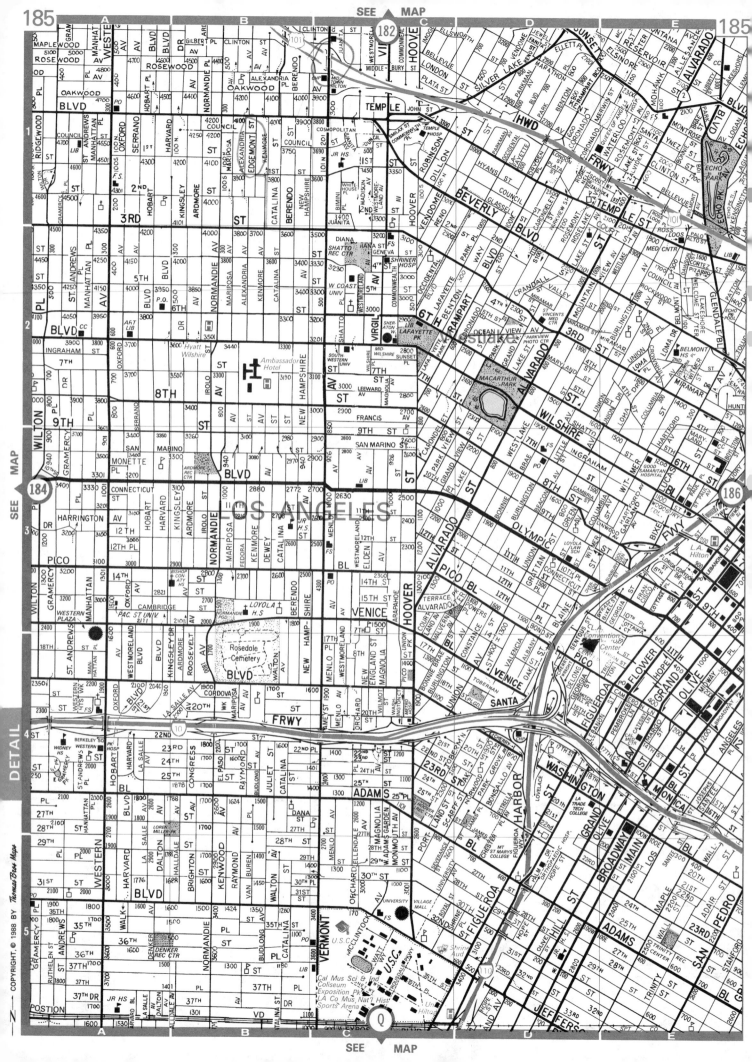

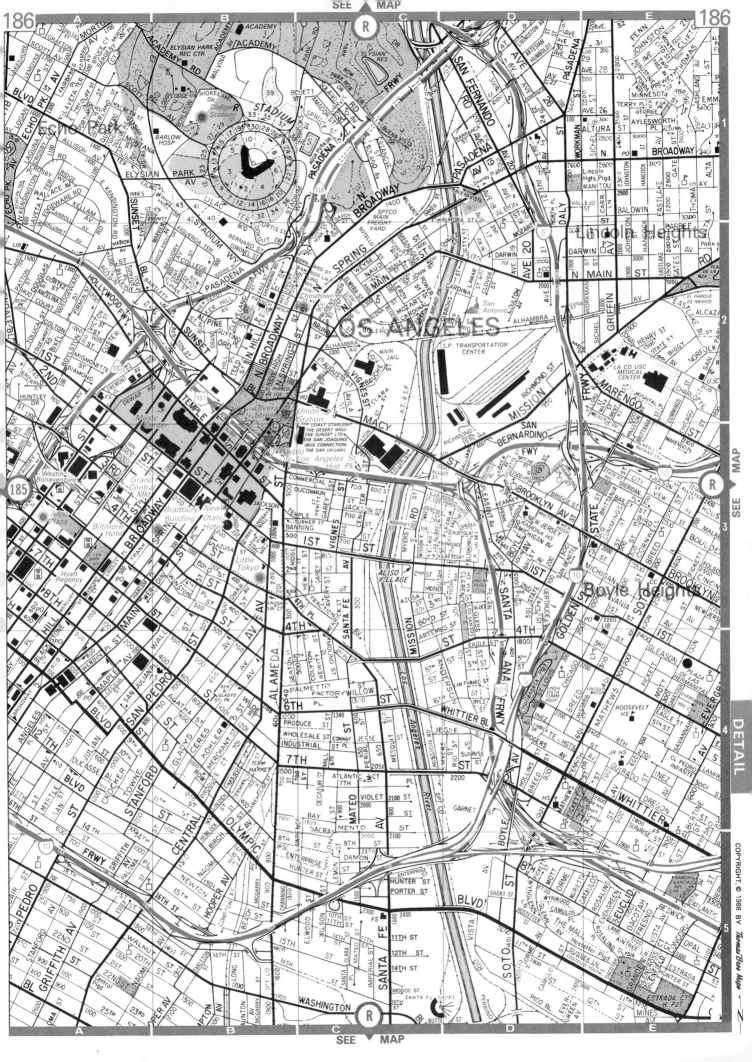

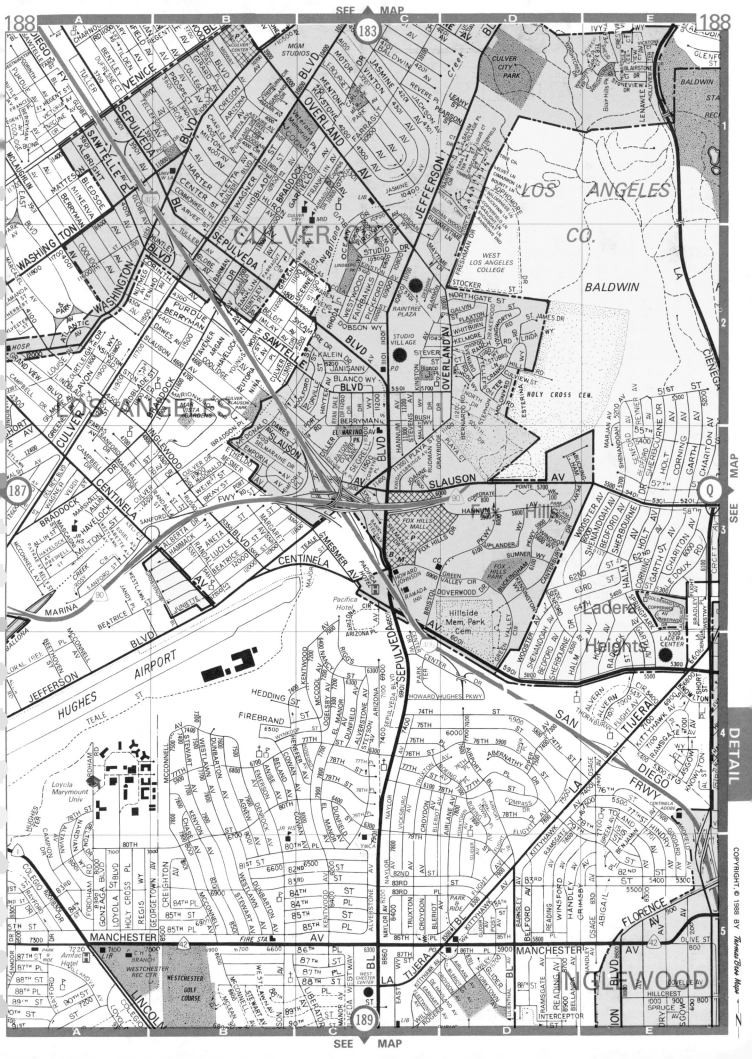

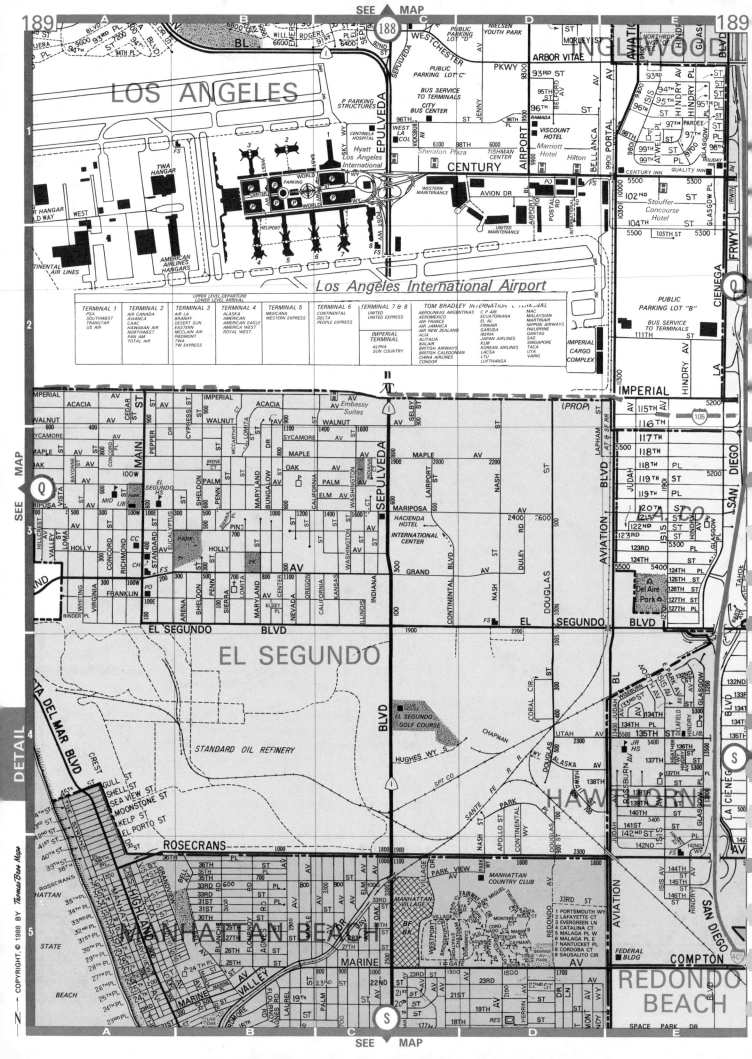

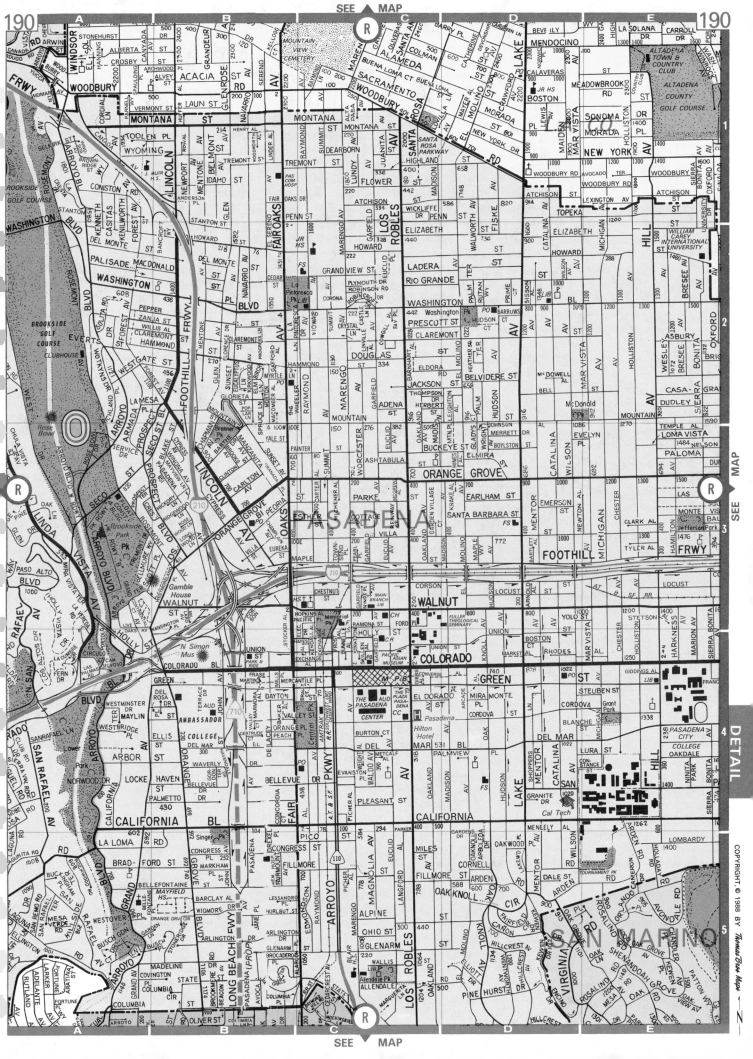

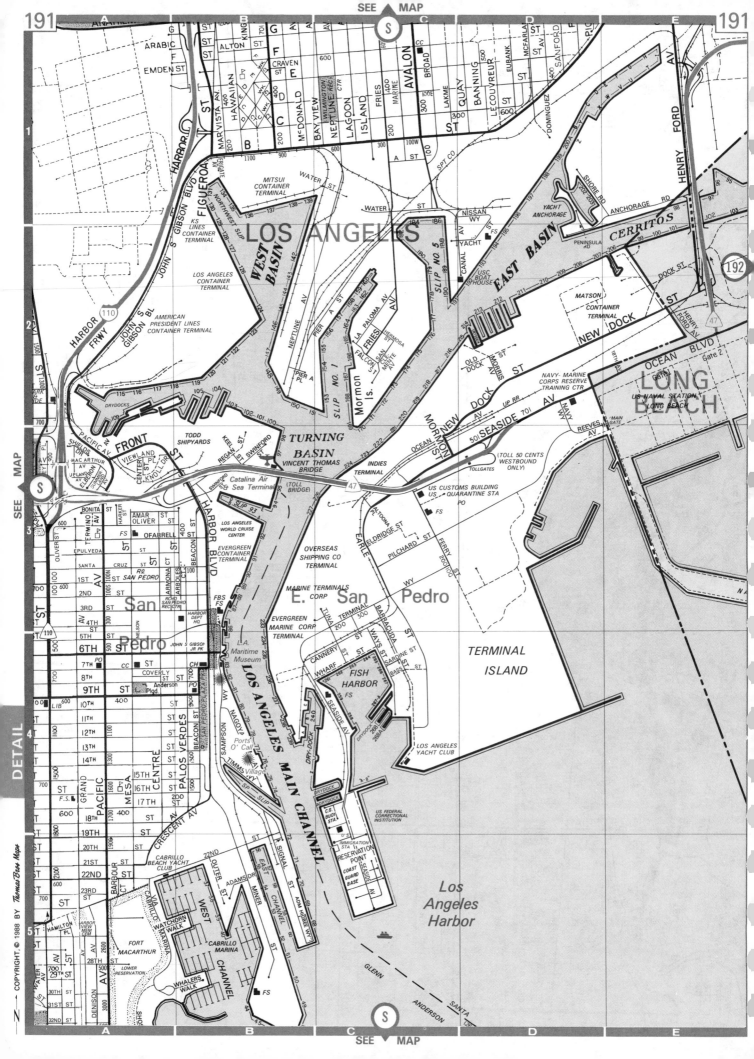

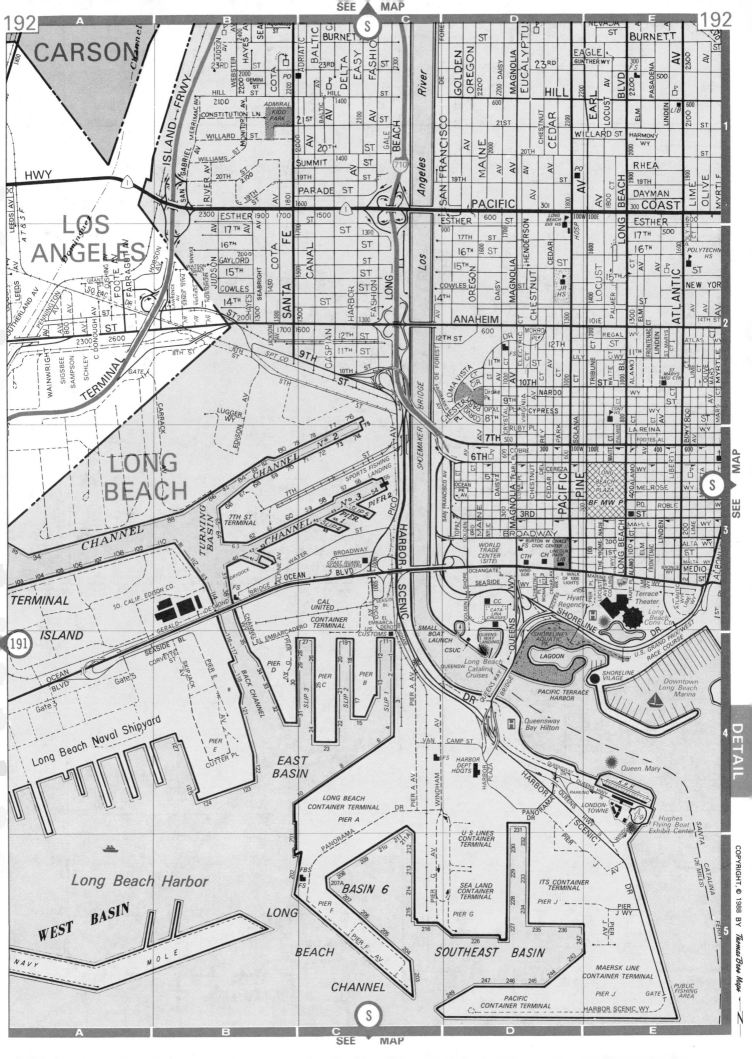

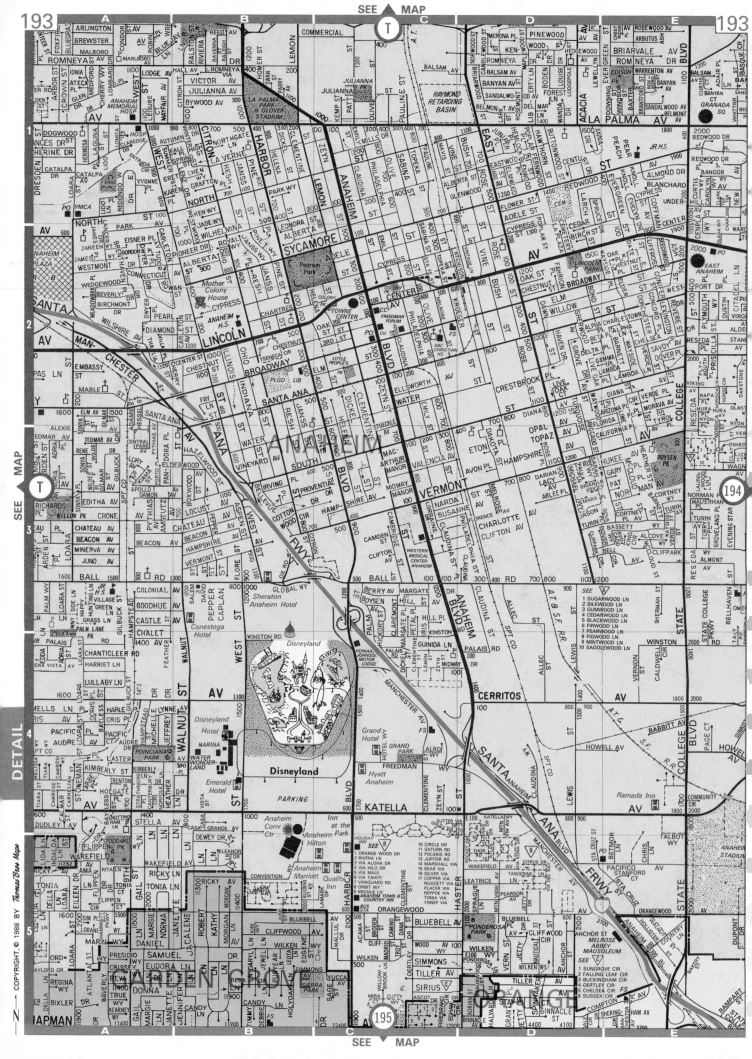

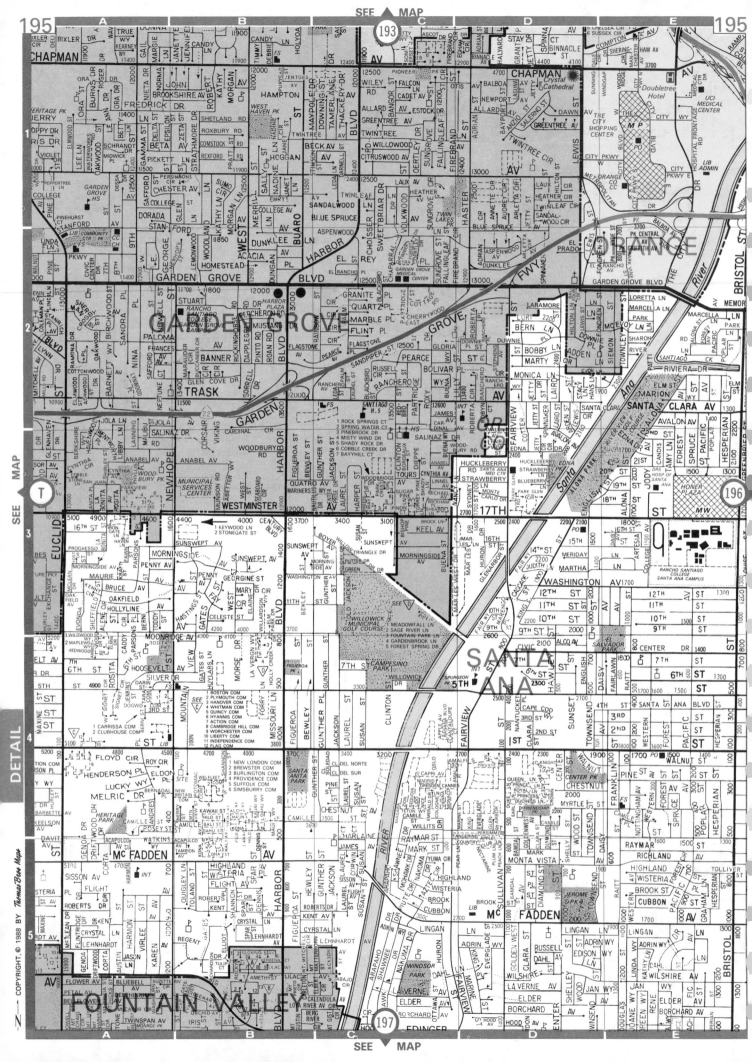

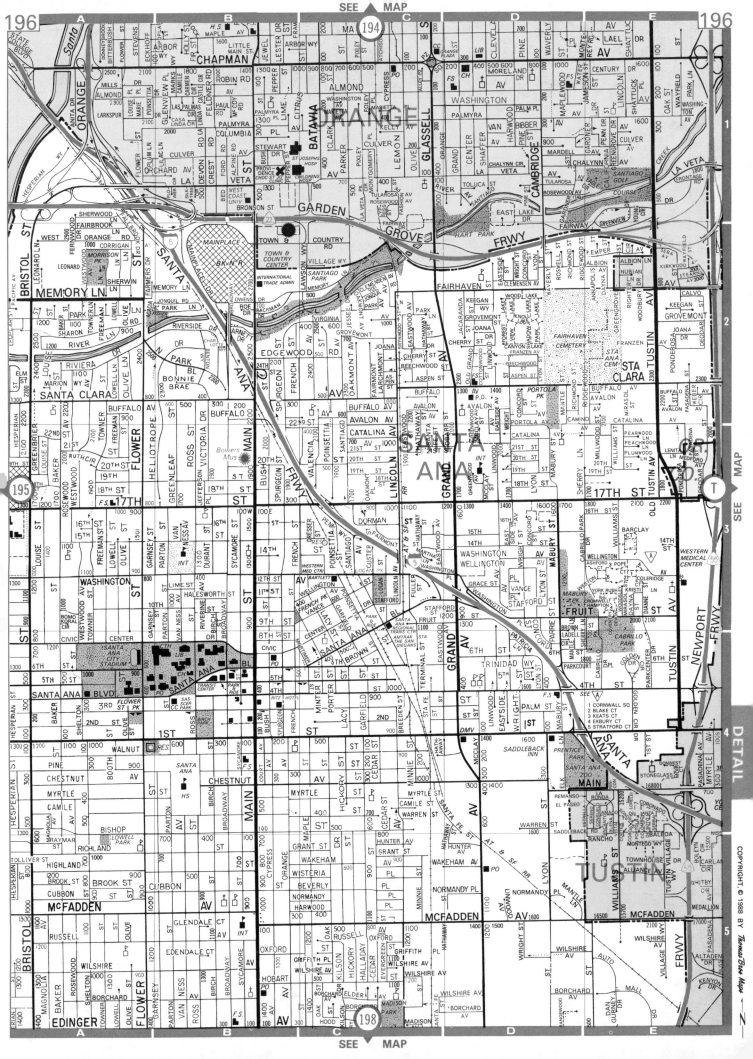

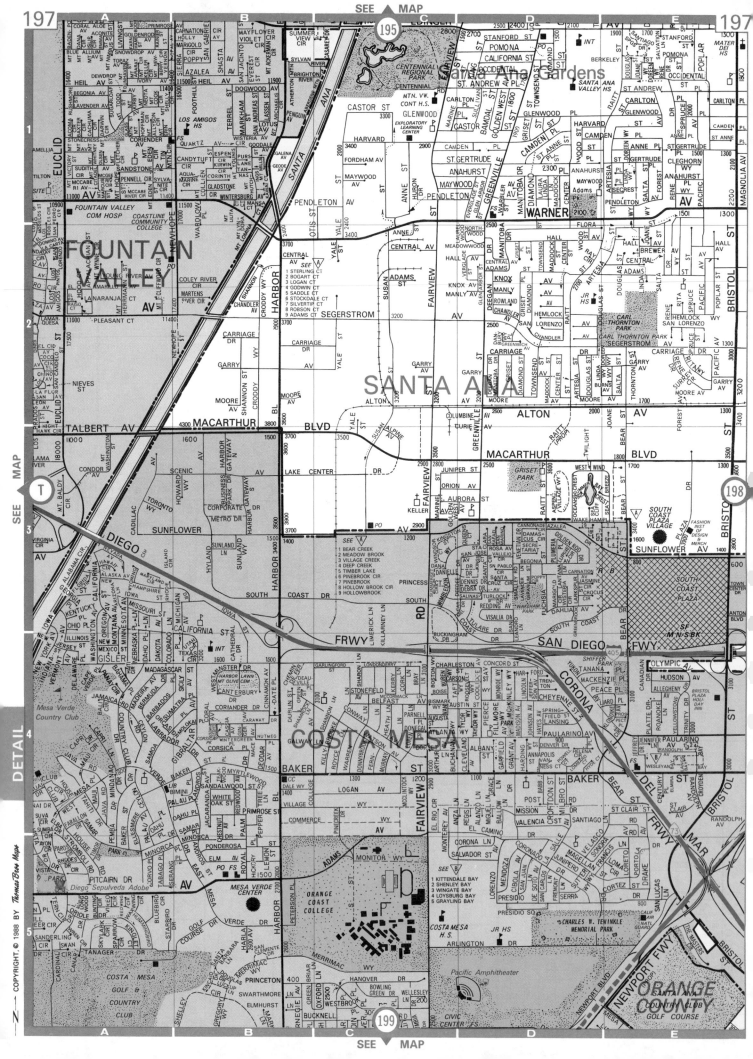

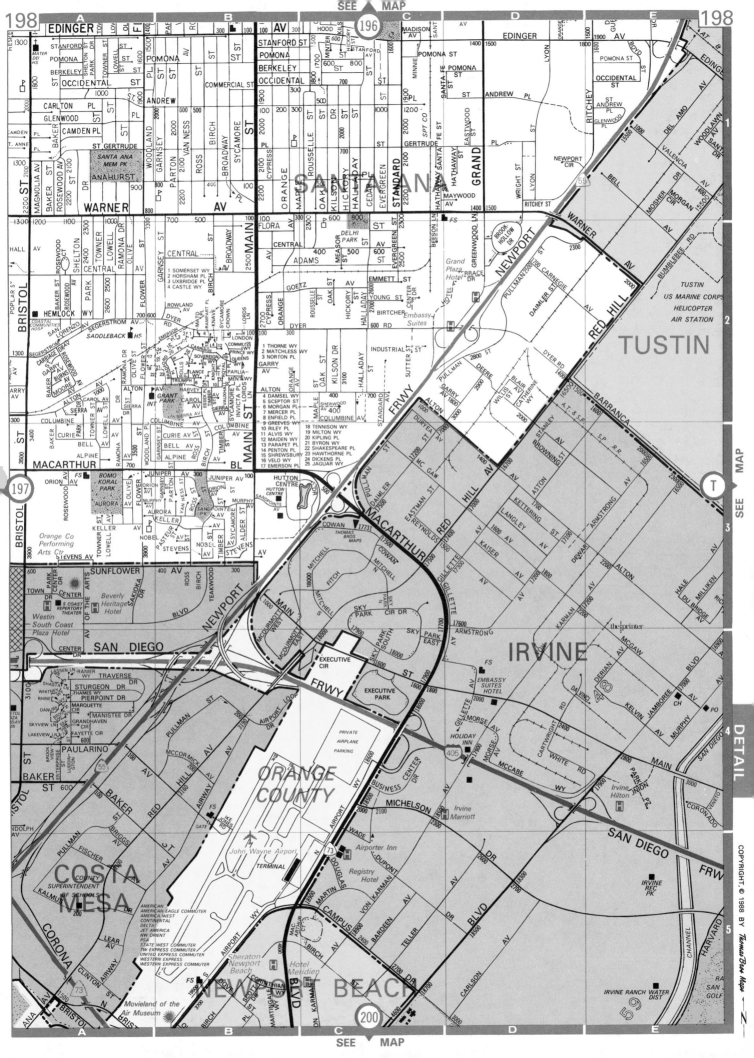

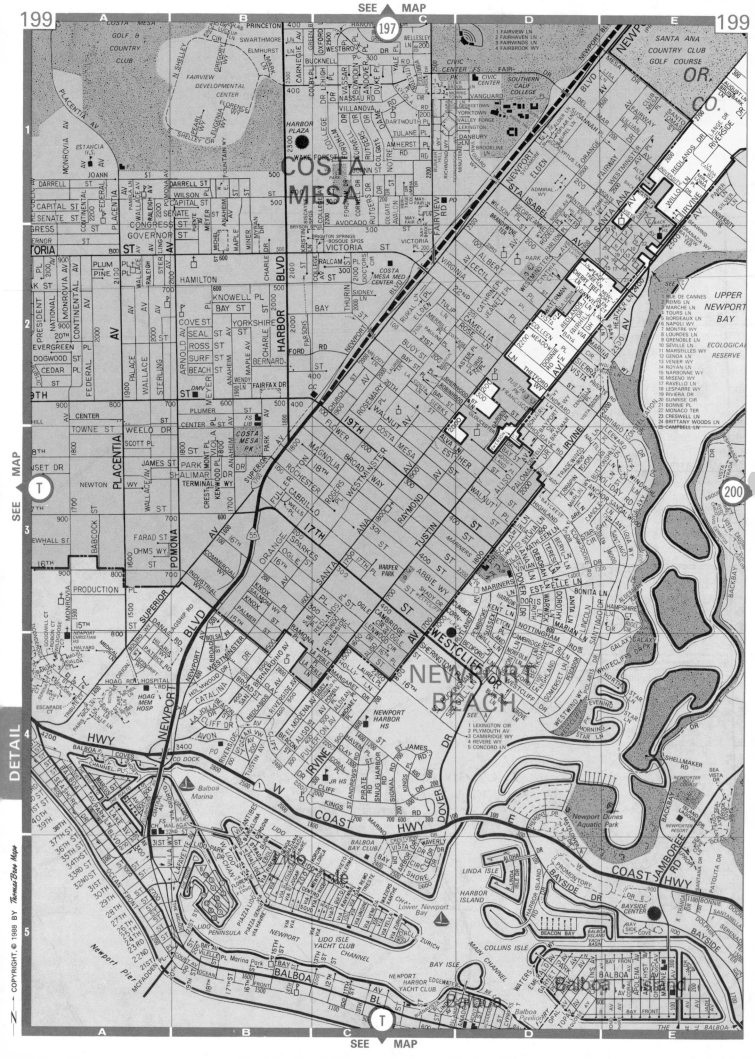

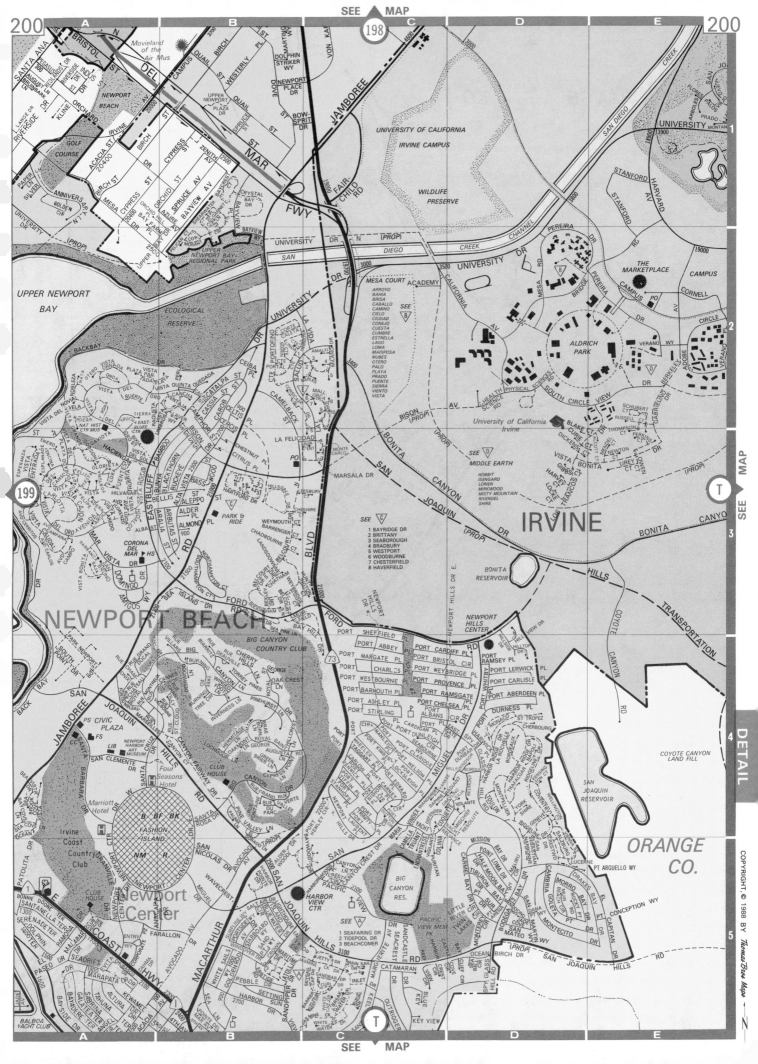

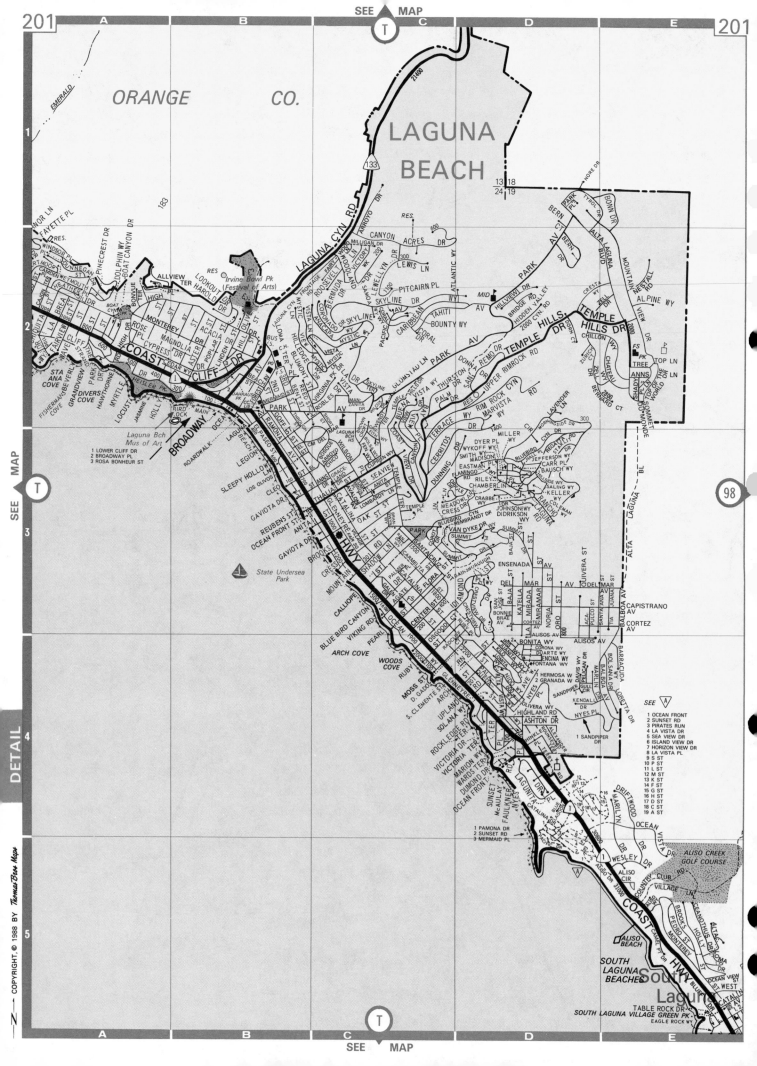

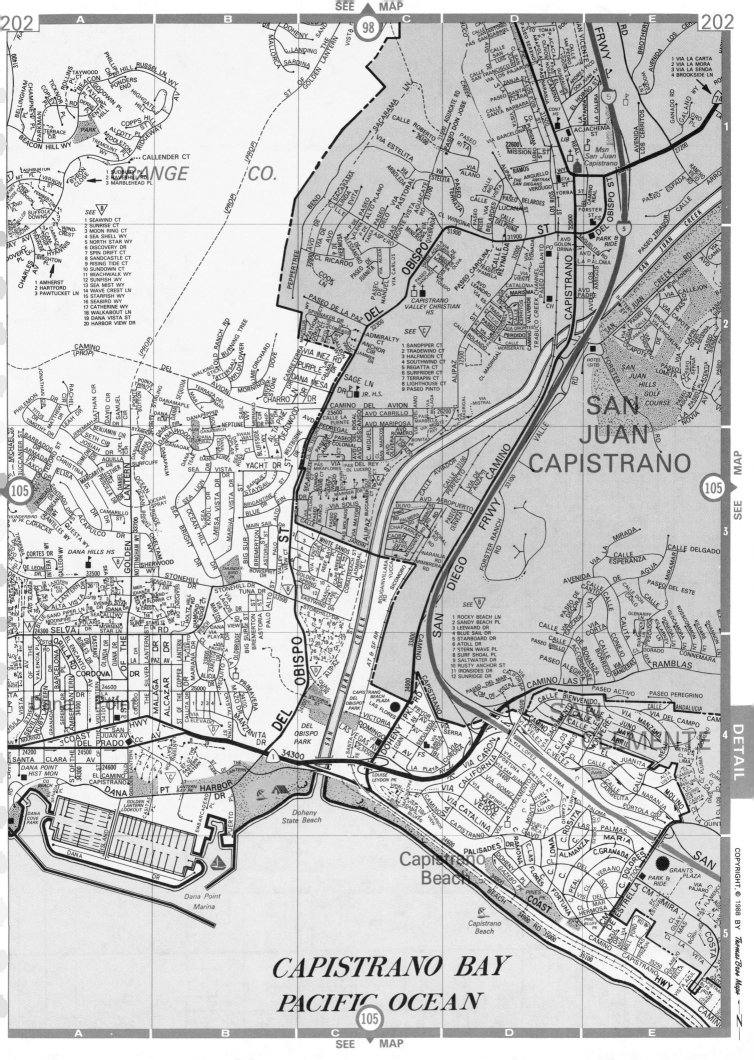

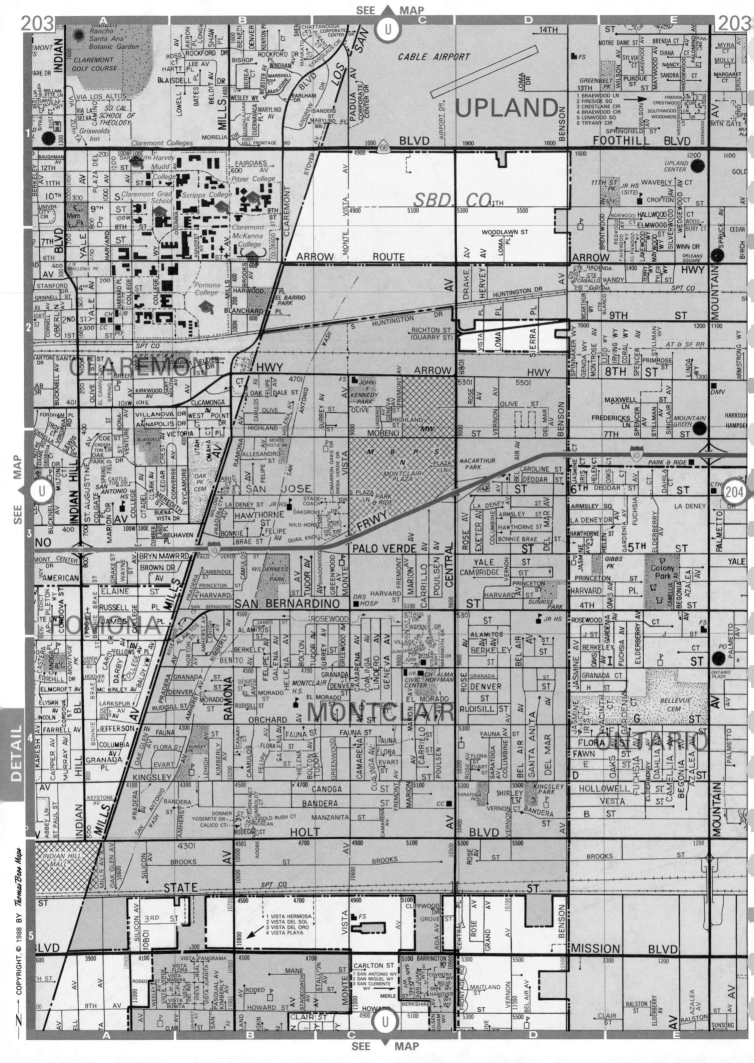

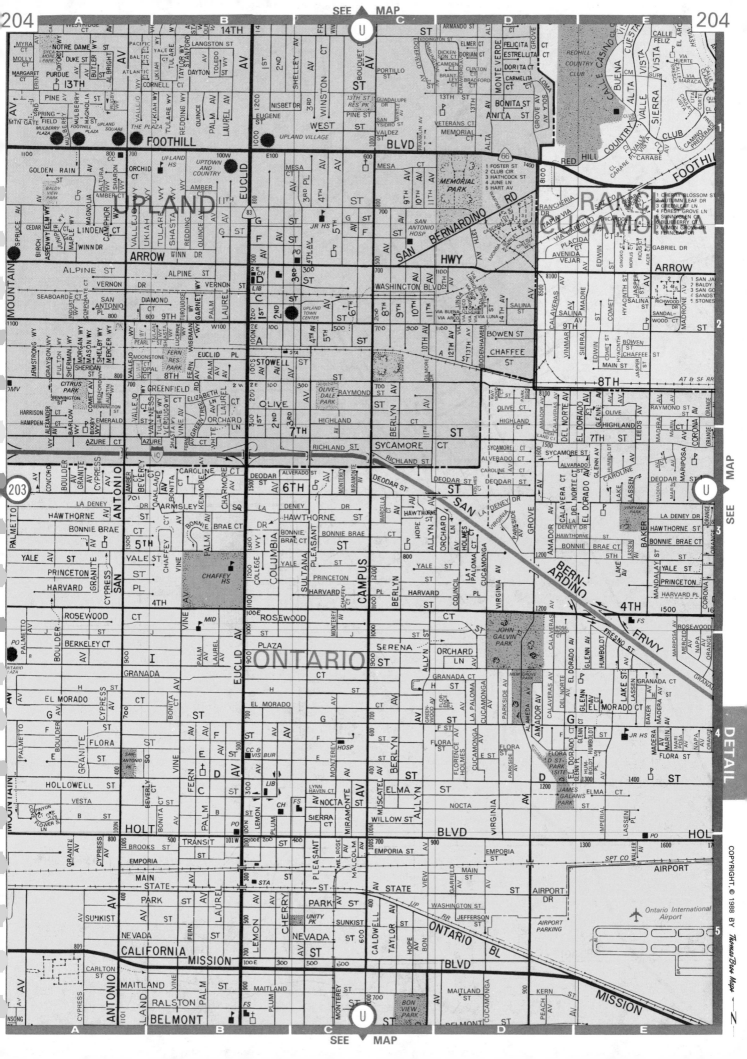

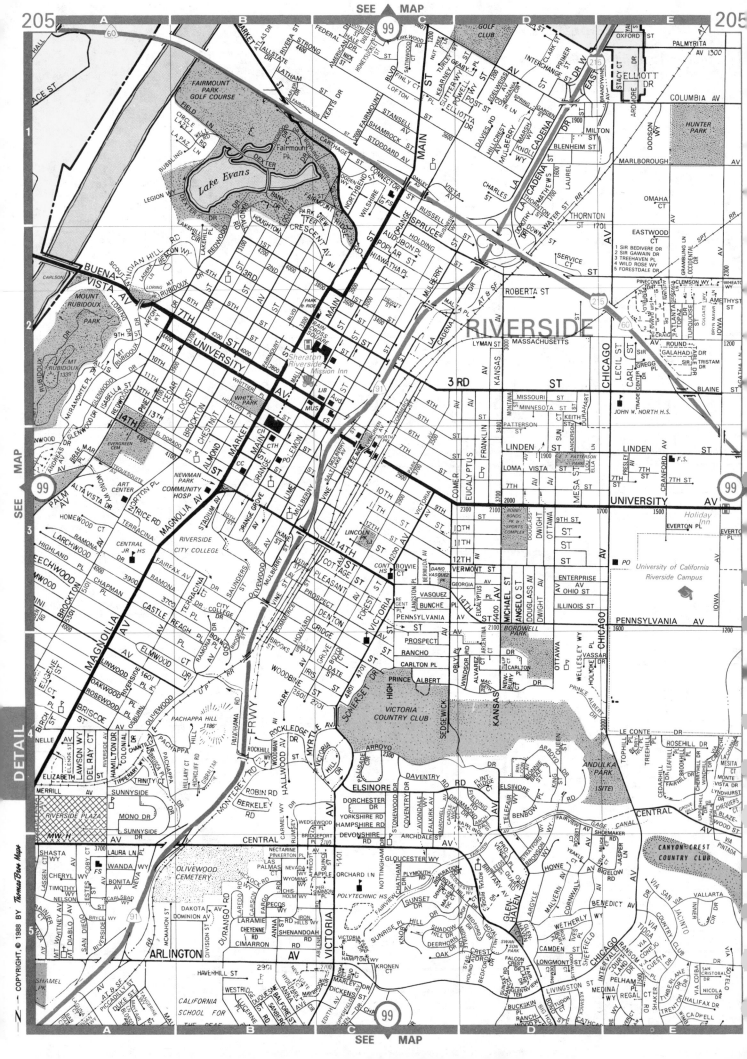

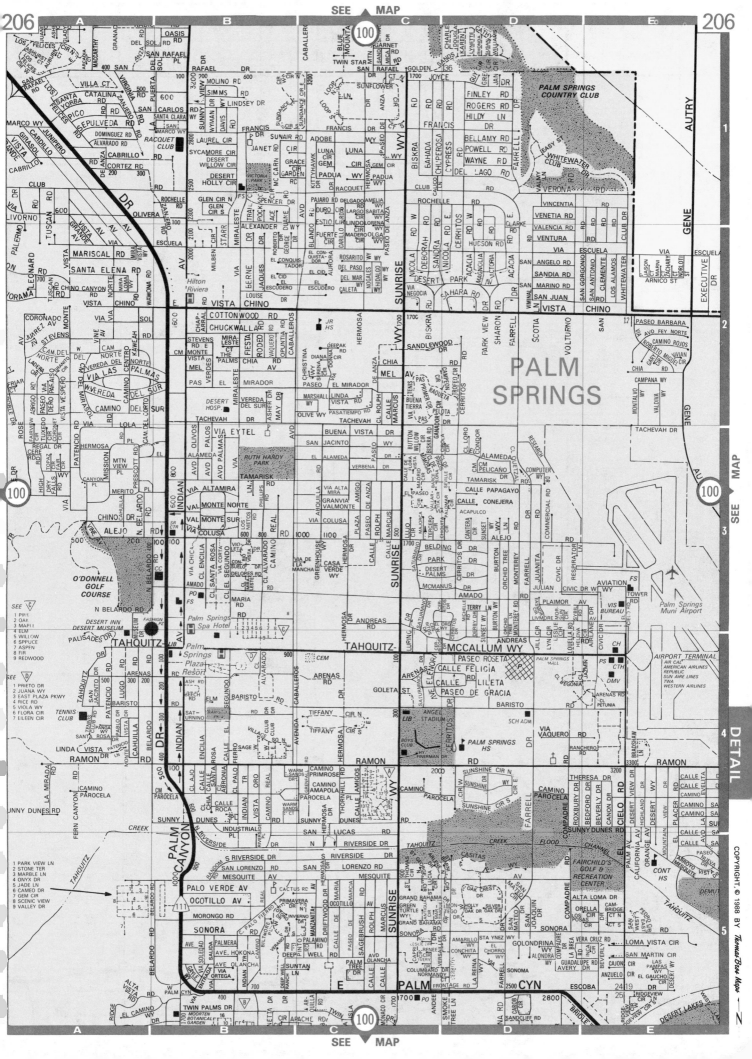

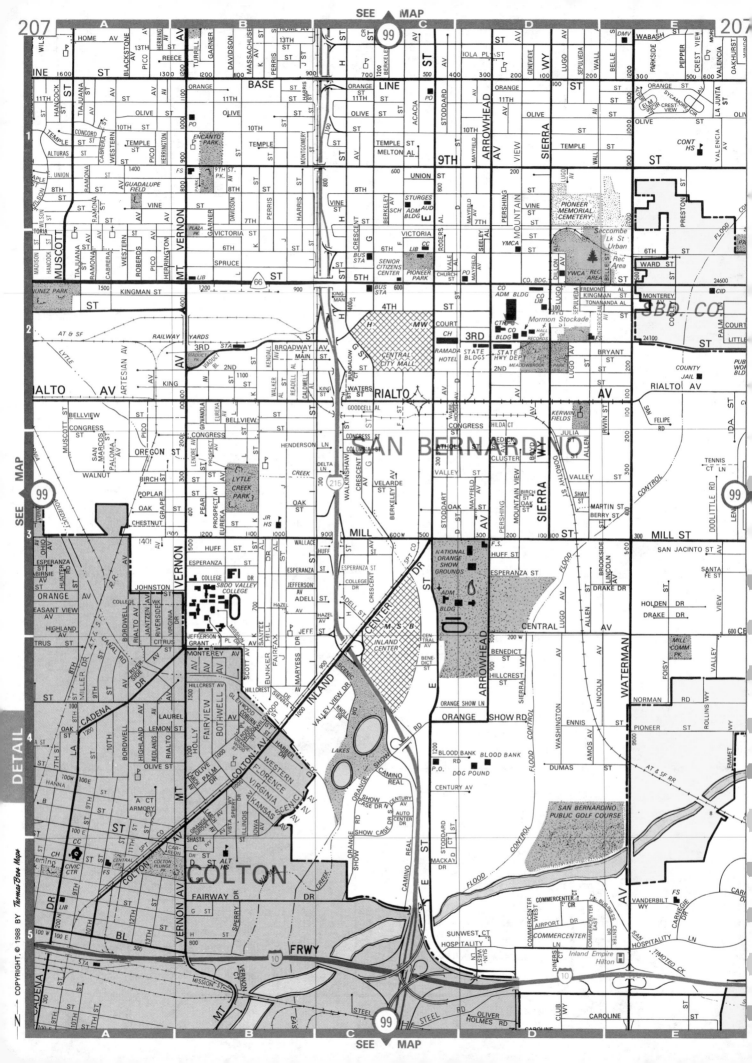

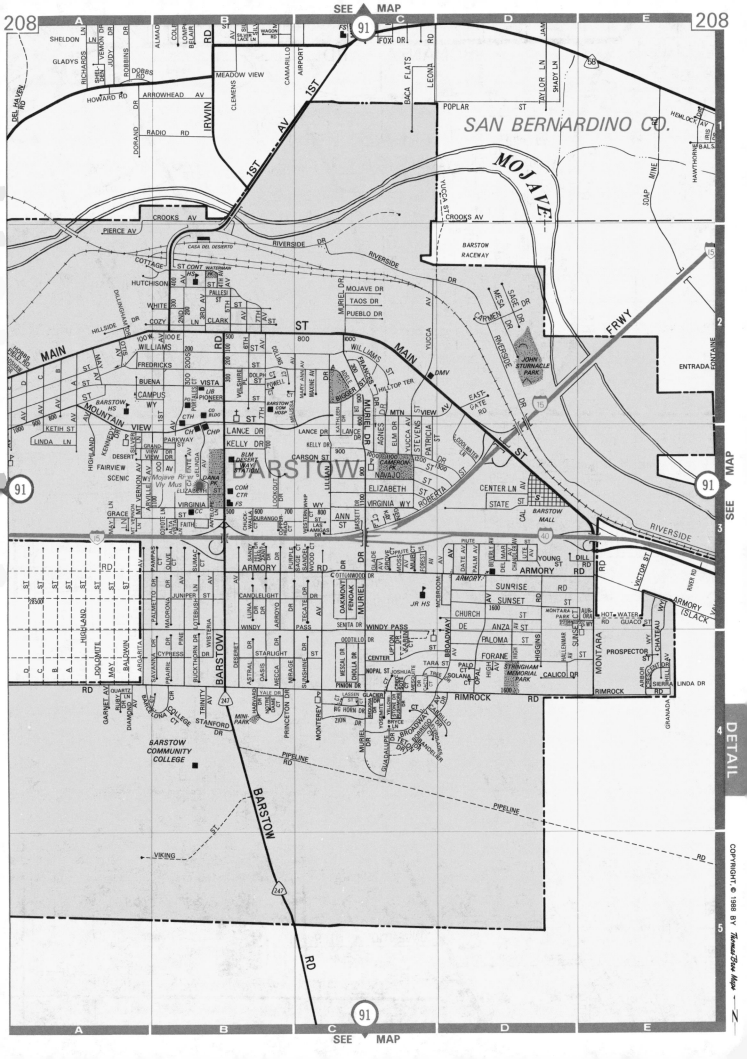

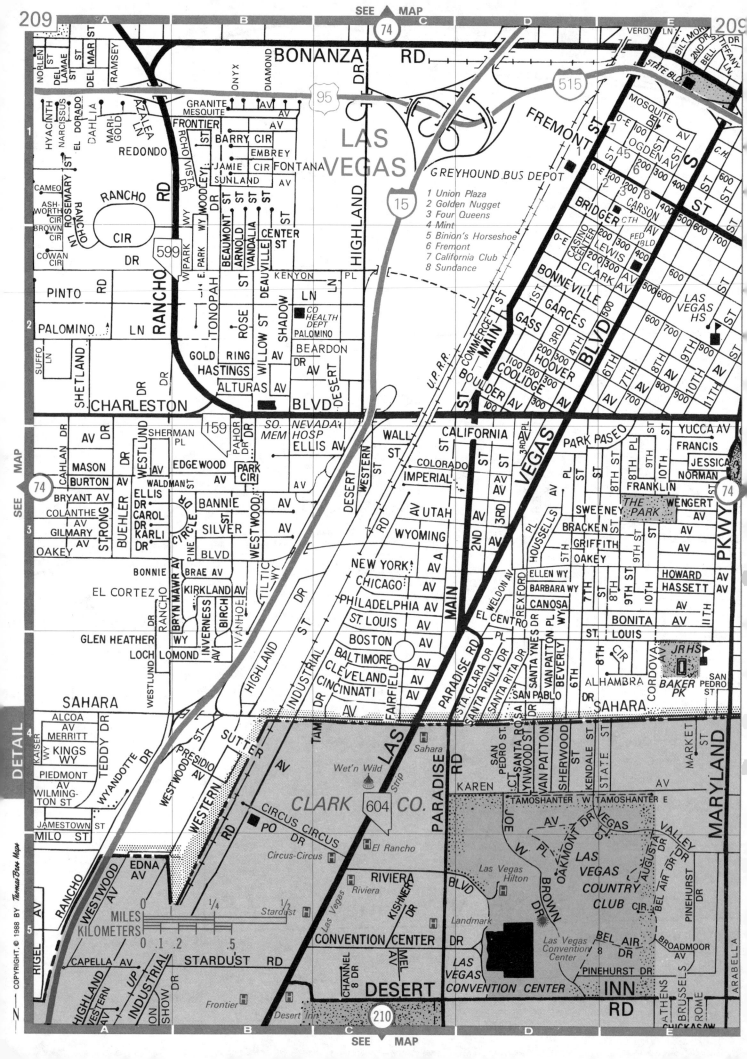

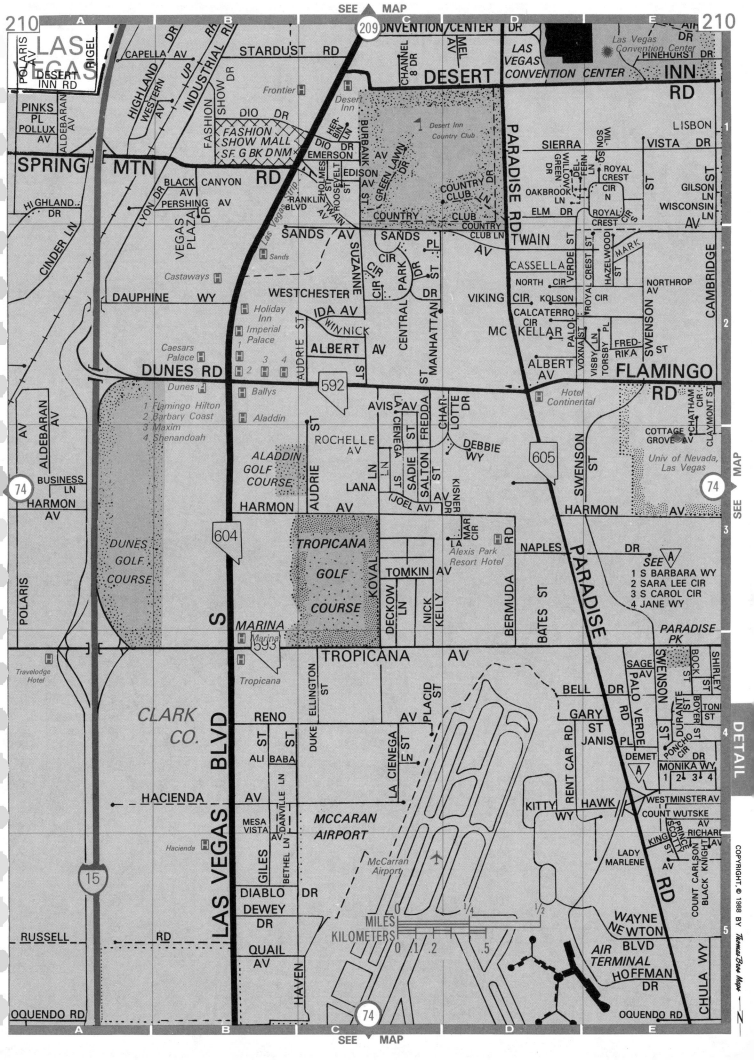

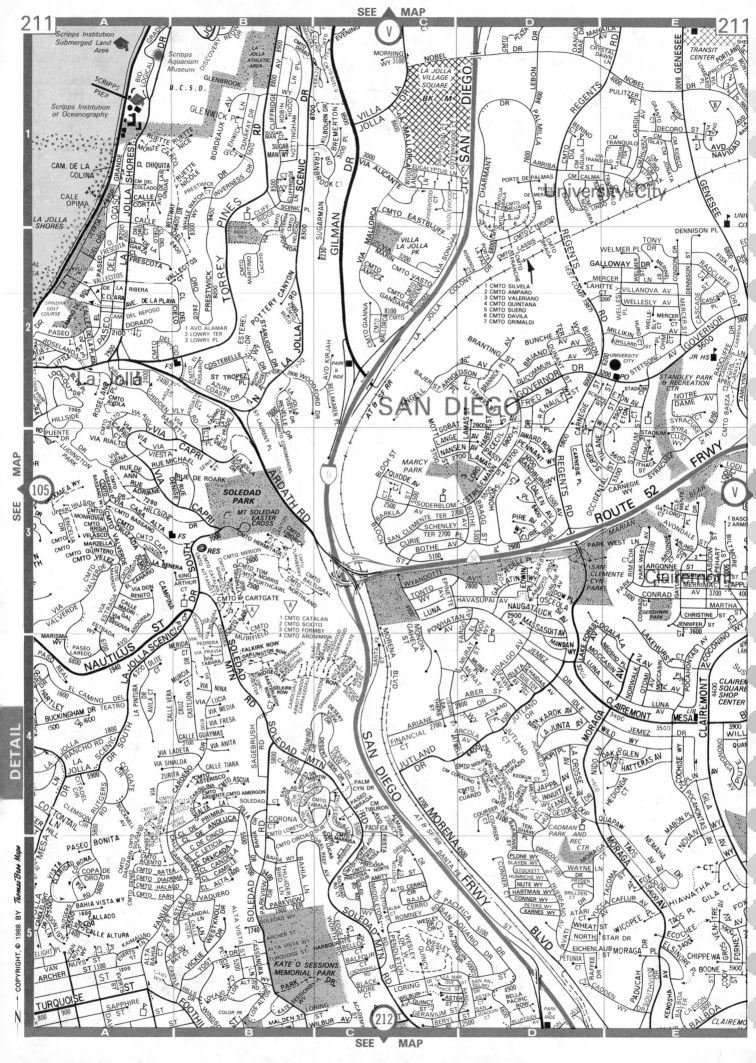

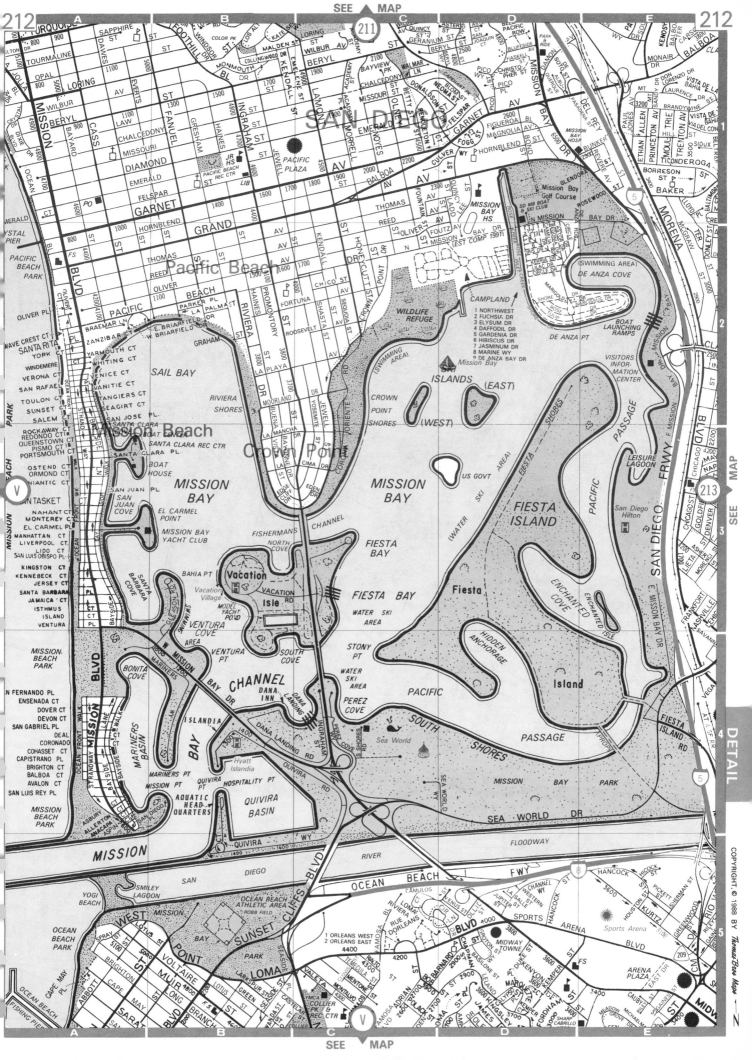

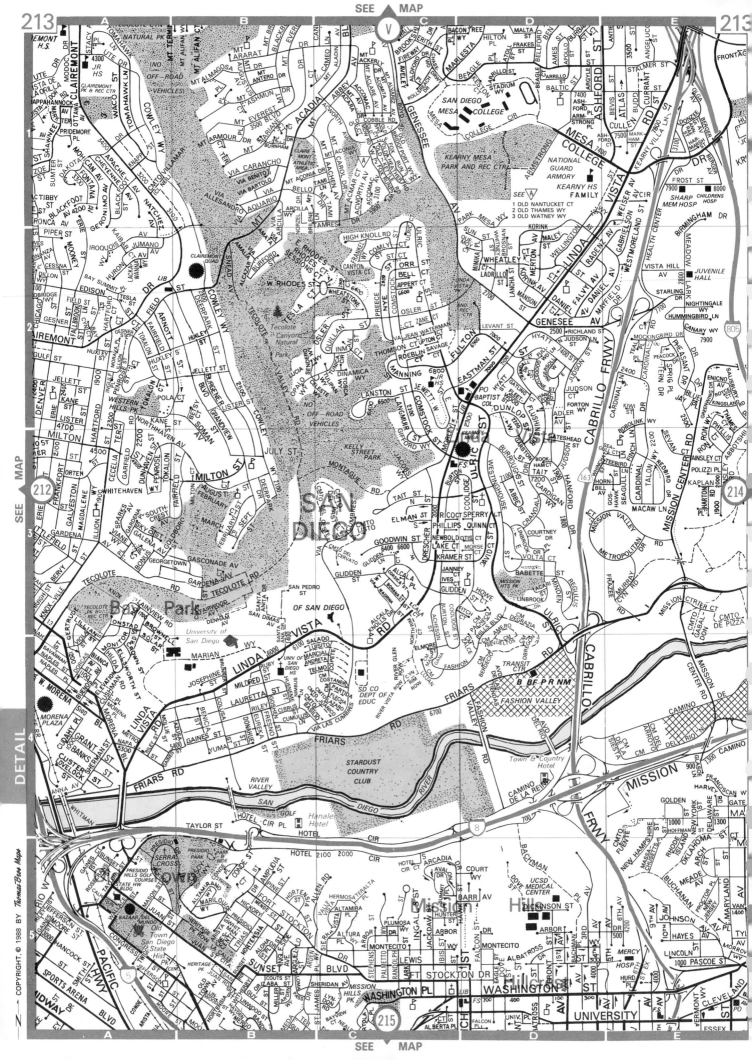

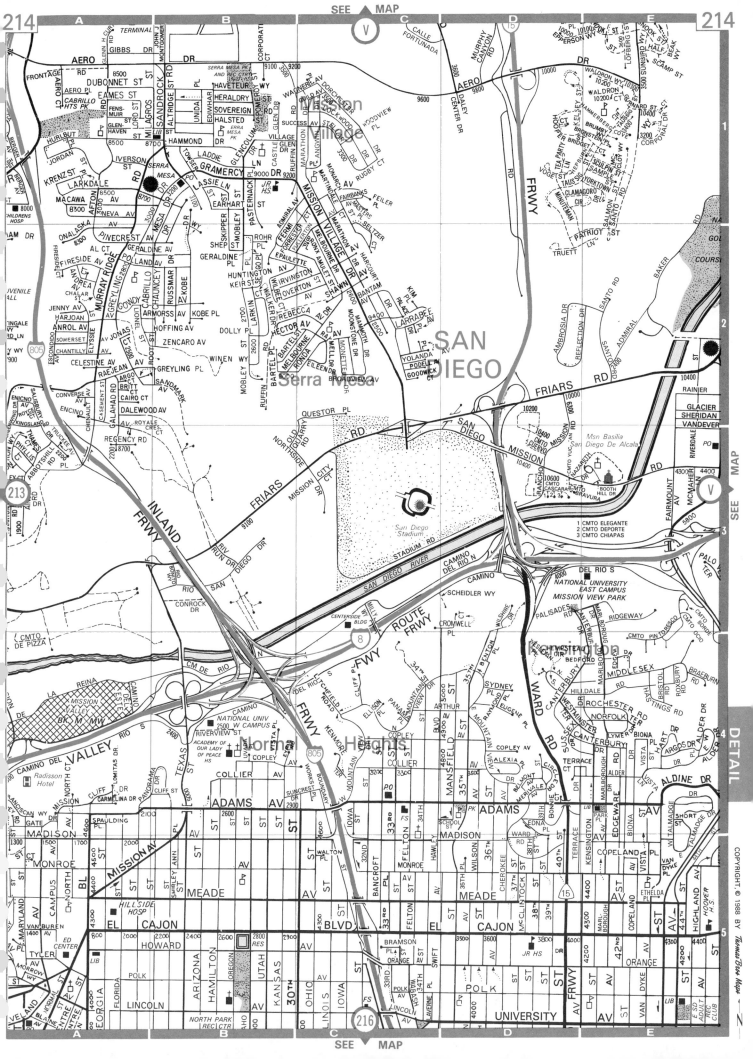

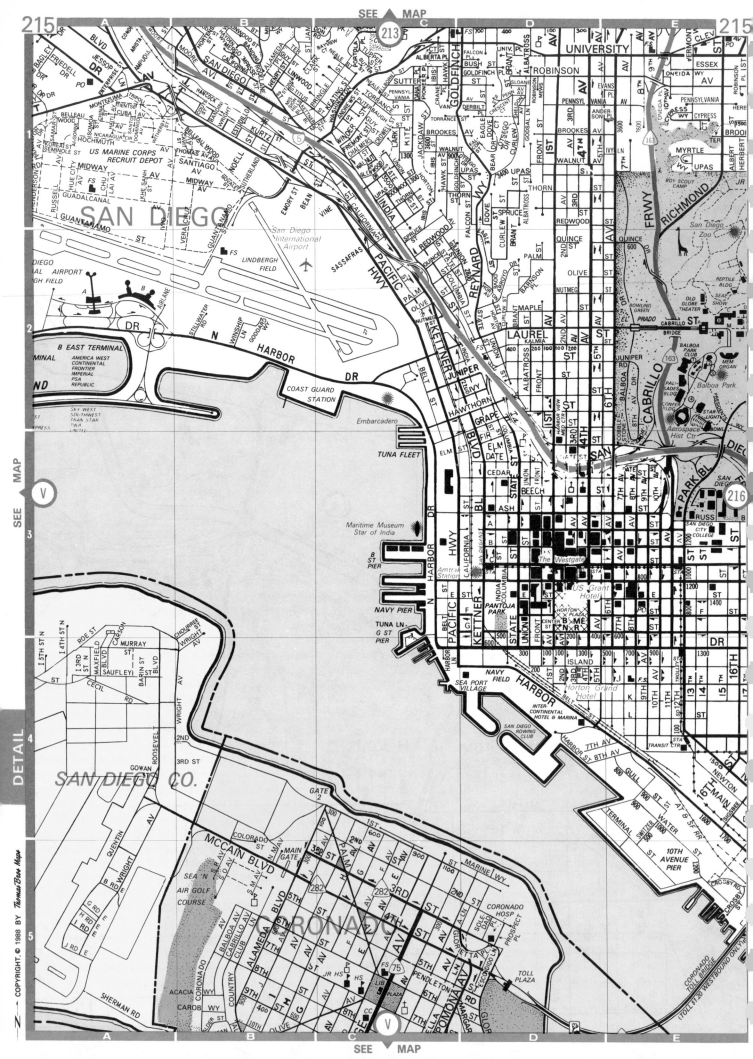

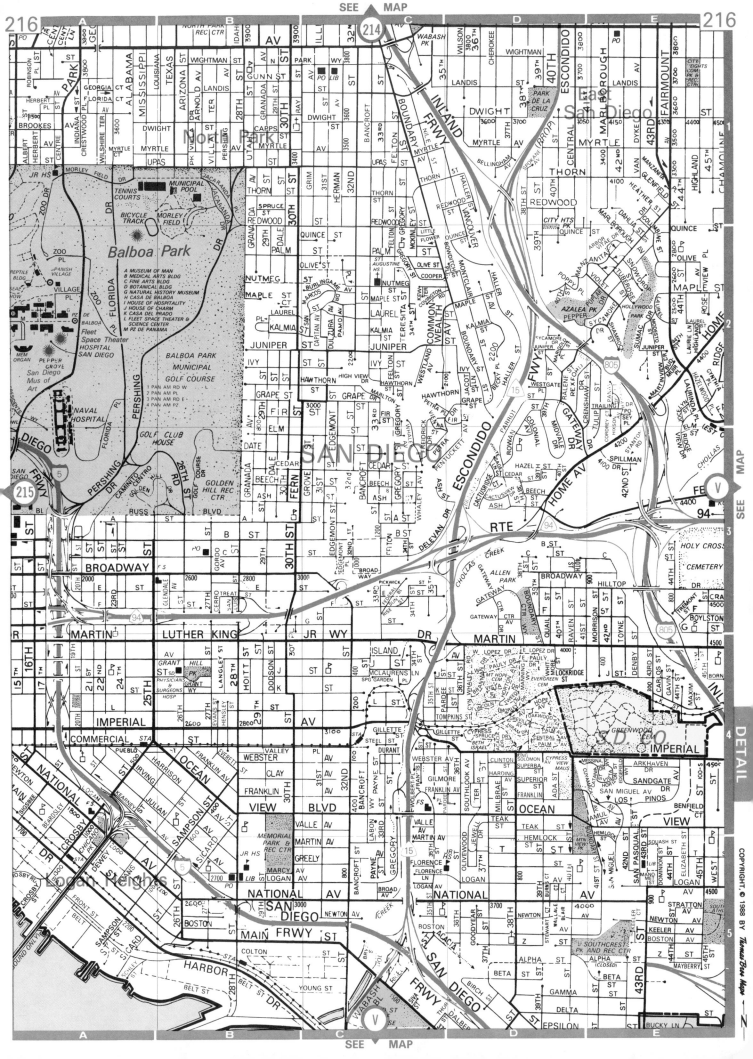

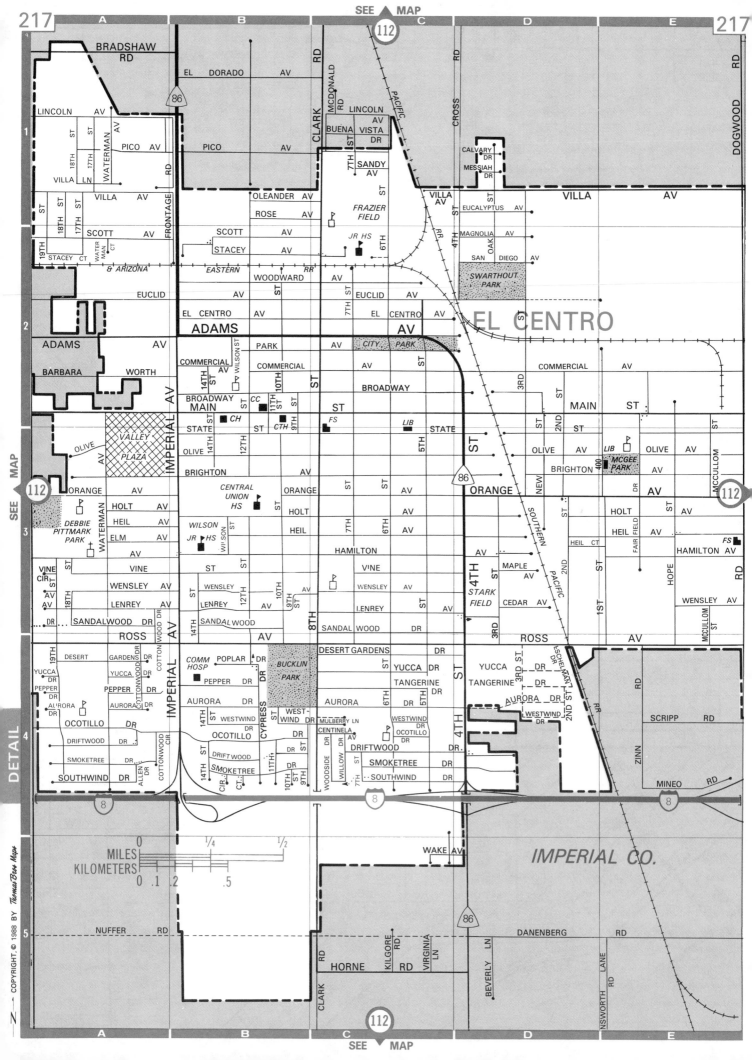

# LIST OF ABBREVIATIONS

| | | | |
|---|---|---|---|
| AL............ALLEY | CR............CRESCENT | KPN.....KEY PENINSULA NORTH | RDG............RIDGE |
| AR............ARROYO | CRES............CRESCENT | KPS.....KEY PENINSULA SOUTH | RES............RESERVOIR |
| ARR............ARROYO | CSWY............CAUSEWAY | L............LA | RIV............RIVER |
| AV............AVENUE | CT............COURT | LN............LANE | RV............RIVER |
| AVD............AVENIDA | CTE............CORTE | LP............LOOP | RO............RANCHO |
| AVD D LS......AVENIDA DE LOS | CTO............CUT OFF | LS............LAS, LOS | S............SOUTH |
| BCH............BEACH | CTR............CENTER | MDW............MEADOW | SN............SAN |
| BL............BOULEVARD | CV............COVE | MHP........MOBILE HOME PARK | SPG............SPRING |
| BLVD............BOULEVARD | CY............CANYON | MNR............MANOR | SPGS............SPRINGS |
| CEM............CEMETERY | CYN............CANYON | MT............MOUNT | SQ............SQUARE |
| CIR............CIRCLE | D............DE | MTN............MOUNTAIN | SRA............SIERRA |
| CK............CREEK | DL............DEL | MTWY............MOTORWAY | ST............SAINT |
| CL............CALLE | DR............DRIVE | MTY............MOTORWAY | ST............STREET |
| CL DL............CALLE DEL | DS............DOS | N............NORTH | STA............SANTA |
| CL D LS............CALLE DE LAS | E............EAST | PAS............PASEO | STA............STATION |
| CALLE DE LOS | EST............ESTATE | PAS DE............PASEO DE | TER............TERRACE |
| CL EL............CALLE EL | EXPWY............EXPRESSWAY | PAS DL............PASEO DEL | THTR............THEATER |
| CLJ............CALLEJON | EXT............EXTENSION | PAS D LS........PASEO DE LAS | TK TR............TRUCK TRAIL |
| CL LA............CALLE LA | FRWY............FREEWAY | PASEO DE LOS | TR............TRAIL |
| CL LS............CALLE LAS | FRW............FREEWAY | PGD............PLAYGROUND | VIA D............VIA DE |
| CALLE LOS | FY............FREEWAY | PK............PARK | VIA D LS............VIA DE LAS |
| CM............CAMINO | GN............GLEN | PK............PEAK | VIA DE LOS |
| CM D............CAMINO DE | GRDS............GROUNDS | PKWY............PARKWAY | VIA DL............VIA DEL |
| CM D LA........CAMINO DE LA | GRN............GREEN | PL............PLACE | VIS............VISTA |
| CM D LS............CAMINO DE LAS | GRV............GROVE | PT............POINT | VLG............VILLAGE |
| CAMINO DE LOS | HTS............HEIGHTS | PY............PARKWAY | VLY............VALLEY |
| CMTO............CAMINITO | HWY............HIGHWAY | PZ............PLAZA | VW............VIEW |
| CN............CANAL | HY............HIGHWAY | RCH............RANCH | W............WEST |
| COM............COMMON | JCT............JUNCTION | RCHO............RANCHO | WK............WALK |
| | | RD............ROAD | WY............WAY |

# INDEX OF CITIES

# INDEX OF COUNTIES

**STREETS**

219
A ST

# STREET INDEX

219
ARTISTS DR




| STREET | CO. | PAGE & GRID |
|---|---|---|
| A | | |
| A ST | ALA | L E5 |
| A ST | ALA | 45 E2 |
| A ST | DVS | 136 C3 |
| A ST | DN | 1 D4 |
| A ST | H | 146 E2 |
| A ST | SBD | 92 A1 |
| A ST | SD | 215 D3 |
| A ST | TEH | 18 E5 |
| A ST W | ALA | L E5 |
| A ST W | ALA | N E1 |
| A ST W | H | 146 B3 |
| ABBOTT DR | KER | 80 B3 |
| ABBOTT RD | LACO | R A5 |
| ABBOTT ST | MON | 54 D4 |
| ABBOTT ST | SAL | 171 D4 |
| ABBY ST | FRE | 165 D3 |
| ABELIA ST | SBD | 92 B3 |
| ABELOR RD | INY | 51 C4 |
| ABERDEEN DR | SBD | 100 E1 |
| ABERDEEN STA RD | INY | 59 E1 |
| ABERNATHY RD | SOL | L E1 |
| ABERNATHY RD | SOL | M A1 |
| ABERNATHY RD | SOL | 38 E3 |
| ABERNATHY RD | YUB | 26 A4 |
| ABLE RD | COL | 32 E2 |
| ABORN RD | SCL | P C3 |
| ABORN RD | SCL | 46 C4 |
| ABRAM DR | RCO | 100 A5 |
| ACACIA AV | ANA | 193 D1 |
| ACACIA AV | STA | 47 C5 |
| ACACIA AV | SUT | 33 C2 |
| ACACIA ST | SAL | 171 A4 |
| ACADEMY AV | FRCO | 57 E4 |
| ACAMPO RD | SJCO | 40 B4 |
| ACARI RD | KER | 78 B3 |
| ACKERMAN LN | HUM | 16 B3 |
| ACME RD | SUT | 33 B3 |
| ACMITE ST | KER | 91 E3 |
| ACOMA TR | SBD | 100 D1 |
| ADA RD | KER | 78 B3 |
| ADAIR RD | IMP | 108 E5 |
| ADAIR RD | STA | 47 C2 |
| ADAM FOX FRM RD | HUM | 9 E4 |
| ADAMS AV | CM | 197 C5 |
| ADAMS AV | EC | 217 B2 |
| ADAMS AV | FRCO | 56 D4 |
| ADAMS AV | FRCO | 57 C4 |
| ADAMS AV | FRCO | 58 A4 |
| ADAMS AV | ORA | T C4 |
| ADAMS AV | SD | 214 B4 |
| ADAMS AV | SDCO | V C3 |
| ADAMS AV | SDCO | 111 D1 |
| ADAMS BLVD | LA | 184 A4 |
| ADAMS BLVD | LA | 185 C4 |
| ADAMS BLVD | LACO | Q D4 |
| ADAMS DR | KER | 79 E1 |
| ADAMS RD | TEH | 18 C4 |
| ADAMS ST | IMP | 109 A5 |
| ADAMS ST | RCO | 99 A2 |
| ADAMS ST | RCO | 101 A4 |
| ADDISON RD | BUT | 25 C1 |
| ADELAIDA RD | SLO | 75 E1 |
| ADELAIDA RD | SLO | 76 A1 |
| ADELINE ST | B | 156 A4 |
| ADELINE ST | O | 157 D2 |
| ADELANTO RD | SBD | 91 B3 |
| ADML CALLAHN LN | VAL | 134 E3 |
| ADOBE DR | KER | 79 E2 |
| ADOBE DR | KER | 80 A2 |
| ADOBE PL | MON | 65 C4 |
| ADOBE RD | BUT | 25 C4 |
| ADOBE RD | COL | 25 A5 |
| ADOBE RD | KER | 78 D4 |
| ADOBE RD | SBD | 101 B1 |
| ADOBE RD | SLO | 76 A1 |
| ADOBE RD | SHA | 18 D3 |
| ADOBE RD | SON | L A1 |
| ADOBE RD | SON | 38 A3 |
| ADOBE RD | TEH | 18 D4 |
| ADOBE CREEK RD | LAK | 31 D3 |
| ADOBE RANCH RD | MNO | 44 A5 |
| ADOHR RD | KER | 78 A3 |
| ADOLFO LOPEZ BL | BAJA | 112 B4 |
| AERO DR | SD | 214 A1 |
| AERO DR | SDCO | V B2 |
| AERO DR | SDCO | 111 D1 |
| AEROPUERTO HWY | BAJA | 111 E2 |
| AFTON BLVD | GLE | 25 A4 |
| AFTON RD | BUT | 25 B5 |
| AFTON CANYON RD | SBD | 82 D5 |
| AGATE RD | SBD | 91 D1 |
| AGER RD | SIS | 4 B3 |
| AGER RD | SIS | 5 D2 |
| AGER BESWICK RD | SIS | 4 C3 |
| AGGEN RD | VEN | 88 C5 |
| AGNES WILSON RD | LPAZ | 104 A2 |
| AGNES WILSON RD | RCO | 103 E2 |
| AGOURA RD | LACO | 96 E1 |
| AGUA CALIENT BL | BAJA | 111 E3 |
| AGUA CALIENT RD | SB | 87 D4 |
| AQUA CALIENT RD | SON | 132 A1 |
| AGUA DULCE CYN | LACO | 89 D4 |
| AGUA FRIA RD | MPA | 49 A3 |
| AGUAJITO RD | MON | 53 E4 |
| AGUAJITO RD | MON | 168 D2 |
| AGUA MANSA RD | RCO | 99 B2 |
| AGUAS FRIAS RD | BUT | 25 B4 |
| AGUEREBERRY PT | INY | 71 D1 |
| AHERN RD | SJCO | 47 A2 |
| AHLF RD | SUT | 33 C2 |
| AINSWORTH PL | RCO | 107 A1 |
| AIR BASE PKWY | FRFD | 135 C2 |
| AIR BASE PKWY | SOL | M A1 |
| AIR BASE PKWY | SOL | 38 E3 |
| AIR BASE PKWY | SOL | 39 A3 |
| AIR BASE RD | SBD | 91 B3 |
| AIRD CIR | BUT | 25 E3 |
| AIROLA | CAL | 41 B4 |
| AIROSA DR | SBD | 90 E3 |
| AIROX RD | SB | 86 B1 |
| AIR PARK DR | IMP | 108 C2 |
| AIRPORT | SJCO | 40 B5 |
| AIRPORT BLVD | KER | 80 A5 |
| AIRPORT BLVD | LA | 188 D5 |
| AIRPORT BLVD | LA | 189 D1 |
| AIRPORT BLVD | LACO | Q D5 |
| AIRPORT BLVD | RCO | 101 A4 |
| AIRPORT BLVD | SAL | 171 E5 |
| AIRPORT BLVD | SMCO | N C1 |
| AIRPORT BLVD | SF | 144 C1 |
| AIRPORT BLVD | SJ | 151 E2 |
| AIRPORT BLVD | SCR | 54 B2 |
| AIRPORT BLVD | SON | 37 E1 |
| AIRPORT BLVD S | SSF | 144 C2 |
| AIRPORT DR | O | 159 D5 |
| AIRPORT RD | ALP | 36 C4 |
| AIRPORT RD | HUM | 9 E4 |
| AIRPORT RD | KER | 78 A4 |
| AIRPORT RD | MEN | 22 C5 |
| AIRPORT RD | MEN | 30 C1 |
| AIRPORT RD | MOD | 8 A1 |
| AIRPORT RD | MOD | 14 E1 |
| AIRPORT RD | MNO | 50 E2 |
| AIRPORT RD | NAPA | L D1 |
| AIRPORT RD | NAPA | 38 C3 |
| AIRPORT RD | O | 159 D4 |
| AIRPORT RD | SLO | 76 B1 |
| AIRPORT RD | SHA | 18 C3 |
| AIRPORT RD | SIS | 4 B3 |
| AIRPORT RD | SOL | M D1 |
| AIRPORT RD | SOL | 39 C3 |
| AIRPORT RD | TRI | 17 D1 |
| AIRPORT WY | SJCO | 40 B5 |
| AIRPORT WY | SJCO | 47 B2 |
| AIRWAY DR | KLAM | 5 C1 |
| AKER AV | STA | 47 D1 |
| AKERS RD | TUL | 68 B1 |
| AKINS RD | SIS | 5 D2 |
| AKRICH ST | SHA | 18 C2 |
| ALABAMA ST | SBD | 99 C2 |
| ALAMEDA AV | BUR | 179 C5 |
| ALAMEDA AV | LACO | Q D3 |
| ALAMEDA AV | O | 159 B1 |
| ALAMEDA AV | SAL | 171 C5 |
| ALAMEDA AV | YOL | 39 D2 |
| ALAMEDA ST | LA | 186 B4 |
| ALAMEDA ST | LACO | 97 E2 |
| ALAMEDA ST | LACO | S D2 |
| ALAMEDA ST | MAN | 161 C3 |
| ALAMEDA ST | VAL | 134 C4 |
| ALAMEDA, THE | SJ | 151 C2 |
| ALAMEDA, THE | SJ | 152 A4 |
| ALAMEDA, THE | SCLR | 151 C2 |
| ALAM D LS PULGS | BLMT | 145 A4 |
| ALAM D LS PULGS | SMCO | N C1 |
| ALAM D LS PULGS | SMCO | N D2 |
| ALAM D LS PULGS | SM | 145 A4 |
| ALAM D LS PULGS | SMCO | 45 D4 |
| ALAMEDA PAD SER | STB | 174 C2 |
| ALAMITOS AV | LACO | S D3 |
| ALAMO DR | MPA | 48 D2 |
| ALAMO RD | IMP | 109 B5 |
| ALAMO ST | LACO | 88 E5 |
| ALAMO ST | SIS | 5 A2 |
| ALAMO ST | VEN | 88 E5 |
| ALAMO ST | VEN | 89 A5 |
| ALAMO CREEK RD | SLO | 76 D5 |
| ALAMO PINTADO | SB | 86 E3 |
| ALBA RD | SCR | N E5 |
| ALBA RD | SCR | 53 E1 |
| ALBAUGH RD | LAS | 14 C3 |
| ALBERS RD | STA | 47 E2 |
| ALBRT ETTER RCH | HUM | 16 A5 |
| ALBERTON AV | BUT | 25 A3 |
| ALBION LTL RIV | MEN | 30 B1 |
| ALBION RIDGE RD | MEN | 30 C1 |
| ALBRIGHT RD | IMP | 109 B3 |
| ALCALDE RD | FRCO | 66 D3 |
| ALCATRAZ AV | ALA | L D4 |
| ALCATRAZ AV | O | 156 B4 |
| ALCOSTA BLVD | CC | M B5 |
| ALDEN ST | KER | 78 E4 |
| ALDER AV | SBD | 80 E1 |
| ALDER AV | SBD | 99 B1 |
| ALDER ST | PAC | 167 B2 |
| ALDER CAMP RD | DN | 1 E5 |
| ALDER CAMP RD | DN | 9 E1 |
| ALDER CAMP RD | DN | 10 A1 |
| ALDER CREEK RD | NEV | 27 D5 |
| ALDER CK BCH RD | MEN | 30 C3 |
| ALDRCRFT HTS RD | SCL | P B5 |
| ALDRCRFT HTS RD | SCL | 54 A1 |
| ALDERPOINT RD | HUM | 16 C3 |
| ALDER PT BLUFF | TRI | 16 D5 |
| ALDER SPGS RD | GLE | 23 D3 |
| ALDER SPGS RD | GLE | 24 A3 |
| ALDERPOINT RD | HUM | 16 C3 |
| ALDERWOOD DR | SIS | 4 A4 |
| ALDINE DR | SD | 214 E4 |
| ALDINE DR | SDCO | V C3 |
| ALDINE DR | SDCO | 111 D1 |
| ALDRIDGE RD | SHA | 19 A2 |
| ALEJO DR | RCO | 100 C3 |
| ALESSANDRO BLVD | RCO | 99 B3 |
| ALEXANDER AV | BUT | 33 C1 |
| ALEXANDER AV | SHA | 18 C3 |
| ALEXANDER LN | LAS | 21 C3 |
| ALEXANDR VLY RD | SON | 31 D5 |
| ALFALFA AV | STA | 47 C4 |
| ALFRD HARRL HWY | KER | 78 D2 |
| ALGERINE RD | TUO | 41 C5 |
| ALGODON RD | YUB | 33 D3 |
| ALGRN WRDS FRRY | TUO | 41 C5 |
| ALGOMAN AV | SBD | 91 E3 |
| ALHAMBRA | CC | 38 E5 |
| ALHAMBRA AV | CC | L E3 |
| ALHAMBRA AV | M | 154 B1 |
| ALHAMBRA BLVD | SCTO | 137 E3 |
| ALHAMBRA RD | LACO | R B3 |
| ALHAMBRA WY | M | 154 C3 |
| ALHAMBRA VLY RD | CC | L D3 |
| ALHAMBRA VLY RD | CC | 38 D5 |
| ALHAMBRA VLY RD | CC | 154 C5 |
| ALHAMBRA VLY RD | M | 154 C4 |
| ALICE AV | HUM | 16 C5 |
| ALICIA AV | YUB | 33 D2 |
| ALICIA PKWY | ORA | 98 D5 |
| ALISAL RD | MON | 54 D4 |
| ALISAL RD | SB | 86 E3 |
| ALISAL ST E | SAL | 171 D4 |
| ALISAL ST W | SAL | 171 B4 |
| ALISO CANYON RD | LACO | 89 E4 |
| ALISO CANYON RD | SB | 87 C1 |
| ALISO CANYON RD | VEN | 88 B5 |
| ALISO PARK RD | SB | 87 C1 |
| ALISOS AV | SB | 87 A3 |
| ALISOS CYN RD | SB | 86 D2 |
| ALLAN RD | AMA | 41 A1 |
| ALLEGHANY RD | YUB | 26 C5 |
| ALLEN AV | LACO | R C2 |
| ALLEN AV | MCO | 48 C3 |
| ALLEN RD | IMP | 108 D3 |
| ALLEN RD | KER | 78 C3 |
| ALLEN RD | SJCO | 47 C1 |
| ALLENDALE RD | SOL | 39 A2 |
| ALLERTON AV | SSF | 144 D1 |
| ALLIANCE RD | HUM | 9 E5 |
| ALLIANCE RD | HUM | 10 A5 |
| ALLISON RCH RD | NEV | 34 C2 |
| ALLUVIAL AV | FRCO | 57 C3 |
| ALMA AV | KER | 79 D5 |
| ALMA ST | PA | 147 A2 |
| ALMA ST | SJ | 152 C5 |
| ALMA ST | SCL | N E2 |
| ALMA ST | SCL | 45 D4 |
| ALMADEN AV | SJ | 152 B4 |
| ALMADEN BLVD | SJ | 152 B4 |
| ALMADEN EXPWY | SCL | P B4 |
| ALMADEN EXPWY | SCL | 46 B5 |
| ALMANOR DR W | PLU | 20 B4 |
| ALMER RD | COL | 32 D2 |
| ALMOND AV | CLO | 32 E3 |
| ALMOND AV | MCO | 48 A4 |
| ALMOND AV | STA | 47 C3 |
| ALMOND DR | MCO | 55 D2 |
| ALMOND DR | MCO | 56 A2 |
| ALMOND DR | SLO | 76 B2 |
| ALMOND RD | KER | 77 B1 |
| ALMND ORCHRD RD | SUT | 33 B1 |
| ALMONDWOOD DR | SJCO | 47 B2 |
| ALMONTE BLVD | MAR | 140 B4 |
| ALOHA ST | TEH | 18 D5 |
| ALONA ST | KER | 80 A4 |
| ALONDRA | LACO | 97 E3 |
| ALONDRA BLVD | LACO | 98 A3 |
| ALOSTA AV | LACO | 98 C1 |
| ALOSTA AV | LACO | U A2 |
| ALPHA RD | NEV | 26 E5 |
| ALPINE AV | FRCO | 56 D4 |
| ALPINE AV | SJCO | 40 A5 |
| ALPINE AV | S | 160 A3 |
| ALPINE BLVD | SDCO | 107 A5 |
| ALPINE RD | MOD | 7 C5 |
| ALPINE RD | MOD | 8 C1 |
| ALPINE RD | SJCO | 40 B4 |
| ALPINE RD | SMCO | N D3 |
| ALPINE RD | SMCO | 45 D4 |
| ALPINE MINE RD | ALP | 36 A5 |
| ALPS DR | KER | 79 C5 |
| ALT CT | RCO | 107 C1 |
| ALTA | FRCO | 58 A4 |
| ALTA ST | MON | 54 E5 |
| ALTA ST | NEV | 34 C1 |
| ALTA BONNY NOOK | PLA | 34 D1 |
| ALTADENA DR | LACO | 98 A1 |
| ALTADENA DR | LACO | R B2 |
| ALTAMONT PS RD | ALA | M D5 |
| ALTA SIERRA DR | NEV | 34 C2 |
| AL TAHOE BLVD | SLT | 129 A4 |
| ALTAIR AV | SDCO | 106 D5 |
| ALTA LOMA DR | SBD | 100 E1 |
| ALTA MESA DR | SHA | 18 C2 |
| ALTA MESA RD | SAC | 40 B2 |
| ALTAMONT PSS RD | ALA | 46 C2 |
| ALTA VISTA | AVLN | 105 A4 |
| ALTA VISTA | BKD | 166 E2 |
| ALTA VISTA DR | KER | 78 D3 |
| ALTHEA AV | FRCO | 56 D2 |
| ALTON AV | SA | 197 D3 |
| ALTUS AV | KER | 80 B5 |
| ALUM ROCK AV | SCL | P C3 |
| ALUM ROCK AV | SCL | 46 B4 |
| ALVARADO BLVD | ALA | N E1 |
| ALVARADO BLVD | ALA | P A1 |
| ALVARADO BLVD | ALA | 45 E3 |
| ALVARADO RD | MON | 65 D4 |
| ALVARADO RD | STA | 47 E2 |
| ALVARADO ST | LA | 185 D1 |
| ALVARADO ST | LACO | Q E4 |
| ALVARADO ST | SDCO | 106 C2 |
| ALVARADO TR | MCO | 55 D2 |
| ALVARADO-NILES | ALA | 45 E3 |
| ALVARADO NLS RD | ALA | P A1 |
| ALVES RD | MCO | 48 A3 |
| ALVIN AV | SMA | 173 B2 |
| ALVIN DR E | SAL | 171 D1 |
| ALVIN DR W | SAL | 171 C1 |
| ALVISO-MLPTS RD | SCL | 46 A4 |
| ALVORD MTN RD | SBD | 82 C5 |
| ALWARD RD | SHA | 19 B3 |
| AMADOR AV | FRCO | 56 D5 |
| AMADOR ST | FRE | 165 B4 |
| AMADOR ST | VAL | 134 D4 |
| AMADOR CREEK RD | AMA | 40 E2 |
| AMAR RD | LACO | 98 B2 |
| AMAR RD | LACO | R E4 |
| AMARGOSA RD | SBD | 91 B3 |
| AMARGOSA ST | SBD | 92 C2 |
| AMBOY RD | SBD | 93 D4 |
| AMBOY RD | SBD | 101 C1 |
| AMBOY RD | SBD | 101 E1 |
| AMBROSE DR | SAL | 171 A4 |
| AMBOY CUTOFF | SBD | 93 E3 |
| AMEDEE RD | LAS | 21 D4 |
| AMELIA AV | LACO | U B1 |
| AMEN LN | TEH | 18 C3 |
| AMERICAN AV | FRCO | 57 D4 |
| AMERICAN AV | FRCO | 58 B4 |
| AMERICAN AV | MCO | 47 D4 |
| AMERICAN AV | STA | 47 C2 |
| AMERICAN CYN RD | NAPA | L D2 |
| AMERICAN CYN RD | NAPA | 38 D4 |
| AMERICN FLAT RD | AMA | 40 E2 |
| AMRICAN FLT SDE | AMA | 40 E1 |
| AMERICN GIRL MN | IMP | 110 B5 |
| AMERICN MINE RD | SHA | 18 A1 |
| AMERIGO | SJCO | 40 C5 |
| AMES ST | ALA | M D5 |
| AMES ST | ALA | 46 C2 |
| AMESTI RD | SCR | 54 B2 |
| AMOROSE ST | RCO | 99 B4 |
| AMOUR RD | SUT | 33 C4 |
| AMSTERDAM RD | MCO | 48 B3 |
| ANAHEIM BLVD | ANA | 193 C1 |
| ANAHEIM BLVD | ORA | 98 C3 |
| ANAHEIM BLVD | ORA | T C2 |
| ANAHEIM ST | LB | 192 D2 |
| ANAHEIM ST | LA | 191 A1 |
| ANAHEIM ST | LA | 192 D2 |
| ANAHEIM ST | LACO | 97 D4 |
| ANAHEIM ST | LACO | S C2 |
| ANAPAMU ST | STB | 174 C3 |
| ANCHO ERIE MINE | NEV | 26 E5 |
| ANCHO MINE RD | NEV | 26 E5 |
| ANCHOR | FRCO | 58 B4 |
| ANDERHOLT RD | IMP | 112 B4 |
| ANDERSON DR W | SHA | 18 C3 |
| ANDERSON LN | HUM | 15 E2 |
| ANDERSON RD | DVS | 136 B3 |
| ANDERSON RD | SLO | 76 A1 |
| ANDERSON RD | SOL | 39 C4 |
| ANDERSON RD | STA | 47 C4 |
| ANDERSON RD | TUL | 68 C2 |
| ANDERSON ST | SBD | 99 C2 |
| ANDERSON CK RD | JKSN | 3 D1 |
| ANDERSON GRADE | SIS | 4 A4 |
| ANDERSON RCH RD | LAS | 14 D4 |
| ANDERSON VLY WY | MEN | 30 E3 |
| ANDESITE RD | SIS | 4 D5 |
| ANDESITE RD | SIS | 12 D1 |
| ANDESITE LOG RD | SIS | 12 D1 |
| ANDRADE RD | ALA | P B1 |
| ANDRADE RD | ALA | 46 B3 |
| ANDRE RD | IMP | 109 A4 |
| ANDRESSEN RD | PLA | 33 E3 |
| ANDREW AV | SB | 86 C1 |
| ANDREWS RD | LAS | 14 C3 |
| ANDREWS RD | SIS | 4 E3 |
| ANGELES CRST HY | LACO | R B1 |
| ANGELES FRST HY | LACO | 90 A4 |
| ANGELES FRST HY | LACO | R B1 |
| ANITA RD | BUT | 25 A2 |
| ANNADALE AV | FRCO | 57 B4 |
| ANNADALE AV | FRCO | 58 A3 |
| ANNAPOLIS RD | SON | 30 E5 |
| ANNAPOLIS RD | SON | 31 A5 |
| ANNETTE RD | KER | 76 E1 |
| ANNIN AV | KER | 78 B1 |
| ANTELOPE DR | LAS | 8 B4 |
| ANTELOPE HWY | LACO | 90 D4 |
| ANTELOPE RD | MNO | 42 E1 |
| ANTELOPE RD | MNO | 43 A1 |
| ANTELOPE RD | RCO | 99 C4 |
| ANTELOPE RD | SAC | 34 A5 |
| ANTELOPE RD | SLO | 66 E5 |
| ANTELOPE SPGS | MNO | 50 E2 |
| ANTELOPE VLY FY | LACO | 89 E2 |
| ANTELOPE VLY RD | SIE | 27 C3 |
| ANTONIO RD | SCL | N E2 |
| ANTHONY RD | LACO | 89 D4 |
| ANTOLA RD | LAS | 21 C3 |
| ANZA RD | IMP | 112 A4 |
| ANZA RD | RCO | 106 D1 |
| ANZAR RD | SBT | 54 D2 |
| ANZA TRAIL RD | IMP | 111 C4 |
| APACHE TR | RCO | 100 B3 |
| APACHE CYN RD | VEN | 88 A2 |
| APPALOOSA RD | CAL | 41 A3 |
| APPIAN WY | CC | L C3 |
| APPIAN WY | CC | 38 C5 |
| APPLE AV | STA | 47 C3 |
| APPLE RD | TEH | 24 C2 |
| APPLE CANYON RD | RCO | 100 C4 |
| APPLE COLONY RD | TUO | 41 D5 |
| APPLEGATE RD | MCO | 48 B4 |
| APPLE RANCH RD | TUO | 41 E4 |
| APPLE SEED LN | RCO | 100 A5 |
| APPLE VALLEY RD | SBD | 91 C3 |
| APPLEWHITE | SBD | 91 A5 |
| APRICOT AV | STA | 47 C3 |
| APRIL LN | VEN | 88 C4 |
| AQUEDUCT RD | KER | 79 E5 |
| AQUEDUCT RD | KER | 80 A5 |
| AQUEDUCT RD | SBD | 103 A2 |
| AQUEDUCT RD | SBD | 104 A4 |
| ARAMAYO WY | TEH | 24 E1 |
| ARASTRADERO RD | PA | 147 E5 |
| ARATA LN | SON | 37 E1 |
| ARBINI RD | STA | 47 E1 |
| ARBOGA RD | YUB | 33 D2 |
| ARBOLEDA DR | MCO | 48 C5 |
| ARBOR AV | BLMT | 145 B5 |
| ARBOR RD | SLO | 76 A1 |
| ARBOR WY | MCO | 56 C1 |
| ARBORETUM RD | PA | 147 A3 |
| ARBOR VITAE ST | ING | 189 D1 |
| ARBOR VITAE ST | LA | 189 D1 |
| ARBOR VITAE ST | LACO | Q D5 |
| ARBURUA RD | MCO | 55 D2 |
| ARC RD | INY | 51 D5 |
| ARCH RD | SJCO | 40 B5 |
| ARCH AIRPORT RD | SJCO | 40 B5 |
| ARCHER AV | SUT | 33 C1 |
| ARCHER RD | SHA | 18 B3 |
| ARCHERDALE RD | SJCO | 40 C5 |
| ARCHIBALD AV | RCO | 98 E3 |
| ARCHIBALD AV | SBD | U E4 |
| ARCHIE BROWN RD | SHA | 13 D4 |
| ARDATH RD | SD | 211 B3 |
| ARDATH RD | SDCO | V A2 |
| ARDATH RD | SDCO | 106 C5 |
| ARDEN DR | LACO | R C3 |
| ARDEN WY | SAC | 40 A1 |
| ARDENWOOD BLVD | ALA | N E1 |
| ARDENWOOD BLVD | ALA | P A1 |
| ARENA WY | MCO | 48 A4 |
| ARGO ST | KER | 80 D1 |
| ARGONAUT RD | LAK | 31 D3 |
| ARGONNE DR | S | 160 B4 |
| ARGUELLO BL | SF | 141 D2 |
| ARGYLE RD | MON | 65 B3 |
| ARLINGTON AV | CC | L C3 |
| ARLINGTON AV | LA | 184 E5 |
| ARLINGTON AV | LACO | Q D4 |
| ARLINGTON AV | LACO | S C2 |
| ARLINGTON AV | RIV | 205 A5 |
| ARLINGTON AV | RCO | 99 A2 |
| ARLINGTON AV S | RENO | 130 A5 |
| ARLINGTON RD | PLU | 20 D5 |
| ARLINGTON MN RD | RCO | 103 B3 |
| ARMORY RD | BARS | 208 B3 |
| ARMOUR RD | SUT | 33 C4 |
| ARMOUR RANCH RD | SB | 86 E3 |
| ARMOUR RANCH RD | SB | 87 A3 |
| ARMSTRONG | SJCO | 40 A4 |
| ARMSTRONG AV | FRCO | 57 D2 |
| ARMSTRONG AV | FRCO | 57 D3 |
| ARMSTRONG RD | CAL | 41 C3 |
| ARMSTRONG RD | LAS | 14 D3 |
| ARMSTRONG RD | RCO | 99 A2 |
| ARMSTRONG RD | STA | 47 C4 |
| ARMSTRONG RD | YUB | 33 D1 |
| ARMSTRNG WDS RD | SON | 37 C1 |
| ARMY RD | RCO | 110 B1 |
| ARNOLD DR | SON | 132 A3 |
| ARMY ST | SFCO | L B5 |
| ARNOLD RD | IMP | 112 C5 |
| ARMY ST | SFCO | 45 C2 |
| ARNO RD | SAC | 40 A3 |
| ARNOLD DR | SON | L B2 |
| ARNOLD DR | SON | 38 B3 |
| ARNOLD WY | SDCO | 107 B5 |
| AROSA RD | KER | 79 C4 |
| ARQUES AV | SVL | 148 E5 |
| ARQUES RD | SCL | P A3 |
| ARRECHE RD | MOD | 7 D5 |
| ARRELLAGA ST | STB | 174 B3 |
| ARROW HWY | CLA | 203 C2 |
| ARROW HWY | LACO | 98 B1 |
| ARROW HWY | LACO | U B2 |
| ARROW HWY | MTCL | 203 C2 |
| ARROW HWY | ROC | 204 B2 |
| ARROW HWY | SBD | U D2 |
| ARROW HWY | SBD | 98 E1 |
| ARROW HWY | UPL | 204 A2 |
| ARROW ROUTE | SBD | 203 B2 |
| ARROWHEAD AV | SBDO | 207 D4 |
| ARROWHEAD BLVD | RCO | 103 D5 |
| ARROWHEAD BLVD | RCO | 110 D1 |
| ARROWHEAD RD | LAK | 32 A3 |
| ARROWHEAD ST | CAL | 41 A5 |
| ARROWHEAD TR | SBD | 82 E4 |
| ARROWHEAD TR | SBD | 83 A4 |
| ARROWHEAD LK RD | SBD | 91 C5 |
| ARROYA AV | MCO | 56 A1 |
| ARROYO AV | KER | 79 E5 |
| ARROYO AV | KER | 80 A5 |
| ARROYO BLVD | LACO | R B2 |
| ARROYO BLVD | PAS | 190 A4 |
| ARROYO PKWY | PAS | 190 C5 |
| ARROYO RD | ALA | P C1 |
| ARROYO RD | ALA | 46 C2 |
| ARROYO RD | SBD | 92 A4 |
| ARROYO BURRO RD | SB | 87 C4 |
| ARROYO GR GUADL | SLO | 76 B5 |
| ARROYO GR GUADL | SLO | 86 A1 |
| AROYO GR HUASNA | SLO | 76 D4 |
| ARROYO SECO RD | MON | 64 E2 |
| ARROYO SECO RD | MON | 65 A1 |
| ARTESIA AV | SB | 86 B3 |
| ARTESIA BLVD | LACO | 97 D3 |
| ARTESIA BLVD | LACO | 98 A3 |
| ARTESIA BLVD | LACO | S B1 |
| ARTESIA FRWY | LACO | 98 A3 |
| ARTESIA FRWY | LACO | S D1 |
| ARTESIA FRWY | LACO | T A1 |
| ARTHUR | SJCO | 47 C1 |
| ARTHUR RD | CC | L E3 |
| ARTHUR RD | CC | M A3 |
| ARTHUR ST | RCO | 101 C5 |
| ARTICHOKE RD | SMCO | N C4 |
| ARTICHOKE RD | SMCO | 45 C5 |
| ARTIC MINE RD | NEV | 26 E5 |
| ARTISTS DR | INY | 72 A1 |


STREETS

| STREET | CO. | PAGE & GRID |
|---|---|---|
| ASH AV | SHA | 13 C5 |
| ASH AV | STA | 47 C3 |
| ASH ST | SD | 215 D3 |
| ASH ST | SDCO | 107 A4 |
| ASHBY AV | ALA | L D4 |
| ASHBY AV | B | 156 B3 |
| ASHBY RD | SHA | 18 C2 |
| ASH CREEK RD | INY | 60 B5 |
| ASH CREEK RD | SHA | 18 E3 |
| ASH CREEK RD | SIS | 4 A3 |
| ASH CK SINK RD | SIS | 13 A2 |
| ASHE RD | KER | 78 D4 |
| ASHLAN AV | FRCO | 56 C3 |
| ASHLAN AV | FRCO | 57 A5 |
| ASHLEY LN | SJCO | 40 B4 |
| ASH VALLEY RD | LAS | 8 A3 |
| ASH VALLEY RD | LAS | 14 D3 |
| ASHWORTH RD | MPA | 49 B3 |
| ASILOMAR AV | PAC | 167 A2 |
| ASPEN VALLEY RD | TUO | 49 C1 |
| ASPEN VALLEY RD | TUO | 63 A4 |
| ASSOCIATED RD | SB | 86 B1 |
| ASSOCIATED RD | SIS | 4 E3 |
| ASSOCIATED RD | SIS | 5 A3 |
| ASTER RD | SBD | 91 A3 |
| ASTORIA AV | KER | 89 C1 |
| ATEN RD | IMP | 109 A5 |
| ATHEL ST | KER | 80 C1 |
| ATHERTON AV | MAR | L A2 |
| ATHERTON BLVD | MAR | 38 B4 |
| ATHERTON ST | LACO | S E2 |
| ATHERTON ST | LACO | T A2 |
| ATHLONE RD | MCO | 48 D5 |
| ATKINS RD | SJCO | 40 C4 |
| ATLANTIC AV | A | 157 D5 |
| ATLANTIC AV | FRFD | 135 C1 |
| ATLANTIC AV | LB | 192 E2 |
| ATLANTIC AV | LACO | 97 E3 |
| ATLANTIC AV | LACO | S D1 |
| ATLANTIC AV E | FRFD | 135 D1 |
| ATLANTIC BLVD | LACO | 98 A2 |
| ATLANTIC BLVD | LACO | R B4 |
| ATLANTIC BLVD | LACO | S D2 |
| ATLAS | CC | 38 C5 |
| ATLAS RD | CC | L C3 |
| ATLAS PEAK RD | NAPA | 38 D2 |
| ATTERBERRY CT | KER | 79 E2 |
| ATTILA RD | SBD | 84 C4 |
| ATWATER | MCO | 47 E4 |
| ATWELL AV | TUL | 67 E4 |
| ATWELL AV | TUL | 68 A4 |
| ATWOOD | PLA | 34 C3 |
| AUBERRY RD | FRCO | 57 E1 |
| AUBERRY RD | FRCO | 58 A1 |
| AUBERRY RD | MAD | 49 E5 |
| AUBREY AV | MCO | 56 A2 |
| AUBURN BLVD | SAC | 34 A5 |
| AUBURN RD | NEV | 34 C2 |
| AUBURN RD | PLA | 34 B3 |
| AUBURN FRST HLL | PLA | 34 D3 |
| AUBURN RAVNE RD | AUB | 126 C3 |
| AUBURN RAVNE RD | PLA | 126 C3 |
| AUCTION SNIVELY | TEH | 18 D4 |
| AUDUBON DR | FRCO | 57 C2 |
| AUGUST AV | MCO | 47 D4 |
| AUGUST RD | STA | 47 D4 |
| AUGUSTINE RD | RCO | 109 C1 |
| AUKLET RD | SBD | 92 C1 |
| AULD RD | RCO | 99 D5 |
| AURORA CYN RD | MNO | 43 B3 |
| AUSTIN RD | IMP | 109 A5 |
| AUSTIN RD | SJCO | 40 B5 |
| AUSTIN RD | SJCO | 47 B1 |
| AUSTIN CREEK RD | SON | 37 C2 |
| AUSTIN MDWS RD | NEV | 27 A4 |
| AUSTRIAN RD | CAL | 41 B4 |
| AUTOPSTA TIJ-EN | BAJA | 111 D3 |
| AVALON AV | SBD | 100 E1 |
| AVALON BLVD | LA | 191 C1 |
| AVALON BLVD | LACO | 97 E3 |
| AVALON BLVD | LACO | S C1 |
| AVALON CYN RD | AVLN | 105 A5 |
| AVENA | SJCO | 47 C1 |
| AVENAL CUTOFF | KIN | 67 A3 |
| AVD BERMUDAS | RCO | 100 E4 |
| AVD DEL CAPITAN | SB | 87 A4 |
| AVD D LS ARBLES | VEN | 88 D5 |
| AVD D LS ARBLES | VEN | 96 D1 |
| AVD DL PRESIDNT | ORA | 105 E1 |
| AVENIDA DEL SOL | KER | 80 C1 |
| AVENIDA ENCINO | RCO | 100 D5 |
| AVD LA CUMBRE | RCO | 100 D5 |
| AVD LOS FELIZ | RCO | 100 D5 |
| AVENIDA OBREGON | RCO | 100 E4 |
| AVENUE A | KER | 89 E1 |
| AVENUE A | YUMA | 112 D5 |
| AVENUE B | LACO | 89 D2 |
| AVENUE B | LACO | 90 C2 |
| AVENUE C | LACO | 89 D2 |
| AVENUE C | LACO | 90 D2 |
| AVENUE C | YUMA | 112 C5 |
| AVENUE D | LACO | 90 B2 |
| AVENUE E | LACO | 89 E2 |
| AVENUE E | LACO | 90 A2 |
| AVENUE E | RCO | 99 B3 |
| AVENUE E | YUMA | 112 C5 |
| AVENUE E-8 | LACO | 90 B2 |
| AVENUE F | LACO | 89 B2 |
| AVENUE F | LACO | 89 D2 |
| AVENUE F | LACO | 90 C2 |
| AVENUE F | SBD | 99 D2 |
| AVENUE F-4 | LACO | 89 E2 |
| AVENUE F-4 | LACO | 90 A2 |
| AVENUE F-8 | LACO | 89 C2 |
| AVENUE F-8 | LACO | 90 D2 |
| AVENUE G | LACO | 89 E2 |
| AVENUE G-2 | LACO | 90 C2 |

| STREET | CO. | PAGE & GRID |
|---|---|---|
| AVENUE G-3 | LACO | 90 C2 |
| AVENUE G-4 | LACO | 90 C2 |
| AVENUE G-6 | LACO | 90 C2 |
| AVENUE G-8 | LACO | 90 B2 |
| AVENUE H | LACO | 89 E2 |
| AVENUE I | LACO | 89 E2 |
| AVENUE J | LACO | 89 E3 |
| AVENUE J | LACO | 90 C2 |
| AVENUE J-8 | LACO | 90 A2 |
| AVENUE K | LACO | 89 E3 |
| AVENUE K | LACO | 90 C3 |
| AVENUE K-8 | LACO | 89 D3 |
| AVENUE L | LACO | 89 E3 |
| AVENUE L | LACO | 90 B3 |
| AVENUE L | RCO | 99 D2 |
| AVENUE M | LACO | 89 E3 |
| AVENUE M | LACO | 90 B3 |
| AVENUE M-8 | LACO | 89 E3 |
| AVENUE N | LACO | 89 E3 |
| AVENUE N | LACO | 90 C3 |
| AVENUE O | LACO | 90 A3 |
| AVENUE ONE | MCO | 48 B4 |
| AVENUE P | LACO | 89 E3 |
| AVENUE P | LACO | 90 A3 |
| AVENUE P | LACO | 90 D3 |
| AVENUE P-8 | LACO | 90 A3 |
| AVENUE P-8 | LACO | 90 C3 |
| AVENUE Q | LACO | 90 C3 |
| AVENUE Q | LACO | 90 C3 |
| AVENUE R-8 | LACO | 90 D3 |
| AVENUE S | LACO | 89 E3 |
| AVENUE S | LACO | 90 A3 |
| AVENUE SAN LUIS | LA | 177 B4 |
| AVENUE STANFORD | LACO | 89 B4 |
| AVENUE T | LACO | 90 B3 |
| AVENUE T | LACO | 90 C3 |
| AVENUE TWO | MCO | 48 B4 |
| AVENUE U | LACO | 90 C3 |
| AVENUE Z | LACO | 90 D4 |
| AVENUE 2 | TUL | 68 D5 |
| AVENUE 4 1/2 | MAD | 56 E3 |
| AVENUE 5 | MAD | 56 E3 |
| AVENUE 5 1/2 | MAD | 56 E3 |
| AVENUE 5 1/2 | MAD | 57 A3 |
| AVENUE 6 | MAD | 56 E3 |
| AVENUE 6 | MAD | 57 A3 |
| AVENUE 6 1/2 | MAD | 57 A3 |
| AVENUE 7 1/2 | MAD | 56 D3 |
| AVENUE 7 1/2 | MAD | 56 E3 |
| AVENUE 7 1/2 | MAD | 57 C3 |
| AVENUE 8 | MAD | 56 E3 |
| AVENUE 8 | MAD | 57 A2 |
| AVENUE 8 | MAD | 57 C2 |
| AVENUE 8 | TUL | 68 B5 |
| AVENUE 8 1/2 | MAD | 57 A2 |
| AVENUE 9 | MAD | 56 E2 |
| AVENUE 9 | MAD | 57 C2 |
| AVENUE 9 1/2 | MAD | 56 E2 |
| AVENUE 10 | MAD | 56 E2 |
| AVENUE 10 | MAD | 57 B2 |
| AVENUE 10 1/2 | MAD | 56 E2 |
| AVENUE 10 1/2 | MAD | 57 A2 |
| AVENUE 11 | MAD | 56 E2 |
| AVENUE 11 | MAD | 57 A2 |
| AVENUE 11 1/2 | MAD | 56 E2 |
| AVENUE 11 1/2 | MAD | 57 A2 |
| AVENUE 12 | MAD | 56 E2 |
| AVENUE 12 | MAD | 57 B2 |
| AVENUE 12 | TUL | 68 B5 |
| AVENUE 12 | TUL | 68 C5 |
| AVENUE 12 1/2 | MAD | 57 B2 |
| AVENUE 13 | MAD | 56 E2 |
| AVENUE 13 1/2 | MAD | 56 E2 |
| AVENUE 13 1/2 | MAD | 57 A2 |
| AVENUE 14 | MAD | 56 D2 |
| AVENUE 14 | MAD | 57 C2 |
| AVENUE 14 1/2 | MAD | 56 E2 |
| AVENUE 14 1/2 | MAD | 57 A2 |
| AVENUE 14 1/2 | MAD | 57 C2 |
| AVENUE 15 | MAD | 56 E2 |
| AVENUE 15 1/2 | MAD | 56 E2 |
| AVENUE 15 1/2 | MAD | 57 B2 |
| AVENUE 16 | MAD | 56 E2 |
| AVENUE 16 | TUL | 68 B4 |
| AVENUE 16 | TUL | 68 C4 |
| AVENUE 16 1/2 | MAD | 56 E2 |
| AVENUE 17 | MAD | 56 D2 |
| AVENUE 17 1/2 | MAD | 56 E2 |
| AVENUE 18 | MAD | 56 D2 |
| AVENUE 18 1/2 | MAD | 56 D2 |
| AVENUE 19 | MAD | 56 D1 |
| AVENUE 19 1/2 | MAD | 56 D1 |
| AVENUE 20 | LA | 186 D2 |
| AVENUE 20 | MAD | 56 D1 |
| AVENUE 20 1/2 | MAD | 56 D1 |
| AVENUE 21 | MAD | 56 D1 |
| AVENUE 21 | MAD | 57 A1 |
| AVENUE 21 1/2 | MAD | 56 D1 |
| AVENUE 22 | MAD | 56 D1 |
| AVENUE 22 1/2 | MAD | 56 D1 |
| AVENUE 23 1/2 | MAD | 56 D1 |
| AVENUE 24 | MAD | 56 D1 |
| AVENUE 24 | TUL | 68 B4 |
| AVENUE 24 1/2 | MAD | 56 E1 |
| AVENUE 25 | MAD | 56 D1 |
| AVENUE 25 1/2 | MAD | 56 D1 |
| AVENUE 26 | MAD | 56 D1 |
| AVENUE 26 1/2 | MAD | 56 E1 |
| AVENUE 27 | MAD | 48 D5 |
| AVENUE 27 1/2 | MAD | 48 E5 |
| AVENUE 28 | MAD | 48 E5 |
| AVENUE 28 | TUL | 68 C4 |
| AVENUE 32 | TUL | 68 B4 |
| AVENUE 40 | TUL | 68 C4 |
| AVENUE 42 | TUL | 67 E4 |
| AVENUE 42 | TUL | 68 C4 |
| AVENUE 42 | TUL | 68 A4 |

| STREET | CO. | PAGE & GRID |
|---|---|---|
| AVENUE 44 | TUL | 68 B4 |
| AVENUE 46 | TUL | 67 E4 |
| AVENUE 46 | TUL | 68 C4 |
| AVENUE 50 | TUL | 67 E4 |
| AVENUE 52 | TUL | 68 B4 |
| AVENUE 52 | TUL | 68 C4 |
| AVENUE 54 | TUL | 67 E4 |
| AVENUE 56 | TUL | 68 B4 |
| AVENUE 58 | TUL | 68 A4 |
| AVENUE 62 | TUL | 68 A4 |
| AVENUE 64 | TUL | 68 D4 |
| AVENUE 66 | TUL | 68 D4 |
| AVENUE 68 | TUL | 68 A4 |
| AVENUE 68 | TUL | 68 D4 |
| AVENUE 70 | TUL | 68 D4 |
| AVENUE 74 | TUL | 68 D4 |
| AVENUE 76 | TUL | 68 D4 |
| AVENUE 78 | TUL | 68 D4 |
| AVENUE 80 | TUL | 68 B4 |
| AVENUE 80 | TUL | 68 C4 |
| AVENUE 84 | TUL | 68 A4 |
| AVENUE 86 | TUL | 68 D4 |
| AVENUE 88 | TUL | 67 E4 |
| AVENUE 88 | TUL | 68 A4 |
| AVENUE 88 | TUL | 68 D4 |
| AVENUE 90 | TUL | 68 D4 |
| AVENUE 92 | TUL | 68 D4 |
| AVENUE 94 | TUL | 68 D4 |
| AVENUE 95 | TUL | 68 C4 |
| AVENUE 96 | TUL | 68 D4 |
| AVENUE 100 | TUL | 68 D3 |
| AVENUE 102 | TUL | 68 D3 |
| AVENUE 104 | TUL | 67 E3 |
| AVENUE 104 | TUL | 68 C3 |
| AVENUE 108 | TUL | 68 A3 |
| AVENUE 108 | TUL | 68 D3 |
| AVENUE 112 | TUL | 67 E3 |
| AVENUE 112 | TUL | 68 D3 |
| AVENUE 116 | TUL | 68 B3 |
| AVENUE 116 | TUL | 68 D3 |
| AVENUE 120 | TUL | 67 E3 |
| AVENUE 120 | TUL | 68 D3 |
| AVENUE 124 | TUL | 68 C3 |
| AVENUE 128 | TUL | 67 E3 |
| AVENUE 128 | TUL | 68 C3 |
| AVENUE 132 | TUL | 68 C3 |
| AVENUE 136 | TUL | 67 E3 |
| AVENUE 136 | TUL | 68 C3 |
| AVENUE 138 | TUL | 68 E3 |
| AVENUE 144 | TUL | 68 A3 |
| AVENUE 152 | TUL | 68 B3 |
| AVENUE 152 | TUL | 68 C3 |
| AVENUE 156 | TUL | 68 D3 |
| AVENUE 160 | TUL | 68 A3 |
| AVENUE 160 | TUL | 68 D3 |
| AVENUE 164 | TUL | 68 B3 |
| AVENUE 168 | TUL | 68 A3 |
| AVENUE 168 | TUL | 68 C3 |
| AVENUE 169 | TUL | 68 D3 |
| AVENUE 172 | TUL | 68 C3 |
| AVENUE 176 | TUL | 68 A3 |
| AVENUE 176 | TUL | 68 C3 |
| AVENUE 178 | TUL | 68 D3 |
| AVENUE 180 | TUL | 68 B3 |
| AVENUE 182 | TUL | 68 D3 |
| AVENUE 184 | TUL | 68 C2 |
| AVENUE 188 | TUL | 68 D2 |
| AVENUE 190 | TUL | 68 A2 |
| AVENUE 192 | TUL | 68 A2 |
| AVENUE 192 | TUL | 68 B2 |
| AVENUE 196 | TUL | 68 B2 |
| AVENUE 196 | TUL | 68 D2 |
| AVENUE 198 | TUL | 68 A2 |
| AVENUE 199 | TUL | 67 E2 |
| AVENUE 200 | TUL | 68 A2 |
| AVENUE 200 | TUL | 68 C2 |
| AVENUE 204 | TUL | 67 E2 |
| AVENUE 204 | TUL | 68 A2 |
| AVENUE 204 | TUL | 68 C2 |
| AVENUE 204 | TUL | 68 C4 |
| AVENUE 206 | TUL | 68 D2 |
| AVENUE 208 | TUL | 67 E2 |
| AVENUE 208 | TUL | 68 A2 |
| AVENUE 208 | TUL | 68 C2 |
| AVENUE 212 | TUL | 68 B2 |
| AVENUE 212 | TUL | 68 D2 |
| AVENUE 216 | TUL | 68 A2 |
| AVENUE 216 | TUL | 68 D2 |
| AVENUE 222 | TUL | 68 D2 |
| AVENUE 224 | TUL | 68 B2 |
| AVENUE 226 | TUL | 68 D2 |
| AVENUE 228 | TUL | 68 B2 |
| AVENUE 232 | TUL | 68 D2 |
| AVENUE 236 | TUL | 68 A2 |
| AVENUE 236 | TUL | 68 D2 |
| AVENUE 240 | TUL | 68 A2 |
| AVENUE 244 | TUL | 68 A2 |
| AVENUE 248 | TUL | 68 A2 |
| AVENUE 252 | TUL | 68 A2 |
| AVENUE 256 | TUL | 67 E2 |
| AVENUE 260 | TUL | 68 A2 |
| AVENUE 264 | TUL | 68 B2 |
| AVENUE 268 | TUL | 68 A2 |
| AVENUE 271 | TUL | 68 B1 |
| AVENUE 272 | TUL | 68 A1 |
| AVENUE 272 | TUL | 68 D1 |
| AVENUE 276 | TUL | 68 C1 |
| AVENUE 280 | TUL | 68 A1 |
| AVENUE 300 | TUL | 68 C1 |
| AVENUE 304 | TUL | 68 A1 |
| AVENUE 306 | TUL | 68 D1 |
| AVENUE 308 | TUL | 68 A1 |
| AVENUE 312 | TUL | 68 D1 |
| AVENUE 318 | TUL | 68 C1 |
| AVENUE 320 | TUL | 68 A1 |
| AVENUE 320 | TUL | 68 D1 |
| AVENUE 324 | TUL | 68 C1 |

| STREET | CO. | PAGE & GRID |
|---|---|---|
| AVENUE 328 | TUL | 68 A1 |
| AVENUE 328 | TUL | 68 C1 |
| AVENUE 332 | TUL | 68 C1 |
| AVENUE 332 | TUL | 58 C5 |
| AVENUE 334 | TUL | 58 D5 |
| AVENUE 334 | TUL | 68 D1 |
| AVENUE 336 | TUL | 68 B1 |
| AVENUE 336 | TUL | 58 C5 |
| AVENUE 337 | TUL | 68 C1 |
| AVENUE 340 | TUL | 68 B1 |
| AVENUE 340 | TUL | 58 C5 |
| AVENUE 344 | TUL | 68 B1 |
| AVENUE 344 | TUL | 58 C5 |
| AVENUE 346 | TUL | 68 D1 |
| AVENUE 348 | TUL | 68 C1 |
| AVENUE 350 | TUL | 58 D5 |
| AVENUE 352 | TUL | 57 E5 |
| AVENUE 352 | TUL | 58 C5 |
| AVENUE 356 | TUL | 58 B5 |
| AVENUE 356 | TUL | 58 C5 |
| AVENUE 360 | TUL | 57 E5 |
| AVENUE 360 | TUL | 58 C5 |
| AVENUE 364 | TUL | 58 C5 |
| AVENUE 368 | TUL | 58 B5 |
| AVENUE 368 | TUL | 58 C5 |
| AVENUE 376 | TUL | 57 E5 |
| AVENUE 376 | TUL | 58 C5 |
| AVENUE 380 | TUL | 58 C5 |
| AVENUE 384 | TUL | 58 A5 |
| AVENUE 386 | TUL | 58 C5 |
| AVENUE 388 | TUL | 58 C5 |
| AVENUE 390 | TUL | 57 E5 |
| AVENUE 390 | TUL | 58 C5 |
| AVENUE 392 | TUL | 58 A5 |
| AVENUE 394 | TUL | 58 C5 |
| AVENUE 396 | TUL | 57 E5 |
| AVENUE 396 | TUL | 58 A5 |
| AVENUE 398 | TUL | 58 C5 |
| AVENUE 400 | TUL | 58 B5 |
| AVENUE 404 | TUL | 58 B5 |
| AVENUE 404 | TUL | 58 C5 |
| AVENUE 408 | TUL | 57 E5 |
| AVENUE 408 | TUL | 58 B5 |
| AVENUE 410 | TUL | 57 E5 |
| AVENUE 416 | TUL | 58 C5 |
| AVENUE 424 | TUL | 58 A4 |
| AVENUE 428 | TUL | 58 B4 |
| AVENUE 432 | TUL | 58 B4 |
| AVENUE 436 | TUL | 58 B4 |
| AVENUE 438 | TUL | 58 B4 |
| AVENUE 440 | TUL | 58 B4 |
| AVENUE 444 | TUL | 58 B4 |
| AVENUE 448 | TUL | 58 B4 |
| AVENUE 450 | TUL | 58 B4 |
| AVENUE 452 | TUL | 58 B4 |
| AVENUE 456 | TUL | 58 B4 |
| AVENUE 460 | TUL | 58 B4 |
| AVENUE 464 | TUL | 58 B4 |
| AVENUE 468 | TUL | 58 B4 |
| AVENUE 472 | TUL | 58 B4 |
| AVERY RD | FRCO | 55 E3 |
| AVERY RD | MCO | 55 D3 |
| AVERY SHEEP RCH | CAL | 41 C3 |
| AVIATION BLVD | ELS | 189 E3 |
| AVIATION BLVD | HAW | 189 E3 |
| AVIATION BLVD | ING | 189 E3 |
| AVIATION BLVD | LA | 188 E5 |
| AVIATION BLVD | LA | 189 E3 |
| AVIATION BLVD | LACO | 97 D3 |
| AVIATION BLVD | LACO | S B1 |
| AVIATION BLVD | RB | 189 E3 |
| AVOCADO BLVD | SDCO | V E3 |
| AVOCADO BLVD | SDCO | 111 E1 |
| AVOCADO RD | BUT | 25 E5 |
| AYERS AV | SJCO | 47 C1 |
| AYRES HOLMES RD | PLA | 34 B3 |
| AZALEA TR | RCO | 100 B3 |
| AZEVEDO | MCO | 47 D5 |
| AZEVEDO RD | SOL | 39 C4 |
| AZEVEDO RD | STA | 47 C4 |
| AZTEC AV | RCO | 102 C4 |
| AZUSA AV | LACO | 98 B2 |
| AZUSA AV | LACO | R E4 |
| AZUSA CANYON RD | LACO | R E3 |
| B | | |
| B ST | BUT | 25 C5 |
| B ST | DVS | 136 C3 |
| B ST | FRE | 165 C4 |
| B ST | H | 146 E2 |
| B ST | IMP | 109 A4 |
| B ST | KER | 68 B5 |
| B ST | LA | 191 B1 |
| B ST | LACO | 97 E4 |
| B ST | LACO | 98 C2 |
| B ST | LACO | S C2 |
| B ST | SCTO | 137 C2 |
| B ST | SD | 215 D3 |
| B ST | SJCO | 40 B5 |
| B ST | YUBA | 125 D3 |
| B ST | YUB | 33 D2 |
| B ST N | SCTO | 137 B2 |
| BABCOCK RD | LAS | 14 B4 |
| BABCOCK CNDR RD | LAS | 14 B4 |
| BABEL SLOUGH RD | YOL | 39 D2 |
| BACHELOR VLY RD | LAK | 31 C2 |
| BACK BONE RD | NEV | 26 D5 |
| BACKBONE RD | SHA | 13 A5 |
| BACKBONE RD | SHA | 18 E1 |
| BACKES LN | KER | 79 C4 |
| BACKUS RD | KER | 79 E5 |
| BACON RD | STA | 47 B4 |
| BACON ST | SDCO | V A3 |
| BACON ST | SDCO | 111 C1 |
| BACON ISLAND | SJCO | 39 E5 |
| BADDAGE RD | RCO | 107 B1 |
| BADENOUGH CY RD | SIE | 27 D3 |
| BADGER RD | SON | 37 E2 |

| STREET | CO. | PAGE & GRID |
|---|---|---|
| BADGER RD | SON | 38 A2 |
| BADGER FLAT | MCO | 55 D1 |
| BAGDAD HWY | SBD | 93 C4 |
| BAGDAD HWY | SBD | 101 C1 |
| BAGDAD WY | SBD | 93 D4 |
| BAGDAD CHASE RD | SBD | 93 B2 |
| BAGGTT MARYSVLL | BUT | 25 D5 |
| BAILEY AV | KER | 70 A5 |
| BAILEY AV | MCO | 48 B4 |
| BAILEY AV | SB | 86 B3 |
| BAILEY AV | SCL | P D4 |
| BAILEY RD | COL | 32 E3 |
| BAILEY RD | CC | M B3 |
| BAILEY RD | CC | 39 A5 |
| BAILEY RD | DN | 1 E3 |
| BAILEY RD | IMP | 110 D5 |
| BAILEY RD | RCO | 107 B1 |
| BAILEY RD | SBD | 84 A2 |
| BAILEY RD | SCL | 46 C5 |
| BAILEY RD | SUT | 33 C3 |
| BAILEY FLATS RD | MAD | 49 B5 |
| BAILEY HILL RD | SIS | 4 A2 |
| BAILY RD | KER | 79 B4 |
| BAILY RIDGE RD | CAL | 41 C2 |
| BAIN ST | RCO | 99 A2 |
| BAIR RD | HUM | 10 B4 |
| BAIRD RD | SON | 38 A2 |
| BAKER AV | ONT | 204 E3 |
| BAKER AV | ORA | T C3 |
| BAKER AV | ROC | 204 E3 |
| BAKER RD | COL | 32 C2 |
| BAKER RD | MCO | 55 E1 |
| BAKER RD | PLCV | 138 B2 |
| BAKER RD | SJCO | 40 B4 |
| BAKER RD | STA | 47 C3 |
| BAKER RD | TEH | 18 D5 |
| BAKER RD | SUT | 33 C4 |
| BAKER RD | YUB | 26 B5 |
| BAKER ST | CM | 197 B4 |
| BAKER ST | CM | 198 A4 |
| BAKER CREEK RD | INY | 51 D5 |
| BAKER RCH SODA | PLA | 34 E2 |
| BAKER RCH SODA | PLA | 35 B2 |
| BAKER RILEY WY | CAL | 41 B3 |
| BKRSFLD-GLNVLLE | KER | 68 E5 |
| BKRSFLD-GLNVLLE | KER | 69 A5 |
| BKRSFLD-GLNVLLE | KER | 78 D2 |
| BAKRSFLD-MCKITT | KER | 78 A3 |
| BALBOA AV | SD | 211 E5 |
| BALBOA AV | SD | 212 C1 |
| BALBOA AV | SDCO | V A2 |
| BALBOA AV | SDCO | 106 C5 |
| BALBOA BLVD | LACO | 97 C1 |
| BALBOA BLVD | NB | 199 B5 |
| BALBOA BLVD | ORA | T C4 |
| BALCH PARK RD | TUL | 69 A2 |
| BALCOM CYN RD | VEN | 88 D5 |
| BALDERSTON | ED | 34 E3 |
| BALD HILL RD | PLA | 34 C3 |
| BALD HILLS RD | DN | 1 E4 |
| BALD HILLS RD | DN | 2 A4 |
| BALD HILLS RD | HUM | 10 A2 |
| BALD MTN RD | CAL | 41 B2 |
| BALD MTN RD | HUM | 10 B5 |
| BALD MTN RD | MEN | 23 A2 |
| BALD MTN RD | MNO | 50 D1 |
| BALD MTN RD | SHA | 13 E4 |
| BALD MTN RD | YUB | 33 E1 |
| BALD MTN RD N | CAL | 41 C2 |
| BALD MTN LKOUT | SIS | 3 D4 |
| BALD MT SPGS RD | MNO | 50 E1 |
| BALD ROCK RD | BUT | 25 E3 |
| BALDWIN AV | LACO | R C3 |
| BALDWIN RD | STA | 47 D2 |
| BALDWIN RD | STA | 47 B3 |
| BALDWIN RD | VEN | 88 A4 |
| BALDWIN ST | CAL | 40 D4 |
| BALDWIN PARK BL | LACO | R D4 |
| BALDY RD | SBD | 90 E5 |
| BALDY MCCULY RD | SHA | 13 E4 |
| BALDY MESA RD | SBD | 91 A4 |
| BALE LN | NAPA | 29 B2 |
| BALFOUR RD | CC | M C3 |
| BALFOUR RD | CC | 39 C5 |
| BALIS BELL RD | TEH | 18 B5 |
| BALL RD | ANA | 193 A3 |
| BALL RD | ANA | 194 A3 |
| BALL RD | ORA | 98 B3 |
| BALL RD | ORA | T B2 |
| BALL RD | TEH | 17 E4 |
| BALL MT LTL SHA | SIS | 4 B4 |
| BALL MT LTL SHA | SIS | 5 A4 |
| BALL MTN LKOUT | SIS | 4 D3 |
| BALL ROCK RD | TEH | 23 E1 |
| BALLANTREE LN | NEV | 34 B2 |
| BALLARAT RD | INY | 71 C3 |
| BALLARD RD | TEH | 24 E2 |
| BALLICO AV | MCO | 48 A4 |
| BALLINGER RD | RCO | 99 E5 |
| BALLINGR CYN RD | VEN | 87 E1 |
| BALLIS RD | TEH | 18 C5 |
| BALLS FERRY RD | SHA | 18 D3 |
| BALL FERY PK RD | SHA | 18 D3 |
| BALSAM RD | SBD | 91 B4 |
| BALSAMO RD | SBD | 81 A5 |
| BALTIMORE MN RD | PLA | 34 E3 |
| BANCROFT AV | O | 159 D1 |
| BANCROFT DR | SDCO | V D3 |
| BANCROFT DR | SDCO | 111 E1 |
| BANCROFT RD | CC | M A3 |
| BANCROFT RD | STA | 47 C3 |
| BANCROFT WY | ALA | L D4 |
| BANCROFT WY | B | 156 A3 |
| BANDERILLA DR | MPA | 48 D2 |
| BANDINI BLVD | LACO | R A4 |
| B & R LN | SOL | 39 C3 |
| BANDUCCI RD | KER | 79 B4 |

| STREET | CO. | PAGE & GRID |
|---|---|---|
| BANGOR AV | KIN | 57 E5 |
| BANGOR PARK RD | BUT | 25 D5 |
| BANGOR PARK CTO | BUT | 25 E5 |
| BANGS AV | STA | 47 C2 |
| BANNER RD | CAL | 41 B3 |
| BANNER QUAKR HL | NEV | 34 D1 |
| BANNER RDG LAVA | NEV | 34 C1 |
| BANNING IDYLLWD | RCO | 100 A3 |
| BANNISTER AV | SCL | P E5 |
| BANNISTER RD | IMP | 108 E4 |
| BANTA RD | SJCO | 47 E2 |
| BAR RD | MAD | 49 E5 |
| BAR RD | MAD | 50 A5 |
| BARBARA WRTH RD | IMP | 112 B4 |
| BARBER | SJCO | 39 E3 |
| BARBER LN | RCO | 107 B1 |
| BARBER RD | ALP | 36 B4 |
| BARBER RD | TEH | 25 A2 |
| BARBER MTN RD | SDCO | 112 B1 |
| BARD RD | IMP | 110 D5 |
| BARDSDALE AV | VEN | 88 D4 |
| BARGLEY RD | COL | 32 C2 |
| BARHAM AV | TEH | 24 D2 |
| BARHAM BLVD | LA | 181 C1 |
| BARHAM BLVD | LACO | Q D3 |
| BAR K RD | TRI | 17 C2 |
| BARKER RD | KER | 67 B5 |
| BARKER CREEK RD | TRI | 17 B2 |
| BARKER MINE RD | MNO | 51 C2 |
| BARKHOUSE CK RD | SIS | 3 D3 |
| BARKSHANTY RD | SIS | 10 D1 |
| BARLOW LN | INY | 51 D4 |
| BAR MTN LOOKOUT | SIS | 3 C4 |
| BARNES LN | MEN | 23 B2 |
| BARNES RD | KER | 90 B1 |
| BARNES RD | SBD | 92 D4 |
| BARNES RD | SLO | 66 A5 |
| BARNES RD | SLO | 76 A1 |
| BARNETT AV | SDCO | V B3 |
| BARNETT RD | STA | 48 B2 |
| BARNEY GULCH RD | TRI | 11 B5 |
| BARNHART RD | STA | 47 C3 |
| BARNY OLDFLD RD | IMP | 110 C5 |
| BARR RD | HUM | 10 B5 |
| BARRANCA AV | LACO | U C2 |
| BARRANCA RD | ORA | 98 C4 |
| BARRANCA RD | ORA | T D3 |
| BARRANCA RD | TUS | 198 E2 |
| BARREL SPGS RD | LACO | 90 A3 |
| BARREL SPGS RD | MOD | 7 E3 |
| BARRETT | CC | 38 C5 |
| BARRETT AV | FRCO | 57 B5 |
| BARRETT AV | FRCO | 57 C5 |
| BARRETT LAKE RD | SDCO | 112 B2 |
| BARRINGTON AV | LACO | 180 B2 |
| BARRINGTON LN | SIE | 27 C4 |
| BARRY RD | SUT | 33 D2 |
| BARRYS RD | HUM | 16 A1 |
| BARSTOW AV | FRCO | 57 A3 |
| BARSTOW AV | FRCO | 57 C3 |
| BARSTOW AV | KIN | 57 E5 |
| BARSTOW FRWY | SBD | 91 A5 |
| BARSTOW FRWY | SBD | 99 B1 |
| BARSTOW RD | BARS | 208 B3 |
| BARSTOW RD | KER | 80 D5 |
| BARSTOW RD | SBD | 91 E2 |
| BARSTOW RD | SBD | 92 A4 |
| BARTEL ST | SHA | 13 C5 |
| BARTELL RD | INY | 51 E5 |
| BARTH RD | IMP | 108 E3 |
| BARTLE GAP RD | SIS | 13 B3 |
| BARTLETT RD | SOL | 39 C3 |
| BARTLETTE RD | INY | 60 B5 |
| BARTLETT SPG RD | LAK | 31 E2 |
| BARTLETT SPG RD | LAK | 31 E2 |
| BARTOLOMEI | SJCO | 40 C5 |
| BARTOLOMEI | SJCO | 47 C1 |
| BARTON | PLA | 34 B5 |
| BARTON RD | SBD | 99 C2 |
| BARTON ST | RCO | 99 B3 |
| BARTON HILL RD | YUB | 26 B4 |
| BAR W RD | HUM | 16 B3 |
| BASCOM AV | SCL | 46 B5 |
| BASCOM AV | SJ | 151 C4 |
| BASCOM AV | SCL | P B3 |
| BASE LINE AV | SB | 86 E3 |
| BASELINE RD | LACO | 98 E1 |
| BASE LINE RD | LACO | U A2 |
| BASE LINE RD | PLA | 33 E5 |
| BASELINE RD | SBD | U D2 |
| BASELINE RD | SBD | 98 E1 |
| BASELINE RD | SBD | 101 C1 |
| BASELINE ST | SBDO | 207 B1 |
| BASELINE ST | SBD | 102 C1 |
| BASIC SCHOOL RD | KER | 78 B5 |
| BASILONE RD | SDCO | 105 E1 |
| BASIN RD | SBD | 82 E5 |
| BASIN ST | KER | 79 C2 |
| BASLER RD | TEH | 18 B4 |
| BASS | FRCO | 56 C3 |
| BASSET RD | LAS | 14 C3 |
| BASSETT AV | KER | 68 C5 |
| BASS HILL RD | LAS | 21 A4 |
| BASS LAKE RD | ED | 34 C5 |
| BASS VALLEY RD | MAD | 49 D4 |
| BASTANCHURY RD | ORA | T E1 |
| BATAVIA RD | SOL | 39 B2 |
| BATCHELDER RD | SB | 86 C2 |
| BATEMAN RD | SHA | 19 B2 |
| BATES | SUT | 33 C4 |
| BATTL CK BTM RD | SHA | 19 A3 |
| BAUGHMAN RD | IMP | 108 E4 |
| BAUMBACH AV | KER | 79 B4 |
| BAUTISTA RD | RCO | 100 A4 |
| BAXTER AV | NAP | 133 B2 |
| BAXTER RD | MCO | 48 E5 |
| BAXTER RD | RCO | 99 C5 |
| BAXTERS RD | MNO | 43 E5 |
| BAXTERS RD | MNO | 50 E1 |
| BAY DR | SC | 169 A3 |
| BAY HWY | SON | 37 C3 |
| BAY RD | SMCO | N D2 |
| BAY RD | SMCO | 45 D3 |
| BAY ST | SF | 142 B1 |
| BAY ST | SF | 143 A2 |
| BAY ST | SC | 169 B4 |
| BAYLEY RES RD | MOD | 8 A2 |
| BAYLIS BLUE GUM | GLE | 24 D4 |
| BAYOU RD | SAC | 33 D5 |
| BAYSHORE BLVD | SMCO | L C5 |
| BAYSHORE BLVD | SMCO | 45 C2 |
| BAYSHORE FRWY | BLMT | 145 B3 |
| BAYSHORE FRWY | BURL | 144 C3 |
| BAYSHORE FRWY | MLBR | 144 C3 |
| BAYSHORE FRWY | MVW | 148 A3 |
| BAYSHORE FRWY | SJ | 151 D1 |
| BAYSHORE FRWY | SJ | 152 B1 |
| BAYSHORE FRWY | SM | 145 B3 |
| BAYSHORE FRWY | SMCO | 45 D3 |
| BAYSHORE FRWY | SMCO | 144 C3 |
| BAYSHORE FRWY | SMCO | 145 B3 |
| BAYSHORE FRWY | SSF | 144 C1 |
| BAYSHORE FRWY | SVL | 148 D3 |
| BAYSIDE DR | NB | 199 D5 |
| BAYSIDE DR | NB | 200 A5 |
| BAY VIEW AV | NAPA | 38 C3 |
| BAY VIEW RD | MCO | 55 C1 |
| BEACH BLVD | ORA | 98 B3 |
| BEACH BLVD | ORA | T B1 |
| BEACH RD | HUM | 22 A1 |
| BEACH RD | IMP | 109 A2 |
| BEACH RD | MPA | 49 B4 |
| BEACH RD | SCR | 54 B3 |
| BEACH ST | SF | 143 A2 |
| BEACH PARK BL | FCTY | 145 D3 |
| BEACON RD | SLO | 76 B1 |
| BEACON ST | AVLN | 105 B5 |
| BEAL RD | IMP | 109 B2 |
| BEALE RD N | YUB | 33 D2 |
| BEALE RD S | YUB | 33 E3 |
| BEALE ST | SF | 143 D4 |
| BEAL RANCH RD | CAL | 40 E3 |
| BEAL RANCH RD | CAL | 41 A3 |
| BEALEVILLE RD | KER | 79 B3 |
| BEAMER ST | YOL | 33 B5 |
| BEAN CLIPPER RD | YUB | 26 B4 |
| BEAN CREEK RD | BUT | 25 E4 |
| BEAN CREEK RD | SCR | P A5 |
| BEAN CREEK RD | SCR | 54 A1 |
| BEAN HOLLOW RD | SMCO | N C4 |
| BEAN HOLLOW RD | SMCO | 45 C5 |
| BEAR ST | CM | 197 E4 |
| BEAR ST | ORA | T D3 |
| BEAR BASIN RD | DN | 2 B3 |
| BEAR BUTTE RD | HUM | 16 B5 |
| BEAR CANYON RD | FRCO | 66 B2 |
| BEAR CREEK DR N | MCO | 48 C4 |
| BEAR CREEK DR S | MCO | 48 C4 |
| BEAR CREEK LOOP | TRI | 12 A3 |
| BEAR CREEK RD | CC | L D3 |
| BEAR CREEK RD | CC | 38 D5 |
| BEAR CREEK RD | LAK | 31 D1 |
| BEAR CREEK RD | SCL | P A4 |
| BEAR CREEK RD | SCR | N E5 |
| BEAR CREEK RD | SCR | P A5 |
| BEAR CREEK RD | SCR | 45 E5 |
| BEARD RD | NAP | 133 C2 |
| BEAR GULCH RD | SMCO | N C3 |
| BEAR MTN BLVD | KER | 78 D4 |
| BEAR MTN RD | FRCO | 58 B3 |
| BEAR MTN RD | SHA | 18 C1 |
| BEAR MTN RD | SIS | 13 C2 |
| BEAR MTN LKOUT | SHA | 18 C1 |
| BEAR MT WINE RD | KER | 78 E3 |
| BEAR MT WINE RD | KER | 79 A3 |
| BEAR RANCH HILL | BUT | 25 E2 |
| BEAR RIVER | AMA | 41 D1 |
| BEAR RIVER S | AMA | 41 D1 |
| BEAR RIVER DR | SUT | 33 D3 |
| BEAR RIV RDG RD | HUM | 15 D3 |
| BEAR SPRINGS RD | LAS | 14 A3 |
| BEAR TRAP DR | MPA | 49 A3 |
| BEAR TRAP RD | NEV | 26 C5 |
| BEAR VALLEY | MPA | 48 E3 |
| BEAR VLY PKWY | SDCO | 106 D4 |
| BEAR VALLEY RD | COL | 32 B2 |
| BEAR VALLEY RD | KER | 79 B4 |
| BEAR VALLEY RD | SBD | 90 E4 |
| BEAR VALLEY RD | SIE | 27 D4 |
| BEAR VLY CUTOFF | SBD | 91 B4 |
| BEASON ST | KER | 78 A1 |
| BEASORE RD | MAD | 49 E4 |
| BEATIE RD | SHA | 18 D3 |
| BEAUCHAMP RD | COL | 32 D2 |
| BEAUMONT AV | RCO | 99 E3 |
| BEAUMONT ST | SBD | 91 E3 |
| BEAVER CREEK RD | SIS | 3 D3 |
| BECHELLI LN | RED | 122 E2 |
| BECHELLI LN | SHA | 18 C2 |
| BECK AV | SOL | L E1 |
| BECK AV | SOL | M A1 |
| BECKER | SUT | 33 C4 |
| BECKER RD | SOL | 39 C1 |
| BECKET CT | KER | 79 C5 |
| BECKWITH RD | SIE | 27 D3 |
| BECKWITH RD | STA | 47 B2 |
| BECKWRTH CALPNE | PLU | 27 C3 |
| BECKWRTH GENESE | PLU | 26 E1 |
| BECKWRTH GENESE | PLU | 27 B1 |
| BECKWRTH LOYLTN | PLU | 27 C3 |
| BCKWRTH TYLRSVL | PLU | 26 D1 |
| BCKWRTH TYLRSVL | PLU | 27 B2 |
| BEDFORD DR | SBD | 92 B1 |
| BEE CANYON RD | RCO | 100 A4 |
| BEECH AV | KER | 78 B2 |
| BEECH AV | SBD | 99 A2 |
| BEECH ST | BKD | 166 B2 |
| BEECH ST | SDCO | 106 C2 |
| BEECHER RD | SJCO | 40 B5 |
| BEE GULCH RD | ALP | 42 A1 |
| BEEGUM RD | SHA | 17 D4 |
| BEEGUM GORGE RD | SHA | 17 D4 |
| BEEKLEY RD | RCO | 102 C4 |
| BEEKLEY RD | SBD | 90 E4 |
| BEEROCK RD | SLO | 65 D5 |
| BEHYMER | FRCO | 56 C2 |
| BEHYMER AV | FRCO | 57 D2 |
| BELCHER AV | MCO | 48 B4 |
| BELFAST RD | LAS | 21 B3 |
| BELL | MCO | 48 A4 |
| BELL LN | PLU | 26 D1 |
| BELL RD | AMA | 40 E1 |
| BELL RD | BUT | 25 A3 |
| BELL RD | KER | 77 E2 |
| BELL RD | KER | 78 A2 |
| BELL RD | PLA | 34 B3 |
| BELL RD | SB | 87 C1 |
| BELL RD | STA | 47 C4 |
| BELL ST | SB | 86 D2 |
| BELLA ROSA DR | HUM | 16 C4 |
| BELLA VISTA DR | KER | 79 D1 |
| BELLE TER | KER | 166 D5 |
| BELLE GRAVE AV | RCO | 99 A2 |
| BELLEVUE AV | SUT | 33 D3 |
| BELLEVUE RD | MCO | 48 B4 |
| BELLFLOWER BLVD | LACO | 98 A3 |
| BELLFLOWER BLVD | LACO | S E2 |
| BELLFLOWER BLVD | LACO | T A2 |
| BELLFLOWER ST | SBD | 91 B3 |
| BELL HILL RD | LAK | 31 D3 |
| BELL MTN RD | SBD | 91 C3 |
| BELL SPRINGS RD | HUM | 16 C5 |
| BELL SPRINGS RD | MEN | 22 D1 |
| BELLVIEW RD | MAD | 57 C1 |
| BELMONT AV | FRE | 165 C3 |
| BELMONT AV | FRCO | 56 C3 |
| BELMONT AV | FRCO | 57 C3 |
| BELOMY ST | SCLR | 151 B3 |
| BELSBY AV | RCO | 102 C4 |
| BELTLINE RD | SHA | 18 C2 |
| BENA RD | KER | 79 A3 |
| BENBOW DR | HUM | 22 C1 |
| BEND | TEH | 18 D4 |
| BENDER | SJCO | 40 A3 |
| BENDER AV | KER | 78 B2 |
| BENDER RD | SHA | 18 A3 |
| BENDLER RD | STA | 47 E2 |
| BENEDICT CYN DR | LACO | Q C3 |
| BENHAM LN | CUR | 1 D2 |
| BEN HUR RD | MPA | 49 B4 |
| BENICIA AV | KIN | 57 E5 |
| BENICIA RD | SOL | 38 D4 |
| BENICIA RD | VAL | 134 D5 |
| BENIT JUAREZ BL | BAJA | 112 B4 |
| BENNER AV | KER | 68 B5 |
| BENNET RD | LACO | 89 A5 |
| BENNET RD | VEN | 88 E5 |
| BENNETS WELL RD | INY | 72 A2 |
| BENNETT RD | BUT | 25 A2 |
| BENNETT RD | MCO | 55 E2 |
| BENNETT RD | NEV | 34 C1 |
| BENNETT RD | RCO | 100 D3 |
| BENNETT VLY RD | SON | 38 A2 |
| BENNETT VLY RD | STR | 131 D4 |
| BENSON AV | MTCL | 203 D3 |
| BENSON AV | ONT | 203 D5 |
| BENSON AV | SBD | U D3 |
| BENSON AV | SBD | 98 D2 |
| BENSON AV | SBD | 203 D3 |
| BENSON AV | UPL | 203 D1 |
| BENSON DR | SHA | 18 B2 |
| BENSON RD | TEH | 18 C4 |
| BENT RD | STA | 47 D2 |
| BENTLEY RD | STA | 47 D2 |
| BENTON DR | SHA | 18 C2 |
| BENTON RD | RCO | 99 D5 |
| BENTON RD E | RCO | 99 E5 |
| BENTON ST | SCLR | 150 C3 |
| BENTON CROSSING | MNO | 51 B2 |
| BENTN GBG PT RD | MNO | 51 C1 |
| BERDOO CYN RD | RCO | 101 B3 |
| BERKELEY AV | STA | 47 E3 |
| BERKSHIRE RD | KER | 79 A3 |
| BERMUDA DR | SM | 145 B2 |
| BERNAL AV | ALA | M B5 |
| BERNAL AV | ALA | P B1 |
| BERNAL DR E | SAL | 171 C3 |
| BERNARD ST | KER | 78 D3 |
| BERNARD WY | SHA | 18 C1 |
| BERRELLESA ST | M | 154 B2 |
| BERRY AV | H | 146 E4 |
| BERRY RD | SUT | 33 D3 |
| BERRY CREEK RD | BUT | 25 E3 |
| BERRYESSA RD | SJ | 152 C1 |
| BERRYESSA RD | SCL | P B3 |
| BERRYESSA RD | SCL | 46 B4 |
| BERRYSSA KNX RD | NAPA | 32 C4 |
| BERT RD | LAS | 27 E1 |
| BERTAS RD | HUM | 15 E1 |
| BERT CRANE RD | MCO | 48 B5 |
| BERTRAM CIR | KER | 79 C4 |
| BERYL ST | LACO | 97 D3 |
| BERYL ST | LACO | S B1 |
| BERYL ST | SD | 212 A1 |
| BERYLWOOD RD | VEN | 88 C5 |
| BESSEMR MINE RD | SBD | 92 B4 |
| BEST RD | IMP | 109 B4 |
| BEST RD | MPA | 49 C3 |
| BEST RD | RCO | 99 E5 |
| BEST RD | SUT | 33 C3 |
| BETHANY RD | SJCO | 46 D1 |
| BETHEL AV | FRCO | 57 E4 |
| BETHEL RD | SLO | 76 A2 |
| BETHEL ISLND RD | CC | M D3 |
| BETHEL ISLND RD | CC | 39 C5 |
| BETTERAVIA RD | STB | 173 C5 |
| BETTERAVIA RD | SB | 86 B1 |
| BETTERAVIA RD | SMA | 173 C5 |
| BETTS RD | TRI | 23 A1 |
| BETTY WY | SIS | 4 B4 |
| BETZ RD | SUT | 33 D3 |
| BEVERLY | LACO | 98 A2 |
| BEVERLY BLVD | BH | 183 C1 |
| BEVERLY BLVD | LA | 183 C1 |
| BEVERLY BLVD | LA | 184 B1 |
| BEVERLY BLVD | LA | 185 C1 |
| BEVERLY BLVD | LACO | 97 D2 |
| BEVERLY BLVD | LACO | 183 C1 |
| BEVERLY BLVD | LACO | Q D4 |
| BEVERLY DR | BH | 183 B1 |
| BEVERLY DR | LAS | 20 E3 |
| BEVERLY DR | LA | 183 B1 |
| BEVERLY DR | LACO | Q C3 |
| BEVERLY GLEN BL | LA | 180 E2 |
| BEVERLY GLEN BL | LA | 183 A3 |
| BEVERLY GLEN BL | LACO | 97 C1 |
| BEVERLY GLEN BL | LACO | Q C3 |
| BEVERWIL DR | BH | 183 C3 |
| BEVERWIL DR | LA | 183 C3 |
| BEYER BLVD | SDCO | V D5 |
| BEYER BLVD | SDCO | 111 D2 |
| BEYER LN | SJCO | 40 B5 |
| BEYER WY | SDCO | V C5 |
| BEYER WY | SDCO | 111 D2 |
| BEYERS LN | NEV | 34 B2 |
| BIANCHI RD | S | 160 B4 |
| BIDDLE | SLO | 76 B1 |
| BIDWELL RD | SHA | 13 D5 |
| BIDWELL CK RD | MOD | 7 D3 |
| BIEBER LKOUT RD | LAS | 14 B3 |
| BIG BAR DUMP RD | TRI | 17 A1 |
| BIG BAR MTN RD | BUT | 25 E2 |
| BIG BEN | PLA | 34 B3 |
| BIG BEND RD | BUT | 25 D3 |
| BIG BEND RD | SHA | 13 A4 |
| BIG CANYON | LAK | 32 A4 |
| BIG CREEK RD | PLU | 26 B2 |
| BIG CREEK RD | TRI | 17 B2 |
| BIG CK SHAFT RD | TUO | 48 E1 |
| BIG DIPPER | PLA | 34 D2 |
| BIGELOW RD | SIS | 13 A2 |
| BIGELOW RD | SUT | 33 B1 |
| BIG FLAT RD | DN | 2 B4 |
| BIG FRCH CK RD | TRI | 11 A5 |
| BIGGAR LN | MEN | 23 A2 |
| BIGGS EAST HWY | BUT | 25 C5 |
| BIG HILL RD | TUO | 41 D4 |
| BIG HILL LKOUT | HUM | 10 C3 |
| BIG HORN DR | RCO | 100 D5 |
| BIG INCH PIPELN | KER | 79 E5 |
| BIG INCH PIPELN | KER | 80 A5 |
| BIG LAKES RD | MOD | 14 D2 |
| BIG MEADOWS RD | SIS | 3 C5 |
| BIG OAK DR | MEN | 31 B3 |
| BIG PN REPTR RD | INY | 51 E5 |
| BIG RANCH RD | NAPA | 29 E5 |
| BIG RANCH RD | NAPA | 38 C2 |
| BIG RANCH RD | NAPA | 133 C2 |
| BIG RESRVOIR RD | PLA | 34 C2 |
| BIG ROCK CK RD | LACO | 90 C4 |
| BIG SAGE RD | MOD | 6 E5 |
| BIG SAGE RD | MOD | 7 A5 |
| BIG SANDY RD | MON | 66 B4 |
| BIG SPRING DR | NEV | 34 B2 |
| BIG SPRING RD | SHA | 19 A2 |
| BIG SPRINGS RD | MNO | 50 D1 |
| BIG SPRINGS RD | SIS | 4 C5 |
| BIG SPRINGS RD | SIS | 12 C1 |
| BIG SPRINGS RD | SIS | 13 A2 |
| BIG SPRINGS CTO | PLU | 20 B4 |
| BIG STUMP RD | SIS | 5 A2 |
| BIG TRAILS DR | MEN | 22 E4 |
| BIG TRAILS DR | MEN | 23 A4 |
| BIG TREES RD | INY | 51 C4 |
| BIG TUJUNGA BL | LACO | Q E1 |
| BIG TUJUNGA CYN | LACO | 89 E5 |
| BIG VALLEY RD | LAK | 31 D3 |
| BILBY RD | SAC | 39 E2 |
| BILLE RD | BUT | 25 C3 |
| BILLIE ST | KER | 78 D4 |
| BILLINGS AV | KER | 78 B1 |
| BILLINGS LN | RCO | 99 B4 |
| BILLY WRIGHT RD | MCO | 55 C2 |
| BINET RD | BUT | 26 B4 |
| BINGHAMTON RD | SOL | 39 B2 |
| BIOLA AV | FRCO | 57 B3 |
| BIR RD | INY | 51 C4 |
| BIRCH AV | MON | 65 A1 |
| BIRCH ST | ORA | 98 C3 |
| BIRCH ST | ORA | T D1 |
| BIRCH ST | ORA | U A4 |
| BIRCH CREEK RD | INY | 59 E1 |
| BIRCHIM LN | INY | 51 C3 |
| BIRCHIN FLAT RD | MNO | 42 E2 |
| BIRCHIN FLAT RD | MNO | 43 A2 |
| BIRCHVILLE RD | NEV | 26 B5 |
| BIRD AV | SJ | 152 B5 |
| BIRD RD | SJCO | 47 A2 |
| BIRDS LANDNG RD | SOL | 39 B4 |
| BIRD SPG CYN RD | KER | 80 A1 |
| BIRKHEAD | FRCO | 57 C2 |
| BIRMINGHAM DR | SDCO | 106 B4 |
| BISCH CT | KER | 79 E2 |
| BISHOP AV | FRCO | 57 B4 |
| BISHOP AV | FRCO | 67 B1 |
| BISHOP AV | SUT | 33 C1 |
| BISHOP ST | SNLO | 172 D4 |
| BISHOP CK RD E | INY | 51 C4 |
| BISHOP CK RD W | INY | 51 C4 |
| BISIGNANI RD | MCO | 55 E1 |
| BISSET STN RD | MAD | 49 D4 |
| BITNEY SPGS RD | NEV | 34 B1 |
| BITTERWATER RD | MON | 65 C2 |
| BITTRWTR VLY RD | KER | 77 A1 |
| BIXBY RD | VEN | 88 D5 |
| BIXLER RD | CC | 39 D5 |
| BLACK RD | SB | 86 B1 |
| BLACK BART RD | BUT | 25 E4 |
| BLACK BEAR RD | SIS | 11 B2 |
| BLACK BUTTE RD | GLE | 24 B3 |
| BLACK BUTTE RD | SHA | 19 A3 |
| BLACK BUTTE RD | TEH | 24 C2 |
| BLACK CANYON RD | INY | 51 E4 |
| BLACK CANYON RD | MNO | 44 B5 |
| BLACK CANYON RD | MNO | 51 B1 |
| BLACK CANYON RD | SBD | 81 C5 |
| BLACK CANYON RD | SBD | 84 B5 |
| BLACK CANYON RD | SBD | 94 C1 |
| BLACK CANYON RD | SDCO | 107 A3 |
| BLACK DIAMND WY | CC | 39 B5 |
| BLACK DIAMND MN | BUT | 25 C2 |
| BLK EAGLE MN RD | RCO | 101 E3 |
| BLACK FOX MTN | SIS | 13 B2 |
| BLACK GULCH RD | KER | 79 C1 |
| BLACK GULCH RD | LAS | 14 A5 |
| BLACK HAWK RD | CC | M B4 |
| BLACK HAWK RD | CC | 46 B1 |
| BLACKHAWK RD | PLU | 26 C1 |
| BLACK HILLS RD | RCO | 100 D4 |
| BLACKIE RD | MON | 54 C3 |
| BLACK LAKE RD | LAS | 14 B5 |
| BLACKMER RD | SUT | 33 B2 |
| BLACKMORE | SJCO | 47 C1 |
| BLACK MTN RD | IMP | 110 B3 |
| BLACK MTN RD | SDCO | 106 D4 |
| BLACK MTN RD | SMCO | N C2 |
| BLACK MTN RD | SMCO | 45 C3 |
| BLACK MTN RD | SIS | 4 B3 |
| BLACK MTN TR | RCO | 100 B3 |
| BLACK MTN LO RD | SLO | 76 D3 |
| BLACK RANCH RD | SHA | 13 C4 |
| BLACK ROCK RD | RCO | 103 C5 |
| BLACK ROCK CYN | SBD | 100 E2 |
| BLACK RCK MN RD | MNO | 51 C2 |
| BLACK ROCK SPGS | INY | 59 E2 |
| BLACKS CYN RD | MOD | 14 D1 |
| BLACKS RDG LKOT | LAS | 14 B5 |
| BLACKSTONE AV | FRE | 165 D1 |
| BLACKSTONE ST | TUL | 68 B2 |
| BLACKWELL LN | DN | 1 D4 |
| BLAGEN RD | CAL | 41 C3 |
| BLAINE ST | RCO | 99 B2 |
| BLAIR RD | IMP | 109 B3 |
| BLAIS RD | IMP | 109 A4 |
| BLAKE RD | SAC | 40 B2 |
| BLAKE ST | SBD | 99 B1 |
| BLAKER RD | STA | 47 D3 |
| BLANCHARD FT RD | TRI | 17 D2 |
| BLANCO | MON | 54 C4 |
| BLANCO RD | MPA | 48 D2 |
| BLANCO RD E | MON | 171 C5 |
| BLANCO RD E | SAL | 171 C5 |
| BLANCO RD W | MON | 171 A5 |
| BLANCO RD W | SAL | 171 A5 |
| BLAND RD | SHA | 17 E3 |
| BLANEY AV | CPTO | 149 E5 |
| BLANKENSHIP AV | KER | 78 A1 |
| BLANKO RD | SBD | 90 E4 |
| BLATCHLEY RD | TEH | 24 D2 |
| BLAZING STAR AV | SBD | 91 A3 |
| BLEDSOE RD | MCO | 48 B3 |
| BLEVENS RD | LPAZ | 104 C5 |
| BLEWETT RD | STA | 47 B2 |
| BLICKENSTAFF RD | LAS | 21 B4 |
| BLISS DR | RCO | 107 C1 |
| BLISS RD | MCO | 48 C5 |
| BLISS RD | YUB | 33 D2 |
| BLITHEDALE AV | MAR | L B4 |
| BLITHEDALE AV | MAR | 45 B1 |
| BLITHEDALE AV E | MV | 140 A3 |
| B L M DUMP RD | LAS | 20 E1 |
| BLOCK RD | BUT | 25 C5 |
| BLOCK RD | BUT | 33 C1 |
| BLODGETT RD | IMP | 109 B5 |
| BLOODY CAMP RD | HUM | 10 C3 |
| BLOOMR HLL LKOT | BUT | 25 D3 |
| BLOOMFIELD AV | LACO | T A2 |
| BLOOMFIELD AV | SCL | 54 D2 |
| BLOOMFIELD RD | SON | 37 D3 |
| BLOOMFLD GRNTVL | NEV | 26 D5 |
| BLOOMINGTON RD | SBD | 99 B2 |
| BLOSS AV | MCO | 47 D4 |
| BLOSSER RD | STB | 173 A2 |
| BLOSSER RD | SB | 86 B1 |
| BLOSSER RD | SMA | 173 A4 |
| BLOSSOM | SJCO | 39 E3 |
| BLOSSOM AV | MCO | 56 A2 |
| BLOSSOM RD | STA | 47 E2 |
| BLOSSOM HILL RD | SCL | P B4 |
| BLOSSOM HILL RD | SCL | 46 A5 |
| BLOWERS DR | RCO | 99 A4 |
| BLUE GILL RD | SIS | 4 B3 |
| BLUE GULCH RD | SIS | 11 B3 |
| BLUE GUM AV | STA | 47 C2 |
| BLUE LAKE BLVD | HUM | 10 A5 |
| BLUE LAKE RD | LAS | 8 D3 |
| BLUE LAKE RD | MOD | 8 C3 |
| BLUE LK MPLE CK | HUM | 16 B1 |
| BLUE LAKES RD | ALP | 36 B5 |
| BLUE LAKES RD | LAK | 31 C2 |
| BLUE MTN RD | CAL | 41 C2 |
| BLUE MTN RD | KER | 69 A5 |
| BLUE MTN LKT RD | CAL | 41 C2 |
| BLUE RIDGE RD | SOL | 38 E2 |
| BLUE RIDGE RD | TEH | 19 B3 |

STREETS

222
BLUE SLIDE RD
STREET INDEX
BYSTRUM RD


| STREET | CO. | PAGE & GRID |
|---|---|---|
| BLUE SLIDE RD | HUM | 15 E3 |
| BLUFF ST | RCO | 100 A2 |
| BLUFF CREEK RD | TRI | 16 E5 |
| BLYTHE AV | FRCO | 57 C3 |
| BLYTHE AV | FRCO | 67 B1 |
| BOARDER ST | RCO | 100 A3 |
| BOARTS RD | IMP | 109 A4 |
| BOAT HARBOR RD | LAS | 20 E2 |
| BOBCAT TR | RCO | 100 A5 |
| BOB HOPE DR | RCO | 100 E4 |
| BOBS GAP RD | LACO | 90 C4 |
| BOB WHITE WY | INY | 73 A4 |
| BOCA RD | NEV | 27 E5 |
| BOCA SPRINGS RD | NEV | 27 E5 |
| BOCA SPGS RD E | NEV | 27 E5 |
| BOCKMAN RD | ALA | 146 A2 |
| BODEGA AV | SON | 38 A3 |
| BODEGA HWY | SON | 37 D2 |
| BODEM ST | MDO | 162 D2 |
| BODFISH CYN RD | KER | 79 D1 |
| BODIE RD | MNO | 43 C3 |
| BODIE MASONC RD | MNO | 43 C3 |
| BOESSOW RD | SAC | 40 B3 |
| BOGARD RD | LAS | 14 B5 |
| BOGGS RD | COL | 24 E5 |
| BOGGS & CHAMLIN | TEH | 24 C2 |
| BOGUE RD | STA | 47 E3 |
| BOGUE RD | STA | 48 A3 |
| BOGUE RD | SUT | 33 C2 |
| BOHAN DILLON RD | SON | 37 B1 |
| BOHEMIAN HWY | SON | 37 C2 |
| BOHN BLVD | SHA | 18 C3 |
| BOLAM RD | SIS | 4 D5 |
| BOLAM RD | SIS | 12 D1 |
| BOLAM LOGGNG RD | SIS | 12 D1 |
| BOLES RD | COL | 32 E3 |
| BOLEY RD | IMP | 108 E5 |
| BOLLINGER CY RD | CC | M A4 |
| BOLLINGER CY RD | CC | M B5 |
| BOLINGER CYN RD | CC | 45 E1 |
| BOLINGER CYN RD | CC | 46 A1 |
| BOLO RD | SBD | 94 A3 |
| BOLSA AV | ORA | 98 B4 |
| BOLSA CHICA RD | ORA | 98 B4 |
| BOLSA CHICA RD | ORA | T B3 |
| BON ST | MCO | 48 D5 |
| BONANZA AV | TRI | 17 D1 |
| BONANZA RD | CLK | 74 D2 |
| BONANZA RD | LV | 209 B1 |
| BONANZA RD | SBD | 101 A1 |
| BONANZA TR | SBD | 91 C2 |
| BONANZA WY | NEV | 34 B1 |
| BONANZA KING RD | TRI | 12 A4 |
| BOND RD | SJCO | 40 A2 |
| BOND RD | STA | 47 E2 |
| BONDS CORNER RD | IMP | 112 C4 |
| BONDS FLAT RD | TUO | 48 C2 |
| BONDURANT | MPA | 49 A2 |
| BONE STEEL RD | IMP | 112 C4 |
| BONETTI RD | SJCO | 46 D1 |
| BONITA AV | LACO | 98 C1 |
| BONITA AV | LACO | U B2 |
| BONITA RD | MCO | 55 D2 |
| BONITA RD | SDCO | V D4 |
| BONITA RD | SDCO | 111 D2 |
| BONITA CYN DR | IRV | 200 C3 |
| BONITA CYN DR | ORA | 98 C4 |
| BONITA CYN DR | ORA | T D4 |
| BONITA LATERAL | SB | 76 C5 |
| BONITA LATERAL | SB | 86 B1 |
| BONITA SCHL RD | SLO | 76 C5 |
| BONITA SCHL RD | SB | 76 C5 |
| BONITA SCHL RD | SB | 86 B1 |
| BONITA VISTA RD | RCO | 100 C4 |
| BONNER RD | MCO | 48 D4 |
| BONNEYVIEW RD E | SHA | 18 C2 |
| BONNIE CT | KER | 79 C3 |
| BONNY LN | RCO | 107 B1 |
| BONNY DOON RD | SCR | 53 D2 |
| BONNYVIEW RD S | SHA | 18 C2 |
| BONVIEW AV | SBD | 98 D2 |
| BOOKER RD | TUO | 41 D5 |
| BOONE LN | FRCO | 66 B3 |
| BOONE ST | SMA | 173 A3 |
| BOOTH RD | LPAZ | 104 B2 |
| BOOT JACK | MPA | 49 C3 |
| BORAX RD | KER | 80 D5 |
| BORAX MILL RD | INY | 62 A5 |
| BORBA | SJCO | 40 A5 |
| BORBA | SJCO | 47 A1 |
| BORCHARD | VEN | 96 D1 |
| BORDEN RD | SAC | 40 B3 |
| BORDEN ST | MAD | 57 A2 |
| BORDER AV | RCO | U E5 |
| BORDER AV | RCO | 98 E3 |
| BORDER AV | SBD | 100 E1 |
| BOREL RD | RCO | 99 D5 |
| BORMAN LN | LAK | 32 B4 |
| BORNT RD | IMP | 112 C4 |
| BORON AV | KER | 80 E5 |
| BORRGO SLTN SEA | SDCO | 108 A2 |
| BORREGO SPGS RD | SDCO | 107 E2 |
| BORREGO VLY RD | SDCO | 107 E2 |
| BOSCOVICH RD | IMP | 112 D5 |
| BOSTON AV | LACO | Q E2 |
| BOTTINI | TUO | 41 E4 |
| BOTTLE CREEK RD | BUT | 25 D1 |
| BOTTLE HILL RD | BUT | 25 D1 |
| BOTTLE ROCK RD | LAK | 31 E4 |
| BOUCHO RD | COL | 32 E3 |
| BOULDER AV | SBD | 99 C1 |
| BOULDER HWY | CLK | 74 D2 |
| BOULDER CK RD | SDCO | 107 C5 |
| BOULDER CK RD | SIS | 3 C5 |
| BOULEVARD, THE | GLE | 24 E4 |
| BL D L AMERICAS | BAJA | 112 B4 |
| BOULTON RD | SUT | 33 C3 |
| BOUNDARY ST | SD | 216 C1 |
| BOUNDARY TR | DN | 2 A4 |
| BOUQUET CYN RD | LACO | 89 C4 |
| BOUSE QUARTZITE | LPAZ | 104 C4 |
| BOW AV | KER | 80 C1 |
| BOWEN RD | COL | 32 D1 |
| BOWEN RANCH RD | SBD | 91 C4 |
| BOWERS AV | SCL | P B3 |
| BOWERS AV | SCLR | 150 D1 |
| BOWKER RD | IMP | 112 B3 |
| BOWKER RD | IMP | 112 B4 |
| BOWL PL | SB | 86 E3 |
| BOWMAN RD | KER | 80 D1 |
| BOWMAN RD | MOD | 7 B5 |
| BOWMAN RD | SBDO | 81 A1 |
| BOWMAN RD | SJCO | 47 A1 |
| BOWMAN RD | TEH | 18 B4 |
| BOWMAN LAKE RD | NEV | 27 A5 |
| BOWMAN LAKE RD | NEV | 35 A1 |
| BOX CANYON RD | RCO | 101 C5 |
| BOX CAR RD | MCO | 55 E1 |
| BOX ELDER ST | RCO | 100 C4 |
| BOX SPRINGS BL | RCO | 99 B2 |
| BOX SPRINGS RD | RCO | 99 C2 |
| BOYCE RD | SOL | 39 A1 |
| BOYD | CC | 38 E5 |
| BOYD DR | TUL | 58 C4 |
| BOYD RD | IMP | 109 B5 |
| BOYD SPRINGS RD | LAS | 14 B4 |
| BOYER RD | MPA | 49 C3 |
| BOYER RD | YUB | 33 D1 |
| BOYES BLVD | SON | 132 A2 |
| BOYLE RD | IMP | 109 A3 |
| BOYLE RD | SHA | 18 D2 |
| BOYLES AV | LAK | 32 A3 |
| BOY SCOUT CP RD | VEN | 88 B2 |
| BRACE RD | PLA | 34 B4 |
| BRACK RD | SON | 31 D5 |
| BRACK RD | SON | 37 D1 |
| BRADBURY RD | MCO | 47 E3 |
| BRADBURY RD | MCO | 48 A3 |
| BRADBURY RD | STA | 47 C3 |
| BRADFORD AV | ORA | T D1 |
| BRADFORD RD | BUT | 25 B4 |
| BRADFORD RD | RCO | 107 B1 |
| BRADLEY AV | SDCO | V E2 |
| BRADLEY AV | SDCO | 106 E5 |
| BRADLEY RD | MON | 65 E4 |
| BRADLEY RD | RCO | 99 C4 |
| BRADLEY RD | VEN | 88 C5 |
| BRADLY HENLY RD | SIS | 4 B3 |
| BRADLEY LOCK RD | MON | 65 C4 |
| BRADSHAW RD | IMP | 109 A5 |
| BRADSHAW RD | SAC | 40 A2 |
| BRADSHAW RD | YUB | 33 E3 |
| BRADSHW TR, THE | RCO | 102 A5 |
| BRADSHW TR, THE | RCO | 110 B1 |
| BRADY RD | TRI | 17 B2 |
| BRAGG RD | RCO | 100 A5 |
| BRAMLETT RCH RD | MNO | 44 C5 |
| BRAMLOT RD | TRI | 17 B3 |
| BRANCH RD | SLO | 76 B1 |
| BRANCH RD E | HUM | 22 C1 |
| BRANCH RD W | SIS | 3 D4 |
| BRANCH CAMP W | BUT | 25 D1 |
| BRANCH MILL RD | SLO | 76 B4 |
| BRANCIFORTE DR | SCR | 54 A2 |
| BRANCO RD | MCO | 55 E1 |
| BRAND BLVD | LACO | Q E2 |
| BRANDON RD | ED | 40 D1 |
| BRANDT | IMP | 109 A3 |
| BRANDT RD | SJCO | 40 C4 |
| BRANDT RD | KER | 78 A2 |
| BRANDY CITY RD | SIE | 26 A3 |
| BRANDY CREEK RD | SHA | 18 A2 |
| BRANFORD ST | LACO | Q C2 |
| BRANHAM LN | SCL | P B4 |
| BRANHAM LN | SCL | 46 B5 |
| BRANNAN ST | SF | 143 D5 |
| BRANNAN ISL RD | SAC | 39 C4 |
| BRANNAN ISLD RD | SAC | M D2 |
| BRANNAN MTN RD | RD | 10 C4 |
| BRANNIGAN MN RD | SBD | 83 C4 |
| BRANNIN RD | TEH | 24 C2 |
| BRANNON AV | FRCO | 56 B2 |
| BRANSCOMB RD | MEN | 22 D4 |
| BRANSTETTER LN | SHA | 18 C2 |
| BRANT RD | SBD | 84 C3 |
| BRANT CIMA RD | SBD | 84 B3 |
| BRAWLEY | IMP | 108 C2 |
| BRAWLEY AV | FRCO | 57 C5 |
| BRAY AV | TEH | 18 D5 |
| BRAZO RD | MCO | 47 C4 |
| BREA BLVD | ORA | 98 C3 |
| BREA BLVD | ORA | U A4 |
| BREA BLVD | ORA | T C1 |
| BREA CANYON RD | LACO | 98 C2 |
| BREA CYN CUTOFF | LACO | U A3 |
| BREA CYN CUTOFF | LACO | 98 C2 |
| BRECKENRIDGE RD | KER | 78 E3 |
| BRECKENRIDGE RD | KER | 79 A2 |
| BREEDLOVE RD | ED | 34 E3 |
| BRENDA ST | KER | 70 A5 |
| BRENT RD | TEH | 18 D4 |
| BRENTWOOD AV | CC | M D3 |
| BREUING RD | MCO | 55 D1 |
| BRENNAN | SJCO | 47 C1 |
| BRENTWOOD AV | CC | 39 C5 |
| BRETZ RD | FRCO | 58 B1 |
| BREUNER AV | COL | 32 E3 |
| BREWER RD | NEV | 34 C2 |
| BREWER RD | PLA | 33 E4 |
| BREWER CREEK RD | SIS | 12 E1 |
| BRICELAND RD | HUM | 16 B5 |
| BRICELAND RD | MEN | 22 B1 |
| BRICELND THORNE | HUM | 16 B5 |
| BRIDESTEIN RD | IMP | 109 C5 |
| BRIDGE RD | VEN | 88 C4 |
| BRIDGE ST | COL | 33 A2 |
| BRIDGE ST | RCO | 99 D3 |
| BRIDGE ST | SUT | 33 C2 |
| BRIDGE ST | SUT | 125 A3 |
| BRIDGE ST | YUBA | 125 D3 |
| BRIDGE ARBOR | LAK | 31 D2 |
| BRIDGE CK SPGS | LAS | 20 C2 |
| BRIDGE GULCH RD | TRI | 17 B3 |
| BRDGPORT SCH RD | ED | 41 A1 |
| BRIDGEWAY | MAR | 140 D5 |
| BRIDLE PATH DR | SCL | P E5 |
| BRIGGS AV | LACO | R A2 |
| BRIGGS RD | RCO | 99 D4 |
| BRIGGS RD | VEN | 88 C5 |
| BRIGGS GRIDLY W | BUT | 25 C5 |
| BRIGGSMORE AV | STA | 47 C2 |
| BRIGHTON AV | MDO | 162 E1 |
| BRIGHTWOOD | MAD | 57 B1 |
| BRIM RD | COL | 32 B2 |
| BRIMHALL RD | KER | 78 B3 |
| BRINKERHOFF AV | SB | 86 E3 |
| BRINKERHOFF AV | SB | 87 A3 |
| BRIONES VLY RD | CC | 39 B5 |
| BRISTOL RD | VEN | 88 B5 |
| BRISTOL ST | CM | 197 E4 |
| BRISTOL ST | CM | 198 A4 |
| BRISTOL ST | ORA | 98 C4 |
| BRISTOL ST | ORA | 197 E4 |
| BRISTOL ST | ORA | T D3 |
| BRISTOL ST | SA | 195 E5 |
| BRISTOL ST | SA | 196 A2 |
| BRISTOL ST | SA | 197 E2 |
| BRISTOL ST | SA | 198 A2 |
| BRISTOL ST N | NB | 200 B1 |
| BRITE RD | KER | 78 A3 |
| BRITTO RD | MCO | 56 A2 |
| BROAD ST | NEVC | 128 B2 |
| BROAD ST | SNLO | 172 C3 |
| BROAD ST | SLO | 172 C3 |
| BROAD ST W | NEVC | 128 B2 |
| BROADWAY | A | 157 E3 |
| BROADWAY | ALA | L D4 |
| BROADWAY | ALA | 45 D1 |
| BROADWAY | AMA | 40 E2 |
| BROADWAY | ANA | 193 B2 |
| BROADWAY | EUR | 121 A4 |
| BROADWAY | FRE | 165 C3 |
| BROADWAY | LB | 192 D3 |
| BROADWAY | LA | 185 E5 |
| BROADWAY | LA | 186 A3 |
| BROADWAY | LACO | Q E3 |
| BROADWAY | LACO | S C1 |
| BROADWAY | LACO | S E2 |
| BROADWAY | O | 156 C5 |
| BROADWAY | O | 158 A2 |
| BROADWAY | SCTO | 137 A4 |
| BROADWAY | SBD | 92 D5 |
| BROADWAY | SD | 215 E3 |
| BROADWAY | SD | 216 A3 |
| BROADWAY | SDCO | V E2 |
| BROADWAY | SDCO | V B3 |
| BROADWAY | SDCO | 106 D3 |
| BROADWAY | SDCO | 106 E5 |
| BROADWAY | SDCO | 111 D1 |
| BROADWAY | SDCO | 111 D2 |
| BROADWAY | SF | 143 A3 |
| BROADWAY | SFCO | L B4 |
| BROADWAY | SMCO | N C1 |
| BROADWAY | SB | 76 C5 |
| BROADWAY | SC | 169 E3 |
| BROADWAY | SMA | 173 C3 |
| BROADWAY | SMON | 180 A4 |
| BROADWAY | SOL | 134 C1 |
| BROADWAY | SNMA | 132 D5 |
| BROADWAY | SON | L B1 |
| BROADWAY | SUT | 33 C2 |
| BROADWAY | VAL | 134 C2 |
| BROADWAY | YUB | 33 D3 |
| BROADWAY N | LA | 186 C1 |
| BROADWAY N | LACO | R A3 |
| BROADWAY RD | LACO | R C5 |
| BROADWAY RD | VEN | 88 D5 |
| BROADWAY ST | FRFD | 135 B4 |
| BROADWAY ST | SBD | 101 A1 |
| BROADWAY TER | O | 156 C5 |
| BROCK RD | IMP | 112 A3 |
| BROCKMAN LN | INY | 51 D4 |
| BROCKMAN RD | KER | 78 C1 |
| BROCKMAN RD | LAS | 8 A4 |
| BROCKMAN MLL RD | AMA | 41 A1 |
| BROCK MTN LKOUT | SHA | 12 E5 |
| BROKAW RD | SJ | 151 D1 |
| BROKAW RD | SCL | P B3 |
| BROKAW RD | SCL | 46 B4 |
| BROKEOFF MDWS | SHA | 19 C2 |
| BROOKDALE RD | SHA | 18 D2 |
| BROOKHILL RD | MAD | 57 C2 |
| BROOKHURST ST | ORA | 98 B4 |
| BROOKHURST ST | ORA | T C2 |
| BROOKLYN AV | LA | 186 D3 |
| BROOKLYN ST | LACO | R A4 |
| BROOKS RD | MCO | 48 B4 |
| BROOKS RD | NEV | 34 C2 |
| BROOKS ST | SB | 86 D1 |
| BROOKSIDE | FRCO | 58 D4 |
| BROOKSIDE AV | RCO | 99 E2 |
| BROOKSIDE AV | SBD | 99 C2 |
| BROOKSIDE DR | SP | 155 A1 |
| BROOKSIDE RD | CAL | 41 C2 |
| BROOKSIDE RD | S | 160 A2 |
| BROPHY RD | YUB | 33 D2 |
| BROWN RD | KER | 70 C5 |
| BROWN RD | KER | 80 C1 |
| BROWN RD | SB | 86 A1 |
| BROWN RD | SHA | 13 D4 |
| BROWN RD | SOL | 39 B3 |
| BROWN RD | SUT | 33 C3 |
| BROWN ST | NAP | 133 C3 |
| BROWN ST | RCO | 99 B3 |
| BROWNLL LAVA BD | SIS | 5 C3 |
| BROWNING | PLA | 33 E5 |
| BROWNING RD | COL | 33 B3 |
| BROWNING RD | KER | 68 C5 |
| BROWNING RD | SUT | 33 C3 |
| BROWN MATRL RD | KER | 77 C1 |
| BROWNS CREEK RD | TRI | 17 D2 |
| BROWNS MTN RD | TRI | 17 D1 |
| BROWNS RANCH RD | TRI | 17 D1 |
| BROWNS RAVINE | BUT | 25 D1 |
| BROWNS VALLEY | SBT | 55 B4 |
| BROWNS VLY RD | NAP | 133 A5 |
| BROWN VALLEY RD | SOL | 39 A2 |
| BROWN VALLEY RD | SCR | 54 B2 |
| BROYLE RD | STA | 47 C3 |
| BROYLES RD | BUT | 25 A2 |
| BROYLES RD | STA | 47 C2 |
| BRUCE RD | BUT | 25 B3 |
| BRUCE CRUM | SHA | 13 E4 |
| BRUCEVILLE RD | SAC | 40 A3 |
| BRUCITE ST | KER | 91 E3 |
| BRUELLA RD | SJCO | 40 B5 |
| BRUGGA LN | HUM | 15 D2 |
| BRUNDAGE LN | BKD | 166 C5 |
| BRUNDAGE LN | KER | 166 C5 |
| BRUNSWICK AV | LA | 182 E2 |
| BRUNSWICK RD | NEV | 34 C1 |
| BRUS | MOD | 8 B3 |
| BRUSH LN | STA | 47 C3 |
| BRUSH CREEK RD | SIS | 4 B3 |
| BRUSH CREEK RD | SON | 37 E2 |
| BRUSH CREEK RD | SON | 38 A2 |
| BRUSHY MTN LKOT | HUM | 10 C5 |
| BRYAN AV | FRCO | 57 B5 |
| BRYANT | FRCO | 56 B2 |
| BRYANT ST | SBD | 99 D2 |
| BRYANT ST | SF | 142 D4 |
| BRYANT ST | SF | 143 D5 |
| BRYANT RAVIN RD | BUT | 26 A4 |
| BRYANTS CYN RD | MON | 55 A5 |
| BRYANTS CYN RD | MON | 65 A1 |
| BUARO ST | GGR | 195 B2 |
| BUCHANAN RD | CC | M B3 |
| BUCHANAN RD | CC | 39 B5 |
| BUCHANAN RD | MAD | 49 B5 |
| BUCHANAN RD | TUO | 41 E5 |
| BUCHANAN ST | RCO | 101 B5 |
| BUCHANAN HLW RD | MCO | 48 D5 |
| BUCK RD | RCO | 99 D5 |
| BUCK RD | SJCO | 40 B3 |
| BUCKEYE RD | MPA | 49 A3 |
| BUCKEYE RD | NEV | 34 D1 |
| BUCKEYE ARM RD | TRI | 11 D5 |
| BUCKEYE CK RD | SON | 31 A5 |
| BUCKEYE CK RD | TRI | 11 D5 |
| BUCKEYE CK RD | TRI | 12 A4 |
| BUCKEYE CK RD | TRI | 17 E1 |
| BUCKEYE RDG RD | TRI | 11 D5 |
| BUCKHORN | TEH | 24 C2 |
| BUCKHORN AV | KER | 89 C1 |
| BUCKHORN RD | SIS | 4 C5 |
| BUCKHORN RDG RD | AMA | 41 B2 |
| BUCKHORN STA LP | TRI | 17 E1 |
| BUCKLEY RD | SLO | 76 B4 |
| BUCKMAN FUNCK | SJCO | 40 D5 |
| BUCK MEADOWS | MPA | 49 A1 |
| BUCKNELL RD | KER | 80 D3 |
| BUCKS BAR RD | ED | 34 E5 |
| BUCKS FLAT RD | TEH | 19 B4 |
| BUCKSKIN RD | CAL | 41 A4 |
| BUCKS LAKE RD | PLU | 26 C1 |
| BUCKWHEAT RD | SBD | 90 E4 |
| BUDDY CT | KER | 79 B3 |
| BUELL RD | SHA | 18 A3 |
| BUENA CREEK RD | SDCO | 106 C3 |
| BUENA VISTA | AMA | 40 D3 |
| BUENA VISTA | LACO | 97 D1 |
| BUENA VISTA | SCL | 54 D1 |
| BUENA VISTA AV | A | 157 D5 |
| BUENA VISTA AV | A | 158 B5 |
| BUENA VISTA AV | MV | 140 A2 |
| BUENA VISTA AV | RIV | 205 A2 |
| BUENA VISTA AV | RCO | U E5 |
| BUENA VISTA AV | SCL | P E5 |
| BUENA VISTA BL | KER | 78 D4 |
| BUENA VISTA BL | KER | 79 A4 |
| BUENA VISTA DR | MER | 170 C1 |
| BUENA VISTA DR | SBD | 100 E1 |
| BUENA VISTA DR | SLO | 76 A1 |
| BUENA VISTA DR | SCR | 54 B2 |
| BUENA VISTA RD | AMA | 40 C3 |
| BUENA VISTA RD | KER | 78 C3 |
| BUENA VISTA RD | SBD | 91 E4 |
| BUENA VISTA RD | SJCO | 40 C3 |
| BUENA VISTA ST | BUR | 179 C2 |
| BUENA VISTA ST | LACO | Q D2 |
| BUENA VISTA ST | LACO | R D3 |
| BUENA VISTA ST | VEN | 88 D5 |
| BUERER LN | SJCO | 47 C1 |
| BUERKLE RD | KER | 78 A3 |
| BUFFALO RUN RD | RCO | 102 C4 |
| BUFFUM LN | LAS | 21 B3 |
| BUFFUM RD | SHA | 13 B5 |
| BUHACH RD | MCO | 48 B5 |
| BUHNE ST | EUR | 121 C2 |
| BULKLEY RD | SOL | 39 C2 |
| BULLARD AV | FRCO | 56 C3 |
| BULLARD AV | FRCO | 57 B3 |
| BULL CANYON RD | SLO | 76 D5 |
| BULL CREEK RD | MPA | 49 B2 |
| BULLION MTN RD | SBD | 101 C1 |
| BULLIS RD | LACO | S D1 |
| BULLRIDGE WHEEL | KIN | 67 B4 |
| BULL RUN ST | KER | 80 C1 |
| BULL SKIN RIDGE | SHA | 19 A1 |
| BULLY CHOOP RD | SHA | 17 E3 |
| BULS RD | KER | 87 E1 |
| BUMMERVILLE RD | CAL | 41 B2 |
| BUNCE RD | SUT | 33 D2 |
| BUNCH GRASS LKT | SHA | 13 B5 |
| BUNDY DR | LA | 180 B4 |
| BUNDY DR | LACO | Q C4 |
| BUNDY CANYON RD | RCO | 99 C5 |
| BUNKER RD | MCO | 47 C5 |
| BUNKER RD | MCO | 55 C1 |
| BUNKER HILL RD | SIE | 26 D3 |
| BUNKER STATN RD | SOL | 39 C3 |
| BUNNY LN | RCO | 100 C5 |
| BUNSELMEIER RD | LAS | 14 B3 |
| BUNTE RD | MON | 65 C3 |
| BUNTGVLL CUMMGS | LAS | 21 B4 |
| BURBANK BLVD | BUR | 179 B3 |
| BURBANK BLVD | LA | 179 B3 |
| BURBANK BLVD | LACO | 97 C1 |
| BURBANK BLVD | LACO | Q C2 |
| BURBANK ST | KER | 78 A2 |
| BURCH RD | SUT | 33 C3 |
| BURCHELL AV | MCO | 48 D5 |
| BURCHELL RD | SCL | 54 C1 |
| BURCH HAVEN RD | MCO | 55 B2 |
| BURGESS RCH RD | TRI | 16 E5 |
| BURKE LN | SOL | 39 B3 |
| BURLANDO RD | KER | 69 D5 |
| BURLINGAME AV | SMCO | N C1 |
| BURLNGTN RDG RD | NEV | 34 E1 |
| BURMA RD | NEV | 34 C2 |
| BURNES VALLEY | LAK | 32 A3 |
| BURNETT | PLA | 34 B3 |
| BURNHAM RD | VEN | 88 A4 |
| BURNS AV | KER | 78 C1 |
| BURNS FRWY | HUM | 9 E5 |
| BURNS FRWY | HUM | 10 A5 |
| BURNS RD | LPAZ | 104 A2 |
| BURNS CANYON RD | SBD | 100 B1 |
| BURNS CUTOFF | SJCO | 40 A5 |
| BURNSIDE LK RD | ALP | 36 B4 |
| BURNT RCH DUMP | TRI | 10 E5 |
| BURNT TREE RD | SBD | 81 C5 |
| BURRELL RD | HUM | 15 E4 |
| BURRIS LN | MEN | 31 C1 |
| BURRIS RD | SUT | 33 B2 |
| BURROUGH N RD | FRCO | 58 A2 |
| BURROUGH VLY RD | FRCO | 58 A2 |
| BURSON RD | CAL | 40 D4 |
| BURTON WY | BH | 183 C1 |
| BURTON WY | LA | 183 C1 |
| BURTON MESA BL | SB | 86 B2 |
| BURWOOD RD | SJCO | 47 D2 |
| BUSCH LN | MEN | 23 B5 |
| BUSH ST | AMA | 40 D2 |
| BUSH ST | SF | 142 A3 |
| BUSH ST | SF | 143 C4 |
| BUSHARD ST | ORA | T C3 |
| BUSHEY RD | MOD | 14 C1 |
| BUSSEL RD | KER | 78 B2 |
| BUSTER RD | COL | 33 A2 |
| BUTANO CUTOFF | SMCO | N C4 |
| BUTANO CUTOFF | SMCO | 45 C5 |
| BUTCHER RCH RD | SIE | 26 E3 |
| BUTLER AV | FRCO | 57 C3 |
| BUTLER RD | COL | 25 A5 |
| BUTLER RD | STA | 47 B2 |
| BUTLER VLY RD | HUM | 16 A1 |
| BUTTE AV | FRCO | 66 E1 |
| BUTTE AV | SUT | 33 C2 |
| BUTTE RD | LAS | 14 D3 |
| BUTTE RD E | SUT | 33 C2 |
| BUTTE RD N | SUT | 33 B1 |
| BUTTE RD S | SUT | 33 B2 |
| BUTTE RD W | SUT | 33 B1 |
| BUTTE CREEK RD | HUM | 16 B2 |
| BUTTE HOUSE RD | SUT | 33 C2 |
| BUTTE HOUSE RD | YUBA | 125 A2 |
| BUTTEMER RD | SBD | 90 E4 |
| BUTTE MTN RD | AMA | 40 E2 |
| BUTTE MTN RD | AMA | 41 A2 |
| BUTTE MTN RD | TEH | 24 C2 |
| BUTTERBREAD CYN | KER | 79 E2 |
| BUTTERBREAD CYN | KER | 80 A2 |
| BUTTERCUP CT | KER | 79 C4 |
| BUTTERFIELD RD | MAR | L A3 |
| BUTTRFLD STG RD | MAD | 49 D5 |
| BUTTRFLD STG RD | MAD | 57 D1 |
| BUTTRFLD STG RD | RCO | 99 D5 |
| BUTTERFLY PK RD | RCO | 100 C5 |
| BTRFLY VLY TWAN | PLU | 26 C1 |
| BUTTERMILK RD | INY | 51 B4 |
| BUTTERS RD | IMP | 109 C4 |
| BUTTE SLOUGH RD | COL | 33 A2 |
| BUTTE VALLEY RD | INY | 72 A3 |
| BUTTE VLY RD E | SIS | 5 A3 |
| BUTTE VLY RD W | SIS | 4 E3 |
| BUTTE VLY AIRPT | SIS | 5 A3 |
| BUTTONHOOK RD | SB | 86 D3 |
| BUTTONWILLOW AV | FRCO | 58 A4 |
| BUTTONWILLOW DR | KER | 77 E3 |
| BUTTONWILLOW DR | KER | 78 A3 |
| BUTTS RD | MCO | 47 C5 |
| BUTTS RD | MCO | 55 C1 |
| BUTTS CANYON RD | LAK | 32 B5 |
| BUZZARD ROOST | SHA | 19 A1 |
| BVD AV | MCO | 48 C5 |
| BYERS PASS RD | LAS | 21 B3 |
| BYINGTON RD | SUT | 33 C4 |
| BYOFF RD | TRI | 10 E5 |
| BYRON HWY | CC | M D3 |
| BYRON HWY | CC | 39 D5 |
| BYRON RD | SJCO | 46 D1 |
| BYRON RD | CC | M E4 |
| BYRON RD | CC | 46 D1 |
| BYSTRUM RD | STA | 47 D3 |




STREETS

223
BYWOOD DR
# STREET INDEX
CHAPULNIK RD

COPYRIGHT, © 1988 BY Thomas Bros Maps


| STREET | CO. | PAGE & GRID |
|---|---|---|
| BYWOOD DR | TEH | 18 C4 |
| C | | |
| C ST | KER | 68 B5 |
| C ST | SD | 215 D3 |
| C ST | YOL | 137 A2 |
| CABALLERO CT | LAK | 32 A4 |
| CABIN RD | LAS | 14 B4 |
| CABRILLO AV | LACO | S C2 |
| CABRILLO BLVD | STB | 174 E4 |
| CABRILLO DR | AVLN | 105 B5 |
| CABRILLO FRWY | SD | 213 D3 |
| CABRILLO FRWY | SD | 215 E2 |
| CABRILLO FRWY | SDCO | V B3 |
| CABRILLO HWY | MONT | 167 D5 |
| CABRILLO HWY | MONT | 168 C2 |
| CABRILLO HWY | MON | 53 E5 |
| CABRILLO HWY | MON | 54 B4 |
| CABRILLO HWY | MON | 168 C2 |
| CABRILLO HWY | SNLO | 172 A1 |
| CABRILLO HWY | SLO | 75 B1 |
| CABRILLO HWY | SLO | 76 B5 |
| CABRILLO HWY | SLO | 172 A1 |
| CABRILLO HWY | SMCO | N B2 |
| CABRILLO HWY | SMCO | 45 B3 |
| CABRILLO HWY | SB | 86 B1 |
| CABRILLO HWY | SC | 169 A4 |
| CABRILLO HWY | SCR | N D5 |
| CABRILLO HWY | SCR | 53 D1 |
| CABRILLO HWY | SCR | 54 A2 |
| CACHAGUA RD | MON | 54 C5 |
| CACHAGUA RD | MON | 64 C1 |
| CACHUMA RD | SB | 87 A2 |
| CACTUS AV | RCO | 99 C3 |
| CACTUS AV | SBD | 99 B1 |
| CACTUS DR | MCO | 55 D2 |
| CACTUS FLATS | INY | 70 B2 |
| CACTUS VLY RD | RCO | 99 E4 |
| CADET RD | KER | 78 A4 |
| CADILLAC AV | LA | 183 D4 |
| CADIZ DR | SBD | 102 C1 |
| CADIZ RD | SBD | 94 B3 |
| CADIZ RD | SBD | 103 A1 |
| CADY RD | IMP | 109 A4 |
| CAHUENGA BLVD | LA | 179 A3 |
| CAHUENGA BLVD | LA | 181 D5 |
| CAHUENGA BLVD | LACO | Q D3 |
| CAHUENGA BLVD W | LA | 181 B2 |
| CAHUILLA RD | RCO | 100 B5 |
| CAHUILLA RD | SBD | 91 C3 |
| CAHUILLA HTS RD | RCO | 100 A5 |
| CAIRO | KIN | 57 D5 |
| CAJALCO RD | RCO | 99 A3 |
| CAJON BLVD | SBD | 91 A5 |
| CAJON ST | SBD | 99 C2 |
| CALAVERAS AV | FRCO | 56 D4 |
| CALAVERAS AV | FRCO | 66 D2 |
| CALAVERAS RD | ALA | P C1 |
| CALAVERAS RD | ALA | 46 B3 |
| CALAVERAS RD | SCL | 46 B4 |
| CALAVERITAS RD | CAL | 41 A3 |
| CALDOR RD | ED | 41 B1 |
| CALICO BLVD | SBD | 92 A1 |
| CALICO RD | SBD | 92 A1 |
| CALIENT-BODF RD | KER | 79 B3 |
| CALIENT-BODF RD | KER | 79 C2 |
| CALIENTE CK RD | KER | 79 C3 |
| CALIFORNIA AV | BKD | 166 B3 |
| CALIFORNIA AV | COL | 32 E3 |
| CALIFORNIA AV | FRE | 165 A5 |
| CALIFORNIA AV | FRCO | 56 C3 |
| CALIFORNIA AV | FRCO | 57 C3 |
| CALIFORNIA AV | KER | 78 D3 |
| CALIFORNIA AV | LACO | R A5 |
| CALIFORNIA AV | MDO | 162 A4 |
| CALIFORNIA AV | RENO | 130 A3 |
| CALIFORNIA AV | RCO | 98 E2 |
| CALIFORNIA AV | RCO | 99 D4 |
| CALIFORNIA AV | SCL | P D5 |
| CALIFORNIA AV | SCL | 54 C1 |
| CALIFORNIA AV | SC | 169 C4 |
| CALIFORNIA AV | STA | 47 B2 |
| CALIFORNIA BLVD | LACO | R B3 |
| CALIFORNIA BLVD | NAP | 133 B2 |
| CALIFORNIA BLVD | PAS | 190 A4 |
| CALIFORNIA BLVD | SNLO | 172 B1 |
| CALIFORNIA BLVD | SLO | 172 B1 |
| CALIFORNIA DR | IMP | 108 C2 |
| CALIFORNIA DR | NAPA | 29 D4 |
| CALIFORNIA ST | BUR | 179 C3 |
| CALIFORNIA ST | EUR | 121 C2 |
| CALIFORNIA ST | LACO | 98 A1 |
| CALIFORNIA ST | ONT | 204 A5 |
| CALIFORNIA ST | SBD | 99 B1 |
| CALIFORNIA ST | SDCO | 106 B3 |
| CALIFORNIA ST | SF | 141 C3 |
| CALIFORNIA ST | SF | 142 A3 |
| CALIFORNIA ST | SF | 143 D4 |
| CALIFORNIA ST | SFCO | L B4 |
| CALIFORNIA ST | SFCO | 45 B1 |
| CALIFORNIA ST | SJCO | 40 A5 |
| CALIFORNIA ST | S | 160 D2 |
| CALIF CITY BLVD | KER | 80 B4 |
| CALIFRNIA FARMS | SJCO | 47 C1 |
| CALIF PINES BL | MOD | 14 E2 |
| CALISTOGA RD | SON | 38 A1 |
| CALKINS RD | FRCO | 57 E1 |
| CALLAHAN RD | TEH | 18 C5 |
| CALLAHAN RD E | SIS | 11 D1 |
| CALLE DEL SOL | AVLN | 105 B5 |
| CALLE ECUESTRE | SB | 87 A4 |
| CALLEGUAS RD | VEN | 96 C1 |
| CALLE H COLEGIO | BAJA | 112 B4 |
| CALLE LIPPIZANA | SB | 87 A4 |
| CALLENDR BLK LK | SLO | 76 B5 |
| CALLE QUEBRADA | SB | 87 A4 |
| CALLE REAL | SB | 86 E4 |
| CALLE REAL | SB | 87 A4 |
| CALLOWAY DR | KER | 78 C3 |
| CALNEVA RD | LAS | 21 E5 |
| CALPACK RD | SJCO | 46 E1 |
| CALPINE RD | SIE | 27 B3 |
| CALPINE LO RD | SIE | 27 B3 |
| CALVIN CREST RD | MAD | 49 D4 |
| CALVINE RD | SAC | 39 E2 |
| CALVINE RD | SAC | 40 A2 |
| CALZ | BAJA | 112 B4 |
| CALZADA AV | SB | 86 E3 |
| CAMANCHE PKWY | CAL | 40 D3 |
| CAMANCHE PKWY N | AMA | 40 C3 |
| CAMANCHE PKWY S | CAL | 40 D3 |
| CAMARES DR | LACO | 90 A3 |
| CAMARILLO ST | LA | 179 B4 |
| CAMARILLO ST | LACO | Q D3 |
| CAMBRIA AV | FRCO | 56 A2 |
| CAMBRIA RD | SBD | 91 E4 |
| CAMBRIDGE DR | BUR | 179 E2 |
| CAMBRIDGE RD | SHA | 18 C3 |
| CAMBRIDGE ST | OR | 196 D1 |
| CAMBRIDGE ST | SA | 196 D1 |
| CAMDEN AV | SCL | P B4 |
| CAMDEN AV | SCL | 46 B5 |
| CAMERON AV | LACO | 98 C2 |
| CAMERON AV | LACO | U A2 |
| CAMERON RD | MEN | 30 C2 |
| CAMERON CYN RD | KER | 79 D5 |
| CAMERON PARK DR | ED | 34 C5 |
| CAMINO AV | IMP | 108 C2 |
| CAMINO ALTO | MAR | L B4 |
| CAMINO ALTO | MV | 140 B3 |
| CM CAPISTRANO | SJC | 202 D3 |
| CAMINO CIELO | SB | 87 A3 |
| CM DE FLORES | AVLN | 105 B4 |
| CAMINO DL MONTE | AVLN | 105 A4 |
| CAMINO DL MONTE | CAR | 53 D5 |
| CAMINO DL MONTE | CAR | 168 C3 |
| CAMINO DL MONTE | MON | 168 C3 |
| CAMINO DIABLO | CC | M D4 |
| CAMINO DIABLO | CC | 46 C1 |
| CM DOS RIOS | VEN | 96 D1 |
| CM LAS RAMBLAS | SJC | 202 D4 |
| CM MIRA COSTA | SCL | 202 E5 |
| CAMINO ORO | SHA | 19 A2 |
| CAMINO PABLO | CC | L D4 |
| CAMINO PABLO | CC | L E4 |
| CAMINO REAL | LACO | S A2 |
| CAMINO REAL | SHA | 19 A3 |
| CAMINO SANTA FE | SDCO | 106 C5 |
| CM SANTA FE DR | SDCO | V B2 |
| CM TASSAJARA RD | ALA | M B5 |
| CM TASSAJARA RD | ALA | 46 B2 |
| CM TASSAJARA RD | CC | M B4 |
| CM TASSAJARA RD | CC | 46 A1 |
| CAMINO VISTA | SHA | 19 A2 |
| CAMMATTI-SHN RD | SLO | 76 D1 |
| CAMP RD | SAC | 39 E3 |
| CAMP RD E | COL | 32 D2 |
| CAMPBELL | SJCO | 47 D1 |
| CAMPBELL AV | BUT | 33 C1 |
| CAMPBELL AV | SCL | P B4 |
| CAMPBELL AV | SCL | 46 A5 |
| CAMPBELL DR | KER | 78 E4 |
| CAMPBELL RD | IMP | 111 E3 |
| CAMPBELL RD | SBD | 101 D1 |
| CAMPBELL RD | SB | 86 C3 |
| CAMPBELL RD | SOL | 39 B1 |
| CAMPBL HOT SPGS | SIE | 27 C4 |
| CAMPBELL RDG RD | TRI | 10 D4 |
| CAMPBLLS FLT RD | TUO | 41 C5 |
| CAMP CREEK RD | BUT | 25 E2 |
| CAMP CREEK RD | SIS | 4 B2 |
| CAMP FAR WST RD | PLA | 34 A3 |
| CAMP FAR WST RD | YUB | 34 A2 |
| CAMPHORA RD | MON | 54 E5 |
| CAMPHORA RD | MON | 55 A5 |
| CAMP KIMTU RD | HUM | 16 C5 |
| CAMP NINE RD | CAL | 41 C4 |
| CAMPO RD | SDCO | V D3 |
| CAMPO RD | SDCO | 111 E1 |
| CAMPODONICA RD | MCO | 48 A3 |
| CAMPOS LN | SOL | 39 A2 |
| CAMP ROCK RD | SBD | 92 A1 |
| CAMPO SECO RD | CAL | 40 D3 |
| CAMPO SECO RD | TUO | 41 C5 |
| CAMP THREE RD | SIS | 10 E1 |
| CAMPTON RD | EUR | 121 D4 |
| CAMPTON RD | HUM | 15 E1 |
| CAMPTONVILLE RD | SIE | 26 C5 |
| CAMPUS AV | ONT | 204 C3 |
| CAMPUS AV | SBD | 98 D1 |
| CAMPUS AV | UPL | 204 C3 |
| CAMPUS DR | IRV | 198 C5 |
| CAMPUS DR | KER | 78 E4 |
| CAMPUS DR | ORA | 198 C5 |
| CAMPUS DR | SCL | 147 A3 |
| CAMP WEOTT RD | HUM | 15 D2 |
| CMP 1 TEN MI RD | MEN | 22 C4 |
| CMP 2 TEN MI RD | MEN | 22 C4 |
| CAMP 8 RD | SLO | 76 C2 |
| CAMUESA RD | SB | 87 D3 |
| CANA HWY | BUT | 25 A2 |
| CANADA BLVD | LACO | 97 E1 |
| CANADA BLVD | LACO | R A2 |
| CANADA RD | SMCO | N D2 |
| CANADA RD | SMCO | 45 C3 |
| CANADA RD | SCL | 54 D2 |
| CANAL AV | FRCO | 57 E1 |
| CANAL BLVD | SJCO | 46 E1 |
| CANAL BLVD | SJCO | 47 A1 |
| CANAL DR | MCO | 47 E4 |
| CANAL DR | MCO | 48 A4 |
| CANAL RD | GLE | 24 E3 |
| CANAL RD | KER | 77 E2 |
| CANAL RD | KER | 78 A2 |
| CANAL ST | PLCV | 138 C3 |
| CANAL BANK RD | STA | 47 E2 |
| CANAL BANK RD | STA | 48 A2 |
| CANAL GULCH RD | SIS | 4 A4 |
| CANAL SCHOOL RD | MCO | 47 C4 |
| CANA PINE CREEK | BUT | 25 A2 |
| C AND D BLVD | RCO | 103 D5 |
| CANFIELD RD | SDCO | 107 A2 |
| CANFIELD RD | SON | 37 E3 |
| CANNIBAL RD | HUM | 15 D2 |
| CANNON RD | SDCO | 106 B3 |
| CANNON RD | TEH | 18 B5 |
| CANNON ST | SDCO | V A3 |
| CANOGA AV | LA | 177 C3 |
| CANON DR | BH | 183 B1 |
| CANON RD | SOL | 39 A3 |
| CANON ST | SDCO | 111 C1 |
| CANON PERDIDO | STB | 174 C4 |
| CANRIGHT RD | SOL | 39 C3 |
| CANTELOW RD | SOL | 38 E2 |
| CANTELOW RD | SOL | 39 A2 |
| CANTON RD | MCO | 48 C5 |
| CANYON DR | RCO | 100 C3 |
| CANYON DR | SBD | 82 A5 |
| CANYON RD | INY | 52 B3 |
| CANYON RD | MEN | 23 A5 |
| CANYON RD | MNO | 52 B3 |
| CANYON RD | SBD | 93 B5 |
| CANYON RD | SBD | 100 C2 |
| CANYON RD | SMCO | N C4 |
| CANYON RD | SMCO | 45 C5 |
| CANYON RD | SR | 139 B4 |
| CANYON RD | SHA | 18 C3 |
| CANYON RD | SON | 31 D5 |
| CANYON WY | PLA | 34 D3 |
| CANYON CREEK RD | MOD | 14 E1 |
| CANYON CREEK RD | SIS | 3 B5 |
| CANYON CREEK RD | TRI | 17 C1 |
| CANYON CREST DR | RCO | 99 B2 |
| CANYON VW LOOP | TEH | 19 B4 |
| CANYON VIEW RD | SBD | 91 D4 |
| CAPAY AV | GLE | 24 E3 |
| CAPAY RD | TEH | 24 D2 |
| CAPE GLOUCESTER | SBD | 91 E2 |
| CAPEZZOLI LN | LAS | 21 C4 |
| CAPITAL BLVD | GLE | 24 E4 |
| CAPITAN TK TR | SDCO | 107 B5 |
| CAPITOL AV | SCTO | 137 C3 |
| CAPITOL AV | SCL | P C3 |
| CAPITOL AV | SCL | 46 B4 |
| CAPITOL AV | YOL | 137 A2 |
| CAPITOL AV | YOL | 39 D1 |
| CAPITOL EXPWY | SCL | P C4 |
| CAPITOL EXPWY | SCL | 46 B5 |
| CAPITOL ST | SAL | 171 B3 |
| CAPITOLA RD | SCR | 54 A2 |
| CAPPELL RD | HUM | 10 C2 |
| CAPPS CROSSING | ED | 35 B5 |
| CAPRI AV | MCO | 55 D1 |
| CARBINE TR | KER | 79 D5 |
| CARBON CYN RD | ORA | 98 C3 |
| CARBON CYN RD | ORA | T E1 |
| CARBON CYN RD | ORA | U B4 |
| CARBON CYN RD | SBD | 98 C3 |
| CARBON CYN RD | SBD | U C3 |
| CARBONDALE RD | AMA | 40 C2 |
| CARBONDALE RD | SAC | 40 C2 |
| CARDELLA RD | MCO | 48 B4 |
| CARDIFF ST | SDCO | V D3 |
| CAREY RD | IMP | 109 A4 |
| CARGIL LN | RCO | 107 C1 |
| CARIBOU RD | SIS | 11 C3 |
| CARLETON RD | MPA | 49 B3 |
| CARLIN RD | SJCO | 46 E1 |
| CARLSBAD BLVD | SDCO | 106 B3 |
| CARLSON | CC | 38 C5 |
| CARLSON BLVD | CC | L C3 |
| CARLSON BLVD | R | 155 B3 |
| CARLSON RD | BUT | 25 B4 |
| CARLSON RD | SUT | 33 C3 |
| CARLTON RD | SCR | 54 C2 |
| CARLTON RD | SIS | 4 B4 |
| CARLUCCI RD | MCO | 56 A1 |
| CARLYLE RD | NEV | 27 A5 |
| CARMEL RD | KER | 77 D1 |
| CARMELLIA AV | FRCO | 56 B2 |
| CARMEL MTN RD | SDCO | 106 D4 |
| CARMEL RCHO BL | MON | 168 D5 |
| CARMEL VLY RD | MON | 54 B5 |
| CARMEL VLY RD | MON | 64 C1 |
| CARMEL VLY RD | MON | 168 E4 |
| CARMEL VLY RD | SDCO | V A1 |
| CARMEL VLY RD | SDCO | 106 C4 |
| CARMEN LN | BUT | 25 A3 |
| CARMENCITA AV | SJCO | 40 A2 |
| CARMENITA AV | LACO | T B1 |
| CARNATION RD | MCO | 47 D5 |
| CARNELIAN BAY | PLA | 35 E1 |
| CARNEROS AV | NAPA | 38 C3 |
| CARPENTER RD | HUM | 10 D5 |
| CARPENTER RD | SJCO | 40 B5 |
| CARPENTER RD | STA | 47 C3 |
| CARPENTER ST | CAR | 53 D5 |
| CARPENTER ST | CAR | 168 C3 |
| CARPENTER ST | MON | 168 C3 |
| CARPENTERIA | MON | 54 C3 |
| CARPINTERIA ST | STB | 174 E3 |
| CARPENTER RIDGE | BUT | 25 D1 |
| CARQUINEZ SC DR | CC | L E3 |
| CARR AV | SBT | 54 C2 |
| CARRIAGE LN | SHA | 18 B3 |
| CARRIER GLCH RD | TRI | 17 C3 |
| CARRILLO ST | STB | 174 B4 |
| CARRIZO GRGE RD | SDCO | 111 A4 |
| CARROLL RD | SAC | 40 A3 |
| CARROLL CK RD | INY | 60 B5 |
| CARROLTON | SJCO | 47 C1 |
| CARROT LN | RCO | 107 B1 |
| CARRVILLE LOOP | TRI | 11 E4 |
| CARRVILLE LOOP | TRI | 12 A4 |
| CARSON RD | ED | 34 E5 |
| CARSON ST | LACO | 97 D3 |
| CARSON ST | LACO | S B2 |
| CARSTENS RD | MPA | 49 B3 |
| CARTER RD | MPA | 49 B3 |
| CARTER ST | SBD | 99 D2 |
| CARTMILL AV | TUL | 68 A2 |
| CARUTHERS AV | FRCO | 57 C5 |
| CARVER LN | RCO | 99 B4 |
| CASADEL RD | MAD | 49 E5 |
| CASADEL RD | MAD | 50 A5 |
| CASA DIABLO CTO | MNO | 51 B2 |
| CASA DIABLO MN | MNO | 51 B2 |
| CASA GRANDE RD | SON | L A1 |
| CASALE RD | TEH | 18 D5 |
| CASA LOMA RD | SCL | P C5 |
| CASA LOMA RD | SCL | 54 B1 |
| CASCADE BLVD | SHA | 18 C2 |
| CASCADE RD | SBD | 101 A1 |
| CASCADIAN AV | SBD | 91 D3 |
| CASE RD | RCO | 99 C4 |
| CASEY AV | KER | 68 B5 |
| CASEY AV | SB | 86 E3 |
| CASEY RD | IMP | 109 B5 |
| CASEY RD | SOL | 39 B2 |
| CASITAS VIS RD | VEN | 88 A5 |
| CASPR LTL LK RD | MEN | 22 C5 |
| CASS ST | MONT | 167 E4 |
| CASS ST | MON | 53 E3 |
| CASS ST | SDCO | V A2 |
| CASS ST | SDCO | 106 C5 |
| CASSEL RD | SHA | 13 D5 |
| CASSEL FALL RIV | SHA | 13 D4 |
| CASSERLY RD | SCR | 54 C2 |
| CASSIDY ST | SDCO | 106 B3 |
| CASTAIC RD | LACO | 89 B4 |
| CASTAIC CYN RD | LACO | 89 B3 |
| CASTERLINE RD | HUM | 16 D4 |
| CASTLE CT | BUT | 25 C3 |
| CASTLE ST | S | 160 C3 |
| CASTLE CREEK RD | SHA | 12 C3 |
| CASTLE LAKE RD | SIS | 12 C2 |
| CASTRO | CC | 38 C5 |
| CASTRO RD | CC | 38 D5 |
| CASTRO RD | RCO | 99 D4 |
| CASTRO RANCH RD | CC | L D3 |
| CASTRO VLY BL | ALA | 146 D1 |
| CASTROVILLE BL | MON | 54 C3 |
| CATALINA AV | AVLN | 105 B5 |
| CATALINA BLVD | SDCO | V A3 |
| CATALINA DR | DVS | 136 C1 |
| CAT CANYON RD | SB | 86 D2 |
| CATERPILLAR RD | SHA | 18 C2 |
| CATFISH BCI RD | PLU | 20 B4 |
| CATHEDRAL RD | ED | 35 E3 |
| CATHEY RD | HUM | 16 B4 |
| CATLETT RD W | SUT | 33 D4 |
| CATRINA RD | MCO | 56 B1 |
| CATTARAUGUS AV | CUL | 183 C4 |
| CATTARAUGUS AV | LA | 183 C4 |
| CATTLE DR | TUL | 68 E3 |
| CATTLE DRIVE RD | MNO | 51 C1 |
| CATTLEMEN RD | MON | 65 D3 |
| CATWAY RD | SB | 87 A2 |
| CAUGHLIN RD | SBD | 91 A3 |
| CAVE CITY RD | CAL | 41 B3 |
| CAVEDALE RD | SON | 38 B2 |
| CAVIN RD | VEN | 88 E4 |
| CAVITT & STLLMN | PLA | 34 B4 |
| CAWELTI RD | VEN | 96 C1 |
| CAWSTON AV | RCO | 99 E4 |
| CAYLEY DR | KER | 79 C4 |
| CAYTON VLY RD | SHA | 13 C4 |
| CAYUCOS CK RD | SLO | 75 D2 |
| CAZADERO HWY | SON | 37 C1 |
| CCMO RD | KER | 77 D3 |
| CEBADA CYN RD | SB | 86 C3 |
| CECIL AV | KER | 68 B5 |
| CECIL RD | COL | 33 B3 |
| CECILVILLE RD | SIS | 11 C3 |
| CEDAR AV | FRCO | 57 C3 |
| CEDAR AV | FRCO | 57 C5 |
| CEDAR AV | RCO | 100 C4 |
| CEDAR AV | SBD | 99 B2 |
| CEDAR DR | MOD | 14 B3 |
| CEDAR ST | SBD | 80 E1 |
| CEDAR ST | SDCO | 107 A4 |
| CEDAR CAMP RD | HUM | 10 C2 |
| CEDAR CAMP RD | SIS | 10 C1 |
| CEDAR CAMP RD | TRI | 17 A4 |
| CEDAR CANYON RD | SBD | 84 B4 |
| CEDAR CREEK RD | ED | 40 E1 |
| CEDAR CREEK RD | ED | 41 A1 |
| CEDAR CREEK RD | HUM | 10 C5 |
| CEDAR CK LP RD | BUT | 25 C1 |
| CEDAR GROVE RD | SIS | 5 A2 |
| CEDAR RAVINE RD | ED | 34 E5 |
| CEDAR RAVINE ST | PLCV | 138 E3 |
| CEDARVILLE DUMP | MOD | 8 E1 |
| CEDAR WELL | SIS | 5 A4 |
| CEDARWOOD CT | SHA | 19 A3 |
| CEDROS DR | SBD | 90 E2 |
| CEMENT HILL RD | FRFD | 135 C1 |
| CEMENT HILL RD | NEV | 34 C1 |
| CEMETERY DR | MOD | 14 C3 |
| CEMETERY RD | COL | 32 D1 |
| CEMETERY RD | HUM | 16 D4 |
| CEMETERY RD | MCO | 47 D4 |
| CEMETERY RD | MNO | 43 C4 |
| CEMETERY RD | SBD | 82 A5 |
| CEMETERY RD | SHA | 19 B2 |
| CEMETERY RD | SIS | 5 A2 |
| CENTENNIAL RD | HUM | 15 D3 |
| CENTER AV | MCO | 56 B2 |
| CENTER RD | LAS | 21 A3 |
| CENTER RD | STA | 47 B2 |
| CENTER ST | CAL | 41 A3 |
| CENTER ST | MAN | 161 A4 |
| CENTER ST | RCO | 99 B2 |
| CENTER ST | SBD | 99 C2 |
| CENTER ST | SC | 169 D3 |
| CENTER ST | S | 160 D3 |
| CENTER ST EXT | RCO | 99 C2 |
| CENTER ST S | TEH | 24 E1 |
| CTR SCH HOUSE | LAS | 14 C3 |
| CENTERVILLE LN | DGL | 36 B3 |
| CENTERVILLE RD | BUT | 25 C3 |
| CENTERVILLE RD | HUM | 15 D2 |
| CENTERVILLE RD | MOD | 8 A1 |
| CENTERVILLE RD | MOD | 14 E1 |
| CENTINELA AV | CUL | 187 D1 |
| CENTINELA AV | ING | 188 B3 |
| CENTINELA AV | LA | 187 D1 |
| CENTINELA AV | LACO | Q C4 |
| CENTINELLA RD | MCO | 55 C1 |
| CENTRAL AV | A | 158 A5 |
| CENTRAL AV | A | 159 A1 |
| CENTRAL AV | FRCO | 56 D4 |
| CENTRAL AV | FRCO | 57 B4 |
| CENTRAL AV | HUM | 9 E4 |
| CENTRAL AV | HUM | 10 A4 |
| CENTRAL AV | KER | 78 A2 |
| CENTRAL AV | LA | 186 B5 |
| CENTRAL AV | LACO | 97 E2 |
| CENTRAL AV | LACO | Q E2 |
| CENTRAL AV | LACO | S C1 |
| CENTRAL AV | MCO | 47 D4 |
| CENTRAL AV | MON | 65 B2 |
| CENTRAL AV | MTCL | 203 C3 |
| CENTRAL AV | ORA | T C1 |
| CENTRAL AV | ORA | U A4 |
| CENTRAL AV | PAC | 167 C2 |
| CENTRAL AV | RCO | 99 B2 |
| CENTRAL AV | RCO | 205 B5 |
| CENTRAL AV | SAL | 171 A4 |
| CENTRAL AV | SBD | U D3 |
| CENTRAL AV | SBD | 98 D2 |
| CENTRAL AV | RCO | 99 B4 |
| CENTRAL AV | SBD | 203 C3 |
| CENTRAL AV | SB | 86 B3 |
| CENTRAL AV | STA | 47 D3 |
| CENTRAL AV | SUT | 33 B3 |
| CENTRAL AV | TEH | 24 D1 |
| CENTRAL AV | VEN | 88 C5 |
| CENTRAL AV | YOL | 39 D2 |
| CENTRAL RD | SBD | 91 C3 |
| CENTRAL EXPWY | MVW | 148 B4 |
| CENTRAL EXPWY | SCL | N E2 |
| CENTRAL EXPWY | SCL | P B3 |
| CENTRAL EXPWY | SVL | 148 B4 |
| CENTRAL FRWY | SF | 143 A5 |
| CENTRAL SKYWAY | SF | 142 C4 |
| CENTRAL ST | RCO | 99 C5 |
| CENTRAL CAMP RD | MAD | 49 E4 |
| CENTRAL HILL RD | CAL | 40 E3 |
| CENTRAL HILL RD | CAL | 41 A3 |
| CENTRL HOUSE RD | BUT | 25 D5 |
| CENTRALIA ST | LACO | S E2 |
| CENTRALIA ST | LACO | T A2 |
| CENTRAL VLY HWY | KER | 78 B1 |
| CENTURY BLVD | LA | 189 D1 |
| CENTURY BLVD | LACO | 97 D2 |
| CENTURY BLVD | LACO | Q D5 |
| CERINI AV | FRCO | 57 B5 |
| CERINI AV | FRCO | 57 C5 |
| CERRITOS AV | ANA | 193 D4 |
| CERRITOS AV | ORA | T B2 |
| CERRO GORDO RD | INY | 60 C5 |
| CERRO GORDO RD | INY | 60 D4 |
| CERRO NOROESTE | KER | 78 A5 |
| CERRO NOROESTE | KER | 87 E1 |
| CERVANTES BLVD | SF | 142 A1 |
| CHABOT RD | VAL | 134 D1 |
| CHADBOURNE RD | CC | 39 B5 |
| CHADBOURNE RD | SOL | 38 E3 |
| CHADWICK RD | SBD | 101 E1 |
| CHAHLIP LN | FRCO | 58 C1 |
| CHALET DR | KER | 79 C4 |
| CHALFANT RD | MNO | 51 D3 |
| CHALFANT LP RD | MNO | 51 D3 |
| CHALK BLUFF RD | INY | 51 C4 |
| CHALK BLUFF RD | NEV | 34 D1 |
| CHALK HILL RD | SON | 37 E1 |
| CHALLNGE CTO RD | YUB | 26 A4 |
| CHALONE RD | SBT | 55 A5 |
| CHAMBERLAIN | PLA | 34 A3 |
| CHAMBERLAIN RD | MCO | 48 B5 |
| CHAMBERS RD | HUM | 15 D4 |
| CHAMBERS WLS RD | SBD | 103 E1 |
| CHAMPAGNE AV | KER | 89 C1 |
| CHAMPS FLAT RD | LAS | 20 C2 |
| CHANAC RD | KER | 79 B4 |
| CHANDLER | YUB | 33 D1 |
| CHANDLER BLVD | BUR | 179 C3 |
| CHANDLER BLVD | LA | 179 A4 |
| CHANDLER BLVD | LACO | Q C2 |
| CHANDLER RD | PLU | 26 D1 |
| CHANDON AV | BUT | 33 C1 |
| CHANNEL ISLD BL | VEN | 96 B1 |
| CHAPARAJOS ST | CAL | 41 A4 |
| CHAPARRAL DR | SHA | 18 B2 |
| CHAPMAN AV | GGR | 195 A1 |
| CHAPMAN AV | OR | 195 D1 |
| CHAPMAN AV | OR | 196 B1 |
| CHAPMAN AV | ORA | 98 C3 |
| CHAPMAN AV | ORA | T B2 |
| CHAPMAN AV | ORA | T C1 |
| CHAPMAN DR | CRTM | 140 B2 |
| CHAPMAN RD | RCO | 107 C1 |
| CHAPPIUS LN N | LAS | 21 B3 |
| CHAPPIUS LN S | LAS | 21 B4 |
| CHAPULNIK RD | IMP | 109 B4 |


STREETS

CHARD AV

# STREET INDEX

224

COPPEROPOLIS RD




| STREET | CO. | PAGE & GRID |
|---|---|---|
| CHARD AV | TEH | 18 D5 |
| CHARLEBOIS RD | MNO | 42 E1 |
| CHARLES ST | KER | 80 D1 |
| CHARLES ST | SHA | 18 C3 |
| CHARLES HILL RD | CC | L D4 |
| CHARLESTON BLVD | LV | 209 A2 |
| CHARLESTON BL E | CLK | 74 D2 |
| CHARLESTON RD | MCO | 55 D2 |
| CHARLESTON RD | SCL | N E3 |
| CHARLESTON RD | SCL | P A3 |
| CHARLESTON RD | SCL | 45 E4 |
| CHARLESTON RD W | PA | 147 E5 |
| CHRLSTN VOLCANO | AMA | 41 A2 |
| CHAROLAIS RD | SLO | 76 A1 |
| CHARTER WY | SJCO | 40 B5 |
| CHARTER OAK DR | TUL | 68 C1 |
| CHASE AV | KER | 79 E2 |
| CHASE AV | KER | 80 A2 |
| CHASE AV | SDCO | V E3 |
| CHASE AV | SDCO | 111 E1 |
| CHASE AV | TEH | 24 D2 |
| CHASE DR | RCO | 98 E3 |
| CHASE SCHOOL RD | RCO | 100 E3 |
| CHATEAU DR | SMCO | 45 C3 |
| CHATEAU RD | ML | 164 D3 |
| CHATEAU FRESNO | FRCO | 57 B4 |
| CHATEAU FRESNO | FRCO | 57 B5 |
| CHATSWORTH BLVD | SDCO | V A3 |
| CHATSWORTH BLVD | SDCO | 111 C1 |
| CHECKMATE RD | RCO | 100 A5 |
| CHELSEY AV | CC | L C3 |
| CHEMEHUEVI BLVD | MOH | 96 B4 |
| CHEMISE MTN RD | HUM | 22 A1 |
| CHEROKEE LN | SAC | 40 B3 |
| CHEROKEE LN | SJCO | 40 B3 |
| CHEROKEE RD | BUT | 25 D4 |
| CHEROKEE RD | MCO | 55 D1 |
| CHEROKEE RD | SBD | 82 C5 |
| CHEROKEE RD | SJCO | 40 B5 |
| CHERRY AV | FRCO | 57 C4 |
| CHERRY AV | FRCO | 57 C5 |
| CHERRY AV | KER | 78 B2 |
| CHERRY AV | LACO | 97 E4 |
| CHERRY AV | LACO | S E2 |
| CHERRY AV | RCO | 99 E3 |
| CHERRY AV | SBD | 99 A2 |
| CHERRY AV | STA | 47 C4 |
| CHERRY ST | SUT | 33 C2 |
| CHERRY CREEK RD | SON | 31 C4 |
| CHERRY GLEN RD | SOL | 38 E3 |
| CHERRY VLY BLVD | RCO | 99 E2 |
| CHERT RD | RCO | 107 B1 |
| CHESEBORO RD | LACO | 90 B4 |
| CHESTER AV | BKD | 166 C4 |
| CHESTER AV | KER | 78 D3 |
| CHESTER LN | BKD | 166 B4 |
| CHESTR JUNPR LK | PLU | 20 A3 |
| CHESTER SKI RD | PLU | 20 A4 |
| CHESTR WRNR VLY | PLU | 19 E3 |
| CHESTR WRNR VLY | PLU | 20 A3 |
| CHESTNUT AV | FRCO | 57 C2 |
| CHESTNUT AV | FRCO | 57 C5 |
| CHESTNUT AV | SMCO | N B1 |
| CHESTNUT AV | SA | 196 B4 |
| CHESTNUT AV | TEH | 18 D5 |
| CHESTNUT ST | SF | 143 A3 |
| CHESTNUT ST | SHA | 18 C3 |
| CHESTNUT WY | CAL | 41 B5 |
| CHEVALIER RD | KER | 78 D4 |
| CHEVY CHASE DR | LACO | 97 E1 |
| CHEVY CHASE DR | LACO | R A3 |
| CHEZEM RD | HUM | 10 B5 |
| CHICAGO AV | RIV | 205 E4 |
| CHICAGO AV | STA | 47 C2 |
| CHICK RD | IMP | 112 B3 |
| CHICK RD | RCO | 108 E1 |
| CHICKEN HAWK RD | PLA | 34 E2 |
| CHICKEN RCH RD | TUO | 41 C5 |
| CHICO AV | KIN | 57 E5 |
| CHICO CANYON RD | BUT | 25 C2 |
| CHICORB LN | SOL | 39 B2 |
| CHICO RIVER RD | BUT | 25 A3 |
| CHIDAGO LOOP | MNO | 51 C2 |
| CHIDAGO CYN RD | MNO | 51 B2 |
| CHIHUAHUA VLY | SDCO | 107 B2 |
| CHILDS AV | MER | 170 B5 |
| CHILDS AV | MCO | 48 C4 |
| CHILE CAMP RD | CAL | 40 D3 |
| CHILENO VLY RD | SON | 37 E3 |
| CHILENO VLY RD | SON | 38 A3 |
| CHILES RD | YOL | 39 C1 |
| CHILES POPE VLY | NAPA | 29 D1 |
| CHILES POPE VLY | NAPA | 38 C1 |
| CHILI HILL | PLA | 34 B3 |
| CHIMNEY ROCK RD | SLO | 75 D1 |
| CHINA CAMP RD | MCO | 55 D1 |
| CHINA CREEK RD | MAD | 49 D4 |
| CHINA GRADE | SIS | 3 A4 |
| CHINA GRADE LP | KER | 78 D2 |
| CHINA GRADE RD | PLU | 26 D1 |
| CHINA GULCH DR | SHA | 18 B3 |
| CHINA LAKE BLVD | KER | 80 D1 |
| CHINA PK LO RD | SIS | 3 A3 |
| CHINA POINT RD | BUT | 25 D2 |
| CHINA RANCH RD | INY | 73 A5 |
| CHINO AV | SBD | U C3 |
| CHINO AV | SBD | 98 D2 |
| CHINO-CORONA RD | SBD | 98 E2 |
| CHINQUAPIN RD | MAD | 49 E4 |
| CHINQUAPIN RD | MAD | 50 A4 |
| CHINQUAPIN DR | MEN | 23 A5 |
| CHIRIACO RD | RCO | 101 E4 |
| CHITTENDEN RD | TEH | 24 C2 |
| CHLORIDE RD | SBD | 92 B1 |
| CHLORIDE CLF RD | INY | 62 A3 |
| CHOLAME RD | MON | 66 C4 |
| CHOLAME VLY RD | SLO | 66 D5 |
| CHOLLA RD | SBD | 91 C4 |
| CHOLLA RD | SBD | 92 C5 |
| CHORRO ST N | SNLO | 172 A1 |
| CHORRO ST S | SNLO | 172 B2 |
| CHOWCHILLA | MAD | 56 D3 |
| CHOWCHILLA BLVD | MAD | 56 D1 |
| CHOWCHILLA MTN | MPA | 49 C3 |
| CHRISMAN RD | SJCO | 47 A2 |
| CHRISTENSEN RD | SAC | 40 A3 |
| CHRISTIAN RD | TEH | 24 D2 |
| CHRISTN VLY RD | PLA | 34 C3 |
| CHROME MINE RD | TRI | 17 B3 |
| CHUALAR RD | MON | 54 D4 |
| CHUALAR CYN RD | MON | 54 E4 |
| CHUALAR RIV RD | MON | 54 D5 |
| CHUCKWAGON DR | CAL | 41 A5 |
| CHUCKWALLA RD | SBD | 91 D3 |
| CHUCKWL SPGS RD | RCO | 102 D5 |
| CHUCKWLA VLY RD | RCO | 102 D4 |
| CHUCKWLA VLY RD | RCO | 103 A5 |
| CHURCH AV | FRE | 165 B5 |
| CHURCH AV | FRCO | 57 A3 |
| CHURCH AV | FRCO | 57 D3 |
| CHURCH AV | SCL | P E5 |
| CHURCH AV | SCL | 54 D1 |
| CHURCH LN | HUM | 15 E2 |
| CHURCH LN | SCL | P E5 |
| CHURCH RD | SOL | M D2 |
| CHURCH RD | SOL | 39 C4 |
| CHURCH ST | HUM | 16 D4 |
| CHURCH ST | SBD | 99 C2 |
| CHURCH ST | STA | 47 D2 |
| CHURCH ST | S | 160 C5 |
| CHURCH HILL RD | CAL | 41 A3 |
| CHURCHILL MN RD | INY | 51 D3 |
| CHURCH SPGS RD | STA | 48 A1 |
| CHURN CREEK RD | SHA | 18 C2 |
| CIBOLA RD | LPAZ | 103 E5 |
| CIBOLA RD | LPAZ | 110 D1 |
| CIENAGA RD | KER | 78 A5 |
| CIENEGA RD | SBT | 54 E3 |
| CIENEGA RD | SBT | 55 A4 |
| CIMA RD | SBD | 83 E2 |
| CIMA RD | SBD | 84 A2 |
| CIMA MESA RD | LACO | 90 B4 |
| CINCHA ST | CAL | 41 A4 |
| CINDER RD | INY | 70 C3 |
| CINDER PIT RD | MOD | 14 D1 |
| CIRCLE DR | INY | 70 E1 |
| CIRCLE DR | RCO | 100 B4 |
| CIRCLEA CT | BUT | 25 C3 |
| CIRCLE C LN | SOL | 39 B2 |
| CITRACADO PKWY | SDCO | 106 D3 |
| CITRON ST | ANA | 193 B1 |
| CITRUS AV | LACO | 98 C2 |
| CITRUS AV | LACO | U A2 |
| CITRUS AV | SBD | 99 A2 |
| CITRUS AV | SBD | 99 D2 |
| CITRUS AV | SDCO | 106 C3 |
| CITRUS AV | SDCO | 106 D3 |
| CITY DR, THE | OR | 195 E2 |
| CITY CAMP | MNO | 43 C5 |
| CITY CREEK RD | SBD | 99 C1 |
| CIVIC CENTER DR | SR | 139 C1 |
| CIVIC CENTER DR | SA | 196 A3 |
| CLAIREMONT DR | SD | 211 E4 |
| CLAIREMONT DR | SD | 213 A1 |
| CLAIREMONT DR | SDCO | V B2 |
| CLAIREMONT DR | SDCO | 106 C5 |
| CLAIREMONT MESA | SD | 211 D4 |
| CLAIRMNT MSA BL | SDCO | V B2 |
| CLAIREMONT MESA | SDCO | 106 C5 |
| CLARATINA AV | STA | 47 D2 |
| CLAREMONT AV | ALA | L D4 |
| CLAREMONT AV | B | 156 C4 |
| CLAREMONT AV | O | 156 B5 |
| CLAREMONT BLVD | CLA | 203 B2 |
| CLARIBEL RD | STA | 47 D2 |
| CLARISSA AV | AVLN | 105 B5 |
| CLARK AV | COL | 24 E5 |
| CLARK AV | LACO | S E2 |
| CLARK AV | SB | 86 C1 |
| CLARK AV | TEH | 24 E2 |
| CLARK AV | YUBA | 125 C4 |
| CLARK RD | BUT | 25 C3 |
| CLARK RD | IMP | 109 A5 |
| CLARK RD | IMP | 112 A4 |
| CLARK RD | MEN | 30 D2 |
| CLARK RD | MON | 65 A1 |
| CLARK RD | SLO | 76 C1 |
| CLARK RD | SOL | 39 B2 |
| CLARK RD | STA | 47 C2 |
| CLARK RD | SUT | 33 C1 |
| CLARK ST | NAP | 133 E3 |
| CLARKE RD | HUM | 15 D4 |
| CLARK MTN RD | SBD | 84 A2 |
| CLARK RANCH RD | MNO | 51 C1 |
| CLARKSBURG | YOL | 39 D2 |
| CLARKS FORK RD | ALP | 42 B2 |
| CLARKSON AV | FRCO | 56 D5 |
| CLARKSON AV | FRCO | 57 C5 |
| CLARKS VLY RD | GLE | 24 B4 |
| CLAUS RD | STA | 47 D2 |
| CLAUSEN RD | MCO | 48 E5 |
| CLAWITER RD | ALA | N E1 |
| CLAWITER RD | ALA | 45 E2 |
| CLAWITER RD | ALA | 146 B4 |
| CLAWITER RD | H | 146 B4 |
| CLAY RD | INY | 72 D1 |
| CLAY ST | SAL | 171 B4 |
| CLAY ST | U | 123 B3 |
| CLAY BANK RD | SOL | 39 A3 |
| CLAY MINE RD | KER | 80 C5 |
| CLAY RIVER RD | SBD | 91 E1 |
| CLAY STATION RD | SAC | 40 B3 |
| CLAYTON AV | FRCO | 56 D4 |
| CLAYTON AV | FRCO | 58 A4 |
| CLAYTON RD | CC | 39 A5 |
| CLAYTON RD | NEV | 34 B2 |
| CLAYTON RD | SON | 32 A5 |
| CLAYTON RD | SON | 38 A1 |
| CLAYTON RD | STA | 47 D3 |
| CLAYTON CREEK | LAK | 32 A4 |
| CLEAR CREEK RD | KER | 79 B4 |
| CLEAR CREEK RD | SBT | 65 E1 |
| CLEAR CREEK RD | SBT | 66 A1 |
| CLEAR CREEK RD | SHA | 18 B3 |
| CLEARFIELD DR | MLBR | 144 B5 |
| CLEAR LAKE RD | MOD | 6 C3 |
| CLEGHORN RD | LAS | 14 D5 |
| CLEGHORN CYN RD | SBD | 91 B5 |
| CLEM | SJCO | 40 C4 |
| CLEMENCEAU AV | FRCO | 57 D5 |
| CLEMENTE AV | AVLN | 105 B5 |
| CLEMENTS RD | SJCO | 40 C4 |
| CLEMENTS RD | SUT | 33 C2 |
| CLEVELAND AV | MAD | 57 A2 |
| CLEVELAND AV | SBD | U E3 |
| CLEVELAND AV | SBD | 98 E2 |
| CLEVELAND AV | SD | 213 E5 |
| CLEVELAND AV | STA | 47 D1 |
| CLEVELAND RD | MCO | 56 C1 |
| CLEVELAND ST | RCO | 101 C5 |
| CLIFF DR | LAG | 201 B2 |
| CLIFF DR | STB | 174 A5 |
| CLIFF DR W | SC | 169 D4 |
| CLIFF RIDGE RD | MEN | 30 C2 |
| CLIFTON CT RD | SJCO | 46 D1 |
| CLINE GULCH RD | SHA | 18 A1 |
| CLINTON AV | FRE | 165 B1 |
| CLINTON AV | FRCO | 56 E3 |
| CLINTON AV | FRCO | 57 A3 |
| CLINTON AV | KIN | 57 E5 |
| CLINTON AV S | SJCO | 47 B1 |
| CLINTON RD | AMA | 41 A2 |
| CLINTON RD | ED | 41 A2 |
| CLINTON RD | STA | 47 D2 |
| CLINTON RD E | AMA | 41 A2 |
| CLINTON RD W | AMA | 41 A2 |
| CLINTN KEITH RD | RCO | 99 C5 |
| CLIO STATE RD | PLU | 27 B3 |
| CLOSE AV | TUL | 68 D1 |
| CLOUGH RD | HUM | 15 D2 |
| CLOUTIER ST | DN | 1 D3 |
| CLOVER LN | SB | 86 E2 |
| CLOVER LN | SB | 87 A2 |
| CLOVER LN | SHA | 18 B3 |
| CLOVER CREEK RD | KLAM | 5 A1 |
| CLOVERDALE DR | SHA | 18 B3 |
| CLOVERDALE RD | RCO | U E3 |
| CLOVERDALE RD | RCO | 98 E2 |
| CLOVERDALE RD | SMCO | N C4 |
| CLOVERDALE RD | SMCO | 45 C5 |
| CLOVERFIELD BL | SMON | 180 A5 |
| CLOVERLEAF DR | MAD | 57 B2 |
| CLOVER VLY RD | LAK | 31 D2 |
| CLOVIS AV | FRCO | 57 D5 |
| CLUB DR | DN | 1 E3 |
| CLYDE AV | MCO | 48 B5 |
| COACHELLA CANAL | RCO | 108 D1 |
| COACHLA CNAL RD | IMP | 109 B2 |
| COACHLLA CYN RD | RCO | 101 D5 |
| COAL RD | RCO | 99 B4 |
| COAL CANYON RD | BUT | 25 C4 |
| COAL CANYON RD | ORA | U D5 |
| COAL CANYON RD | ORA | 98 D3 |
| COALINGA RD | SBT | 65 D1 |
| COAL MINE RD | AMA | 40 D3 |
| COALINGA RD | SBT | 66 A1 |
| COALNGA MNL SPG | FRCO | 66 B3 |
| COAST HWY | LAG | 201 A2 |
| COAST HWY | ORA | 98 C5 |
| COAST HWY | ORA | 201 A2 |
| COAST HWY | ORA | 202 D5 |
| COAST HWY | SON | 30 D5 |
| COAST HWY E | NB | 199 D4 |
| COAST HWY E | NB | 200 A5 |
| COAST HWY W | NB | 199 C4 |
| COAST RD | MON | 64 B1 |
| COAST RIDGE TR | MON | 64 E4 |
| COCHRANE RD | SCL | P D4 |
| COCHRAN RD | SCL | 54 C1 |
| COCK RBN ISL RD | HUM | 15 D2 |
| COCOPAH RD | IMP | 112 D5 |
| COD DR | SIS | 4 B3 |
| CODONI AV | STA | 47 D2 |
| COFFEE RD | KER | 78 C2 |
| COFFEE RD | MDO | 162 E2 |
| COFFEE RD | STA | 47 D2 |
| COFFEE ST | MCO | 48 C5 |
| COFFEE CREEK RD | HUM | 15 D2 |
| COFFEE CREEK RD | TRI | 11 D3 |
| COGSWELL RD | STA | 47 E2 |
| COGSWELL RD | STA | 48 A2 |
| COHASSET RD | BUT | 25 C2 |
| COHASSET RD | C | 124 A2 |
| COHEN RD | SJCO | 47 A1 |
| COHN AV | FRCO | 66 D3 |
| COLBY RD | IMP | 110 D5 |
| COLBY MTN LKOUT | TEH | 19 D5 |
| COLDEN AV | LACO | Q E5 |
| COLD CANYON RD | LACO | 97 B2 |
| COLD CREEK RD | TRI | 17 B3 |
| COLD SPRINGS RD | ED | 34 D4 |
| COLD SPRINGS RD | LAS | 8 C4 |
| COLDWATR CYN AV | LACO | 97 C1 |
| COLDWATR CYN AV | LACO | Q C2 |
| COLDWATR CYN DR | LACO | 97 D1 |
| COLDWELL AV | MDO | 162 A2 |
| COLDWELL LN | FRCO | 66 B3 |
| COLE RD | IMP | 112 B4 |
| COLE RD | MPA | 49 B3 |
| COLE GRADE RD | SDCO | 106 D2 |
| COLEMAN AV | MP | 147 A1 |
| COLEMAN AV | SMCO | 147 A1 |
| COLEMAN AV | SCL | P B3 |
| COLEMAN AV | SCLR | 151 C2 |
| COLEMN FSH HTCH | SHA | 18 D3 |
| COLEMAN VLY RD | SON | 37 C2 |
| COLES RD | SUT | 33 B3 |
| COLES LEVEE RD | KER | 78 B4 |
| COLEY RD | IMP | 112 D5 |
| COLFAX | PLA | 34 D2 |
| COLFAX AV | GV | 127 C4 |
| COLFAX AV | LACO | Q D3 |
| COLFAX AV | NEV | 127 C4 |
| COLFAX FRST HLL | PLA | 34 D2 |
| COLGATE RD | KER | 80 D3 |
| COLIMA RD | LACO | 98 B3 |
| COLIMA RD | LACO | R D5 |
| COLIN RD | SBD | 80 E1 |
| COLLEGE AV | ALA | L D4 |
| COLLEGE AV | B | 156 B3 |
| COLLEGE AV | MAR | 139 B5 |
| COLLEGE AV | MDO | 162 A2 |
| COLLEGE AV | O | 156 B5 |
| COLLEGE AV | SDCO | V C3 |
| COLLEGE AV | SDCO | 111 D1 |
| COLLEGE AV | SIS | 12 C1 |
| COLLEGE AV | SON | 37 E2 |
| COLLEGE AV | SON | 38 A2 |
| COLLEGE AV | STR | 131 C3 |
| COLLEGE AV W | STR | 131 B3 |
| COLLEGE BLVD | PLA | 34 B4 |
| COLLEGE BLVD | SDCO | 106 B3 |
| COLLEGE DR | SAL | 171 A4 |
| COLLEGE DR | SMA | 173 D4 |
| COLLEGE CITY RD | COL | 33 A3 |
| COLLEGE HTS BL | KER | 80 E1 |
| COLLIER RD | MCO | 47 E4 |
| COLLIER RD | MCO | 48 A4 |
| COLLIER RD | SJCO | 40 B3 |
| COLLIER CYN RD | ALA | 46 B2 |
| COLLINS AV | OR | 194 D4 |
| COLLINS AV | ORA | T D2 |
| COLLINS RD | IMP | 110 D5 |
| COLLINS RD | INY | 51 D4 |
| COLLINSVILLE RD | SOL | M B2 |
| COLLINSVILLE RD | SOL | 39 B4 |
| COLLYER DR | SHA | 18 C2 |
| COLOMA RD | ED | 34 D4 |
| COLOMA RD | ED | 138 B1 |
| COLOMA RD | SAC | 40 A1 |
| COLOMA ST | PLCV | 138 C2 |
| COLOMBERO DR | SIS | 12 D2 |
| COLOMBO MINE RD | SIE | 26 E4 |
| COLOMBO MINE RD | SIE | 27 A4 |
| COLOMBUS AV | MCO | 47 D4 |
| COLONY RD | BUT | 25 B4 |
| COLONY RD | MON | 64 E1 |
| COLONY RD | MON | 65 A1 |
| COLONY RD | SAC | 40 B2 |
| COLORADO AV | RCO | 99 A3 |
| COLORADO AV | SCL | N E2 |
| COLORADO AV | SMON | 180 A5 |
| COLORADO BLVD | LACO | 97 E1 |
| COLORADO BLVD | LACO | 98 A1 |
| COLORADO BLVD | LACO | R D3 |
| COLORADO BLVD | PAS | 190 B4 |
| COLORADO RD | FRCO | 57 A5 |
| COLORADO RD | MPA | 49 B3 |
| COLORADO ST | GLEN | 182 E1 |
| COLORADO ST | LACO | Q E3 |
| COLORADO ST | LACO | S E2 |
| COLORADO ST | LACO | T A2 |
| COLORADO RV RD | RCO | 103 D4 |
| COLOSEUM | INY | 59 E2 |
| COLSEN CYN RD | SB | 86 D1 |
| COLT LN | CAL | 41 A5 |
| COLTON AV | CLTN | 207 B4 |
| COLTON AV | SBD | 99 B2 |
| COLUMBIA AV | RCO | 99 B2 |
| COLUMBIA RD N | KER | 80 D3 |
| COLUMBIA RD S | KER | 80 D4 |
| COLUMBINE RD | SIS | 12 C2 |
| COLUMBUS AV | SF | 143 B2 |
| COLUMBUS AV | SFCO | 45 C1 |
| COLUMBUS PKWY | SOL | L D2 |
| COLUMBUS PKWY | SOL | 38 D4 |
| COLUMBUS ST | KER | 78 D3 |
| COLUSA AV | CC | L D4 |
| COLUSA AV | FRCO | 56 E4 |
| COLUSA AV | FRCO | 66 E1 |
| COLUSA AV | SUT | 125 A2 |
| COLUSA AV | YUBA | 125 A2 |
| COLUSA RD | SBD | 91 B3 |
| COLUSA CO RD | COL | 31 E1 |
| COLUSA-PRNTN RD | COL | 32 E1 |
| COLYEAR SPGS RD | TEH | 17 E5 |
| COMANCHE DR | KER | 78 E4 |
| COMANCHE DR | KER | 79 A3 |
| COMANCHE PT RD | KER | 79 A4 |
| COMBIE RD | NEV | 34 C3 |
| COMBIE RD | PLA | 34 C3 |
| COMETA RD | SJCO | 47 D1 |
| COMM BLVD | SBD | 91 C1 |
| COMMERCE AV | LACO | Q E1 |
| COMMERCIAL ST | SD | 216 A4 |
| COMMONS RD | STA | 47 D3 |
| COMMONWEALTH | ORA | 98 B3 |
| COMMONWEALTH AV | ORA | T B1 |
| COMMONWEALTH AV | RCO | 99 E4 |
| COMPTCHE UKIAH | MEN | 30 B1 |
| COMPTON AV | LACO | Q E5 |
| COMPTON BLVD | LACO | S B1 |
| COMSTOCK | WSH | 130 B3 |
| COMSTOCK RD | SBT | 55 A2 |
| COMSTOCK RD | SJCO | 40 C4 |
| CONARD RD | LAS | 20 D3 |
| CONCHO ST | CAL | 41 A4 |
| CONCORD AV | CC | 39 C5 |
| CONCORD BLVD | CC | M A3 |
| CONCORD BLVD | CC | 39 A5 |
| CONCOW RD | BUT | 25 D1 |
| CONDIT AV | STA | 47 B3 |
| CONDOR RD | SBD | 92 B1 |
| CONDOR RD | SBD | 101 C1 |
| CONDUIT | SUT | 33 C3 |
| CONE RD | INY | 51 D5 |
| CONE RD 3 | LAS | 20 B1 |
| CONE GROVE RD | TEH | 18 D5 |
| CONEJO AV | FRCO | 57 B5 |
| CONEJO AV | FRCO | 57 C5 |
| CONEJO DR | SBD | 90 E3 |
| CONE PEAK RD | MON | 64 E3 |
| CONFER RD | SJCO | 40 B5 |
| CONGRESS AV | MONT | 53 D3 |
| CONGRESS AV | PAC | 167 B3 |
| CONGRESS ST | SD | 213 A5 |
| CONGRSS SPGS RD | SCL | N E4 |
| CONGRSS SPGS RD | SCL | P A4 |
| CONGRSS SPGS RD | SCL | 45 E5 |
| CONKLIN BLVD | KER | 80 C4 |
| CONKLIN RD | MOD | 8 D1 |
| CONKLIN CK RD | HUM | 15 D4 |
| CONKLING RD | IMP | 112 A3 |
| CONN CREEK RD | NAPA | 29 D4 |
| CONNECTION | LAS | 21 E4 |
| CONNELLY RD | IMP | 112 C3 |
| CONRAD GROVE LP | TEH | 19 D3 |
| CONSTANCE AV | STB | 174 A2 |
| CONSTANTIA RD | LAS | 27 E1 |
| CONSTELLATN AV | KER | 89 C1 |
| CONSUMNES MINE | ED | 35 B5 |
| CONTADAS | CC | 38 D5 |
| CONTOUR AV | RCO | 99 D3 |
| CONTRA COSTA AV | FRCO | 56 D4 |
| CONTRA COSTA BL | CC | L E3 |
| CONTRA COSTA BL | CC | M A3 |
| CONTRA LOMA BL | CC | M C3 |
| CONVENTN CTR DR | CLK | 209 C5 |
| CONVICT CPGD RD | MNO | 50 E2 |
| CONVICT CPGD RD | MNO | 51 A2 |
| CONVICT CK EXP | MNO | 51 A2 |
| CONVICT LAKE RD | MNO | 50 E2 |
| CONVICT LAKE RD | MNO | 51 A2 |
| CONVOY ST | SDCO | V B2 |
| CONVOY ST | SDCO | 106 D5 |
| CONWAY RANCH RD | MNO | 43 B4 |
| COOK LN | SOL | 39 B3 |
| COOK RD | AMA | 40 C3 |
| COOK ST | RCO | 100 E4 |
| COOK ST | SMA | 173 A3 |
| COOK CAMPBLL RD | SIS | 4 E4 |
| COOK PEAK LKOUT | KER | 79 D1 |
| COOKS CAMP RD | CAL | 41 C2 |
| COOKS SPRING RD | COL | 32 B1 |
| COOLEY RD | IMP | 109 B5 |
| COOLEY RD | SIS | 4 B3 |
| COOLGARDIE RD | SBD | 81 D4 |
| COOLIDGE AV | O | 158 E4 |
| COOLIDGE AV | SCL | P D5 |
| COOMBSVILLE RD | NAPA | L D1 |
| COOMBSVILLE RD | NAPA | 38 D3 |
| COON HOLLOW CK | BUT | 25 D1 |
| COOPER RD | IMP | 109 C5 |
| COOPER RD | MON | 54 C4 |
| COOPER RD | NEV | 34 C1 |
| COOPR CIENG T T | RCO | 100 B5 |
| COOPERSTOWN RD | STA | 48 B2 |
| COPA DE ORA AV | MCO | 55 D1 |
| COPCO RD | SIS | 4 B3 |
| COPENHAGEN | HUM | 15 D2 |
| COPP AV | KER | 89 B1 |
| COPPER | FRCO | 57 D2 |
| COPPER AV | FRCO | 56 A2 |
| COPPER CYN RD | SHA | 18 C1 |
| COPPER CITY RD | SBD | 81 D4 |
| COPPER COVE DR | CAL | 41 A5 |
| COPPER HEAD RD | MON | 65 C4 |
| COPPER MTN RD | SBD | 101 B1 |
| COPPEROPOLIS | SJCO | 40 D5 |
| COPPER VISTA WY | SDCO | 106 C3 |
| COPP PIT RD | MOD | 14 D2 |
| COPUS RD | KER | 78 B4 |
| CORAL RD | MCO | 47 E5 |
| CORAL RD | MCO | 55 E1 |
| CORAN RD | SHA | 18 B1 |
| CORBETT CYN RD | SLO | 76 B4 |
| CORBIN AV | LA | 178 B3 |
| CORBIN RD | COL | 32 D1 |
| CORCORAN RD | KER | 77 E1 |
| CORD | SJCO | 40 C3 |
| CORDA RD | MON | 54 E5 |
| CORDELIA RD | SOL | L E1 |
| CORDELIA RD | SOL | M A1 |
| CORDELIA RD | SOL | 38 E3 |
| CORDELIA RD | SOL | 135 B5 |
| CORDELIA RD | SUIS | 135 B5 |
| CORE RD | SAC | 39 E2 |
| CORKILL RD | RCO | 100 D3 |
| CORN CAMP RD | KER | 77 E3 |
| CORNELIA AV | FRCO | 57 B4 |
| CORNELIUS AV | SUT | 33 D3 |
| CORNING RD | TEH | 24 C2 |
| CORN SPRINGS RD | RCO | 102 C5 |
| CORONA AV | KIN | 57 E5 |
| CORONA EXPWY | RCO | 98 D3 |
| CORONA EXPWY | SBD | 98 D2 |
| CORONA FRWY | RCO | 98 E3 |
| CORONA RD | SON | L A1 |
| CORONA RD | SON | 38 A3 |
| CORONA D MAR FY | CM | 197 D4 |
| CORONA D MAR FY | ORA | 98 C4 |
| CORONADO AV | SDCO | V C5 |
| CORONADO AV | SDCO | 111 D2 |
| CORRAL RD | SHA | 19 E2 |
| COPPEROPOLIS RD | TRI | 17 B5 |


STREETS

| STREET | CO. | PAGE | GRID |
|---|---|---|---|
| CORRL DE TIERRA | MON | 54 | C5 |
| CORRAL HOLLW RD | SJCO | 46 | E2 |
| CORRALITOS RD | SCR | 54 | B2 |
| CORREIA RD | SJCO | 39 | E4 |
| CORRELL RD | SUT | 33 | B3 |
| CORTE MADERA AV | CRTM | 140 | B1 |
| CORTEZ AV | MCO | 47 | E3 |
| CORTEZ AV | MCO | 48 | A3 |
| CORTEZ WY | KER | 79 | E2 |
| CORTINA SCH RD | COL | 32 | D3 |
| CORTINA VNYD RD | COL | 32 | D3 |
| CORTO RD | SBD | 91 | D4 |
| CORWIN RD | SBD | 91 | C3 |
| CORWIN RANCH RD | RCO | 99 | B5 |
| CORYDON RD | RCO | 99 | B5 |
| COSGROVE | CAL | 41 | B4 |
| COSTA RD | YUB | 26 | A4 |
| COSTNER RD | STA | 47 | C2 |
| COTA ST | STB | 174 | C4 |
| COTHARIN RD | VEN | 96 | D2 |
| COTTA RD | SJCO | 39 | E4 |
| COTTAGE AV | MAN | 161 | E1 |
| COTTAGE AV | SJCO | 161 | E1 |
| COTTLE RD | STA | 47 | D1 |
| COTTON RD | MCO | 55 | E2 |
| COTTON CREEK | MPA | 48 | D2 |
| COTTON GIN RD | MCO | 55 | E2 |
| COTTNTAIL CK RD | SLO | 75 | D2 |
| COTTONWOOD AV | RCO | 99 | C3 |
| COTTONWOOD AV | RCO | 99 | D4 |
| COTTONWOOD DR | SBD | 92 | C1 |
| COTTONWOOD RD | BUT | 25 | C4 |
| COTTONWOOD RD | INY | 60 | B5 |
| COTTONWOOD RD | KER | 78 | D3 |
| COTTONWOOD RD | MCO | 47 | C5 |
| COTTONWOOD RD | RCO | 100 | A2 |
| COTTONWOOD RD | SBT | 55 | B4 |
| COTTONWD CYN RD | MNO | 43 | C4 |
| COTTONWD CYN RD | RCO | 99 | C4 |
| COTTONWD CYN RD | SB | 77 | B5 |
| COTTONWD CK RD | SIS | 4 | A2 |
| COTTONWD SPG RD | RCO | 101 | D4 |
| COUCH ST | VAL | 134 | C3 |
| COUGHLAN ST | VAL | 134 | B3 |
| COULTERVILLE RD | MPA | 49 | C2 |
| COUNCIL HILL RD | SIE | 26 | C4 |
| COUNCILMAN RD | HUM | 10 | D5 |
| COUNTRY | SJCO | 40 | C5 |
| COUNTRY RD | SIS | 4 | C5 |
| COUNTRY CLUB BL | SJCO | 40 | A5 |
| COUNTRY CLUB BL | SJCO | 160 | A3 |
| COUNTRY CLUB DR | RCO | 100 | D4 |
| COUNTRY CLUB RD | AVLN | 105 | A5 |
| COUNTRY CLUB RD | HUM | 10 | D4 |
| COUNTRY CLUB RD | YUB | 33 | D3 |
| COUNTRYMAN DR | PLU | 26 | B2 |
| COUNTY RD | INY | 51 | D5 |
| COUNTY RD | MOD | 8 | A1 |
| COUNTY RD | MOD | 14 | E1 |
| COUNTY RD B | GLE | 24 | C4 |
| COUNTY RD BB | GLE | 24 | C4 |
| COUNTY RD C | GLE | 24 | C3 |
| COUNTY RD D | GLE | 24 | D4 |
| COUNTY RD F | GLE | 24 | D3 |
| COUNTY RD H | GLE | 24 | D3 |
| COUNTY RD H | GLE | 24 | D4 |
| COUNTY RD I | GLE | 24 | D3 |
| COUNTY RD J | GLE | 24 | D3 |
| COUNTY RD M | GLE | 24 | D4 |
| COUNTY RD MM | GLE | 24 | D3 |
| COUNTY RD N | GLE | 24 | D4 |
| COUNTY RD NN | GLE | 24 | D3 |
| COUNTY RD P | GLE | 24 | D4 |
| COUNTY RD PP | GLE | 24 | D4 |
| COUNTY RD QQ | GLE | 24 | D3 |
| COUNTY RD R | GLE | 24 | E4 |
| COUNTY RD RR | GLE | 24 | E3 |
| COUNTY RD S | GLE | 24 | E4 |
| COUNTY RD SS | GLE | 24 | E4 |
| COUNTY RD T | GLE | 24 | E4 |
| COUNTY RD TT | GLE | 24 | E4 |
| COUNTY RD U | GLE | 24 | E3 |
| COUNTY RD V | GLE | 24 | E3 |
| COUNTY RD V | GLE | 24 | E4 |
| COUNTY RD VV | GLE | 24 | E3 |
| COUNTY RD VV | GLE | 24 | E4 |
| COUNTY RD W | GLE | 24 | E4 |
| COUNTY RD WW | GLE | 24 | E4 |
| COUNTY RD XX | GLE | 24 | E3 |
| COUNTY RD XX | GLE | 25 | A5 |
| COUNTY RD Y | GLE | 25 | A5 |
| COUNTY RD YY | GLE | 25 | A5 |
| COUNTY RD Z | GLE | 25 | A4 |
| COUNTY RD ZZ | GLE | 25 | A4 |
| COUNTY RD 5 | YOL | 33 | A4 |
| COUNTY RD 6 | YOL | 33 | A4 |
| COUNTY RD 7 | YOL | 33 | A4 |
| COUNTY RD 8 | YOL | 32 | E4 |
| COUNTY RD 9 | GLE | 24 | D3 |
| COUNTY RD 10 | YOL | 32 | E4 |
| COUNTY RD 11 | GLE | 24 | E3 |
| COUNTY RD 11 | YOL | 32 | E4 |
| COUNTY RD 11 | YOL | 33 | A4 |
| COUNTY RD 11A | YOL | 33 | B4 |
| COUNTY RD 11B | YOL | 33 | B4 |
| COUNTY RD 12 | YOL | 33 | B4 |
| COUNTY RD 12A | YOL | 33 | A4 |
| COUNTY RD 13 | YOL | 32 | E4 |
| COUNTY RD 14 | YOL | 33 | A4 |
| COUNTY RD 14A | YOL | 33 | B4 |
| COUNTY RD 15 | GLE | 24 | E3 |
| COUNTY RD 15 | YOL | 33 | B4 |
| COUNTY RD 15B | YOL | 32 | E4 |
| COUNTY RD 15B | YOL | 33 | A4 |
| COUNTY RD 16 | GLE | 24 | E3 |
| COUNTY RD 16 | YOL | 33 | A5 |
| COUNTY RD 16A | YOL | 32 | E5 |

| STREET | CO. | PAGE | GRID |
|---|---|---|---|
| COUNTY RD 17 | YOL | 33 | A5 |
| COUNTY RD 18 | GLE | 24 | E3 |
| COUNTY RD 18 | YOL | 33 | B5 |
| COUNTY RD 18B | YOL | 33 | C5 |
| COUNTY RD 18C | YOL | 33 | C5 |
| COUNTY RD 19 | GLE | 24 | E3 |
| COUNTY RD 19 | GLE | 24 | E3 |
| COUNTY RD 19 | YOL | 33 | B5 |
| COUNTY RD 19A | YOL | 33 | A5 |
| COUNTY RD 20 | GLE | 24 | E3 |
| COUNTY RD 20 | YOL | 33 | C5 |
| COUNTY RD 20A | YOL | 32 | E5 |
| COUNTY RD 21 | GLE | 24 | E3 |
| COUNTY RD 21 | GLE | 24 | E3 |
| COUNTY RD 21A | YOL | 32 | E5 |
| COUNTY RD 23 | GLE | 25 | A3 |
| COUNTY RD 23 | YOL | 33 | A5 |
| COUNTY RD 24 | GLE | 24 | D3 |
| COUNTY RD 24 | YOL | 33 | B5 |
| COUNTY RD 25 | GLE | 24 | D3 |
| COUNTY RD 25 | YOL | 33 | A5 |
| COUNTY RD 25A | YOL | 33 | A5 |
| COUNTY RD 26 | GLE | 24 | C3 |
| COUNTY RD 26 | YOL | 33 | A5 |
| COUNTY RD 26A | YOL | 33 | C5 |
| COUNTY RD 27 | GLE | 24 | D3 |
| COUNTY RD 27 | YOL | 33 | B5 |
| COUNTY RD 28 | GLE | 24 | D3 |
| COUNTY RD 28 | YOL | 33 | A5 |
| COUNTY RD 28H | YOL | 39 | C1 |
| COUNTY RD 29 | GLE | 24 | E3 |
| COUNTY RD 29 | GLE | 25 | A3 |
| COUNTY RD 29 | YOL | 39 | A1 |
| COUNTY RD 29A | YOL | 39 | A1 |
| COUNTY RD 30 | GLE | 24 | D3 |
| COUNTY RD 30 | GLE | 25 | A3 |
| COUNTY RD 30 | YOL | 39 | B1 |
| CO RD 30 1/2 | GLE | 25 | A3 |
| COUNTY RD 31 | GLE | 24 | D4 |
| COUNTY RD 31 | GLE | 25 | A3 |
| COUNTY RD 31 | YOL | 39 | A1 |
| COUNTY RD 32 | GLE | 24 | E4 |
| COUNTY RD 32 | GLE | 25 | A4 |
| COUNTY RD 32 | YOL | 39 | B1 |
| CO RD 32 1/2 | GLE | 24 | E4 |
| COUNTY RD 33 | GLE | 24 | D4 |
| COUNTY RD 33 | GLE | 25 | A4 |
| COUNTY RD 34 | GLE | 24 | E4 |
| COUNTY RD 34 | GLE | 25 | A4 |
| COUNTY RD 35 | GLE | 24 | D4 |
| COUNTY RD 36 | GLE | 24 | E4 |
| COUNTY RD 36 | YOL | 39 | C2 |
| COUNTY RD 37 | GLE | 24 | E4 |
| COUNTY RD 38 | GLE | 24 | E4 |
| COUNTY RD 38 | YOL | 39 | C2 |
| COUNTY RD 38A | YOL | 39 | C2 |
| COUNTY RD 39 | GLE | 24 | D4 |
| COUNTY RD 40 | GLE | 24 | E4 |
| COUNTY RD 41 | GLE | 24 | E4 |
| COUNTY RD 43 | GLE | 24 | E4 |
| COUNTY RD 43 | YOL | 32 | D4 |
| COUNTY RD 44 | GLE | 24 | E4 |
| COUNTY RD 44 | YOL | 32 | D4 |
| COUNTY RD 45 | GLE | 24 | D4 |
| COUNTY RD 45 | YOL | 32 | D4 |
| COUNTY RD 46 | GLE | 24 | E4 |
| COUNTY RD 47 | YOL | 32 | D4 |
| COUNTY RD 48 | GLE | 24 | D4 |
| COUNTY RD 49 | GLE | 24 | D4 |
| COUNTY RD 50 | GLE | 24 | E4 |
| COUNTY RD 50 | GLE | 25 | A4 |
| COUNTY RD 53 | GLE | 24 | E4 |
| COUNTY RD 57 | GLE | 24 | D4 |
| COUNTY RD 58 | GLE | 24 | C4 |
| COUNTY RD 59 | GLE | 24 | C5 |
| COUNTY RD 59 | YOL | 32 | D4 |
| COUNTY RD 60 | GLE | 24 | D5 |
| COUNTY RD 61 | GLE | 24 | E5 |
| COUNTY RD 61 | YOL | 32 | D4 |
| COUNTY RD 62 | GLE | 24 | C5 |
| COUNTY RD 63 | GLE | 25 | A5 |
| COUNTY RD 63 | YOL | 32 | D4 |
| COUNTY RD 64 | GLE | 24 | E5 |
| COUNTY RD 65A | GLE | 24 | E5 |
| COUNTY RD 65B | GLE | 24 | E5 |
| COUNTY RD 65C | GLE | 24 | C5 |
| COUNTY RD 66A | GLE | 24 | D5 |
| COUNTY RD 66B | GLE | 24 | E5 |
| COUNTY RD 67 | GLE | 25 | A5 |
| COUNTY RD 68 | GLE | 24 | D5 |
| COUNTY RD 69 | GLE | 24 | C5 |
| COUNTY RD 69 | GLE | 25 | A5 |
| COUNTY RD 70 | GLE | 25 | A5 |
| COUNTY RD 70 | YOL | 32 | D4 |
| COUNTY RD 71 | GLE | 24 | D5 |
| COUNTY RD 71 | YOL | 32 | D4 |
| COUNTY RD 75A | YOL | 32 | D4 |
| COUNTY RD 76 | YOL | 32 | D5 |
| COUNTY RD 78 | YOL | 32 | D5 |
| COUNTY RD 78A | YOL | 32 | D5 |
| COUNTY RD 79 | YOL | 32 | E5 |
| COUNTY RD 79A | YOL | 32 | E5 |
| COUNTY RD 79B | YOL | 32 | E5 |
| COUNTY RD 80 | YOL | 32 | E5 |
| COUNTY RD 81 | YOL | 32 | E5 |
| COUNTY RD 82 | YOL | 32 | E5 |
| COUNTY RD 82B | YOL | 32 | E5 |
| COUNTY RD 84A | YOL | 32 | E4 |
| COUNTY RD 84B | YOL | 32 | E4 |
| COUNTY RD 85 | YOL | 32 | E5 |
| COUNTY RD 85B | YOL | 32 | E5 |
| COUNTY RD 86 | YOL | 32 | E4 |
| COUNTY RD 86A | YOL | 33 | A5 |
| COUNTY RD 87 | YOL | 33 | A5 |
| COUNTY RD 87B | YOL | 32 | E5 |
| COUNTY RD 88 | YOL | 33 | A4 |
| COUNTY RD 88A | YOL | 33 | A5 |

| STREET | CO. | PAGE | GRID |
|---|---|---|---|
| COUNTY RD 88B | YOL | 33 | A5 |
| COUNTY RD 89 | YOL | 33 | A4 |
| COUNTY RD 90 | YOL | 39 | A1 |
| COUNTY RD 90A | YOL | 33 | A5 |
| COUNTY RD 91 | YOL | 33 | A5 |
| COUNTY RD 91A | YOL | 39 | A1 |
| COUNTY RD 91B | YOL | 33 | A4 |
| COUNTY RD 92 | YOL | 33 | B4 |
| COUNTY RD 92B | YOL | 33 | A4 |
| COUNTY RD 92C | YOL | 33 | B5 |
| COUNTY RD 92D | YOL | 33 | B5 |
| COUNTY RD 92F | YOL | 39 | B1 |
| COUNTY RD 93 | YOL | 33 | B5 |
| COUNTY RD 93A | YOL | 33 | B4 |
| COUNTY RD 93B | YOL | 33 | B4 |
| COUNTY RD 94 | YOL | 33 | B4 |
| COUNTY RD 94A | YOL | 33 | B5 |
| COUNTY RD 94B | YOL | 33 | B5 |
| COUNTY RD 95 | YOL | 33 | B4 |
| COUNTY RD 95A | YOL | 39 | B1 |
| COUNTY RD 96 | YOL | 33 | B5 |
| COUNTY RD 96B | YOL | 33 | B5 |
| COUNTY RD 97 | YOL | 33 | B5 |
| COUNTY RD 97D | YOL | 39 | B1 |
| COUNTY RD 98 | YOL | 33 | B5 |
| COUNTY RD 99 | YOL | 33 | B5 |
| COUNTY RD 99E | YOL | 33 | C5 |
| COUNTY RD 100 | YOL | 33 | C5 |
| COUNTY RD 101 | YOL | 33 | C5 |
| COUNTY RD 101A | YOL | 39 | C1 |
| COUNTY RD 102 | YOL | 33 | C5 |
| COUNTY RD 102B | YOL | 33 | C5 |
| COUNTY RD 103 | YOL | 33 | C5 |
| COUNTY RD 104 | YOL | 39 | C1 |
| COUNTY RD 105 | YOL | 39 | C2 |
| COUNTY RD 106 | YOL | 39 | C2 |
| COUNTY RD 107 | YOL | 33 | C5 |
| COUNTY RD 107A | YOL | 33 | D4 |
| COUNTY RD 108 | YOL | 33 | B4 |
| COUNTY RD 116 | YOL | 33 | C4 |
| COUNTY RD 119 | YOL | 33 | D5 |
| COUNTY RD 122 | YOL | 33 | D5 |
| COUNTY RD 124 | YOL | 33 | D5 |
| COUNTY RD 152 | YOL | 39 | C2 |
| COUNTY RD 155 | YOL | 39 | C2 |
| COUNTY RD 126 | YOL | 33 | D5 |
| COUNTY RD 128A | YOL | 39 | D1 |
| COUNTY RD 200 | GLE | 24 | D3 |
| COUNTY RD 303 | GLE | 24 | B4 |
| COUNTY RD 304 | GLE | 24 | B4 |
| COUNTY RD 307 | GLE | 24 | A3 |
| COUNTY RD 310 | GLE | 23 | E4 |
| COUNTY RD 314 | GLE | 24 | B3 |
| COUNTY RD 315 | GLE | 24 | A3 |
| COUNTY RD 400 | GLE | 24 | B5 |
| COUNTY HOSP RD | PLU | 26 | C2 |
| COUNTY LINE RD | KER | 68 | B5 |
| CO LINE RD E | TRI | 17 | E2 |
| CO LINE RD E | TRI | 17 | E2 |
| CO LINE CK RD | TRI | 16 | E3 |
| COURCHEVEL RD | PLA | 35 | D2 |
| COURSE RD | KER | 78 | B4 |
| COURT ST | RED | 122 | B2 |
| COURTLAND RD N | YOL | 39 | D2 |
| COURTLANDT CT | KER | 79 | C4 |
| COUTOLENC RD | BUT | 25 | D2 |
| COVE AV | FRCO | 58 | B4 |
| COVE RD | SBD | 91 | E4 |
| COVE RD | SHA | 13 | A5 |
| COVELL BL | DVS | 136 | B2 |
| COVELO RD | MEN | 23 | A3 |
| COVELO RD | MEN | 22 | E4 |
| COVELO REFUS RD | MEN | 23 | A2 |
| COVERT RD | STA | 47 | C2 |
| COVINA BLVD | LACO | R | E3 |
| COWBOY CNTRY TR | RCO | 107 | B1 |
| COWBOY JOE RD | LAS | 21 | D5 |
| COW CAMP RD | BUT | 25 | E2 |
| COW CAMP RD | MNO | 43 | C3 |
| COW CREEK RD S | SHA | 18 | E2 |
| COW CREEK RD S | SHA | 19 | A2 |
| COWEL RD | CC | 38 | E5 |
| COW GULCH RD | SHA | 17 | D3 |
| COW HAVEN CY RD | KER | 80 | B1 |
| COW MTN ACCESS | MEN | 31 | B2 |
| COX AV | SCL | P | A4 |
| COX AV | SCL | 45 | E5 |
| COX LN | BUT | 25 | D5 |
| COX RD | IMP | 109 | A3 |
| COX RD | SJCO | 40 | C4 |
| COX RD | SHA | 18 | B3 |
| COX RD | STA | 47 | B3 |
| COX ST | RCO | 99 | C4 |
| COXCOMB TR | SBD | 102 | C1 |
| COXEY | SBD | 91 | D4 |
| COX FERRY RD | MCO | 48 | B3 |
| COYOTE RD | MCO | 56 | B1 |
| COYOTE RD | SBD | 101 | A2 |
| COYOTE #1 RD | IMP | 111 | C4 |
| COYOTE #2 RD | IMP | 111 | C4 |
| COYOTE CYN RD | INY | 71 | D4 |
| COYOTE CYN RD | RCO | 107 | C1 |
| COYOTE GAP RD | BUT | 25 | E2 |
| COYOTE LAKE RD | SBD | 82 | B5 |
| COYOTE RES RD | SCL | P | E5 |
| COYOTE SPGS RD | MNO | 43 | C4 |
| COYOTE VLY RD | INY | 51 | C4 |
| COYOTE VLY RD | SBD | 93 | A5 |
| COYOTE VLY RES | LAS | 14 | C5 |
| COZZI AV | MCO | 56 | A1 |
| CRABTREE RD | LAS | 8 | D4 |
| CRABTREE RD | STA | 48 | B2 |
| CRAFTON AV | SBD | 99 | D2 |
| CRAIG | SJCO | 47 | C1 |
| CRAIG AV | SON | 132 | B3 |
| CRAIG AV | TEH | 18 | E5 |
| CRAIG RD | SUT | 33 | B1 |

| STREET | CO. | PAGE | GRID |
|---|---|---|---|
| CRAMER | PLA | 34 | B3 |
| CRAM GULCH RD | SIS | 4 | B5 |
| CRANE AV | MCO | 47 | D4 |
| CRANE RD | STA | 47 | D2 |
| CRANE CANYON RD | SON | 38 | A2 |
| CRANE FLAT | MPA | 63 | B5 |
| CRANE FLAT RD | MPA | 49 | C2 |
| CRANE VALLEY RD | MAD | 49 | E5 |
| CRANMORE RD | SUT | 33 | B3 |
| CRANMORE RD | SUT | 33 | B4 |
| CRANNELL RD | HUM | 9 | E4 |
| CRANNELL RD | HUM | 10 | A4 |
| CRATER RD | SBD | 93 | E3 |
| CRATER HILL RD | PLA | 34 | B3 |
| CRAWFORD AV | FRCO | 58 | A4 |
| CRAWFORD RD | CLO | 32 | E2 |
| CRAWFORD RD | MEN | 23 | A2 |
| CRAWFORD RD | STA | 47 | D2 |
| CRAY CROFT RDG | SIE | 26 | D4 |
| CRAZY HORSE CYN | MON | 54 | D3 |
| CREED RD | SOL | 39 | B3 |
| CREEK RD | MCO | 55 | D2 |
| CREEK RD | RED | 122 | A4 |
| CREEK RD | VEN | 88 | B4 |
| CREEKSIDE CT | KER | 79 | C4 |
| CREEKSIDE LN | STA | 47 | E2 |
| CREIGHTON DR | SHA | 13 | D3 |
| CRENSHAW BLVD | LACO | 97 | D3 |
| CRENSHAW BLVD | LACO | Q | D5 |
| CRENSHAW BLVD | LACO | S | B2 |
| CREOLE MINE RD | SBD | 92 | E4 |
| CRESCENT AV | AVLN | 105 | B5 |
| C RESERVOIR RD | MOD | 6 | D4 |
| CRESSEY WY | MCO | 48 | A4 |
| CRESSMAN RD | FRCO | 58 | B1 |
| CREST DR | RCO | 99 | B2 |
| CREST RD | LACO | S | B2 |
| CRESTLINE RD | SDCO | 107 | A2 |
| CRESTON RD | SLO | 76 | B1 |
| CRESTON EUREKA | SLO | 76 | B2 |
| CRESTN ODONOVAN | SLO | 76 | C2 |
| CRESTVIEW DR | MNO | 51 | D2 |
| CRESTVIEW ST | KER | 80 | C1 |
| CREWS RD | SCL | 54 | D2 |
| CRIPE RD | FRCO | 58 | A1 |
| CRIPPEN AV | SBD | 91 | A3 |
| CRIPPLE CK RD | SLO | 76 | B2 |
| CRISPIN RD | MEN | 30 | C3 |
| CRISS RD | SIS | 4 | E3 |
| CRISS RD | SIS | 5 | A3 |
| CRISTIANITOS RD | SDCO | 105 | E1 |
| CRISWELL AV | MCO | 55 | E1 |
| CROCKER RD | SJCO | 46 | E1 |
| CROCKER SPGS RD | KER | 77 | D4 |
| CRONESE LAKE RD | SBD | 82 | E4 |
| CRONESE LAKE RD | SBD | 83 | A4 |
| CROOKED MDW RD | MNO | 50 | E1 |
| CROSBY RD | HUM | 15 | D2 |
| CROSBY ST | SD | 216 | A5 |
| CROSBY HAROLD | PLA | 34 | B3 |
| CROSS RD | COL | 32 | E3 |
| CROSS RD | MON | 65 | C4 |
| CROSS CYNS RD | SLO | 66 | B5 |
| CROSS CTRVILLE | MEN | 31 | B1 |
| CROSS CNTRY RD | MON | 66 | B4 |
| CROUCH AV | BUT | 25 | A3 |
| CROW RD | STA | 47 | E2 |
| CROW CANYON RD | ALA | M | A5 |
| CROW CANYON RD | ALA | 45 | E2 |
| CROWDER | PLA | 33 | E5 |
| CROWDER FLAT RD | MOD | 6 | E5 |
| CROWLEY RD | SUT | 33 | C3 |
| CROWLEY LAKE DR | MNO | 51 | A3 |
| CROWLEY LAKE PL | MNO | 51 | A2 |
| CROWLY LK DM RD | MNO | 51 | B2 |
| CROWN RD | MCO | 48 | C4 |
| CROWN & PICKLE | SBD | 92 | D5 |
| CROWN POINT RD | BUT | 25 | C2 |
| CROWN VLY PKWY | ORA | 98 | D5 |
| CROWN VALLEY RD | LACO | 89 | E4 |
| CROWS LANDNG RD | MDO | 162 | C5 |
| CROWS LANDNG RD | STA | 47 | C4 |
| CROWS LANDNG RD | STA | 162 | C5 |
| CROY RD | SCL | P | C5 |
| CROY RD | SCL | 54 | C1 |
| CRUCERO RD | SBD | 83 | A5 |
| CRUCERO RD | SBD | 93 | B1 |
| CRUICKSHANK RD | IMP | 112 | B3 |
| CRUMP LN | FRCO | 66 | B3 |
| CRUZON GRADE RD | NEV | 26 | C5 |
| CRYSTAL AV | MOH | 96 | A3 |
| CRYSTAL CK RD | SHA | 18 | A2 |
| CRYSTAL SPGS AV | SBR | 144 | A4 |
| CRYSTAL SPGS DR | LA | 182 | C1 |
| CRYSTAL SPGS DR | LACO | Q | E3 |
| CRYSTAL SPGS RD | KLAM | 5 | C1 |
| CRYSTAL SPGS RD | SMCO | N | C2 |
| CRYSTAL SPGS RD | SMCO | 45 | C3 |
| CUDA DR | KER | 78 | E4 |
| CUDDEBACK RD | SBD | 80 | E3 |
| CUDDEBACK RD | SBD | 81 | A3 |
| CUDDY VALLEY RD | KER | 88 | C1 |
| CUDDY VALLEY RD | VEN | 88 | C2 |
| CUFF RD | IMP | 109 | B2 |
| CUIN RD | IMP | 108 | E5 |
| CULL CANYON RD | ALA | M | A5 |
| CULL CANYON RD | ALA | 45 | E2 |
| CULLEN AV | SCL | P | E5 |
| CULVER BLVD | CUL | 183 | C5 |
| CULVER BLVD | CUL | 188 | A3 |
| CULVER BLVD | LA | 183 | C5 |
| CULVER BLVD | LA | 188 | A3 |
| CULVER BLVD | LACO | 97 | C2 |
| CULVER BLVD | LACO | 187 | D5 |
| CULVER DR | ORA | 98 | C4 |
| CULVER DR | ORA | T | E4 |
| CUMMINGS RD | HUM | 15 | E1 |

| STREET | CO. | PAGE | GRID |
|---|---|---|---|
| CUMMINGS RD | VEN | 88 | B5 |
| CUMMINGS SKYWAY | CC | 38 | D4 |
| CUMMINGS VLY RD | KER | 79 | B4 |
| CUNEO RD | MPA | 48 | E1 |
| CUNNINGHAM LN | MNO | 42 | E1 |
| CUNNINGHAM RD | CAL | 41 | C3 |
| CUNNINGHAM RD | MCO | 48 | D5 |
| CUNNINGHAM RD | MEN | 31 | B2 |
| CURLEW ST | SD | 215 | D1 |
| CURRAN RD | AMA | 40 | D3 |
| CURREY RD | SOL | 39 | B1 |
| CURRIE RD | SOL | 39 | C4 |
| CURRIER RD | BUT | 25 | C4 |
| CURRY AV | SJCO | 40 | B4 |
| CURTIS ST | SM | 145 | B3 |
| CURTIS ST W | SAL | 171 | C2 |
| CURTNER AV | SCL | P | B4 |
| CURTNER AV | SCL | 46 | B5 |
| CUSTER AV | FRCO | 56 | B2 |
| CUSTER AV | SBD | 91 | E4 |
| CUTCA TRUCK TR | RCO | 106 | E1 |
| CUTLER AV | GLE | 24 | E3 |
| CUT OFF RD | LAS | 21 | C3 |
| CUTOFF RD | MEN | 23 | C5 |
| CUTTING | CC | 38 | C5 |
| CUTTING AV | GLE | 24 | E3 |
| CUTTING BLVD | CC | L | C3 |
| CUTTING BLVD | R | 155 | A4 |
| CUTTING WHRF RD | NAPA | L | C1 |
| CUTTNGS WHRF RD | NAPA | 38 | C3 |
| CUYAMA ST | SB | 87 | D1 |
| CYA RD | MPA | 49 | A3 |
| CYPRESS AV | LACO | R | E3 |
| CYPRESS AV | SHA | 18 | C2 |
| CYPRESS AV | SUT | 33 | D3 |
| CYPRESS RD | CC | M | D3 |
| CYPRESS RD | CC | 39 | C5 |
| CYPRESS RD | MCO | 56 | A1 |
| CYPRESS RD | SBD | 80 | E1 |
| CYPRESS ST | C | 124 | C4 |
| CYPRESS ST | LACO | 98 | B2 |
| CYPRESS MTN DR | SLO | 75 | D1 |
| CYPRUS AV | U | 123 | B2 |
| CYRMIC RD | KER | 77 | D3 |
| CYRUS CANYON RD | KER | 79 | D1 |
| D | | | |
| D ST | MAR | L | B3 |
| D ST | MDO | 162 | C4 |
| D ST | ONT | 203 | D4 |
| D ST | SR | 139 | C4 |
| D ST | SON | L | A1 |
| D ST | SON | 38 | A3 |
| DAGGETT YERMO | SBD | 92 | A1 |
| DAGNINO RD | ALA | M | C5 |
| DAGNINO RD | ALA | 46 | C2 |
| DAHLIN RD | SJCO | 47 | C1 |
| DAHLSTROM RD | COL | 32 | E3 |
| DAILEY RD | KER | 79 | C2 |
| DAINTY AV | CC | M | D3 |
| DAINTY AV | CC | 39 | C5 |
| DAIRY AV | LACO | S | D1 |
| DAIRY LN | MCO | 56 | A1 |
| DAIRY RD | BUT | 25 | A3 |
| DAIRY RD | KER | 78 | A3 |
| DAIRY RD | STA | 47 | B2 |
| DAIRY RD | YUB | 33 | E3 |
| DAIRY MART RD | SDCO | V | C5 |
| DAIRY MART RD | SDCO | 111 | D2 |
| DAKIN RD | LAS | 21 | C4 |
| DAKOTA AV | FRCO | 57 | C3 |
| DAKOTA AV | FRCO | 56 | E3 |
| DAKOTA AV | STA | 47 | C2 |
| DALBY | PLA | 33 | E3 |
| DALE LN | SHA | 18 | B3 |
| DALE RD | KER | 79 | B4 |
| DALE RD | STA | 47 | C2 |
| DALE RD | TEH | 24 | E2 |
| DALE TR | SBD | 101 | E1 |
| DALE VISTA RD | SBD | 101 | E1 |
| DALLY RD | SOL | 39 | B3 |
| DALTON AV | ALA | M | D5 |
| DALTON AV | ALA | 46 | C2 |
| DALY ST | LA | 186 | D1 |
| DAMIEN AV | LACO | 98 | C1 |
| DANA DR | SHA | 18 | C2 |
| DANA FOOTHLL RD | SLO | 76 | C5 |
| DANBY RD | SBD | 101 | D1 |
| DANENBERG RD | IMP | 112 | B3 |
| DANIELS AV | VAL | 134 | A3 |
| DANLEY LATERAL | COL | 32 | C1 |
| DANLEY RD | COL | 32 | D1 |
| DAN MCNAMARA RD | MCO | 48 | A5 |
| DANTES VIEW | INY | 72 | B1 |
| DANVILLE BLVD | CC | M | A4 |
| DANVILLE BLVD | CC | 45 | E1 |
| DARBY RD | BUT | 25 | E5 |
| DARBY RD | CAL | 41 | C3 |
| DARGATE RD | KER | 77 | E2 |
| DARK CANYON RD | BUT | 25 | D3 |
| DARLING RD | LACO | 89 | D4 |
| DARLING RDG RD | ED | 34 | E4 |
| DARMS LN | NAPA | 38 | C1 |
| DARRAH RD | MPA | 49 | B3 |
| DATE ST | SB | 86 | C1 |
| DATE PALM DR | RCO | 100 | D4 |
| DATONI RD | YUB | 33 | D2 |
| DAUBENBERGER RD | STA | 47 | E3 |
| DAULTON RD | MAD | 56 | B1 |
| DAULTON RD | MAD | 57 | B1 |
| DA VALL DR | RCO | 100 | D3 |
| DAVENPORT RD | LACO | 89 | D4 |
| DAVEY GLEN RD | SM | 145 | C4 |
| DAVID AV | MONT | 53 | C3 |
| DAVID AV | MONT | 167 | B3 |
| DAVID AV | PAC | 167 | B3 |
| DAVID RD | KER | 78 | E5 |
| DAVIDSON | FRCO | 56 | B2 |

STREETS

| STREET | CO. | PAGE & GRID |
|---|---|---|
| DAVIDSON RD | HUM | 9 E2 |
| DAVIDSON RD | HUM | 10 A2 |
| DAVIS AV | FRCO | 57 A5 |
| DAVIS AV | FRCO | 57 C5 |
| DAVIS AV | KER | 78 B1 |
| DAVIS RD | BUT | 25 B5 |
| DAVIS RD | IMP | 109 A2 |
| DAVIS RD | KER | 76 E1 |
| DAVIS RD | MON | 54 C4 |
| DAVIS RD | MON | 171 A4 |
| DAVIS RD | RCO | 99 D3 |
| DAVIS RD | SJCO | 40 A4 |
| DAVIS RD | SIS | 4 C4 |
| DAVIS RD | SIS | 5 B4 |
| DAVIS RD | STA | 47 C4 |
| DAVIS RD | STA | 48 B3 |
| DAVIS RD | SUT | 33 B2 |
| DAVIS ST | ALA | L D5 |
| DAVIS ST | ALA | 45 D2 |
| DAVIS ST | LAK | 32 A3 |
| DAVIS CK CEM RD | MOD | 7 C4 |
| DVS CK TRNS STA | MOD | 7 C4 |
| DAWN RD | KER | 89 E1 |
| DAWN RD | KER | 90 A1 |
| DAWSON RD | RCO | 99 C3 |
| DAWSON RANCH RD | MNO | 51 D2 |
| DAY AV | SHA | 19 E1 |
| DAY RD | MOD | 13 E3 |
| DAY RD | SCL | 54 C1 |
| DAY RD | SHA | 13 E3 |
| DAY ST | RCO | 99 C3 |
| DAY RD | SCL | P E5 |
| DAYLIGHT PASS | INY | 61 E4 |
| DAYLIGHT PS CTO | INY | 61 E3 |
| DAYTON RD | BUT | 25 B3 |
| DAYTON WEST RD | BUT | 25 B3 |
| DEAD HRSE CY RD | SIS | 13 B3 |
| DEAD INDIAN RD | JKSN | 4 A1 |
| DEADMAN CK RD | MNO | 50 D2 |
| DEAD MANS GULCH | MON | 65 E4 |
| DEADWOOD RD | BUT | 25 D3 |
| DEADWOOD RD | PLA | 35 A2 |
| DEADWOOD RD | TRI | 17 E1 |
| DEADWOOD LO RD | SIS | 3 D4 |
| DEALWOOD RD | IMP | 109 B5 |
| DEAN CREEK RD | HUM | 16 C5 |
| DE ANGELIS RD | MCO | 47 D4 |
| DE ANZA BLVD | CPTO | 149 D4 |
| DE ANZA DR | RCO | 99 E3 |
| DEARBORN RD | IMP | 111 E3 |
| DEARDORFF RD | CAL | 41 B2 |
| DEARWOOD DR | MEN | 31 B2 |
| DEATH VALLEY RD | INY | 52 B5 |
| DEAVER AV | KER | 70 A5 |
| DECPTION CYN RD | RCO | 100 E3 |
| DECKER AV | SBD | 92 E5 |
| DECKER RD | SUT | 33 B2 |
| DECORD DR | LACO | 89 A4 |
| DECOTO RD | ALA | P A1 |
| DECOTO RD | ALA | 45 E3 |
| DEE KNOCH RD | SHA | 13 E4 |
| DEEP CREEK RD | MOD | 8 D1 |
| DEEP CREEK RD | SBD | 91 C5 |
| DEEP SPRINGS RD | SBD | 84 A3 |
| DEEP SPGS RANCH | INY | 52 B4 |
| DEEP WELL RD | MCO | 55 E1 |
| DEER WY | RCO | 100 B5 |
| DEER CREEK AV | TUL | 68 B5 |
| DEER CREEK RD | SBD | 91 C4 |
| DEER CREEK RD | VEN | 96 D2 |
| DEER FLAT RD | SHA | 19 C2 |
| DEERHORN VLY RD | SDCO | 112 B1 |
| DEER LICK KNOB | TRI | 17 D2 |
| DEER LICK SPGS | TRI | 17 D3 |
| DEER MTN RD | SIS | 4 D5 |
| DEER PARK RD | BUT | 26 A3 |
| DEER PARK RD | NAPA | 29 B2 |
| DEER PARK RD | NAPA | 38 B1 |
| DEER SPRING RD | MNO | 51 B2 |
| DEER VALLEY | ED | 34 C5 |
| DEER VALLEY RD | CC | M C3 |
| DEER VALLEY RD | CC | 39 C5 |
| DEER VALLEY RD | CC | 46 C1 |
| DEETZ RD | SIS | 12 C2 |
| DEFENDER GRADE | AMA | 41 B2 |
| DEFRAIN BLVD | RCO | 103 D5 |
| DE HARVEY ST | KER | 78 D4 |
| DEHESA RD | SDCO | 107 A5 |
| DE LA CRUZ BL | SCL | P B3 |
| DE LA CRUZ BL | SCLR | 151 C2 |
| DE LA GUERRA ST | STB | 174 D3 |
| DEL AMO BLVD | LACO | 98 A3 |
| DEL AMO BLVD | LACO | S D2 |
| DE LA VINA ST | STB | 174 B3 |
| DELAWARE AV | SC | 169 A5 |
| DELAWARE RD | STA | 47 E2 |
| DELAWARE ST | SM | N C1 |
| DELCERRO BLVD | SDCO | V C3 |
| DELCERRO BLVD | SDCO | 111 D1 |
| DEL DIOS HWY | SDCO | 106 D4 |
| DELEVAN RD | COL | 32 D1 |
| DELFATTI LN | KLAM | 5 B1 |
| DELFERN RD | KER | 77 D2 |
| DELFIND RD | KER | 77 D2 |
| DELHI RD | SOL | 39 C2 |
| DELIMA RD | SJCO | 47 A1 |
| DEL MAR AV | LACO | R C4 |
| DEL MAR AV | VAL | 134 D3 |
| DEL MAR BLVD | PAS | 190 C4 |
| DEL MAR HTS RD | SDCO | 106 C4 |
| DEL MAR HTS RD | SDCO | V A1 |
| DEL MONTE AV | SUT | 33 C4 |
| DEL MONTE BLVD | MONT | 167 B1 |
| DEL NORTE AV | FRCO | 57 A4 |
| DEL NORTE DR | TEH | 18 C4 |
| DEL NORTE ST | EUR | 121 B2 |
| DEL OBISPO ST | ORA | 98 D5 |
| DEL OBISPO ST | ORA | 202 B4 |
| DEL OBISPO ST | SJC | 202 C2 |
| DEL ORO RD | SBD | 91 C4 |
| DEL ORTO RD | CAL | 40 E3 |
| DEL ORTO RD | CAL | 41 A3 |
| DEL PASO RD | SAC | 33 D5 |
| DELPHOS RD | CLO | 32 D2 |
| DEL PUERTO AV | STA | 47 C3 |
| DEL PUERTO CYN | STA | 46 E4 |
| DEL PUERTO CYN | STA | 47 A3 |
| DEL REY AV | FRCO | 57 E3 |
| DEL REY AV | FRCO | 57 E5 |
| DEL ROSA AV | SBD | 99 C1 |
| DELTA AV | SJCO | 46 E1 |
| DELTA AV | SJCO | 47 A1 |
| DELTA RD | CC | M D3 |
| DELTA RD | CC | 39 C5 |
| DELTA RD | MCO | 55 E1 |
| DE LUZ RD | SDCO | 106 B1 |
| DEMAREE RD | TUL | 68 B1 |
| DEMAREST MNE RD | CAL | 41 A4 |
| DEMPSEY RD | SCL | P B2 |
| DENISE AV | KER | 80 A5 |
| DENNETT ST | PAC | 167 B2 |
| DENNISON RD | KER | 79 D4 |
| DENNY RD | TRI | 10 E5 |
| DENNY RD | TRI | 11 A4 |
| DENTON RD | MCO | 56 A1 |
| DENTON RD | STA | 48 A2 |
| DENTN & LEAK RD | MCO | 56 B1 |
| DENVER AV | FRCO | 56 E4 |
| DENVER AV | KIN | 57 E5 |
| DENVERTON RD | SOL | 39 B3 |
| DE PORTOLA RD | RCO | 99 E5 |
| DEPOT AV | SB | 86 C1 |
| DEPOT RD | ALA | 146 B5 |
| DEPOT RD | H | 146 B5 |
| DEPOT ST | SMA | 173 B3 |
| DERBY ST | B | 156 B3 |
| DERRICK BLVD | FRCO | 66 C2 |
| DERRICK RD | BUT | 25 D4 |
| DERRICK RD | IMP | 111 E3 |
| DERRICK RD | LAS | 14 B3 |
| DERRICK FT RD N | TRI | 11 E3 |
| DERRICK FT RD N | TRI | 12 A3 |
| DERRICK FT RD S | TRI | 12 A3 |
| DERSCH RD | SHA | 18 C3 |
| DESCANSO AV | AVLN | 105 B5 |
| DESCHUTES RD | SHA | 18 D2 |
| DESERT RD | IMP | 112 D3 |
| DESERT CTR RICE | RCO | 102 C4 |
| DESERT INN RD | CLK | 209 C5 |
| DESERT INN RD | CLK | 210 C1 |
| DESERT SHORS DR | IMP | 108 C1 |
| DESERT VIEW AV | SBD | 91 D4 |
| DESERT WILLW TR | SBD | 100 D2 |
| DESEVADO RD | SIS | 4 C3 |
| DE SOTO AV | LA | 177 D3 |
| DE SOTO AV | LACO | 177 D4 |
| DESSIE DR | LAK | 31 C3 |
| DETLOW RD | BUT | 25 D3 |
| DETOUR RD | GLE | 24 D3 |
| DETWEILER RD | MPA | 48 D2 |
| DEVILS CORRL RD | LAS | 20 D3 |
| DEVILS DEN RD | KIN | 67 B5 |
| DEVOE RD | SUT | 33 C4 |
| DEVONSHIRE BLVD | LACO | 97 C1 |
| DEVORE FRWY | SBD | 99 A1 |
| DEVORE RD | SBD | 99 B1 |
| DEVOSE DR | LAS | 8 A4 |
| DE VRIES | SJCO | 40 A4 |
| DEWITT RD | STA | 47 D2 |
| DE WOLF AV | FRCO | 57 D2 |
| DE WOLF AV | FRCO | 57 D5 |
| DE WOLF AV | SB | 86 B3 |
| DE 1 FIRST ST | COL | 32 D1 |
| DIABLO RD | CC | M B4 |
| DIABLO RD | CC | 46 A1 |
| DIABLO MINE RD | INY | 51 C3 |
| DIABLO MINE RD | MNO | 51 C3 |
| DIABLO OASIS DR | RCO | 100 C3 |
| DIAGONAL 7 | MAD | 56 C3 |
| DIAGONAL 11 | MAD | 56 D1 |
| DIAGONAL 232 | TUL | 68 D4 |
| DIAGONAL 252 | TUL | 68 D3 |
| DIAGONAL 254 | TUL | 68 D3 |
| DIAMOND RD | ED | 138 C5 |
| DIAMOND BAR BL | LACO | 98 C2 |
| DIAMOND BAR BL | LACO | U B3 |
| DIAMOND MTN RD | PLU | 20 E4 |
| DIAMOND VLY RD | ALP | 36 C4 |
| DIAZ LN | INY | 51 D4 |
| DIAZ ST | KER | 80 A4 |
| DICK COOK | PLA | 34 B4 |
| DICKERMAN RD | IMP | 109 B4 |
| DICKINSON AV | FRCO | 57 B4 |
| DICKINSON AV | FRCO | 67 B1 |
| DICKNSN FRRY RD | MCO | 48 B5 |
| DIDO AV | SBD | 92 A3 |
| DIEHL RD | IMP | 111 E3 |
| DIEHL RD | STA | 47 C4 |
| DIENSTAG RD | STA | 48 A2 |
| DIERSSEN RD | SAC | 39 E3 |
| DIETRICH | SJCO | 40 C5 |
| DIETRICH RD | IMP | 109 B4 |
| DIGGER RAVNE RD | PLU | 26 C1 |
| DI GIORGIO RD | KER | 78 D3 |
| DI GIORGIO RD | KER | 79 A3 |
| DILLARD RD | SAC | 40 B2 |
| DILLION RD | SIS | 10 D1 |
| DILLON RD | HUM | 15 D2 |
| DILLON RD | RCO | 100 E3 |
| DILLON RD | RCO | 100 C3 |
| DILLON BEACH RD | MAR | 37 D3 |
| DINKELSPIEL RD | SOL | 39 B4 |
| DINKEY CREEK RD | FRCO | 58 B1 |
| DINKY AV | KER | 89 B1 |
| DINUBA AV | FRCO | 56 E4 |
| DINUBA AV | FRCO | 57 C4 |
| DINUBA AV | FRCO | 58 A4 |
| DIPS RD | TRI | 17 B3 |
| DIRKS RD | COL | 24 D5 |
| DISCH RD | SJCO | 40 C4 |
| DISTELRATH DR | DN | 1 D3 |
| DISTRICT CTR DR | BUT | 25 D5 |
| DITCH RD | KER | 78 A5 |
| DITCH RD | SIE | 26 C4 |
| DITCH CREEK RD | SIS | 4 A3 |
| DIVISADERO ST | FRE | 165 B3 |
| DIVISADERO ST | SF | 142 A2 |
| DIVISION ST | LACO | 89 E2 |
| DIVISION ST | SDCO | V C4 |
| DIVISION ST | SDCO | 111 D1 |
| DIVISION ST | SLO | 76 B5 |
| DIVISION CK RD | INY | 59 E2 |
| DIXIE RD | BUT | 25 D2 |
| DIXIE RD | SBD | 91 D1 |
| DIXIE CYN RND VY | PLU | 20 C5 |
| DIXIE VALLEY RD | LAS | 14 D4 |
| DIXON AV E | SOL | 39 B2 |
| DIXON AV W | SOL | 39 B2 |
| DIXON LN | INY | 51 D4 |
| DIXON HILL RD | YUB | 26 A5 |
| DIXON MINE RD | ALP | 42 C1 |
| DOBBINS ST | KER | 70 A5 |
| DOBIE LN | MEN | 23 B3 |
| DOBIE MEADOWS | MNO | 43 D4 |
| DOBIE MEADOWS | MNO | 43 E4 |
| DOBIE MEADOWS | MNO | 44 A4 |
| DOBSON RD | SBD | 81 E4 |
| DODDS | SJCO | 40 C5 |
| DODDS | SJCO | 47 C1 |
| DODDS RD | STA | 47 C4 |
| DODGE RD | COL | 24 E5 |
| DODGE RDG LP RD | TUO | 42 A3 |
| DOE MILL RD | BUT | 25 C2 |
| DOERKSEN RD | STA | 47 E3 |
| DOG BAR RD | NEV | 34 C2 |
| DOG CREEK RD | SHA | 12 B4 |
| DOGGIE TR | SBD | 101 A2 |
| DOGTOWN RD | CAL | 41 B4 |
| DOGTOWN RD | MPA | 48 E2 |
| DOGTOWN RD | MPA | 49 A2 |
| DOG VALLEY RD | SIE | 27 E5 |
| DOGWOOD DR | EC | 217 E4 |
| DOGWOOD RD | ALP | 36 A5 |
| DOGWOOD RD | IMP | 109 A5 |
| DOGWOOD RD | IMP | 112 A4 |
| DOHENY DR | BH | 183 D2 |
| DOHENY DR | LA | 183 D2 |
| DOHENY DR | LACO | Q D4 |
| DOHENY PARK RD | ORA | 202 C4 |
| DOLAN RD | MON | 54 B3 |
| DOLAN HARDNG RD | YUB | 34 A1 |
| DOLLARHIDE RD | NAPA | 38 C1 |
| DOLORES ST | SF | 142 C5 |
| DOLPHIN AV | KER | 80 C1 |
| DOLPHIN DR | IMP | 108 C2 |
| DOME AV | TUL | 68 D3 |
| DOME ST | SB | 86 D1 |
| DOMINION RD | SB | 86 C1 |
| DOMINO CT | KER | 79 B4 |
| DON RD | SBD | 101 D1 |
| DONAHUE RD | SUT | 33 C4 |
| DONKIN RD | STA | 47 B3 |
| DONLON, JAMES BL | CC | M C3 |
| DONNER PASS RD | NEV | 27 B5 |
| DONOVAN RD | SMA | 173 A2 |
| DON PEDRO RD | STA | 47 C3 |
| DONS RD | MOD | 8 B2 |
| DOOLITTLE DR | A | 159 A3 |
| DOOLITTLE DR | ALA | L D5 |
| DOOLITTLE DR | ALA | 45 D2 |
| DOOLITTLE DR | O | 159 C3 |
| DOOLITTLE CK RD | SIS | 2 E3 |
| DOON GRADE | BUT | 25 D2 |
| DORA RD | SUT | 33 B2 |
| DORA ST | U | 123 C3 |
| DORAN SCENIC DR | SBD | 82 A5 |
| DORFF LN | HUM | 15 D2 |
| DORIS AV | VEN | 96 B1 |
| DORNES RD | PLA | 34 A3 |
| DORRETT DR | BUT | 25 C2 |
| DORRIS AV | FRCO | 66 E2 |
| DORRIS BROWNELL | SIS | 5 B3 |
| DORRIS TEHNER | SIS | 5 A3 |
| DORSEY RD | STA | 47 D1 |
| DOS CABEZA RD | IMP | 111 B3 |
| DOSE RD | TRI | 10 E5 |
| DOS PALMAS RD | SBD | 90 E4 |
| DOS REIS RD | SJCO | 47 A1 |
| DOS RIOS DR | SBD | 90 E3 |
| DOS RIOS LN | STA | 47 B3 |
| DOS RIOS RD | BUT | 25 C5 |
| DOSTER RD | CAL | 41 A3 |
| DOTTA LN | PLU | 27 D3 |
| DOTTA GUIDCI RD | PLU | 27 D2 |
| DOTY RD | SHA | 13 D5 |
| DOUBLE SPGS RD | CAL | 40 E3 |
| DOUGHERTY RD | CC | M B4 |
| DOUGHERTY RD | CC | 46 B1 |
| DOUGHERTY RD | SUT | 33 C3 |
| DOUGLAS | KIN | 67 D1 |
| DOUGLAS AV | FRCO | 56 C4 |
| DOUGLAS AV | SB | 86 B3 |
| DOUGLAS LN | SBD | 100 E1 |
| DOUGLAS RD | SAC | 40 B1 |
| DOUGLAS ST | ELS | 189 D3 |
| DOUGLAS RGR STA | MAD | 49 E5 |
| DOVE | SJCO | 47 D1 |
| DOVER AV | FRFD | 135 D3 |
| DOVER AV | KIN | 67 E1 |
| DOVER DR | NB | 199 C4 |
| DOVER DR | ORA | T C4 |
| DOVER CANYON RD | SLO | 75 E1 |
| DOVE SPG CYN RD | KER | 80 A2 |
| DOW BUTTE RD | LAS | 20 D1 |
| DOW BUTTE LO RD | LAS | 20 D1 |
| DOWD RD | PLA | 34 A3 |
| DOWD RD | PLA | 33 E4 |
| DOWD CAMP RD | PLA | 34 A3 |
| DOWDEN RD | IMP | 109 B3 |
| DOWER AV | FRCO | 57 B3 |
| DOWER AV | FRCO | 57 B5 |
| DOW FLAT RD | LAS | 20 D1 |
| DOWNEY AV | LACO | S E1 |
| DOWNEY RD | INY | 73 A4 |
| DOWNEY RD | LACO | R A4 |
| DOWNEY ST | MDO | 162 C3 |
| DOWNIE RD | STA | 47 E3 |
| DOWNIE RD | STA | 48 A3 |
| DOWS PRAIRIE RD | HUM | 9 E4 |
| DOYLE DR | SF | 141 D1 |
| DOYLE GRADE | LAS | 27 D1 |
| DOYLE RD | MCO | 47 C5 |
| DOYLE RANCH RD | KER | 69 E5 |
| DOYLE RANCH RD | KER | 79 E1 |
| DRAIN 10 RD | SIS | 5 E2 |
| DRAIS AV | SJCO | 40 C5 |
| DRAKE AV | COL | 32 E3 |
| DRAKE RD | HUM | 15 E2 |
| DRAPER RD | STA | 47 C4 |
| DRAPER RD | TEH | 18 C3 |
| DREDGR CP MORGN | TRI | 17 C1 |
| DRESSER AV | KER | 78 A2 |
| DREW RD | IMP | 111 E3 |
| DREXLER | SUT | 33 B2 |
| DRIVE 212 | TUL | 58 C5 |
| DRIVE 244 | TUL | 68 D2 |
| DRIVE 254 | TUL | 58 D4 |
| DRIVER AV | LACO | 97 A1 |
| DRIVER RD | KER | 68 C5 |
| DRIVER RD | KER | 78 C1 |
| DRIVER RD | KER | 78 C2 |
| DROBISH RD | BUT | 25 E5 |
| DROGE | SJCO | 47 C1 |
| DRUM CANYON RD | SB | 86 D3 |
| DRUMMOND AV | KER | 80 C1 |
| DRY CREEK RD | LAK | 32 A5 |
| DRY CREEK RD | MCO | 48 B3 |
| DRY CREEK RD | MNO | 50 D2 |
| DRY CREEK RD | NAPA | 29 C4 |
| DRY CREEK RD | NAPA | 38 B2 |
| DRY CREEK RD | PLA | 34 C3 |
| DRY CREEK RD | SJCO | 40 B3 |
| DRY CREEK RD | SLO | 76 B1 |
| DRY CREEK RD | SHA | 18 D2 |
| DRY CREEK RD | SIS | 4 B3 |
| DRY CREEK RD | SON | 31 C5 |
| DRY CREEK RD | TUL | 58 D5 |
| DRY CREEK RD W | SON | 31 D5 |
| DRY CREEK RD W | SON | 37 D1 |
| DRY CK BASIN RD | MOD | 8 C1 |
| DRY CK CMP GRND | LAS | 8 B3 |
| DRY CREEK CTOFF | MNO | 50 D2 |
| DRYDEN AV | SCL | P E5 |
| DRY GENESEO RD | SLO | 76 B1 |
| DRY SLOUGH RD | COL | 33 A3 |
| DRYTOWN AMADOR- | | |
| -VIA BUNKERHILL | AMA | 40 E2 |
| DU BOIS ST | SR | 139 D4 |
| DUBOIS TK TR | SDCO | 107 B5 |
| DUCK CREEK RD | AMA | 40 C3 |
| DUCK LAKE RD | LAS | 21 E4 |
| DUDLEY RD | MON | 65 D3 |
| DUFAU | VEN | 96 C1 |
| DUGGANS RD | NEV | 34 C2 |
| DUMETZ RD | LA | 177 C5 |
| DUMP RD | HUM | 16 B3 |
| DUMP RD | INY | 60 A3 |
| DUMP RD | LAK | 31 D2 |
| DUNAWAY RD | IMP | 111 D3 |
| DUNAWEAL LN | NAPA | 29 A2 |
| DUNBAR LN | SDCO | 107 A5 |
| DUNCAN RD | SBD | 90 E4 |
| DUNCAN RD | SJCO | 40 C5 |
| DUNCAN ST | KER | 78 E4 |
| DUNCAN CYN RD | SBD | 99 A1 |
| DUNCAN CREEK RD | SHA | 17 E3 |
| DUNDERBURG MDW | MNO | 43 B4 |
| DUNE RD | SBD | 92 B1 |
| DUNES RD | CLK | 210 B2 |
| DUNFORD RD | KER | 78 A3 |
| DUNLAP DR | RCO | 99 C3 |
| DUNLAP RD | FRCO | 58 C3 |
| DUNLAP RD | KER | 69 B5 |
| DUNN LN | CAL | 41 B5 |
| DUNN RD | MCO | 48 C4 |
| DUNN RD | STA | 47 B2 |
| DUNNE AV | SCL | P D5 |
| DUNNE AV E | SCL | P D5 |
| DUNSTONE DR | BUT | 25 D5 |
| DUNTON RD | STA | 40 E5 |
| DUPONT RD | RCO | 102 D5 |
| DURANT AV | B | 156 A3 |
| DURFEE AV | LACO | R C4 |
| DURHAM RD | ALA | P B2 |
| DURHAM RD | SIS | 5 A3 |
| DURHAM DAYTN HY | BUT | 25 B3 |
| DURHAM FERRY RD | SJCO | 47 A2 |
| DURKEE RD | LAS | 14 A3 |
| DURNEL RD | BUT | 25 B4 |
| DUSTIN RD | SJCO | 40 B4 |
| DUSTIN AKERS RD | KER | 78 A4 |
| DUSTY LN | STA | 47 D2 |
| DUSTY WY | TEH | 18 D5 |
| DUSTY MILE RD | SBD | 92 D5 |
| DUTCH CREEK RD | SIS | 3 E3 |
| DUTCH CREEK RD | TRI | 17 C2 |
| DUTCHER CK RD | SON | 31 C5 |
| DUTCH MINE RD | TUO | 41 C5 |
| DUTTON AV | SON | 131 C4 |
| DUTTON AV N | STR | 131 B3 |
| DUVALL ST | KER | 78 A4 |
| DUZEL CREEK RD | SIS | 3 E5 |
| DUZEL CREEK RD | SIS | 11 E1 |
| DUZEL RCK LO RD | SIS | 3 E5 |
| DUZEL RCK LO RD | SIS | 11 E1 |
| DWIGHT WY | MCO | 48 A4 |
| DWINNELL WY | SIS | 4 C5 |
| DWINNELL WY | SIS | 12 C1 |
| DYE RD | SDCO | 107 A4 |
| DYER DR | PLU | 20 C4 |
| DYER LN | PLA | 33 E5 |
| DYER RD | ORA | T D3 |
| DYER ST | ALA | N E1 |
| DYER ST | ALA | P A1 |
| DYER ST | ALA | 45 E3 |
| DYERVILLE LOOP | HUM | 16 B4 |
| DYERVILLE LP RD | HUM | 16 C4 |
| DYSERT RD | SIS | 4 E3 |
| DYSON LN | PLU | 27 C3 |
| **E** | | |
| E ST | DVS | 136 D3 |
| E ST | EUR | 121 C1 |
| E ST | FRE | 165 C4 |
| E ST | H | 146 E2 |
| E ST | SCTO | 137 C2 |
| E ST | SBDO | 207 C4 |
| E ST | SBD | 99 B2 |
| E ST | SDCO | V C4 |
| E ST | SDCO | 111 D2 |
| E ST | YUB | 33 D2 |
| EABY RD | SBD | 90 E4 |
| EADY RD | IMP | 112 A4 |
| EAGER RD | SUT | 33 C2 |
| EAGLE AV | FRCO | 56 A2 |
| EAGLE BORAX WLL | INY | 72 A2 |
| EAGLE CK LP RD | TRI | 11 E3 |
| EAGLE CK LP RD | TRI | 12 A3 |
| EAGLE FIELD RD | MCO | 55 E2 |
| EAGLE LAKE RD | NEV | 27 A5 |
| EAGLE MTN RD | RCO | 102 B4 |
| EAGLE PK LKOUT | TEH | 24 A2 |
| EAGLE ROCK BLVD | LACO | R A3 |
| EAGLE ROCK RD | TRI | 17 A1 |
| EAGLE RCK LKOUT | SIS | 4 D3 |
| EAGLES NEST RD | MNO | 43 A4 |
| EAGLES NEST RD | SAC | 40 B2 |
| EAGLEVL DUMP RD | MOD | 8 E2 |
| EAGLEVILLE LOOP | MOD | 8 E2 |
| EARDLEY AV | PAC | 167 C2 |
| EARHART RD | O | 159 D4 |
| EARLHAM ST | SDCO | 107 A4 |
| EARP RD | COL | 33 A2 |
| EAST AV | ALA | M D5 |
| EAST AV | ALA | 46 C2 |
| EAST AV | BUT | 25 B3 |
| EAST AV | BUT | 124 B1 |
| EAST AV | C | 124 A1 |
| EAST AV | FRCO | 57 C5 |
| EAST AV | MCO | 48 A3 |
| EAST AV | TEH | 24 D2 |
| EAST LN | MEN | 23 B3 |
| EAST RD | LACO | R E5 |
| EAST ST | ANA | 193 D1 |
| EAST ST | AUB | 126 C3 |
| EAST ST | ORA | T D2 |
| EAST ST | RED | 122 B1 |
| EASTBLUFF DR | NB | 200 A3 |
| EAST END AV | SBD | 98 D2 |
| EAST END RD | SBD | 92 A4 |
| EASTERN AV | LACO | 98 A2 |
| EASTERN AV | LACO | R B5 |
| EAST FORK RD | SHA | 18 A1 |
| EAST FORK RD | TRI | 11 B5 |
| EAST FORK RD | TRI | 17 C3 |
| EAST FORK RD | TRI | 12 A4 |
| EAST GRADE RD | SDCO | 107 A2 |
| EAST GRADE RD | TRI | 16 E2 |
| E FK HAYFORD RD | TRI | 17 C3 |
| E FK INDIAN CK | SHA | 2 E3 |
| E FK STUART CPG | TRI | 11 E5 |
| EASTIN RD | STA | 47 C5 |
| EAST LEVEE RD | SAC | M D2 |
| EASTMAN RD | STA | 40 D5 |
| EASTMAN RD | STA | 47 D1 |
| EASTMONT RD | KER | 78 E2 |
| EASTSHORE FRWY | ELC | 155 D3 |
| EASTSHORE FRWY | R | 155 D3 |
| EASTSHORE FRWY | SP | 155 D3 |
| EASTSHORE RD | SHA | 18 B2 |
| EAST SIDE | PLU | 20 D5 |
| EASTSIDE LN | MNO | 42 E1 |
| EASTSIDE RD | INY | 51 D4 |
| EASTSIDE RD | MEN | 23 A5 |
| EAST SIDE RD | MEN | 31 B2 |
| EASTSIDE RD | MNO | 42 E1 |
| EASTSIDE RD | RED | 122 B4 |
| EASTSIDE RD | SHA | 18 C2 |
| EASTSIDE RD | SHA | 18 C3 |
| EASTSIDE RD | SIS | 3 D5 |
| EASTSIDE RD | SIS | 11 D1 |
| EAST SIDE RD | TRI | 12 A4 |
| E SIDE CALPELLA | MEN | 31 B2 |
| E SDE PORTR VLY | MEN | 31 B1 |
| E SDE REDWD VLY | MEN | 31 B1 |
| EAST WEST RD | SIS | 5 D2 |
| EASY ST | KER | 79 C4 |
| EASY ST | SHA | 18 D2 |
| EATON RD | BUT | 25 B3 |
| EATON RD | STA | 47 E1 |
| EBERLE RD | KER | 78 C4 |
| ECHO PARK AV | LA | 185 E1 |
| ECHO PARK AV | LA | 186 A1 |
| ECHO VALLEY RD | MON | 54 C3 |
| EDDINS RD | IMP | 109 A3 |
| EDDY RD | COL | 33 A3 |

227
EDDY RD
STREET INDEX
FILLMORE ST




| STREET | CO. | PAGE & GRID | |
|---|---|---|---|
| EDDY RD | LPAZ | 104 | A2 |
| EDDY ST | SF | 143 | B5 |
| EDDY GULCH RD | SIS | 11 | B2 |
| EDDY GLH LKOUT | SIS | 11 | B3 |
| EDEN PLAINS RD | CC | M | D3 |
| EDGAR AV | BUT | 25 | B3 |
| EDGEMONT ST | LA | 182 | B5 |
| EDGER RD | IMP | 108 | E5 |
| EDGEWATER BLVD | FCTY | 145 | D2 |
| EDGEWATER RD | SMCO | N | C2 |
| EDGEWOOD AV | MAR | L | A4 |
| EDGEWOOD AV | MAR | 45 | B1 |
| EDGEWOOD RD | SMCO | 45 | D3 |
| EDGEWOOD RD | SIS | 12 | C1 |
| EDGEWD BIG SPGS | SIS | 12 | C1 |
| EDINGER AV | ORA | 98 | B4 |
| EDINGER AV | ORA | T | B3 |
| EDINGER AV | SA | 196 | A5 |
| EDINGER AV | SA | 197 | C1 |
| EDINGER AV | SA | 198 | A1 |
| EDINGER ST | FTNV | 195 | C5 |
| EDINGER ST | SA | 195 | C5 |
| EDISON AV | SBD | 98 | D2 |
| EDISON BLVD | BUR | 179 | B3 |
| EDISON HWY | KER | 78 | E3 |
| EDISON HWY | KER | 79 | A3 |
| EDISON AV | SBD | U | D3 |
| EDISON RD | KER | 78 | E3 |
| EDISON ST | SB | 86 | E3 |
| EDITH AV | TEH | 24 | D2 |
| EDMINSTER RD | MCO | 47 | D4 |
| EDMUNDSON AV | SCL | P | D5 |
| EDMUNDSON AV | SCL | 54 | C1 |
| EDNA RD | SLO | 172 | D5 |
| ED POWERS RD | INY | 51 | C4 |
| ED RAU RD | SAC | 39 | E2 |
| EDSEL LN | STA | 47 | C2 |
| EDWARD ST | KER | 79 | B5 |
| EDWARDS | SJCO | 47 | D1 |
| EDWARDS ST | ORA | T | B3 |
| EEL RIVER RD | MEN | 23 | B5 |
| EEL RIVER RD | MEN | 31 | C1 |
| EEL ROCK RD | HUM | 16 | C4 |
| EGAN RD | TUO | 41 | C5 |
| EGGERT RD | SOL | 39 | C2 |
| EHRLICH RD | STA | 47 | C3 |
| EICKHOFF RD | LAK | 31 | D2 |
| EIGHMY RD | TEH | 18 | C4 |
| EIGHTH ST | C | 124 | C5 |
| EIGHT MILE RD | SJCO | 39 | E4 |
| EIGHT MILE RD | SJCO | 40 | A4 |
| EISENHOWER DR | RCO | 100 | E5 |
| EISENHOWER ST | FRFD | 135 | D3 |
| ELBERTA ST | KER | 89 | E1 |
| EL CAJON BLVD | SD | 214 | A5 |
| EL CAJON BLVD | SDCO | V | D3 |
| EL CAJON BLVD | SDCO | 111 | D1 |
| EL CAMINO AV | SAC | 40 | A1 |
| EL CAMINO DR | SHA | 18 | C3 |
| EL CAMINO RD | SBD | 101 | D1 |
| EL CAMINO CIELO | SB | 87 | C4 |
| EL CAMINO REAL | BLMT | 145 | C4 |
| EL CAMINO REAL | BURL | 144 | B3 |
| EL CAMINO REAL | MP | 147 | A2 |
| EL CAMINO REAL | MLBR | 144 | C4 |
| EL CAMINO REAL | MON | 54 | D4 |
| EL CAMINO REAL | MON | 65 | A1 |
| EL CAMINO REAL | MON | 66 | A5 |
| EL CAMINO REAL | MON | 171 | B1 |
| EL CAMINO REAL | MVW | 148 | B5 |
| EL CAMINO REAL | ORA | 105 | E1 |
| EL CAMINO REAL | PA | 147 | B3 |
| EL CAMINO REAL | SAL | 171 | D3 |
| EL CAMINO REAL | SBT | 54 | D2 |
| EL CAMINO REAL | SBR | 144 | B3 |
| EL CAMINO REAL | SDCO | 106 | B3 |
| EL CAMINO REAL | SNLO | 172 | A4 |
| EL CAMINO REAL | SLO | 66 | A5 |
| EL CAMINO REAL | SLO | 76 | B2 |
| EL CAMINO REAL | SLO | 172 | E1 |
| EL CAMINO REAL | SM | 145 | A3 |
| EL CAMINO REAL | SMCO | N | D2 |
| EL CAMINO REAL | SMCO | 45 | C3 |
| EL CAMINO REAL | STB | 173 | D5 |
| EL CAMINO REAL | SB | 86 | C1 |
| EL CAMINO REAL | SCL | P | A3 |
| EL CAMINO REAL | SCLR | 150 | B2 |
| EL CAMINO REAL | SCLR | 151 | A2 |
| EL CAMINO REAL | SCL | 46 | A4 |
| EL CAMINO REAL | SCL | 54 | D2 |
| EL CAMINO REAL | SMA | 173 | C1 |
| EL CAMINO REAL | SSF | 144 | B3 |
| EL CAMINO REAL | SVL | 150 | B2 |
| EL CAMPO RD | MCO | 55 | E2 |
| EL CAMPO RD | RCO | 100 | C5 |
| EL CAMPO RD | SLO | 76 | B5 |
| EL CAPITAN WY | MCO | 47 | E4 |
| EL CAPITAN WY | MCO | 48 | A3 |
| EL CAPTN SCH RD | MCO | 48 | B5 |
| EL CARISO TK TR | RCO | 99 | B4 |
| EL CENTRO AV | NAPA | 38 | C3 |
| EL CENTRO BLVD | SUT | 33 | D3 |
| EL CENTRO RD | SAC | 33 | D5 |
| EL CENTRO ST | IMP | 111 | E3 |
| EL CERRITO RD | RCO | 98 | E3 |
| EL CERRO BLVD | CC | M | A4 |
| EL CIELITO RD | STB | 174 | D1 |
| EL CIELO DR | RCO | 100 | D3 |
| EL CIELO RD | PMSP | 206 | E5 |
| EL CONQUISTA RD | RCO | 107 | A1 |
| ELDER AV | KIN | 67 | B1 |
| ELDER CREEK RD | RCO | 107 | B1 |
| ELDER CREEK RD | SAC | 40 | A1 |
| EL DIABLO RD | SBD | 92 | E5 |
| EL DORADO AV | FRCO | 56 | E4 |
| EL DORADO AV | FRCO | 66 | E2 |
| EL DORADO AV | S | 160 | C1 |

| STREET | CO. | PAGE & GRID | |
|---|---|---|---|
| EL DORADO DR | RCO | 100 | C3 |
| EL DORADO DR | SBD | 102 | C1 |
| EL DORADO ST | AUB | 126 | D3 |
| EL DORADO ST | FRE | 165 | C3 |
| EL DORADO ST | MONT | 167 | E4 |
| EL DORADO ST | SJCO | 40 | A5 |
| EL DRDO HLLS RD | ED | 34 | C5 |
| EL DORADO MN RD | RCO | 101 | C2 |
| ELDRIDGE RD | LAS | 14 | A5 |
| ELEANOR AV | STA | 47 | D2 |
| ELEVADO AV | BH | 183 | A2 |
| ELEVADO RD | SBD | 91 | B3 |
| ELDER ST | SDCO | 106 | C2 |
| ELDER CREEK RD | SAC | 39 | E1 |
| ELECTRA RD | AMA | 41 | A3 |
| ELEVATOR RD | SOL | 39 | D3 |
| ELFERS RD | STA | 47 | B3 |
| ELGIN | MCO | 56 | B1 |
| ELGIN AV | KIN | 67 | B1 |
| ELHOLM RD | MCO | 47 | C5 |
| ELINOR RD N | HUM | 16 | A3 |
| ELINOR RD S | HUM | 16 | A3 |
| ELIZA GULCH RD | SIS | 3 | E4 |
| ELIZABETH LK RD | LACO | 89 | C3 |
| ELZBTH LK P CYN | LACO | 89 | B2 |
| ELK | MCO | 48 | A4 |
| ELK AV | BUT | 25 | B3 |
| ELK CT | KER | 79 | B4 |
| ELK CREEK RD | HUM | 16 | B4 |
| ELK CREEK RD | SIS | 3 | A4 |
| ELK GROVE BLVD | SAC | 39 | E2 |
| ELK GROVE BLVD | SAC | 40 | A2 |
| ELK GRV FLRN RD | SAC | 39 | E2 |
| ELK GRV FLRN RD | SAC | 40 | A2 |
| ELK HILLS RD | KER | 77 | E3 |
| ELK HILLS RD | KER | 78 | A3 |
| ELKHORN AV | FRCO | 56 | D5 |
| ELKHORN AV | FRCO | 57 | D5 |
| ELKHORN BLVD | SAC | 33 | D5 |
| ELKHORN RD | MEN | 31 | A4 |
| ELKHORN RD | MON | 54 | C3 |
| ELKHORN GRAD RD | KER | 78 | A5 |
| ELKHORN GRADE | FRCO | 57 | B5 |
| ELK MOUNTAIN RD | LAK | 23 | C5 |
| ELK MOUNTAIN RD | LAK | 31 | C1 |
| ELK RIVER RD | HUM | 121 | A5 |
| ELK RIVER RD | HUM | 15 | E1 |
| ELK VALLEY RD | DN | 1 | D4 |
| ELK VALLEY RD | SIS | 10 | D1 |
| ELK VLY CRSS RD | DN | 1 | E4 |
| ELLA AV | YUB | 33 | D2 |
| ELLA RICHTER RD | SHA | 18 | A3 |
| ELLENA ST | FRCO | 57 | B5 |
| ELLEN SPGS DR | LAK | 32 | A4 |
| ELLENWOOD DR | STA | 47 | E2 |
| ELLENWOOD RD | STA | 48 | A2 |
| ELLER LN | SIS | 3 | D5 |
| ELLER LN | SIS | 11 | D1 |
| ELLIOT | SJCO | 40 | B3 |
| ELLIOT AV | MCO | 48 | B4 |
| ELLIOT ST | SBD | 93 | B2 |
| ELLIOT RCH RD | PLA | 34 | E2 |
| ELLIOTT RD | BUT | 25 | C3 |
| ELLIOTT CK RD | SIS | 3 | B2 |
| ELLIOTT RCH RD | SAC | 39 | E2 |
| ELLIS AV | RCO | 99 | C4 |
| ELLIS RD | AMA | 41 | C1 |
| ELLIS RD | YUB | 33 | D2 |
| ELLIS ST | SF | 143 | B5 |
| ELLSWORTH ST | B | 156 | A3 |
| ELM AV | FRCO | 57 | C4 |
| ELM AV | MON | 65 | B1 |
| ELM AV | SBR | 144 | B3 |
| ELM AV | SDCO | 106 | B3 |
| ELM ST | BKD | 166 | B2 |
| ELM ST | RCO | 99 | C5 |
| ELM ST | SDCO | 107 | A4 |
| ELM ST | TUL | 68 | B3 |
| EL MARGARITA RD | SUT | 33 | C2 |
| EL MEDIO RD | SBD | 90 | E3 |
| ELMER AV | SUT | 33 | C2 |
| ELMER ST | RCO | 99 | B4 |
| ELMIRA RD | SOL | 39 | A2 |
| EL MIRAGE RD | SBD | 90 | E3 |
| EL MIRAGE RD | SBD | 91 | A3 |
| ELMO HWY | KER | 78 | A1 |
| EL MONTE AV | LACO | R | D3 |
| EL MONTE AV | TUL | 58 | A4 |
| EL MONTE RD | SCL | N | E3 |
| EL MONTE RD | SCL | 45 | E4 |
| ELNA RD | INY | 59 | E1 |
| EL NIDO RD | MCO | 48 | C5 |
| EL NORTE PKWY | SDCO | 106 | D3 |
| ELORDY LN | SUT | 33 | E4 |
| EL PASTA RD | RCO | 107 | A1 |
| EL POMAR AV | STA | 47 | E2 |
| EL POMAR DR | SLO | 76 | A2 |
| EL POMAR RD | SLO | 76 | B2 |
| EL POMAR RO RD | SLO | 76 | B2 |
| EL PORTAL | CC | 38 | C5 |
| EL POZO GRADE | SLO | 76 | D3 |
| EL RANCHO DR | KER | 79 | C4 |
| EL REPOSO RD | RCO | 107 | A1 |
| EL RIO DR | TUL | 68 | C1 |
| EL ROBLAR | VEN | 88 | A4 |
| EL ROBLAR ST | SB | 87 | E1 |
| EL SEGUNDO BLVD | ELS | 189 | D4 |
| EL SEGUNDO BLVD | LACO | 97 | D3 |
| EL SEGUNDO BLVD | LACO | Q | D5 |
| EL SEGUNDO BLVD | LACO | S | C1 |
| EL SERENO RD | MCO | 55 | C2 |
| EL SOBRANTE RD | RCO | 99 | B3 |
| EL TEJON HWY | KER | 78 | E4 |
| EL TEJON HWY | KER | 79 | A4 |
| EL TORO DR | BKD | 166 | C5 |
| EL TORO RD | ORA | 98 | D5 |
| ELVAS FRWY | SCTO | 137 | E2 |

| STREET | CO. | PAGE & GRID | |
|---|---|---|---|
| ELVERTA RD | SAC | 33 | D5 |
| EL VICINO AV | MDO | 162 | D2 |
| ELWOOD RD | FRCO | 58 | B3 |
| ELY RD | SON | L | A1 |
| ELY RD | SUT | 33 | C4 |
| ELYSIAN VLY RD | LAS | 21 | A4 |
| EMBARCADRO, THE | SF | 143 | B2 |
| EMBARCADERO RD | PA | 147 | C2 |
| EMBARCADERO RD | SCL | N | E2 |
| EMBRCDRO SKYWAY | SF | 143 | D3 |
| EMERALD AV | RCO | 100 | E3 |
| EMERALD AV | STA | 47 | C2 |
| EMERALD DR | SDCO | 106 | C3 |
| EMERALD RD | SBD | 91 | E4 |
| EMERSON RD | MOD | 8 | D2 |
| EMERSON RD | TEH | 18 | D4 |
| EMERY RD | STA | 47 | E2 |
| EMERY RD | STA | 48 | A2 |
| EMIGH RD | SOL | 39 | C4 |
| EMIGRANT RD | PLU | 26 | D1 |
| EMIGRANT TR | SHA | 19 | B3 |
| EMMERT RD | COL | 33 | A3 |
| EMMIGRANT TR | ALP | 36 | B4 |
| EMPIRE | CC | 39 | C5 |
| EMPIRE AV | BUR | 179 | B2 |
| EMPIRE AV | CC | M | D3 |
| EMPIRE ST | GV | 127 | B4 |
| EMPIRE ST | NEV | 127 | C4 |
| EMPIRE CREEK RD | SIS | 3 | E3 |
| EMPIRE GRADE | SCR | N | E5 |
| EMPIRE GRADE | SCR | 53 | D1 |
| EMPIRE MINE RD | CC | M | C3 |
| EMPIRE MINE RD | CC | 39 | B5 |
| ENCHNTD FRST RD | RCO | 100 | A4 |
| ENCINAL | MON | 54 | D4 |
| ENCINAL AV | ALA | L | D5 |
| ENCINAL AV | ALA | 45 | D1 |
| ENCINAL RD | SUT | 33 | C1 |
| ENCINITAS BLVD | SDCO | 106 | C4 |
| ENCINITAS RD | SDCO | 106 | C3 |
| END RD W | HUM | 10 | A5 |
| ENDERTS BCH RD | DN | 1 | E4 |
| ENGLEHART AV | FRCO | 58 | A4 |
| ENGLISH RD | IMP | 109 | A3 |
| ENGLISH COLONY | PLA | 34 | B4 |
| ENGLISH HILLS | SOL | 39 | A2 |
| ENNIS RD | FRCO | 58 | C3 |
| ENNIS RD | SUT | 33 | B2 |
| ENOS LN | KER | 78 | B3 |
| ENSLEY RD | SUT | 33 | C4 |
| ENTERPRISE | SJCO | 47 | D1 |
| ENTERPRISE RD | BUT | 25 | E4 |
| ENTERPRISE ST | TUL | 68 | A2 |
| ERBES RD | VEN | 96 | E1 |
| EREISTIN DR | SBD | 92 | D5 |
| ERHIT RD | TUO | 48 | E1 |
| ERHIT RD | TUO | 49 | A1 |
| ERICKSON RD | BUT | 25 | B4 |
| ERLE RD | MCO | 48 | E5 |
| ERNST | MPA | 48 | E2 |
| ERNST | MPA | 49 | A2 |
| ERRECA RD | MCO | 48 | A5 |
| ERRINGER RD | VEN | 88 | E5 |
| ERRINGER RD | VEN | 89 | A5 |
| ERRINGER RD | VEN | 96 | E1 |
| ERRINGER RD | VEN | 97 | A1 |
| ERSKINE RD | IMP | 108 | E5 |
| ERSKINE CK RD | KER | 79 | D1 |
| ERTESZEK DR | KER | 79 | C4 |
| ERWIN ST | LA | 178 | C3 |
| ESCALON BELLOTA | SJCO | 40 | C5 |
| ESCALON BELLOTA | SJCO | 47 | C1 |
| ESCHINGER RD | SAC | 39 | E2 |
| ESCHINGER RD | SAC | 40 | A2 |
| ESCOBAR ST | M | 154 | A2 |
| ESCOLLE RD | MON | 54 | D5 |
| ESCONDIDO AV | SDCO | 106 | C3 |
| ESCONDIDO FRWY | RCO | 99 | C3 |
| ESCONDIDO FRWY | SD | 216 | D3 |
| ESCONDIDO FRWY | SDCO | 106 | D2 |
| ESCONDIDO RD | LACO | 89 | D4 |
| ESMERALDA RD | CAL | 41 | B4 |
| ESPERANZA AV | RCO | 100 | B3 |
| ESPERANZA RD | MON | 54 | D4 |
| ESPERANZA RD | SIS | 13 | A2 |
| ESPINOSA RD | MON | 54 | C3 |
| ESPINOSA RD | MON | 65 | B1 |
| ESPLANADE | BUT | 25 | A2 |
| ESPLANADE AV | RCO | 99 | D4 |
| ESPLANADE, THE | C | 124 | B3 |
| ESPOLA RD | SDCO | 106 | D4 |
| ESQUON RD | BUT | 25 | B4 |
| ESSEX LN | HUM | 10 | A5 |
| ESSEX RD | SBD | 94 | D2 |
| ESTHER AV | MCO | 56 | B2 |
| ESTRELLA RD | SLO | 66 | A5 |
| ESTRELLA RD | SLO | 76 | B1 |
| ESTUDILLO AV | ALA | L | E5 |
| ETHANAC RD | RCO | 99 | C4 |
| ETHEREDGE ST | KER | 68 | D5 |
| ETIWANDA AV | SBD | 98 | E2 |
| ETTERBG HONEYDW | HUM | 16 | A5 |
| ETTING RD | VEN | 96 | C1 |
| ETZEL RD | SOL | 39 | C2 |
| EUCALYPTUS AV | MCO | 48 | A4 |
| EUCALYPTUS AV | RCO | 99 | C3 |
| EUCALYPTUS AV | SBD | U | E3 |
| EUCALYPTUS AV | SBD | 98 | E2 |
| EUCALYPTUS AV | STA | 47 | B3 |
| EUCALYPTUS RD | BUT | 25 | B5 |
| EUCALYPTUS RD | MCO | 56 | A2 |
| EUCALYPTUS ST | AVLN | 105 | B5 |
| EUCALYPTUS ST | SBD | 91 | B4 |
| EUCLID AV | ALA | L | D4 |
| EUCLID AV | ONT | 204 | B4 |
| EUCLID AV | SBD | U | D3 |
| EUCLID AV | SBD | 98 | D2 |

| STREET | CO. | PAGE & GRID | |
|---|---|---|---|
| EUCLID AV | SDCO | V | C3 |
| EUCLID AV | SDCO | 111 | D1 |
| EUCLID AV | SF | 141 | E3 |
| EUCLID AV | STA | 47 | E3 |
| EUCLID AV | UPL | 204 | B1 |
| EUCLID ST | FTNV | 197 | A3 |
| EUCLID ST | GGR | 195 | A3 |
| EUCLID ST | ORA | 98 | B3 |
| EUCLID ST | ORA | T | C2 |
| EUCLID ST | SA | 195 | A5 |
| EUREKA RD | PLA | 34 | B5 |
| EUREKA RD S | INY | 52 | D5 |
| EUREKA WY | RED | 122 | B1 |
| EUREKA WY | SHA | 18 | C2 |
| EUREKA CYN RD | SCR | P | C5 |
| EUREKA CYN RD | SCR | 54 | B1 |
| EUREKA HILL RD | MEN | 30 | C3 |
| EUREKA MINE RD | SIE | 26 | C4 |
| EUREKA VLY RD | INY | 52 | D4 |
| EUROPE AV | KER | 79 | D5 |
| EVAN HEWES HWY | IMP | 111 | D3 |
| EVAN HEWES HWY | IMP | 112 | D3 |
| EVANS | TUL | 68 | D1 |
| EVANS AV | FRCO | 56 | B2 |
| EVANS RD | COL | 32 | D2 |
| EVANS RD | RCO | 107 | C1 |
| EVANS RD | SIS | 4 | E3 |
| EVANS REIMER RD | BUT | 25 | B5 |
| EVELYN AV | MVW | 148 | B4 |
| EVELYN AV | SCL | P | A3 |
| EVELYN AV | SVL | 148 | E5 |
| EVELYN AV | SVL | 150 | A1 |
| EVERETT AV | KIN | 67 | C1 |
| EVERETT ST | KER | 80 | D1 |
| EVERETT MEM HWY | SIS | 12 | C2 |
| EVERGLADE | SUT | 33 | C3 |
| EVERGREEN RD | CAL | 40 | D4 |
| EVERGREEN RD | TEH | 18 | C4 |
| EVERGREEN RD | TUO | 42 | B5 |
| EVERGREEN RD | TUO | 63 | A3 |
| EVERITT RD | SUT | 33 | C2 |
| EXCELSIOR AV | FRCO | 66 | E1 |
| EXCELSIOR AV | FRCO | 67 | C1 |
| EXCELSIOR AV | KIN | 67 | D1 |
| EXCELSIOR RD | SAC | 40 | A2 |
| EXCELSIOR MN RD | SBD | 73 | D5 |
| EXCELSIOR MN RD | SBD | 83 | D1 |
| EXCELSIOR PT RD | NEV | 34 | E1 |
| EXCHEQUER | MPA | 48 | D3 |
| EXCHEQUER DR | FRCO | 58 | C1 |
| EXCHEQUER DAM | MPA | 48 | D3 |
| EXP MINE RD | TUO | 41 | C4 |
| EXPOSITION BLVD | LA | 184 | C5 |
| EXPOSITION BLVD | LA | 185 | C5 |
| EXPOSITION BLVD | LACO | 97 | D2 |
| EXPOSITION BLVD | LACO | Q | D4 |
| EXPOSITION BLVD | SAC | 39 | E1 |
| F | | | |
| F ST | DVS | 136 | D2 |
| F ST | EUR | 121 | D3 |
| F ST | FRE | 165 | D4 |
| F ST | HUM | 15 | E1 |
| F ST | SBD | 99 | B1 |
| F ST | SDCO | V | C4 |
| F ST | SDCO | 111 | D2 |
| FABRY RD | MON | 55 | B5 |
| FAHEY RD | MCO | 55 | C1 |
| FAIR ST | BUT | 25 | B3 |
| FAIR ST | BUT | 124 | E5 |
| FAIRBANKS RD | MEN | 23 | B3 |
| FAIRCHILD LN | SJCO | 40 | B5 |
| FAIRFAX | FRCO | 56 | B3 |
| FAIRFAX AV | KIN | 67 | C1 |
| FAIRFAX AV | LA | 181 | A4 |
| FAIRFAX AV | LA | 184 | A3 |
| FAIRFAX AV | LACO | Q | D4 |
| FAIRFAX AV | LACO | 181 | A4 |
| FAIRFAX RD | KER | 78 | E3 |
| FAIRFAX BOLINAS | MAR | 38 | A5 |
| FAIRFIELD AV | FRFD | 135 | B3 |
| FAIRFIELD AV | SBD | 91 | C3 |
| FAIRFIELD ST | EUR | 121 | B3 |
| FAIRGROUND DR | NAPA | L | D1 |
| FAIRGROUNDS DR | VAL | 134 | E2 |
| FAIRHAVEN AV | OR | 196 | C2 |
| FAIRHAVEN AV | ORA | T | E2 |
| FAIRHAVEN AV | SA | 196 | C2 |
| FAIRLANE RD | SBD | 92 | A4 |
| FAIRMEAD BLVD | MAD | 56 | E1 |
| FAIRMONT AV | SDCO | V | C3 |
| FAIRMONT AV | SDCO | 111 | D1 |
| FAIRMONT AV E | MDO | 162 | D1 |
| FAIRMONT RD | LACO | 89 | C3 |
| FAIRMOUNT AV | SD | 214 | E5 |
| FAIRMOUNT AV | SD | 216 | E1 |
| FAIROAKS AV | LACO | R | B2 |
| FAIR OAKS AV | LACO | 190 | B2 |
| FAIR OAKS AV | PAS | 190 | B4 |
| FAIR OAKS AV | SCL | 45 | E4 |
| FAIR OAKS AV | SCL | 46 | A4 |
| FAIR OAKS AV | SVL | 149 | E1 |
| FAIR OAKS BLVD | SAC | 40 | A1 |
| FAIR OAKS BLVD | SAC | 34 | A5 |
| FAIR PLAY RD | ED | 41 | A1 |
| FAIRVIEW AV | ALA | P | A1 |
| FAIRVIEW AV | CC | M | D3 |
| FAIRVIEW AV | CC | 39 | C5 |
| FAIRVIEW AV | RCO | 100 | A4 |
| FAIRVIEW AV | SB | 87 | B4 |
| FAIRVIEW RD | COL | 32 | D1 |
| FAIRVIEW RD | CM | 199 | C1 |
| FAIRVIEW RD | MON | 54 | E5 |
| FAIRVIEW RD | ORA | 98 | C4 |
| FAIRVIEW RD | ORA | T | C4 |
| FAIRVIEW RD | SBT | 54 | E2 |
| FAIRVIEW RD | SBT | 55 | A2 |
| FAIRVIEW RD | SBD | 92 | C1 |

| STREET | CO. | PAGE & GRID | |
|---|---|---|---|
| FAIRVIEW RD | VEN | 88 | B4 |
| FAIRWAY DR | CLTN | 207 | B5 |
| FAIRWAY DR | EUR | 121 | C5 |
| FAIRWAY PL | SB | 86 | E3 |
| FAITH HOME RD | MCO | 47 | D4 |
| FAITH HOME RD | STA | 47 | D3 |
| FALL RD | INY | 70 | B2 |
| FALLBROOK AV | LA | 177 | A4 |
| FALL CREEK RD | SIS | 4 | C2 |
| FALLEN LEAF RD | ED | 35 | E3 |
| FALLING LEAF RD | SHA | 18 | C2 |
| FALLON RD | SBT | 54 | E2 |
| FALLON RD | SBT | 55 | A2 |
| FALL RIVER RD | SHA | 13 | E4 |
| FALLS CYN RD | AVLN | 105 | A5 |
| FAMOSO HWY | KER | 78 | A1 |
| FAMOSO-PRTVL HY | KER | 78 | C1 |
| FANDANGO PSS RD | MOD | 7 | C3 |
| FANNING | SJCO | 40 | B5 |
| FANOE RD | MON | 54 | E5 |
| FARGO AV | KIN | 67 | C1 |
| FARGO CANYON RD | RCO | 101 | B4 |
| FARINA ST | RCO | 100 | A5 |
| FARLEY MINE RD | SBD | 91 | D3 |
| FARMER RANCH RD | TRI | 17 | B2 |
| FARMERSVILLE RD | TUL | 68 | C2 |
| FARM HILL BLVD | SMCO | N | D2 |
| FARM HILL BLVD | SMCO | 45 | D4 |
| FARMLAN RD | SUT | 33 | B2 |
| FARMLAND AV | MCO | 48 | C4 |
| FARNHAM RDG RD | ED | 41 | A1 |
| FARQUHAR RD | TEH | 18 | B4 |
| FARRIS DR | CAL | 40 | D4 |
| FARRIS RD | BUT | 25 | B5 |
| FARRIS RD | BUT | 33 | B1 |
| FASIG RD | SUT | 33 | B3 |
| FAUST RD | STA | 47 | C2 |
| FAWCETT RD | IMP | 112 | A3 |
| FAWN LODGE RD | TRI | 17 | D1 |
| FAXON RD | COL | 33 | B3 |
| FAY LN | SIS | 11 | D1 |
| FAY RD | MCO | 47 | D4 |
| FAY RANCH RD | KER | 69 | E5 |
| FAY RANCH RD | KER | 79 | E1 |
| FAY RIDGE RD | KER | 78 | C1 |
| FEATHER LAKE HY | LAS | 20 | A2 |
| FEATHER LAKE HY | LAS | 20 | D3 |
| FEATHER LAKE RD | SHA | 19 | E1 |
| FEATHER RIV BL | YUB | 33 | D3 |
| FEDERAL BLVD | SDCO | V | C3 |
| FEDERAL BLVD | SDCO | 111 | D1 |
| FEE RD | MOD | 7 | D3 |
| FEENSTRA RD | SLO | 76 | B2 |
| FEE RESRVOIR RD | MOD | 7 | D3 |
| FELCIANA MTN RD | MPA | 49 | B3 |
| FELDMILLER RD | TRI | 16 | E3 |
| FELDSPAR AV | KER | 80 | D1 |
| FELICITA RD | SDCO | 106 | D3 |
| FELIZ CREEK RD | MEN | 31 | B3 |
| FELL ST | SFCO | L | B5 |
| FELL ST | SF | 141 | E4 |
| FELL ST | SF | 142 | B4 |
| FELL ST | SFCO | 45 | B1 |
| FELLOWSHIP RD | STB | 174 | A5 |
| FELTER RD | SCL | 46 | B4 |
| FELTN EMPIRE RD | SCR | N | E5 |
| FELTON EMPRE RD | SCR | 53 | E1 |
| FENDERS FERRY | SHA | 13 | A5 |
| FENSLER RD | SIS | 5 | D2 |
| FENTEM RD | MCO | 47 | C5 |
| FERGUSON RD | IMP | 110 | E4 |
| FERN RD | SHA | 19 | A2 |
| FERN RD E | SHA | 19 | A1 |
| FERN ST | SD | 216 | B3 |
| FERN ST | SDCO | V | C3 |
| FERN ST | SDCO | 111 | D1 |
| FERN CANYON DR | MEN | 31 | B2 |
| FERNDALE DMP RD | HUM | 15 | D2 |
| FERRELL RD | IMP | 112 | A4 |
| FERRETTI RD | TUO | 41 | D5 |
| FERRETTI RD | TUO | 48 | D1 |
| FERRY RD | TEH | 18 | D4 |
| FERRY RD E | HUM | 15 | E2 |
| FESLER ST | SMA | 173 | B2 |
| FICKLE HILL RD | HUM | 10 | A5 |
| FIDDLETOWN RD | AMA | 40 | E2 |
| FIDLTWN QTZ MTN | AMA | 40 | E1 |
| FIDLTWN SHNDOAH | AMA | 40 | E1 |
| FIDDLTWN SLV LK | AMA | 41 | A1 |
| FIDDYMENT | PLA | 33 | E4 |
| FIELD RD | SBD | 82 | C5 |
| FIELDBROOK RD | HUM | 10 | A4 |
| FIELDS RD | MCO | 48 | C3 |
| FIELDS RD | RCO | 100 | A3 |
| FIELDS RIDGE RD | BUT | 26 | B4 |
| FIESTA ISLND RD | SD | 212 | E4 |
| FIFIELD RD | IMP | 109 | B4 |
| FIFIELD RD | SUT | 33 | D4 |
| FIFTH AV | C | 124 | B3 |
| FIFTH ST | C | 124 | B5 |
| FIG AV | FRE | 165 | C5 |
| FIG AV | FRCO | 57 | C4 |
| FIG AV | FRCO | 57 | C5 |
| FIG AV | STA | 47 | C3 |
| FIGMOND AV | MCO | 48 | C3 |
| FIG TREE LN | SHA | 18 | C3 |
| FIGUEROA ST | LA | 185 | D5 |
| FIGUEROA ST | LA | 191 | B1 |
| FIGUEROA ST | LACO | R | A3 |
| FIGUEROA ST | LACO | S | C2 |
| FIGUEROA ST | MONT | 167 | E3 |
| FIGUEROA MTN RD | SB | 87 | B2 |
| FILBURN ST | KER | 78 | A1 |
| FILIPPINI RD | SIE | 27 | C3 |
| FILLMAN RD | LAS | 8 | A4 |
| FILLMORE ST | RCO | 101 | B5 |
| FILLMORE ST | SF | 142 | B2 |


STREETS

| STREET | CO. | PAGE & GRID | |
|---|---|---|---|
| FILLY LN | CAL | 41 | B5 |
| FIMPLE RD | BUT | 25 | B3 |
| FINCK RD | SJCO | 46 | E1 |
| FINE AV | SJCO | 40 | C5 |
| FINE AV | STA | 47 | D2 |
| FINK RD | STA | 47 | C4 |
| FINKS RD | COL | 32 | D1 |
| FINLEY LN | LAS | 14 | C3 |
| FINNEL AV | TEH | 24 | D1 |
| FINNEY RD | IMP | 109 | B5 |
| FINNEY RD | STA | 47 | C2 |
| FINNING HILL RD | PLA | 34 | E2 |
| FIR ST | C | 124 | E4 |
| FIR ST | RCO | 100 | C4 |
| FIRE CAMP RD | BUT | 25 | E4 |
| FIRESTONE | FRCO | 66 | C3 |
| FIRESTONE BLVD | LACO | 97 | E2 |
| FIRESTONE BLVD | LACO | R | A5 |
| FIRETHORN RD | SBD | 92 | B3 |
| FIRST AV | C | 124 | B3 |
| FIRST AV | STA | 47 | C3 |
| FIRST AV E | C | 124 | D3 |
| FIRST ST | SIS | 12 | D3 |
| FISCHER RD | IMP | 111 | E4 |
| FISH & GAME RD | LAS | 21 | C3 |
| FISHER AV | KER | 89 | C1 |
| FISHER DR | TUL | 68 | C1 |
| FISHER RD | HUM | 15 | E2 |
| FISHER RD | IMP | 110 | D5 |
| FISHER RD | LPAZ | 104 | A2 |
| FISHER RD | MCO | 48 | B4 |
| FISHER RD | TRI | 10 | E5 |
| FISHERS LANDING | YUMA | 110 | E4 |
| FISH HATCHRY RD | INY | 59 | E3 |
| FISH ROCK RD | MEN | 31 | A4 |
| FISH ROCK RD | MEN | 30 | D4 |
| FISH SLOUGH RD | MNO | 51 | D2 |
| FISH SPRINGS RD | INY | 59 | E1 |
| FISKE | MPA | 48 | E1 |
| FISKE | MPA | 49 | A1 |
| FITCH MTN RD | SON | 37 | D1 |
| FITZGERALD DR | BUT | 25 | C2 |
| FITZGERALD RD | SCL | P | E5 |
| FITZGERALD RD | SCL | 54 | D1 |
| FITZHUGH CK RD | MOD | 8 | B2 |
| FIVE BRIDGES RD | INY | 51 | D4 |
| FIVE MILE DR | AMA | 40 | D2 |
| FIVE MILE CK RD | TUO | 41 | D4 |
| FIVE MI STA RD | SBD | 95 | D2 |
| FLAMINGO RD | CLK | 210 | C2 |
| FLANAGAN RD | SHA | 18 | C1 |
| FLANNERY RD | SOL | 39 | B3 |
| FLATTOP MTN RD | KIN | 67 | A4 |
| FLEA VALLEY RD | BUT | 25 | D2 |
| FLEMING AV E | VAL | 134 | E3 |
| FLEMING RD | PLA | 34 | A3 |
| FLETCHER DR | LACO | Q | E3 |
| FLETCHER PKWY | SDCO | V | D3 |
| FLETCHER PKWY | SDCO | 111 | E1 |
| FLINT AV | KIN | 67 | C1 |
| FLINT AV | MCO | 47 | E4 |
| FLINT AV | MCO | 48 | A4 |
| FLINT ST | KER | 80 | C5 |
| FLOOD RD | IMP | 110 | D5 |
| FLOOD RD | SJCO | 40 | C5 |
| FLORADALE AV | SB | 86 | B3 |
| FLORAL AV | C | 124 | D1 |
| FLORAL AV | FRCO | 56 | D4 |
| FLORAL AV | FRCO | 57 | B4 |
| FLORENCE AV | ING | 188 | E5 |
| FLORENCE AV | LACO | 97 | D2 |
| FLORENCE AV | LACO | Q | D5 |
| FLORES AV | TEH | 18 | D5 |
| FLORES RD | YUB | 34 | A1 |
| FLORIDA AV | RCO | 99 | D4 |
| FLORIDA DR | SD | 216 | A2 |
| FLORIDA ST | VAL | 134 | C4 |
| FLORIN RD | SAC | 40 | A1 |
| FLORIN MILL RD | SHA | 13 | D3 |
| FLORIN PERKINS | SAC | 40 | A2 |
| FLOURNOY AV | TEH | 24 | D2 |
| FLOWER ST | LA | 185 | E4 |
| FLOWER ST | SA | 196 | A3 |
| FLOWERS LN | SHA | 18 | C3 |
| FLOWING WELLS | IMP | 109 | B3 |
| FLOYD AV | FRCO | 57 | B3 |
| FLOYD AV | STA | 47 | D2 |
| FLYNN RD | INY | 51 | D4 |
| FLYNN CREEK RD | MEN | 30 | D2 |
| FOAM ST | MONT | 167 | D2 |
| FOAM ST | MON | 53 | E2 |
| FOGARTY RD | STA | 47 | E1 |
| FOGARTY RD | STA | 48 | A1 |
| FOGG RD | SAC | 39 | E2 |
| FOLETTA RD | MON | 54 | D5 |
| FOLEY AV | KER | 79 | D3 |
| FOLSOM AV | FRCO | 56 | B2 |
| FOLSOM BLVD | SAC | 34 | B5 |
| FOLSOM BLVD | SAC | 39 | E1 |
| FOLSOM BLVD | SAC | 40 | A1 |
| FOLSOM BLVD | SCTO | 137 | E4 |
| FONSECA RD | COL | 24 | E5 |
| FONTANA AV | SBD | 99 | A2 |
| FOOLISH PLSR RD | RCO | 107 | A1 |
| FOOTE RD | SIE | 26 | C5 |
| FOOTHILL AV | O | 159 | D1 |
| FOOTHILL BLVD | ALA | 146 | D1 |
| FOOTHILL BLVD | BUT | 25 | D4 |
| FOOTHILL BLVD | CLA | 203 | C1 |
| FOOTHILL BLVD | CPTO | 149 | A5 |
| FOOTHILL BLVD | H | 146 | E2 |
| FOOTHILL BLVD | LACO | 89 | C5 |
| FOOTHILL BLVD | LACO | 89 | E5 |
| FOOTHILL BLVD | LACO | 98 | B1 |
| FOOTHILL BLVD | LACO | Q | B1 |
| FOOTHILL BLVD | LACO | U | A1 |
| FOOTHILL BLVD | NAP | 133 | B4 |

| STREET | CO. | PAGE & GRID | |
|---|---|---|---|
| FOOTHILL BLVD | O | 158 | B3 |
| FOOTHILL BLVD | ORA | T | E3 |
| FOOTHILL BLVD | ROC | 204 | B1 |
| FOOTHILL BLVD | SBD | 99 | A1 |
| FOOTHILL BLVD | SD | 212 | B1 |
| FOOTHILL BLVD | SDCO | V | A2 |
| FOOTHILL BLVD | SDCO | 106 | C5 |
| FOOTHILL BLVD | SNLO | 172 | A2 |
| FOOTHILL BLVD | UPL | 203 | C1 |
| FOOTHILL BLVD | UPL | 204 | B1 |
| FOOTHILL DR | SBD | 102 | C1 |
| FOOTHILL DR | SIS | 4 | A4 |
| FOOTHILL DR | SOL | 39 | A2 |
| FOOTHILL EXPWY | PA | 147 | C5 |
| FOOTHILL EXPWY | SCL | N | E3 |
| FOOTHILL EXPWY | SCL | 45 | E4 |
| FOOTHILL EXPWY | SCCO | 149 | A4 |
| FOOTHILL FRWY | LACO | 97 | D1 |
| FOOTHILL FRWY | LACO | 98 | A1 |
| FOOTHILL FRWY | LACO | R | B2 |
| FOOTHILL FRWY | LACO | R | C3 |
| FOOTHILL FRWY | PAS | 190 | B2 |
| FOOTHILL RD | ALA | P | B1 |
| FOOTHILL RD | ALA | 46 | B2 |
| FOOTHILL RD | DGL | 36 | B3 |
| FOOTHILL RD | INY | 59 | E3 |
| FOOTHILL RD | MNO | 51 | C1 |
| FOOTHILL RD | MON | 64 | E1 |
| FOOTHILL RD | MON | 65 | A1 |
| FOOTHILL RD | SBD | 91 | D4 |
| FOOTHILL RD | SBD | 92 | A4 |
| FOOTHILL RD | SLO | 76 | A3 |
| FOOTHILL RD | STB | 174 | B1 |
| FOOTHILL RD | SB | 87 | D1 |
| FOOTHILL RD | SB | 174 | B1 |
| FOOTHILL RD | SCL | P | E5 |
| FOOTHILL RD | SCL | 54 | D1 |
| FOOTHILL RD | TEH | 18 | E5 |
| FOOTHILL RD | VEN | 88 | B4 |
| FOOTHILL RD | VEN | 88 | B5 |
| FOPPIANO LN | SJCO | 40 | B5 |
| FORBES N | PLA | 34 | B3 |
| FORBES S | PLA | 34 | A3 |
| FORBES AV | SR | 139 | C3 |
| FORBES RANCH RD | RCO | 100 | C4 |
| FORBESTOWN RD | BUT | 25 | E4 |
| FORBESTOWN RD | BUT | 26 | A4 |
| FRBSTOWN RES RD | BUT | 26 | A4 |
| FORD RD | NB | 200 | B3 |
| FORD ST | RCO | 100 | E3 |
| FORD ST | SBD | 99 | C2 |
| FORDYCE LAKE RD | NEV | 27 | B5 |
| FOREMAN CIR RD | BUT | 25 | D4 |
| FOREST | MPA | 49 | D3 |
| FOREST AV | MONT | 53 | D2 |
| FOREST AV | PAC | 167 | C5 |
| FOREST BLVD | KER | 80 | B4 |
| FOREST CIR | BUT | 25 | C2 |
| FOREST DR | BUT | 25 | C2 |
| FOREST RD | CAR | 168 | C4 |
| FOREST TR | ML | 164 | B1 |
| FOREST HOME BL | SBD | 99 | E2 |
| FORST HM CRBNDL | AMA | 40 | D2 |
| FOREST HOUSE | SIS | 3 | E4 |
| FOREST LAKE | SJCO | 40 | A3 |
| FOREST LAWN DR | LA | 179 | E5 |
| FOREST LAWN DR | LA | 181 | C1 |
| FOREST LAWN DR | LACO | Q | D3 |
| FOREST RANCH RD | BUT | 25 | C2 |
| FOREST RANCH WY | BUT | 25 | C2 |
| FORGAY RD | PLU | 20 | D5 |
| FORREST ST | BKD | 166 | C4 |
| FORRESTER RD | IMP | 109 | A4 |
| FORSYTHE RD | YUB | 26 | A5 |
| FT BRAGG SHERWD | MEN | 22 | C5 |
| FT CADY RD | SBD | 92 | C1 |
| FORT INDEPNDNCE | INY | 59 | E3 |
| FORTNA RD | SUT | 33 | C2 |
| FORT ROMIE RD | MON | 64 | E1 |
| FORT ROMIE RD | MON | 65 | A1 |
| FORT ROSS RD | SON | 37 | B1 |
| FORT SAGE RD | LAS | 21 | E5 |
| FORT SEWARD RD | HUM | 16 | C5 |
| FORT STOCKTN DR | SD | 213 | B5 |
| FORT STOCKTN DR | SDCO | V | B3 |
| FORT STOCKTN DR | SDCO | 111 | C1 |
| FORT TEJON RD | LACO | 90 | B3 |
| FT TEJON CHSBRO | LACO | 90 | B3 |
| FORTUNA BLVD | HUM | 15 | E2 |
| FORTY MILE RD | YUB | 33 | D3 |
| FORTYNINE LN | MOD | 7 | D5 |
| FORTYNINE PALMS | SBD | 101 | B1 |
| FORWARD RD | TEH | 19 | B3 |
| FORWARDS MILL | SHA | 19 | C3 |
| FOSS RD | JKSN | 3 | D1 |
| FOSS HILL | SON | 32 | A5 |
| FOSSIL BED RD | SBD | 81 | C5 |
| FOSTER | MON | 54 | C4 |
| FOSTER RD | LACO | R | B5 |
| FOSTER RD | LACO | S | E1 |
| FOSTER RD | LACO | T | A1 |
| FOSTER RD | NAP | 133 | B5 |
| FOSTER RD | SHA | 18 | B3 |
| FOSTER RD | SIS | 4 | C3 |
| FOSTER CITY BL | FCTY | 145 | D2 |
| FOSTER CITY BL | SMCO | N | D1 |
| FOSTER CITY BL | SMCO | 45 | D3 |
| FOSTER MTN RD | MEN | 23 | B5 |
| FOULDS RD | IMP | 108 | E3 |
| FOULKE LN | SIS | 4 | B5 |
| FOUNTAIN AV | LA | 182 | A4 |
| FOUNTN HOUSE RD | YUB | 26 | B5 |
| FOUR CORNERS RD | LAS | 14 | B3 |
| FOUR MILE RD | COL | 24 | E5 |
| FOUR MILE RD | COL | 32 | E1 |
| FOUR MIL RDG RD | BUT | 25 | E3 |
| FOURTEENTH ST | EUR | 121 | B2 |

| STREET | CO. | PAGE & GRID | |
|---|---|---|---|
| FOURTH AV | SUT | 33 | D3 |
| FOURTH ST | C | 124 | B5 |
| FOUSSAT RD | SDCO | 106 | B3 |
| FOUTS SPRGS RD | COL | 24 | A5 |
| FOWLER AV | FRCO | 57 | D2 |
| FOWLER AV | FRCO | 57 | D5 |
| FOWLER RD | PLA | 34 | B3 |
| FOWLER PBLC CMP | SIS | 13 | A2 |
| FOX RD | LAS | 21 | B4 |
| FOX RD | MCO | 48 | B4 |
| FOX RD | STA | 47 | D2 |
| FOX RD | SOL | 39 | B2 |
| FOXEN CANYON RD | SB | 86 | D1 |
| FOXWORTHY AV | SCL | P | B4 |
| FOXWORTHY AV | SCL | 46 | B5 |
| FRAGUERO RD | TUO | 41 | C5 |
| FRANCESCHI RD | KER | 79 | D3 |
| FRANCISCO ST | SF | 143 | A3 |
| FRANCISQUITO AV | LACO | R | E4 |
| FRANCISQUITO CYN | LACO | 89 | C3 |
| FRANCIS SPGS RD | SBD | 83 | C2 |
| FRANCO WSTRN RD | KER | 77 | D3 |
| FRANK AV | KER | 70 | A5 |
| FRANK COX RD | STA | 47 | B3 |
| FRANKENHEIMR RD | STA | 47 | E1 |
| FRANKLIN AV | LA | 181 | E4 |
| FRANKLIN AV | LA | 182 | A4 |
| FRANKLIN AV | LACO | Q | E3 |
| FRANKLIN AV | YUBA | 125 | C4 |
| FRANKLIN BLVD | SAC | 39 | E2 |
| FRANKLIN BLVD | SCTO | 137 | D5 |
| FRANKLIN RD | MCO | 48 | B4 |
| FRANKLIN RD | SBD | 84 | C4 |
| FRANKLIN RD | SUT | 33 | B2 |
| FRANKLIN RD | SUT | 125 | A4 |
| FRANKLIN ST | MDO | 162 | A4 |
| FRANKLIN ST | MONT | 167 | D3 |
| FRANKLIN ST | MON | 53 | E3 |
| FRANKLIN ST | SF | 143 | A4 |
| FRANKLIN CYN RD | M | 154 | A3 |
| FRANKLIN LEVEE | SUT | 33 | B2 |
| FRANK SNATRA DR | RCO | 100 | D4 |
| FRANKWOOD AV | FRCO | 58 | A4 |
| FRANZ VALLEY RD | SON | 38 | A1 |
| FRANZ VLY SCHL | SON | 38 | A1 |
| FRASER RD | KER | 78 | C3 |
| FRATES RD | SON | L | A1 |
| FRATES RD | SON | 38 | A3 |
| FRAZIER LN | MEN | 23 | B2 |
| FRAZIER RD | FRCO | 57 | E1 |
| FRAZIER RD | SJCO | 40 | C4 |
| FRAZIER MTN RD | VEN | 88 | C2 |
| FRAZR MTN PK RD | KER | 88 | C2 |
| FRAZIER PK RD | SCL | 54 | D2 |
| FRAZINE RD | STA | 47 | D2 |
| FREDERICK AV | SJCO | 47 | B2 |
| FREDERICK ST | RCO | 99 | C3 |
| FREDERICKSBURG | ALP | 36 | C4 |
| FREDERICKSON LN | CC | M | C3 |
| FREDERICKSON RD | LAS | 8 | D5 |
| FRED HAIGHT DR | DN | 1 | E3 |
| FREDRICKS RD | IMP | 109 | A4 |
| FREEBORN RD | KER | 78 | A3 |
| FREEDOM BLVD | SCR | 54 | B2 |
| FREEMAN FLAT RD | MON | 65 | C2 |
| FREEMN SCH HSE | TEH | 24 | C2 |
| FREEMONT BLVD | ALA | P | B2 |
| FREEPORT BLVD | SCTO | 137 | C5 |
| FREITAS PKWY | MAR | 38 | B5 |
| FREITAS RD | STA | 47 | C4 |
| FREMONT AV | KER | 79 | E2 |
| FREMONT AV | KIN | 67 | B1 |
| FREMONT AV | LSAL | 149 | B2 |
| FREMONT AV | LACO | R | B4 |
| FREMONT AV | SCL | P | A3 |
| FREMONT AV | SCL | 45 | E4 |
| FREMONT AV | SVL | 149 | B2 |
| FREMONT BLVD | ALA | 46 | A3 |
| FREMONT DR | SON | L | B1 |
| FREMONT RD | SBD | 92 | C1 |
| FREMONT RD | SJCO | 40 | B5 |
| FREMONT ST | CLK | 74 | D2 |
| FREMONT ST | LV | 209 | D1 |
| FREMONT ST | SBD | 99 | D2 |
| FREMONT ST | SF | 143 | D4 |
| FREMONT ST | S | 160 | A4 |
| FREMONT PEAK RD | SBD | 81 | A4 |
| FRENCH AV | BUT | 33 | C1 |
| FRENCH RD | HUM | 16 | B5 |
| FRENCH&SUGAR CK | SIS | 11 | D2 |
| FRENCH BAR RD | AMA | 40 | E3 |
| FRENCH CAMP RD | HUM | 10 | C3 |
| FRENCH CAMP RD | SJCO | 40 | B5 |
| FRENCH CAMP RD | SJCO | 47 | B1 |
| FRENCH CREEK RD | BUT | 25 | E3 |
| FRENCH CREEK RD | ED | 40 | D1 |
| FRENCH CREEK RD | SIS | 11 | D2 |
| FRENCH FLAT RD | TUO | 41 | B5 |
| FRENCH GULCH RD | CAL | 41 | B4 |
| FRENCH GULCH RD | SHA | 18 | A1 |
| FRENCH HILL RD | DN | 2 | A3 |
| FRENCHMAN LK RD | PLU | 27 | D2 |
| FRENCHTOWN RD | YUB | 26 | A5 |
| FRENZEN RD | COL | 32 | E3 |
| FRESH WATER RD | COL | 32 | C2 |
| FRESHWTR KNEELD | HUM | 15 | E1 |
| FRESHWTR LGN RD | HUM | 9 | E3 |
| FRESHWATER POOL | HUM | 16 | A1 |
| FRESNO AV | KER | 78 | B2 |
| FRESNO AV | KER | 78 | C2 |
| FRESNO AV | SJCO | 40 | A5 |
| FRESNO RD | MCO | 48 | D5 |
| FRESNO ST | FRE | 165 | E2 |
| FRESNO ST | FRCO | 57 | C3 |
| FRESNO-COALINGA | FRCO | 66 | E1 |
| FRESNO FLAT RD | MAD | 49 | D4 |
| FRESZ RD | RCO | 106 | E1 |

| STREET | CO. | PAGE & GRID | |
|---|---|---|---|
| FREWERT RD | SJCO | 47 | A1 |
| FREY AV | KER | 77 | E2 |
| FREY AV | KER | 78 | A2 |
| FREY RANCH RD | BUT | 26 | B3 |
| FRIANT RD | FRCO | 57 | C2 |
| FRIANT RD | MAD | 57 | D2 |
| FRIARS RD | SD | 213 | A4 |
| FRIARS RD | SD | 214 | D2 |
| FRIARS RD | SDCO | V | B3 |
| FRIARS RD | SDCO | 111 | D1 |
| FRIARS RD | SDCO | 214 | B3 |
| FRICOT CITY RD | CAL | 41 | B4 |
| FRIDAY RIDGE RD | HUM | 10 | C5 |
| FRIEDRICH RD | TRI | 10 | E5 |
| FRIEDRICH RD | TRI | 16 | E1 |
| FRIEL RD | CLO | 33 | A3 |
| FRINK RD | IMP | 109 | D3 |
| FRISBY RD | SHA | 19 | A1 |
| FRITZ DR | TUL | 68 | D1 |
| FRONT ST | DN | 1 | D4 |
| FRONT ST | LA | 191 | A3 |
| FRONT ST | SAL | 171 | C4 |
| FRONT ST | SF | 143 | D3 |
| FRONT ST | SC | 169 | D3 |
| FRONT ST | SOL | 39 | C4 |
| FRONTAGE RD | CAL | 40 | E3 |
| FRONTAGE RD | CAL | 41 | A3 |
| FRONTIER RD | SBD | 91 | C2 |
| FRUCHTENICHT RD | COL | 33 | B3 |
| FRUDDEN RD | MON | 65 | D4 |
| FRUIT AV | FRE | 165 | B2 |
| FRUIT AV | FRCO | 57 | C4 |
| FRUIT AV | FRCO | 57 | C5 |
| FRUIT AV | STA | 47 | B3 |
| FRUIT ST | SA | 196 | D3 |
| FRUITLAND AV | MCO | 48 | A4 |
| FRUITLAND RD | YUB | 33 | D1 |
| FRUITRIDGE RD | SAC | 39 | E1 |
| FRUITRIDGE RD | SAC | 40 | A1 |
| FRUITVALE AV | ALA | L | D4 |
| FRUITVALE AV | ALA | 45 | D1 |
| FRUITVALE AV | KER | 78 | D3 |
| FRUITVALE AV | O | 158 | E4 |
| FRUITVALE AV | O | 159 | B1 |
| FRUITVALE AV | SCL | P | A4 |
| FRUITVALE RD | BUT | 25 | B4 |
| FRUITVALE RD | PLA | 34 | B3 |
| FRY RD | SOL | 39 | B3 |
| FRYMIRE RD | STA | 48 | A1 |
| FUENTE ST | ORA | T | C1 |
| FUERTE DR | SDCO | V | E3 |
| FUERTE DR | SDCO | 111 | E1 |
| FUGLER RD | SB | 86 | C1 |
| FULKERTH RD | STA | 47 | C3 |
| FULLEN RD | CAL | 41 | C3 |
| FULLER LN | AMA | 40 | C3 |
| FULLER RD | INY | 59 | E1 |
| FULLERTON RD | LACO | 98 | B2 |
| FULLERTON RD | LACO | R | E5 |
| FULMOR RD | HUM | 15 | D2 |
| FULMOR TOPPEN | HUM | 15 | D2 |
| FULTON AV | SAC | 40 | A1 |
| FULTON LN | NAPA | 29 | C2 |
| FULTON RD | SON | 37 | E2 |
| FULTON ST | B | 156 | A3 |
| FULTON ST | SF | 141 | D4 |
| FULTON ST | SF | 142 | A3 |
| FULTON ST | SF | 143 | A5 |
| FULTON ST | SFCO | L | B5 |
| FULTON ST | SFCO | 45 | B1 |
| FULTON ST | S | 160 | B3 |
| FULTON ST N | FRE | 165 | C3 |
| FULWEILER AV | AUB | 126 | B3 |
| FURLONG AV | SCL | 54 | D2 |
| FURNACE CK RD | SBD | 91 | E4 |
| FURNC CK WSH RD | INY | 72 | C2 |
| FURNC CK WSH RD | INY | 73 | A4 |
| FUZZY LN | SHA | 18 | C3 |
| G | | | |
| G ST | DVS | 136 | D3 |
| G ST | FRE | 165 | C4 |
| G ST | HUM | 9 | E5 |
| G ST | HUM | 10 | A5 |
| G ST | MER | 170 | D4 |
| G ST | MCO | 48 | C4 |
| G ST | MCO | 48 | C4 |
| G ST | SCTO | 137 | C2 |
| GABY AV | COL | 32 | E3 |
| GADDINI | SOL | 39 | A1 |
| GAFFERY RD | STA | 47 | A3 |
| GAFFEY ST | LA | 191 | A3 |
| GAFFEY ST | LACO | S | C3 |
| GAFFNEY RD | YOL | 39 | D2 |
| GAGE AV | LACO | Q | E5 |
| GAGE RD | BUT | 25 | C4 |
| GAINES LN | SHA | 18 | D3 |
| GALE AV | FRCO | 66 | C2 |
| GALE RD | SBD | 91 | E2 |
| GALENA ST | RCO | 99 | A2 |
| GALENA CYN RD | INY | 72 | A3 |
| GALEPPI RD | LAS | 21 | C4 |
| GALLAGHER AV | TEH | 24 | D2 |
| GALLAGHER RD | SUT | 33 | E3 |
| GALLATIN RD | LAS | 20 | E2 |
| GALLATIN RD | TEH | 18 | C5 |
| GALLAWAY RD | SIE | 26 | D4 |
| GALLINAS AV | SR | 139 | B1 |
| GALLOPADE TR | SBD | 80 | E1 |
| GALVEZ AV | FRCO | 56 | B2 |
| GAMBLE RD | MCO | 48 | B3 |
| GAMMEL RD | SBD | 101 | C1 |
| GANESHA BLVD | LACO | 98 | C2 |
| GANESHA BLVD | LACO | U | B2 |
| GANGER RD | SIS | 5 | D2 |
| GANN RD | CAL | 40 | E4 |
| GAP FOLSOM RD | CAL | 41 | C2 |
| GARAPATOS RD | MON | 64 | B1 |

| STREET | CO. | PAGE & GRID | |
|---|---|---|---|
| GARATE RD | LAS | 8 | C5 |
| GARBAGE DUMP RD | LAS | 14 | B3 |
| GARBAGE PIT RD | MNO | 43 | B3 |
| GARBAGE PIT RD | MNO | 50 | D1 |
| GARBONI RD | RCO | 99 | D4 |
| GARCES HWY | KER | 67 | E5 |
| GARCES HWY | KER | 68 | C5 |
| GARCES HWY | KER | 69 | A5 |
| GARCIA RIVER RD | MEN | 30 | C3 |
| GARDEN HWY | SAC | 39 | D1 |
| GARDEN HWY | SUT | 33 | D2 |
| GARDEN HWY | SUT | 125 | D5 |
| GARDEN HWY | YUBA | 125 | E4 |
| GARDEN RD | SDCO | 106 | E4 |
| GARDEN ST | STB | 174 | B3 |
| GARDENA BLVD | LACO | S | C1 |
| GARDEN BAR | PLA | 34 | B3 |
| GARDEN BAR RD | NEV | 34 | B3 |
| GARDENDALE ST | LACO | R | B5 |
| GARDENDALE ST | LACO | S | E1 |
| GARDEN GROVE BL | GGR | 195 | A2 |
| GARDEN GROVE BL | OR | 195 | D2 |
| GARDEN GROVE BL | ORA | 98 | B4 |
| GARDEN GROVE BL | ORA | T | C2 |
| GARDEN GROVE FY | GGR | 195 | B2 |
| GARDEN GROVE FY | OR | 195 | B2 |
| GARDEN GROVE FY | OR | 196 | C1 |
| GARDEN GROVE FY | ORA | 98 | B4 |
| GARDEN GROVE FY | ORA | T | C2 |
| GARDEN VLY RD | ED | 34 | D4 |
| GARDEN VLY RD | YUB | 26 | B5 |
| GARDINER FRY RD | TEH | 24 | E2 |
| GARDNER AV | MCO | 48 | C4 |
| GARDNER LN | CAL | 41 | B4 |
| GARDNER ST | LA | 184 | B1 |
| GARDNER ST | VAL | 134 | B3 |
| GARDNER FLD RD | KER | 78 | A4 |
| GAREY AV | LACO | 98 | D2 |
| GAREY AV | LACO | U | C3 |
| GAREY AV | SB | 86 | C1 |
| GARFIELD AV | FRCO | 57 | B3 |
| GARFIELD AV | FRCO | 57 | B5 |
| GARFIELD AV | LACO | 98 | A2 |
| GARFIELD AV | LACO | R | B5 |
| GARFIELD AV | LACO | S | D1 |
| GARFIELD AV | ORA | 98 | B4 |
| GARFIELD AV | ORA | T | B3 |
| GARFIELD AV | SAC | 34 | A5 |
| GARFIELD ST | RCO | 101 | C5 |
| GARIN RD | MON | 54 | C2 |
| GARLAND RD | BUT | 25 | C2 |
| GARLOCK RD | KER | 80 | C2 |
| GARMIRE RD | SUT | 33 | B2 |
| GARNER LN | BUT | 25 | B2 |
| GARNER PL | CAL | 40 | D4 |
| GARNER RD | STA | 47 | D2 |
| GARNET AV | SD | 212 | A1 |
| GARNET AV | SDCO | V | A2 |
| GARNET AV | SDCO | 106 | C5 |
| GARNET ST | SBD | 99 | D2 |
| GARNETT LN | SOL | 39 | B2 |
| GARNIER RD | LAS | 21 | D5 |
| GARRARD | CC | 38 | C5 |
| GARRET | PLA | 34 | D2 |
| GARRETT DR | RCO | 100 | A5 |
| GARRISON AV | STA | 47 | C2 |
| GARST RD | IMP | 109 | A3 |
| GARST RD | STA | 47 | D2 |
| GARVEY AV | LACO | 98 | A2 |
| GARVEY AV | LACO | R | C4 |
| GARVEY RD | IMP | 108 | E4 |
| GARWOOD RD | SUT | 33 | D4 |
| GARZOLI AV | KER | 78 | B1 |
| GAS COMPANY RD | KER | 78 | A4 |
| GASKELL RD | KER | 78 | B2 |
| GASKELL RD | KER | 89 | D1 |
| GAS LINE RD | RCO | 102 | B5 |
| GASPERS RD | SHA | 18 | D2 |
| GAS POINT RD | SHA | 18 | B3 |
| GASQUET FLAT RD | DN | 2 | A3 |
| GASTENBIDE RD | MCO | 55 | C2 |
| GASTON RD | NEV | 26 | E5 |
| GATES RD | STA | 47 | B2 |
| GATES RD | TRI | 16 | D1 |
| GATES CANYON RD | SOL | 38 | E2 |
| GATES CANYON RD | SOL | 39 | A2 |
| GATEWAY | CC | 39 | D5 |
| GATEWAY BLVD | LA | 180 | D5 |
| GATEWAY BLVD | KER | 80 | E1 |
| GATEWAY RD | CC | M | D3 |
| GATOS TR | SBD | 100 | E1 |
| GAVILAN DR | RCO | 99 | B3 |
| GAVIOTA | AVLN | 105 | A4 |
| GAVIOTA BCH RD | SB | 86 | D4 |
| GAVIOTA STA RD | SB | 86 | D4 |
| GAVILAN RD | SDCO | 106 | C1 |
| GAWNE CARTER RD | SJCO | 40 | C5 |
| GAWNE CARTER RD | SJCO | 47 | C1 |
| GAZELLE CALLAHN | SIS | 4 | B5 |
| GAZELLE CALLAHN | SIS | 11 | E2 |
| GAZELLE CALLAHN | SIS | 12 | A1 |
| GAZELLE MTN LKT | SIS | 12 | A1 |
| GAZOS CREEK RD | SMCO | N | C4 |
| GAZOS CREEK RD | SMCO | 45 | C5 |
| G-BAR-T RCH RD | MNO | 44 | C5 |
| G-BAR-T RCH RD | MNO | 51 | C1 |
| GEARY BLVD | SF | 141 | A3 |
| GEARY BLVD | SF | 142 | A3 |
| GEARY BLVD | SFCO | L | B4 |
| GEARY BLVD | SFCO | 45 | B1 |
| GEARY RD | CC | L | E3 |
| GEARY RD | CC | M | A3 |
| GEARY RD | CC | 38 | E5 |
| GEARY ST | SF | 143 | A4 |
| GEER AV | MCO | 47 | D4 |
| GEER RD | STA | 47 | E3 |
| GELDING RD | CAL | 41 | B4 |

COPYRIGHT, © 1988 BY Thomas Bros Maps

STREETS

229
GENASCI RD
STREET INDEX
HALL RD




| STREET | CO. | PAGE & GRID |
|---|---|---|
| GENASCI RD | SIE | 27 C3 |
| GENE AUTRY TR | PMSP | 206 E2 |
| GENERL BEALE RD | KER | 79 A3 |
| GENRL PETROLEUM | KER | 79 E5 |
| GENRL PETROLEUM | KER | 80 A5 |
| GENRL PETROLEUM | KER | 89 C1 |
| GENERALS HWY | TUL | 58 E3 |
| GENERALS HWY | TUL | 59 A5 |
| GENESEE AV | SD | 211 E1 |
| GENESEE AV | SD | 213 C1 |
| GENESEE AV | SDCO | V B2 |
| GENESEE AV | SDCO | 106 C5 |
| GENESEE INDN CK | PLU | 26 E1 |
| GENESEO RD | SLO | 76 B1 |
| GENEVA AV | KIN | 67 C1 |
| GENOA LN | DGL | 36 B3 |
| GENTRY RD | IMP | 109 A3 |
| GENTRY RD | INY | 72 E4 |
| GENTRY RD | INY | 73 A4 |
| GEORGE RD | IMP | 112 A4 |
| GEORGE SMITH RD | FRCO | 58 B3 |
| GEORGETOWN | ED | 34 E3 |
| GEORGETOWN RD | ED | 34 E4 |
| GEORGETOWN RD | PLCV | 138 C1 |
| GEO WSHNTN BL S | SUT | 33 C3 |
| GEORGIA LN | STA | 47 E2 |
| GEORGIA RD | SBD | 81 C5 |
| GEORGIA ST | VAL | 134 C4 |
| GEORGIA ST | SOL | L D2 |
| GEORGIA SLID RD | ED | 34 D3 |
| GEPHART RD | KER | 80 D5 |
| GERARD AV | MCO | 48 C4 |
| GERBER RD | SAC | 40 A2 |
| GERBER RD | TEH | 18 D5 |
| GERKIN RD | INY | 51 D4 |
| GERRIE LN | RCO | 107 C1 |
| GETTYSBURG AV | FRCO | 56 C3 |
| GETTYSBURG AV | FRCO | 57 A3 |
| GEYSERS RD | SON | 31 D4 |
| GEYSRS RESRT RD | SON | 31 D4 |
| GHOST TOWN RD | SBD | 92 A1 |
| GIANT RD | CC | L C3 |
| GIANT ROCK RD | SBD | 92 E5 |
| GIANT ROCK RD | SBD | 93 A5 |
| GIBRALTAR RD | SB | 87 C3 |
| GIBSON LN | MEN | 23 B5 |
| GIBSON RD | COL | 32 D2 |
| GIBSON RD | YOL | 33 B5 |
| GIBSON CYN RD | SOL | 39 A2 |
| GIDDINGS AV | TUL | 68 B1 |
| GIELOW LN | MEN | 31 B2 |
| GIFFORD RD | SUT | 33 C4 |
| GILBERT RD | STA | 47 D1 |
| GILLAM RD | CAL | 40 E3 |
| GILLESPIE RD | IMP | 109 A2 |
| GILLESPIE ST | STB | 174 A4 |
| GILLETT RD | IMP | 109 B5 |
| GILLETT RD | MON | 65 C4 |
| GILLETTE RD | KER | 79 D3 |
| GILLETTE RD | MCO | 48 D5 |
| GILLILAND RD | LAS | 8 C5 |
| GILLIS CYN RD | SLO | 76 D1 |
| GILLMAN AV | KER | 89 D1 |
| GILL RANCH RD | PLU | 26 E2 |
| GILL STA COSO | INY | 70 C3 |
| GILMAN DR | SD | 211 C2 |
| GILMAN DR | SDCO | V A2 |
| GILMAN DR | SDCO | 106 C5 |
| GILMAN RD | SCL | 54 D2 |
| GILMAN RD | SHA | 12 D4 |
| GILMAN SPGS RD | RCO | 99 D3 |
| GILMORE | SJCO | 40 C4 |
| GILMOR RANCH RD | TEH | 18 D5 |
| GILROY HT SP RD | SCL | 54 D1 |
| GIRARD LO RD | SHA | 12 C3 |
| GIRARD LOOKOUT | SHA | 12 C3 |
| GIRARD RIDGE RD | SHA | 12 C4 |
| GIRAUDO RD | KER | 79 B4 |
| GIRD RD | SDCO | 106 C2 |
| GIRDNER RD | SUT | 33 B2 |
| GIRVAN RD | SHA | 18 C2 |
| GISH ST | SJ | 152 A2 |
| GIVENS LUSTR RD | MCO | 48 C5 |
| GLACIER LODG RD | INY | 51 D5 |
| GLACIER PT RD | MPA | 63 C5 |
| GLADDING RD | PLA | 34 A3 |
| GLADSTONE ST | LACO | U A2 |
| GLASSCOCK RD | SJCO | 39 E4 |
| GLASSELL ST | OR | 194 C4 |
| GLASSELL ST | OR | 196 C1 |
| GLASSELL ST | ORA | 98 C3 |
| GLASSELL ST | ORA | T D2 |
| GLASS FLOW RD | MNO | 50 D1 |
| GLEASON RD | SBD | 92 D5 |
| GLEN AV | MER | 170 E4 |
| GLEN RD | SB | 87 B4 |
| GLEN ALPINE RD | ED | 35 E4 |
| GLEN ANNIE RD | SB | 87 B4 |
| GLEN ARBOR RD | SCR | N E5 |
| GLEN ARBOR RD | SCR | P A5 |
| GLEN ARBOR RD | SCR | 53 E1 |
| GLENBURN RD | SHA | 13 D4 |
| GLEN CANYON RD | SCR | 54 A1 |
| GLENCO AV | GLE | 24 D3 |
| GLENDALE AV | LACO | 97 E1 |
| GLENDALE AV | LACO | Q E3 |
| GLENDALE BLVD | LA | 182 E3 |
| GLENDALE BLVD | LA | 185 E2 |
| GLENDALE BLVD | LACO | Q E3 |
| GLENDALE DR | HUM | 10 A5 |
| GLENDALE FRWY | LACO | R A3 |
| GLENDORA AV | LACO | 98 B2 |
| GLENDORA AV | LACO | U A2 |
| GLENDORA MTN RD | LACO | 98 C1 |
| GLENDORA MTN RD | LACO | U A1 |
| GLENISON GAP RD | TRI | 17 C1 |
| GLENN AV | FRCO | 66 E3 |
| GLENN DR | GLE | 24 A4 |
| GLENN RD | TEH | 24 C2 |
| GLENN RD W | COL | 24 D5 |
| GLENN-ALLEN AV | KER | 68 D5 |
| GLENN COOLDG DR | SC | 169 A2 |
| GLENN COOLDG DR | SCR | 169 A2 |
| GLENNDENNING RD | SIS | 3 D5 |
| GLENOAKS BLVD | BUR | 179 C1 |
| GLENOAKS BLVD | LA | 179 C1 |
| GLENOAKS BLVD | LACO | 89 D5 |
| GLENOAKS BLVD | LACO | 97 D1 |
| GLENOAKS BLVD | LACO | Q C1 |
| GLENOAKS RD | RCO | 99 D5 |
| GLENSHIRE DR | NEV | 27 D5 |
| GLENWOOD DR | SCR | 54 A1 |
| GLENWOOD LN | FRCO | 58 B1 |
| GLOBE DR | TUL | 69 A3 |
| GLOBE MINE RD | SBD | 84 A5 |
| GLORIA RD | MON | 54 E5 |
| GLORIA RD | MON | 55 A5 |
| GLORIETTA BLVD | CC | L E4 |
| GLORIETTA BLVD | CC | 45 D1 |
| G-O RD | DN | 2 B4 |
| GOAT MTN RD | COL | 32 A1 |
| GOBBI ST | U | 123 C4 |
| GOBLE LN | HUM | 15 D2 |
| GODDELL RD | CAL | 40 E3 |
| GODFREY AV | SCL | P E5 |
| GODFREY RCH RD | SLO | 75 E1 |
| GODLEY | PLA | 34 B3 |
| GODWIN RD | SBD | 101 C1 |
| GOETZ RD | RCO | 99 C4 |
| GOFFS RD | SBD | 94 D2 |
| GOFFS RD | SBD | 95 A1 |
| GOGNA | SJCO | 40 B5 |
| GOLD CROWN RD | RCO | 101 E2 |
| GOLD CROWN RD | SBD | 101 E1 |
| GOLDEN AV | SBD | 99 C1 |
| GOLDEN RD | SIS | 5 D2 |
| GOLDEN ST | SBD | 100 E1 |
| GOLDEN CYN RD | INY | 72 A1 |
| GOLDEN CTR FRWY | GV | 127 E2 |
| GOLDEN CTR FRWY | NEV | 127 E2 |
| GOLDEN EAGLE AV | PLU | 26 C1 |
| GOLDEN GATE AV | SF | 142 A3 |
| GOLDEN GATE AV | SF | 143 A5 |
| GOLDEN GATE DR | HUM | 16 B3 |
| GOLDEN GATE RD | MNO | 42 D1 |
| GOLDN LK FOREST | PLU | 26 E3 |
| GOLDENROD AV | FRCO | 57 A4 |
| GOLDEN SPGS DR | LACO | U B3 |
| GOLDEN STATE AV | BKD | 166 C2 |
| GOLDEN STATE BL | FRCO | 57 E5 |
| GOLDEN STATE BL | STA | 47 D3 |
| GOLDEN STATE DR | MAD | 57 A2 |
| GOLDEN STATE FY | BUR | 179 C1 |
| GOLDEN STATE FY | LA | 179 C1 |
| GOLDEN STATE FY | LA | 182 D1 |
| GOLDEN STATE FY | LA | 186 D3 |
| GOLDEN STATE FY | LACO | 89 B4 |
| GOLDEN STATE FY | LACO | 97 D1 |
| GOLDEN STATE FY | LACO | Q B1 |
| GOLDN TROUT CRS | BUT | 26 B4 |
| GOLDENWEST AV | ORA | 98 B4 |
| GOLDEN WEST ST | ORA | T B3 |
| GOLD HILL | ED | 34 D4 |
| GOLDHILL RD | PLA | 34 B3 |
| GOLD HILL RD | SOL | 38 D4 |
| GOLD LAKE RD | PLU | 27 A3 |
| GOLD LAKE RD | SIE | 27 A3 |
| GOLD PARK | SBD | 101 C2 |
| GOLD RCK RCH RD | IMP | 110 B5 |
| GOLD RUN RD | LAS | 20 E4 |
| GOLDRUSH RD | RCO | 107 B1 |
| GOLDSBOROUGH GL | SHA | 17 D3 |
| GOLD STONE LN | SHA | 18 B2 |
| GOLDSTONE RD | SBD | 81 E3 |
| GOLD STRIKE RD | CAL | 41 A3 |
| GOLER RD | KER | 80 E2 |
| GOLF RD | MCO | 48 C4 |
| GOLF CLUB RD | CC | L E3 |
| GOLF CLUB RD | CC | M A3 |
| GOLF COURSE RD | HUM | 10 A5 |
| GOLF LINK RD | AVLN | 105 B5 |
| GOLF LINK RD | MCO | 47 E4 |
| GOLF LINKS RD | ALA | L E5 |
| GOLF LINKS RD | ALA | 45 E2 |
| GOMAN AV | TUL | 70 A3 |
| GOMER AV | KER | 78 A1 |
| GOMEZ RD | SHA | 13 D4 |
| GONDER RD | IMP | 109 B4 |
| GONSALVES RD | TEH | 18 C5 |
| GONZAGA RD | MCO | 55 C1 |
| GONZALES RD | MCO | 55 C2 |
| GONZALES RD | VEN | 88 B5 |
| GONZALES RD | VEN | 96 B1 |
| GONZALES RIV RD | MON | 54 E5 |
| GOODALE RD | INY | 59 E2 |
| GOODE HILL RD | LACO | 89 E3 |
| GOODENOUGH RD | VEN | 88 D4 |
| GOODFELLOW AV | FRCO | 57 E4 |
| GOODWATER AV | SHA | 18 C2 |
| GOODWIN DR | SBD | 91 A4 |
| GOODWIN RD | STA | 47 D2 |
| GOODWIN RD | VEN | 88 B4 |
| GOODYEAR RD | SOL | 38 E4 |
| GOODYEAR CK RD | SIE | 26 D4 |
| GOOLSBY RCH RD | MNO | 51 C1 |
| GOOSE CREEK RD | AMA | 40 C3 |
| GOOSE HAVEN RD | SOL | 39 B3 |
| GOOSE RANCH RD | TRI | 17 D1 |
| GOOSE VALLEY RD | SHA | 13 C4 |
| GOPHER CYN RD | SDCO | 106 C2 |
| GOPHR HLL LNDFL | PLU | 26 C1 |
| GORDEN RD | HUM | 16 C2 |
| GORDONS FRRY RD | SIS | 3 A3 |
| GORDON TRACT RD | CC | L C3 |
| GORDON VLY RD | NAPA | 38 E2 |
| GORDON VLY RD | SOL | L E1 |
| GORDON VLY RD | SOL | 38 E2 |
| GORGE RD | INY | 51 C3 |
| GORMAN RANCH | PLA | 34 E3 |
| GOSFORD RD | KER | 78 C3 |
| GOSS RD | SBD | 90 E4 |
| GOUDIE TRUCK TR | SDCO | 107 C5 |
| GOUGER NECK RD | MOD | 14 B3 |
| GOUGH ST | SF | 142 C2 |
| GOUGH ST | SF | 143 A4 |
| GOULD AV | LACO | S B1 |
| GOULD RD | COL | 25 A5 |
| GOULD RD | LPAZ | 104 A2 |
| GOVE RD | MCO | 48 B5 |
| GOVER RD | SHA | 18 D3 |
| GOVERNOR DR | SD | 211 D2 |
| GOVERNOR DR | SDCO | V B2 |
| GOVERNOR DR | SDCO | 106 C5 |
| GOVERNOR MN RD | LACO | 89 E4 |
| GOWER ST | LA | 181 E5 |
| GOWLING RD | IMP | 109 B5 |
| G P RD | KER | 77 C1 |
| GRACE RESORT RD | SHA | 19 B3 |
| GRACIE RD | NEV | 34 C1 |
| GRACIOSA RD | SB | 86 C2 |
| GRAEAGLE RD | SIE | 26 E3 |
| GRAEAGLE RD | SIE | 27 A3 |
| GRAEAGL JHNSVLL | PLU | 26 E2 |
| GRAESER RD | IMP | 112 C3 |
| GRAHAM | SIS | 12 C1 |
| GRAHAM AV | RCO | 99 B4 |
| GRAHAM RD | FRCO | 57 A4 |
| GRAHAM RD | IMP | 111 E3 |
| GRAHAM RD | SJCO | 40 B3 |
| GRAHAM RD | TEH | 19 B3 |
| GRAHAM HILL RD | SC | 169 D1 |
| GRAHAM HILL RD | SCR | 54 A1 |
| GRAHAM HILL RD | SCR | 169 D1 |
| GRAHAM PASS RD | RCO | 109 E1 |
| GRAINLAND RD | BUT | 25 A4 |
| GRAMERCY DR | SD | 214 B1 |
| GRAMERCY DR | SDCO | V C2 |
| GRAMERCY DR | SDCO | 111 D1 |
| GRANADA AV | SAL | 171 D2 |
| GRAND AV | ALA | L D4 |
| GRAND AV | BUT | 25 C4 |
| GRAND AV | ELS | 189 A3 |
| GRAND AV | LA | 185 D4 |
| GRAND AV | LACO | 97 E2 |
| GRAND AV | LACO | 98 C2 |
| GRAND AV | LACO | Q C5 |
| GRAND AV | LACO | U A2 |
| GRAND AV | LACO | S A1 |
| GRAND AV | O | 158 A2 |
| GRAND AV | ORA | 98 C4 |
| GRAND AV | ORA | T D3 |
| GRAND AV | PAS | 190 A5 |
| GRAND AV | P | 158 C1 |
| GRAND AV | RCO | 99 D4 |
| GRAND AV | RCO | 99 B4 |
| GRAND AV | RCO | 99 E4 |
| GRAND AV | SA | 196 D4 |
| GRAND AV | SA | 198 D1 |
| GRAND AV | SD | 212 B2 |
| GRAND AV | SDCO | V A3 |
| GRAND AV | SNLO | 172 C1 |
| GRAND AV | SLO | 76 B4 |
| GRAND AV | SMCO | L B5 |
| GRAND AV | SMCO | N B1 |
| GRAND AV | SMCO | 45 C2 |
| GRAND AV | SR | 139 D3 |
| GRAND AV | SB | 86 E3 |
| GRAND AV | TUL | 68 D3 |
| GRAND AV | VEN | 88 D4 |
| GRAND AV | YUB | 33 D2 |
| GRAND AV E | SSF | 144 C1 |
| GRAND AV W | O | 157 D2 |
| GRAND ST | MDO | 162 C3 |
| GRAND CIRCLE BL | RCO | U E5 |
| GRAND CIRCLE BL | RCO | 98 E3 |
| GRANDE AV | DVS | 136 C1 |
| GRANDE PUMICE | MOD | 8 A1 |
| GRANDE PUMICE | MOD | 14 E1 |
| GRAND ISLAND RD | SAC | M D1 |
| GRAND ISLAND RD | SAC | 39 D4 |
| GRANDON RD | RCO | 107 C1 |
| GRAND VIEW AV | LACO | R C2 |
| GRANDVILLE RD | MCO | 56 B2 |
| GRANGE RD | LAK | 32 B4 |
| GRANGE AV | PLA | 34 B4 |
| GRANGE RD | SOL | M A1 |
| GRANGE RD | SON | 38 A2 |
| GRANGE RD | TEH | 24 D2 |
| GRANGER CK RD | MOD | 8 D1 |
| GRANGEVILLE BL | KIN | 67 C1 |
| GRANGEVILLE BYPS | KIN | 67 B1 |
| GRANITE RD | KER | 78 D1 |
| GRANITE RD | KER | 79 A1 |
| GRANITE RD | MAD | 49 B5 |
| GRANITE RD | SBD | 92 A4 |
| GRANITE RD | TUO | 41 C5 |
| GRANITE CK RD | SCR | 54 A2 |
| GRNIT MTN VW RD | SDCO | 107 D3 |
| GRANITE PARK RD | TRI | 11 D5 |
| GRANITE SPGS RD | MPA | 48 D2 |
| GRANITE VIEW RD | INY | 60 A4 |
| GRANITEVILLE RD | NEV | 27 A4 |
| GRANIT WELLS RD | SBD | 81 A3 |
| GRANT AV | ALCO | 146 E4 |
| GRANT AV | COL | 32 E3 |
| GRANT AV | SF | 143 C2 |
| GRANT RD | LSAL | 149 A3 |
| GRANT RD | MCO | 56 C1 |
| GRANT RD | MVW | 148 A5 |
| GRANT RD | SCL | N E3 |
| GRANT RD | SCL | P A3 |
| GRANT RD | SCL | 45 E4 |
| GRANT ST | RCO | 101 C5 |
| GRANT ST | SM | 145 A2 |
| GRANT ST | SMA | 173 B1 |
| GRANT LAKE RD | MNO | 50 C1 |
| GRANTLAND AV | FRCO | 57 B2 |
| GRANTLAND AV | FRCO | 67 B1 |
| GRANT LINE RD | SAC | 40 A2 |
| GRANT LINE RD | SJCO | 47 A2 |
| GRAPE WY | BUT | 25 A3 |
| GRAPEFRUIT BLVD | RCO | 101 B4 |
| GRAPEVNE CYN RD | KER | 70 C5 |
| GRAPEVNE CYN RD | SBD | 91 D5 |
| GRAPEVINE GULCH | AMA | 40 D3 |
| GRAPP LN | RCO | 107 C1 |
| GRASS RD | SBD | 100 A1 |
| GRASSHOPPR RD S | LAS | 8 A5 |
| GRASSHOPPR RD S | LAS | 14 E5 |
| GRASSHOPPER FLT | TRI | 11 C5 |
| GRASS VALLEY RD | SBT | 54 E3 |
| GRASS VALLEY RD | SBT | 55 A3 |
| GRATON RD | SON | 37 D2 |
| GRATTON RD | STA | 47 E3 |
| GRAVEL PIT RD | RCO | 103 C5 |
| GRAVEN RES RD | MOD | 8 A2 |
| GRAVEN RES RD | MOD | 14 E2 |
| GRAVES RD | SJCO | 47 B1 |
| GRAVEYARD GULCH | SIS | 3 C5 |
| GRAY AV | YUBA | 125 C2 |
| GRAYSON | CC | 38 E5 |
| GRAYSON RD | STA | 47 B3 |
| GREAT CIR DR | KER | 80 B4 |
| GREAT HWY | SFCO | L B5 |
| GREAT HWY | SFCO | 45 B2 |
| GREAT NORTHERN | MOD | 5 E3 |
| GREAT SO OVRLND | SDCO | 108 A5 |
| GREELEY RD | KER | 78 C3 |
| GREELY HILL RD | MPA | 48 E1 |
| GREELY HILL RD | MPA | 49 A1 |
| GREEN RD | COL | 32 D3 |
| GREEN RD | IMP | 109 C4 |
| GREEN RD | SAC | 40 B2 |
| GREEN RD | SBD | 90 D4 |
| GREENBACK LN | SAC | 34 B5 |
| GREENBAY RD | COL | 32 E3 |
| GREENFIELD AV | VAL | 134 D3 |
| GREENFIELD DR | SDCO | 107 A5 |
| GREEN HILL RD | SON | 37 D2 |
| GREENHORN RD | NEV | 34 C1 |
| GREENHORN RD | SIS | 4 A4 |
| GREEN HOUSE RD | MCO | 47 E5 |
| GREEN HOUSE RD | MCO | 48 A5 |
| GREEN LAKES RD | MNO | 43 B4 |
| GREENLEAF AV | LACO | R D5 |
| GREENLEY RD | TUO | 41 C5 |
| GREENLEY RD | TUO | 163 D3 |
| GREEN MTN RD | MAD | 49 B5 |
| GREEN MTN LKOUT | MPA | 49 B5 |
| GREEN RIVER RD | RCO | U D5 |
| GREEN RIVER RD | RCO | 98 D3 |
| GREENSPOT RD | SBD | 99 C1 |
| GREENSPOT RD | SBD | 99 D2 |
| GREEN SPRING RD | TUO | 48 B1 |
| GREENSTONE | ED | 34 D5 |
| GREENTREE BLVD | SBD | 91 B4 |
| GREEN VALLEY RD | CC | M B4 |
| GREEN VALLEY RD | CC | 46 A1 |
| GREEN VALLEY RD | ED | 34 D5 |
| GREEN VALLEY RD | SCR | 54 B2 |
| GREEN VALLEY RD | SOL | L E1 |
| GREEN VALLEY RD | SOL | 38 D3 |
| GREEN VALLEY RD | SON | 37 D2 |
| GREENVILLE RD | ALA | 46 C2 |
| GREENVILLE ST | ORA | T C3 |
| GREENVILLE ST | SA | 197 D3 |
| GRNVLL RND VLY | PLU | 20 C5 |
| GREENVLL WLF CK | PLU | 20 C5 |
| GREENWALD AV | RCO | 99 B4 |
| GREENWOOD AV | FRCO | 57 E4 |
| GREENWOOD AV | LACO | R B4 |
| GREENWOOD RD | ED | 34 D4 |
| GREENWOOD RD | SJCO | 47 A2 |
| GREENWD HTS DR | HUM | 10 A5 |
| GREEN, W S RD | COL | 32 E2 |
| GREGORY AV | YOL | 39 D1 |
| GREGORY RD | CAL | 40 D4 |
| GREGORY CK RD | SHA | 12 C5 |
| GREILICH RD | AMA | 40 D2 |
| GRIDER RD | SIS | 3 B3 |
| GRIDER CREEK RD | SIS | 3 B4 |
| GRIDLEY RD | COL | 25 B5 |
| GRIDLEY-COLUSA | BUT | 25 B5 |
| GRIEVE RD | COL | 33 A3 |
| GRIFFIN AV | LA | 186 E2 |
| GRIFFIN RD | IMP | 109 B4 |
| GRIFFIN RD | STA | 47 C2 |
| GRIFFIN ST | SAL | 171 D3 |
| GRIFFITH AV | KER | 78 B2 |
| GRIFFITH AV | MCO | 47 E4 |
| GRIFFITH AV | YUB | 33 D2 |
| GRIFFITH PK BL | LA | 182 D3 |
| GRIFFITH PK DR | LA | 182 D3 |
| GRIFFITH PK DR | LACO | Q E3 |
| GRIMES AV | STA | 47 C2 |
| GRIMES RD | SJCO | 46 E1 |
| GRIMES-ARBKL RD | CLU | 33 A3 |
| GRIMES CYN RD | VEN | 88 D5 |
| GRIMSEL DR | KER | 79 C5 |
| GRINDSTONE RD | GLE | 23 E3 |
| GRINDSTONE RD | GLE | 24 A3 |
| GRIZZLY RD | PLU | 27 B2 |
| GRIZZLY RD | TUO | 48 D1 |
| GRIZZLY BLUF RD | HUM | 15 D2 |
| GRIZZLY GLCH RD | SHA | 18 A2 |
| GRIZLY HLL RD N | NEV | 26 C5 |
| GRIZZLY ISLD RD | SOL | M A1 |
| GRIZZLY ISLD RD | SOL | 38 E3 |
| GRIZZLY ISLD RD | SOL | 39 A3 |
| GRIZZLY ISLD RD | SOL | 135 D5 |
| GRIZZLY PEAK BL | B | 156 B1 |
| GRIZZLY PEAK BL | CC | 156 E2 |
| GRIZZLY PEAK BL | O | 156 B1 |
| GRZZLY PK LKOUT | SIS | 13 B3 |
| GROOMS | SJCO | 47 D1 |
| GROSJEAN | MPA | 49 B3 |
| GROTTO CANYON | INY | 61 D4 |
| GROUSE CREEK RD | SIS | 11 E2 |
| GROUSE RIDGE RD | NEV | 27 A5 |
| GROVE AV | GLE | 24 D3 |
| GROVE AV | MCO | 48 B4 |
| GROVE AV | ONT | 204 D3 |
| GROVE AV | ROC | 204 D3 |
| GROVE AV | SBD | U D3 |
| GROVE AV | SBD | 98 E2 |
| GROVE AV | U | 123 B3 |
| GROVE RD | SUT | 33 D3 |
| GROVE ST | ALA | L D4 |
| GROVE ST | ALA | M A5 |
| GROVE ST | SON | 132 A3 |
| GROVE WY | ALA | L E5 |
| GROVE WY | ALA | P A1 |
| GROVE WY | ALCO | 146 D2 |
| GROVE SHFTR FWY | O | 156 B5 |
| GROVE SHFTR FWY | O | 157 E3 |
| GROVE SHFTR FWY | O | 158 A2 |
| GRUB GULCH RD | MAD | 49 B5 |
| GRUBBS RD | BUT | 25 D5 |
| GSCHWEND RD | MEN | 30 D2 |
| GUADALUPE PKWY | SJ | 151 D1 |
| GUADALUPE PKWY | SJ | 152 A3 |
| GUADALUPE ST | SB | 86 A1 |
| GUALALA LOOKOUT | MEN | 30 D4 |
| GUALALA RDG RD | MEN | 30 D4 |
| GUERNEVILLE HWY | SON | 37 C1 |
| GUERNEVILLE RD | STR | 131 A2 |
| GUERNEVILLE RD | SON | 37 E2 |
| GUERRERO ST | SF | 142 C4 |
| GUERRERO ST | SFCO | L B5 |
| GUERRERO ST | SFCO | 45 C2 |
| GUIBAL AV | SCL | P E5 |
| GUIBERSON RD | VEN | 88 D4 |
| GUIDIVILLE RES | MEN | 31 B2 |
| GUINTOLI LN | HUM | 9 E5 |
| GUINTOLI LN | HUM | 10 A5 |
| GULCH RD | TRI | 17 B3 |
| GULLETT RD | IMP | 109 A5 |
| GULLEY VIEW DR | RCO | 107 C1 |
| GULLING ST N | PLU | 27 B2 |
| GULLING ST S | PLU | 27 B2 |
| GUM AV | GLE | 25 A4 |
| GUN CLUB RD | KER | 77 E2 |
| GUN CLUB RD | MCO | 47 D5 |
| GUNN AV | LACO | R C5 |
| GUNST RD | HUM | 9 E2 |
| GUNST RD | HUM | 10 A2 |
| GURR RD | MCO | 48 B5 |
| GUTHERIE RD | IMP | 108 E5 |
| GUTIERREZ ST | STB | 174 C4 |
| GUTTRY RD | LAS | 14 B3 |
| GUY KERR RCH RD | HUM | 10 C5 |
| GUYS GULCH RD | SIS | 4 A5 |
| GWIN MINE RD | CAL | 40 E3 |
| GYLE RD | TEH | 24 D1 |
| GYPSUM CYN RD | ORA | U C5 |
| GYPSUM CYN RD | ORA | 98 D3 |
| H | | |
| H ST | BKD | 166 C4 |
| H ST | BEN | 153 C5 |
| H ST | EUR | 121 D1 |
| H ST | FRE | 165 B3 |
| H ST | IMP | 109 A4 |
| H ST | KER | 78 D3 |
| H ST | MCO | 55 D1 |
| H ST | SCTO | 137 B2 |
| H ST | SAC | 39 E1 |
| H ST | SBD | 91 D1 |
| H ST | SDCO | V C4 |
| H ST | SDCO | 106 B4 |
| H ST | SDCO | 111 D2 |
| H ST | SR | 139 C3 |
| H ST | SB | 86 B3 |
| HAAS RD | COL | 32 D2 |
| HACIENDA AV | RCO | 100 D2 |
| HACIENDA AV | SM | 145 A3 |
| HACIENDA BLVD | LACO | 98 B2 |
| HACIENDA BLVD | LACO | R D5 |
| HACIENDA BLVD | KER | 80 B4 |
| HACIENDA RD | SHA | 18 D3 |
| HACKAMORE PL | MNO | 43 A3 |
| HACKETT RD | STA | 47 C3 |
| HACKLEMAN RD | IMP | 109 A5 |
| HACKMAN RD | SOL | 39 C2 |
| HACKNEY DR | MNO | 42 E1 |
| HACKSTAFF RD | LAS | 21 E5 |
| HAGATA RD | LAS | 21 A2 |
| HAGEMAN RD | KER | 78 C3 |
| HAGEMAN RD | SUT | 33 B2 |
| HAGEN RD | NAPA | 38 D3 |
| HAGEN RD | NAPA | 133 E2 |
| HAGEN FLAT RD | SHA | 13 A4 |
| HAHN RD | COL | 32 D3 |
| HAIGHT MTN RD | SIS | 5 A5 |
| HAILES RD | VEN | 96 C1 |
| HAILLE RD | TEH | 25 A2 |
| HALE AV | COL | 32 E3 |
| HALE AV | SCL | P D4 |
| HALE RD | AMA | 41 A2 |
| HALEY RD | IMP | 109 C3 |
| HALEY RD | MCO | 47 C5 |
| HALEY ST | STB | 174 C4 |
| HALF MOON BY RD | SMCO | 45 C3 |
| HALFWAY RD | SDCO | 107 B2 |
| HALL AV | SJCO | 47 D1 |
| HALL RD | LAS | 27 E1 |
| HALL RD | MON | 54 C3 |
| HALL RD | SON | 37 E2 |


STREETS

HALL RD

# STREET INDEX

HOLLYWOOD WY

230




| STREET | CO. | PAGE & GRID |
|---|---|---|
| HALL RD | STA | 47 E3 |
| HALL RD | STA | 48 A2 |
| HALL RD | TEH | 24 D2 |
| HALL RD | VEN | 88 D4 |
| HALL WY | SHA | 19 E2 |
| HALL CITY CK RD | TRI | 17 C3 |
| HALLEY RD | SOL | 39 A2 |
| HALLOCK | VEN | 88 C5 |
| HALLORAN SPG RD | SBD | 83 B3 |
| HALLORAN SUMMIT | SBD | 83 D2 |
| HALLOWELL RD | STA | 47 C4 |
| HALLS FLAT RD | LAS | 20 A2 |
| HALLS GRADE RD | RCO | 100 B3 |
| HALLWOOD BLVD | YUB | 33 D2 |
| HALLWOOD BLVD W | YUB | 33 D2 |
| HALSTEAD | SBD | 81 C5 |
| HAM LN | SJCO | 40 A4 |
| HAMBONE RD | SIS | 13 C2 |
| HAMBURG RD | MCO | 55 E2 |
| HAMES RD | SCR | 54 B2 |
| HAMILTON | YOL | 39 D2 |
| HAMILTON AV | ORA | T B4 |
| HAMILTON AV | SCL | P B3 |
| HAMILTON AV | SCL | 46 A5 |
| HAMILTON AV | TEH | 24 D1 |
| HAMILTON RD | DN | 1 E4 |
| HAMILTON RD | KER | 89 D1 |
| HAMILTON RD | STA | 47 B3 |
| HAMILTON RD E | BUT | 25 C5 |
| HAMILTON RD W | BUT | 25 C5 |
| HAMLTN NORD CNA | BUT | 25 A3 |
| HAMILTN VICTORA | ORA | 98 B4 |
| HAMLIN RD | BUT | 25 C3 |
| HAMLIN GULCH RD | SIS | 3 E5 |
| HAMLOW RD | STA | 47 E3 |
| HAMMER LN | SJCO | 40 A5 |
| HAMMER LOOP RD | TEH | 18 A5 |
| HAMMETT RD | STA | 47 C2 |
| HAMMIL RD | MNO | 51 D2 |
| HAMMONTON RD | YUB | 33 E2 |
| HAMMNTN SMRTVLL | YUB | 33 E2 |
| HAMNER AV | RCO | U E4 |
| HAMNER AV | RCO | 98 E3 |
| HAMPTON RD | CC | L D3 |
| HANAUPAH CYN RD | INY | 72 A2 |
| HANAWALT AV | KER | 78 A1 |
| HANCOCK RD | SBD | 84 C4 |
| HANEY VIEW DR | SHA | 13 E4 |
| HANFORD ARMONA | KIN | 67 C1 |
| HANKINS RD | COL | 32 D2 |
| HANKS RD | MOD | 7 D4 |
| HANSEN | FRCO | 58 B4 |
| HANSEN AV | RCO | 99 D3 |
| HANSEN RD | LAS | 21 B1 |
| HANSEN RD | SJCO | 46 D2 |
| HANSEN ST | SAL | 171 E5 |
| HAPGOOD RD | SB | 86 C3 |
| HAPPY TR | SBD | 92 D5 |
| HAPPY CAMP LKOT | MOD | 14 B1 |
| HAPPY CAMP RD | VEN | 88 D5 |
| HAPPY CAMP DUMP | SIS | 3 A3 |
| HAPPY CANYON RD | SB | 87 A3 |
| HAPPY GAP RD | TUL | 58 D3 |
| HAPPY VALLEY RD | ALA | P B1 |
| HAPPY VALLEY RD | CC | L E4 |
| HAPPY VALLEY RD | CC | 45 D1 |
| HAPPY VALLEY RD | ED | 35 A5 |
| HAPPY VALLEY RD | SHA | 18 C3 |
| HARBERS LN | HUM | 15 E2 |
| HARBISON RD | COL | 32 E1 |
| HARBISON CYN RD | SDCO | 107 A5 |
| HARBOR | YOL | 39 D1 |
| HARBOR BLVD | ANA | 193 B1 |
| HARBOR BLVD | CM | 197 B5 |
| HARBOR BLVD | CM | 199 B2 |
| HARBOR BLVD | FTNV | 195 B5 |
| HARBOR BLVD | FTNV | 197 B2 |
| HARBOR BLVD | GGR | 195 B3 |
| HARBOR BLVD | LA | 191 B3 |
| HARBOR BLVD | LACO | S C3 |
| HARBOR BLVD | ORA | 98 B3 |
| HARBOR BLVD | ORA | T C2 |
| HARBOR BLVD | SMCO | N D2 |
| HARBOR BLVD | SA | 195 B5 |
| HARBOR BLVD | SA | 197 B2 |
| HARBOR BLVD | VENT | 175 E4 |
| HARBOR BLVD | VEN | 96 B1 |
| HARBOR DR | IMP | 108 C2 |
| HARBOR DR | SD | 215 D4 |
| HARBOR DR | SD | 216 B5 |
| HARBOR DR | SDCO | V B4 |
| HARBOR DR N | SD | 215 B2 |
| HARBOR FRWY | LA | 185 D4 |
| HARBOR FRWY | LA | 191 A2 |
| HARBOR FRWY | LACO | 97 D4 |
| HARBOR FRWY | LACO | S C2 |
| HARBOR WY | R | 155 A3 |
| HARBOR SCNIC DR | LB | 192 C3 |
| HARDEN FLAT | TUO | 49 B1 |
| HARDER RD | ALA | N E1 |
| HARDER RD | ALA | P A1 |
| HARDER RD | ALA | 45 E2 |
| HARDER RD W | H | 146 D4 |
| HARDIN RD | NAPA | 32 C5 |
| HARDIN RD | NAPA | 38 C1 |
| HARDING AV | STA | 47 D3 |
| HARDING RD | MCO | 47 E3 |
| HARDING RD | MCO | 48 A3 |
| HARDING WY | SJCO | 40 A5 |
| HARDING WY | S | 160 A4 |
| HARDMAN AV | NAPA | 38 C2 |
| HARDRK DAVIS RD | SBD | 91 B3 |
| HARDY RD | IMP | 111 E3 |
| HARE CANYON RD | MON | 65 E4 |
| HARE CANYON RD | MON | 66 A4 |
| HARKINS | MON | 54 C4 |
| HARKINS RD | SAL | 171 E5 |

| STREET | CO. | PAGE & GRID |
|---|---|---|
| HARKINS SLGH RD | SCR | 54 B2 |
| HARKNESS DR | PLU | 20 A3 |
| HARKNESS ST | NAP | 133 A2 |
| HARLAN AV | FRCO | 66 D1 |
| HARLAN AV | FRCO | 57 C5 |
| HARLAN RD | COL | 32 C2 |
| HARLAN MTN RD | SBT | 54 E4 |
| HARLAN MTN RD | SBT | 55 A4 |
| HARLEY LEIGHTON | SHA | 18 C2 |
| HARMON RD | MCO | 56 B1 |
| HARMON RD | TUL | 67 E2 |
| HARMONY GRVE RD | SDCO | 106 C3 |
| HARMONY VLY RD | SLO | 75 C2 |
| HARNEY | SJCO | 40 A4 |
| HARP RD | TEH | 18 C3 |
| HARPER LN | MCO | 55 C2 |
| HARPER LN | SOL | 39 B2 |
| HARPER RD | IMP | 112 D5 |
| HARPER LAKE RD | SBD | 81 B5 |
| HARPOLD RD | KLAM | 5 D1 |
| HARRIGAN RD | IMP | 111 E3 |
| HARRINGTON AV | COL | 32 E3 |
| HARRIS | MPA | 49 C3 |
| HARRIS RD | BUT | 25 B4 |
| HARRIS RD | HUM | 16 D5 |
| HARRIS RD | IMP | 109 B5 |
| HARRIS RD | MON | 54 C4 |
| HARRIS RD | SUT | 33 C3 |
| HARRIS ST | EUR | 121 B3 |
| HARRIS ST | HUM | 9 E5 |
| HARRIS ST | HUM | 15 E1 |
| HARRISON AV | HUM | 9 E5 |
| HARRISON AV | HUM | 15 E1 |
| HARRISON RD | TRI | 17 B2 |
| HARRISON ST | O | 158 B2 |
| HARRISON ST | RCO | 101 B5 |
| HARRISON ST | SF | 143 D5 |
| HARRISN GLCH RD | SHA | 17 C3 |
| HARRIS RANCH RD | MNO | 51 D2 |
| HARROD RD | SBD | 92 A4 |
| HARROLD RD | SJCO | 47 D1 |
| HARRY CASH RD | SIS | 4 C4 |
| HART AV | KER | 68 C5 |
| HART RD | IMP | 109 C4 |
| HART RD | SIS | 4 C4 |
| HART RD | STA | 47 C2 |
| HART FLAT RD | KER | 79 B3 |
| HARTLEY DR | BUT | 25 C2 |
| HARTMANN RD | LAK | 32 B4 |
| HART MINE RD | SBD | 84 D3 |
| HARTNELL | RED | 122 E4 |
| HARTNELL AV | SHA | 18 C2 |
| HART OAKS DR | KER | 79 B3 |
| HARTSHORN RD | IMP | 109 C5 |
| HARTS MEADOW | SIS | 12 E1 |
| HARTS MTN RD | SIS | 4 E5 |
| HARTVICKSON LN | CAL | 40 E4 |
| HARVARD AV | IRV | 200 E1 |
| HARVARD AV | ORA | T E3 |
| HARVARD RD | SBD | 92 C1 |
| HARVARD MINE RD | TUO | 41 C5 |
| HARVEY RD | BUT | 25 C2 |
| HARVEY RD | SAC | 40 A3 |
| HARVEY RD | STA | 47 C4 |
| HARVEY RD 1 | LAS | 20 C1 |
| HARVEY RD 2 | LAS | 20 C1 |
| HARVEY RD 4 | LAS | 20 C1 |
| HARVY MTN LO RD | LAS | 20 C1 |
| HARVY PETTIT RD | MCO | 48 D5 |
| HARVEY VLY RD | LAS | 20 C1 |
| HARWOOD RD | SCL | P B4 |
| HARWOOD RD | SCL | 46 B5 |
| HASKELL AV | LACO | Q B2 |
| HASKINS RD | SIS | 5 D2 |
| HASKINS VALLEY | BUT | 26 A3 |
| HASLEY CYN RD | LACO | 89 A4 |
| HASSLER RD | ED | 34 E4 |
| HASTAIN RD | IMP | 109 B4 |
| HASTE ST | B | 156 A3 |
| HASTER ST | ANA | 193 D5 |
| HASTER ST | ANA | 195 C1 |
| HASTER ST | ORA | T C2 |
| HATCHET CK RD | TRI | 11 E4 |
| HAT CREEK PK RD | SHA | 13 D4 |
| HAT CK PWRHOUSE | SHA | 13 D4 |
| HAT CK PWRHS #2 | SHA | 13 D4 |
| HATCH RD | BUT | 25 B5 |
| HATCH RD | MCO | 48 C4 |
| HATCH RD | STA | 47 C2 |
| HATCHET CK RD | NEV | 34 B2 |
| HATCHET CK RD | TRI | 12 A4 |
| HATHAWAY ST | RCO | 100 A3 |
| HAUSER BLVD | LA | 184 B3 |
| HAUSER BR RD | SON | 37 A1 |
| HAVASU LAKE RD | SBD | 95 D4 |
| HAVEN AV | SBD | U E2 |
| HAVEN AV | SBD | 98 E2 |
| HAVEN RD | SBD | 80 E5 |
| HAVENS RD | IMP | 108 E5 |
| HAVERFORD RD | SDCO | 107 A4 |
| HAVLINA ST | SIS | 5 D2 |
| HAWEE CANYON RD | INY | 70 B2 |
| HAWKEYE AV | STA | 47 E3 |
| HAWKINS RD | SOL | 39 B2 |
| HAWKINS RD | STA | 48 A3 |
| HAWKINS BAR RD | TRI | 10 D5 |
| HAWKNSVLLE HMBG | SIS | 3 E4 |
| HAWKNSVLLE HMBG | SIS | 4 A4 |
| HAWKS HILL RD | HUM | 15 D2 |
| HAWLEY GRADE | ED | 36 A4 |
| HAWTHORNE AV | C | 124 D3 |
| HAWTHORNE AV | SHA | 18 B3 |
| HAWTHORNE BLVD | LACO | 97 D3 |
| HAWTHORNE BLVD | LACO | S B2 |
| HAWTHORNE ST | MONT | 167 D3 |
| HAWTHORNE ST | RCO | 99 C5 |
| HAWVER RD | CAL | 41 A3 |

| STREET | CO. | PAGE & GRID |
|---|---|---|
| HAYDEN RD | MCO | 48 D4 |
| HAYDEN HILL RD | LAS | 14 C4 |
| HAYDN HLL CTOFF | LAS | 14 D4 |
| HAYDN HLL LKOUT | LAS | 14 D4 |
| HAYES AV | FRCO | 57 B3 |
| HAYES AV | FRCO | 57 B5 |
| HAYES ST | NAP | 133 C3 |
| HAYES ST | RCO | 101 C5 |
| HAYNES RD | SBD | 91 E3 |
| HAYNES RD | SHA | 13 C5 |
| HAYS CANYON RD | MOD | 8 E2 |
| HAYWARD BLVD | ALA | M A5 |
| HAYWARD BLVD | ALA | P A1 |
| HAYWARD RD | MCO | 48 C2 |
| HAZEL AV | SAC | 34 B5 |
| HAZELDEAN RD | STA | 48 A2 |
| HAZEL DELL RD | SCR | 54 C2 |
| HAZEL VALLEY RD | ED | 35 B4 |
| HAZELTINE AV | LACO | Q C2 |
| HAZELTON AV | S | 160 E5 |
| HAZEN RD | TEH | 19 B3 |
| HEACOCK ST | RCO | 99 C2 |
| HEAD DAM RD | BUT | 25 D1 |
| HEALDSBURG AV | SON | 37 E2 |
| HEALY RD | MCO | 48 C5 |
| HEARST RD | MCO | 47 D5 |
| HEARST RD | MCO | 55 D1 |
| HEARST POST OFC | MEN | 23 B4 |
| HEARST WLLTS RD | MEN | 23 A5 |
| HEATH RD | KER | 78 C3 |
| HEATHER AV | KER | 70 C5 |
| HEATHER AV | MAD | 57 B1 |
| HEATHER DR | FRFD | 135 C2 |
| HEBER RD | IMP | 112 B3 |
| HECKER PASS HWY | SCL | 54 C2 |
| HECTOR RD | SBD | 92 D2 |
| HEDDING ST | SJ | 151 C4 |
| HEDDING ST | SJ | 152 B2 |
| HEDDING ST | SCL | P B3 |
| HEDGER RD | SUT | 33 C1 |
| HEFFERNAN AV | IMP | 112 A4 |
| HEGAN LN | BUT | 25 B3 |
| HEGENBRGR EXPWY | ALA | 45 D2 |
| HEGENBRGR EXPWY | O | 159 E2 |
| HEGENBERGER RD | ALA | L D5 |
| HEGENBERGER RD | ALA | 45 D2 |
| HEGENBURGER RD | O | 159 E3 |
| HEIDI RD | TUL | 68 E1 |
| HEINSEN RD | MON | 65 D4 |
| HEINZELMAN DR | SIS | 4 C5 |
| HEISKELL DR | MAD | 57 B1 |
| HEITT AV | KER | 68 B5 |
| HELEN DR | MLBR | 144 B5 |
| HELENA AV | STA | 47 E2 |
| HELENDALE RD | SBD | 91 B2 |
| HELLMAN AV | RCO | U E4 |
| HELLMAN AV | RCO | 98 E2 |
| HELLS HALF ACRE | SIE | 26 D4 |
| HELLS HALF ACRE | TUO | 41 D3 |
| HELLS HALF ACRE | TUO | 42 A3 |
| HELLS HOLLOW RD | TUO | 48 E1 |
| HELMS CT | KER | 79 C3 |
| HEMET LAKE RD | RCO | 100 B4 |
| HEMPHILL RD | LAS | 21 B4 |
| HENDERSON AV | TUL | 68 D3 |
| HENDERSON RD | FRCO | 57 B4 |
| HENDERSON RD | FRCO | 57 C4 |
| HENDERSON RD | RED | 122 D3 |
| HENDERSON ST | EUR | 121 C3 |
| HENDRICKS DR | SBD | 101 E1 |
| HENDRICKS RD | LAK | 31 C2 |
| HENLEY RD | KLAM | 5 C1 |
| HENNESSEY RD | HUM | 10 D5 |
| HENNESSEY RD | TRI | 10 E5 |
| HENNESS PASS RD | SIE | 26 D4 |
| HENNESS PASS RD | SIE | 27 A4 |
| HENRY RD | SBD | 101 D1 |
| HENRY RD | SJCO | 40 D5 |
| HENRY RD | SJCO | 47 D1 |
| HENRY ST | B | 156 A1 |
| HENRY DOTA RD | SIE | 27 C4 |
| HENRY FORD AV | LA | 191 E1 |
| HENRY FORD AV | LB | 191 E2 |
| HENRY MILLER AV | MCO | 56 A1 |
| HENRY MILLER RD | MCO | 55 C1 |
| HENSLEY RD | MAD | 57 B1 |
| HEREFORD RD | MCO | 47 E5 |
| HEREFORD RD | MCO | 48 A5 |
| HEREFORD RD | MCO | 55 E1 |
| HEREFORD RD | SBD | 92 B1 |
| HERIOT LN | PLU | 27 C3 |
| HERIOT LN | SIE | 27 C3 |
| HERITAGE CT | SHA | 18 B2 |
| HERITAGE RD | SDCO | V D5 |
| HERITAGE RD | SDCO | 111 E2 |
| HERLONG ACCESS | LAS | 21 D5 |
| HERMOSA AV | LACO | S A1 |
| HERMOSA RD | KER | 78 E3 |
| HERMOSA RD | VEN | 88 B4 |
| HERNANDEZ DR | LACO | 90 A3 |
| HERNANDEZ DR | MPA | 48 C2 |
| HERNDON AV | FRCO | 56 B3 |
| HERNDON AV | FRCO | 57 C3 |
| HERNLEY RD | RCO | 107 B1 |
| HERON AV | SBD | 101 A1 |
| HERRICK RD | HUM | 121 B5 |
| HERRING RD | KER | 78 C4 |
| HERZOG RD | SAC | M D1 |
| HERZOG RD | SAC | 39 D3 |
| HESPELER RD | SOL | 38 E2 |
| HESPERIA RD | MON | 65 C5 |
| HESPERIA RD | SBD | 91 B4 |
| HESPERIAN BLVD | ALA | N E1 |
| HESPERIAN BLVD | ALA | P A1 |
| HESPERIAN BLVD | ALA | 45 E2 |
| HESPERIAN BLVD | ALCO | 146 A2 |
| HESPERIAN BLVD | H | 146 A2 |

| STREET | CO. | PAGE & GRID |
|---|---|---|
| HESSE RD | TEH | 18 B5 |
| HETTENSHAW RD | TRI | 16 E4 |
| HETZEL RD | IMP | 108 E5 |
| HEWES AV | ORA | 98 C4 |
| HEWES AV | ORA | T E3 |
| HEWITT | SJCO | 40 C5 |
| HEWLTT STURTVNT | MEN | 31 B3 |
| HEYSER RD | IMP | 110 D5 |
| HIALEAH WY | RCO | 100 C5 |
| HIATT RD | SUT | 33 B4 |
| HIAWATHA AV | AVLN | 105 A4 |
| HIBBARD RD | MEN | 31 A4 |
| HIBBARD RD | SJCO | 40 B4 |
| HICKEY BLVD | SMCO | N B1 |
| HICKEY BLVD | SMCO | 45 B2 |
| HICKMAN LN | TEH | 18 C4 |
| HICKMAN RD | STA | 47 E3 |
| HICKMAN RD | STA | 48 A3 |
| HICKS | LAS | 21 B4 |
| HICKS LN | BUT | 25 B2 |
| HICKS RD | SUT | 33 E3 |
| HIDALGO ST | MPA | 48 C2 |
| HIDDEN HILLS RD | SBD | 94 A2 |
| HIDDEN OAKS DR | KER | 79 B4 |
| HIDDEN VLY RD | SB | 87 B4 |
| HIDEAWAY HAVEN | SHA | 13 D3 |
| HIEROGLYPH RD | MNO | 51 C2 |
| HIETT AV | KER | 78 B1 |
| HIGDON RD | CAL | 41 B2 |
| HIGGINS AV | BUT | 33 C1 |
| HIGGNS PRSMA RD | SMCO | N B2 |
| HIGGNS PRSMA RD | SMCO | 45 C3 |
| HIGH RD | SBD | 91 D4 |
| HIGH RD | SIS | 3 E4 |
| HIGH ST | ALA | L D4 |
| HIGH ST | A | 159 A2 |
| HIGH ST | AUB | 126 D3 |
| HIGH ST | MONT | 167 D3 |
| HIGH ST | MON | 53 E3 |
| HIGH ST | O | 159 B1 |
| HIGH ST | SC | 169 B3 |
| HIGH ST | SCR | 53 E2 |
| HIGHGRADE RD | MOD | 7 E2 |
| HIGHLAND AV | FRCO | 57 D2 |
| HIGHLAND AV | LA | 181 C4 |
| HIGHLAND AV | LA | 184 C1 |
| HIGHLAND AV | LACO | 97 D3 |
| HIGHLAND AV | LACO | Q D4 |
| HIGHLAND AV | LACO | S A1 |
| HIGHLAND AV | MB | 189 A5 |
| HIGHLAND AV | SBD | 98 E1 |
| HIGHLAND AV | SBD | 99 C2 |
| HIGHLAND AV | SDCO | V C4 |
| HIGHLAND AV | SDCO | 111 D1 |
| HIGHLAND AV | U | 123 B3 |
| HIGHLAND BLVD | RCO | 99 D2 |
| HIGHLAND DR | CLK | 209 A5 |
| HIGHLAND DR | LACO | R A2 |
| HIGHLAND DR | SNLO | 172 A1 |
| HIGHLAND RD | CC | M C5 |
| HIGHLAND RD | CC | 46 B1 |
| HIGHLAND WY | SCR | P B5 |
| HIGHLAND WY | SCR | 54 B1 |
| HIGHLND HOME RD | RCO | 99 E3 |
| HIGHLAND LK RD | ALP | 42 B1 |
| HIGHLAND SPG RD | LAK | 31 D3 |
| HIGHLND SPGS RD | RCO | 99 E3 |
| HIGHLAND VLY RD | SDCO | 106 E4 |
| HIGHLANDS LK RD | SHA | 12 B4 |
| HIGHLINE RD | IMP | 109 C5 |
| HIGHLINE RD | KER | 79 B4 |
| HIGHLINE RD | KER | 79 C4 |
| HIGH PRAIRIE RD | HUM | 10 C5 |
| HIGHRIDGE RD | LACO | S B3 |
| HIGH ROCK RD | LAS | 21 E4 |
| HIGH SCHOOL RD | SON | 37 D2 |
| HIGH VALLEY RD | KER | 88 D1 |
| HIGH VALLEY RD | LAK | 31 E2 |
| HIGH VALLEY RD | LAK | 31 E3 |
| HIGH VALLEY RD | LAK | 32 A3 |
| HY TO THE STARS | SDCO | 107 A2 |
| HIGUERA ST | SLO | 76 A4 |
| HIGUERA ST | SNLO | 172 B3 |
| HILDRETH LN | SJCO | 40 B4 |
| HILDRETH RD | MAD | 57 D1 |
| HILL | FRCO | 58 B4 |
| HILL AV | PAS | 190 E2 |
| HILL RD | COL | 32 D2 |
| HILL RD | CC | 38 E5 |
| HILL RD | KER | 78 C4 |
| HILL RD | KLAM | 5 C2 |
| HILL RD | MEN | 23 B3 |
| HILL RD | SMCO | N C4 |
| HILL RD | SCL | P D5 |
| HILL RD | SCL | 54 D1 |
| HILL RD | SIS | 5 D3 |
| HILL RD | YUB | 33 E1 |
| HILL RD E | MEN | 23 A5 |
| HILL ST | AVLN | 105 B4 |
| HILL ST | LA | 185 D5 |
| HILL ST | LA | 186 A3 |
| HILL ST | LACO | S D2 |
| HILL ST | ML | 164 C4 |
| HILL ST | SDCO | V A3 |
| HILL ST | SDCO | 106 B3 |
| HILL ST | SDCO | 111 C1 |
| HILLCREST AV | BEN | 153 C4 |
| HILLCREST AV | CC | 39 C5 |
| HILLCREST BLVD | LACO | R D3 |
| HILLCREST BLVD | MLBR | 144 D5 |
| HILLCREST BLVD | SMCO | N C1 |
| HILLCREST BLVD | SMCO | 45 B3 |
| HILLCREST RD | CC | M C3 |
| HILLCREST ST | KER | 80 E1 |
| HILLDALE AV | MCO | 55 E1 |
| HILLDALE AV | MCO | 86 E1 |
| HILLER RD | HUM | 9 E4 |

| STREET | CO. | PAGE & GRID |
|---|---|---|
| HILLER ST | BLMT | 145 C4 |
| HILLGATE RD | COL | 32 E3 |
| HILLHURST AV | LA | 182 C3 |
| HILLMAN AV | BLMT | 145 B4 |
| HILLSBORO AV | LA | 183 D3 |
| HILLSDALE AV | SCL | P B4 |
| HILLSDALE BLVD | SMCO | N C2 |
| HILLSDALE BL E | FCTY | 145 D2 |
| HILLSDALE BL E | SM | 145 B3 |
| HILLSDALE BL W | SM | 145 A4 |
| HILLS FERRY RD | MCO | 47 C4 |
| HILLSIDE AV | RCO | 98 E3 |
| HILLSIDE BLVD | SMCO | L B5 |
| HILLSIDE BLVD | SMCO | N B1 |
| HILLSIDE BLVD | SMCO | 45 B2 |
| HILLSIDE DR | MPA | 49 C3 |
| HILLSIDE DR | SMCO | N C1 |
| HILLSIDE DR | SMCO | 45 C3 |
| HILLSIDE DR | SHA | 18 D2 |
| HILL SIDE STA | LAS | 14 B3 |
| HILLSIDE VIS RD | RCO | 107 C1 |
| HILLS VALLEY RD | FRCO | 58 B4 |
| HILLTOP | SHA | 18 C2 |
| HILLTOP DR | CC | L C3 |
| HILLTOP RD | SIS | 5 A2 |
| HILL VIEW TK TR | SBD | 91 C2 |
| HILMAR RD | STA | 47 D4 |
| HILT RD | SIS | 4 A2 |
| HILT HUNGRY RD | SIS | 4 A2 |
| HILTON PACK STA | MNO | 51 A3 |
| HILTONS RD | HUM | 9 E2 |
| HILTONS RD | HUM | 10 A2 |
| HIME RD | IMP | 112 A3 |
| HI MOUNTAIN RD | SLO | 76 C3 |
| HINDS RD | STA | 47 D1 |
| HINKLEY RD | SBD | 81 C5 |
| HINTON AV | MCO | 47 E4 |
| HIRSCH RD | MPA | 49 B4 |
| HIRSCHDALE RD | NEV | 27 E5 |
| HITCHCOCK RD | MON | 54 C4 |
| HI YOU GULCH RD | SIS | 3 D4 |
| HOADLEY PKS RD | SHA | 17 E1 |
| HOAG RD | TEH | 24 D2 |
| HOAGLAND RD | HUM | 16 D5 |
| HOAGLIN RD | TRI | 16 D5 |
| HOAGLIN SCH RD | TRI | 16 E5 |
| HOBART AV | FRCO | 56 B2 |
| HOBART MILLS RD | NEV | 27 D5 |
| HOBBS RD | IMP | 109 A2 |
| HOBBS RD | SUT | 33 C3 |
| HOBO GULCH RD | TRI | 11 B5 |
| HOBSON AV | MON | 65 B2 |
| HOBSON WY | RCO | 103 C5 |
| HOFFMAN BLVD | R | 155 A4 |
| HOFFMAN LN | CC | 39 C5 |
| HOFFMAN RD | SBD | 80 E3 |
| HOFFMAN RD | SBD | 81 A3 |
| HOFFMAN RD | YUB | 33 D3 |
| HOFFMAN ST | AMA | 40 E2 |
| HFMN PLUMAS RD | YUB | 33 D3 |
| HOGAN | FRCO | 58 A4 |
| HOGAN LN | SJCO | 40 B4 |
| HOGAN DAM RD | CAL | 40 E4 |
| HOGAN DAM RD | CAL | 40 E4 |
| HOGBACK RD | INY | 60 A4 |
| HOG CANYON RD | KER | 79 D3 |
| HOG CANYON RD | SLO | 76 B1 |
| HOG CANYON EXT | SLO | 66 B5 |
| HOGIN RD | STA | 47 C4 |
| HOG LAKE TK TR | RCO | 100 B5 |
| HOGSBACK RD | TEH | 18 D5 |
| HOGSBACK RD | TEH | 19 B4 |
| HOKE RD | SUT | 33 C2 |
| HOLBROOK RD | MCO | 48 D5 |
| HOLCOMB CK RD | SBD | 91 E5 |
| HOLCOMB VLY RD | SBD | 91 E5 |
| HOLCOMBS RD | SIE | 27 D4 |
| HOLDEN | SJCO | 40 C5 |
| HOLDNER RD | SOL | 39 B2 |
| HOLDRIDGE DR | TUL | 68 E3 |
| HOLDRIDGE RD | IMP | 112 C3 |
| HOLE AV | RCO | 99 A3 |
| HOLENBECK | SJCO | 40 C5 |
| HOLIDAY AV | KER | 89 C1 |
| HOLIDAY RD | DN | 2 B3 |
| HOLLAND | YOL | 39 D2 |
| HOLLAND AV | BUT | 25 B3 |
| HOLLAND RD | RCO | 99 C4 |
| HOLLAND RD | SOL | 39 C3 |
| HOLLND TRACT RD | CC | 39 D5 |
| HOLLENBECK AV | LACO | U A3 |
| HOLLENBECK AV | SVL | 149 D2 |
| HOLLISTER AV | SB | 87 B4 |
| HOLLISTER ST | SDCO | V C5 |
| HOLLISTER ST | SDCO | 111 D2 |
| HOLLOW LN | SHA | 18 C2 |
| HOLLOW RD | CC | 39 A5 |
| HOLLOWAY RD | COL | 32 E1 |
| HOLLOWAY RD | KER | 77 C1 |
| HOLLOW LOG RD | PLA | 34 E2 |
| HOLLY AV | LACO | R C3 |
| HOLLY RD | SBD | 91 A3 |
| HOLLY RD | TRI | 17 A4 |
| HOLLY ST | SMCO | N D2 |
| HOLLYWOOD BLVD | LA | 181 A4 |
| HOLLYWOOD BLVD | LA | 182 A4 |
| HOLLYWOOD BLVD | LACO | 97 D2 |
| HOLLYWOOD BLVD | LACO | Q D3 |
| HOLLYWOOD FRWY | LA | 181 B2 |
| HOLLYWOOD FRWY | LA | 185 D1 |
| HOLLYWOOD FRWY | LA | 186 A2 |
| HOLLYWOOD FRWY | LACO | 97 D1 |
| HOLLYWOOD FRWY | LACO | Q D3 |
| HOLLYWOOD LN | SBD | 101 D1 |
| HOLLYWOOD WY | BUR | 179 B3 |
| HOLLYWOOD WY | LA | 179 B3 |
| HOLLYWOOD WY | LACO | 97 D1 |


STREETS

| STREET | CO. | PAGE | GRID |
|---|---|---|---|
| HOLLYWOOD WY | LACO | Q | D2 |
| HOLMAN HWY | MONT | 167 | C5 |
| HOLMAN HWY | MON | 53 | D4 |
| HOLMAN HWY | MON | 168 | C1 |
| HOLMES AV | KER | 78 | B5 |
| HOLMES LN | SOL | 39 | A2 |
| HOLMES RD | SBD | 84 | C4 |
| HOLMES RD | TEH | 24 | E1 |
| HOLMES ST | ALA | P | C1 |
| HOLMES ST | ALA | 46 | C2 |
| HOLMS FLAT RD | HUM | 16 | B3 |
| HOLOHAN RD | SCR | 54 | C2 |
| HOLSTEAD RD | SBD | 81 | C5 |
| HOLT | SJCO | 39 | E5 |
| HOLT AV | LACO | U | A2 |
| HOLT BLVD | MTCL | 203 | B5 |
| HOLT BLVD | ONT | 203 | B5 |
| HOLT BLVD | ONT | 204 | A5 |
| HOLT BLVD | POM | 203 | B5 |
| HOLT BLVD | SBD | U | C2 |
| HOLT BLVD | SBD | 98 | D2 |
| HOLT RD | IMP | 109 | C5 |
| HOLT RD | KER | 79 | E5 |
| HOLT RD | KER | 80 | A5 |
| HOLTON RD | IMP | 109 | B5 |
| HOLTVLE DUMP RD | IMP | 109 | C5 |
| HOLTZWL | MPA | 48 | E2 |
| HOLTZWL | MPA | 49 | A2 |
| HOLWORTHY DR | TUL | 68 | D2 |
| HOLZHAUSER LN | SIS | 11 | D1 |
| HOME AV | SD | 216 | D3 |
| HOME AV | SDCO | V | C3 |
| HOME AV | SDCO | 111 | D1 |
| HOMEDALE RD | KLAM | 5 | C1 |
| HOMES RD | SBD | 91 | E4 |
| HOMESTEAD AV | SAL | 171 | B4 |
| HOMESTEAD RD | SLO | 76 | B2 |
| HOMESTEAD RD | SCL | P | A3 |
| HOMESTEAD RD | SCL | 45 | E4 |
| HOMESTEAD RD | SCLR | 150 | C3 |
| HOMESTEAD RD | SCLR | 151 | A3 |
| HOMESTEAD RD | SVL | 150 | C3 |
| HOMEWOOD CYN RD | INY | 71 | B4 |
| HONDA RD | SB | 86 | B3 |
| HONEY BEE RD | SHA | 18 | B3 |
| HONEY RUN RD | BUT | 25 | C3 |
| HONEY SPGS RD | SDCO | 112 | B1 |
| HONEY WAGON RD | IMP | 108 | E2 |
| HONOLULU AV | IMP | 108 | C2 |
| HONOLULU AV | LACO | Q | E2 |
| HONOLULU RD | KER | 78 | A4 |
| HOOD FRANKLN RD | SAC | 39 | E2 |
| HOOKER CREEK RD | HUM | 16 | C5 |
| HOOKER CREEK RD | TEH | 18 | C4 |
| HOOKTON RD | HUM | 15 | D1 |
| HOOPER RD | SUT | 33 | C2 |
| HOOPER RD | YUB | 33 | D2 |
| HOOVER RD | MCO | 56 | C1 |
| HOOVER ST | LA | 185 | C3 |
| HOOVER ST | LACO | Q | E4 |
| HOOVER FLAT RD | LAS | 14 | C4 |
| HOPE ST | KLAM | 5 | C1 |
| HOPE ST | LA | 185 | E4 |
| HOPKINS ST | ALA | L | C4 |
| HOPLAND ST | SBD | 91 | B3 |
| HOPPER RD | STA | 47 | E2 |
| HOPYARD RD | ALA | M | B5 |
| HOPYARD RD | ALA | 46 | B2 |
| HORIZON RD | SBD | 91 | B3 |
| HORIZON ST | SBD | 91 | C4 |
| HORN LN | SIS | 11 | D1 |
| HORN RD | LAS | 8 | C5 |
| HORNBROOK RD | SIS | 4 | B3 |
| HORNITOS RD | MPA | 48 | D3 |
| HORR RD | SHA | 13 | D3 |
| HORSE CANYON RD | KER | 80 | B1 |
| HORSE CREEK RD | SIS | 3 | C3 |
| HORSE LAKE RD | LAS | 21 | C1 |
| HORSE LINTO RD | HUM | 10 | D4 |
| HORSE RDG LKOUT | TRI | 17 | A4 |
| HORSESHOE RD | STA | 47 | E1 |
| HORSESHOE RD | STA | 48 | A1 |
| HORSESHOE BR RD | PLA | 34 | B4 |
| HORSESHOE HL RD | MAR | 37 | E5 |
| HORSESHOE MDWS | INY | 60 | A4 |
| HORTON CREEK RD | INY | 51 | C4 |
| HOSFIELD DR | TUL | 68 | B2 |
| HOSKING RD | KER | 78 | D3 |
| HOSLER AV | BUT | 25 | A3 |
| HOSPITAL LN | RED | 122 | C5 |
| HOSTETTER RD | SCL | P | B3 |
| HOTCHKISS RD | TRI | 22 | E1 |
| HOT CK RANCH RD | MNO | 50 | E2 |
| HOT CK RANCH RD | MNO | 51 | A2 |
| HOTLUM | SIS | 12 | C1 |
| HOT SPRINGS RD | ALP | 36 | B5 |
| HOT SPRINGS RD | RCO | 108 | D1 |
| HOT SPRINGS RD | TUL | 68 | E4 |
| HOT SPRINGS RD | TUL | 69 | A4 |
| HOUGHTON AV | TEH | 24 | D2 |
| HOUGHTON RD | KER | 78 | C4 |
| HOUSE RD | IMP | 108 | E5 |
| HOUSE RD | LAS | 14 | C3 |
| HOUSTON AV | KIN | 67 | D1 |
| HOUSTON AV | TUL | 68 | B1 |
| HOUT RD | AMA | 40 | D2 |
| HOVLEY RD | IMP | 109 | A4 |
| HOWARD | SJCO | 47 | A1 |
| HOWARD AV | FRCO | 57 | A5 |
| HOWARD AV | FRCO | 57 | A3 |
| HOWARD AV | MCO | 47 | E4 |
| HOWARD AV | MCO | 48 | A4 |
| HOWARD AV | SD | 214 | A5 |
| HOWARD RD | MCO | 47 | E4 |
| HOWARD RD | RCO | 107 | B1 |
| HOWARD RD | STA | 47 | B3 |
| HOWARD RD | TUL | 68 | B4 |

| STREET | CO. | PAGE | GRID |
|---|---|---|---|
| HOWARD ST | MEN | 23 | A3 |
| HOWARD CREEK RD | SIE | 27 | A3 |
| HOWARD MTHWS RD | SJCO | 40 | A5 |
| HOWRDS GLCH FTG | MOD | 14 | C1 |
| HOWE RD | CC | L | E3 |
| HOWE CREEK RD | HUM | 15 | E3 |
| HOWELL AV | KER | 80 | C1 |
| HOWELL AV | SIS | 11 | D1 |
| HOWELL RD | IMP | 109 | A2 |
| HOWELL MTN RD | NAPA | 29 | C2 |
| HOWELL MTN RD | NAPA | 38 | B1 |
| HOWELLS RD | PLU | 26 | B1 |
| HOWLAND HILL RD | DN | 1 | D4 |
| HOWSLEY RD | SUT | 33 | D4 |
| HOY RD | SIS | 12 | C1 |
| HOY RD | TEH | 18 | D5 |
| HOYER RD | STA | 47 | C4 |
| HUASNA RD | SLO | 76 | C4 |
| HUASNA TOWNSITE | SLO | 76 | D4 |
| HUB CT | CAL | 41 | A5 |
| HUBBARD | PLA | 34 | B3 |
| HUBBARD RD | LACO | 89 | E4 |
| HUBBARD ST | LACO | 89 | C5 |
| HUBBARD ST | LACO | Q | C1 |
| HUDSON AV | FRCO | 56 | B2 |
| HUDSON RD | CAL | 41 | A5 |
| HUDSON RD | MON | 65 | A1 |
| HUDSON ST | SMCO | N | D2 |
| HUDSON RD | SIS | 4 | A3 |
| HUDSON RD | SUT | 33 | E3 |
| HUDSON ST | SHA | 13 | C5 |
| HUERHUERO L PNZ | SLO | 76 | C2 |
| HUEY RD | SLO | 76 | A1 |
| HUFF RD | IMP | 108 | E5 |
| HUFF RD | SBD | 91 | E3 |
| HUFF ST | RCO | 107 | C1 |
| HUFFAKER RD | SUT | 33 | E3 |
| HUFFMEISTER RD | COL | 32 | C2 |
| HUFFORD RD | HUM | 9 | E2 |
| HUFFORD RD | HUM | 10 | A2 |
| HUGHES AV | CUL | 183 | C5 |
| HUGHES AV | FRCO | 57 | C4 |
| HUGHES AV | FRCO | 67 | C1 |
| HUGHES AV | LA | 183 | C5 |
| HUGHES LN | KER | 78 | D3 |
| HUGHES RD | GV | 127 | C2 |
| HUGHES RD | NEV | 127 | C2 |
| HUGHES RD | SUT | 33 | C2 |
| HULEN RD | MCO | 47 | C5 |
| HULEN RD | MCO | 55 | C1 |
| HULL AV | MCO | 48 | B4 |
| HULL RD | GLE | 24 | A3 |
| HULL CREEK RD | TRI | 23 | A1 |
| HULL MTN RD | LAK | 23 | D5 |
| HULL VALLEY RD | MEN | 23 | A2 |
| HULTBERG RD | MCO | 47 | D4 |
| HULTBERG RD | STA | 47 | D3 |
| HUMBOLDT AV | FRCO | 56 | E3 |
| HUMBOLDT AV | FRCO | 57 | A3 |
| HUMBOLDT RD | BUT | 19 | D5 |
| HUMBOLDT RD | BUT | 25 | B3 |
| HUMBOLDT RD | C | 124 | E4 |
| HUMBOLDT RD | DN | 1 | E4 |
| HUMBOLDT RD | PLU | 19 | E5 |
| HUMBOLDT RD | PLU | 20 | A5 |
| HUMBLDT HILL RD | HUM | 15 | E1 |
| HUMBUG RD | PLU | 19 | E5 |
| HUMBUG RD | PLU | 20 | A5 |
| HUMBUG CREEK RD | SIS | 4 | A4 |
| HUMBUG HUMBOLDT | PLU | 20 | B4 |
| HUME AV | KIN | 67 | E1 |
| HUME RD | FRCO | 58 | E3 |
| HUMPHREY CIR | PLU | 20 | D5 |
| HUMPHREY RD | SUT | 33 | C2 |
| HUN RD | SBD | 84 | C4 |
| HUNEWILL RCH RD | MNO | 43 | B3 |
| HUNGRY CK MTRWY | PLU | 20 | E5 |
| HUNGRY CK LO RD | SIS | 4 | A2 |
| HUNGRY VLY RD | VEN | 88 | D2 |
| HUNT RD | CAL | 40 | E4 |
| HUNT RD | CAL | 41 | A4 |
| HUNT RD | IMP | 112 | B3 |
| HUNT RD | LAS | 14 | C3 |
| HUNT RD | MCO | 47 | C5 |
| HUNTER | MON | 54 | C4 |
| HUNTER BLVD | RCO | 103 | D4 |
| HUNTER ST | CAL | 41 | A5 |
| HUNTER CREEK RD | DN | 1 | E5 |
| HUNTER CREEK RD | DN | 2 | A5 |
| HUNTER MTN RD | INY | 61 | A4 |
| HUNTERS VLY RD | MPA | 48 | E2 |
| HUNTINGTON AV | SBR | 144 | C3 |
| HUNTINGTON DR | LACO | 97 | E2 |
| HUNTINGTON DR | LACO | R | B3 |
| HUNTINGTON RD | MAD | 57 | C2 |
| HUNTINGTON RD | STA | 47 | B2 |
| HUTCHINS ST | SJCO | 40 | A4 |
| HUTCHINSON RD | SJCO | 47 | B2 |
| HUTCHINSON RD | SUT | 33 | C3 |
| HUNTLEY MINE RD | MNO | 50 | E2 |
| HUNTSMAN AV | FRCO | 56 | E4 |
| HUNTSMAN AV | FRCO | 57 | C4 |
| HUNTSMAN AV | FRCO | 58 | A4 |
| HUPP COUTOLENC | BUT | 25 | D2 |
| HURDS GULCH RD | SIS | 3 | D5 |
| HURLES CIR | BUT | 25 | E4 |
| HURLETON RD | BUT | 25 | E4 |
| HURLTN SWDS FLT | BUT | 25 | E4 |
| HURLEY FLATS RD | RCO | 100 | B3 |
| HURRICANE RD | SLO | 77 | D4 |
| HUSMAN RD | MCO | 47 | C5 |
| HUSMAN RD | MCO | 55 | C1 |
| HUSTED RD | COL | 32 | E2 |
| HUSTON RD | IMP | 109 | B5 |
| HUTCHINS | MCO | 56 | B1 |
| HUTSELL RD | MEN | 30 | E3 |
| HYAMPOM RD | TRI | 17 | A2 |

| STREET | CO. | PAGE | GRID |
|---|---|---|---|
| HYDE RD | IMP | 111 | E3 |
| HYDE ST | FRCO | 57 | B5 |
| HYDRIL RD | KIN | 67 | A3 |
| HYPERION AV | LA | 182 | D4 |
| I | | | |
| I AV | SBD | 91 | C4 |
| I ST | BEN | 153 | A4 |
| I ST | EUR | 121 | D1 |
| I ST | MDO | 162 | B3 |
| IBEX SPRING RD | SBD | 72 | D5 |
| ICE HOUSE RD | ED | 35 | C3 |
| ICE HOUSE RD | ED | 35 | C4 |
| ICELAND RD | NEV | 27 | E5 |
| IDAHO AV | KIN | 67 | D2 |
| IDAHO RD | STA | 47 | D3 |
| IDAHO ST | SDCO | V | C3 |
| IDAHO ST | SDCO | 111 | D1 |
| IDAHO-MARYLAND | NEV | 34 | C1 |
| IDAHO-MARYLD RD | GV | 127 | D3 |
| IDAHO-MARYLD RD | NEV | 127 | D3 |
| IDALEONA DR | RCO | 99 | B3 |
| IDLEWOOD LN | HUM | 9 | E3 |
| IDLEWOOD LN | HUM | 10 | A3 |
| IGNACIO BLVD | MAR | L | A2 |
| IKE CROW RD | STA | 47 | C4 |
| ILLINOIS AV | STA | 47 | C2 |
| ILLINOIS AV | TEH | 24 | E2 |
| ILLINOIS VLY RD | DN | 2 | D2 |
| IMLER RD | IMP | 108 | E4 |
| IMOLA AV | NAPA | L | D1 |
| IMOLA AV | NAP | 133 | C5 |
| IMOLA AV W | NAP | 133 | B5 |
| IMPERIAL AV | EC | 217 | B4 |
| IMPERIAL AV | IMP | 109 | A5 |
| IMPERIAL AV | SD | 216 | A4 |
| IMPERIAL AV | SDCO | V | C3 |
| IMPERIAL AV | SDCO | 111 | D1 |
| IMPERIAL HWY | IMP | 111 | B3 |
| IMPERIAL HWY | LA | 189 | B2 |
| IMPERIAL HWY | LACO | 97 | D3 |
| IMPERIAL HWY | LACO | 98 | B3 |
| IMPERIAL HWY | LACO | Q | C5 |
| IMPERIAL HWY | LACO | R | E5 |
| IMPERIAL HWY | LACO | S | A1 |
| IMPERIAL HWY | ORA | R | E5 |
| IMPERIAL HWY | ORA | T | C1 |
| IMPERIAL ST | KER | 77 | E2 |
| IMPERIAL ST | KER | 78 | B2 |
| IMPERIAL DAM RD | IMP | 110 | E5 |
| IMPERL GABLS RD | IMP | 110 | B3 |
| INCLINE RD | MPA | 49 | B2 |
| INCLINE RD | MPA | 63 | A5 |
| INDEPENDENCE RD | CAL | 41 | B2 |
| INDPNDCE CEM RD | CAL | 41 | B2 |
| INDEPNDNC LK RD | SIE | 27 | C5 |
| INDEPNDNCIA MAT | BAJA | 112 | B4 |
| INDIA ST | SD | 215 | C1 |
| INDIAN AV | PMSP | 206 | B4 |
| INDIAN AV | RCO | 100 | C3 |
| INDIAN RD | LAS | 21 | A4 |
| INDIANA AV | MCO | 56 | B1 |
| INDIANA AV | STA | 47 | E2 |
| INDIANA ST | LACO | R | B4 |
| INDIANA RCH RD | YUB | 26 | A5 |
| INDIANA SCH RD | YUB | 26 | A5 |
| INDIAN CYN RD | KER | 70 | C5 |
| INDIAN CYN RD | KER | 80 | C1 |
| INDIAN CEM RD | ALP | 36 | B4 |
| INDIAN COVE CIR | SBD | 101 | B2 |
| INDIAN CV E RD | SBD | 101 | B2 |
| INDIAN CV W RD | SBD | 101 | B2 |
| INDIAN CV MT RD | SBD | 101 | B2 |
| INDIAN CREEK RD | ALP | 36 | C5 |
| INDIAN CREEK RD | KER | 79 | D3 |
| INDIAN CREEK RD | MNO | 51 | D2 |
| INDIAN CREEK RD | PLU | 20 | E5 |
| INDIAN CREEK RD | RCO | 100 | A4 |
| INDIAN CREEK RD | SIS | 2 | D2 |
| INDIAN CREEK RD | SIS | 3 | D4 |
| INDIAN CREEK RD | TRI | 17 | D2 |
| INDIAN DIGGINS | ED | 41 | B1 |
| INDIAN FLAT RD | NEV | 34 | C1 |
| INDIAN GUIDE | FRCO | 58 | B3 |
| INDIAN GULCH RD | MPA | 48 | E3 |
| INDIAN GULCH RD | MPA | 49 | A4 |
| INDIAN GLCH EXT | MPA | 48 | D4 |
| INDIAN HILL BL | CLA | 203 | A3 |
| INDIAN HILL BL | LACO | 98 | D2 |
| INDIAN HILL BL | POM | 203 | A5 |
| INDIAN HILL RD | RCO | 100 | C5 |
| INDIAN HILL RD | SIE | 26 | C4 |
| INDIAN HILL RD | STA | 48 | C2 |
| INDIANOLA AV | FRCO | 57 | E4 |
| INDIANOLA CTOFF | HUM | 9 | E5 |
| INDIANOLA CTOFF | HUM | 10 | A5 |
| INDIANOLA RESRV | HUM | 15 | D2 |
| INDIAN OLE RD | LAS | 20 | C4 |
| INDIAN PAINT DR | RCO | 100 | C5 |
| INDIAN PASS RD | IMP | 110 | B4 |
| INDIAN PEAK RD | MPA | 49 | B3 |
| INDIAN POINT RD | KER | 79 | B4 |
| INDIAN RANCH RD | INY | 71 | C2 |
| INDIAN RES RD | AMA | 40 | D3 |
| INDIAN ROCK RD | IMP | 112 | D5 |
| INDIANS RD | MON | 64 | D2 |
| INDIAN SCHL RD | LPAZ | 104 | A2 |
| INDIAN SRVCE RD | TUL | 69 | A3 |
| INDIAN SPGS RD | ALP | 36 | D5 |
| INDIAN SPGS RD | NEV | 34 | B2 |
| INDIAN SPGS RD | SBD | 81 | D4 |
| INDIAN TOM LAKE | SIS | 5 | B2 |
| INDIAN VLY RD | MAR | 38 | A4 |
| INDIAN VLY RD | MON | 66 | A5 |
| INDIAN VLY RD | SIE | 26 | C4 |
| INDIAN VLY RD | SLO | 66 | A5 |
| INDIAN VLY RD | TRI | 17 | A2 |
| INDIAN WELLS ST | KER | 80 | D1 |

| STREET | CO. | PAGE | GRID |
|---|---|---|---|
| INDIO AV | SBDO | 100 | E1 |
| INDUSTRIAL BLVD | MOH | 96 | B4 |
| INDUSTRIAL PKWY | ALA | N | E1 |
| INDUSTRIAL PKWY | ALA | P | A1 |
| INDUSTRIAL PKWY | ALA | 45 | E2 |
| INDSTRL FARM RD | KER | 78 | C2 |
| INGHRAM RD | TEH | 24 | D2 |
| INGLEWOOD AV | LACO | S | B1 |
| INGLEWOOD BLVD | LA | 188 | A2 |
| INGOMAR GRADE | MCO | 55 | D1 |
| INGOMAR RD | MCO | 47 | D5 |
| INGOMAR RD | MCO | 55 | D1 |
| INGRAHAM ST | SD | 212 | B1 |
| INGRAHAM ST | SDCO | V | A3 |
| INGRAM LN | SUT | 33 | B1 |
| INGRAM CREEK RD | STA | 47 | A3 |
| INK GRADE | NAPA | 32 | B5 |
| INK GRADE | NAPA | 38 | B1 |
| INLAND DR | SJCO | 40 | A5 |
| INLAND FRWY | SD | 214 | A3 |
| INLAND FRWY | SD | 216 | C1 |
| INLAND FRWY | SDCO | V | D4 |
| INLAND FRWY | SDCO | 106 | C5 |
| INLAND FRWY | SDCO | 111 | D2 |
| INLAND CTR DR | SBDO | 207 | B4 |
| INSKIP RD | TEH | 19 | A4 |
| INTAKE BLVD | RCO | 103 | D5 |
| INTERLAKE RD | SLO | 65 | D5 |
| INTERNATIONL AV | FRCO | 57 | D2 |
| INTERNATIONL AV | IMP | 109 | B3 |
| INVESTOR AV | RCO | 102 | C4 |
| INWOOD RD | SHA | 19 | A3 |
| INYO N | INY | 51 | D3 |
| INYO ST | DN | 1 | D4 |
| INYOKERN RD | KER | 80 | D1 |
| IONA AV | KIN | 67 | D2 |
| IONE RD | SAC | 40 | C2 |
| IONE BUENA VIS | AMA | 40 | D3 |
| IONE MICHIGN BR | AMA | 40 | C2 |
| IOWA AV | RCO | 99 | B2 |
| IOWA AV | STA | 47 | C3 |
| IOWA CITY RD | YUB | 33 | D1 |
| IOWA HILL | PLA | 34 | D2 |
| IRIS AV | RCO | 99 | B3 |
| IRIS CT | KER | 79 | C1 |
| IRIS DR | SAL | 171 | C2 |
| IRIS LN | SDCO | 106 | D3 |
| IRIS RD | LAS | 13 | E3 |
| IRIS RD | LAS | 14 | A3 |
| IRIS WY | CAL | 41 | B2 |
| IRIS CANYON RD | MONT | 167 | E5 |
| IRIS CANYON RD | MONT | 168 | E1 |
| IRISH HILL RD | AMA | 40 | D2 |
| IRISH TOWN PNE- | | | |
| -GRV WIELAND RD | AMA | 41 | A2 |
| IRMULCO RD | MEN | 22 | E5 |
| IRONAGE RD | SBD | 101 | E1 |
| IRONE AV | KER | 89 | C1 |
| IRON MTN RD | SBD | 91 | C1 |
| IRON MTN RD | SHA | 18 | B1 |
| IRON MTN PUMPNG | SBD | 102 | E1 |
| IRONWOOD AV | RCO | 99 | C2 |
| IRONWOOD CT | KER | 79 | B4 |
| IRVINE AV | CM | 199 | C4 |
| IRVINE AV | NB | 199 | C4 |
| IRVINE AV | ORA | 199 | E1 |
| IRVINE BLVD | ORA | 98 | C4 |
| IRVINE BLVD | ORA | T | E3 |
| IRVINE RD | IMP | 109 | C4 |
| IRVINE CENTR DR | ORA | 98 | C4 |
| IRVINE CENTR DR | ORA | T | E3 |
| IRVINE LODGE RD | MEN | 22 | E4 |
| IRWIN RD | SBD | 81 | E5 |
| IRWIN RD | SBD | 82 | A5 |
| IRWIN RD | SBD | 208 | B1 |
| IRWIN RD | TEH | 24 | C2 |
| IRWINDALE AV | LACO | R | E3 |
| ISABELLA BLVD | KER | 80 | B4 |
| ISABELA-WLKR PS | KER | 79 | D1 |
| ISABELA-WLKR PS | KER | 80 | B1 |
| ISHI PISHI RD | HUM | 10 | D2 |
| ISLAND RD | SHA | 13 | D3 |
| ISLAND RD | SIS | 3 | D5 |
| ISLAND RD | SIS | 11 | D1 |
| ISLAND BAR HILL | BUT | 25 | E4 |
| ISLAND MTN RD | HUM | 22 | D1 |
| ISLAND MTN RD | TRI | 22 | D1 |
| ISLAND PARK RD | FRCO | 58 | B2 |
| ISLETON RD | SAC | M | E1 |
| ISPEN AV | MCO | 48 | E5 |
| ITALIAN BAR RD | FRCO | 50 | A5 |
| ITALIAN BAR RD | TUO | 41 | C4 |
| IVANHOE RD | SBD | 91 | E4 |
| IVANPAH RD | SBD | 84 | C3 |
| IVANPAH CIMA RD | SBD | 84 | B3 |
| IVERSON LN | LAS | 14 | B3 |
| IVERSON RD | MEN | 30 | D4 |
| IVERSON RD | MON | 54 | E5 |
| IVERSON ST | SAL | 171 | B4 |
| IVESGROVE DR | LACO | 89 | D3 |
| IVORY MILL RD | GLE | 24 | A4 |
| IVY AV | MCO | 56 | C1 |
| J | | | |
| J ST | DVS | 136 | D2 |
| J ST | MDO | 162 | B3 |
| J ST | MER | 170 | C5 |
| J ST | SCTO | 137 | E3 |
| J ST | SDCO | V | C4 |
| J ST | SDCO | 111 | D2 |
| JACALITOS CK RD | FRCO | 66 | D3 |
| JACARANDA DR | KER | 79 | B4 |
| JACK AV | KER | 78 | B2 |
| JACKASS FLTS RD | NEV | 26 | C5 |
| JACKASS FLTS RD | NEV | 34 | C1 |
| JACKASS GRADE | SBT | 55 | E4 |
| JACKASS GRADE | SBT | 56 | A4 |
| JACKASS HILL RD | TUO | 41 | C5 |

| STREET | CO. | PAGE | GRID |
|---|---|---|---|
| JACK CREEK RD | SLO | 75 | E2 |
| JACK CREEK RD | SLO | 76 | A2 |
| JACKLIN RD | SCL | P | B2 |
| JACKLIN RD | SCL | 46 | B4 |
| JACK PINE AV | KER | 79 | E5 |
| JACK RABBIT TR | RCO | 99 | D3 |
| JACK RANCH RD | KER | 69 | B5 |
| JACK RANCH RD | KER | 80 | D1 |
| JACKS RD | MON | 54 | E5 |
| JACK SHAW RD | HUM | 16 | B2 |
| JACK SLOUGH RD | YUB | 33 | D2 |
| JACKSNIPE RD | SOL | 38 | E3 |
| JACKSON | PLA | 33 | E4 |
| JACKSON AV | KER | 77 | E1 |
| JACKSON AV | KER | 78 | B1 |
| JACKSON AV | KIN | 67 | D2 |
| JACKSON AV | SJCO | 47 | D1 |
| JACKSON DR | SDCO | V | D2 |
| JACKSON DR | SDCO | 106 | D5 |
| JACKSON RD | IMP | 109 | B4 |
| JACKSON RD | SAC | 40 | A1 |
| JACKSON RD | SBD | 91 | D3 |
| JACKSON RD | STA | 47 | C2 |
| JACKSON ST | ALA | L | E5 |
| JACKSON ST | ALA | M | A5 |
| JACKSON ST | ALA | N | E1 |
| JACKSON ST | ALA | P | A1 |
| JACKSON ST | ALA | 45 | E2 |
| JACKSON ST | RCO | 99 | A3 |
| JACKSON ST | RCO | 101 | A4 |
| JACKSON ST | SF | 143 | D3 |
| JACKSON ST | TEH | 18 | D5 |
| JACKSON ST W | ALA | N | E1 |
| JACKSON ST W | H | 146 | D4 |
| JACKSON GATE RD | AMA | 40 | E2 |
| JACKSON MDWS RD | SIE | 27 | C4 |
| JACKSON RCH RD | HUM | 9 | E5 |
| JACKSON SLGH RD | SAC | M | D2 |
| JACKSON VLY RD | AMA | 40 | D3 |
| JACKSONVILLE RD | TUO | 41 | C5 |
| JACK TONE RD | SJCO | 40 | B4 |
| JACOBS | FRCO | 58 | B4 |
| JACOBS RD | SJCO | 40 | A5 |
| JACOBS WY | RCO | 99 | B4 |
| JACOBY CREEK RD | HUM | 10 | A5 |
| JACQUELINE | SIS | 4 | C2 |
| JADE AV | SIS | 4 | C4 |
| JAHANT | SJCO | 40 | A3 |
| JAHANT RD | SJCO | 40 | B3 |
| JAIL RD | AVLN | 105 | B5 |
| JAKE RD | RCO | 100 | A5 |
| JALAMA RD | SB | 86 | B4 |
| JAMACHA BLVD | SDCO | V | D3 |
| JAMACHA RD | SDCO | V | E3 |
| JAMACHA RD | SDCO | 111 | D1 |
| JAMAICA BLVD | MOH | 96 | B4 |
| JAMBOREE BLVD | IRV | 198 | E4 |
| JAMBOREE BLVD | IRV | 200 | C1 |
| JAMBOREE BLVD | ORA | T | D4 |
| JAMBOREE RD | IRV | 198 | E4 |
| JAMBOREE RD | NB | 200 | A4 |
| JAMBOREE RD | ORA | 98 | C5 |
| JAMES RD | FRCO | 56 | E4 |
| JAMES RD | IMP | 109 | B5 |
| JAMES RD | KER | 78 | D2 |
| JAMES DONLON BL | CC | M | C3 |
| JAMES LICK FRWY | SF | 142 | E5 |
| JAMES LICK FRWY | SFCO | 45 | C2 |
| JAMES LICK SKWY | SF | 142 | D4 |
| JAMES LICK SKWY | SF | 143 | D5 |
| JAMESON AV | FRCO | 57 | B5 |
| JAMESON AV | FRCO | 57 | B4 |
| JAMESON RD | COL | 32 | E1 |
| JAMESON RD | KER | 79 | D4 |
| JAMISON CK RD | SCR | N | D5 |
| JAMISON CK RD | SCR | 53 | D1 |
| JANE RD | SBD | 92 | D4 |
| JANES RD | HUM | 10 | A5 |
| JANESVLLE GRADE | LAS | 21 | B4 |
| JANICE AV | KER | 79 | E1 |
| JANICE AV | KER | 80 | A1 |
| JANICE RD | SIS | 4 | C2 |
| JANICE ST | KER | 80 | A4 |
| JANOPAUL AV | STA | 162 | C5 |
| JANSS RD | VEN | 96 | D1 |
| JAPATUL LN | SDCO | 107 | B5 |
| JAPATUL LN | SDCO | 112 | B1 |
| JAPATUL RD | SBD | 91 | C4 |
| JAPATUL RD | SBD | 91 | D3 |
| JAPATUL RD | SDCO | 107 | B5 |
| JAPATUL RD | SDCO | 112 | B1 |
| JAPATUL VLY RD | SDCO | 107 | C5 |
| JAPATUL VLY RD | SDCO | 112 | C1 |
| JAQUIMA DR | CAL | 41 | A4 |
| JARDINE RD | SLO | 76 | B1 |
| JARED LN | SB | 86 | E2 |
| J ARTHR YNGR FY | SMCO | 45 | D3 |
| J ARTHR YNGR FY | FCTY | 145 | D1 |
| J ARTHR YNGR FY | SM | 145 | D1 |
| JARVIS AV | ALA | N | E2 |
| JARVIS AV | ALA | P | A2 |
| JARVIS AV | ALA | 45 | E3 |
| JARVIS RD | ALP | 36 | C4 |
| JASMINE RD | SBD | 92 | B3 |
| JASPER LN | YUB | 33 | E2 |
| JASPER RD | IMP | 112 | B4 |
| JASPER RD | TUO | 48 | B1 |
| JASPER SEARS BR | MCO | 55 | C1 |
| JASPER SEARS RD | MCO | 55 | C1 |
| JAVA AV | KIN | 67 | C2 |
| JAVA DR | SVL | 148 | E2 |
| JAVIS AV | KER | 80 | C1 |
| JAVIS AV | KER | 80 | E1 |
| JAWBONE CYN RD | KER | 79 | E2 |
| JAWBONE CYN RD | KER | 80 | B3 |
| JAY DEE LN | RCO | 100 | C5 |
| JAYMAR RD | HUM | 16 | B3 |

JAYNE AV
232
LAKE AV

# STREET INDEX


| STREET | CO. | PAGE & GRID | |
|---|---|---|---|
| JAYNE AV | FRCO | 66 | D3 |
| JAYNE AV | FRCO | 67 | A2 |
| JEAN BLANC RD | INY | 51 | D3 |
| JEANESE | TUO | 41 | C5 |
| JEAN NICHOLS RD | RCO | 99 | D5 |
| JEFF ST | KER | 80 | C1 |
| JEFFERSON AV | FRCO | 56 | E4 |
| JEFFERSON AV | FRCO | 57 | C4 |
| JEFFERSON AV | FRCO | 58 | A4 |
| JEFFERSON AV | RCO | 99 | C5 |
| JEFFERSON AV | SM | N | D2 |
| JEFFERSON BLVD | CUL | 183 | D5 |
| JEFFERSON BLVD | CUL | 188 | C1 |
| JEFFERSON BLVD | LA | 183 | D5 |
| JEFFERSON BLVD | LA | 185 | A5 |
| JEFFERSON BLVD | LACO | 97 | D2 |
| JEFFERSON BLVD | LACO | Q | D4 |
| JEFFERSON BLVD | LACO | 187 | D4 |
| JEFFERSON BLVD | LACO | 188 | A4 |
| JEFFERSON BLVD | YOL | 39 | D2 |
| JEFFERSON ST | MONT | 167 | D4 |
| JEFFERSON ST | NAP | 133 | C4 |
| JEFFERSON ST | ORA | T | D1 |
| JEFFERSON ST | RCO | 101 | A4 |
| JEFFERSON ST | SDCO | 106 | B3 |
| JEFFERSON ST | SF | 143 | A2 |
| JEFFERSON ST N | NAP | 133 | B1 |
| JEFFERY RD | IMP | 111 | E3 |
| JEFFREY RD | ORA | 98 | C4 |
| JEFFREY RD | ORA | T | E4 |
| JEFFREY RCH RD | MNO | 51 | D2 |
| JELLYS FERRY RD | TEH | 18 | D4 |
| JENEVEIN AV | SBR | 144 | B3 |
| JENKINS RD | KER | 78 | C3 |
| JENKS LAKE RD | SBD | 100 | A1 |
| JENNINGS RD | STA | 47 | C3 |
| JENNY LIND RD | CAL | 40 | D4 |
| JENSEN AV | COL | 32 | E3 |
| JENSEN AV | FRCO | 56 | C4 |
| JENSEN AV | FRCO | 57 | A3 |
| JENSEN RD | SLO | 75 | E1 |
| JERROLD AV | FRCO | 56 | B2 |
| JERRY COLLNS AV | MCO | 48 | B5 |
| JERSEY | MCO | 55 | E2 |
| JERSEY AV | KIN | 67 | C2 |
| JERSEYDALE RD | MPA | 49 | C3 |
| JERSEY ISLAND | CC | 39 | C4 |
| JERSEY ISLND RD | CC | M | D3 |
| JERUSALEM GRADE | LAK | 32 | B4 |
| JESS VALLEY RD | MOD | 8 | B3 |
| JESUS MARIA RD | CAL | 41 | A3 |
| JETTY RD S | HUM | 15 | D1 |
| JEWELL AV | PAC | 167 | A1 |
| JEWELL RD | TEH | 18 | C4 |
| JEWELL VLY RD | SDCO | 111 | A4 |
| JEWETT RD | HUM | 16 | D5 |
| JEWETT RD | SUT | 33 | D2 |
| JEWETTA AV | KER | 78 | C3 |
| J HELT RD | HUM | 15 | D2 |
| JIM DAY RD | SHA | 13 | E4 |
| JIM HARVEY RD | SHA | 18 | C2 |
| JIMMY DURNTE BL | SDCO | 106 | C4 |
| JIM NEGRA RD | MCO | 55 | C2 |
| JOAQUIN RD | ML | 164 | D2 |
| JOAQUIN RDG LKT | FRCO | 66 | C2 |
| JOEGER | PLA | 34 | C3 |
| JOE SMITH RD | INY | 51 | D4 |
| JOHANSEN RD | STA | 47 | D2 |
| JOHN ST | RCO | 100 | E3 |
| JOHN ST | SAL | 171 | C4 |
| JOHN DALY BLVD | SMCO | L | B5 |
| JOHN DALY BLVD | SMCO | 45 | B2 |
| J F KENNEDY DR | RCO | 99 | C3 |
| J F KENNEDY DR | SF | 141 | B4 |
| JOHN FOX RD | STA | 47 | E2 |
| JOHN GIBSON BL | LA | 191 | A2 |
| JOHN LADD CHROM | SIS | 3 | B3 |
| JOHN MUIR PKWY | CC | L | D3 |
| JOHN MUIR PKWY | CC | 38 | D5 |
| JOHNNY MDW RD | MNO | 43 | E5 |
| JOHNNY MDW RD | MNO | 50 | E1 |
| JOHNNY MDW RD | MNO | 51 | A1 |
| JOHNS DR | TUL | 68 | D3 |
| JOHNS RD | KER | 79 | C3 |
| JOHN SCHOOL RD | COL | 33 | A3 |
| JOHN SCHOOL RD | YOL | 33 | A3 |
| JOHN SMITH RD | SBT | 55 | A3 |
| JOHNSON AV | MCO | 47 | D4 |
| JOHNSON AV | SDCO | V | E2 |
| JOHNSON AV | SDCO | 106 | E5 |
| JOHNSON AV | SNLO | 172 | C3 |
| JOHNSON AV | SLO | 76 | B3 |
| JOHNSON CT | KER | 79 | C4 |
| JOHNSON DR | TUL | 58 | B4 |
| JOHNSON RD | HUM | 10 | B3 |
| JOHNSON RD | HUM | 15 | E2 |
| JOHNSON RD | KER | 78 | C3 |
| JOHNSON RD | LAS | 21 | B3 |
| JOHNSON RD | LACO | 89 | D3 |
| JOHNSON RD | LACO | 89 | D4 |
| JOHNSON RD | MCO | 55 | E1 |
| JOHNSON RD | SBD | 90 | E3 |
| JOHNSON RD | SBD | 90 | E4 |
| JOHNSON RD | SBD | 91 | C3 |
| JOHNSON RD | SJCO | 40 | C4 |
| JOHNSON RD | TEH | 18 | B5 |
| JOHNSON RD | TEH | 18 | D4 |
| JOHNSON RD N | MCO | 55 | D1 |
| JOHNSON ST | RCO | 101 | B5 |
| JOHNSON ST | RCO | 108 | B1 |
| JOHNSON ST | SBD | 91 | E3 |
| JOHNSON ST | SB | 87 | D1 |
| JOHNSON CYN RD | INY | 72 | A3 |
| JOHNSON CYN RD | MON | 54 | E5 |
| JOHNSON CYN RD | MON | 55 | A5 |
| JOHNSON RCH RD | PLU | 20 | D5 |
| JOHNSON SCH RD | LAS | 21 | B3 |

| STREET | CO. | PAGE & GRID | |
|---|---|---|---|
| JOHNSTON AV | KER | 80 | D1 |
| JOHNSTON AV | RCO | 99 | E4 |
| JOHNSVILLE RD | SIE | 26 | D3 |
| JOHNSVLL MCCREA | PLU | 26 | E3 |
| JOHN WEST RD | MAD | 49 | D4 |
| JOINES RD | YUB | 33 | E1 |
| JOINT HWY 14 | LAS | 20 | E3 |
| JOINT HWY 14 | LAS | 21 | A3 |
| JOINT RD | TEH | 18 | B5 |
| JOJOBA RD | RCO | 107 | A1 |
| JOJOBA RD E | RCO | 107 | A1 |
| JOJOBA ST | RCO | 102 | C4 |
| JOLON RD | MON | 65 | B3 |
| JOLON PLEYTO | MON | 65 | B4 |
| JONATA PARK RD | SB | 86 | D3 |
| JONATHAN ST | SBD | 91 | B3 |
| JONES AV | COL | 32 | E3 |
| JONES LN | MOD | 8 | B1 |
| JONES RD | LAS | 8 | B5 |
| JONES RD | MCO | 48 | B4 |
| JONES RD | SJCO | 47 | D1 |
| JONES ST | FRCO | 57 | B5 |
| JONES ST | SF | 143 | B2 |
| JONES ST | SMA | 173 | D3 |
| JONES BAR RD | NEV | 34 | C1 |
| JONES BRADWAY | SBD | 92 | A3 |
| JONES VALLEY RD | SIE | 27 | E4 |
| JORDAN RD | HUM | 16 | A3 |
| JORDAN RD | MCO | 47 | E4 |
| JORDAN RD | MCO | 48 | A4 |
| JORDAN CREEK RD | MPA | 48 | E1 |
| JORDAN CREEK RD | MPA | 49 | A1 |
| JORDON HILL RD | BUT | 25 | D2 |
| JORGENSEN RD | MCO | 47 | C5 |
| JORGENSEN RD | STA | 47 | C4 |
| JOSE RD | SCR | P | B5 |
| JOSE BASIN RD | FRCO | 50 | A5 |
| JOSE BASIN RD | MAD | 58 | A1 |
| JOSEPH PL | SIS | 4 | C2 |
| JOSEPH CREEK RD | MOD | 7 | C5 |
| JOSHUA BLVD | KER | 80 | C5 |
| JOSHUA DR | SBD | 100 | D2 |
| JOSHUA LN | SBD | 100 | E2 |
| JOSHUA RD | SBD | 91 | C3 |
| JOSHUA RD | SBD | 91 | D4 |
| JOSHUA WY | KER | 79 | D5 |
| JOSHUA TREE RD | SBD | 92 | C5 |
| JOY RD | SON | 37 | C2 |
| JOY ST | KER | 70 | A5 |
| J T CROW RD | STA | 47 | C4 |
| JUAN ST | SD | 213 | A5 |
| JUAN ST | SDCO | V | B3 |
| JUAN DIEGO- | | | |
| -FLATS RD | RCO | 100 | A5 |
| JUBILEE PASS RD | INY | 72 | C4 |
| JUDSON ST | SBD | 99 | C2 |
| JULIAN AV | KER | 89 | D1 |
| JULIAN AV | SDCO | 107 | A5 |
| JULIAN RD | SDCO | 107 | D4 |
| JULIAN ST | SCL | P | C3 |
| JULIAN ST | SCL | 46 | B4 |
| JULIAN ST | SJ | 152 | A4 |
| JULIE ST | KER | 79 | C3 |
| JUMAR CT | RCO | 107 | B1 |
| JUMPER AV | KER | 78 | A2 |
| JUNCAL RD | SB | 87 | D4 |
| JUNE ST | SBD | 99 | B1 |
| JUNE LK BCH RD | MNO | 50 | C1 |
| JUNIPER AV | MCO | 48 | B4 |
| JUNIPER LN | SIS | 4 | C5 |
| JUNIPER RD | LAS | 14 | B3 |
| JUNIPER RD | RCO | 99 | B3 |
| JUNIPER ST | SDCO | 106 | C2 |
| JUNIPER FLTS RD | RCO | 99 | D4 |
| JUNIPER FLTS RD | RCO | 101 | A2 |
| JUNIPER HILL RD | LACO | 90 | B4 |
| JUNIPR KNOLL RD | SIS | 5 | A3 |
| JUNIPER LAKE RD | LAS | 20 | A3 |
| JUNIPERO ST | CAR | 168 | C4 |
| JUNIPERO SRA BL | SCL | N | D3 |
| JUNIPERO SRA BL | SCL | 45 | D4 |
| JUNIPERO SRA FY | CPTO | 149 | C4 |
| JUNIPERO SRA FY | CPTO | 150 | A4 |
| JUNIPERO SRA FY | MLBR | 144 | A5 |
| JUNIPERO SRA FY | SJ | 150 | A4 |
| JUNIPERO SRA FY | SMCO | 45 | C3 |
| JUNIPERO SRA FY | SCL | 149 | C4 |
| JUNIPER STA RD | MOD | 7 | B5 |
| JUNKANS RD | SHA | 18 | A3 |
| JURS RD | CAL | 41 | B2 |
| JURUPA AV | RCO | 99 | A2 |
| JURUPA AV | SBD | 99 | A2 |
| JURUPA RD | RCO | 99 | A2 |
| JUSTICE CT | KER | 79 | D2 |
| JUSTICE RD | TRI | 16 | E5 |
| JUTLAND DR | SD | 211 | C4 |
| J W BARR | SIS | 12 | C2 |
| K | | | |
| K ST | BEN | 153 | A4 |
| K ST | MDO | 162 | B3 |
| KADOTA AV | MCO | 48 | D5 |
| KAGEL CANYON RD | LACO | Q | D1 |
| KAISER | SJCO | 40 | B5 |
| KAISER RD | IMP | 109 | C3 |
| KAISER RD | RCO | 102 | C4 |
| KAISER RD | STA | 47 | D3 |
| KALIN RD | IMP | 109 | A4 |
| KAMM AV | FRCO | 56 | E3 |
| KAMM AV | FRCO | 57 | C5 |
| KAMM AV | TUL | 57 | D5 |
| KAMM RD | IMP | 109 | C5 |
| KANDRA RD | SIS | 5 | D2 |
| KANE RD | HUM | 9 | E3 |
| KANE RD | HUM | 10 | A3 |
| KANE RD | SBD | 91 | E2 |
| KANSAS AV | KIN | 67 | D2 |
| KANSAS AV | MDO | 162 | A3 |

| STREET | CO. | PAGE & GRID | |
|---|---|---|---|
| KANSAS AV | STA | 47 | C2 |
| KANSAS AV | TEH | 18 | E5 |
| KAPAPA RD | SBD | 80 | E1 |
| KAPRANOS RD | LAK | 23 | C5 |
| KARCHNER RD | PLA | 34 | A3 |
| KAREN AV | RCO | 100 | C3 |
| KARLO RD | LAS | 21 | C2 |
| KARNAK RD | SUT | 33 | C4 |
| KASSON RD | SJCO | 47 | A2 |
| KATELLA AV | ANA | 193 | C4 |
| KATELLA AV | ANA | 194 | B4 |
| KATELLA AV | OR | 194 | B4 |
| KATELLA AV | ORA | 98 | B3 |
| KATELLA AV | ORA | T | D2 |
| KATHERINE RD | VEN | 97 | A1 |
| KAUFENBERG RD | LAS | 14 | A4 |
| KAUFFMAN AV | TEH | 18 | E5 |
| KAUFMAN RD | STA | 47 | E2 |
| KAUT RD | TRI | 10 | E5 |
| KAVANAUGH RD | IMP | 112 | C3 |
| KEARNEY AV | FRCO | 57 | A3 |
| KEARNEY BLVD | FRE | 165 | B4 |
| KEARNY ST | SF | 143 | C2 |
| KEARNY VILLA RD | SD | 213 | E1 |
| KEARNY VILLA RD | SD | 214 | A1 |
| KEARNY VILLA RD | SDCO | V | C2 |
| KEARNY VILLA RD | SDCO | 106 | D5 |
| KEATON RD | MCO | 47 | D4 |
| KECKS RD | KER | 77 | A1 |
| KEEFER RD | BUT | 25 | A2 |
| KEEGAN RD | COL | 32 | C2 |
| KEELE RD | RCO | 110 | C1 |
| KEIM BLVD | RCO | 110 | C1 |
| KELBAKER RD | SBD | 83 | C3 |
| KELBAKER RD | SBD | 84 | A5 |
| KELBAKER RD | SBD | 93 | E2 |
| KELBAKER RD | SBD | 94 | A1 |
| KELLEMS LN | SIS | 3 | D5 |
| KELLEMS LN | SIS | 11 | D1 |
| KELLER RD | RCO | 99 | C5 |
| KELLEY RD | SBD | 101 | D1 |
| KELLOG RD | SUT | 33 | B2 |
| KELLOGG DR | ORA | 98 | C3 |
| KELLOGG DR | ORA | T | E1 |
| KELLOGG RD | DN | 1 | D3 |
| KELLOGG SRRA BL | RCO | 100 | C3 |
| KELLY | SJCO | 47 | D1 |
| KELLY RD | HUM | 16 | C2 |
| KELLY RD | NAPA | L | D1 |
| KELLY RD | NAPA | 38 | D3 |
| KELLY RD | TEH | 24 | A2 |
| KELLY RD | YUB | 26 | B5 |
| KELLY GULCH RD | SIS | 11 | B2 |
| KELSEY CREEK RD | SIS | 3 | B5 |
| KELSEY CREEK RD | LAK | 31 | D3 |
| KELSO AV | KER | 79 | E1 |
| KELSO RD | ALA | M | E4 |
| KELSO RD | ALA | 46 | D1 |
| KELSO RD | KER | 79 | E1 |
| KELSO RD | SBD | 83 | C4 |
| KELSO AMBOY RD | SBD | 93 | E1 |
| KELSO AMBOY RD | SBD | 94 | A1 |
| KELSO CIMA RD | SBD | 83 | E5 |
| KELSO CIMA RD | SBD | 84 | A4 |
| KELSO CK VLY RD | KER | 79 | E1 |
| KELSO VALLEY RD | KER | 79 | E2 |
| KELSO VALLEY RD | KER | 80 | A2 |
| KEMP CT | HUM | 16 | B3 |
| KEMPER RD | KER | 80 | A5 |
| KEMPER RD | STA | 47 | D2 |
| KEMPTON RD | SUT | 33 | D3 |
| KENDALL AV | KER | 80 | D1 |
| KENDALL DR | SBD | 99 | B1 |
| KENDLE RD | IMP | 109 | C4 |
| KENMAR LN | KER | 79 | A4 |
| KENMAR RD | HUM | 15 | E2 |
| KENNEBRAW LN | HUM | 16 | C4 |
| KENNEDY AV | BUT | 25 | A3 |
| KENNEDY RD | STA | 48 | A1 |
| KENNEDY RD | TRI | 17 | B1 |
| KENNEDY MEADOW | TUL | 70 | A3 |
| KENNEDY MEM DR | SHA | 18 | B2 |
| KENNEFICK RD | SJCO | 40 | B4 |
| KENNETH AV | SAC | 34 | B5 |
| KENNETH RD | LACO | Q | D2 |
| KENNETT RD | SHA | 18 | C1 |
| KENNEY AV | TEH | 18 | C4 |
| KENNY AV | MCO | 48 | B4 |
| KENNY CAMP RD | TRI | 11 | D5 |
| KENO WORDEN RD | KLAM | 5 | A1 |
| KENSINGTON WY | S | 160 | B2 |
| KENT AV | KIN | 67 | B2 |
| KENT AV | KIN | 67 | C2 |
| KENT AV | MAR | 139 | B5 |
| KENT AV | SUT | 33 | C1 |
| KENTUCKY AV | YOL | 33 | B5 |
| KENTUCKY ST | FRFD | 135 | B3 |
| KENWOOD | SDCO | 111 | A4 |
| KENWOOD DR | SDCO | V | D3 |
| KEOUGH HOT SPGS | INY | 51 | D5 |
| KERN RD | SBD | 101 | D1 |
| KERN ST | SAL | 171 | D4 |
| KERN CANYON RD | KER | 79 | A2 |
| KERN RIV CYN RD | KER | 79 | B2 |
| KERTO RD | KER | 78 | A5 |
| KERSHAW RD | IMP | 109 | B4 |
| KESTER AV | LACO | Q | C3 |
| KESWICK DAM RD | SHA | 18 | B2 |
| KETTLEMAN LN | SJCO | 40 | A4 |
| KETTNER BLVD | SD | 215 | D4 |
| KETTNER BLVD | SDCO | V | B3 |
| KEYES RD | MCO | 48 | B3 |
| KEYES RD | STA | 47 | D3 |
| KEYES RD | STA | 48 | A3 |
| KEYES ST | SJ | 152 | D5 |
| KEYS RD | SUT | 33 | D4 |
| KEYSTONE RD | IMP | 109 | A5 |

| STREET | CO. | PAGE & GRID | |
|---|---|---|---|
| KEYSVILLE RD | KER | 79 | C1 |
| KEZAR DR | SF | 141 | D4 |
| KIBBE RD | YUB | 33 | D1 |
| KICKAPOO TR | SBD | 100 | D2 |
| KIDDER AV | FRFD | 135 | C3 |
| KIDDER CREEK RD | SIS | 3 | C5 |
| KIDDER CK RD S | SIS | 3 | D5 |
| KIDDER CK RD S | SIS | 11 | D1 |
| KID LAKES | PLA | 35 | C1 |
| KIDWELL RD | SOL | 39 | B1 |
| KIEFER BLVD | SAC | 39 | E1 |
| KIEFER BLVD | SAC | 40 | B1 |
| KIEFER RD | IMP | 112 | C4 |
| KIELY BLVD | SJ | 150 | E5 |
| KIELY BLVD | SCLR | 150 | D3 |
| KIERNAN AV | STA | 47 | B2 |
| KIETZKE LN | RENO | 130 | E3 |
| KIFER RD | SCLR | 150 | D1 |
| KIFER RD | SVL | 150 | E1 |
| KILAGA SPGS RD | PLA | 34 | B3 |
| KILAGA SPG RD N | PLA | 34 | B3 |
| KILBURN AV | NAP | 133 | A4 |
| KILBURN RD | STA | 47 | C4 |
| KILE RD | SJCO | 39 | E3 |
| KILER CANYON RD | SLO | 75 | E1 |
| KILER CANYON RD | SLO | 76 | A1 |
| KILGORE RD | SUT | 33 | A2 |
| KILKARE RD | ALA | 46 | B2 |
| KILLGORE HLS RD | SIS | 4 | A4 |
| KILROY | STA | 47 | D3 |
| KILROY RD | MCO | 47 | D4 |
| KIMBALL AV | SBD | 98 | D2 |
| KIMBALL LN | YUB | 33 | D2 |
| KIMBALL RD | TEH | 18 | D5 |
| KIMBERLINA RD | KER | 78 | B1 |
| KIMBERLY CT | KER | 79 | C5 |
| KIMBERLY DR | KER | 79 | C5 |
| KIMBERLY RD | SHA | 18 | D3 |
| KIMTU CT | HUM | 16 | B5 |
| KINCAID RD | SCL | P | D3 |
| KINCAID RD | SCL | 46 | C4 |
| KINE AV | RCO | 99 | C3 |
| KINEVAN RD | SB | 87 | B4 |
| KING AV | KIN | 67 | C2 |
| KING RD | COL | 32 | C2 |
| KING RD | IMP | 112 | C3 |
| KING RD | KER | 67 | C5 |
| KING RD | PLA | 34 | B4 |
| KING RD | SJ | 152 | D1 |
| KING RD | SCL | P | C3 |
| KING RD | SCL | 46 | B4 |
| KING RD | SCL | 152 | D1 |
| KING RD | SOL | 39 | C2 |
| KING RD | TEH | 18 | C5 |
| KING RD | TRI | 12 | A4 |
| KING ST | BKD | 166 | E4 |
| KING CITY RD | SBT | 65 | C1 |
| KINGDON | SJCO | 40 | A4 |
| KING RANCH RD | BUT | 25 | E5 |
| KING RIDGE RD | SON | 37 | A1 |
| KINGS AV | FRCO | 66 | D2 |
| KINGS RD | SBD | 90 | E4 |
| KINGS RD | TUO | 48 | E1 |
| KINGS RD | TUO | 49 | A1 |
| KINGSBURY RD | TRI | 17 | B2 |
| KINGS CANYON RD | FRCO | 58 | A3 |
| KINGS HILL RD | PLA | 34 | D2 |
| KINGSLEY ST | MTCL | 203 | A4 |
| KINGS MTN RD | SMCO | N | D2 |
| KINGS MTN RD | SMCO | 45 | C4 |
| KINGS PEAK RD | HUM | 16 | A5 |
| KINGSTON RD | SBD | 83 | E2 |
| KINGS VALLEY RD | DN | 1 | E3 |
| KINNEY RD | MEN | 30 | C3 |
| KIOWA BLVD | MOH | 96 | B4 |
| KIOWA RD | RCO | 102 | C3 |
| KIOWA RD | SBD | 91 | C4 |
| KIP ST | KER | 80 | C1 |
| KIRBY RD | MCO | 48 | C4 |
| KIRBY ST | CAL | 40 | D4 |
| KIRK RD | SCL | P | B4 |
| KIRKER PASS RD | CC | M | B3 |
| KIRKVILLE RD | SUT | 33 | C3 |
| KIRSCHENMANN RD | SB | 87 | D1 |
| KIT CARSON RD | AMA | 35 | E5 |
| KIT CARSON CPGD | ALP | 36 | B4 |
| KLAMATH BCH RD | DN | 1 | E5 |
| KLAMATH BCH RD | DN | 9 | E1 |
| KLAMATH BCH RD | DN | 10 | A1 |
| KLAMATH MILL RD | DN | 2 | A5 |
| KLAMATH MILL RD | DN | 10 | A1 |
| KLAMATHON RD | SIS | 4 | B3 |
| KLAMATH RIV RD | SIS | 3 | D3 |
| KLASSETTE ST | KER | 80 | A4 |
| KLAU MINE RD | SLO | 75 | D1 |
| KLIPSTEIN ST | KER | 78 | A5 |
| KLIPSTEIN CY RD | KER | 78 | A5 |
| KLOKE RD | IMP | 112 | B4 |
| KLONDIKE RD | SBD | 93 | C3 |
| KLONDKE MINE RD | TRI | 17 | A3 |
| KNEELAND RD | HUM | 16 | B1 |
| KNIEBES RD | MCO | 47 | D5 |
| KNIGHTON RD | SHA | 18 | C3 |
| KNIGHTS RD | SUT | 33 | C3 |
| KNIGHTSEN AV | CC | M | D3 |
| KNIGHTSEN AV | CC | 39 | C5 |
| KNOB HILL RD | MEN | 31 | B2 |
| KNOB PK LKOT RD | SHA | 17 | D3 |
| KNOTT AV | ORA | 98 | B3 |
| KNOTT AV | ORA | T | B2 |
| KNOW | PLA | 33 | E5 |
| KNOWLES RD | MAD | 49 | B5 |
| KNOWLES RD | MCO | 56 | C1 |
| KNOX RD | STA | 47 | E1 |
| KNOXVL DVLHD RD | NAPA | 32 | C4 |
| KOALA RD | SBD | 91 | A3 |
| KOCH RD | KER | 78 | B2 |

| STREET | CO. | PAGE & GRID | |
|---|---|---|---|
| KOENIGSTEIN RD | VEN | 88 | C4 |
| KOESTER RD | KER | 79 | D3 |
| KONOCTI RD | LAK | 31 | D3 |
| KOPTA RD | TEH | 24 | E2 |
| KOSTER RD | SJCO | 47 | A2 |
| KOSTER ST | EUR | 121 | B1 |
| KOWOLOWSKI RD | MOD | 6 | A2 |
| KRAEMER BLVD | ORA | T | D1 |
| KRAFFT RD | MCO | 48 | D4 |
| KRAFT RD | KER | 78 | E5 |
| KRAMAR RD | IMP | 111 | E3 |
| KRAMER BLVD | ORA | 98 | C3 |
| KRAMER RD | LAS | 14 | B3 |
| KRAMER RD | SBD | 91 | A1 |
| KRATZMEYER RD | KER | 78 | C2 |
| KREHE RD | SUT | 33 | C1 |
| KROSENS RD | YUB | 25 | E5 |
| KRUSE RD | COL | 32 | D1 |
| KT RD | SBT | 54 | E3 |
| KT RD | SBT | 55 | A3 |
| KUBLER RD | IMP | 111 | E4 |
| KUCK RD | SIS | 4 | B4 |
| KUENZLI ST | RENO | 130 | D2 |
| KUMBERG RD | IMP | 112 | C4 |
| KUNA AV | SBD | 92 | E5 |
| KURT RD | KER | 77 | E1 |
| KUTZ RD | IMP | 108 | E5 |
| KYLE AV | KER | 70 | A5 |
| KYTE AV | KER | 78 | C2 |
| L | | | |
| L ST | CC | M | C3 |
| L ST | DVS | 136 | D3 |
| L ST | DN | 1 | D4 |
| L ST | MDO | 162 | B3 |
| L ST | SCTO | 137 | B3 |
| L ST | SDCO | V | C4 |
| L ST | SDCO | 111 | D2 |
| LA BARR MDWS RD | NEV | 34 | C2 |
| LABP & L RD | SBD | 91 | A4 |
| LA BREA AV | LA | 181 | C4 |
| LA BREA AV | LA | 184 | C3 |
| LA BREA AV | LACO | 97 | D2 |
| LA BREA AV | LACO | Q | D5 |
| LA BREA CK RD | SB | 77 | A5 |
| LA BRISA DR | SBD | 100 | E1 |
| LA BRISTA DR | SBD | 100 | D1 |
| LA BRUCHERIE RD | IMP | 112 | A3 |
| LA CADENA DR | CLTN | 207 | A4 |
| LA CADENA DR | SBD | 90 | E3 |
| LA CADENA DR | SBD | 99 | B2 |
| LACEY BLVD | KIN | 67 | C1 |
| LA CIENEGA BLVD | BH | 183 | E2 |
| LA CIENEGA BLVD | CUL | 183 | E5 |
| LA CIENEGA BLVD | ING | 188 | E4 |
| LA CIENEGA BLVD | ING | 189 | E2 |
| LA CIENEGA BLVD | LA | 183 | E4 |
| LA CIENEGA BLVD | LACO | 97 | D2 |
| LA CIENEGA BLVD | LACO | Q | D4 |
| LA CIENEGA BLVD | LACO | 183 | E2 |
| LA CIENEGA BLVD | LACO | 188 | E1 |
| LA CIENEGA BLVD | LACO | 189 | E2 |
| LAC JAC | FRCO | 58 | A4 |
| LACK RD | IMP | 109 | A4 |
| LA COLINA | TUL | 68 | E3 |
| LA COLINA LN | RCO | 107 | C1 |
| LA CONTENTA RD | SBD | 100 | E2 |
| LA COSTA AV | SDCO | 106 | C3 |
| LA CRESCENTA AV | LACO | R | A2 |
| LA CRESTA DR | SDCO | 107 | A5 |
| LA CUARTA ST | LACO | R | D5 |
| LADD RD | STA | 47 | C2 |
| LADDER RIDGE RD | LAK | 31 | D2 |
| LADINO AV | MCO | 48 | B4 |
| LA ENTRADA AV | LACO | R | D5 |
| LAFAYETTE RD | SIE | 26 | D5 |
| LAFAYETTE ST | SCLR | 151 | B1 |
| LAFAYETTE ST | S | 160 | D5 |
| LA GLORIA RD | SBT | 55 | B5 |
| LAGOMARSINO AV | MON | 65 | B2 |
| LAGOON DR | KER | 78 | A2 |
| LA GRANADA | SDCO | 106 | C4 |
| LA GRANDE RD | COL | 32 | C2 |
| LA GRANGE RD | MCO | 48 | C2 |
| LA GRANGE RD | STA | 48 | C2 |
| LA GRANGE RD | TUO | 48 | C1 |
| LA GRANGE DM RD | STA | 48 | C2 |
| LAGUE RD | YUB | 26 | A5 |
| LAGUNA AV | FRCO | 67 | B1 |
| LAGUNA FRWY | ORA | 98 | D4 |
| LAGUNA FRWY | ORA | T | E4 |
| LAGUNA RD | SON | 37 | D2 |
| LAGUNA RD | VEN | 96 | C1 |
| LAGUNA CYN RD | LAG | 201 | B2 |
| LAGUNA CYN RD | ORA | 98 | D5 |
| LAGUNA CYN RD | ORA | T | E5 |
| LAGUNA CREEK TR | SOL | 38 | E3 |
| LAGUNA MTN RD | SDCO | 107 | D5 |
| LAGUNA SECA DR | SBD | 91 | D4 |
| LAGUNA SECA RD | MCO | 55 | D3 |
| LA HABRA BLVD | ORA | R | E5 |
| LA HABRA BLVD | ORA | T | B1 |
| LA HONDA RD | SMCO | N | C3 |
| LA HONDA RD | SMCO | 45 | C4 |
| LAIRD RD | PLA | 34 | B4 |
| LAIRD RD | STA | 47 | C3 |
| LAIRO RED ROCK | SIS | 5 | B3 |
| LA JOLLA AV | SDCO | 106 | C5 |
| LA JOLLA BLVD | SDCO | V | A2 |
| LA JOLLA BLVD | SDCO | 106 | C5 |
| LA JOLLA AMAGO | SDCO | 107 | A2 |
| LA JOLLA S DR N | SD | 211 | B2 |
| LA JOLLA S RD S | SD | 211 | A4 |
| LA JOLLA SHR DR | SD | 211 | C2 |
| LA JOLLA VLG RD | SDCO | V | A2 |
| LAKE AV | FRCO | 56 | E3 |
| LAKE AV | FRCO | 57 | A3 |
| LAKE AV | KER | 79 | C2 |


COPYRIGHT, © 1988 BY Thomas Bros Maps

STREETS

# STREET INDEX





| STREET | CO. | PAGE & GRID |
|---|---|---|
| LAKE AV | LACO | 98 A1 |
| LAKE AV | LACO | R B3 |
| LAKE AV | PAS | 190 D4 |
| LAKE AV | SCR | 54 C2 |
| LAKE BLVD | SHA | 18 C2 |
| LAKE DR | SBD | 91 C5 |
| LAKE RD | FRCO | 50 B5 |
| LAKE RD | KER | 80 C3 |
| LAKE RD | MCO | 48 C4 |
| LAKE RD | STA | 47 E2 |
| LAKE RD | STA | 48 A2 |
| LAKE RD N | INY | 51 B5 |
| LAKE RD S | INY | 51 C5 |
| LAKE RD S | KER | 78 B4 |
| LAKE RD S | KER | 78 C4 |
| LAKE ST | MAD | 57 A2 |
| LAKE ST | RCO | 99 B4 |
| LK ALMANOR W DR | PLU | 20 B4 |
| LK ALMANR RD E | PLU | 20 C4 |
| LK ALPINE RD E | ALP | 42 A1 |
| LK ALPINE RD W | ALP | 42 A2 |
| LAKE ANNIE RD | MOD | 7 D3 |
| LK BRITTON LOOP | SHA | 13 D4 |
| LK BRITTON RAMP | SHA | 13 D4 |
| LAKE CALIF DR | TEH | 18 D3 |
| LAKE CANYON RD | LACO | 89 B3 |
| LAKE CANYON RD | LACO | 89 C3 |
| LAKE CITY RD | NEV | 26 C5 |
| LK CITY DUMP RD | MOD | 7 D5 |
| LAKE CREST RD | LAS | 21 B4 |
| LAKE DAVIS RD | PLU | 27 B2 |
| LAKE EARL DR | DN | 1 D4 |
| LAKE FOREST DR | ORA | 98 D4 |
| LAKE FRANCES RD | YUB | 26 B5 |
| LAKE HERMAN RD | SOL | L E2 |
| LAKE HERMAN RD | SOL | 38 D4 |
| LAKE HERMAN RD | SOL | 153 C1 |
| LK JENNINGS PK | SDCO | 107 A5 |
| LAKELAND RD | LACO | R C5 |
| LAKELAND RD | LACO | T A1 |
| LAKE LEAVITT RD | LAS | 21 B3 |
| LAKE MARY RD | ML | 164 A4 |
| LAKE MARY RD | MNO | 50 D2 |
| LAKE MATHEWS DR | RCO | 99 B3 |
| LAKE MCCUMBER | SHA | 19 B2 |
| LAKE MEAD DR | CLK | 74 E3 |
| LAKE MORENA DR | SDCO | 112 D1 |
| LAKE MURRAY BL | SDCO | V D3 |
| LAKE MURRAY BL | SDCO | 106 D5 |
| LAKEPORT BLVD | LAK | 31 D3 |
| LAKE POWAY RD | SDCO | 106 D4 |
| LAKERIDGE RD | SHA | 19 A3 |
| LAKE SHORE AV | O | 158 B3 |
| LAKESHORE BLVD | LAK | 31 D3 |
| LAKESHORE DR | KLAM | 5 B1 |
| LAKESHORE DR | LAK | 32 A3 |
| LAKESHORE DR | SHA | 12 C5 |
| LAKE SHORE DR | SIS | 4 C5 |
| LAKESHORE RD | MOD | 7 B4 |
| LAKESIDE DR | O | 158 A3 |
| LAKE SIDE LN | SIS | 4 C2 |
| LAKE STATION RD | KER | 78 B4 |
| LAKE TAHOE BLVD | SLT | 129 A4 |
| LAKEVIEW | KIN | 67 C2 |
| LAKEVIEW | PLA | 34 A3 |
| LAKEVIEW AV | ORA | T E2 |
| LAKEVIEW AV | RCO | 99 D3 |
| LAKEVIEW DR | AMA | 40 D3 |
| LAKEVIEW DR | LAK | 31 D2 |
| LAKE VIEW DR | LAS | 21 B4 |
| LAKE VIEW DR | SLO | 75 D1 |
| LAKEVIEW RD | MPA | 49 B3 |
| LAKEVIEW RD | SCR | 54 C2 |
| LAKEVIEW RD | SDCO | 107 A5 |
| LAKE VIEW RD | SIS | 4 C3 |
| LAKEVIEW RD | SON | 38 B3 |
| LAKEVIEW CEM RD | SIS | 5 A3 |
| LAKEVILLE HWY | SON | L A1 |
| LAKEVILLE RD | SON | L B2 |
| LK WILDWOOD DR | NEV | 34 B1 |
| LAKEWOOD BLVD | LACO | 98 A3 |
| LAKEWOOD BLVD | LACO | S E2 |
| LAKEWOOD DR | MEN | 23 A5 |
| LAKIN DAM RD | SIS | 13 A2 |
| LA LOMA AV | B | 156 B2 |
| LA LOMA AV | MDO | 162 C3 |
| LA LOMA AV | VEN | 88 C5 |
| LA LOMA RD | LACO | R B3 |
| LA LOMA RD | PAS | 190 A5 |
| LAMB BLVD | CLK | 74 E2 |
| LAMB CANYON RD | RCO | 99 E3 |
| LAMBERT LN | LAS | 21 C4 |
| LAMBERT RD | LACO | R D5 |
| LAMBERT RD | ORA | U A4 |
| LAMBERT RD | ORA | T C1 |
| LAMBERT RD | SAC | 39 E3 |
| LAMBERT BRDG RD | SON | 31 D5 |
| LAMBIE RD | SOL | 39 B3 |
| LAMBUTH RD | STA | 47 D1 |
| LAMERT LN | GLE | 24 D5 |
| LA MESA RD | SBD | 90 E4 |
| LA MIRADA AV | LACO | R D5 |
| LA MIRADA AV | LACO | T B1 |
| LA MIRADA BLVD | LACO | 98 B3 |
| LAMMERS RD | SJCO | 46 E2 |
| LAMPLEY RD | STA | 48 A2 |
| LAMPSON AV | GGR | 195 A1 |
| LAMPSON AV | ORA | T B2 |
| LANCASTER BLVD | KER | 90 B1 |
| LANCASTER BLVD | LACO | 90 A2 |
| LANCASTER RD | LACO | 88 E2 |
| LANCASTER RD | LACO | 89 A2 |
| LANCASTER RD | STA | 47 E1 |
| LANCASTER RD | STA | 48 A1 |
| LANCHA PLANA- | | |
| -BUENA VISTA RD | AMA | 40 D3 |
| LANDACRE RD | TRI | 17 B2 |
| LANDAU BLVD | RCO | 100 D3 |
| LANDECENA DR | TRI | 17 D1 |
| LANDER AV | MCO | 47 D5 |
| LANDER AV | STA | 47 E3 |
| LANDERGEN RD | HUM | 15 E4 |
| LANDES RD | TEH | 18 C4 |
| LANDESS RD | SCL | 46 B4 |
| LANDIS GULCH | TRI | 17 C3 |
| LANDRAM AV | MCO | 48 B4 |
| LANES RD | FRCO | 57 C2 |
| LANES VALLEY RD | TEH | 19 A3 |
| LANFAIR RD | SBD | 84 D3 |
| LANFAIR RD | SBD | 94 E1 |
| LANGDON RD | MCO | 55 D2 |
| LANGLL VLY RD E | KLAM | 5 E1 |
| LANGLL VLY RD E | KLAM | 6 A1 |
| LANGLL VLY RD W | KLAM | 5 E1 |
| LANGLL VLY RD W | KLAM | 6 A1 |
| LANGWORTH RD | STA | 47 D2 |
| LANINI RD | MON | 54 E5 |
| LANINI RD | MON | 55 A5 |
| LANKERSHIM BLVD | LA | 179 A5 |
| LANKERSHIM BLVD | LACO | 97 D1 |
| LANKERSHIM BLVD | LACO | Q D2 |
| LANNAGAN RD | TRI | 11 B5 |
| LANNAGAN RD | TRI | 17 B1 |
| LANPHERE RD | HUM | 9 E5 |
| LANSING AV | KIN | 67 C2 |
| LA PALMA AV | ANA | 193 D1 |
| LA PALMA AV | ANA | 194 A1 |
| LA PALMA AV | KER | 80 A5 |
| LA PALMA AV | ORA | 98 A3 |
| LA PALMA AV | ORA | T B2 |
| LA PALOMA | AVLN | 105 A4 |
| LA PALOMA DR | TUL | 68 E3 |
| LA PALOMA RD | MCO | 48 C4 |
| LA PANZA AV | SB | 87 E2 |
| LA PAZ RD | ORA | 98 D5 |
| LA PORTE RD | BUT | 25 D5 |
| LA PORTE RD | BUT | 26 B4 |
| LA PORTE RD | YUB | 26 A5 |
| LA POSTA RD | SDCO | 112 D1 |
| LA PUENTE RD | LACO | U A3 |
| LARCHMONT BLVD | LA | 184 E1 |
| LARGO GRANDE | RCO | 107 B1 |
| LARGO VISTA RD | LACO | 90 D4 |
| LARKELLEN AV | LACO | R E4 |
| LARKIN RD | BUT | 25 C4 |
| LARKIN RD | SUT | 33 C1 |
| LARKIN VALLEY | SCR | 54 B2 |
| LARKMEAD LN | NAPA | 29 B2 |
| LARKSPUR DR | MLBR | 144 B5 |
| LARREA AV | SBD | 101 B1 |
| LARRY FLAT | MOD | 7 D3 |
| LARSEN RD | IMP | 109 A5 |
| LARSON LN | MNO | 42 E1 |
| LARSON RD | RCO | 107 C1 |
| LA RUE RD | YOL | 136 B3 |
| LA SALLE CANYON | SB | 86 B3 |
| LAS AMIGAS RD | NAPA | 38 C3 |
| LAS ANIMAS RD | SCL | 46 C5 |
| LAS FLORES AV | KER | 80 C1 |
| LA SIERRA AV | RCO | 99 A3 |
| LAS LOMAS AV | AVLN | 105 A5 |
| LAS PALMAS AV | STA | 47 C3 |
| LAS PASOS | VEN | 96 C1 |
| LASPINA DR | TUL | 68 B2 |
| LAS PLUMAS AV | BUT | 25 D4 |
| LS PULGAS CY RD | SDCO | 106 A2 |
| LAS ROCAS | RCO | 100 D4 |
| LASSELLE ST | RCO | 99 C3 |
| LASSEN AV | BUT | 25 B3 |
| LASSEN AV | FRCO | 67 A1 |
| LASSEN AV | FRCO | 57 A3 |
| LASSEN LN | SIS | 12 C2 |
| LASSEN RD | TEH | 25 A2 |
| LASSEN ST | LAS | 8 B4 |
| LASSEN ST | NAP | 133 A1 |
| LASSEN TRAIL | TEH | 19 D4 |
| LASSEN CREEK RD | MOD | 7 C4 |
| LASSEN PARK HWY | SHA | 19 D2 |
| LASSICS LKOT RD | TRI | 16 E4 |
| LAST CHANCE CYN RD | KER | 80 C2 |
| LAST CHANCE MNE | NEV | 26 E5 |
| LAST CHANCE MNE | NEV | 35 A1 |
| LAS TUNAS DR | LACO | R C3 |
| LAS VARAS RD | SB | 87 A4 |
| LAS VEGAS BLVD | CLK | 74 D3 |
| LAS VEGAS BL S | CLK | 209 C4 |
| LAS VEGAS BL S | CLK | 210 B5 |
| LAS VEGAS BL S | LV | 209 C4 |
| LAS VIRGENES RD | LACO | 97 A1 |
| LATHAM RD | SUT | 33 B3 |
| LATHROP RD | MAN | 161 A1 |
| LATHROP RD | SJCO | 47 A1 |
| LATHROP RD | SJCO | 161 D1 |
| LATIGO CYN RD | LACO | 97 A2 |
| LA TIJERA BLVD | LA | 188 C5 |
| LA TIJERA BLVD | LACO | Q D5 |
| LATKA LN | TEH | 19 B4 |
| LATROBE RD | AMA | 40 D1 |
| LATROBE RD | ED | 40 C1 |
| LATROBE RD | SAC | 40 B1 |
| LA TUNA CYN RD | LACO | 97 D1 |
| LA TUNA CYN RD | LACO | Q D2 |
| LAUFFER RD | HUM | 22 D1 |
| LAUGHLIN RD | STA | 47 E2 |
| LAURA DR | LAS | 27 E1 |
| LAUREL AV | KIN | 67 B2 |
| LAUREL AV | ML | 164 C4 |
| LAUREL AV | MLBR | 144 C5 |
| LAUREL AV | SUT | 33 D3 |
| LAUREL DR E | MON | 171 E2 |
| LAUREL DR E | SAL | 171 E2 |
| LAUREL DR W | MON | 171 A2 |
| LAUREL DR W | SAL | 171 A2 |
| LAUREL LN | YUB | 33 D1 |
| LAUREL ST | NAP | 133 A4 |
| LAUREL ST | SD | 215 D2 |
| LAUREL ST | SDCO | V C3 |
| LAUREL ST | SC | 169 C3 |
| LAUREL WY | TEH | 18 C4 |
| LAUREL CYN BLVD | LACO | 97 D1 |
| LAUREL CYN BLVD | LACO | Q C1 |
| LAUREL DELL RD | LAK | 31 C2 |
| LAURELES GRADE | MON | 54 C5 |
| LAUREL GLEN RD | SCR | P B5 |
| LAUREL GLEN RD | SCR | 54 A1 |
| LAUREL GROVE AV | MAR | 139 B4 |
| LAUREL GROVE AV | MAR | L A3 |
| LAUREL GROVE AV | ROSS | 139 A4 |
| LAURELLEN RD | YUB | 33 D2 |
| LAURENT ST | SC | 169 B3 |
| LAURJOE RD | SBD | 91 E3 |
| LAUSTEN RD | COL | 32 D1 |
| LAUX RD | COL | 33 A1 |
| LAVA BED RD | BUT | 25 B3 |
| LAVA BDS NAT MN | MOD | 6 A4 |
| LAVA BDS MED LK | SIS | 5 C5 |
| LAVAL RD | KER | 78 E5 |
| LAVER CROSSING | LAS | 21 E5 |
| LAVERNE AV | MAR | 140 A3 |
| LA VETA AV | OR | 196 B1 |
| LAVEZZOLA RD | SIE | 26 D4 |
| LAVIC RD | SBD | 92 E2 |
| LA VISTA AV | VEN | 88 C5 |
| LAWNCREST RD | SHA | 18 C2 |
| LAWRENCE | AMA | 41 A1 |
| LAWRENCE EXPWY | SCL | P A3 |
| LAWRENCE EXPWY | SCLR | 150 C4 |
| LAWRENCE EXPWY | SJ | 150 C4 |
| LAWRENCE EXPWY | SVL | 150 C4 |
| LAWRENCE RD | AMA | 40 E1 |
| LAWSON LN | HUM | 15 E2 |
| LAXAQUE RD | MOD | 8 D1 |
| LAYTNVL DOS RIO | MEN | 22 E3 |
| LAZARO CARDENAS | BAJA | 112 B4 |
| LAZARUS LN | RCO | 100 A5 |
| L B CROW RD | STA | 47 C4 |
| LEACH RD | YUB | 33 D3 |
| LEAR AV | SBD | 101 B1 |
| LEARY RD | SAC | M D1 |
| LEARY RD | SAC | 39 D3 |
| LEASTALK AV | SBD | 84 C3 |
| LEATHER RD | IMP | 110 D5 |
| LEAVENWORTH ST | SF | 143 B2 |
| LEAVESLEY RD | SCL | P E5 |
| LEAVESLEY RD | SCL | 54 D1 |
| LEAVITT RD | LAS | 21 B3 |
| LEE RD | MCO | 48 A3 |
| LEE RD | PLU | 26 D1 |
| LEE RD | SHA | 13 E4 |
| LEE RD | SUT | 33 D4 |
| LEEDS | MCO | 48 C4 |
| LEEGE AV | SB | 86 B3 |
| LEEK RD | STA | 47 D2 |
| LEE SCHOOL RD | SAC | 40 B2 |
| LEESVILLE RD | COL | 32 C2 |
| LEESVL-LODGA RD | COL | 32 B1 |
| LEFF RD | RCO | 107 B1 |
| LEFFINGWELL RD | LACO | R C5 |
| LEFFINGWELL RD | LACO | T B1 |
| LEGION AV | MCO | 47 E4 |
| LEGION AV | MCO | 48 A4 |
| LEGION PARK DR | MDO | 162 E5 |
| LE GRAND RD | MCO | 48 D5 |
| LEGRAY RD | KER | 78 E5 |
| LEIGHTON, H RD | SHA | 18 C2 |
| LEILA LN | SBD | 101 E1 |
| LEIMERT BLVD | LACO | Q D4 |
| LEININGER RD | TEH | 25 A1 |
| LEISER RD | SUT | 33 C4 |
| LEISURE TOWN RD | SOL | 39 A2 |
| LELITER RD | KER | 70 C5 |
| LEMON AV | SDCO | V D3 |
| LEMON AV | SDCO | 111 E1 |
| LEMON AV | SJCO | 47 D1 |
| LEMON AV | STA | 47 B3 |
| LEMON RD | SBD | 91 C4 |
| LEMON ST | ORA | T C1 |
| LEMON ST | VAL | 134 D5 |
| LEMON CANYON RD | SIE | 27 C4 |
| LEMOS RD | SIS | 4 A2 |
| LENAHAN RD | COL | 32 D1 |
| LENARD RD | LAS | 14 C3 |
| LENINGER RD | BUT | 25 A2 |
| LENTELL RD | HUM | 15 E1 |
| LENWOOD RD | SBD | 91 D1 |
| LEO RD | RCO | 107 A1 |
| LEON AV | MCO | 56 B2 |
| LEON RD | RCO | 99 D4 |
| LEONA AV | LACO | 89 D3 |
| LEONARD AV | FRCO | 57 D4 |
| LEONARD AV | KER | 78 A2 |
| LEONARD RD | MPA | 49 C3 |
| LEONI RD | ED | 41 B1 |
| LEOTA ST | MCO | 55 D1 |
| LEPRECHAUN LN | RCO | 107 B1 |
| LERDO HWY | KER | 77 D2 |
| LERDO HWY | KER | 78 A2 |
| LEROY AV | SJCO | 47 B1 |
| LESSING ST | SBD | 91 A3 |
| LETTS VALLEY RD | COL | 31 E1 |
| LEVEE RD | FRCO | 56 E4 |
| LEVEE RD | IMP | 112 D5 |
| LEVEE RD | YOL | 39 C2 |
| LEVERONI RD | SON | L B1 |
| LEVERONI RD | SON | 38 B3 |
| LEVERONI RD | SON | 132 B5 |
| LEVIATHAN LKOUT | ALP | 36 D5 |
| LEVIATHAN RD | ALP | 36 D5 |
| LEWELLING BLVD | ALA | 146 B1 |
| LEWELLING BL E | ALA | L E5 |
| LEWIS RD | MON | 54 C2 |
| LEWIS RD | SHA | 13 E4 |
| LEWIS RD | SOL | 39 B3 |
| LEWIS RD | STA | 47 C4 |
| LEWIS RD | VEN | 96 C1 |
| LEWIS RD | YUB | 33 E3 |
| LEWIS CREEK RD | MON | 65 D2 |
| LEWIS RIDGE RD | BUT | 26 B4 |
| LEWISTON AV | FRCO | 67 C1 |
| LEWISTON RD | SHA | 18 A1 |
| LEWISTON RD | TRI | 17 D1 |
| LEWISTON TURNPK | TRI | 17 E1 |
| LEXINGTON AV | MCO | 56 A2 |
| LEXINGTON AV | SDCO | 106 E5 |
| LEXINGTON ST | SCLR | 151 B3 |
| LEXINGTN HLL RD | PLU | 26 C3 |
| LIBERAL AV | TEH | 24 D2 |
| LIBERTY AV | MCO | 48 A4 |
| LIBERTY RD | SJCO | 40 B3 |
| LIBERTY RD W | BUT | 25 B5 |
| LIBERTY ISLD RD | SOL | M D1 |
| LIBERTY ISLD RD | SOL | 39 C3 |
| LIBRAMIENTO SUR | BAJA | 111 D3 |
| LIBRAMNT ORIENT | BAJA | 111 D2 |
| LICHEN WY | RCO | 107 B1 |
| LICHENS RD | SIS | 4 B4 |
| LIEBERT RD | IMP | 111 E3 |
| LIGGET AV | COL | 32 E3 |
| LIGHTHILL RD | SIS | 3 D5 |
| LIGHTHOUSE AV | MONT | 167 D2 |
| LIGHTHOUSE AV | MON | 53 E2 |
| LIGHTHOUSE AV | PAC | 167 B2 |
| LIGHTHOUSE RD | HUM | 15 D4 |
| LIGHTHOUSE RD | MEN | 30 C3 |
| LILI VALLEY WY | CAL | 41 C2 |
| LILLEY MTN DR | MAD | 49 C5 |
| LILY GAP RD | CAL | 41 C2 |
| LIM RD | LAS | 14 C3 |
| LIME CREEK RD | CAL | 40 E3 |
| LIMEDYKE LKOUT | TRI | 16 E2 |
| LIMEKILN RD | MON | 54 D5 |
| LIME KILN RD | NEV | 34 C2 |
| LIMEKILN RD | SBT | 54 E4 |
| LIMEKILN RD | SBT | 55 A4 |
| LIME KILN RD | TUO | 41 C5 |
| LIME SADDLE RD | BUT | 25 C3 |
| LIMONITE AV | RCO | 99 A2 |
| LINCOLN | LACO | 97 C2 |
| LINCOLN | MCO | 48 B5 |
| LINCOLN AV | ANA | 193 B2 |
| LINCOLN AV | ANA | 194 B2 |
| LINCOLN AV | FRCO | 56 D4 |
| LINCOLN AV | FRCO | 57 A4 |
| LINCOLN AV | FRCO | 58 A4 |
| LINCOLN AV | KIN | 67 C2 |
| LINCOLN AV | LACO | R B2 |
| LINCOLN AV | LACO | 190 B1 |
| LINCOLN AV | OR | 194 E2 |
| LINCOLN AV | ORA | 98 B3 |
| LINCOLN AV | ORA | T B2 |
| LINCOLN AV | PAS | 190 B1 |
| LINCOLN AV | RCO | U E5 |
| LINCOLN AV | RCO | 98 E3 |
| LINCOLN AV | SAL | 171 C4 |
| LINCOLN AV | SD | 214 A5 |
| LINCOLN AV | SDCO | 106 D3 |
| LINCOLN AV | SR | 139 D3 |
| LINCOLN AV | SA | 196 C3 |
| LINCOLN AV | SCL | P B3 |
| LINCOLN AV | SCL | 46 B4 |
| LINCOLN AV | YUB | 33 E1 |
| LINCOLN AV W | NAP | 133 A3 |
| LINCOLN BLVD | BUT | 25 D5 |
| LINCOLN BLVD | LA | 187 A1 |
| LINCOLN BLVD | LA | 189 A1 |
| LINCOLN BLVD | LACO | Q B4 |
| LINCOLN BLVD | LACO | 187 D3 |
| LINCOLN BLVD | MCO | 47 E4 |
| LINCOLN BLVD | MCO | 48 A4 |
| LINCOLN BLVD | SF | 141 B2 |
| LINCOLN BLVD | SMON | 187 A1 |
| LINCOLN RD | SBD | 91 E4 |
| LINCOLN RD | SUT | 33 C2 |
| LINCOLN RD | SUT | 125 A5 |
| LINCOLN RD | YUBA | 125 A5 |
| LINCOLN ST | NAPA | 29 A1 |
| LINCOLN ST | RCO | 101 B5 |
| LINCOLN ST | SC | 169 D3 |
| LINCOLN ST | S | 160 D5 |
| LINCOLN ST N | KER | 77 E4 |
| LINCOLN ST N | KER | 78 A4 |
| LINCOLN WY | AUB | 126 D2 |
| LINCOLN WY | SFCO | L B5 |
| LINCOLN WY | SF | 141 C4 |
| LINCOLN WY | SFCO | 45 B1 |
| LINCOLN WY E | AUB | 126 D2 |
| LINCOLN WY E | PLA | 126 D2 |
| LINDA DR | SIS | 4 B2 |
| LINDA VISTA AV | LACO | 98 A1 |
| LINDA VISTA AV | LACO | R B3 |
| LINDA VISTA AV | NAP | 133 A2 |
| LINDA VISTA AV | PAS | 190 A3 |
| LINDA VISTA AV | TUL | 68 D3 |
| LINDA VISTA DR | SB | 87 A3 |
| LINDA VISTA RD | SBD | 91 D1 |
| LINDA VISTA RD | SD | 213 B4 |
| LINDA VISTA RD | SDCO | V B3 |
| LINDA VISTA RD | SDCO | 111 C1 |
| LINDBERGH BLVD | KER | 80 B4 |
| LINDBLOOM RD | MCO | 55 D3 |
| LINDEN AV | MCO | 56 A1 |
| LINDEN AV | SBD | 99 B2 |
| LINDEN AV | SSF | 144 B1 |
| LINDENBERGER RD | RCO | 99 D4 |
| LINDERO CYN RD | LACO | 96 E1 |
| LINDLEY AV | LA | 178 E4 |
| LINDLEY AV | LACO | 97 C1 |
| LINDLEY RD | HUM | 15 E4 |
| LINDSAY RD | IMP | 109 A3 |
| LINDSAY RD | KER | 78 C4 |
| LINDSEY AV | GLE | 24 E3 |
| LINE RD | YOL | 39 D2 |
| LINEA DEL CIELO | SDCO | 106 C4 |
| LINGARD RD | MCO | 48 C5 |
| LINN RD | SJCO | 40 C4 |
| LINNE RD | SJCO | 46 E2 |
| LINNE RD | SLO | 76 B1 |
| LINSON AV | SBD | 91 A3 |
| LINWOOD AV | STA | 47 C3 |
| LINWOOD RD | MCO | 47 E3 |
| LINWOOD RD | MCO | 48 A3 |
| LISBON ST | MCO | 48 A5 |
| LISBON ST | SDCO | V D3 |
| LISCOMB HILL RD | HUM | 10 A5 |
| LIST AV | TUL | 68 C1 |
| LITT RD | STA | 47 D2 |
| LITTLE AV | BUT | 33 C1 |
| LITTLE RD | LPAZ | 104 A2 |
| LITTLE BEAR RD | RCO | 102 C4 |
| LITL BLACK ROCK | TRI | 17 C4 |
| LTL BRWNS CK RD | TRI | 11 D5 |
| LTL BRWNS CK RD | TRI | 17 D1 |
| LITTLE GIANT ML | TEH | 19 B4 |
| LITTL GRASS VLY | PLU | 26 C3 |
| LITTL HONKR BAY | SOL | 39 B3 |
| LITTLE JOHN | SJCO | 40 C5 |
| LITTLE JOHN RD | CAL | 41 A5 |
| LITTLE LAKE RD | INY | 70 C4 |
| LITTLE LAKE RD | MEN | 30 C1 |
| LITL MORONGO DR | SBD | 100 D1 |
| LITL PANOCHE RD | FRCO | 55 D4 |
| LITL PANOCHE RD | SBT | 55 D4 |
| LITTLE RIVER | MEN | 30 B1 |
| LTL SLATE CK RD | SHA | 12 B4 |
| LTL SYCAMOR CYN | LACO | 96 D2 |
| LITL TUJUNGA RD | LACO | 89 D5 |
| LITTLE VLY RD | LAS | 14 A4 |
| LITTLE VLY RD | MEN | 22 C4 |
| LITTLE VLY DUMP | LAS | 14 B5 |
| LITL VIRGNIA LK | MNO | 43 B4 |
| LITTLE WALKR RD | MNO | 42 E5 |
| LITTLE WALKR RD | MNO | 43 A3 |
| LIVELY RD | BUT | 25 B5 |
| LIVE OAK | FRCO | 58 B3 |
| LIVE OAK AV | LACO | 98 B1 |
| LIVE OAK AV | SBD | 99 A2 |
| LIVE OAK AV | SCL | P D5 |
| LIVE OAK AV | SCL | 54 C1 |
| LIVEOAK DR | BUT | 25 B3 |
| LIVE OAK DR | SBD | 99 D1 |
| LIVE OAK RD | ORA | 98 E4 |
| LIVE OAK RD | SBT | 55 B4 |
| LIVE OAK RD | SJCO | 40 A4 |
| LIVEOAK RD | SLO | 76 A1 |
| LIVE OAK RD | TEH | 18 C5 |
| LIVE OAK CYN RD | SBD | 99 D2 |
| LIVERMORE RD | NAPA | 32 A5 |
| LIVNGSTN CRESSY | MCO | 47 E4 |
| LIVNGSTN CRESSY | MCO | 48 A4 |
| LIVORNA RD | CC | M A4 |
| LLAGAS RD | SCL | P D5 |
| LLAGAS RD | SCL | 54 C1 |
| LLANO RD | SON | 37 E2 |
| LLOYD LN | SHA | 18 C3 |
| LOBATA RD | YUB | 33 E1 |
| LOCAN AV | FRCO | 57 D3 |
| LOCH LOMOND RD | LAK | 31 E4 |
| LOCKHART RD | SBD | 81 B4 |
| LOCKWOOD RD | STA | 47 D3 |
| LOCKWOOD CEM RD | MON | 65 C4 |
| LOCKWD JOLON RD | MON | 65 C4 |
| LOCKWD SAN ARDO | MON | 65 C4 |
| LOCKWD SN LUCAS | MON | 65 C3 |
| LOCKWOOD VLY RD | VEN | 88 C2 |
| LOCO BILL RD | KER | 79 D3 |
| LOCUST AV | RCO | 99 C2 |
| LOCUST AV | SBD | 81 A5 |
| LOCUST AV | SBD | 91 E4 |
| LOCUST AV | STA | 47 C3 |
| LOCUST RD | SHA | 18 D3 |
| LOCUST TREE RD | SJCO | 40 B4 |
| LODGE RD | FRCO | 58 A1 |
| LODI LN | NAPA | 29 B2 |
| LODI RD | COL | 33 A3 |
| LOFGREN RD | BUT | 25 B4 |
| LOGAN AV | SD | 216 E5 |
| LOGAN LN | MEN | 23 B2 |
| LOG CABIN MINE | MNO | 43 C5 |
| LOGGING CAMP RD | MNO | 50 E1 |
| LOG HOUSE RD | SIS | 4 E2 |
| LOKERN RD | KER | 77 D3 |
| LOKOYA RD | NAPA | 38 B2 |
| LOLETA AV | TEH | 24 D2 |
| LOLETA RD | HUM | 15 D2 |
| LOMA AV | MCO | 56 B1 |
| LOMA ALTA DR | LACO | 98 A1 |
| LOMA ALTA DR | LACO | R B2 |
| LOMA ALTA DR | STB | 174 B4 |
| LOMA PRIETA AV | SCR | P B5 |
| LOMA PRIETA RD | SCR | 54 A1 |
| LOMA RICA DR | NEV | 34 C1 |
| LOMA RICA RD | YUB | 33 D1 |
| LOMAS CONTADAS | CC | 45 D1 |
| LOMAS CANTADAS | CC | 156 E2 |
| LOMAS SANTA FE | SDCO | 106 C4 |
| LOMA VERDE RD | RCO | 102 C4 |
| LOMA VISTA DR | NAPA | 38 C2 |
| LOMBARD ST | SFCO | L B4 |
| LOMBARD ST | SF | 142 A2 |
| LOMBARD ST | SF | 143 A3 |
| LOMBARD ST | SFCO | 45 B1 |
| LOMBARDY AV | MCO | 47 E3 |
| LOMBARDY AV | MCO | 48 A3 |
| LOMITA | VEN | 88 A4 |
| LOMITA AV | MLBR | 144 B4 |

234
LOMITA BLVD
STREET INDEX
MARICOPA HWY




| STREET | CO. | PAGE & GRID |
|---|---|---|
| LOMITA BLVD | LACO | 97 D3 |
| LOMITA BLVD | LACO | S B2 |
| LOMITAS DR | TUL | 58 D5 |
| LOMITAS DR | TUL | 68 D1 |
| LOMPOC-CASML RD | SB | 86 B2 |
| LONDALE RD | STA | 47 D1 |
| LONE BUTTE RD | KER | 80 A5 |
| LONE COMPANY RD | MNO | 42 E1 |
| LONE HILL AV | LACO | U B2 |
| LONE MTN RD | JOS | 2 C2 |
| LONE OAK AV | STA | 47 E2 |
| LONE PINE LN | SON | 38 A1 |
| LONE PINE CYN | SBD | 90 E5 |
| LONE PN NRRW GG | INY | 60 B4 |
| LONE STAR MN RD | MNO | 51 C2 |
| LONE STAR RD | COL | 32 E2 |
| LONE STAR RD | MNO | 51 C2 |
| LONE STAR RD | PLA | 34 B3 |
| LONE STAR RD | SBD | 91 C2 |
| LONE TREE | SJCO | 47 C1 |
| LONE TREE RD | BUT | 25 D5 |
| LONE TREE RD | MCO | 48 B5 |
| LONE TREE RD | SBT | 55 A2 |
| LONE TREE RD | SHA | 18 D3 |
| LONE TREE WY | CC | M C3 |
| LONE TREE WY | CC | 39 B5 |
| LONG BARN | TUO | 41 E4 |
| LONG BEACH BLVD | LB | 192 E3 |
| LONG BEACH BLVD | LACO | 97 E3 |
| LONG BEACH BLVD | LACO | S D1 |
| LONG BEACH BL N | LACO | S D1 |
| LONG BEACH FRWY | LB | 192 C2 |
| LONG BEACH FRWY | LACO | 97 E3 |
| LONG CANYON RD | SB | 86 D1 |
| LONG CANYON RD | RCO | 100 D3 |
| LONGCOR RD | TEH | 18 C3 |
| LONGDEN AV | LACO | R C3 |
| LONG FELLOW AV | BUT | 25 B3 |
| LONG GULCH RD | SIS | 4 A4 |
| LONG HAY FLAT | SHA | 19 B3 |
| LONG HOLLOW DR | MAD | 49 C5 |
| LONG HOLLOW DR | TEH | 24 C2 |
| LONGHORN DR | LAS | 8 B4 |
| LONGHORN LN | KER | 79 B4 |
| LONG PRAIRIE RD | SIS | 5 A5 |
| LONG RAVINE RD | NEV | 34 B2 |
| LONG RIDGE RD | TRI | 16 E5 |
| LONG VALLEY RD | ALP | 36 C4 |
| LONG VALLEY RD | LAK | 32 A3 |
| LONG VALLEY RD | SIE | 27 E3 |
| LONG VALLEY RD | PLU | 20 C5 |
| LONGVIEW AV | MCO | 47 E4 |
| LONGVIEW AV | MCO | 48 A4 |
| LONGVIEW RD | LACO | 90 C3 |
| LONOAK RD | MON | 65 C2 |
| LOOKOUT RD | CAL | 41 C2 |
| LOOKOUT ADIN RD | LAS | 14 B3 |
| LKOUT-HACKMR RD | MOD | 6 B5 |
| LKOUT-HACKMR RD | MOD | 14 B1 |
| LKOUT INDIAN RD | MOD | 14 B3 |
| LOOKOUT MTN RD | SLO | 76 C3 |
| LOONEY RD | MCO | 48 B3 |
| LOOP BLVD N | KER | 80 B4 |
| LOOP BLVD S | KER | 80 B4 |
| LOOP RD | HUM | 16 A2 |
| LOOP RD | RCO | 101 B2 |
| LOOP RD | SHA | 19 C2 |
| LOPES RD | SOL | 38 E4 |
| LOPEZ DR | SLO | 76 B4 |
| LOPEZ CANYON RD | LACO | Q C1 |
| LOPEZ CANYON RD | SLO | 76 C4 |
| LOQUAT AV | STA | 47 B3 |
| LORAINE AV | LACO | U A1 |
| LORENSON | PLA | 34 B3 |
| LORENTZ RD | AMA | 40 D1 |
| LORENZEN RD | SJCO | 47 A2 |
| LORETZ RD | CLO | 32 D1 |
| LORRAINE RD | SBD | 92 E5 |
| LORT DR | TUL | 68 C1 |
| LOS ALAMITOS BL | ORA | T A2 |
| LOS ALAMOS RD | RCO | 99 C5 |
| LOS ALTOS DR | LACO | R D4 |
| LOS ANGELES AV | VEN | 89 A5 |
| LOS ANGELES ST | KER | 78 A2 |
| LOS ANGELES ST | LA | 185 E5 |
| LS ANGLS AQDUCT | KER | 80 B2 |
| LS BERROS ARRYO | SLO | 76 B4 |
| LOS BURROS RD | MON | 64 E4 |
| LOS BURROS RD | MON | 65 A4 |
| LOS CERRITOS RD | MCO | 48 B3 |
| LOS CERRITOS RD | STA | 48 B2 |
| LOS COCHES RD | MON | 65 A1 |
| LOS COCHES RD | SDCO | V E2 |
| LOS COCHES RD | SDCO | 107 A5 |
| LS COYOTES DIAG | LACO | S E2 |
| LS COYOTES DIAG | LACO | T A2 |
| LOS FELIZ BLVD | GLEN | 182 E2 |
| LOS FELIZ BLVD | LA | 182 B3 |
| LOS FELIZ BLVD | LACO | 97 D1 |
| LOS FELIZ BLVD | LACO | Q E3 |
| LOS FLORES RD | SBD | 91 B5 |
| LOS GATOS BLVD | SCL | P B4 |
| LOS GATOS BLVD | SCL | 46 A5 |
| LOS GATOS RD | FRCO | 66 C2 |
| LOS LOBOS RD | MON | 65 D4 |
| LOS NIETOS RD | LACO | 98 A2 |
| LOS NIETOS RD | LACO | R C5 |
| LOS OLIVOS ST | STB | 174 A3 |
| LOS OSOS VLY RD | SLO | 75 E3 |
| LOS OSOS VLY RD | SLO | 76 A3 |
| LOS PADRES RD | SBD | 91 C3 |
| LOS PALOS DR | SAL | 171 D5 |
| LOS PINOS DR | RCO | 100 D5 |
| LOS PRADOS | SM | 145 C3 |
| LS RANCHITOS RD | SR | 139 B1 |
| LOS ROBLES RD | LACO | 98 A1 |
| LOS ROBLES AV | LACO | R B3 |

| STREET | CO. | PAGE & GRID |
|---|---|---|
| LOS ROBLES AV | PAS | 190 C2 |
| LOST RD | RCO | 99 C4 |
| LOST CREEK RD | TEH | 19 E4 |
| LOST CK DAM RD | YUB | 26 B4 |
| LOST HILLS AV | FRCO | 66 D3 |
| LOST HILLS RD | KER | 77 D2 |
| LOST LAKE RD | ALP | 36 A5 |
| LOST LAKE RD | FRCO | 57 D2 |
| LOST SECTION S | INY | 72 C3 |
| LOST SECTION RD | INY | 72 C3 |
| LOS VERJELES RD | BUT | 25 E5 |
| LOS VERJELES RD | YUB | 25 E5 |
| LOTT RD | BUT | 25 B3 |
| LOTUS RD | ED | 34 D5 |
| LOUIE RD | SIS | 4 C5 |
| LOUIS AV | BUT | 25 D5 |
| LOUISE AV | MAN | 161 A2 |
| LOUISE AV | SJCO | 47 C1 |
| LOUISIANA ST | SUIS | 135 C4 |
| LOUISIANA ST | VAL | 134 C4 |
| LOUMAS LN | KER | 79 C4 |
| LOUPE AV | SCL | P C3 |
| LOUPE AV | SCL | 46 B4 |
| LOVE CREEK RD | CAL | 41 C3 |
| LOVEKIN BLVD | RCO | 103 D5 |
| LOVELAND RD | IMP | 109 A4 |
| LOVELOCK RD | BUT | 25 D2 |
| LOVENESS RD | MOD | 14 B1 |
| LOW RD | IMP | 111 E3 |
| LOWDEN RD | RED | 122 E3 |
| LOWDEN RD | SHA | 122 E3 |
| LOW DIVIDE RD | DN | 1 E3 |
| LOW DIVIDE RD | DN | 2 A3 |
| LOWE RD | IMP | 110 B3 |
| LOWELL ST | SDCO | V A3 |
| LOWELL HILL RD | NEV | 34 D1 |
| LOWER RD | AVLN | 105 B5 |
| LOWER TER | AVLN | 105 B5 |
| LOWER AZUSA RD | LACO | 98 B2 |
| LOWER AZUSA RD | LACO | R D3 |
| LOWR CHILES VLY | NAPA | 29 E2 |
| LOWR CHILES VLY | NAPA | 38 C1 |
| LOWER COLFAX RD | NEV | 34 C2 |
| LOWER DORRAY RD | CAL | 41 A2 |
| LOWR ENTRPRS RD | BUT | 25 E4 |
| LOWER FIRE RD | SIS | 4 D5 |
| LOWER FORBESTWN | BUT | 26 A4 |
| LOWER GAS PT RD | SHA | 18 B3 |
| LOWR GLACIER RD | INY | 51 E5 |
| LOWER HONCUT RD | BUT | 25 D5 |
| LOWER JONES | SJCO | 39 D5 |
| LOWER KLAMTH HY | KLAM | 5 B1 |
| LOWER KUCK RD | SIS | 4 C3 |
| LOWER LAKE RD | DN | 1 D3 |
| LOWER LAKE RD | LAK | 31 E3 |
| LOWER LAKE RD | LAK | 32 A3 |
| LWR LITL SHASTA | SIS | 4 B4 |
| LOWER MAD RIVER | TRI | 16 E3 |
| LOWER RATLSNAKE | TRI | 17 A3 |
| LOWER SACRAMNTO | SJCO | 40 A4 |
| LOWER SPGS RD | SHA | 18 B2 |
| LOWER WSIDE RD | TRI | 16 E4 |
| LOWR WYANDTT RD | BUT | 25 D5 |
| LOWERY RD | HUM | 15 D3 |
| LOWERY RD | TEH | 18 B5 |
| LOWERY CEM RD | TEH | 24 A1 |
| LOWES CANYON RD | SLO | 66 B5 |
| LOW GAP RD | MEN | 30 D1 |
| LOW GAP RD | MEN | 31 A2 |
| LOW GAP RD | MEN | 123 A2 |
| LOW GAP RD | U | 123 A2 |
| LOYALTON RD | SIE | 27 D3 |
| LOYALTON RD | SIE | 27 C3 |
| LOZANO RD | MPA | 48 D2 |
| LOZANOS RD | PLA | 34 B4 |
| LUBKEN RD | INY | 60 B4 |
| LUCAS | SJCO | 40 A4 |
| LUCAS VALLEY RD | MAR | L A3 |
| LUCAS VALLEY RD | MAR | 38 A4 |
| LUCE GRISWLD RD | TEH | 18 B4 |
| LUCERNE VLY CTF | SBD | 91 D2 |
| LUCILLE | FRCO | 66 D3 |
| LUCILLE LN | RCO | 107 C1 |
| LUCINDA RD | SBD | 81 C5 |
| LUCKEHE RD | SUT | 33 C1 |
| LUCKY HILL RD | SIE | 26 C3 |
| LUCY BROWN RD | SLO | 76 D1 |
| LUDLOW RD | SBD | 93 A2 |
| LUDY BLVD | RCO | 110 C1 |
| LUIS AV | MCO | 55 C1 |
| LUISENO RD | RCO | 107 B1 |
| LUKENS LN | RCO | 99 C3 |
| LULU MINE RD | TUO | 41 C5 |
| LULU MINE RD | TUO | 48 C1 |
| LUMGREY RD | SIS | 3 E3 |
| LUMPKIN RD | BUT | 25 E4 |
| LUMPKIN RD | BUT | 26 B4 |
| LUMPKIN- | | |
| -LA PORTE RD | BUT | 26 A4 |
| LUMPKIN RDG RD | BUT | 26 B3 |
| LUNA RD | IMP | 109 B3 |
| LUNDY AV | SCL | P B3 |
| LUNDY LAKE RD | MNO | 43 B4 |
| LUNING AV | TEH | 24 D1 |
| LUNT RD | BUT | 25 D3 |
| LUPE RD | AMA | 41 A2 |
| LUPIN AV | MCO | 48 B4 |
| LUPINE | FRCO | 58 B3 |
| LUPINE LN | RCO | 100 C5 |
| LURLINE AV | COL | 32 D2 |
| LUTHER RD | PLA | 34 C3 |
| LUTHER RD | TEH | 18 D5 |
| LUTHER E GIBSON | SOL | 38 E4 |
| LUTHER GIBSN FY | BEN | 153 D4 |
| LUTIE AV | KER | 80 A4 |
| LUX AV | MCO | 56 B1 |
| LYERLY RD | IMP | 109 B3 |

| STREET | CO. | PAGE & GRID |
|---|---|---|
| LYNCH RD | NAPA | 38 D3 |
| LYNCH CANYON DR | SLO | 65 D5 |
| LYNCH MDWS RD | BUT | 25 D2 |
| LYNN RD | VEN | 96 D1 |
| LYON AV | FRCO | 56 C2 |
| LYON AV | RCO | 99 E3 |
| LYON RD | STA | 47 E2 |
| LYON RD | STA | 48 A2 |
| LYONS AV | LACO | 89 B4 |
| LYONS AV | SLT | 129 A3 |
| LYONS RD | IMP | 111 E4 |
| LYONS RD | IMP | 112 A4 |
| LYONS ST | SNRA | 163 C3 |
| LYTLE AV | KER | 68 B5 |
| LYTLE CREEK RD | SBD | 90 E5 |
| LYTLE CREEK RD | SBD | 99 A1 |
| LYTTON ST | SDCO | V A3 |
| LYTTON SPG RD | SON | 31 D5 |
| M | | |
| M ST | EUR | 121 D1 |
| M ST | FRE | 165 D3 |
| M ST | MCO | 48 C4 |
| M ST | MER | 170 C5 |
| M 1 | TUL | 69 A5 |
| M 3 | TUL | 69 B5 |
| M 8 | LACO | 90 C3 |
| M 9 | TUL | 69 B5 |
| M 10 | TUL | 69 B5 |
| M 15 | TUL | 69 A4 |
| M 33 | TUL | 68 E4 |
| M 52 | TUL | 69 A4 |
| M 56 | TUL | 69 B4 |
| M 99 | TUL | 69 C4 |
| M 107 | TUL | 69 C3 |
| M 109 | TUL | 68 E4 |
| M 109 | TUL | 69 A4 |
| M 112 | TUL | 69 A4 |
| M 117 | TUL | 68 D3 |
| M 120 | TUL | 68 E3 |
| M 176 | TUL | 68 E3 |
| M 220 | TUL | 69 A2 |
| M 231 | TUL | 69 A2 |
| M 240 | TUL | 68 E2 |
| M 276 | TUL | 69 A1 |
| M 296 | TUL | 68 D1 |
| M 348 | TUL | 68 E1 |
| M 357 | TUL | 58 E5 |
| M 357 | TUL | 59 A4 |
| M 375 | TUL | 59 B5 |
| M 453 | TUL | 58 D4 |
| M 461 | TUL | 58 D4 |
| M 465 | TUL | 58 D4 |
| M 468 | TUL | 58 D4 |
| M 469 | TUL | 58 D4 |
| MABURY RD | SJ | 152 D1 |
| MABURY ST | SA | 196 D3 |
| MAC RD | RCO | 107 C1 |
| MACARTHUR BLVD | ALA | L D5 |
| MACARTHUR BLVD | ALA | 45 D1 |
| MACARTHUR BLVD | CM | 197 B3 |
| MACARTHUR BLVD | IRV | 198 C3 |
| MACARTHUR BLVD | IRV | 200 B5 |
| MACARTHUR BLVD | NB | 198 C3 |
| MACARTHUR BLVD | NB | 200 B5 |
| MACARTHUR BLVD | O | 157 E1 |
| MACARTHUR BLVD | O | 158 B2 |
| MACARTHUR BLVD | ORA | 98 C4 |
| MACARTHUR BLVD | ORA | T C3 |
| MACARTHUR BLVD | ORA | 198 C3 |
| MACARTHUR BLVD | SA | 197 D3 |
| MACARTHUR BLVD | SA | 198 A3 |
| MACARTHUR FRWY | ALA | 45 D1 |
| MACARTHUR FRWY | O | 157 D1 |
| MACARTHUR FRWY | O | 158 B2 |
| MACDOEL DIST RD | SIS | 4 E4 |
| MACDOEL DIST RD | SIS | 5 A3 |
| MACDONALD AV | CC | L C3 |
| MACDONALD AV | R | 155 B3 |
| MACDONALD LN | SIS | 4 C5 |
| MACE BLVD | YOL | 39 C1 |
| MACHADO LN | SIS | 4 C5 |
| MACHADO ST | RCO | 99 B4 |
| MACKERT RD | SUT | 33 C4 |
| MACKS GULCH RD | SIS | 4 A5 |
| MACKS GULCH RD | SIS | 12 A1 |
| MACKVILLE RD | SJCO | 40 C3 |
| MACLAY AV | LACO | 89 D5 |
| MACLAY AV | LACO | Q C1 |
| MACY ST | LA | 186 C3 |
| MACY ST | LACO | 97 E2 |
| MACY ST | LACO | R A4 |
| MADDALENA RD | PLU | 27 C2 |
| MADDEN AV | SUT | 33 C2 |
| MADDOCK RD | SUT | 33 C4 |
| MADEIRA AV N | MON | 171 D3 |
| MADEIRA AV N | SAL | 171 D3 |
| MADERA AV | FRCO | 57 A4 |
| MADERA AV | KER | 78 B2 |
| MADERA AV | KER | 78 C2 |
| MADERA AV | MAD | 57 A2 |
| MADERA RD | MCO | 55 D1 |
| MADERA RD | SBD | 90 E3 |
| MADERA ST | SDCO | V D3 |
| MADERA ST | SDCO | 111 D1 |
| MADISON AV | KIN | 67 C2 |
| MADISON AV | SAC | 34 A5 |
| MADISON AV | SAC | 34 B5 |
| MADISON AV | SBR | 144 A4 |
| MADISON AV | SD | 214 A4 |
| MADISON ST | KER | 166 E5 |
| MADISON ST | RCO | 99 B2 |
| MADISON ST | RCO | 101 A4 |
| MADISON ST | S | 160 D3 |
| MADONNA RD | SLO | 76 A4 |
| MADONNA RD | SNLO | 172 A5 |
| MADRE BLVD | LACO | 98 A1 |
| MAD RIVER RD | HUM | 9 E5 |

| STREET | CO. | PAGE & GRID |
|---|---|---|
| MAD RIVER ROCK | TRI | 16 E3 |
| MADRONA ST | NAPA | 29 B3 |
| MADRONE RD | SON | 38 B3 |
| MADSEN | FRCO | 57 E2 |
| MADSEN AV | FRCO | 57 E5 |
| MAGEE CANYON RD | MNO | 44 A5 |
| MAGEE CANYON RD | MNO | 51 B1 |
| MAGEE HILLS RD | RCO | 99 E5 |
| MAGIC MTN PKWY | LACO | 89 B4 |
| MAGNOLIA | MAR | 38 B5 |
| MAGNOLIA | SJCO | 47 D1 |
| MAGNOLIA AV | FRCO | 57 C5 |
| MAGNOLIA AV | GLE | 24 D3 |
| MAGNOLIA AV | KER | 78 A2 |
| MAGNOLIA AV | LB | 192 D3 |
| MAGNOLIA AV | MAR | L A3 |
| MAGNOLIA AV | MCO | 47 E4 |
| MAGNOLIA AV | MCO | 48 A4 |
| MAGNOLIA AV | ONT | 203 E5 |
| MAGNOLIA AV | ORA | 98 B4 |
| MAGNOLIA AV | ORA | T C2 |
| MAGNOLIA AV | RCO | 99 A3 |
| MAGNOLIA AV | RIV | 205 A4 |
| MAGNOLIA AV | SDCO | V E2 |
| MAGNOLIA AV | SDCO | 106 E5 |
| MAGNOLIA AV | SDCO | 107 A4 |
| MAGNOLIA AV | MLBR | 144 C4 |
| MAGNOLIA AV | STA | 47 B3 |
| MAGNOLIA BLVD | BUR | 179 B4 |
| MAGNOLIA BLVD | LA | 179 B4 |
| MAGNOLIA BLVD | LACO | Q C3 |
| MAGNOLIA RD | YUB | 33 D1 |
| MAGNUS ORCHD RD | SIE | 26 D5 |
| MAGONIGAL RD | NEV | 27 B5 |
| MAHER RD | MON | 54 C3 |
| MAHOGANY WY | LAS | 20 E2 |
| MAHOGANY FLAT | INY | 71 C2 |
| MAHOGANY PK RD | SIS | 5 B3 |
| MAHON AV | SJCO | 47 D1 |
| MAHONEY RD | SLO | 75 E1 |
| MAHONEY RD | SB | 86 B1 |
| MAIDEN LN | AVLN | 105 A4 |
| MAIDU DR | AUB | 126 C5 |
| MAIL RD | SB | 86 D3 |
| MAIL RT | LAS | 8 C5 |
| MAIN AV E | SCL | P D5 |
| MAIN AV E | SCL | 54 C1 |
| MAIN RD N | KLAM | 5 E2 |
| MAIN RD S | MOD | 7 A3 |
| MAIN ST | A | 157 C4 |
| MAIN ST | AMA | 40 D2 |
| MAIN ST | BARS | 208 A2 |
| MAIN ST | CC | L E4 |
| MAIN ST | CC | M A3 |
| MAIN ST | CC | M A4 |
| MAIN ST | EC | 217 B2 |
| MAIN ST | ELS | 189 A3 |
| MAIN ST | GV | 127 C3 |
| MAIN ST | HUM | 15 E3 |
| MAIN ST | IMP | 109 A5 |
| MAIN ST | IMP | 109 B2 |
| MAIN ST | INY | 51 D4 |
| MAIN ST | IRV | 198 B3 |
| MAIN ST | KER | 78 E3 |
| MAIN ST | LAK | 31 D3 |
| MAIN ST | LAS | 8 B4 |
| MAIN ST | LAS | 21 B4 |
| MAIN ST | LV | 209 C3 |
| MAIN ST | LA | 185 E5 |
| MAIN ST | LA | 186 A3 |
| MAIN ST | LACO | 88 E4 |
| MAIN ST | LACO | Q C5 |
| MAIN ST | LACO | Q E5 |
| MAIN ST | LACO | R B3 |
| MAIN ST | LACO | S A1 |
| MAIN ST | LACO | S C2 |
| MAIN ST | MAN | 161 C4 |
| MAIN ST | MEN | 30 C4 |
| MAIN ST | MOD | 14 B3 |
| MAIN ST | NAP | 133 C2 |
| MAIN ST | NAPA | 38 A1 |
| MAIN ST | ORA | 98 B4 |
| MAIN ST | ORA | T D3 |
| MAIN ST | PLCV | 138 D3 |
| MAIN ST | RCO | U E5 |
| MAIN ST | RCO | 98 E3 |
| MAIN ST | RCO | 99 B4 |
| MAIN ST | RCO | 99 E4 |
| MAIN ST | RCO | 205 C2 |
| MAIN ST | SAL | 171 C4 |
| MAIN ST | SBD | 91 B4 |
| MAIN ST | SBD | 91 D1 |
| MAIN ST | SBD | 93 B2 |
| MAIN ST | SCL | P B3 |
| MAIN ST | SD | 216 B5 |
| MAIN ST | SDCO | V C5 |
| MAIN ST | SDCO | V E3 |
| MAIN ST | SDCO | 106 C2 |
| MAIN ST | SDCO | 107 A4 |
| MAIN ST | SDCO | 111 D2 |
| MAIN ST | SF | 143 E4 |
| MAIN ST | SJCO | 40 B5 |
| MAIN ST | SLO | 75 C2 |
| MAIN ST | SLO | 76 A2 |
| MAIN ST | SA | 196 B4 |
| MAIN ST | SA | 198 B3 |
| MAIN ST | SB | 76 C5 |
| MAIN ST | SB | 86 B1 |
| MAIN ST | STB | 173 A3 |
| MAIN ST | SMA | 173 A3 |
| MAIN ST | SHA | 18 C1 |
| MAIN ST | SIE | 26 D4 |
| MAIN ST | SIS | 3 D5 |
| MAIN ST | SON | 37 C2 |
| MAIN ST | STA | 47 E3 |
| MAIN ST | S | 160 E4 |
| MAIN ST | SUIS | 135 C4 |

| STREET | CO. | PAGE & GRID |
|---|---|---|
| MAIN ST | TEH | 18 D3 |
| MAIN ST | TUL | 68 B1 |
| MAIN ST | TUL | 68 D3 |
| MAIN ST | VENT | 175 A2 |
| MAIN ST | YUBA | 125 D5 |
| MAIN ST E | STA | 47 E3 |
| MAIN ST N | AMA | 40 E2 |
| MAIN ST N | LA | 186 C2 |
| MAIN ST N | LACO | R A4 |
| MAIN ST N | MON | 54 C4 |
| MAIN ST N | SAL | 171 C2 |
| MAIN ST S | SAL | 171 B5 |
| MAIN ST W | GV | 127 A3 |
| MAIN ST W | SB | 76 B5 |
| MAIN ST W | SB | 86 A1 |
| MAIN ST W | STA | 47 D3 |
| MAIN DRAIN RD | KER | 77 D2 |
| MAINE AV | LACO | R E3 |
| MAINE ST | SOL | 38 C4 |
| MAINE ST | VAL | 134 C4 |
| MAIN EAST WEST | MOD | 5 E3 |
| MAIN PRAIRIE RD | SOL | 39 B3 |
| MAJESTC OAK CIR | SHA | 18 C3 |
| MAJESTIC VW DR | SHA | 18 C3 |
| MALAGA AV | FRCO | 56 E4 |
| MALAGA AV | FRCO | 57 C4 |
| MALAGA RD | KER | 78 E3 |
| MALIBU CYN RD | LACO | 97 A2 |
| MALIN HWY | MOD | 5 E2 |
| MALLARD RD | MCO | 55 E2 |
| MALLARD RD | YOL | 39 D2 |
| MALLOTT RD | SUT | 33 C2 |
| MALTON AV | TEH | 24 D2 |
| MALUM RIDGE RD | MAD | 49 E4 |
| MALVERN AV | ORA | T C1 |
| MAMELUKE HLL RD | ED | 34 E3 |
| MAMMTH POOL RD | MAD | 49 E5 |
| MAMMTH POOL RD | MAD | 50 A5 |
| MAMMTH SCNC LP | MNO | 50 D2 |
| MAMMOTH TVRN RD | ML | 164 D2 |
| MANCHESTER AV | ANA | 193 A2 |
| MANCHESTER AV | ING | 188 D5 |
| MANCHESTER AV | LA | 187 D5 |
| MANCHESTER AV | LA | 188 A5 |
| MANCHESTER AV | LACO | 97 D2 |
| MANCHESTER AV | LACO | Q E5 |
| MANCHESTER AV | SDCO | 106 C4 |
| MANDEVLL CYN RD | LACO | 97 C2 |
| MANDRAPA RD | IMP | 111 E4 |
| MANGALAR RD | RCO | 100 C5 |
| MANGO ST | SBD | 80 E5 |
| MANGROVE AV | BUT | 124 B2 |
| MANGROVE AV | C | 124 C3 |
| MANHATTAN AV | LACO | 97 D3 |
| MANHATTAN AV | LACO | S A1 |
| MANHATTAN BLVD | LACO | 97 D3 |
| MANHATTAN BLVD | LACO | S B1 |
| MANIER DR | TUL | 69 A3 |
| MANILLA AV | AVLN | 105 B5 |
| MANKAS CORNR RD | SOL | L E1 |
| MANKAS CORNR RD | SOL | M A1 |
| MANKAS CORNR RD | SOL | 38 E3 |
| MANLY RD | KER | 89 D1 |
| MANN RD | ALA | M C5 |
| MANNEL AV | KER | 78 B2 |
| MANNER MTN TR | NEV | 34 C1 |
| MANNING AV | FRCO | 56 B4 |
| MANNING AV | FRCO | 57 E4 |
| MANNING RD | ALA | 46 C2 |
| MANOR RD | COL | 32 C2 |
| MANOR ST | KER | 78 D2 |
| MANTECA AV | KIN | 67 C2 |
| MANTECA RD | SJCO | 47 B2 |
| MANTON RD | TEH | 18 E4 |
| MANTON RD | TEH | 19 A3 |
| MANTON SCH RD | TEH | 19 B3 |
| MANUAL DOMINGOS | SB | 86 C3 |
| MANZANA DR | RCO | 100 D3 |
| MANZANITA AV | BUT | 25 B3 |
| MANZANITA AV | BUT | 124 C2 |
| MANZANITA AV | RCO | 99 C2 |
| MANZANITA RD | ML | 164 D2 |
| MANZANITA RD | RCO | 100 B5 |
| MANZANITA RD | TRI | 16 D1 |
| MANZANITA LK RD | MAD | 49 E5 |
| MANZANITA LKOUT | MOD | 14 D2 |
| MANZNR REWRD RD | INY | 60 A3 |
| MAPES RD | LAS | 21 C3 |
| MAPES RD | RCO | 99 C4 |
| MAPLE AV | FRCO | 57 C2 |
| MAPLE AV | FRCO | 67 C1 |
| MAPLE AV | SBD | 91 B4 |
| MAPLE AV | STR | 131 D4 |
| MAPLE LN | NAPA | 29 B2 |
| MAPLE LN | SBD | 100 A1 |
| MAPLE ST | RCO | 98 E3 |
| MAPLE ST | SAL | 171 C4 |
| MAPLE ST | SDCO | 107 A4 |
| MAPLE CREEK RD | HUM | 10 B5 |
| MAPLE HILLS RD | HUM | 16 B5 |
| MARCH LN | S | 160 A1 |
| MARCIEL DR | MAD | 57 B2 |
| MARCONI AV | SAC | 40 A1 |
| MARCO POLO AV | RCO | 100 A5 |
| MARCUM RD | SUT | 33 D4 |
| MARCUSE RD | SUT | 33 D3 |
| MAR DE CORTEZ | AVLN | 105 A4 |
| MARE ISLAND BL | VAL | 134 B4 |
| MARE ISL CAUSWY | VAL | 134 B3 |
| MARENGO AV | LACO | R B3 |
| MARENGO RD | COL | 32 D2 |
| MARENGO ST | LA | 186 E2 |
| MARGUERITE AV | TEH | 24 D2 |
| MARGUERITE PKWY | ORA | 98 D5 |
| MARGUERITE RD | MCO | 48 E5 |
| MARGUERTE MN RD | AUB | 126 C2 |
| MARICOPA HWY | KER | 78 B5 |


STREETS

235
MARIE AV
# STREET INDEX
MINERET RD




| STREET | CO. | PAGE & GRID |
|---|---|---|
| MARIE AV | KER | 89 E1 |
| MARIE DR | PLU | 20 D5 |
| MARIN AV | FRCO | 56 D4 |
| MARIN ST | VAL | 134 C4 |
| MARINA AV | ALA | P C1 |
| MARINA AV | ALA | 46 C2 |
| MARINA BLVD | ALA | L D5 |
| MARINA BLVD | ALA | 45 D2 |
| MARINA BLVD | SF | 142 A1 |
| MARINA BLVD | SUIS | 135 C4 |
| MARINA DR | IMP | 108 C2 |
| MARINA DR | MEN | 31 B1 |
| MARINA EXPWY | LACO | 187 D3 |
| MARINA FRWY | CUL | 188 A3 |
| MARINA FRWY | LA | 188 A3 |
| MARINA FRWY | LACO | 97 C2 |
| MARINA VISTA | M | 154 B2 |
| MARIPOSA ST | VAL | 134 E3 |
| MARINE AV | COL | 32 E3 |
| MARINE AV | MB | 189 C5 |
| MARINE AV | RB | 189 C5 |
| MARINE PKWY | RC | 145 E4 |
| MARINERS ISL BL | SM | 145 C2 |
| MARINETTE | TUL | 68 B1 |
| MARINE WORLD PY | SMCO | N D2 |
| MARINE WORLD PY | SMCO | 45 D3 |
| MARINO LN | KER | 79 E2 |
| MARIPOSA AV | BUT | 25 B3 |
| MARIPOSA AV | C | 124 D2 |
| MARIPOSA AV | RCO | 99 B3 |
| MARIPOSA AV | TUL | 68 B1 |
| MARIPOSA RD | SJCO | 40 B5 |
| MARIPOSA RD | SJCO | 47 C1 |
| MARIPOSA RD | STA | 47 D2 |
| MARIPOSA ST | SFCO | 142 E4 |
| MARIPOSA WY | MCO | 48 C5 |
| MARIPOSA DUMP | MPA | 49 B3 |
| MARITIME ST | O | 157 B2 |
| MARKET AV | CC | L C3 |
| MARKET ST | COL | 33 A2 |
| MARKET ST | O | 157 E2 |
| MARKET ST | RIV | 205 B3 |
| MARKET ST | RCO | 99 B2 |
| MARKET ST | SD | 215 E4 |
| MARKET ST | SD | 216 A4 |
| MARTN L KING WY | SDCO | V C3 |
| MARKET ST | SFCO | L B5 |
| MARKET ST | SF | 142 B4 |
| MARKET ST | SF | 143 D4 |
| MARKET ST | SFCO | 45 B2 |
| MARKET ST | SJ | 152 B3 |
| MARKET ST | SCLR | 151 B3 |
| MARKET ST | S | 160 E5 |
| MARKET ST | YUBA | 125 D1 |
| MARKET ST W | MON | 171 B3 |
| MARKET ST W | SAL | 171 B3 |
| MARKHAM ST | RCO | 99 B3 |
| MARK HOPKINS AV | SUT | 33 D3 |
| MARKLEEVLLE LKT | ALP | 36 C5 |
| MARKS | FRCO | 57 C5 |
| MARKS AV | FRCO | 57 C4 |
| MARKS RD | SBD | 101 D1 |
| MARK SPGS W RD | SON | 37 E1 |
| MARKWEST STA RD | SON | 37 D1 |
| MARLAY AV | SBD | 99 A2 |
| MAR MONTE AV | SCR | 54 B2 |
| MARNI CT | KER | 79 C4 |
| MAROA AV | FRE | 165 C1 |
| MAROA AV | FRCO | 57 C3 |
| MARQUARDT AV | LACO | T B1 |
| MARR RD | LAS | 8 D5 |
| MARSH RD | SCL | 46 B3 |
| MARSH RD | SMCO | N D2 |
| MARSH ST | SNLO | 172 B3 |
| MARSH ST | SLO | 76 A3 |
| MARSHALL RD | ED | 34 D4 |
| MARSHALL RD | MCO | 55 C1 |
| MARSHALL RD | STA | 47 C4 |
| MARSHALL ST | RCO | 99 C4 |
| MARSHAL-PETALMA | MAR | 37 D4 |
| MARSHALL RCH RD | TRI | 17 C2 |
| MARSH CREEK RD | CC | M B3 |
| MARSH CREEK RD | CC | M D4 |
| MARSH CREEK RD | CC | 39 B5 |
| MARSH CREEK RD | CC | 46 B1 |
| MARSHES FLAT RD | TUO | 48 D1 |
| MARSHVIEW RD | SOL | 38 D4 |
| MART AV | STA | 47 E2 |
| MARTIN AV | FRE | 165 C5 |
| MARTIN AV | KER | 78 B2 |
| MARTIN LN | AMA | 40 D3 |
| MARTIN RD | FRCO | 56 D4 |
| MARTIN RD | IMP | 109 A4 |
| MARTIN RD | MON | 64 D1 |
| MARTIN RD | YUB | 25 E5 |
| MARTIN ST | LAK | 31 D3 |
| MARTIN ST | MONT | 167 D4 |
| MARTIN ST | MON | 53 E3 |
| MARTIN ST | RCO | 99 B3 |
| MARTINEZ RD | MON | 65 C4 |
| MARTINEZ CYN RD | LACO | 89 A4 |
| MARTINGALE LN | CAL | 41 A4 |
| MRTN LTHR KG BL | LA | 184 C5 |
| MRTN LTHR KG BL | LACO | Q D4 |
| MARTIS PEAK RD | PLA | 35 E1 |
| MARTY RD | SUT | 33 A2 |
| MARVIN RANCH RD | SIE | 26 C4 |
| MAR VISTA | SDCO | 106 C3 |
| MAR VISTA DR | MONT | 168 D1 |
| MAR VISTA DR | MONT | 167 D4 |
| MAR VISTA DR | MON | 53 E3 |
| MARX RD NO 1 | SHA | 18 A3 |
| MARX RD NO 2 | SHA | 18 A3 |
| MARYLAND ST | VAL | 134 B5 |
| MARYSVILLE BLVD | SAC | 33 E5 |
| MARYSVILLE RD | YUB | 26 A5 |
| MARYSVILLE RD | YUB | 33 E1 |

| STREET | CO. | PAGE & GRID |
|---|---|---|
| MASON ST | SF | 143 B2 |
| MASON ST | STB | 174 E3 |
| MASON DIXON RD | SBD | 100 E1 |
| MASONIC AV | SFCO | L B5 |
| MASONIC AV | SF | 142 A3 |
| MASONIC RD | MNO | 43 C2 |
| MASSACHUSTTS AV | SDCO | V D3 |
| MASSACHUSTTS AV | SDCO | 111 D1 |
| MASSACK RD | PLU | 26 D2 |
| MASSEY RD | MPA | 49 C3 |
| MAST AV | KER | 78 B1 |
| MASTEN AV | SCL | P E5 |
| MASTEN RD | TEH | 18 B5 |
| MASTERS AV | FRCO | 56 D4 |
| MASTERSONS RD | SIS | 11 E2 |
| MATHER ST | O | 158 B1 |
| MATHER FIELD RD | SAC | 40 A1 |
| MATHESON RD | SHA | 18 B2 |
| MATHEWS RD | LAS | 14 B4 |
| MATHEWS RD | SJCO | 40 A5 |
| MATHEWS RD | SJCO | 47 A1 |
| MATHEWS RD | SIS | 5 A2 |
| MATHILDA AV | SCL | P A3 |
| MATHILDA AV | SCL | 45 E4 |
| MATHILDA AV | SVL | 148 D5 |
| MATILIJA RD | VEN | 88 A4 |
| MATLOCK LP | TEH | 18 C4 |
| MATTERHORN DR | KER | 79 C5 |
| MATTHEWS LN | YUB | 33 D1 |
| MATTOLE RD | HUM | 15 C3 |
| MATTOLE RD | HUM | 16 E4 |
| MAUI RD | SBD | 92 C1 |
| MAURICO AV | RCO | 99 C4 |
| MAWSON RD | SUT | 33 A2 |
| MAXSON RD | FRCO | 58 B2 |
| MAXWELL LN | SOL | 39 C2 |
| MAXWELL RD | AMA | 40 C2 |
| MAXWELL CYN RD | NAPA | 38 C1 |
| MAXWLL SITES RD | COL | 32 C1 |
| MAY | CC | 38 C5 |
| MAYARADA | SBD | 101 E1 |
| MAYARO LODGE RD | BUT | 25 E2 |
| MAYBECK | SJCO | 40 A5 |
| MAYBERT RD | NEV | 26 E5 |
| MAYER AV | KER | 78 B2 |
| MAYER RD | YUB | 33 D2 |
| MAYFIELD RD | RCO | 102 A4 |
| MAYHEW AV | TEH | 24 D2 |
| MAYNARD RD | SHA | 18 D2 |
| MAY SCHOOL RD | ALA | M C5 |
| MAY SCHOOL RD | ALA | 46 C2 |
| MAYS CANYON RD | SON | 37 C2 |
| MAYTEN RD | SIS | 4 C5 |
| MAZE BL | MDO | 162 A3 |
| MAZE BLVD | STA | 47 C2 |
| MAZOURKA CANYON | INY | 60 A3 |
| MCADAMS CK RD | SIS | 3 D5 |
| MCADAMS INDN CK | SIS | 3 D4 |
| MCARTHUR RD | SHA | 13 C3 |
| MCARTHUR RD | SUT | 33 B2 |
| MCAULIFFE RD | SHA | 18 A3 |
| MCAUSLAND RD | COL | 24 E5 |
| MCBEAN PKWY | LACO | 89 B4 |
| MCCABE RD | IMP | 112 A3 |
| MCCABE RD | MCO | 47 B5 |
| MCCABE RD | MCO | 55 B1 |
| MCCAHILL LN | HUM | 15 E2 |
| MCCAIN BLVD | COR | 215 B5 |
| MCCAIN VLY RD | SDCO | 111 A4 |
| MCCALL AV | FRCO | 57 D3 |
| MCCALL BLVD | RCO | 99 C4 |
| MCCANN RD | HUM | 16 B4 |
| MCCART RD | KER | 68 A5 |
| MCCARTHY RES RD | CAL | 41 B2 |
| MCCARTY RD | RCO | U D4 |
| MCCARTY RD | RCO | 98 E3 |
| MCCARTY RD | SBD | 98 E3 |
| MCCARTY RD | TEH | 24 B2 |
| MCCATER RD | MCO | 48 E5 |
| MCCAY | MPA | 48 E3 |
| MCCLAIN LN | RCO | 107 B1 |
| MCCLATCHY RD | SUT | 33 B2 |
| MCCLELLAN RD | CPTO | 149 B5 |
| MCCLELLAN RD | LAS | 14 C3 |
| MCCLELLAN RD | LAS | 21 C3 |
| MCCLELLN MTN RD | HUM | 16 C3 |
| MCCLINTOCK RD | STA | 47 C4 |
| MCCLOSKEY RD | SBT | 54 E3 |
| MCCLOSKEY RD | SBT | 55 A3 |
| MCCLOSKEY RD | SOL | 39 C3 |
| MCCLOUD AV | SIS | 12 C2 |
| MCCLOUD DUMP RD | SIS | 12 E2 |
| MCCLURE AV | TEH | 24 D1 |
| MCCLURE RD | STA | 47 D2 |
| MCCLURE SUB RD | MEN | 31 B2 |
| MCCOMBS RD | KER | 77 E1 |
| MCCOMBS RD | KER | 78 B1 |
| MCCONAHUE GL RD | SIS | 11 E1 |
| MCCONNELL RD | IMP | 109 B5 |
| MCCORMACK RD | SOL | 39 B3 |
| MCCOURTNEY RD | NEV | 34 B2 |
| MCCOURTNEY RD | NEV | 127 A5 |
| MCCOURTNEY RD | PLA | 34 A3 |
| MCCOY AV | KER | 77 E1 |
| MCCOY RD | LAS | 20 C3 |
| MCCOY RD | MON | 54 E5 |
| MCCOY RD | MON | 55 A5 |
| MCCOY RD | TEH | 18 C4 |
| MCCRACKEN RD | STA | 47 B3 |
| MCCREERY RCH RD | SBT | 55 C3 |
| MCCRORY RD | SOL | 39 A3 |
| MCCULLACH RD | MCO | 47 D4 |
| MCCULLOCK BLVD | MOH | 96 B4 |
| MCCULLY RD | MOD | 7 D5 |
| MCCUNE RD | SOL | 39 A2 |
| MCDANIEL RD | IMP | 112 D5 |
| MCDERMOTT RD | COL | 32 D1 |

| STREET | CO. | PAGE & GRID |
|---|---|---|
| MCDERMOTT RD | RCO | 99 E4 |
| MCDOEL DIST | SIS | 4 E3 |
| MCDOEL DORRS RD | SIS | 5 A3 |
| MCDONALD | SJCO | 39 D5 |
| MCDONALD AV | STA | 47 C2 |
| MCDONALD RD | IMP | 109 A3 |
| MCDOWELL BLVD | SON | L A1 |
| MCEWEN RD | CC | L D3 |
| MCEWEN RD | CC | 38 D4 |
| MCEWEN RD | STA | 47 E2 |
| MCFADDEN | MON | 54 C4 |
| MCFADDEN AV | SA | 195 A5 |
| MCFADDEN AV | SA | 196 C5 |
| MCFARLND-WDY RD | KER | 78 C1 |
| MCGARY RD | SOL | 38 D4 |
| MCGEE AV | STA | 47 D2 |
| MCGEE CREEK RD | MNO | 51 A3 |
| MCGOWAN | YUB | 33 D2 |
| MCGRATH RD | SUT | 33 B2 |
| MCHENRY AV | MDO | 162 C3 |
| MCHENRY AV | SJCO | 47 C2 |
| MCHENRY RD | MCO | 48 C5 |
| MCINTIRE RD | SJCO | 40 C3 |
| MCINTOSH RD | HUM | 10 D4 |
| MCKEAN RD | SCL | P C4 |
| MCKEAN RD | SCL | 46 C5 |
| MCKEE RD | MCO | 48 C4 |
| MCKEE RD | SJ | 152 E2 |
| MCKEE RD | SCL | P C3 |
| MCKEE RD | SCL | 46 B4 |
| MCKEE ST | MCO | 48 D5 |
| MCKEEN RD | SIS | 11 D2 |
| MCKELL RD | LAK | 32 A5 |
| MCKENZIE AV | FRE | 165 D3 |
| MCKENZIE RD | SAC | 40 A3 |
| MCKERNIE ST | RCO | 99 E4 |
| MCKIBBEN RD | KER | 78 A1 |
| MCKIM RD | IMP | 109 B5 |
| MCKINLEY AV | FRE | 165 B2 |
| MCKINLEY AV | FRCO | 57 A3 |
| MCKINLEY AV | SJCO | 47 A1 |
| MCKINLEY ST | RCO | 99 A3 |
| MCKINLEYVLLE AV | HUM | 9 E4 |
| MCKINNEY CK RD | SIS | 3 D4 |
| MCKNNEY RUBICN- | | |
| -SPRING RD | PLA | 35 D2 |
| MCLAIN RD | YUB | 26 B4 |
| MCLAUGHLIN AV | LA | 187 E1 |
| MCLAUGHLIN AV | SCL | P C3 |
| MCMASTER RD | MCO | 48 C5 |
| MCMILLAN CYN RD | SLO | 76 C4 |
| MCMULLIN | SJCO | 47 A2 |
| MCMULLIN GRADE | FRCO | 57 A4 |
| MCMURRY MDWS RD | INY | 59 D1 |
| MCNAMARA RD | MCO | 48 C5 |
| MCNEILL LN | SOL | 39 B1 |
| MCNELLA LN | PLU | 27 C3 |
| MCNERNEY RD | IMP | 109 A3 |
| MCRAE RD | BUT | 25 B4 |
| MCRAE RD | TUO | 41 C5 |
| MCSWAIN RD | MER | 170 A3 |
| MCSWAIN RD | MCO | 170 A3 |
| MEACHAM RD | KER | 78 B3 |
| MEAD RD | IMP | 109 B4 |
| MEADE AV | SD | 214 B5 |
| MEADOW DR | AMA | 41 B2 |
| MEADOW DR | MCO | 48 A4 |
| MEADOW RD | TRI | 17 D1 |
| MEADOW GLEN RD | CAL | 41 C2 |
| MEADOW LAKE RD | NEV | 26 E5 |
| MEADOW LAKE RD | NEV | 27 B4 |
| MEADOW LAKE RD | SIE | 27 B5 |
| MEADOW RIDGE RD | MAD | 49 D5 |
| MEADOWS DR | VAL | 134 A1 |
| MEADOWS RD | IMP | 112 B4 |
| MEADOWSWEET DR | CRTM | 140 C1 |
| MEADOW VLY RD | YUB | 26 A5 |
| MEADOW VIEW DR | SHA | 18 C3 |
| MEADOWVIEW RD | SAC | 39 E2 |
| MEADOW VISTA RD | PLA | 34 C3 |
| MEALEY RD | IMP | 108 E5 |
| MEAMBER CK RD | SIS | 3 C4 |
| MEARS RIDGE RD | SHA | 12 C3 |
| MECCA DALE RD | RCO | 101 E3 |
| MECHAM RD | SON | 37 E3 |
| MEDFORD AV | KIN | 67 C2 |
| MEDFORD RD | FRCO | 57 E1 |
| MEDICINE LK HWY | MOD | 5 E5 |
| MEDICINE LK HWY | SIS | 5 D5 |
| MEDICINE LK RD | SIS | 5 C5 |
| MEDICINE LK RD | SIS | 13 B2 |
| MEDLIN RD | STA | 47 D4 |
| MEEKLAND AV | ALA | L E5 |
| MEEKLAND AV | ALA | M A5 |
| MEEKLAND AV | ALA | N E1 |
| MEEKLAND AV | ALA | P A1 |
| MEEKS RD | SBD | 92 D5 |
| MEHRING RD | IMP | 110 D5 |
| MEHRTEN DR | TUL | 68 D1 |
| MEIER RD | STA | 47 E2 |
| MEIER RD | STA | 48 A2 |
| MEIGS RD | STB | 174 A5 |
| MEIKLE RD | STA | 47 E2 |
| MEIKLE RD | STA | 48 A2 |
| MEISS RD | SAC | 40 B2 |
| MEISS LAKE- | | |
| -SAMS NECK RD | SIS | 4 E3 |
| MEISS LAKE- | | |
| -SAMS NECK RD | SIS | 5 A3 |
| MELCHER RD | KER | 78 B1 |
| MELLA DR | AMA | 41 A2 |
| MELLO AV | SJCO | 47 C1 |
| MELLOR RD | STA | 48 A2 |
| MELODY CT | HUM | 10 A5 |
| MELOLANO RD | IMP | 109 B5 |
| MELON ST | RCO | 102 C4 |
| MELONES CT | TUO | 41 B5 |

| STREET | CO. | PAGE & GRID |
|---|---|---|
| MELROSE AV | LA | 181 B5 |
| MELROSE AV | LA | 182 C5 |
| MELROSE AV | LACO | Q AV |
| MELROSE AV | LACO | 183 D1 |
| MELROSE DR | SDCO | 106 C3 |
| MEMORY LN | SA | 195 E2 |
| MEMORY LN | SA | 196 A2 |
| MENALTO AV | MP | 147 C1 |
| MENDENHALL RD | TEH | 18 C5 |
| MENDIBOURE RD | LAS | 8 B4 |
| MENDIBURN | KER | 79 D5 |
| MENDIBURN RD | KER | 80 B4 |
| MENDOCINO AV | FRCO | 57 E2 |
| MENDOCINO AV | STR | 131 C1 |
| MENDOCINO PASS | MEN | 23 B2 |
| MENIFEE RD | RCO | 99 C4 |
| MENLO AV | RCO | 99 E4 |
| MERCED AV | FRCO | 66 D3 |
| MERCED AV | KER | 78 A2 |
| MERCED AV | LACO | R E4 |
| MERCED AV | MCO | 47 E4 |
| MERCEDES AV | MCO | 48 B4 |
| MERCED FALLS RD | MPA | 48 D3 |
| MERCED FALLS RD | TUO | 48 D2 |
| MERIDIAN AV | SCL | 151 E5 |
| MERIDIAN BLVD | ML | 164 C3 |
| MERIDIAN RD | BUT | 25 A3 |
| MERIDIAN RD | SBD | 91 E2 |
| MERIDIAN RD | SCL | P B3 |
| MERIDIAN RD | SCL | 46 B5 |
| MERIDIAN RD | SOL | 39 B3 |
| MERIDIAN RD | SUT | 33 A2 |
| MERIDIAN ST | SJ | 151 E5 |
| MERLE AV | STA | 47 D2 |
| MERRIAM RD | STA | 47 E3 |
| MERRIAM RD | YUB | 26 B5 |
| MERRILL AV | FRCO | 56 B2 |
| MERRILL AV | SBD | 98 D2 |
| MERRILL RD | TEH | 24 E2 |
| MERRILL RD S | KLAM | 5 C2 |
| MERRILL ST | SBD | 99 A2 |
| MERRILL FLAT RD | LAS | 20 D2 |
| MERRILLVILLE RD | LAS | 20 E2 |
| MERRIMAC CTO RD | BUT | 25 E3 |
| MERRITT | LAK | 31 D3 |
| MERRITT DR | TUL | 57 E5 |
| MERRITT DR | TUL | 58 A5 |
| MERRITT LN | PLA | 34 A3 |
| MERVEL AV | MCO | 55 E2 |
| MESA DR | RCO | 103 C5 |
| MESA DR | RCO | 110 C1 |
| MESA DR | SBD | 100 E1 |
| MESA DR | SDCO | 106 B3 |
| MESA RD | MAR | 37 E5 |
| MESA RD | SBD | 92 E5 |
| MESA TK TR W | SDCO | 107 C5 |
| MESA COLLEGE DR | SD | 213 D1 |
| MESA COLLEGE DR | SDCO | V B2 |
| MESA GRANDE RD | SDCO | 107 B3 |
| MESQUITE RD | INY | 61 B2 |
| MESQUITE CYN RD | KER | 80 C2 |
| MESQUITE SPG RD | SBD | 101 B1 |
| MESQUITE VLY RD | INY | 73 C3 |
| MESSICK | SJCO | 40 C4 |
| MESSICK RD | SUT | 33 D3 |
| MESSILLA VLY RD | BUT | 25 D3 |
| MESSING RD | CAL | 40 D4 |
| MESTMAKER ST | KER | 68 D5 |
| METCALF RD | NEV | 34 B2 |
| METCALFE RD | SCL | P D4 |
| METCALFE RD | SCL | 46 C5 |
| METROPOLE AV | AVLN | 105 B5 |
| METROPOLITAN RD | HUM | 15 E2 |
| METTER RD | SUT | 33 C1 |
| METTLER AV | KER | 68 B5 |
| METTLER AV | KER | 78 B2 |
| METTLER RD | SJCO | 40 A4 |
| METTLER RD | STA | 47 D1 |
| METZ RD | MON | 65 B1 |
| METZGER RD | SHA | 13 D3 |
| MEXICAN LAKE RD | SBT | 66 B1 |
| MEYER RD | LACO | R D5 |
| MEYER RD | LACO | T B1 |
| MEYERS LN | SUT | 33 B1 |
| MEYERS GRADE RD | SON | 37 B1 |
| MICA RD | RCO | 107 C1 |
| MICHAEL RD | MCO | 48 B5 |
| MICHEL RD | CAL | 41 B3 |
| MICHELSON DR | IRV | 198 C4 |
| MICHELTORENA ST | STB | 174 B3 |
| MICHIGAN BAR RD | SAC | 40 C2 |
| MICHILLINDA BL | LACO | R C2 |
| MICHOACAN AVD | BAJA | 112 B4 |
| MICKE GROVE RD | SJCO | 40 B4 |
| MIDDLE AV | SCL | P E5 |
| MIDDLE AV | SCL | 54 D1 |
| MIDDLE RD | BLMT | 145 C4 |
| MIDDLE RD | MAR | 37 D3 |
| MIDDLE RD | SJCO | 46 E1 |
| MIDDLE TER | AVLN | 105 B5 |
| MIDDLE BAR RD | AMA | 40 E3 |
| MIDDLE BAR RD | AMA | 41 A3 |
| MIDDLE CREEK RD | SHA | 18 B2 |
| MIDDLE CREEK RD | SIS | 3 C3 |
| MIDDLE CK RCH | SIS | 3 C3 |
| MIDDLEFIELD RD | MP | 147 A1 |
| MIDDLEFIELD RD | PA | 147 E3 |
| MIDDLEFIELD RD | SCL | N E2 |
| MIDDLEFLD RD E | MVW | 148 B4 |
| MIDDLE FORK RD | MON | 66 B4 |
| MDDL FK GASQUET | DN | 2 A3 |
| MID FK HUMBG RD | SIS | 3 E4 |
| MIDDLE HARBR RD | O | 157 C3 |
| MIDDL HONCUT RD | BUT | 25 D5 |
| MIDDLE RIDGE RD | MEN | 30 B2 |
| MIDDLETON DR | DN | 1 D3 |
| MIDDLETON RD | SUT | 33 B2 |

| STREET | CO. | PAGE & GRID |
|---|---|---|
| MIDDLETON RD | TRI | 11 E3 |
| MIDDLETOWN RD | PLCV | 138 B2 |
| MIDDLETWN PK DR | SHA | 18 B2 |
| MDL TWO ROCK RD | SON | 37 E3 |
| MDL TWO ROCK RD | SON | 38 A3 |
| MIDLAND AV | SDCO | 106 D4 |
| MIDLAND RD | RCO | 103 B2 |
| MIDLAND TR | KER | 80 C2 |
| MIDOIL RD | KER | 77 E4 |
| MIDWAY | BUT | 25 B4 |
| MIDWAY DR | SD | 213 A5 |
| MIDWAY DR | SDCO | V A3 |
| MIDWAY RD | ALA | M E5 |
| MIDWAY RD | KER | 77 E4 |
| MIDWAY RD | SBD | 101 D1 |
| MIDWAY RD | SOL | 39 B2 |
| MIDWAY WELLS | INY | 61 D3 |
| MIKISHA BLVD | SBD | 92 D5 |
| MILAN RD | KER | 77 E2 |
| MILE END | MON | 64 E1 |
| MILE END | MON | 65 A1 |
| MILES RD | MCO | 48 C5 |
| MILFORD RD | SBDO | 81 A1 |
| MILFORD CEM RD | LAS | 21 C5 |
| MILFORD GRADE | LAS | 21 C5 |
| MILGEO RD | SJCO | 47 C2 |
| MIL-GOR RD | SBD | 101 E1 |
| MILHAM AV | KIN | 67 B3 |
| MILITAR | BAJA | 112 B4 |
| MILITARY E | BEN | 153 C4 |
| MILITARY W | BEN | 153 B4 |
| MILITARY W | SOL | 38 D4 |
| MILITARY RD | SIS | 13 A2 |
| MILITARY PASS | SIS | 12 D1 |
| MILITARY PASS | SIS | 13 A2 |
| MILL AV | KER | 78 B1 |
| MILL RD | BUT | 26 B4 |
| MILL RD | MNO | 52 C3 |
| MILL RD | SLO | 76 B1 |
| MILL RD | TEH | 19 C4 |
| MILL RD | YUB | 26 B4 |
| MILL ST | GV | 127 B4 |
| MILL ST | NEV | 34 C1 |
| MILL ST | RENO | 130 C3 |
| MILL ST | SBD | 99 C2 |
| MILL ST | SBDO | 207 C3 |
| MILL ST | U | 123 C3 |
| MILLARD CYN RD | RCO | 100 B2 |
| MILLBRAE AV | MLBR | 144 D5 |
| MILLBRAE AV | SMCO | N C1 |
| MILLBRAE AV | SMCO | 45 B3 |
| MILLBROOK AV | FRCO | 57 C2 |
| MILL CANYON RD | MNO | 42 E2 |
| MILL CREEK RD | HUM | 10 C3 |
| MILL CREEK RD | MEN | 31 B2 |
| MILL CREEK RD | SBD | 99 E1 |
| MILL CREEK RD | SIS | 3 C5 |
| MILL CREEK RD | SIS | 3 E4 |
| MILL CREEK RD | SON | 31 C5 |
| MILL CREEK RD | SON | 37 D1 |
| MILL CK PWR HS | MNO | 43 B4 |
| MILLER | MAR | 45 B1 |
| MILLER AV | CPTO | 150 A5 |
| MILLER AV | FRCO | 56 B2 |
| MILLER AV | MAR | L B4 |
| MILLER AV | MV | 140 A3 |
| MILLER AV | VAL | 134 E4 |
| MILLER RD | COL | 33 A3 |
| MILLER RD | IMP | 112 C3 |
| MILLER RD | MCO | 48 D4 |
| MILLER RD | TRI | 23 A1 |
| MILLER RD | YOL | 39 C2 |
| MILLER ST | SMA | 173 C3 |
| MILLER RANCH RD | SIE | 26 D4 |
| MILLERTON RD | FRCO | 57 D2 |
| MILLERTON RD | MAD | 57 D1 |
| MILLIKEN AV | SBD | U E3 |
| MILLIKEN AV | SBD | 98 E2 |
| MIL POTRERO HWY | KER | 88 B1 |
| MILLS AV | CLA | 203 A4 |
| MILLS AV | LACO | R D5 |
| MILLS AV | MTCL | 203 A4 |
| MILLS RD | MCO | 47 C5 |
| MILLS RD | SOL | 39 C2 |
| MILLS RD | SUT | 33 B2 |
| MILLS ORCHDS RD | COL | 32 C1 |
| MILLS PARK RD | SIE | 27 A3 |
| MILLUX AV | FRCO | 56 B2 |
| MILLUX RD | KER | 78 C4 |
| MILLVL PLAIN RD | SHA | 18 D3 |
| MILLWOOD DR | TUL | 58 C5 |
| MILLWOOD RD | FRCO | 58 C3 |
| MILNES RD | STA | 47 D2 |
| MILPAS DR | SBD | 91 D4 |
| MILPAS ST | STB | 174 D3 |
| MILPITAS RD | MON | 64 E3 |
| MILPITAS RD | MON | 65 B3 |
| MILPITAS WSH RD | IMP | 110 B2 |
| MILSAP BAR RD | BUT | 25 E3 |
| MILSAP BAR RD | BUT | 26 A3 |
| MILSTEAD RD | MEN | 22 D1 |
| MILTON RD | CAL | 40 E5 |
| MILTON RD | NAPA | L C1 |
| MILTON RD | NAPA | 38 C3 |
| MILTON RD | SJCO | 40 C5 |
| MILTON RD | STA | 40 E5 |
| MINA RD | MEN | 23 A1 |
| MINE RD | VEN | 89 A5 |
| MINER RD | CC | L D4 |
| MINER RD | CC | 45 D1 |
| MINER ST | S | 160 E4 |
| MINERAL RD | IMP | 108 E1 |
| MINERAL RD | SHA | 19 C3 |
| MINERAL KING AV | TUL | 68 A1 |
| MINERAL KING RD | TUL | 59 B5 |
| MINERAL SCHOOL | SHA | 19 A1 |
| MINERET RD | ML | 164 C2 |


STREETS

| STREET | CO. | PAGE & GRID | |
|---|---|---|---|
| MINERS CREEK RD | SIS | 11 | D2 |
| MINES RD | ALA | P | D1 |
| MINES RD | ALA | 46 | D3 |
| MINES RD | SCL | 46 | D3 |
| MING AV | KER | 78 | C3 |
| MINI DR | VAL | 134 | C1 |
| MINNEOLA RD | SBD | 92 | B1 |
| MINNESOTA ST | SDCO | 106 | C2 |
| MINNEWAWA AV | FRCO | 57 | D2 |
| MINNEWAWA AV | FRCO | 57 | D5 |
| MINNIEAR RD | STA | 47 | B3 |
| MINNIETTA RD | INY | 71 | B2 |
| MINT RD | MCO | 56 | B1 |
| MINTURN RD | MCO | 48 | D5 |
| MIRABEL RD | SON | 37 | D2 |
| MIRAMAR RD | SDCO | V | B1 |
| MIRAMAR RD | SDCO | 106 | D5 |
| MIRAMAR WY | SDCO | V | B2 |
| MIRAMAR WY | SDCO | 106 | D5 |
| MIRA MESA BLVD | SDCO | V | B1 |
| MIRA MESA BLVD | SDCO | 106 | C5 |
| MIRANDA AV | CC | M | A4 |
| MIRASOL AV | KER | 77 | E3 |
| MIRASOL AV | KER | 78 | A3 |
| MISSION AV | MCO | 48 | C5 |
| MISSION AV | SD | 214 | A5 |
| MISSION AV | SDCO | 106 | B3 |
| MISSION AV | SR | 139 | C3 |
| MISSION BLVD | ALA | 45 | E2 |
| MISSION BLVD | ALA | 146 | C1 |
| MISSION BLVD | H | 146 | D2 |
| MISSION BLVD | MTCL | 203 | A5 |
| MISSION BLVD | ONT | 203 | D5 |
| MISSION BLVD | ONT | 204 | B5 |
| MISSION BLVD | POM | 203 | A5 |
| MISSION BLVD | RCO | 99 | A2 |
| MISSION BLVD | SBD | U | D2 |
| MISSION BLVD | SBD | 98 | D2 |
| MISSION BLVD | SBD | 203 | A5 |
| MISSION BLVD | SD | 212 | A1 |
| MISSION BLVD | SDCO | V | A2 |
| MISSION BLVD | SDCO | 106 | C5 |
| MISSION DR | LACO | R | B3 |
| MISSION FRWY | SDCO | V | A3 |
| MISSION RD | LA | 186 | D2 |
| MISSION RD | LACO | 98 | A2 |
| MISSION RD | LACO | R | B3 |
| MISSION RD | MON | 65 | B3 |
| MISSION RD | SDCO | 106 | C2 |
| MISSION RD | SMCO | L | B5 |
| MISSION RD | SMCO | N | B1 |
| MISSION RD | SMCO | 45 | B2 |
| MISSION ST | SFCO | L | B5 |
| MISSION ST | SF | 142 | C5 |
| MISSION ST | SF | 143 | C5 |
| MISSION ST | STB | 174 | A3 |
| MISSION ST | SC | 169 | A4 |
| MISSION TR | RCO | 99 | B5 |
| MISSION BAY DR | SD | 212 | D1 |
| MISSN BAY DR W | SD | 212 | B4 |
| MISSION CTR RD | SD | 213 | E3 |
| MISSION CK RD | RCO | 100 | C2 |
| MISSION GRGE RD | SDCO | V | C2 |
| MISSION GRGE RD | SDCO | 106 | E5 |
| MISSION LKS BL | RCO | 100 | C2 |
| MISSN OLIVE RD | BUT | 25 | E5 |
| MISSION RDGE RD | STB | 174 | D2 |
| MISSION VLY FWY | SD | 213 | C5 |
| MISSION VLY FWY | SD | 214 | A4 |
| MISSION VLGE DR | SD | 214 | C1 |
| MISSION VLGE DR | SDCO | V | C2 |
| MISSION VLGE DR | SDCO | 106 | D5 |
| MISSOURI AV | STA | 47 | E2 |
| MISTLETOE DR | VEN | 88 | C4 |
| MITCHELL RD | HUM | 10 | C3 |
| MITCHELL RD | HUM | 15 | E1 |
| MITCHELL RD | LAS | 8 | A5 |
| MITCHELL RD | LAS | 14 | E5 |
| MITCHELL RD | STA | 47 | D4 |
| MITCHLLS CMP RD | IMP | 110 | C2 |
| MIX CANYON RD | SOL | 38 | E2 |
| MOANING CAVE RD | CAL | 41 | B4 |
| MOBLEY | SJCO | 40 | C5 |
| MOBLEY | SJCO | 47 | C1 |
| MOCAL RD | KER | 77 | E4 |
| MOCAL RD | KER | 78 | D4 |
| MOCKINGBIRD CYN | RCO | 99 | B3 |
| MODJESKA CYN RD | ORA | 98 | E4 |
| MODOC AV | FRCO | 57 | A3 |
| MODOC COUNTY RD | MOD | 5 | D3 |
| MOFFAT BLVD | MAN | 161 | C4 |
| MOFFAT BLVD | SJCO | 161 | C4 |
| MOFFAT RANCH RD | INY | 60 | A4 |
| MOFFATT RD | MCO | 47 | D5 |
| MOFFETT BLVD | MVW | 148 | A4 |
| MOFFETT BLVD | SCL | N | E3 |
| MOFFETT BLVD | SCL | P | A3 |
| MOFFETT DR | TUL | 68 | D1 |
| MOFFETT RD | STA | 47 | D3 |
| MOFFETT CK RD E | SIS | 3 | E5 |
| MOFFETT CK RD W | SIS | 3 | E5 |
| MOHAVE RD | LPAZ | 103 | E3 |
| MOHAVE ROSE DR | LACO | 89 | D3 |
| MOHAVE VLY HWY | MOH | 85 | D5 |
| MOHLER RD | SJCO | 47 | B2 |
| MOJAVE AV | KER | 89 | C1 |
| MOJAVE DR | SBD | 91 | B3 |
| MOJAVE RD | SBD | 91 | B4 |
| MOJAVE RD | SBD | 101 | C1 |
| MOJAVE-RANDSBRG | KER | 80 | C4 |
| MOJVE TRPICO RD | KER | 79 | E5 |
| MOJVE TRPICO RD | KER | 80 | A5 |
| MOJVE TRPICO RD | KER | 89 | E1 |
| MOKELUMNE HILL- | | | |
| -CMP SECO TP RD | CAL | 41 | C3 |
| MOLERA RD | MON | 54 | B3 |
| MOLINO AV | MV | 140 | A3 |

| STREET | CO. | PAGE & GRID | |
|---|---|---|---|
| MOLLER AV | TEH | 24 | E2 |
| MONARCH MINE RD | SIE | 26 | E4 |
| MONARCH MINE RD | SIE | 27 | A4 |
| MONO DR E | MONO | 43 | C4 |
| MONO WY | TUO | 163 | D4 |
| MONROE | MCO | 55 | D1 |
| MONROE AV | FRCO | 57 | B3 |
| MONROE AV | FRCO | 57 | B5 |
| MONROE AV | TEH | 18 | D5 |
| MONROE ST | RCO | 101 | A4 |
| MONROE ST | SCLR | 150 | C1 |
| MONSON | FRCO | 58 | B4 |
| MONTGUE AGER RD | SIS | 4 | B4 |
| MONTAGUE EXPWY | SCL | P | B3 |
| MONTAGUE GRNADA | SIS | 4 | B4 |
| MONTANA AV | LA | 180 | A3 |
| MONTANA AV | LACO | 97 | C2 |
| MONTANA AV | SHA | 18 | C2 |
| MONTANA ST | PAS | 190 | A1 |
| MONTARA RD | SBD | 91 | E1 |
| MONTE RD | IMP | 109 | A4 |
| MONTEBELLO BLVD | LACO | R | C4 |
| MONTE BELLO RD | SCL | N | E3 |
| MONTE BELLO RD | SCL | 45 | D4 |
| MONTE BLOYD RD | MEN | 30 | D2 |
| MONTECITO RD | SDCO | 107 | A4 |
| MONTECITO RD | SLO | 75 | E2 |
| MONTECITO ST | STB | 174 | D3 |
| MONTE DIABLO AV | S | 160 | A4 |
| MONTEREY AV | FRCO | 56 | D4 |
| MONTEREY AV | FRCO | 66 | D2 |
| MONTEREY AV | MDO | 162 | D4 |
| MONTEREY AV | RCO | 100 | E4 |
| MONTEREY BLVD | SFCO | L | B5 |
| MONTEREY BLVD | SFCO | 45 | B2 |
| MONTEREY HWY | SCL | P | D4 |
| MONTEREY HWY | SCL | 54 | D1 |
| MONTEREY RD | LACO | R | B3 |
| MONTEREY RD | SLO | 76 | A1 |
| MONTEREY RD | SLO | 76 | A2 |
| MONTEREY RD | SCL | 46 | B4 |
| MONTEREY ST | SAL | 171 | C4 |
| MONTEREY ST | SNLO | 172 | C3 |
| MONTEREY PSS RD | LACO | R | B4 |
| MONTE VERDE AV | CAR | 168 | B3 |
| MONTE VISTA AV | MCO | 48 | A3 |
| MONTE VISTA AV | SBD | U | C2 |
| MONTE VISTA AV | SBD | 80 | E1 |
| MONTE VISTA AV | SBD | 98 | D1 |
| MONTE VISTA AV | STA | 47 | C3 |
| MONTE VISTA AV | STA | 48 | A3 |
| MONTE VISTA DR | SDCO | 106 | C3 |
| MONTE VISTA RD | SHA | 18 | B3 |
| MONTEZUMA RD | SDCO | V | C3 |
| MONTEZUMA RD | SDCO | 111 | D1 |
| MONTEZUMA HL RD | SOL | 39 | B4 |
| MONTFORD AV | MV | 140 | A3 |
| MONTGOMERY AV | BUT | 25 | A3 |
| MONTGOMERY DR | STR | 131 | D3 |
| MONTGOMERY RD | IMP | 109 | B3 |
| MONTGOMERY RD | TRI | 11 | B5 |
| MONTGOMERY ST | SF | 143 | C2 |
| MONTGOMERY ST | MCO | 48 | C3 |
| MONTGOMRY CK RD | TRI | 11 | D5 |
| MONTGMRY RCH RD | SHA | 18 | B2 |
| MONTICELLO RD | NAPA | 133 | E1 |
| MONTPELIER RD | STA | 47 | E3 |
| MONTPELIER RD | STA | 48 | A3 |
| MONUMENT BLVD | CC | M | A3 |
| MONUMENT RD | HUM | 15 | E3 |
| MOODY RD | MEN | 22 | B2 |
| MOODY ST | ORA | T | B2 |
| MOON BEND RD | COL | 32 | A2 |
| MOON BEND RD | COL | 33 | A2 |
| MOONEY BLVD | TUL | 68 | B2 |
| MOONEY RD | LAS | 20 | C2 |
| MOONEY RD | LAS | 20 | C3 |
| MOONEY FLAT RD | NEV | 34 | A1 |
| MOONRIDGE RD | SBD | 100 | A1 |
| MOONSHINE RD | YUB | 26 | B5 |
| MOONWIND ST | KER | 80 | D1 |
| MOORE RD | LAS | 21 | E4 |
| MOORE RD | PLA | 33 | E4 |
| MOORE RD | PLA | 34 | A4 |
| MOORE RD | SUT | 33 | B2 |
| MOOREHEAD RD | STA | 47 | C5 |
| MOORES FLAT RD | NEV | 26 | D5 |
| MOORPARK FRWY | VEN | 88 | E5 |
| MOORPARK RD | VEN | 96 | D1 |
| MOORPARK ST | LACO | Q | C3 |
| MOORVILL RDG RD | BUT | 26 | B4 |
| MOOSE CAMP RD | SHA | 13 | B5 |
| MORADA LN | SJCO | 40 | B4 |
| MORAGA AV | ALA | L | D4 |
| MORAGA AV | ALA | 45 | D1 |
| MORAGA AV | MCO | 55 | D1 |
| MORAGA AV | O | 158 | E1 |
| MORAGA AV | P | 158 | D1 |
| MORAGA AV | SD | 211 | E5 |
| MORAGA RD | CC | L | E4 |
| MORAGA RD | CC | 45 | E1 |
| MORAGA WY | CC | L | E4 |
| MORAN AV | MCO | 48 | A4 |
| MORAN RD | CAL | 41 | C3 |
| MORAN RD | STA | 47 | C4 |
| MORAN RD | TEH | 24 | D1 |
| MORCOURT AV | KER | 80 | C1 |
| MOREHEAD RD | DN | 1 | D3 |
| MOREHEAD RD | SUT | 33 | B2 |
| MORELLO AV | CC | L | E3 |
| MORELLO AV | CC | 154 | E3 |
| MORELLO AV | M | 154 | E4 |
| MORENA BLVD | SD | 211 | C4 |
| MORENA BLVD | SD | 212 | E1 |
| MORENA BLVD | SD | 213 | A4 |
| MORENA BLVD | SDCO | V | A2 |
| MORENA BLVD | SDCO | 111 | C1 |

| STREET | CO. | PAGE & GRID | |
|---|---|---|---|
| MORENA BLVD W | SD | 213 | A4 |
| MORENA RES DR | SDCO | 112 | D1 |
| MORENO AV | SDCO | V | E1 |
| MORENO AV | SDCO | 106 | E5 |
| MORENO RD | STB | 174 | C2 |
| MORENO ST | MTCL | 203 | C3 |
| MORENO BEACH DR | RCO | 99 | C2 |
| MORGAN RD | CAL | 41 | B5 |
| MORGAN RD | HUM | 15 | D2 |
| MORGAN RD | LAS | 21 | C1 |
| MORGAN RD | SBD | 101 | D1 |
| MORGAN RD | STA | 47 | D3 |
| MORGAN WY | LPAZ | 104 | A5 |
| MORGAN CYN RD | FRCO | 57 | E2 |
| MORGAN TERRITRY | CC | 39 | B5 |
| MORGAN TERRITRY | CC | 46 | B1 |
| MORGAN VLY RD | LAK | 32 | B4 |
| MORLEY AV | MCO | 48 | D5 |
| MORMON ST | LA | 191 | C3 |
| MORMN EMGRNT TR | ED | 35 | C5 |
| MORNING DR | KER | 78 | E3 |
| MORNING STAR RD | ALP | 36 | C5 |
| MORNING STR CTO | SBD | 84 | B3 |
| MORNING STAR MN | SBD | 84 | B3 |
| MORONGO RD | RCO | 100 | A3 |
| MORONGO RD | SBD | 101 | B1 |
| MORONI RD | SUT | 33 | B2 |
| MORRETTI CYN RD | SLO | 76 | B4 |
| MORRILL RD | STA | 47 | D2 |
| MORRIS AV W | MDO | 162 | A2 |
| MORRIS RD | COL | 33 | A2 |
| MORRIS RD | KER | 78 | A3 |
| MORRIS RD | STA | 47 | C4 |
| MORRIS MINE RD | MNO | 51 | C2 |
| MORRISON RD | STA | 48 | A1 |
| MORRISN BRYN RD | TEH | 24 | B2 |
| MORRISON CYN RD | ALA | P | B1 |
| MORRISON CYN RD | ALA | 46 | A3 |
| MORRIS RANCH RD | RCO | 100 | C5 |
| MORRO RD | KER | 91 | C3 |
| MORSE RD | SJCO | 40 | B4 |
| MORSE RD | YOL | 39 | D3 |
| MORTON AV | TUL | 68 | D3 |
| MORTON BL S | MDO | 162 | C4 |
| MOSAIC CANYON | INY | 61 | D4 |
| MOSELEY RD | DN | 1 | D3 |
| MOSHER | MPA | 49 | A3 |
| MOSQUITO RD | ED | 34 | E4 |
| MOSQUITO RDG RD | PLA | 34 | E3 |
| MOSS OLD MLL RD | TRI | 10 | E5 |
| MOTHER DR | ED | 34 | D5 |
| MOTHER LODE TR | MAD | 49 | C4 |
| MOTOR AV | LA | 183 | B3 |
| MOTOR AV | LACO | Q | C4 |
| MOTT AIRPORT RD | SIS | 12 | D2 |
| MOULTAN LOOP | TEH | 19 | A3 |
| MOULTON PKWY | ORA | 98 | C4 |
| MOUND SPGS RD | SBD | 100 | C1 |
| MT ACADIA BLVD | SD | 213 | B2 |
| MT ADA RD | AVLN | 105 | B5 |
| MOUNTAIN AV | LACO | R | D2 |
| MOUNTAIN AV | RCO | 100 | A4 |
| MOUNTAIN AV | SBD | U | D2 |
| MOUNTAIN AV | SBD | 98 | D1 |
| MOUNTAIN AV | UPL | 203 | E2 |
| MOUNTAIN BLVD | O | 156 | E5 |
| MOUNTAIN DR | STB | 174 | B2 |
| MOUNTAIN RD | SBD | 90 | D4 |
| MOUNTAIN RD S | VEN | 88 | C5 |
| MOUNTAIN ST | LACO | Q | E2 |
| MTN CLIMBER WY | KER | 79 | C5 |
| MTN HOME CK RD | SBD | 99 | E1 |
| MTN HOME RCH RD | SON | 38 | A1 |
| MTN HOUSE RD | ALA | M | E4 |
| MTN HOUSE RD | ALA | 46 | D1 |
| MTN HOUSE RD | MEN | 31 | C4 |
| MTN HOUSE RD | SIE | 26 | D4 |
| MTN LEMON RD S | VEN | 88 | C5 |
| MTN MEADOW RD | SHA | 19 | C2 |
| MTN QUAIL LN | MOD | 7 | B5 |
| MOUNTAIN RCH RD | CAL | 41 | B3 |
| MTN SCHOOL RD | SHA | 13 | B5 |
| MTN SPRINGS RD | SBD | 94 | E1 |
| MTN SPRINGS RD | SLO | 76 | A1 |
| MOUNTAIN VW AV | FRCO | 56 | C5 |
| MOUNTAIN VW AV | FRCO | 57 | D5 |
| MOUNTAIN VW AV | SBD | 99 | C2 |
| MOUNTAIN VW AV | RCO | 99 | E2 |
| MOUNTAIN VW RD | HUM | 16 | B1 |
| MOUNTAIN VW RD | KER | 78 | E3 |
| MOUNTAIN VW RD | KER | 79 | A3 |
| MOUNTAIN VW RD | MEN | 30 | E3 |
| MOUNTAIN VW RD | RCO | 100 | D3 |
| MOUNTAIN VW RD | SBD | 92 | B1 |
| MOUNTAIN VW RD | SBD | 91 | C1 |
| MOUNTAIN VW RD | STB | 174 | A4 |
| MOUNTAIN VW RD | SCR | P | B5 |
| MOUNTAIN VW RD | SCR | 54 | A1 |
| MOUNTAIN VW RD | SHA | 13 | C5 |
| MOUNTAIN VW RD | STA | 47 | D3 |
| MOUNTAIN VW ST | BARS | 208 | A2 |
| MTN VW-ALVSO RD | MVW | 148 | A5 |
| MTN VW-ALVSO RD | SCL | P | B3 |
| MTN VIEW RCH RD | SON | 31 | C5 |
| MT AUKUM RD | ED | 40 | E1 |
| MT AUKUM RD | ED | 41 | A1 |
| MT BALDY LKOUT | SIS | 2 | D3 |
| MT BULLION CTFF | MPA | 49 | A3 |
| MT DIABLO SC BL | CC | M | B4 |
| MT EATON RD | TUO | 41 | D5 |
| MT EDEN RD | SCL | N | E4 |
| MT EDEN RD | SCL | P | A4 |
| MT EDEN RD | SCL | 45 | E5 |
| MT EMMA RD | LACO | 90 | A4 |
| MT GAINES | MPA | 48 | E3 |
| MT GLEASON AV | LACO | Q | E2 |
| MT HAMILTON RD | SCL | P | C3 |

| STREET | CO. | PAGE & GRID | |
|---|---|---|---|
| MT HAMILTON RD | SCL | 46 | C4 |
| MT HERMON RD | SCR | P | A5 |
| MT HERMON RD | SCR | 53 | E1 |
| MT HOUGH CRYSTL | PLU | 26 | D1 |
| MT HOLLYWOOD DR | LA | 182 | A2 |
| MT HOUSE RD | YUB | 26 | C5 |
| MT MADONNA RD | SCL | 54 | C2 |
| MT OLIVE RD | NEV | 34 | C2 |
| MT OPHIR RD | MPA | 49 | A3 |
| MT PIERCE LKOUT | HUM | 15 | E3 |
| MT PINOS RD | KER | 88 | D2 |
| MT PINOS RD | VEN | 88 | A1 |
| MT PINOS RD | VEN | 88 | C2 |
| MT REBA RD | ALP | 42 | A1 |
| MT SHASTA DR | SIS | 12 | E2 |
| MT VEEDER RD | NAPA | 29 | C4 |
| MT VEEDER RD | NAPA | 38 | B2 |
| MT VERNON AV | CLTN | 207 | B4 |
| MT VERNON AV | KER | 78 | D3 |
| MT VERNON AV | RCO | 99 | B2 |
| MT VERNON AV | SBD | 91 | D1 |
| MT VERNON AV | SBD | 99 | B2 |
| MT VERNON AV | SBDO | 207 | B2 |
| MT VERNON RD | PLA | 34 | B3 |
| MT WHITNEY | FRCO | 57 | C5 |
| MT WHITNEY AV | FRCO | 66 | D1 |
| MT WHITNEY ST | KER | 70 | C5 |
| MT WILSON | LACO | 98 | A1 |
| MT WILSON RD | LACO | R | C1 |
| MT ZION RD | AMA | 41 | A2 |
| MOVIE RD | INY | 60 | A4 |
| MOWRY AV | ALA | P | A2 |
| MOWRY AV | ALA | 46 | A3 |
| M T FREITAS PKY | SR | 139 | A1 |
| MUCK VALLEY RD | LAS | 14 | B4 |
| MUDD RD | IMP | 109 | A5 |
| MUD LAKE RD | ALP | 36 | C4 |
| MUD LAKE RD | MOD | 6 | A5 |
| MUD LAKE RD | MOD | 14 | A1 |
| MUELLER | SJCO | 40 | A5 |
| MUELLER | SJCO | 47 | A1 |
| MUIR AV | BUT | 25 | A3 |
| MUIR MILL RD | MEN | 22 | E5 |
| MUIR MILL RD | MEN | 23 | A5 |
| MUIR MILL RD | MEN | 30 | E1 |
| MUIR MILL RD | MEN | 31 | A1 |
| MUIR WOODS RD | MAR | L | A4 |
| MUIR WOODS RD | MAR | 45 | A1 |
| MULBERRY AV | MCO | 48 | B4 |
| MULBERRY AV | RCO | 99 | A2 |
| MULBERRY DR | LACO | R | D5 |
| MULBERRY ST | C | 124 | D5 |
| MULE BRIDGE RD | SIS | 11 | C2 |
| MULE CANYON RD | SBD | 92 | A1 |
| MULE CREEK RD | TRI | 11 | D5 |
| MULE DEER LN | MOD | 7 | B5 |
| MULE TOWN RD | SHA | 18 | B2 |
| MULHOLLAND DR | LA | 177 | A5 |
| MULHOLLAND DR | LA | 181 | A2 |
| MULHOLLAND DR | LACO | 97 | C1 |
| MULHOLLAND DR | LACO | Q | C3 |
| MULHOLLAND HWY | LACO | 97 | A1 |
| MULLER LN | DGL | 36 | B3 |
| MULLER RD | KER | 78 | E3 |
| MULLER RD | KER | 79 | A3 |
| MULLOY RD | SIS | 4 | C3 |
| MUMMA RD | COL | 33 | A3 |
| MUMY RD | INY | 51 | C4 |
| MUNCY RD | STA | 47 | C3 |
| MUNJAR RD | BUT | 25 | A2 |
| MUNRAS AV | MONT | 167 | D5 |
| MUNRAS AV | MON | 53 | E4 |
| MUNSEY RD | KER | 80 | C3 |
| MUNRAS AV | MONT | 168 | D1 |
| MUNZER RD | KER | 78 | B3 |
| MURCHISON DR | MLBR | 144 | D5 |
| MURIEL DR | BARS | 208 | C2 |
| MURPHY AV | SCL | P | B3 |
| MURPHY LN | SCL | P | E5 |
| MURPHY LN | SCL | 54 | D1 |
| MURPHY LN | SHA | 19 | A1 |
| MURPHY RD | IMP | 112 | A3 |
| MURPHY RD | MON | 54 | C2 |
| MURPHY RD | NEV | 26 | C5 |
| MURPHY RD | SBT | 55 | B3 |
| MURPHY RD | SCR | 54 | C2 |
| MURPHY RD | SJCO | 47 | C1 |
| MURPHY RD | STA | 47 | C2 |
| MURPHY RD | TUO | 41 | C5 |
| MURPHYS GRD RD | CAL | 41 | B4 |
| MURRAY RD | HUM | 9 | E4 |
| MURRAY RD | HUM | 10 | A4 |
| MURRAY RD | SJCO | 40 | C5 |
| MURRAY RD | SUT | 33 | C3 |
| MURRAY CK RD E | CAL | 41 | B3 |
| MURRAY CK RD W | CAL | 41 | A3 |
| MURRAY RIDGE RD | SD | 214 | A2 |
| MURRIETA HT SPG | RCO | 99 | C5 |
| MURRIETTA RD | RCO | 99 | C3 |
| MUSCAT AV | FRCO | 57 | B4 |
| MUSCAT AV | FRCO | 57 | D4 |
| MUSCOTT ST | SBDO | 207 | A2 |
| MUSTANG RD | RCO | 100 | A5 |
| MUSTANG SPGS RD | SLO | 76 | A1 |
| MUTAU FLAT RD | VEN | 88 | C2 |
| MYER AV | TUL | 68 | C2 |
| MYERS LN | COL | 32 | E2 |
| MYERS RD | COL | 32 | D2 |
| MYERS RD | SIS | 4 | E3 |
| MYERS RD | SIS | 5 | A3 |
| MYERS ST | BUT | 25 | D4 |
| MYFORD RD | ORA | T | E3 |
| MYKLE OAKS RD | MPA | 49 | A3 |
| MYRA AV | LA | 182 | C5 |
| MYRTLE AV | DN | 1 | E5 |
| MYRTLE AV | EUR | 121 | E1 |
| MYRTLE AV | HUM | 9 | E5 |

| STREET | CO. | PAGE & GRID | |
|---|---|---|---|
| MYRTLE AV | HUM | 15 | E1 |
| MYRTLE AV | LACO | R | D2 |
| MYRTLEWOOD DR | MAD | 57 | C2 |
| N | | | |
| NABORLY RD | SBD | 101 | D1 |
| NACIMNTO-FER RD | MON | 64 | E3 |
| NACIMNTO-FER RD | MON | 65 | A3 |
| NACIMIENTO LAKE | MON | 65 | E4 |
| NACMIENTO LK DR | SLO | 75 | E1 |
| NACMIENTO LK DR | SLO | 76 | A1 |
| NACIONAL ST | SAL | 171 | A3 |
| NADEAU RD | INY | 71 | B1 |
| NADER RD | PLA | 34 | A3 |
| NAGEL CANYON RD | KER | 79 | D3 |
| NAGLEE AV | SJ | 151 | D4 |
| NANTES AV | MCO | 55 | E1 |
| NAPA AV | FRCO | 56 | E5 |
| NAPA RD | SBD | 92 | E5 |
| NAPA RD | SON | 38 | B3 |
| NAPA RD | SON | L | B1 |
| NAPA RD | SON | 132 | D5 |
| NAPA ST | SON | L | B1 |
| NAPA ST E | SNMA | 132 | E4 |
| NAPA ST E | SON | 38 | B3 |
| NAPA ST W | SNMA | 132 | C4 |
| NARANJO BLVD | TUL | 58 | D5 |
| NARANJO BLVD | TUL | 68 | D1 |
| NARBONNE AV | LACO | S | B2 |
| NARRAGANSETT AV | SDCO | V | A3 |
| NARRAGANSETT AV | SDCO | 111 | C1 |
| NASHUA RD | MON | 54 | C3 |
| NASON RD | MON | 64 | C1 |
| NASON ST | RCO | 99 | C3 |
| NATIONAL AV | SD | 216 | A4 |
| NATIONAL AV | SDCO | V | C4 |
| NATIONAL AV | SDCO | 111 | D1 |
| NATIONAL BLVD | CUL | 183 | D5 |
| NATIONAL BLVD | LA | 180 | E5 |
| NATIONAL BLVD | LA | 183 | C4 |
| NATIONAL BLVD | LACO | Q | C4 |
| NATL TRAILS HWY | SBD | 91 | B2 |
| NATL TRAILS HWY | SBD | 92 | A1 |
| NATL TRAILS HWY | SBD | 93 | A2 |
| NATL TRAILS HWY | SBD | 94 | A3 |
| NATIVIDAD RD | MON | 54 | D4 |
| NATOMAS RD | SUT | 33 | D4 |
| NATURAL BRDG RD | INY | 72 | B1 |
| NAUMAN RD | VEN | 96 | B1 |
| NAUTILUS ST | SD | 211 | A4 |
| NAVAJO DR | SAL | 171 | C1 |
| NAVAJO RD | RCO | 99 | C4 |
| NAVAJO RD | SBD | 91 | C3 |
| NAVAJO RD | SDCO | V | D2 |
| NAVAJO RD | SDCO | 111 | D1 |
| NAVARO ST | SDCO | V | A3 |
| NAVARRO RDG RD | MEN | 30 | C2 |
| NAVELENCIA AV | FRCO | 58 | A4 |
| NAVY DR | SJCO | 40 | A5 |
| NEAL SPRING RD | SLO | 76 | B1 |
| NEBO ST | SBD | 92 | A1 |
| NEBRASKA AV | FRCO | 57 | B4 |
| NEBRASKA AV | FRCO | 57 | C4 |
| NEBRASKA AV | TUL | 58 | A4 |
| NEBRASKA ST | VAL | 134 | C3 |
| NECKLE RD | IMP | 112 | A3 |
| NECTAR RD | RCO | 107 | B1 |
| NEEDHAM RD | STA | 47 | B3 |
| NEEDHAM ST | MDO | 162 | A3 |
| NEEDLE PEAK RD | SLT | 129 | D4 |
| NEELEY | SJCO | 40 | A4 |
| NEENACH RD | LACO | 89 | E2 |
| NEES AV | FRCO | 56 | C3 |
| NEES AV | FRCO | 57 | C3 |
| NEGRO CREEK DR | TUL | 58 | C4 |
| NEGRO HOLE RD | SIS | 5 | C4 |
| NEIGHBORS BLVD | RCO | 103 | D5 |
| NEIGHBORS BLVD | RCO | 110 | D1 |
| NEILSON RD | CAL | 40 | E3 |
| NELANDER | MCO | 47 | E4 |
| NELSON | SJCO | 47 | C1 |
| NELSON AV | BUT | 25 | C4 |
| NELSON DR | TUL | 69 | B2 |
| NELSON RD | BUT | 25 | B4 |
| NELSON RD | TRI | 17 | C2 |
| NELSON BAR RD | BUT | 25 | D3 |
| NELSON CREEK RD | SHA | 13 | B4 |
| NELSON PIT RD | IMP | 112 | C3 |
| NELSON RES RD | LAS | 8 | B3 |
| NELSONS CROSSNG | BUT | 26 | A3 |
| NELSN SHPPEE RD | BUT | 25 | B4 |
| NEROLY RD | CC | 39 | C5 |
| NEROLY RD | CC | M | C3 |
| NESTLE AV | LA | 178 | D5 |
| NETHERLANDS RD | YOL | 39 | D2 |
| NETHERTON RD | MCO | 47 | C5 |
| NEUGERBAUER | SJCO | 39 | E5 |
| NEUMARKEL RD | KER | 79 | A3 |
| NEURALIA RD | KER | 80 | B4 |
| NEVA AV | TEH | 24 | D2 |
| NEVADA AV | KIN | 67 | B2 |
| NEVADA AV | KIN | 67 | C2 |
| NEVADA ST | AUB | 126 | B3 |
| NEVADA ST | NEVC | 128 | C2 |
| NEVADA ST | NEV | 128 | D2 |
| NEVADA CITY HWY | GV | 127 | D2 |
| NEVADA CITY HWY | NEV | 127 | D2 |
| NEVADA CITY HWY | NEV | 128 | A5 |
| NEVIS AV | KER | 78 | C1 |
| NEW AV | LACO | R | C4 |
| NEW AV | SCL | P | E5 |
| NEW AV | SCL | 54 | D1 |
| NEWARK BLVD | ALA | P | A2 |
| NEWARK BLVD | ALA | 45 | E3 |
| NEWBERRY RD | SBD | 92 | C1 |
| NEW BIG OAK FLT | MPA | 49 | C1 |
| NEW BIG OAK FLT | MPA | 63 | B4 |
| NEWCASTLE | PLA | 34 | B4 |



STREETS

237
NEWCASTLE RD
STREET INDEX
OLYMPIC BLVD




| STREET | CO. | PAGE & GRID |
|---|---|---|
| NEWCASTLE RD | SJCO | 40 B5 |
| NEW CEMETERY RD | LAS | 14 B3 |
| NEW CHESTR DUMP | PLU | 20 B4 |
| NW CHG QRTZ MTN | AMA | 40 E2 |
| NEWCOMB AV | FRCO | 56 C4 |
| NEWCOMB ST | TUL | 68 D3 |
| NEW DOCK ST | LA | 191 C2 |
| NEW DOCK ST | LACO | S C3 |
| NEWHALL AV | LACO | 89 B4 |
| NEWHALL RD | MCO | 48 B5 |
| NEWHALL RD | SUT | 33 B2 |
| NEWHALL ST | SJ | 151 D3 |
| NEW HOPE RD | SAC | 39 E3 |
| NEW HOPE RD | SAC | 40 A3 |
| NEWHOPE ST | FTNV | 197 B2 |
| NEWHOPE ST | GGR | 195 A3 |
| NEWHOPE ST | ORA | T C3 |
| NEWHOPE ST | SA | 195 A3 |
| NEW IDRIA RD | SBT | 55 E5 |
| NEW IDRIA RD | SBT | 56 A4 |
| NEWLAND ST | ORA | T B3 |
| NEWMARK AV | FRCO | 57 E4 |
| NEW PLEYTO RD | MON | 65 D4 |
| NEW PEORIA FLAT | TUO | 41 B5 |
| NEWPORT AV | GLE | 24 D3 |
| NEWPORT AV | ORA | 98 C4 |
| NEWPORT AV | ORA | T E2 |
| NEWPORT BLVD | CM | 199 C2 |
| NEWPORT BLVD | NB | 199 A4 |
| NEWPORT BLVD | ORA | 98 C4 |
| NEWPORT BLVD | ORA | T E2 |
| NEWPORT FRWY | CM | 197 E5 |
| NEWPORT FRWY | CM | 198 B3 |
| NEWPORT FRWY | OR | 194 E3 |
| NEWPORT FRWY | OR | 196 E3 |
| NEWPORT FRWY | ORA | 98 C4 |
| NEWPORT FRWY | ORA | T C4 |
| NEWPORT FRWY | ORA | 196 E3 |
| NEWPORT FRWY | SA | 196 E4 |
| NEWPORT FRWY | TUS | 196 E4 |
| NEWPORT RD | MCO | 48 A3 |
| NEWPORT RD | RCO | 99 C4 |
| NEWPORT RD | RCO | 99 D4 |
| NEWRIVER RD | TRI | 11 A4 |
| NEW ROME RD | NEV | 34 C1 |
| NEWSOM RD | MCO | 47 C5 |
| NEWSOM RD | MCO | 55 C1 |
| NEWTON AV | KIN | 67 C3 |
| NEWTOWN RD | ED | 34 E5 |
| NEWVILLE RD | GLE | 24 B3 |
| NEWVILLE RD | TEH | 24 A2 |
| NEW YORK DR | LACO | R B2 |
| NEW YORK DR | LACO | R B2 |
| NEW YRK FLAT RD | YUB | 26 A4 |
| NEW YRK HOUS RD | YUB | 26 A5 |
| NEW YORK MTN RD | SBD | 84 C4 |
| NEW YORK RCH RD | AMA | 40 E2 |
| NEW YORK RCH RD | AMA | 41 A2 |
| NICASIO VLY RD | MAR | 37 E4 |
| NICE LUCERNE | LAK | 31 D2 |
| NICHOLAS RD | MAD | 57 E2 |
| NICHOLLS RD | NEV | 34 B2 |
| NICHOLS RD | IMP | 112 A3 |
| NICHOLS RD | RCO | 99 B4 |
| NICHOLS CYN RD | LA | 181 A3 |
| NICHOLS MILL RD | SIE | 27 B4 |
| NICKEL RD | MCO | 48 A5 |
| NICOLAS RD | RCO | 99 D5 |
| NICOLAUS | PLA | 33 E4 |
| NICOLAUS AV | SUT | 33 D3 |
| NIDER RD | IMP | 109 B3 |
| NIDERER RD | SLO | 75 E1 |
| NIDERER RD | SLO | 76 A1 |
| NIELSON | SJCO | 40 C5 |
| NIELSON AV | FRE | 165 A3 |
| NIELSEN AV | FRCO | 57 A3 |
| NIELSON RD | CAL | 41 A3 |
| NIESTRATH RD | SON | 37 B1 |
| NILAND AV | IMP | 109 B3 |
| NILAND MRINA RD | IMP | 109 A2 |
| NILE AV | SJCO | 47 B1 |
| NILE RD | SJCO | 47 B1 |
| NILES AV | KIN | 67 D3 |
| NILES ST | BKD | 166 C2 |
| NILES ST | KER | 78 E3 |
| NILES CANYON RD | ALA | P B1 |
| NILES CANYON RD | ALA | 46 A3 |
| NILL AV | KER | 78 C1 |
| NIMITZ BLVD | SD | 212 C5 |
| NIMITZ BLVD | SDCO | V A3 |
| NIMITZ BLVD | SDCO | 111 C1 |
| NIMITZ FRWY | ALA | 45 D2 |
| NIMITZ FRWY | ALA | 146 C4 |
| NIMITZ FRWY | H | 146 C4 |
| NIMITZ FRWY | O | 157 D1 |
| NIMITZ FRWY | O | 158 B4 |
| NIMITZ FRWY | O | 159 C1 |
| NIMITZ FRWY | SJ | 152 A1 |
| NINE RD | CAL | 41 C4 |
| NINE MILE CYN | INY | 70 B4 |
| NINTH ST | C | 124 C5 |
| NIPOMO ST | SNLO | 172 B3 |
| NIPTON RD | SBD | 84 C2 |
| NIPTON DESRT RD | SBD | 84 C2 |
| NIPTON MOORE RD | SBD | 84 C2 |
| NISQUALLY RD | SBD | 91 B4 |
| NISSEN RD | HUM | 15 D2 |
| NM 1 | TUL | 68 E5 |
| NM 14 | TUL | 68 E4 |
| NM 18 | TUL | 69 C4 |
| NM 23 | TUL | 69 B4 |
| NM 24 | TUL | 69 B4 |
| NM 45 | TUL | 69 C4 |
| NM 50 | TUL | 69 B4 |
| NM 88 | TUL | 69 C4 |
| NM 93 | TUL | 69 C4 |
| NM 112 | TUL | 69 C3 |
| NM 117 | TUL | 70 A3 |
| NM 121 | TUL | 69 B3 |
| NM 127 | TUL | 69 B3 |
| NM 133 | TUL | 70 A3 |
| NM 163 | TUL | 69 B3 |
| NM 175 | TUL | 69 B3 |
| NM 231 | TUL | 69 B2 |
| NM 232 | TUL | 69 A2 |
| NM 276 | TUL | 69 A1 |
| NOBLE RD | YUB | 33 D2 |
| NOFFSINGER RD | IMP | 109 B3 |
| NOLAN RD | IMP | 109 B4 |
| NOLINA CIR | RCO | 100 D4 |
| NO NINE | MPA | 48 E3 |
| NONPAREIL AV | COL | 32 E3 |
| NOPEL AV | BUT | 25 C2 |
| NORD AV | BUT | 124 A4 |
| NORD AV | KER | 78 C3 |
| NORD HWY | BUT | 25 A3 |
| NORDAHL RD | IMP | 110 D5 |
| NORD GIANELLA | BUT | 25 A3 |
| NORDOFF ST | LACO | 97 C1 |
| NORFOLK ST | SM | 145 A1 |
| NORHAM PL | SBD | 101 A1 |
| NORIEGA RD | KER | 78 C3 |
| NORIEGA ST | SF | 141 C5 |
| NORMA ST S | KER | 80 E1 |
| NORMAL ST | SD | 214 A5 |
| NORMAL ST | SDCO | V B3 |
| NORMAL ST | SDCO | 111 D1 |
| NORMAN | SUT | 33 B2 |
| NORMAN AV | KER | 80 B5 |
| NORMAN RD | COL | 24 E5 |
| NORMANDIE AV | LA | 182 B5 |
| NORMANDIE AV | LA | 185 B5 |
| NORMANDIE AV | LACO | Q E5 |
| NORMANDIE AV | LACO | S C2 |
| NORMAN HILLS RD | RCO | 107 C1 |
| NORRBOM RD | SON | 38 B3 |
| NORRBOM RD | SON | 132 D3 |
| NORRIS RD | KER | 78 C2 |
| NORRIS CYN RD | CC | M A5 |
| NORRIS CYN RD | CC | 46 A2 |
| NORRISH RD | IMP | 109 C5 |
| NORTH AV | FRCO | 56 C4 |
| NORTH AV | FRCO | 57 B4 |
| NORTH AV | KIN | 57 D5 |
| NORTH AV | MCO | 47 E3 |
| NORTH AV | MCO | 48 A3 |
| NORTH AV | ORA | T C2 |
| NORTH AV | SDCO | 106 D3 |
| NORTH AV | STA | 47 C2 |
| NORTH HWY | INY | 61 E4 |
| NORTH HWY | INY | 62 A5 |
| NORTH HWY | INY | 72 B1 |
| NORTH RD | STA | 47 B2 |
| NORTH ST | MAN | 161 C3 |
| NORTH ARM | PLU | 20 D5 |
| N BNK CHETKO RD | CUR | 1 D2 |
| NORTH BUSCH RD | MEN | 23 B5 |
| NORTH BUSCH RD | MEN | 31 B1 |
| NORTHCREST DR | DN | 1 D4 |
| NORTHRLY BR GRN | SLO | 75 D2 |
| NORTH FORK RD | HUM | 15 D4 |
| NORTH FORK RD | MAD | 49 D5 |
| NORTH FORK RD | SBT | 66 A2 |
| NORTH FORK RD | TUO | 41 E4 |
| N FK MAD RIV RD | TRI | 17 B5 |
| NORTHGATE BLVD | SAC | 33 E5 |
| NORTH GATE RD | CC | M B4 |
| NORTH GATE RD | CC | 39 A5 |
| NORTH GATE RD | SOL | 39 A3 |
| NORTH LIVERMORE | ALA | 46 C2 |
| NORTH RIDGE RD | SBD | 100 C2 |
| NORTHRUP RD | MCO | 47 D4 |
| NORTHRUP RD | MOD | 8 A1 |
| NORTHRUP RD | MOD | 14 E1 |
| NORTH SHORE | PLA | 35 E1 |
| NORTH SHORE DR | SBD | 92 A5 |
| NORTH SHORE RD | SIS | 12 C2 |
| NORTHSIDE DR | MPA | 63 B2 |
| NORTH SIDE RD | SBD | 91 E3 |
| NORTH STAR TR | SBD | 100 C2 |
| NORTH VALLEY RD | PLU | 20 D5 |
| NORTHWOODS BLVD | NEV | 27 D5 |
| NORTHWOODS BLVD | NEV | 35 D1 |
| NORTON RD | KER | 80 B3 |
| NORTON RD | SBT | 55 E4 |
| NORTON RD | SOL | 39 C3 |
| NORTONVILLE | CC | 39 B5 |
| NORVEL RD | LAS | 20 C3 |
| NORWALK BLVD | LACO | 98 A3 |
| NORWALK BLVD | LACO | R C5 |
| NORWALK BLVD | LACO | T A1 |
| NORWGIAN RCH RD | TRI | 11 E4 |
| NORWOOD AV | SR | 139 A4 |
| NOTRE DAME AV | BLMT | 145 B5 |
| NOVATO BLVD | MAR | L A2 |
| NOVATO BLVD | MAR | 38 A4 |
| NOYES VALLEY RD | SIS | 11 E2 |
| NTU RD | SB | 86 B1 |
| NUESTRO RD | SUT | 33 C2 |
| NUEVO RD | RCO | 99 C3 |
| NUNES LN | SHA | 19 C2 |
| NUNNIEMAKER RD | HUM | 16 C4 |
| NURSE SLOUGH LN | SOL | 39 A3 |
| NYON RD | SBD | 100 B1 |
| O | | |
| O ST | FRE | 165 D3 |
| OAHU RD | SBD | 92 C1 |
| OAK AV | DVS | 136 C3 |
| OAK AV | LAKE | 7 B1 |
| OAK AV | MCO | 48 B4 |
| OAK AV | SUT | 33 D3 |
| OAK AV | TRI | 17 B2 |
| OAK DR | SDCO | 112 D1 |
| OAK RD | MPA | 49 B3 |
| OAK ST | BKD | 166 A4 |
| OAK ST | MCO | 47 E4 |
| OAK ST | MCO | 48 A4 |
| OAK ST | SF | 141 E4 |
| OAK ST | SF | 142 A4 |
| OAK ST | SHA | 18 B3 |
| OAK ST | S | 160 B4 |
| OAK ST | U | 123 C2 |
| OAK WY | BUT | 25 A3 |
| OAK CREEK RD | KER | 79 D5 |
| OAK CREEK RD N | INY | 59 E3 |
| OAK CREEK RD S | INY | 59 E3 |
| OAKDALE RD | MCO | 48 A3 |
| OAKDALE RD | MCO | 48 B3 |
| OAKDALE RD | STA | 47 D2 |
| OAKDALE CYN RD | LACO | 89 A2 |
| OAKDL WTRFRD HY | STA | 47 E2 |
| OAK FLAT RD | SLO | 75 E1 |
| OAK FLAT RD | SLO | 76 A1 |
| OAK FLAT RD | STA | 47 B4 |
| OAK GLENN AV | SCL | P D5 |
| OAK GLEN AV | SCL | 54 C1 |
| OAK GLEN RD | RCO | 100 A5 |
| OAK GLEN RD | SBD | 99 E2 |
| OAK GROVE | CC | 38 E5 |
| OAK GROVE | MPA | 49 B4 |
| OAK GROVE RD | CC | M A3 |
| OAK GRV SCHOOL | MPA | 49 B4 |
| OAK HILL RD | ED | 34 E5 |
| OAK HILL RD | SBD | 91 A4 |
| OAK KNOLL AV | LACO | R B3 |
| OAK KNOLL AV | NAPA | 29 E5 |
| OAK KNOLL AV | NAPA | 38 C2 |
| OAK KNL RNG STA | SIS | 3 D3 |
| OAKLAND AV | FRCO | 67 A1 |
| OAKLAND AV | O | 158 B2 |
| OAKLAND AV | P | 158 C1 |
| OAKLAND RD | SJ | 152 B1 |
| OAKLAND CP RD | PLU | 26 D1 |
| OAKLEA RD | STA | 47 B3 |
| OAKLEY LN | YUB | 33 E3 |
| OAK MEADOW RD | NEV | 34 B2 |
| OAKMONT TR | SHA | 18 C1 |
| OAKMORE ST | TUL | 68 B2 |
| OAK PARK BLVD | CC | L E3 |
| OAK PARK BLVD | CC | M A3 |
| OAK RANCH RD | SIE | 26 D4 |
| OAK RIDGE RD | SCL | P D2 |
| OAK RIDGE RD | TRI | 17 A2 |
| OAK RUN RD | SHA | 18 D2 |
| OAK RUN RD | SHA | 19 A1 |
| OAK RUN TO FERN | SHA | 19 A1 |
| OAK SPG RNCH RD | SBD | 90 E4 |
| OAK SPRINGS RD | SBD | 91 D4 |
| OAKS AV | ONT | 203 D5 |
| OAKS RANCHO RD | KER | 79 B4 |
| OAK TREE RD | NEV | 26 B5 |
| OAK VALLEY DR | SIS | 4 A4 |
| OAK VALLEY RD | YUB | 26 A4 |
| OAK VIEW CT | KER | 79 B4 |
| OAKVILLE CROSS | NAPA | 29 D3 |
| OAKVLLE CRSS RD | NAPA | 38 C2 |
| OAKVILLE GRADE | NAPA | 29 C4 |
| OAKVILLE GRADE | NAPA | 38 B2 |
| OAKWAY | BUT | 25 D2 |
| OAKWOOD | SJCO | 40 C5 |
| OAKWOOD | SJCO | 47 C1 |
| OASIS RD | MON | 65 C3 |
| OASIS RD | INY | 52 C3 |
| OASIS RD | RCO | 102 C4 |
| OASIS RD | SBD | 90 D4 |
| OASIS RD | SHA | 18 C2 |
| OAT GAP RD | MEN | 23 C5 |
| OAT HILL RD | LAK | 32 B5 |
| OAT HILL RD N | NAPA | 32 B5 |
| OATMAN RD | MOH | 85 D5 |
| OATMN TOPOCK HY | MOH | 95 E1 |
| OBANION RD | SUT | 33 C3 |
| OBERLIN RD | SIS | 4 A4 |
| OBRIEN RD | JOS | 2 C2 |
| OBSIDAN DOME RD | MNO | 50 D1 |
| O'BYRNES FERRY | TUO | 41 B5 |
| OCCIDENTAL RD | SON | 37 D2 |
| OCEAN AV | CAR | 53 D5 |
| OCEAN AV | CAR | 168 B3 |
| OCEAN AV | SFCO | L B5 |
| OCEAN AV | SFCO | 45 B2 |
| OCEAN AV | SB | 86 B3 |
| OCEAN BLVD | LB | 191 E2 |
| OCEAN BLVD | LB | 192 B3 |
| OCEAN BLVD | LACO | 98 A4 |
| OCEAN BLVD | LACO | S D2 |
| OCEAN DR | DN | 1 D3 |
| OCEAN DR | HUM | 9 E4 |
| OCEAN DR | MEN | 22 C4 |
| OCEAN BEACH FWY | SD | 212 C5 |
| OCEAN PARK BLVD | LA | 180 C5 |
| OCEAN PARK BLVD | LACO | Q C4 |
| OCEAN PARK BLVD | SMON | 180 C5 |
| OCEAN PARK BLVD | SMON | 187 A1 |
| OCEAN PARK RD | SB | 86 A2 |
| OCEANSIDE BLVD | SDCO | 106 B3 |
| OCEAN VIEW AV | INY | 51 B3 |
| OCEAN VIEW BLVD | LACO | R A2 |
| OCEAN VIEW BLVD | PAC | 167 A1 |
| OCEAN VIEW BLVD | SD | 216 B4 |
| OCEAN VIEW BLVD | SDCO | V C4 |
| OCEAN VIEW BLVD | SDCO | 111 D1 |
| OCEANVIEW DR | CUR | 1 D2 |
| OCEAN VIEW DR | DN | 1 D3 |
| OCONNOR WY | SLO | 76 A3 |
| OCOTILLO WY | SBD | 91 C4 |
| ODD FELLW PK RD | HUM | 16 A3 |
| ODOM LN | MEN | 22 C5 |
| O'FARRELL ST | SF | 143 A5 |
| OFFAL RD | MNO | 42 E1 |
| OFFIELD LOOKOUT | SIS | 10 E1 |
| OFFUTT RD | KER | 78 B1 |
| OGBURN CEM RD | SHA | 19 A2 |
| OGIER RD | IMP | 112 C3 |
| OGILBY RD | IMP | 110 B4 |
| OGULIN CANYON | LAK | 32 A3 |
| O'HARA AV | CC | M D3 |
| O'HARA AV | CC | 39 C5 |
| OHIO AV | FRCO | 56 C3 |
| OHIO AV | LA | 180 B4 |
| OHM RD | COL | 32 E2 |
| OHM RD | TEH | 18 D5 |
| OIL CANYON RD | FRCO | 66 D2 |
| OIL CITY RD | FRCO | 66 D2 |
| OILER CT | KER | 79 C3 |
| OILFIELDS RD | KER | 78 D2 |
| OIL PLANT RD | MNO | 43 C5 |
| OIL WELL RD | HUM | 15 E2 |
| OJAI DR | SHA | 18 C3 |
| OJAI FRWY | VEN | 88 A5 |
| OJAI FRWY | VENT | 175 A2 |
| OJAI FRWY | VEN | 175 A2 |
| OJAI ST | VEN | 88 B4 |
| O'KEEFE ST | MP | 147 B1 |
| O'KEEFE ST E | SMCO | 147 C1 |
| OKEEFFE RD | SIS | 5 D2 |
| OKLAHOMA AV | TEH | 18 D5 |
| OKLAHOMA SCH RD | SIS | 5 B3 |
| OLANCHA DRWN RD | INY | 70 E1 |
| OLD HWY | COL | 32 D1 |
| OLD HWY | LAS | 21 D5 |
| OLD HWY | MPA | 49 A4 |
| OLD HWY | PLU | 26 D1 |
| OLD AIRLINE HWY | SBT | 55 B4 |
| OLD ALLRED RD | MPA | 49 B3 |
| OLD ALTURAS HWY | MOD | 5 E2 |
| OLD ALTURAS HWY | MOD | 6 A2 |
| OLD ALTURAS RD | SHA | 18 D2 |
| OLD ARCATA RD | HUM | 9 E5 |
| OLD ARCATA RD | HUM | 10 A5 |
| OLD AUBURN RD | SAC | 34 A5 |
| OLD BANNING- | | |
| -IDYLLWILD RD | RCO | 100 A3 |
| OLD BAYSHRE HWY | SJ | 152 A1 |
| OLD BREA CYN RD | LACO | U A3 |
| OLD CAMP TWO RD | SIS | 13 C2 |
| OLD CASTLE RD | SDCO | 106 D2 |
| OLD CEMETERY RD | LAS | 14 B3 |
| OLD CHAMPS FLAT | LAS | 20 D1 |
| OLD CHISHOLM DR | SBD | 101 B1 |
| OLD COAST HWY | SB | 86 D3 |
| OLD COPPER CITY | SBD | 81 D3 |
| OLD CORNING RD | TEH | 24 D2 |
| OLD COULTRVLLE- | | |
| -YOSEMITE RD | MPA | 49 C1 |
| OLD COULTRVLLE- | | |
| -YOSEMITE RD | MPA | 63 A4 |
| OLD CUTOFF RD | LAS | 21 B4 |
| OLD DAVIS RD | SOL | 39 C1 |
| OLD DON PDRO RD | TUO | 48 C1 |
| OLD DRYTOWN- | | |
| -PLYMOUTH RDYMT | AMA | 40 D2 |
| OLD EEL RIV RD | LAK | 23 C5 |
| OLD EEL ROCK | HUM | 16 C4 |
| OLD EL MIRAGE | SBD | 90 D3 |
| OLD ELSINORE RD | RCO | 99 C3 |
| OLDENBERG RD | SBD | 91 D3 |
| OLD FRIANT RD | FRCO | 57 C2 |
| OLD GASQUET TLL | DN | 2 B3 |
| OLD GULCH RD | CAL | 41 B4 |
| OLD HRLD PLM RD | LACO | 90 A3 |
| OLD HAUN RD | PLU | 20 C4 |
| OLD HERNANDZ RD | SBT | 55 C5 |
| OLD HWY RD | LAS | 14 A4 |
| OLD HWY RD | PLU | 26 C1 |
| OLD HWY RT 29 | LAS | 21 C5 |
| OLD HWY S FORK | DN | 2 A3 |
| OLD HIGHWAY 99 | SIS | 12 B1 |
| OLD HWY 138 | LACO | 89 D2 |
| OLD HONEY RUN | BUT | 25 C3 |
| OLD KANE SPG RD | SDCO | 108 A3 |
| OLD KNOX RD | YUB | 26 B4 |
| OLD LAMBERT RD | AMA | 40 C2 |
| OLD LANDMARK DR | SBD | 91 D1 |
| OLD LEESVL GRAD | COL | 32 C2 |
| OLD LOMA RD | BUT | 25 C1 |
| OLD LONG VLY RD | LAK | 32 A3 |
| OLD MAIL RT | LAS | 8 C5 |
| OLD MAMMOTH RD | ML | 164 A5 |
| OLD MAMMOTH RD | MNO | 50 D2 |
| OLD MATTOLE RD | HUM | 15 D4 |
| OLD MIDLAND RD | KLAM | 5 B1 |
| OLD MILL RD | DN | 1 D4 |
| OLD MINE RD | SBD | 101 A1 |
| OLD MINE TR | RCO | 100 B5 |
| OLD MIRAMAR RD | SDCO | V B2 |
| OLD MIRAMAR RD | SDCO | 106 C5 |
| OLD MORGN HL RD | TRI | 17 B2 |
| OLD MORRO RD | SLO | 76 A2 |
| OLD NATL TR HWY | SBD | 94 D2 |
| OLD OAK FLAT RD | MPA | 49 C1 |
| OLD PARKER RD | SBD | 103 E2 |
| OLD PIEDMONT RD | SCL | 46 B4 |
| OLD PLYMTH SAC- | | |
| -VIA FIN RCH RD | AMA | 40 D2 |
| OLD PONY EXPRSS | ALP | 36 B4 |
| OLD RAILROAD GR | SHA | 12 B4 |
| OLD RANCH RD | KER | 79 C5 |
| OLD REDWOOD HWY | SON | 37 D1 |
| OLD RENO RD | NEV | 27 D5 |
| OLD RIDGE RD | LACO | 89 A2 |
| OLD RIVER RD | KER | 78 C3 |
| OLD RIVER RD | KER | 78 C4 |
| OLD RIV SCHL RD | LACO | R B5 |
| OLD SN FRANCSCO | SVL | 150 A1 |
| OLD SCHOOL RD | SHA | 13 D3 |
| OLD SCH HOUS RD | TRI | 22 E1 |
| OLD SEIAD HWY | SIS | 3 B3 |
| OLD SEIAD CK RD | SIS | 3 B3 |
| OLD SHASTA RIV | SIS | 4 A3 |
| OLD SHERWIN GRD | INY | 51 B3 |
| OLD SHERWOOD RD | MEN | 22 E4 |
| OLD SKYLINE | KIN | 67 A3 |
| OLD SONOMA RD | NAP | 133 B4 |
| OLD SONOMA RD | NAPA | L C1 |
| OLD SONOMA RD | NAPA | 38 C3 |
| OLD SONOMA RD | NAPA | 133 A5 |
| OLD SPANISH TR | INY | 72 E4 |
| OLD SPANISH TR | INY | 73 B4 |
| OLD STAGE RD | MEN | 30 D4 |
| OLD STAGE RD | MON | 54 D3 |
| OLD STAGE RD | SIS | 12 C2 |
| OLD STAGE RD N | SIS | 12 C1 |
| OLD STAGEROAD | MEN | 30 D4 |
| OLD STATE HWY | HUM | 9 E2 |
| OLD STATE HWY | HUM | 10 A2 |
| OLD STATE HWY | INY | 72 E3 |
| OLD STATE HWY | INY | 73 A3 |
| OLD STATE HWY | KIN | 67 B4 |
| OLD STATE HWY | LAK | 31 C2 |
| OLD STATE HWY | MNO | 43 C5 |
| OLD STATE HWY | MNO | 50 D2 |
| OLD STATE HWY | SIS | 4 E3 |
| OLD STATE HWY | SIS | 5 A4 |
| OLD STEWRTS PT- | | |
| -SKAGGS SPGS RD | SON | 31 B5 |
| OLD STOCKTON RD | AMA | 40 D3 |
| OLD STOCKTON- | | |
| -IONE HWY | AMA | 40 D2 |
| OLD STRWBRRY RD | TUO | 41 E3 |
| OLD STRWBRRY RD | TUO | 42 A3 |
| OLD SUTTER CK- | | |
| -AMADOR CITY HY | AMA | 40 E2 |
| OLD STTR HLL RD | AMA | 40 E2 |
| OLD TELEGRPH RD | VEN | 88 E4 |
| OLD TELEGRPH RD | VEN | 89 A4 |
| OLD THREE CK RD | HUM | 10 C5 |
| OLD TIM BELL RD | STA | 47 E2 |
| OLD TOLL | MPA | 49 A3 |
| OLD TOLL RD | INY | 71 A1 |
| OLD TOLL RD | LAS | 14 A3 |
| OLD TOLL RD | MEN | 31 C3 |
| OLD TOLL RD | YUB | 26 B5 |
| OLD TOPANGA CYN | LACO | 97 B2 |
| OLD TRUCKEE RD | SIE | 27 C4 |
| OLD WESTSIDE RD | SIS | 4 B5 |
| OLD WILBUR RD | COL | 32 C2 |
| OLD WITR SPG RD | LAK | 31 C2 |
| OLD WOMAN SPGS | SBD | 100 D1 |
| OLD WOMN SPG RD | SBD | 92 A4 |
| OLD YERMO CTOFF | SBD | 91 E1 |
| OLD YOSEMITE RD | MPA | 49 A1 |
| OLD 44 DR | SHA | 18 C2 |
| OLEANDER | SJCO | 47 B2 |
| OLEANDER AV | BKD | 166 C4 |
| OLEANDER AV | RCO | 99 B3 |
| OLEMA ST | SBD | 80 E1 |
| OLINDA RD | SHA | 18 C3 |
| OLIVAS LN | SOL | 39 A2 |
| OLIVE AV | BUR | 179 C5 |
| OLIVE AV | COR | 215 B5 |
| OLIVE AV | FRE | 165 B2 |
| OLIVE AV | FRCO | 57 A3 |
| OLIVE AV | FRCO | 57 C3 |
| OLIVE AV | GLE | 24 D3 |
| OLIVE AV | MAR | L A2 |
| OLIVE AV | MCO | 48 A4 |
| OLIVE AV | MCO | 48 C4 |
| OLIVE AV | RCO | 99 B5 |
| OLIVE AV | RCO | 99 D4 |
| OLIVE AV | SDCO | 106 C3 |
| OLIVE AV | SJCO | 47 B2 |
| OLIVE AV | STA | 47 B3 |
| OLIVE AV | STA | 47 E1 |
| OLIVE AV | STA | 48 A1 |
| OLIVE AV | TEH | 24 D1 |
| OLIVE AV | TUL | 68 D3 |
| OLIVE AV W | MER | 170 B2 |
| OLIVE DR | KER | 78 D2 |
| OLIVE DR E | DVS | 136 D3 |
| OLIVE HWY | BUT | 25 D4 |
| OLIVE LN | GLE | 25 A4 |
| OLIVE RD | TEH | 24 D2 |
| OLIVE RD | VEN | 88 B5 |
| OLIVE ST | AVLN | 105 A4 |
| OLIVE ST | LA | 185 E4 |
| OLIVE ST | LACO | R C3 |
| OLIVE ST | MAR | 38 B4 |
| OLIVE ST | RCO | 99 B4 |
| OLIVE ST | SDCO | 107 A4 |
| OLIVE ST | SHA | 18 B3 |
| OLIVEHURST | YUB | 33 D2 |
| OLIVE LAKE BLVD | RCO | 103 D5 |
| OLIVENHAIN RD | SDCO | 106 C4 |
| OLIVE ORCHRD RD | CAL | 40 D4 |
| OLIVER RD | SBT | 55 D4 |
| OLIVERA DR | TUL | 58 C5 |
| OLIVE SCHOOL LN | SOL | 39 A2 |
| OLIVET RD | SON | 37 D2 |
| OLIVEWOOD AV | TEH | 24 D2 |
| OLNEY PARK DR | SHA | 18 B2 |
| OLSEN RD | MCO | 48 B3 |
| OLSEN RD | VEN | 88 D5 |
| OLSEN CREEK RD | TRI | 16 E2 |
| OLSON RD | LAS | 8 B4 |
| OLYMPIC | LAK | 32 A3 |
| OLYMPIC BLVD | BH | 183 B2 |
| OLYMPIC BLVD | LA | 183 B2 |
| OLYMPIC BLVD | LA | 184 B2 |
| OLYMPIC BLVD | LA | 185 B3 |
| OLYMPIC BLVD | LA | 186 B4 |
| OLYMPIC BLVD | LA | 180 C4 |
| OLYMPIC BLVD | LACO | 97 D2 |
| OLYMPIC BLVD | LACO | Q D4 |
| OLYMPIC BLVD | SMON | 180 A5 |


STREETS

OLYMPIC RD

238

PEORIA RD

# STREET INDEX




| STREET | CO. | PAGE & GRID |
|---|---|---|
| OLYMPIC RD | MAD | 57 B1 |
| OLYMPIC RD | SBD | 100 E1 |
| OMAHA AV | KIN | 67 B3 |
| OMAHA AV | KIN | 67 E3 |
| OMEGA RD | NEV | 26 E5 |
| OMO RANCH RD | ED | 40 E1 |
| OMO RANCH RD | ED | 41 B1 |
| ONEAL RD | BUT | 25 C4 |
| ONEAL RD | MAD | 57 D1 |
| ONE HOLE SPG RD | SBD | 92 C5 |
| ONION VALLEY RD | ED | 35 B4 |
| ONION VALLEY RD | INY | 59 E3 |
| ONSTOTT RD | SUT | 33 C2 |
| ONTARIO AV | RCO | U E5 |
| ONTARIO AV | RCO | 98 E3 |
| ONYX AV | SIS | 4 C5 |
| OPAL RD | MCO | 48 D4 |
| OPAL WY | SHA | 18 C1 |
| OPAL FERRY RD | KER | 88 D1 |
| OPAL MTN RD | SBD | 81 C4 |
| OPENSHAW RD | BUT | 25 C4 |
| OPEN SHAW RD | PLU | 20 D5 |
| OPHIR RD | BUT | 25 D5 |
| OPHIR RD | INY | 71 A2 |
| ORANGE AV | BUT | 25 E5 |
| ORANGE AV | EC | 217 D3 |
| ORANGE AV | FRCO | 57 C4 |
| ORANGE AV | FRCO | 57 D4 |
| ORANGE AV | KIN | 67 A3 |
| ORANGE AV | KIN | 67 D3 |
| ORANGE AV | LACO | Q E2 |
| ORANGE AV | LACO | R D4 |
| ORANGE AV | LACO | S D2 |
| ORANGE AV | ORA | T B2 |
| ORANGE AV | RCO | 99 C3 |
| ORANGE AV | SD | 214 C5 |
| ORANGE AV | SDCO | V B4 |
| ORANGE AV | SDCO | V D5 |
| ORANGE AV | SDCO | 111 C1 |
| ORANGE AV | SDCO | 111 D2 |
| ORANGE AV | SJCO | 47 D1 |
| ORANGE AV | SON | 132 A4 |
| ORANGE AV | STA | 47 C3 |
| ORANGE AV W | SSF | 144 A1 |
| ORANGE FRWY | ANA | 194 A4 |
| ORANGE FRWY | OR | 196 A1 |
| ORANGE FRWY | ORA | 98 C3 |
| ORANGE FRWY | ORA | 194 A4 |
| ORANGE FRWY | ORA | T D1 |
| ORANGE RD | SDCO | 107 A3 |
| ORANGE ST | KER | 78 B2 |
| ORANGE ST | RCO | 99 B2 |
| ORANGE ST | SBD | 99 C2 |
| ORANGE BLOSM RD | STA | 48 A1 |
| ORANGEBURG AV E | MDO | 162 D1 |
| ORANGEBURG AV W | MDO | 162 B1 |
| ORANGE GROVE AV | LACO | 98 C2 |
| ORANGE GROVE AV | LACO | R C3 |
| ORANGE GROVE AV | LACO | U B2 |
| ORANGE GROVE BL | LACO | R B3 |
| ORANGE GROVE BL | PAS | 190 C3 |
| ORANGE-OLIVE RD | OR | 194 C3 |
| ORANGE-OLIVE RD | ORA | 98 C3 |
| ORANGE-OLIVE RD | ORA | T D2 |
| ORANGE PARK BL | ORA | T E2 |
| ORANGE SHOW RD | CLTN | 207 C5 |
| ORANGE SHOW RD | SBDO | 207 C5 |
| ORANGETHORPE AV | ORA | 98 B3 |
| ORANGETHORPE AV | ORA | 98 C3 |
| ORANGETHORPE AV | ORA | T B1 |
| ORANGEWOOD AV | ORA | T B2 |
| ORANGEWOOD RD | TEH | 24 D1 |
| ORCHARD AV | H | 146 E4 |
| ORCHARD AV | SLO | 76 A5 |
| ORCHARD AV | TEH | 24 D2 |
| ORCHARD DR | FRCO | 58 D4 |
| ORCHARD DR | MCO | 48 C5 |
| ORCHARD RD | IMP | 112 C3 |
| ORCHARD RD | MCO | 47 C5 |
| ORCHARD RD | SJCO | 40 B4 |
| ORCHARD RD | STA | 47 B2 |
| ORCHARD ST | RCO | 99 E2 |
| ORCHARD WY | MCO | 56 C1 |
| ORCHARD PARK AV | MCO | 48 B4 |
| ORCHARD SPGS RD | NEV | 34 D2 |
| ORCUTT RD | SLO | 76 B4 |
| ORCUTT RD | SLO | 172 D5 |
| ORCUTT RD | SNLO | 172 D5 |
| ORCUTT RD | VEN | 88 C4 |
| ORCUTT-GAREY RD | SB | 86 C1 |
| ORD ST | SB | 86 B2 |
| ORD FERRY RD | BUT | 25 A4 |
| ORD MOUNTAIN RD | SBD | 91 E2 |
| ORD RANCH RD | BUT | 25 C5 |
| ORDWAY RD | SIS | 12 C1 |
| OREGON AV | SCL | N E2 |
| OREGON DR | MDO | 162 D4 |
| OREGON CREEK RD | SIE | 26 D4 |
| OREGON GULCH RD | BUT | 25 D4 |
| OREGON HILL RD | YUB | 26 B5 |
| OREGON MTN RD | DN | 2 C3 |
| OREGON-PAGE MLL | PA | 147 D3 |
| OREGON-PAGE MLL | SCL | 45 E4 |
| ORESTIMBA RD | STA | 47 C4 |
| ORINDA DR | SM | 145 C4 |
| ORLEANS AV | FRCO | 55 E3 |
| ORMONDE RD | SLO | 76 B4 |
| ORMSBY AV | FRCO | 56 C2 |
| ORNBAUN RD | MEN | 30 E3 |
| ORO FINO RD | SIS | 3 D5 |
| OROVILLE BANGOR | BUT | 25 D4 |
| OROVLL CHICO HY | BUT | 25 B3 |
| OROVLL DAM BL E | BUT | 25 D4 |
| OROVLLE GRIDLEY | BUT | 25 C5 |
| OROVLE QUNCY HY | BUT | 25 D4 |
| OROVLE QUNCY HY | BUT | 25 E3 |
| OROVLE QUNCY HY | BUT | 26 A3 |

| STREET | CO. | PAGE & GRID |
|---|---|---|
| ORR RD | SAC | 40 A3 |
| ORR & DAY RD | LACO | R C5 |
| ORR & DAY RD | LACO | T A1 |
| ORR CREEK LN | PLA | 34 B3 |
| ORRIS RD | RCO | 102 A4 |
| ORRLAND AV | TUL | 68 B3 |
| ORR MTN LOOKOUT | SIS | 5 A4 |
| ORR SPRINGS RD | MEN | 30 E1 |
| ORR SPRINGS RD | MEN | 31 A1 |
| ORSI RD | STA | 47 E1 |
| ORTEGA HWY | ORA | 98 E5 |
| ORTEGA HWY | SCL | 202 E1 |
| ORTIGALITA RD | MCO | 55 D2 |
| OSAGE RD | SOL | 39 B2 |
| OSBORN RD | SIS | 5 D2 |
| OSBORN RD | TEH | 24 B2 |
| OSBORNE AV | RCO | 102 C4 |
| OSBORNE RD | SBD | 91 D2 |
| OSBORNE ST | LACO | 97 C1 |
| OSBORNE ST | LACO | Q C2 |
| OSBORNE PARK RD | IMP | 109 D4 |
| OSDICK RD | SBD | 80 E3 |
| OSGOOD RD | ALA | P B2 |
| OSO PKWY | ORA | 98 D5 |
| OSO FLACO LK RD | SLO | 76 B5 |
| OSOS ST | SNLO | 172 C3 |
| OSPITAL RD | CAL | 40 D4 |
| OSTROM RD | YUB | 33 E2 |
| OSWALD RD | SUT | 33 B2 |
| OSWELL ST | KER | 78 D3 |
| OTAY LAKES RD | SDCO | V D4 |
| OTAY LAKES RD | SDCO | 111 E2 |
| OTAY MESA RD | SDCO | V D5 |
| OTAY MESA RD | SDCO | 111 E2 |
| OTAY VALLEY RD | SDCO | V D5 |
| OTAY VALLEY RD | SDCO | 111 E2 |
| OTIS DR | A | 159 A2 |
| OTIS ST | LACO | R A5 |
| OTOE RD | SBD | 91 C3 |
| OUR HOUS DAM RD | SIE | 26 C5 |
| OUTINGDALE | ED | 40 E1 |
| OUTINGDALE | ED | 41 A1 |
| OUTLAW MINE RD | RCO | 102 A2 |
| OUTPOST DR | LA | 181 C3 |
| OVERLAND AV | CUL | 188 C1 |
| OVERLAND AV | LA | 183 B5 |
| OVERLAND AV | LACO | Q C4 |
| OVERLAND AV | MCO | 55 D1 |
| OVERLAND DR | SHA | 18 C3 |
| OWENS | SJCO | 47 D1 |
| OWENS AV | CLK | 74 E2 |
| OWENS RD | INY | 51 D4 |
| OWENS RD | SIS | 5 A2 |
| OWENS GORGE RD | MNO | 51 B2 |
| OWENS RIVER RD | MNO | 50 E1 |
| OWENS RV RCH RD | MNO | 50 E1 |
| OWENYO LONE PNE | INY | 60 B4 |
| OWL HOLE SPG RD | SBD | 82 B1 |
| OXALIS AV | FRCO | 56 B2 |
| OXBOW PL | SB | 86 E3 |
| OXFORD AV | FRCO | 56 A2 |
| OXFORD RD | SOL | 39 D3 |
| OXFORD ST | B | 156 A2 |
| OXNARD BLVD | OXN | 176 C1 |
| **P** | | |
| P ST | BKD | 166 D5 |
| P ST | FRE | 165 E3 |
| P ST | KER | 166 D5 |
| P ST | SCTO | 137 A3 |
| P ST | SBD | 91 D1 |
| PACHECO BLVD | CC | L E3 |
| PACHECO BLVD | CC | 38 E5 |
| PACHECO BLVD | CC | 154 C2 |
| PACHECO BLVD | M | 154 C2 |
| PACHECO RD | KER | 78 D3 |
| PACHECO PASS HY | SCL | 54 E2 |
| PACHECO PASS RD | SCL | 54 D2 |
| PACIFIC AV | DN | 1 D4 |
| PACIFIC AV | LB | 192 D3 |
| PACIFIC AV | LA | 187 A2 |
| PACIFIC AV | LA | 191 A4 |
| PACIFIC AV | LACO | 97 D4 |
| PACIFIC AV | LACO | S C3 |
| PACIFIC AV | LACO | S D2 |
| PACIFIC AV | PAC | 167 C2 |
| PACIFIC AV | SC | 169 D3 |
| PACIFIC AV | S | 160 B1 |
| PACIFIC AV | SUT | 33 D3 |
| PACIFIC AV | SUT | 33 D4 |
| PACIFIC AV | TUL | 68 B2 |
| PACIFIC BLVD | LACO | 97 E2 |
| PACIFIC BLVD | LACO | R A4 |
| PACIFIC BLVD | SM | 145 B4 |
| PACIFIC HWY | SD | 213 A5 |
| PACIFIC HWY | SD | 215 C2 |
| PACIFIC ST | MONT | 167 E4 |
| PACIFIC ST | SBD | 99 C1 |
| PACIFIC BCH DR | SD | 212 A2 |
| PACIFIC BCH DR | SDCO | V A3 |
| PACIFIC CST HWY | LB | 192 D1 |
| PACIFIC CST HWY | LA | 192 D1 |
| PACIFIC CST HWY | LACO | 97 B2 |
| PACIFIC CST HWY | LACO | S B1 |
| PACIFIC CST HWY | LACO | T A3 |
| PACIFIC CST HWY | ORA | T A3 |
| PACIFIC CST HWY | VEN | 96 C2 |
| PACIFC GRV-CRML | MONT | 167 B4 |
| PACIFC GRV-CRML | MON | 53 D3 |
| PACIFC GRV-CRML | MON | 167 B4 |
| PACIFC GRV-CRML | PAC | 167 B4 |
| PACIFIC HTS RD | BUT | 25 C5 |
| PACIFIC LUMBER | HUM | 16 A1 |
| PACIFIC MINE RD | SIE | 26 C3 |
| PACIFIC VIEW DR | MEN | 30 C3 |
| PACIFIC VIEW RD | VEN | 96 C2 |
| PACKER RD | COL | 32 E1 |
| PACKER LAKE RD | SIE | 26 E3 |

| STREET | CO. | PAGE & GRID |
|---|---|---|
| PACKER LAKE RD | SIE | 27 A3 |
| PAC MINE RD | SIE | 26 D3 |
| PADUA AV | CLA | 203 C1 |
| PADUA AV | LACO | 98 D1 |
| PADUA AV | UPL | 203 C1 |
| PAGE AV | FRCO | 67 B1 |
| PAGE RD | STA | 47 B2 |
| PAGE MILL RD | PA | 147 C5 |
| PAGE MILL RD | SCL | N E3 |
| PAGE MILL RD | SCL | 45 D4 |
| PA HA LN | INY | 51 D4 |
| PAIGE AV | TUL | 68 B2 |
| PAIGE BAR RD | SHA | 18 B2 |
| PAINE RD | AMA | 40 D2 |
| PAINT RD | CAL | 41 B4 |
| PAINTED CAVE | SB | 87 C4 |
| PAINTED GORG RD | IMP | 111 C3 |
| PAINTER AV | LACO | 98 B2 |
| PAINTER AV | LACO | R D4 |
| PAJARO ST | SAL | 171 C4 |
| PALA RD | DN | 1 D3 |
| PALA RD | RCO | 106 D1 |
| PALA TEMECLA RD | SDCO | 106 D1 |
| PALAZZO RD | MCO | 47 E5 |
| PALAZZO RD | MCO | 48 A5 |
| PALAZZO RD | MCO | 55 E1 |
| PALERMO RD | BUT | 25 D5 |
| PALRMO HONCT HY | BUT | 25 D5 |
| PALISADE AV | SBD | 91 E3 |
| PALISADES AV | RED | 122 E1 |
| PALISADES DR | LACO | 97 C2 |
| PALLETT CK RD | LACO | 90 C4 |
| PALM AV | AUB | 126 C3 |
| PALM AV | COR | 215 C5 |
| PALM AV | FRE | 165 C2 |
| PALM AV | FRCO | 57 C3 |
| PALM AV | KER | 78 B1 |
| PALM AV | KER | 78 C3 |
| PALM AV | LACO | R C5 |
| PALM AV | MCO | 48 A4 |
| PALM AV | RCO | 99 B2 |
| PALM AV | RCO | 99 E4 |
| PALM AV | SBD | 99 B1 |
| PALM AV | SDCO | V C5 |
| PALM AV | SDCO | V D3 |
| PALM AV | SDCO | 111 D2 |
| PALM AV | SDCO | 111 E1 |
| PALM AV | SCL | P D4 |
| PALM AV | SCL | 54 C1 |
| PALM AV | SHA | 18 B3 |
| PALM DR | RIV | 206 E1 |
| PALM DR | RCO | 100 D3 |
| PALM DR | SDCO | 106 C4 |
| PALM DR | SCL | N E2 |
| PALM ST | BKD | 166 B4 |
| PALM CANYON DR | PMSP | 206 B5 |
| PALM CANYON DR | RCO | 100 D4 |
| PALM CANYON DR | SDCO | 107 E2 |
| PALM CYN DR E | PMSP | 206 C5 |
| PALM CYN DR N | PMSP | 206 A1 |
| PALMDALE BLVD | LACO | 90 B3 |
| PALMDALE RD | SBD | 90 E4 |
| PALMDALE RD | SBD | 91 A3 |
| PALMER AV | FRCO | 66 C2 |
| PALMER RD | SB | 86 C2 |
| PALMER CREEK RD | HUM | 15 E2 |
| PALMETTO AV | BUT | 124 C3 |
| PALMETTO AV | C | 124 C3 |
| PALMETTO AV | ONT | 203 E5 |
| PALMETTO AV | ONT | 204 A5 |
| PALMETTO ST | SBD | 80 E5 |
| PALMETTO ST | SBD | 81 A5 |
| PALMETTO WY | LAS | 20 D2 |
| PALMS TO PINES | RCO | 100 E4 |
| PALO COLORDO RD | MON | 64 B1 |
| PALOMA RD | CAL | 40 E3 |
| PALOMAR AV | SDCO | V C5 |
| PALOMAR AV | SDCO | 111 D2 |
| PALOMAR ST | RCO | 99 C5 |
| PALOMAR APRT RD | SDCO | 106 B3 |
| PALOMAR DIV TK | RCO | 106 D1 |
| PALOMARES RD | ALA | M A5 |
| PALOMARES RD | ALA | P A1 |
| PALOMARES RD | ALA | 46 A2 |
| PALOMAS AV | KER | 77 E3 |
| PALOMAS AV | KER | 78 A3 |
| PALOMINO RD | SDCO | 106 C2 |
| PALOMINO WY | HUM | 22 C1 |
| PALO PRIETA CHO | SLO | 76 D1 |
| PALOS VERDES BL | LACO | S B2 |
| PALOS VRDS DR E | LACO | 97 D4 |
| PALOS VRDS DR E | LACO | S B3 |
| PALOS VRDS DR N | LACO | 97 D3 |
| PALOS VRDS DR N | LACO | S B2 |
| PALOS VRDS DR S | LACO | S A3 |
| PALOS VRDS DR S | LACO | 97 D4 |
| PALOS VRDS DR W | LACO | 97 D4 |
| PALOS VRDS DR W | LACO | S B2 |
| PALO VERDE AV | LACO | S E2 |
| PALO VERDE BLVD | MOH | 96 B4 |
| PALO VERDE RD | IMP | 110 C1 |
| PALO VERDE RD | SBD | 100 C2 |
| PALO VERDE ST | MTCL | 203 C3 |
| PAMELA ST | KER | 79 C2 |
| PAMO RD | SDCO | 107 A3 |
| PAMPA RD | KER | 79 A3 |
| PANAMA LN | KER | 78 B3 |
| PANAMA LN | KER | 79 A3 |
| PANAMA RD | KER | 78 D3 |
| PANAMA RD | KER | 79 A3 |
| PANAMINT VLY RD | INY | 71 B1 |
| PANCHO RD | RCO | 107 A1 |
| PANCHORICO RD | MON | 65 E3 |
| PANGBORN LN | INY | 60 B4 |
| PANOCHE RD | FRCO | 56 D3 |
| PANOCHE RD | SBT | 55 B4 |
| PANOCHE RD | SBT | 56 A4 |

| STREET | CO. | PAGE & GRID |
|---|---|---|
| PANORAMA DR | KER | 78 E2 |
| PANORAMA PT RD | SHA | 18 D3 |
| PANORAMIC HWY | MAR | 38 A5 |
| PANORAMIC HWY | MAR | L A4 |
| PANORAMIC HWY | MAR | 45 A1 |
| PANTHER CK RD | TEH | 19 C3 |
| PANTHER GAP RD | HUM | 16 A4 |
| PAPPAS RD | KER | 80 C3 |
| PARADISE AV | MDO | 162 A4 |
| PARADISE AV | STA | 47 C3 |
| PARADISE DR | CRTM | 140 D1 |
| PARADISE DR | MAR | L B3 |
| PARADISE DR | MAR | 45 B1 |
| PARADISE DR | RCO | 100 C5 |
| PARADISE RD | CLK | 74 D2 |
| PARADISE RD | CLK | 209 C4 |
| PARADISE RD | CLK | 210 E3 |
| PARADISE RD | COL | 24 E5 |
| PARADISE RD | LV | 209 C4 |
| PARADISE RD | SJCO | 46 E1 |
| PARADISE RD | SJCO | 47 A1 |
| PARADISE RD | SB | 87 B3 |
| PARADISE RD | STA | 47 C2 |
| PARADISE SPG RD | SBD | 81 E4 |
| PARADISE SPG RD | SBD | 82 B5 |
| PARADISE VLY RD | SDCO | V D4 |
| PARADISE VLY RD | SDCO | 111 D1 |
| PARAISO SPGS RD | MON | 64 E1 |
| PARAISO SPGS RD | MON | 65 A1 |
| PARAMOUNT BLVD | LACO | 98 A3 |
| PARAMOUNT BLVD | LACO | R C4 |
| PARAMOUNT BLVD | LACO | S E1 |
| PARDEE DAM RD | CAL | 40 D3 |
| PARDOES | AMA | 41 D1 |
| PARIS AV | KIN | 67 D3 |
| PARIS VALLEY RD | MON | 65 D3 |
| PARK AV | BUT | 25 B3 |
| PARK AV | C | 124 C5 |
| PARK AV | LAG | 201 C2 |
| PARK AV | O | 157 D1 |
| PARK AV | SJ | 151 D3 |
| PARK AV | SJ | 152 B4 |
| PARK AV | SCLR | 151 C3 |
| PARK AV | TRI | 17 D2 |
| PARK AV W | NAP | 133 A3 |
| PARK BLVD | ALA | L D4 |
| PARK BLVD | ALA | 45 D1 |
| PARK BLVD | CC | L C3 |
| PARK BLVD | O | 158 D3 |
| PARK BLVD | SD | 214 A5 |
| PARK BLVD | SD | 215 E3 |
| PARK BLVD | SD | 216 A1 |
| PARK BLVD | SDCO | V B3 |
| PARK BLVD N | SA | 196 B2 |
| PARK DR S | CC | 156 D1 |
| PARK RD | BEN | 153 D4 |
| PARK RD | IMP | 109 B4 |
| PARK RD | SBT | 55 A3 |
| PARK RD E | COL | 24 B5 |
| PARK ST | ALA | L D5 |
| PARK ST | HUM | 9 E5 |
| PARK ST | S | 160 B4 |
| PARK ST | TUL | 68 B3 |
| PARK WY | LAK | 31 D2 |
| PARK CREEK RD | ED | 35 B4 |
| PARKER AV | CC | L D3 |
| PARKER RD | SBD | 101 E1 |
| PARKER RD | STA | 47 D2 |
| PARKER CREEK RD | MOD | 7 B2 |
| PARKER CREEK RD | MOD | 8 B1 |
| PARKER CK RD W | MOD | 8 B1 |
| PARKER DAM RD | SBD | 104 B1 |
| PARKER LAKE RD | MNO | 43 C5 |
| PARKER LAKE RD | MNO | 50 C1 |
| PARKER-POSTN RD | LPAZ | 103 E4 |
| PARKFIELD GRADE | FRCO | 66 C3 |
| PARKFLD CEM RD | MON | 66 C4 |
| PARKFLD-COALNGA | FRCO | 66 C4 |
| PARK HILL RD | SLO | 76 B3 |
| PARKMAN RD | IMP | 110 D5 |
| PARK MARINA DR | RED | 122 D1 |
| PARK MOABI | SBD | 95 E2 |
| PARKMONT DR | LACO | 89 D3 |
| PK PRESIDIO BL | SF | 141 C3 |
| PARKS RD | SUT | 33 C3 |
| PARKSIDE DR | RCO | 101 D5 |
| PARKSIDE DR N | CC | M B3 |
| PARKVIEW LN | KER | 79 C5 |
| PARKVILLE RD | SHA | 18 D3 |
| PARKWAY DR | DN | 1 D4 |
| PARKWAY DR | TEH | 18 D4 |
| PARLIER AV | FRCO | 56 E4 |
| PARLIER AV | FRCO | 57 D4 |
| PARLIER AV | FRCO | 58 B4 |
| PARNASSUS BLVD | SF | 141 D5 |
| PARR | CC | 38 C5 |
| PARROTTS FERRY | TUO | 41 C4 |
| PARSONS RD | FRCO | 66 C2 |
| PASADENA AV | LA | 186 D1 |
| PASADENA FRWY | LA | 186 B2 |
| PASADENA FRWY | LACO | 97 E2 |
| PASADENA FRWY | LACO | R A3 |
| PASCOE RD | KER | 69 B5 |
| PASEO AV | SUT | 33 C1 |
| PASEO DEL MAR | LACO | 97 D4 |
| PASEO DEL MAR | LACO | S B3 |
| PASKENTA RD | TEH | 18 D5 |
| PASKENTA RD | TEH | 24 C1 |
| PASKENTA CEM RD | TEH | 24 B2 |
| PASO ST | KER | 78 A5 |
| PASO NOGAL | CC | 38 E5 |
| PASO ROBLES BL | SLO | 76 A1 |
| PASO ROBLES HWY | KER | 77 A1 |
| PASQUALE RD | NEV | 34 C1 |
| PASS RD | SUT | 33 A2 |
| PASSONS BLVD | LACO | R C5 |
| PASSONS BLVD | LACO | R C5 |

| STREET | CO. | PAGE & GRID |
|---|---|---|
| PAST TIME LN | RCO | 100 A5 |
| PATHFINDER RD | LACO | U B3 |
| PATRICIA AV | SIS | 4 C2 |
| PATRICIA LN | CAL | 41 C3 |
| PATRICIA LN | MNO | 42 E1 |
| PATRICIA LN | MNO | 43 A1 |
| PATRICK RD | LPAZ | 104 A2 |
| PATRICK WY | SBD | 100 E1 |
| PATRICKS CK RD | DN | 2 B3 |
| PATRICKS PT | HUM | 9 E3 |
| PATTERSON AV | SB | 87 B4 |
| PATTERSON LN | MOD | 8 D1 |
| PATTERSON RD | HUM | 10 D4 |
| PATTERSON RD | KER | 89 B1 |
| PATTERSON RD | STA | 47 D2 |
| PATTERSON RD | VEN | 96 B1 |
| PATTERSON CK RD | SIS | 3 C5 |
| PATTERSON CK RD | SIS | 11 D1 |
| PATTRSN MILL RD | MOD | 8 E3 |
| PATTERSON PS RD | ALA | M D5 |
| PATTERSON PS RD | ALA | 46 C2 |
| PATTERSON PS RD | SJCO | 46 D2 |
| PATTERSN RCH RD | TRI | 17 A1 |
| PATTERSN SAWMLL | LAS | 8 D3 |
| PATTISON RD | CAL | 40 D3 |
| PATTON | MCO | 55 E1 |
| PATTON MILLS RD | TEH | 24 A2 |
| PATTYMOCUS- | | |
| PATWIN RD | SBD | 90 E3 |
| PAUBA RD | RCO | 106 D1 |
| PAUI RD | RCO | 107 B1 |
| PAULARINO AV | CM | 197 E4 |
| PAULINE AV | STA | 47 C2 |
| PAUL NEGRA RD | MCO | 55 E3 |
| PAXTON RD | SBDO | 100 E1 |
| PAXTON ST | LACO | Q C1 |
| PAYEN RD | SAC | 40 C1 |
| PAYMASTER MN RD | SBD | 83 C4 |
| PAYNE AV | CC | 39 C5 |
| PAYNE RD | IMP | 108 E5 |
| PAYNE RD | SUT | 33 B2 |
| PAYNE WY | KER | 79 D3 |
| PAYNES CK LOOP | TEH | 19 A4 |
| PAYNES CREEK RD | TEH | 19 A4 |
| PAYNES CREEK RD | TEH | 18 D4 |
| PEABODY RD | SOL | M B1 |
| PEABODY RD | SOL | 39 A3 |
| PEACEFUL GLEN | SOL | 39 A2 |
| PEACH AV | FRCO | 57 D2 |
| PEACH AV | FRCO | 57 D5 |
| PEACH AV | GLE | 24 E4 |
| PEACH AV | MCO | 47 E4 |
| PEACH AV | MCO | 48 A4 |
| PEACH TREE RD | MON | 65 E2 |
| PEACH TREE RD | MON | 66 A2 |
| PEACHY CYN RD | SLO | 75 E1 |
| PEACHY CYN RD | SLO | 76 A1 |
| PEAK RD | TRI | 16 E5 |
| PEAR AV | GLE | 25 A4 |
| PEAR AV | STA | 47 C4 |
| PEARBLOSSOM HWY | LACO | 90 A4 |
| PEARL RD | SJCO | 40 B3 |
| PEARL ST | SDCO | V A2 |
| PEARL ST | SDCO | 106 C5 |
| PEAR MAIN ST | SBD | 91 B3 |
| PEARSON RD | BUT | 25 C3 |
| PEARSON RD | INY | 70 C5 |
| PEASE RD | SUT | 33 C2 |
| PEAVINE RDG RD | ED | 35 B4 |
| PEBBLE BEACH DR | DN | 1 D4 |
| PEBBLY BEACH RD | AVLN | 105 B5 |
| PECHO VALLEY RD | SLO | 75 E3 |
| PECK RD | LACO | 98 B1 |
| PECK RD | LACO | R D4 |
| PEDERSON | FRCO | 58 A3 |
| PEDLEY RD | RCO | 99 A2 |
| PEDRICK RD | SOL | 39 B2 |
| PEDRICK RD | SOL | 39 B1 |
| PEDRO RANCH RD | MNO | 51 C1 |
| PEDROS RD | STA | 47 D3 |
| PEGASUS DR | KER | 78 D2 |
| PEGASUS ST | KER | 79 B4 |
| PELGER RD | SUT | 33 B3 |
| PELICAN RD | STA | 47 B2 |
| PELLERIN RD | STA | 47 E2 |
| PELLET RD | IMP | 108 E4 |
| PELLISER RD | KER | 79 B4 |
| PELTIER RD | SJCO | 39 E3 |
| PELTIER RD | SJCO | 40 A3 |
| PENCIL RD | MOD | 7 B5 |
| PENDLETON RD | SBD | 92 A1 |
| PENDOLA RD | YUB | 26 B4 |
| PENDOLA EXT | YUB | 26 C4 |
| PENDOLA GARDEN | MPA | 49 A3 |
| PENFIELD AV | LA | 178 A4 |
| PENINSULA AV | SMCO | N C1 |
| PENINSULA DR | HUM | 15 E5 |
| PENINSULA DR | PLU | 20 B4 |
| PENMAN SPGS RD | SLO | 76 B1 |
| PENNINGTON RD | BUT | 25 B5 |
| PENNINGTON RD | SUT | 33 B1 |
| PENNSYLVANIA AV | FRFD | 135 B3 |
| PENNSYLVANIA AV | LACO | Q E2 |
| PENNSYLVANIA AV | RIV | 205 E3 |
| PENNSYLVANIA AV | RCO | 99 E3 |
| PENNSYLVANIA AV | SOL | L E1 |
| PENNSYLVANIA AV | SOL | M A1 |
| PENNSYLVANIA AV | SOL | 135 B4 |
| PENNSYLV GCH RD | CAL | 41 C4 |
| PENON LOOKOUT | MPA | 48 D1 |
| PENOYAR GRAS LK | SIS | 4 E5 |
| PENOYAR TENNANT | SIS | 5 A5 |
| PENROSE ST | LACO | Q D2 |
| PENTLAND RD | KER | 78 B5 |
| PENTZ RD | BUT | 25 C3 |
| PENTZ MAGALIA | BUT | 25 D3 |
| PEORIA RD | YUB | 34 A1 |


STREETS

| STREET | CO. | PAGE & GRID |
|---|---|---|
| PEPPER AV | SBD | 99 B2 |
| PEPPER DR | KER | 78 E3 |
| PEPPER RD | SON | 37 E3 |
| PEPPER RD | SON | 38 A3 |
| PEPPER ST | MCO | 47 E4 |
| PEPPER ST | MCO | 48 A4 |
| PEPPER ST | SBD | 80 E5 |
| PEPPER ST | SBD | 81 A5 |
| PERALTA BLVD | ALA | P A1 |
| PERALTA BLVD | ALA | 46 A3 |
| PERALTA ST | ALA | L C4 |
| PERALTA ST | O | 157 C2 |
| PERCH ST | KER | 79 C4 |
| PERCY AV | YUBA | 125 D3 |
| PERCY RD | KER | 79 D1 |
| PEREZ RD | IMP | 112 D5 |
| PERI RD | MON | 65 D4 |
| PERIMETER RD | NEV | 34 B2 |
| PERINI RD | LAK | 32 A4 |
| PERKINS AV | KER | 78 B1 |
| PERKINS RD | CLO | 33 A3 |
| PERKINS RD | SB | 87 C1 |
| PERKINS ST | U | 123 B3 |
| PERRAL RD | KER | 77 D2 |
| PERRIN AV | FRCO | 57 D2 |
| PERRIN RD | SJCO | 47 B2 |
| PERRIS BLVD | RCO | 99 C3 |
| PERRY RD | COL | 32 D1 |
| PERRY RD | RCO | 99 B4 |
| PERRY CREEK RD | ED | 41 A1 |
| PERSHING AV | S | 160 A1 |
| PERSHING AV | SJCO | 40 A5 |
| PERSHING DR | LA | 187 D5 |
| PERSHING DR | LACO | Q C5 |
| PERSHING DR | SD | 216 A3 |
| PERSHING DR | SDCO | V C3 |
| PESCADERO RD | SMCO | N C4 |
| PESCADERO CK RD | SMCO | 45 C5 |
| PETALUMA AV | SON | 132 B4 |
| PETALUMA HLL RD | STR | 131 D4 |
| PETALUMA HLL RD | SON | 38 A2 |
| PETALUMA HLL RD | SON | 131 D4 |
| PETE MILLER RD | STA | 47 C5 |
| PETERSBOURGH S | CAL | 40 E3 |
| PETERSBURG RD | SIS | 11 B3 |
| PETERSON DR | NAPA | 29 B2 |
| PETERSON LN | LAK | 31 D3 |
| PETERSON RD | COL | 32 C1 |
| PETERSON RD | FRCO | 58 B1 |
| PETERSON RD | IMP | 109 B3 |
| PETERSON RD | KER | 68 C5 |
| PETERSON RD | KER | 77 E1 |
| PETERSON RD | KER | 78 B1 |
| PETERSON RD | LPAZ | 104 A3 |
| PETERSON RD | LACO | 89 D4 |
| PETERSON RDG RD | YUB | 26 B5 |
| PETRIFIED FORST | NAPA | 38 A1 |
| PETRIFIED FORST | SON | 38 A1 |
| PETRO RD | INY | 72 C2 |
| PETROGLYPH RD | MNO | 51 D3 |
| PETRLEUM CLB RD | KER | 78 A4 |
| PETTINGER RD | CAL | 40 D4 |
| PETTYJOHN RD | TEH | 17 E5 |
| PEW RD | SBD | 85 C5 |
| PEZZI RD | SJCO | 40 B4 |
| PFE RD | PLA | 33 E5 |
| PFITZER RD | MCO | 47 D5 |
| PHEASANT CT | KER | 79 B4 |
| PHEASANT DR | MOD | 7 B5 |
| PHEASANT LN | SIS | 4 B4 |
| PHELAN RD | HUM | 15 D1 |
| PHELAN RD | SBD | 91 A4 |
| PHELPS AV | FRCO | 66 D2 |
| PHILADELPHIA ST | LACO | 98 E2 |
| PHILADELPHIA ST | SBD | U C3 |
| PHILADELPHIA ST | SBD | 98 E2 |
| PHILBRIC RD | SB | 86 C1 |
| PHILBROOK RD | BUT | 25 D1 |
| PHILDOW RD | LAS | 20 E3 |
| PHILIP | PLA | 33 E4 |
| PHILIPS RD | MCO | 55 E1 |
| PHILLIPE LN | SIS | 4 A4 |
| PHILLIPS | LAK | 32 A3 |
| PHILLIPS BLVD | SBD | U C3 |
| PHILLIPS DR | SBD | 82 A5 |
| PHILLIPS RD | KER | 78 C1 |
| PHILLIPS RD | KER | 78 D4 |
| PHILLIPS RD | KER | 80 B4 |
| PHILLIPS RD | SHA | 19 A1 |
| PHILLIPS RD | SOL | 39 B1 |
| PHILLIPSVLLE RD | HUM | 16 C4 |
| PHILO GRNWD RD | MEN | 30 C2 |
| PHOENIX LAKE RD | TUO | 41 D5 |
| PHYLLIS RD | TEH | 18 C4 |
| PICACHO RD | IMP | 110 D5 |
| PICADOR BLVD | SDCO | V D5 |
| PICADOR BLVD | SDCO | 111 D2 |
| PICARD RD | SIS | 4 E2 |
| PICARD RD | SIS | 5 A2 |
| PICRD SAMS NECK | SIS | 4 E2 |
| PICARDY DR | S | 160 B4 |
| PICAYUNE RD | MAD | 49 D5 |
| PICKENS RD | LAS | 21 D5 |
| PICKERING AV | LACO | R C5 |
| PICKETT RD | IMP | 109 B4 |
| PICO BLVD | LA | 180 D4 |
| PICO BLVD | LA | 183 B3 |
| PICO BLVD | LA | 184 C3 |
| PICO BLVD | LA | 185 A3 |
| PICO BLVD | LACO | Q C4 |
| PICO BLVD | SMON | 180 B5 |
| PICO BLVD | SMON | 187 A1 |
| PICO CANYON RD | LACO | 89 B4 |
| PIEDMONT AV | B | 156 B3 |
| PIEDMONT AV | O | 158 B1 |
| PIEDMONT RD | SCL | P C3 |
| PIEDRA RD | FRCO | 58 A3 |
| PIEDRA AZUL | MCO | 55 D3 |
| PIEDRAS DR | RCO | 99 B3 |
| PIER AV | LACO | S B1 |
| PIERCE LN | SOL | 38 E4 |
| PIERCE RD | SCL | P A4 |
| PIERCE RD | SCL | 45 E5 |
| PIERCE RD | SUT | 33 C3 |
| PIERCE ST | BKD | 166 A2 |
| PIERCE ST | RCO | 99 A3 |
| PIERCE ST | RCO | 101 B4 |
| PIERCE CK MTWY | PLU | 20 E4 |
| PIERCE POINT RD | MAR | 37 D4 |
| PIERI RD | KER | 78 B4 |
| PIERLE RD | IMP | 108 E5 |
| PIERSON BLVD | RCO | 100 C2 |
| PIGEON PASS RD | RCO | 99 C2 |
| PIGEON POINT RD | HUM | 15 E1 |
| PIGEON SPG RD | KER | 79 C5 |
| PIKE RD | STA | 47 D3 |
| PIKE CITY RD | SIE | 26 C5 |
| PIKE CITY RD | YUB | 26 C5 |
| PILAR RD | SIS | 4 D5 |
| PILE ST | SDCO | 107 A4 |
| PILGRIM CK RD | SIS | 12 E2 |
| PILITAS HUERHRO | SLO | 76 C2 |
| PILOT SPRING RD | MNO | 43 D5 |
| PILOT SPRING RD | MNO | 50 E1 |
| PIMLICO DR | RCO | 100 C5 |
| PINAL ST | SB | 86 D1 |
| PINE AV | BUT | 25 B3 |
| PINE AV | LB | 192 D3 |
| PINE AV | MEN | 31 C1 |
| PINE AV | PAC | 167 C2 |
| PINE AV | SBD | U D4 |
| PINE AV | SBD | 98 D2 |
| PINE AV | TRI | 17 B2 |
| PINE DR | HUM | 16 B4 |
| PINE DR | LAS | 20 E2 |
| PINE DR | MPA | 48 E1 |
| PINE ST | C | 124 C4 |
| PINE ST | CC | L E3 |
| PINE ST | MONT | 167 D2 |
| PINE ST | MON | 53 E2 |
| PINE ST | NAP | 133 B4 |
| PINE ST | RED | 122 B1 |
| PINE ST | RCO | 100 C4 |
| PINE ST | SDCO | 107 A4 |
| PINE ST | SF | 142 A3 |
| PINE ST | SF | 143 C4 |
| PINE ST | SHA | 18 C3 |
| PINE ST | U | 123 C2 |
| PINE CANYON RD | MON | 65 B3 |
| PINE CANYON RD | SB | 76 E5 |
| PINE COVE TR | KER | 79 D2 |
| PINE CREEK BLVD | MOD | 8 B1 |
| PINE CREEK RD | INY | 51 B4 |
| PINE CREEK RD | HUM | 10 C3 |
| PINE CREEK RD | SIS | 2 E3 |
| PINE FLAT | SON | 31 E5 |
| PINE FLAT RD | SBD | 91 E5 |
| PINE FLAT RD | SCR | N E5 |
| PINE FLAT RD | SCR | 53 D1 |
| PINE GROVE | VEN | 88 C4 |
| PINE GROVE RD | KLAM | 5 C1 |
| PINE GRV TABEAU | AMA | 41 A2 |
| PINE GRV VOLCNO | AMA | 41 A2 |
| PINE GULCH RD | AMA | 40 E2 |
| PINE HILLS RD | SDCO | 107 C4 |
| PINE HOLLOW RD | CC | M B3 |
| PINEHURST RD | CC | 45 D1 |
| PINE MTN DR | TUO | 48 E1 |
| PINE MTN RD | KER | 78 E1 |
| PINE MTN RD | KER | 79 A1 |
| PINE MTN RD | MEN | 31 D4 |
| PINE NUT RD | MNO | 42 E1 |
| PINE RIDGE | FRCO | 58 C3 |
| PINE RIDGE RD | HUM | 10 C3 |
| PINE RIDGE RD | MEN | 31 A2 |
| PNES TO PLMS HY | RCO | 100 B4 |
| PINE TREE CY RD | KER | 80 A4 |
| PINE VALLEY RD | MON | 65 D3 |
| PINEVISTA CIR | RCO | 100 A3 |
| PINEWOOD LN | FRCO | 58 B1 |
| PINEY CK LOOP | MON | 64 D2 |
| PINKSTON CYN RD | BUT | 25 D3 |
| PINNACLE RD | SBD | 81 A1 |
| PINOLE VLY RD | CC | L D3 |
| PINOLI RIDGE RD | NEV | 26 E4 |
| PINOLI RIDGE RD | NEV | 27 A4 |
| PINON CANYON RD | KER | 79 C4 |
| PINON VILLGE RD | TUL | 70 A3 |
| PINTO DR | CAL | 41 B4 |
| PINTO RD | RCO | 101 E4 |
| PINTO BASIN RD | RCO | 101 D4 |
| PINTO MTN RD | SBD | 101 C1 |
| PIONEER AV | STA | 47 D1 |
| PIONEER BLVD | LACO | 98 A3 |
| PIONEER BLVD | LACO | T A1 |
| PIONEER DR | KER | 78 E3 |
| PIONEER RD | DN | 2 B3 |
| PIONEER RD | MCO | 55 D1 |
| PIONEER RD | STA | 47 D3 |
| PIONEER TR | SLT | 129 C4 |
| PIONEER CK RD | AMA | 41 B2 |
| PIONEERTOWN RD | SBD | 100 D1 |
| PIONEER TR RD | ED | 36 A4 |
| PIPE CREEK RD | RCO | 100 C5 |
| PIPE LINE AV | SBD | U C3 |
| PIPE LINE AV | SBD | 98 D2 |
| PIPER RD | CC | M D3 |
| PIPES RD | SBD | 100 C1 |
| PIPES CANYON RD | SBD | 100 D1 |
| PIPI RD | ED | 41 C1 |
| PIRCEN RD | LAS | 14 B3 |
| PIRU CANYON RD | LACO | 89 A4 |
| PIRU CANYON RD | VEN | 88 E4 |
| PISGAH CRATR RD | SBD | 92 E2 |
| PISTACHIO RD | KER | 77 B1 |
| PIT RD | MNO | 51 A2 |
| PIT #1 PWRHS RD | SHA | 13 D4 |
| PITTMAN HILL RD | FRCO | 58 A2 |
| PITT RIV CYN RD | LAS | 14 A4 |
| PITT SCHOOL RD | SOL | 39 B2 |
| PITTVILLE RD | LAS | 20 A1 |
| PITTVILLE RD | SHA | 13 E4 |
| PITTVILLE BENCH | LAS | 14 A4 |
| PITTZER RD | IMP | 112 B3 |
| PIUMA RD | LACO | 97 A2 |
| PIUTE MTN RD | KER | 79 D2 |
| PIUTE PINES RD | KER | 79 D3 |
| PLACENTIA AV | CM | 199 A3 |
| PLACENTIA AV | NB | 199 A3 |
| PLACENTIA AV | ORA | T C4 |
| PLACER AV | FRCO | 56 E4 |
| PLACER CT | KER | 79 D2 |
| PLACER RD | SHA | 18 B3 |
| PLACER RD | SUT | 33 E3 |
| PLACER ST | RED | 122 A2 |
| PLACER ST | SHA | 18 B2 |
| PLACER ST | TRI | 17 D1 |
| PLACER HILLS RD | PLA | 34 C3 |
| PLACERITA CYN | LACO | 89 C5 |
| PLACERVILLE DR | PLCV | 138 A3 |
| PLACERVILLE RD | SAC | 34 B5 |
| PLAINS RD | CC | 39 C5 |
| PLAINSBURG RD | MCO | 48 D5 |
| PLANO ST | TUL | 68 D3 |
| PLANTATION ST | RCO | 102 C4 |
| PLANT FIVE RD | INY | 51 C4 |
| PLANZ RD | KER | 78 D3 |
| PLASKETT RDG RD | MON | 64 E4 |
| PLATEAU CIR | SHA | 18 B2 |
| PLATEAU PINE RD | SHA | 19 B3 |
| PLATFORM RD | MAR | 37 E4 |
| PLATINA RD | SHA | 18 A3 |
| PLATINA RD | SHA | 17 D3 |
| PLATINA SCH RD | SHA | 17 D4 |
| PLAYA AZUL | AVLN | 105 B4 |
| PLAZA ST | SDCO | 106 C4 |
| PLEASANT | CC | 38 E5 |
| PLEASANT AV | SON | 37 E1 |
| PLEASANT RD | SLO | 66 B5 |
| PLEASANT GROVE | PLA | 33 D4 |
| PLEASANT GROVE | SUT | 33 E4 |
| PLEASANT GRV LN | BUT | 25 E5 |
| PLEASANT HILL | SON | 37 D2 |
| PLEASANT HLL RD | CC | L E4 |
| PLEASANT HLL RD | CC | M A3 |
| PLEASNT HL RD E | M | 154 C4 |
| PLEASANT OAK DR | TUL | 68 E3 |
| PLEASNTN SNL RD | ALA | P B1 |
| PLEASNTN SNL RD | ALA | 46 B2 |
| PLEASANT PT RD | HUM | 15 E2 |
| PLEASNTS VLY RD | SOL | 38 E2 |
| PLEASNTS VLY RD | SOL | 39 A2 |
| PLEASANT VLY AV | O | 156 B5 |
| PLEASANT VLY RD | ALP | 36 B5 |
| PLEASANT VLY RD | ED | 34 E5 |
| PLEASANT VLY RD | NEV | 34 B1 |
| PLEASANT VLY RD | STA | 47 D1 |
| PLEASANT VLY RD | VEN | 96 B1 |
| PLEASNT VLY DAM | INY | 51 C3 |
| PLESANTE RD | MON | 54 C3 |
| PLEYTO CEM RD | MON | 65 C4 |
| PLINCO MINE RD | PLU | 21 C5 |
| PLUMAS AV | FRCO | 57 A3 |
| PLUMAS ST | RENO | 130 B4 |
| PLUMAS ARBGA RD | YUB | 33 D3 |
| PLUMB LN E | RENO | 130 D5 |
| PLUMB LN W | RENO | 130 C5 |
| PLUMBAGO RD | SIE | 26 D5 |
| PLUM CREEK RD | TEH | 19 A4 |
| PLUMMER LKOT RD | TRI | 17 B3 |
| PLUM VALLEY RD | MOD | 7 C4 |
| PLUNKETT RD | HUM | 10 A5 |
| PLYMIRE RD | TEH | 18 C5 |
| PLYMOUTH AV | KIN | 67 A3 |
| PLYMOUTH RD | SBD | 80 E5 |
| PLYMTH SHNDOAH | AMA | 40 B1 |
| POCK LN | SJCO | 40 B5 |
| POCKET RD | SAC | 39 D2 |
| POE RD | IMP | 108 E3 |
| POE POWERHOUSE | BUT | 25 E3 |
| POINSETTIA LN | SDCO | 106 B3 |
| PT LAKEVIEW RD | LAK | 32 A3 |
| POINT LOMA AV | SDCO | V A3 |
| POINT LOMA AV | SDCO | 111 C1 |
| POINT LOMA BL W | SDCO | V A3 |
| POINT LOMA BL W | SD | 212 B5 |
| PT OF TIMBER RD | CC | 39 D5 |
| PT PLEASANT RD | SAC | 39 E3 |
| POINT RANCH RD | MNO | 43 B3 |
| PT REYES RD | MAR | 37 E4 |
| PT REYES PETLMA | MAR | 37 E4 |
| POINT SAL RD | SB | 86 A1 |
| PT SAN PEDRO RD | MAR | L B3 |
| POKER BAR RD | TRI | 17 D1 |
| POKER FLAT RD | SIE | 26 D3 |
| POLE LINE RD | LAS | 20 A1 |
| POLE LINE RD | MCO | 55 E2 |
| POLELINE RD | SBD | 93 A5 |
| POLE LINE RD | SHA | 13 E5 |
| POLETA RD | INY | 51 D4 |
| POLETA LAWS RD | INY | 51 D4 |
| POLHEMUS RD | SMCO | N C2 |
| POLI ST | VENT | 175 E2 |
| POLK AV | FRCO | 57 B3 |
| POLK AV | FRCO | 67 B1 |
| POLK AV | FRCO | 57 B5 |
| POLK ST | LACO | Q C1 |
| POLK ST | RCO | 101 B5 |
| POLLACK FLAT | SIS | 5 A5 |
| POLSON RD | NAPA | 38 D3 |
| POMEGRANATE AV | STA | 47 C3 |
| POMELO AV | STA | 47 C3 |
| POMERADO RD | SDCO | V C1 |
| POMERADO RD | SDCO | 106 D5 |
| POMEROY AV | SCLR | 150 C3 |
| POMEROY LS BERS | SLO | 76 C5 |
| POMONA AV | COR | 215 C5 |
| POMONA AV | CM | 199 B3 |
| POMONA AV | TEH | 24 D1 |
| POMONA BLVD | LACO | R B4 |
| POMONA FRWY | LACO | 98 A2 |
| POMONA FRWY | LACO | R E4 |
| POMONA ST | CC | 38 D4 |
| POMPONIO CK RD | SMCO | N C3 |
| POND RD | KER | 68 A5 |
| PONDER WY | SHA | 18 B3 |
| PONDEROSA BLVD | LAS | 21 B4 |
| PONDEROSA RD | CAL | 41 C4 |
| PONDEROSA WY | AMA | 41 B3 |
| PONDEROSA WY | BUT | 25 C2 |
| PONDEROSA WY | BUT | 25 D3 |
| PONDEROSA WY | BUT | 26 A4 |
| PONDEROSA WY | CAL | 41 B3 |
| PONDEROSA WY | MPA | 49 B3 |
| PONDEROSA WY | PLA | 34 D3 |
| PONDEROSA WY | SHA | 19 B2 |
| PONDEROSA WY | TEH | 19 B3 |
| PONDOSA WY | SIS | 13 C3 |
| PONY RD | SBD | 92 C4 |
| PONY WY | CAL | 41 A4 |
| PONY EXPRESS TR | ED | 35 A4 |
| POOLE AV | KER | 80 C1 |
| POOLE LN | SIE | 27 D3 |
| POOLE RD | HUM | 15 D2 |
| POOLE RD | MCO | 48 D5 |
| POOL STATION RD | CAL | 41 A3 |
| POONKINNEY RD | MEN | 23 A3 |
| POOP OUT HL RD | SBD | 100 A1 |
| POOR BOY CK RD | ALP | 36 C5 |
| POORE RD | IMP | 109 C4 |
| POPE ST | NAPA | 29 C2 |
| POPE CANYON RD | NAPA | 38 C1 |
| POPE VALLEY RD | NAPA | 29 C1 |
| POPE VALLEY RD | NAPA | 32 B5 |
| POPE VALLEY RD | NAPA | 38 B1 |
| POPLAR AV | KER | 78 B2 |
| POPLAR AV | MLBR | 144 D5 |
| POPLAR AV | SMCO | N C1 |
| POPPET FLAT RD | RCO | 100 A3 |
| POPPY BLVD | KER | 80 B4 |
| PORTAL RD W | MNO | 43 C5 |
| PORT CHICAGO HY | CC | M A3 |
| PORTER | FRCO | 58 A4 |
| PORTER AV | RCO | 99 C3 |
| PORTER RD | SOL | 39 B2 |
| PORTER CREEK RD | SON | 37 E1 |
| PORTER CREEK RD | SON | 38 A1 |
| PORTERVILLE HWY | KER | 68 D5 |
| PORTERVILLE HWY | KER | 78 D1 |
| PORTERVILLE WY | KER | 78 C1 |
| PORT KENYON RD | HUM | 15 D2 |
| PORTOLA AV | ALA | M C5 |
| PORTOLA AV | RCO | 100 E4 |
| PORTOLA BLVD | ALA | 46 C2 |
| PORTOLA DR | SFCO | L B5 |
| PORTOLA DR | SFCO | 45 B2 |
| PORTOLA RD | SLO | 76 A2 |
| PORTOLA RD | SMCO | N D3 |
| PORTOLA RD | SMCO | 45 D4 |
| PORTOLA STAT PK | SMCO | 45 D5 |
| PORTOLA S PK RD | SMCO | N D4 |
| PORTOLA MCLEARS | PLU | 27 B3 |
| PORTUGUESE BEND | SUT | 33 C4 |
| PORTUGUESE CYN | MON | 66 B4 |
| PORT WINE RIDGE | PLU | 26 C3 |
| PORT WINE RIDGE | SIE | 26 C4 |
| PORTY ST | KER | 78 D4 |
| POSO AV | KER | 77 E1 |
| POSO AV | KER | 78 A1 |
| POSO FLAT RD | KER | 79 A1 |
| POST AV | TEH | 24 E2 |
| POST RD | RCO | 99 B4 |
| POST ST | SF | 142 B3 |
| POST ST | SF | 143 A4 |
| POST MTN RD | TRI | 17 B3 |
| POTRERO AV | SF | 142 D4 |
| POTRERO RD E | VEN | 96 D1 |
| POTRERO RD W | VEN | 96 C1 |
| POTRERO ST | SFCO | L C5 |
| POTRERO GRDE BL | LACO | R C4 |
| POTTER RD | MON | 54 D4 |
| POTTEROFF RD | CAL | 41 B3 |
| POUND RD | IMP | 109 A3 |
| POUNDSTONE RD | COL | 33 B3 |
| POURROY RD | RCO | 99 D5 |
| POVERTY RD | SAC | M D1 |
| POVERTY RD | SAC | 39 D3 |
| POVERTY HILL RD | SIE | 26 C4 |
| POWAY RD | SDCO | V C1 |
| POWAY RD | SDCO | 106 D4 |
| POWDER HILL RD | SIS | 5 C5 |
| POWDER HILL RD | SIS | 13 C1 |
| POWELL AV | SON | 37 D1 |
| POWELL RD | SBD | 92 D5 |
| POWELL RD | SUT | 33 B1 |
| POWELL RD | VEN | 88 E4 |
| POWELLTOWN RD | BUT | 25 D2 |
| POWER RD | TRI | 17 C1 |
| POWER HOUSE RD | FRCO | 57 E1 |
| POWER HOUSE RD | MEN | 23 B5 |
| POWERHOUSE RD | STA | 11 E5 |
| POWERHOUSE RD S | TEH | 19 B3 |
| POWER HSE HL RD | BUT | 25 C5 |
| POWER INN RD | SAC | 40 A1 |
| POWER LINE RD | MNO | 52 C3 |
| POWER LINE RD | RCO | 106 E1 |
| POWER LINE RD | SAC | 33 D5 |
| POWER LINE RD | SBD | 83 A3 |
| POWER LINE RD | SBD | 91 C3 |
| POWER LINE RD | SHA | 18 B2 |
| POWER LINE RD | SUT | 33 D4 |
| POWERS AV | MAN | 161 D3 |
| POZOS RD | RCO | 99 C3 |
| PRADO RD | SNLO | 172 A5 |
| PRAHSER RD | SJCO | 40 C5 |
| PRAIRE WY | MEN | 22 C5 |
| PRAIRE WY | MEN | 30 B1 |
| PRAIRIE AV | LACO | S B1 |
| PRAIRIE AV | SBD | 91 C1 |
| PRAIRIE DR | LAS | 8 A5 |
| PRAIRIE CK RD | TRI | 17 A1 |
| PRAIRIE FLOWER | STA | 47 D4 |
| PRAIRIE FLWR RD | STA | 47 D3 |
| PRATT RD | TUL | 68 B1 |
| PRATT RANCH RD | MEN | 31 C3 |
| PRATVLL BTT RES | PLU | 20 B5 |
| PREFUMO CYN RD | SLO | 75 E4 |
| PREFUMO CYN RD | SLO | 76 A4 |
| PRELL RD | SB | 86 C1 |
| PRESCOTT AV | MONT | 167 C3 |
| PRESCOTT AV | MON | 53 D3 |
| PRESCOTT AV | PAC | 167 C3 |
| PRESCOTT RD | SJCO | 47 B1 |
| PRESIDIO AV | SF | 142 A2 |
| PRESIDIO BLVD | SFCO | L B5 |
| PRESIDIO BLVD | SFCO | 45 B1 |
| PRESSLEY RD | SON | 38 A2 |
| PRESTON | MPA | 49 A5 |
| PRESTON RD | BUT | 25 C4 |
| PRESTON RD | IMP | 111 E4 |
| PRESTON RD | MCO | 47 C4 |
| PREVITALI RD | AMA | 41 A2 |
| PRICE CREEK RD | HUM | 15 E3 |
| PRICE CK CAMPBL | TRI | 17 B1 |
| PRICE CK SCH RD | HUM | 15 E2 |
| PRICE CANYON RD | SLO | 76 B4 |
| PRIEST COLTRVLL | MPA | 48 D1 |
| PRIEST COLTRVLL | TUO | 48 E1 |
| PRIEST VLY RD | MON | 66 A2 |
| PRIM RD | IMP | 109 B5 |
| PRIMROSE MN RD | SIE | 26 E4 |
| PRINCE AV | FRCO | 56 A2 |
| PRINCE RD | MCO | 47 C4 |
| PRINCESS PAT MN | SBD | 90 E2 |
| PRINCETON | FRCO | 58 A3 |
| PRINCETON RD | MCO | 48 B3 |
| PROGRESS RD | SUT | 33 B2 |
| PROSPECT AV | KER | 78 A1 |
| PROSPECT AV | ORA | T E2 |
| PROSPECT AV | SDCO | V E2 |
| PROSPECT BLVD | PAS | 190 A3 |
| PROSPECT RD | SCL | 45 E4 |
| PROSPECT RD | SCL | P A3 |
| PROSPECT ST | SDCO | V A2 |
| PROSPECT ST | SDCO | 106 C5 |
| PROSPERITY AV | TUL | 68 A2 |
| PROSSER DAM RD | NEV | 27 D5 |
| PROUTY RD | SJCO | 40 B3 |
| PROVIDENCE RCH | SBD | 84 B4 |
| PRUNE AV | STA | 47 C3 |
| PRUNERIDGE AV | CPTO | 150 A4 |
| PRUNERIDGE AV | SJ | 151 A4 |
| PRUNERIDGE AV | SCLR | 150 C4 |
| PRUNERIDGE AV | SCL | 151 A4 |
| PUDDING CK RD | MEN | 22 C5 |
| PRUSSIAN HLL RD | CAL | 41 B3 |
| PUEBLO AV | KIN | 67 C3 |
| PUEBLO AV | NAP | 133 B2 |
| PUENTE AV | LACO | 98 B2 |
| PUENTE AV | LACO | R D4 |
| PULGA RD | BUT | 25 D2 |
| PULLMAN RD | IMP | 111 E4 |
| PUMICE MINE RD | MNO | 50 D1 |
| PUMICE MINE RD | MNO | 51 C1 |
| PUMICE MILL RD | MNO | 51 D3 |
| PUMP RD | MCO | 55 E2 |
| PUMP RD | STA | 47 C4 |
| PUMPHOUSE RD | COL | 32 D2 |
| PUMPHOUSE RD | SIS | 4 B5 |
| PUMPHOUSE RD | YOL | 39 D2 |
| PUNKIN CTR RD | LAS | 14 B4 |
| PURDON RD | NEV | 26 C5 |
| PURDY AV | KER | 80 A5 |
| PURISIMA RD | SB | 86 B3 |
| PURISIMA CK RD | SMCO | 45 C4 |
| PURITAN MINE RD | LACO | 89 E4 |
| PUTAH LN | LAK | 32 A4 |
| PUTAH CREEK RD | SOL | 39 A1 |
| PUTNAM RD | COL | 25 A5 |
| PUTNAM WY | COL | 32 E3 |
| PYLE RD | CAL | 41 B5 |
| PYLE RD | LAK | 31 D2 |
| PYRAMID HILLS | KIN | 67 A5 |
| PYRITE RD | RCO | 99 A2 |
| Q | | |
| QUAIL AV | KIN | 67 B3 |
| QUAIL DR | RCO | 100 B5 |
| QUAIL HILL RD | HUM | 16 A2 |
| QUAIL ST | KER | 80 C1 |
| QUAIL WY | RCO | 100 A5 |
| QUAIL HILL RD | CAL | 41 A5 |
| QUAIL HOLLOW RD | SCR | N E5 |
| QUAIL SPGS RD | SBD | 101 A1 |
| QUAIL SPGS SPUR | SBD | 101 A2 |
| QUAKER ST | HUM | 9 E5 |
| QUAKR HL CRS RD | NEV | 34 D1 |
| QUALITY RD | KER | 68 C5 |
| QUARRY RD | HUM | 9 E4 |
| QUARRY RD | MAD | 49 B5 |
| QUARRY RD | PA | 147 A3 |
| QUARRY RD | SDCO | V D4 |
| QUARRY RD | SDCO | 111 E1 |
| QUARRY RD S | HUM | 10 A5 |
| QUARTZ AV | SIS | 4 C4 |
| QUARTZ ST | BUT | 25 D2 |

STREETS

# STREET INDEX

| STREET | CO. | PAGE & GRID |
|---|---|---|
| QUARTZ ST | SBD | 84 C3 |
| QUARTZ ST | TUO | 41 C5 |
| QUARTZ HILL RD | SHA | 18 C2 |
| QUARTZ MT LKOUT | SIS | 3 D5 |
| QUARTZ MTN RD | MAD | 49 D5 |
| QUARTZ VLY DR | SIS | 3 C5 |
| QUARTZ VLY RD | SIS | 3 C5 |
| QUARTZ VLY RD E | SIS | 3 C5 |
| QUATAL CYN RD | KER | 87 E2 |
| QUATAL CYN RD | SB | 87 E2 |
| QUATAL CYN RD | VEN | 88 A1 |
| QUEBEC AV | KIN | 67 E3 |
| QUEBEC AV | KIN | 67 A3 |
| QUEEN OF SHEBA | INY | 72 A3 |
| QUEENS AV | YUBA | 125 A1 |
| QUEENS WY | LB | 192 D4 |
| QUESTHAVEN RD | SDCO | 106 C3 |
| QUICK RD | IMP | 112 C5 |
| QUIEN SABE RD | SBT | 55 B3 |
| QUIEN SABE RCH | SBT | 55 B3 |
| QUIMBY RD | SCL | P C3 |
| QUIMBY RD | SCL | 46 C4 |
| QUINCY RD | SIE | 26 D3 |
| QUINCY RD | STA | 47 E3 |
| QUINCY JCT RD | PLU | 26 D1 |
| QUINCY LA PORTE | PLU | 26 D2 |
| QUINCY LA PORTE | PLU | 26 C4 |
| QUINLEY AV | MCO | 48 B5 |
| QUINN RD | HUM | 15 D1 |
| QUINN RD | KER | 68 D5 |
| QUISENBERRY RD | STA | 47 C3 |
| QUITO RD | SCL | P A4 |
| QUITO RD | SCL | 46 A5 |
| R | | |
| R ST | FRE | 165 E3 |
| R ST | MER | 170 B4 |
| RABBIT BRUSH LN | SIS | 4 B4 |
| RABBIT RANCH RD | MNO | 51 C2 |
| RABBIT SPGS RD | SBD | 91 E4 |
| RABBIT SPGS RD | SBD | 92 A4 |
| RABER ST | KER | 80 A5 |
| RACE ST | SJ | 151 E4 |
| RACE ST | SCL | P B3 |
| RACE TRACK RD | SAC | M E1 |
| RACE TRACK RD | SAC | 39 D3 |
| RACE TRACK RD | TUO | 163 A3 |
| RACETRACK VLY | INY | 61 A2 |
| RACINE AV | KIN | 67 E3 |
| RACQUET CLUB DR | SR | 139 B3 |
| RADIO LN | RED | 122 C5 |
| RADIO STATN RD | SOL | 39 B2 |
| RAGAN MEADWS RD | TRI | 17 A3 |
| RAG DUMP RD | BUT | 25 D2 |
| RAGLIN RIDGE RD | TEH | 23 E1 |
| RAGLIN RIDGE RD | TEH | 24 A1 |
| RAGSDALE RD | RCO | 102 B4 |
| RAHILLY RD | MCO | 48 B5 |
| RAIL CANYON RD | COL | 24 B5 |
| RAIL CANYON RD | GLE | 24 B5 |
| RAIL CREEK RD | SIS | 12 A2 |
| RAILROAD AV | CC | M B3 |
| RAILROAD AV | DN | 1 D4 |
| RAILROAD AV | HUM | 16 D4 |
| RAILROAD AV | RED | 122 B3 |
| RAILROAD AV | SMA | 173 B2 |
| RAILROAD AV | SOL | 135 E3 |
| RAILROAD AV | SUT | 33 C2 |
| RAILROAD AV | VAL | 134 A4 |
| RAILROAD ST | SBD | 84 C3 |
| RAILROAD CYN RD | RCO | 99 C4 |
| RAILRD FLAT RD | CAL | 41 B3 |
| RAINBOW | FRCO | 57 E3 |
| RAINBOW BASN RD | SBD | 81 D5 |
| RAINBOW CYN RD | SBD | 93 B4 |
| RAINBOW GLEN RD | SDCO | 106 C1 |
| RAINBOW LAKE RD | SHA | 18 A3 |
| RAINES RD | STA | 47 B3 |
| RAIN TREE LN | BUT | 25 A2 |
| RAJNUS RD | KLAM | 5 E2 |
| RALPH RD | IMP | 109 A5 |
| RALSTON AV | BLMT | 145 C5 |
| RALSTON AV | SMCO | N C2 |
| RALSTON AV | SMCO | 45 C3 |
| RAMAL RD | SON | 38 C3 |
| RAMBLA PACIFICO | LACO | 97 B2 |
| RAMELI GREIG RD | PLU | 27 D2 |
| RAMIREZ RD | YUB | 33 D1 |
| RAMON RD | PMSP | 206 C4 |
| RAMON RD | RCO | 100 D3 |
| RAMONA AV | LACO | U B2 |
| RAMONA AV | MTCL | 203 B5 |
| RAMONA AV | SBD | U C3 |
| RAMONA AV | SBDO | 203 B5 |
| RAMONA AV | SBD | 91 C3 |
| RAMONA AV | SBD | 98 D2 |
| RAMONA BLVD | LACO | R D3 |
| RAMONA BLVD | RCO | 99 E3 |
| RAMONA DR | SNLO | 172 A2 |
| RAMONA EXPWY | RCO | 99 C3 |
| RAMONA EXPWY | RCO | 99 D3 |
| RAMONA FRWY | SDCO | V D3 |
| RAMONA FRWY | SDCO | 106 E5 |
| RAMOS RD | MCO | 55 D1 |
| RAMP RD | MNO | 43 B3 |
| RAMSEY RD | RCO | 107 B1 |
| RAMSEY RD | SOL | 38 E3 |
| RAMSEY MINE RD | LPAZ | 104 D4 |
| RAMS HILL DR | SDCO | 107 E3 |
| RAMSHORN RD | TRI | 12 A3 |
| RAMS HORN GRADE | AMA | 41 E2 |
| RAMSHN MUMBO CK | TRI | 12 B3 |
| RANCH RD | HUM | 15 E2 |
| RANCH RD | MCO | 48 C5 |
| RANCH RD | MNO | 52 C3 |
| RANCH RD | SBD | 92 E5 |
| RANCHERIA RD | KER | 69 C5 |
| RANCHERIA RD | KER | 78 E2 |
| RANCHERIA RD | KER | 79 A2 |
| RANCHERIA RD | MEN | 30 C3 |
| RANCHERIA CK RD | SIS | 4 A3 |
| RANCHERIAS RD | SBD | 91 C3 |
| RANCHERIA-SAWML | KER | 79 B1 |
| RANCHERO | SBD | 91 B4 |
| RANCHITA CYN RD | MON | 66 C5 |
| RANCHITA CYN RD | SLO | 66 B5 |
| RANCHITO RD | MPA | 48 D2 |
| RANCHITOS RD | MAR | L A3 |
| RANCHLAND DR | SHA | 18 B2 |
| RANCH LAND RD | SDCO | 106 E4 |
| RANCHO AV | SBD | 99 B2 |
| RANCHO DR | KER | 78 E4 |
| RANCHO DR | KER | 79 A4 |
| RANCHO DR | SBD | 91 A3 |
| RANCHO RD | KER | 78 E5 |
| RANCHO RD | KER | 79 A5 |
| RANCHO RD | LV | 209 A2 |
| RANCHO RD | SB | 76 C5 |
| RANCHO RD | SB | 86 B1 |
| RANCHO RD | SHA | 18 C2 |
| RNCHO ALISAL RD | SB | 86 E3 |
| RCHO BAUTSTA RD | RCO | 100 B5 |
| RO BERNARDO RD | SDCO | 106 D4 |
| RANCHO CALIF RD | RCO | 99 D5 |
| RANCHO CALIF RD | RCO | 106 C1 |
| RANCHO CANADA | SDCO | 107 A5 |
| RNCHO CONEJO BL | VEN | 96 D1 |
| RO SANTA FE RD | SDCO | 106 C3 |
| RANCHO VIEJO RD | SJC | 202 E1 |
| RANDALL AV | SBD | 99 A2 |
| RANDALL RD | KER | 77 E4 |
| RANDOLPH RD | MCO | 47 E4 |
| RANDOLPH RD | SAC | 40 A2 |
| RANDSBURG RD | SBD | 81 C2 |
| RANDSBRG CUTOFF | KER | 80 A4 |
| RANDSBRG CUTOFF | SBD | 80 E3 |
| RANDSBG INYOKRN | KER | 80 D1 |
| RANDSBG WASH RD | SBD | 80 E1 |
| RANDSBG WASH RD | SBD | 81 A1 |
| RANGE RD | MCO | 48 B5 |
| RANGER STA RD | INY | 51 B3 |
| RANGER STA RD | INY | 60 A4 |
| RANGER STA RD | TRI | 17 B1 |
| RANNELS BLVD | RCO | 103 C5 |
| RANNELS BLVD | RCO | 110 C1 |
| RASOR RD | SBD | 83 A4 |
| RATTLESNAKE RD | NEV | 34 C2 |
| RATTLESNAKE RD | TRI | 17 B3 |
| RATTLSNK BTT RD | MOD | 14 E1 |
| RATTLSNK CYN RD | SBD | 92 C5 |
| RATTLSNAK CK RD | SIS | 3 D5 |
| RAWHIDE RD | TUO | 41 C5 |
| RAWSON RD | TEH | 18 D5 |
| RAY | SJCO | 40 A3 |
| RAY | SJCO | 40 A4 |
| RAY RD | SB | 86 B1 |
| RAYHOUSE RD | YOL | 32 C4 |
| RAYMOND AV | ORA | T C1 |
| RAYMOND RD | ALA | M D5 |
| RAYMOND RD | ALA | 46 C2 |
| RAYMOND RD | MAD | 49 C5 |
| RAYMOND RD | MAD | 57 B1 |
| RAYNOR RANCH | MCO | 48 E5 |
| READING RD | TEH | 18 D5 |
| REAL RD | BKD | 166 A4 |
| REAL RD | KER | 166 A5 |
| REALTY RD | SJCO | 40 B4 |
| REATA RD | INY | 51 D4 |
| RECALDE RD | SBT | 55 E4 |
| RECHE RD | SBD | 92 D5 |
| RECHE RD | SDCO | 106 C2 |
| RECHE CANYON RD | RCO | 99 C2 |
| RECLAMATION RD | LAK | 31 D2 |
| RECLAMATION RD | SUT | 33 C3 |
| RECTOR RD | NEV | 34 C1 |
| RED BANK RD | TEH | 18 B5 |
| RED BANK RD | TEH | 24 C1 |
| RED BOX RD | LACO | R C2 |
| RED CAP RD | HUM | 10 D2 |
| RED CLOUD MN RD | RCO | 102 B4 |
| REDDING AV | KIN | 67 D3 |
| REDDING CYN RD | INY | 51 E4 |
| REDDING CK RD | TRI | 17 D2 |
| REDDINGTON AV | COL | 32 E3 |
| RED DOG RD | NEV | 34 D1 |
| RED GRADE RD | TRI | 17 D1 |
| RED HEAD CYN RD | MON | 65 D3 |
| RED HILL AV | CM | 198 A4 |
| RED HILL AV | IRV | 198 D3 |
| RED HILL AV | ORA | T D3 |
| RED HILL BLVD | ORA | 98 C4 |
| REDHILL RD | CAL | 41 B4 |
| RED HILL RD | IMP | 109 A3 |
| RED HILL RD | INY | 51 C4 |
| RED HILL RD | TRI | 17 C1 |
| REDHILL RD | TUO | 48 C1 |
| REDINGER LK RD | MAD | 49 E5 |
| REDINGER LK RD | MAD | 50 A5 |
| REDLANDS BLVD | RCO | 99 C2 |
| REDLANDS BLVD | SBDO | 207 D5 |
| REDLANDS BLVD | SBD | 99 C2 |
| REDLANDS FRWY | RCO | 99 D2 |
| REDLANDS FRWY | SBD | 99 D2 |
| REDLANDS ST | SBD | 99 D2 |
| REDMEYER RD | MEN | 31 B2 |
| REDMOND RD | HUM | 9 E5 |
| RED MOUNTAIN RD | KER | 80 E3 |
| RED MOUNTAIN RD | MCO | 55 B1 |
| RED MOUNTAIN RD | RCO | 100 A5 |
| RED MOUNTAIN RD | SBD | 80 E3 |
| RED MOUNTAIN RD | SHA | 13 C3 |
| RED MOUNTAIN RD | TRI | 17 B4 |
| RED MTN LKOUT | GLE | 24 A3 |
| RED MTN MTWY | TRI | 17 B4 |
| RED MTN TK TR | RCO | 106 C1 |
| RED OAK CYN RD | SIE | 26 E3 |
| REDONDO AV | LACO | 98 A4 |
| REDONDO AV | LACO | S E2 |
| REDONDO BLVD | LA | 184 B4 |
| REDONDO BCH BL | LACO | S B1 |
| REDPARK RD | HUM | 9 A1 |
| RED ROCK RD | LAS | 8 D4 |
| RED ROCK RD | LAS | 27 E2 |
| RED ROCK RD | SIS | 5 A3 |
| REDROCK-INYOKRN | KER | 80 C1 |
| REDROCK-INYOKRN | KER | 80 C2 |
| REDROCK-RANDSBG | KER | 80 B3 |
| RED ROVER MN RD | LACO | 89 E4 |
| RED SHANK LN | RCO | 100 A5 |
| REDSTONE AV | KER | 79 C3 |
| RED TOP RD | SOL | 38 D3 |
| RED TOP MTN RD | MAD | 57 C1 |
| RED VISTA RD | ALP | 36 A5 |
| REDWING RD | SBD | 91 D3 |
| REDWOOD BLVD | KER | 80 B4 |
| REDWOOD DR | HUM | 16 C5 |
| REDWOOD DR | TUL | 69 B2 |
| REDWOOD HWY | CRTM | 140 C2 |
| REDWOOD HWY | DN | 1 E3 |
| REDWOOD HWY | DN | 2 A5 |
| REDWOOD HWY | DN | 9 E3 |
| REDWOOD HWY | HUM | 15 E3 |
| REDWOOD HWY | HUM | 16 A3 |
| REDWOOD HWY | HUM | 16 B4 |
| REDWOOD HWY | MAR | L A2 |
| REDWOOD HWY | MAR | 38 A4 |
| REDWOOD HWY | MAR | 140 C2 |
| REDWOOD HWY | MEN | 22 D2 |
| REDWOOD HWY | SR | 139 D2 |
| REDWOOD HWY | STR | 131 C2 |
| REDWOOD HWY | SON | 31 C4 |
| REDWOOD HWY | SON | 37 E2 |
| REDWOOD HWY | SON | 38 A3 |
| REDWOOD RD | ALA | L E4 |
| REDWOOD RD | ALA | 47 E1 |
| REDWOOD RD | NAPA | 29 D5 |
| REDWOOD RD | NAPA | 38 C2 |
| REDWOOD RD | STA | 47 D3 |
| REDWOOD ST | SOL | L D2 |
| REDWOOD ST | VAL | 134 B3 |
| REDWD HOUSE RD | HUM | 16 B3 |
| REDWOOD RTRT RD | SCL | P D5 |
| REDWOOD RTRT RD | SCL | 54 C1 |
| REED | FRCO | 58 A4 |
| REED AV | KER | 80 A5 |
| REED AV | SVL | 150 B1 |
| REED LN | SCL | P A3 |
| REED RD | KER | 68 C5 |
| REED RD | SUT | 33 C2 |
| REEDER RD | KLAM | 5 C1 |
| REED MTN RD | HUM | 22 C1 |
| REED ORCHARD RD | TEH | 25 A1 |
| REEDS CREEK RD | TEH | 18 B5 |
| REEDS TURNPIKE | CAL | 41 A5 |
| REED VALLEY RD | RCO | 100 A5 |
| REESE AV | COL | 33 A1 |
| REESE RD | BUT | 25 A2 |
| REEVES RD | VEN | 88 B4 |
| REEVES CYN RD | MEN | 31 A1 |
| REFUGIO RD | SB | 86 E3 |
| REGENTS RD | SD | 211 D2 |
| REGENTS RD | SDCO | V A2 |
| REGENTS RD | SDCO | 106 C5 |
| REGLI LN | HUM | 15 E2 |
| REICHART RCH RD | MNO | 51 C1 |
| REID AV | TUL | 68 D3 |
| REID RD | KER | 79 E2 |
| REID RD | KER | 80 A2 |
| REILLY RD | MCO | 48 C5 |
| REINA RD | KER | 78 C2 |
| REINO RD | VEN | 96 D1 |
| REIS AV | VAL | 134 E5 |
| RELIEF HILL RD | NEV | 26 D5 |
| RELIEZ RD | CC | 38 E5 |
| RELIZ CANYON RD | MON | 65 A2 |
| RELIEZ VLY RD | CC | L E3 |
| REMANN AV | SHA | 19 E1 |
| REMBACH WY | KER | 79 C1 |
| RENFRO RD | KER | 78 C3 |
| RENGSTORFF RD | SCL | N E2 |
| RENGSTORFF RD | SCL | P A2 |
| RENO AV | TEH | 24 D1 |
| RENWICK AV | SB | 86 B3 |
| REQUA RD | DN | 1 E5 |
| REQUA RD | DN | 2 A5 |
| RESEDA BLVD | LA | 178 D3 |
| RESEDA BLVD | LACO | 97 C1 |
| RESERVATION RD | COL | 32 E1 |
| RESERVATION RD | MON | 54 B4 |
| RESERVATION RD | TUL | 68 E3 |
| RESERVE RD | KER | 77 D3 |
| RESERVOIR RD | BUT | 25 D5 |
| RESERVOIR RD | ED | 34 D3 |
| RESERVOIR RD | SOL | 38 D4 |
| RESERVOIR RD | STA | 48 A2 |
| RESERVOIR ST | LACO | 98 D2 |
| RETRAC WY | NEV | 34 B2 |
| RETSON RD | BUT | 25 D2 |
| REVIS RD | MAD | 49 C5 |
| REWARD RD | KER | 77 D3 |
| REYES ADOBE RD | LACO | 96 E1 |
| REYNARD WY | SD | 215 D2 |
| REYNOLDS AV | MCO | 56 B2 |
| REYNOLDS HWY | MEN | 23 A5 |
| REYNOLDS RD | SHA | 13 E4 |
| REYNLDS FRRY RD | TUO | 41 B5 |
| RHEEM BLVD | CC | L E4 |
| RHELM | CC | 38 C5 |
| RHONDA RD | SHA | 18 C3 |
| RIALTO AV | SBD | 99 B1 |
| RIALTO AV | SBDO | 207 C2 |
| RIATA RD | LAK | 32 A4 |
| RIATA WY | CAL | 41 A4 |
| RICE AV | SBD | 101 A1 |
| RICE AV | VEN | 96 B1 |
| RICE RD | FRCO | 57 C2 |
| RICE RD | MCO | 48 B5 |
| RICE RD | STA | 47 E2 |
| RICE RD | VEN | 88 A4 |
| RICE CANYON RD | LAS | 21 B3 |
| RICE CANYON RD | LAS | 21 B3 |
| RICE CREEK RD | LAK | 23 D5 |
| RICE CREEK RD | LAK | 31 D1 |
| RICES CROSNG RD | NEV | 34 B1 |
| RICES CROSNG RD | YUB | 26 A5 |
| RICES TEX HL RD | YUB | 26 A5 |
| RICETON HWY | BUT | 25 C5 |
| RICH LN | RCO | 106 E1 |
| RICH RD | KER | 68 C5 |
| RICHARD RD | SIS | 4 D5 |
| RICHARD ST | KER | 70 A5 |
| RICHARDS AV | BUT | 33 C1 |
| RICHARDS BLVD | DVS | 136 D3 |
| RICHARDSON AV | SF | 142 A1 |
| RICHARDSON RD | SBD | 91 A3 |
| RICHARDSON RD | SIS | 4 E3 |
| RICHARDSON RD | SIS | 5 A2 |
| RICHARDSON SPGS | BUT | 25 B2 |
| RICH BAR RD | PLU | 26 B1 |
| RICHEY RD | CLO | 33 A3 |
| RICHFIELD RD | TEH | 24 D1 |
| RICH GULCH RD | PLU | 26 B1 |
| RICHLAND RD | SUT | 125 B5 |
| RICHMOND RD | LAS | 21 A3 |
| RICHMOND ST | SD | 215 E1 |
| RICHVALE HWY | BUT | 25 B4 |
| RIDER ST | RCO | 99 B3 |
| RIDGE DR | SHA | 18 B2 |
| RIDGE RD | AMA | 40 E2 |
| RIDGE RD | CAL | 41 B2 |
| RIDGE RD | NEV | 34 C1 |
| RIDGE RD | NEV | 127 A2 |
| RIDGE RD | NEV | 128 A4 |
| RIDGE RD | SIE | 26 C5 |
| RIDGE RD | SIS | 3 E4 |
| RIDGE RD | TEH | 18 C5 |
| RIDGECREST BLVD | KER | 80 D1 |
| RIDGE ROUTE RD | ED | 34 E4 |
| RIDGEWAY DR | ED | 35 B4 |
| RIDGEWAY HWY | MEN | 23 B5 |
| RIDGEWOOD | MEN | 23 A5 |
| RIDGEWOOD DR | HUM | 15 E1 |
| RIDGEWOOD RD | SHA | 18 C2 |
| RIEBLI RD | SON | 37 E1 |
| RIEBLI RD | SON | 38 A1 |
| RIEFF RD | LAK | 32 B4 |
| RIEGO RD | SUT | 33 D5 |
| RIGGIN AV | TUL | 68 A1 |
| RIGGINS RD | SUT | 33 C4 |
| RIGGS RD | LAK | 31 D3 |
| RIGGS RD | SBD | 83 B2 |
| RIKER ST | SAL | 171 B5 |
| RILEY RD | BUT | 25 B5 |
| RILEY RD | SB | 86 E3 |
| RILEY RD | SAC | 40 A2 |
| RIM O T WRLD HY | SBD | 91 C5 |
| RIM O T WRLD HY | SBD | 99 D1 |
| RIMPAU BLVD | LA | 184 C3 |
| RIMROCK RD | BARS | 208 D4 |
| RIM ROCK RD | RCO | 107 C1 |
| RIMROCK RD | SBD | 91 D1 |
| RIMROCK RD | SBD | 100 C1 |
| RIM ROCK CANYON | RCO | 107 C1 |
| RINCON AV | SDCO | 106 D3 |
| RINCON AV | SON | 38 A2 |
| RINCON RD | SBD | 91 C4 |
| RINCNADA LS PIL | SLO | 76 C3 |
| RINGWOOD AV | SMCO | N D2 |
| RIO RD | CAR | 168 C4 |
| RIO RD | MON | 168 C4 |
| RIO BLANCO | SJCO | 40 A4 |
| RIO BONITO RD E | BUT | 25 C5 |
| RIO BONITO RD W | BUT | 25 C5 |
| RIO DEL SOL RD | RCO | 100 E3 |
| RIOLINDA AV | FRCO | 57 B4 |
| RIO LINDA BLVD | SAC | 33 E5 |
| RIO OSO RD | SUT | 33 D3 |
| RIORDON RD | COL | 32 D1 |
| RIOSA RD | PLA | 33 E3 |
| RIOSA RD | PLA | 34 A3 |
| RIO VISTA AV | FRCO | 58 A4 |
| RIO VISTA AV W | TEH | 18 D4 |
| RIO VISTA RD | SUIS | 135 C4 |
| RIO VISTA ST | ORA | T D2 |
| RIPONE RD | STA | 47 C2 |
| RIPPON RD N | SJCO | 47 C1 |
| RIPPON RD W | SJCO | 47 B2 |
| RISING HILL RD | SIS | 4 C5 |
| RITCHEY ST | SA | 198 E1 |
| RITTER RD | SHA | 13 D3 |
| RITTS MILL RD | SHA | 19 B2 |
| RIVER AV | BUT | 33 C1 |
| RIVER BLVD | KER | 78 D3 |
| RIVER RD | BUT | 25 A3 |
| RIVER RD | COL | 33 A1 |
| RIVER RD | HUM | 15 D3 |
| RIVER RD | HUM | 16 D5 |
| RIVER RD | MAD | 49 C5 |
| RIVER RD | MAD | 57 B1 |
| RIVER RD | MCO | 47 D4 |
| RIVER RD | MON | 54 D4 |
| RIVER RD | RCO | U E4 |
| RIVER RD | RCO | 98 E3 |
| RIVER RD | RCO | 99 C4 |
| RIVER RD | SAC | M D1 |
| RIVER RD | SBD | 85 C5 |
| RIVER RD | SBD | 95 D1 |
| RIVER RD | SJCO | 47 C1 |
| RIVER RD | SLO | 66 A5 |
| RIVER RD | SLO | 76 A1 |
| RIVER RD | SLO | 76 C3 |
| RIVER RD | SON | 37 D2 |
| RIVER RD | STA | 47 B3 |
| RIVER RD | STA | 47 D1 |
| RIVER RD | TEH | 24 D1 |
| RIVER RD S | YOL | 39 D2 |
| RIVER ST | SC | 169 C1 |
| RIVER ST | SCR | 169 C1 |
| RIVER ST | SON | 31 C4 |
| RIVER BENCH RD | LAS | 20 E3 |
| RIVERBEND AV | FRCO | 57 E3 |
| RIVERCREST DR | HUM | 16 B5 |
| RIVEREDGE RD | SDCO | 106 C1 |
| RIVERFORD RD | SDCO | V E2 |
| RIVERFORD RD | SDCO | 106 E5 |
| RIVER GRADE RD | LACO | R D3 |
| RIV JCT FRMS RD | SJCO | 47 B2 |
| RIVER RANCH RD | SHA | 18 C3 |
| RIVER ROCK RD | TRI | 17 D1 |
| RIVERSIDE | WSH | 130 B3 |
| RIVERSIDE AV | MCO | 47 D4 |
| RIVERSIDE AV | RCO | 103 C5 |
| RIVERSIDE AV | SBD | 99 B1 |
| RIVERSIDE AV | SHA | 18 C3 |
| RIVERSIDE AV | TEH | 18 D5 |
| RIVERSIDE BLVD | SCTO | 137 B4 |
| RIVERSIDE BLVD | SAC | 39 D1 |
| RIVERSIDE DR | LA | 179 B5 |
| RIVERSIDE DR | LA | 182 D3 |
| RIVERSIDE DR | LACO | Q E3 |
| RIVERSIDE DR | LACO | Q C3 |
| RIVERSIDE DR | RED | 122 A1 |
| RIVERSIDE DR | RCO | 99 B4 |
| RIVERSIDE DR | SBD | U C3 |
| RIVERSIDE DR | SBD | 98 D2 |
| RIVERSIDE DR | SDCO | V E2 |
| RIVERSIDE DR | SDCO | 106 E5 |
| RIVERSIDE DR | SHA | 18 C2 |
| RIVERSIDE DR | SON | 132 B3 |
| RIVERSIDE DR | STA | 47 D2 |
| RIVERSIDE FRWY | ANA | 194 C1 |
| RIVERSIDE FRWY | ORA | 98 C3 |
| RIVERSIDE FRWY | ORA | T E1 |
| RIVERSIDE FRWY | RCO | 99 A3 |
| RIVERSIDE RD | HUM | 10 A5 |
| RIVERSIDE RD | INY | 51 D4 |
| RIVERSIDE RD | SBD | 92 C1 |
| RIVERSIDE ST | KER | 78 A2 |
| RIVERSIDE PK RD | HUM | 16 A3 |
| RIVER SPRINGS | MNO | 44 B5 |
| RIVERVIEW DR | SHA | 12 C5 |
| RIVER VIEW RD | SBD | 91 C1 |
| RIVERVIEW RD | TRI | 17 B2 |
| RIVER WAY DR | TUL | 68 B1 |
| RIVIERA | RED | 122 A5 |
| RIVIERA DR | SD | 212 B2 |
| RIVIERA DR | SDCO | V A3 |
| RIVIERA DR | SHA | 18 C2 |
| RIVIERA RD | SUT | 33 C1 |
| ROAD 1 | LAS | 20 B1 |
| ROAD 1 | MAD | 56 B1 |
| ROAD 4 | LAS | 20 B1 |
| ROAD 4 | MAD | 56 C1 |
| ROAD 5 | MAD | 56 C1 |
| ROAD 5 1/2 | MAD | 56 C2 |
| ROAD 6 | MAD | 56 C1 |
| ROAD 7 | MAD | 56 C1 |
| ROAD 8 | MAD | 56 C1 |
| ROAD 8 1/2 | MAD | 56 C3 |
| ROAD 9 | LAS | 20 B1 |
| ROAD 9 | MAD | 56 C1 |
| ROAD 10 | MAD | 56 D1 |
| ROAD 10 1/2 | MAD | 56 D2 |
| ROAD 11 | MAD | 56 D1 |
| ROAD 12 | MAD | 56 D1 |
| ROAD 12 | TUL | 57 E5 |
| ROAD 13 | MAD | 56 D1 |
| ROAD 14 | MAD | 56 D1 |
| ROAD 14 1/2 | MAD | 56 D1 |
| ROAD 15 | MAD | 56 D1 |
| ROAD 15 1/2 | MAD | 56 D1 |
| ROAD 16 | MAD | 56 D2 |
| ROAD 16 | TUL | 57 E5 |
| ROAD 16 1/2 | MAD | 56 D2 |
| ROAD 17 | MAD | 56 D2 |
| ROAD 18 | MAD | 56 E1 |
| ROAD 18 1/2 | MAD | 56 E1 |
| ROAD 19 | MAD | 56 E1 |
| ROAD 19 1/2 | MAD | 56 E2 |
| ROAD 20 | MAD | 56 E2 |
| ROAD 20 1/2 | MAD | 56 E2 |
| ROAD 21 | MAD | 56 E2 |
| ROAD 21 1/2 | MAD | 56 E2 |
| ROAD 22 | MAD | 48 E5 |
| ROAD 22 1/2 | MAD | 48 E5 |
| ROAD 23 | MAD | 48 E5 |
| ROAD 23 1/2 | MAD | 56 E1 |
| ROAD 24 | MAD | 56 E1 |
| ROAD 24 | TUL | 57 E5 |
| ROAD 24 | TUL | 67 E2 |
| ROAD 24 1/2 | MAD | 56 E2 |
| ROAD 24 1/2 | MAD | 57 A2 |
| ROAD 25 | LAS | 20 B1 |
| ROAD 25 | MAD | 57 A2 |
| ROAD 26 | MAD | 57 A2 |
| ROAD 26 1/2 | MAD | 57 A2 |
| ROAD 27 | MAD | 57 A1 |
| ROAD 28 | MAD | 57 A2 |
| ROAD 28 | TUL | 57 E5 |
| ROAD 28 | TUL | 67 E2 |
| ROAD 28 1/2 | MAD | 57 A2 |
| ROAD 29 | MAD | 49 B5 |
| ROAD 29 1/2 | MAD | 57 B2 |
| ROAD 30 | MAD | 57 B2 |
| ROAD 30 1/2 | MAD | 57 B2 |
| ROAD 31 | MAD | 57 B3 |

241
ROAD 31½ STREET INDEX SAN DIEGO FRWY




| STREET | CO. | PAGE & GRID |
|---|---|---|
| ROAD 31 1/2 | MAD | 57 B2 |
| ROAD 32 | MAD | 57 B2 |
| ROAD 32 | TUL | 57 E5 |
| ROAD 33 | MAD | 57 B2 |
| ROAD 33 1/2 | MAD | 57 B2 |
| ROAD 34 | MAD | 57 B3 |
| ROAD 34 | TUL | 67 E4 |
| ROAD 34 | TUL | 68 A4 |
| ROAD 34 1/2 | MAD | 57 B2 |
| ROAD 35 | MAD | 57 B2 |
| ROAD 36 | MAD | 57 B2 |
| ROAD 36 | TUL | 57 E5 |
| ROAD 37 | MAD | 57 B2 |
| ROAD 37 1/2 | MAD | 57 C2 |
| ROAD 38 | MAD | 57 C2 |
| ROAD 38 | TUL | 67 E4 |
| ROAD 39 | MAD | 57 C2 |
| ROAD 39 1/2 | MAD | 57 C2 |
| ROAD 40 | MAD | 57 C2 |
| ROAD 40 | TUL | 57 E5 |
| ROAD 40 1/2 | MAD | 57 C2 |
| ROAD 42 | TUL | 57 E4 |
| ROAD 44 | TUL | 57 E5 |
| ROAD 46 | TUL | 68 A4 |
| ROAD 48 | TUL | 57 E4 |
| ROAD 48 | TUL | 68 A1 |
| ROAD 50 | TUL | 68 A4 |
| ROAD 52 | TUL | 58 A4 |
| ROAD 52 | TUL | 68 A1 |
| ROAD 56 | TUL | 58 A5 |
| ROAD 56 | TUL | 68 A1 |
| ROAD 60 | TUL | 58 A5 |
| ROAD 60 | TUL | 68 A1 |
| ROAD 64 | TUL | 58 A4 |
| ROAD 64 | TUL | 68 A1 |
| ROAD 68 | TUL | 58 A5 |
| ROAD 68 | TUL | 68 A1 |
| ROAD 72 | TUL | 58 A4 |
| ROAD 74 | TUL | 58 A5 |
| ROAD 76 | TUL | 58 A5 |
| ROAD 76 | TUL | 68 A1 |
| ROAD 78 | TUL | 58 A4 |
| ROAD 80 | TUL | 58 A5 |
| ROAD 80 | TUL | 68 A2 |
| ROAD 84 | TUL | 58 A5 |
| ROAD 84 | TUL | 68 A1 |
| ROAD 88 | TUL | 58 A5 |
| ROAD 88 | TUL | 68 A3 |
| ROAD 92 | TUL | 68 A2 |
| ROAD 96 | TUL | 58 A4 |
| ROAD 100 | TUL | 58 B5 |
| ROAD 100 | TUL | 68 B1 |
| ROAD 104 | TUL | 58 B5 |
| ROAD 108 | TUL | 68 B1 |
| ROAD 109 | TUL | 58 B4 |
| ROAD 110 | MEN | 31 B3 |
| ROAD 112 | TUL | 58 B5 |
| ROAD 114 | TUL | 58 B4 |
| ROAD 116 | TUL | 58 B5 |
| ROAD 120 | TUL | 58 B5 |
| ROAD 124 | TUL | 58 B4 |
| ROAD 124 | TUL | 68 B2 |
| ROAD 128 | TUL | 58 B4 |
| ROAD 128 | TUL | 68 B3 |
| ROAD 132 | TUL | 58 B4 |
| ROAD 132 | TUL | 68 B1 |
| ROAD 136 | TUL | 58 B4 |
| ROAD 136 | TUL | 68 B3 |
| ROAD 138 | TUL | 68 B1 |
| ROAD 140 | TUL | 58 B4 |
| ROAD 140 | TUL | 68 B1 |
| ROAD 143 | TUL | 58 B4 |
| ROAD 144 | TUL | 58 B5 |
| ROAD 148 | TUL | 58 B5 |
| ROAD 148 | TUL | 68 B1 |
| ROAD 152 | TUL | 58 B4 |
| ROAD 152 | TUL | 68 B1 |
| ROAD 156 | TUL | 58 B5 |
| ROAD 156 | TUL | 68 B1 |
| ROAD 158 | TUL | 68 B1 |
| ROAD 164 | TUL | 68 C1 |
| ROAD 166 | TUL | 68 C1 |
| ROAD 168 | TUL | 68 C1 |
| ROAD 172 | TUL | 68 C2 |
| ROAD 176 | TUL | 68 C3 |
| ROAD 180 | TUL | 58 C5 |
| ROAD 180 | TUL | 68 C1 |
| ROAD 182 | TUL | 58 C5 |
| ROAD 182 | TUL | 68 C1 |
| ROAD 184 | TUL | 58 C5 |
| ROAD 188 | TUL | 68 C3 |
| ROAD 190 | TUL | 68 C1 |
| ROAD 192 | TUL | 68 C1 |
| ROAD 194 | TUL | 58 C5 |
| ROAD 196 | TUL | 58 C5 |
| ROAD 196 | TUL | 68 C1 |
| ROAD 197 | TUL | 58 C5 |
| ROAD 200 | TUL | 58 C5 |
| ROAD 200 | TUL | 68 C1 |
| ROAD 202 | TUL | 68 C3 |
| ROAD 204 | MAD | 57 C2 |
| ROAD 204 | TUL | 58 C5 |
| ROAD 205 | MAD | 57 C2 |
| ROAD 206 | TUL | 58 C5 |
| ROAD 208 | TUL | 58 C5 |
| ROAD 208 | TUL | 68 C1 |
| ROAD 209 | MAD | 57 C1 |
| ROAD 210 | TUL | 68 C1 |
| ROAD 212 | TUL | 58 C5 |
| ROAD 212 | TUL | 68 C1 |
| ROAD 216 | MAD | 57 D1 |
| ROAD 216 | TUL | 68 C2 |
| ROAD 220 | TUL | 58 D5 |
| ROAD 220 | TUL | 68 D1 |
| ROAD 222 | TUL | 68 D1 |
| ROAD 224 | TUL | 68 D4 |
| ROAD 228 | TUL | 68 D1 |
| ROAD 232 | TUL | 68 D2 |
| ROAD 235 | MAD | 50 A5 |
| ROAD 236 | TUL | 68 D1 |
| ROAD 240 | TUL | 68 D4 |
| ROAD 244 | TUL | 68 D1 |
| ROAD 248 | TUL | 68 D1 |
| ROAD 252 | TUL | 68 D2 |
| ROAD 256 | TUL | 68 D3 |
| ROAD 260 | TUL | 68 D2 |
| ROAD 264 | TUL | 68 D3 |
| ROAD 266 | TUL | 68 D4 |
| ROAD 268 | TUL | 68 D3 |
| ROAD 272 | TUL | 68 D4 |
| ROAD 276 | TUL | 68 D2 |
| ROAD 296 | TUL | 68 E3 |
| ROAD 320 | TUL | 68 E3 |
| ROAD 406 | MAD | 57 C1 |
| ROAD 434 | MAD | 49 D4 |
| ROAD 601 | MAD | 49 D4 |
| ROAD 602 | MAD | 57 B1 |
| ROAD 612 | MAD | 49 C5 |
| ROAD 810 | MAD | 49 C4 |
| ROAD 812 | MAD | 49 C4 |
| ROAN RD | CAL | 41 B4 |
| ROBB RD | RCO | 99 B4 |
| ROBBEN RD | SOL | 39 B3 |
| ROBBEN RD | SOL | 39 B2 |
| ROBBINS RD | SUT | 33 B3 |
| ROBBINS RNCH RD | NEV | 26 D5 |
| ROBBY RD | KER | 79 B4 |
| ROBERTA AV | LAKE | 7 C1 |
| ROBRTNO RIGHETI | SLO | 76 B4 |
| ROBERTS LN | KER | 78 D2 |
| ROBERTS RD | SJCO | 40 A5 |
| ROBERTS RD | SJCO | 47 A1 |
| ROBERTS RD | SON | 38 A3 |
| ROBERTS FRRY RD | STA | 48 B2 |
| ROBERTSON BLVD | BH | 183 D2 |
| ROBERTSON BLVD | CUL | 183 D5 |
| ROBERTSON BLVD | LA | 183 D4 |
| ROBERTSON BLVD | LACO | Q D4 |
| ROBERTSON BLVD | LACO | 183 D2 |
| ROBERTSON BLVD | MAD | 56 D1 |
| ROBERTS RES RD | MOD | 14 B3 |
| ROBIN AV | MCO | 47 E4 |
| ROBIN AV | MCO | 48 A4 |
| ROBINSON | SJCO | 47 C1 |
| ROBINSON RD | IMP | 109 A5 |
| ROBINSON RD | MCO | 48 C3 |
| ROBINSON RD | SOL | 39 B3 |
| ROBINSON CYN RD | MON | 54 B5 |
| ROBINSON CK RD | MEN | 31 A2 |
| ROBINSN MILL RD | BUT | 25 E5 |
| ROBNSN RCHRIA W | LAK | 31 D2 |
| ROBLAR AV | SB | 86 E3 |
| ROBLAR RD | SON | 37 D3 |
| ROBLEY POINT RD | BUT | 25 D2 |
| ROBS RD | MOD | 8 B3 |
| ROCA LN | SBD | 90 E2 |
| ROCK CANYON RD | LAS | 14 A3 |
| ROCK CANYON RD | RCO | 107 C1 |
| ROCK CREEK DR | BUT | 25 B2 |
| ROCK CREEK RD | CAL | 40 E4 |
| ROCK CREEK RD | CAL | 41 A4 |
| ROCK CREEK RD | ED | 34 E4 |
| ROCK CREEK RD | INY | 51 A3 |
| ROCK CREEK RD | MNO | 51 A3 |
| ROCK CREEK RD | NEV | 34 C1 |
| ROCK CREEK RD | SHA | 18 B2 |
| ROCK CREEK RD | SHA | 19 B3 |
| ROCK CK GRBG PT | MNO | 51 B3 |
| ROCKERFELLER RD | BUT | 25 E3 |
| ROCKHAVEN | SBD | 101 A2 |
| ROCKING CHR RD | SBD | 101 A2 |
| ROCKE RD | BUT | 25 C3 |
| ROCKLIN | PLA | 34 B4 |
| ROCK PILE RD | KER | 79 A4 |
| ROCKPILE RD | SON | 31 B4 |
| ROCKRIDGE RD | RCO | 100 A5 |
| ROCK RIVER RD | STA | 48 B1 |
| ROCK RIVER RD | TUO | 48 B1 |
| ROCK SPRINGS RD | SBD | 91 C4 |
| ROCKVILLE RD | SOL | L E1 |
| ROCKVILLE RD | SOL | 38 D3 |
| ROCKWOOD RD | IMP | 112 A4 |
| ROCKY CT | KER | 79 D5 |
| ROCKY LN | KER | 79 D3 |
| ROCKY RD | RCO | 99 B5 |
| ROCKY BAR RD | ED | 41 A1 |
| ROCKY BLUFF RD | RCO | 99 B4 |
| ROCKY CANYON RD | SLO | 76 B2 |
| ROCKYDALE RD | JOS | 2 C1 |
| ROCKY PT CMPGRD | PLU | 20 B5 |
| RODDEN RD | STA | 47 E1 |
| RODEO AV | TEH | 24 D1 |
| RODEO BLVD | LACO | Q D4 |
| RODEO RD | LA | 184 A5 |
| RODEO RD | SBD | 91 C2 |
| RODEO GULCH RD | SCR | 54 A2 |
| RODUNER RD | MCO | 48 B5 |
| ROEDING RD | STA | 47 D3 |
| ROEN RD | STA | 48 A2 |
| ROGERS RD | KER | 80 B3 |
| ROGERS RD | STA | 47 B3 |
| ROGERS CREEK RD | SIS | 10 E1 |
| ROHNERVILLE RD | HUM | 15 E2 |
| ROLAND DR | SIS | 4 C5 |
| ROLINDA AV | FRCO | 57 B5 |
| ROLLING HLLS RD | LACO | S B2 |
| ROLLINS RD | MLBR | 144 E5 |
| ROLLINS LAKE RD | PLA | 34 D2 |
| ROMEL ST | CAL | 41 A4 |
| ROMERO | MCO | 55 C1 |
| ROMERO RD | MCO | 47 C5 |
| ROMERO CYN RD | SB | 87 D4 |
| ROMERS DAIRY RD | MEN | 31 B2 |
| ROMIE LN E | SAL | 171 C5 |
| RONNIE AV | KER | 79 B5 |
| ROOP RD | SCL | P E5 |
| ROOP RD | SCL | 54 D1 |
| ROOSEVELT RD | MCO | 48 C5 |
| ROOST AV | KER | 79 B4 |
| ROOT AV | KER | 78 B1 |
| ROOT RD | RCO | 99 E5 |
| ROOT RD | STA | 47 D2 |
| ROSA RD | MCO | 47 D4 |
| ROSAMOND BLVD | KER | 89 D1 |
| ROSAMOND BLVD | KER | 90 B1 |
| ROSAMND HLLS RD | RCO | 107 C1 |
| ROSAMUND BLVD | KER | 80 C5 |
| ROSARITA DR | SAL | 171 D2 |
| ROSCOE BLVD | LACO | 97 C1 |
| ROSCOE RD | HUM | 15 E4 |
| ROSCOE RD | STA | 47 E2 |
| ROSE AV | FRCO | 56 E4 |
| ROSE AV | FRCO | 57 C4 |
| ROSE AV | LA | 187 A2 |
| ROSE AV | MCO | 47 E4 |
| ROSE AV | MCO | 48 B4 |
| ROSE AV | VEN | 88 B5 |
| ROSE AV | VEN | 96 B1 |
| ROSE DR | ORA | T D1 |
| ROSE RD | KER | 79 E2 |
| ROSE RD | KER | 80 A2 |
| ROSE RD | SIS | 5 D2 |
| ROSE RD | TRI | 17 B1 |
| ROSE RD | YOL | 39 D2 |
| ROSE ST | SDCO | 106 D3 |
| ROSEBURG AV | MDO | 162 A1 |
| ROSECRANS | LACO | 97 D3 |
| ROSECRANS AV | ELS | 189 B5 |
| ROSECRANS AV | MB | 189 B5 |
| ROSECRANS AV | ORA | 98 B3 |
| ROSECRANS AV | ORA | T C1 |
| ROSECRANS BLVD | SDCO | 111 C1 |
| ROSECRANS ST | SDCO | V A3 |
| ROSE GARDEN RD | MCO | 47 C5 |
| ROSEDALE HWY | KER | 78 C3 |
| ROSE HILLS RD | LACO | R D4 |
| ROSE LAWN AV | MCO | 47 E3 |
| ROSELAWN AV | MDO | 162 A5 |
| ROSE LAWN AV | STA | 47 E3 |
| ROSELLE AV | STA | 47 D2 |
| ROSE MARIE LN | S | 160 A1 |
| ROSEMARY RD | SB | 86 C1 |
| ROSEMEAD BLVD | LACO | 98 A2 |
| ROSEMEAD BLVD | LACO | R C5 |
| ROSE MINE RD | SBD | 92 B5 |
| ROSEMORE AV | STA | 47 C2 |
| ROSER RD | TEH | 24 C2 |
| ROSES RD | LACO | R C3 |
| ROSE VALLEY RD | VEN | 88 B3 |
| ROSEWOOD AV | VEN | 96 C1 |
| ROSEWOOD BLVD | KER | 80 B5 |
| ROSITA ST | LA | 178 B5 |
| ROSS AV | EC | 217 A4 |
| ROSS RD | IMP | 111 E3 |
| ROSS RD | IMP | 112 D5 |
| ROSSI ST | SAL | 171 C3 |
| ROSSMORE AV | LA | 184 D2 |
| ROSSMORE AV | LACO | Q D4 |
| ROSY RIDGE RD | RCO | 107 B1 |
| ROUGH&READY RD | NEV | 34 B1 |
| ROULTS RD | MNO | 51 B3 |
| ROUND HOUSE RD | MAD | 49 D4 |
| ROUND MTN LKOUT | SIS | 13 D1 |
| ROUND MTN RD | KER | 78 D2 |
| ROUND MTN RD | MNO | 51 B2 |
| ROUND ROBIN DR | RCO | 100 B4 |
| ROUND VALLEY RD | SBD | 100 B1 |
| ROUND VALLEY RD | TEH | 23 D2 |
| ROUND VLY RD N | INY | 51 B4 |
| ROUND VLY RD S | INY | 51 C4 |
| RND VLY TUNGSTN | INY | 51 C4 |
| ROUNDY RD | TRI | 11 D5 |
| ROUNDY RD | TRI | 17 D1 |
| ROUSE AV | STA | 162 A5 |
| ROUSE RD | RCO | 99 C4 |
| RT OLYMPC TORCH | LAS | 20 D2 |
| ROUTE 4 FRWY | CC | 154 D3 |
| ROUTE 4 FRWY | M | 154 D3 |
| ROUTE 47 FRWY | LB | 191 E2 |
| ROUTE 47 FRWY | LB | 192 A2 |
| ROUTE 47 FRWY | LA | 191 E2 |
| ROUTE 47 FRWY | LA | 192 A2 |
| ROUTE 47 FRWY | LACO | 97 E4 |
| ROUTE 47 FRWY | LACO | S D2 |
| ROUTE 52 FRWY | SD | 211 E3 |
| ROUTE 94 FRWY | SD | 216 C3 |
| ROUTE 101 FRWY | STB | 173 D5 |
| ROUTE 101 FRWY | SB | 86 D4 |
| ROUTE 101 FRWY | SB | 87 D4 |
| ROUTE 101 FRWY | SMA | 173 C1 |
| ROWDY CREEK RD | DN | 1 E3 |
| ROWENA AV | LA | 182 D3 |
| ROWLEE RD | KER | 77 E2 |
| ROWLEE RD | KER | 78 A2 |
| ROWLES RD | TEH | 24 E2 |
| ROXBURY DR | SIS | 3 C4 |
| ROXBURY RD | MCO | 56 B1 |
| ROXFORD ST | LACO | 89 C5 |
| ROXFORD ST | LACO | Q B1 |
| ROYAL AV | VEN | 88 E5 |
| ROYAL AV | VEN | 89 A5 |
| ROYAL OAKS DR | LACO | R D3 |
| ROY JONES RD | SIS | 4 B3 |
| ROYO RNCHERO DR | SUT | 33 C2 |
| RUBIDOUX BLVD | RCO | 99 B2 |
| RUBLE RD | STA | 47 C3 |
| RUCKER AV | SCL | P E5 |
| RUCKER AV | SCL | 54 D1 |
| RUDD RD | KER | 78 C3 |
| RUDDICK | MEN | 31 B2 |
| RUDGEAR RD | CC | M A4 |
| RUDNICK RD | KER | 80 C4 |
| RUDOLPH DR | KER | 79 C4 |
| RUDOLPH RD | INY | 51 D3 |
| RUEGGER RD | IMP | 109 A3 |
| RUFF LN | GLE | 24 E5 |
| RUFFIN RD | SDCO | V C2 |
| RUFFIN RD | SDCO | 106 D5 |
| RUGGED TRAIL RD | RCO | 107 C1 |
| RUMBLE RD | STA | 47 C2 |
| RUNGE RD | SOL | 39 C2 |
| RUSH ST | RCO | 107 C1 |
| RUSH CREEK DR | TRI | 11 D5 |
| RUSH CREEK RD | MNO | 43 C5 |
| RUSH CREEK RD | TRI | 17 D1 |
| RUSH CK SHORTCT | TRI | 17 D1 |
| RUSH CK CAMP RD | TRI | 11 D5 |
| RUSHNG HILL LKT | TUO | 48 B1 |
| RUSS LN | HUM | 15 D2 |
| RUSSEL AV | KER | 79 A4 |
| RUSSELL AV | FRCO | 56 A3 |
| RUSSELL BLVD | DVS | 136 B3 |
| RUSSELL BLVD | YOL | 38 E1 |
| RUSSELL BLVD | YOL | 39 A1 |
| RUSSELL RD | CAL | 41 A3 |
| RUSSELL RD | SAC | 39 D3 |
| RUSSELL RD | STA | 47 B2 |
| RUSSELL RD | TEH | 18 C3 |
| RUTH AV | BLMT | 145 C4 |
| RUTH DUMP RD | TRI | 17 A4 |
| RUTHERFORD | NAPA | 29 D3 |
| RUTHERFORD RD | IMP | 109 A4 |
| RUTH HILL RD | FRCO | 58 C3 |
| RUTH HILL RD | FRCO | 58 B3 |
| RUTH ZENIA RD | TRI | 16 E4 |
| RYAN AV | KER | 80 A4 |
| RYAN RD | LAS | 21 B3 |
| RYAN RD | SLO | 76 C2 |
| RYAN CREEK RD | MEN | 23 A5 |
| RYE CANYON RD | LACO | 89 B4 |
| RYE GRASS SWALE | MOD | 8 A1 |
| RYE GRASS SWALE | MOD | 14 E1 |
| RYER RD E | SOL | 39 D3 |
| RYER ISLAND RD | SOL | M D1 |
| S | | |
| S ST | EUR | 121 E2 |
| SABINANA RD | YUB | 33 E1 |
| SABODAN ST | KER | 78 D5 |
| SACHREITER RD | COL | 33 A2 |
| SACRAMENTO AV | BUT | 25 A3 |
| SACRAMENTO AV | C | 124 A4 |
| SACRAMENTO AV | FRCO | 56 D4 |
| SACRAMENTO AV | SUT | 33 D3 |
| SACRAMENTO BLVD | SCTO | 137 E5 |
| SACRAMENTO DR | SHA | 18 C2 |
| SACRAMNTO FWY N | SCTO | 137 D1 |
| SACRAMENTO ST | AUB | 126 C4 |
| SACRAMENTO ST | PLA | 34 D1 |
| SACRAMENTO ST | PLCV | 138 C3 |
| SACRAMENTO ST | VAL | 134 B2 |
| SACRMNTO VLY RD | SUT | 33 C3 |
| SACRMNTO VLY BL | SUT | 33 C4 |
| SADDLE CT | KER | 79 C5 |
| SADDLEBACK RD | SIE | 26 D4 |
| SADDLEHORN RD | SBD | 84 C3 |
| SADDLE PEAK RD | LACO | 97 B2 |
| SADDLE TRAIL RD | SHA | 18 B3 |
| SADDLE VIEW CT | SHA | 13 E4 |
| SAGE AV | SBD | 100 D1 |
| SAGE RD | HUM | 15 D2 |
| SAGE RD | RCO | 99 E4 |
| SAGEBRUSH LN | SIS | 4 E3 |
| SAGE CANYON RD | KER | 80 B1 |
| SAGE FLATS DR | INY | 70 B2 |
| SAGE HEN RD | MNO | 51 A2 |
| SAGE HEN RD | NEV | 27 D5 |
| SAGE HN MDWS RD | MNO | 43 E5 |
| SAGE HN MDWS RD | MNO | 50 E1 |
| SAGE HN MDWS RD | MNO | 51 A1 |
| SAGEHORN RD | MOD | 7 D3 |
| SAGELAND CT | KER | 79 B4 |
| SAGE VALLEY RD | LAS | 21 D5 |
| SAGINAW AV | FRCO | 57 E4 |
| SAHARA AV | LV | 209 A4 |
| SAHARA AV E | CLK | 74 D2 |
| SAHARA AV W | CLK | 74 C2 |
| ST CATHERINE WY | AVLN | 105 B4 |
| ST FRANCIS AV | STA | 47 C2 |
| ST GEORGE ST | LA | 182 D3 |
| ST HELENA HWY | NAPA | 29 D4 |
| ST HELENA RD | SON | 38 A1 |
| ST JAMES ST | SJ | 152 C3 |
| ST JOHN RD | TRI | 16 E2 |
| ST JOHN LOOP RD | TRI | 16 E2 |
| ST LOUIS AV | KER | 80 A4 |
| ST LOUIS RD | HUM | 9 E5 |
| ST LOUIS RD | HUM | 10 A5 |
| ST LOUIS RD | PLU | 26 C3 |
| ST MARYS AV | TEH | 18 D5 |
| ST MARYS RD | CC | L E4 |
| ST MARYS RD | CC | M A4 |
| ST MARYS RD | CC | 45 E1 |
| SALE LN | TEH | 18 D5 |
| SALEM AV | KIN | 67 E3 |
| SALEM RD | SOL | 39 B3 |
| SALINAS RD | MON | 54 C2 |
| SALINAS ST | STB | 174 E3 |
| SALINE VLY ALT | INY | 70 E1 |
| SALINE VLY RD | INY | 60 C3 |
| SALINE VLY RD | INY | 60 D5 |
| SALMON CREEK RD | HUM | 16 B4 |
| SALMON FALLS RD | ED | 34 C5 |
| SALMON LAKE RD | SIE | 26 E3 |
| SALMON LAKE RD | SIE | 27 A3 |
| SALMON RIVER RD | SIS | 10 E2 |
| SALMON RIVER RD | SIS | 11 A2 |
| SALT RD N | SHA | 12 C4 |
| SALT CREEK RD | MCO | 55 D2 |
| SALT CREEK RD | SHA | 12 D5 |
| SALTDALE RD | KER | 80 C3 |
| SALTON DR | IMP | 108 C2 |
| SALTON RD | SBD | 80 E5 |
| SALTON RD | SBD | 81 A5 |
| SALTON BAY DR | IMP | 108 C2 |
| SALTON VIEW RD | RCO | 101 B3 |
| SALT POOL RD | INY | 72 A1 |
| SALT SPG VLY RD | CAL | 40 E4 |
| SALT SPG VLY RD | CAL | 41 A4 |
| SALTUS RD | SBD | 93 E3 |
| SALTUS RD | SBD | 94 A3 |
| SALVADORI RD | SIS | 4 B5 |
| SAM ALLEY RIDGE | LAK | 31 D2 |
| SAMEL DR | SBD | 100 D2 |
| SAMPLE RD | FRCO | 57 E2 |
| SAMPSON ST | SD | 216 B5 |
| SAMSON AV | TEH | 18 D5 |
| SAMSON AV | TEH | 24 D2 |
| SAN ANDREAS RD | SCR | 54 B2 |
| SAN ANDREAS RD | SBD | 100 E2 |
| SAN ANDREAS ST | STB | 174 A3 |
| SN ANTONE CP RD | CAL | 41 B4 |
| SAN ANTONIO AV | CAR | 53 D5 |
| SAN ANTONIO AV | ONT | 204 A3 |
| SAN ANTONIO AV | SBD | 98 D1 |
| SAN ANTONIO AV | UPL | 204 A3 |
| SN ANTONIO AV N | CAR | 168 B4 |
| SAN ANTONIO DR | LACO | S D2 |
| SAN ANTONIO DR | LACO | T A1 |
| SAN ANTONIO RD | MON | 65 D5 |
| SAN ANTONIO RD | SB | 86 B2 |
| SAN ANTONIO RD | SCL | N E3 |
| SAN ANTONIO RD | SCL | P A3 |
| SAN ANTONIO RD | SCL | P E3 |
| SAN ANTONIO RD | SCL | 45 E4 |
| SAN ANTONIO ST | SJ | 152 E3 |
| SAN ANTONIO VLY | SCL | 46 D4 |
| SAN BENACIO RD | MON | 54 C4 |
| SAN BENITO AV | FRCO | 56 D4 |
| SAN BENITO AV | TEH | 18 D5 |
| SN BERNARDNO AV | FRCO | 56 C3 |
| SN BERNARDNO AV | SBD | 98 D2 |
| SN BERNARDNO FY | CLA | 203 A3 |
| SN BERNARDNO FY | LA | 186 D3 |
| SN BERNARDNO FY | LACO | 98 B2 |
| SN BERNARDNO FY | LACO | R D4 |
| SN BERNARDNO FY | MTCL | 203 A3 |
| SN BERNARDNO FY | ONT | 203 A3 |
| SN BERNARDNO FY | ONT | 204 B3 |
| SN BERNARDNO FY | SBD | 98 E2 |
| SN BERNARDNO FY | UPL | 204 B3 |
| SN BERNARDNO RD | LACO | U A2 |
| SN BERNARDNO RD | SBD | 80 E1 |
| SN BERNARDNO RD | UPL | 204 C2 |
| SN BERNARDNO ST | MTCL | 203 B3 |
| SN BERNARDNO ST | POM | 203 C3 |
| SN BERNARDNO ST | SBD | U D2 |
| SN BERNARDNO CK | SLO | 75 E3 |
| SN BERNARDNO CK | SLO | 76 A3 |
| SANBORN RD | SUT | 33 C2 |
| SANBORN RD S | SAL | 171 E5 |
| SAN BRUNO AV | SBR | 144 B3 |
| SAN BRUNO AV | SMCO | 45 B2 |
| SAN CARLOS AV | SMCO | N D2 |
| SAN CARLOS AV | SMCO | 45 D3 |
| SAN CARLOS RD | MCO | 55 D2 |
| SAN CARLOS ST | CAR | 168 B4 |
| SAN CARLOS ST | SJ | 151 D5 |
| SAN CARLOS ST | SJ | 152 C4 |
| SAN CARLOS ST | SCL | 151 D5 |
| SANCHES RD | MCO | 47 C4 |
| SANCHEZ RD | MON | 54 E5 |
| SAND CANYON AV | ORA | 98 C4 |
| SAND CANYON AV | ORA | T E4 |
| SAND CANYON RD | INY | 51 C4 |
| SAND CANYON RD | KER | 70 C5 |
| SAND CANYON RD | KER | 79 D4 |
| SAND CANYON RD | LACO | 89 C4 |
| SAND CANYON RD | SBD | 99 D2 |
| SAND CREEK RD | COL | 32 D3 |
| SAND CREEK RD | FRCO | 58 B4 |
| SAND CREEK RD | TUL | 58 B4 |
| SAND CREST DR | IMP | 108 C2 |
| SANDERS RD | STA | 47 C3 |
| SANDERS RD | SUT | 33 C2 |
| SANDERSON AV | RCO | 99 E4 |
| SAND FLAT RD | SIS | 12 D2 |
| SAND FLAT CTOFF | MNO | 50 E1 |
| SAND HILL RD | SMCO | N D3 |
| SAND HILL RD | SMCO | 45 D4 |
| SANDIA CREEK DR | SDCO | 106 C1 |
| SAN DIEGO AV | FRCO | 56 C4 |
| SAN DIEGO AV | SD | 213 B5 |
| SAN DIEGO FRWY | CUL | 188 A1 |
| SAN DIEGO FRWY | HAW | 189 E3 |
| SAN DIEGO FRWY | ING | 188 D4 |
| SAN DIEGO FRWY | IRV | 198 E5 |
| SAN DIEGO FRWY | LA | 180 C2 |
| SAN DIEGO FRWY | LA | 188 D4 |
| SAN DIEGO FRWY | LACO | 97 C2 |
| SAN DIEGO FRWY | LACO | 180 C2 |
| SAN DIEGO FRWY | LACO | 189 E3 |
| SAN DIEGO FRWY | LACO | S B1 |
| SAN DIEGO FRWY | ORA | 98 D4 |
| SAN DIEGO FRWY | ORA | 197 A3 |
| SAN DIEGO FRWY | ORA | 198 A4 |
| SAN DIEGO FRWY | ORA | 202 C4 |
| SAN DIEGO FRWY | ORA | T B3 |
| SAN DIEGO FRWY | SD | 211 D1 |
| SAN DIEGO FRWY | SD | 212 E3 |
| SAN DIEGO FRWY | SD | 215 D3 |
| SAN DIEGO FRWY | SD | 216 A3 |
| SAN DIEGO FRWY | SDCO | V A2 |
| SAN DIEGO FRWY | SDCO | 106 B3 |
| SAN DIEGO FRWY | SDCO | 111 D2 |
| SAN DIEGO FRWY | SJC | 202 C4 |


STREETS

| STREET | CO. | PAGE & GRID |
|---|---|---|
| SAN DIEGO ST | KER | 78 B2 |
| SN DIEGO MSN RD | SD | 214 D2 |
| SAN DIMAS AV | LACO | U B2 |
| SN DIMAS CYN RD | LACO | U B1 |
| SANDMOUND BLVD | CC | 39 D5 |
| SAN DOMINGO RD | CAL | 41 B4 |
| SAND RIDGE RD | ED | 34 E5 |
| SAND RIDGE RD | ED | 40 E1 |
| SANDRINI RD | KER | 78 D4 |
| SANDROCK RD | SD | 214 B1 |
| SANDROCK RD | SDCO | V B3 |
| SANDROCK RD | SDCO | 106 D5 |
| SAND SLOUGH RD | MCO | 47 E5 |
| SAND SLOUGH RD | MCO | 48 A5 |
| SANDY AV | KER | 80 C1 |
| SANDY DR | RCO | 107 C1 |
| SANDY RD | MON | 66 B4 |
| SANDY ST | KER | 80 C1 |
| SANDY HILLS RD | RCO | 107 C1 |
| SANDY MUSH RD | MCO | 48 B5 |
| SANDY PRAIRIE | HUM | 15 E2 |
| SAN FELIPE RD | SBT | 54 E2 |
| SAN FELIPE RD | SBT | 55 A2 |
| SAN FELIPE RD | SDCO | 107 C2 |
| SAN FELIPE RD | SCL | P C3 |
| SAN FELIPE RD | SCL | 46 C4 |
| SAN FERNANDO BL | BUR | 179 C1 |
| SAN FERNANDO BL | LA | 179 C1 |
| SAN FERNANDO RD | BUR | 179 E2 |
| SAN FERNANDO RD | GLEN | 182 D1 |
| SAN FERNANDO RD | LA | 186 D1 |
| SAN FERNANDO RD | LACO | 89 B5 |
| SAN FERNANDO RD | LACO | 89 C5 |
| SAN FERNANDO RD | LACO | 97 E1 |
| SAN FERNANDO RD | LACO | Q C1 |
| SANFORD RD | SON | 37 D2 |
| SANFORD RCH RD | MEN | 31 B2 |
| SN FRANCSQT CYN | LACO | 89 B4 |
| SAN GABRIEL BL | LACO | 98 A2 |
| SAN GABRIEL BL | LACO | R C3 |
| SAN GABRIEL FWY | LACO | 98 A3 |
| SAN GABRIEL FWY | LACO | S E1 |
| SAN GABRIEL RD | LACO | R E3 |
| SAN GABRIEL CYN | LACO | 98 C1 |
| SN GABRL CYN RD | LACO | R E3 |
| SN GABRL RV FWY | LACO | T A1 |
| SN GABRL RIV PY | LACO | R C4 |
| SAN GORGONIO AV | RCO | 100 A3 |
| SN GUILLERMO RD | VEN | 88 B2 |
| SANHEDRIN RD | GLE | 24 A4 |
| SAN IGNACIO RD | RCO | 99 E5 |
| SANITARIUM RD | NAPA | 29 C2 |
| SAN JACINTO RD | RCO | 99 C4 |
| SAN JACINTO ST | SBD | 100 C2 |
| SAN JACINTO RDG | RCO | 100 A4 |
| SAN JOAQUIN AV | FRCO | 66 D3 |
| SAN JOAQUIN AV | LAK | 32 A3 |
| SAN JOAQUIN RD | ORA | T E3 |
| SAN JOAQUIN ST | S | 160 D3 |
| SN JQUIN HLS RD | NB | 200 A4 |
| SAN JOSE BLVD | MAR | 38 A4 |
| SAN JOSE RD | CLO | 32 E2 |
| SN JOSE AVNALES | SLO | 76 D3 |
| SN JOSE L PANZA | SLO | 76 C3 |
| SN JOSE-STA MAR | SLO | 76 B3 |
| SN JS ST MAR LK | SLO | 76 C3 |
| SN JS ST MAR MT | SLO | 76 D3 |
| SAN JUAN AV | SAC | 34 A5 |
| SAN JUAN HWY | SBT | 54 D2 |
| SAN JUAN RD | MCO | 56 B1 |
| SAN JUAN RD | MON | 54 C2 |
| SAN JUAN CYN RD | SBT | 54 D3 |
| SAN JUSTO RD | SBT | 54 D3 |
| SANKEY RD | SUT | 33 D4 |
| SAN LUCAS RD | MON | 65 C3 |
| SAN LUIS BAY DR | SLO | 76 A4 |
| SAN LUISITO CK | SLO | 75 E3 |
| SAN LUISITO CK | SLO | 76 A3 |
| SAN MARCOS RD | SLO | 76 A1 |
| SAN MARCOS RD | SB | 87 B4 |
| SN MARCOS PS RD | SB | 87 B3 |
| SAN MARIN DR | MAR | L A2 |
| SAN MARTIN AV | SCL | P E5 |
| SAN MARTIN AV | SCL | 54 D1 |
| SN MARTNZ CHQT | LACO | 89 A4 |
| SN MARTNZ GD CN | LACO | 89 A4 |
| SAN MATEO AV | FRCO | 56 D5 |
| SAN MATEO AV | SBR | 144 B1 |
| SAN MATEO AV | SSF | 144 B1 |
| SAN MATEO RD | SDCO | 105 E1 |
| SAN MATEO ST | SBD | 99 C2 |
| SAN MIGUEL | CC | 45 E1 |
| SAN MIGUEL AV | SAL | 171 C5 |
| SAN MIGUEL DR | CC | M A4 |
| SAN MIGUEL DR | NB | 200 C5 |
| SN MGUEL CYN RD | MON | 54 C3 |
| SN MIGUELITO RD | SB | 86 B3 |
| SAN PABLO AV | ALA | L D4 |
| SAN PABLO AV | ALA | 45 D1 |
| SAN PABLO AV | CC | L C3 |
| SAN PABLO AV | CC | 38 C5 |
| SAN PABLO AV | ELC | 155 E4 |
| SAN PABLO AV | O | 157 E2 |
| SAN PABLO AV | R | 155 D2 |
| SAN PABLO AV | SP | 155 B1 |
| SN PABLO DAM RD | CC | L D3 |
| SN PABLO DAM RD | CC | 38 C5 |
| SN PABLO DAM RD | SP | 155 C1 |
| SAN PASQUAL RD | SDCO | 106 D3 |
| SAN PASQUAL RD | SB | 86 B3 |
| SAN PASQUAL VLY | SDCO | 106 E3 |
| SAN PEDRO AV | SBD | 84 C3 |
| SAN PEDRO RD N | MAR | L B3 |
| SAN PEDRO RD N | MAR | 38 B5 |
| SAN PEDRO RD N | MAR | 139 C2 |
| SAN PEDRO RD N | SR | 139 C2 |
| SAN PEDRO ST | LA | 185 E5 |

| STREET | CO. | PAGE & GRID |
|---|---|---|
| SAN PEDRO ST | LA | 186 A4 |
| SAN PEDRO ST | LACO | S C1 |
| SAN RAFAEL AV | PAS | 190 A4 |
| SAN RAFAEL DR | RCO | 100 C3 |
| SN RAMON VLY BL | CC | M B5 |
| SN RAMON VLY BL | CC | 46 A2 |
| SANS BAKER RD | FRCO | 58 C3 |
| SN SIMEON CK RD | SLO | 75 C1 |
| SANTA ANA AV | CM | 199 C3 |
| SANTA ANA AV | NB | 199 C3 |
| SANTA ANA AV | ORA | T C4 |
| SANTA ANA AV | ORA | 199 E1 |
| SANTA ANA AV | SBD | 99 A2 |
| SANTA ANA BLVD | SA | 196 A4 |
| SANTA ANA FRWY | ANA | 193 D4 |
| SANTA ANA FRWY | LA | 186 D3 |
| SANTA ANA FRWY | LACO | 98 A2 |
| SANTA ANA FRWY | LACO | T B1 |
| SANTA ANA FRWY | ORA | 98 A2 |
| SANTA ANA FRWY | ORA | T B1 |
| SANTA ANA FRWY | SA | 196 B2 |
| SANTA ANA RD | VEN | 88 A5 |
| SANTA ANA ST | ANA | 193 B2 |
| STA ANA CYN RD | ORA | 98 C3 |
| STA ANA CYN RD | ORA | T E2 |
| STA ANA VLY RD | SBT | 55 A3 |
| SANTA ANITA AV | LACO | 98 B2 |
| SANTA ANITA AV | LACO | R C4 |
| SANTA ANITA AV | LACO | R D2 |
| SANTA ANITA RD | SBT | 55 B3 |
| STA BARBARA ST | SDCO | 111 C1 |
| STA BARBARA ST | STB | 174 B2 |
| STA BARBARA ST | SDCO | V A3 |
| STA BARB CYN RD | SB | 87 D1 |
| SANTA CLARA | A | 159 A1 |
| SANTA CLARA AV | O | 158 B2 |
| SANTA CLARA AV | SA | 195 E2 |
| SANTA CLARA AV | SA | 196 A2 |
| SANTA CLARA AV | VEN | 88 B5 |
| SANTA CLARA ST | SJ | 152 C3 |
| SANTA CLARA ST | SCL | P C3 |
| SANTA CLARA ST | SCL | 46 B4 |
| SANTA CLARA ST | VAL | 134 B4 |
| SANTA CLARA WY | SM | 145 C3 |
| SANTA CRUZ AV | SCL | P A4 |
| STA CRZ GUN CLB | MCO | 55 E2 |
| STA CRZ GUN CLB | MCO | 56 A2 |
| SANTA FE | MCO | 48 C4 |
| SANTA FE AV | KIN | 67 E3 |
| SANTA FE AV | LB | 192 B2 |
| SANTA FE AV | LA | 186 C5 |
| SANTA FE AV | LACO | R A4 |
| SANTA FE AV | LACO | S D2 |
| SANTA FE AV | MCO | 48 D5 |
| SANTA FE AV | SBD | 81 B5 |
| SANTA FE AV | SDCO | 106 C2 |
| SANTA FE AV | SJCO | 47 D1 |
| SANTA FE AV | STA | 47 D2 |
| SANTA FE BLVD | MAD | 57 B2 |
| SANTA FE DR | MCO | 48 A3 |
| SANTA FE DR | SDCO | 106 C4 |
| SANTA FE GRADE | FRCO | 56 C3 |
| SANTA FE GRADE | MCO | 47 D4 |
| SANTA FE RD | SBD | 92 B4 |
| SANTA FE ST | SBD | 92 A1 |
| SANTA FE WY | KER | 78 B2 |
| STA FE FIRE RD | SBD | 91 A5 |
| STA FE SPGS RD | LACO | R C5 |
| SANTA INEZ AV | SMCO | 45 C3 |
| SANTA ISABEL | CM | 199 D1 |
| SANTA LUCIA | SBR | 144 B4 |
| SANTA LUCIA AV | CAR | 168 B4 |
| SANTA LUCIA AV | MCO | 55 D1 |
| SANTA LUCIA RD | SLO | 76 A2 |
| SANTA MARIA WY | SB | 86 C1 |
| STA MAR MESA RD | SB | 86 C1 |
| SANTA MONICA BL | BH | 183 A2 |
| SANTA MONICA BL | LA | 180 C3 |
| SANTA MONICA BL | LA | 181 C5 |
| SANTA MONICA BL | LA | 182 A5 |
| SANTA MONICA BL | LA | 183 A2 |
| SANTA MONICA BL | LACO | 97 D2 |
| SANTA MONICA BL | LACO | 181 C5 |
| SANTA MONICA BL | LACO | 183 A2 |
| SANTA MONICA BL | SMON | 180 C3 |
| SANTA MONICA FY | LA | 184 A4 |
| SANTA MONICA FY | LA | 185 A4 |
| SANTA MONICA FY | LA | 186 A4 |
| SANTA MONICA FY | LACO | 97 C2 |
| SANTA MONICA FY | LACO | Q C4 |
| SANTA MONICA FY | SMON | 180 B5 |
| SANTA PAULA FWY | VEN | 88 B5 |
| SANTA PAULA ST | VEN | 88 C5 |
| STA RITA GRADE | MCO | 56 B1 |
| SANTA RITA RD | ALA | M B5 |
| SANTA RITA RD | ALA | 46 B2 |
| STA RITA OLD CK | SLO | 75 E2 |
| SANTA ROSA AV | SON | 37 E2 |
| SANTA ROSA AV | STR | 131 D4 |
| SANTA ROSA RD | INY | 60 D5 |
| SANTA ROSA RD | RCO | 99 B4 |
| SANTA ROSA RD | SBD | 91 D4 |
| SANTA ROSA RD | SB | 86 C3 |
| SANTA ROSA RD | VEN | 88 D5 |
| SANTA ROSA ST | SNLO | 172 C2 |
| STA ROSA CK RD | SLO | 75 C2 |
| STA ROSA MTN TK | RCO | 100 D5 |
| SANTA TERESA BL | SCL | P C4 |
| SANTA TERESA BL | SCL | 46 B5 |
| SANTA TERESA BL | SCL | 54 D2 |
| SANTA YSABEL RD | SLO | 75 E3 |
| SANTIAGO BLVD | OR | 194 E2 |
| SANTIAGO BLVD | ORA | 98 C3 |
| SANTIAGO BLVD | ORA | T E2 |
| SANTIAGO CYN RD | ORA | 98 D3 |
| SANTIAGO CYN RD | ORA | T E2 |
| SN TIMTEO CY RD | RCO | 99 D2 |

| STREET | CO. | PAGE & GRID |
|---|---|---|
| SN TIMTEO CY RD | SBD | 99 D2 |
| SAN TOMAS EXPWY | SJ | 150 E5 |
| SAN TOMAS EXPWY | SCL | P B3 |
| SAN TOMAS EXPWY | SCLR | 150 E2 |
| SAN TOMAS EXPWY | SCLR | 151 A1 |
| SAN TOMAS EXPWY | SCL | 46 A5 |
| SANTOS AV | SJCO | 47 C1 |
| SANTOS RD | SB | 86 D3 |
| SANTOS ST | SB | 86 B1 |
| SAN VICENTE BL | LA | 180 A3 |
| SAN VICENTE BL | LA | 183 E2 |
| SAN VICENTE BL | LA | 184 B3 |
| SAN VICENTE BL | LACO | 97 C2 |
| SAN VICENTE BL | LACO | Q D4 |
| SAN VICENTE RD | MON | 55 A5 |
| SAN VICENTE RD | MON | 65 A1 |
| SAN VICENTE RD | SDCO | 107 A4 |
| SAN VINCENTE AV | SAL | 171 B4 |
| SAPAQUE RD | MON | 65 C5 |
| SARATOGA AV | KER | 80 E1 |
| SARATOGA AV | SJ | 150 E5 |
| SARATOGA AV | SCL | P A4 |
| SARATOGA AV | SCLR | 150 E5 |
| SARATOGA AV | SCLR | 151 A4 |
| SARATOGA AV | SCL | 45 E5 |
| SARATGA-LS G RD | SCL | P A4 |
| SARTGA-LS GATOS | SCL | 45 E5 |
| SARATOGA SPGS | LAK | 31 C2 |
| SARATOGA SPG RD | SBD | 72 D5 |
| SARATOGA SPG RD | SBD | 82 D1 |
| SARATOGA-SVL RD | SCL | P A4 |
| SARATOGA-SVL RD | SCL | 45 E5 |
| SARATOGA-SVL RD | SVL | 149 D2 |
| SARBO RD | MCO | 55 D1 |
| SARDINE LAKE RD | SIE | 27 A4 |
| SARGENT RD | SJCO | 40 A4 |
| SARGENTS RD | MON | 65 E4 |
| SARGENTS RD | MON | 66 A4 |
| SARIDA AV | KER | 79 C4 |
| SARINA RD | DN | 1 D3 |
| SARON FRUIT COL | TEH | 18 D4 |
| SASIA RD | KER | 79 B4 |
| SATICOY AV | VEN | 88 B5 |
| SATICOY ST | LA | 177 A1 |
| SATICOY ST | LA | 178 C1 |
| SAUGUS VNTRA RD | LACO | 89 A4 |
| SAVANA | MCO | 48 D5 |
| SAVIERS RD | OXN | 176 C5 |
| SAWMILL | INY | 51 C4 |
| SAW MILL RD | ALP | 36 B5 |
| SAWMILL RD | BUT | 25 C3 |
| SAWMILL RD | KER | 69 C5 |
| SAWMILL RD | KER | 79 C1 |
| SAWMILL RD | MNO | 50 E2 |
| SAW MILL CREEK | SBT | 66 B1 |
| SAWMILL CRSSOVR | MNO | 51 B1 |
| SAWMILL CUTOFF | MNO | 50 D2 |
| SAWMILL FLAT RD | TUO | 41 C4 |
| SAWMILL MDWS RD | MNO | 51 B1 |
| SAWTELLE AV | SUT | 33 C3 |
| SAWTELLE BLVD | CUL | 188 A1 |
| SAWTELLE BLVD | LA | 180 C3 |
| SAWTELLE BLVD | LA | 188 B2 |
| SAWTOOTH PEAK | KER | 80 C1 |
| SAWYER AV | STA | 47 D1 |
| SAWYERS BAR RD | SIS | 11 C1 |
| SAYLOR RD | STA | 47 E3 |
| SAYRE ST | LACO | Q C1 |
| SCALA LN | SIS | 4 B4 |
| SCALES RD | YUB | 26 C4 |
| SCANDIA RD | SOL | M B1 |
| SCANDIA RD | SOL | 39 A3 |
| SCARFACE RD | SIS | 3 E5 |
| SCARFACE RD | SIS | 4 A5 |
| SCARLT BUGLE RD | RCO | 100 C5 |
| SCARONI AV | KER | 78 B2 |
| SCENIC DR | STA | 47 D2 |
| SCENIC DR | MDO | 162 D2 |
| SCENIC DR | STA | 162 D2 |
| SCENIC RD | CAR | 168 B4 |
| SCHAAD RD | COL | 32 D2 |
| SCHADD RD | CAL | 41 C2 |
| SCHAEFER AV | SBD | 98 E2 |
| SCHAEFFER RD | SB | 87 D1 |
| SCHAFER AV | TEH | 18 E5 |
| SCHAGLE RD | SUT | 33 C3 |
| SCHALLOCK RD | KER | 78 C5 |
| SCHARTZ RD | IMP | 109 B4 |
| SCHATZ RD | KER | 79 C4 |
| SCHEAFER | MPA | 49 B3 |
| SCHEIBER RD | SUT | 33 D3 |
| SCHELL RD | IMP | 112 C3 |
| SCHILLING | MPA | 48 E2 |
| SCHILLING AV | FRCO | 67 B1 |
| SCHLAG RD | SUT | 33 C2 |
| SCHLEISMAN RD | RCO | 98 E2 |
| SCHMIDT DR | RCO | 107 A1 |
| SCHMIDT RD | MCO | 47 C5 |
| SCHOBER LN | INY | 51 D4 |
| SCHOOL RD | IMP | 112 D5 |
| SCHOOL RD | MNO | 50 E2 |
| SCHOOL RD | MNO | 51 A2 |
| SCHOOL ST | HUM | 15 E2 |
| SCHOOL ST | MEN | 30 C3 |
| SCHOOL ST | U | 123 C2 |
| SCHOOLER RD | SBD | 101 D1 |
| SCHOOL HOUSE RD | LAS | 8 C5 |
| SCHOOL HOUSE RD | MPA | 49 A4 |
| SCHLHOUSE HL RD | SIS | 4 D3 |
| SCHOTT RD | BUT | 25 C2 |
| SCHOTT RD | LAS | 14 B3 |
| SCHROEDER AV | SUT | 33 C1 |
| SCHROEDER MINE | SIS | 3 E4 |
| SCHUETTE RD | LAK | 31 C2 |
| SCHULMEYER RD | SIS | 4 A4 |
| SCHULTE RD | SJCO | 46 E2 |
| SCHULTZ RD | KER | 80 D5 |

| STREET | CO. | PAGE & GRID |
|---|---|---|
| SCHUSTER RD | KER | 68 B5 |
| SCIARONE RD | ED | 35 B5 |
| SCOFIELD AV | KER | 78 A1 |
| SCOTT AV | LACO | R D5 |
| SCOTT BLVD | SCL | P B3 |
| SCOTT BLVD | SCLR | 151 A2 |
| SCOTT RD | CAL | 41 C3 |
| SCOTT RD | LAS | 27 E2 |
| SCOTT RD | MPA | 49 C3 |
| SCOTT RD | RCO | 99 C4 |
| SCOTT RD | SAC | 40 C1 |
| SCOTT RD | SIS | 5 D2 |
| SCOTT BAR RD | SIS | 3 D4 |
| SCOTT CREEK RD | ALA | P B2 |
| SCOTT CREEK RD | ALA | 46 B3 |
| SCOTT DAM RD | LAK | 23 C5 |
| SCOTT FORBES RD | YUB | 34 A1 |
| SCOTT LUMBER RD | SHA | 19 C1 |
| SCOTT MTN RD | SIS | 11 E2 |
| SCOTT RIVER RD | SIS | 3 B4 |
| SCOTTS CREEK RD | LAK | 31 C3 |
| SCOTTS FLAT RD | NEV | 34 D1 |
| SCOTTS VLY RD | LAK | 31 C2 |
| SCOTT VALLEY DR | SCR | P A5 |
| SCOTTS VLY RD | SCR | 54 A1 |
| SCOTT VALLEY RD | SIS | 3 D5 |
| SCOTT VALLEY RD | SIS | 11 D1 |
| SCOTT VLY AIRPT | SIS | 3 D5 |
| SCOUT RD | BUT | 19 D5 |
| SCOUT ST | SHA | 18 B3 |
| SCOVELL AV | RCO | 99 E4 |
| SCRANTON AV | TUL | 68 D3 |
| SEAL BEACH BLVD | ORA | 98 A4 |
| SEAL BEACH BLVD | ORA | T A3 |
| SEARLES STA RD | KER | 80 E2 |
| SEARLES STA RD | SBD | 80 E2 |
| SEARLES STA CTO | SBD | 80 E2 |
| SEARS RD | LAS | 21 B4 |
| SEARS RD | SOL | L D2 |
| SEARS POINT RD | SOL | 38 C4 |
| SEARS POINT RD | SOL | 134 B2 |
| SEARS POINT RD | SON | L B2 |
| SEARS POINT RD | VAL | 134 B2 |
| SEASIDE AV | LA | 191 D3 |
| SEASIDE BLVD | LACO | S C3 |
| SEATTLE AV | KIN | 67 D3 |
| SEA VIEW DR | IMP | 108 C2 |
| SEAVIEW RD | SON | 37 A1 |
| SEAVW QUARRY RD | SON | 37 B1 |
| SEAWARD AV | VENT | 175 D3 |
| SEBASTIAN RD | KER | 78 E5 |
| SEBASTIAN RD | KER | 79 A5 |
| SEBASTOPOL AV | STR | 131 C4 |
| SEBASTOPOL FRWY | STR | 131 B4 |
| SEBASTOPOL FRWY | SON | 131 B4 |
| SEBASTOPOL RD | SON | 131 B4 |
| SECO ST | PAS | 190 A3 |
| SECOND ST | C | 124 B5 |
| SECRETARIAT RD | KER | 79 B4 |
| SECRET SPGS RD | SIS | 4 E3 |
| SECTION OLD RED | PLU | 19 E3 |
| SEE CANYON RD | SLO | 75 E4 |
| SEE CANYON RD | SLO | 76 A4 |
| SEE VEE LN | INY | 51 D4 |
| SEIAD CREEK | SIS | 3 B3 |
| SEIAD OAKS RD | SIS | 3 B3 |
| SEIDNER | SJCO | 47 D1 |
| SEIGLER CYN RD | LAK | 32 A4 |
| SEIGLER SPGS RD | LAK | 31 E4 |
| SELLERS AV | CC | M D4 |
| SELLERS AV | CC | 39 C5 |
| SELMADOLPH ST | SBD | 91 E3 |
| SELVA RD | ORA | 202 A4 |
| SEMINARY AV | ALA | L D5 |
| SEMINARY AV | ALA | 45 D1 |
| SEMINARY AV | O | 159 E1 |
| SEMINARY DR | MAR | 140 C4 |
| SEMINARY DR | MV | 140 C4 |
| SENATOR WASH RD | IMP | 110 E5 |
| SENECA RD | PLU | 20 B5 |
| SENECA RD | SBD | 91 B4 |
| SENECA RD | SBD | 91 E3 |
| SENILIS AV | SBD | 100 C2 |
| SENTER RD | SJ | 152 E5 |
| SENTER RD | SCL | P C3 |
| SENTER RD | SCL | 46 B4 |
| SEPULVEDA BLVD | CUL | 188 A1 |
| SEPULVEDA BLVD | ELS | 189 C3 |
| SEPULVEDA BLVD | LA | 180 D3 |
| SEPULVEDA BLVD | LA | 183 A5 |
| SEPULVEDA BLVD | LA | 188 C4 |
| SEPULVEDA BLVD | LA | 189 C3 |
| SEPULVEDA BLVD | LACO | 97 C1 |
| SEPULVEDA BLVD | LACO | Q C2 |
| SEPULVEDA BLVD | LACO | S B2 |
| SEPULVEDA BLVD | LACO | 180 B2 |
| SEPULVEDA BLVD | MB | 189 C3 |
| SEQUOIA BLVD | KER | 80 B4 |
| SEQUOIA RD | FRCO | 58 D3 |
| SEQUOIA RD | HUM | 16 C4 |
| SERENADE DR | SBD | 80 E1 |
| SERENE DR | SHA | 18 B2 |
| SERENO DR | VAL | 134 C2 |
| SERFAS CLUB DR | RCO | U D5 |
| SERFAS CLUB DR | RCO | 98 E3 |
| SERPA LN | SIS | 3 D5 |
| SERPA LN | SOL | 39 B2 |
| SERRAMONTE BLVD | SMCO | L B5 |
| SERRAMONTE BLVD | SMCO | N B1 |
| SERRANO RD | VEN | 96 C2 |
| SERVICE RD | SIE | 26 C4 |
| SERVICE RD | STA | 47 C3 |
| SESPE ST | VEN | 88 D5 |
| SESPE RIVER RD | VEN | 88 B3 |
| SEVEN HILLS RD | ALA | L E5 |
| SEVEN HILLS RD | ALA | M A5 |
| SEVEN MILE LN | BUT | 25 A4 |

| STREET | CO. | PAGE & GRID |
|---|---|---|
| SEVEN MI SLOUGH | HUM | 15 D2 |
| SEVEN OAK RD | SBD | 100 A1 |
| SEVERE RD | IMP | 109 A3 |
| SEWARD DR | HUM | 16 C4 |
| SEXTON | SJCO | 47 C1 |
| SEYMOUR RD | SUT | 33 B4 |
| SEYMOUR CK RD | VEN | 88 C2 |
| SHABELL LN | INY | 59 E3 |
| SHACKELFORD RD | STA | 47 B2 |
| SHADOW CYN RD | SLO | 75 E2 |
| SHADOW MTN RD | SBD | 83 D2 |
| SHADOW MTN RD | SBD | 90 E2 |
| SHADOW MTN RD | SBD | 91 A2 |
| SHADOW MTN RD | SBD | 101 D1 |
| SHADY LN | SR | 139 A4 |
| SHADY DELL RD | SIS | 5 A3 |
| SHAFFER RD | MCO | 48 B3 |
| SHAFFER ST | OR | 194 D3 |
| SHAFTER AV | KER | 78 B2 |
| SHAFTER RD | KER | 78 C4 |
| SHAIN AV | FRCO | 56 B2 |
| SHAKELEY LN | AMA | 40 D2 |
| SHAKE RIDGE RD | AMA | 40 E2 |
| SHAKE RIDGE RD | AMA | 41 A2 |
| SHALE RD | KER | 77 E4 |
| SHAMROCK RD | SIS | 4 A4 |
| SHANDON CEM RD | SLO | 76 D1 |
| SHANDON-SN JUAN | SLO | 76 D1 |
| SHANK RD | IMP | 109 B4 |
| SHANNON DR | SBD | 101 D1 |
| SHANNONDALE RD | LACO | 89 E4 |
| SHANNON VLY RD | LACO | 89 E4 |
| SHARON RD | MCO | 55 E2 |
| SHARON RD | YOL | 136 A1 |
| SHARPE RD | SON | 38 A1 |
| SHARP PARK RD | SMCO | N B1 |
| SHARP PARK RD | SMCO | 45 B2 |
| SHASTA AV | FRCO | 56 E3 |
| SHASTA AV | FRCO | 57 A3 |
| SHASTA BLVD | TEH | 18 E5 |
| SHASTA BLVD | TEH | 24 E1 |
| SHASTA ST | VAL | 134 D4 |
| SHASTA WY | C | 124 B4 |
| SHASTA WY | KLAM | 5 C1 |
| SHASTA CO RD | MOD | 13 E3 |
| SHA DAM ACCS RD | SHA | 18 B1 |
| SHA SPG MCCLOUD | SIS | 12 D2 |
| SHASTA VIEW DR | MOD | 14 E1 |
| SHASTA VIEW DR | SHA | 18 C2 |
| SHASTA VISTA DR | SIS | 4 C5 |
| SHATTUCK AV | B | 156 A2 |
| SHATTUCK AV | O | 156 A4 |
| SHAVES AV | SBD | 91 C1 |
| SHAW AV | FRCO | 57 C3 |
| SHAWMUT RD | TUO | 41 C5 |
| SHAWMUT RD | TUO | 48 C1 |
| SHAW PIT RD | MOD | 14 B2 |
| SHAWS FLAT RD | SNRA | 163 A2 |
| SHAWS FLAT RD | TUO | 163 A2 |
| SHAWS FLAT RD | TUO | 41 C5 |
| SHAWS FT JMSTWN | TUO | 41 C5 |
| SHAY CREEK RD | ALP | 36 B5 |
| SHEE CAMP RD | MNO | 51 B2 |
| SHEEP CREEK RD | SBD | 90 E4 |
| SHEEP CK SPG RD | SBD | 82 E1 |
| SHEEP CK TK TR | SBD | 90 E5 |
| SHEEP MTN RD | SIS | 5 A3 |
| SHEEP RANCH RD | CAL | 41 B3 |
| SHEEPY CREEK RD | SIS | 5 B2 |
| SHEEPY ISLND RD | SIS | 5 B2 |
| SHEFFIELD RD | SUT | 33 C3 |
| SHEKELL | VEN | 88 D5 |
| SHELBY ST | KER | 78 B5 |
| SHELDON RD | SAC | 39 E2 |
| SHELDON ST | LACO | Q C2 |
| SHELL AV | CC | L E3 |
| SHELL AV | MCO | 56 A1 |
| SHELL BLVD | CC | 38 E5 |
| SHELL BLVD | FCTY | 145 D2 |
| SHELL RD | FRCO | 66 D2 |
| SHELL RD | TUO | 41 C5 |
| SHELL CANYON RD | IMP | 111 C3 |
| SHELLCO RD | KER | 67 C5 |
| SHELL GULCH RD | SIS | 11 D1 |
| SHELL NO 2 | YUB | 33 D1 |
| SHELLEY | SJCO | 40 D4 |
| SHELLEY RD | SIS | 4 B4 |
| SHELTER COVE RD | HUM | 22 A1 |
| SHELTER ISLD DR | SDCO | V A3 |
| SHELTON RD | SBD | 101 D1 |
| SHELTON RD | SJCO | 40 C4 |
| SHELTN BUTTE RD | HUM | 10 D2 |
| SHENANDOAH SCHL | AMA | 40 E1 |
| SHEPHERD AV | FRCO | 57 C2 |
| SHEPHERD RD | MOD | 14 B3 |
| SHEPPARD RD | VEN | 88 C5 |
| SHERIDAN | FRCO | 58 A4 |
| SHERIDAN RD | ALA | P B2 |
| SHERIDAN RD | ALA | 46 B3 |
| SHERIDAN RD | SLO | 76 B5 |
| SHERMAN RD | SBD | 100 C2 |
| SHERMAN WY | LA | 177 B1 |
| SHERMAN WY | LA | 178 C1 |
| SHERMAN WY | LACO | 97 C1 |
| SHERMAN ISLD RD | SAC | M C2 |
| SHERWIN CK RD | MNO | 50 E2 |
| SHERWOOD AV | KER | 77 E1 |
| SHERWOOD AV | KER | 78 B1 |
| SHERWOOD BLVD | TEH | 24 E1 |
| SHERWOOD DR | SAL | 171 C3 |
| SHERWOOD RD | MEN | 22 E4 |
| SHERWD RNCHERIA | MEN | 22 E4 |
| SHETLAND CT | CAL | 41 B5 |
| SHIELDS AV | FRCO | 56 A3 |
| SHIELDS AV | FRCO | 57 A3 |
| SHIELDS RD | SHA | 17 C3 |
| SHIELLS RD | STA | 47 C4 |

| STREET | CO. | PAGE & GRID |
|---|---|---|
| SHILOH RD | SOL | 39 B4 |
| SHILOH RD | SON | 37 E1 |
| SHIMMINS RDG RD | MEN | 22 E4 |
| SHIMMINS RDG RD | MEN | 23 A4 |
| SHINGLE RD S | ED | 40 C1 |
| SHINGLETWN DUMP | SHA | 19 B3 |
| SHINGLETOWN RDG | SHA | 19 A3 |
| SHINN RANCH RD | LAS | 21 D2 |
| SHIPPEE RD | BUT | 25 C4 |
| SHIPPEE RD | MCO | 48 B5 |
| SHIRK RD | TUL | 68 A1 |
| SHIRLAND | PLA | 34 C4 |
| SHIRLEY RD | CAL | 41 A5 |
| SHIRLEY MDWS RD | KER | 79 C1 |
| SHIRT TAIL CYN | PLA | 34 D2 |
| SHIVELY RD | HUM | 16 A3 |
| SHOEMAKE AV | STA | 47 B2 |
| SHOEMAKER AV | LACO | T B1 |
| SHOEMAKER RD | HUM | 10 C4 |
| SHOEMAKER RD | SIS | 4 E4 |
| SHOP RD | MNO | 42 E1 |
| SHOP ST | INY | 70 B2 |
| SHORE RD | SBT | 54 E2 |
| SHORELINE DR | LB | 192 D3 |
| SHORELINE DR | STB | 174 C5 |
| SHORELINE HWY | MAR | L A4 |
| SHORELINE HWY | MAR | 37 D4 |
| SHORELINE HWY | MEN | 22 C3 |
| SHORELINE HWY | MEN | 30 C4 |
| SHORELINE HWY | MAR | 140 B4 |
| SHORT AV | KER | 91 C3 |
| SHORT RD | KER | 78 A5 |
| SHORT CREEK RD | MEN | 23 B2 |
| SHORTYS WELL RD | INY | 72 A2 |
| SHOSHONE VLY RD | SBD | 93 B5 |
| SHOSHONI LOOP | SHA | 13 E4 |
| SHOUP AV | LA | 177 B3 |
| SHOUP RD | SHA | 18 A3 |
| SHOWER PASS RD | HUM | 16 B2 |
| SHRODE LN | LAS | 21 C4 |
| SHULTZ RD | MCO | 56 C1 |
| SHUMWAY RCH RD | RCO | 100 D5 |
| SHUTE MTN RD | BUT | 25 E3 |
| SHUTT ST | DN | 1 D3 |
| SHY ST | MCO | 47 C5 |
| SHY ST | MCO | 55 C1 |
| SICARD FLAT RD | YUB | 34 A1 |
| SIDDING RD | KER | 78 B3 |
| SIDEWINDER RD | IMP | 110 C5 |
| SIDEWINDER RD | RCO | 102 C3 |
| SIDEWINDER RD | SBD | 91 D2 |
| SIDNEY GULCH RD | TRI | 17 D1 |
| SIEGLER SPGS RD | LAK | 32 A4 |
| SIERRA AV | FRCO | 57 C3 |
| SIERRA AV | NAP | 133 A1 |
| SIERRA AV | SBD | 99 A2 |
| SIERRA DR | MPA | 48 E1 |
| SIERRA DR | MDO | 162 B4 |
| SIERRA HWY | KER | 80 A5 |
| SIERRA HWY | KER | 90 A1 |
| SIERRA HWY | LACO | 89 C4 |
| SIERRA PKWY | CAL | 41 D3 |
| SIERRA RD | LAS | 20 E3 |
| SIERRA RD | SCL | P C3 |
| SIERRA RD | SCL | 46 B4 |
| SIERRA RD | STA | 47 E1 |
| SIERRA ST | RENO | 130 B2 |
| SIERRA WY | KER | 69 D5 |
| SIERRA WY | KER | 79 D1 |
| SIERRA WY | SBDO | 207 D3 |
| SIERRA WY | SBD | 99 C1 |
| SIERRA WY | TUL | 58 A5 |
| SIERRA CTR DR | SHA | 13 E4 |
| SRA COLLEGE BL | PLA | 34 B5 |
| SIERRA DEL SOL | RCO | 100 E3 |
| SIERRA MADRE AV | LACO | 98 C1 |
| SIERRA MADRE AV | LACO | U A1 |
| SIERRA MADRE BL | LACO | R C3 |
| SIERRA MADRE BL | LACO | R C2 |
| SIERRA VISTA AV | TEH | 24 D1 |
| SIERRA VISTA ST | KER | 80 C1 |
| SIERRA VLY RD | PLU | 27 C3 |
| SIEVERS RD | SOL | 39 B2 |
| SIGNAL RD | IMP | 111 E4 |
| SIGNAL BUTTE RD | LAS | 20 E1 |
| SIGNAL RIDGE RD | MEN | 30 D3 |
| SIKES RD | SOL | 39 C2 |
| SILAXO AV | FRCO | 56 C2 |
| SILLS RD | COL | 32 D3 |
| SILSBEE RD | IMP | 112 A3 |
| SILURIAN LK RD | SBD | 83 B2 |
| SILVA RD | MPA | 49 B3 |
| SILVA RD | SIS | 4 C3 |
| SILVERA CT | BUT | 25 C3 |
| SILVERADO TR | NAP | 133 E4 |
| SILVERADO TR | NAPA | 29 A1 |
| SILVERADO TR | NAPA | 38 C2 |
| SILVER BAR RD | MPA | 49 B4 |
| SILVER BRDG RD | SHA | 18 D2 |
| SILVER CYN RD | INY | 51 E4 |
| SILVRADO CYN RD | ORA | 98 E4 |
| SILVER CREEK RD | MOH | 85 D4 |
| SILVER CREEK RD | SCL | P C4 |
| SILVER CREEK RD | SCL | 46 B4 |
| SILVER CK CMPGD | ALP | 42 C1 |
| SILVER HILL RD | ALP | 36 C5 |
| SILVER KING RD | SHA | 18 B2 |
| SILVER LAKE BL | LA | 182 E4 |
| SILVER LAKE BL | LA | 185 D1 |
| SILVER LAKE BL | LACO | Q E4 |
| SILVER LAKE RD | LAS | 20 B3 |
| SILVER BAR RD | MPA | 49 B4 |
| SILVER PUFF DR | KER | 89 E3 |
| SILVER QUEEN RD | KER | 79 E5 |
| SILVER QUEEN RD | KER | 80 A5 |
| SILVR RAPIDS RD | CAL | 40 D4 |
| SILVR STRAND BL | SDCO | V B4 |

| STREET | CO. | PAGE & GRID |
|---|---|---|
| SILVR STRAND BL | SDCO | 111 D2 |
| SILVERTHORN RD | SHA | 18 D1 |
| SLVR TIP CPGRD | ALP | 42 A2 |
| SILVER VLY RD | SBD | 92 B1 |
| SILVEYVILLE RD | SOL | 39 B2 |
| SIMAS ST | SB | 86 B1 |
| SIMI VALLEY- | | |
| -SN FERN VLY FY | LA | 89 B5 |
| SIMI VALLEY- | | |
| -SN FERN VLY FY | VEN | 88 E5 |
| SIMMERHORN RD | SAC | 40 A3 |
| SIMMLER RD | SLO | 77 A2 |
| SIMMLR BITTRWTR | SLO | 76 E1 |
| SIMMLR BITTRWTR | SLO | 77 A1 |
| SIMMLR SN DIEGO | SLO | 77 B3 |
| SIMMLR SN DIEGO | SLO | 77 C4 |
| SIMMLER SODA LK | SLO | 77 C3 |
| SIMMONS RD | LAK | 23 C5 |
| SIMMONS RD | SHA | 18 B2 |
| SIMMONS RD | STA | 47 C3 |
| SIMPSON LN | MEN | 22 C5 |
| SIMPSON LN | YUB | 33 D2 |
| SIMPSON RD | IMP | 109 B3 |
| SIMPSON RD | RCO | 99 D4 |
| SIMPSON RD | TEH | 24 C1 |
| SIMPSN DATNI RD | YUB | 33 D2 |
| SIMS RD | TUO | 41 C5 |
| SIMS RD | TUO | 48 C1 |
| SIMS CREEK RD | TRI | 17 C3 |
| SIMS LOOKOUT RD | SHA | 12 C4 |
| SINCLAIR FRWY | ALA | 46 B3 |
| SINCLAIR FRWY | SJ | 151 D5 |
| SINCLAIR FRWY | SCL | 46 B3 |
| SINCLAIR FRWY | SCL | 151 D5 |
| SINCLAIR RD | IMP | 109 A3 |
| SINEX AV | PAC | 167 B2 |
| SINGLE SPRINGS | SIS | 4 E5 |
| SINGLETON RD | RCO | 99 D2 |
| SINGLE TREE | SBD | 100 E2 |
| SINGLETREE DR | CAL | 41 A5 |
| SINGLEY RD | HUM | 15 E2 |
| SINNARD AV | SUT | 33 C1 |
| SINTON RD | SB | 86 B1 |
| SIR F DRAKE BL | MAR | 37 E4 |
| SIR F DRAKE BL | MAR | 38 A5 |
| SIR F DRAKE BL | MAR | L A3 |
| SIR F DRAKE BL | ROSS | 139 A4 |
| SIR F DRAKE BL | SANS | 139 A4 |
| SISK RD | STA | 47 C2 |
| SISKIYOU AV | FRCO | 57 A3 |
| SISKIYOU AV | FRCO | 67 A2 |
| SITES-LODOGA RD | COL | 24 B5 |
| SITES-LODOGA RD | COL | 32 B1 |
| SIX MILE RD | CAL | 41 B4 |
| SKAGGS ISLND RD | SOL | 38 C4 |
| SKAGGS SPGS RD | SON | 31 C5 |
| SKIDOO RD | INY | 71 D1 |
| SKI HILL RD | MOD | 7 C5 |
| SKI RUN BLVD | SLT | 129 C3 |
| SKITTONE RD | STA | 47 D2 |
| SKULL FLAT RD | CAL | 41 B2 |
| SKUNK RANCH RD | CAL | 41 C4 |
| SKYLINE BLVD | ALA | L D4 |
| SKYLINE BLVD | ALA | 45 D1 |
| SKYLINE BLVD | KIN | 67 A3 |
| SKYLINE BLVD | SMCO | N B1 |
| SKYLINE BLVD | SMCO | N C2 |
| SKYLINE BLVD | SMCO | 45 C3 |
| SKYLINE BLVD | SCL | N E4 |
| SKYLINE DR | KER | 79 B4 |
| SKYLINE DR | MONT | 167 C4 |
| SKYLINE DR | MON | 53 D3 |
| SKYLINE DR | SBD | 100 E1 |
| SKYLINE DR | SDCO | V D4 |
| SKYLINE DR | SDCO | 111 D1 |
| SKYLINE MTWY | PLU | 20 D4 |
| SKYLINE RD | KER | 77 E3 |
| SKYLINE RD | KIN | 67 A3 |
| SKYLINE RD | SON | 31 A5 |
| SKY LINE DR | VAL | 134 E3 |
| SKYLINE FRST DR | MONT | 167 C5 |
| SKYLINE FRST DR | MONT | 168 C1 |
| SKYLINE FRST DR | MON | 53 D4 |
| SKYLINE RCH RD | SBD | 100 D1 |
| SKY RANCH RD | MON | 54 C5 |
| SKY VALLEY RD | RCO | 100 E3 |
| SKY VALLEY RD | SOL | 38 D4 |
| SKY VIEW DR | IMP | 108 C2 |
| SKYVIEW RD | MAD | 57 C2 |
| SKYWAY | BUT | 25 C2 |
| SKYWAY DR | SB | 86 B1 |
| SKYWAY RD | BUT | 19 D5 |
| SKYWAY RD | BUT | 25 D1 |
| SLACKS CYN RD | MON | 66 B3 |
| SLASH X RCH RD | SBD | 91 C2 |
| SLATE RD | YUB | 26 A4 |
| SLATE CREEK RD | SHA | 12 B4 |
| SLATE CREEK RD | TRI | 11 D5 |
| SLATE GULCH | MPA | 48 E3 |
| SLATE MTN RD | TRI | 12 A4 |
| SLATE MTN LO RD | SHA | 12 B4 |
| SLATER AV | ORA | T B3 |
| SLATER RD | HUM | 16 B2 |
| SLATE RANGE | INY | 71 B2 |
| SLATER BUTTE LO | SIS | 2 E3 |
| SLAUGHTERHOUSE | MPA | 49 B3 |
| SLAUSON AV | CUL | 188 D3 |
| SLAUSON AV | LACO | 97 D2 |
| SLAUSON AV | LACO | Q E4 |
| SLAUSON AV | LACO | R C5 |
| SLAUSON AV | LACO | 188 D3 |
| SLAYTON RD | IMP | 109 C5 |
| SLIGER MINE RD | ED | 34 D3 |
| SLOAT BLVD | SFCO | L B5 |
| SLOAT BLVD | SFCO | 45 B2 |
| SLOAT RD | PLU | 26 E2 |
| SLOUGH RD | SIS | 4 B5 |

| STREET | CO. | PAGE & GRID |
|---|---|---|
| SLOUGH RD | SIS | 12 B1 |
| SLOUGHHOUSE RD | SAC | 40 B2 |
| SLOVER AV | SBD | 99 A2 |
| SLUG GULCH RD | ED | 41 A1 |
| SLUSSER RD | SON | 37 D2 |
| SLY PARK RD | ED | 35 A5 |
| SMALLEY RD | FRCO | 57 E1 |
| SMARTS RANCH RD | SBD | 92 B5 |
| SMARTVILLE RD | YUB | 34 A1 |
| SMITH | YUB | 33 E1 |
| SMITH AV | FRCO | 57 E4 |
| SMITH AV | KER | 78 B1 |
| SMITH AV | KER | 70 A5 |
| SMITH GRADE | SCR | 53 D1 |
| SMITH RD | MON | 65 C5 |
| SMITH RD | SBD | 80 E1 |
| SMITH MTN RD | MON | 66 B3 |
| SMITH PK LKOUT | TUO | 48 E1 |
| SMITH PK LKOUT | TUO | 49 A1 |
| SMITHNECK RD | SIE | 27 D4 |
| SMITHSON RD | SBD | 91 B2 |
| SMITH STA RD | MPA | 48 E1 |
| SMITH STA RD | MPA | 49 A1 |
| SMITH STA RD | TUO | 48 E1 |
| SMITH STA RD | TUO | 49 A1 |
| SMOKE CK RCH RD | LAS | 21 D3 |
| SMOKE TREE RD | SBD | 90 E4 |
| SNAVELY RD | DN | 1 E3 |
| SNEATH LN | SMCO | N B1 |
| SNEATH LN | SMCO | 45 B2 |
| SNEATH LN | SBR | 144 A2 |
| SNELL ST | SNRA | 163 B3 |
| SNELLING HWY | MER | 170 A3 |
| SNELLING RD | MCO | 48 C3 |
| SNELL VALLEY RD | NAPA | 32 B5 |
| SNOW RD | KER | 77 E2 |
| SNOW RD | KER | 78 C2 |
| SNOW ST | KER | 79 E1 |
| SNOW ST | KER | 80 A1 |
| SNOW CAMP RD | HUM | 10 B5 |
| SNOWDN HOVEY GL | SIS | 4 C4 |
| SNOWS RD | ED | 35 A5 |
| SNOWSHOE SPGS | ALP | 36 B4 |
| SNOW TENT RD | NEV | 26 D5 |
| SNYDER RD | IMP | 109 C5 |
| SNYDER RD | MCO | 47 C5 |
| SOAP CREEK RD | SIS | 3 E5 |
| SOBOBA RD | RCO | 99 E3 |
| SOBOBA ST | RCO | 100 A4 |
| SOBRANTE AV | CC | L D3 |
| SOBRANTE AV | CC | 38 C5 |
| SODA BAY RD | LAK | 31 D3 |
| SODA CANYON RD | NAPA | 38 C2 |
| SODA CREEK RD | SHA | 12 C3 |
| SODA LAKE RD | KER | 78 A5 |
| SODA LAKE RD | KER | 87 E1 |
| SODA LAKE CK RD | SLO | 77 B3 |
| SODA LK SN DIEG | SLO | 77 B3 |
| SODA LK SN DIEG | SLO | 77 D4 |
| SODA ROCK LN W | SON | 31 D5 |
| SODA SPRINGS RD | BUT | 19 D5 |
| SODA SPRINGS RD | SON | 30 E5 |
| SOETH RD | GLE | 24 B5 |
| SOLANO AV | ALA | L D4 |
| SOLANO AV | NAP | 133 A2 |
| SOLANO AV | VAL | 134 C5 |
| SOLANO WY | CC | M A3 |
| SOLDIER MTN DR | SHA | 13 D3 |
| SOLDIER MTN RD | SHA | 13 D3 |
| SOLEDAD DR | MONT | 167 D4 |
| SOLEDAD DR | MONT | 168 D1 |
| SOLEDAD DR | MON | 53 E4 |
| SOLEDAD FRWY | SDCO | V B2 |
| SOLEDAD FRWY | SDCO | 106 C5 |
| SOLEDAD CYN RD | LACO | 89 E4 |
| SOLEDAD MTN RD | SD | 211 B4 |
| SOLOMAN RD | SB | 86 B1 |
| SOMAVIA RD | MON | 54 D4 |
| SOMEO ST | SB | 86 B1 |
| SOMERSVILLE RD | CC | M B3 |
| SOMERSVILLE RD | CC | 39 B5 |
| SONOMA AV | FRCO | 56 D4 |
| SONOMA AV | FRCO | 66 D1 |
| SONOMA AV | STR | 131 E3 |
| SONOMA BLVD | NAPA | L D2 |
| SONOMA BLVD | VAL | 134 C4 |
| SONOMA HWY | SNMA | 132 C3 |
| SONOMA MTN RD | SON | 38 A2 |
| SONORA | SJCO | 40 D5 |
| SONORA | STA | 41 A5 |
| SONORA RD | STA | 40 D5 |
| SONORA RD | STA | 47 D1 |
| SONORA RD | STA | 48 A1 |
| SONORA ELEM SCH | TUO | 163 D4 |
| SOPHIE ST | RCO | 99 C4 |
| SOQUEL AV | SC | 169 D3 |
| SOQUEL DR | SCR | 54 A2 |
| SOQUEL-SAN JOSE | SCR | 54 A2 |
| SORENSON RD | HUM | 16 B3 |
| SORENSON RD | RCO | 107 B1 |
| SORREL WY | CAL | 41 A4 |
| SORRENTO VLY RD | SDCO | 106 C4 |
| SORRENTO VLY RD | SDCO | V A1 |
| SOSCOL AV | NAP | 133 D3 |
| SOSCOL RD | NAPA | 38 C3 |
| SOTO ST | LA | 186 D5 |
| SOTO ST | LACO | R A4 |
| SOULE LN | SIS | 4 C4 |
| SOULSBYVILLE RD | TUO | 41 D5 |
| SOUTH AV | FRCO | 56 E4 |
| SOUTH AV | FRCO | 57 B4 |
| SOUTH AV | MCO | 47 E4 |
| SOUTH AV | MCO | 48 A4 |
| SOUTH AV | TEH | 24 E2 |
| SOUTH DR | SF | 141 B4 |
| SOUTH RD | MNO | 51 C1 |
| SOUTH RD | BLMT | 145 C5 |

| STREET | CO. | PAGE & GRID |
|---|---|---|
| SOUTH ST | ANA | 193 B3 |
| SOUTH ST | ANA | 194 A2 |
| SOUTH ST | GLE | 24 D3 |
| SOUTH ST | LACO | 98 A3 |
| SOUTH ST | LACO | S D1 |
| SOUTH ST | LACO | T A1 |
| SOUTH ST | ORA | T C2 |
| SOUTH ST | RED | 122 B2 |
| SOUTH ST | SBD | 90 E4 |
| SOUTH ST | SNLO | 172 B4 |
| SOUTH ST | SHA | 18 C3 |
| SOUTHAM RD | COL | 24 E5 |
| SOUTHAMPTON RD | BEN | 153 A3 |
| SOUTH BANK RD | DN | 1 E3 |
| S BNK CHETKO RD | CUR | 1 D2 |
| SOUTH BAY FRWY | SDCO | V D4 |
| SOUTH BAY FRWY | SDCO | 111 D1 |
| SOUTHBAY FRWY | SVL | 148 C4 |
| SOUTHERN AV | SIS | 12 E2 |
| S EMBARCADRO FY | SF | 142 E4 |
| S EMBARCADRO FY | SFCO | 45 C2 |
| SOUTH FORK DR | TUL | 58 E5 |
| SOUTH FORK DR | TUL | 68 E1 |
| SOUTH FORK DR | TUL | 69 A1 |
| SOUTH FORK RD | DN | 1 E4 |
| SOUTH FORK RD | DN | 2 A4 |
| SOUTH FORK RD | SHA | 18 B3 |
| SOUTH FORK RD | SIS | 2 E3 |
| SOUTH FORK RD | TRI | 10 D5 |
| SOUTH FORK RD | TRI | 16 E2 |
| SOUTH FORK RD | TUO | 41 D4 |
| S FK LOOKOUT RD | SHA | 18 B2 |
| S FK MAD RIV RD | TRI | 17 B5 |
| S FORK MTN RD | LAS | 8 B3 |
| S FORK MTN RD | TRI | 16 E3 |
| S FK SALMON RIV | SIS | 11 B2 |
| SOUTH GRADE RD | SDCO | 107 A2 |
| SOUTH GRADE RD | SDCO | 107 B5 |
| SOUTHSIDE DR | MPA | 63 B2 |
| SOUTHSIDE RD | SBT | 54 E3 |
| SOUTHSIDE RD | SBT | 55 A3 |
| SOUTH VLY FRWY | SCL | 54 C1 |
| SW EXPWY | SCL | P B3 |
| SOUTHWORTH RD | CAL | 40 D4 |
| SOUZA RD | TRI | 17 A4 |
| SOWLES RD | SJCO | 40 B3 |
| SPA RD | IMP | 108 E1 |
| SPACER DR | TUL | 68 B2 |
| SPALDING RD | LAS | 20 D1 |
| SPANGLE GOLD RD | MAD | 49 C5 |
| SPANGLER RD | KER | 68 C5 |
| SPANISH DAGGER | RCO | 100 C5 |
| SPANISH DRY DGN | ED | 34 D3 |
| SPANISH RCH RD | PLU | 26 B1 |
| SPANSH RCH BUTE | PLU | 25 E2 |
| SPANSH RCH BUTE | PLU | 26 A2 |
| SPANISH VALLEY | NAPA | 32 C5 |
| SPARKS RD | MCO | 47 C5 |
| SPARKS RANCH RD | SOL | 39 B1 |
| SPEAR AV | HUM | 10 A5 |
| SPECIMAN SPG RD | MAD | 49 B4 |
| SPENCE RD | MON | 54 D4 |
| SPENCER LN | SON | 32 A5 |
| SPENCER LN | SON | 38 A1 |
| SPENCER RD | COL | 24 E5 |
| SPENCER RD | STA | 47 A2 |
| SPENCEVILLE RD | NEV | 34 B2 |
| SPENCEVILLE RD | YUB | 33 E3 |
| SPERRY AV | STA | 47 B3 |
| SPERRY RD | STA | 47 E3 |
| SPGNOLI MINE RD | AMA | 41 A2 |
| SPILLWAY RD | MNO | 51 B2 |
| SPINELLI RD | MAD | 49 C5 |
| SPINK RD | CAL | 41 B2 |
| SPLICER RD | COL | 33 A3 |
| SPOONER RD | LAS | 8 A4 |
| SPOONER RD | LAS | 14 E4 |
| SPORTS ARENA BL | SD | 212 D5 |
| SPORTS ARENA BL | SD | 213 A5 |
| SPRECKELS BLVD | MON | 54 C4 |
| SPRING RD | VAL | 134 C4 |
| SPRING ST | LACO | S E2 |
| SPRING ST | NAPA | 29 C3 |
| SPRING ST | U | 123 B3 |
| SPRING ST N | LA | 186 B2 |
| SPRING TR | LAK | 31 D2 |
| SPRING BRNCH RD | TEH | 18 D3 |
| SPRING BRNCH RD | TEH | 19 A3 |
| SPRINGBROOK RD | CC | L E4 |
| SPRINGBROOK RD | CC | M A4 |
| SPRING CREEK RD | SHA | 13 D3 |
| SPRINGDALE ST | ORA | T B3 |
| SPRINGER RD | SCL | N E3 |
| SPRINGFIELD AV | FRCO | 56 E4 |
| SPRINGFIELD AV | FRCO | 57 B4 |
| SPRING GAP RD | TUO | 41 E3 |
| SPRING GAP RD | TUO | 42 A3 |
| SPRING GARDEN | PLA | 34 D3 |
| SPRING GULCH RD | LAS | 14 B4 |
| SPRING GULCH RD | SHA | 18 C3 |
| SPRING HILL RD | LAS | 14 E4 |
| SPRING HILL RD | SON | 37 E3 |
| SPRING HILL RD | SON | 38 A3 |
| SPRING LAKE RD | KLAM | 5 B1 |
| SPRING MDWS RD | SIS | 12 E3 |
| SPRING MTN RD | NAPA | 29 A2 |
| SPRING MTN RD | NAPA | 38 B1 |
| SPRINGS RD | SOL | L D2 |
| SPRINGS RD | SOL | 38 D4 |
| SPRING VLY LTRL | COL | 32 D2 |
| SPRING VLY RD | COL | 32 C2 |
| SPRING VLY RD | MEN | 31 B1 |
| SPRING VLY RD | YUB | 33 E1 |
| SPRINGVILLE AV | TUL | 68 D3 |
| SPRINGVLLE MILO | TUL | 69 A2 |
| SPROUL CREEK RD | HUM | 22 B1 |
| SPRUCE AV | SSF | 144 B1 |

| STREET | CO. | PAGE & GRID |
|---|---|---|
| SPRUCE RD | TUL | 68 C2 |
| SPRUCE RD EXT | LAK | 32 A4 |
| SPRUCE ST | B | 156 A1 |
| SPRUCE CAMP RD | MCO | 55 E2 |
| SPRUCE GROVE RD | LAK | 32 B4 |
| SPUNKY CYN RD | LACO | 89 C3 |
| SPUR ST | CAL | 41 A4 |
| SPYROCK RD | MEN | 22 D2 |
| SQUAW BUSH RD | SBD | 92 B4 |
| SQUAW FLAT RD | VEN | 88 D3 |
| SQUAW GULCH RD | SIS | 11 D2 |
| SQUAW VALLEY RD | SIS | 12 D3 |
| SQUAW VLY LP RD | SIS | 12 D3 |
| SQUIRREL CK RD | PLU | 26 D2 |
| STADIUM WY | LACO | Q E3 |
| STADIUM WY | SD | 214 B3 |
| STADIUM WY | SDCO | V B3 |
| STADIUM WY | SDCO | 111 D1 |
| STAFFORD RD | HUM | 16 A3 |
| STAG RD | AVLN | 105 B4 |
| STAGE RD | BUT | 25 C2 |
| STAGE RD | LAS | 8 D5 |
| STAGE RD | LACO | T B1 |
| STAGE RD | SMCO | N C4 |
| STAGE RD | SMCO | 45 C5 |
| STAGE COACH LN | SDCO | 106 C2 |
| STAGECOACH RD | HUM | 9 E4 |
| STAGECOACH RD | SB | 87 B3 |
| STAGECOACH CYN | NAPA | 32 C5 |
| STAGE GULCH RD | SON | L A1 |
| STAGHORN RD | RCO | 107 C1 |
| STAHL RD | IMP | 109 B4 |
| STALLARD RD | IMP | 110 C2 |
| STALLION WY | CAL | 41 B4 |
| STAMPEDE DAM RD | SIE | 27 E5 |
| STAMPFLI LN RD | PLU | 20 D5 |
| STANDARD RD | TUO | 41 D5 |
| STANDARD MNE RD | PLU | 20 C5 |
| STANDIFORD AV | STA | 47 C2 |
| STANDISH PIT RD | LAS | 21 B3 |
| STANDLEY ST | U | 123 B3 |
| STANISLAUS AV | FRCO | 66 D1 |
| STANISLAUS RD W | STA | 47 B3 |
| STANLEY | SJCO | 40 C5 |
| STANLEY AV | VEN | 88 A5 |
| STANLEY BLVD | ALA | M C5 |
| STANLEY BLVD | ALA | P C1 |
| STANLEY BLVD | ALA | 46 B2 |
| STANLEY RD | CAL | 41 B2 |
| STANLEY RD | IMP | 109 B3 |
| STANLEY RD | RCO | 100 A5 |
| STANWOOD DR | STB | 174 E2 |
| STANYAN ST | SF | 141 E3 |
| STAPP RD | HUM | 16 C2 |
| STAR AV | STA | 47 E2 |
| STARBRIGHT MINE | SBD | 82 A4 |
| STARDUST RD | CLK | 210 B1 |
| STAR HILL RD | SMCO | N C3 |
| STARK | SJCO | 40 A5 |
| STARK | SJCO | 47 A1 |
| STARK RD | STA | 47 B3 |
| STARKEY RD | SLO | 76 C1 |
| STARLING ST | LACO | 90 C2 |
| STARLITE DR | INY | 51 C4 |
| STARLITE DR | INY | 51 C4 |
| STARR RD | IMP | 109 C5 |
| STATE LN | SBD | 100 B1 |
| STATE ST | LACO | R A5 |
| STATE ST | MTCL | 203 B5 |
| STATE ST | ONT | 203 B5 |
| STATE ST | POM | 203 B5 |
| STATE ST | RCO | 99 E4 |
| STATE ST | SB | 87 C4 |
| STATE ST | SD | 215 D4 |
| STATE ST | SDCO | V B4 |
| STATE ST | STB | 174 B3 |
| STATE ST N | MEN | 31 B2 |
| STATE ST N | U | 123 C2 |
| STATE ST S | MEN | 123 D3 |
| STATE ST S | U | 123 D3 |
| STATE COLLGE BL | ORA | 98 C3 |
| STATE COLLGE BL | ORA | T D2 |
| STATE COL BL N | ANA | 193 E5 |
| STATE COL BL N | OR | 193 E5 |
| STATE COL PKWY | SBD | 99 B1 |
| STATE FRSTRY RD | SON | 31 A5 |
| STATE LINE RD | MOD | 5 E2 |
| STATE LINE RD | MNO | 52 C3 |
| STATE LINE RD | INY | 72 D1 |
| STATE LINE RD | SIS | 5 B2 |
| STATEN ISLND RD | SJCO | 39 D4 |
| STATE RANCH RD | SUT | 33 C3 |
| STATION RD | KER | 78 A3 |
| STAVERVILLE RD | SIE | 27 D3 |
| STEARNS RD | STA | 47 E2 |
| STEARNS ST | LACO | S E2 |
| STEARNS ST | VEN | 89 A5 |
| STEEG RD | SBD | 101 D1 |
| STEEL BRIDGE RD | TRI | 17 D1 |
| STEELE LN | MEN | 22 E3 |
| STEELE LN W | STR | 131 B2 |
| STEELE CYN RD | NAPA | 38 D2 |
| STEELHEAD CIR | TRI | 17 D1 |
| STEELHEAD RD | HUM | 16 D5 |
| STEEL SWAMP RD | MOD | 6 C3 |
| STEFFAN ST | VAL | 134 E5 |
| STEIDLMAYER RD | CLU | 33 A2 |
| STEINEGUL | SJCO | 47 D1 |
| STEINER RD | AMA | 40 E1 |
| STEINER RD | SUT | 33 B3 |
| STEINER FLAT RD | TRI | 17 C1 |
| STELLAR RD | SBD | 92 A4 |
| STELLING RD N | CPTO | 149 C4 |
| STELLING RD S | CPTO | 149 D5 |
| STENT CUTOFF | TUO | 41 C5 |
| STEPHENS MNE RD | SBD | 80 E2 |
| STEPHENS MNE RD | SBD | 81 A2 |



STREETS

| STREET | CO. | PAGE & GRID |
|---|---|---|
| STEPHENSON BLVD | RCO | 110 C1 |
| STEPHENS RIDGE | BUT | 25 E3 |
| STERCHI LN | SIS | 4 C4 |
| STERLING AV | SBD | 99 C2 |
| STERLING RD | INY | 70 C4 |
| STERLING LAKE | NEV | 27 B5 |
| STETSON AV | RCO | 99 E4 |
| STEVEN ST | KER | 78 B5 |
| STEVENS RD | IMP | 111 E3 |
| STEVENS CK BLVD | CPTO | 149 C5 |
| STEVENS CK BLVD | CPTO | 150 A5 |
| STEVENS CK BLVD | SCL | P B3 |
| STEVENS CK BLVD | SCLR | 150 A5 |
| STEVENS CK BLVD | SCL | 46 A4 |
| STEVENS CK FRWY | MVW | 148 A4 |
| STEVENS CK RD | SCL | N E3 |
| STEVENS CK RD | SCL | P A3 |
| STEVENS CK RD | SCL | 45 E5 |
| STEVENSON BLVD | ALA | P A2 |
| STEVENSN BDG RD | SOL | 39 B1 |
| STEVENS PASS RD | SIS | 5 A5 |
| STEVENS PASS RD | SIS | 13 B1 |
| STEWART | MOD | 14 D1 |
| STEWART AV | BUT | 124 A5 |
| STEWART LN | INY | 51 E5 |
| STEWART LN | SOL | 39 C4 |
| STEWART RD | HUM | 16 C4 |
| STEWART RD | INY | 51 D4 |
| STEWART RD | SJCO | 47 A1 |
| STEWART RD | SUT | 33 D2 |
| STEWART RD | TEH | 18 C5 |
| STEWART ST | SB | 86 C1 |
| STEWARTS POINT- | | |
| -SKAGGS SPGS RD | SON | 30 E5 |
| STEWARTS POINT- | | |
| -SKAGGS SPGS RD | SON | 31 A5 |
| STEWART RCH RD | HUM | 16 D4 |
| STEWART SPGS RD | SIS | 12 B1 |
| STICE RD | TEH | 18 D4 |
| STIERLIN RD | SCL | N E2 |
| STIERLIN RD | SCL | P A2 |
| STILLWELL AV | MONT | 167 D3 |
| STILLWELL AV | MON | 53 E3 |
| STILSON CYN RD | BUT | 25 B3 |
| STIMPSON RD | BUT | 25 D5 |
| STIMPSON RD | BUT | 33 D1 |
| STINE RD | BKD | 166 A5 |
| STINE RD | KER | 78 D3 |
| STINGY LN | SHA | 18 C3 |
| STOCKDALE HWY | KER | 78 A3 |
| STOCKDALE RD | SLO | 76 A1 |
| STOCKER ST | LACO | Q D4 |
| STOCKTON AV | MCO | 48 B4 |
| STOCKTON AV | SJ | 151 E3 |
| STOCKTON BLVD | SCTO | 137 E4 |
| STOCKTON BLVD | SAC | 39 E1 |
| STOCKTON RD | VEN | 88 D5 |
| STOCKTON ST | SF | 143 C2 |
| STOCKTON ST | SNRA | 163 A5 |
| STOCKWLL MNE RD | INY | 71 B4 |
| STODDARD RD | STA | 47 C2 |
| STODDARD RD | STA | 47 E2 |
| STODDARD MTN RD | SBD | 91 C2 |
| STODDARD WELLS | SBD | 91 D2 |
| STOEKEL RD | SHA | 18 B3 |
| STONE AV | STA | 47 C2 |
| STONE RD | LAS | 20 E1 |
| STONE RD | MCO | 55 D1 |
| STONEBORO RD | MEN | 30 C3 |
| STONE CANYON RD | MON | 66 B3 |
| STONE COAL RD | MOD | 14 B2 |
| STONEHEDGE DR | YUB | 25 E5 |
| STONEHILL DR | ORA | 202 B3 |
| STONE HOUSE RD | SAC | 40 C1 |
| STONEHURST AV | LACO | Q D2 |
| STONERIDGE DR | ALA | 46 A2 |
| STONE VALLEY RD | CC | M A4 |
| STONE VALLEY RD | CC | 46 A1 |
| STONEWLL CYN RD | MON | 65 A1 |
| STONEY CREEK RD | LAS | 21 D2 |
| STONY CREEK RD | AMA | 40 D3 |
| STONYFD-LDGA RD | COL | 24 B5 |
| STONY POINT RD | STR | 131 A3 |
| STONY POINT RD | SON | 38 A3 |
| STONY POINT RD | SON | 37 E2 |
| STONY POINT RD | SON | 37 E3 |
| STONY POINT RD | SON | 131 A4 |
| STOREY | FRCO | 56 C2 |
| STORRIE RD | PLU | 25 E2 |
| STORY RD | SJ | 152 E4 |
| STORY RD | SCL | P C3 |
| STORY RD | SCL | 46 B4 |
| STORY RD | STA | 47 E3 |
| STOVALL RD | COL | 32 D2 |
| STOVEPIPE WELLS | INY | 61 D4 |
| STOVER RD | HUM | 10 B4 |
| STOW | SJCO | 40 C5 |
| STOW | SJCO | 47 C1 |
| STOWELL RD | STB | 173 B4 |
| STOWELL RD | SB | 86 B1 |
| STOWELL RD | SMA | 173 B4 |
| STRADLEY AV | KER | 68 B5 |
| STRAND, THE | LAS | 20 E1 |
| STRATTON LN | SOL | 39 B4 |
| STRAWBERRY DR | MAR | 140 D3 |
| STRAWBERRY LN | SHA | 18 C3 |
| STRAWBERRY RD | MON | 54 C3 |
| STREETER AV | RCO | 99 B2 |
| ST OF GL LNTERN | ORA | 202 A4 |
| STREET 200 | MAD | 57 D1 |
| STREET 225 | MAD | 50 A5 |
| STREET 600 | MAD | 49 B1 |
| STREET 600 | MAD | 49 C4 |
| STREET 603 | MAD | 57 B1 |
| STREIBY RD | IMP | 109 B4 |
| STRINGTOWN RD | BUT | 25 E4 |
| STRIPLIN RD | SUT | 33 D4 |

| STREET | CO. | PAGE & GRID |
|---|---|---|
| STROUD AV | FRCO | 57 C5 |
| STRUCKMAN RD | CAL | 41 B3 |
| STUBBLEFIELD RD | KER | 78 A5 |
| STUBBLEFIELD RD | KER | 87 E1 |
| STUBBY SPRGS TR | RCO | 101 A2 |
| STUDEBAKER RD | LACO | 98 A3 |
| STUDEBAKER RD | LACO | S E1 |
| STUDEBAKER RD | LACO | S E2 |
| STUDEBAKER RD | LACO | T A1 |
| STUHR RD | STA | 47 C4 |
| STUKEY ST | DN | 1 D3 |
| STUMPFIELD MTN | MPA | 49 C3 |
| STUMPTOWN RD | HUM | 9 E4 |
| STUNT RD | LACO | 97 B2 |
| STURGIS RD | VEN | 96 B1 |
| STURM RD | HUM | 16 C3 |
| SUBACO RD | SUT | 33 B3 |
| SUBSTATION RD | MNO | 50 E2 |
| SUCCESS DR | TUL | 68 D3 |
| SUCCESS VLY DR | TUL | 68 E3 |
| SUCKER RUN RD | BUT | 26 A4 |
| SUCKOW RD | KER | 80 D5 |
| SUDDEN RD | SB | 86 B3 |
| SUE AV | KER | 89 C1 |
| SUE ST | KER | 80 B5 |
| SUEY RD | SMA | 173 E3 |
| SUEY CREEK RD | SLO | 76 D5 |
| SUGAR CREEK RD | SIS | 11 D2 |
| SUGARLOAF RD | FRCO | 58 A1 |
| SUGAR LOAF RD | INY | 51 D5 |
| SUGRLF LKSHR RD | SHA | 12 B5 |
| SUGRLOAF LKT RD | SHA | 12 B5 |
| SUGARLOAF TK TR | SBD | 99 E1 |
| SUGAR PINE | PLA | 34 E2 |
| SUGAR PINE PL | BUT | 25 C2 |
| SUGAR PINE RD | TUO | 41 E4 |
| SUGAR PINE SPG | LAS | 14 A3 |
| SUISUN VLY RD | SOL | L E1 |
| SUISUN VLY RD | SOL | 38 E3 |
| SULFUR RD | INY | 52 D5 |
| SULKEY CT | CAL | 41 A5 |
| SULLENGER RD | SUT | 33 B2 |
| SULLIVAN RD | KER | 78 A2 |
| SULLIVAN RD | MPA | 49 B3 |
| SULLIVAN RD | STA | 47 C5 |
| SULLIVAN ST | ORA | T C3 |
| SULLIVAN ST | SA | 195 D5 |
| SULPHUR BANK DR | LAK | 32 A3 |
| SULPHUR MTN RD | VEN | 88 B4 |
| SULPHR MTN RD E | VEN | 83 B4 |
| SULPHUR SPGS RD | MON | 65 B3 |
| SULTANA DR | MCO | 48 A4 |
| SULTZE AV | KER | 78 B5 |
| SUMMERHILL DR | TUO | 42 A3 |
| SUMMER HOMES RD | ML | 164 C2 |
| SUMMERS LN | KLAM | 5 C1 |
| SUMMERS RD | LAS | 21 E5 |
| SUMMERSET RD | SBD | 91 C1 |
| SUMMIT AV | GLE | 24 D3 |
| SUMMIT AV | SBD | 99 A1 |
| SUMMIT RD | BUT | 25 D5 |
| SUMMIT RD | KER | 79 C4 |
| SUMMIT RD | SCL | P C5 |
| SUMMIT RD | SCR | P A5 |
| SUMMIT RD | SCR | 54 B1 |
| SUMMIT CREEK RD | TRI | 17 C2 |
| SUMMIT LAKE DR | NAPA | 38 B1 |
| SUMMIT LEVEL RD | CAL | 41 C3 |
| SUMMITROSE ST | LACO | Q E1 |
| SUMMIT TRUCK TR | SBD | 91 B5 |
| SUMMY | SUT | 33 B2 |
| SUMNER AV | AVLN | 105 B5 |
| SUMNER AV | FRCO | 56 E4 |
| SUMNER AV | FRCO | 58 B4 |
| SUMNER AV | RCO | 98 E2 |
| SUMNER ST | BKD | 166 E3 |
| SUNBURST AV | SBD | 100 E1 |
| SUNEVER RD | SBD | 101 A1 |
| SUNFAIR RD | SBD | 101 A1 |
| SUNFLOWER AV | CM | 197 D3 |
| SUNFLOWER AV | CM | 198 A3 |
| SUNFLOWER AV | LACO | U A2 |
| SUNFLOWR SPG RD | SBD | 94 D2 |
| SUNFLR SPGS SPR | SBD | 94 E3 |
| SUNKIST ST | ANA | 194 A2 |
| SUNKIST ST | ORA | T D2 |
| SUNKIST TR | LPAZ | 104 C4 |
| SUNLAND BLVD | LACO | 97 D1 |
| SUNLAND BLVD | LACO | Q D2 |
| SUNLAND DR | INY | 51 D4 |
| SUNNY LN | AVLN | 105 B5 |
| SUNNY ACRES AV | MCO | 47 E3 |
| SUNNY ACRES AV | MCO | 48 A3 |
| SUNNYBRAE BLVD | SM | 145 A2 |
| SUNNY BRAE LN | HUM | 10 A5 |
| SUNNY HILL RD | SHA | 18 A3 |
| SUNNYSIDE AV | FRCO | 57 D3 |
| SUNNYSIDE AV | FRCO | 57 D4 |
| SUNNYSIDE AV | MAD | 57 A1 |
| SUNNYSIDE AV | MV | 140 A2 |
| SUNNYSIDE RD | LAS | 21 B4 |
| SUNNYSLOPE | FRCO | 58 B2 |
| SUNNYSLOPE RD | SBD | 90 E4 |
| SUNNYVALE AV | CPTO | 149 D1 |
| SUNNYVALE AV | SVL | 148 E5 |
| SUNNY VISTA RD | SBD | 100 E1 |
| SUNOL BLVD | ALA | P B1 |
| SUNRISE | SBD | 101 B1 |
| SUNRISE BLVD | SAC | 34 A5 |
| SUNRISE BLVD | SJCO | 40 B2 |
| SUNRISE HWY | SDCO | 107 D4 |
| SUNRISE HWY | SDCO | 107 D5 |
| SUNRISE WY | PMSP | 206 C5 |
| SUNRISE WY | RCO | 100 D3 |
| SUNRISE SPGS RD | SBD | 93 A5 |
| SUNSET | SAC | 34 B5 |
| SUNSET AV | FRFD | 135 D3 |

| STREET | CO. | PAGE & GRID |
|---|---|---|
| SUNSET AV | KER | 79 E5 |
| SUNSET AV | LACO | R D4 |
| SUNSET AV | MAD | 57 A2 |
| SUNSET AV | MCO | 55 D1 |
| SUNSET AV | RCO | 99 E3 |
| SUNSET AV | SOL | 135 D3 |
| SUNSET BLVD | BH | 183 A1 |
| SUNSET BLVD | KER | 79 A4 |
| SUNSET BLVD | LA | 181 B4 |
| SUNSET BLVD | LA | 182 A4 |
| SUNSET BLVD | LA | 185 D1 |
| SUNSET BLVD | LA | 186 A1 |
| SUNSET BLVD | LACO | 97 C2 |
| SUNSET BLVD | LACO | Q D2 |
| SUNSET BLVD | SD | 213 B5 |
| SUNSET BLVD | SDCO | V B3 |
| SUNSET BLVD | SFCO | L B5 |
| SUNSET BLVD | SF | 141 A5 |
| SUNSET BLVD | SFCO | 45 B2 |
| SUNSET BLVD | LA | 180 C1 |
| SUNSET BLVD W | PLA | 33 E4 |
| SUNSET BLVD W | PLA | 34 A4 |
| SUNSET DR | IMP | 108 C2 |
| SUNSET DR | INY | 60 B4 |
| SUNSET DR | MCO | 47 E4 |
| SUNSET DR | MCO | 48 A4 |
| SUNSET DR | MONT | 53 C2 |
| SUNSET DR | PAC | 167 B2 |
| SUNSET DR | SDCO | 106 C3 |
| SUNSET PKWY | MAR | 38 A4 |
| SUNSET RD | CC | M D3 |
| SUNSET RD | CC | 39 C5 |
| SUNSET RD | CLK | 74 D3 |
| SUNSET RD | GLE | 24 D3 |
| SUNSET RD | SBD | 100 E1 |
| SUNSET ST | FRCO | 66 D2 |
| SUNSET CYN DR | LACO | Q D2 |
| SUNSET CLIFFS BL | SD | 212 B5 |
| SUNSET CLIFFS BL | SDCO | V A3 |
| SUNSET CLIFFS BL | SDCO | 111 C1 |
| SUNSET CRSNG RD | LACO | U B3 |
| SUNSET LAKE RD | ALP | 42 B1 |
| SUNSHINE MNE RD | KER | 80 E3 |
| SUPERIOR AV | CM | 199 A3 |
| SUPERIOR AV | NB | 199 A3 |
| SUPERIOR RD | KER | 78 B3 |
| SURPRISE CYN RD | INY | 71 C3 |
| SURPRISE SPG RD | SBD | 100 E1 |
| SURPRISE VLY RD | LAS | 8 E3 |
| SURPRISE VLY RD | MOD | 7 E3 |
| SURPRISE VLY RD | MOD | 8 E3 |
| SUSAN HILLS DR | LAS | 20 E3 |
| SUSANVILLE RD | LAS | 14 B3 |
| SUSQUEHANNA RD | SIS | 4 D3 |
| SUTLIFF RD | SJCO | 47 D1 |
| SUTTENFIELD RD | SJCO | 40 B3 |
| SUTTER AV | FRCO | 56 E4 |
| SUTTER AV | FRCO | 66 E3 |
| SUTTER AV | MDO | 162 A5 |
| SUTTER LN | AMA | 40 D2 |
| SUTTER RD | HUM | 9 E4 |
| SUTTER RD | HUM | 10 A4 |
| SUTTER RD | YOL | 39 D3 |
| SUTTER ST | AMA | 40 E2 |
| SUTTER ST | SF | 142 B3 |
| SUTTER ST | SF | 143 C4 |
| SUTTER CK IONE- | | |
| -BACK CUTOFF RD | AMA | 40 D2 |
| SUTTR CK VOLCNO | AMA | 40 E2 |
| SUTTR CK VOLCNO | AMA | 41 A2 |
| SUTTER ISLND RD | SAC | M D1 |
| SUTTER ISLND RD | SAC | 39 D3 |
| SUTTERVILLE RD | SAC | 39 D1 |
| SWAN RD | MCO | 48 B4 |
| SWAN RD | SOL | 39 C2 |
| SWAN MTN RD | PLU | 20 B3 |
| SWANSEA RD | LPAZ | 104 D3 |
| SWANSON AV | FRCO | 57 B5 |
| SWANSON AV | FRCO | 57 C5 |
| SWANSON RD | STA | 47 E3 |
| SWANTON RD | SCR | N D5 |
| SWANTON RD | SCR | 53 D1 |
| SWARTHOT CYN RD | SBD | 91 A5 |
| SWASEY DR | SHA | 18 B2 |
| SWEDE CREEK RD | SHA | 18 D2 |
| SWEDE CREEK RD | TRI | 11 A5 |
| SWEDES FLAT RD | BUT | 25 E5 |
| SWEENEY RD | ED | 35 B5 |
| SWEENEY RD | SB | 86 C3 |
| SWEENEY RD | SOL | 39 A2 |
| SWEENEY PASS RD | SDCO | 108 A5 |
| SWEENY RD | MCO | 55 C2 |
| SWEET RD | IMP | 109 A5 |
| SWEETEN LN | SBD | 91 D1 |
| SWEETLAND RD | NEV | 26 B5 |
| SWEETSER RD | KER | 89 E1 |
| SWEETWATER RD | SDCO | V C4 |
| SWEETWATER RD | SDCO | 111 E1 |
| SWEETWATER RD | SDCO | 111 D2 |
| SWEETWTR SPGS BL | SDCO | V E3 |
| SWEETWTR SPG RD | SON | 37 D1 |
| SWEITZER LN | SBD | 92 D5 |
| SWENSEN RD | MCO | 47 D4 |
| SWETZER RD | SUT | 33 E3 |
| SWIFT AV | MCO | 56 A2 |
| SWIFT RD | SBD | 80 E5 |
| SWIFT ST | SC | 169 A4 |
| SWIFT CREEK | TRI | 11 E4 |
| SWIGART RD | SIS | 4 B4 |
| SWISS RANCH RD | CAL | 41 B3 |
| SX RD | MOD | 14 E1 |
| SYCAMORE AV | FRCO | 57 A4 |
| SYCAMORE AV | SDCO | 106 C3 |
| SYCAMORE DR | LACO | 88 E5 |
| SYCAMORE LN | DVS | 136 B3 |
| SYCAMORE RD | ALA | P B1 |
| SYCAMORE RD | KER | 78 E4 |

| STREET | CO. | PAGE & GRID |
|---|---|---|
| SYCAMORE RD | KER | 79 A4 |
| SYCAMORE RD | SDCO | V C5 |
| SYCAMORE RD | SDCO | 111 D2 |
| SYCAMORE RD | VEN | 88 D4 |
| SYCAMORE ST | ANA | 193 B2 |
| SYCAMORE ST | MCO | 47 E3 |
| SYCAMORE ST | MCO | 48 A3 |
| SYCAMORE CYN RD | SB | 87 C4 |
| SYCAMORE CYN RD | STB | 174 E3 |
| SYCAMORE CUTOFF | CLU | 33 A2 |
| SYCAMRE FLAT RD | MON | 65 A2 |
| SYCAMORE SL RD | COL | 33 A2 |
| SYCAMORE VLY RD | CC | M B4 |
| SYCAMORE VLY RD | CC | 46 A1 |
| SYDNOR AV | KER | 80 D1 |
| SYKES RD | INY | 70 B3 |
| SYLVAN AV | STA | 47 D2 |
| SYLVESTER RD | MCO | 55 D1 |
| SYMMES RD | INY | 59 E3 |
| T | | |
| T ST | BKD | 166 D4 |
| T ST | STA | 47 C4 |
| TABL MTN OVRCRS | BUT | 25 C4 |
| TABLE BLUFF RD | HUM | 15 D1 |
| TABLE MTN BL | BUT | 25 C4 |
| TABLE MTN RD | FRCO | 57 D2 |
| TABLE MTN RD | RCO | 100 C5 |
| TABLE MTN TK TR | RCO | 107 C1 |
| TABLEROCK RD | SIS | 4 C4 |
| TABOOSE CK RD | INY | 59 E1 |
| TABOR AV | FRFD | 135 B2 |
| TABOR AV | SOL | 39 A3 |
| TABOR AV E | FRFD | 135 C2 |
| TAECKER RD | IMP | 109 B4 |
| TAFT AV | OR | 194 C3 |
| TAFT AV | ORA | 98 C3 |
| TAFT AV | ORA | T D2 |
| TAFT HWY | KER | 78 C3 |
| TAFT ST | TEH | 24 E1 |
| TAGE RD | SBD | 101 D1 |
| TAGLIO RD | MCO | 47 D5 |
| TAHOE ST | MCO | 48 B4 |
| TAHQTZ-MCCLM WY | PMSP | 206 A4 |
| TALBERT AV | FTNV | 197 A3 |
| TALBERT AV | ORA | 98 B4 |
| TALBERT AV | ORA | T B3 |
| TALBERT LN | SOL | 39 B4 |
| TALBOT ST | SDCO | V A3 |
| TALC CITY RD | INY | 70 D1 |
| TALMAGE RD | U | 123 D4 |
| TAMALPAIS AV | MAR | 38 B5 |
| TAMALPAIS DR | CRTM | 140 B1 |
| TAMARACK AV | SDCO | 106 B3 |
| TAMARACK RD | SHA | 13 C5 |
| TAMARACK RD | SHA | 19 C1 |
| TAMARACK RD | TEH | 19 C4 |
| TAMARACK LK RD | TRI | 12 B3 |
| TAMARACK PK RD | SHA | 13 C5 |
| TAMPA AV | LA | 178 B3 |
| TAMPA AV | LACO | 97 B1 |
| TANABE RD | YUB | 33 D1 |
| TANATEA ST | RCO | 107 C1 |
| TANK FARM RD | KER | 78 A4 |
| TANK FARM RD | SLO | 76 B4 |
| TANNERY GLCH RD | TRI | 11 D5 |
| TAPADERO ST | CAL | 41 A4 |
| TAPIA LN | SBD | 90 E2 |
| TAPLIN RD | NAPA | 29 C3 |
| TAPO RD | VEN | 89 A5 |
| TAPO CANYON RD | VEN | 89 A5 |
| TARA AV | KER | 69 B5 |
| TAR CANYON RD | KIN | 66 E4 |
| TARKE RD | SUT | 33 B2 |
| TARPON DR | SIS | 4 B3 |
| TASSAJARA RD | MON | 64 D2 |
| TATE CREEK RD | SIS | 13 A2 |
| TAVERN RD | SDCO | 107 B5 |
| TAVERNETTI RD | MON | 54 E5 |
| TAVERNETTI RD | MON | 55 A5 |
| TAVERNOR RD | SAC | 40 B2 |
| TAYLOR AV | KER | 78 B1 |
| TAYLOR BLVD | CC | L E3 |
| TAYLOR BLVD | CC | M A3 |
| TAYLOR BLVD | CC | 38 E5 |
| TAYLOR BLVD | MLBR | 144 C5 |
| TAYLOR LN | SIS | 5 B4 |
| TAYLOR RD | CC | 39 C4 |
| TAYLOR RD | STA | 47 C3 |
| TAYLOR ST | SF | 143 B2 |
| TAYLOR ST | SJ | 152 B2 |
| TAYLORSVL TRANS | PLU | 20 D5 |
| TEAFORD SDLE RD | MAD | 49 E4 |
| TEAGUE AV | FRCO | 57 D2 |
| TEAGUE AV | MON | 65 B2 |
| TEAL DR | MOD | 7 A5 |
| TEALE RD | KER | 78 D4 |
| TEALE RD | KER | 79 A4 |
| TEAPOT | TUL | 68 C3 |
| TECHNR RBSN RD | SIS | 5 A4 |
| TECOLOTE RD | SDCO | V B3 |
| TECOLOTE RD | SDCO | 111 C1 |
| TECOPA HOT SPGS | INY | 73 A4 |
| TED ELDER RD | SHA | 13 D3 |
| TED KIPF RD | IMP | 109 C3 |
| TED KIPF RD | IMP | 110 A4 |
| TEDOC RD | TEH | 17 D4 |
| TEFFT ST | SLO | 76 C5 |
| TEGAN RD | SAC | 39 E2 |
| TEGNER RD | MCO | 47 D4 |
| TEHACHAPI BLVD | KER | 79 D4 |
| TEHACHP-WLW SPG | KER | 79 D5 |
| TEHAMA AV | KIN | 67 A4 |
| TEHAMA AV | TEH | 24 D1 |
| TEHAMA ST | GLE | 24 D4 |
| TEHAMA & VNA RD | TEH | 24 E1 |
| TEJON RD | LACO | 90 C4 |
| TELEGRAPH AV | B | 156 B3 |

| STREET | CO. | PAGE & GRID |
|---|---|---|
| TELEGRAPH AV | O | 156 B3 |
| TELEGRAPH AV | S | 160 A2 |
| TELEGRAPH RD | CAL | 40 E5 |
| TELEGRAPH RD | CAL | 41 A5 |
| TELEGRAPH RD | LACO | 89 A4 |
| TELEGRAPH RD | LACO | 98 A2 |
| TELEGRAPH RD | LACO | R B4 |
| TELEGRAPH RD | MPA | 49 B3 |
| TELEGRAPH RD | VEN | 88 E4 |
| TELEGRPH CYN RD | SDCO | V D5 |
| TELEGRPH CYN RD | SDCO | 111 D2 |
| TELEGRAPH CK RD | HUM | 22 A1 |
| TELEGRAPH MN RD | SBD | 83 D3 |
| TELEPHONE RD | SB | 86 C1 |
| TELEPHONE RD | VEN | 88 B5 |
| TELESCOPE PK RD | RD | 10 C4 |
| TELL BLVD | DN | 1 D3 |
| TEMESCAL CYN RD | RCO | 99 A3 |
| TEMPERANCE AV | FRCO | 57 D2 |
| TEMPERANCE AV | FRCO | 57 D5 |
| TEMPLE AV | LACO | R D4 |
| TEMPLE AV | LACO | S E2 |
| TEMPLE ST | LA | 185 C1 |
| TEMPLE ST | LA | 186 B2 |
| TEMPLE CITY BL | LACO | R C3 |
| TEMPLE CREEK | SJCO | 40 C5 |
| TEMPLE CREEK | SJCO | 47 C1 |
| TEMPLE HILLS DR | LAG | 201 D2 |
| TEMPLETON RD | SLO | 76 A2 |
| TENAJA RD | RCO | 99 B5 |
| TENAJA TRUCK TR | RCO | 99 B5 |
| TENMILE RD | MEN | 30 D4 |
| TENMILE CUTF RD | MEN | 30 D4 |
| TENNANT AV | SCL | P E5 |
| TENNANT AV | SCL | 54 D1 |
| TENNANT RD | SIS | 4 E5 |
| TENNANT RD | SIS | 5 A5 |
| TENNANT LAVA BD | MOD | 5 E4 |
| TENNANT LAVA BD | SIS | 5 B5 |
| TENNANT MT HRBN | SIS | 5 A4 |
| TENNESSEE ST | SBD | 99 C2 |
| TENNESSEE ST | VAL | 134 C4 |
| TENNESSEE ST E | FRFD | 135 C3 |
| TENNYSON RD | ALA | N E1 |
| TENNYSON RD | ALA | P A1 |
| TENNYSON RD | ALA | 45 E2 |
| TEPUSQUET RD | SB | 86 D1 |
| TEQUEPIS CYN RD | SB | 87 A3 |
| TERCEIRA RD | MCO | 55 E2 |
| TERMINAL RD | AVLN | 105 B5 |
| TERMINOUS RD | SAC | 39 D4 |
| TERMO GRASSHPPR | LAS | 8 A5 |
| TERMO GRASSHPPR | LAS | 14 E5 |
| TERRA BELLA ST | LACO | Q C2 |
| TERRACE | FRCO | 58 A3 |
| TERRACE RD | RCO | 100 D4 |
| TERRY MILL RD | SHA | 13 A5 |
| TERWER RIFFL RD | DN | 10 A1 |
| TERWILLIGER RD | RCO | 107 C1 |
| TESLA RD | ALA | M D5 |
| TESLA RD | ALA | P D1 |
| TESLA RD | ALA | 46 C2 |
| TESORO RD | SBD | 90 E3 |
| TEST STATION | MNO | 43 C5 |
| TEXAS AV | KER | 79 E5 |
| TEXAS AV | KER | 80 A5 |
| TEXAS RD | STA | 47 C2 |
| TEXAS ST | FRFD | 135 A3 |
| TEXAS ST | SD | 216 B1 |
| TEXAS ST | SDCO | V B3 |
| TEXAS ST | SDCO | 111 D1 |
| TEXAS ST N | SOL | M A1 |
| TEXAS ST N | SOL | 38 E3 |
| TEXAS ST N | FRFD | 135 C3 |
| TEXAS HILL | MPA | 48 E2 |
| TEXAS HILL RD | YUB | 26 A5 |
| TEXAS SPGS RD | SHA | 18 B2 |
| THATCHER RD | SHA | 19 C2 |
| THATCHER MLL RD | SHA | 19 C2 |
| THATCHER RDG RD | BUT | 25 D1 |
| THE BRADSHAW TR | RCO | 102 A5 |
| THEDA ST | RCO | 99 C4 |
| THE INDIAN RD | MOD | 8 B3 |
| THEODORE ST | RCO | 99 D3 |
| THEODORIC RD | SBD | 84 C4 |
| THING RD | SDCO | 112 C2 |
| THIRD ST | C | 124 B5 |
| THISSELL RD | SOL | 39 B2 |
| THOMAS | SON | 31 E5 |
| THOMAS | SON | 37 E1 |
| THOMAS RD | HUM | 16 B5 |
| THOMAS RD | KER | 90 C1 |
| THOMAS RD | MCO | 55 C2 |
| THOMAS RD | SBT | 55 A3 |
| THOMAS RD | SHA | 18 B3 |
| THOMAS RD | SHA | 19 A1 |
| THOMAS ST | KER | 80 A4 |
| THOME RD | YUB | 33 D1 |
| THOMES AV | TEH | 24 D1 |
| THOMPSON AV | FRCO | 57 D3 |
| THOMPSON AV | FRCO | 57 D5 |
| THOMPSON BLVD | VENT | 175 B2 |
| THOMPSON RD | IMP | 109 A5 |
| THOMPSON RD | LAS | 14 B4 |
| THOMPSON RD | MNO | 43 B4 |
| THOMPSON RD | SBD | 81 C5 |
| THOMPSON RD | SLO | 76 C5 |
| THOMPSON RD | SUT | 33 C3 |
| THOMPSON CYN AV | KER | 79 C2 |
| THOMPSON CYN RD | MON | 65 B2 |
| THOMSEN RD | SOL | 39 C2 |
| THORNBERRY RD | MAD | 49 D4 |
| THORNBURG ST | SMA | 173 B3 |
| THORNE AV | FRE | 165 B4 |
| THORNTON AV | ALA | P A1 |
| THORNTON AV | ALA | 45 E3 |
| THORNTON AV | ALA | 46 A3 |

245
THORNTON RD
STREET INDEX
VENZKE RD




| STREET | CO. | PAGE & GRID |
|---|---|---|
| THORNTON RD | MCO | 48 B4 |
| THORNTON RD | SJCO | 40 A4 |
| THOUSND OAKS BL | LACO | 96 E1 |
| THOUSND OAKS BL | VEN | 96 D1 |
| THOUSND PLMS RD | RCO | 100 E3 |
| THOUSAND SPGS | SHA | 13 D3 |
| THREE CHOP RD | MEN | 22 D5 |
| THREE FLAGS HWY | KER | 80 D1 |
| THREE PINES CYN | KER | 80 B1 |
| THREE SLASHS RD | IMP | 110 C2 |
| THRIFT RD | MCO | 48 C5 |
| THRUSH DR | SIS | 4 B3 |
| THUNDER | SDCO | 106 B3 |
| THUNDERBIRD BL | KER | 80 C4 |
| THUNDERBIRD RD | SBD | 91 C3 |
| THUNDER CYN RD | SLO | 75 D2 |
| TIBURON BLVD | MAR | L B4 |
| TIBURON BLVD | MAR | 140 E3 |
| TICE VALLEY BL | CC | L E4 |
| TICE VALLEY BL | CC | M A4 |
| TICE VALLEY BL | CC | 45 E1 |
| TICINO ST | SB | 86 B1 |
| TIEDEMAN RD | STA | 47 B2 |
| TIERNEY RD | HUM | 16 B3 |
| TIERRA BUENA RD | SUT | 33 C2 |
| TIERRA DEL SOL | SDCO | 112 E2 |
| TIERRA RJADA RD | VEN | 88 E5 |
| TIERRA SANTA BL | SDCO | V C2 |
| TIERRA SANTA BL | SDCO | 106 D5 |
| TIFFANY RCH RD | SLO | 76 B4 |
| TIGER CREEK RD | SIS | 11 D2 |
| TILTON AV | SCL | P D4 |
| TILTON DR | LACO | 89 E3 |
| TIM BELL RD | STA | 48 A2 |
| TIMBER COVE RD | SON | 37 A1 |
| TIMBER CRATER | SHA | 13 D3 |
| TIMBUCTOO RD | YUB | 34 A1 |
| TIMM RD | SOL | 39 A2 |
| TIMMONS AV | KER | 68 B5 |
| TIMMONS RD | SIS | 4 B5 |
| TIM MULLEN RD | HUM | 16 B1 |
| TIMS RD | SB | 86 E2 |
| TIN BARN RD | SON | 31 A5 |
| TIN BARN RD | SON | 37 A1 |
| TINDALL RCH RD | MEN | 31 B2 |
| TINNEMAHA RD | INY | 59 E1 |
| TIOGA PASS RD | MPA | 42 E5 |
| TIOGA PASS RD | MPA | 43 A5 |
| TIOGA PASS RD | MPA | 50 A1 |
| TIOGA PASS RD | MPA | 63 D3 |
| TIOGA PASS RD | MNO | 43 A5 |
| TIOGA PASS RD | TUO | 42 E5 |
| TIOGA PASS RD | TUO | 50 A1 |
| TIOGA PASS RD | TUO | 63 A4 |
| TIONESTA RD | MOD | 5 E5 |
| TIONESTA RD | MOD | 6 A4 |
| TIONESTA RD | SIS | 5 D5 |
| TIPPECANOE ST | SBD | 99 C2 |
| TIPTOP RD | MPA | 49 C3 |
| TISDALE | SUT | 33 B3 |
| TITLOW HILL RD | HUM | 10 C5 |
| TITSWORTH RD | IMP | 109 C4 |
| TIZON RD | RCO | 107 B1 |
| TOBACCO | SJCO | 40 C5 |
| TOBIN DR | VAL | 134 B1 |
| TODAYANA WY | PLA | 34 D2 |
| TODCO RD | KER | 69 B5 |
| TODD RD | SON | 37 E2 |
| TODD EYMANN RD | FRCO | 58 D3 |
| TODD VALLEY | PLA | 34 D3 |
| TOEWS AV | MCO | 48 D4 |
| TOFT DR | RCO | 99 A4 |
| TOKAY COLONY RD | SJCO | 40 C4 |
| TOLAND LN | SOL | 39 C4 |
| TOLAND RD | VEN | 88 C4 |
| TOLAND PARK RD | VEN | 88 C4 |
| TOLL GATE WY | BUT | 25 C2 |
| TOLL HOUSE RD | FRCO | 57 D2 |
| TOLL HOUSE RD | FRCO | 58 A2 |
| TOMALES RD | SON | 37 E3 |
| TOMALES PETALMA | MAR | 37 D3 |
| TOM GREEN MN RD | SHA | 18 A1 |
| TOMKI RD | MEN | 23 B5 |
| TOMPKNS HILL RD | HUM | 15 E2 |
| TOM SHAW RD | HUM | 16 B2 |
| TOM WELLS RD | LPAZ | 104 A5 |
| TONNER CYN RD | ORA | U A4 |
| TONZI RD | AMA | 40 D2 |
| TOOBY DR | FRFD | 135 A3 |
| TOOME CAMP | TEH | 24 A2 |
| TOOMES RD | STA | 47 C2 |
| TOPA LN | VEN | 88 C4 |
| TOPANGA CYN BL | LA | 177 B3 |
| TOPANGA CYN BL | LACO | 97 B1 |
| TOPAZ LN | MNO | 42 E1 |
| TOPAZ RD | SBD | 91 B3 |
| TOPEKA DR | LA | 178 C4 |
| TOPO RD | MON | 65 B1 |
| TOPO VALLEY RD | SBT | 65 C1 |
| TOPOCK DAVIS DM | MOH | 95 E1 |
| TOPPEN DORFF LN | HUM | 15 D2 |
| TORO CANYON RD | SB | 87 D4 |
| TORO CREEK RD | SLO | 75 E2 |
| TORO CREEK RD | SLO | 76 A2 |
| TORRANCE BLVD | LACO | 97 D3 |
| TORRANCE BLVD | LACO | S B2 |
| TORREY PINES RD | SD | 211 B2 |
| TORREY PINES RD | SDCO | V A2 |
| TORREY PINES RD | SDCO | 106 C5 |
| TORREY RD N | VEN | 88 E4 |
| TORREY RD S | VEN | 88 E4 |
| TOTH RD | HUM | 22 A1 |
| TOTTEN RD | SHA | 13 E4 |
| TOVEY AV | LACO | 90 A3 |
| TOWER RD | MCO | 48 C4 |
| TOWER RD | SLO | 76 B1 |
| TOWER LINE RD | KER | 79 A4 |

| STREET | CO. | PAGE & GRID |
|---|---|---|
| TOWNE AV | LACO | U C2 |
| TOWNSEND RD | IMP | 109 C5 |
| TOWNSEND RD | SIS | 4 C4 |
| TOWNSEND ST | SBD | 91 D1 |
| TOWNSHIP AV | VEN | 88 E5 |
| TOWNSHIP AV | VEN | 89 A5 |
| TOWNSHIP RD | KLAM | 5 B2 |
| TOWNSHIP RD | YUB | 34 A1 |
| TOWNSHIP RD N | SUT | 33 C2 |
| TOWNSHIP RD S | SUT | 33 C3 |
| TOZER ST | MAD | 57 A2 |
| TRABUCO RD | ORA | 98 D4 |
| TRABUCO RD | ORA | T E3 |
| TRACTOR AV | FRCO | 66 D2 |
| TRACY AV | KER | 78 A2 |
| TRACY BLVD | SBD | 100 D1 |
| TRACY BLVD | SJCO | 39 E5 |
| TRACY BLVD | SJCO | 46 E1 |
| TRAGEDY SPGS RD | AMA | 35 E5 |
| TRAIL CANYON RD | INY | 72 A1 |
| TRAILS END LN | RCO | 107 C1 |
| TRAILS END RD | SIS | 4 C5 |
| TRAILS END CAMP | SBD | 96 B5 |
| TRAMPA CYN RD | MON | 64 C1 |
| TRAMWAY RD | TEH | 19 C4 |
| TRANCAS ST | NAP | 133 C2 |
| TRANCAS ST | NAPA | 133 D2 |
| TRASK AV | GGR | 195 B2 |
| TRASK AV | ORA | T B3 |
| TRAUTWEIN RD | RCO | 99 B3 |
| TRAVIS BL | FRFD | 135 B3 |
| TRAVIS BLVD | SOL | L E1 |
| TRAVIS BLVD | SOL | M A1 |
| TRAYNHAM RD | COL | 33 A3 |
| TREAT BLVD | CC | M A3 |
| TREAT BLVD | CC | 38 E5 |
| TREAT BLVD | CC | 39 A5 |
| TREDWAY | SJCO | 40 A4 |
| TREFOIL LN | SHA | 18 D3 |
| TREMONT RD | SOL | 39 C1 |
| TREMONT ST | AVLN | 105 B5 |
| TRENTHAM RD | IMP | 109 B5 |
| TRES CERITOS AV | RCO | 99 D4 |
| TRESTLE GLEN | MAR | 45 B1 |
| TRESTLE GLEN RD | O | 158 C3 |
| TRETHEWAY RD | SJCO | 40 B4 |
| TRIANGLE RD | MPA | 49 B3 |
| TRIANGLE RCH RD | MOD | 6 D4 |
| TRIANGLE RCH RD | STA | 47 D2 |
| TRIMBLE RD | SCL | P B3 |
| TRIMMER SPGS RD | FRCO | 58 A3 |
| TRIMMER SPGS RD | INY | 58 C2 |
| TRINDADE RD | MCO | 48 B4 |
| TRNIDAD SCNC DR | HUM | 9 E4 |
| TRINITY | TEH | 18 D5 |
| TRINITY AV | FRCO | 56 E3 |
| TRINITY AV | FRCO | 57 A4 |
| TRINITY RD | SON | 38 B2 |
| TRINITY ST | FRE | 165 C4 |
| TRINITY ALPS RD | TRI | 11 D5 |
| TRINITY DAM BL | TRI | 11 D5 |
| TRINITY DAM BL | TRI | 17 E1 |
| TRINITY MTN RD | SHA | 12 A5 |
| TRINITY PINE DR | TRI | 17 B3 |
| TRIPP FLATS RD | RIV | 100 B5 |
| TRIUNFO CYN RD | LACO | 96 E1 |
| TRONA RD | SBD | 80 E2 |
| TRONA RD | SBD | 81 A1 |
| TRONA AIRPRT RD | INY | 71 B4 |
| TRONA WLDRSE RD | INY | 71 B4 |
| TROPICANA AV | CLK | 74 D3 |
| TROPICANA AV | CLK | 210 C4 |
| TROWER | MPA | 49 A3 |
| TROWER AV | NAP | 133 A1 |
| TROY RD | SBD | 92 C2 |
| TRUCKEE AV | TEH | 24 D1 |
| TRUCKE ARPRT RD | NEV | 27 D5 |
| TRUCKE-TAHO ARP | NEV | 35 E1 |
| TRUESDALE RD | SLO | 76 D1 |
| TRUEX RD | BUT | 25 D3 |
| TRUMAN RD | KER | 89 D1 |
| TRUMAN MDWS RD | MNO | 44 C5 |
| TRUMBULL RD | LAS | 21 D2 |
| TRUXTUN AV | BKD | 166 B3 |
| TRUXTUN AV | KER | 78 D3 |
| TSCHIRKY RD | SIS | 5 D2 |
| TUBBS RD | SOL | 39 A2 |
| TUCACOTA HLS RD | RCO | 99 E5 |
| TUCKER RD | KER | 79 C4 |
| TUCKER RD | LAS | 21 D5 |
| TUCKER CYN RD | SLO | 76 D1 |
| TUCSON AV | KIN | 67 D4 |
| TUDOR RD | SUT | 33 C3 |
| TUGG WY | CAL | 41 A5 |
| TUJUNGA AV | LACO | Q D3 |
| TUJUNGA CYN BL | LACO | Q E1 |
| TULARE AV | KER | 77 E2 |
| TULARE AV | FRCO | 57 C3 |
| TULARE AV | TUL | 68 B1 |
| TULARE ST | FRE | 165 D4 |
| TULAROSA RD | SB | 86 C3 |
| TULE LN | CC | 39 C5 |
| TULE LN | GLE | 24 E4 |
| TULE RD | COL | 33 A3 |
| TULE RD | YOL | 39 D2 |
| TULE CYN TK TR | RCO | 107 C1 |
| TULE CREEK RD | TRI | 17 B2 |
| TULEDAD RD | LAS | 8 D5 |
| TULE PEAK RD | RCO | 107 B1 |
| TULE SPRING RD | INY | 72 A2 |
| TULE SPGS TK TR | SDCO | 107 B4 |
| TULIP AV | STA | 47 C4 |
| TULLOCH RD | MCO | 48 B1 |
| TULLOCH RD | TUO | 41 B5 |
| TULLY RD | MDO | 162 A2 |
| TULLY RD | SJCO | 40 C4 |
| TULLY RD | SCL | P C3 |

| STREET | CO. | PAGE & GRID |
|---|---|---|
| TULLY RD | SCL | 46 B4 |
| TULLY RD | STA | 47 C2 |
| TULLY CREEK RD | HUM | 10 C3 |
| TUMBLEWEED RD | LACO | 90 C4 |
| TUNA CANYON RD | LACO | 97 B2 |
| TUNGSTEN RD | MNO | 51 D3 |
| TUNGSTEN CTY RD | INY | 51 C4 |
| TUNITAS CK RD | SMCO | N C3 |
| TUNITAS CK RD | SMCO | 45 C4 |
| TUNNEL RD | B | 156 C4 |
| TUOLUMNE AV | FRCO | 56 D4 |
| TUOLUMNE BLVD | MDO | 162 A4 |
| TUOLUMNE DR | MLBR | 144 B5 |
| TUOLUMNE RD | STA | 47 C3 |
| TUOLUMNE ST | SOL | L D2 |
| TUOLUMNE ST | VAL | 134 D2 |
| TUPMAN RD | KER | 78 B3 |
| TURK ST | SF | 142 A3 |
| TURK ST | SF | 143 B5 |
| TURKEY AV | BUT | 25 D5 |
| TURKEY FLAT RD | MON | 66 D4 |
| TURKEY HILL RD | KLAM | 5 E2 |
| TURLOCK AV | SCL | P E5 |
| TURLOCK AV | SCL | 54 D1 |
| TURLOCK RD | MCO | 48 B3 |
| TURNBULL CYN RD | LACO | 98 B2 |
| TURNBULL CYN RD | LACO | R D4 |
| TURNELL RD | TEH | 18 C4 |
| TURNER AV | BUT | 33 C1 |
| TURNER AV | MCO | 47 D4 |
| TURNER AV | SBD | U E2 |
| TURNER AV | SBD | 98 E2 |
| TURNER DR | TUL | 68 B2 |
| TURNER RD | AMA | 40 E2 |
| TURNER RD | MCO | 47 D4 |
| TURNER RD | SJCO | 39 E4 |
| TURNER RD | SJCO | 40 A4 |
| TURNER RD | STA | 47 D3 |
| TURNER ISLND RD | MCO | 56 A1 |
| TURQUOISE ST | SD | 211 A5 |
| TURQUOISE ST | SDCO | V A2 |
| TURQUOISE ST | SDCO | 106 C5 |
| TURRI RD | SLO | 75 E3 |
| TURRI RD | SLO | 76 A3 |
| TURTLE MTN RD | SBD | 95 C4 |
| TURTLE VLY RD | SBD | 91 C2 |
| TUSCAN SPGS RD | TEH | 18 D4 |
| TUSSING RCH RD | SBD | 91 C4 |
| TUSTIN AV | CM | 199 C3 |
| TUSTIN AV | NB | 199 C3 |
| TUSTIN AV | OR | 194 E3 |
| TUSTIN AV | OR | 196 E2 |
| TUSTIN AV | ORA | 98 C4 |
| TUSTIN AV | ORA | 196 E4 |
| TUSTIN AV | ORA | 199 C3 |
| TUSTIN AV | SA | 196 E4 |
| TUSTIN AV | ORA | T D2 |
| TU SU LN | INY | 51 D4 |
| TUTTLECREEK RD | INY | 60 A4 |
| TUTTLETOWN RD | TUO | 41 C5 |
| TUXEDO AV N | S | 160 C3 |
| TUXFORD ST | LACO | Q D2 |
| TWEEDY BLVD | LACO | R A5 |
| TWENTIETH ST | C | 124 E5 |
| TWENTY-EIGHT MI | STA | 47 E1 |
| TWNTY MULE TEAM | INY | 72 A1 |
| TWNTY MULE TEAM | KER | 80 C4 |
| TWNTYNINE PALMS | SBD | 100 E1 |
| TWNTYNINE PALMS | SBD | 101 D1 |
| TWENTY-SIX MILE | STA | 47 D1 |
| TWIN RD S | MNO | 43 A5 |
| TWIN CITIES RD | SAC | 39 E3 |
| TWIN CITIES RD | SAC | 40 A3 |
| TWIN LAKES RD | MNO | 43 B3 |
| TWIN LAKES RD | TRI | 12 B3 |
| TWIN LKS CMPST | ALP | 35 E5 |
| TWIN OAKES RD | KER | 79 D3 |
| TWIN OAKS VLY | SDCO | 106 C5 |
| TWIN PEAKS RD | SDCO | 106 D4 |
| TWIN PINES RD | RCO | 100 A3 |
| TWIN VALLEY RD | LAK | 31 E2 |
| TWIN VIEW BLVD | SHA | 18 C2 |
| TWISSELMAN RD | KER | 67 B5 |
| TWIST RD | TUO | 41 C5 |
| TWIST RD | TUO | 48 C1 |
| TWITCHLL ISL RD | SAC | M D2 |
| TWITCHLL ISL RD | SAC | 39 C4 |
| TWO MILE RD | COL | 32 D1 |
| TWO MILE RD | SBD | 101 B1 |
| TYLER AV | LACO | R C4 |
| TYLER RD | AMA | 40 E1 |
| TYLER RD | TEH | 18 D5 |
| TYLER ST | MONT | 167 E3 |
| TYLER ST | RCO | 99 A3 |
| TYLER ST | RCO | 101 B4 |
| TYLER ST | SAL | 171 B2 |
| TYLER ST | SDCO | V D3 |
| TYLER ST | SDCO | 111 D1 |
| TYLER FOOT CRSG | NEV | 26 B5 |
| TYLER GULCH RD | SIS | 3 D4 |
| TYLER ISLAND RD | SAC | M E2 |
| TYLER ISLAND RD | SAC | 39 D4 |
| U | | |
| U ST | FRE | 165 E3 |
| UBEHEBE RD | INY | 60 E4 |
| UGO ST | MCO | 48 A4 |
| UKIAH RD | MEN | 31 B2 |
| UKIAH BOONVILLE | MEN | 30 E3 |
| UKIAH BOONVILLE | MEN | 31 A3 |
| UKONOM LKOUT RD | SIS | 2 E5 |
| ULLREY AV | SJCO | 47 C1 |
| ULRIC ST | SD | 213 D3 |
| ULRIC ST | SDCO | V B3 |
| ULRIC ST | SDCO | 111 C1 |
| UNDERPASS RD | MEN | 22 E4 |
| UNDERSTOCK DR | BUT | 25 C2 |
| UNDERWOOD LN | INY | 51 D4 |

| STREET | CO. | PAGE & GRID |
|---|---|---|
| UNDERWOOD RD | MON | 54 C5 |
| UNDERWD MTN RD | TRI | 16 E1 |
| UNDINE RD | SJCO | 46 E1 |
| UNION AV | BKD | 166 E3 |
| UNION AV | KER | 166 E5 |
| UNION AV | FRFD | 135 C4 |
| UNION AV | SB | 86 C1 |
| UNION AV | SCL | P B4 |
| UNION AV | SCL | 46 B5 |
| UNION AV | SOL | 38 E3 |
| UNION RD | KER | 78 B4 |
| UNION RD | MAN | 161 A3 |
| UNION RD | SBT | 54 E3 |
| UNION RD | SJCO | 47 B1 |
| UNION RD | SLO | 76 B1 |
| UNION ST | EUR | 121 C2 |
| UNION ST | HUM | 15 E1 |
| UNION CITY BLVD | ALA | N E1 |
| UNION CITY BLVD | ALA | P A1 |
| UNION CITY BLVD | ALA | 45 E3 |
| UNION HILL RD | TRI | 17 D2 |
| UNION RIDGE RD | ED | 34 E5 |
| UNION SCHOOL RD | SHA | 18 C1 |
| UNION SUGAR AV | SB | 86 B3 |
| UNITED ST | KER | 80 A5 |
| UNIVERSITY AV | ALA | L D4 |
| UNIVERSITY AV | KER | 78 E2 |
| UNIVERSITY AV | PA | 147 B2 |
| UNIVERSITY AV | RIV | 205 B2 |
| UNIVERSITY AV | RCO | 99 B2 |
| UNIVERSITY AV | SAL | 171 A4 |
| UNIVERSITY AV | SD | 214 D5 |
| UNIVERSITY AV | SD | 215 D1 |
| UNIVERSITY AV | SD | 216 D1 |
| UNIVERSITY AV | SDCO | V B3 |
| UNIVERSITY AV | SDCO | 111 D1 |
| UNIVERSITY AV | SMCO | N E2 |
| UNIVERSITY DR | IRV | 200 C2 |
| UNIVERSITY DR | ORA | 98 C4 |
| UNIVERSITY DR | ORA | T D4 |
| UPAS ST | SD | 216 A1 |
| UPHAM RD | BUT | 25 E5 |
| UPHILL RD | SBD | 101 A1 |
| UPJOHN RD W | KER | 80 D1 |
| UPLAND RD | VEN | 88 C5 |
| UPPER TER | AVLN | 105 B5 |
| UPPER BEAR RIV | HUM | 15 D3 |
| UPPR COUGR FIRE | SIS | 4 D5 |
| UPPR COUGR FIRE | SIS | 12 D1 |
| UPPER DIVISN CK | INY | 59 E2 |
| UPPER DORRAY RD | CAL | 41 A2 |
| UPPER FALL RD | SIS | 13 A2 |
| UPPER LK CTY RD | MOD | 7 D5 |
| UPR MAD RIV RD | TRI | 17 A4 |
| UPPER PALMRO RD | BUT | 25 D5 |
| UPPER SHOTGN RD | SHA | 12 C4 |
| UPPER S FORK RD | TRI | 16 E2 |
| UPPR SUMMRS MDW | MNO | 43 B3 |
| UPPER TOBY RCH | HUM | 16 C5 |
| UPPER WILLOW CK | SIS | 4 C3 |
| UPTON RD | AMA | 40 E1 |
| USAL RD | MEN | 22 B2 |
| USFS CAMP RD | TRI | 17 A1 |
| USONA RD | MPA | 49 C4 |
| USTICK RD | STA | 47 C3 |
| UTAH AV | SSF | 144 C1 |
| UTAH DR | INY | 70 E1 |
| UTAH ST | FRFD | 135 B3 |
| UTAH TR | SBD | 101 C1 |
| UTAH MINE RD | BUT | 25 D2 |
| UTICA AV | KIN | 67 D4 |
| UTICA PWRHSE RD | CAL | 41 C4 |
| UVAS RD | SCL | 54 C1 |
| UXMAL | BAJA | 112 B4 |
| V | | |
| V ST | MER | 170 A4 |
| VADNEY AV | TEH | 24 E2 |
| VAIL | SJCO | 39 E3 |
| VAIL RD | IMP | 109 A3 |
| VAIRA RANCH RD | AMA | 40 D2 |
| VALDOR RD | TRI | 17 C1 |
| VALENCIA AV | LACO | 89 B4 |
| VALENCIA AV | ORA | 98 C3 |
| VALENCIA AV | ORA | T D1 |
| VALENCIA BLVD | TUL | 58 C5 |
| VALENCIA BLVD | TUL | 68 C1 |
| VALENCIA DR | SCR | 54 B2 |
| VALENSIN RD | SAC | 40 A3 |
| VALENTINE AV | FRCO | 57 C4 |
| VALENTINE AV | FRCO | 67 C1 |
| VALERIA AV | FRCO | 56 B2 |
| VALERIO ST | STB | 174 B3 |
| VALK RD | STA | 47 E2 |
| VALLECITO ST | SHA | 18 C1 |
| VALLECITOS RD | ALA | P C1 |
| VALLECITOS RD | ALA | 46 B2 |
| VALLE VISTA AV | VAL | 134 C3 |
| VALLE VISTA RD | SBD | 101 B1 |
| VALLEY AV | ALA | M B5 |
| VALLEY AV | ALA | P B1 |
| VALLEY AV | ALA | 46 B2 |
| VALLEY BLVD | LACO | 97 E2 |
| VALLEY BLVD | LACO | 98 B2 |
| VALLEY BLVD | LACO | R C3 |
| VALLEY BLVD | SBD | 99 A2 |
| VALLEY PKWY | SDCO | 106 D3 |
| VALLEY RD | ED | 34 C5 |
| VALLEY RD | KER | 80 C3 |
| VALLEY RD | MEN | 23 A5 |
| VALLEY RD | PLA | 34 A3 |
| VALLEY RD | SAC | 34 C5 |
| VALLEY RD E | SB | 87 D4 |
| VALLEY RD W | MOD | 8 B3 |
| VALLEY CTR RD | SBD | 92 B1 |
| VALLEY CTR RD | SDCO | 106 E3 |
| VALLEY CIR BL | LACO | 97 B1 |
| VALLEY CTOFF RD | LAS | 14 B3 |

| STREET | CO. | PAGE & GRID |
|---|---|---|
| VALLEY FORD RD | SON | 37 D3 |
| VLY FRD/FRNKLN- -MARSH RD | MAR | 37 D3 |
| VLY FRD/FRNKLN- -SCHOOL RD | MAR | 37 D3 |
| VALLEY HOME RD | STA | 47 D1 |
| VALLEY SAGE RD | LACO | 89 D4 |
| VALLEY VIEW DR | CAL | 41 C3 |
| VALLEY VIEW DR | SBD | 102 C1 |
| VALLEY VIEW RD | JKSN | 3 E1 |
| VALLEY VIEW RD | SBD | 91 C1 |
| VALLEY VIEW ST | ORA | 98 B3 |
| VALLEY VIEW ST | ORA | T B2 |
| VALLEY VW LKOUT | TEH | 24 A2 |
| VALLEY VISTA BL | LA | 178 E5 |
| VALLEY WELLS RD | INY | 71 B4 |
| VALLEY WELLS RD | SBD | 81 C5 |
| VALLEY WEST RD | KER | 78 A4 |
| VALLOMBROSA AV | BUT | 25 B3 |
| VALLOMBROSA AV | BUT | 124 D4 |
| VALLOMBROSA AV | C | 124 D4 |
| VALOS RD | KER | 78 E5 |
| VALPARAISO AV | SMCO | N D2 |
| VALPARAISO AV | SCL | 45 D4 |
| VALPICO RD | SJCO | 46 E2 |
| VALPREDO AV | KER | 78 D5 |
| VAL VERDE | PLA | 34 B4 |
| VALYERMO | LACO | 90 C4 |
| VAN ALDEN AV | LA | 178 C4 |
| VAN ALLEN | SJCO | 40 C5 |
| VAN ALLEN | SJCO | 47 C1 |
| VAN ARSDALE RD | MEN | 23 B5 |
| VAN BRMMR LKOUT | SIS | 5 B4 |
| VAN BUREN BLVD | RCO | 99 A2 |
| VAN BUREN ST | MONT | 167 E4 |
| VAN BUREN ST | RCO | 101 A4 |
| VANCE AV | HUM | 15 D5 |
| VAN CLIFF | MCO | 47 E5 |
| VANDEGRIFT BLVD | SDCO | 106 B2 |
| VANDEGRIFT RD | SDCO | 106 B2 |
| VANDEN RD | SOL | 39 A3 |
| VANDENBERG RD | SB | 86 B2 |
| VANDER LINDN RD | IMP | 112 C3 |
| VANDER POEL RD | IMP | 112 A3 |
| VANDER VEER RD | RCO | 101 C5 |
| VAN DOLLEN RD | SLO | 66 B5 |
| VAN DUSEN CYN | SBD | 92 A5 |
| VAN DUZEN RD | TRI | 16 E4 |
| VAN DUZEN RD E | TRI | 16 E3 |
| VAN GORDN CK RD | SLO | 75 C1 |
| VAN LOON CUTOFF | MNO | 51 D2 |
| VAN NESS AV | FRE | 165 D3 |
| VAN NESS AV | FRCO | 57 C3 |
| VAN NESS AV | LACO | Q D5 |
| VAN NESS AV | SF | 143 A4 |
| VAN NESS AV | SFCO | L B4 |
| VAN NESS AV | SFCO | 45 C1 |
| VAN NESS AV S | SF | 142 C4 |
| VAN NESS RD | TRI | 12 A5 |
| VAN NUYS BLVD | LACO | 89 C5 |
| VAN NUYS BLVD | LACO | 97 C1 |
| VAN NUYS BLVD | LACO | Q C1 |
| VANOWEN ST | BUR | 179 B2 |
| VANOWEN ST | LA | 177 A2 |
| VANOWEN ST | LA | 178 B2 |
| VANOWEN ST | LA | 179 B2 |
| VAN SICKLE RD | SOL | 39 A4 |
| VARGAS RD | ALA | P B1 |
| VARGAS RD | ALA | 46 B3 |
| VARNER RD | RCO | 100 D3 |
| VARNI RD | SCR | 54 B2 |
| VASCO RD | ALA | M D5 |
| VASCO RD | ALA | 46 C2 |
| VASCO RD | CC | M D4 |
| VASCO RD | CC | 46 C1 |
| VASQUEZ CYN RD | LACO | 89 C4 |
| VASQUEZ CK RD | SBT | 55 D4 |
| VASSAR AV | MCO | 48 C5 |
| VASSAR ST | RENO | 130 C4 |
| VAUGHN AV | MCO | 48 B4 |
| VAUGHN RD | RCO | 108 E1 |
| VAUGHN RD | SOL | 39 B2 |
| VAWTER RD | COL | 32 E3 |
| VAWTER RANCH RD | RCO | 99 E5 |
| VEDDER RD | SHA | 13 C5 |
| VEE BEE ST | RCO | 100 E3 |
| VENCILL RD | IMP | 112 C3 |
| VENDEL RD | IMP | 108 E4 |
| VENICE BLVD | LA | 183 C5 |
| VENICE BLVD | LA | 184 C3 |
| VENICE BLVD | LA | 185 C3 |
| VENICE BLVD | LA | 187 C2 |
| VENICE BLVD | LA | 188 A1 |
| VENICE BLVD | LACO | 97 C2 |
| VENICE BLVD | LACO | Q C4 |
| VENTURA AV | FRCO | 57 D3 |
| VENTURA AV | MAD | 56 D1 |
| VENTURA AV | VEN | 88 A5 |
| VENTURA AV | VENT | 175 B2 |
| VENTURA BLVD | LA | 177 D4 |
| VENTURA BLVD | LA | 178 A4 |
| VENTURA BLVD | LACO | 97 C1 |
| VENTURA FRWY | BUR | 179 C5 |
| VENTURA FRWY | LA | 177 C4 |
| VENTURA FRWY | LA | 178 B4 |
| VENTURA FRWY | LA | 179 C5 |
| VENTURA FRWY | LACO | 97 A1 |
| VENTURA FRWY | VENT | 175 C2 |
| VENTURA FRWY | VEN | 88 A5 |
| VENTURA FRWY | VEN | 96 C1 |
| VENTURA RD | MCO | 48 B5 |
| VENTURA RD | OXN | 176 A4 |
| VENTURA RD | VEN | 96 B1 |
| VENTURA ST | FRE | 165 D5 |
| VENTURA ST | VEN | 88 D4 |
| VENTURE VLY RD | SDCO | 107 C3 |
| VENZKE RD | SHA | 18 D3 |


STREETS

# STREET INDEX

| STREET | CO. | PAGE & GRID |
|---|---|---|
| VERA AV | KER | 80 D1 |
| VERANO AV | SON | 132 C3 |
| VERBENA AV | C | 124 E2 |
| VERBENA AV | SBD | 91 B3 |
| VERBENA DR | RCO | 100 D2 |
| VERDE AV | MCO | 47 D4 |
| VERDEMNT RCH RD | SBD | 99 B1 |
| VERDE SCHOOL RD | IMP | 112 C3 |
| VERDI PEAK RD | SIE | 27 E4 |
| VERDUGO AV | BUR | 179 B4 |
| VERDUGO AV | LACO | Q D3 |
| VERDUGO BLVD | LACO | R A2 |
| VERDUGO LN | KER | 78 C2 |
| VERDUGO RD | LACO | R A3 |
| VERMICULITE MN | SBD | 100 E2 |
| VERMONT AV | ANA | 193 C3 |
| VERMONT AV | LA | 182 B5 |
| VERMONT AV | LA | 185 C5 |
| VERMONT AV | LACO | 97 D3 |
| VERMONT AV | LACO | S C2 |
| VERMONT CYN RD | LA | 182 B2 |
| VERNON AV | LACO | 97 D2 |
| VERNON AV | LACO | Q E4 |
| VERNON AV | LACO | U A1 |
| VERNON RD | SUT | 33 D4 |
| VERSAILLES AV | A | 159 A2 |
| VESTA ST | SDCO | 111 D1 |
| VESTA ST | SDCO | V C4 |
| VESTAL RD | TEH | 18 A4 |
| VETERAN AV | LACO | Q C5 |
| VETERANS HALL | TRI | 10 E5 |
| VIA CAPRI | SD | 211 A3 |
| VIA DE LA VALLE | SDCO | 106 C4 |
| VIA DEL REY | MONT | 167 D4 |
| VIA DEL REY | MON | 53 E3 |
| VIADUCT BLVD | SBDO | 207 B2 |
| VIA GAYUBA | MONT | 167 D4 |
| VIA PARAISO | MONT | 167 D4 |
| VIA RANCHO PKWY | SDCO | 106 D4 |
| VIA SECO ST | SBD | 92 A3 |
| VIA VERDE | LACO | U A2 |
| VICHY SPGS RD | MEN | 31 B2 |
| VICKREY LN | SOL | 38 E2 |
| VICTOR AV | SHA | 18 C2 |
| VICTOR RD | SJCO | 40 B4 |
| VICTOR ST | KER | 80 D1 |
| VICTORIA AV | RCO | 99 A3 |
| VICTORIA AV | RIV | 205 C4 |
| VICTORIA CT | KER | 79 C4 |
| VICTORIA DR | SDCO | 107 B5 |
| VICTORIA DR | SHA | 18 B2 |
| VICTORIA ST | LACO | 97 E3 |
| VICTORIA ST | LACO | S C1 |
| VICTORIA ST | ORA | T C4 |
| VICTORIA ST | SM | 199 A2 |
| VICTORIA ST | STB | 174 B4 |
| VICTORY AV | STA | 47 D1 |
| VICTORY BLVD | BUR | 179 B2 |
| VICTORY BLVD | LA | 177 C2 |
| VICTORY BLVD | LA | 178 B3 |
| VICTORY BLVD | LA | 179 B2 |
| VICTORY BLVD | LACO | 97 D1 |
| VICTORY BLVD | LACO | Q C2 |
| VICTORY HWY | CC | M C3 |
| VICTORY HWY | CC | 39 C5 |
| VICTORY HWY | SAC | M D1 |
| VICTORY PL | BUR | 179 D2 |
| VICTORY PL | LACO | Q D2 |
| VICTORY RD | SJCO | 47 D1 |
| VIEJAS GRADE | SDCO | 107 B5 |
| VIERRA RD | YUB | 26 A5 |
| VIEUDELOU AV | AVLN | 104 B4 |
| VIEW DR | TUL | 58 B4 |
| VIEW LAND RD | LAS | 21 D3 |
| VILAS RD | BUT | 25 C2 |
| VILLA AV | EC | 217 C1 |
| VILLA AV | SR | 139 D3 |
| VILLA RD | IMP | 109 B5 |
| VILLA ST | SAL | 171 B3 |
| VILLA CREEK RD | SLO | 75 D2 |
| VILLAGE DR | AMA | 40 D3 |
| VILLAGE RD | SDCO | 106 C5 |
| VLLA L JOLLA DR | SD | 211 C1 |
| VLLA MANUCHA RD | STA | 47 C4 |
| VILLA PARK RD | ORA | T E2 |
| VINA RD | TEH | 24 E2 |
| VINCENT AV | LACO | R E3 |
| VINCENT RD | MCO | 47 E3 |
| VINCENT RD | MCO | 48 A3 |
| VINCENT RD | STA | 47 E3 |
| VINCENT RD | STA | 48 A3 |
| VINE AV | MCO | 48 B4 |
| VINE AV | SJCO | 47 D1 |
| VINE ST | LA | 181 D5 |
| VINE ST | LACO | Q D3 |
| VINE ST | SDCO | V E2 |
| VINE ST | SDCO | 107 A5 |
| VINE ST | SJ | 152 B4 |
| VINE WY | KER | 79 C1 |
| VINE HILL RD | SCR | P B5 |
| VINE HILL RD | SCR | 54 A1 |
| VINELAND AV | FRCO | 57 A4 |
| VINELAND AV | LACO | 97 D1 |
| VINELAND AV | LACO | Q D2 |
| VINELAND RD | KER | 78 E4 |
| VINEWOOD AV | MCO | 47 E4 |
| VINEWOOD AV | MCO | 48 A4 |
| VINEYARD AV | ALA | M C5 |
| VINEYARD AV | ALA | P C1 |
| VINEYARD AV | ALA | 46 B2 |
| VINEYARD AV | OXN | 176 D1 |
| VINEYARD AV | SBD | 98 E2 |
| VINEYARD AV | SBD | U E3 |
| VINEYARD AV | VEN | 176 D1 |
| VINEYARD DR | SLO | 75 E1 |
| VINEYARD DR | SLO | 76 A1 |
| VINEYARD RD | PLA | 34 A5 |

| STREET | CO. | PAGE & GRID |
|---|---|---|
| VINEYARD RD | SJCO | 40 A2 |
| VINEYARD RD | STA | 47 B3 |
| VINEYARD RD | YUB | 34 A2 |
| VINEYARD WY | MCO | 56 B1 |
| VINEYARD CYN RD | MON | 66 B4 |
| VINNUM RD | HUM | 16 B4 |
| VINTON GULCH RD | BUT | 25 D3 |
| VINTON LOYALTON | PLU | 27 D3 |
| VIOLA AV | TEH | 24 D2 |
| VIOLA MINERAL | TEH | 19 C3 |
| VIRGIL AV | LACO | Q E4 |
| VIRGINIA | SBD | 92 D5 |
| VIRGINIA AV | KIN | 67 E4 |
| VIRGINIA AV | MDO | 162 B2 |
| VIRGINIA RD | LACO | R B3 |
| VIRGINIA RD | STA | 47 E2 |
| VIRGINIA RD | STA | 48 A2 |
| VIRGINIA RD | YUB | 33 E1 |
| VIRGINIA ST | RCO | 99 D3 |
| VIRGINIA ST N | RENO | 130 B2 |
| VIRGINIA ST S | RENO | 130 B3 |
| VIRGINIA LK RD | MNO | 43 B4 |
| VIRGINIATOWN RD | PLA | 34 B3 |
| VISALIA RD | FRCO | 58 D4 |
| VISALIA RD | TUL | 68 C1 |
| VISTA AV | MCO | 48 D5 |
| VISTA AV | RCO | 98 E3 |
| VISTA AV | SBD | 98 D1 |
| VISTA LN | LAS | 21 B4 |
| VISTA RD | SBD | 91 B2 |
| VISTA WY | SDCO | 106 B3 |
| VISTA CHINO | PMSP | 206 A2 |
| VISTA CHINO | RCO | 100 D3 |
| VISTA DEL MAR | LACO | 97 C2 |
| VISTA DL MAR BL | ELS | 189 A4 |
| VISTA DL MAR BL | LACO | Q C5 |
| VISTA DEL VALLE | LA | 182 B1 |
| VISTA DE ORO | RCO | 100 E3 |
| VISTA ENCINA AV | MDO | 162 D3 |
| VISTA GRANDE DR | KER | 79 D1 |
| VISTA MINE RD | IMP | 110 A4 |
| VIVIAN RD | STA | 47 C3 |
| VLASNIK RD | KER | 77 E2 |
| VOGEL RD | IMP | 111 E3 |
| VOGEL RD | KER | 79 D5 |
| VOLCANO CIR | BUT | 25 B3 |
| VOLCANO PIONEER | AMA | 41 A2 |
| VOLCANOVILLE RD | ED | 34 E3 |
| VOLLEY RD | PLA | 34 C3 |
| VOLTA RD | MCO | 55 D1 |
| VOLTAIRE ST | SDCO | V A3 |
| VOLTAIRE ST | SDCO | 111 C1 |
| VON GLAHN | SJCO | 47 C1 |
| VOORHESS RD | MCO | 48 D5 |
| VORDEN RD | SAC | M D1 |
| VORDEN RD | SAC | 39 D3 |
| VOTAW RD | AMA | 40 E1 |
| VULCAN MINE RD | SBD | 84 A5 |
| VULCAN MINE RD | SBD | 94 A1 |
| **W** | | |
| WAALEW RD | SBD | 91 C3 |
| W A BARR RD | SIS | 12 C2 |
| WABASH AV | SBD | 99 D2 |
| WABASH BLVD | SD | 214 C5 |
| WABASH BLVD | SD | 216 C5 |
| WABASH BLVD | SDCO | 111 D1 |
| WABASH BLVD | SDCO | V C4 |
| WACHTEL WY | SAC | 34 B5 |
| WACKERMAN RD | TEH | 24 C2 |
| WADDELL ST | TUL | 68 C2 |
| WADDINGTON RD | HUM | 15 E2 |
| WADE AV | MCO | 48 E5 |
| WADLEIGH RD | COL | 32 D1 |
| WAGNER | SJCO | 47 C1 |
| WAGNER AV | ANA | 194 A3 |
| WAGNER AV | COL | 32 E3 |
| WAGON RD | BUT | 25 C2 |
| WAGON WHEEL | SBD | 101 A1 |
| WAGSTAFF RD | BUT | 25 C3 |
| WAHL RD | IMP | 112 A3 |
| WAINWRIGHT RD | MCO | 47 D4 |
| WAKEFIELD | FRCO | 58 A4 |
| WALCH AV | TEH | 24 E2 |
| WALDO RD | YUB | 34 A2 |
| WALERGA | PLA | 33 E5 |
| WALGROVE AV | LA | 187 C1 |
| WALKER DR | SHA | 13 D4 |
| WALKER PL | MNO | 51 C1 |
| WALKER RD | DN | 1 E3 |
| WALKER RD | IMP | 108 E3 |
| WALKER RD | LAS | 14 C3 |
| WALKER RD | MEN | 23 A5 |
| WALKER RD | MEN | 31 A1 |
| WALKER RD | NAPA | 32 B5 |
| WALKER RD | SBD | 92 C5 |
| WALKER RD | SIS | 3 C3 |
| WALKER RD | SON | 37 E3 |
| WALKER ST | GLE | 24 D3 |
| WALKER ST | ORA | T B2 |
| WALKER WY | IMP | 110 B5 |
| WALKER BASIN RD | KER | 79 C3 |
| WALKER CREEK RD | INY | 70 B2 |
| WALKER CREEK RD | SIS | 3 B3 |
| WALKR LANDNG RD | SAC | M D1 |
| WALKR LANDNG RD | SAC | 39 D3 |
| WALKER MINE RD | PLU | 26 E1 |
| WALKER MINE RD | SHA | 18 B1 |
| WALKER PLAINS | BUT | 25 E2 |
| WALKUP RD | COL | 32 B1 |
| WALL RD | SJCO | 40 C4 |
| WALLACE AV | VAL | 134 D4 |
| WALLACE RD | KER | 78 C1 |
| WALLACE RD | SON | 37 E2 |
| WALLACE RD | SON | 38 A2 |
| WALLACE CK RD | SON | 37 D1 |
| WALLEN RD | TEH | 18 D4 |
| WALLER ST | SF | 141 E4 |

| STREET | CO. | PAGE & GRID |
|---|---|---|
| WALLER ST | SF | 142 A4 |
| WALLIS RD | STA | 48 A3 |
| WALLY HILL RD | CAL | 41 B4 |
| WALMORT RD | SAC | 40 A2 |
| WALNUT AV | CC | M A3 |
| WALNUT AV | CC | 38 E5 |
| WALNUT AV | FRE | 165 C5 |
| WALNUT AV | FRCO | 57 C4 |
| WALNUT AV | LACO | Q E2 |
| WALNUT AV | MCO | 48 A4 |
| WALNUT AV | ORA | T E3 |
| WALNUT AV | STA | 47 C3 |
| WALNUT AV | STA | 47 D1 |
| WALNUT AV | TUL | 68 B1 |
| WALNUT AV | U | 123 B3 |
| WALNUT AV | YUB | 33 D2 |
| WALNUT BLVD | CC | M A4 |
| WALNUT BLVD | CC | M D4 |
| WALNUT BLVD | CC | 39 C5 |
| WALNUT BLVD | CC | 46 C1 |
| WALNUT DR | COL | 32 D2 |
| WALNUT DR | HUM | 15 E1 |
| WALNUT DR | NAPA | 29 D4 |
| WALNUT DR | SJCO | 40 C4 |
| WALNUT LN | GLE | 25 A4 |
| WALNUT RD | TEH | 24 D2 |
| WALNUT ST | ANA | 193 B4 |
| WALNUT ST | C | 124 A5 |
| WALNUT ST | ORA | T C1 |
| WALNUT ST | PAS | 190 B3 |
| WALNUT ST | TEH | 18 C5 |
| WALNUT ST | VAL | 134 C1 |
| WALNUT GROVE AV | LACO | R C4 |
| WALNUT GROVE RD | SJCO | 39 E3 |
| WALSER RD | KER | 79 C2 |
| WALTERS RD | LAS | 14 C3 |
| WALTERS RD | SOL | 39 A3 |
| WALTERS CAMP RD | IMP | 110 C2 |
| WALTERS MINE RD | BUT | 26 B3 |
| WALTHERS RD | SOL | M A1 |
| WALTON AV | SUT | 33 C2 |
| WALTON AV | SUT | 125 A5 |
| WALTZ RD | PLA | 33 E3 |
| WAMBLE RD | STA | 47 E1 |
| WAMBLE RD | STA | 48 A1 |
| WANGENHEIM RD | STA | 47 C4 |
| WARD AV | STA | 47 B4 |
| WARD RD | HUM | 10 B5 |
| WARD RD | LACO | 89 E4 |
| WARD RD | MCO | 55 E1 |
| WARD CREEK RD | PLU | 26 E1 |
| WARD LAKE RD | LAS | 21 B3 |
| WARDLOW RD | LACO | 98 A3 |
| WARDLOW RD | LACO | S E2 |
| WARDLOW RD | LACO | T A2 |
| WARDROBE AV | MCO | 48 B4 |
| WARDS FERRY RD | TUO | 41 D5 |
| WARDS FERRY RD | TUO | 48 D1 |
| WARE RD | COL | 32 E2 |
| WARE RD | IMP | 112 B4 |
| WARING RD | SDCO | V C3 |
| WARING RD | SDCO | 111 D1 |
| WARING RD | STA | 47 E3 |
| WARM SPRINGS BL | ALA | P B2 |
| WARM SPGS BLVD | ALA | 46 B3 |
| WARM SPRINGS RD | INY | 51 D4 |
| WARM SPRINGS RD | SON | 38 B2 |
| WARNER AV | FTNV | 197 D2 |
| WARNER AV | ORA | 98 B4 |
| WARNER AV | ORA | T C3 |
| WARNER AV | ORA | T E3 |
| WARNER AV | SA | 197 D2 |
| WARNER AV | SA | 198 A1 |
| WARNER AV | TUS | 198 D2 |
| WARNER RD S | LAS | 8 C3 |
| WARNER RD W | MOD | 8 C1 |
| WARNER ST | C | 124 A3 |
| WARNERVILLE RD | STA | 47 E2 |
| WARNERVILLE RD | STA | 48 A2 |
| WARREGARD RD | CAL | 41 B3 |
| WARREN AV | RCO | 99 D4 |
| WARREN AV | TEH | 18 C4 |
| WARREN FRWY | ALA | 45 D1 |
| WARREN FRWY | O | 156 E5 |
| WARREN RD | CAL | 40 D4 |
| WARREN RD | RCO | 99 D5 |
| WARREN RD | RCO | 99 D4 |
| WARREN VISTA AV | SBD | 100 E1 |
| WASCO WY | KER | 78 A3 |
| WASCO POND RD | KER | 69 B5 |
| WASHBURN WY | KLAM | 5 B1 |
| WASHINGTON AV | RCO | 99 C5 |
| WASHINGTON AV | SBD | 99 B2 |
| WASHINGTON AV | SDCO | V E3 |
| WASHINGTON AV | SDCO | 106 E5 |
| WASHINGTON AV | SA | 195 D3 |
| WASHINGTON AV | SA | 196 A3 |
| WASHINGTON BLVD | ALA | P B2 |
| WASHINGTON BLVD | CUL | 183 D5 |
| WASHINGTON BLVD | CUL | 187 C3 |
| WASHINGTON BLVD | CUL | 188 A2 |
| WASHINGTON BLVD | DN | 1 D4 |
| WASHINGTON BLVD | LA | 183 D5 |
| WASHINGTON BLVD | LA | 184 D4 |
| WASHINGTON BLVD | LA | 185 B4 |
| WASHINGTON BLVD | LA | 186 C5 |
| WASHINGTON BLVD | LA | 187 A3 |
| WASHINGTON BLVD | LACO | 97 E2 |
| WASHINGTON BLVD | LACO | 98 A2 |
| WASHINGTON BLVD | LACO | R B2 |
| WASHINGTON BLVD | LACO | R C4 |
| WASHINGTON BLVD | MCO | 47 E4 |
| WASHINGTON BLVD | MCO | 48 A4 |
| WASHINGTON BLVD | PAS | 190 A2 |
| WASHINGTON PL | CUL | 188 A2 |
| WASHINGTON PL | LA | 188 A2 |
| WASHINGTON PL | SD | 213 C5 |

| STREET | CO. | PAGE & GRID |
|---|---|---|
| WASHINGTON RD | MCO | 56 B1 |
| WASHINGTON RD | NEV | 26 D5 |
| WASHINGTON RD | SBD | 92 A3 |
| WASHINGTON RD | STA | 47 D3 |
| WASHINGTON ST | SB | 87 C1 |
| WASHINGTON ST | FRCO | 66 D3 |
| WASHINGTON ST | LA | 187 B3 |
| WASHINGTON ST | MONT | 167 E4 |
| WASHINGTON ST | RCO | 99 B3 |
| WASHINGTON ST | RCO | 100 E4 |
| WASHINGTON ST | RIV | 99 D5 |
| WASHINGTON ST | SD | 213 D5 |
| WASHINGTON ST | SD | 215 C1 |
| WASHINGTON ST | SDCO | V B3 |
| WASHINGTON ST | SDCO | 111 C1 |
| WASHINGTON ST | SCLR | 151 C3 |
| WASHINGTON ST | SNRA | 163 B2 |
| WASHINGTON ST | S | 160 C5 |
| WASHINGTON ST | TUO | 163 B2 |
| WASHINGTON ST E | SON | L A1 |
| WASHINGTON ST E | SON | 38 A3 |
| WASHOE | FRCO | 56 C4 |
| WASHOE AV | FRCO | 56 C3 |
| WASIOJA RD | SB | 77 C5 |
| WASIOJA RD | SB | 87 B1 |
| WATER LN | SMCO | N C4 |
| WATER ST | AMA | 40 E2 |
| WATER ST | SC | 169 D2 |
| WATER ST | SCR | 54 A2 |
| WATER CANYON RD | KER | 80 B3 |
| WATER CANYON RD | KER | 79 C5 |
| WATERFRONT RD | CC | L E3 |
| WATERFRONT RD | CC | M A3 |
| WATERFRONT RD | CC | 154 E1 |
| WATERLOO LN | DGL | 36 C3 |
| WATERLOO RD | SJCO | 40 B5 |
| WATERMAN AV | SBD | 99 C2 |
| WATERMAN AV | SBD | 207 E3 |
| WATERMAN AV | SBDO | 207 E3 |
| WATERMAN BLVD | FRFD | 135 A2 |
| WATERMAN RD | AMA | 40 D2 |
| WATERMAN RD | SAC | 40 A2 |
| WATERS RD | VEN | 88 D5 |
| WATERS END RD | SLO | 76 C4 |
| WATERTOWN RD | CAL | 40 E3 |
| WATER TROUGH RD | SON | 37 D2 |
| WATKINS DR | RCO | 99 B2 |
| WATKINS RD | TEH | 24 D2 |
| WATKINS TR | KER | 79 C5 |
| WATKINSON RD | SJCO | 40 B3 |
| WATMAUGH RD | SON | L B1 |
| WATSON RD | MEN | 31 B2 |
| WATSONVILLE RD | SCL | P D5 |
| WATSONVILLE RD | SCL | 54 C1 |
| WATT AV | SAC | 34 A5 |
| WATT AV | SAC | 40 A1 |
| WATT LN | BUT | 25 C5 |
| WATTENBURG RD | MEN | 23 A3 |
| WATTRSN TROUGHS | MNO | 51 B2 |
| WATTS AV | SUT | 33 D3 |
| WATTS DR | KER | 79 C3 |
| WATTS VALLEY RD | FRCO | 57 E3 |
| WATTS VALLEY RD | FRCO | 58 A3 |
| WAUCOBA SALINE | INY | 60 C2 |
| WAUKEENA RD | YOL | 39 D2 |
| WAVERLY | SBD | 91 D1 |
| WAVERLY | SJCO | 40 D5 |
| WAY RD | MCO | 55 E1 |
| WAYBUR RD | SUT | 33 C3 |
| WEAVER CREEK E | TRI | 17 D1 |
| WEAVER CT | KER | 79 D3 |
| WEAVER RD | IMP | 109 A4 |
| WEAVER HILLS DR | RCO | 107 A1 |
| WEAVERVLL SCOTT | TRI | 12 A2 |
| WEAVERVLL SCOTT | TRI | 11 D5 |
| WEAVERVLL SCOTT | TRI | 11 E3 |
| WEBB RD | IMP | 109 C5 |
| WEBB RD | SHA | 18 D3 |
| WEBB RD | SUT | 33 C4 |
| WEBER AV | FRE | 165 A2 |
| WEBER AV | S | 160 C5 |
| WEBER RD | SOL | 39 B2 |
| WEBSTER AV | RCO | 99 C3 |
| WEBSTER RD | SBD | 91 E1 |
| WEBSTER ST | A | 157 E5 |
| WEBSTER ST | ALA | 45 D1 |
| WEBSTER ST | FRFD | 135 B4 |
| WEBSTER ST | O | 158 A3 |
| WEDEL AV | KER | 77 E1 |
| WEED RD | IMP | 112 A4 |
| WEEDPATCH HWY | KER | 78 E3 |
| WEEDS POINT RD | YUB | 26 C4 |
| WEEKS RD | SCL | P C5 |
| WEEMASOUL RD | TEH | 18 A5 |
| WEGIS RD | KER | 78 C3 |
| WEIMAR CROSS RD | PLA | 34 C3 |
| WEINERT RD | IMP | 109 A5 |
| WEIR AV | MCO | 47 E4 |
| WEIR CANYON RD | ORA | U C5 |
| WEIR CANYON RD | ORA | 98 D3 |
| WEISS RD | SUT | 33 B2 |
| WEISER RD | KER | 77 C1 |
| WEITCHER RD | MOD | 14 E1 |
| WELCH CT | CAL | 41 B5 |
| WELCOME AV | KER | 80 D1 |
| WELDON | FRCO | 58 A3 |
| WELLBARN AV | FRCO | 57 E1 |
| WELLOCK RD | TRI | 17 D1 |
| WELLS AV | RENO | 130 C3 |
| WELLS AV N | RENO | 130 C2 |
| WELLS DR | LA | 178 C4 |
| WELLS LN | SJCO | 40 B4 |
| WELLS RD | COL | 32 D1 |
| WELLS RD | MAD | 49 C5 |
| WELLS RD | RCO | 103 D4 |
| WELLS RD | VEN | 88 B5 |
| WELLSFORD RD | STA | 47 D2 |

| STREET | CO. | PAGE & GRID |
|---|---|---|
| WELLSONA RD | SLO | 76 A1 |
| WELTY RD | STA | 47 A3 |
| WENDEL RD | LAS | 21 D3 |
| WENGLER HILL RD | SHA | 19 A2 |
| WENTE ST | ALA | P C1 |
| WENTE ST | ALA | 46 C2 |
| WENTWORTH ST | LACO | 89 D5 |
| WENTWORTH ST | LACO | Q D1 |
| WENTWTH SPGS RD | ED | 34 E3 |
| WENTWTH SPGS RD | ED | 35 B3 |
| WERICK RD | RCO | 99 A3 |
| WESCOTT RD | COL | 33 A2 |
| WEST AV | FRE | 165 A1 |
| WEST AV | FRCO | 57 C4 |
| WEST AV | FRCO | 67 C1 |
| WEST AV | RCO | 110 C1 |
| WEST DR | RCO | 100 D2 |
| WEST LN | S | 160 E1 |
| WEST LN | SJCO | 40 A4 |
| WEST LN | MCO | 48 B4 |
| WEST LN | SJCO | 160 E1 |
| WEST RD | COL | 33 A3 |
| WEST RD | LACO | R D5 |
| WEST RD | MEN | 31 B1 |
| WEST RD | STA | 47 C4 |
| WEST ST | ANA | 193 B4 |
| WEST ST | EUR | 121 E1 |
| WEST ST | O | 157 E2 |
| WEST ST | ORA | T C2 |
| WEST ST | TUL | 68 A2 |
| WESTBOROUGH | SMCO | N B1 |
| WESTBROOK LN | DN | 1 E3 |
| WESTCLIFF DR | NB | 199 C4 |
| WEST COAST RD | HUM | 16 C5 |
| W END OREGN MTN | TRI | 17 C1 |
| WESTERN AV | KER | 78 A2 |
| WESTERN AV | LA | 182 A4 |
| WESTERN AV | LA | 185 A5 |
| WESTERN AV | LACO | 97 D3 |
| WESTERN AV | LACO | Q D5 |
| WESTERN AV | LACO | Q E2 |
| WESTERN AV | LACO | S C3 |
| WESTERN AV | ORA | T B2 |
| WESTERN CYN RD | LA | 182 A3 |
| WESTERN HILL RD | RCO | 100 B5 |
| WESTERN MINE | LAK | 32 A5 |
| WESTRN MINERALS | KER | 78 A5 |
| WESTFALL | MPA | 49 C3 |
| WESTFALL W | MPA | 49 A4 |
| WESTGATE AV | HUM | 9 E3 |
| WESTGATE DR | HUM | 15 E1 |
| WESTGATE DR | NAPA | 38 D2 |
| WESTHAVEN DR | HUM | 9 E4 |
| WESTLAKE BLVD | VEN | 96 E1 |
| WEST LAWN AV | FRCO | 57 B4 |
| WEST LAWN AV | FRCO | 57 B5 |
| WESTMINSTER AV | GGR | 195 B3 |
| WESTMINSTER AV | ORA | 98 A4 |
| WESTMINSTER AV | ORA | T A3 |
| WESTMINSTER AV | SA | 195 B3 |
| WESTMORELAND RD | IMP | 108 E5 |
| WESTON RD | TEH | 24 B2 |
| WESTOVER DR | TEH | 18 D5 |
| WESTOVER DR | TEH | 24 D1 |
| WEST PORTAL RD | MNO | 50 D1 |
| WESTRIDGE RD | TRI | 17 B3 |
| WESTSIDE BLVD | MCO | 47 E4 |
| WESTSIDE BLVD | MCO | 48 A4 |
| WESTSIDE FRWY | FRCO | 56 B4 |
| WESTSIDE FRWY | FRCO | 66 E2 |
| WEST SIDE FRWY | KER | 77 D1 |
| WEST SIDE FRWY | KER | 78 D4 |
| WESTSIDE FRWY | KIN | 67 B4 |
| WESTSIDE FRWY | MCO | 55 D1 |
| WESTSIDE FRWY | STA | 47 B3 |
| WEST SIDE HWY | INY | 72 A1 |
| WEST SIDE HWY | KER | 67 B5 |
| WEST SIDE HWY | KER | 78 A4 |
| WESTSIDE RD | IMP | 111 E3 |
| WEST SIDE RD | JOS | 2 C1 |
| WEST SIDE RD | LAS | 8 A5 |
| WESTSIDE RD | MOD | 7 B3 |
| WESTSIDE RD | MOD | 8 A2 |
| WESTSIDE RD | SHA | 18 B1 |
| WESTSIDE RD | SIE | 27 B3 |
| WESTSIDE RD | SON | 37 D1 |
| WSIDE POTTR VLY | MEN | 31 B1 |
| WESTWOOD BLVD | LA | 183 A4 |
| WESTWOOD BLVD | LACO | Q C4 |
| WESTWOOD ST | TUL | 68 D3 |
| WET MEADOW RD | MNO | 50 E1 |
| WETMORE RD | ALA | P C1 |
| WETMORE RD | ALA | 46 C2 |
| WEYER RD | STA | 47 E2 |
| WEYMOUTH BLUFF | HUM | 15 E2 |
| WHEALAN RD | MCO | 48 D5 |
| WHEATLAND RD | SUT | 33 E3 |
| WHEDBEE DR | SOL | 38 E3 |
| WHEELER RD | IMP | 108 E5 |
| WHEELER RD | SBD | 91 C2 |
| WHEELER CYN RD | VEN | 88 B5 |
| WHEELER NURSERY | SHA | 12 E5 |
| WHEELER RDG RD | KER | 78 E5 |
| WHEEL GULCH RD | TRI | 17 B1 |
| WHEELOCK RD | BUT | 25 C3 |
| WHIPPLE AV | SMCO | N D2 |
| WHIPPLE RD | ALA | P A1 |
| WHISKEY CK RD | COL | 32 E3 |
| WHISKEY CK RD | SHA | 18 B2 |
| WHSKEY SLIDE RD | CAL | 41 B3 |
| WHISLER RD | KER | 78 B1 |
| WHITAKER BLF RD | MAR | 37 D3 |
| WHITE AV | LACO | U C2 |
| WHITE DR | BUT | 25 B4 |
| WHITE LN | KER | 78 D3 |
| WHITE LN | NAPA | 29 C3 |
| WHITE LN | SJCO | 40 B5 |

| STREET | CO. | PAGE & GRID |
|---|---|---|
| WHITE RD | COL | 33 A3 |
| WHITE RD | MCO | 47 D3 |
| WHITE RD | MON | 66 C4 |
| WHITE RD | SBD | 91 A4 |
| WHITE RD | SCL | P C3 |
| WHITE RD | SCL | 46 B4 |
| WHITE COTTGE RD | NAPA | 29 C2 |
| WHITE COTTGE RD | NAPA | 38 B1 |
| WHITE CRANE RD | MCO | 47 E4 |
| WHITE CRANE RD | MCO | 48 A4 |
| WHITEHORSE RD | MOD | 13 E2 |
| WHITEHORSE RD | MOD | 14 A2 |
| WHITEHURST RD | SCL | 54 C2 |
| WHITE MTN RD | INY | 51 E4 |
| WHITE MTN RD | INY | 60 D4 |
| WHITE OAK DR | SHA | 18 C3 |
| WHITE PINE LN | SB | 86 E2 |
| WHITE PINE LN | SB | 87 A2 |
| WHITEPINE ST | SIS | 4 B3 |
| WHITE RIVER RD | KER | 69 A5 |
| WHITE ROCK RD | ED | 40 C1 |
| WHITE ROCK RD | MPA | 49 A4 |
| WHITE ROCK RD | MPA | 48 E5 |
| WHITE ROCK RD | MCO | 48 E5 |
| WHITE ROCK RD | SAC | 40 A1 |
| WHITE ROCK RD | SHA | 17 C3 |
| WHTE ROCK LK RD | NEV | 27 B5 |
| WHITES BRDGE AV | FRCO | 56 D3 |
| WHITES BRDGE AV | FRCO | 57 C3 |
| WHITES GULCH RD | SIS | 11 C2 |
| WHITES MILL RD | KER | 69 B5 |
| WHITES MILL RD | KER | 79 B1 |
| WHITEWTR CYN RD | RCO | 100 C2 |
| WHITE WOLF RD | TUO | 42 D5 |
| WHITE WOLF RD | TUO | 63 C3 |
| WHITLEY AV | KIN | 67 D3 |
| WHITLOCK RD | IMP | 109 C5 |
| WHITLOCK RD | MPA | 49 A3 |
| WHITLOCK RD E | MPA | 49 B3 |
| WHITLOW RD | HUM | 16 C4 |
| WHITMORE AV | STA | 47 D2 |
| WHITMORE RD | SHA | 18 E2 |
| WHITMORE RD | SHA | 19 A2 |
| WHITMRE TUBS RD | MNO | 50 E2 |
| WHITMRE TUBS RD | MNO | 51 A2 |
| WHITNEY AV | VAL | 134 D1 |
| WHITNY PORTL RD | INY | 60 A4 |
| WHITSETT AV | LACO | Q C3 |
| WHITTIER AV | RCO | 99 E4 |
| WHITTIER BLVD | LA | 186 D4 |
| WHITTIER BLVD | LACO | 98 A2 |
| WHITTIER BLVD | LACO | R B4 |
| WHITTIER BLVD | LACO | R D5 |
| WHITTIER BLVD | ORA | R D5 |
| WHITTLE AV E | AVLN | 105 B5 |
| WHITTLE RD | CAL | 41 B4 |
| WHITWELL WY | RCO | 107 C1 |
| WHITWORTH RD | MCO | 47 C5 |
| WHITWORTH RD | MCO | 55 C1 |
| WIASMUL RD | RCO | 107 B1 |
| WIBLE RD | KER | 166 B5 |
| WIBLE RD | KER | 78 D4 |
| WICKENDEN WAY | MOD | 8 A1 |
| WICKMAN RD | BUT | 25 B5 |
| WICKS ST | SB | 86 C1 |
| WIDGEON RD | YOL | 39 D3 |
| WIDOW SPGS DR | SIS | 12 E2 |
| WIDOW VALLEY RD | MOD | 13 E3 |
| WIDOW VALLEY RD | MOD | 14 A3 |
| WIGHT WY | LAK | 31 D3 |
| WILBUR | CC | 39 B5 |
| WILBUR AV | LA | 178 C3 |
| WILBUR RD | BUT | 25 C4 |
| WILBUR SPRGS RD | COL | 32 B3 |
| WILCOX RD | SHA | 19 D1 |
| WILCOX RD | TEH | 18 D4 |
| WILCOX RANCH RD | TUO | 41 C5 |
| WILD RD | SBD | 91 B2 |
| WILDASS RD | SBT | 66 B1 |
| WILDCAT RD | MCO | 55 C2 |
| WILDCAT RD | SHA | 18 E3 |
| WILDCAT RD | SHA | 19 A3 |
| WILDCAT RD | TEH | 19 A3 |
| WILD CAT TR | RCO | 100 A5 |
| WILDCAT CK RD | SIS | 11 D2 |
| WILDCAT CYN RD | CC | L D4 |
| WILDCAT CYN RD | CC | 45 D1 |
| WILDCAT CYN RD | SDCO | 107 A5 |
| WILD DUCK RD | MCO | 55 E2 |
| WILDER RD | HUM | 16 A2 |
| WILDER RD | TEH | 18 D5 |
| WLDRNSS LDGE RD | MEN | 22 D3 |
| WILDER RIDGE RD | HUM | 16 A4 |
| WILDHORSE RD | SBD | 92 B1 |
| WILDHORSE CY RD | MON | 65 C2 |
| WILDMAN RD | KER | 78 E4 |
| WILD PLUM RD | SIE | 27 A4 |
| WILDROSE RD | INY | 61 C5 |
| WILD WASH RD | SBD | 91 C2 |
| WILDWOOD AV | SLT | 129 D3 |
| WILDWOOD RD | COL | 32 E3 |
| WILDWOOD RD | KER | 78 A2 |
| WILDWOOD RD | SJCO | 47 C1 |
| WILDWOOD RD | TRI | 17 C2 |
| WILDWOOD CYN RD | SBD | 99 E2 |
| WILEY WELLS RD | RCO | 103 B5 |
| WILFRED CYN RD | MNO | 51 B2 |
| WILHOLT RD | SJCO | 40 A5 |
| WILKIE AV | SUT | 33 D3 |
| WILKINS AV | STA | 47 D1 |
| WILKINS RD | IMP | 109 B2 |
| WILKINS RD | IMP | 112 D5 |
| WILKINSON RD | IMP | 109 A3 |
| WILLARD RD | TEH | 18 C5 |
| WILLARD CK RD | LAS | 20 E3 |
| WILLIAM RD | BUT | 25 C3 |
| WILLIAM ST | SJ | 152 C4 |
| WILLIAMS | SJCO | 47 C1 |
| WILLIAMS AV | MCO | 47 D4 |
| WILLIAMS RD | IMP | 109 B4 |
| WILLIAMS RD | KER | 79 C2 |
| WILLIAMS RD | KER | 80 D4 |
| WILLIAMS RD | LAS | 8 B4 |
| WILLIAMS RD | MON | 54 D4 |
| WILLIAMS RD | SHA | 13 E4 |
| WILLIAMS CK RD | HUM | 15 D2 |
| WILLIAMSON RD | KER | 79 D4 |
| WILLIAMSON RD | RCO | 107 A1 |
| WILLIAMSON RD | TUO | 41 B5 |
| WILLIAM TELL TR | KER | 79 C5 |
| WILLIAMS VLY RD | PLU | 20 C5 |
| WILLIAMS WLL RD | SBD | 81 E5 |
| WILLIS RD | MCO | 56 B1 |
| WILLISTON RD | SUT | 33 C1 |
| WILLMOTT RD | MCO | 55 D1 |
| WILLMS RD | STA | 48 A1 |
| WILLOUGHBY RD | IMP | 112 A4 |
| WILLOW AV | CRTM | 140 B1 |
| WILLOW AV | FRCO | 57 D2 |
| WILLOW AV | GLE | 24 E5 |
| WILLOW AV | KER | 89 C1 |
| WILLOW DR | KER | 78 A2 |
| WILLOW DR | MAD | 57 B1 |
| WILLOW RD | MP | 147 A2 |
| WILLOW RD | SBD | 91 C4 |
| WILLOW RD | SDCO | 107 A5 |
| WILLOW RD | SLO | 76 B5 |
| WILLOW RD | SMCO | N E2 |
| WILLOW RD | SMCO | 45 D3 |
| WILLOW ST | LACO | 97 E3 |
| WILLOW ST | LACO | S D2 |
| WILLOW ST | SJ | 152 C5 |
| WILLOW WY | LAS | 20 E2 |
| WILLOW CREEK RD | AMA | 40 D2 |
| WILLOW CREEK RD | INY | 52 D4 |
| WILLOW CREEK RD | SBT | 55 C5 |
| WILLOW CREEK RD | SLO | 75 E1 |
| WILLOW CREEK RD | SLO | 76 A1 |
| WILLOW CREEK RD | SIS | 4 C3 |
| WILLOW CREEK RD | YUB | 26 B5 |
| WLLW CK RED RCK | SIS | 5 B3 |
| WILLOW GLEN DR | SDCO | 111 E1 |
| WILLOW GLEN RD | YUB | 26 A5 |
| WILLOW PASS RD | CC | M A3 |
| WILLOW PASS RD | CC | M B3 |
| WILLOW PASS RD | CC | 39 A5 |
| WILLOW POINT RD | YOL | 39 D2 |
| WILLOW RCH RD S | MOD | 7 C3 |
| WILLOWS RD | SDCO | 107 B5 |
| WILLOW SPGS EXT | SIS | 13 A2 |
| WILLOW SPGS RD | KER | 79 D5 |
| WILLOW SPGS RD | KER | 89 D1 |
| WILLOW SPGS RD | KER | 90 A1 |
| WILLOW SPGS RD | LAS | 14 A5 |
| WILLOW SPGS RD | LACO | 89 C3 |
| WILLOW SPGS RD | SCL | P D5 |
| WILLOW SPGS RD | SCL | 54 C1 |
| WILLOW VLY RD | NEV | 34 C1 |
| WILL S GREEN RD | COL | 32 E2 |
| WILMINGTON AV | LACO | 97 E3 |
| WILMINGTON AV | LACO | S D2 |
| WILMINGTON BLVD | LA | 191 B1 |
| WILMINGTON BLVD | LACO | S C2 |
| WILSHIRE AV | SBD | 101 C1 |
| WILSHIRE BLVD | BH | 183 B2 |
| WILSHIRE BLVD | LA | 180 D2 |
| WILSHIRE BLVD | LA | 183 B2 |
| WILSHIRE BLVD | LA | 185 A2 |
| WILSHIRE BLVD | LACO | 97 D2 |
| WILSHIRE BLVD | LACO | Q D4 |
| WILSHIRE BLVD | LACO | 180 D2 |
| WILSHIRE BLVD | SMON | 180 A4 |
| WILSHIRE RD | SBD | 92 A4 |
| WILSON AV | COL | 32 E3 |
| WILSON AV | MAR | 38 A4 |
| WILSON AV | VAL | 134 A3 |
| WILSON DR | LA | 181 A2 |
| WILSON DR | TUL | 68 E3 |
| WILSON RD | IMP | 112 D5 |
| WILSON RD | KER | 78 D3 |
| WILSON RD | MCO | 55 D1 |
| WILSON RD | SUT | 33 D3 |
| WILSON ST | KER | 79 C3 |
| WILSON ST | RIV | 100 A3 |
| WILSON ST | TEH | 24 E1 |
| WILSON WY | PLA | 34 B3 |
| WILSON WY | SJCO | 40 B5 |
| WILSON BEND RD | COL | 33 B3 |
| WILSON CREEK RD | DN | 1 E5 |
| WILSON HILL RD | MAR | 37 E4 |
| WILSON HILL RD | SHA | 19 A3 |
| WILSON LAKE RD | TEH | 19 D4 |
| WILSON LANDING | BUT | 25 A2 |
| WILSON RANCH RD | SBD | 90 E4 |
| WILSON SPGS RD | LAS | 14 A5 |
| WILSON VLY RD | RCO | 107 A1 |
| WILTON PL | LA | 181 E5 |
| WILTON PL | LA | 182 A5 |
| WILTON PL | LA | 184 E3 |
| WILTON PL | LA | 185 A3 |
| WILTON RD | SAC | 40 A2 |
| WIMER RD | SJCO | 40 D4 |
| WINCHESTER BLVD | SCL | P B3 |
| WINCHESTER BLVD | SCL | 46 A5 |
| WINCHESTER RD | RCO | 99 D4 |
| WINCHUCK RD | CUR | 1 D2 |
| WINDING WY | SR | 139 B4 |
| WINDING WY | SHA | 18 D2 |
| WINDING WY | SIS | 12 E2 |
| WINDLASS DR | RCO | 101 C5 |
| WINDSONG WY | RCO | 107 B1 |
| WINDSOR AV | LACO | R B2 |
| WINDSOR RD | SON | 37 D1 |
| WINDSOR RIV RD | SON | 37 D1 |
| WINE CREEK RD | SON | 31 D5 |
| WINE CREEK RD | SON | 37 D1 |
| WINEMAN RD | SLO | 76 C5 |
| WINEVILLE AV | SBD | 99 A2 |
| WINGATE RD | INY | 71 C3 |
| WINGFIELD RD | LAS | 21 A3 |
| WING LEVEE RD | SJCO | 46 E1 |
| WINNETKA AV | LA | 178 A3 |
| WINNETKA AV | LACO | 97 B1 |
| WINSHIP RD | SOL | 39 C2 |
| WINSHIP RD | YUBA | 125 D4 |
| WINSLOW RD | IMP | 109 A2 |
| WINSOME WY | SHA | 18 B2 |
| WINTER GRDNS BL | SDCO | V E2 |
| WINTER GRDNS BL | SDCO | 106 E5 |
| WINTERGREEN RD | SBD | 90 E4 |
| WINTERS RD | SBD | 100 E1 |
| WINTERS RD | SOL | 39 A1 |
| WINTRS GULCH RD | SIS | 4 A5 |
| WINTON AV W | ALA | 45 E2 |
| WINTON AV W | H | 146 C4 |
| WINTON AV W | ALA | L E5 |
| WINTON AV W | ALA | N E1 |
| WINTON RD | CAL | 41 B2 |
| WINTON WY | MCO | 48 B4 |
| WINTOON WY | SIS | 12 E2 |
| WIRT RD | IMP | 109 B3 |
| WISCONSIN AV | COL | 32 E3 |
| WISCONSIN AV | TEH | 24 E2 |
| WISE RD | PLA | 33 E3 |
| WISE RD | PLA | 34 A3 |
| WISHON AV | FRE | 165 C2 |
| WISHON DR | TUL | 69 B2 |
| WISTOS LN | LAS | 21 B3 |
| WITHERS AV | CC | L E3 |
| WITHERS AV | CC | 38 E5 |
| WITHROW RD | SHA | 19 A2 |
| WITTER SPG E RD | LAK | 31 C2 |
| WIXOM RD | IMP | 111 E3 |
| WOHLFORD RD | SDCO | 106 E3 |
| WOLF RD | NEV | 34 C2 |
| WOLF CREEK RD | ALP | 36 C5 |
| WOLF CREEK RD | NEV | 34 C2 |
| WOLFE RD | CPTO | 150 A4 |
| WOLFE RD | SCL | P A3 |
| WOLFE RD | SCL | 45 E4 |
| WOLFE RD | SCL | 46 A4 |
| WOLFE RD | SVL | 150 A3 |
| WOLFE RD | VEN | 96 C1 |
| WOLFE GRADE | MAR | L B3 |
| WOLFE GRADE | MAR | 139 C5 |
| WOLFSEN | MCO | 47 E5 |
| WOLFSEN | MCO | 55 E1 |
| WOLFSKILL | SOL | 39 A1 |
| WONDER AV | KER | 80 A4 |
| WONDERLAND BLVD | SHA | 18 C1 |
| WONDERLAND DR | RCO | 100 A3 |
| WONDER STUMP RD | DN | 1 E3 |
| WONDERVIEW RD | RCO | 100 A3 |
| WOO RD | MCO | 55 E2 |
| WOOD RD | RCO | 99 B3 |
| WOOD RD | SUT | 33 B2 |
| WOOD RD | VEN | 96 C1 |
| WOOD ST | GLE | 24 D4 |
| WOODBINE RD | RCO | 100 C5 |
| WOODBRIDGE RD | SJCO | 39 E4 |
| WOODBRIDGE RD | SJCO | 40 B4 |
| WOODBURY RD | LACO | R B2 |
| WOODBURY RD | PAS | 190 A1 |
| WOOD CANYON RD | INY | 71 D1 |
| WOODCUTTERS WY | SHA | 19 B3 |
| WOODEN VLY RD | NAPA | 38 D2 |
| WOODFORD-TEH RD | KER | 79 C4 |
| WOODHILL DR | SHA | 13 A5 |
| WOODHOUSE MINE | CAL | 41 B2 |
| WOODLAND AV | MCO | 48 C4 |
| WOODLAND AV | SR | 139 E5 |
| WOODLAND AV | STA | 47 C2 |
| WOODLAND AV | TEH | 24 D1 |
| WOODLAND DR | MPA | 49 C3 |
| WOODLAND WY | SHA | 19 B3 |
| WOODLF TUNNL RD | BUT | 26 B4 |
| WOODLEY RD | SDCO | 106 C4 |
| WOOLEY RD E | VEN | 96 B1 |
| WOODMAN AV | LACO | 97 C1 |
| WOODMAN AV | LACO | Q C2 |
| WOOD RANCH RD | LAS | 21 B2 |
| WOODRIDGE RD | SHA | 19 B3 |
| WOODROW AV | SC | 169 C5 |
| WOODRUFF AV | LACO | S E2 |
| WOODRUFF AV | LACO | T A2 |
| WOODRUFF LN | YUB | 33 D1 |
| WOODSBRO RD | SJCO | 40 A5 |
| WOODSIDE AV | SDCO | V E2 |
| WOODSIDE AV | SDCO | 106 E5 |
| WOODSIDE RD | SMCO | 45 D3 |
| WOODSIDE RD | SMCO | N D2 |
| WOODS LAKE RD | ALP | 36 A5 |
| WOODSON AV | TEH | 24 D2 |
| WOODSON RD | SJCO | 40 A3 |
| WOOD VALLEY RD | SDCO | 106 E3 |
| WOODVIEW LN | MPA | 49 B4 |
| WOODWARD AV | SJCO | 47 A1 |
| WOODY RD | KER | 78 D1 |
| WOODY ST | KER | 78 E1 |
| WOODY-GRANIT RD | KER | 68 E5 |
| WOODY-GRANIT RD | KER | 69 A5 |
| WOODY-GRANIT RD | KER | 78 E1 |
| WOODY-GRANIT RD | KER | 79 A1 |
| WOOKEY RD | BUT | 25 A2 |
| WOOLEY RD | OXN | 176 A4 |
| WOOLLOMES AV | KER | 68 A5 |
| WOOLNER AV | FRFD | 135 A4 |
| WORDEN AV | MCO | 48 C5 |
| WORDEN RD | CAL | 41 B3 |
| WORK RD | KER | 90 B1 |
| WORKMAN ST | LACO | Q C1 |
| WORKMAN MILL RD | LACO | 98 A2 |
| WORKMAN MILL RD | LACO | R C4 |
| WORMWOOD RD | IMP | 111 E4 |
| WORSLEY RD | RCO | 100 C2 |
| WORTH AV | TUL | 68 D3 |
| WORTH RD | SUT | 33 D4 |
| WORTHINGTON RD | IMP | 108 E5 |
| WORTHINGTON RD | MCO | 47 C5 |
| WORTHINGTON ST | KER | 79 E1 |
| WRAGG CANYON RD | NAPA | 38 D2 |
| WRAN RD | LAS | 21 C4 |
| WREN RD | STA | 47 E2 |
| WRIGHT AV | SVL | 149 B3 |
| WRIGHT AV | TUL | 68 B3 |
| WRIGHT RD | IMP | 109 C5 |
| WRIGHT RD | SIS | 5 D3 |
| WRIGHTS LAKE RD | ED | 35 D4 |
| WRIGLEY RD | HUM | 15 E1 |
| WRIGLEY TER RD | AVLN | 105 B5 |
| WUNPOST RD | MCO | 65 E4 |
| WYANDOTTE AV | BUT | 25 D4 |
| WYNDTT MNRS RCH | BUT | 25 D4 |
| WYE RD | INY | 51 D4 |
| WYER RD | COL | 32 E3 |
| WYLIE DR | MDO | 162 E1 |
| WYLIE ST | SB | 87 D1 |
| WYMAN CREEK RD | INY | 52 A3 |
| WYNCOOP RD | SUT | 33 B2 |
| WYNDAM LN | RED | 122 C4 |
| WYNDHAVEN DR | TEH | 18 D4 |
| WYO AV | GLE | 24 E3 |
| WYSE RD | LACO | 89 D4 |
| X | | |
| XIMENO AV | LACO | S E3 |
| Y | | |
| YAJOME ST | NAP | 133 C2 |
| YANKEE HILL RD | TUO | 41 C4 |
| YAQUI GULCH RD | MPA | 49 B3 |
| YAQUI PASS RD | SDCO | 107 E3 |
| YARD RD | TEH | 18 D4 |
| YELLOW BUTTE RD | SIS | 4 D5 |
| YELLW JACKET RD | MNO | 51 C1 |
| YELLW JACKET RD | TEH | 19 C4 |
| YERBA BLVD | KER | 80 B4 |
| YERBA BUENA RD | VEN | 96 D2 |
| YERMO RD | SBD | 82 C5 |
| YERMO RD | SBD | 92 A1 |
| YERMO CUTOFF | SBD | 81 E5 |
| YERMO CUTOFF | SBD | 82 A5 |
| YGNACIO VLY RD | CC | M A3 |
| YGNACIO VLY RD | CC | 45 E1 |
| YGNACIO VLY RD | CC | 39 A5 |
| YMCA RD | FRCO | 58 D3 |
| YOAKIM BRDG RD | SON | 31 C5 |
| YOCUM RD | IMP | 109 B3 |
| YOKE ST | SHA | 18 C3 |
| YOLANDA AV | KER | 89 C2 |
| YOLANO RD | SOL | 39 C2 |
| YOLO AV | FRCO | 56 E4 |
| YOLO ST | STA | 47 C4 |
| YOLO CO LINE RD | COL | 32 E3 |
| YOLO CO LINE RD | COL | 33 A3 |
| YORBA LN | SBD | 90 E3 |
| YORBA LINDA BL | ORA | 98 C3 |
| YORBA LINDA BL | ORA | T D1 |
| YORK AV | KIN | 67 A5 |
| YORK BLVD | LACO | 97 E1 |
| YORK BLVD | LACO | R A3 |
| YORK RD | IMP | 110 D5 |
| YORK RD | SIS | 4 C3 |
| YORK ST | NAP | 133 C3 |
| YOSEMITE AV | MAN | 161 A4 |
| YOSEMITE AV | MCO | 48 C4 |
| YOSEMITE AV | SJCO | 47 B1 |
| YOSEMITE BLVD | MDO | 162 E3 |
| YOSEMITE BLVD | STA | 47 D2 |
| YOSEMITE BLVD | STA | 48 B2 |
| YOSEMITE RD | TUO | 41 D5 |
| YOSEMITE OAKS RD | MPA | 49 B3 |
| YSMTE SPGS PKWY | MAD | 49 C5 |
| YOU BET RD | NEV | 34 D2 |
| YOUD RD | MCO | 48 B3 |
| YOUNG AV | COL | 32 E3 |
| YOUNG RD | COL | 24 E5 |
| YOUNG RD | IMP | 109 B3 |
| YOUNG RD | STA | 47 C3 |
| YOUNG ST | RCO | 99 E4 |
| YOUNG LOVE AV | SC | 169 B4 |
| YOUNGS HILL RD | YUB | 26 C4 |
| YOUNGSTOWN RD | MCO | 47 E4 |
| YOUNT ST | NAPA | 29 D4 |
| YOUNTVLL CRS RD | NAPA | 29 D4 |
| YOUNTVLL CRS RD | NAPA | 38 C2 |
| YOWELL RD | MOD | 14 B3 |
| YREKA AGER RD | SIS | 4 B4 |
| YREKA MONO | SIS | 4 A4 |
| YREKA WALKER RD | SIS | 3 D3 |
| YREKA WALKER RD | SIS | 4 A4 |
| YTURRIARTE RD | SBT | 55 D4 |
| YUBA AV | FRCO | 56 E3 |
| YUBA NEVADA RD | YUB | 26 B5 |
| YUBA PASS RD | SIE | 27 B4 |
| YUCAIPA BLVD | SBD | 99 D2 |
| YUCCA RD | RCO | 107 C1 |
| YUCCA RD | SBD | 90 E3 |
| YUCCA TR | SBD | 100 E1 |
| YUCCA LOMA RD | SBD | 91 C4 |
| YUCCA MESA RD | SBD | 100 E1 |
| Z | | |
| ZABALA RD | MON | 54 D4 |
| ZABRISKIE PT RD | INY | 72 A1 |
| ZACA STATION RD | SB | 86 E2 |
| ZACHARIAS RD | STA | 47 B3 |
| ZACHARY AV | KER | 78 C1 |
| ZANES RD | HUM | 15 E1 |
| ZAPPONE RD | IMP | 110 A4 |
| ZAYANTE RD | SCR | 54 A1 |
| ZAYANTE RD E | SCR | P A5 |
| ZEDIKER AV | FRCO | 57 E3 |
| ZEDIKER AV | FRCO | 57 E4 |
| ZEERING RD | STA | 47 C3 |
| ZEIGLER PT RD | HUM | 10 D5 |
| ZELDA LN | SBD | 101 E1 |
| ZENIA RD | MEN | 23 A2 |
| ZENIA BLUFF RD | HUM | 16 D5 |
| ZENIA LK MTN RD | TRI | 17 A5 |
| ZENIA LK MTN RD | TRI | 23 A1 |
| ZENO RD | LAK | 31 D2 |
| ZERKER RD | KER | 78 C2 |
| ZERMATT DR | KER | 79 C5 |
| ZINC HILL RD | INY | 70 E1 |
| ZINC MINE RD | SBD | 84 A3 |
| ZINFANDEL DR | SAC | 40 A1 |
| ZINFANDEL LN | NAPA | 29 C3 |
| ZINK RD | BUT | 25 E3 |
| ZITZMAN RD | SIS | 3 C5 |
| ZLABEK RD | SIS | 5 D2 |
| ZOGG MINE RD | SHA | 18 B2 |
| ZOO DR | LACO | Q E3 |
| ZULU QUEN MN RD | RCO | 102 A2 |
| ZUMWALT | SJCO | 47 C1 |
| ZUMWALT AV | TUL | 68 A2 |
| ZUMWALT RD | COL | 32 D2 |
| ZZYZX RD | SBD | 83 B4 |
| NUMERIC STREETS | | |
| 1ST AV | BARS | 208 B1 |
| 1ST AV | BUT | 25 B3 |
| 1ST AV | GLE | 24 E3 |
| 1ST AV | IMP | 112 D5 |
| 1ST AV | LPAZ | 104 B2 |
| 1ST AV | LACO | R D5 |
| 1ST AV | LACO | T B1 |
| 1ST AV | MCO | 47 E4 |
| 1ST AV | PLU | 20 A4 |
| 1ST AV | SBD | 208 C1 |
| 1ST AV | SD | 215 D4 |
| 1ST AV | SDCO | V B3 |
| 1ST AV | SDCO | V C4 |
| 1ST AV | SDCO | 111 D2 |
| 1ST ST | ALA | M C5 |
| 1ST ST | ALA | 46 C2 |
| 1ST ST | BEN | 153 B4 |
| 1ST ST | DN | 1 D3 |
| 1ST ST | DVS | 136 D3 |
| 1ST ST | FRCO | 57 C3 |
| 1ST ST | LA | 186 A2 |
| 1ST ST | LACO | Q E4 |
| 1ST ST | NAPA | L C1 |
| 1ST ST | NAP | 133 C4 |
| 1ST ST | ORA | 98 B4 |
| 1ST ST | ORA | T D3 |
| 1ST ST | RCO | U E4 |
| 1ST ST | RCO | 98 E3 |
| 1ST ST | SF | 143 D4 |
| 1ST ST | SCL | P B3 |
| 1ST ST | SJ | 151 E1 |
| 1ST ST | SJ | 152 B3 |
| 1ST ST | SA | 195 A4 |
| 1ST ST | SA | 196 A4 |
| 1ST ST | SCL | 46 A4 |
| 1ST ST | SCL | 54 D2 |
| 1ST ST | SHA | 18 C3 |
| 1 1/2 AV | KIN | 68 A1 |
| 2ND AV | COL | 33 B3 |
| 2ND AV | GLE | 24 E3 |
| 2ND AV | KIN | 68 A1 |
| 2ND AV | LPAZ | 104 B1 |
| 2ND AV | MCO | 47 D4 |
| 2ND AV | RCO | 103 D4 |
| 2ND AV S | MCO | 48 A4 |
| 2ND ST | FRFD | 135 A3 |
| 2ND ST | KER | 68 B5 |
| 2ND ST | LA | 186 A2 |
| 2ND ST | LACO | S E3 |
| 2ND ST | MER | 170 A5 |
| 2ND ST | SDCO | V E3 |
| 2ND ST | SDCO | 106 B3 |
| 2ND ST | SDCO | 106 E5 |
| 2ND ST | SR | 139 C4 |
| 2ND ST E | BEN | 153 C4 |
| 2ND ST E | RENO | 130 B3 |
| 2ND ST E | SOL | 38 D4 |
| 2ND ST W | RENO | 130 A3 |
| 2 1/2 AV | KIN | 67 E2 |
| 3RD AV | FCTY | 145 C1 |
| 3RD AV | GLE | 24 E3 |
| 3RD AV | LPAZ | 104 B1 |
| 3RD AV | MCO | 47 D4 |
| 3RD AV | NAPA | 38 D3 |
| 3RD AV | RCO | 103 D4 |
| 3RD AV | SBD | 99 B1 |
| 3RD AV | SDCO | V C4 |
| 3RD AV | SDCO | 111 D2 |
| 3RD AV | SMCO | N C1 |
| 3RD AV | SMCO | 45 C3 |
| 3RD AV | TEH | 18 E5 |
| 3RD AV | TEH | 24 E1 |
| 3RD ST | BH | 183 C1 |
| 3RD ST | CC | 38 C5 |
| 3RD ST | COR | 215 B5 |
| 3RD ST | DVS | 136 D3 |
| 3RD ST | EUR | 121 C1 |
| 3RD ST | LB | 192 D3 |
| 3RD ST | LA | 183 C1 |
| 3RD ST | LA | 184 B1 |
| 3RD ST | LA | 185 A1 |
| 3RD ST | LA | 186 A3 |
| 3RD ST | LACO | Q D4 |
| 3RD ST | NAP | 133 C4 |
| 3RD ST | RIV | 205 C2 |
| 3RD ST | SBDO | 207 D2 |
| 3RD ST | SBD | 99 C1 |
| 3RD ST | SFCO | L C5 |
| 3RD ST | SF | 143 D4 |

# STREET INDEX

| STREET | CO. | PAGE | GRID |
|---|---|---|---|
| 3RD ST | SR | 139 | C4 |
| 3RD ST | SHA | 18 | C3 |
| 3RD ST | TEH | 24 | D2 |
| 3RD ST | YOL | 137 | A2 |
| 4TH AV | CAR | 168 | C3 |
| 4TH AV | GLE | 24 | E3 |
| 4TH AV | KIN | 67 | E1 |
| 4TH AV | MCO | 47 | D4 |
| 4TH AV | MON | 168 | C3 |
| 4TH AV | RCO | 103 | D4 |
| 4TH AV | SD | 215 | D3 |
| 4TH AV | SDCO | V | C4 |
| 4TH AV | SDCO | 111 | D2 |
| 4TH ST | ALA | L | D4 |
| 4TH ST | BKD | 166 | C4 |
| 4TH ST | COR | 215 | C5 |
| 4TH ST | EC | 217 | D4 |
| 4TH ST | EUR | 121 | C1 |
| 4TH ST | KER | 166 | C4 |
| 4TH ST | LA | 186 | A3 |
| 4TH ST | MAR | L | A3 |
| 4TH ST | MAR | 38 | B5 |
| 4TH ST | MOD | 8 | B1 |
| 4TH ST | ONT | 203 | D5 |
| 4TH ST | ONT | 204 | B3 |
| 4TH ST | RCO | 99 | C4 |
| 4TH ST | SBD | 99 | D2 |
| 4TH ST | SDCO | V | C4 |
| 4TH ST | SDCO | 111 | C1 |
| 4TH ST | SJ | 152 | B2 |
| 4TH ST | SR | 139 | B3 |
| 4TH ST | SA | 196 | B4 |
| 4TH ST | SCL | 54 | E3 |
| 4TH ST | SHA | 18 | D3 |
| 4TH ST | STR | 131 | D3 |
| 4TH ST E | RENO | 130 | B2 |
| 4TH ST W | RENO | 130 | A2 |
| 5TH AV | CAR | 168 | B3 |
| 5TH AV | GLE | 24 | E3 |
| 5TH AV | GLE | 24 | E3 |
| 5TH AV | KIN | 67 | E1 |
| 5TH AV | LPAZ | 104 | A2 |
| 5TH AV | LACO | R | D3 |
| 5TH AV | SBD | 92 | D5 |
| 5TH AV | SBD | 99 | D2 |
| 5TH AV | SDCO | 106 | D3 |
| 5TH AV | SR | 139 | B3 |
| 5TH AV E | SIS | 4 | B4 |
| 5TH ST | DVS | 136 | C3 |
| 5TH ST | EUR | 121 | C1 |
| 5TH ST | HUM | 9 | E5 |
| 5TH ST | LA | 186 | A3 |
| 5TH ST | RCO | 99 | A3 |
| 5TH ST | SCTO | 137 | A3 |
| 5TH ST | SBD | 99 | C1 |
| 5TH ST | SBD | 207 | C2 |
| 5TH ST | SBDO | 207 | C2 |
| 5TH ST | SF | 143 | C5 |
| 5TH ST | SA | 195 | C4 |
| 5TH ST | SOL | L | D2 |
| 5TH ST | TEH | 24 | E1 |
| 5TH ST | VAL | 134 | D5 |
| 5TH ST | VEN | 96 | B1 |
| 5TH ST E | BEN | 153 | C5 |
| 5TH ST E | OXN | 176 | D4 |
| 5TH ST E | VEN | 176 | D4 |
| 5TH ST W | LACO | 90 | A2 |
| 5 1/2 AV | KIN | 67 | E2 |
| 6TH AV | CAR | 168 | B3 |
| 6TH AV | GLE | 24 | E3 |
| 6TH AV | KIN | 67 | E1 |
| 6TH AV | MCO | 47 | E4 |
| 6TH AV | RCO | 103 | D4 |
| 6TH AV | SD | 215 | E3 |
| 6TH AV | SDCO | V | B3 |
| 6TH ST | GLE | 24 | D3 |
| 6TH ST | LB | 192 | D3 |
| 6TH ST | LA | 184 | C2 |
| 6TH ST | LA | 185 | C2 |
| 6TH ST | LA | 186 | A3 |
| 6TH ST | ONT | 203 | D4 |
| 6TH ST | RCO | 99 | A3 |
| 6TH ST | YUB | 33 | E2 |
| 6 1/2 AV | KIN | 67 | E2 |
| 7TH | CC | 38 | C5 |
| 7TH AV | CAR | 168 | B3 |
| 7TH AV | KIN | 67 | E1 |
| 7TH AV | LPAZ | 104 | A2 |
| 7TH AV | LACO | R | D4 |
| 7TH AV | SF | 141 | D4 |
| 7TH AV | SFCO | L | B5 |
| 7TH AV | SFCO | 45 | B2 |
| 7TH AV | SCR | 54 | A2 |
| 7TH AV | YUB | 33 | D2 |
| 7TH ST | EUR | 121 | C1 |
| 7TH ST | IMP | 109 | A4 |
| 7TH ST | KER | 78 | B1 |
| 7TH ST | LB | 192 | D3 |
| 7TH ST | LA | 185 | C2 |
| 7TH ST | LA | 186 | A3 |
| 7TH ST | LACO | 97 | C2 |
| 7TH ST | LACO | 98 | A4 |
| 7TH ST | LACO | S | E2 |
| 7TH ST | O | 157 | C3 |
| 7TH ST | O | 158 | A4 |
| 7TH ST | RIV | 205 | B2 |
| 7TH ST | RCO | 99 | B2 |
| 7TH ST | RCO | 99 | E4 |
| 7TH ST | SBD | 91 | B4 |
| 7TH ST | SBD | 99 | B2 |
| 7TH ST | SBD | 99 | D2 |
| 7TH ST | SJ | 152 | B3 |
| 7TH ST | SLO | 75 | E3 |
| 7TH ST | STA | 47 | E3 |
| 7TH ST | UPL | 203 | E3 |
| 7TH ST N | MDO | 162 | B3 |
| 7TH ST S | MDO | 162 | C4 |
| 7TH ST S | STA | 162 | C4 |
| 7TH ST W | BEN | 153 | B4 |
| 7TH STANDARD RD | KER | 77 | C2 |
| 7 1/2 AV | KIN | 57 | E5 |
| 8TH AV | CAR | 53 | D5 |
| 8TH AV | CAR | 168 | B3 |
| 8TH AV | KIN | 67 | D1 |
| 8TH AV | RCO | 103 | D4 |
| 8TH AV | SD | 215 | E3 |
| 8TH ST | ALA | L | C4 |
| 8TH ST | BKD | 166 | C4 |
| 8TH ST | BUT | 25 | C5 |
| 8TH ST | EC | 217 | C3 |
| 8TH ST | IMP | 112 | A3 |
| 8TH ST | LA | 185 | A2 |
| 8TH ST | LA | 186 | A3 |
| 8TH ST | O | 157 | C3 |
| 8TH ST | RCO | 99 | E3 |
| 8TH ST | SBD | U | E2 |
| 8TH ST | SBD | 98 | E2 |
| 8TH ST | SDCO | V | C4 |
| 8TH ST | SDCO | 106 | B3 |
| 8TH ST | SDCO | 111 | D1 |
| 8TH ST | SJCO | 40 | B5 |
| 8TH ST | SON | L | B1 |
| 8TH ST | UPL | 203 | E2 |
| 8TH ST E | DVS | 136 | C3 |
| 8TH ST W | DVS | 136 | B3 |
| 8 1/2 AV | KIN | 57 | D5 |
| 9TH AV | KER | 68 | C5 |
| 9TH AV | KIN | 67 | D1 |
| 9TH AV | LPAZ | 104 | A2 |
| 9TH AV | SD | 215 | E4 |
| 9TH AV | SDCO | 106 | D3 |
| 9TH ST | GGR | 195 | A2 |
| 9TH ST | LB | 192 | C2 |
| 9TH ST | LA | 185 | A3 |
| 9TH ST | LA | 186 | A4 |
| 9TH ST | LA | 191 | A4 |
| 9TH ST | LACO | S | C3 |
| 9TH ST | MDO | 162 | B3 |
| 9TH ST | SBD | 203 | E2 |
| 9TH ST | SBDO | 207 | C1 |
| 9TH ST | SF | 143 | B5 |
| 9TH ST | UPL | 203 | E2 |
| 9TH ST | UPL | 204 | B2 |
| 9TH ST | YUMA | 112 | C5 |
| 9TH ST S | MDO | 162 | C4 |
| 9TH ST S | STA | 162 | C4 |
| 9 1/2 AV | KIN | 67 | D1 |
| 10 MI HOUSE TR | BUT | 25 | C2 |
| 10TH | CC | 38 | C5 |
| 10TH AV | KIN | 67 | D1 |
| 10TH AV | RCO | 103 | D5 |
| 10TH ST | LB | 192 | D2 |
| 10TH ST | RCO | 99 | D3 |
| 10TH ST | SF | 142 | D4 |
| 10TH ST | SJ | 152 | B2 |
| 10TH ST | UPL | 203 | E2 |
| 10TH ST | YUB | 33 | D2 |
| 10TH ST | YUMA | 112 | C5 |
| 10TH ST E | LACO | 90 | A3 |
| 10TH ST W | BEN | 153 | A3 |
| 10TH ST W | CC | M | C3 |
| 10TH ST W | LACO | 89 | E3 |
| 10 1/2 AV | KIN | 67 | D2 |
| 11TH AV | KIN | 67 | D1 |
| 11TH AV | LPAZ | 104 | A2 |
| 11TH AV | RCO | 103 | D5 |
| 11TH AV | SBD | 91 | E1 |
| 11TH AV | SD | 215 | E4 |
| 11TH AV | SDCO | V | B3 |
| 11TH ST | LAK | 31 | D3 |
| 11TH ST | MDO | 162 | B3 |
| 11TH ST | SBD | 91 | B4 |
| 11TH ST | SJCO | 47 | A2 |
| 11TH ST | YUMA | 112 | C5 |
| 12TH AV | KIN | 67 | D1 |
| 12TH AV | LPAZ | 104 | A2 |
| 12TH AV | SD | 215 | E4 |
| 12TH AV | SDCO | V | B3 |
| 12TH ST | BUT | 25 | C4 |
| 12TH ST | HUM | 15 | E2 |
| 12TH ST | MOD | 8 | A1 |
| 12TH ST | O | 157 | C2 |
| 12TH ST | SCTO | 137 | C3 |
| 12TH ST | YUB | 33 | D2 |
| 12TH ST E | O | 159 | C1 |
| 12TH ST N | SCTO | 137 | C2 |
| 12 3/4 AV | KIN | 67 | D1 |
| 13TH AV | ALA | L | D4 |
| 13TH AV | ALA | 45 | D1 |
| 13TH AV | CAR | 168 | B4 |
| 13TH AV | KIN | 67 | D1 |
| 13TH AV | LPAZ | 104 | A2 |
| 13TH AV | O | 158 | C4 |
| 13TH ST | CC | 38 | C5 |
| 13TH ST | SJ | 152 | B2 |
| 13 1/4 AV | KIN | 67 | D1 |
| 14 MILE HOUSE | BUT | 25 | C2 |
| 14TH AV | KIN | 67 | D1 |
| 14TH AV | LPAZ | 104 | A2 |
| 14TH AV | O | 158 | C4 |
| 14TH AV | RCO | 100 | D3 |
| 14TH AV | RCO | 103 | D5 |
| 14TH ST E | ALA | L | E5 |
| 14TH ST E | ALA | L | E5 |
| 14TH ST E | CC | M | C3 |
| 14TH AV E | O | 158 | D5 |
| 14TH ST | ALA | 146 | B1 |
| 14TH ST | CC | 39 | B5 |
| 14TH ST | EUR | 121 | B2 |
| 14TH ST | MDO | 162 | B3 |
| 14TH ST | O | 157 | C2 |
| 14TH ST | RIV | 99 | E2 |
| 14TH ST | RIV | 205 | C3 |
| 14TH ST | RCO | 99 | B2 |
| 14TH ST | SBD | 99 | D2 |
| 14TH ST E | ALA | 45 | E2 |
| 14TH ST E | DVS | 136 | C2 |
| 14TH ST E | O | 159 | D1 |
| 14TH ST W | DVS | 136 | C2 |
| 14 1/2 AV | KIN | 67 | D2 |
| 15TH AV | KIN | 67 | D1 |
| 15TH AV | RCO | 103 | C5 |
| 15TH AV | SDCO | 106 | D3 |
| 15TH ST | KER | 80 | A5 |
| 15TH ST | MDO | 162 | B3 |
| 15TH ST | SCTO | 137 | B4 |
| 15 1/2 AV | KIN | 67 | C1 |
| 16TH AV | KIN | 67 | C1 |
| 16TH AV | RCO | 100 | D3 |
| 16TH AV | RCO | 103 | D5 |
| 16TH ST | MER | 170 | B3 |
| 16TH ST | SCTO | 137 | C4 |
| 16TH ST | SBD | 98 | D1 |
| 16TH ST | SBD | 99 | D2 |
| 16TH ST | SD | 215 | E4 |
| 16TH ST | SD | 216 | A4 |
| 16TH ST | SDCO | V | B3 |
| 17 MILE DR | MON | 53 | B3 |
| 17 MILE DR | MON | 167 | A3 |
| 17 MILE DR | PAC | 167 | B2 |
| 17TH AV | KIN | 67 | C1 |
| 17TH AV | SCR | 54 | A2 |
| 17TH ST | CM | 199 | B3 |
| 17TH ST | MDO | 162 | C3 |
| 17TH ST | ORA | 98 | C4 |
| 17TH ST | ORA | T | B4 |
| 17TH ST | ORA | T | C4 |
| 17TH ST | ORA | T | D3 |
| 17TH ST | SF | 141 | E5 |
| 17TH ST | SF | 142 | A5 |
| 17TH ST | SJ | 152 | C2 |
| 17TH ST | SA | 195 | D3 |
| 17TH ST | SA | 196 | A3 |
| 18TH AV | KIN | 67 | C1 |
| 18TH AV | RCO | 100 | D3 |
| 18TH AV | RCO | 103 | D5 |
| 18TH ST | BKD | 166 | B3 |
| 18TH ST | LAK | 32 | A3 |
| 18TH ST | SDCO | V | C4 |
| 18TH ST | SDCO | 111 | D2 |
| 18 3/4 AV | KIN | 67 | C1 |
| 19TH AV | KIN | 67 | C3 |
| 19TH AV | SFCO | L | B5 |
| 19TH AV | SFCO | 45 | B2 |
| 19TH ST | BKD | 166 | B3 |
| 19TH ST | CM | 199 | A2 |
| 19TH ST | KER | 80 | A5 |
| 19TH ST | ORA | T | C4 |
| 19TH ST | SBD | 98 | D1 |
| 20TH AV | KIN | 67 | C1 |
| 20TH AV | RCO | 100 | D3 |
| 20TH AV | RCO | 103 | C5 |
| 20TH ST | KER | 80 | B5 |
| 20TH ST | KIN | 80 | A5 |
| 20TH ST E | LACO | 90 | A3 |
| 20TH ST W | KER | 89 | E1 |
| 20 1/2 AV | KIN | 67 | C2 |
| 21ST AV | KIN | 67 | C3 |
| 21ST ST | BKD | 166 | B3 |
| 21ST ST | MER | 170 | D3 |
| 21ST ST | SCTO | 137 | C4 |
| 21ST ST | SJ | 152 | C2 |
| 21 1/2 AV | KIN | 67 | C1 |
| 22ND AV | KIN | 67 | C1 |
| 22ND AV | RCO | 100 | B3 |
| 22ND AV | RCO | 103 | C5 |
| 22ND ST | RCO | 100 | A3 |
| 22ND ST | YUB | 33 | D2 |
| 22 1/2 AV | KIN | 67 | C1 |
| 23RD AV | KIN | 67 | C1 |
| 23RD AV | O | 158 | C4 |
| 23RD ST | BKD | 166 | C3 |
| 23RD ST | CC | L | C3 |
| 23RD ST | CC | 38 | C5 |
| 23RD ST | R | 155 | B3 |
| 23RD ST | SP | 155 | B3 |
| 23RD ST | SMON | 187 | B1 |
| 23 1/2 AV | KIN | 67 | B1 |
| 24TH AV | KIN | 67 | B1 |
| 24TH AV | RCO | 100 | E3 |
| 24TH AV | RCO | 103 | C5 |
| 24TH ST | BKD | 166 | C2 |
| 24TH ST | KER | 78 | C3 |
| 24TH ST | SAC | 39 | E1 |
| 24TH ST | SBD | 98 | D1 |
| 24TH ST | SDCO | V | C4 |
| 24TH ST | SDCO | 111 | D2 |
| 24TH ST | SJ | 152 | D2 |
| 24 1/2 AV | KIN | 67 | B1 |
| 25TH AV | KIN | 67 | B1 |
| 25TH AV | KIN | 67 | B4 |
| 25TH AV | RCO | 103 | C5 |
| 25TH AV | SF | 141 | B3 |
| 25TH AV | SM | 145 | B3 |
| 25TH ST | LACO | S | C3 |
| 25TH ST | SD | 216 | A4 |
| 25TH ST | SDCO | V | B3 |
| 25TH ST E | LACO | 90 | A3 |
| 25TH ST W | KER | 89 | E1 |
| 26TH AV | RCO | 101 | A3 |
| 26TH AV | RCO | 103 | C5 |
| 26TH ST | SD | 216 | B5 |
| 26 1/4 AV | KIN | 67 | B1 |
| 27TH AV | KIN | 67 | B1 |
| 27TH ST | SDCO | V | C5 |
| 27TH ST | SDCO | 111 | D2 |
| 28TH AV | KIN | 67 | B2 |
| 28TH AV | RCO | 101 | A3 |
| 28TH AV | RCO | 110 | D1 |
| 28TH AV | SM | 145 | A3 |
| 28TH ST | SD | 216 | B4 |
| 28TH ST | SDCO | V | C3 |
| 28TH ST | SDCO | 111 | D1 |
| 29TH AV | ALA | L | D4 |
| 29TH ST | SCTO | 137 | D4 |
| 30TH AV | KIN | 67 | B3 |
| 30TH AV | RCO | 100 | D3 |
| 30TH AV | RCO | 110 | C1 |
| 30TH ST | BKD | 166 | D2 |
| 30TH ST | KER | 80 | B5 |
| 30TH ST | SD | 214 | B5 |
| 30TH ST | SD | 216 | B4 |
| 30TH ST | SDCO | V | C4 |
| 30TH ST | SDCO | 111 | D1 |
| 30TH ST | SDCO | 111 | D2 |
| 30TH ST E | LACO | 90 | A3 |
| 30TH ST W | KER | 89 | E1 |
| 30TH ST W | LACO | 89 | E2 |
| 31ST AV | SM | 145 | A4 |
| 32ND AV | RCO | 101 | A3 |
| 32ND AV | RCO | 110 | C1 |
| 32ND ST | KER | 80 | B5 |
| 32ND ST | LAK | 32 | A3 |
| 32ND ST | SD | 216 | C4 |
| 32ND ST | SDCO | 111 | D1 |
| 34TH AV | RCO | 100 | D3 |
| 34TH AV | RCO | 110 | C1 |
| 34TH ST | BKD | 166 | C2 |
| 35TH AV | ALA | L | D4 |
| 35TH AV | O | 158 | E5 |
| 35TH AV | RCO | 110 | C1 |
| 36TH AV | KIN | 67 | A4 |
| 36TH AV | RCO | 100 | D4 |
| 36TH AV | RCO | 110 | D1 |
| 36TH ST | LAK | 32 | A3 |
| 37TH ST | KER | 80 | B5 |
| 38TH AV | RCO | 101 | A4 |
| 38TH AV | RCO | 110 | D1 |
| 38TH ST | SD | 216 | D5 |
| 39TH AV | SM | 145 | C3 |
| 40TH AV | RCO | 101 | A4 |
| 40TH AV | SF | 141 | A3 |
| 40TH AV | SM | 145 | B4 |
| 40TH ST | SBD | 99 | B1 |
| 40TH ST | SD | 214 | D5 |
| 40TH ST | SDCO | V | C4 |
| 40TH ST E | LACO | 90 | A3 |
| 40TH ST W | KER | 89 | E1 |
| 40TH ST W | LACO | 89 | E2 |
| 41ST AV | SCR | 54 | A2 |
| 41ST ST | LACO | Q | E4 |
| 42ND AV | RCO | 101 | A4 |
| 42ND AV | SM | 145 | B4 |
| 43RD ST | SD | 214 | E5 |
| 43RD ST | SD | 216 | E1 |
| 44TH AV | RCO | 100 | E4 |
| 47TH AV | RCO | 101 | A4 |
| 47TH AV | SAC | 39 | E1 |
| 47TH ST E | LACO | 90 | A3 |
| 48TH AV | RCO | 101 | A4 |
| 50TH AV | RCO | 101 | A4 |
| 50TH ST E | LACO | 90 | A3 |
| 50TH ST W | KER | 89 | E1 |
| 50TH ST W | LACO | 89 | E2 |
| 51ST ST | LACO | Q | E4 |
| 52ND AV | RCO | 101 | A4 |
| 54TH AV | RCO | 101 | A4 |
| 54TH ST | RCO | 99 | A2 |
| 54TH ST | SDCO | V | C3 |
| 54TH ST | SDCO | 111 | D1 |
| 55TH ST E | LACO | 90 | B3 |
| 57TH ST E | LACO | 90 | B3 |
| 58TH AV | RCO | 101 | A5 |
| 60TH AV | RCO | 101 | A5 |
| 60TH ST | SDCO | V | C4 |
| 60TH ST E | LACO | 90 | B2 |
| 60TH ST W | KER | 89 | E2 |
| 60TH ST W | LACO | 89 | E2 |
| 62ND AV | RCO | 101 | B5 |
| 64TH AV | RCO | 101 | B5 |
| 65TH EXPWY | SAC | 39 | E1 |
| 65TH ST E | LACO | 90 | B2 |
| 65TH ST W | LACO | 89 | E2 |
| 66TH AV | RCO | 101 | B5 |
| 67TH ST | RCO | 101 | A5 |
| 68TH AV | RCO | 101 | B5 |
| 68TH AV | TEH | 18 | E5 |
| 70TH AV | RCO | 101 | B5 |
| 70TH ST | SDCO | V | D3 |
| 70TH ST | SDCO | 111 | D1 |
| 70TH ST E | LACO | 90 | B3 |
| 70TH ST W | LACO | 89 | E2 |
| 72ND AV | RCO | 101 | B5 |
| 73RD AV | ALA | L | D5 |
| 74TH AV | RCO | 101 | B5 |
| 76TH AV | RCO | 101 | B5 |
| 76TH ST E | LACO | 90 | B3 |
| 78TH AV | RCO | 108 | B1 |
| 80TH AV | RCO | 107 | C1 |
| 80TH AV | RCO | 108 | B1 |
| 80TH ST E | LACO | 90 | B3 |
| 80TH ST W | KER | 89 | D2 |
| 80TH ST W | LACO | 89 | D3 |
| 81ST AV | RCO | 108 | B1 |
| 82ND AV | RCO | 108 | B1 |
| 84TH AV | RCO | 108 | B1 |
| 85TH ST W | LACO | 89 | D3 |
| 87TH ST E | LACO | 90 | B4 |
| 87TH ST W | LACO | 89 | D3 |
| 90TH ST E | LACO | 90 | B3 |
| 90TH ST W | KER | 89 | D2 |
| 90TH ST W | LACO | 89 | D3 |
| 92ND ST | LACO | Q | E5 |
| 92ND ST W | LACO | 89 | D3 |
| 95TH ST W | LACO | 89 | D3 |
| 96TH ST E | LACO | 90 | B4 |
| 97TH ST W | LACO | 89 | D3 |
| 98TH AV | ALA | L | E5 |
| 98TH AV | ALA | 45 | D2 |
| 98TH AV | O | 159 | D4 |
| 98TH ST W | LACO | 89 | D3 |
| 99-97 CUTOFF | SIS | 4 | B4 |
| 100TH ST E | LACO | 90 | B2 |
| 100TH ST W | KER | 89 | D2 |
| 103RD ST | LACO | Q | E5 |
| 105TH ST E | LACO | 90 | B3 |
| 106TH ST E | LACO | 90 | B4 |
| 110TH ST E | LACO | 90 | B3 |
| 110TH ST W | KER | 79 | D5 |
| 110TH ST W | LACO | 89 | D2 |
| 115TH ST W | KER | 79 | D5 |
| 120TH ST E | LACO | 90 | B2 |
| 120TH ST W | LACO | 89 | D2 |
| 121ST ST E | LACO | 90 | B4 |
| 130TH ST E | LACO | 90 | C2 |
| 130TH ST W | LACO | 89 | D2 |
| 131ST ST E | LACO | 90 | C4 |
| 135TH ST | LACO | S | C1 |
| 137TH ST E | LACO | 90 | C2 |
| 140TH ST E | LACO | 90 | C2 |
| 140TH ST W | KER | 89 | D1 |
| 145TH ST | KER | 89 | D1 |
| 145TH ST E | LACO | 90 | C3 |
| 146TH ST | KER | 89 | D1 |
| 147TH ST | KER | 89 | C1 |
| 149TH ST | KER | 89 | C1 |
| 150TH ST E | LACO | 90 | C3 |
| 152ND ST W | KER | 89 | C1 |
| 155TH ST | KER | 89 | C1 |
| 157TH ST W | KER | 89 | C1 |
| 160TH ST W | LACO | 89 | C2 |
| 164TH ST | LACO | S | B1 |
| 165TH ST E | LACO | 90 | C3 |
| 170TH ST E | LACO | 90 | C3 |
| 170TH ST W | KER | 89 | C2 |
| 170TH ST W | LACO | 89 | C2 |
| 175TH ST E | LACO | 90 | C3 |
| 176TH ST | KER | 89 | C1 |
| 177TH ST | KER | 89 | C1 |
| 180TH ST E | LACO | 90 | C3 |
| 180TH ST W | LACO | 89 | C2 |
| 182ND ST | LACO | S | C1 |
| 185TH ST E | LACO | 90 | C3 |
| 185TH ST W | KER | 89 | C2 |
| 190TH ST | LACO | 97 | D3 |
| 190TH ST | LACO | S | B1 |
| 190TH ST E | LACO | 90 | C2 |
| 190TH ST W | LACO | 89 | C2 |
| 195TH ST | LACO | S | E1 |
| 195TH ST | LACO | T | A1 |
| 195TH ST E | LACO | 90 | C2 |
| 195TH ST W | KER | 89 | C2 |
| 200TH ST E | LACO | 90 | D2 |
| 200TH ST E | LACO | 90 | C3 |
| 204TH ST E | LACO | 90 | D4 |
| 210TH ST | KER | 89 | C1 |
| 210TH ST E | LACO | 90 | D3 |
| 215TH ST W | KER | 89 | C2 |
| 220TH ST | LACO | S | C2 |
| 220TH ST E | LACO | 90 | D3 |
| 223RD ST | LACO | S | C2 |
| 223RD ST E | LACO | 90 | D4 |
| 225TH ST E | LACO | 90 | D2 |
| 228TH ST | LACO | S | C2 |
| 230TH ST E | LACO | 90 | D3 |
| 230TH ST W | KER | 89 | B2 |
| 233RD ST E | LACO | 90 | D4 |
| 235TH ST W | KER | 89 | B2 |
| 235TH ST W | LACO | 89 | B2 |
| 240TH ST E | LACO | 90 | D3 |
| 295TH ST W | KER | 89 | B2 |
| 300TH ST W | KER | 89 | B2 |
| 8001 | MAD | 50 | A5 |
| 8003 | MAD | 50 | A4 |
| 8004 | MAD | 50 | A4 |
| 8005 | MAD | 50 | A4 |
| 8006 | MAD | 50 | A4 |
| 8007 | MAD | 50 | A4 |
| 8008 | MAD | 50 | A5 |
| 8009 | MAD | 50 | A4 |
| 8009 | MAD | 50 | A5 |
| 8013 | MAD | 50 | B4 |
| 8014 | MAD | 50 | B4 |
| 8015 | MAD | 50 | B4 |
| 8016 | MAD | 50 | A4 |
| 8020 | MAD | 50 | A4 |
| 8021 | MAD | 49 | E4 |
| 8023 | MAD | 50 | B3 |
| 8024 | MAD | 50 | A3 |
| 8026 | MAD | 50 | B3 |
| 8027 | MAD | 50 | B3 |
| 8029 | MAD | 50 | A4 |
| 8041 | MAD | 49 | E4 |
| 8042 | MAD | 49 | D3 |
| 8046 | MAD | 49 | D3 |
| 8063 | MAD | 57 | C1 |
| 8066 | MAD | 57 | D1 |
| 8067 | MAD | 57 | E1 |
| 8080 | MAD | 57 | D1 |
| 8081 | MAD | 49 | D5 |
| 8082 | MAD | 49 | D5 |
| 8083 | MAD | 49 | D5 |
| 8086 | MAD | 49 | C5 |
| 8087 | MAD | 57 | C1 |
| 8089 | MAD | 49 | D4 |

17540

# HIGHWAY INDEX



| ROUTE NO. | CO. | PAGE & GRID |
|---|---|---|
| **FEDERAL** | | |
| 6 | ESM | 44 E4 |
| 6 | MIN | 44 D5 |
| 6 | MNO | 51 C1 |
| 50 | CRSN | 36 B2 |
| 50 | DGL | 36 B2 |
| 50 | ED | 35 B4 |
| 50 | ED | 36 A3 |
| 50 | LYON | 36 D1 |
| 50 | SAC | 40 A1 |
| 60 | LPAZ | 104 D4 |
| 93 | CLK | 74 E2 |
| 93 | MOH | 85 E1 |
| 95 | CLK | 74 D2 |
| 95 | LPAZ | 103 E5 |
| 95 | MIN | 44 A1 |
| 95 | NYE | 62 B2 |
| 95 | RCO | 103 E2 |
| 95 | SBD | 85 B4 |
| 95 | SBD | 95 B1 |
| 95 | SBD | 103 D1 |
| 95 | YUMA | 112 E5 |
| 97 | KLAM | 5 B1 |
| 97 | SIS | 4 D5 |
| 97 | SIS | 5 A3 |
| 97 | SIS | 12 C1 |
| 101 | CUR | 1 C1 |
| 101 | DN | 10 A1 |
| 101 | HUM | 9 E3 |
| 101 | HUM | 10 A2 |
| 101 | HUM | 15 D2 |
| 101 | HUM | 16 B4 |
| 101 | HUM | 22 C1 |
| 101 | LACO | 97 B1 |
| 101 | LACO | Q D3 |
| 101 | MAR | 38 B5 |
| 101 | MAR | 45 B1 |
| 101 | MAR | L B2 |
| 101 | MEN | 22 C2 |
| 101 | MEN | 31 A1 |
| 101 | MON | 54 C3 |
| 101 | MON | 55 A5 |
| 101 | MON | 65 B2 |
| 101 | SB | 86 C1 |
| 101 | SB | 87 A4 |
| 101 | SBT | 54 D3 |
| 101 | SCL | 46 A4 |
| 101 | SFCO | 45 B1 |
| 101 | SFCO | L B4 |
| 101 | SLO | 76 A1 |
| 101 | SMCO | 45 C2 |
| 101 | SMCO | L C5 |
| 101 | SMCO | N C1 |
| 101 | SCL | 54 D1 |
| 101 | SCL | P C3 |
| 101 | SON | 32 D5 |
| 101 | SON | 37 E1 |
| 101 | SON | 33 A3 |
| 101 | VEN | 88 A5 |
| 101 | VEN | 96 D1 |
| 197 | DN | 1 E3 |
| 199 | DN | 1 E3 |
| 199 | DN | 2 C3 |
| 395 | CRSN | 36 C2 |
| 395 | DGL | 36 C3 |
| 395 | INY | 51 C3 |
| 395 | INY | 59 E1 |
| 395 | INY | 60 A3 |
| 395 | INY | 70 B1 |
| 395 | KER | 70 C5 |
| 395 | KER | 80 D1 |
| 395 | LAKE | 7 C1 |
| 395 | LAS | 8 B3 |
| 395 | LAS | 21 B3 |
| 395 | LAS | 27 E1 |
| 395 | MOD | 7 C3 |
| 395 | MOD | 8 B2 |
| 395 | MNO | 42 E2 |
| 395 | MNO | 43 A2 |
| 395 | MNO | 50 D1 |
| 395 | SBD | 80 E3 |
| 395 | SBD | 91 A2 |
| 395 | WSH | 28 A3 |
| **INTERSTATE** | | |
| 5 | COL | 32 D1 |
| 5 | COL | 33 A3 |
| 5 | FRCO | 55 E3 |
| 5 | FRCO | 56 B4 |
| 5 | FRCO | 66 D1 |
| 5 | GLE | 24 D3 |
| 5 | JKSN | 4 A1 |
| 5 | KER | 77 E2 |
| 5 | KER | 78 B3 |
| 5 | KER | 88 D1 |
| 5 | KIN | 67 C4 |
| 5 | LACO | 88 E2 |
| 5 | LACO | 89 A3 |
| 5 | LACO | 97 E1 |
| 5 | LACO | 98 B3 |
| 5 | LACO | Q D2 |
| 5 | LACO | R C5 |
| 5 | MCO | 47 C5 |
| 5 | MCO | 55 E2 |
| 5 | ORA | 98 B3 |
| 5 | ORA | 105 E1 |
| 5 | ORA | T E3 |
| 5 | ORA | U A5 |
| 5 | SAC | 39 E2 |
| 5 | SDCO | 106 A2 |
| 5 | SDCO | 111 D2 |
| 5 | SDCO | V A2 |
| 5 | SJCO | 39 E4 |
| 5 | SJCO | 40 A4 |
| 5 | SJCO | 47 A2 |
| 5 | SHA | 12 C3 |
| 5 | SHA | 18 C2 |
| 5 | SIS | 4 B3 |
| 5 | SIS | 12 D2 |
| 5 | STA | 47 A3 |
| 5 | TEH | 18 D4 |
| 5 | TEH | 24 D1 |
| 5 | YOL | 33 A4 |
| 8 | IMP | 111 B4 |
| 8 | SDCO | 107 A5 |
| 8 | SDCO | 111 C1 |
| 8 | SDCO | 112 D1 |
| 8 | SDCO | V B3 |
| 8 | YUMA | 112 D5 |
| 10 | LPAZ | 103 E5 |
| 10 | LACO | 97 D2 |
| 10 | LACO | 98 A2 |
| 10 | LACO | Q D4 |
| 10 | LACO | U B2 |
| 10 | RCO | 99 E3 |
| 10 | RCO | 100 A3 |
| 10 | RCO | 101 A4 |
| 10 | RCO | 102 D4 |
| 10 | RCO | 103 B5 |
| 10 | SBD | 99 A1 |
| 10 | SBD | U E2 |
| 15 | CLK | 74 E1 |
| 15 | RCO | 99 B4 |
| 15 | SBD | 82 C5 |
| 15 | SBD | 83 D3 |
| 15 | SBD | 84 A2 |
| 15 | SBD | 91 D2 |
| 15 | SBD | 92 B1 |
| 15 | SDCO | 106 D3 |
| 15 | SDCO | V C1 |
| 15 | SBD | 99 A1 |
| 40 | SBD | 92 A1 |
| 40 | SBD | 93 D2 |
| 40 | SBD | 94 D2 |
| 40 | SBD | 95 D1 |
| 80 | ALA | L C4 |
| 80 | CC | 38 C5 |
| 80 | CC | L C3 |
| 80 | NEV | 27 C6 |
| 80 | NEV | 35 D1 |
| 80 | PLA | 34 D2 |
| 80 | PLA | 35 A1 |
| 80 | SAC | 33 E5 |
| 80 | SAC | 34 A5 |
| 80 | SAC | 39 E1 |
| 80 | SFCO | 45 C1 |
| 80 | SFCO | L C4 |
| 80 | SOL | 38 E3 |
| 80 | SOL | 39 A2 |
| 80 | WSH | 28 A4 |
| 80 | YOL | 39 D1 |
| 105 | LACO | Q D5 |
| 105 | LACO | S B1 |
| 110 | LACO | 97 D3 |
| 110 | LACO | Q E5 |
| 110 | LACO | S C1 |
| 205 | SJCO | 46 D2 |
| 210 | LACO | 89 E5 |
| 210 | LACO | 97 E1 |
| 210 | LACO | 98 B1 |
| 210 | LACO | Q C1 |
| 210 | LACO | R A2 |
| 210 | LACO | U A2 |
| 215 | SBD | 99 B1 |
| 238 | ALA | 45 E2 |
| 238 | ALA | L E5 |
| 280 | SCL | 45 E4 |
| 280 | SCL | N E3 |
| 280 | SCL | P A3 |
| 280 | SFCO | 45 B2 |
| 280 | SFCO | L C5 |
| 280 | SMCO | 45 B2 |
| 280 | SMCO | N C2 |
| 380 | SMCO | 45 C2 |
| 380 | SMCO | N C1 |
| 405 | LACO | 97 C1 |
| 405 | LACO | Q B3 |
| 405 | LACO | S C2 |
| 405 | ORA | 98 B4 |
| 405 | ORA | T A2 |
| 480 | SFCO | 45 C1 |
| 505 | SOL | 39 A2 |
| 505 | YOL | 33 A4 |
| 505 | YOL | 39 A1 |
| 580 | ALA | 45 A1 |
| 580 | ALA | 46 A2 |
| 580 | ALA | L D4 |
| 580 | ALA | M A5 |
| 580 | CC | L C3 |
| 580 | MAR | 38 B5 |
| 580 | SJCO | 46 D2 |
| 605 | LACO | 98 B2 |
| 605 | LACO | R D4 |
| 605 | LACO | S E2 |
| 605 | LACO | T A2 |
| 680 | ALA | 46 B2 |
| 680 | ALA | P B1 |
| 680 | CC | 38 E5 |
| 680 | CC | 46 A1 |
| 680 | CC | L E4 |
| 680 | CC | M A3 |
| 680 | SCL | 46 B4 |
| 680 | SCL | P B2 |
| 680 | SOL | 38 E4 |
| 680 | SOL | L E2 |
| 780 | SOL | 38 D4 |
| 780 | SOL | L E2 |
| 805 | SDCO | 106 C5 |
| 805 | SDCO | 111 D2 |
| 805 | SDCO | V B1 |
| 880 | ALA | P B2 |
| 980 | ALA | 45 D1 |
| 980 | ALA | L D4 |
| **STATE** | | |
| 1 | HUM | 15 D3 |
| 1 | LACO | 96 D2 |
| 1 | LACO | 97 B2 |
| 1 | LACO | Q C4 |
| 1 | LACO | S B2 |
| 1 | MAR | 37 E4 |
| 1 | MAR | 45 A1 |
| 1 | MAR | L B4 |
| 1 | MEN | 22 C2 |
| 1 | MEN | 30 C3 |
| 1 | MON | 54 B3 |
| 1 | MON | 64 B2 |
| 1 | MON | 65 A4 |
| 1 | ORA | 98 C5 |
| 1 | ORA | 105 D1 |
| 1 | ORA | T B3 |
| 1 | SFCO | 45 B1 |
| 1 | SFCO | L B4 |
| 1 | SLO | 65 A5 |
| 1 | SLO | 75 B1 |
| 1 | SLO | 76 A4 |
| 1 | SMCO | 45 B2 |
| 1 | SMCO | L B5 |
| 1 | SMCO | N B1 |
| 1 | SB | 86 B2 |
| 1 | SCR | 53 C1 |
| 1 | SCR | 54 B2 |
| 1 | SCR | N D5 |
| 1 | SON | 30 D5 |
| 1 | SON | 37 B1 |
| 1 | VEN | 96 C1 |
| 2 | LACO | 90 C4 |
| 2 | LACO | 97 E1 |
| 2 | LACO | Q C4 |
| 2 | LACO | R A1 |
| 2 | SBD | 90 E5 |
| 3 | SIS | 3 D5 |
| 3 | SIS | 4 A4 |
| 3 | SIS | 11 D1 |
| 3 | SIS | 12 A2 |
| 3 | TRI | 11 E4 |
| 3 | TRI | 12 A3 |
| 3 | TRI | 17 B2 |
| 4 | ALP | 36 C5 |
| 4 | ALP | 42 B1 |
| 4 | CAL | 41 D2 |
| 4 | CC | 38 D5 |
| 4 | CC | 39 C5 |
| 4 | CC | L E3 |
| 4 | CC | M B3 |
| 4 | SJCO | 39 E5 |
| 4 | SJCO | 40 B5 |
| 4 | STA | 40 E5 |
| 9 | SCL | 45 E5 |
| 9 | SCL | N E4 |
| 9 | SCL | P A4 |
| 9 | SCR | 53 D1 |
| 9 | SCR | N E4 |
| 9 | SCR | P A5 |
| 12 | CAL | 40 D4 |
| 12 | CAL | 41 A3 |
| 12 | NAPA | 38 C3 |
| 12 | NAPA | L C1 |
| 12 | SAC | 39 C4 |
| 12 | SAC | M E2 |
| 12 | SJCO | 39 E4 |
| 12 | SJCO | 40 A1 |
| 12 | SOL | 38 E3 |
| 12 | SOL | 39 A3 |
| 12 | SOL | M B1 |
| 12 | SON | 37 E2 |
| 12 | SON | 38 A2 |
| 13 | ALA | 45 D1 |
| 13 | ALA | L D4 |
| 14 | KER | 80 C1 |
| 14 | KER | 89 E1 |
| 14 | LACO | 89 E2 |
| 15 | SDCO | V C3 |
| 16 | COL | 32 C3 |
| 16 | SAC | 39 E1 |
| 16 | SAC | 40 A1 |
| 16 | YOL | 32 D4 |
| 17 | SCR | 54 A1 |
| 17 | SCR | P B5 |
| 18 | LACO | 90 D4 |
| 18 | SBD | 91 A4 |
| 18 | SBD | 92 A4 |
| 18 | SBD | 99 C1 |
| 19 | LACO | 98 A3 |
| 19 | LACO | R C3 |
| 19 | LACO | S E1 |
| 20 | COL | 32 E2 |
| 20 | COL | 33 A2 |
| 20 | LAK | 31 E3 |
| 20 | LAK | 32 A3 |
| 20 | MEN | 22 D5 |
| 20 | MEN | 31 C2 |
| 20 | NEV | 34 C1 |
| 20 | SUT | 33 C2 |
| 20 | YUB | 33 E1 |
| 22 | ORA | 98 B4 |
| 22 | ORA | T A3 |
| 23 | LACO | 96 E2 |
| 23 | VEN | 88 D5 |
| 23 | VEN | 96 E1 |
| 24 | ALA | L D4 |
| 24 | CC | 38 E5 |
| 24 | CC | 45 E1 |
| 24 | CC | L E4 |
| 24 | CC | M A3 |
| 25 | MON | 65 D2 |
| 25 | SBT | 55 A3 |
| 25 | SBT | 65 D1 |
| 26 | CAL | 41 B2 |
| 26 | SJCO | 40 D4 |
| 27 | LACO | 97 B1 |
| 27 | LACO | Q A2 |
| 28 | CRSN | 36 B2 |
| 28 | PLA | 35 E1 |
| 28 | WSH | 36 A1 |
| 29 | LAK | 31 D2 |
| 29 | LAK | 32 A4 |
| 29 | NAPA | 38 B1 |
| 29 | NAPA | L D1 |
| 29 | SOL | 38 D4 |
| 30 | LACO | 98 D1 |
| 30 | LACO | U C2 |
| 30 | SBD | 98 E1 |
| 30 | SBD | 99 B1 |
| 30 | SBD | U E1 |
| 31 | RCO | 98 E2 |
| 31 | RCO | U E4 |
| 32 | BUT | 25 A3 |
| 32 | GLE | 24 D3 |
| 32 | TEH | 19 E4 |
| 33 | FRCO | 56 B2 |
| 33 | FRCO | 66 D2 |
| 33 | KER | 67 B5 |
| 33 | KER | 77 B1 |
| 33 | KER | 78 A5 |
| 33 | KIN | 67 A4 |
| 33 | MCO | 47 C5 |
| 33 | MCO | 55 C1 |
| 33 | SJCO | 47 A2 |
| 33 | SLO | 87 E1 |
| 33 | SB | 87 E1 |
| 33 | STA | 47 B3 |
| 33 | VEN | 88 A2 |
| 34 | VEN | 88 C5 |
| 34 | VEN | 96 C1 |
| 35 | LACO | T A1 |
| 35 | SFCO | 45 B2 |
| 35 | SFCO | L B5 |
| 35 | SMCO | 45 C3 |
| 35 | SMCO | L B5 |
| 35 | SMCO | N B1 |
| 35 | SCL | 46 A5 |
| 36 | HUM | 15 E2 |
| 36 | HUM | 16 C3 |
| 36 | LAS | 20 E3 |
| 36 | LAS | 21 A3 |
| 36 | PLU | 20 A4 |
| 36 | SHA | 17 E4 |
| 36 | TEH | 17 E4 |
| 36 | TEH | 18 C4 |
| 36 | TEH | 19 C4 |
| 36 | TRI | 16 E3 |
| 36 | TRI | 17 A3 |
| 37 | MAR | L B2 |
| 37 | SOL | 38 D4 |
| 37 | SOL | L C2 |
| 37 | SON | 38 C4 |
| 38 | SBD | 91 E5 |
| 38 | SBD | 92 A5 |
| 38 | SBD | 99 E1 |
| 38 | SBD | 100 B1 |
| 39 | KLAM | 5 C1 |
| 39 | LACO | 98 C1 |
| 39 | LACO | R E3 |
| 39 | LACO | U A2 |
| 39 | ORA | 98 B4 |
| 39 | ORA | R D5 |
| 39 | ORA | T C1 |
| 41 | FRCO | 57 C3 |
| 41 | KIN | 67 C2 |
| 41 | MAD | 49 D4 |
| 41 | MAD | 57 C2 |
| 41 | MPA | 63 C5 |
| 41 | SLO | 66 D5 |
| 41 | SLO | 76 A2 |
| 42 | LACO | 97 E2 |
| 42 | LACO | Q C5 |
| 42 | LACO | R B5 |
| 43 | FRCO | 57 D5 |
| 43 | KER | 68 B5 |
| 43 | KER | 78 B2 |
| 43 | KIN | 67 E2 |
| 43 | TUL | 68 A3 |
| 44 | LAS | 20 A2 |
| 44 | SHA | 18 C2 |
| 44 | SHA | 19 C2 |
| 45 | COL | 32 E1 |
| 45 | COL | 33 A2 |
| 45 | GLE | 24 E3 |
| 45 | YOL | 33 C4 |
| 46 | JOS | 2 D1 |
| 46 | KER | 77 A1 |
| 46 | KER | 78 B1 |
| 46 | SLO | 66 D5 |
| 46 | SLO | 75 E2 |
| 46 | SLO | 76 B1 |
| 47 | LACO | 191 C3 |
| 48 | LACO | 89 A2 |
| 49 | AMA | 40 D1 |
| 49 | CAL | 41 A3 |
| 49 | ED | 34 D4 |
| 49 | MAD | 49 D4 |
| 49 | MPA | 48 E2 |
| 49 | MPA | 49 A3 |
| 49 | NEV | 34 C1 |
| 49 | PLA | 34 C3 |
| 49 | PLU | 27 D3 |
| 49 | SIE | 26 C4 |
| 49 | SIE | 27 C4 |
| 49 | TUO | 41 C5 |
| 49 | TUO | 48 D1 |
| 49 | YUBA | 26 C4 |
| 50 | ED | 34 C5 |
| 50 | SAC | 39 E1 |
| 50 | SAC | 40 A1 |
| 52 | SDCO | 106 C5 |
| 52 | SDCO | V B2 |
| 53 | LAK | 32 A3 |
| 54 | SDCO | 111 E1 |
| 54 | SDCO | V D4 |
| 55 | ORA | 98 C4 |
| 55 | ORA | T D3 |
| 56 | SDCO | 106 D4 |
| 57 | LACO | 98 C2 |
| 57 | LACO | U B3 |
| 57 | ORA | 98 C3 |
| 57 | ORA | T D1 |
| 58 | KER | 77 E3 |
| 58 | KER | 78 B3 |
| 58 | KER | 80 A4 |
| 58 | SBD | 91 C1 |
| 58 | SLO | 76 B3 |
| 58 | SLO | 77 A3 |
| 59 | MCO | 48 C4 |
| 60 | LACO | 98 B2 |
| 60 | LACO | R D4 |
| 60 | RCO | 99 B2 |
| 60 | SBD | 98 D2 |
| 60 | SBD | U E3 |
| 61 | ALA | 45 D2 |
| 61 | ALA | L D5 |
| 62 | RCO | 100 C2 |
| 62 | RCO | 102 E2 |
| 62 | SBD | 101 A1 |
| 62 | SBD | 102 A2 |
| 62 | SBD | 103 B2 |
| 63 | FRCO | 58 B4 |
| 63 | TUL | 58 B5 |
| 63 | TUL | 68 B2 |
| 65 | KER | 68 D6 |
| 65 | KER | 78 D2 |
| 65 | PLA | 34 A3 |
| 65 | TUL | 68 C2 |
| 65 | YUB | 33 D3 |
| 66 | JKSN | 4 A1 |
| 66 | KLAM | 4 D1 |
| 66 | SBD | 98 E1 |
| 66 | SBD | 99 B1 |
| 66 | SBD | U D2 |
| 67 | SDCO | 106 E4 |
| 67 | SDCO | 107 A4 |
| 67 | SDCO | V E2 |
| 68 | MOH | 85 D4 |
| 68 | MON | 54 B4 |
| 70 | BUT | 25 D3 |
| 70 | KLAM | 5 D1 |
| 70 | LAS | 27 E2 |
| 70 | PLU | 26 A1 |
| 70 | SUT | 33 D4 |
| 70 | YUB | 33 D1 |
| 71 | LACO | 98 D2 |
| 71 | LACO | U C3 |
| 71 | RCO | 98 D2 |
| 71 | SBD | 98 D2 |
| 71 | SBD | U C3 |
| 72 | LPAZ | 104 B2 |
| 72 | LACO | 97 E2 |
| 72 | LACO | 98 A2 |
| 72 | LACO | R B4 |
| 73 | ORA | 98 C4 |
| 73 | ORA | T D4 |
| 74 | ORA | 98 E5 |
| 74 | ORA | 99 A5 |
| 74 | RCO | 99 C4 |
| 74 | RCO | 100 A4 |
| 75 | SDCO | 111 C1 |
| 75 | SDCO | V B4 |
| 76 | SDCO | 106 D2 |
| 76 | SDCO | 107 B2 |
| 77 | ALA | L D5 |
| 77 | ALA | 45 D1 |
| 77 | ALA | 159 C1 |
| 78 | IMP | 108 C3 |
| 78 | IMP | 109 A4 |
| 78 | IMP | 110 C2 |
| 78 | RCO | 103 D5 |
| 78 | RCO | 110 C1 |
| 78 | SDCO | 106 C3 |
| 78 | SDCO | 107 C3 |
| 78 | SDCO | 108 A3 |
| 79 | RCO | 99 E3 |
| 79 | RCO | 106 D1 |
| 79 | SDCO | 107 B1 |
| 80 | SFCO | L C5 |
| 82 | SCL | 46 A4 |
| 82 | SCL | P A3 |
| 82 | SMCO | 45 C2 |
| 82 | SMCO | N B1 |
| 83 | SBD | 98 D2 |
| 83 | SBD | U D3 |
| 84 | ALA | 45 E3 |
| 84 | ALA | 46 B3 |
| 84 | ALA | M C5 |
| 84 | SMCO | 45 D4 |
| 84 | SMCO | N D3 |
| 84 | YOL | 39 D1 |
| 85 | SCL | 45 E4 |
| 85 | SCL | P A3 |
| 86 | IMP | 108 C2 |
| 86 | IMP | 109 A4 |
| 86 | RCO | 101 B4 |
| 86 | RCO | 108 B1 |
| 87 | SCL | 46 B4 |
| 87 | SCL | P B3 |
| 88 | ALP | 36 C4 |
| 88 | AMA | 35 D5 |
| 88 | AMA | 41 A2 |
| 88 | DGL | 36 C3 |
| 88 | SJCO | 40 C3 |
| 89 | ALP | 36 B4 |
| 89 | ED | 35 E3 |
| 89 | ED | 36 A4 |
| 89 | MNO | 36 D5 |
| 89 | NEV | 27 D5 |
| 89 | PLA | 35 D1 |
| 89 | PLU | 20 A4 |
| 89 | PLU | 26 C1 |
| 89 | SHA | 13 C3 |
| 89 | SHA | 19 E1 |
| 89 | SIE | 27 C4 |
| 89 | SIS | 12 E2 |
| 89 | SIS | 13 B3 |
| 89 | TEH | 19 D3 |
| 90 | LACO | Q D4 |
| 90 | ORA | 98 C3 |
| 90 | ORA | T E1 |
| 91 | LACO | 97 E3 |
| 91 | LACO | S C1 |
| 91 | ORA | 98 C3 |
| 91 | ORA | T C2 |
| 91 | RCO | 99 A3 |
| 91 | RCO | U D5 |
| 92 | ALA | 45 D3 |
| 92 | ALA | N E1 |
| 92 | SMCO | 45 D3 |
| 92 | SMCO | N C2 |
| 94 | SDCO | 111 E1 |
| 94 | SDCO | 112 D2 |
| 94 | SDCO | V D3 |
| 95 | LPAZ | 104 B2 |
| 95 | MOH | 85 D5 |
| 95 | MOH | 95 D1 |
| 95 | MOH | 96 B3 |
| 96 | HUM | 10 C3 |
| 96 | SIS | 2 E4 |
| 96 | SIS | 3 C3 |
| 96 | SIS | 10 E1 |
| 98 | IMP | 111 C3 |
| 98 | IMP | 112 C4 |

| ROUTE NO. | CO. | PAGE & GRID |
|---|---|---|
| 99 | BUT | 25 B3 |
| 99 | FRCO | 57 B3 |
| 99 | JKSN | 3 E1 |
| 99 | KER | 68 B5 |
| 99 | KER | 78 C2 |
| 99 | MAD | 56 D1 |
| 99 | MAD | 57 B2 |
| 99 | MCO | 48 B4 |
| 99 | MCO | 56 D1 |
| 99 | SAC | 39 E2 |
| 99 | SAC | 40 A2 |
| 99 | SJCO | 40 B4 |
| 99 | SJCO | 47 B1 |
| 99 | STA | 47 D3 |
| 99 | SUT | 33 C3 |
| 99 | TEH | 18 D5 |
| 99 | TUL | 57 E5 |
| 100 | CRSN | 36 C2 |
| 103 | LACO | 97 E4 |
| 103 | LACO | S D2 |
| 104 | SAC | 40 C2 |
| 107 | LACO | 97 D3 |
| 107 | LACO | S B2 |
| 108 | MNO | 42 E2 |
| 108 | STA | 47 D2 |
| 108 | TUO | 41 D4 |
| 108 | TUO | 42 B2 |
| 110 | LACO | 97 E2 |
| 110 | LACO | R B3 |
| 111 | IMP | 108 D1 |
| 111 | IMP | 109 B3 |
| 111 | IMP | 112 B3 |
| 111 | RCO | 100 C3 |
| 111 | RCO | 101 A4 |
| 111 | RCO | 108 D1 |
| 112 | ALA | 45 D2 |
| 112 | ALA | L E5 |
| 113 | SOL | 39 B2 |
| 113 | SOL | M C1 |
| 113 | SUT | 33 C3 |
| 113 | YOL | 33 C5 |
| 114 | SMCO | N D2 |
| 115 | IMP | 109 B3 |
| 115 | IMP | 112 C3 |
| 116 | SON | 37 D2 |
| 116 | SON | 38 A3 |
| 116 | SON | L A1 |
| 117 | SDCO | 111 E2 |
| 117 | SDCO | V D5 |
| 118 | LACO | 89 B5 |
| 118 | LACO | Q C1 |
| 118 | VEN | 88 C5 |
| 118 | VEN | 89 A5 |
| 119 | KER | 78 B3 |
| 120 | MNO | 43 C5 |
| 120 | MNO | 51 B1 |
| 120 | SJCO | 47 B1 |
| 120 | STA | 48 A1 |
| 120 | TUO | 41 C5 |
| 120 | TUO | 48 C1 |
| 120 | TUO | 49 B1 |
| 121 | NAPA | 38 D2 |
| 121 | NAPA | L C1 |
| 121 | SON | 38 B3 |
| 121 | SON | L B1 |
| 123 | ALA | L D4 |
| 124 | AMA | 40 D2 |
| 125 | SDCO | 106 E4 |
| 125 | SDCO | V D2 |
| 126 | LACO | 89 A4 |
| 126 | VEN | 88 D4 |
| 126 | VEN | 89 A4 |
| 127 | INY | 72 D2 |
| 127 | SBD | 72 E5 |
| 127 | SBD | 83 B2 |
| 128 | MEN | 30 C2 |
| 128 | MEN | 31 B4 |
| 128 | NAPA | 38 B2 |
| 128 | SON | 31 D5 |
| 128 | SON | 38 A1 |
| 128 | YOL | 39 A1 |
| 129 | SCR | 54 D2 |
| 130 | SCL | 46 C4 |
| 130 | SCL | P C3 |
| 131 | MAR | 38 B5 |
| 131 | MAR | 45 B1 |
| 131 | MAR | L B4 |
| 132 | MPA | 48 D2 |
| 132 | SJCO | 47 A2 |
| 132 | STA | 47 B2 |
| 132 | STA | 48 B2 |
| 133 | ORA | 98 D5 |
| 133 | ORA | T E4 |
| 134 | LACO | 97 D1 |
| 134 | LACO | Q E3 |
| 134 | LACO | R A3 |
| 135 | SB | 86 C1 |
| 136 | INY | 60 B4 |
| 137 | TUL | 68 B2 |
| 138 | LACO | 88 E2 |
| 138 | LACO | 89 A2 |
| 138 | LACO | 90 A3 |
| 138 | SBD | 91 A5 |
| 139 | LAS | 14 C3 |
| 139 | LAS | 20 E1 |
| 139 | LAS | 21 A3 |
| 139 | MOD | 5 E3 |
| 139 | MOD | 6 A4 |
| 139 | MOD | 14 D1 |
| 139 | SIS | 5 E3 |
| 140 | KLAM | 5 C1 |
| 140 | LAKE | 7 A1 |
| 140 | MCO | 47 D4 |
| 140 | MCO | 48 A4 |
| 140 | MPA | 48 E4 |
| 140 | MPA | 49 C2 |
| 142 | ORA | T E1 |
| 142 | ORA | U B4 |
| 142 | SBD | 98 D2 |
| 144 | SB | 87 C4 |
| 145 | FRCO | 57 A4 |
| 145 | FRCO | 66 E1 |
| 145 | MAD | 57 B2 |
| 146 | CLK | 74 E3 |
| 146 | MON | 55 B5 |
| 146 | SBT | 55 C5 |
| 147 | PLU | 20 C4 |
| 149 | BUT | 25 C4 |
| 150 | SB | 87 E4 |
| 150 | VEN | 88 B4 |
| 151 | SHA | 18 C1 |
| 152 | MAD | 56 C1 |
| 152 | MCO | 55 E1 |
| 152 | MCO | 56 B1 |
| 152 | SCL | 54 D2 |
| 152 | SCR | 54 C2 |
| 154 | SB | 87 A3 |
| 155 | KER | 68 B5 |
| 155 | KER | 69 B5 |
| 155 | KER | 79 C1 |
| 156 | CLK | 72 E1 |
| 156 | CLK | 74 A1 |
| 156 | MON | 54 C3 |
| 156 | SBT | 54 E2 |
| 156 | SBT | 55 A2 |
| 157 | CLK | 73 E2 |
| 157 | CLK | 74 A2 |
| 158 | CLK | 73 E1 |
| 158 | CLK | 74 A1 |
| 160 | CLK | 73 E3 |
| 160 | CLK | 74 B3 |
| 160 | NYE | 73 C2 |
| 160 | SAC | 39 E1 |
| 160 | SAC | M D2 |
| 161 | CLK | 74 C5 |
| 161 | SIS | 5 B2 |
| 162 | BUT | 25 B5 |
| 162 | GLE | 24 B4 |
| 162 | GLE | 25 B5 |
| 162 | MEN | 22 E4 |
| 162 | MEN | 23 A3 |
| 163 | CLK | 85 C4 |
| 163 | SDCO | 106 D5 |
| 163 | SDCO | V B3 |
| 164 | CLK | 84 E2 |
| 164 | LACO | 98 A1 |
| 165 | MCO | 47 E5 |
| 165 | MCO | 55 E2 |
| 166 | KER | 77 A4 |
| 166 | KER | 78 B5 |
| 166 | SB | 86 B1 |
| 166 | SLO | 76 D5 |
| 167 | MNO | 43 E4 |
| 168 | FRCO | 50 B5 |
| 168 | FRCO | 57 E2 |
| 168 | FRCO | 58 A1 |
| 168 | INY | 51 E5 |
| 168 | INY | 52 C3 |
| 168 | MNO | 52 C3 |
| 169 | DN | 1 E5 |
| 169 | DN | 2 A5 |
| 169 | DN | 10 A1 |
| 169 | HUM | 10 C3 |
| 170 | LACO | 97 D1 |
| 170 | LACO | Q C2 |
| 172 | TEH | 19 D4 |
| 173 | SBD | 91 C5 |
| 174 | NEV | 34 D2 |
| 175 | LAK | 31 E3 |
| 175 | LAK | 32 A5 |
| 175 | MEN | 31 C3 |
| 176 | SB | 86 C1 |
| 177 | RCO | 102 D2 |
| 178 | INY | 72 D3 |
| 178 | INY | 73 A3 |
| 178 | KERN | 69 E5 |
| 178 | KER | 70 A5 |
| 178 | KER | 78 E2 |
| 178 | KER | 79 A2 |
| 178 | KER | 80 B1 |
| 178 | SBD | 81 A1 |
| 180 | FRCO | 56 E3 |
| 180 | FRCO | 57 C3 |
| 180 | FRCO | 58 B3 |
| 180 | FRCO | 59 A3 |
| 182 | MNO | 43 C2 |
| 183 | MON | 54 C3 |
| 184 | KER | 78 E3 |
| 185 | ALA | 45 D1 |
| 185 | ALA | L D5 |
| 188 | SDCO | 112 C2 |
| 189 | SBD | 91 C5 |
| 190 | INY | 61 D4 |
| 190 | INY | 70 C1 |
| 190 | INY | 72 C1 |
| 190 | TUL | 68 B3 |
| 190 | TUL | 69 A3 |
| 191 | BUT | 25 C3 |
| 192 | SB | 87 C4 |
| 193 | ED | 34 E4 |
| 193 | PLA | 34 B3 |
| 195 | RCO | 101 B5 |
| 198 | FRCO | 66 E2 |
| 198 | KIN | 67 C2 |
| 198 | MON | 65 D2 |
| 198 | MON | 66 A2 |
| 198 | TUL | 58 E5 |
| 198 | TUL | 59 A5 |
| 198 | TUL | 68 B1 |
| 200 | HUM | 9 E5 |
| 200 | HUM | 10 A5 |
| 201 | TUL | 58 B5 |
| 202 | KER | 79 C4 |
| 203 | MNO | 50 D2 |
| 204 | KER | 78 D3 |
| 206 | DGL | 36 B3 |
| 206 | SBD | 99 B1 |
| 207 | DGL | 36 B3 |
| 208 | DGL | 36 E4 |
| 208 | MEN | 22 B2 |
| 209 | SDCO | 111 C1 |
| 209 | SDCO | V A4 |
| 213 | LACO | S C3 |
| 213 | LACO | 97 D3 |
| 215 | RCO | 99 C3 |
| 216 | TUL | 68 C1 |
| 217 | SB | 87 B4 |
| 218 | MON | 54 B4 |
| 219 | STA | 47 C2 |
| 220 | SOL | 39 D3 |
| 221 | NAPA | L D1 |
| 221 | NAPA | 38 D3 |
| 223 | KER | 78 D4 |
| 223 | KER | 79 A4 |
| 224 | SB | 87 E4 |
| 225 | SB | 87 C4 |
| 227 | SLO | 76 B4 |
| 229 | SLO | 76 B2 |
| 232 | VEN | 88 B5 |
| 233 | MAD | 56 D1 |
| 236 | SCR | 53 D1 |
| 236 | SCR | N D4 |
| 237 | SCL | 46 B4 |
| 237 | SCL | P A3 |
| 238 | ALA | 46 A2 |
| 238 | ALA | P A1 |
| 243 | RCO | 100 A3 |
| 245 | TUL | 58 C4 |
| 245 | TUL | 68 C1 |
| 246 | SB | 86 C3 |
| 247 | SBD | 91 E2 |
| 247 | SBD | 92 B4 |
| 247 | SBD | 100 D1 |
| 249 | FRCO | 58 D4 |
| 250 | ORA | 98 C3 |
| 253 | MEN | 31 A3 |
| 254 | HUM | 16 B4 |
| 255 | HUM | 9 E5 |
| 255 | HUM | 10 A5 |
| 259 | SBD | 99 B1 |
| 262 | ALA | 46 A3 |
| 262 | ALA | P B2 |
| 263 | SIS | 4 A4 |
| 264 | ESM | 52 A1 |
| 265 | ESM | 52 E1 |
| 266 | ESM | 52 E3 |
| 266 | MNO | 52 C3 |
| 267 | ESM | 61 C1 |
| 267 | PLA | 35 E1 |
| 267 | PLA | 36 A1 |
| 269 | FRCO | 67 A1 |
| 270 | MNO | 43 B3 |
| 271 | MEN | 22 C1 |
| 273 | SHA | 18 C2 |
| 274 | SDCO | 106 C5 |
| 274 | SDCO | V B2 |
| 281 | LAK | 31 E3 |
| 282 | SDCO | 111 C1 |
| 282 | SDCO | V B4 |
| 284 | PLU | 27 D2 |
| 299 | HUM | 10 B4 |
| 299 | LAS | 14 A3 |
| 299 | MOD | 7 C5 |
| 299 | MOD | 8 B1 |
| 299 | MOD | 14 D1 |
| 299 | SHA | 13 B5 |
| 299 | SHA | 18 B2 |
| 299 | TRI | 10 D5 |
| 299 | TRI | 16 E1 |
| 299 | TRI | 17 D1 |
| 330 | SBD | 99 C1 |
| 338 | LYON | 43 B1 |
| 341 | LYON | 36 D1 |
| 341 | WSH | 28 C5 |
| 359 | MIN | 44 B2 |
| 360 | MIN | 44 E3 |
| 371 | RCO | 100 B5 |
| 372 | NYE | 73 B2 |
| 373 | NYE | 62 D5 |
| 374 | NYE | 62 A3 |
| 380 | SMCO | N B1 |
| 428 | WSH | 36 C1 |
| 429 | WSH | 36 B1 |
| 430 | WSH | 28 B4 |
| 431 | WSH | 28 B5 |
| 431 | WSH | 36 B1 |
| 445 | WSH | 28 D1 |
| 446 | WSH | 28 E2 |
| 447 | WSH | 28 E2 |
| 480 | SFCO | L C4 |
| 512 | CRSN | 36 C2 |
| 513 | CRSN | 36 C2 |
| 604 | CLK | 74 E2 |
| 666 | WSH | 28 B4 |
| 710 | LACO | 97 E2 |
| 710 | LACO | R B5 |
| 710 | LACO | S D2 |
| 880 | ALA | 45 E2 |
| 880 | SCL | 46 B4 |
| COUNTY | | |
| 1 | LPAZ | 103 E3 |
| 1 | LPAZ | 104 A1 |
| 3 | LPAZ | 104 B2 |
| 10 | LPAZ | 104 A2 |
| 14 | LPAZ | 103 E2 |
| 14 | LPAZ | 104 A2 |
| 17 | LPAZ | 103 E2 |
| 17 | LPAZ | 104 A2 |
| 21 | LPAZ | 103 E3 |
| 21 | LPAZ | 104 A3 |
| 25 | LPAZ | 103 E3 |
| 29 | LPAZ | 103 E2 |
| 30 | LPAZ | 103 E3 |
| 30 | LPAZ | 104 A3 |
| 34 | LPAZ | 103 E3 |
| 38 | LPAZ | 103 E3 |
| 44 | LPAZ | 103 E3 |
| 44 | LPAZ | 104 A3 |
| 50 | LPAZ | 103 E4 |
| 56 | LPAZ | 103 E4 |
| A 1 | LAS | 20 D2 |
| A 2 | LAS | 14 C3 |
| A 3 | LAS | 21 B4 |
| A 5 | TEH | 18 C3 |
| A 6 | TEH | 18 E4 |
| A 6 | TEH | 19 B3 |
| A 7 | TEH | 18 D5 |
| A 8 | TEH | 18 D5 |
| A 9 | TEH | 24 D2 |
| A10 | SIS | 12 C2 |
| A11 | TEH | 24 D1 |
| A12 | SIS | 4 B5 |
| A13 | PLU | 20 B4 |
| A14 | PLU | 27 A3 |
| A15 | PLU | 27 B2 |
| A16 | SHA | 17 E3 |
| A16 | SHA | 18 A3 |
| A16 | SHA | 122 A2 |
| A17 | SHA | 18 D3 |
| A17 | SHA | 19 A3 |
| A18 | SHA | 18 C2 |
| A19 | SHA | 13 D3 |
| A21 | LAS | 20 C2 |
| A22 | PLU | 20 D5 |
| A23 | PLU | 27 C2 |
| A23 | SIE | 27 C3 |
| A24 | PLU | 27 D3 |
| A25 | LAS | 21 D5 |
| A26 | LAS | 21 D5 |
| A27 | LAS | 21 B3 |
| B 2 | BUT | 25 D4 |
| D 1 | DN | 1 E3 |
| D 2 | DN | 1 D4 |
| D 3 | DN | 1 D3 |
| D 5 | DN | 1 D2 |
| E 1 | ALP | 36 C5 |
| E 4 | YOL | 32 E4 |
| E 4 | YOL | 33 A4 |
| E 6 | YOL | 39 B1 |
| E 6 | YOL | 136 A2 |
| E 7 | SOL | 39 B1 |
| E 7 | YOL | 33 B5 |
| E 8 | YOL | 33 C4 |
| E 8 | YOL | 39 C1 |
| E 8 | YOL | 136 E1 |
| E 9 | YOL | 39 D2 |
| E10 | YOL | 33 B4 |
| E11 | YOL | 33 B4 |
| E13 | SAC | 39 D3 |
| E16 | AMA | 40 E1 |
| E16 | ED | 35 B4 |
| G 1 | SBT | 54 E3 |
| G 2 | SCL | 46 A4 |
| G 2 | SCL | P A3 |
| G 2 | SCLR | 150 C2 |
| G 3 | PA | 147 D3 |
| G 3 | SCL | 45 D4 |
| G 3 | SCL | 147 B6 |
| G 3 | SCL | N E3 |
| G 4 | SCL | 46 A4 |
| G 4 | SCL | P B3 |
| G 4 | SCLR | 150 E1 |
| G 4 | SCLR | 151 A1 |
| G 5 | PA | 147 C6 |
| G 5 | SCL | 45 E4 |
| G 5 | SCL | 147 A5 |
| G 5 | SCL | 149 A3 |
| G 5 | SCL | N E3 |
| G 6 | MVW | 148 C5 |
| G 6 | SCL | 45 E4 |
| G 6 | SCL | 46 A4 |
| G 6 | SCL | 148 C5 |
| G 6 | SCLR | 151 B1 |
| G 6 | SVL | 148 C5 |
| G 7 | SCL | 54 D2 |
| G 8 | SCL | 46 B5 |
| G 8 | SCL | 54 C1 |
| G 8 | SCL | P B4 |
| G 9 | SCL | 54 D2 |
| G10 | SCL | 46 B5 |
| G10 | SCL | P B4 |
| G11 | MON | 54 C3 |
| G12 | MON | 54 C3 |
| G13 | MON | 65 C2 |
| G13 | SBT | 65 C1 |
| G14 | MON | 65 B3 |
| G15 | MON | 65 B1 |
| G16 | MON | 54 B5 |
| G16 | MON | 64 C1 |
| G16 | MON | 65 B1 |
| G16 | MON | 168 E4 |
| G17 | MON | 54 C4 |
| G17 | MON | 65 A1 |
| G18 | MON | 65 D4 |
| G19 | MON | 65 E5 |
| G20 | MON | 54 C5 |
| J 1 | FRCO | 55 E3 |
| J 1 | FRCO | 56 A3 |
| J 1 | SBT | 55 B4 |
| J 2 | ALA | 46 C2 |
| J 2 | ALA | M D5 |
| J 2 | ALA | P D1 |
| J 2 | SJCO | 46 E1 |
| J 3 | S | 160 E2 |
| J 3 | SJCO | 47 B2 |
| J 3 | SJCO | 160 E2 |
| J 4 | CC | 46 D1 |
| J 4 | SJCO | 46 E2 |
| J 4 | SJCO | 47 A2 |
| J 5 | SJCO | 40 B4 |
| J 5 | SJCO | 47 C1 |
| J 6 | SJCO | 40 C5 |
| J 6 | SJCO | 47 D1 |
| J 7 | MCO | 47 E3 |
| J 7 | MCO | 48 A3 |
| J 7 | SJCO | 40 B5 |
| J 7 | SJCO | 47 C1 |
| J 7 | STA | 47 D2 |
| J 8 | SCTO | 137 D5 |
| J 9 | SJCO | 47 C1 |
| J 9 | STA | 47 D1 |
| J 9 | STA | 48 A3 |
| J11 | SAC | 39 D3 |
| J11 | SJCO | 39 D3 |
| J12 | SJCO | 40 C3 |
| J13 | SJCO | 46 E1 |
| J14 | STA | 40 E5 |
| J14 | STA | 47 E1 |
| J15 | TUL | 68 B2 |
| J16 | MPA | 48 E3 |
| J16 | MCO | 48 B3 |
| J16 | STA | 47 D3 |
| J17 | MCO | 48 A3 |
| J17 | STA | 47 C3 |
| J18 | STA | 47 C4 |
| J19 | FRCO | 58 B4 |
| J19 | TUL | 58 A5 |
| J20 | MPA | 48 E2 |
| J20 | TUO | 48 E1 |
| J21 | TUL | 58 D5 |
| J22 | TUL | 68 B4 |
| J23 | TUL | 58 C5 |
| J23 | TUL | 68 C2 |
| J24 | TUL | 68 B4 |
| J25 | TUL | 68 A1 |
| J27 | TUL | 68 C2 |
| J28 | TUL | 68 C2 |
| J29 | TUL | 68 D2 |
| J30 | TUL | 68 B1 |
| J32 | TUL | 68 A1 |
| J34 | TUL | 68 A1 |
| J38 | TUL | 57 E5 |
| J38 | TUL | 58 B5 |
| J40 | TUL | 58 A5 |
| J41 | TUL | 70 B4 |
| J42 | TUL | 68 E3 |
| J42 | TUL | 69 A3 |
| J44 | TUL | 68 C5 |
| J59 | MCO | 48 C2 |
| J59 | TUO | 48 C1 |
| N 1 | LACO | 97 B2 |
| N 2 | LACO | 89 A2 |
| N 3 | LACO | 89 E5 |
| N 3 | LACO | 90 A4 |
| N 5 | LACO | 90 A2 |
| N 6 | LACO | 90 C4 |
| N 7 | LACO | S B3 |
| N 8 | LACO | 98 C2 |
| N 8 | LACO | R D5 |
| N 8 | LACO | U A3 |
| N 8 | LACO | T B1 |
| N 9 | LACO | 96 E2 |
| N 9 | LACO | 97 A2 |
| R 2 | RCO | 102 B4 |
| R 3 | RCO | 99 E5 |
| R 3 | RCO | 100 A5 |
| R 3 | RCO | 106 E1 |
| R 3 | RCO | 107 A1 |
| S 1 | SDCO | 107 D4 |
| S 1 | SDCO | 112 D1 |
| S 2 | IMP | 111 B3 |
| S 2 | SDCO | 107 C3 |
| S 2 | SDCO | 108 A4 |
| S 2 | SDCO | 111 B3 |
| S 3 | SDCO | 107 E3 |
| S 4 | SDCO | 106 D4 |
| S 4 | SDCO | V C1 |
| S 5 | SDCO | 106 D4 |
| S 6 | SDCO | 106 E2 |
| S 6 | SDCO | 107 A2 |
| S 7 | SDCO | 107 A2 |
| S 8 | SDCO | 106 C4 |
| S 9 | SDCO | 106 C4 |
| S10 | SDCO | 106 C3 |
| S11 | SDCO | 106 C3 |
| S12 | SDCO | 106 D3 |
| S13 | SDCO | 106 C1 |
| S14 | SDCO | 106 C3 |
| S15 | SDCO | 106 C2 |
| S16 | RCO | 106 D1 |
| S16 | SDCO | 106 D1 |
| S17 | SDCO | V E3 |
| S17 | SDCO | 111 E1 |
| S17 | SDCO | 112 A1 |
| S18 | ORCO | 98 D4 |
| S19 | ORCO | 98 E4 |
| S20 | SB | 86 B2 |
| S21 | SDCO | V A1 |
| S21 | SDCO | 106 C5 |
| S22 | IMP | 108 C2 |
| S22 | SDCO | 107 E2 |
| S22 | SDCO | 108 B2 |
| S24 | IMP | 112 D5 |
| S24 | IMP | 110 D5 |
| S26 | IMP | 109 A4 |
| S27 | IMP | 109 A5 |
| S28 | IMP | 109 A5 |
| S28 | IMP | 112 C3 |
| S29 | IMP | 108 E5 |
| S29 | IMP | 111 E3 |
| S30 | IMP | 109 A3 |
| S30 | IMP | 112 A3 |
| S31 | IMP | 109 B4 |
| S31 | IMP | 112 B3 |
| S32 | IMP | 109 C4 |
| S32 | IMP | 112 C3 |
| S33 | IMP | 109 C4 |
| S33 | IMP | 112 C4 |
| S34 | IMP | 110 B4 |
| S80 | IMP | 108 C5 |
| S80 | IMP | 109 A5 |
| S80 | IMP | 111 D3 |
| S80 | IMP | 112 A3 |

# CALIFORNIA SCENIC DRIVES

# POINTS OF INTEREST INDEX

| NAME & ADDRESS | PAGE & GRID |
|---|---|
| AIRPORTS | 251 |
| AMUSEMENT PARKS | 252 |
| BEACHES | 252 |
| CAMPGROUNDS | 253 |
| COLLEGES & UNIVERSITIES | 255 |
| GOLF COURSES | 255 |
| HARBORS | 256 |
| HISTORICAL SITES | 256 |
| HOTELS | 258 |
| MISSIONS | 262 |
| PARKS & NATIONAL FORESTS | 262 |
| POINTS OF INTEREST | 264 |
| RECREATION LAKES, RIVERS & MARINAS | 269 |
| SKI AREAS | 271 |
| THEATER | 271 |
| WINERIES | 272 |

**\*\*\*\*\*\*\*\*\*\*\*\*\*\*\*\*\*\*\*\*\*\*\*\*\*\*\*\*\*\*\*\*\*\*\*\*\*\*\*\*\*\*\*\*\*\*\*\*\*\*\*\*\*\***

### AIRPORTS

**\*\*\*\*\*\*\*\*\*\*\*\*\*\*\*\*\*\*\*\*\*\*\*\*\*\*\*\*\*\*\*\*\*\*\*\*\*\*\*\*\*\*\*\*\*\*\*\*\*\*\*\*\*\***

| NAME & ADDRESS | PAGE | GRID |
|---|---|---|
| ALTURAS MUNICIPAL AIRPORT, 1 mi W of Alturas | 8 | A1 |
| AMADOR COUNTY AIRPORT, near Amador | 40 | D2 |
| ANTIOCH AIRPORT, Lone Tree Wy, Antioch | M | C3 |
| ARCATA AIRPORT, off Hwy 101 at Airport Rd | 10 | A4 |
| AUBURN AIRPORT, 4 mi N of Auburn | 34 | C3 |
| BAKERSFIELD AIRPARK, Watts Dr & Union Av | 78 | D3 |
| BARSTOW-DAGGETT, Nat'l Trails Hwy, Barstow | 92 | B1 |
| BENTON AIRPORT, Gold St, Redding | 122 | A3 |
| BISHOP AIRPORT, 2 mi E of Bishop | 51 | D4 |
| BRACKETT FIELD, McKinley Av, La Verne | U | C2 |
| BUCHANAN FIELD AIRPORT, John Glenn Dr, Concord | M | A3 |
| BURBANK-GLENDALE-PASADENA, 2627 N Hollywood Wy | 179 | B1 |
| CALAVERAS CO AIRPORT, Hwy 49 S of San Andreas | 41 | A4 |
| CANNON INTERNATIONAL AIRPORT, 2 of Reno | 28 | C4 |
| CARSON AIRPORT, Carson City, Nevada | 36 | C1 |
| CATALINA AIR & SEA TERMINAL, Harbor Blvd | 191 | B3 |
| CHICO MUNICIPAL AIRPORT, 5 mi NW of Chico | 25 | B2 |
| CHINO AIRPORT, Hwy 83, Chino | U | D3 |
| COLUSA COUNTY AIRPORT, 3 mi S of Colusa | 33 | A2 |
| DELANO MUNICIPAL AIRPORT, Hwy 99, Delano | 68 | B5 |
| DOUGLAS COUNTY AIRPORT, Minden, Nevada | 36 | C3 |
| FANTASY HAVEN AIRPORT, 2 mi SE of Tehachapi | 79 | D4 |
| FRESNO AIR TERMINAL, 5175 E Clinton Av | 57 | D3 |
| FRESNO-CHANDLER DOWNTOWN AIRPORT, Amador & Thorne | 165 | B4 |
| IMPERIAL COUNTY AIRPORT, Hwy 86 at Main, Imperial | 109 | A5 |
| INYOKERN COUNTY AIRPORT, Hwy 395, Inyokern | 80 | D1 |

| NAME & ADDRESS | PAGE | GRID |
|---|---|---|
| JOHN MCNAMARA FIELD, nr Crescent City | 1 | C4 |
| JOHN WAYNE AIRPORT, MacArthur Blvd | 198 | B5 |
| KERN VALLEY AIRPORT, Sierra Wy N of Lake Isabella | 69 | D5 |
| LAKEVIEW MUNICIPAL AIRPORT, near jct of 140 & 395 | 7 | B1 |
| LAMPSON AIRPORT, SW of Clear Lake off Hwy 175 | 31 | D3 |
| LIVERMORE AIRPORT, Stanley Blvd, Livermore | M | C5 |
| LONE PINE AIRPORT, 1 mile south of Lone Pine | 60 | B4 |
| LONG BEACH MUNICIPAL, 4100 Donald Douglas Dr | S | E2 |
| LOS ANGELES INTERNATIONAL, 1 World Wy | 189 | C2 |
| MADERA AIRPORT, Hwy 99 & Av 17 | 57 | A2 |
| MARIPOSA YOSEMITE AIRPORT, near Mariposa | 49 | A3 |
| McCARRAN INTERNATIONAL, 5 miles S of Las Vegas | 210 | C5 |
| MEADOWS FIELD, Skyway & Airport Drs | 78 | D2 |
| MENDOCINO COUNTY AIRPORT, Hwy 1 S of Little River | 30 | B1 |
| MERCED MUNICIPAL AIRPORT, 2 mi SW of Merced | 170 | A5 |
| MONTEREY PENINSULA AIRPORT, off Hwy 68 | 54 | B1 |
| NEEDLES MUNICIPAL, Airport Rd & Hwy 95, Needles | 95 | D2 |
| NORTH LAS VEGAS AIR TERMINAL, 3.5 miles NW of L V | 74 | D2 |
| OAKDALE AIRPORT, 8191 Laughlin Rd, Oakdale | 47 | E1 |
| OAKLAND INTERNATIONAL, Doolittle & Airport Wy | 159 | B4 |
| OCOTILLO WELLS AIRPORT, HWY 78, Ocotillo | 108 | B3 |
| ONTARIO INTERNATIONAL AIRPORT, 2 mi E of Ontario | 204 | E5 |
| OROVILLE AIRPORT, 3 mi SW of Oroville | 25 | C4 |
| PALMDALE AIRPORT, Sierra Hwy | 90 | A3 |
| PALM SPRINGS MUNICIPAL, 2 mi E of Palm Springs | 206 | E3 |
| PEARCE AIRPORT, Hwy 53 S of Clearlake | 32 | A3 |
| PLACERVILLE AIRPORT, S of Hwy 50 near Smithflat | 34 | E5 |
| REDDING MUNICIPAL AIRPORT, 7 miles SE of Redding | 18 | C2 |
| SACRAMENTO CO METRO ARPRT, 12 mi NW of Sacramento | 33 | D5 |
| SACRAMENTO EXECUTIVE AIRPORT, 6151 Freeport Blvd | 39 | D1 |
| SALINAS MUNICIPAL AIRPORT, off Hwy 101 | 54 | D4 |
| SAN DIEGO INTERNATIONAL AIRPORT, Lindbergh Field | 215 | B2 |
| SAN FRANCISCO INTL, Airport Wy off Bayshore Fwy | 144 | D3 |
| SAN JOSE INTERNATIONAL AIRPORT, 1661 Airport Bl | 151 | C1 |
| SANTA BARBARA AIRPORT, James Fowler Rd | 87 | B4 |
| SANTA MARIA PUBLIC AIRPORT, Skyway Dr, Sta Maria | 86 | B1 |
| SANTA MONICA MUNICIPAL AIRPORT | 187 | C1 |
| SHAFTER-KERN COUNTY AIRFIELD, Lerdo Hwy | 78 | B2 |
| SISKIYOU COUNTY AIRPORT, Montague | 4 | C4 |
| STOCKTON METRO AIRPORT, 5000 S Airport Wy | 40 | B5 |
| SUSANVILLE AIRPORT, 5 mi SE of Susanville | 21 | B3 |
| SUTTER COUNTY AIRPORT, off Samuel Dr | 125 | E4 |
| TAFT-KERN AIRPORT, West Side Hwy, Taft | 78 | A4 |
| TAHOE AIRPORT, Pioneer Trail Rd | 36 | A3 |
| TEHACHAPI-KERN CO AIRPORT, Green & J Sts | 79 | D4 |
| TRUCKEE AIRPORT, 4 miles E of Truckee | 35 | E1 |
| TULELAKE MUNI AIRPORT, N of Hw 139 near Newell | 5 | E3 |

| NAME & ADDRESS | PAGE & GRID | | NAME & ADDRESS | PAGE & GRID | |
|---|---|---|---|---|---|
| UKIAH AIRPORT, State St | 123 | D5 | CASPER HEADLANDS STATE RESERVE, Hwy 1 near Casper | 22 | A5 |
| VENTURA COUNTY AIRPORT, Oxnard | 176 | A4 |   Scenic environment with good fishing. | | |
| YUBA COUNTY AIRPORT, Olivehurst | 33 | D2 | CASPER STATE BEACH, off Hwy 1 near Casper | 22 | B5 |
| YUCCA VALLEY AIRPORT, Hwys 62 & 247, Yucca Valley | 100 | D1 |   Scenic area for picnicking and fishing. | | |

****************************************** AMUSEMENT PARKS ******************************************

| NAME & ADDRESS | PAGE & GRID | | NAME & ADDRESS | PAGE & GRID | |
|---|---|---|---|---|---|
| | | | CAYUCOS STATE BEACH, on Ocean Front Rd | 75 | D2 |
| | | |   Fishing pier, barbeque & picnic facilities. | | |
| DISNEYLAND, Harbor Blvd, Anaheim | 193 | B4 | CORAL BEACH, Hwy 1 W of Malibu Beach | 97 | A2 |
|   Amusement park-7 theme sections, rides, shops. | | |   Fishing, swimming and picnicking. | | |
| KNOTTS BERRY FARM, 8039 Beach Bl, Buena Park | T | B2 | CORONA DEL MAR STATE BEACH, Corona Del Mar | T | D5 |
|   Ride 'Corkscrew' & 'Log Ride'; shops, rstrnts. | | |   Sandy beach, tidepools, body surfng, picnckng. | | |
| MARINE WORLD AFRICA, 1000 Fairgrounds, Vallejo | 134 | E1 | DOCKWEILER STATE BEACH, Venice | 187 | A4 |
|   Land & sea animal shows; natural setting | | |   Swimming, picnicking, fishing. | | |
| MARRIOTT'S GREAT AMERICA, 1 Great America Pkwy | P | B3 | DOHENY STATE BEACH, Puerto & Del Obispo Sts | 202 | B4 |
|   Family amusement park, American history theme. | | |   Surfing, camping, fire rings & picnic areas. | | |
| RAGING WATERS, 111 Via Verde, San Dimas | U | B2 | EAST BEACH, E Cabrillo Blvd, Santa Barbara | 174 | E4 |
|   Pools, slides, picnic area. | | |   BBQ & picnic facilities, volleyball courts. | | |
| RAGING WATERS, off Capitol Expwy, San Jose | P | C3 | EL CAPITAN STATE BEACH, Avenida del Capitan | 87 | A4 |
|   Pools, slides, picnic area. | | |   Surfing, hiking, camping, boat rentals. | | |
| SAN DIEGO WILD ANIMAL PARK, 5 mi W of Escondido | 106 | D3 | EL DORADO BEACH, off Hwy 50, South Lake Tahoe | 129 | A3 |
|   Tour through preserve for endangered species. | | |   On the south shore of lovely Lake Tahoe. | | |
| SEA WORLD, 1720 S Shores Rd, Mission Bay Park | 212 | C4 | EMMA WOOD STATE BEACH, Hwy 101 & Hwy 33 | 88 | A5 |
|   Marine life amusement pk, shows; Japanese Vlg. | | |   Camping, fishing and swimming. | | |
| SIX FLAGS MAGIC MOUNTAIN, I-5 at Valencia Av | 89 | B4 | GAZO CREEK ANGLING ACCESS, Gazo Creek Rd | N | C4 |
|   Family amusement park; thrill rides and shops. | | |   Beach access for fishing. | | |
| SPLASHDOWN WATERSLIDE, 200 Dempsey, Milpitas | P | C2 | GOLETA BEACH COUNTY PARK, 5990 Sandspit Rd | 87 | B4 |
|   Water flumes; picnic area. | | |   Fishing pier, swimming, boat hoist. | | |
| UNIVERSAL STUDIOS & AMPHITHEATER, Univ City Plaza | 181 | B1 | GRAYWHALE COVE STATE BEACH, N of Half Moon Bay | N | A1 |
|   Features tours of movie and TV sets; shows. | | |   Good beach for fishing. | | |
| WET 'N WILD, 2600 Las Vegas Blvd, Las Vegas | 209 | C4 | HALF MOON BAY STATE BEACH, near Half Moon Bay | N | B2 |
|   Wave pool, flumes, water roller coaster. | | |   Camp on bluffs above beaches, hike, picnic. | | |
| WILD RIVERS, Irvine Center Dr, Irvine | 98 | D4 | HERMOSA BEACH, btwn Redondo & Manhattan Beaches | S | A1 |
|   Water slides and activities. | | |   Public fishing pier, swimming, surfing. | | |
| WINDSOR WATERWORKS, 8225 Conde, Windsor | 37 | E1 | HUNTINGTON BEACH STATE PARK, Huntington Beach | T | B4 |
|   Pool, flumes, picnic area. | | |   Sandy beach, good surfing, picnicking. | | |

****************************************** BEACHES ******************************************

| NAME & ADDRESS | PAGE & GRID | | NAME & ADDRESS | PAGE & GRID | |
|---|---|---|---|---|---|
| | | | ISLA VISTA COUNTY BEACH PARK, Camino Del Sur | 87 | B4 |
| | | |   Sandy beach, tidepools. | | |
| | | | J D PHELAN BEACH, El Camino del Mar, Sn Francisco | 141 | A2 |
| | | |   Swimming cove protected from the wind. | | |
| ARROYO BURRO BEACH COUNTY PARK, 2981 Cliff Dr | 87 | C4 | LAS TUNAS STATE BEACH, near Jct Hwy 1 & Hwy 27 | Q | A4 |
|   Swimming, picnicking, surf fishing. | | |   Swimming in the surf, fishing, and picnicking. | | |
| ASILOMAR STATE BEACH, Sunset Dr, Pacific Grove | 167 | A1 | LEADBETTER BEACH, Shoreline Dr, Santa Barbara | 174 | C5 |
|   Conference facilities in a beautiful setting. | | |   Very wide, sandy beach; picnic facilities. | | |
| ATASCADERO STATE BEACH, Jct Hwy 1 and Hwy 41 | 75 | D3 | LEO CARRILLO STATE BEACH, S of Hwy 101 | 96 | D2 |
|   Swimming, fishing and camping. | | |   Good surfing, diving and swimming. | | |
| AVILA STATE BEACH, Front St | 76 | A4 | LEUCADIA STATE BEACH, Leucadia | 106 | B4 |
|   Fishing, fire rings, swimming. | | |   Scenic beach for fishing and swimming. | | |
| BAKER BEACH, NW shore Presidio, San Francisco | 141 | B2 | LITTLE RIVER STATE BEACH, South of Trinidad | 9 | E4 |
|   Fishing, hiking nearby, no swimming. | | |   Beautiful beaches, delta, nature trails. | | |
| BEAN HOLLOW STATE BEACH, S of Half Moon Bay | N | B4 | MALIBU LAGOON STATE BEACH, near Malibu | 97 | B2 |
|   Fishing and camping on the beach. | | |   Site of famous surfrider beach, swimming. | | |
| BOLSA CHICA STATE BEACH, N of Huntington Beach | T | A3 | MANCHESTER STATE BEACH, near Point Arena | 30 | B3 |
|   Sandy beach, body surfing, picnicking. | | |   Beaches, sand dunes, Point Arena Lighthouse. | | |
| BOOMER BEACH, Coast Blvd, La Jolla | 105 | B2 | MANHATTAN STATE BEACH, Manhattan Beach | S | A1 |
|   Scenic beach, swimming and fishing. | | |   Public fishing pier, swimming, surfing. | | |
| CABRILLO BEACH, E of Pacific Av, San Pedro | S | C3 | MANRESA STATE BEACH, off San Andreas Rd | 54 | B2 |
|   Public boat ramp, surf fishing, barbeque pits. | | |   Sandy beach, tide pools. | | |
| CAPISTRANO BEACH, San Juan Capistrano | 202 | D5 | MARINA STATE BEACH, 10 mi N of Monterey | 54 | B4 |
|   Sandy beach, body surfing, picnicking. | | |   Good fishing area. | | |
| CAPITOLA CITY BEACH, 30th Av, Capitola | 54 | A2 | MARINE STREET BEACH, La Jolla | 105 | A3 |
|   Swimming and fishing. | | |   Fishing, swimming and sunbathing. | | |
| CARDIFF STATE BEACH, Cardiff | 106 | B4 | MCGRATH STATE BEACH, S of Santa Clara River | 96 | A1 |
|   Fine beach for fishing or swimming. | | |   Hiking, camping, fishing. | | |
| CARLSBAD STATE BEACH, 3 mi S of Carlsbad Bl | 106 | A3 | MONTARA STATE BEACH, N of Half Moon Bay | N | A2 |
|   Fish, swim, surf, camp, store, concessions. | | |   Fishing beach. | | |
| CARMEL RIVER STATE BEACH, Scenic Rd | 168 | B4 | MONTEREY STATE BEACH, Park Av | 54 | B4 |
|   Skin diving, fishing, bird watching sites. | | |   Sandy beach, fishing, swimming in summer. | | |
| CARPINTERIA STATE BEACH, Linden Av | 87 | D4 | MOONLIGHT STATE BEACH, Encinitas | 106 | B4 |
|   Camping, picnicking, fishing pier, boat ramp. | | |   Sandy beach for swimming and fishing. | | |
| CASA BEACH, Coast Blvd, La Jolla | 105 | A3 | MORRO STRAND STATE BEACH, end of Yerba Buena Rd | 75 | D2 |
|   Swimming and fishing. | | |   Sand dunes, streams; camping permitted. | | |
| | | | MOSS LANDING STATE BEACH, off Hwy 1 | 54 | B3 |
| | | |   Fishing and equestrian trails. | | |

| NAME & ADDRESS | PAGE & GRID | NAME & ADDRESS | PAGE & GRID |
|---|---|---|---|
| FOREST OF NISENE MARKS, 4 miles N of Aptos<br>Camping, picnicking, hiking trails. | P B5 | PAUL M. DIMMICK WAYSIDE CAMPGROUND, W of Navarro<br>Primitive campgrounds; swim, fish, picnic. | 30 C2 |
| FREMONT PEAK STATE PARK, S of San Juan Bautista<br>Camping, hiking trails, picnicking. | 54 D3 | PFEIFFER BIG SUR STATE PARK, E of Hwy 1, Big Sur<br>Hiking, camping, swimming and fishing. | 64 B2 |
| FURNACE CREEK CAMPGROUND, Furnace Creek Ranch<br>Camping facilities in the heart of Death Vly. | 62 A5 | PICACHO STATE RECREATION AREA, W of Picacho<br>Camping, fishing, hiking and sailing. | 110 C4 |
| GAVIOTA STATE PARK, Gaviota Beach Rd<br>Camping, fishing, boat launch, picnic areas. | 86 D4 | PISMO DUNES STATE VEHICULAR REC AREA, Pismo Beach<br>Off-road, 4-wheel drive trails; camp & picnic. | 76 B5 |
| GEORGE HATFIELD STATE REC AREA, 28 mi W of Merced<br>Camping, hiking, fishing, and picnicking. | 47 D4 | PISMO STATE BEACH, off Hwy 101, Pismo Beach<br>Camping & hiking along sandy beaches & dunes. | 76 B5 |
| GRIZZLY CREEK REDWOODS STATE PARK, E of Fortuna<br>Scenic; camp, fish, nature trails, creeks. | 16 B3 | PLUMAS EUREKA STATE PARK, Hwy A14 at Johnsville<br>Camping, scenic creeks, trails, lakes & mtns. | 26 E2 |
| GROVER HOT SPRINGS STATE PARK, W of Markleeville<br>Camping; fishing and swimming in hot creeks. | 36 B5 | POINT MUGU STATE PARK, Hwy 1<br>Camp near the ocean; hiking, swimming&fishing. | 96 C2 |
| HENDY WOODS STATE PARK, near Philo on Hwy 128<br>Camp, picnic, fish, hike, swim. | 30 D3 | PORTOLA STATE PARK, W of Hwy 35<br>Camping, recreational facilities. | N D4 |
| HENRY COE STATE PARK, 14 mi NE of Morgan Hill<br>Picturesque camping and picnic grounds. | P E4 | PRAIRIE CREEK REDWOODS STATE PARK, N of Orick<br>Camping, fishing, picnic areas, hiking. | 10 A1 |
| HENRY COWELL REDWOODS STATE PARK, N of Santa Cruz<br>Equestrian trails, camping, hiking, fishing. | N E5 | PROVIDENCE MTNS STATE REC AREA, Essex Rd<br>Camping facilities in scenic surroundings. | 94 B1 |
| HIDDEN VIEW, 17 miles N of Madera<br>Scenic area to camp, swim and fish. | 49 B5 | RED ROCK CANYON STATE PARK, Hwy 14 at Ricardo<br>Camping, picnicking, hiking and exhibits. | 80 B3 |
| HOLLISTER HILLS VEHICULAR REC AREA, Cienega Rd<br>Camping, motorcycling & 4-wheel drive trails. | 54 E3 | REFUGIO STATE BEACH, Refugio Rd<br>Tidepools; camping and fishing. | 86 E4 |
| HUMBOLDT REDWOODS STATE PARK, Redwood Highway<br>Tallest redwoods; camp, fish, hike, picnic. | 16 A4 | RICHARDSON GROVE STATE PARK, S of Garberville<br>Scenic camping area; fish, swim, hike. | 22 B1 |
| HUNGRY VALLEY STATE VEHICULAR REC AREA, Gorman<br>Primitive camping; off-road vehicle use. | 88 E2 | RUSSIAN GULCH STATE PARK, S of Fort Bragg<br>Camp, hike to waterfall, rocky headlands. | 30 A1 |
| INDIAN GRINDING ROCK STATE HIST PK, S of Volcano<br>Restored Miwok Indian Vlg; camping facilities. | 41 A2 | SADDLEBACK BUTTE STATE PARK, E of Lancaster<br>Camping, picnicking, and hiking trails. | 90 C3 |
| J SMITH REDWOODS STATE PARK, NE of Crescent City<br>Camping, picnicking, hiking, fishing&exhibits. | 1 E4 | SALTON SEA STATE RECREATION AREA, off Hwy 111<br>Good area to camp, boat, waterski, or hike. | 108 E2 |
| LAKE ELSINORE STATE REC AREA, near I-5 & Hwy 74<br>Camping, swimming, fishing and boating. | 99 B4 | SALT POINT STATE PARK, N of Fort Ross off Hwy 1<br>Camping, beaches, underwater preserve, trails. | 37 A1 |
| LAKE OROVILLE STATE REC AREA, NE of Oroville<br>Camp, fish, boat, waterski, horseback ride. | 25 D4 | SAMUEL P. TAYLOR STATE PARK, off Hwy 1 near Olema<br>Camping, fishing, winter sports, riding. | 37 E4 |
| LAKE PERRIS STATE REC AREA, off Ramona Expwy<br>Camping, bicycle trails, boat rentals. | 99 C3 | SAN CLEMENTE STATE BEACH, San Clemente<br>Surfing, camping; barbeque, picnic facilities. | 105 D1 |
| LEO CARRILLO STATE BEACH, S of Hwy 101<br>Good surfing, diving and swimming. | 96 D2 | SAN ELIJO STATE BEACH, Cardiff<br>Camping & picnicking on the beach; swimming. | 106 B4 |
| LITTLE GRASS VALLEY RESERVOIR, W of Gibsonville<br>Camping and recreational facilities. | 26 C3 | SAN LUIS RES STATE REC AREA, 16 mi W of Los Banos<br>Lovely area to camp, waterski, fish & hike. | 55 C1 |
| MACKERRICHER STATE PARK, N of Fort Bragg<br>Rocky beaches, sand dunes, nature trails. | 22 B5 | SAN ONOFRE STATE BEACH, San Onofre<br>Surf fishing, clamming, surfing and camping. | 105 E2 |
| MALAKOFF DIGGINS STATE HIST PK, NE of Nevada City<br>Camping along colorful slopes. | 26 D5 | SAN SIMEON STATE BEACH, Hwy 1, Morro Bay<br>Camping and hiking; sand dunes to explore. | 75 B1 |
| MANCHESTER STATE BEACH, near Point Arena<br>Camping on sandy beaches among sand dunes. | 30 B3 | SILVERWOOD LAKE STATE RECREATION AREA, Hwy 138<br>Camping, swimming, boating and fishing. | 91 B5 |
| McARTHUR-BURNEY FALLS MEM STATE PK, NE of Burney<br>Well developed park with camping and fishing. | 13 C4 | SINKYONE WILDERNESS ST PK, Humboldt & Mendocno Co<br>Tent camping, picnicking, hiking and fishing. | 22 A1 |
| McCONNELL STATE RECREATION AREA, 5 mi SE of Delhi<br>Camping, picnicking, fishing and swimming. | 48 A3 | SONOMA COAST STATE BEACH, N of Bodega Bay<br>Camp, hike, picnic; scenic beaches. | 37 B2 |
| MILLERTON LAKE REC AREA, 22 miles E of Madera<br>Camping, boating, fishing & horseback riding. | 57 D1 | SOUTH CARLSBAD STATE BEACH, S of Carlsbad<br>Scenic beach for camping, fishing or swimming. | 106 B3 |
| MONTANA DE ORO STATE PARK, Pecho Valley Rd<br>Barbeque facilities; camping, riding & hiking. | 75 E3 | STANDISH HICKEY STATE REC AREA, 1 mi N of Leggett<br>Camping, fishing, hiking trails, swimming. | 22 C2 |
| MORRO BAY STATE PARK, on Morro Bay<br>Camping, fishing, clam digging, boating. | 75 D3 | STOVEPIPE WELLS CAMPGROUND, Death Valley Natl Mon<br>200 campsites (RV & tents) in the valley. | 61 C4 |
| MT SAN JACINTO STATE PARK, Hwy 111 near Palm Spgs<br>Hiking, picnicking and limited camping. | 100 B3 | SUGARLOAF RIDGE STATE PARK, Adobe Canyon Rd<br>Camping, fishing and riding. | 38 A2 |
| MOUNT TAMALPAIS STATE PARK, 6 mi N of Hwy 1<br>Camping, hiking, equestrian trails. | L A3 | SUGAR PINE POINT STATE PARK, N of Meeks Bay<br>Camping, swimming, fishing and hiking. | 35 E2 |
| NEW BRIGHTON STATE BEACH, off Hwy 1<br>Scenic camping; fishing and swimming. | 54 A2 | SUNSET CAMPGROUND, Furnace Creek Ranch, Death Vly<br>Campsites near the heart of Death Valley. | 62 A5 |
| OAKWOOD LAKE RESORT, off I-5 S of Manteca<br>Camping, watersports and shopping. | 47 A1 | SUNSET STATE BEACH, W of Watsonville<br>Scenic beach to camp, fish, dig for clams. | 54 B2 |
| OCOTILLO WELLS STATE VEHICULAR REC AREA, Hwy 78<br>Off-road 4-wheel drive vehicle trails. | 108 B3 | TAHOE STATE RECREATION AREA, N of Tahoe City<br>Camp, swim, fish, boat, picnic. | 35 E2 |
| PALOMAR MOUNTAIN STATE PARK, Birch Hill Rd<br>Beautiful area to camp or enjoy a picnic. | 107 A2 | TEXAS SPRINGS CAMPGROUND, Furnace Creek Ranch<br>RV and tent campsites in scenic Death Valley. | 62 A5 |
| PATRICKS POINT STATE PARK, N of Trinidad<br>Camping, hiking, biking, picnicking. | 9 D3 | TUOLUMNE MEADOWS, Tioga Pass Rd<br>Camp, fish, backpack, mtn climb, horses. | 43 A5 |

# POINTS OF INTEREST INDEX

| NAME & ADDRESS | PAGE & GRID | | NAME & ADDRESS | PAGE & GRID | |
|---|---|---|---|---|---|

**HARBORS**

| | | |
|---|---|---|
| ALAMEDA HARBOR, Embarcadero & 9th Av | 158 | B4 |
| Major shipping center of northern California. | | |
| BODEGA HARBOR, Hwy 1 at Bodega Bay | 37 | C3 |
| Small but busy harbor; parks nr harbor & bay. | | |
| INNER HARBOR, between Oakland & Alameda | 157 | D4 |
| Busy commercial section of SF Bay. | | |
| LONG BEACH HARBOR, Ocean Blvd | 192 | A5 |
| Shares largest man-made harbr with Ls Angeles. | | |
| LOS ANGELES HARBOR, Seaside Av | 191 | C5 |
| Busy commercial port of state's largest city. | | |
| PORT HUENEME HARBOR, end of Hueneme Rd | 96 | B1 |
| Dominated by US Naval installation. | | |
| PORT OF SACRAMENTO, off Lake Washington | 39 | D1 |
| Furthest inland port of Sac deep-watr channel. | | |
| PORT OF STOCKTON, off Hwy 5 in Stockton | 160 | A5 |
| Busy inland agricultural seaport. | | |
| RICHMOND INNER HARBOR, Richmond | 155 | B5 |
| Commercial port in San Francisco Bay. | | |
| SAN DIEGO BAY, W of I-5 | V | C4 |
| Busy deepwater port, home of USN 11th Fleet. | | |
| SAN FRANCISCO HARBOR, Fisherman's Wharf | L | B4 |
| Major commercial port; 1st in W Coast shippng. | | |
| SANTA CRUZ HARBOR | 169 | E4 |
| Small commercial harbor in Monterey Bay. | | |

**HISTORICAL SITES**

| | | |
|---|---|---|
| ALPINE COUNTY HIST COMPLEX, Hwy 89, Markleeville | 36 | C5 |
| Historic museum and restored buildings. | | |
| ANDERSON MARSH STATE HIST PARK, near Clear Lake | 32 | A3 |
| Buildings from Anderson Ranch & Indian site. | | |
| ANGELS HOTEL, Angels Camp | 41 | B4 |
| Hotel in Twain's 'The Jumpng Frog of Calv Co'. | | |
| ARROYO DE CANTUA, off Hwy 5 | 66 | D1 |
| Headqrtrs of notorious bandit Jquin Murieta. | | |
| ASTRONOMICAL OBSERVATORY, off Shake Ridge Rd | 41 | A2 |
| 1st observ in Cal - discvrd Great Comet 1861. | | |
| AVERY HOTEL, Moran Rd, Avery | 41 | C3 |
| Wooden hotel built in 1853. | | |
| BALE GRIST MILL ST HISTORIC PARK, on Hwy 29 | 38 | B1 |
| Restored mill was built in 1846. | | |
| BANNING PARK, 401 E M St, Wilmington | S | C2 |
| House built in 1850s by Gen Phineas Banning. | | |
| BARNSDALL PARK, 4800 Hollywood Bl | 182 | B4 |
| Site of Frank Lloyd Wright's Hollyhock House. | | |
| BENICIA CAPITOL STATE HISTORIC PARK, H & 1st Sts | 153 | B4 |
| Capitol of California in 1853. | | |
| BIDWELL MANSION ST HIST PK, 525 Esplanade, Chico | 124 | B4 |
| Restored Victorian home of Chico founder. | | |
| BODIE STATE HISTORICAL PARK, Bodie, off Hwy 395 | 43 | C3 |
| Gold boom town, now a restored ghost town. | | |
| BOK KAI TEMPLE (CHINESE JOSS HOUSE), Marysville | 33 | D2 |
| Only temple in USA for worship of River God. | | |
| BORAX MUSEUM, Furnace Creek Ranch, Death Valley | 62 | A5 |
| Memorabilia from the old borax mine. | | |
| BOWERS MANSION, Washoe Valley | 36 | B1 |
| Granite home built 1864 wth rewards of mining. | | |
| BRAND PARK, San Fernando Bl, Los Angeles | Q | D2 |
| Picturesque atmosphere of early Cal missions. | | |
| BRIDGEPORT COVERED BRIDGE, Bridgeport | 34 | B1 |
| Longest single-span wood-covered bridge in US. | | |
| BURBANK MEMORIAL GARDENS, Santa Rosa Av | 131 | D4 |
| A living memorial dedicated to the naturalist. | | |
| CALICO GHOST TOWN, 10.5 miles NE of Barstow | 92 | A1 |
| Restored mining town - tour of mine & museum. | | |
| CALIFORNIA STANDARD OIL WELL, McKittrick Field | 77 | E3 |
| Discovery well started new oil field in 1899. | | |

| | | |
|---|---|---|
| CAMP CURTIS, 1 mi N of Arcata. | 9 | E5 |
| Estab for the protection of white settlers. | | |
| CAMP SALVATION, Calexico | 112 | B4 |
| Refugee ctr for emigrants in search of gold. | | |
| CAMRON STANFORD HOUSE, 14418 Lakeside Dr | 158 | A3 |
| Built in 1876 it serves as the Oakland Museum. | | |
| THE CASTLE, 70 S B St, Virginia City | 36 | D1 |
| Built 1868 - restored; antique furnishings. | | |
| CATALINA ISLAND MUSEUM, Casino Building | 97 | B4 |
| Features displays on the island's history. | | |
| CHARCOAL KILNS, near Wildrose, Death Vly Natl Mon | 71 | D2 |
| Large old kilns used during the mining days. | | |
| CHILDREN'S PARK, S Morton Bl, Modesto | 162 | D4 |
| Childrens playground wth old train & airplane. | | |
| CHINESE TEMPLE, E of Oroville | 25 | D4 |
| A temple of worship for over 10,000 Chinese. | | |
| CHUMASH PAINTED CAVES STATE HISTORIC PK, Hwy 154 | 87 | C4 |
| Indian art can be seen on the cave walls. | | |
| COL THOMAS BAKER MEMORIAL, City Hall, Bakersfield | 166 | C3 |
| Civic Center commemorates friend of travelers. | | |
| COLUMBIA CITY HOTEL, Main St, Columbia | 41 | C4 |
| Hotel built in 1856 which is still in use. | | |
| COLUMBIA STATE HISTORIC PARK, N of Columbia | 41 | C4 |
| Gold boom town in 1850s, now preserved. | | |
| CONCANNON VINEYARD, S of Livermore | P | D1 |
| Estab Livermore Vly as a select wine district. | | |
| CONGREGATIONAL CHURCH, Jesus Maria Rd | 41 | A3 |
| Built 1853 - oldest Congregtnl Church in Ca. | | |
| COTTONWOOD CHARCOAL KILNS, N of Cartago | 70 | B1 |
| Blt 1870s to char wood for mines at Owens Lk. | | |
| DEATH VALLEY GATEWAY, mouth of Furnace Creek | 72 | B1 |
| Natural entrance to Death Vly used by settlrs. | | |
| DE LA GUERRA PLAZA, 15 E De La Guerra St | 174 | C4 |
| Shopping arcade in historic adobes. | | |
| DEL NORTE COUNTY HISTORICAL MUSEUM, Crescent City | 1 | D4 |
| Largest museum in Northern California. | | |
| DIEGO SEPULVEDA ADOBE, 1900 Adams Av, Costa Mesa | 197 | A5 |
| Old ranch adobe now houses a museum. | | |
| DRYTOWN, N of Amador | 40 | E2 |
| 1st town in Ama, in which gold was discvrd. | | |
| D STEWART COUNTY STORE, in Ione | 40 | C2 |
| The 1st brick bldg, built in Lone Vly, 1856. | | |
| DUNSMUIR HOME & GARDENS, 2960 Peralta Oaks Ct | L | E5 |
| Blt 1899, Greek revival mansion, 48 acre grdn. | | |
| EL PRESIDIO DE SANTA BARBARA, 210 E Canon Perdido | 174 | C3 |
| One of four presidios built in Calif, 1782. | | |
| EL PUEBLO DE LOS ANGELES, Main & Arcadia Sts | 186 | B3 |
| State historic pk with many historic landmrks. | | |
| EMPIRE MINE STATE HIST PK, Colfax Rd | 127 | D4 |
| Oldst quartz mine in operatn for over 100 yrs. | | |
| ESTUDILLO HOME, S of San Leandro | L | E5 |
| Home of the family which founded San Leandro. | | |
| FELTON COVERED BRIDGE, off Graham Hill Rd, Felton | P | A5 |
| 1 of 3 remaining coverd bridgs in Sta Cruz Co. | | |
| FERNANDO PACHECO ADOBE, Concord | M | B3 |
| Restored adobe house originally built in 1843. | | |
| FORESTIERE UNDERGROUND GARDENS, Shaw Av, Fresno | 57 | B3 |
| 7 acres of grottos, vines and courts. | | |
| FORT HUMBOLDT STATE HISTORIC PARK, Eureka | 121 | A3 |
| Exhibits of logging & military life. | | |
| FORT JANESVILLE, near Janesville | 21 | B4 |
| Fort built for protection from Indian attacks. | | |
| FORT MASON, Golden Gate National Recreation Area | 143 | A1 |
| Former army hdqurtrs houses mus; cultural ctr. | | |
| FORT POINT NATL HISTORIC PARK, Golden Gate Park | 141 | C1 |
| Built in 1861 to control access to SF Bay. | | |
| FORT TEJON STATE HISTORIC PARK, Ft Tejon Rd | 88 | D1 |
| Former military center; summer programs. | | |
| FRESNO FLATS HISTORIC PARK, Rd 427, Oakhurst | 49 | D4 |
| Historic buildings and artifacts of Madera Co. | | |
| FT ROSS STATE HIST PARK, at Fort Ross | 37 | A1 |
| Restored American outpost; museum and beach. | | |

# POINTS OF INTEREST INDEX

| NAME & ADDRESS | PAGE & GRID | NAME & ADDRESS | PAGE & GRID |
|---|---|---|---|
| GIANT DESERT FIGURES, 18 miles north of Blythe<br>3 giant figures - 2 animals, 1 coiled serpent. | 103 C3 | METHODIST CHURCH, S of Ione<br>Dedicatd 'Lone City Centenary Church' in 1866. | 40 C3 |
| GOLD BUG MINE, off Bedford Rd, Placerville<br>Exposed gold veins in old mine shaft; tours. | 138 E1 | MONO COUNTY HISTORICAL MUSEUM, Bridgeport City Pk<br>Restored ele sch, houses many histrcl artfcts. | 43 B3 |
| GOLD COUNTRY, HIGHWAY 49, from Mariposa to Vinton<br>300 mi drive through the historic Mother Lode. | 41 A3 | MONTEREY STATE HIST PARK, 210 Olivier St<br>Includes many buildings of historic interest. | 167 E3 |
| GRANVILLE P SWIFT ADOBE, N of Orland<br>Rodeos were held annually at this site. | 24 D3 | MORMON STATION STATE HIST MON, N of Gardnerville<br>Museum has pioneer items & displays; old fort. | 36 B3 |
| HARMONY BORAX WORKS, Furnace Creek, Death Valley<br>Preserved processing plant nr borax discovery. | 62 A5 | MORMON STOCKADE, Court St, San Bernardino<br>Site of 1851 stockade built for protection. | 207 D2 |
| HAROLD LLOYD ESTATE, 1740 Greenacres, Beverly Hls<br>Once home to the silent screen actor. | Q C3 | MORRO ROCK, off the coast of Morro Bay<br>Important navigational landmark for 300+ yrs. | 75 D3 |
| HERITAGE HILL, Lake Forest Dr & Serrano, El Toro<br>Restored historicl bldgs of central Orange Co. | 98 D4 | MOTHER COLONY HOUSE, 400 N West St, Anaheim<br>First house built in Anaheim. | 193 B2 |
| INDIAN GRINDING ROCK STATE HIST PK, S of Volcano<br>Restored Miwok Indian village, museum. | 41 A2 | MT SHASTA MUSEUM, off Hwy 5 north of Dunsmuir<br>Features the geology & history of gold mining. | 12 C2 |
| IOOF HALL, Mokelumne Hill<br>1st 3-story bldg in the interior of the state. | 41 A3 | MURPHYS, 9 mi NE of Angels Camp<br>Victorian houses, old jail, hotels, church. | 41 C4 |
| JACK LONDON STATE HISTORIC PARK, Broadway<br>Museum is in House of Happy Walls. | 38 B2 | MURPHY'S HOTEL, off Hwy 4 in Murphys<br>Early guests included Mark Twain & Gen Grant. | 41 C4 |
| JACOBY BUILDING, 8th & H, Arcata<br>Princpl supply store for Klmth-Trnty miners. | 10 A5 | MUSEUM OF NATURAL HIST, State Pk Rd, Sta Barbara<br>Displays, films & lectures. | 174 B2 |
| JOHN MUIR NATIONAL HISTORIC SITE, 4204 Alhambra<br>House built 1882; visitor's center & tours. | 154 B4 | NAPA COUNTY HISTORICAL MUSEUM, in Calistoga<br>County history of the late 1800s. | 38 A1 |
| KEANE WONDER MINE & MILL, off Daylight Pass Ctoff<br>Well-preserved historic remains of silvr mine. | 61 E4 | NAPA VALLEY RAILROAD DEPOT, Calistoga<br>Built 1868, is now the Southern Pacfic depot. | 38 B1 |
| KENTUCKY MINE HISTORIC PARK, NE of Sierra City<br>Restored stamp mill & old gold mine buildngs. | 27 A4 | NATIONAL HISTORIC SHIPS, Hyde St Pier, Aquatic Pk<br>Museum of 5 ships; includes the Balclutha. | 143 B1 |
| KERN CO MUSEUM & PIONEER VILLAGE, 3801 Chester<br>Exhibits of pioneer and Indian history. | 166 C2 | NEVADA STATE HIST MUS, 1650 N Virginia St, Reno<br>Indian, pioneer, mineral, gambling exhibits. | 28 B4 |
| KEYESVILLE, 4 miles W of Isabella<br>Center of placer & quartz gold mining,1853-70. | 79 C1 | OCTAGON HOUSE, 2645 Gough St, San Francisco<br>Eary San Francisco home built in 1861. | 143 A2 |
| KIT CARSON MARKER, Kit Carson<br>Replica of orig instriptn cut from Kit's tree. | 35 D5 | ODD FELLOWS MEMORIAL, Kirkwood<br>Here rests the Unknown Pioneer, 1849. | 36 A5 |
| LAKE COUNTY MUSEUM, 255 N Forbes St, Lakeport<br>In old courthouse, Indian & pioneer displays. | 31 D3 | OLD CUSTOM HOUSE, Fisherman's Wharf<br>Oldest government building in California. | 167 E3 |
| LAKEPORT HISTORICAL MUSEUM, 175 3rd St, Lakeport<br>Displays of indian baskets & other artifacts. | 31 C3 | OLDEST HOUSE NORTH OF SF BAY, N of Novato<br>Built 1776 by an Indian chief. | L A2 |
| LARKIN HOUSE, Jefferson St & Calle Principal<br>Served as American Consulate 1843 to 1846. | 167 E4 | OLD FIREHOUSE No 1, 214 Main St, Nevada City<br>Indian baskets, pioneer and Donner Party itms. | 128 C2 |
| LAWS RAILROAD MUSEUM & HIST SITE, NE of Bishop<br>Restored 1880's RR depot, locomotive, equip. | 51 D3 | OLD FOLSOM POWERHOUSE, Folsom<br>Long distance generating plant built in 1890s. | 34 B5 |
| LELAND STANFORD WINERY, off Hwy 680<br>Founder of Stanfrd Uni, operated here in 1869. | P B2 | OLD HOMESTEAD, Crockett<br>Built in 1867 - 1st American home in Crockett. | L D3 |
| LIVERMORE MEMORIAL MONUMENT, Livermore<br>Remembrance of the 1st settler of Livermore. | P C1 | OLD SACRAMENTO STATE HISTORIC PARK, 2nd & I Sts<br>Business district during Gold Rush; restored. | 137 A2 |
| L A CO MUSEUM OF NATURAL HIST, 900 Exposition Bl<br>Exhibits include Indian artfcts, gems & mummy. | 185 C5 | OLD SPANISH LIGHTHOUSE, Point Loma<br>Lighthouse constructed 1854 - 1855. | V A4 |
| LOS ENCINOS STATE HIST PK, 16756 Moorpark St<br>This historic park features 1849 Osa Adobe. | Q B3 | OLD STOVEPIPE WELL, off Hwy 190, Death Valley<br>Site of underground well marked by stovepipe. | 61 D4 |
| LOS ROBLES ADOBE, 3 mi N of Lemoore<br>Restored adobe house, built in 1849. | 67 C1 | OLD TOWN SAN DIEGO STATE HISTORIC PARK<br>Restored Spanish-style bldgs; museums, shops. | 213 A5 |
| LOTT HOME, 1735 Montgomery St, Oroville<br>Restored; furnished 1856 home of Judse C Lott. | 25 C4 | OLVERA STREET, 130 Paseo de la Plaza<br>Shopping & dining in birthplace of Ls Angeles. | 186 B2 |
| LOWER LAKE STONE JAIL, Lower Lake<br>Claimed to be smallest jail in US, built 1876. | 32 A3 | PEPPARD CABIN, off Hwy 70 in Quincy<br>Cabin built in 1888; made of hand hewn logs. | 26 C2 |
| LUMMIS HOME STATE HISTORIC MNT, 200 E Av 43, LA<br>Built 1895 by Charles F Lummis. | R B3 | PERALTA HOME, W of Castro Valley<br>The first brick home built in Alameda County. | L E5 |
| MARIPOSA COUNTY COURTHOUSE, Mariposa<br>Built 1854 after Mariposa became the Co seat. | 49 B3 | PETALUMA ADOBE ST HISTORIC PARK, Adobe Ranch Rd<br>Relics displayed in 1836 adobe house. | L A1 |
| MARIPOSA COUNTY HIST CENTER, 12th St & Jessie St<br>Early Gold Rush equip, stamp mill, buildngs. | 49 B3 | PETER LASSEN GRAVE, 5 mi E of Susanville<br>In memory of a pioneer killed by Indians. | 21 A4 |
| MARSHALL'S BLACKSMITH SHOP, Gold Trail Pk<br>Marshall was a smithy & qualified carpenter. | 34 E4 | PETER L TRAVER BUILDING, off Hwy 4<br>Served as a generl store & Wells Fargo Office. | 41 C4 |
| MARY AARON MUSEUM, 704 D St, Marysville<br>Restored home - gold rush tools, pictures. | 33 D2 | PIGEON PT LIGHTHOUSE, Pigeon Pt Rd, San Mateo Co.<br>Constructed in 1872 and still in use. | N C4 |
| MARY AUSTIN'S HOUSE, Independence<br>Wrote books depicting beauty of Owens Valley. | 59 E3 | PIONEER YOSEMITE HISTORY CENTER, Wawona<br>Historical buildings, covered bridge, cabins. | 49 C3 |
| McKITTRICK BREA PIT, 1/2 mi W of McKittrick<br>Animals were trapped in ancient asphalt pit. | 77 E3 | PIONEER SCHOOLHOUSE, 2 mi E of Quincy<br>1st schoolhouse in Plumas Co, built in 1857. | 26 C1 |
| MENDOCINO PRESBYTERIAN CHURCH, Main St, Mendocino<br>Blt 1868 of redwood, 1 of oldest still in use. | 30 C1 | PLUMAS COUNTY MUSEUM, 500 Jackson Street, Quincy<br>Artifacts of early Plumas County | 26 C2 |

| NAME & ADDRESS | PAGE & GRID | NAME & ADDRESS | PAGE & GRID |
|---|---|---|---|
| PLYMOUTH TRADING POST, Plymouth<br>Office & commissary of the many small mines. | 40 E2 | VALLECITO BELL MONUMENT, Vallecito<br>Used to call the town together until 1939. | 41 B4 |
| POINT FERMIN HISTORIC LIGHTHOUSE, Paseo Del Mar<br>Located in Angels Gate Park. | S C3 | VIRGINIA CITY, NE of Carson City, Nevada<br>Old mining town - churches, hotels, homes. | 36 D1 |
| POINT SUR STATE HISTORIC PARK, Monterey County<br>Ranger-guided tours of lighthouse & Moro Rock. | 64 A1 | VOLCANO, 12 mi NE of Jackson<br>Gold rush bldgs - hotel, jail, brewery, PO. | 41 A2 |
| PONY EXPRESS REMOUNT STATION, off Hwy 88<br>An important remount station in the 1860s. | 36 B4 | WATTS TOWER STATE HISTORIC PARK, 1765 E 107th St<br>Unusual tower studded with glass & shell. | R A5 |
| PRESIDIO OF MONTEREY, Pacific St<br>Now House Defense Language Institute. | 167 E3 | WEAVERVILLE JOSS HOUSE STATE HIST PK, Weaverville<br>Chinese worship house built in 1874. | 17 C1 |
| PRESIDIO OF SAN FRANCISCO, NW end Lombrd<br>Active Army Post fr 1776; 1450 Acres, hikng. | 141 C2 | WILL ROGERS STATE HISTORIC PARK, Sunset Blvd<br>Will Rogers' home located in 186 acre park. | Q B4 |
| RAILTOWN 1897 STATE HISTORIC PARK, Jamestown<br>26 acre park with trains on exhibit. | 41 B5 | WOODLAND OPERA HOUSE STATE HIST PARK, Woodland<br>Built in 1895 to serve Sacramento Valley. | 33 C5 |
| RED BRICK GRAMMAR SCHOOL, Altaville<br>Built 1848 - it is one of the oldest in Ca. | 41 A4 | YORBA-SLAUGHTER ADOBE, 5.5 miles south of Chino<br>Early American architecture, built in 1850s. | U D3 |
| RENEGADE CANYON NATURL HIST LNDMRK, nr China Lake<br>Remarkable prehistoric rockpile collection. | 70 D5 | YUCAIPA ADOBE, Yucaipa<br>Oldest house in San Bernardino Co, built 1842. | 99 D2 |
| RHYOLITE, off Hwy 374, Nevada<br>Once a booming silver town, now in ruins. | 62 A2 | ****************************************************<br>**H**                  HOTELS<br>**************************************************** | |
| RICHARDSON ADOBE, 2.5 mi S of Soledad<br>Built 1843, later used as stage station & PO. | 65 B1 | | |
| ROCKVILLE STONE CHAPEL, Rockville<br>Volunteer pioneers built chapel in 1856. | L D1 | * Indicates information obtained from AAA. | |
| ROOP'S FORT, Weatherlow St, Susanville<br>Built in 1854 - Emigrant trains stopped here. | 20 E3 | *ADOBE INN-CARMEL, Dolores St & 8th Av<br>19 units; fireplaces, pool, sauna; restaurant. | 168 B3 |
| ST JAMES EPISCOPAL CHURCH, Sonora<br>Oldest Episcopal Church in California. | 163 C3 | *AHWAHNEE HOTEL, E end of Yosemite Valley<br>An elegant hotel built in the 1920's. | 63 D1 |
| SAINT TERESA'S CHURCH, Bodega<br>Built of redwood in 1859; still in use. | 37 C3 | *AIRPORTER INN, 18700 MacArthur Blvd<br>Across from John Wayne Airport. | 198 C5 |
| SAINT VINCENT'S SCHOOL, north of San Rafael<br>Founded in 1855. | L B3 | *ALADDIN, 3667 Las Vegas Bl, Las Vegas<br>Casino, restaurants, entertainment, shops. | 210 B2 |
| SALVIO PACHECO ADOBE, Concord<br>Two-story home was the 1st built in the vly. | M B3 | ALEXIS PARK RESORT, 375 E Harmon Av, Las Vegas<br>500 rooms; pools, putting green, tennis. | 210 D3 |
| SAN DIEGO PLAZA, Old Town, San Diego<br>Center of Mexican Pueblo, blt 1830s; restored. | 213 A5 | *AMBASSADOR HOTEL, 3400 Wilshire Blvd<br>Classic hotel; spacious landscaped grounds. | 185 B2 |
| SAN JUAN BAUTISTA STATE HIST PARK, 2nd St, SJB<br>Incl mission, Plaza Hotel, & house built 1841. | 54 D3 | AMFAC HOTEL, 8601 Lincoln Blvd, Los Angeles<br>750 rooms; pool, entertainment, diningroom. | 188 A5 |
| SAN PASQUAL BATTLEFIELD STATE HIST PARK, Hwy 78<br>Battle site between Dragoons & Californios. | 106 E3 | ANAHEIM HILTON & TOWERS, 777 N Convention Wy<br>1600 units; restaurants, entertainment. | 193 C5 |
| SAN RAFAEL ADOBE, 1330 Dorothy Dr, Glendale<br>Adobe and hacienda built in 1865. | Q E2 | *ANAHEIM MARRIOTT HOTEL, 700 W Convention Wy<br>1043 units;pool,whirlpool, balconies & patios. | 193 C5 |
| SANTA BARBARA HISTORICAL MUS, 136 E De La Guerra<br>Exhibits of state & local history. | 174 C3 | ARROWHEAD HILTON, in Lake Arrowhead Village<br>257 rooms; pool, whirlpool, boat dock. | 91 C5 |
| SANTA CRUZ CITY MUSEUM, 1305 E Cliff Dr<br>Natural history of Santa Cruz County. | 169 E3 | BAKERSFIELD HILTON INN, Rosedale Hwy, Bakersfield<br>197 units; pool, whirlpool, disco. | 166 A2 |
| SANTA CRUZ COUNTY HIST MUS, Cooper & Front Sts<br>Artifacts & history of early Santa Cruz Co. | 169 D3 | *BALLY'S, 3645 Las Vegas Blvd, Las Vegas<br>Casino, restaurants, entertainment. | 210 B2 |
| SANTA MARIA VALLEY HIST MUSEUM, 616 S Broadway<br>Pioneer Indian & Spanish historical exhibits. | 173 C3 | *BALLYS HOTEL - RENO, 2500 E 2nd St, Reno<br>Casino, restaurants, theatres, shows, shops. | 28 C4 |
| SCOTT MUSEUM, off Hwy 3 in Trinity Center<br>Features Indian artifacts and antiques. | 11 E4 | *BARBARY COAST HOTEL, 3595 Las Vegas Blvd S<br>Casino, restaurant, entertainment. | 210 B2 |
| SKIDOO, off Skidoo Rd in Death Valley<br>Ruins of mining town that once flourished. | 61 D5 | BARNEY'S, Hwy 50 in South Lake Tahoe<br>Casino, shows and restaurant. | 129 E1 |
| SNELLING COURTHOUSE, Snelling<br>1st courthouse in Merced County, built 1857. | 48 C3 | *BEST WESTERN CAMERON PARK INN, on US Hwy 50<br>61 rooms; pool. Restaurant adjacent. | 34 C5 |
| SONOMA HISTORIC PARK, W Spain St & 3rd St W<br>Home of General Vallejo built in 1850. | 132 D3 | *BEST WESTERN CAVALIER INN, 3.5 mi S of Sn Simeon<br>66 rooms; oceanfront, pool, restaurant. | 75 C1 |
| STEVENSON HOUSE, 530 Houston St, Monterey<br>Living quarters of Robert Louis Stevenson. | 167 E4 | *BEST WESTERN DANISH INN LODGE, 1455 Mission Dr<br>81 rooms; pool, garage, dining room. | 86 E3 |
| STONE HOUSE, 6 mi N of Middleton<br>Oldest building in Lake County, 1st blt 1854. | 32 A4 | *BEST WESTERN FLAGWAVER, 937 North H St, Lompoc<br>72 rooms; pool, coffeeshop opposite. | 86 B3 |
| SULPHUR BANK MINE, S of Clearlake Oaks<br>Sulphur & quicksilver mine from 1800s - 1900s. | 32 A3 | *BEST WESTERN LAWRENCE WELK VILLAGE INN, Escndido<br>132 rooms; pool, golf, tennis, entertainment. | 106 D3 |
| SUSPENSION BRIDGE, S of Chico<br>Bidwell Bar Bridge was the 1st in Calif, 1856. | 25 B3 | *BEST WESTERN PONDEROSA MOTOR INN, H St near 11th<br>98 units; pool & sauna, 3 blocks from capitol. | 137 C2 |
| SUTTER'S FORT STATE HIST PARK, 28th & L Sts, Sact<br>Features relics of Gold Rush Era. | 137 D3 | *BEST WESTERN ROYAL LAS VEGAS, 99 Convention Ctr<br>237 units; pool, restaurant and casino. | 209 D5 |
| TEMPLE OF KUAN TI, Albion St, Mendocino<br>Chinese house of worship. | 30 B1 | *BEST WESTERN ROYAL SCOT, 1680 Oceanside Blvd<br>80 rooms; pool & sauna, movies, dining room. | 106 B3 |
| TUMCO MINES, 4 mi NE of Ogilby<br>Largest stamp mill in US was located here. | 110 C5 | *BEST WESTERN STATION HOUSE INN, S Lake Tahoe<br>100 rooms; near beach, casinos and skiing. | 36 A3 |

# POINTS OF INTEREST INDEX

| NAME & ADDRESS | PAGE & GRID | NAME & ADDRESS | PAGE & GRID |
|---|---|---|---|
| HOLIDAY INN, 222 W Houston, Fullerton<br>Close to freeway and nearby major attractions. | T C1 | LA SIESTA VILLAS, Hwy 111, Palm Springs<br>18 luxurious villas; swimming pool. | 100 C3 |
| *HOLIDAY INN, 3475 Las Vegas Bl, Las Vegas<br>Casino, entertainment, shops. | 210 B2 | *LAS VEGAS HILTON, 3000 Paradise Rd<br>Casino, restaurants, star entertainment. | 209 D5 |
| *HOLIDAY INN, 1000 E 6th St, Reno<br>286 units; casino, pool, dining room. | 130 C2 | LE BARON HOTEL, 1350 N First St, San Jose<br>327 rooms; pool, steamroom, entertainment. | 151 E1 |
| HOLIDAY INN, 1200 University Av, Riverside<br>207 units; sauna, whirlpool, dining room. | 205 E3 | *L'ERMITAGE, 9291 Burton Wy, Beverly Hills<br>Elegant suites in the European tradition. | 183 C1 |
| HOLIDAY INN, STOCKTON, Center St, Stockton<br>194 rooms; pool, sauna, restaurant. | 160 D4 | THE LODGE AT PEBBLE BEACH, on the 17 Mile Drive<br>159 units; pool, sauna, golf course. | 53 B5 |
| *HOLIDAY INN-UNION SQUARE, Powell & Sutter Sts<br>400 units; restaurant & coffee shop. | 143 C3 | LOS ANGELES AIRPORT HILTON, Century Bl,Ls Angeles<br>1281 rooms; pool, diningroom, entertainment. | 189 D1 |
| HOTEL CONTINENTAL, Flamingo & Paradise Rds, L V<br>400 units; pool, restaurant, slot casino. | 210 D2 | *LOS ANGELES HILTON HOTEL, Wilshire at Figueroa<br>900 units; pool, shopping; public facilities. | 185 E3 |
| *HOTEL DEL CORONADO, on Coronado Peninsula<br>Elegant beachfront hotel built in the 1880's. | V B4 | *MADONNA INN, US 101 at Madonna Rd, Sn Luis Obspo<br>109 unusually decorated rooms; restaurnt,cafe. | 172 A4 |
| HOTEL LA JOLLA, 7766 Fay Av, La Jolla<br>78 rooms; pools, exercise room, dining room. | 105 B3 | MARINA DEL REY MARRIOTT, Maxella Av,Marina dl Rey<br>283 rooms; whirlpool & pool, dining room. | 187 D3 |
| HOTEL MERIDIEN, 4500 MacArthur Bl, Newport Beach<br>440 rooms; whirlpool & pool, sauna, tennis. | 198 C5 | *MARINA HOTEL, 3805 Las Vegas Blvd<br>870 units; pool, 2 restaurants, casino. | 210 B4 |
| HYATT ANAHEIM, 1700 S Harbor Blvd, Anaheim<br>301 rooms; pool, dining room. | 193 C4 | *MARINA INTERNATIONAL HOTEL, 4200 Admiralty Wy<br>136 units; patios/balconies, pool; LAX trans. | 187 C3 |
| HYATT BURLINGAME, 1333 Old Bayshore Hy,Burlingame<br>304 rooms; swimming pool, beautiful grounds. | 45 C3 | *MARINERS INN, 6180 Moonstone Beach Dr, Cambria<br>26 rooms; whirlpool. Across from the beach. | 75 C2 |
| HYATT ISLANDIA, 1441 Quivira Rd, San Diego<br>349 rooms; pool & whirlpool, dining room. | 212 B4 | *MARK HOPKINS HOTEL, 1 Nob Hill, San Francisco<br>Elegnt lndmrk htl, panoramic vw 'Top of Mark'. | 143 C3 |
| *HYATT LAKE TAHOE RESORT HOTEL, Country Club Dr<br>460 rooms; pool, beach, sauna, tennis. | 36 B1 | *MARRIOTT INN, 200 Marina Blvd, Berkeley<br>376 rooms; indoor pool, sauna, restaurant. | L C4 |
| *HYATT LOS ANGELES INTERNATIONAL, 6225 W Century<br>603 rooms; pool, dining; across from LAX. | 189 C1 | MARRIOTT HOTEL, 18000 Von Karman, Irvine<br>502 rooms; tennis, exercise room, pool. | 198 D4 |
| HYATT-OAKLAND INT'L AIRPORT, Hegenberger, Oakland<br>335 rooms; pool & wading pool, dining room. | 159 D3 | *MARRIOTT HOTEL, 5855 W Century Bl, Los Angeles<br>Very large hotel, transport to airport. | 189 D1 |
| HYATT PALO ALTO, 4290 El Camino Real<br>200 units; pool, putting green, restaurant. | 147 E5 | *MARRIOTT'S RANCHO LAS PALMAS RESORT, Bob Hope Dr<br>456 rooms; pools, golf, tennis, bicycles. | 100 E4 |
| HYATT REGENCY, 200 S Pine, Long Beach<br>531 rooms; pool & whirlpool, exercise room. | 192 D3 | *MARRIOTT'S SANTA BARBARA BILTMORE, 1260 Channel<br>229 rooms; overlooks ocean, pool, restaurant. | 87 D4 |
| *HYATT REGENCY LOS ANGELES, Hope & 7th Sts<br>487 units; at Broadway Plaza; LAX transport. | 186 A3 | *MAXIM, 160 E Flamingo, Las Vegas<br>Casino, restaurant, entertainment, shops. | 210 B3 |
| *HYATT REGENCY, 1 Old Golf Course Rd, Monterey<br>579 rooms; pools & whirlpool, golf, tennis. | 54 B4 | MENDOCINO HOTEL, 45080 Main St, Mendocino<br>Restored 1878 Victorian hotel. | 30 B1 |
| *HYATT REGENCY, 5 Embarcadero Ctr, San Francisco<br>Striking arch, glss elvatr, revolvng rftp bar. | 143 E3 | *MINT, 100 E Fremont St, Las Vegas<br>Casino, restaurant, entertainment, arcade. | 209 C2 |
| HYATT RICKEYS, 4219 El Camino Real, Palo Alto<br>350 units; health club, pool, putting green. | 147 E5 | MONTECITO INN, 1295 Coast Vlg Rd, Montecito<br>60 rooms & suites; restored historic inn. | 87 D4 |
| *HYATT SAN JOSE, 1740 N 1st St<br>475 rooms; putting green, dining room. | 151 E1 | *MOONSTONE INN, 5860 Moonstone Beach Dr, Cambria<br>9 rooms with an ocean view from each. | 75 B2 |
| HYATT SUNSET, 8401 Sunset Blvd, Hollywood<br>262 rooms; rooftop pool, dining, entertainmnt. | Q D3 | MURPHY'S HOTEL, off Hwy 4 in Murphys<br>Historical monument still in full operation. | 41 C4 |
| *HYATT ON UNION SQUARE, 345 Stockton St, SF<br>693 units; 3 restaurants, entertainment. | 143 C3 | *NAPA VALLEY LODGE BEST WESTERN, Yountville<br>55 rooms; lovely view, pool & whirlpool. | 38 C2 |
| HYATT WILSHIRE, 3515 Wilshire Blvd, Los Angeles<br>400 rooms; entertainment, diningroom, pool. | 185 B2 | NEWARK HILTON, 39900 Balentine, Newark<br>318 rooms; pool, sauna, whirlpool, dining. | P A2 |
| IMPERIAL PALACE, 3535 Las Vegas Blvd, Las Vegas<br>1500 rooms; pools, entertainment, casino. | 210 B2 | NEW OTANI HOTEL, Los Angeles St, Los Angeles<br>448 rooms; beautiful garden, pool & sauna. | 186 B3 |
| INLAND EMPIRE HILTON, Waterman Av, San Bernardino<br>247 units; dining room, pool & whirlpool. | 207 D5 | NEWPORT BCH MARRIOTT, Newport Ctr Dr, Newport Bch<br>603 rooms; 2 pools, tennis, dining. | 200 A4 |
| INN AT THE PARK, 1855 S Harbor Blvd, Anaheim<br>500 units; pool, restaurant & coffee shop. | 193 C4 | OAKLAND AIRPORT HILTON, Hegenberger Rd, Oakland<br>367 rooms; pool, restaurant, entertainment. | 159 D4 |
| *THE INN AT RANCHO SANTA FE, Linea del Cielo<br>80 rooms and cottages on tree-shaded grounds. | 106 C4 | ONTARIO AIRPORT HILTON, 700 'G' St, Ontario<br>309 rooms; dining, whirlpool & swimming pool. | U E2 |
| IRVINE HILTON, 17900 Jamboree Blvd, Irvine<br>550 units; close to John Wayne Airport. | 198 E4 | PACIFICA HOTEL, 6161 Centinela Av, Culver City<br>375 rooms; swimming pool, restaurant. | 188 C3 |
| *JADE TREE INN, Junipero St near 5th, Carmel<br>55 units; ocean view, fireplace, pool, lanais. | 168 C3 | *PACIFIC PLAZA, 501 Post St, San Francisco<br>140 units; restaurant, pay valet garage. | 143 C3 |
| LA CASA DEL ZORRO, Borrego Springs<br>Studios, suites and casitas. | 107 E2 | PALA MESA RESORT, Jct I-15 & Hwy 76, Fallbrook<br>135 rooms; pool, whirlpool, golf, tennis. | 106 C2 |
| *LA COSTA HOTEL & SPA, Costa del Mar Rd, Carlsbad<br>547 rooms & houses; golf, tennis, health spa. | 106 C3 | PALM SPRINGS HILTON RIVIERA, Palm Springs<br>467 rooms; 2 pools, wading pool, tennis. | 206 B2 |
| LANDMARK HOTEL, Paradise Rd, Las Vegas<br>Lovely rooms; restaurant, showrooms & casino. | 209 D5 | *PALM SPRINGS PLAZA RESORT, 400 E Tahquitz-McC<br>258 units; pool, saunas, whirlpools, tennis. | 206 B4 |
| *LA QUINTA HOTEL, Eisenhower Dr, La Quinta<br>269 rooms; lovely grounds, pool, tennis, golf. | 100 E4 | *PALM SPRINGS SPA HOTEL, Indian Av N & Tahquitz-M<br>230 units; pool, 2 hot minerl pools, steam rm. | 206 B3 |

| NAME & ADDRESS | PAGE & GRID | | NAME & ADDRESS | PAGE & GRID | |
|---|---|---|---|---|---|
| PASADENA HILTON, 150 Los Robles Av, Pasadena<br>253 rooms; entertainment, dining room, pool. | 190 | C4 | SHERATON HOTEL, Industry Hills Pkwy, Industry<br>298 rooms; golf, tennis, 2 swimming pools. | R | E4 |
| *PEPPER TREE INN, 3850 State St, Santa Barbara<br>150 rooms; patios, 2 pools & sauna, restaurnt. | 87 | C4 | SHERATON INN, 1177 Airport Blvd, Burlingame<br>316 rooms; dining room & coffee shop; pools. | N | D1 |
| *PICADILLY INN AIRPORT, 5115 E McKinley, Fresno<br>185 rooms; pool, whirlpool, restaurant. | 57 | D3 | *SHERATON NEWPORT BEACH, 4545 MacArthur Blvd<br>Beautiful facilities, entertainment. | 198 | B5 |
| *PICADILLY INN-SHAW, 2305 W Shaw Av, Fresno<br>203 rooms; pool, airport trans, restaurant. | 57 | C3 | *SHERATON PLAZA, 6101 W Century Blvd<br>Beautiful facilities, easy access to LAX. | 189 | C1 |
| PINE INN, Ocean Av, Carmel<br>49 rooms; Victorian decor, beautiful view. | 168 | B3 | SHERATON PREMIERE, off Lankershim, Universal City<br>450 rooms; exercise room, pool & whirlpool. | 181 | A1 |
| PLEASANTON HILTON, Johnson Dr, Pleasanton<br>298 rooms; racquetball, tennis, swimming pool. | M | B5 | SHERATON RIVERSIDE, 3400 Market, Riverside<br>296 units; dining room and entertainment. | 205 | B2 |
| *QUAIL LODGE, 8205 Valley Greens Dr, Carmel Vly<br>100 rooms; scenic grounds, golf, tennis. | 54 | B5 | *SHERATON SANTA BARBARA HOTEL, 1111 E Cabrillo<br>174 rooms; ocean view, pool, dining room. | 87 | D4 |
| QUALITY INN, 616 Convention Wy, Anaheim<br>281 rooms; pool, dining & entertainment. | 193 | C5 | *SHERATON SUNNYVALE INN, 1100 N Mathilda Av<br>174 rooms; pool, restaurant, cocktail lounge. | 148 | D4 |
| QUALITY ROYALE, 1433 Camino del Rio, San Diego<br>265 rooms; pool, sauna, putting green. | 214 | A4 | SHERATON SUNRISE, Point East Dr, Rancho Cordova<br>265 rooms; dining room, swimming pool. | 40 | B1 |
| *QUEEN MARY, Pier J, Long Beach<br>British liner now serves as hotel & restrnt. | 192 | E4 | SHERATON UNIVERSAL, off Lankershim, Universal City<br>475 rooms; entertainment, pool & sauna. | 181 | A1 |
| *QUEENSWAY BAY HILTON, 700 Queenswy Dr, Long Bch<br>Located on the waterfront next to Queen Mary. | 192 | D4 | SHERATON VALLEY INN, 5101 California Av, Bakrsfld<br>200 rooms; pool and restaurant. | 78 | C3 |
| *RAMADA HOTEL, 6th & Lake St, Reno<br>250 units; casino and restaurant. | 130 | B2 | *SHORE CLIFF LODGE, 2555 Price St, Pismo Beach<br>99 rooms; ocean view, heated pool, restaurant. | 76 | B4 |
| RAMADA INN, 1331 Katella Av, Anaheim<br>240 rooms; pool, jacuzzi, restaurant & lounge. | 193 | E4 | *SILVERADO COUNTRY CLUB RESORT, 1600 Atlas Peak<br>260 rooms; 8 pools, golf, tennis, bicycles. | 38 | D2 |
| *RAMADA INN, 114 E Highway 246, Buellton<br>98 rooms; pool, convention & conference facil. | 86 | D3 | *SMUGGLERS INN, 3737 N Blackstone Av, Fresno<br>210 rooms; beautiful landscape, pool, restrnt. | 57 | C3 |
| *RANCHO BERNARDO INN, 17550 Bernardo Oaks Dr<br>236 rooms; 2 pools, golf, bicycling, tennis. | 106 | D4 | *SOUTH COAST PLAZA HOTEL, 666 Anton Bl, Costa Msa<br>400 rooms; pool, putting green, tennis. | 198 | A3 |
| RED LION INN, Camino del Rio Ct, Bakersfield<br>262 units; pool, whirlpool. | 166 | A2 | *STANFORD COURT, 905 California St, Nob Hill<br>Gracious 1900s decor in Old Stanford House. | 143 | C3 |
| *RED LION MOTOR INN, 1830 Hilltop Dr, Redding<br>194 rooms; pool, putting green, dining room. | 18 | C2 | STARDUST HOTEL, 3000 Las Vegas Blvd S<br>Casino, restaurant, entertainment, pool. | 209 | B5 |
| *RED LION MOTOR INN, 2001 Point West Wy, Sacto<br>448 rooms; pools, airport trans, dining room. | 39 | E1 | *STOCKTON HILTON, 2323 Grand Canal<br>202 rooms; 3 pools, dining room & coffee shop. | 40 | A5 |
| *REGISTRY HOTEL, 18800 MacArthur Blvd<br>296 units; across from John Wayne Airport. | 198 | C5 | STOUFFER CONCOURSE, 5400 Century Bl, Los Angeles<br>750 rooms; restaurant, swimming pool. | 189 | E1 |
| *RENO HILTON, 255 N Sierra<br>Lovely hotel with pool, casino & restaurants. | 130 | B3 | SUNDANCE HOTEL, 301 E Fremont St, Las Vegas<br>650 units; restaurant, buffet and casino. | 209 | C2 |
| *RIO BRAVO RESORT, 11200 Lake Ming Rd, Rio Bravo<br>112 rooms; tennis, golf, pools, airstrip. | 78 | E2 | *SUNNYVALE HILTON INN, 1250 Lakeside Dr<br>372 rooms; pool, restaurant, airport trans. | P | A3 |
| RITZ CARLTON, 33533 Shoreline Dr, Laguna Niguel<br>393 rooms; golf, tennis, pools, ocean view. | 105 | D1 | *TAHOE SEASONS RESORT, Saddle & Keller, Lk Tahoe<br>160 rooms; tennis courts and restaurant. | 129 | E3 |
| *RIVIERA, 2901 Las Vegas Bl, Las Vegas<br>Casino, restaurants, entertainment, shops. | 209 | C5 | THE CHATEAU, 4195 Solano Av, Napa<br>115 rooms; Country-French atmosphere, pool. | 38 | C2 |
| *SACRAMENTO INN, 1401 Arden Wy<br>387 rooms; pools, putting green, dining room. | 39 | E1 | *TICKLE PINK MOTOR INN, 155 Highland Dr, Carmel<br>35 rooms; beautiful view and lovely location. | 54 | A5 |
| *SAHARA (DEL WEBB'S), 2535 Las Vegas Bl, Ls Vegas<br>Casino, restaurants, entertainment, shops. | 209 | C4 | TORRANCE MARRIOTT, 3635 Fashion Wy, Torrance<br>487 rooms; 2 pools, sauna, whirlpool. | S | B2 |
| *SAN DIEGO HILTON, 1775 E Mission Bay Dr<br>356 units; pool, beach, rental boats & bikes. | 212 | E3 | TOWN & COUNTRY, Hotel Circle, San Diego<br>966 rooms; 4 pools, sauna & whirlpool. | 213 | D4 |
| *SANDS, 3355 Las Vegas Bl, Las Vegas<br>Casino, restaurants, star entertainment. | 210 | B2 | *THE TREE HOUSE BEST WESTERN, off I-5, Mt Shasta<br>94 rooms; indoor pool, bicycles, dining room. | 12 | C2 |
| *SANDS REGENT, Arlington & 3rd Sts, Reno<br>Casino, restaurants, entertainment, shops. | 130 | A2 | *TROPICANA, 3801 Las Vegas Bl, Las Vegas<br>Casino, cafe, entertainment, theater, shops. | 210 | B4 |
| SAN FRAN AIRPORT MARRIOTT, Bayshore Hy, Burlingame<br>689 rooms; dining, health club, pool. | N | C1 | *UNION PLAZA HOTEL, 1 Main St, Las Vegas<br>Casino, restaurant, entertainment. | 209 | C1 |
| *SAN LUIS BAY INN, Avila Beach<br>76 rooms; ocean view, golf, swim, dining room. | 76 | A4 | *UNIVERSITY HILTON, 3540 E Figueroa St, LA<br>241 units; next to USC campus; pool. | 185 | C5 |
| *SANTA CLARA MARRIOTT, Great America Parkway<br>764 rooms; near Great America Theme Park. | P | B3 | *VACATION VILLAGE, Mission Bay Pk, San Diego<br>449 bungalows, rooms & suites; 5 pools. | 212 | B3 |
| *THE SHASTA INN, 2180 Hilltop Dr, Redding<br>148 rooms; pool & whirlpool, restaurant. | 18 | C2 | WAWONA HOTEL, S entrance to Yosemite Valley<br>A grand mountain resort built in the 1800's. | 49 | D3 |
| SHENANDOAH HOTEL, 120 E Flamingo Rd, Las Vegas<br>Casino, shows and restaurant. | 210 | B3 | *WEST BEACH MOTOR LODGE, Cabrillo Bl & Bath St<br>45 units; across from yacht harbor & beach. | 174 | C4 |
| SHERATON-ANAHEIM, 1015 W Ball Rd, Anaheim<br>500 rooms; entertainment, dining, pool. | 193 | B3 | *THE WESTGATE, 2nd Av at C St, San Diego<br>223 units; elegant decor, restaurant. | 215 | D3 |
| *SHERATON AT FISHERMAN'S WHARF, 2500 Mason St, SF<br>525 units; pool, restaurant and coffee shop. | 143 | B1 | *WESTIN BONAVENTURE, 6th & Flower, Los Angeles<br>Rooftop restaurnt & revolvng cocktl lounge. | 186 | A3 |
| *SHERATON HOTEL, 45 John Glenn Dr, Concord<br>331 rooms; conference center, entertainment. | M | A3 | *WESTIN ST FRANCIS, Union Square, San Francisco<br>Fashionable shops, skyline view from elevator. | 143 | C3 |

# POINTS OF INTEREST INDEX

| NAME & ADDRESS | PAGE & GRID |
|---|---|
| *WESTWOOD MARQUIS, Hilgard Av near Wilshire Bl,LA  250 elegant suites; pool, sauna, whirlpool. | 180 D2 |

**MISSIONS**

| NAME & ADDRESS | PAGE & GRID |
|---|---|
| MSN BASILICA SAN DIEGO DE ALCALA, 10818 SD Msn Rd  1769, 1st missn estblshd along El Camino Real. | 214 E3 |
| MISSION LA PURIMISA CONCEPCION, 15 mi W of US 101  1787, 11th missn, rebuilt by original methods. | 86 B2 |
| MISSION NUESTRA SENORA DE LA SOLEDAD, off US 101  1791, 13th missn, stood in ruins for 100 yrs. | 65 A1 |
| MISSION SAN ANTONIO DE PADUA, off U S 101  1771, 3rd msn, one of largest restored missns. | 65 B3 |
| MISSION SAN ANTONIO DE PALA, off Hwy 76  Built in 1816 to help the Sn Luis Rey Mission. | 106 E2 |
| MISSION SAN BUENAVENTURA, Main & Figueroa Sts  1782, 9th missn, last founded by Father Serra. | 175 B2 |
| MISSION SAN CARLOS BORROMEO, Lasuen Dr, Carmel  1770, 2nd missn, burial place of Father Serra. | 168 B4 |
| MSN SAN FERNANDO REY DE ESPANA, 15151 SF Msn Bl  1797, 17th msn, destroyed by '71 quake; rstrd. | Q C1 |
| MISSION SAN FRANCISCO DE ASIS, Dolores & 16th Sts  1776, 6th missn, chapel unchanged for 175 yrs. | 142 C4 |
| MISSION SAN FRANCISCO SOLANO, Spain & 1st Sts  1823, 21st missn, northernmost & last of msns. | 132 D3 |
| MISSION SAN GABRIEL ARCANGEL, 1120 Old Mill Rd  1771, 4th missn, at crossroads in early Calif. | R C3 |
| MISSION SAN JOSE, 43300 Mission Blvd  1777, 14th missn, noted for outstanding music. | P B2 |
| MISSION SAN JUAN BAUTISTA, off US 101  1797, 15th msn, near othr buildngs of msn era. | 54 D3 |
| MISSION SAN JUAN CAPISTRANO, off I-5 at Ortega  1776, 7th mission, swallows return annually. | 202 E1 |
| MISSION SAN LUIS OBISPO, Chorro & Monterey Sts  1772, 5th mission, 1st misn to use tile tools. | 172 C3 |
| MISSION SAN LUIS REY DE FRANCIA, on Hwy 76  1798, 18th missn, most successful of all msns. | 106 B3 |
| MISSION SAN MIGUEL ARCANGEL, 801 Mission St  1797, 16th missn, last msn secularized - 1834. | 66 A5 |
| MISSION SAN RAFAEL ARCANGEL, A St & 5th Av  1817, 20th missn, founded to aid sick Indians. | 139 D3 |
| MISSION SANTA BARBARA, Laguna & Los Olivos Sts  1786, 10th missn, famed as most beautiful msn. | 174 B2 |
| MISSION SANTA CLARA DE ASIS, Grant & Franklin St  1777, 8th missn, bell dated 1798 still clangs. | 151 B2 |
| MISSION SANTA CRUZ, School & Emmet Sts  1791, 12th msn, destroyed, replica built 1931. | 169 D2 |
| MISSION SANTA INES, 1760 Mission Dr  1804, 19th mission, favorite mission of many. | 86 E3 |

**PARKS (STATE & FEDERAL) & NATIONAL FORESTS**

| NAME & ADDRESS | PAGE & GRID |
|---|---|
| ADM WILLIAM STANDLEY STATE REC AREA, Laytonville  Beautiful scenery; no camping facilities. | 22 C3 |
| AHJUMAWI LAVA SPRINGS STATE PARK, Island Rd  Accessible by boat only. | 13 E3 |
| ALAMEDA PARK, Micheltorea & Anacapa Sts  Displays 280 species of plants and shrubs. | 174 C3 |
| AMERICAN RIVER PARKWAY, from Nimbus Dam  23 mi long greenbelt along banks of Sacto Riv. | 137 B1 |
| ANCIENT BRISTLECONE PINE FOREST, White Mountn Rd  4600 yr old pine forest, nature trails. | 52 A3 |
| ANDREW MOLERA STATE PARK, W of Hwy 1, Big Sur  50 campsites, sandy beach, hiking, meadows. | 64 B2 |
| ANGELES NATIONAL FOREST, N of Los Angeles  In rugged mtns of LA, hiking & winter sports. | Q D1 |
| ANGEL ISLAND STATE PARK, E San Francisco Bay  Isl pk has hiking, bike rentl, picnc, day use. | L B4 |
| ANNADEL STATE PARK, Channel Dr  Riding & hiking. | 38 A2 |

| NAME & ADDRESS | PAGE & GRID |
|---|---|
| ANTELOPE VALLEY CAL POPPY RESERVE, W of Lancaster  Scenic area for picnicking. | 89 D2 |
| ANZA BORREGO DESERT STATE PARK, San Diego County  Beautiful wildflowers in spring; camp, hike. | 108 A4 |
| ARMSTRONG REDWOODS STATE RESERVE, E of Fort Ross  Giant redwoods, picnicking, hiking trails. | 37 C1 |
| AUSTIN CREEK STATE RECREATION AREA, E of Ft Ross  Camp, horseback ride, meadows, vllys, forests. | 37 C1 |
| AZALEA STATE RESERVE, off Hwy 101, Arcata  Beautiful azaleas bloom late May - early June. | 10 A4 |
| BENBOW LAKE STATE REC AREA, 2 mi S of Garberville  Horse trails, fish, hike, swim, picnic. | 22 B1 |
| BENICIA STATE RECREATION AREA, W of Benicia  Good fishing; picnicking facilities. | L D2 |
| BIG BASIN REDWOODS STATE PARK, on Hwy 236  First state park to preserve redwoods. | N D4 |
| BOGGS MOUNTAIN STATE FOREST, N of Hwy 175  Picnicking; hiking trails. | 32 A4 |
| BONELLI REGIONAL COUNTY PARK, Park Rd, San Dimas  Picnicking facilities and hiking trails. | U B2 |
| BORDER FIELD STATE PARK, 15 mi S of San Diego  Good area to picnic, fish, swim, or hike. | V B5 |
| BOTHE-NAPA VALLEY STATE PARK, on Hwy 29  Hiking, picnic & camping areas, swimming pool. | 38 A1 |
| BRANNAN ISLAND, South of Rio Vista  Boat, fish, camp, hike; visitors center. | M D2 |
| BROOKSIDE PARK, Rosemont Av, Pasadena  Site of Rosebowl; swimming, hiking, golfing. | 190 A3 |
| BUCKSKIN MOUNTAIN STATE PARK, Hwy 95, Arizona  Scenic area to hike and picnic. | 104 C1 |
| BURTON CREEK STATE PARK, E of Tahoe State Park  Camping and picnicking. | 35 E1 |
| BUTANO STATE PARK, E of Hwy 1 at Gazos Creek Rd  Camping, recreational facilities. | N C4 |
| CALAVERAS BIG TREES STATE PARK, E of Arnold  2 giant Redwood groves - self-guided tours. | 41 D3 |
| CANDLESTICK POINT RECREATION AREA, US 101  Scenic hiking trails; picnicking & fishing. | L C5 |
| CASTLE CRAG STATE PARK, S of Dunsmuir  Pinnacles, crags, cliffs, green pines, rec. | 12 D3 |
| CASTLE ROCK STATE PARK, near Jct Hwy 9 and Hwy 35  Nature & hiking trails; picnicking & camping. | N E4 |
| CASWELL MEMORIAL STATE PARK, Hwy 99 S of Manteca  Camp, fish, swim, hike, picnic. | 47 B2 |
| CHABOT REGIONAL PARK, Lake Chabot  5000 acre park; fish, picnic, moto-X, boat. | L E5 |
| CHANNEL ISLANDS NATIONAL PARK, off Santa Barbara  Consists of 5 islands, 20 to 60 mi offshore. | 87 C5 |
| CHINA CAMP STATE PARK, N of San Rafael  Recreational facilities and camping. | L B3 |
| CHINO HILLS STATE PARK, off Hwy 71, Orange Co  Hiking trails, picnic areas. | U C4 |
| CLEAR LAKE STATE PARK, near Lakeport  Camp, boat, wtrski, hike, fish, swim, picnic. | 31 D3 |
| CLEVELAND NATL FOREST, San Diego & Orange Co's  Hiking, boating, riding, fishing, camping. | 107 B4 |
| COL. ALLENWORTH STATE HIST PARK, 20 mi N of Wasco  Historical exhibits; picnicking facilities. | 68 B4 |
| CRYSTAL COVE STATE PARK, N of Laguna Beach  3 miles of beaches for swimming & picnicking. | T D5 |
| CUYAMACA RANCHO STATE PARK, on Hwy 79, Julian  In old Indian territory; camp, hike; horses. | 107 C4 |
| DAYTON STATE PARK, Hwy 50 near Dayton  Hiking and picnicking facilities. | 36 D1 |
| DEL NORTE COAST REDWOODS ST PK, S of Crescent Cty  Dense forests, giant redwoods, good camping. | 1 E4 |
| DEVIL'S POSTPILE NATL MONUMNT, Mammoth Lakes Area  Spectacular mass of hexagonal basalt columns. | 50 C2 |
| D. L. BLISS STATE PARK, North of Emerald Bay  Dense forest, trails, camping, beach area. | 35 E3 |
| DONNER MEMORIAL STATE PARK, 2 mi W of Truckee  Rec at Donner Lake, Donner Prty memorial, mus. | 35 D1 |

# POINTS OF INTEREST INDEX

# POINTS OF INTEREST INDEX

| NAME & ADDRESS | PAGE & GRID | NAME & ADDRESS | PAGE & GRID |
|---|---|---|---|
| BALBOA PAVILION, Balboa Bl, Newport Beach<br>Beautiful landmark of Newport Bay; cruises. | 199 D5 | CEDAR GROVE, Kings Canyon National Park<br>Base for trail trips by horseback or backpack. | 59 B3 |
| BATTERY POINT LIGHTHOUSE, Crescent City<br>Tours & museum include history of lighthouse. | 1 D4 | CHINATOWN, 900 N Broadway, Los Angeles<br>Authentic Chinese shops and restaurants. | 186 C2 |
| BAY MEADOWS RACETRACK, S Delaware, San Mateo<br>Thoroughbred, harness & quarter horse racing. | 145 B3 | CHINATOWN, between Stockton & Kearny Sts, SF<br>Largest Chinese settlement in America. | 143 C2 |
| BERKELEY AQUATIC PARK, Polk St, San Francisco<br>Curved fishing pier creates cold swim lagoon. | L C4 | CHURCH BUILT FROM ONE TREE, Santa Rosa<br>Built from a single redwood tree. | 131 D4 |
| BERKELEY ROSE GARDENS, Euclid Av & Bayview<br>1000's of different varieties of roses. | 156 A1 | CHURCH FINE ARTS BUILDING, University of Nevada<br>Art exhibits & theater productions. | 130 B1 |
| BIDWELL PARK, E 4th St, Chico<br>Swimming pool, picnic, golf, nature trails. | 124 D4 | CIVIC MEMORIAL AUDITORIUM, Center St, Stockton<br>Various shows, conventions, exhibits&displays. | 160 D4 |
| BIRD ROCK, Bird Rock Av, La Jolla<br>Birdwatching in a natural coastal setting. | 105 B5 | CLARK BIRD REFUGE, E of Santa Barbara<br>Wild birds in their natural habitat. | 87 C4 |
| BOWERS MUSEUM, 2002 N Main St, Santa Ana<br>Historical pioneer, Indian & Spanish displays. | 196 B3 | CLARK MEMORIAL MUSEUM, 240 E St, Eureka<br>Victorian furniture & clothing, antique guns. | 121 C1 |
| BRADBURY BUILDING, 304 Broadway, Los Angeles<br>Distinguished 19th Century structure. | 186 B3 | CLEAR LAKE WILDLIFE REFUGE, off Hwy 139<br>Hunting of waterfowl, good photography. | 6 B3 |
| BRIDALVEIL FALL, Yosemite National Park<br>Beautifl waterfall drops 600' to Yosemite Vly. | 63 A2 | CLIFF HOUSE, 1066 Point Lobos Av<br>Famous restaurant with magnificent view. | L A4 |
| BROOKS HALL, under San Francisco Civic Center<br>Subterranean hall built in 1958 for shows. | 143 B4 | COIT TOWER, top of Telegraph Hill<br>Volunteer firefighter mem, good view of city. | 143 C2 |
| BUFFALO PRESERVE, Golden Gate Park<br>10 acres downtown SF used for bison preserve. | 141 A4 | COLEMAN FISH STATION, 12 mi SE of Anderson<br>Large salmon hatchery; spawning fall & winter. | 18 D3 |
| BURBANK STUDIOS, 4000 Warner Blvd<br>Offers tours of day's activity on the lot. | 179 C5 | COLUSA NATL WILDLIFE REFUGE, on Hwy 20<br>1000's of birds to view on self-guided tour. | 32 E2 |
| CABOTS PUEBLO MUSEUM, 67624 Desert View<br>Indian, Eskimo & early settler artifacts. | 100 C3 | COMMUNITY MEMORIAL MUS, Butte House Rd, Yuba City<br>Memorabilia of early Indians and Pioneers. | 125 B2 |
| CABRILLO MARINE MUSEUM, 3720 Stephen M White Dr<br>Beautiful exhibits of fish, birds & whales. | S B3 | COW MOUNTAIN REC AREA, near Cow Mountain<br>Camp, boat, wtrski, hike, fish, swim, hunt. | 31 C2 |
| CALAVERAS COUNTY MUSEUM, 30 N Main, San Andreas<br>In old courthouse; Indian arts, guns, gems. | 41 A3 | COW PALACE, Geneva Av & Santos St, Daly City<br>Arena, exhibition center; sports events. | L B5 |
| CALICO MTNS ARCHAEOLOGICAL PROJ, Hwy 15, Barstow<br>Tours available Wednesday through Sunday. | 82 B5 | CROCKER ART MUSEUM, 210 O Street, Sacramento<br>Paintings, furniture, sculpture. | 137 A3 |
| CALIFORNIA ALMOND GROWERS EXCHANGE, 216 O Street<br>Offers tours and films daily. | 137 C2 | CRYSTAL CATHEDRAL, Chapman Av, Garden Grove<br>Features religious and secular concerts. | 195 D1 |
| CALIFORNIA CAVERNS, Cave City Rd, San Andreas<br>Tours of the caves available. | 41 B3 | DAFFODIL HILL, 3 mi N of Volcano<br>Blossoms from late March through mid-April. | 41 B2 |
| CALIFORNIA RAILWAY MUSEUM, E of Fairfield, Hwy 12<br>Restored rail cars, rides, exhibits & museum. | M B1 | DANTES VIEW, above Badwater, Death Vly Nat'l Mon<br>Beautiful vw of Badwater & Death Vly from mtn. | 72 B2 |
| CALIFORNIA LIVING MUSEUM, Hwy 178, Rio Bravo<br>Informative contemporary museum. | 78 E2 | DEATH VALLEY NATIONAL MONUMENT, Hwy 190<br>Vast & colorful desert; record summer temps. | 61 B3 |
| CALIF MUSEUM OF SCIENCE & INDUSTRY, 700 State Dr<br>Fascinating do-it-yourself mus in Expositn Pk. | 185 C5 | DELEVAN NATIONAL WILDLIFE REFUGE, SE of Delevan<br>Nesting area for migrating waterfowl. | 32 E1 |
| CALIFORNIA OIL MUSEUM, 1003 Main St, Santa Paula<br>History of discovery & drilling of oil in Cal. | 88 B5 | DESCANSO GARDENS, 1418 Descanso Dr<br>1000s of beautifl flowrs frm around the world. | R A2 |
| CALIFORNIA RAILROAD MUSEUM, E of I-5 on Front St<br>Exhibits housed in restored railway station. | 137 A2 | DESERT MINING MUSEUM, Butte St, Randsburg<br>Large gem & mineral exhibits, mine guides. | 80 D3 |
| CALIFORNIA RODEO GROUNDS, 1034 N Main St<br>Parades & sqaure dancing at rodeo. | 171 C2 | DEVIL'S GOLF COURSE, S of Hwy 190, Death Valley<br>Unusual salt formations from ancient lakebed. | 72 A1 |
| CALIFORNIA STATE ARCHIVES, 1020 O St<br>Features historical documents of California. | 137 B3 | DEVIL'S HOLE, DEATH VALLEY NATIONAL MONUMENT<br>A deep water-filled cave, preserves pupfish. | 72 E1 |
| CALIFORNIA WESTERN RAILROAD, Laurel St, Ft Bragg<br>Train trips through picturesque redwoods. | 22 B5 | DE YOUNG MEMORIAL MUSEUM, Golden Gate Park<br>Oldst municipl US art mus; hses wrld of art. | 141 C4 |
| CAMPANILE, center of Univ of Berkeley campus<br>Landmark chimes hourly from 12 bronze bells. | 156 B2 | DISNEY STUDIOS, Alameda Av at Buena Vista, Burbnk<br>Creative team for Disney Productions. | 179 D4 |
| CANDLESTICK PARK, Gilman Av east of Bayshore Fwy<br>Home of San Francisco 49ers & Giants. | L C5 | DODGER STADIUM, 1000 Elysian Park<br>Home of the Los Angeles Dodgers | 186 B1 |
| CANNERY ROW, south of Pt Alones, Monterey<br>Famous location of John Steinbeck's novels. | 167 E2 | EASTERN CALIFORNIA MUSEUM, Hwy 395, Independence<br>Exhibits of local and natural history. | 60 A3 |
| CARIZZO GORGE RAILROAD TRESTLE, N of Jacumba<br>Highest wooden trestle still in use. | 111 A4 | EMBARCADERO, Embarcadero Center on the waterfront<br>Centers on 4 towers; shops, hotels & restrnts. | 143 D2 |
| CARSON MANSION, 143 M St, Eureka<br>Fabulous Victorian home; carved redwood walls. | 121 D1 | EMBARCADERO, Harbor Drive, San Diego<br>Restored old ships, maritime mus, restaurants. | 215 C2 |
| CASINO, St Catherine Wy, Catalina Island<br>Features grand ballroom where big bands play. | 97 B4 | EMPIRE COMPANY FIRE MUSEUM, Curry St, Carson City<br>Old firefighting trucks, equipment & pictures. | 36 B2 |
| CASTLE AIR MUSEUM, Heritage Wy, Atwater<br>Air Force museum; open daily. | 48 B4 | EQUESTRIAN CENTER, 34th Av & Kennedy Dr<br>Horses for rent for use in Golden Gate Park. | 141 B4 |
| CATALINA ISLAND, 21 mi SW of Los Angeles.<br>Boats depart from Long Beach & LA Harbors. | 97 D5 | EUREKA VALLEY SAND DUNES, S Eureka Rd<br>Home to a variety of rare plants & animals. | 60 D1 |
| CEC SEABEE MUSEUM, Naval Battalion Center<br>History of the Naval Construction Battalion. | 96 A1 | EXPLORATORIUM & PALACE OF FINE ARTS, Goldn Gate Pk<br>A fascinating 'hands on' science museum. | 142 A1 |

| NAME & ADDRESS | PAGE & GRID | | NAME & ADDRESS | PAGE & GRID | |
|---|---|---|---|---|---|
| EXPOSITION PARK, Exposition B1 | Q | E4 | HAVASU NATIONAL WILDLIFE REFUGE, Lake Havasu | 96 | A3 |
| Includes memorial coliseum & sports arena. | | | Good fishing, many beaches along river. | | |
| FARMER'S MARKET, 3rd St & Fairfax Av | 184 | A1 | HAYWARD AREA HISTORICAL SOCIETY MUS, 22701 Main | 146 | E2 |
| Acres of markets, restaurants & gift shops. | | | California & local historical exhibits. | | |
| FEATHER RIVER HATCHERY, Lake Oroville | 25 | E4 | HEARST SAN SIMEON STATE HIST MONUMENT, off Hwy 1 | 75 | B1 |
| View millions of salmon & steelhead. | | | Tours of fabulous estate of William R Hearst. | | |
| FEATHER RIVER RAILROAD MUSEUM, Portola | 27 | B2 | HERSHEY CHOCOLATE CO, 1400 S Yosemite, Oakdale | 47 | E1 |
| Over 50 trains; summer train rides. | | | Visitors center, tours of chocolate factory. | | |
| FERRY BUILDING EMBARCADERO, foot of Market St | 143 | E2 | HOLLYWOOD BOULEVARD, Los Angeles | 181 | D4 |
| Bay trafic hist, world trade ctr, mineral mus. | | | Possibly the best known street in L A. | | |
| FISHERMAN'S WHARF, off Foam St, Monterey | 167 | E3 | HOLLYWOOD PARK RACE TRACK, 1050 Prairie St | Q | D5 |
| Art gallery, shopping & theater. | | | Features thoroughbred & harness racing. | | |
| FISHERMAN'S WHARF, ft of Taylor at Jefferson, S F | 143 | B1 | HOLLYWOOD WAX MUSEUM, 6767 Hollywood B1 | 181 | C4 |
| Open air markets, restaurants, vw fshng fleet. | | | Life-sized figures of many famous moviestars. | | |
| FLEET SPACE THEATER & SCIENCE CENTER, Balboa Park | 216 | A2 | HONEY LAKE, SE of Susanville | 21 | C4 |
| Exquisite celestial displays and films. | | | Sierra Ordnance Depot - military facility. | | |
| FLYING LADY MUS, 15060 Foothill Rd, Morgan Hill | P | E5 | HUNTINGTON LIBRARY, 1151 Oxford Rd | R | C3 |
| Features vintage airplanes and cars. | | | Includes an art gallery & botanical gardens. | | |
| FOREST LAWN MEMORIAL PARK, 1712 S Glendale Av | 179 | D5 | HURD CANDLE FACTORY, 3020 St Helena Hwy North | 38 | B1 |
| Large collection of stained glass & statuary. | | | Distinctive hand-made candles. | | |
| THE FORUM, Manchester & Prairie Sts | Q | D5 | INDIAN CULTURAL CENTER, Yosemite Village | 63 | D1 |
| Popular center for sports & entertainment. | | | Indian history in the area, displays, relics. | | |
| FRESNO CONVENTION CENTER, Tulare & M Sts | 165 | E4 | INDIAN VALLEY MUSEUM, Taylorsville | 20 | D5 |
| Various shows, conventions, exhib & displays. | | | Located near an original Maidu settlement. | | |
| FRESNO METROPOLITAN MUSEUM, Van Ness Av, Fresno | 165 | D3 | IRVINE BOWL PARK, off Laguna Canyon Rd | 201 | B2 |
| Natural and historical exhibits. | | | Natural amphitheater-Pageant of the Masters. | | |
| FRONTIER MUSEUM, Rancho California Rd, Temecula | 99 | C5 | JACK LONDON SQUARE, foot of Broadway | 157 | E4 |
| Collection of artifacts of early settlers. | | | Site of the 1st & Last Chance Saloon. | | |
| FROST AMPHITHEATER, Stanford University | 147 | A3 | JACKSON SQUARE, Jackson & Montgomery Sts | 143 | D2 |
| Outdoor theater which seats 9,500. | | | Former 'Barbary Coast'; now shopping plaza. | | |
| FURNACE CREEK VISITOR CENTER, Death Valley | 62 | A5 | JAPAN CENTER, Post & Geary Sts, Japantown | 143 | A3 |
| Ranger talks, museum, information & gift shop. | | | Hub of growing Japantown; traditional culture. | | |
| GAMBLE HOUSE, 4 Westmoreland Pl, Pasadena | 190 | B3 | JAPANESE TEA GARDEN, Golden Gate Park | 141 | C4 |
| Great architectural work, originl furnishings. | | | Creatd 1894; oriental landscape, cherry trees. | | |
| GENERAL GRANT GROVE, Redwd Mtn Kings Cyn Nat'l Pk | 58 | E4 | KELLY GRIGGS MUSEUM, 311 Washington, Red Bluff | 18 | D5 |
| Seasonal festivities, horse & foot trails. | | | Restored Victorian home; furnshd wth antiques. | | |
| GHIRARDELLI SQUARE, N Point, Beach & Larkin Sts | 143 | A1 | KINGS RIVER, Kings Canyon National Park | 59 | B2 |
| Shops, outdoor cafes by old chocolate factory. | | | Middle fork runs thru natl pk; exclnt fishing. | | |
| GIANT FOREST, Sequoia National Forest | 59 | A4 | KNIGHT MARITIME MUSEUM, 550 Calle Principal | 167 | E4 |
| One of largest & finest Sequoia groves. | | | Exhibits feature history of whaling industry. | | |
| GLACIER POINT, S of Curry Village | 63 | D2 | LA BREA TAR PITS, 5801 Wilshire B1, Los Angeles | 184 | B2 |
| 3200' abve the vly, vw vly & snow-covrd peaks. | | | Displys of prehistoric animals found in pits. | | |
| GOLDEN CANYON, S of Hwy 190, Death Valley | 62 | A5 | LAGUNA BEACH MUSEUM OF ART, 307 Cliff Dr | 201 | A3 |
| Hike through dramatically colored, scenic cyn. | | | Features continually changing collections. | | |
| GOLDEN GATE BRIDGE, on Hwy 101 | 141 | C1 | LA JOLLA CAVES, 1325 Coast Blvd, La Jolla | 105 | C2 |
| Famous bridge offers spectacular view. | | | Formed by wave action; curio shop. | | |
| GOLD COUNTRY, HIGHWAY 49, Mariposa to Vinton | 27 | D3 | LA JOLLA MUSEUM CONTEMPORARY ART, 700 Prospect St | 107 | B5 |
| Historic 300 mi drive through the Mother Lode. | | | Collection of architecture, photos & films. | | |
| GOLDEN GATE PROMENADE, along SF Bay shoreline | 141 | D1 | LAKE COUNTY DIAMONDS, 875 Lakeport Blvd, Lakeport | 32 | A4 |
| Walkway along marina green. | | | Largest open-pick diamond field. | | |
| GRAND CANYON OF THE TUOLUMNE, N of White Wolf | 42 | C5 | LAKE SHASTA CAVERNS, Shasta Caverns Rd E of I-5 | 18 | C1 |
| Trails to deep-cut canyons, waterfalls, mdws. | | | Colorful rock formatns; boat tours available. | | |
| GRAND CENTRAL MARKET, Hill & 4th Sts | 186 | A3 | LA MESA/PACIFIC RR MUSEUM, 4695 Nebo Dr, La Mesa | V | D3 |
| Food bazaar specializing in foods of Mexico. | | | Memorabilia of the Pacific SW Railroad. | | |
| GREAT PETALUMA MILL, 6 Petaluma B1 N | L | A1 | LAS VEGAS CONVENTION CENTER | 209 | D5 |
| Shops & restaurants in restored grain mill. | | | Conventions & exhibits, banquets. | | |
| GREYSTONE MANSION, 501 N Doheny Rd, Beverly Hills | Q | C3 | LAVA BEDS NATIONAL MONUMENT, 30 mi S of Tulelake | 5 | D4 |
| Historic mansion and surrounding park. | | | Cooled lava forming cones, canyons & caves. | | |
| GRIFFITH OBSERVATORY, 2800 Observatory Rd | 182 | B3 | LAWRENCE LIVERMORE NAT LAB, East Av, Livermore | M | D5 |
| Features displys, planetarium, laserium shows. | | | Energy research project conducted in this lab. | | |
| GRIFFITH PARK, Los Feliz B1 & Riverside Dr | 182 | B2 | LEGION OF HONOR MUSEUM, Lincoln Park | 141 | A3 |
| One of nation's largest municipal parks. | | | Modeled after French Legn; fine art, graphics. | | |
| HALL OF FLOWERS, Golden Gate Park | 141 | C4 | LEONIS ADOBE & PLUMMER HOUSE, Calabasas | 97 | B1 |
| Suberb seasonal flower displays. | | | Restored pioneer homes. | | |
| HANCOCK PARK, 5801 Wilshire B1, Los Angeles | 184 | A2 | LICK OBSERVATORY, Mt Hamilton | P | D3 |
| La Brea Tar Pits, LA County Museum of Art. | | | 120" reflecting telescope. | | |
| HAPPY ISLES NATURE CENTER, Yosemite Valley | 63 | D2 | LITTLE TOKYO, Central Av & 2nd St, Los Angeles | 186 | B3 |
| Mus, ranger explains vly featres & Indn caves. | | | Teahouses, sushi bars, shops & hotels. | | |
| HARRAH'S AUTO COLLECTION, Glendale Rd, Sparks | 28 | C4 | LIVING DESERT, 47900 Portola Av, Palm Desert | 100 | E4 |
| Grand collection of automobiles. | | | Botanical garden and wild animal park. | | |
| HASTINGS BUILDING, 2nd & J Sts | 137 | A2 | LODGE POLE, Sequoia National Forest | 59 | B4 |
| Museum featuring the history of Sacramento. | | | Visitors center has geologic displays in park. | | |

# POINTS OF INTEREST INDEX

| NAME & ADDRESS | PAGE & GRID | NAME & ADDRESS | PAGE & GRID |
|---|---|---|---|
| LOG CABIN MUSEUM, 980 Star Lake Av at Hwy 50<br>Displays the history of the Lake Tahoe area. | 129 A4 | MOVIELAND OF THE AIR, John Wayne Airport<br>Large collectn of authentic antique airplanes. | 198 A5 |
| LOMBARD STREET, between Hyde & Leavenworth Sts<br>'Worlds Crookedest Street'; picturesque. | 143 B2 | MOVIELAND WAX MUSEUM, 7711 Beach Bl, Buena Park<br>Wax displays of celebrities & movie scenes. | T B2 |
| LONG BEACH CATALINA CRUISES, Golden Shore<br>Boats depart daily for 22 mile trip to island. | 192 D4 | MUD BATHS, in Calistoga<br>Attracts visitors year around. | 38 A1 |
| LONG BEACH CONVENTION CENTER, Shoreline Dr<br>Hosts many shows and concerts. | 192 E3 | MUSIC CONCOURSE, Golden Gate Park<br>Free opn air concrts givn alng tree lined wlk. | 141 D4 |
| LONDON BRIDGE, at Lake Havasu<br>Moved from the Thames River to Lake Havasu. | 96 A4 | MUSEUM OF MINING, Johnsville<br>Historical museum of mining in California. | 26 E3 |
| LOS ANGELES STATE & COUNTY ARBORETUM, Arcadia<br>Beautiful gardens featuring numerous plants. | R C3 | NATIONAL MARITIME MUSEUM, foot of Polk Street<br>Displays nautical models, figureheads, photos. | 143 A1 |
| LOS ANGELES COLISEUM, Exposition Pk, Los Angeles<br>Major sports events; UCLA vs USC football. | Q E4 | NATURAL BRIDGE, Death Valley National Monument<br>Colorful hike to natural arch in Black Mtns. | 72 B1 |
| LOS ANGELES CONVENTION CENTER, 1201 S Figueroa<br>A variety of large exhibits and shows. | 185 D3 | NBC STUDIOS, 3000 W Alameda Av, Burbank<br>A look at behind-the-scenes TV production. | 179 D5 |
| LOS ANGELES CO MUSEUM OF ART, 5905 Wilshire Blvd<br>Large collection of impressionist paintings. | 184 A2 | NEVADA STATE CAPITOL, N Carson St, Carson City<br>Built 1871, silver dome caps large stone bldg. | 36 B2 |
| LOS ANGELES COUNTY MUSEUMS, Exposition Park<br>Natural history, science & many more exhibits. | Q E4 | NEVADA ST MUS, N Carson at Robinson, Carson City<br>Mining, pioneer, R R objects & exhibits. | 36 B2 |
| LOS ANGELES ZOO, 5333 Zoo Dr<br>15 acre park features more than 2000 animals. | 182 B1 | NOB HILL, at Calif, Sacramento, Jones & Tyler Sts<br>Symbolic of elegant living; cable car access. | 143 C3 |
| LOWER KLAMATH NATIONAL WILDLIFE REFUGE, Tulelake<br>Great stopping point for migrating waterfowl. | 5 C3 | NORTON SIMON MUSEUM, 411 W Colorado Blvd<br>Outstanding collection of art & sculpture. | 190 B4 |
| MARCH FIELD MUSEUM, March Air Force Base<br>Exhibits of aircraft & memorabilia. | 99 C3 | OAKDALE MUSEUM, 1st & F Sts, Oakdale<br>Features local and natural history artifacts. | 47 E2 |
| MARIPOSA GROVE, Southern Yosemite Natl Pk<br>Giant Sequoias; Grizzly Giant is oldest here. | 49 D3 | OAKLAND-ALAMEDA COUNTY COLISEUM, Nimitz Fy, Av 66<br>2 bldg sprts complex, indr arena, outdr stadm. | 159 D2 |
| MARITIME MUSEUM STAR OF INDIA, 1306 N Harbor Dr<br>Restored windjammer - oldest iron ship afloat. | 215 C3 | OAKLAND MUSEUM, 1000 Oak St at 10th St<br>Unusual environmtl mus follows Calif history. | 158 A3 |
| McHENRY MUSEUM, 1402 I St, Modesto<br>Historical displays, photos & models. | 162 B3 | OAKWOOD LAKE RESORT, off I-5 S of Manteca<br>Water theme park with camping facilities. | 47 A1 |
| MENDOCINO COAST BOTANICAL GARDENS, S of Ft Bragg<br>Gardens open daily; admission charged. | 22 B5 | OAKLAND WORLD TRADE CENTER, Embarcadero<br>Busy trade center near Inner Harbor at SF Bay. | 157 E4 |
| MENDOCINO COUNTY MUSEUM, 400 E Commrcial, Willts<br>Indian, pioneer, art & logging exhibits. | 23 A5 | OAKLAND ZOO, Knowland Dr & 98th Av<br>Picinic area, amusmt pk, aerail trm, baby zoo. | L E5 |
| MERCED COUNTY FAIRGROUNDS, nr Jct of Hwy 99 & 59<br>Hosts Merced County Fair in mid-July. | 170 D4 | OIL MUSEUM, Hwy 33, Taft<br>History of oil industry & processing methods. | 78 A5 |
| MERCER CAVERNS, 1 mi N of Murphys<br>Colorful limestone formations found in 1885. | 41 B4 | OLD EAGLE THEATER, J & Front Sts<br>First theater in California, opened in 1849. | 137 B2 |
| MINING MUSEUM, Univ of Nevada, Reno<br>History of mining, equipment & minerals. | 130 B1 | OLD FAITHFUL GEYSER OF CALIFORNIA, on Tubbs Rd<br>Eruptions occur every 50 minutes. | 38 A1 |
| MOANING CAVE, 5150 Moaning Cave Rd<br>Limestone formations, Indian relics & bones. | 41 B4 | OLD GOVERNOR'S MANSION, 16th & H Sts, Sacramento<br>Victorian gothic mansion built in 1877; tours. | 137 C3 |
| MODOC COUNTY MUSEUM, 600 S Main St, Alturas<br>Displays of Indian objects & old firearms. | 7 B5 | OLD TOWN ART GUILD, G & 2nd Sts, Eureka<br>Galleries, gift shops, art supplies. | 121 C1 |
| MODOC NATIONAL WILDLIFE REFUGE, south of Alturas<br>Popular nesting area for a variety of birds. | 8 B1 | ONE LOG HOUSE, Phillipsville<br>2000 year old log home hewn from 40 ton tree. | 16 C4 |
| MOJAVE RIVER VLY MUSEUM, 270 Virginia Wy, Barstow<br>Mining, railroad & Indian artifacts displayed. | 208 B3 | ORANGE EMPIRE RAILWAY MUSEUM, Perris<br>An extensive collection of early trains. | 99 B4 |
| MONO HOT SPRINGS, northeast of Lakeshore<br>Hot and cold currents, beach, near campsites. | 50 D4 | OREGON CAVES NATIONAL MONUMENT, off Hwy 46<br>Spectacular formations of mineral deposits. | 2 E2 |
| MONTEREY BAY AQUARIUM, Cannery Row, Monterey<br>Unique aquarium with 'hands on' exhibits. | 167 E2 | PACIFIC SW RAILWAY MUSEUM, Highway 94, Campo<br>Exhibits of the Pacific SW Railway. | 112 D2 |
| MORETON BAY FIG TREE, Chapala & Montecito<br>Largest fig tree of its kind in the nation. | 174 D4 | PAGE MUSEUM, 5801 Wilshire Blvd<br>Exhibits of prehistoric animals from tar pits. | 184 B2 |
| MORMON TEMPLE, 10777 Santa Monica Bl<br>One of the largest Mormon temples in the US. | 180 D3 | PAINTED GORGE, off Hwy 195, N of Salton Sea<br>Bluffs of colorfully layered rock. | 101 C5 |
| MORRISON PLANETARIUM, in Golden Gate Park<br>Interesting celestial films and displays. | 141 D4 | PALM SPRINGS AERIAL TRAMWAY, Tramway Dr<br>Spectacular view of desert floor below. | 100 C3 |
| MORRO BAY AQUARIUM, 595 Embarcadero<br>More than 300 fish & marine animal displays. | 75 D3 | PALOMAR OBSERVATORY, Hwy 56, Mt Palomar<br>Operated by Cal Tech; tours; 200" telescope. | 107 A2 |
| MORRO BAY NATURAL HISTORY MUS, Morro Bay State Pk<br>Chumash Indians, wildlife & marine displays. | 64 A4 | PAULEY PAVILION, U C L A Campus<br>Features many sports events. | 180 C1 |
| MT SHASTA, off Hwy 5 N of Dunsmuir<br>Mighty 14,162 ft mtn covered by 5 glaciers. | 12 D1 | PELTON WHEEL MINING MUSEUM, Allison Ranch Rd<br>Pelton waterwheel, old mining tools. | 127 B4 |
| MT SHASTA FISH HATCHERY, 1 mi W of Mt Shasta<br>Trout produced to stock Northern Cal streams. | 12 C2 | PIER 39, northern waterfront, San Francisco<br>Recreates old SF street scene; shops, rstrnts. | 143 C1 |
| MT WHITNEY, Whitney Portal Rd<br>At 14,495' it is highest mtn in contiguous US. | 59 E4 | PIONEER MUSEUM & HAGGIN GALLERIES, Stockton<br>Historical displays, paintings & art objects. | 160 B4 |
| MOUNT WILSON OBSERVATORY, Mt Wilson Rd<br>Famous for huge Hooker telescope & camera. | R C2 | PLACER COUNTY MUSEUM, 1273 High St, Auburn<br>Displays of early mining equipment. | 126 C4 |

# POINTS OF INTEREST INDEX

***\*******************************************\*******

## RECREATION LAKES, RIVERS & MARINAS
**\*********************************************\*******

| NAME & ADDRESS | PAGE & GRID | NAME & ADDRESS | PAGE & GRID |
|---|---|---|---|
| GOLDEN GATE NATL REC AREA, San Francisco & Marin<br>Beaches & gardens; hiking and picnicking. | 141 A2 | LAKE MERRITT, downtown Oakland<br>Large natural salt water lake. | 158 B3 |
| GOLDEN GATE YACHT CLUB, off Marina Bl, SF<br>Private yacht club at SF yacht harbor. | 142 A1 | LAKE MOHAVE, E of Searchlight, Nevada<br>Boat, fish, swim, camp, beaches, marinas. | 85 C2 |
| HELL HOLE RESERVOIR, NE of Michigan Bluff<br>50+ dev sites - boat, waterski, fish, hike. | 35 C2 | LAKE NACIMIENTO, 40 mi NW of Paso Robles<br>350+ dev sites - waterski, boat, swim, hike. | 65 D5 |
| HENSLEY LAKE PARK & REC AREA, 17 mi N of Madera<br>Camping, picnicking, waterskiing & swimming. | 49 B5 | LAKE OROVILLE STATE REC AREA, NE of Oroville<br>200+ dev sites - boat, waterski, fish, horses. | 25 D4 |
| HOGAN RESERVOIR, 3 mi W of San Andreas<br>Dev & undev sites - boat, fish, hike, swim. | 40 E4 | LAKE PERRIS STATE REC AREA, off Ramona Expressway<br>Fish, water ski, camp; boat & bicycle rentals. | 99 C3 |
| HUNTINGTON HARBOUR, Huntington Beach<br>Waterfront homes & marina facilities. | T A3 | LAKE PILLSBURY, near Scott Dam<br>100+ dev sites - boat, waterski, fish, hike. | 23 D5 |
| HUNTINGTON LAKE, north of Camp Sierra<br>300+ dev sites - boat, waterski, fish, horses. | 50 B5 | LAKE SABRINA, 18 mi SW of Bishop<br>Dev sites - boat, fish, backpack, picnic. | 51 B5 |
| ICE HOUSE RESERVOIR, 12 mi N of Riverton<br>80+ dev sites - boat, fish, swim, hike. | 35 C4 | LAKE SAN ANTONIO RECREATION AREA, W of Bradley<br>650+ dev sites-boat, fish, swim, hike, horses. | 65 D4 |
| INDIAN CREEK RESERVOIR, east of Markleeville<br>20+ dev sites - boat, fish, backpack, picnic. | 36 C4 | LAKE SHASTA, off I-5 north of Redding<br>400+ sites - houseboating, fishing, wtrskiing. | 18 C1 |
| IRON GATE RESERVOIR & LAKE COPCO, NE of Henley<br>Camp, picnic, fish, swim, raft, hike, hunt. | 4 C2<br>25 A3 | LAKE SHASTINA, 7 mi N of Weed<br>70+ dev sites - boat, waterski, fish, hike. | 4 C5 |
| IRVINE FINCH RIVER ACCESS, Hwy 32 & Sacto River<br>River Access, boat launch & picnic facilities. | | LAKE SISKIYOU, 3 mi W of Mt Shasta<br>280+ dev sites - boat, fish, windsurf. | 12 C2 |
| JACK LONDON MARINA, Embarcadero, Oakland<br>Pleasure boat marina in the Inner Harbor. | 157 D4 | LAKE SPAULDING, N of Emigrant Gap<br>20+ dev sites - boat, waterski, hike, fish. | 35 B1 |
| JACKSON MEADOW RESERVOIR, SE of Sierra City<br>120+ dev sites - boat, waterski, fish, hike. | 27 B4 | LAKE SUCCESS, 20 mi E of Tipton via Hwy 190<br>100+ dev sites - boat, fish, swim, hike. | 68 D3 |
| JENKINSON LAKE, 18 mi E of Placerville<br>290+ dev sites - boat, fish, swim, hike. | 35 B4 | LAKE TAHOE, California-Nevada border<br>Dev camps, boat, wtrski, fish, swim, horses. | 35 E2 |
| JUNE LAKE LOOP, 18 miles north of Mammoth Lakes<br>280+ dev sites - boat, fish, backpack, horses. | 50 C1 | LAKE TURLOCK STATE REC AREA, SW of La Grange<br>60+ dev sites - boat, waterski, fish, hike. | 48 B2 |
| JUNIPER LAKE, Lassen Volcanic National Park<br>Sail, swim, backpack, hike, picnic, horses. | 20 A3 | LAKE VALLEY RESERVOIR, E of Emigrant Gap<br>Camp, boat, fish, swim, hike, picnic. | 35 B1 |
| LAKE ALMANOR, southwest of Susanville<br>170+ dev sites - boat, waterski, fish, hike. | 20 B4 | LEWISTON LAKE, 35 mi NW of Redding<br>90+ dev sites - sail, canoe, fish, hunt. | 17 E1 |
| LAKE AMADOR, 7 mi S of Ione<br>Dev camps - boat, fish, waterslide, hike. | 40 D3 | LITTLE GRASS VALLEY RESERVOIR, W of Gibsonville<br>240+ dev sites - boat, waterski, fish, hike. | 26 C3 |
| LAKE ARROWHEAD, Hwy 173<br>Charming resort area; fishing, winter sports. | 91 C5 | LONG BEACH MARINA & MARINE STADIUM, Long Beach<br>One of the largest marinas on the west coast. | S D3 |
| LAKE BERRYESSA, on Hwy 128, Napa County<br>Camping, fishing, waterskiing, resorts. | 32 D5 | LOON LAKE, NW of Emerald Bay<br>50+ dev sites - boat, fish, hike, picnic. | 35 D3 |
| LAKE BRITTON, 13 mi N of Burney<br>120+ dev sites - boat, waterski, fish, horses. | 13 C4 | LOPEZ LAKE, 23 mi N of Santa Maria<br>300+ sites - boat, waterski, fish, picnic. | 76 C4 |
| LAKE CACHUMA RECREATION AREA, 11 mi S of Solvang<br>Fishing, boating, camping; no swimming. | 87 A3 | LOWER NEWPORT BAY, Newport Beach<br>Leads to vast estuary in Upper Newport Bay. | 199 C5 |
| LAKE CASITAS RECREATION AREA, 11311 Santa Ana Rd<br>Fishing, boating, camping. | 88 A4 | LUNDY LAKE, 12 miles north of Lee Vining<br>30+ dev sites - boat, fish, picnic, backpack. | 43 B4 |
| LAKE CROWLEY, 35 miles north of Bishop<br>Dev campsites - boat, waterski, fish, picnic. | 51 A2 | MAMMOTH POOL RESERVOIR, east of Bass Lake<br>60+ dev sites - boat, waterski, fish, hike. | 50 B4 |
| LAKE DAVIS, north of Portola<br>110+ dev sites - boat, fish, hike, picnic. | 27 A2 | MANZANITA LAKE, Lassen Volcanic National Park<br>170+ dev sites - sail, fish, hike, horses. | 19 D2 |
| LAKE DEL VALLE STATE REC AREA, off Hwy 84<br>Boating and recreation facilities. | P D1 | MARINA DEL REY, Via Marina<br>Berths more than 10,000 yachts. | 187 C4 |
| LAKE ELSINORE STATE RECREATION AREA, Lk Elsinore<br>Area to swim, fish, camp, water ski and boat. | 99 B4 | MARTINEZ YACHT HARBOR, Martinez<br>Small pleasure craft marina. | 154 B1 |
| LAKE HENSHAW, off CA 76, Santa Ysabel<br>400+ dev sites - fish, boat, hike. | 107 B2 | MARTIS CREEK RESERVOIR, SE of Truckee<br>20+ dev sites - sail, fish, swim, hike. | 35 E1 |
| LAKE HODGES, off S6 on Lake Dr, Escondido<br>Owned by SD City for day use only; fish, boat. | 106 D4 | MEDICINE LAKE, 48 miles NE of McCloud<br>70+ dev sites - boat, waterski, fish, horses. | 5 D5 |
| LAKE ISABELLA, 48 mi NE of Bakersfield<br>One of the most complete rec lakes in Calif. | 79 D1 | MILLERTON LAKE REC AREA, 22 miles East of Madera<br>130+ dev sites - boat, waterski, fish, horses. | 57 D1 |
| LAKE JENNINGS, Jennings Pk Rd N off I-8<br>RV & tent camping; boat, limited fishing. | 107 A5 | MISSION BAY, Mission Bay Park, W of I-5<br>Separate courses for diverse water sports. | 212 D2 |
| LAKE KAWEAH, 17 mi E of Visalia via Hwy 198<br>Campsites, boating, fishing, swimming. | 68 D1 | MONO LAKE TUFA STATE RESERVE, Hy 395 @ Lee Vining<br>Interesting salt formatns surround saltwtr lk. | 43 D4 |
| LAKE McCLOUD, 12 mi S of McCloud<br>Undev campsites - boat, fish, picnic, hike. | 12 E3 | MONTEREY MARINA, Ocean View Blvd<br>Small craft harbor near Fisherman's Wharf. | 167 E3 |
| LAKE McCLURE, S of Coulterville<br>550+ dev sites - housebt, fish, swim, picnic. | 48 D2 | MORENA LAKE, Oak Dr & Buckman Spgs Rd, W of I-8<br>Campsites, fishing, boating, hiking, horses. | 112 D1 |
| LAKE MEAD NATL RECREATION AREA, Hwy 93 & Lakeshre<br>One of largest artificial lakes in the world. | 85 C1 | NOYO HARBOR, south of Fort Bragg<br>Small, scenic eastern-like fishing village. | 22 B5 |
| LAKE MENDOCINO, N of Ukiah<br>300+ dev sites - boat, waterski, fish, hike. | 31 B2 | OCEANSIDE HARBOR, 1540 Harbor Dr N<br>Deep sea & sport fishing; pier fishng; sailng. | 106 A3 |

# POINTS OF INTEREST INDEX

# POINTS OF INTEREST INDEX

| NAME & ADDRESS | PAGE & GRID | | NAME & ADDRESS | PAGE & GRID |
|---|---|---|---|---|
| DOROTHY CHANDLER PAVILION, 135 N Grand Av<br>Part of the Music Center; musical performnces. | 186 A2 | | BARGETTO WINERY, 700 Cannery Row, Monterey<br>Tasting room and gift shop. | 167 E2 |
| GEARY THEATER, 415 Geary St at Mason St<br>The Amer Conservatory Theatr performs nightly. | 143 C3 | | BARGETTO WINERY, 3535 N Main St, Soquel<br>Wine tasting room and gift shop. | 54 A2 |
| GREEK THEATER, 2700 N Vermont Av, Los Angeles<br>Natural amphitheatre in Griffith Park. | 182 B3 | | BEAULIEU VINEYARD, 1960 St Helena Hwy, Rutherford<br>Open daily for tasting and guided tours. | 29 C3 |
| HOLLYWOOD BOWL, 2301 N Highland Av<br>Natural amphitheater, seats 20,000. | 181 C3 | | BELLA ROSA WINERY, Hwy 99 & Pond Rd, McFarland<br>Winery and tasting room are open daily. | 68 B5 |
| HUNTINGTON HARTFORD THEATRE, 1615 N Vine St<br>More serious drama of well known stars. | 181 D4 | | BELVEDERE WINERY, 4035 Westside Rd, Healdsburg<br>Tasting room open daily; group tours by appt. | 37 D1 |
| IRVINE MEADOWS AMPHITHEATER, 8800 Irvine Ctr Dr<br>Concerts under the stars. | 98 D5 | | BERINGER VINEYARDS, 2000 Main St, St Helena<br>Tours of Rhine House, Beringer caves; tasting. | 29 B3 |
| JOHN ANSON FORD THEATER, 2580 Cahuenga Blvd<br>Features occasional outdoor jazz concerts. | 181 D3 | | BERNARDO WINERY, 13330 Pas Dl Verano N, Escondido<br>Wine tasting, sales & gift shop; picnic area. | 106 D4 |
| L A STAGE WEST, Canon Dr, Beverly Hills<br>Features off-Broadway plays. | 183 C2 | | BIANCHI VINEYARDS, 5806 N Modoc Av, Kerman<br>Winery and tasting room are open daily. | 57 A3 |
| MANN'S CHINESE THEATRE, 6925 Hollywood Bl<br>Famed forecourt with footprints of stars. | 181 C4 | | BOEGER WINERY, 1709 Carson, Placerville<br>Wine tasting. | 35 A4 |
| MARK TAPER FORUM, 135 N Grand Av<br>Part of the Music Center; experimental drama. | 186 A2 | | BRANDER VINEYARD, 2620 W Highway 154, Los Olivos<br>Open Monday-Saturday for wine tasting & tours. | 86 E3 |
| THE MUSIC CENTER, 135 N Grand Av, Los Angeles<br>3 theatre complex for drama, music & opera. | 186 A2 | | BRITTON CELLARS, 40620 Calle Contento, Temecula<br>Daily tasting & sales; picnic area. | 99 D5 |
| PACIFIC AMPHITHEATER, Fairview Rd, Costa Mesa<br>Outdoor concerts & entertainment. | 197 D5 | | BROOKSIDE VINEYARD, 2801 E Guasti Rd, Guasti<br>Tasting room & tours open daily; picnic area. | U E2 |
| PANTAGES THEATER, 6233 Hollywood Blvd<br>Features many Broadway productions. | 181 D4 | | BUENA VISTA WINERY, Old Winery Rd, Sonoma<br>Historic landmark of Cal's first wine cellars. | L C1 |
| PARAMOUNT THEATER, 2025 Broadway<br>30's movie house is now performing arts centr. | 158 A2 | | BYRON WINERY, 5230 Tepusquet Rd, Santa Maria<br>Daily tours, wine tasting and retail sales. | 86 D1 |
| PERFORMING ARTS CTR, 600 Town Ctr Dr, Costa Mesa<br>Features musical and theatrical performances. | 198 A3 | | CACHE CELLARS, Pedrick Rd, Davis<br>Tasting room open daily; groups by appointmnt. | 39 B2 |
| SHRINE AUDITORIUM, Jefferson & Figueroa, L A<br>A variety of musical programs & exhibits. | 185 D5 | | CADENASSO WINERY, 1955 W Texas St, Fairfield<br>Winery and tasting room are open daily. | 135 A4 |
| SHUBERT THEATRE, 2020 Avenue of the Stars<br>The stage for many broadway plays. | 183 A2 | | CADLOLO WINERY, 1124 California St, Escalon<br>Tasting room and tours available. | 47 D1 |
| TERRACE THEATER, Ocean Blvd, Long Beach<br>Features drama, opera, dance & symphony. | 192 E3 | | CAKEBREAD CELLARS, Hwy 29 btwn Oakville & Ruthrfd<br>Tours by appointment only. | 29 D3 |
| WILSHIRE THEATER, Wilshire & La Cienega<br>Classic theater - features plays & musicals. | 183 E2 | | CALIFORNIA CELLAR MASTERS, 212 W Pine St, Lodi<br>Winery and tasting room are open daily. | 40 A4 |

********************** WINERIES **********************

Many of the wineries located in the Napa Valley are shown on Page 29 in this Driver's Guide.

| NAME & ADDRESS | PAGE & GRID | | NAME & ADDRESS | PAGE & GRID |
|---|---|---|---|---|
| ADELAIDA CELLARS, Von Dollen Rd, Paso Robles<br>Winery and tasting room are open daily. | 66 B5 | | CALLAWAY WINERY, Rancho California Rd, Temecula<br>Tours and tasting room; picnic facilities. | 99 D5 |
| ALDERBROOK WINERY, 2306 Magnolia Dr, Healdsburg<br>Tasting room open daily; tours by appointment. | 37 D1 | | CAMBIASO VINEYARDS, 1141 Grant Av, Healdsburg<br>Winery is open daily for retail sales. | 37 E1 |
| ALEXANDER VLY VINEYARDS, 8644 Hwy 128, Healdsburg<br>Wine tasting; tours by appointment. | 31 E5 | | CAPARONE WINERY, San Marcos Rd, Paso Robles<br>Tasting and sales available daily. | 66 A5 |
| ALMADEN VINEYARDS, 1530 Blossom Hill Rd, San Jose<br>Historic museum, sparkling wine cellar; tour. | P C4 | | J CAREY VINEYARDS, 1711 Alamo Pintado Rd, Solvang<br>Open for tours and tasting. | 86 E3 |
| ALMADEN VINEYARDS, 8090 Pacheco Pass Hy, Hollistr<br>Open daily for wine tasting; picnic area. | 54 E2 | | CASA DE FRUTA, 6680 Pacheco Pass Hy, Hollister<br>Open daily; gourmet deli. | 54 E2 |
| ALTAMURA WINERY, 4240 Silverado Tr, Napa<br>Tasting room open daily; appointmnt suggested. | 29 E4 | | CASSAYRE-FORNI CELLARS, 1271 Manley Ln, Rutherfrd<br>Retail sales and tasting room. | 29 C3 |
| AMADOR CITY WINERY, Hwy 49 & O'Neill Al, Amador<br>Winery and tasting room are open daily. | 40 D2 | | CAYMUS VINEYARDS, 8700 Conn Creek Rd, Rutherford<br>Guided tours and tasting by appointment. | 29 D3 |
| A. NONINI WINERY, 2450 N Dickenson, Fresno<br>Winery tours, tasting and retail sales. | 57 B3 | | CHAMISAL VINEYARD, 7525 Orcutt Rd, Sn Luis Obispo<br>Wine tasting & retail sales; picnic area. | 76 B4 |
| ARCIERO WINERY, Hwy 46 & Jardine Rd, Paso Robles<br>Winery and tasting room are open daily. | 76 B1 | | CHARLES F SHAW VINEYRDS, 1010 Big Tree, St Helena<br>Tasting room open daily; groups by appointmnt. | 29 B2 |
| AUSTIN CELLARS, 2923 Grand Av, Solvang<br>Tasting room and retail sales; picnic area. | 86 E3 | | CHARLES KRUG WINERY, off Hwy 29, St Helena<br>Guided tours and wine tasting daily. | 29 C2 |
| BALLARD CANYON WINERY, Ballard Cyn Rd, Solvang<br>Tours by appointment only. | 86 E3 | | CHATEAU DE LEU, 1635 W Mason Rd, Suisun<br>Wine tasting & sales; picnic facilities. | L E1 |
| BANDIERA WINERY, 155 Cherry Creek Rd, Cloverdale<br>Tasting & sales open Tuesday through Sunday. | 31 C4 | | CHATEAU DIANA, 6195 Dry Creek Rd, Healdsburg<br>Tasting room and picnic area. | 31 D5 |
| BARENGO LOST HILLS WINERY, 1 mi W on Acampo Rd<br>Tasting room and picnic area. | 40 A4 | | CHATEAU JULIEN WINERY, 8940 Carmel Vly Rd, Carmel<br>Tasting room open daily; groups by appointmnt. | 54 B5 |
| | | | CHATEAU MONTELENA, 1429 Tubbs Ln, Calistoga<br>Tours by appointment; store open daily. | 29 A1 |
| | | | CHATEAU ST JEAN, 8555 Sonoma Hwy, Kenwood<br>Tasting, self-guided tours. | 38 A2 |
| | | | CHRISTIAN BROTHERS, 2555 Main St, St Helena<br>Open daily for champagne tasting & tours. | 29 B2 |
| | | | CILURZO VINEYARD, 41220 Calle Contento, Temecula<br>Informal tours and wine tasting; picnic area. | 99 D5 |

# POINTS OF INTEREST INDEX

| NAME & ADDRESS | PAGE & GRID | NAME & ADDRESS | PAGE & GRID |
|---|---|---|---|
| ROBERT STEMMLER, 3805 Lambert Bridge Rd, Healdsbg<br>  Wine tasting and retail sales; picnicking. | 31 D5 | STRINGER'S ORCHARDS, 3/4 mile S of New Pine Creek<br>  Daily tours and tasting; gift shop. | 7 D2 |
| RODNEY STRONG, 11455 Old Redwood Hwy, Healdsburg<br>  Tasting & sales; concerts & cultural events. | 37 D1 | STUERMER WINERY, Highway 29, Lower Lake<br>  Tasting room open Thurs-Sun; groups req appts. | 32 A4 |
| ROSENBLUM CELLARS, 1401 Stanford Av, Emeryville<br>  Tasting room open weekdays; annual open house. | L D4 | SUMMER HILL VINEYDS, 3920 Hecker Pass Hwy, Gilroy<br>  Wine tasting & retail sales; picnic area. | 54 D2 |
| ROSS-KELLER WINERY, 900 McMurray Rd, Buellton<br>  Tours and tasting daily. | 86 D3 | SUNRISE WINERY, 13100 Montebello Rd, Cupertino<br>  Open weekdays for wine tasting. | N E4 |
| ROSS-KELLER, 985 Orchard Av, Nipomo<br>  Tasting room and sales daily; picnic area. | 76 C5 | SUSINE CELLARS, 301 Spring St, Suisun<br>  Tasting and sales available Tuesday-Saturday. | 135 C4 |
| ROUND HILL CELLARS, Lodi Ln, St Helena<br>  Tours by appointment; retail sales. | 29 B2 | SUTTER HOME, 227 St Helena Hwy S, St Helena<br>  Tasting room and gift shop. | 29 C3 |
| RUTHERFORD HILL WINERY, End of Rutherford Hill Rd<br>  Tours daily; tasting 2nd Saturday each month. | 29 D3 | THOMAS VINEYARD, 8916 Foothill Blvd, Cucamonga<br>  Wine tasting & sales; picnic; historic landmk. | U E2 |
| RUTHERFORD VINTNERS, 1673 St Helena Hwy S<br>  Tasting room; group tours by appointment. | 29 C3 | THOMAS KRUSE WINERY, 4390 Hecker Pass Hwy, Gilroy<br>  Retail sales & wine tasting; picnic area. | 54 C2 |
| ST FRANCIS WINERY, 8450 Sonoma Hwy, Kenwood<br>  Tasting & sales daily; tours by appointment. | 38 B2 | TONIO CONTI, Von Dollen Rd, Paso Robles<br>  Tasting room is open daily. | 66 B5 |
| SAN ANTONIO WINERY, 737 Lamar St, Los Angeles<br>  Tours, wine tasting, restaurant; picnic area. | 186 D2 | TOPOLOS AT RUSSIAN RIVER, 5700 Gravenstein Hwy<br>  Tasting room; tours by appointment. | 37 D2 |
| SANFORD WINERY, 7250 Santa Rosa Rd, Buellton<br>  Tours, tasting & sales Monday-Saturday;picnic. | 86 D3 | TRENTADUE, 19170 Redwood Hwy, Geyserville<br>  Open all week for tasting. | 31 D5 |
| SAN MARTIN WINERY, 13000 Depot Av, San Martin<br>  Tasting room open year around. | P D5 | VALLEY OF THE MOON, Madrone Rd, Glen Ellen<br>  Tasting room, retail sales; no tours. | 38 B2 |
| SAN PASQUAL, 13455 San Pasqual Rd, San Diego<br>  Wine tasting & retail sales; tours by appt. | 106 E3 | VEGA VINEYARDS, 9495 Santa Rosa Rd, Buellton<br>  Tours and tasting available. | 86 D3 |
| SANTA BARBARA, 202 Anacapa St, Santa Barbara<br>  Tasting room open. | 86 C2 | VENTANA VINEYARDS, Los Coches Rd W of Greenfield<br>  New Monterey district winery. | 65 B1 |
| SANTA YNEZ VALLEY, 365 N Refugio Rd, Santa Ynez<br>  Tours and tasting on Saturday; M-F by appoint. | 86 E3 | VIANO VINEYARDS, 150 Morello Av, Martinez<br>  Tasting room open daily; appt req for groups. | 154 E2 |
| SANTINO WINERY, Steiner Rd, Plymouth<br>  Informal tours and tasting room. | 40 E1 | VICHON WINERY, 1595 Coombsville Rd, Napa<br>  Tours by appt; wine tasting & retail sales. | 29 C4 |
| SATIETY, Highways 113 & 25A, Yolo<br>  Tasting room and winery are open daily. | 33 C5 | VILLA MT EDEN, Oakville Cross Rd, Oakville<br>  Tours weekdays by appointment. | 29 D3 |
| SAUSAL WINERY, 7370 Highway 128, Healdsburg<br>  Winery and tasting room are open daily. | 31 E5 | VINTAGE WINE CELLARS, 28237 River Rd, Cloverdale<br>  Tasting room is open daily. | 31 C4 |
| SCHARFFENBERGER CELLARS, 7000 Highway 128, Philo<br>  Winery & tasting room open daily except Wed. | 30 D3 | VOSE VINEYARDS, 4035 Mt Veeder Rd, Napa<br>  Tasting room is open daily. | 29 C4 |
| SEBASTIANI VINEYARDS & WINERY, 389 4th St E<br>  1st vineyard in Sonoma Vly; tours and tasting. | 132 E4 | V SATTUI WINERY, White Ln at Hwy 29 S, St Helena<br>  Tasting room, tours, gift shop; founded 1885. | 29 C3 |
| SEQUOIA GROVE, 8338 St Helena Hwy, Napa<br>  Winery tours by appointment; tasting & sales. | 29 D3 | WEIBEL CHAMPAGNE, Stanford Av, Mission San Jose<br>  Champagne tasting room. | P B2 |
| SHENANDOAH VINEYARDS, 12300 Steiner Rd, Plymouth<br>  Winery and tasting room are open daily. | 40 E1 | WEIBEL VINEYARDS, 7051 N State St, Redwood Valley<br>  Tasting room and gift shop; no tours. | 31 B1 |
| SHOWN & SONS VINEYARDS, 3514 St Helena, Rutherfrd<br>  Winery is open daily; appointments suggested. | 29 D3 | WENTE BROS, 5555 Tesla Rd, Livermore<br>  4th generation winery; excellent tour/tasting. | P D1 |
| SIERRA WINERY, 1925 N Mooney Blvd, Tulare<br>  Tasting and sales daily; picnic area. | 68 B2 | WENTE BROS SPARKLING WINE CELLARS, Livermore<br>  Hourly tours available; restaurant. | P D1 |
| SILVERADO VINEYARDS, 6121 Silverado Tr, Napa<br>  Winery and tasting room are open daily. | 29 E4 | WHALER VINEYARD, 6200 Eastside Rd, Ukiah<br>  Tasting room open daily; appointmnts suggestd. | 31 B2 |
| SIMI WINERY, 16275 Healdsburg Av, Healdsburg<br>  Wine tasting, guided tours. | 31 D5 | WHITEHALL LANE WINERY, St Helena Hwy S<br>  Retail sales. | 29 C3 |
| SODA ROCK, 8015 Hwy 128, Healdsburg<br>  Wine tasting; historic stone winery building. | 31 D5 | WHITE OAK VINEYARDS, 208 Haydon St, Healdsburg<br>  Open daily for wine tasting. | 37 E1 |
| SOUVERAIN, Independence Ln & Hwy 101, Geyserville<br>  Open daily for tasting and tours; restaurant. | 31 D5 | WILLIAM WHEELER WINERY, 130 Plaza St, Healdsburg<br>  Open Thursday - Monday for tours and tasting. | 37 E1 |
| SPRING MOUNTAIN VINEYARDS, 2805 Spring Mtn Rd<br>  Tours by appointment only. | 29 B3 | WINDSOR VINEYARDS, 11455 Old Redwood Hwy, Hldsbrg<br>  Tasting room is open daily. | 37 D1 |
| STAG'S LEAP WINE CELLARS, 5766 Silverado Tr, Napa<br>  Tasting room open daily; appt req for tours. | 29 E4 | WINTERS WINERY, 15 Main St, Winters<br>  Wine tasting and retail sales daily. | 39 A1 |
| STEARNS WHARF VINTNERS, Santa Barbara<br>  Retail sales. | 174 D4 | WOODBURY WINERY, 32 Woodland Av, San Rafael<br>  By appointment only. | 139 E4 |
| STEPHEN ZELLERBACH, 14350 Chalk Hill Rd, Healdsbg<br>  Picnic, tasting, retail sales; tours by appt. | 32 B5 | WOODEN VALLEY WINERY, 4756 Suisun Vly Rd, Suisun<br>  Tasting room and sales area are open Tues-Sun. | L E1 |
| STEPHEN ZELLERBACH VINEYARD, 4611 Thomas, Hldsbrg<br>  Tasting room open daily; appt req for groups. | 37 E1 | YANKEE HILL WINERY, Yankee Hill Rd, Columbia<br>  Wine tasting; tours by appointment. | 41 C4 |
| STERLING VINEYARDS, 1111 Dunaweal Ln, Calistoga<br>  Tasting & tours; aerial tramway to hlltp wnry. | 29 A2 | YORK MOUNTAIN WINERY, Hwy 46, Templeton<br>  Tasting room; tours by appointment only. | 75 E2 |
| STEVENOT WINERY, San Domingo Rd near Murphys<br>  Tasting room and retail sales. | 41 B4 | ZACA MESA WINERY, Foxen Cyn Rd, Los Olivos<br>  Tour provides a good overview of winemaking. | 86 E2 |
| STONEGATE WINERY, 1183 Dunaweal Ln, Calistoga<br>  Tours by appointment; retail sales most days. | 29 A2 | | |